D1198907

Annual Review of
Psychology

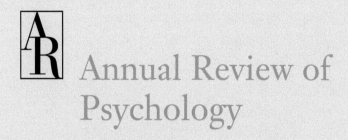

Annual Review of Psychology

Volume 68, 2017

Susan T. Fiske, *Editor*

Princeton University

Daniel L. Schacter, *Associate Editor*

Harvard University

Shelley E. Taylor, *Associate Editor*

University of California, Los Angeles

www.annualreviews.org • science@annualreviews.org • 650-493-4400

Annual Reviews

4139 El Camino Way • P.O. Box 10139 • Palo Alto, California 94303-0139

Annual Reviews
Palo Alto, California, USA

International Standard Serial Number: 0066-4308
International Standard Book Number: 978-0-8243-0268-9
Library of Congress Control Number: 50013143

All Annual Reviews and publication titles are registered trademarks of Annual Reviews.

♾ The paper used in this publication meets the minimum requirements of American National Standards for Information Sciences—Permanence of Paper for Printed Library Materials, ANSI Z39.48-1992.

Annual Reviews and the Editors of its publications assume no responsibility for the statements expressed by the contributors to this *Annual Review*.

TYPESET BY APTARA
PRINTED AND BOUND BY SHERIDAN BOOKS, INC., CHELSEA, MICHIGAN

Introduction

Wisdom does not often appear in rapid-fire social media posts. Wisdom takes time and thought, the accumulation of knowledge informed by evidence and expertise, and the crafting of careful prose. Although wisdom can be pithy, more often scientific insight requires some room to explain and develop.

Annual Review of Psychology articles offer expert, integrative reviews that go beyond top-of-the-head sound bites or click bait, instead examining a topic's nuances and pros and cons, the weight of the evidence, and gaps in our knowledge to date. As such, they provide lasting insights about the current state of the field and ways forward.

What's more, our authors and topics are vetted by the expert Editorial Committee. Our articles are carefully reviewed by devoted colleagues and by the editors. So, take the time to experience some curated wisdom from hand-picked experts. It's time well spent.

Susan T. Fiske
Princeton, New Jersey

Daniel L. Schacter
Cambridge, Massachusetts

Shelley E. Taylor
Los Angeles, California

Annual Review of
Psychology

Volume 68, 2017

Contents

Indexes

Errata

An online log of corrections to *Annual Review of Psychology* articles may be found at
http://www.annualreviews.org/errata/psych

Related Articles

From the *Annual Review of Anthropology*, Volume 45 (2016)

From the *Annual Review of Political Science*, Volume 19 (2016)

Elizabeth Loftus

Eavesdropping on Memory

Elizabeth F. Loftus

Department of Psychology and Social Behavior and Department of Criminology, Law, and Society, University of California, Irvine, California 92697; email: eloftus@uci.edu

Annu. Rev. Psychol. 2017. 68:1–18

The *Annual Review of Psychology* is online at psych.annualreviews.org

This article's doi:
10.1146/annurev-psych-010416-044138

Keywords

memory, false memory, eyewitness testimony

Abstract

For more than four decades, I have been studying human memory. My research concerns the malleable nature of memory. Information suggested to an individual about an event can be integrated with the memory of the event itself, so that what actually occurred, and what was discussed later about what may have occurred, become inextricably interwoven, allowing distortion, elaboration, and even total fabrication. In my writings, classes, and public speeches, I've tried to convey one important take-home message: Just because someone tells you something in great detail, with much confidence, and with emotion, it doesn't mean that it is true. Here I describe my professional life as an experimental psychologist, in which I've eavesdropped on this process, as well as many personal experiences that may have influenced my thinking and choices.

Contents

INTRODUCTION

A few years ago, I received a horrifying email. It came from a woman I'll call Betty, with a subject line in all capital letters: HAVE YOU NO SHAME AT ALL. After learning that I had testified for the defense in a criminal trial involving allegations of abuse by a priest, Betty wrote:

> Loftus, I remember you trying to discredit every single victim of sexual abuse that crossed your line of vision, but this is a new low even for you.. to attack the victims of predatory Catholic priests, who needed every drop of courage they had to come forward in the first place.

> Do NOT send me a reply. All I want is to hold up a mirror to you for an instant and let you see things about yourself that will have you waking up in the middle of the night screaming. And if you contact me, believe me, whore of the press, I will make you wish you had never heard of me. I will make you beg for me to shut the fuck up.

The email continued in this vein, ending by calling me a bitch. I never wrote back to Betty. Her communication was among the most vitriolic that I've received over the past few decades, but it was far from the only attack. Fortunately for me, the Bettys of the world are outnumbered by the Alices.

On June 26, 2014, I received this email from a woman I'll call Alice who lives in Nevada. Alice wrote:

> Dr. Loftus,

> I wanted to take a moment to thank you for your work. Until last year I'd never heard of you, and then suddenly you became someone I desperately needed to hear. I met a wonderful man whose wife (an old friend of mine) had died of cancer and he had the awful task of waiting for the right moment to tell me his middle daughter had accused him of heinous things.

> I went online and researched recovered memories and realized from lots of sources that she was a textbook case of false memory syndrome and

married him. Most of the time he manages to make her accusations irrelevant to his daily life but there are days he still struggles,

especially when he realized he probably lost his first wife due to these troubles..

I found your Ted talk and it was such a relief, such an oasis for those of us in these situations. I just had to let you know that you are a clear voice in our darkness and I hope you continue speaking out for us.

I wrote back to Alice right away and stored her email in my "WhenBlue" file, which contains a collection of letters I can read when the next unexpected Betty decides to send a hateful message my way.

MY CHILDHOOD: IN MEMORY

Growing up in Los Angeles, I never for a moment anticipated that I would become both a target of vitriol and an object of adoration; a bitch to some, but a clear voice in the darkness to others. I never for a moment imagined that I would become a scientist who could alter what people believe about their own histories.

I was born in 1944, while World War II was still raging. Everyone called me Beth. I met my father, Sidney Fishman, about a year later when he returned from the war. I lived with this workaholic physician, my librarian mother Rebecca, and, later, my two brothers, David and Robert. We had a charming, placid life together. I remember ballet classes, although I was never very good. I remember begging to take piano lessons when I was about 8 and then begging to be able to quit them when I was about 9. I remember the scariness of changing elementary schools, required by a family move. I remember bagels at Aunt Pearl's, swimming in Uncle Herman's pool, and visits from Uncle Joe and the Pittsburgh family branch. And I remember when this idyllic childhood ended. My mother drowned in a swimming pool when I was 14 and my younger brothers only 12 and 9. I kept a diary during those years and wrote about that day as "the most tragic day of my life." It still is.[1]

Many teenage girls who keep diaries fear that someone might find and read them, and I was no exception. I could have censored my diary, but I came up with a different idea. When I wanted to write something particularly painful or private, I would jot the thoughts on a separate piece of paper, which I clipped to the page in the diary that contained the date of the thought. Then, if some putative boyfriend begged to read the diary as proof of my genuine affection, I could unclip the little pieces of paper before he got his hands on them. I would later call these my "removable truths." Not all of these removable truths were about matters of childhood romance, such as which boy I had a crush on or who tried to kiss me. One removable truth was titled "My greatest regret." It described in detail how I wished I had been kinder to my mother. It is ironic that I would one day grow up to become a scientist who built her career on removing "truths" from people's memories.

Only two years after my mother died, a raging Southern California fire burned down our family house, along with more than 400 others in our neighborhood in west Los Angeles. I had returned from a normal high school day with my younger brother David to find roadblocks, which we eluded using shortcuts. I actually ran into our burning house to grab the encyclopedia so I could

---

[1]My brothers tease me to this day: "Don't say the M word (mother) or Beth will cry." That teasing, I fear, covers something deeper. When Robert's daughter (whom he named Sydney) turned 10, he called to tell me, "Sydney just turned 10 and still has a mother." Of course I cried.

complete my homework, but it was too dangerous to try to retrieve my diaries. I fretted about these precious possessions: Were they burned, or would they be found with my removable truths still attached? Eventually, when we were able to go back and sift through the charred remains, the diaries were recovered, and so my permanent record of truths, both removable and otherwise, exists today. I consulted them once, 40 years after my mother's death, when I wrote her a letter, titled "Dear Mother," telling her how I felt on the day she died, during the weeks and months in the aftermath, and four decades later (Loftus 2003a).

THE YEARS OF HIGHER EDUCATION

Writing this autobiography wasn't as easy for me as you might think. I was invited 10 years ago to write one for the *History of Psychology in Autobiography* (Loftus 2007a) and another for an edited volume devoted to my contributions to science, law, and academic freedom (Loftus 2007b). I've told my life story before; the past hasn't changed in the past 10 years. Or has it?

Growing up, I loved math. When I was in school, math was the one thing that brought me and my father together; he enjoyed helping me with my homework, and I treasured the time I spent learning from him. In high school, I excelled in algebra and geometry, and when I began college at the University of California, Los Angeles in 1962, I majored in mathematics. In college, I was a bit disheartened to discover that my math classes were taught by only male professors instructing almost exclusively male students. I wasn't as crazy about calculus, but by then, I felt I had invested too much effort in math and was determined to finish a degree in that field. Along the way, I happened to take an introductory psychology course and was utterly fascinated. I finished college in four years with a double major in math and psychology.

What would I do next? My undergraduate professors told me about a subfield in psychology called mathematical psychology, which sounded perfect to me, given my double major. In 1966, I began graduate school at Stanford and majored in psychology, with an emphasis in mathematical psychology. I soon discovered I wasn't particularly interested in mathematical psychology, but I never missed the required Friday seminar sessions where faculty and fellow graduate students discussed their research findings, even though my mind was elsewhere. I would often sit in the back and write letters to my relatives. Sometimes I actually got some sewing done (e.g., hemming skirts that needed to be shortened) to the sound of voices discussing the latest developments in mathematical learning theory.

It was then customary in the Stanford Psychology Department to pair an incoming graduate student with a second-year student who could provide some mentoring. My assigned mentee was a gorgeous graduate of Brown University, named Geoff Loftus, who had driven his black BMW motorcycle across the country to Stanford. I guess you could say I took my mentoring seriously, because nine months later, Beth Fishman became Elizabeth Loftus.[2]

Recently, I found a letter written to me by my soon-to-be father-in-law, Russell Loftus, only two weeks before I married his son. Russ thanked me for a birthday present I had sent him (a 1969 San Francisco calendar). He said I was the "most imaginatively thoughtful person" he had ever met. (I guess he liked the calendar.) The ending of his letter reminded me of an important episode in my past with Geoff. Russ wrote, "Beth dear, I was going to try to get through this letter without being maudlin. I can't. Pete [Geoff's mother] and I constantly think of you and Geoff with more love and affection than we shall ever be able to express . . . also with concern. Concern

---

[2] I married Geoff despite the fact that this Ivy League–educated husband of mine would frequently tease me about word mispronunciations, saying, "You can take the girl out of LA, but you can't take LA out of the girl."

only because of the nature of the times with all of the related implications...." What was that concern? Oh, yes, I remember now: America was in the midst of the Vietnam War, and Geoff was in enormous danger of being drafted and sent to Vietnam. In fact, we decided to get married in the hope of finding a course of joint action that would keep him from fighting in a war that neither of us believed in. It's a long story, but, for roundabout reasons, it worked. We married in my family home in Los Angeles and had a one-day honeymoon so that I could get back to Stanford to study for the comprehensive exams.

I spent my early years at Stanford working on projects that involved computer-assisted instruction. Richard Atkinson chaired my master's thesis committee and helped me complete a thesis on using computerized instruction to learn spelling. Patrick Suppes chaired my doctoral committee and helped me complete a dissertation on using computerized instruction to learn mathematics. I admired these busy professors and wished they could have spent more time with me. It was also satisfying to be able to complete research projects and see them appear in print (Fishman et al. 1968, Loftus & Suppes 1972). But I never got swept off my feet by this line of work.

It wasn't until the later years of graduate school that I was introduced to research that I could truly get excited about. With the social psychologist Jonathan Freedman, I studied semantic memory, i.e., memory for words, concepts, and factual knowledge of the world (Collins & Loftus 1975). It is our repository of general information disassociated from any moment in time. A semantic memory could be knowing that bananas are fruits that are yellow, or that zebra is the name of an animal that is striped. Freedman and I did a number of studies to explore how semantic information is organized in memory. For example, in one study we showed participants the category cue "animal" either before or after the descriptor "striped." We found that participants were a quarter of a second faster to give the response "zebra" when the category cue came before the descriptor. From this we inferred that information in semantic memory is organized according to categories such as animals, rather than attributes such as striped, enabling the mental search for a word to begin sooner when the word's category is given first. Freedman and I published several additional studies together (e.g., Freedman & Loftus 1971, Loftus & Freedman 1972), and I began to give conference talks on semantic memory. I finished graduate school in 1970 and taught for a few years in New York City. Geoff and I had a problem many academic couples face, known as the two-body problem. We wanted to find jobs in the same city. After a few years of job searching, Geoff and I both received offers from the University of Washington, where I would ultimately spend the next several decades.

REAL-WORLD MEMORIES

A few years after my honeymoon with semantic memory, I faced the fact that I wanted to do research with more obvious practical applications. My dad died of cancer at the age of 61 in 1975. I would have loved to do something about the cancer problem, but I obviously lacked the skills and training. My new project would have to involve memory, but how? I decided to study the memories of witnesses to accidents, crimes, and other legal events, combining my experience in memory and my growing interest in legal matters. After obtaining research funding from the US Department of Transportation, I began showing people films of car accidents and noticed that the questions I asked could skew the answers I got from witnesses. Asking, "How fast were the cars going when they smashed into each other?" led to higher estimates of speed than a more neutral question such as, "How fast were the cars going when they hit each other?" The "smashed" question also increased the likelihood that witnesses would say that they saw broken glass at the accident scene, even though there was no broken glass at all. The published paper describing this study has one of my favorite titles: "Reconstruction of Automobile Destruction." I coauthored this paper with

John Palmer, an undergraduate who would go on to become a fantastic researcher himself (Loftus & Palmer 1974). This early study on memory distortion caused by leading questions was followed by others (e.g., Loftus 1975), and it soon became clear that leading questions are one way—though only one of several—by which witnesses' memories can be contaminated. I also found that memories can be contaminated when witnesses talk to one another or when they are exposed to media coverage that contains erroneous detail. Misinformation encountered after the fact can lead to problems with accurate memory, a phenomenon that became known as the misinformation effect (Loftus & Hoffman 1989).

Just for the heck of it, as I was writing this chapter, I searched for "misinformation effect" using Google and discovered that it has a Wikipedia page. Wikipedia tells us that, "The misinformation effect happens when our recall of episodic memories becomes less accurate because of postevent information" (**https://en.wikipedia.org/wiki/Misinformation_effect**). How fun! The entry goes on to describe another of my studies from the 1970s. In this study, subjects saw a simulated accident in which a car stopped at a stop sign. Afterward, some subjects received misinformation that it was a yield sign. Finally, subjects were tested on what they had originally seen. Many subjects reported that they had seen a yield sign, succumbing to the misinformation. A cute cartoon accompanied this description (**Figure 1**).

Studying the misinformation effect has kept me busy because there have been so many interesting questions to ask about the phenomenon (Frenda et al. 2011). When are people particularly prone to having their recollections modified by misinformation? Early on, we showed that people are more susceptible to misinformation about older memories than about more recent ones (Loftus 1992). More recently, we showed that people are also more susceptible when they are sleep deprived than when they are rested (Frenda et al. 2014), to the extent that they can be especially likely to confess to "crimes" that they did not commit (Frenda et al. 2016). These misinformation memories can last for quite a while; in one study, the false memories lasted more than a year (Zhu et al. 2012). What groups of people are especially susceptible to impairments from misinformation? First, we showed that young children were more susceptible to misinformation than adults

Figure 1

Cartoon used by Wikipedia to illustrate the misinformation effect. Figure modified from CaitlinJames/ Wikipedia (**https://en.wikipedia.org/wiki/Misinformation_effect**)/CC-BY-SA-3.0.

(Loftus et al. 1992). Second, we showed that people with low cognitive ability are more susceptible to misinformation than those with high cognitive ability (Zhu et al. 2010). Even people who have superior autobiographical memories are susceptible to misinformation. We conducted a study on a special group of individuals with highly superior autobiographical memory (HSAM). Although these individuals have an extraordinary ability to recall specific dates and autobiographical events, they were as susceptible to memory distortion as their age-matched controls. Taken together, this research invites the speculation that no group of individuals is completely immune to the distorting effects of suggestion and misinformation (Patihis et al. 2013). Finally, we have done numerous studies that show how difficult it is to tell whether a particular memory is authentic or not; one needs independent corroboration (Bernstein & Loftus 2009).

MY FORAY INTO THE WORLD OF LAW

My research on distortions in memory implicitly challenges the credibility and value of memories in a variety of contexts, including eyewitness memories in legal cases. However, eyewitness testimony is typically seen as highly trustworthy evidence by American jurors. In the mid-1970s, I wrote an article for *Psychology Today* magazine titled "Reconstructing Memory: The Incredible Eyewitness" (Loftus 1974). In this article, I wrote about how eyewitness testimony is perceived by jurors and how it can influence the outcome of legal cases. I discussed an unpublished study I had performed with mock jurors. In this study, mock jurors read about a grocery store robbery in which the owner was killed and then had to decide if the defendant was guilty or not. The first group of jurors was told that there had been no eyewitnesses, only circumstantial evidence. The second was told that a store clerk had identified the defendant. The third group was told that the store clerk's identification had been discredited by his poor vision. The results showed that without the eyewitness the evidence for guilt was weak, with only 18% of jurors in the first group voting guilty. Adding a single eyewitness increased the rate of guilty verdicts to 72% in the second group. Discrediting the perceptions of the eyewitness had little impact, with 68% of jurors in the third group supporting a guilty verdict. I also described some of my then-recent studies showing that, in fact, eyewitness testimony is malleable, and leading questions can easily affect what witnesses remember and report. Finally, I talked about a case that I had worked on in which a woman was accused of murder on the basis of eyewitness memory. Perhaps it was due to her acquittal that lawyers began to call me to request case advice and invite me to speak at their conferences.

Attorneys also began asking me to testify in court on the malleability of eyewitness memory. However, at the time, judges were resistant to my work and typically excluded my testimony on the grounds that it invaded the province of the jury or that it was all common knowledge. When one judge finally agreed to let me testify, it came at a terrible time. I will never forget that day—June 3, 1975. My brother David called to tell me that our father had died that morning after a battle with melanoma. I had visited him only a couple of weeks before. I was still wiping away tears when the phone rang again. It was David Allen, a Seattle attorney, who asked me to come to the courthouse right away because it looked like the judge would admit my testimony. Could I really set aside my grief and do this? I somehow managed to collect myself and go to court. Judge Janice Neimi admitted my testimony into trial. Today, when prosecutors try to discredit me by asking how many times I have testified in court (translation: "you're a hired gun"), I often mention the exact date I first began testifying. Then the conversation goes something like this:

Prosecutor: I see you have no trouble remembering that date, even though you've been testifying about difficulties with memory.

Me: I remember that date because it was the day my father died.

Prosecutor: (silence)

I testified at three trials in 1975, five trials in 1976, and seven trials in 1977, and continued testifying at many trials each year. Despite the occasional harsh cross examination, I enjoyed testifying. I felt like I was helping people and spreading the truth about memory. Sometimes my experiences would give me ideas for additional research studies, and the cases were fascinating to my students, enlivening my lectures and writing. I wrote about some of these cases in my presidential address for the American Psychology-Law Society (Loftus 1986b). Some of my scholarship even examined my dual role as an expert witness and an experimental psychologist. Should this role involve being only an impartial educator? Or could it involve some element of advocacy (Loftus 1986a)?

Eventually, I coauthored a book about some of the cases in which I had testified and the role that memory science had played in them (Loftus & Ketcham 1991). My wonderful coauthor, Kathy Ketcham, had been my secretary for years while she was helping put her husband through school. She typed my papers and became fascinated by my work with memory in the process. She is now a successful writer. In writing *Witness for the Defense* (Loftus & Ketcham 1991), Ketcham and I drew material from trial transcripts, police reports, newspaper accounts, and interviews with witnesses, defendants, attorneys, jurors, and family members. We did our best to get accurate information but ultimately had to rely on the memories of people directly involved in the legal dramas, as well as on my own personal memories. We acknowledged in the author's note that "It is unavoidable that these retrospective interpretations will contain memory flaws" (Loftus & Ketcham 1991, p. xiv). Memory, we said, is not always the same thing as truth.

In *Witness for the Defense*, I wrote about some of the more unusual people I met along the way—people involved in criminal and civil cases in which memory was an issue. I've met notorious individuals such as Ted Bundy and Timothy McVeigh. I've also met famous people who got entangled in legal situations in which memory played a role. For example, in my 2007 autobiography (Loftus 2007a), I wrote about Oliver North and, briefly, Martha Stewart as well. I interviewed Martha in New York about a critical phone call with her stockbroker, in which, as she remembered, he told her about ImClone stock. The government thought she was lying when she said she didn't remember being told that the president was selling the stock. I wondered if distractions or other factors could have explained her lack of memory, so I asked her where she was when she received the call. She told me she was on a private plane heading to Mexico for a short vacation and took the call when the aircraft stopped to refuel in San Antonio.

EL: What were you doing just before the call?

MS: Eating lunch.

EL: What did you have for lunch?

MS: Smoked salmon, caviar, and vodka.

EL: Vodka? How much vodka?

MS: Couple of drinks.

EL: Well, two to three drinks are enough to affect the formation of new memories, unless there is some reason you don't want people to know that.

She insisted she didn't care one way or the other, and so the vodka theory was potentially to be offered at trial. When the trial began, her lawyers felt things were going so well that they cut short their defense and dropped the vodka theory. To what I'm sure was her great disappointment, she was convicted. But that one little-known fact might have changed the outcome of her case. I'm pleased to see her smiling face in many magazines today; she obviously bounced back and is a model for how one can hit bottom and survive, even thrive.

I've also met Phil Spector, the famous American music producer, who worked with the Beatles and other talented musicians. *Rolling Stone* magazine had him on their list of the greatest artists of all time. In 2009, he went on trial for murder in the shooting death of an actress in his California home. I testified at his trial about the memory issues surrounding what his driver claimed he had heard Spector say. A few days after testifying, Phil sent me a little card with this message: "Dr. Loftus. Thank you for your amazing and brilliant testimony. I am most grateful and appreciative, and you're prettier than Leslie Stahl." (He was referring to my then-recent interview by Stahl on *60 Minutes*, during which I temporarily tampered with her memory for faces. To her credit, she allowed her memory mistakes to be shown to millions of viewers.) The jury in Spector's case had to decide: Was the actress' death an accident or murder? Ultimately, my testimony did not help his case; he was convicted and began serving a prison sentence of 19 years to life.

THE MEMORY WARS

I was introduced in earnest to the notion of repressed memory in the early 1990s. It began with a phone call from a lawyer who was representing George Franklin, a man accused of murder based on a repressed memory. Franklin's daughter, Eileen, claimed she had recovered a terrible memory, in which she witnessed her dad kill her best friend 20 years earlier. I've written extensively about this case (Loftus 1993, Loftus & Ketcham 1994). At Franklin's trial, Eileen testified in great detail about watching the murder. A prominent psychiatrist vouched for the memory's authenticity. Franklin was convicted, much to my dismay and that of his attorneys and many family members. He became the first American citizen to be convicted of murder based on nothing more than a claim of repressed memory. Five years later, a federal judge reversed his conviction, concluding that the risk of an unreliable outcome was unacceptable.

Because of this case, I started to wonder how such detailed whole memories could grow in someone's mind despite the memories being completely false. If Eileen Franklin's memories were false, she was not simply remembering a detail differently, like a stop sign instead of a yield sign. She was remembering huge events (murders, years of rapes) that didn't happen. How could such elaborate false memories develop in people? I wanted to study this, but what type of false memory could I try to plant in people's minds? It did not seem likely that the Human Subjects Review Committee would appreciate a proposal to plant memories that the subject's father had killed their best friend or raped them repeatedly, so I had to find an analog, something that would have been at least mildly traumatic if it had actually happened to the subjects. Eventually, I had the idea to plant a memory that the subject had been lost in a shopping mall and, after a period of great upset, had been discovered by an elderly person and reunited with their family.[3]

This became our first effort to deliberately plant relatively harmless but rich false memories in volunteers. Along with other researchers, I have been quite successful in getting people to believe and remember that they had all sorts of experiences that would have been at least mildly troubling had they actually happened. Not only have we led ordinary healthy people to believe that they had

---

[3]The idea came to me unexpectedly after trying to solve this puzzle for a couple of years. I was being driven to the airport, after having given a talk at the University of Georgia, by a faculty member, Denise Park, and her two children. Explaining to my host my frustration with trying to think of a memory to plant, it was she who said, "How about getting lost?' We happened to be driving past a huge shopping mall, and the idea just popped into my head. "What about getting lost in a shopping mall?"

been lost in a shopping mall as a child (Loftus & Pickrell 1995), but we and other psychologists have also planted even more bizarre or unusual false memories, such as nearly drowning and being rescued by a lifeguard, witnessing demonic possession, or committing a crime as a teenager (for reviews of some of these memory planting findings, see Loftus 2003b, 2005; Loftus & Davis 2006). In the years after the Franklin case, thousands of other repressed memory cases emerged. The memories often revolved around severe sexual abuse. People were going into therapy with one sort of problem, such as depression or an eating disorder, and coming out with another problem: horrific memories of sexual abuse allegedly perpetrated over years and then repressed into the unconscious until the memory returned. People were suing their family and former neighbors, as well as their doctors, dentists, and teachers. Many families were destroyed in the process, and I found myself deep in the midst of these wars. I tried to speak out about these travesties, the dubious nature of repressed memories, and the injustice of convicting people of crimes based on these memories without additional evidence. I was met with a great deal of anger from people like Betty. The anger came from both the repressed memory patients, convinced of the veracity of their newly "recovered" memories, and the therapists who had helped these patients "find" their memories.

I could endure nasty letters and emails. I could handle death threats made to universities that invited me to speak. But I was not quite prepared for the lengthy battle I would face when I investigated a case that was being touted as solid "proof" of repressed memory, the case of Jane Doe. Jane Doe had accused her mother of sexual abuse when she was a child caught in the midst of an unpleasant divorce and custody battle. A psychiatrist videotaped the "retrieval" of this memory and showed the tapes to others discussing this new "proof." I investigated the case with Mel Guyer, a lawyer and psychologist from the University of Michigan. Our investigation suggested that it was quite possible that no abuse ever occurred to Jane Doe. However, when we published our findings in the *Skeptical Inquirer* (Loftus & Guyer 2002a,b) without identifying Jane Doe, a number of bad things happened. We shielded her identity, but Jane Doe sued us anyway, using her real name, Nicole Taus. She filed her case in 2003, asking for $1.3 million for defamation, invasion of privacy, and other claims. Over the ensuing years of litigation, a trio of California courts threw out 20 of the 21 allegations that she made against me and the other defendants.

My graduate seminar actually traveled from the University of California, Irvine to Los Angeles to watch the oral arguments being made to the California Supreme Court. It would have been a much more fascinating experience for me if there had not been so much personally at stake. Earlier courts had thrown out most of the claims, and the California Supreme Court tossed out all the rest but one. That one claim was that I had misrepresented myself to a foster mother of Taus, allegedly pretending I was a colleague and supervisor of the psychiatrist who was popularizing her case—a claim I completely deny. Ms. Taus's foster mother supported her story by also claiming that she abruptly terminated the interview when she realized my identity, which is not true. Photographs taken of us right after the interview showed the cordial nature of our interaction. Personally, I suspect that after our interview, she regretted what she had told me about Ms. Taus. (Journalists call this source remorse.)

After the California Supreme Court effectively finished gutting her case, Taus offered to withdraw her case against me in return for a payment of $7,500. I would have preferred to have a jury vindicate me, but the insurance company for the magazine decided that the cost of a trial would far exceed $7,500. Insurance companies have a label for this: nuisance settlement. The California Supreme Court also ordered the trial judge to determine how much Taus herself would have to pay for attorney fees and costs incurred by the other defendants who had been cleared of charges along the way. These included my coauthor, Mel Guyer; the *Skeptical Inquirer*, which had published our essay; and Carol Tavris, whom we had thanked in a footnote for her help with the essay.

The trial judge determined that Taus would be responsible for nearly $250,000 in attorney and court fees, and she declared bankruptcy soon after. So, what do I say when people ask me, "Who won the case?" No one won, except perhaps the attorneys; they were well compensated for their time.

During this protracted and miserable legal process, I learned a great deal about the vulnerability of academics to lawsuits. Scholars are not always afforded the full protection of constitutional guarantees, and this is especially true when the scholars work on problems that matter in people's lives and are therefore likely to be sources of controversy or conflict. But these are precisely the kinds of scholarly inquiries in which there is a profound need for our institutions to provide vigilant protection of free speech (Geis & Loftus 2009).

BACK TO RESEARCH

Despite the emotional and financial burden of the Taus complaint, I was able to develop a new line of research with Dan Bernstein, who was a postdoc at the time, and several graduate students at UC Irvine. We wanted to better understand the repercussions of implanted memories—how these false memories impact later thoughts, intentions, and behaviors. In our initial studies, we planted false memories in participants of having gotten sick eating particular foods, such as eggs, pickles, or strawberry ice cream, and found that the participants with the false memories didn't want to eat these foods as much as did participants without false memories (for details, see Bernstein et al. 2005a,b; for a review, see Loftus 2007a). In another study, we planted false memories of having gotten sick on vodka, and the participants were subsequently less interested in drinking a vodka drink. We also planted pleasant memories about white wine and found that people who developed the false memories were more attracted to white wine (Clifasefi et al. 2013, Mantonakis et al. 2013).

This research suggests that it can be disturbingly easy to manipulate people's memories in ways that shape their behavior, a finding that raises a number of ethical concerns. Should we think about banning the use of these mind-manipulating techniques entirely? Could we affirmatively and responsibly use these techniques to help people live happier and healthier lives? These basic ethical questions must be considered carefully in pursuing and applying this line of memory research.

THE TED TALK

By the end of 2012, when I was invited to give a TED talk on false memories (**Figure 2**), I had already been teaching for four decades. When I first started teaching, I wrote out my lectures word for word, even the jokes. Then, if I got nervous, I would have the notes to rely on. By 2012, I was pretty comfortable in the classroom and in front of large one-time audiences. But this did not prepare me for the kind of talk that would be required at TEDGlobal. First I had to submit an outline, and then a script. The TED organizers told me my script was too long for a 16-minute talk, and I had to cut it. When it got to an acceptable length, I began the work of memorizing it. After all, it would be on the Internet and translated into a large number of languages. Exact wording mattered in a way that it never really does in the classroom. I got help from my longtime collaborator, Maryanne Garry, and her students, who found much hipper slides to accompany the talk than I would have found on my own. A few months before the event, I rehearsed the talk via Skype with the TED organizers, and even then I was still reading. I practiced the talk in guest lectures that I volunteered to give for colleagues. To memorize the talk, I used the method of loci, a memorization method developed more than 2,000 years ago in ancient Greece. Specifically, I used familiar locations in my home to remember chunks of the talk. For example, I visualized

Figure 2

Photos of Elizabeth Loftus giving a TED talk at TEDGlobal in 2013. Photo credits: (*a*) J.D. Davidson/TED, (*b*) TED.

Steve Titus, a falsely accused man, greeting me at my front door. That reminded me to start the talk by telling the audience about the sad case of Steve Titus. I visually entered my house and noticed on my right a portrait that my mother-in-law had painted of me at the time I married her son: a reminder to tell them about myself and why I had worked on the Titus case. I noticed on my left a bowl of pine cones: Those became the hundreds of falsely accused people. In all, I placed eight chunks of my talk into eight locations in my home. When I wanted to remember the talk, I took a mental walk through the house, stopping at each location to pick up the chunk of the talk that I had mentally deposited there earlier.

In June 2013, I flew to Edinburgh, Scotland, thumb drive in tow. My former doctoral student Shari Berkowitz joined me for the five-day adventure. Nearly a thousand people had paid thousands of dollars to attend TEDGlobal. Shari and I met and ate and drank with some fascinating people, such as Shonda Rhimes, the wildly successful television producer, and Marlies Carruth, a scouter for the MacArthur Genius Award program. We watched other TED talks that were amazing, such as that given by Apollo Robbins, the American deception specialist, and Arthur Benjamin, the mathematician, who gave a splendid Mathemagic performance. We also watched a brilliant neuroscientist lose her train of thought in the middle of her talk and struggle to finish. My worst nightmare! In the end, I got through my talk without a hitch, and to my amazement the video of it has, as I write this, been viewed more than 2.8 million times (**http://www.ted.com/talks/elizabeth_loftus_the_fiction_of_memory**).

TED AND THE MEMORY WARS

Near the end of my TED Talk in Scotland, I offered the audience a simple take-home message: Just because someone tells you something with confidence, just because they say it with lots of detail, just because they express emotion when they say it, that doesn't mean that it really happened. We can't reliably distinguish true memories from false memories. This weakness in memory has implications for the legal profession, for psychotherapy, and for other aspects of our social lives. Personally, I feel that exposure to this research has made me more tolerant of the everyday memory mistakes and distortions made by my friends and family members. If a sibling or friend tells a story that I know is not accurate, I don't instantly assume they are deliberately fibbing; more typically, I start with the thought that they might have a genuine false memory. I apply the same attitude to public cases of potential lies. When celebrities such as Hillary Clinton or NBC News anchor Brian Williams are shredded by the press for telling inaccurate stories, I sometimes come to their defense with the possibility of a false memory. In the cases of both Clinton and Williams, the spontaneous creation of false memories seems far more plausible to me than the theory that they are deliberately lying, given that both of them told inaccurate stories that had a high chance of being disproven. They had a great deal to lose by lying but very little to gain. To me, this makes the possibility of a false memory in such cases more plausible than lying.

Just to be clear, I don't always assume that a purveyor of falsehoods is honestly mistaken or misremembering. Some people knowingly, consciously lie. Because my research has dramatically challenged the assumptions and therapeutic practices of many repressed-and-recovered-memory practitioners, some of them have repeatedly tried to kill the messenger—me—when they can't kill the data. For example, the Jane Doe case reared its ugly head again in 2014, when a journal published several essays about the case. Virtually all came from people who had found something to complain about in my handling of the case and who were primarily believers in recovered memories of abuse, which they had promoted in their own work for years. They were heavily invested in the Jane Doe story, because they believed it gave their cause credibility. They're entitled to their opinions, of course, but their essays were riddled with distortions of the evidence, which Mel Guyer and I had already addressed in previous publications (Loftus & Guyer 2002a,b). One commenter, whom I'll call K, used his essay as an opportunity to tell a lie about me that dates back two decades, when I resigned from membership in the American Psychological Association (APA) because of the mistreatment of two female colleagues and because of the APA's shift toward becoming more of a guild for practitioners than a home for psychological scientists. In my resignation letter, I wrote that I would be devoting myself to organizations that valued science more highly and more consistently, and I went on to become active in the Association for Psychological Science. At the time of my resignation from the APA, Ray Fowler, then the CEO, urged me to reconsider because he feared more experimental psychologists would join my exodus. But in K's Jane Doe essay, he claimed that Fowler had tipped me off about a pending ethics complaint so that I could resign in time to avoid it. This is a flat-out lie that Fowler himself denied before he died. This rumor still turns up when I'm on the witness stand, being interviewed by prosecutors trying to discredit me. I mention it because it is abhorrent to me when people pass out untruths for applause lines, for attention, or because they don't like scientific work that doesn't jibe with their orthodoxies. Fortunately, the nastiness of people like pants-on-fire K and his allies is outweighed by the Alices of the world.

UNIVERSITY LIFE

I love my job. A colleague once quipped, "Isn't academia great? You get to work any 80 hours a week you want." Yes, I work a lot of hours, but for the most part it is pretty enjoyable work. It's a near-perfect combination of structure and entrepreneurial opportunity. One of my favorite aspects is the interactions with the students, postdocs, and faculty collaborators who help me plan and conduct my research. I wish I had more space to mention them all.[4] I love hearing updates on the students' lives, such as when one becomes chair of a psychology department or another wins a teaching award at her liberal arts college. I like strategizing when one complains about

---

[4]In my 2007 autobiographical chapter, I listed the PhD students whose committees I had chaired or cochaired, ending with the 2006 dissertation of Cara Laney, who recently wrote to tell me that she was chairing the psychology department at her university. Since then, the list has grown to include terrific work by Suzanne Kaasa, Shari Berkowitz, Erin Morris, Tia Peterson, Kally Nelson (Enright), Steven Frenda, Rebecca Nichols, and Lawrence Patihis. Many more are in the pipeline.

being overworked and under-appreciated at her corporate research scientist position or when one complains about his status as a freeway flyer.

One aspect of my professional life that might be different than those of others is the gigantic number of requests for help I routinely receive from people outside the university setting. Some requests come from prisoners and desperate family members; I try to answer all of these. Then there are the weekly requests from far-away college students who want help with papers they are writing, from high school students who want help with assignments, and from elementary students who ask for help with science fair projects. Eighty hours a week isn't enough to answer them all, so I crafted a polite reply that I can easily send back with a few clicks on the keyboard:

> Thanks for your email. I'm so sorry I'm going to have to decline this project. I'm so swamped with work, I barely have time for the things I've already promised to do. So while this sounds exciting, I know I would have trouble meeting any additional obligations. I hope you understand. Best of luck to you and your project.

Sometimes I just couldn't bring myself to send the polite reply, as was the case when a middle school student in Weston, Connecticut, who seemed passionate about human memory, asked for my help. Although she was overly apologetic for intruding on my "busy schedule," she had some questions for me. While asking them, she managed to slip in the fact that her mother was a science reporter for the *New York Times*. I took the time to answer her questions about false memories, the role of trauma in memory, and the processes by which people store and recall memories. Her email arrived just a few months after her mother had written a terrific piece for the *Times* called "Memories Weaken Without Reinforcement," which reported on a new study providing evidence that when a new experience enters memory, it can weaken the ability to remember older experiences (Belluck 2015). This is an issue I had thought deeply about more than three decades ago (Loftus & Loftus 1980). It seemed so cute that the daughter, perhaps a budding science journalist herself, was following in her mother's footsteps, so I answered her right away.

In addition to the interactions with students and colleagues, another great thing about the academic lifestyle is the sabbatical. I used one of those opportunities to spend a year at Harvard University as an American Council on Education fellow working for the President of the university and the Dean of Harvard College. Another year, I spent my sabbatical at the Center for Advanced Study in the Behavioral Sciences at Stanford, where I wrote my first book, *Eyewitness Testimony* (Loftus 1979). I spent another leave at the Georgetown Law Center in Washington, DC, teaching law students and getting a feel for life as a law professor. I spent my last sabbatical in Irvine, using most of my time to write this article. It was not the only thing that I had hoped to accomplish during the sabbatical. My original plan was to spend some time in Tunisia. I had been invited to participate in the International Congress on Cognition, Emotion, and Motivation to be held in Tunisia. In fact, I had been invited not only to present my research at the conference but also to serve as Honorary Chair. I crafted a letter that was posted on the website welcoming people to this important conference, which was dedicated to the proposition that in order to fully understand how we manage everyday tasks in life, such as knowing how to order dinner at a favorite restaurant, or deciding whether to give a B or a B− to a student, or judging whether a defendant is guilty or not guilty, we need to integrate what scientists are discovering about cognition, emotion, and motivation. Tunisia, the furthest north of all countries in Africa, would have been an exciting place to gather and discuss these issues. How moving it would be to discuss psychology while also soaking up some of the geography, politics, and history of a country that held its first free elections only within the past few years. Sadly, I would never get to have this exciting and moving experience. Shortly after my travel plans were firmly in place, three terrorists attacked the Bardo

National Museum in Tunis, the capital city, taking hostages in the process. It was March 18, 2015, and more than 20 people, primarily tourists, were killed, and many others were injured. Three months later, on June 26, 2015, armed terrorists attacked two hotels in a tourist resort area not far from the city of Sousse in Tunisia, killing 40 people, also mostly tourists. These unexpected events likely contributed to the financial difficulties that the conference organizers experienced. In any event, funding was no longer available to bring me to Tunisia. I was able to deliver my presentation and to answer questions in November 2015 via videoconferencing from the terror-free safety of UC Irvine. But I never got the full experience of visiting a beautiful, progressive country that only gave women full legal status, so that they could run their own businesses, deposit money in their own bank accounts, and receive passports that would allow them to travel by themselves, about 50 years ago.

BRIEF CANDLES IN THE ROMANTIC DARK

My marriage to Geoff lasted for 23 years and ended in large part because of my workaholic ways. Happily, we have remained good friends and speak on the phone at least three times a year: on each of our birthdays and on the day of our wedding anniversary.[5]

Since Geoff, I've had a few romantic entanglements, some lasting for days and some for years. I spent time with corporate presidents, film producers, and successful lawyers and academics, but also with mailmen and bakers. I love the beginnings, when you share past memories as you're getting to know each other. I've used these opportunities to dredge up the past and to tell some favored stories, like the ones that had to do with maneuvering a difficult relationship with a stepmother. I cherish some of the wonderful things that have been said to me at the beginning of a new relationship, such as, "If I could make a woman from scratch, she'd be just like you." I've sometimes been the one to end things, but I've had my share of disappointed feelings when he's not as interested as I am. One of the worst breakup lines I have heard was, "When I was in college I dated women who were trim and fit, and, well, you're not that." I can laugh about it now—and even turned it into a Johnny Cochran line: "Trim and fit, and you're not it."

What I've learned is that female friends have the best intentions when they try to offer you an excuse for why he isn't calling, but their comforting words may not be the best medicine. As in the film *He's Just Not That into You*, well-meaning friends might say something like, "Maybe he lost your phone number." "He can't handle your emotional maturity." "You're too pretty; he can't handle that." The film opens with scenes of girlfriends giving these placating excuses to each other all over the world—England, Japan, India—but when I watched two women in Africa having this same conversation, I almost fell off my chair laughing. One woman is distraught that he wasn't calling, and her friend says, "Maybe he was eaten by a lion." After the chair stopped shaking, I thought more. Are these excuse-finding morsels simply helpful white lies that make a friend feel better? Perhaps not if, as my pal Carol Tavris cautioned me, they delay the process of accepting the truth and moving on in life. Maybe we should appreciate our friends when they resist the temptation to make us feel better by suggesting that he was eaten by a lion and tell us, straight, he's just not that into us. They are offering us removable truths—truths worth keeping, even if we temporarily remove them from our diaries.

---

[5] This reminds me of a most unusual Valentine's Day in 2016. Geoff and his lovely third wife, Willa, were visiting a college-going daughter, Emma, that he had with his second wife. Emma wanted to meet me. So Geoff took Wife 3, Wife 1, and the daughter of Wife 2 out for a delicious Italian meal. Just another modern American family!

MEMORY AND SOCIETY

One of the things I'm most pleased to see is how the public understanding about memory has changed, perhaps in part due to the scientific work that I and others have published and publicized. The common understanding that memory is often not reliable has permeated our culture in important ways. Judges who were once resistant to admitting expert testimony from memory scientists into court cases are now more willing to do so. Methods for gathering memory evidence in legal cases have changed, embracing reforms that can lead to greater accuracy. Psychotherapists have become more aware of problematic techniques that can lead their patients into false memories that wreak havoc on the lives of patients and those around them. You can see evidence of the changes in our view of memory over time in a study described in our paper "Are the Memory Wars Over?" (Patihis et al. 2014). It's a thrill for me to be reading some unrelated article in, say, the *New Yorker*, and see heartwarming proclamations, as happened twice in a single day while I was on a long airplane trip. I was catching up with my early 2016 issues of the *New Yorker* and read one piece about child welfare in which the author referred to the "sexual-abuse scandals of the eighties and the recovered-memory travesty of the nineties" (Lepore 2016), and another piece about the series *Making a Murderer* in which the author mentioned that "seventy-two percent of wrongful convictions involve a mistaken eyewitness" (Schulz 2016).

Of course, there is still much educating to do, and we can't remain complacent. While writing this article, the *New York Times* columnist David Brooks published an essay titled "The Year of Unearthed Memories" that made me cringe (Brooks 2015). Brooks has long been a champion for psychological science; he has embraced what our field has to offer and used it to help his readers understand politics, conflict, and even themselves. But in his 2015 essay, he touted worthless theories about how memory works, including the psychobabble that traumatic memories are buried deep in primitive regions of the brain, tucked underneath conscious awareness, yet leaking toxic waste into people's lives. Brooks tied these myths to global racism and oppression. My former postdoc and longtime collaborator, Maryanne Garry, and I wrote a complaining letter to the *Times* that they never published. My favorite part of our letter took Brooks to task for his poor use of metaphor, arguing that he was not helping the world "by drawing a parallel between the culturally-shaped, pseudoscientific operatic plot device that is repressed memory and the culturally-shared, very real burden of painful memories." As Brooks well knows, pseudoscience helped create the beliefs that support racism and oppression. Our short letter ended with a crucial message in three words: "Pseudoscience never helps."

And so, after all these years of studying how we as humans come to be visited by memories that aren't true, I end this review with a message from someone who seems to understand this well and can express it even better. In the words of Harold Pinter in *Old Times*: "The past is what you remember, imagine you remember, convince yourself you remember, or pretend you remember."

In that spirit, I hope this memoire consists more of what I remember than of what I imagine or pretend to remember. But you never know.

DISCLOSURE STATEMENT

The author is not aware of any affiliations, memberships, funding, or financial holdings that might be perceived as affecting the objectivity of this review.

ACKNOWLEDGEMENTS

I would like to thank the many students and colleagues who have helped with my research and publications; even if I didn't have the space to name you all, I deeply appreciate your contributions to our efforts to eavesdrop on memory. I would also like to thank my family and friends, who provided comfort in difficult times. Those times gave me a small taste of the human suffering endured by the falsely accused people I've had a chance to meet.

LITERATURE CITED

Belluck P. 2015. Memories weaken without reinforcement, study finds. *The New York Times*, March 17, p. A8

Bernstein DM, Laney C, Morris EK, Loftus EF. 2005a. False memories about food can lead to food avoidance. *Soc. Cogn.* 23:10–33

Bernstein DM, Laney C, Morris EK, Loftus EF. 2005b. False beliefs about fattening foods can have healthy consequences. *PNAS* 102:13724–31

Bernstein DM, Loftus EF. 2009. How to tell if a particular memory is true or false. *Perspect. Psychol. Sci.* 4:370–74

Brooks D. 2015. The year of unearthed memories. *The New York Times*, Dec. 15, p. A35

Clifasefi SL, Bernstein DB, Mantonakis A, Loftus EF. 2013. "Queasy does it": False alcohol beliefs and memories lead to diminished alcohol preferences. *Acta Psychol.* 143:14–19

Collins AM, Loftus EF. 1975. A spreading activation theory of semantic processing. *Psychol. Rev.* 82:407–28

Fishman EF, Keller L, Atkinson RC. 1968. Massed versus distributed practice in computerized spelling drills. *J. Educ. Psychol.* 59:290–96

Freedman JL, Loftus EF. 1971. Retrieval of words from long-term memory. *J. Verbal Learn. Verbal Behav.* 10:107–15

Frenda SJ, Berkowitz SR, Loftus EF, Fenn KM. 2016. Sleep deprivation and false confessions. *PNAS* 113:2047–50

Frenda SJ, Nichols RM, Loftus EF. 2011. Current issues and advances in misinformation research. *Curr. Dir. Psychol. Sci.* 20:20–23

Frenda SJ, Patihis L, Loftus EF, Lewis HC, Fenn KM. 2014. Sleep deprivation and false memories. *Psychol. Sci.* 25:1674–81

Geis G, Loftus EF. 2009. *Taus v. Loftus*: determining the legal ground rules for scholarly inquiry. *J. Forensic Psychol. Pract.* 9:147–62

Lepore J. 2016. Baby Doe: a political history of tragedy. *The New Yorker*, Feb. 1, **http://www.newyorker.com/magazine/2016/02/01/baby-doe**

Loftus EF. 1974. Reconstructing memory: the incredible eyewitness. *Psychol. Today* 8:116–19

Loftus EF. 1975. Leading questions and the eyewitness report. *Cogn. Psychol.* 7:560–72

Loftus EF. 1979. *Eyewitness Testimony*. Cambridge, MA: Harvard Univ. Press

Loftus EF. 1986a. Experimental psychologist as advocate or impartial educator. *Law Hum. Behav.* 10:63–78

Loftus EF. 1986b. Ten years in the life of an expert witness. *Law Hum. Behav.* 10:241–63

Loftus EF. 1992. When a lie becomes memory's truth. *Curr. Dir. Psychol. Sci.* 1:121–23

Loftus EF. 1993. The reality of repressed memories. *Am. Psychol.* 48:518–37

Loftus EF. 2003a. Dear Mother: facing the loss of a parent. *Psychol. Today*, May 1, pp.68–70

Loftus EF. 2003b. Make-believe memories. *Am. Psychol.* 58:864–73

Loftus EF. 2005. Planting misinformation in the human mind: a 30-year investigation of the malleability of memory. *Learn. Mem.* 12:361–66

Loftus EF. 2007a. Elizabeth F. Loftus (autobiography). In *History of Psychology in Autobiography*, Vol. IX, ed. G Lindzey, M Runyan, pp. 198–227. Washington, DC: Am. Psychol. Assoc. Press

Loftus EF. 2007b. Memory distortions: problems solved and unsolved. In *Do Justice and Let the Skies Fall: Elizabeth Loftus and her Contributions to Science, Law and Academic Freedom*, ed. M Garry, H Hayne, pp. 1–14. Mahwah, NJ: Lawrence Erlbaum Assoc.

Loftus EF, Davis D. 2006. Recovered memories. *Annu. Rev. Clin. Psychol.* 2:469–98

Loftus EF, Freedman JL. 1972. Effect of category-name frequency on the speed of naming an instance of the category. *J. Verbal Learn. Verbal Behav.* 11:343–47

Loftus EF, Guyer M. 2002a. Who abused Jane Doe? The hazards of the single case history. Part I. *Skept. Inq.* 26(3):24–32

Loftus EF, Guyer MJ. 2002b. Who abused Jane Doe? The hazards of the single case history. Part II. *Skept. Inq.* 26(4):37–40

Loftus EF, Hoffman HG. 1989. Misinformation and memory: the creation of memory. *J. Exp. Psychol. Gen.* 118:100–4

Loftus EF, Ketcham K. 1991. *Witness for the Defense: The Accused, the Eyewitness, and the Expert Who Puts Memory on Trial.* New York: St. Martin's Press

Loftus EF, Ketcham K. 1994. *The Myth of Repressed Memory.* New York: St. Martin's Press

Loftus EF, Levidow B, Duensing S. 1992. Who remembers best? Individual differences in memory for events that occurred in a science museum. *Appl. Cogn. Psychol.* 6:93–107

Loftus EF, Loftus GR. 1980. On the permanence of stored information in the human brain. *Am. Psychol.* 35:409–20

Loftus EF, Palmer JC. 1974. Reconstruction of automobile destruction: an example of the interaction between language and memory. *J. Verbal Learn. Verbal Behav.* 13:585–89

Loftus EF, Pickrell JE. 1995. The formation of false memories. *Psychiatr. Ann.* 25:720–25

Loftus EF, Suppes P. 1972. Structural variables that determine problem-solving difficulty in computer-assisted instruction. *J. Educ. Psychol.* 63:531–42

Mantonakis A, Wudarzewski A, Bernstein DM, Clifasefi SL, Loftus EF. 2013. False beliefs can shape current consumption. *Psychology* 4:302–8

Patihis L, Frenda SJ, LePort AKR, Petersen N, Nichols RM, et al. 2013. False memories in highly superior autobiographical memory individuals. *PNAS* 110:20947–52

Patihis L, Ho LY, Tingen IW, Lilienfeld SO, Loftus EF. 2014. Are the "memory wars" over? A scientist-practitioner gap in beliefs about repressed memory. *Psychol. Sci.* 25:519–30

Schulz K. 2016. Dead certainty: how "Making a Murderer" goes wrong. *The New Yorker*, Jan. 25, **http://www.newyorker.com/magazine/2016/01/25/dead-certainty**

Zhu B, Chen C, Loftus EF, He Q, Chen C, et al. 2012. Brief exposure to misinformation can lead to long-term false memories. *Appl. Cogn. Psychol.* 26:301–7

Zhu B, Chen C, Loftus EF, Lin C, He Q, et al. 2010. Individual differences in false memory from misinformation: cognitive factors. *Memory* 18:543–55

Memory: Organization and Control

Howard Eichenbaum

Center for Memory and Brain, Boston University, Boston, Massachusetts 02215;
email: hbe@bu.edu

Annu. Rev. Psychol. 2017. 68:19–45

First published online as a Review in Advance on
September 28, 2016

The *Annual Review of Psychology* is online at
psych.annualreviews.org

This article's doi:
10.1146/annurev-psych-010416-044131

Keywords

memory, cognitive control, hippocampus, prefrontal cortex

Abstract

A major goal of memory research is to understand how cognitive processes
in memory are supported at the level of brain systems and network representations. Especially promising in this direction are new findings in humans
and animals that converge in indicating a key role for the hippocampus in
the systematic organization of memories. New findings also indicate that the
prefrontal cortex may play an equally important role in the active control
of memory organization during both encoding and retrieval. Observations
about the dialog between the hippocampus and prefrontal cortex provide new
insights into the operation of the larger brain system that serves memory.

Contents

INTRODUCTION

There is a long history of tension between the view that memories are stored independently as individual associations and the idea that new information is integrated within systematic organizational structures. In the first half of the 20th century, the association and organization views of memory came into conflict in battles between the characterizations of stimulus-response learning (c.f. Spence 1950) and cognitive maps (Tolman 1948), and the distinction was highlighted in Bartlett's (1932) and Piaget's (1928) ideas on memory organization in schemas. Critics described the organizational views proposed at that time as vague, but the pioneers of modern cognitive science proposed specific forms of systematic organization in which memories are embedded (e.g., Bower 1970, Collins & Quillian 1969, Mandler 1972; see also Holland 2008). Of particular relevance to this review, Mandler (1972, 2011) proposed three types of memory organization (**Figure 1**): an associative structure in which multiple events are linked by direct and indirect associations within a network, a sequential structure involving a temporal organization of serial events, and a schematic structure involving a hierarchical or similarly complex organization of items in memory (Mandler used different names for these organizations). Mandler did not attempt to explain the brain mechanisms that underlie these structures and had no expectation that these organizations could be directly observed. Instead, he based his theory of their existence on results from cleverly designed studies that identified types of memory organization by their consequences in memory

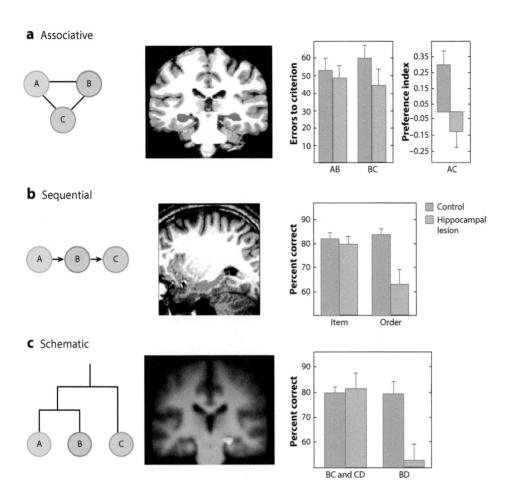

a Associative

b Sequential

c Schematic

Figure 1

Three forms of memory organization and the role of the hippocampus in humans and animals. (*Left column*) Elements A, B, and C are related in ways specific to each type of organization. (*Middle column*) Hippocampal activation in (*a*) associative (Zeithamova et al. 2012), (*b*) sequential (Ezzyat & Davachi 2014), and (*c*) schematic (Zalesak & Heckers 2009) memory organizations. (*Right column*) Graphs depicting the results in memory performance of rats with hippocampal lesions compared to a control group without lesions. (*a*) Rats with hippocampal lesions succeed in learning individual elements and associations (AB and BC) but fail in linking indirectly related elements in an associative organization (reflected in the low preference for the indirectly related element association AC) (Bunsey & Eichenbaum 1996). (*b*) Rats with hippocampal lesions succeed in remembering items in a list but fail in remembering the order of the items in the sequential organization (Fortin et al. 2002). (*c*) Rats with hippocampal lesions succeed in learning trained choices of all pairings in a five-item hierarchy (A–E; B over C and C over D are shown) but fail in inferring relations between indirectly related elements (B and D) in a hierarchical schematic organization (Dusek & Eichenbaum 1997).

judgments. In this review, I argue that new approaches in neuroscience are revealing these organizational structures within neural networks and identifying distinct brain mechanisms that guide encoding and retrieval of information within these organizations. A full understanding of how the brain organizes and controls memory requires a synthesis of findings in humans, in which we can best characterize these organizations and identify the key brain areas involved, with findings in animal models, in which we can examine how networks of neurons—the elements of information processing—support the organization and control processes.

Beginning in the latter half of the twentieth century, neuroscientific research revealed that the hippocampus is the hub of a brain system that supports memory organization. This article begins with an overview of the type of memory organization that is dependent on the hippocampus, then focuses on recent analyses of hippocampal neuronal activity patterns that provide insights about the nature of memory organizations supported by the hippocampus. I then consider additional evidence that memory organization is actively controlled by the prefrontal cortex via its interactions with the hippocampus. Parallels between the findings of behavioral and physiological studies in humans and animals and the resulting conceptual advances about the organization and control of memory by these brain areas are highlighted.

THE HIPPOCAMPUS AND MEMORY ORGANIZATION

In describing the type of memory that is supported by the hippocampus, researchers have emphasized important features of memory impairment in humans with amnesia consequent to hippocampal region damage. Memory dependent on the hippocampal region has been characterized as "declarative" (Cohen & Squire 1980, p. 209) and "explicit" (Graf & Schacter 1985, p. 501), terms that highlight our capacity to remember specific events and facts through direct efforts to access memories via conscious recollection. Characterization of the cognitive processes involved in memory dependent on the hippocampus has distinguished the ability to recognize a previously experienced stimulus via recollection of the stimulus in the context of other information associated with the experience from a sense of familiarity with the stimulus independent of the context in which it was experienced (reviewed in Eichenbaum et al. 2007, Yonelinas & Parks 2007). Furthermore, Tulving (1972) distinguished episodic memory, the ability to recall specific personal experiences that occur in a unique spatial and temporal context, from semantic memory, the accumulated knowledge about the world abstracted from many experiences and not dependent on any specific event during which the information was obtained. Episodic memory is severely impaired following hippocampal damage, even under conditions in which semantic memory is relatively intact (Vargha-Khadem et al. 1997), although the acquisition of new semantic memories is also impaired following hippocampal damage (Bayley et al. 2008, Gabrieli et al. 1988, O'Kane et al. 2004).

Research has also demonstrated properties of recollection that are dependent on the hippocampus in animals. Conscious recollection, typically observed through subjective report in humans, is beyond direct access in animals. However, there are objective measures of memory performance supported by recollection in humans that have been applied to validate animal models of recollection-based memory. One approach examines recognition memory through an analysis of receiver operating characteristics (ROCs) in which subjects study a list of items and are then tested on a larger list. On the larger list, subjects identify old items that were on the original list and new items that were not. The proportion of correct identifications of old items (hits) is compared to the proportion of incorrect identifications of new items as old (false alarms) across a wide range of response biases (Macmillan & Creelman 2005). The ROC function from these data is typically characterized by two prominent dimensions that distinguish recollection and familiarity (for a detailed description, see Yonelinas 2001). Applying the same basic experimental design in an animal model, research has demonstrated that the ROC function for recognition memory in rats is similar to that observed in humans (**Figure 2**) (Fortin et al. 2004; for a review, see Eichenbaum et al. 2010). Furthermore, the ROCs favor recollection in rats under the same conditions that favor recollection in humans (Sauvage et al. 2008); the same is true for conditions favoring familiarity (Sauvage et al. 2010), thus validating the animal model.

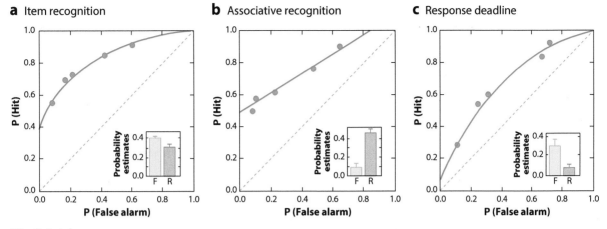

a Item recognition   **b** Associative recognition   **c** Response deadline

F Familiarity index
R Recollection index

Figure 2

Receiver operating characteristic (ROC) analysis of performance on variants of recognition memory in rats. (*a*) Item recognition. The ROC function is characterized by both an offset in the *y* intercept and bowing of the ROC curve, which is strikingly similar to the ROC function for item recognition in humans (Fortin et al. 2004). (*b*) Associative recognition. The ROCs for item pairs are characterized by loss of the bowing of the ROC function while the offset of the *y* intercept is maintained, as is the case when humans are tested in recognition of word pairs (Sauvage et al. 2008). (*c*) Response deadline. When subjects are required to respond rapidly, the offset in the *y* intercept of the ROC is lost and the curvilinear shape is maintained, as is also the case in humans (Sauvage et al. 2010).

Importantly, considerable evidence indicates that the recollection component of the ROCs is differentially impaired by hippocampal damage in humans (reviewed in Eichenbaum et al. 2007, Yonelinas & Parks 2007; for an alternative perspective that focuses on the different contents of memories in recollection and familiarity, see Wixted & Squire 2011). This deficit is also observed in rats such that damage to the hippocampus in rats selectively impairs recollection-based performance, whereas lesions to another part of the medial temporal lobe (the amygdala) selectively impairs familiarity-based performance, confirming in animals the importance of the medial temporal lobe in these features of memory and providing an anatomical double-dissociation of recollection and familiarity processes (Sauvage et al. 2008, 2010; also see Bowles et al. 2007). These observations support the view that the fundamental cognitive processes that underlie recollection and its dependence on the hippocampus are conserved across species.

Notably, Mandler (1972) was among the first to distinguish the two processes in recognition memory that we now call recollection and familiarity. He argued that the most important distinction between these processes is that familiarity for an individual item occurs via the integration of featural elements that compose a single percept, whereas recollection of an item occurs via elaboration of its associates within their organizational structure. In this review, I argue that Mandler's three organizational structures (**Figure 1**) provide a good characterization of the nature of hippocampus-dependent recollective memory.

Associative Organization

In ROC analyses, a demand for memory of specific associations is imposed by using a study list composed of word pairs (e.g., army–table, baseball–saddle) and then testing the ability of the subject to distinguish old pairings (army–table) from new rearranged pairings of the same words (army–saddle). This manipulation strengthens the reliance on recollection of the specific associations for the word pairs because all of the individual words are used in the study phase and are thus equally familiar in the test phase. As a consequence, the ROC function becomes exclusively recollection based in both humans (using word pairs) and animals (using odor pairs), and performance is dramatically impaired following hippocampal damage (Sauvage et al. 2008, Yonelinas & Parks 2007).

In addition to associations between specific items, Mandler (1972) also recognized associations between each item and the larger context of associations into which it fits. Thus, for example, studies on recognition typically employ highly familiar words such that the test does not ask whether one recognizes each word per se (typically all the words are highly familiar) but rather whether one recognizes each word within the context of the studied list. This feature of associative organization in recognition is particularly relevant in a naturalistic test of recognition of items in context that measures the preferential exploration of novel over familiar objects in context in humans and monkeys (Pascalis et al. 2004). In this task, the subject first briefly studies a novel object within a visual context and then, after a delay, is presented with the same object and a new object to view. Humans typically spend more time looking at a novel object than a familiar one, and this simple form of recognition depends on the hippocampus (Pascalis et al. 2004). Importantly, the same test can be applied in monkeys; these studies have shown that the novelty preference depends on the objects being presented in the same background visual context, showing that the object memory is context dependent (Bachevalier et al. 2015). Hippocampal damage also severely impairs this preferential viewing effect in monkeys (Nemanic et al. 2004, Zola et al. 2000), but this deficit occurs only in context-dependent recognition (Bachevalier et al. 2015). In a version of the test developed for rodents, subjects initially explore duplicates of a novel object in a familiar environment and then, following a delay, are presented with one of those objects and a new object replacing the duplicate. Most studies have reported no effect from hippocampal damage when the object is presented in the same context as the original experience. However, hippocampal lesions do impair the ability to identify an object taken out of its context, as is reflected by preferential exploration of a familiar object in a novel spatial context or even in a novel place in the familiar environment, or the ability to identify an object presented out of the initially experienced order of multiple objects, consistent with memory for temporal context being a defining feature of hippocampus-dependent memory (Eacott & Norman 2004, Langston & Wood 2010; see also Cohen et al. 2013).

The associative transitivity test assesses Mandler's (1972) characterization of associative organization structure as a set of items that are directly and indirectly linked such that cuing by a subset of items supports the ability to recall the entire set, an ability known as associative inference. In this test, subjects are trained on associations between pairs of objects that share a common element (AB and BC) and then tested for the existence of the associative network (ABC) via assessment of knowledge about the indirectly related elements (AC). In both humans and animals, the hippocampus is not essential to training on individual associations (AB and BC) but plays a critical role in probe tests in which subjects must infer relations between indirectly related elements (AC) (**Figure 1a**; Bunsey & Eichenbaum 1996, Preston et al. 2004).

Sequential Organization

As introduced by Tulving (1972), episodic memories are defined by the temporal organization of the events that compose personal experiences. There is substantial evidence that the hippocampus is activated in association with memory for temporal order in humans (Howard et al. 2014; reviewed in Eichenbaum 2014). Numerous studies have reported hippocampal activation associated with successful memory for sequences of faces or objects, reconstruction of the order of scenes in a movie clip, identification of items out of order in a familiar sequence, and bridging of a temporal gap between ordered stimuli (**Figure 1*b***; reviewed in Eichenbaum 2014). Correspondingly, selective hippocampal damage in humans results in deficits in remembering the order of words in a list (Mayes et al. 2001) and the order of objects visited in a virtual environment (Spiers et al. 2001) even when recognition memory for individual words and objects was intact.

As in humans, selective hippocampal damage in animals results in impairments in memory for the order of studied object stimuli even when the same animals could recognize the individual stimuli (Fortin et al. 2002, Kesner et al. 2002). In these experiments, animals are presented in each trial with a unique series of odor stimuli, then, following a delay, they are required to judge which of a pair of stimuli arbitrarily selected from the list occurred earlier. Normal rats perform well at the task, but rats with hippocampal damage fail (**Figure 1*b***). Control tests showed that animals with hippocampal damage could distinguish and identify the individual odors on the list even when they could not remember the order in which they had appeared. This contrast strikingly reveals that memory for order is a defining feature of hippocampal memory function in animals, as it is in humans (see also Ergorul & Eichenbaum 2004).

Schematic Organization

Although many tests of semantic memory involve remembering individual facts, it is well known that factual knowledge is embedded within schematic organizations (e.g., Collins & Quillian 1969, Piaget 1928). Studies on human hippocampal function in semantic organization have focused on tasks that require the subject to learn multiple associations or choices between objects when different associations or choice pairings share common elements. The studies then test for a representation that integrates learning about all of the objects by probing for knowledge about indirect relations among elements never experienced together. In some studies, subjects learn a set of overlapping choice problems (choose A over B, B over C, C over D, and D over E) and show acquisition of a hierarchical schematic organization (A over B over C over D over E) by appropriate choices on a probe test of transitive inference between newer experience pairs (e.g., B over D). In both humans and animals, the hippocampus is not essential to learning the individual problems but plays a critical role in probe tests that reveal the establishment of a schematic organization (**Figure 1*c***; Dusek & Eichenbaum 1997, Zalesak & Heckers 2009). In another test, called transverse patterning, subjects are tested for the ability to learn a set of overlapping pairwise choices (choose A over B, B over C, and C over A). Humans and animals with hippocampal damage can learn two unambiguous pairs (e.g., A over B, B over C), but not the full set, which requires a circular schematic organization (Dusek & Eichenbaum 1998, Rickard et al. 2006).

HOW ARE MEMORIES ORGANIZED BY NEURAL NETWORKS WITHIN THE HIPPOCAMPUS?

To begin thinking about how neural networks might support memory organization, we can consider Hebb's (1949) proposal about cell assemblies and phase sequences. Hebb theorized that the unit of perceptual and memory processing was the cell assembly, a set of locally interconnected neurons in which the efficacy of connections was increased when they were activated during a specific event and whose coordinated activity thus represented the concept of that event. Hebb went on to propose that associative learning is based on a linking of cell assemblies via shared neuronal elements and that such a set of overlapping cell assemblies formed a phase sequence. Furthermore, Hebb proposed that networks of concept representations can be organized through shared elements of a larger set of cell assemblies. In his generic example, Hebb described three cell assemblies that were pairwise associated by overlapping elements such that the phase sequences could support an inference between concepts in two cell assemblies that were only indirectly linked by overlapping elements of separate associates. These ideas are being realized in findings, described below, that show how neural networks in the hippocampus support memory for associated items within a context, memory for the order of serially presented items, and memory for a hierarchical structure.

How can we employ Hebb's model to explore memory organization by cell assemblies in real neural networks? Techniques have been developed that examine the activity of populations of neurons, as measured by functional magnetic resonance imaging (fMRI) and by multielectrode single-neuron recording in an approach called representational similarity analysis (RSA) (Kriegeskorte et al. 2008). One popular version of this approach begins by constructing population vectors from the blood-oxygen-level-dependent (BOLD) signal of a large array of voxels [often called multivoxel pattern analysis (MVPA)] or from the firing rates of a set of single neurons within a brain area (Haxby et al. 2014). Population vectors taken under different experimental conditions are then compared by simple correlations (e.g., Pearson's r) that measure the degree of similarity, which is interpreted as reflecting the extent of overlap between cell assemblies that represent specific events. RSA is now widely used in brain imaging studies to test whether activity patterns evoked during the encoding of memories are reinstated during a subsequent delay or retrieval test and whether activity patterns reflect specific memories as associated by similarity in activation patterns or as serially organized by temporally correlated patterns.

In addition, RSA has been further employed in some studies to reveal hierarchical organizations of neural network representation. To accomplish this, the measures of similarity of population vectors for different events are compared and organized to reveal the overall structure of linkages between events. When two events evoke similar population patterns, the functional networks are viewed as close in representational space, forming a very tight phase sequence. When the events evoke less-correlated population patterns, the networks are farther apart in representational space, reflecting indirectly linked cell assemblies; when the events evoke uncorrelated population patterns, the networks are independent. These measures of distances in representational space can then be compared to identify hierarchical structures of organization. This approach has been very successful in revealing the organization of perceptual categories in cortical areas using RSA on fMRI or single-neuron recording data. For example, RSA of multivoxel fMRIs of ventral temporal cortex responses has been employed to identify the hierarchical structure of a representation of the phylogenetic scale (Connolly et al. 2012), and RSA of many single-neuron responses in the temporal cortices of monkeys has been employed to identify a hierarchical organization of representations of species and body parts (Kiani et al. 2007). This approach has also been applied to the organization of memories by the hippocampus, as described in the following sections.

Neural Network Representation of Associative Organizations

Studies on human memory using fMRI have shown that activation of the hippocampus predicts successful memory encoding of face–name (Sperling et al. 2003, Zeineh et al. 2003), face–house (Henke et al. 1997), and word–word associations (Henke et al. 1999) and that even single neurons in the human hippocampus encode specific item–item associations (Ison et al. 2015). Notably, the hippocampus is activated in association with successful memory for both item–item and item–context associations, and the magnitude of hippocampal activation is correlated with the number of associations bound in the memory (Staresina & Davachi 2008).

In addition, considerable evidence shows that specific stimuli are encoded with the spatial context of their experience within the human hippocampus. For example, when human subjects recalled imagined scenes that applied to specific verbal items, the hippocampal activation reflected recall of the item and scene rather than the item alone (Davachi et al. 2003). In a more recent study using RSA, Libby et al. (2014) scanned subjects as they performed a working-memory task that demanded memory for locations of objects presented on a screen. Successful memory was associated with maintenance during the delay of the same hippocampal activation pattern observed during encoding. Supporting theories about the importance of context coding, RSA studies have shown that successful memory is associated with reinstatement of the representation of the relevant spatial or temporal context occupied by the item during initial study (Flegal et al. 2014, Kyle et al. 2015; for reviews, see Davachi 2006, Eichenbaum et al. 2007) and with increased dissimilarity of spatial and temporal context representations between memories (Copara et al. 2014).

Zeithamova et al. (2012) built on Mandler's (1972) assertion that associative organization supports memory for indirect as well as direct associations between elements using Preston and colleagues' (2004) paradigm, in which subjects learn overlapping pairwise associations between objects (e.g., AB and BC) from which they can make inferences between indirectly related elements (AC) (see also Bunsey & Eichenbaum 1996). Zeithamova et al. (2012) used RSA to show that learning the second, overlapping pair (BC) reinstates the specific hippocampal representation of the earlier learned pair (AB) and that this content-specific hippocampal activation signals subsequent success in judgments about the indirect association. These findings indicate that the development of associational networks depends on reinstatement of preexisting associations into which the new information is assimilated and show that the subsequent interleaved network supports novel inferences from memory. A study in which subjects learned partially overlapping associations produced a similar result; in this study, hippocampal activation predicted subsequent integration of these pairings, as revealed by generalization across never-paired but indirectly associated items (Shohamy & Wagner 2008).

Numerous studies on animals report that hippocampal neurons activate during the exploration of specific objects at particular places, suggesting that representations of events are embedded within the spatial firing patterns (place fields) of those neurons. For example, following tone-cued fear conditioning, hippocampal neurons come to be driven by the conditioned tone stimulus when the animal is within the place field of that neuron (Moita et al. 2003). In addition, in rats performing a variant of the novel object exploration task, hippocampal neurons fire in association with specific objects and their familiarity, which are embedded within the spatial firing patterns of these neurons (Manns & Eichenbaum 2009). In rats performing a context-guided object–reward association task, hippocampal neurons fire when animals sample specific objects within particular locations and spatial contexts (Komorowski et al. 2009). These and other studies (e.g., Tse et al. 2007) suggest that the hippocampus associates events within a spatial contextual framework. At the same time, when multiple events share features other than neighborliness within space, a more complex organizational structure emerges (see the section Neural Network Representation of Schematic Organizations; McKenzie et al. 2014, 2016).

Neural Network Representation of Sequential Organizations

RSA of hippocampal activation during sequence memory has revealed that pattern similarity across items in a list is associated with subsequent successful order memory (DuBrow & Davachi 2014). Ezzyat & Davachi (2014) tested whether hippocampal networks could also bridge associations between distinct events that occurred in the same or different contexts (scenes). In this task, subjects report that objects appearing across a contextual boundary are more separated in time than objects appearing within the same context, even when the actual temporal separation is the same. Pattern similarity in hippocampal activation for object cues presented across contexts was correlated with subjects reporting closer temporal proximity, suggesting that the hippocampus binds events across time independent of visual context boundaries. Another study has shown a broad gradient of similarity in hippocampal representations across long periods of time (Nielson et al. 2015), although different mechanisms may support within-experience and between-experience representations (Davachi & DuBrow 2015). In addition, Hsieh et al. (2014) reported that pattern similarity in hippocampal activation signaled the combination of object and temporal position information in sequence learning, indicating that hippocampal activation patterns encode specific items and the order in which they occur (**Figure 3a**). Furthermore, hippocampal activation predicts an accurate estimate of the chronological order of stimuli in a list (Jenkins & Ranganath, 2010). In studies of hippocampal neuronal activity in humans, neurons fire in sequence in association with learning (Paz et al. 2010) and memory (Gelbard-Sagiv et al. 2008) of the flow of events experienced in movie clips.

There is also growing evidence that memory for the flow of events in experiences is mediated directly by representations of time and order in hippocampal neurons in animals (reviewed in Eichenbaum 2014). One study showed that neural ensemble activity patterns in the hippocampus gradually change as rats sample sequences of odors and that this signal of a continuously evolving temporal context predicted success in remembering the odor sequence (Manns et al. 2007). Furthermore, several studies have identified hippocampal principal neurons that fire at a particular moment in time during a temporally structured event (Kraus et al. 2013, Naya & Suzuki 2011, Pastalkova et al. 2008). These time cells compose temporal maps of specific experiences that represent the flow of temporal context and the memories contained within, parallel to the way place cells organize events within a spatial context. In these studies, the location of the animal is held constant or firing patterns associated with elapsed time are distinguished from those associated with spatial and behavioral variables, and the firing patterns of these cells are dependent on the duration of the critical events. Time cells have been observed in a variety of behavioral paradigms that involve bridging a temporal gap, including delay periods in maze tasks, bridging of temporal gaps between associated nonspatial cues, and trace eyelid conditioning (reviewed in Eichenbaum 2014). Furthermore, some of these studies have demonstrated close links between the emergence of time cell sequences and the encoding of specific memories, as well as subsequent memory performance (**Figure 3b**).

Importantly, in some of these studies, the animal is immobilized, and thus space plays no role in ongoing behavior or memory. Nevertheless, the role of the hippocampus in organizing events in time extends even to spatial memories and spatial representations. Thus, in rats performing a spatial alternation task in a T-maze, place cells fire differently depending on whether the animal is executing a left-turn or right-turn trial, even as animals traverse the portion of maze where these routes overlap (reviewed in Shapiro et al. 2006). Furthermore, the activation of these route-specific spatial representations predicts accurate memory performance (Robitsek et al. 2013).

Neural Network Representation of Schematic Organizations

Since the publication of the work of Piaget (1928) and Bartlett (1932), we have known that memories are not stored in isolation but rather are integrated into schematic organizations from which we can extract both direct and indirect associations that are linked via structural rules. The simplest organizations of schematic memories are the associative organizations discussed above (Schlichting & Preston 2016, Zeithamova et al. 2012). In this section, I consider more complex schematic organizations in which the links between elements are operations rather than simple associations.

In an experiment involving the integration of experiences in a naturalistic situation, subjects studied distinct animated scenes that partially overlapped in the inclusion of specific persons,

a Human fMRI

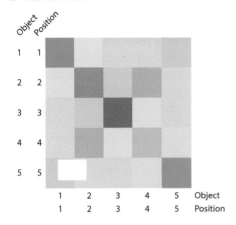

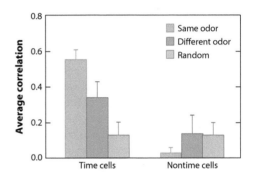

b Rat single neurons

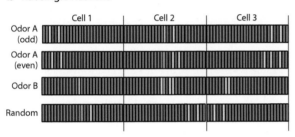

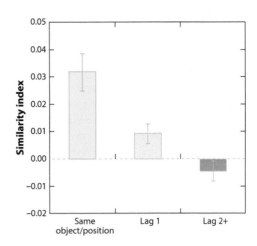

Figure 3

Representational similarity analysis (RSA) of sequential organization in the hippocampus of humans and rats. (*a*) In a human fMRI (*left*), the correlation matrix shows pattern similarity across repetitions of combinations of object and temporal position sequences. The warmest colors, representing the highest similarity for repetition of each object/position element, gradually become cooler with the decreased similarity between elements that are successively more separated. Similarity scores (*right*) are also shown gradually decreasing with increasing temporal distance. Panel adapted with permission from Hsieh et al. (2014). (*b*) In rat single-neuron recordings, animals were required to remember an odor (A or B) that began each trial and match it to an odor presented after a delay. (*Left*) Idealized sequences of binned firing rates of three idealized hippocampal neurons; red indicates a high firing rate, yellow a lower firing rate, and blue no activity. To measure representational similarity for trials beginning with identical odors (e.g., odor A trials), average population vectors for odd- and even-numbered trials are cross-correlated. To measure representational similarity for trials beginning with different odors (A versus B), average population vectors for A trials and B trials are cross-correlated. These correlations were compared to correlations for random ordering of the neurons' activity patterns. (*Right*) The greatest similarity occurred in trials beginning with the same odor. Less, but still above random, similarity occurred for different odors, indicating both coding of temporal organization of each trial type and coding of the general temporal structure common to all trials. Temporal coding was observed in neurons whose activity was temporally modulated but not in cells whose activity was not temporally modulated (nontime cells). Panel adapted with permission from MacDonald et al. (2013).

objects, or scenes of a room, and could thus eventually be integrated into connected narratives that compose the flow of the scenes in time and space (Milivojevic et al. 2015). After the successful integration of the scenes, RSA identified new patterns of hippocampal activation that were more similar than the patterns observed before the integration, indicating a merging of cell assemblies associated with the building of knowledge that integrates the scenes (Milivojevic et al. 2015).

In subjects performing a more complex weather prediction task, Kumaran et al. (2009) reported hippocampal activation associated with abstract knowledge about cue relationships that applied as well to novel stimuli that were linked by the same conceptual relations.

In a yet more complex task, Tavares et al. (2015) designed a role-playing game in which their subjects moved to a new town and sought a job and apartment. To accomplish this, the participants interacted with local people through different responses allowing them to comply with a character's demand or make demands, thereby increasing or decreasing the power of the character, and engage or not engage in personal conversation and physical interaction, thereby increasing or decreasing affiliation with the character. Thus, the composite outcomes of these social interactions positioned each character along axes of power and affiliation, constituting a vector describing the subject's relationship to each character in social space. Tavares et al. then scanned the subjects and found that the fMRI signal in the hippocampus correlated with the vector angle, indicating that the hippocampal network identified each character's position in social space as an interaction of their power and affiliation relations. These findings indicate that the hippocampus plays an important role in the integration of distinct social episodes into a schematic organization along specific relevant dimensions.

In animals, RSA using measures of similarity in neural population coding can also be employed to characterize the organization of multiple memories within the hippocampus. McKenzie et al. (2014) trained rats on a context-dependent object–reward association task in which the rats shuttled between two spatial contexts, in each of which the same two object stimuli (A and B) were presented in one of two positions (**Figure 4a**). Object A was rewarded in one context and object B in the other, such that the rats were required to use the context to guide learning and retrieval of each object–reward association. Subsequently, the animals were trained on the same task with an additional pair of objects, C, which was rewarded in the same context as A, and D, which was rewarded in the same context as B; they were then tested with both pairs of objects. To characterize the structure of the neural network representation for all 16 distinct events (four objects in each of two positions within each of two contexts), similarities between neural population firing patterns in the hippocampus were measured for all pairwise comparisons between events and a hierarchical analysis was applied to iteratively cluster event representations and reveal the organization of the memories. This analysis revealed a highly systematic organization of the hippocampal representations of distinct events (McKenzie et al. 2014). **Figure 4b** illustrates the relationships between representations of each of the events (x axis) as linked (y axis) by specific task dimensions. At the top of this hierarchy, events that occur in different contexts are widely separated in representational space, indicated by anticorrelation between events that occur in different contexts, positioning context as the highest superordinate dimension. Within each context-based network, events are moderately separated by positions within a context, i.e., positions are subordinate to contexts. Next, within each position representation, events that involve different reward valences are associated by positive correlation, and within each reward valence, different objects are associated. Notably, RSA revealed an emergent network representation of the organization of memories that animals acquire in the task that could not be observed from single-neuron firing patterns.

Further insight into the mechanisms by which new information is integrated into an existing schematic organization comes from consideration of the course of learning in this study. RSA on the data from an early stage of training, when only objects A and B were included, showed that the basic organization of those object representations was fully established prior to learning about C and D. When C and D were learned the next day, the hierarchical organization rapidly assimilated the new memories by elaborating only the lowest level of the hierarchy (McKenzie et al. 2014). Notably, within this organization, event representations that were closest together in representational space (A and C, B and D; **Figure 4b**) were never experienced in the same trial.

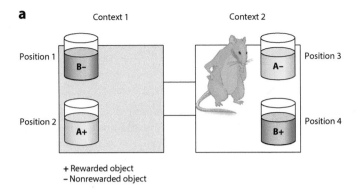

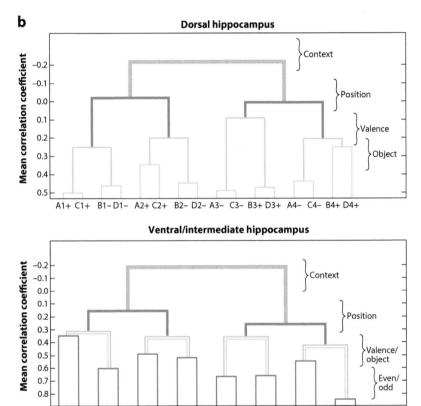

Figure 4

Representational similarity analysis (RSA) of related object memories in the hippocampus of rats.
(*a*) Context-guided object–reward association task. Rats choose between objects A and B in either of two positions in each context. Note that object–reward associations are opposite in the two contexts. Objects were positioned as shown within each context or in the reverse positions in different trials. (*b*) RSA measuring hierarchical ordering of representational similarities (*y* axis) of the 16 object memories (*x* axis). The specific task dimensions are listed on the right. In trials of the dorsal hippocampus (*top graph*), the animals were tested with C and D objects as well as with A and B objects, allowing the distinction of reward valences and object identities, whereas in trials of the ventral and intermediate hippocampus (*bottom graph*) only A and B stimuli were used, so comparisons for identical trial types were made on odd and even numbered trials. Figure adapted with permission from McKenzie et al. (2016).

However, the proximity of their representations in the organization is likely to support strong indirect associations between these items. These findings are consistent with observations from fMRI studies in humans that reveal an integration of new memories into preexisting network representations (Milivojevic et al. 2015, Zeithamova et al. 2012).

A Topography of Organizational Structure

Other studies have extended the observations on memory organization to suggest that there may exist an anatomical topography of the specificity of memory organization within the hippocampus. In the study described in the preceding section, the populations of neurons that encode specific events in particular places in each context were recorded from the dorsal hippocampus. In contrast to those firing patterns, another study showed that the neurons in the ventral hippocampus gradually acquire more generalized representations of events within one of the contexts and that neural ensembles in the ventral hippocampus outperform those in the dorsal hippocampus in discriminating between the contexts in which events occurred (**Figure 5a**; Komorowski et al. 2013). RSA of population firing patterns showed greater similarity of object and position representations in the hierarchical organization of ventral as compared with dorsal hippocampal networks (**Figure 4b**).

Consistent with these observations, studies using a version of RSA to analyze functional imaging patterns in humans have shown that, in a paradigm in which subjects build a narrative from overlapping story elements (as introduced in the preceding section), specific associations (AB and BC) were most strongly represented in the posterior hippocampus (equivalent to the dorsal hippocampus in rodents) and the representation of the full network was more strongly represented in the anterior hippocampus (equivalent to the ventral hippocampus in rats) (**Figure 5b**; Collin et al. 2015). Similarly, in the associative inference paradigm, RSA showed that the posterior hippocampus distinguishes specific learned associations (AB and BC) by using different representations for A and C, whereas the anterior hippocampus integrates these associations by using similarity of A and C representations (Schlichting et al. 2015). Furthermore, whereas the posterior hippocampus is differentially activated during retrieval of the specific details of events in autobiographical memories, the anterior hippocampus is differentially activated during the retrieval of the general context of those memories (Evensmoen et al. 2013).

These and related findings have led to the recent proposal that the dorsal-ventral (posterior-anterior in humans) axis of the hippocampus may contain a topography of more specific to more general features of memories (for reviews, see Poppenk et al. 2013, Strange et al. 2014). Notably, the outputs of the hippocampus to the prefrontal cortex arise in the ventral (anterior in humans) hippocampus, suggesting that these generalized representations provide the prefrontal cortex with information that characterizes the context of a set of related memories. This information may play a major role in prefrontal control of memory organization, as will be discussed in the following sections.

THE COGNITIVE CONTROL OF MEMORY BY THE PREFRONTAL CORTEX

The organization and retrieval of memories is not an automatic or passive product of experience but instead involves distinct control processes that actively guide the encoding and retrieval of memories. Among these active processes are prefrontal–hippocampal interactions, which may direct the structure and selective retrieval of information from memory organizations. In the following sections I consider evidence that interactions between the prefrontal cortex and hippocampus are essential to memory and that the role of the prefrontal cortex is to direct the encoding and retrieval of memory representations in the hippocampus.

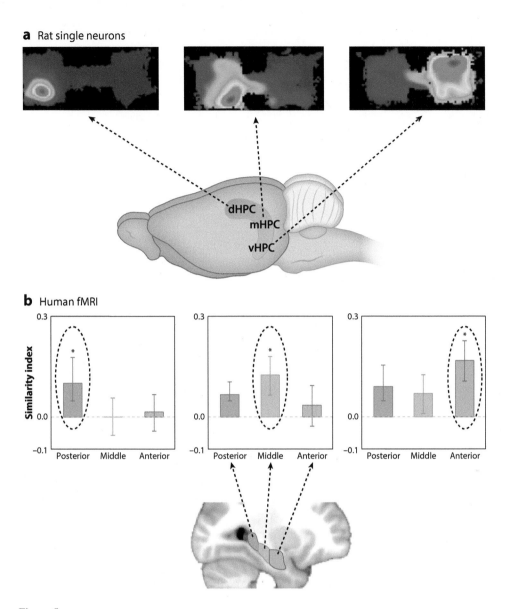

a Rat single neurons

b Human fMRI

Figure 5

Topography of specificity and generality of representations along the long axis of the hippocampus. (*a*) The size of the place fields of hippocampal neurons (as well as the specificity of object and position coding) was graded along the long axis of the hippocampus in rats performing a context-guided object–reward association task. (*Top*) Outline of the two contexts and a typical place field in each panel. Warmer colors indicate higher firing rates. Blue indicates the area of each context explored. (*Bottom*) Areas where place fields of different size are found in the dHPC, mHPC, or vHPC. (*b*) The representational similarities of different scales of association were graded along the long axis of the hippocampus in humans performing an associative inference task. The posterior hippocampus had the highest similarity for one direct association (AB), the middle hippocampus had the highest similarity for both direct associations (AB and BC), and the anterior hippocampus had the highest similarity for the full network of associations (AB, BC, and AC). Panel *b* adapted with permission from Collin et al. (2015). Abbreviations: dHPC, dorsal hippocampus; mHPC, middle hippocampus; vHPC, ventral hippocampus.

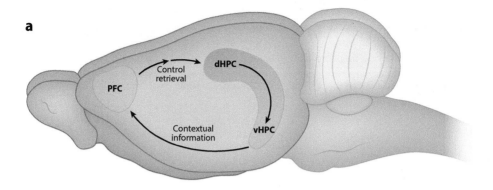

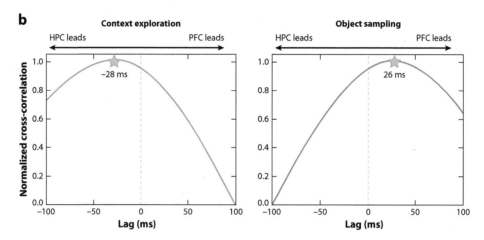

Figure 6

Model of prefrontal–hippocampal interactions in memory. (*a*) The PFC receives direction projections from the vHPC (in rats; anterior HPC in humans) and projects indirectly (via the perirhinal and entorhinal cortices) to the HPC. In this model, when one is cued by context to recall memories, contextual cues are processed by the vHPC, which sends this information to the PFC, which then biases the retrieval of the context-appropriate memories in the dHPC. (*b*) Direction of the flow of information was determined by correlating the amplitude of the theta rhythm in the HPC and PFC across a range of time shifts between the two signals. These correlations reveal that during the exploration of the spatial context, information processing in the HPC leads that in the PFC, whereas during the sampling of the objects, the flow of information reverses, such that the PFC leads the HPC. Abbreviations: dHPC, dorsal hippocampus; HPC, hippocampus; PFC, prefrontal cortex; vHPC, ventral hippocampus.

The Prefrontal Cortex and Hippocampus Work Together in Support of Memory

There are strong anatomical connections between the prefrontal cortex and hippocampus consistent with the view that the prefrontal cortex and hippocampus operate interactively in support of memory (**Figure 6***a*) (for a review, see Simons & Spiers 2003). In humans, functional imaging studies have demonstrated correlations between hippocampal and prefrontal activity in a variety of memory tasks (e.g., Brassen et al. 2006, Bunge et al. 2004, Dickerson et al. 2007, Zeithamova et al. 2012; for a review, see Ritchey et al. 2015). In monkeys, synchronization of theta and beta band oscillations is modulated by trial outcome in a paired associate learning task (Brincat & Miller 2015). In rats, several studies have shown that accurate memory performance in delayed nonmatching to sample is associated with synchronization of prefrontal neural ensembles with hippocampal theta activity (Benchenane et al. 2010, Hyman et al. 2005, Sigurdsson et al. 2010).

Demonstrating the importance of these physiological interactions, lesions that disconnect the prefrontal cortex from the hippocampus impair object–place and object–order memory (Barker et al. 2007). Similarly, lesions that disconnect the prefrontal cortex from the hippocampus result in severe impairment in conditional visual discrimination learning in monkeys (Parker & Gaffan 1998). Taken together, these studies provide evidence from multiple approaches in humans, monkeys, and rats that the prefrontal and hippocampal regions interact in the service of memory. But what is the nature of the conversation between the prefrontal cortex and hippocampus reflected in the physiological and functional interactions between these areas?

The Prefrontal Cortex Performs a Specific Role in the Control of Memory

Considerable converging evidence indicates that the prefrontal cortex contributes to memory through cognitive or strategic control over memory retrieval processes within other brain areas (Anderson & Weaver 2009, Buckner & Wheeler 2001, Dobbins et al. 2002, Kuhl & Wagner 2009, Miller & Cohen 2001, Moscovitch 1992, Postle 2006, Ranganath & Blumenfeld 2008). In humans, evidence indicates that areas of the prefrontal cortex are involved in establishing the organization of relationships among memories and in monitoring retrieval, and functional imaging data have indicated that the memory impairment caused by prefrontal damage can be characterized as a deficit in the suppression of interfering memories. Consistent with this view, patients with prefrontal damage do not have severe impairments in standard tests of event memory. However, deficits resulting from prefrontal damage are apparent when memory for target information must be obtained under conditions of memory interference or distraction. For example, individuals with prefrontal damage successfully learn a set of paired associations (AB) but are severely impaired in learning new associates of original elements (AC), and the impairment is marked by intrusions of the original associations (Shimamura et al. 1995). Similarly, in prefrontal cortex–damaged patients learning two lists of unrelated associations, memory for one list is compromised by intrusions from the other, suggesting that the prefrontal cortex controls memory retrieval by selecting memories relevant to the current context and suppressing irrelevant memories (Depue 2012).

Although the specific homologies between human and animal prefrontal areas are not clear (Vertes 2006), there is substantial evidence that the role of the prefrontal cortex in the control of memory is conserved across mammalian species. Studies on monkeys and rats have extended the classic findings on prefrontal function in set switching determined via the Wisconsin Card Sorting test in humans, showing that prefrontal damage results in severe impairment in animals in switching between learned perceptual sets (Birrell & Brown 2000, Dias et al. 1996). Several studies have also shown that the rodent prefrontal cortex is critical to rule-guided switching between memory strategies (Brown & Bowman 2002, Durstewitz et al. 2010, Marquis et al. 2007, Ragozzino et al. 2003, Rich & Shapiro 2007).

Complementary studies on neuronal activity patterns support the idea that the prefrontal cortex acquires representations of behavioral contexts that determine appropriate memory retrieval. Miller and colleagues (reviewed in Miller 1999, Miller & Cohen 2001) have demonstrated in monkeys the importance of the prefrontal cortex in acquiring prefrontal neural representations that guide perceptions, actions, and cognitive rules. In rats, neuronal ensembles in the prefrontal cortex fire distinctly in different behavioral contexts (Hyman et al. 2012), and patterns of neural activity are altered following a change in contingencies (Durstewitz et al. 2010, Karlsson et al. 2012). In a study directly related to the strategy-switching experiments cited above, Rich & Shapiro (2009) observed that prefrontal neuronal activity patterns predict switching between remembering place and response strategies in the domain of spatial memory. These and other findings have led to a view that the hippocampus creates organizations of memories, whereas the prefrontal cortex extracts a common set of ongoing task rules that govern the selection of memories within the hippocampal organization.

The Mechanism of Prefrontal Control Is Suppression of Competing Memories

Additional evidence suggests that the prefrontal cortex employs contextual representations to control the retrieval of detailed memories in the hippocampus by suppression of context-inappropriate memories. For example, in a study that examined intrusion errors in recognition memory, researchers found that prefrontal damage resulted in a selective increase in false alarms from previous learning in recollection-like memory in rats performing a recognition task, similar to the observation of intrusion errors by humans in the AB versus AC problem described in the preceding section (Farovik et al. 2008). Further evidence for suppression of context-inappropriate memories comes from the studies described in the section Neural Network Representation of Schematic Organizations in which rats used each of two spatial contexts to guide retrieval of otherwise contradictory object–reward associations. In rats performing this task, neurons in the dorsal part of the hippocampus encode these memories as selective firing to specific objects in particular places in each spatial context (**Figure 4b**; Komorowski et al. 2009). However, when the prefrontal cortex is inactivated, dorsal hippocampal neurons indiscriminately retrieve both appropriate and inappropriate object memory representations (Navawongse & Eichenbaum 2013). This observation indicates that the hippocampus is capable of retrieving memories even in the absence of prefrontal input but that the role of the prefrontal cortex is to select the appropriate memory for that context by suppressing alternative representations.

Bidirectional Hippocampal–Prefrontal Interactions Support Context-Guided Memory

The ventral hippocampus projects directly to the prefrontal cortex (Swanson et al. 1978), providing a powerful and immediate route for hippocampal representations of meaningfully distinct spatial contexts to arrive in the prefrontal cortex. This observation, combined with the findings described in the preceding section, suggests a model of bidirectional hippocampal–prefrontal interactions that support memory encoding and context-dependent memory retrieval (**Figure 6a**). According to this model, closely related events that occur within a single context, as well as environmental cues that define the context, are processed by the ventral (anterior in humans) hippocampus as a collection of features and events that define the particular context in which those events occur. This context-defining information is sent via direct projections to the prefrontal cortex, where neural ensembles develop distinct representations that can distinguish contextual rules during the course of learning. When subjects are subsequently cued with the same context, ventral hippocampal signals carrying the contextual information are sent directly to the prefrontal cortex, which then engages the appropriate rules to support retrieval of the context-appropriate memory representations in the dorsal (posterior in humans) hippocampus by suppressing context-inappropriate memories. The dialog between the hippocampus and prefrontal cortex suggested by this model is supported by the recent observations of functional connectivity between the hippocampus and prefrontal cortex in rats performing the context-guided object memory task described in **Figure 6b**. When rats enter a spatial context, hippocampal networks send information about the context to the prefrontal cortex, whereas when the animal subsequently evaluates the object choices, prefrontal networks send information to the hippocampus, presumably to guide retrieval of the appropriate memories (Place et al. 2016).

Prefrontal Control Over the Development and Updating of Memory Organizations

In addition to its role in retrieving memories, cognitive control by the prefrontal cortex may also support the development and updating of memory organizations by guiding the integration of new memories into the organization of preexisting knowledge (Preston & Eichenbaum 2013). McClelland et al. (1995) proposed that new memories are initially represented within the hippocampus and subsequently become interleaved into the semantic organization of existing related memories in the neocortex. This interleaving process incorporates new memories and typically requires modification of the preexisting network structure to add the new memories, consistent with Piaget's (1928) views on assimilation of new information and accommodation of the existing knowledge structure to integrate the new information.

Several studies have reported that the integration of memories into knowledge organizations relies on the prefrontal cortex. In particular, the prefrontal cortex plays an essential role in the acquisition of schematic organizations and in making inferences between indirectly related memories (DeVito et al. 2010). Tse et al. (2011) also showed that prefrontal areas are involved in rapid assimilation of new food–location associations into an organization of preexisting memories of other food locations in the same environment. Conversely, Richards et al. (2014) showed that prefrontal inactivation blocked sensitivity of hippocampal representations to reorganization when the subject was presented with conflicting spatial patterns. In humans, the prefrontal cortex is activated during assimilation of new memories within a schematic organization (Wendelken & Bunge 2010); is essential to transitive inference (Koscik & Tranel 2012); and is activated during assimilation of new memories, inference between indirectly related memories (Zeithamova & Preston 2010, Zeithamova et al. 2012), and updating of a memory organization (Milivojevic et al. 2015). Together, the findings in rodents and humans indicate that the prefrontal cortex plays an important role during integration of new information as well as memory retrieval from schematic organizations.

ORGANIZATION AND CONTROL OF MEMORY: CONCLUDING COMMENTS

Organization of Memories by the Hippocampus

The findings on memory organization discussed in this review share much in common with Tolman's (1948) conception of a cognitive map as a systematic organization of information across multiple domains of life, supporting flexible expression of acquired knowledge in purposeful behavior. O'Keefe & Nadel's (1978) model introduced the idea that cognitive maps are supported by the hippocampus, but later work has focused entirely on how the hippocampus specifically supports geographical maps as they are employed to navigate physical environments. However, Tolman's conceptualization provides a framework for research that would reveal a more comprehensive understanding of hippocampal function in the cognitive maps that organize memories more generally, and several studies have provided evidence that the notion of cognitive maps extends to a broad range of dimensions (Buzsaki & Moser 2013, Eichenbaum & Cohen 2014, Milivojevic & Doeller 2013, Schiller et al. 2015). These findings have inspired a reconciliation of divergent views about the role of the hippocampus in spatial navigation versus memory by revealing the common mechanisms that underlie both functions (Eichenbaum & Cohen 2014, Schiller et al. 2015).

It is also important to consider that all of the forms of memory organization described in this review may be based simply on spatial and temporal contiguities that underlie organizational structures in general. In the 1990s, my colleagues and I proposed that the nature of hippocampal representation is fundamentally relational and can be envisioned as a network of memories—a memory space—that links conceptually distinct events to form a framework of relevant associational dimensions, including spatial and temporal relationships and, potentially, all relationships between events that we experience (Eichenbaum et al. 1992, 1999). Furthermore, we proposed that activation of a subset of elements within a relational network leads to activation of other elements, including those only indirectly connected with the original activated elements. This gives rise to an important property of hippocampus-dependent memory: the ability to use memory flexibly to guide performance in diverse situations outside repetition of the learning event, a property we called representational flexibility. These properties are readily apparent in the examples of associative, sequential, and schematic organization described in this review.

Within this framework, the studies on spatial firing characteristics of hippocampal region neurons in animals can be viewed as both a metaphor and an example of a memory space and can shed light on the mechanisms of this memory space. Thus, the findings on coding of location, direction, speed, and borders by hippocampal region neurons have led some to suggest that the hippocampal system reconciles path integration signals from movement through the representation of physical space with current viewpoints to support navigation (e.g., Cheung et al. 2012, Knierim et al. 2013, Moser et al. 2008); these concepts could apply as broadly to the flexible expression of organized knowledge in any memory organization. Within the framework proposed here, the same computations may reconcile thoughtful movement through a memory space with perception of current events in support of flexible prediction of succeeding events.

Control of Organization and Retrieval from the Memory Organization

The mechanisms of prefrontal control over memory organization could operate via the resolution of conflicts between new experiences and existing memory organization. When new experiences occur, they usually conflict in some way with preexisting associations. For example, in the associative inference paradigm (**Figure 1a**), the preexisting association between B and A is challenged when the subject learns that B is now also (or instead) associated with C. Success in integration of new memories into an already established organization requires some degree of reorganization of the existing structure. The prefrontal cortex could support memory integration by generating the most relevant established structure for reconciliation of the conflicting new information. The key to understanding hippocampal and prefrontal contributions to memory organization therefore lies in understanding how these regions support the representations of new events based on the degree to which those events relate to prior knowledge and how the conflicts in new and existing knowledge are reconciled (Preston & Eichenbaum 2013).

SUMMARY POINTS

1. Two major processes that characterize declarative memory are the elaborate organization of networks of memories supported by the hippocampus and the control of encoding and retrieval of information in the organization by the prefrontal cortex.

2. The hippocampus plays an essential role in memory organization in humans and animals. Correspondingly, networks of neurons in the hippocampus encode associations between events in context, sequential associations that characterize episodes, and complex (e.g., hierarchical) organizations of related memories.

3. The prefrontal cortex supports the cognitive control of memory by developing representations that employ current contextual cues to select context-appropriate memory representations, primarily by suppressing context-inappropriate memories.

4. Context-appropriate retrieval may be supported by a dialog between the hippocampus and prefrontal cortex in which the ventral (in rodents; anterior in humans) hippocampus sends contextual information to the prefrontal cortex, which then identifies contextual rules that direct retrieval of specific memory representations in the hippocampus.

FUTURE ISSUES

1. The full range of memory organization supported by the hippocampus is unknown. Current work highlights spatial and temporal organization, but other findings suggest that the hippocampus supports any systematic dimension of organization (Schiller et al. 2015). In particular, it remains to be determined whether spatial mapping and memory views of hippocampal function can be merged by identifying firing properties of hippocampal region neurons that code direction, speed, and other dimensions of movement through a memory organization.

2. The structure of representations of contexts and rules by networks of neurons in the prefrontal cortex is poorly understood. Current evidence shows distinct network patterns associated with ongoing rules, but the way in which features of rules are represented is unknown.

3. Although there is considerable evidence of a dialog between the hippocampus and prefrontal cortex, it remains unclear how network representations in these areas interact to influence one another. It has yet to be determined how a hippocampal context representation changes rule-related activity in the prefrontal cortex and how prefrontal rule-related activity influences hippocampal memory representations.

DISCLOSURE STATEMENT

The author is not aware of any affiliations, memberships, funding, or financial holdings that might be perceived as affecting the objectivity of this review.

ACKNOWLEDGMENTS

The author's work is supported by National Institute of Mental Health grants MH094263, MH051570, MH52090, and MH095297.

LITERATURE CITED

Anderson MC, Weaver C. 2009. Inhibitory control over action and memory. In *Encyclopedia of Neuroscience*, ed. L Squire, pp. 153–63. Amsterdam, Neth.: Elsevier

Bachevalier J, Nemanic S, Alvarado MC. 2015. The influence of context on recognition memory in monkeys: effects of hippocampal, parahippocampal, and perirhinal lesions. *Behav. Brain Res.* 285:89–98

Barker GRI, Bird F, Alexander V, Warburton EC. 2007. Recognition memory for objects, place, and temporal order: a disconnection analysis of the role of the medial prefrontal cortex and perirhinal cortex. *J. Neurosci.* 27:2948–57

Bartlett FC. 1932. *Remembering.* London: Cambridge Univ. Press

Bayley PJ, O'Reilly RC, Curran T, Squire LR. 2008. New semantic learning in patients with large medial temporal lobe lesions. *Hippocampus* 8:575–83

Benchenane K, Peyrache A, Khamassi M, Tierney PL, Gioanni Y, et al. 2010. Coherent theta oscillations and reorganization of spike timing in the hippocampal-prefrontal network upon learning. *Neuron* 66:921–36

Birrell JM, Brown VJ. 2000. Medial frontal cortex mediates perceptual attentional set shifting in the rat. *J. Neurosci.* 20:4320–24

Bower GH. 1970. Organizational factors in human memory. *Cogn. Psychol.* 1:18–46

Bowles B, Crupi C, Mirsattari SM, Pigott SE, Parrent AG, et al. 2007. Impaired familiarity with reserved recollection after anterior-temporal lobe resection that spares the hippocampus. *PNAS* 104:16382–87

Brassen S, Weber-Fahr W, Sommer T, Lahrnbeck JT, Braus DF. 2006. Research report: Hippocampal-prefrontal encoding activation predicts whether words can be successfully recalled or only recognized. *Behav. Brain Res.* 171:271–78

Brincat SL, Miller EK. 2015. Frequency-specific hippocampal-prefrontal interactions during associative learning. *Nat. Neurosci.* 18:576–81

Brown VJ, Bowman EM. 2002. Rodent models of prefrontal cortical function. *Trends Neurosci.* 25:340–43

Buckner RL, Wheeler ME. 2001. The cognitive neuroscience of remembering. *Nat. Rev. Neurosci.* 2:624–34

Bunge SA, Burrows B, Wagner AD. 2004. Prefrontal and hippocampal contributions to visual associative recognition: interactions between cognitive control and episodic retrieval. *Brain Cogn.* 56:141–52

Bunsey M, Eichenbaum H. 1996. Conservation of hippocampal memory function in rats and humans. *Nature* 379:255–57

Buzsaki G, Moser EI. 2013. Memory, navigation and theta rhythm in the hippocampal-entorhinal system. *Nat. Neurosci.* 16:130–38

Cheung A, Ball D, Milford M, Wyeth G, Wiles J. 2012. Maintaining a cognitive map in darkness: the need to fuse boundary knowledge with path integration. *PLOS Comput. Biol.* 8(8):e1002651

Cohen NJ, Squire LR. 1980. Preserved learning and retention of a pattern-analyzing skill in amnesia: dissociation of knowing how and knowing that. *Science* 210:207–10

Cohen SJ, Munchow AH, Rios LM, Zhang G, Asgeirsdottir HN, Stackman RW. 2013. The rodent hippocampus is essential for nonspatial object memory. *Curr. Biol.* 23:1685–90

Collin SH, Milivojevic B, Doeller CF. 2015. Memory hierarchies map onto the hippocampal long axis in humans. *Nat. Neurosci.* 18:1562–64

Collins AM, Quillian MR. 1969. Retrieval time from semantic memory. *J. Verbal Learn. Verbal Behav.* 8:240–47

Connolly AC, Guntupalli JS, Gors J, Hanke M, Halchenko YO, et al. 2012. The representation of biological classes in the human brain. *J. Neurosci.* 32:2608–18

Copara MS, Hassan AS, Kyle CT, Libby LA, Ranganath C, Ekstrom AD. 2014. Complementary roles of human hippocampal subregions during retrieval of spatiotemporal context. *J. Neurosci.* 34:6834–42

Davachi L. 2006. Item, context and relational episodic encoding in humans. *Curr. Opin. Neurobiol.* 16:693–700

Davachi L, DuBrow S. 2015. How the hippocampus preserves order: the role of prediction and context. *Trends Cogn. Sci.* 19:92–99

Davachi L, Mitchell JP, Wagner AD. 2003. Multiple routes to memory: Distinct medial temporal lobe processes build item and source memories. *PNAS* 100:2157–62

Depue BE. 2012. A neuroanatomical model of prefrontal inhibitory modulation of memory retrieval. *Neurosci. Biobehav. Rev.* 36:1382–99

DeVito LM, Lykken C, Kanter BR, Eichenbaum H. 2010. Prefrontal cortex: role in acquisition of overlapping associations and transitive inference. *Learn. Mem.* 17:161–67

Dias R, Robbins TW, Roberts AC. 1996. Dissociation in prefrontal cortex of affective and attentional shifts. *Nature* 380:69–72

Dickerson BC, Miller SL, Greve DN, Dale AM, Albert MS, et al. 2007. Prefrontal-hippocampal-fusiform activity during encoding predicts intraindividual differences in free recall ability: an event-related functional-anatomic MRI study. *Hippocampus* 17:1060–70

Dobbins IG, Foley H, Schacter DL, Wagner AD. 2002. Executive control during episodic retrieval: Multiple prefrontal processes subserve source memory. *Neuron* 35:989–96

DuBrow S, Davachi L. 2014. Temporal memory is shaped by encoding stability and intervening item reactivation. *J. Neurosci.* 34:13998–4005

Durstewitz D, Vittoz NM, Floresco SB, Seamans JK. 2010. Abrupt transitions between prefrontal neural ensemble states accompany behavioral transitions during rule learning. *Neuron* 66:438–48

Dusek JA, Eichenbaum H. 1997. The hippocampus and memory for orderly stimulus relations. *PNAS* 94:7109–14

Dusek JA, Eichenbaum H. 1998. The hippocampus and transverse patterning guided by olfactory cues. *Behav. Neurosci.* 112:762–71

Eacott MJ, Norman G. 2004. Integrated memory for object, place, and context in rats: a possible model of episodic-like memory? *J. Neurosci.* 24:1948–53

Eichenbaum H. 2014. Time cells in the hippocampus: a new dimension for mapping memories. *Nat. Rev. Neurosci.* 15:732–44

Eichenbaum H, Cohen NJ. 2014. Can we reconcile the declarative memory and spatial navigation views of hippocampal function? *Neuron* 83:764–70

Eichenbaum H, Cohen NJ, Otto T, Wible C. 1992. Memory representation in the hippocampus: functional domain and functional organization. In *Memory: Organization and Locus of Change*, ed. LR Squire, G Lynch, NM Weinberger, JL McGaugh, pp. 163–204. New York: Oxford Univ. Press

Eichenbaum H, Dudchenko P, Wood E, Shapiro M, Tanila H. 1999. The hippocampus, memory, and place cells: Is it spatial memory or a memory space? *Neuron* 23:209–26

Eichenbaum H, Fortin N, Sauvage M, Robitsek RJ, Farovik A. 2010. An animal model of amnesia that uses Receiver Operating Characteristics (ROC) analysis to distinguish recollection from familiarity deficits in recognition memory. *Neuropsychologia* 48:2281–89

Eichenbaum H, Yonelinas AR, Ranganath C. 2007. The medial temporal lobe and recognition memory. *Annu. Rev. Neurosci.* 30:123–52

Ergorul C, Eichenbaum H. 2004. The hippocampus and memory for "what," "where," and "when". *Learn. Mem.* 11:397–405

Evensmoen HR, Lehn H, Xu J, Witter MP, Nadel L, Håberg AK. 2013. The anterior hippocampus supports a coarse, global environmental representation and the posterior hippocampus supports fine-grained, local environmental representations. *J. Cogn. Neurosci.* 25:1908–25

Ezzyat Y, Davachi L. 2014. Similarity breeds proximity: Pattern similarity within and across contexts is related to later mnemonic judgments of temporal proximity. *Neuron* 81:1179–89

Farovik A, Dupont LM, Arce M, Eichenbaum H. 2008. Medial prefrontal cortex supports recollection, but not familiarity, in the rat. *J. Neurosci.* 28:13428–34

Flegal KE, Marín-Gutiérrez A, Ragland JD, Ranganath C. 2014. Brain mechanisms of successful recognition through retrieval of semantic context. *J. Cogn. Neurosci.* 6:1694–704

Fortin NJ, Agster KL, Eichenbaum H. 2002. Critical role of the hippocampus in memory for sequences of events. *Nat. Neurosci.* 5:458–62

Fortin NJ, Wright SP, Eichenbaum H. 2004. Recollection-like memory retrieval in rats is dependent on the hippocampus. *Nature* 431:188–91

Gabrieli JD, Cohen NJ, Corkin S. 1988. The impaired learning of semantic knowledge following bilateral medial temporal-lobe resection. *Brain Cogn.* 7:157–77

Gelbard-Sagiv H, Mukamel R, Harel M, Malach R, Fried I. 2008. Internally generated reactivation of single neurons in human hippocampus during free recall. *Science* 322:96–101

Graf P, Schacter DL. 1985. Implicit and explicit memory for new associations in normal and amnesic subjects. *J. Exp. Psychol. Learn. Mem. Cogn.* 11:501–18

Haxby JV, Connolly AC, Guntupalli JS. 2014. Decoding neural representational spaces using multivariate pattern analysis. *Annu. Rev. Neurosci.* 37:435–56

Hebb DO. 1949. *The Organization of Behavior*. New York: Wiley

Henke K, Buck A, Weber B, Wieser HG. 1997. Human hippocampus establishes associations in memory. *Hippocampus* 7:249–56

Henke K, Weber B, Kneifel S, Wieser HG, Buck A. 1999. Human hippocampus associates information in memory. *PNAS* 96:5884–89

Holland PC. 2008. Cognitive versus stimulus-response theories of learning. *Learn. Behav.* 36:227–41

Howard M, MacDonald C, Tiganj Z, Shankar K, Du Q, et al. 2014. A unified mathematical framework for coding time, space, and sequences in the medial temporal lobe. *J. Neurosci.* 34:4692–707

Hsieh LT, Gruber MJ, Jenkins LJ, Ranganath C. 2014. Hippocampal activity patterns carry information about objects in temporal context. *Neuron* 81:1165–78

Hyman JM, Ma L, Balaguer E, Durstewitz D, Seamans JK. 2012. Contextual encoding by ensembles of medial prefrontal cortex neurons. *PNAS* 109:5086–91

Hyman JM, Zilli EA, Paley AM, Hasselmo ME. 2005. Medial prefrontal cortex cells show dynamic modulation with the hippocampal theta rhythm dependent on behavior. *Hippocampus* 15:739–49

Ison MJ, Quian Quiroga R, Fried I. 2015. Rapid encoding of new memories by individual neurons in the human brain. *Neuron* 87:220–30

Jenkins LJ, Ranganath C. 2010. Prefrontal and medial temporal lobe activity at encoding predicts temporal context memory. *J. Neurosci.* 30:15558–65

Karlsson MP, Tervo DGR, Karpova AY. 2012. Network rests in medial prefrontal cortex mark the onset of behavioral uncertainty. *Science* 338:135–39

Kesner RP, Gilbert PE, Barua LA. 2002. The role of the hippocampus in memory for the temporal order of a sequence of odors. *Behav. Neurosci.* 116:286–90

Kiani R, Esteky H, Mirpour K, Tanaka K. 2007. Object category structure in response patterns of neuronal population in monkey inferior temporal cortex. *J. Neurophysiol.* 97:4296–309

Knierim JJ, Neunuebel JP, Deshmukh SS. 2013. Functional correlates of the lateral and medial entorhinal cortex: objects, path integration and local-global reference frames. *Phil. Trans. R. Soc. Lond. B Biol. Sci.* 369(1635):20130369

Komorowski RW, Garcia CG, Wilson A, Hattori S, Howard MW, Eichenbaum H. 2013. Ventral hippocampal neurons are shaped by experience to represent behaviorally relevant contexts. *J. Neurosci.* 33:8079–87

Komorowski RW, Manns JR, Eichenbaum H. 2009. Robust conjunctive item-place coding by hippocampal neurons parallels learning what happens. *J. Neurosci.* 29:9918–29

Koscik TR, Tranel D. 2012. The human ventromedial prefrontal cortex is critical for transitive inference. *J. Cogn. Neurosci.* 24:1191–204

Kraus BJ, Robinson RJII, White JA, Eichenbaum H, Hasselmo ME. 2013. Hippocampal "time cells": time versus path integration. *Neuron* 78:1090–101

Kriegeskorte N, Mur M, Bandettini P. 2008. Representational similarity analysis—connecting the branches of systems neuroscience. *Front. Syst. Neurosci.* 2:4

Kuhl BA, Wagner AD. 2009. Strategic control of memory. In *Encyclopedia of Neuroscience*, ed. LR Squire, pp. 437–44. Amsterdam: Elsevier

Kumaran D, Summerfield JJ, Hassabis D, Maguire EA. 2009. Tracking the emergence of conceptual knowledge during human decision making. *Neuron* 63:889–901

Kyle CT, Smuda DN, Hassan AS, Ekstrom AD. 2015. Roles of human hippocampal subfields in retrieval of spatial and temporal context. *Behav. Brain Res.* 278:549–58

Langston RF, Wood ER. 2010. Associative recognition and the hippocampus: differential effects of hippocampal lesions on object-place, object-context and object-place-context memory. *Hippocampus* 20:1139–53

Libby LA, Hannula DE, Ranganath C. 2014. Medial temporal lobe coding of item and spatial information during relational binding in working memory. *J. Neurosci.* 34:14233–42

MacDonald CJ, Carrow S, Place R, Eichenbaum H. 2013. Distinct hippocampal time cell sequences represent odor memories in immobilized rats. *J. Neurosci.* 33:14607–16

Macmillan NA, Creelman CD. 2005. *Detection Theory: A User's Guide*. Mahwah, NJ: Lawrence Erlbaum Assoc. 2nd ed.

Mandler G. 1972. Organization, memory, and mental structures. In *Memory Organization and Structure*, ed. CR Puff, pp. 303–19. New York: Academic

Mandler G. 2011. From association to organization. *Curr. Dir. Psych. Sci.* 20:232–35

Manns JR, Eichenbaum H. 2009. A cognitive map for object memory in the hippocampus. *Learn. Mem.* 16:616–24

Manns JR, Howard M, Eichenbaum H. 2007. Gradual changes in hippocampal activity support remembering the order of events. *Neuron* 56:530–40

Marquis J-P, Killcross S, Haddon JE. 2007. Inactivation of the prelimbic, but not infralimbic, prefrontal cortex impairs the contextual control of response conflict in rats. *Eur. J. Neurosci.* 25:559–66

Mayes AR, Isaac CL, Holdstock JS, Hunkin NM, Montaldi D, et al. 2001. Memory for single items, word pairs, and temporal order of different kinds in a patient with selective hippocampal lesions. *Cogn. Neuropsychol.* 18:97–123

McClelland JL, McNaughton BL, O'Reilly RC. 1995. Why there are complementary learning systems in the hippocampus and neocortex: insights from the successes and failures of connectionist models of learning and memory. *Psych. Rev.* 102:419–57

McKenzie S, Frank AJ, Kinsky NR, Porter B, Rivière PD, Eichenbaum. 2014. Hippocampal representation of related and opposing memories develop within distinct, hierarchically-organized neural schemas. *Neuron* 83:202–15

McKenzie S, Keene CS, Farovik A, Bladon J, Place R, et al. 2016. Representation of memories in the cortical-hippocampal system: Results from the application of population similarity analyses. *Neurobiol. Learn. Mem.* 134:178–91

Milivojevic B, Doeller CF. 2013. Mnemonic networks in the hippocampal formation: from spatial maps to temporal and conceptual codes. *J. Exp. Psychol. Gen.* 142:1231–41

Milivojevic B, Vicente-Grabovetsky A, Doeller CF. 2015. Insight reconfigures hippocampal-prefrontal memories. *Curr. Biol.* 25:821–30

Miller EK. 1999. The prefrontal cortex: complex neural properties for complex behavior. *Neuron* 22:15–17

Miller EK, Cohen JD. 2001. An integrative theory of prefrontal cortex function. *Annu. Rev. Neurosci.* 24:167–202

Moita MAP, Moisis S, Zhou Y, LeDoux JE, Blair HT. 2003. Hippocampal place cells acquire location-specific responses to the conditioned stimulus during auditory fear conditioning. *Neuron* 37:485–97

Moscovitch M. 1992. Memory and working-with-memory: a component process model based on modules and central systems. *J. Cogn. Neurosci.* 4:257–67

Moser EI, Kropff E, Moser M-B. 2008. Place cells, grid cells, and the brain's spatial representation system. *Annu. Rev. Neurosci.* 31:69–89

Navawongse R, Eichenbaum H. 2013. Distinct pathways support rule-based memory retrieval and spatial mapping by hippocampal neurons. *J. Neurosci.* 33:1002–13

Naya Y, Suzuki WA. 2011. Integrating what and when across the primate medial temporal lobe. *Science* 333:773–76

Nemanic S, Alvarado MC, Bachevalier J. 2004. The hippocampal/parahippocampal regions and recognition memory: insights from visual paired comparison versus object-delayed nonmatching in monkeys. *J. Neurosci.* 24:2013–26

Nielson DM, Smith TA, Sreekumar V, Dennis S, Sederberg PB. 2015. Human hippocampus represents space and time during retrieval of real-world memories. *PNAS* 112:11078–83

O'Kane G, Kensinger EA, Corkin S. 2004. Evidence for semantic learning in profound amnesia: an investigation with patient H.M. *Hippocampus* 14:417–25

O'Keefe JA, Nadel L. 1978. *The Hippocampus as a Cognitive Map.* New York: Oxford Univ. Press

Parker A, Gaffan D. 1998. Interaction of frontal and perirhinal cortices in visual object recognition memory in monkeys. *Eur. J. Neurosci.* 10:3044–57

Pascalis O, Hunkin NM, Holdstock JS, Isaac CL, Mayes AR. 2004. Visual paired comparison performance is impaired in a patient with selective hippocampal lesions and relatively intact item recognition. *Neuropsychologia* 42:1293–1300

Pastalkova E, Itskov V, Amarasingham A, Buzsáki G. 2008. Internally generated cell assembly sequences in the rat hippocampus. *Science* 321:1322–27

Paz R, Gelbard-Sagiv H, Mukamel R, Harel M, Malach R, Fried I. 2010. A neural substrate in the human hippocampus for linking successive events. *PNAS* 107:6046–51

Piaget J. 1928. *Judgment and Reasoning in the Child.* London: K. Paul, Trench, Trubner & Co.

Place R, Farovik A, Brockmann M, Eichenbaum H. 2016. Bidirectional prefrontal-hippocampal interactions support context-guided memory. *Nat. Neurosci.* 19:992–94

Poppenk J, Evensmoen HR, Moscovitch M, Nadel L. 2013. Long-axis specialization of the human hippocampus. *Trends Cogn. Sci.* 17:230–40

Postle BR. 2006. Working memory as an emergent property of the mind and brain. *Neuroscience* 139:23–38

Preston AR, Eichenbaum H. 2013. Interplay of the hippocampus and prefrontal cortex in memory. *Curr. Biol.* 23:R764–73

Preston AR, Shrager Y, Dudukovic NM, Gabrieli JD. 2004. Hippocampal contribution to the novel use of relational information in declarative memory. *Hippocampus* 14:148–52

Ragozzino ME, Kim J, Hassert D, Minniti N, Kiang C. 2003. The contribution of the rat prelimbic-infralimbic areas to different forms of task switching. *Behav. Neurosci.* 117:1054–65

Ranganath C, Blumenfeld R. 2008. Prefrontal cortex and memory. In *Learning and Memory: A Comprehensive Reference*, ed. J Byrne, pp. 261–79. Oxford, UK: Academic

Rich EL, Shapiro M. 2009. Rat prefrontal cortical neurons selectively code strategy switches. *J. Neurosci.* 29:7208–19

Rich EL, Shapiro ML. 2007. Prelimbic/infralimbic inactivation impairs memory for multiple task switches, but not flexible selection of familiar tasks. *J. Neurosci.* 27:4747–55

Richards BA, Xia F, Santoro A, Husse J, Woodin MA, et al. 2014. Patterns across multiple memories are identified over time. *Nat. Neurosci.* 17:981–86

Rickard TC, Verfaellie M, Grafman J. 2006. Transverse patterning and human amnesia. *J. Cogn. Neurosci.* 18:1723–33

Ritchey M, Libby LA, Ranganath C. 2015. Cortico-hippocampal systems involved in memory and cognition: the PMAT framework. *Prog. Brain Res.* 219:45–64

Robitsek JR, White J, Eichenbaum H. 2013. Place cell activation predicts subsequent memory. *Behav. Brain Res.* 254:65–72

Sauvage MM, Beer Z, Eichenbaum H. 2010. Recognition memory: Adding a response deadline eliminates recollection but spares familiarity. *Learn. Mem.* 17:104–8

Sauvage MM, Fortin NJ, Owens CB, Yonelinas AP, Eichenbaum H. 2008. Recognition memory: opposite effects of hippocampal damage on recollection and familiarity. *Nat. Neurosci.* 11:16–18

Schiller D, Eichenbaum H, Buffalo EA, Davachi L, Foster DJ, et al. 2015. Memory and space: towards an understanding of the cognitive map. *J. Neurosci.* 35:13904–11

Schlichting ML, Mumford JA, Preston AR. 2015. Learning-related representational changes reveal dissociable integration and separation signatures in the hippocampus and prefrontal cortex. *Nat. Commun.* 6:8151

Schlichting ML, Preston AR. 2016. Hippocampal-medial prefrontal circuit supports memory updating during learning and post-encoding rest. *Neurobiol. Learn. Mem.* 134:91–106

Shapiro ML, Kennedy PJ, Ferbinteanu J. 2006. Representing episodes in the mammalian brain. *Curr. Opin. Neurobiol.* 16:701–9

Shimamura AP, Jurica PJ, Mangels JA, Gershberg FB, Knight RT. 1995. Susceptibility to memory interference effects following frontal lobe damage: findings from tests of paired-associate learning. *J. Cogn. Neurosci.* 7:144–52

Shohamy D, Wagner AD. 2008. Integrating memories in the human brain: hippocampal-midbrain encoding of overlapping events. *Neuron* 60:378–89

Sigurdsson T, Stark KL, Karayiurgou M, Gogos JA, Gordon JA. 2010. Impaired hippocampal-prefrontal synchrony in a genetic mouse model of schizophrenia. *Nature* 464:763–67

Simons JS, Spiers HJ. 2003. Prefrontal and medial temporal lobe interactions in long-term memory. *Nat. Rev. Neurosci.* 4:637–48

Spence KW. 1950. Cognitive versus stimulus-response theories of learning. *Psychol. Rev.* 57:159–72

Sperling R, Chua E, Cocchiarella A, Rand-Giovannetti E, Poldrack R, et al. 2003. Putting names to faces: Successful encoding of associative memories activates the anterior hippocampal formation. *NeuroImage* 20:1400–10

Spiers HJ, Burgess N, Hartley T, Vargha-Khadem F, O'Keefe J. 2001. Bilateral hippocampal pathology impairs topographical and episodic memory but not visual pattern matching. *Hippocampus* 11:715–25

Staresina BP, Davachi L. 2008. Selective and shared contributions of the hippocampus and perirhinal cortex to episodic item and associative encoding. *J. Cogn. Neurosci.* 20:1478–89

Strange BA, Witter MP, Lein ES, Moser EI. 2014. Functional organization of the hippocampal longitudinal axis. *Nat. Rev. Neurosci.* 5:655–69

Swanson LW, Wyss JM, Cowan WM. 1978. An autoradiographic study of the organization of intrahippocampal association pathways in the rat. *J. Comp. Neurol.* 181:681–715

Tavares RM, Mendelsohn A, Grossman Y, Williams CH, Shapiro M, et al. 2015. A map for social navigation in the human brain. *Neuron* 7:231–43

Tolman EC. 1948. Cognitive maps in rats and men. *Psychol. Rev.* 55:189–208

Tse D, Langston RF, Kakeyama M, Bethus I, Spooner PA, et al. 2007. Schemas and memory consolidation. *Science* 316:76–82

Tse D, Takeuchi T, Kakeyama M, Kajii Y, Okuno H, et al. 2011. Schema-dependent gene activation and memory encoding in neocortex. *Science* 333:891–95

Tulving E. 1972. Episodic and semantic memory. In *Organization of Memory*, ed. E Tulving, W Donaldson, pp. 381–402. New York: Academic

Vargha-Khadem F, Gadian DG, Watkins KE, Connelly A, Van Paesschen W, Mishkin M. 1997. Differential effects of early hippocampal pathology on episodic and semantic memory. *Science* 277:376–80

Vertes RP. 2006. Interactions among the medial prefrontal cortex, hippocampus and midline thalamus in emotional and cognitive processing in the rat. *Neuroscience* 142:1–20

Wendelken C, Bunge SA. 2010. Transitive inference: distinct contributions of the rostrolateral prefrontal cortex and the hippocampus. *J. Cogn. Neurosci.* 22:837–47

Wixted J, Squire LR. 2011. The medial temporal lobe and attributes of memory. *Trends Cogn. Sci.* 15:210–17

Yonelinas AP. 2001. Components of episodic memory: the contribution of recollection and familiarity. *Philos. Trans. R. Soc. Lond. B Biol. Sci.* 356:1363–74

Yonelinas AP, Parks CM. 2007. Receiver operating characteristics (ROCs) in recognition memory: a review. *Psychol. Bull.* 133:800–32

Zalesak M, Heckers S. 2009. The role of the hippocampus in transitive inference. *Psychiatry Res.* 172:24–30

Zeineh MM, Engel SA, Thompson PM, Brookheimer SY. 2003. Dynamics of the hippocampus during encoding and retrieval of face-name pairs. *Science* 299:577–80

Zeithamova D, Dominick AL, Preston AR. 2012. Hippocampal and ventral medial prefrontal activation during retrieval-mediated learning supports novel inference. *Neuron* 75:168–79

Zeithamova D, Preston AR. 2010. Flexible memories: differential roles for medial temporal lobe and prefrontal cortex in cross-episode binding. *J. Neurosci.* 30:14676–84

Zola SM, Squire LR, Teng E, Stefanacci L, Buffalo EA, Clark RE. 2000. Impaired recognition memory in monkeys after damage limited to the hippocampal region. *J. Neurosci.* 20:451–63

Neural Mechanisms of Selective Visual Attention

Tirin Moore[1,2] and Marc Zirnsak[1,2]

[1]Department of Neurobiology, Stanford University School of Medicine, Stanford, California 94305; email: tirin@stanford.edu, mzirnsak@stanford.edu

[2]Howard Hughes Medical Institute, Stanford, California 94305

Annu. Rev. Psychol. 2017. 68:47–72

The *Annual Review of Psychology* is online at psych.annualreviews.org

This article's doi:
10.1146/annurev-psych-122414-033400

Keywords

orienting, cognition, visual perception, neural circuits, sensory processing

Abstract

Selective visual attention describes the tendency of visual processing to be confined largely to stimuli that are relevant to behavior. It is among the most fundamental of cognitive functions, particularly in humans and other primates for whom vision is the dominant sense. We review recent progress in identifying the neural mechanisms of selective visual attention. We discuss evidence from studies of different varieties of selective attention and examine how these varieties alter the processing of stimuli by neurons within the visual system, current knowledge of their causal basis, and methods for assessing attentional dysfunctions. In addition, we identify some key questions that remain in identifying the neural mechanisms that give rise to the selective processing of visual information.

Contents

INTRODUCTION

Although we experience a complete image of the visual world, our capacity to process all facets of available visual information is extremely limited. These limitations are made compellingly evident in a number of widely popularized perceptual demonstrations, including demonstrations of change blindness (e.g., see **http://cogsci.uci.edu/~ddhoff/cb.html**). However, the limitations in our perception are also apparent when simply considering how much of a typical visual scene we fail to notice or recollect. When considering these limitations in the context of our visual system, which, as in other primates, involves a proportion of subcortical and cortical structures that vastly outstrips that of the other senses, it may seem striking that so much neural machinery frequently goes unused. Visual information that is first transduced in the retina and then conveyed through the visual system is encoded by neurons along numerous spatial and featural dimensions such that the output of populations of neurons at some stages can signal the identity and location of a seemingly infinite number of stimuli. Yet it appears that, under most circumstances, that information goes unused. However, one must also consider the largely adaptive consequences of these limitations, given that what we tend to perceive is the information most relevant to our behavioral goals. Although the visual system carries out a more or less exhaustive extraction of visual information from the environment, at least at early stages, our behavior is driven only by the small subset of that information that is most pertinent. This aspect of visually guided behavior is broadly referred to as selective visual attention, and it is among the more fundamental cognitive functions. In this review, we discuss recent evidence that elucidates the neural mechanisms of visual selective attention. In doing so, we attempt to consider all aspects and types of visual selective attention and discuss how they alter visual processing, their causal basis, and how to assess dysfunctions of attentional control.

VARIETIES OF SELECTIVE VISUAL ATTENTION AND THEIR CORRESPONDING NEURAL CORRELATES

Organisms have a tendency to selectively process only a subset of sensory input. This selective processing comes in multiple forms, and in considering the neural circuitry of attention it is important to consider each of them separately. Although it may seem likely that the different forms of attention should share common mechanisms or consequences at some basic level (e.g., effects on neural coding), as is frequently implied in some models (e.g., Lee & Maunsell 2009, Reynolds & Heeger 2009), the different forms should also be expected to be quite different at other levels (e.g., neuronal source). In the visual modality, a useful starting point is the division of selective attention into three (presumably orthogonal) dichotomies, i.e., three pairs of contrasting types of attention. The first of these is top-down versus bottom-up selective attention, the former describing selective visual processing due to an endogenously generated signal (e.g., representation of a rule, strategy, or motivational state) and the latter describing selective processing based solely on the physical salience of the visual stimulus (e.g., bright or moving objects). In recent years, several investigators have described the combination of top-down and bottom-up factors as stimulus priority, given evidence that neurons in some structures signal both types of attention (Bisley & Goldberg 2010). The second dichotomy distinguishes spatially directed selective attention from attention directed toward particular classes of visual features or objects. The third dichotomy distinguishes between the selective processing of stimuli in the absence of any orienting movements (covert attention) from that which occurs in conjunction with orienting movements (e.g., eye movements, reaching, or grasping). As we discuss in the following sections, by definition these dichotomies already suggest divergent neural mechanisms (e.g., absence of motor commands in covert attention); however, there is still surprisingly little known about the mechanistic basis of these different manifestations of attentional selection.

Top-Down and Bottom-Up Attention

As described above, the deployment of attention can occur either by virtue of the physical salience of a stimulus or according to internal, behavioral goals. Most neurophysiological studies in the past, particularly those aimed at identifying neural circuits controlling attention, have focused primarily on top-down attention. Although it is clear that both top-down and bottom-up attention modulate neuronal activity within the visual system, both the neurophysiological effects and the underlying circuitry of these forms of attention are less understood. In the following sections, we discuss evidence for both forms.

Neural correlates of top-down attention. The primary focus of research on visual selective attention has been on the influence that top-down, covert attention has on visually driven signals throughout the primate visual system, and this research has included parallel work in humans (Corbetta et al. 1991, Hillyard 1993, Heinze et al. 1994, Luck et al. 2000, Pessoa et al. 2003) and nonhuman primates (Desimone & Duncan 1995, Reynolds & Chelazzi 2004, Noudoost et al. 2010). In neurophysiological studies of the latter, the basic observation is that selective visual attention increases visually driven firing rates of neurons encoding the attending stimulus; this modulation is present as early as the dorsal lateral geniculate nucleus (dLGN) (McAlonan et al. 2008) and increases in magnitude at subsequent stages of visual processing (Moran & Desimone 1985, Luck et al. 1997, Maunsell & Cook 2002, Buffalo et al. 2010, Noudoost et al. 2010). The results from human functional brain imaging largely parallel these general observations from neurophysiological studies (Kastner & Ungerleider 2001, Pessoa et al. 2003). In addition, these observations appear to be consistent for both spatial and feature/object-based attention (e.g., Treue & Martínez-Trujillo 1999, Sàenz et al. 2002).

Within the past decade, an increasing number of studies have focused on testing other aspects of neural activity that are affected by selective attention, again largely in the context of top-down, covert attention. Given that selective attention is defined behaviorally as a relative improvement in psychophysical performance for attended versus unattended stimuli (e.g., Carrasco 2011), it is, of course, important to measure the extent to which neural correlates of attention involve corresponding relative improvements in neural coding, particularly because an increase in the neuronal firing rate does not necessarily signify an increase in neural coding. If the objective of attention is to increase the signal-to-noise ratio of the readout from populations of neurons encoding the attended stimulus, then, in theory, this can be accomplished in a number of ways, including strengthening of selected signals, improvements in the efficacy of inputs to the readout stage, and the reduction of noise. A number of studies have measured the influence of selective attention on the coding of visual stimuli by single neurons (e.g., Spitzer et al. 1988; McAdams & Maunsell 1999, 2000; Reynolds & Chelazzi 2004) and populations of single neurons (Cohen & Maunsell 2009, 2010), and they have discovered that attention appears to increase the information conveyed about stimuli. Moreover, attention-driven increases in coding appear to be specific to behavioral conditions in which an animal's perceptual sensitivity per se, rather than simple response bias, is increased (Luo & Maunsell 2015). However, the means by which these increases are accomplished remains somewhat unclear. In addition to changing the firing rate, attention reduces the variability of responses to repeated stimuli (Mitchell et al. 2007) and can reduce the covariability of neuronal responses to repeated stimuli in simultaneously recorded neurons (Cohen & Maunsell 2009, Mitchell et al. 2009). Reductions in firing rate variability increase the information available in stimulus-driven activity by effectively diminishing the noise in the neural signal. Reductions in spiking covariability, by contrast, are expected to reduce the redundancy in signals from populations of neurons (Cohen & Maunsell 2009), at least for neurons with similar stimulus preferences (positive signal correlations) (Averbeck et al. 2006, Ruff & Cohen 2014). However, the relationship between neuronal spiking covariability and the strength of information in the population code is not entirely straightforward (Hu et al. 2014).

In addition to increasing the information available in the spiking activity, attention can potentially enhance signal efficacy via synchrony among neurons encoding the attended stimulus. In particular, some researchers have argued that high frequency (γ-band) synchronization in the spiking output from projection neurons can increase the influence of spikes on downstream neurons (Salinas & Sejnowski 2001, Azouz & Gray 2003; for a contrasting view, see Martin & Schröder 2016). At least within the rodent somatosensory system, evidence exists of a direct influence of γ synchrony among fast-spiking interneurons on both sensory coding (Cardin et al. 2009) and tactile detection (Siegle et al. 2014). In neurophysiological recordings in behaving animals, coherence among spikes and between spikes and local field potentials (LFPs) provides a measure of phase locking within local groups of neurons. A near-zero phase lag in the spiking synchrony among neurons could facilitate the integration of spikes from these populations converging on postsynaptic targets. Studies have generally found increases both in local γ-band LFP power and in synchrony between spiking and the γ-band phase (Fries et al. 2001, Bichot et al. 2005, Fries 2009). Related changes occur within other LFP frequency bands (Fries 2009), and those changes appear to depend on the cortical layer in which they are recorded (Buffalo et al. 2011).

Although observations of increased γ-band synchrony lend support to the notion of a functional role of synchrony in attentional selection, evidence that attentional modulation results in greater postsynaptic efficacy is only now emerging. Briggs et al. (2013) tested the influence of attention on the synaptic efficacy of dLGN inputs to visual area 1 (V1) in monkeys. To accomplish this, they stimulated dLGN neurons while simultaneously measuring the stimulation-evoked responses in V1. They observed that when attention was directed to the receptive fields (RFs) of V1 neurons, those neurons were more likely to be activated by dLGN stimulation. These results are particularly exciting in that they provide a direct approach for testing how attention alters the transmission of signals across stages of the visual system.

Modulation of visual activity by other endogenous factors. Although the evidence in the previous section is largely consistent with the supposition that (top-down) attention should increase the fidelity of neural signals related to the attended stimulus, it nonetheless remains unclear whether the changes that correlate with attentional deployment are actually necessary and sufficient to improve perceptual performance. In fact, this remains one of the more fundamental open questions in study of the neural mechanisms of attention (see the section Future Issues). In recent years, an increased interest in addressing this question has not only necessitated more rigorous measurements of perceptual performance in animal models (e.g., Sridharan et al. 2014) but also prompted investigators to test the degree to which factors other than selective attention modulate visual activity. For example, Baruni et al. (2015) found that, although the relative reward value determined discrimination performance at a given location, the absolute reward amount determined the extent of activity modulation in visual area 4 (V4) (see the section Future Issues). This dissociation indicates that selective attention, or at least its top-down component, is not the only factor contributing to the modulation of sensory responses. Another study demonstrated that the planning of saccadic eye movements to the RFs of V4 neurons was sufficient to modulate visually driven responses, even when saccade planning was spatially dissociated from the direction of covert attention (Steinmetz & Moore 2014) (**Figure 1**). Importantly, the effects of saccade planning on V4 activity were actually greater than the effects associated with attention. The above results demonstrate the potency of endogenous factors other than covert selective attention in regulating sensory driven signals. However, both reward value and motor preparation are generally expected to be coupled with adaptive changes in sensory representations. In later sections of this review (Gaze Control Mechanisms and Their Role in Visual Spatial Attention; Overt Attention and Perisaccadic Perception), we return to the latter of these two factors (motor preparation), as it appears to reveal a great deal about the mechanisms underlying both covert and overt spatial attention.

Neural correlates of bottom-up attention. In contrast to the extensive studies demonstrating the modulation of signals throughout the visual system during top-down attention, details about the influence of bottom-up attention on visual processing are notably less clear. In particular, the degree to which physical, non-task-driven salience can bias visual responses at early stages of the visual system remains ambiguous. Psychophysical studies have established that visual targets composed of features that differ from surrounding distracters are more salient and thus more easily located during visual search (Egeth & Yantis 1997). Such targets are said to pop out from background stimuli, as they can be located more rapidly, even in the presence of many distracters (Treisman & Gelade 1980, Treisman & Sato 1990). Popout stimuli are thus believed to draw attention in an automatic, bottom-up fashion, with search being largely driven via parallel (Treisman & Sato 1990) or preattentive mechanisms (Wolfe 1994). In comparison, targets made up of a unique conjunction of nontarget features are more difficult to locate during search and thus require longer search times as the number of distracters increases (Treisman & Gelade 1980). One report appeared to establish that neurons within V1 exhibit enhanced responses to popout RF stimuli (Knierim & Van Essen 1992). However, a subsequent study showed that V1 responses to popout stimuli

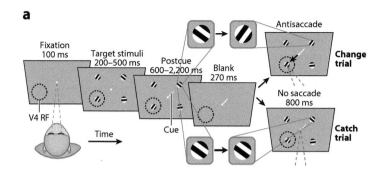

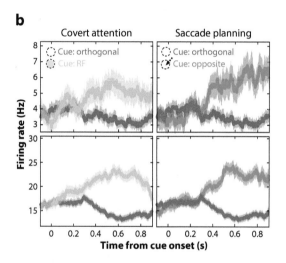

Figure 1

Dissociation of the effects of covert attention and saccade planning on visual area 4 (V4) activity.
(*a*) Antisaccade detection task design and trial sequence (Steinmetz & Moore 2014). Monkeys fixated on a white dot while four peripheral oriented-grating stimuli were presented. After a variable delay, stimuli disappeared then reappeared, either with or without one of the four stimuli rotating (i.e., either change trial or catch trial). Monkeys could earn a reward by making a saccade to the diametrically opposite stimulus from the change in change trials or by maintaining fixation in catch trials. A small, central cue (*white line*) indicated which stimulus, if any, was most likely to change. The panels outlined in green show the change in orientation, or lack of change, across the blank period. The dashed circle indicates V4 receptive field (RF) locations, and the arrow indicates saccade direction. (*b*) Responses of two example neurons in the antisaccade detection task. The left subpanels show a peristimulus time histogram of spiking activity around the time of cue onset for trials in which the monkey was cued to attend to the RF stimulus (*cyan*) and prepare a saccadic response to a distracter stimulus in the opposite direction. Activity is compared to control trials in which the monkey attended to a stimulus orthogonal to the RF (*purple*). The shaded region indicates ±1 standard error of the mean. The right panels show data from the same neuron for trials in which the monkey was cued to attend to a location opposite the RF but had to prepare an antisaccade to a distracter stimulus in the RF. Activity increased under both conditions, indicating that saccade planning modulated V4 responses even when dissociated from covert attention. Figure adapted with permission from Steinmetz & Moore (2014).

do not actually differ substantially from responses to conjunction stimuli (Hegdé & Felleman 2003), whereas neurons within V4 do (Burrows & Moore 2009). Even so, selectivity to popout stimuli is not the sole test of bottom-up modulation. Abrupt onset stimuli also produce transient, involuntary shifts of attention toward the location of the onset (Posner 1980, Carrasco 2011). A recent study reported correlating enhancements in the activity of V1 neurons following such abrupt onsets (Wang et al. 2015). Thus, the way in which bottom-up salience early in the visual system contributes to visual processing may depend critically on the stimulus.

When assessing the influence of bottom-up salience on visual responses, one must also consider the extent to which those influences interact with top-down (endogenous) factors. Although the top-down/bottom-up dichotomy is frequently assumed to reflect independent mechanisms (Corbetta & Shulman 2002), confirmations of that independence tend to yield evidence to the contrary. Numerous neurophysiological and human neuroimaging studies have used passive fixation tasks to probe bottom-up attention (Knierim & Van Essen 1992, Lamme 1995, Nothdurft et al. 1999, Hegdé & Felleman 2003, Beck & Kastner 2005, Constantinidis & Steinmetz 2005). However, other studies, particularly those examining activity in higher order cortical areas, have employed visual search tasks (Chelazzi et al. 1998, Bichot et al. 2005, Thompson et al. 2005, Ogawa & Komatsu 2006, Buschman & Miller 2007, Bichot et al. 2015), and thus the measured activity necessarily included some component of top-down modulation. In fact, popout and conjunction stimuli are most often used in the context of visual search tasks. Some have argued that this task may not be the optimal way to measure purely bottom-up effects (e.g., Prinzmetal & Taylor 2006), as bottom-up and top-down effects clearly interact under these conditions (Einhäuser et al. 2008, Müller et al. 2009). Both psychophysical (e.g., Joseph et al. 1997) and neurophysiological (e.g., Ipata et al. 2006, Burrows & Moore 2009) evidence indicate that the interaction of bottom-up and top-down attention during visual search can lead to a diminution of bottom-up salience and its neural correlates when that salience is not behaviorally relevant (Hamker 2005a).

Major models of visual attention typically involve separate stages for the computation of differences in local features (feature maps) and global salience (salience maps) (Treisman & Sato 1990, Wolfe 1994, Itti & Koch 2001). Recent neurophysiological studies have provided persuasive evidence that global salience is computed, or at least amplified, within the parietal cortex (Balan & Gottlieb 2006, Goldberg et al. 2006, Soltani & Koch 2010) or prefrontal cortex (PFC) (Moore et al. 2003, Thompson & Bichot 2005). Although there is some evidence that neurons in parietal (Constantinidis & Steinmetz 2005, Ipata et al. 2006, Buschman & Miller 2007) and prefrontal (Bichot & Schall 2002, Buschman & Miller 2007) structures are uniquely modulated by popout stimuli, whether this modulation arises de novo in these proposed salience maps, converges there from more feature-selective (feature map) areas, or perhaps does both (Soltani & Koch 2010), remains unknown. The relative contributions of the parietal cortex, the PFC, the feature-selective cortex, and the superior colliculus (SC) (Fecteau & Munoz 2006) to the salience computation persist as one of the more fundamental open questions in attention (see the section Future Issues).

Feature-Based Versus Spatial Attention

The variety of attention whose adaptive significance is perhaps easiest to appreciate is feature-based (or object-based) attention, in which objects are selected on the basis of the degree to which their component features match a behaviorally relevant object. The adaptive significance of feature-based attention is easy to envision because many organisms frequently need to locate important objects within their environment, such as ripe fruit or easy prey. Note also that the selection of such objects is adaptive not only during active search for them, e.g., when hungry, but also under more passive, involuntary circumstances. In classical studies of feature-based attention using visual search tasks, subjects are instructed to localize objects based on their similarity to one that was previously cued (Wolfe 1994). Several classic neurophysiological studies have identified neurons that exhibit correlates of feature-based attention within the primate visual system, beginning, at the latest, within the middle temporal visual area and V4 (Motter 1994a,b; Maunsell and Treue 2006; Bichot et al. 2005) and continuing in later cortical areas (Chelazzi et al. 1993, Bichot & Schall 1999, Sheinberg & Logothetis 2001). Unlike the case of spatial attention, in which the modulation of visually driven activity depends critically on the relationship between a given RF stimulus and the attended location, the modulation of visual activity during feature-based attention specifically depends on the relationship between the RF stimulus and the searched-for (attended) feature. For example, neurons in area V4 respond more vigorously to RF stimuli that more closely match the features that an animal is searching for, and this effect occurs whether or not the stimulus is located at a currently attended location (Bichot et al. 2005). The observation of this effect indicates that representations of stimuli are biased in a spatially invariant manner; that is, the selection of features and objects is spatially global (Treue & Martínez-Trujillo 1999, Sàenz et al. 2002, Martínez-Trujillo & Treue 2004, Cohen & Maunsell 2011). In contrast to the case of spatial attention, few studies have examined the neurophysiological effects of feature-based attention beyond changes in firing rates, the exception being a study finding that the effects of feature-based attention on γ-band LFP power and spike-LFP synchrony in the γ-band are similar to those of spatial attention (Bichot et al. 2005). However, although it is easy to envision how spatial attention should influence perception (e.g., increased detection of all stimuli at relevant locations), it is less straightforward to envision how feature-based attention should affect visual perception. Does feature-based attention simply facilitate the processing of stimuli sharing an attended feature (e.g., Sàenz et al. 2003), or can it cause more complex perceptual biases reflecting task-dependent changes in the encoding or decoding of visual features (Jazayeri & Movshon 2007, Navalpakkam & Itti 2007, Scolari & Serences 2009, Zirnsak & Hamker 2010)?

Covert and Overt Attention

More often than not, the direction of our gaze and the focus of our attention are spatially aligned. This makes it possible to resolve the fine details of fixated stimuli via the fovea, where visual acuity is greatest. Nonetheless, it is also possible to attend to objects of interest in the visual scene without shifting our gaze to them. This covert attention is the form of spatial attention most often studied by visual neuroscientists, as described in the previous sections. The importance of covert spatial attention has been appreciated since at least the nineteenth century, when Hermann von Helmholtz [1867 (1925)] conducted his research. In a classic experiment, von Helmholtz briefly illuminated an array of letters with an electric spark while holding his gaze steady. Von Helmholtz found that he was able to remember only the letters appearing in the area of the screen where his attention was directed, despite his gaze fixating elsewhere. His experiment thus showed that attention and gaze can be dissociated and that the perceptual benefits of attention (in this case, facilitation of memory) can be achieved both at the fovea and in the visual periphery. Since von Helmholtz's time, many psychophysical experiments have demonstrated that covert spatial attention improves the detection (e.g., Bashinski & Bacharach 1980, Hawkins et al. 1990, Müller & Humphreys 1991, Handy et al. 1996, Herrmann et al. 2010), as well as the discrimination (e.g., Downing 1988), of stimulus features at an attended location.

Before the discovery that the effects of covert attention are widespread within the primate visual system, researchers knew that visual activity in a number of brain regions is enhanced when an animal targets a RF stimulus with a saccadic eye movement. This effect was first observed by Goldberg & Wurtz (1972) among neurons within the superficial layers of the SC and subsequently by Mountcastle and colleagues (1981) in the posterior parietal cortex. Later studies demonstrated that the presaccadic visual enhancement is also observed among neurons in V4 (Fischer & Boch 1981) and the inferior temporal cortex (Chelazzi et al. 1993). Moore and colleagues (Moore et al. 1998, Moore & Chang 2009) followed up on the study of Fischer & Boch (1981) and found that, as is observed during covert attention, the presaccadic enhancement of V4 visual responses consists of a reemergence of stimulus selectivity to targeted RF stimuli. When saccades are prepared to non-RF locations, the presaccadic activity and selectivity of V4 neurons are reduced (Moore 1999, Moore & Chang 2009). Thus, the presaccadic response reliably and selectively encodes the stimulus features of the target stimulus. Moreover, the stimulus selectivity present in the presaccadic response correlates significantly with the degree to which saccadic landing points are influenced by the orientation of the RF stimulus (Moore 1999), suggesting that, rather than merely providing a passive perceptual representation of visual attributes (Goodale & Milner 1992), neurons in this ventral stream visual area are instead actively involved in guiding oculomotor commands according to those attributes. In the next section, we describe further studies of the relationship between gaze control mechanisms and visual spatial attention, a relationship that appears to be causal.

GAZE CONTROL MECHANISMS AND THEIR ROLE IN VISUAL SPATIAL ATTENTION

Interdependence of Saccade Planning and Spatial Attention

Perhaps the first evidence of an interdependence of gaze control and attention came from a psychophysical study in which subjects made discriminations about peripherally flashed digits (Crovitz & Daves 1962). This study reported a positive correlation between discrimination performance and the direction of the first saccade subjects made after the stimulus was presented, suggesting that eye movements might facilitate attention. In the 1980s, Rizzolatti and colleagues proposed a premotor theory of attention, which hypothesized that the mechanisms responsible for spatial attention and the mechanisms involved in programming saccades are accomplished by the same neurons, but that in the covert case "the eyes are blocked at a certain peripheral stage" (Rizzolatti et al. 1987, p. 27). Later studies demonstrated that visual detection and discrimination are facilitated at the endpoints of saccades, even when the subject is given a cue to attend elsewhere (Shepherd et al. 1986, Hoffman & Subramaniam 1995, Deubel & Schneider 1996). Thus, it was apparent that planning a saccade is sufficient to facilitate visual perception at targeted locations. These results led to the proposal that a single mechanism drives both the selection of objects for perceptual processing and the preparation needed to produce an appropriate motor response (Schneider 1995).

The Frontal Eye Field in the Prefrontal Cortex

The earliest evidence of a causal role of gaze-control mechanisms in the perceptual benefits of attention comes from Sir David Ferrier (1886), a Scottish physiologist working in the late nineteenth century. Ferrier found that after removal of part of the PFC in a single hemisphere, monkeys were unable to direct their gaze into the affected hemifield and that this movement deficit was accompanied by a "loss of the faculty of attention"; he hypothesized that the "power of attention is intimately related to volitional movements of the head and eyes" (Ferrier 1886, p. 151). Ferrier's approach was subsequently refined by twentieth-century investigators who found that similar deficits in attention resulted from PFC lesions that were restricted to a small band of tissue lying anterior to the arcuate sulcus, which is known as the frontal eye field (FEF) (Welch & Stuteville 1958, Latto & Cowey 1971).

Anatomically, the FEF is appropriately situated for a role in visually guided saccades. FEF neurons receive projections from most of the functionally defined areas within the visual cortex (Schall et al. 1995), and FEF neurons project to both the brainstem saccade generator and the SC, which is a midbrain structure with a known involvement in saccade production (Fries 1984, Stanton et al. 1988, Lynch et al. 1994). However, the FEF also sends feedback projections to much of the visual cortex (Schall et al. 1995, Stanton et al. 1995), suggesting a pathway by which saccade-related signals can influence visual representations. The visually driven responses of some classes of FEF neurons (visual and visuomovement) are enhanced when the RF stimulus is used as a saccade target compared to when no saccade is made to the stimulus (Wurtz & Mohler 1976, Goldberg & Bushnell 1981, Bruce & Goldberg 1985). In addition, neural correlates of visual selection have been observed in the FEF during a search task in which monkeys were required to make a saccade to a singleton embedded among distracters (Bichot & Schall 1999). Although early studies suggested that FEF neuron response enhancement was specifically related to the execution of a saccade (e.g., Goldberg & Bushnell 1981), more recent studies demonstrate that FEF visual responses are enhanced even in the absence of saccades and during purely covert attention (Thompson et al. 2005, Armstrong et al. 2009). Perhaps most compelling is the observation that operantly induced increases in FEF neuronal activity result in both perceptual benefits at spatially specific locations and corresponding enhancements in target selectivity in the visual responses of FEF neurons (Schafer & Moore 2011).

Several studies have employed electrical microstimulation to probe the role of gaze-control structures in the deployment of spatial attention. Moore & Fallah (2001) were the first to examine the effect of intracortical microstimulation on visual attention. They found that when sites within the FEF were stimulated using currents that were too low to evoke saccades (subthreshold), these currents could enhance attentional deployment in a spatially specific manner. Two subsequent studies reported similar enhancements in visual spatial attention following subthreshold microstimulation of the SC (Cavanaugh & Wurtz 2004, Müller et al. 2005). In both cases, the performance-enhancing effects of microstimulation were spatially dependent, as in the FEF studies. In each of the above studies, the effects of microstimulation were measured in the absence of any saccadic eye movements, i.e., during covert attention. Another study examined the effect of FEF microstimulation on the metrics of saccades made to visual stimuli (Schafer & Moore 2007). In control trials, the endpoints of saccades made to drifting gratings were biased in the direction of grating drift even though the grating aperture was stationary. Subthreshold FEF microstimulation augmented this motion-induced saccadic bias for gratings positioned at locations represented at the stimulation site, in addition to increasing the likelihood of saccades to those locations. This result suggests that activation of FEF sites with microstimulation drives the selection of not only retinotopically corresponding visual stimuli (i.e., attention) but also the appropriate saccades needed to fixate those stimuli.

Consistent with the above evidence of the attention-related effects of FEF microstimulation, a number of subsequent studies have observed modulation of visual cortical responses during subthreshold microstimulation of the FEF. FEF microstimulation elicits a brief enhancement of the visually driven responses of V4 neurons with RFs at locations overlapping the stimulated FEF representation (Moore & Armstrong 2003). The magnitude of the enhancement is greater for more effective RF stimuli and when a non-RF (distracter) stimulus is present. Microstimulation of FEF sites that do not overlap the V4 RF suppresses responses, mimicking the effects observed during endogenous attention. Furthermore, the enhancement of V4 responses is confined only to RF stimuli that align with the endpoint of the saccade vector represented at the FEF site. As a result, when two competing stimuli are present within the V4 RF, FEF microstimulation drives the visual responses toward those observed when the aligned stimulus is presented alone (Armstrong et al. 2006, Armstrong & Moore 2007). A subsequent study using functional magnetic resonance imaging (fMRI) examined the influence of FEF microstimulation on visual activation throughout the visual cortex (Ekstrom et al. 2008). FEF microstimulation enhanced the visual activation of retinotopically corresponding foci within multiple visual areas, including V1. Taken together, the above studies provide direct evidence of a robust influence of the FEF on gain of signals within the visual cortex.

OVERT ATTENTION AND PERISACCADIC PERCEPTION

In humans and other primates, the perception of fine detail is limited to a small fraction of the retina, the fovea. To overcome this limitation, we redirect our gaze about three times per second, typically with saccades. These gaze shifts ultimately lead to foveation of important or salient stimuli, yet even before our eyes begin to move, profound changes in perception and neural representations within the visual cortex can be observed. As mentioned above, psychophysical and neurophysiological studies have demonstrated a strong bias in the visual processing of saccadic targets around the time of the movement, and it is now widely believed that shifts of spatial attention precede the actual movement. In psychophysical studies, this belief is supported by observations of enhanced perceptual performance for saccadic targets compared to perceptual performance for nontarget stimuli (Hoffman & Subramaniam 1995, Kowler et al. 1995, Rolfs & Carrasco 2012; for a review, see Zhao et al. 2012).

Psychophysical studies arguing in favor of a presaccadic shift of spatial attention toward saccadic targets in humans are supported by neurophysiological studies in nonhuman primates demonstrating robust enhancements in visually driven neuronal responses prior to saccades to RF stimuli (see the section Covert and Overt Attention). In addition to these enhancements, other studies have reported changes in the RFs of visual cortical neurons. The RFs of V4 neurons, for example, shift closer to the saccadic target when measured around the time of saccades (Tolias et al. 2001). In other words, V4 neurons become more responsive to stimuli appearing closer to the target when an animal is about to make an eye movement as compared to when fixation is stable. This presaccadic convergence of V4 RFs resembles the modulations of V4 RFs measured during covert attention tasks resulting in RF shifts toward the attended target (Connor et al. 1996, 1997). Similar observations of convergent RF shifts around the time of saccades have been reported for FEF neurons as well (Zirnsak et al. 2014). As a result of these convergent RF shifts (**Figure 2**), visual activity within the FEF population is heavily biased toward the saccadic target at the time of the eye movement. This effect leads to a threefold increase in the proportion of RFs near the target region. These observations appear to be at odds with earlier studies reporting a presaccadic shift of FEF RFs toward their postmovement location (Umeno & Goldberg 1997, Sommer & Wurtz 2006, Shin & Sommer 2012). However, similar to studies reporting related RF shifts within other structures (Duhamel et al. 1992, Walker et al. 1995, Nakamura & Colby 2002, Churan et al. 2012), previous reports of FEF RF shifts relied on coarse spatial measurements of presaccadic RFs, making them difficult to distinguish from convergent shifts (Zirnsak et al. 2010, Zirnsak & Moore 2014).

The seemingly biased spatial representations in favor of the movement target within V4 (Tolias et al. 2001) and the FEF (Zirnsak et al. 2014) are reminiscent of the perceptual distortions of space around the time of saccadic eye movements. The ability of human observers to localize briefly presented stimuli at the time of saccades is largely impaired. Typically, human observers perceive such stimuli as if they were presented much closer to the saccadic target than they actually are, resembling a compression of visual space (Ross et al. 1997, Kaiser & Lappe 2004). Hamker et al.

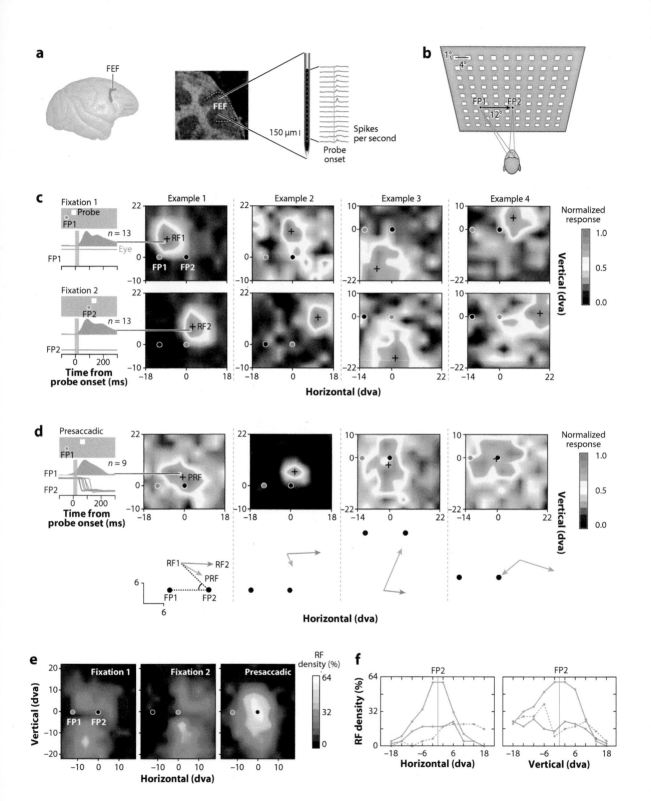

(2008) unified the changes in spatial representations within visual structures and the perceptual distortions at the time of saccades in a computational model. The proposed mechanism is based on the modulation of visual signals around the time of the eye movement. Consistent with the reports of enhanced responses of neurons within extrastriate areas to targets of eye movements, it is assumed that the modulation is strongest for neurons with RFs close to the saccadic target and levels off gradually for neurons with more distant RFs (Armstrong et al. 2006, Hamker & Zirnsak 2006). This gain modulation leads to severe distortions of the neuronal population response to nontarget stimuli, resulting in their mislocalization toward the saccadic target. Moreover, these distorted population responses cause changes in model RFs further downstream. Overall, model RFs converge toward the saccadic target (Zirnsak et al. 2010), leading to an increase in the number of model neurons effectively processing the target region.

Whereas a large body of evidence suggests an interdependence of spatial attention and eye movement preparation, a similar link between eye movement preparation and feature-based attention seems less clear (Born et al. 2012, Jonikaitis & Theeuwes 2013, White et al. 2013). During visual search, feature-based selection is thought to guide subsequent spatial selection both covertly and overtly (Bichot et al. 2005), but effects in the other direction have been given much less consideration. However, in a recent study, Burrows et al. (2014) tested whether spatially directed, overt attention, specifically the preparation of saccades, can produce feature-based-like effects on the responses of neurons in V4 (**Figure 3**). Monkeys made saccades to gratings presented at different orientations at one location while gratings were briefly flashed at another location and in the RF of V4 neurons. Importantly, there was no other task requirement in this paradigm; the orientation of the grating target was unrelated and not important for the completion of the task and the reward. Nonetheless, similar to the classic effects of feature-based attention, V4 responses at the nontarget locations depended reliably on the orientation of the targeted grating. Specifically, responses were greater when the orientation of the targeted grating was the orientation preferred by the recorded neuron. This apparent default initiation of feature-based effects from spatially directed attention is consistent with a computational model of gaze-control influences on visual representations (Hamker 2005b).

In summary, it appears that around the time of gaze shifts, visual representations are largely dominated by the target, in terms of both their spatial and their featural composition. That is, even before a stimulus is foveated, our perception is already biased by it (Pollatsek et al. 1990, Jüttner & Röhler 1993, Ganmor et al. 2015, Herwig et al. 2015).

← ──

Figure 2

Presaccadic changes of frontal eye field (FEF) neuronal receptive fields (RFs). (*a*) The FEF in the macaque cortex (*left*) and in a coronal magnetic resonance image from one macaque (*middle*) are shown (Zirnsak et al. 2014). (*Right*) Linear array microelectrode and traces of FEF visual responses were recorded simultaneously across 16 electrode contacts. (*b*) FEF RFs were mapped with a 10 × 9 array [36 × 32 degrees visual angle (dva)] of probe stimuli (*squares*) flashed during fixation at fixation point (FP) 1 and FP2 and immediately before saccades from FP1 to FP2. (*c*) Four example neuronal RF maps. The far left shows the mean peristimulus response histogram for the most effective probe location during fixation at FP1 (*top*) and FP2 (*bottom*). Blue lines and circles indicate eye position and fixation location, respectively. The black circles represent the FP, which is not fixated. Black crosses indicate RF centers during fixation at FP1 (RF1) and FP2 (RF2). (*d*) Presaccadic RF maps of the same neurons measured immediately before saccades from FP1 to FP2. The far left shows the mean peristimulus response histogram for the most effective probe location. Probe presentation (*vertical gray shading*) was completed before saccade onset in all trials. Black crosses indicate the presaccadic RF (PRF) centers. Below each RF map is the measurement of the changes in RF centers during fixation (RF1 to RF2; *gray vectors*) and saccade preparation (RF1 to PRF; *gold vectors*). (*e*) Subpanels plot the percentage of population RFs (*N* = 179) responsive for a given probe location. Blue circles denote the location of fixation. (*f*) Subpanels show horizontal and vertical cross sections through RF density plots centered on the saccade target (FP2) for fixation 1 (*solid gray*), fixation 2 (*dotted gray*), and presaccadic (*gold*) conditions. Figure adapted with permission from Zirnsak et al. (2014).

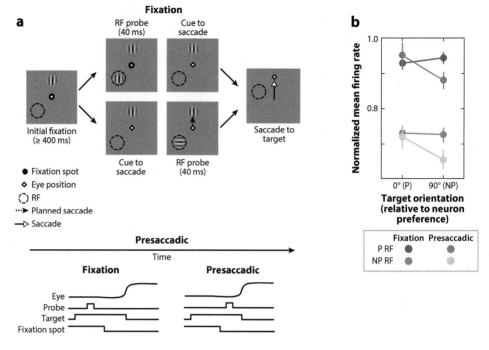

Figure 3

Global selection of saccadic target features by V4 neurons. (*a*) Measurement of target feature-dependent modulation in a delayed saccade task (Burrows et al. 2014). In each trial, the monkey fixated (*diamond*) on a central fixation spot (*black circle*) on the display and was then presented with a saccade target. In the fixation condition (*top*), a probe stimulus appeared briefly in the receptive field (RF) while the monkey continued to fixate, followed by the cue to saccade (the removal of the fixation spot). In the presaccadic condition (*bottom*), the cue to saccade occurred before the probe, and the probe appeared just before saccade initiation. The saccadic target and the RF probe were both gratings, presented at either a neuron's preferred (P) or nonpreferred (NP) orientation. Event traces depict the timelines of the trial events in the two conditions. (*b*) Normalized mean firing rates for all neurons (*N* = 128) during the fixation and presaccadic conditions plotted as a function of target feature (orientation) relative to each neuron's preference. Error bars denote the standard area of the mean. Figure adapted with permission from Burrows et al. (2014).

MECHANISMS OF FEATURE-BASED ATTENTION

As described in the section Feature-Based Versus Spatial Attention, it is relatively easy to appreciate the adaptive significance of feature-based attention. Yet despite the obvious significance of this type of attention to visually guided behavior, remarkably little is understood about its underlying neural basis. In particular, the origin of the clear neural correlates of feature-based attention and the causal basis for its impact on behavior remain elusive. Perhaps one reason for the relative lack of progress in understanding feature-based attention compared to spatial attention is that it is more difficult to envision the type and source of neural signals capable of biasing sensory input in favor of those matching the searched-for object. That is, it has remained unclear where in the brain one should expect the search templates of feature-based attention to reside. By contrast, motor systems, particularly the oculomotor system, have long been considered possible sources of the spatial template employed during spatial attention (for a review, see Moore et al. 2003). It could be that feature- or object-based templates exist somewhere within the visual system (Baldauf & Desimone 2014), yet to date it has remained difficult to identify them.

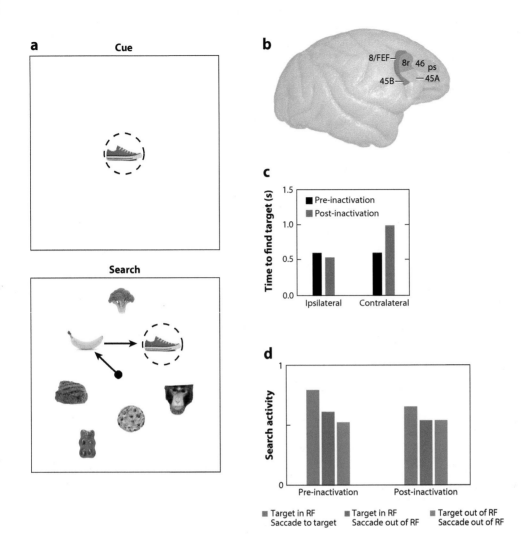

Figure 4

Influence of VPA neurons on visual search and feature selection within the FEF. (*a*) Visual search task (Bichot et al. 2015). The monkey was cued to find a specific object among distracters. The dashed circle represents the current point of fixation, and the arrows represent the monkey's scan path. (*b*) Lateral view of the macaque brain. VPA neurons are likely located within cytoarchitectonic areas 45A and ventral 46. (*c*) Following VPA inactivation, the search times of the animals almost doubled if the target object was presented in the contralateral hemifield but were unaffected if it was presented in the ipsilateral hemifield relative to the inactivated sites. (*d*) Following inactivation of the ventral bank of the principal sulcus, feature selection of target objects by FEF neurons was abolished (compare *red bar* and *blue bar*). Figure adapted with permission from Bichot et al. (2015). Abbreviations: FEF, frontal eye field; ps, principal sulcus; RF, receptive field; VPA, ventral prearcuate.

A recent study by Bichot et al. (2015), however, makes a compelling case for the existence of such a template within the monkey ventral PFC (**Figure 4**). Their data provide evidence that the representation of searched-for object features and the source of feature-based templates reside among neurons within a region of the PFC anterior and ventral to the arcuate sulcus [ventral prearcuate (VPA)], likely within cytoarchitectonic areas 45A and ventral 46. In this study, monkeys performed a standard visual search task in which they were rewarded for localizing, via eye movements, a memorized visual image presented among multiple distracters. On average, monkeys located the remembered target within only approximately three eye movements among eight total images in each behavioral trial, indicating that their search was guided by a memory of the cued stimulus. The authors recorded the responses of neurons within the VPA, as well as the FEF, inferior temporal cortex, and another region of the PFC within the ventral bank of the principal sulcus. Among neurons from these four areas, only neurons in the VPA were selective for the memorized object throughout the entire search period. Neurons in the VPA and the FEF exhibited both feature-based and spatially based attentional modulation. However, the observed feature-based modulation emerged earlier for VPA neurons than it did among neighboring FEF neurons, suggesting that the modulation among VPA neurons was the source of the activity within the other structures, particularly the FEF. To test this hypothesis directly, the authors locally inactivated sites within the VPA. Following local inactivation of the VPA, monkeys exhibited a clear reduction in search performance when the target object appeared within the contralateral (inactivated) visual hemifield. In particular, the average number of saccades required to locate the target object among distracters increased significantly. In addition, following inactivation of the VPA, the feature-based modulation previously observed among neurons within the FEF was no longer present. These results provide compelling evidence that activity within the VPA is necessary for feature-based search behavior as well as the neural correlates of search within other areas of the PFC. The results also raise important questions that may be addressed in future studies. For example, does inactivation of the VPA lead to a loss of feature-based modulation throughout the visual cortex, as it does within the FEF?

NEUROMODULATORS AND ATTENTION

Neuromodulators compose a class of neurotransmitters that influence synaptic transmission broadly within neural circuits, often altering the postsynaptic effects of other transmitters (e.g., glutamate) as well as one another. Generally, researchers have considered, to varying degrees, the roles of three neuromodulators, acetylcholine (Ach), dopamine (DA), and norepinephrine (NE), in attention (Noudoost & Moore 2011a,b). Each of these neuromodulators has a discrete origin from localized brainstem or midbrain nuclei and is released widely throughout other subcortical and cortical structures. Ach is synthesized and released by the nucleus basalis of Meynert, the substantia innominata, and the diagonal band of the basal forebrain. DA is synthesized and released from a set of midbrain nuclei, including the substantia nigra pars compacta and the ventral tegmental area, the latter of which projects broadly to cortical areas. NE is synthesized centrally by neurons within the locus coeruleus (LC) and, like Ach and DA, is released widely throughout subcortical and cortical structures. Importantly, when considering the effects of neuromodulators on specific circuits, like those controlling selective attention, it is necessary to bear in mind the relative breadth of the neuromodulatory projection patterns. In contrast to global arousal and vigilance, selective attention necessarily involves the amplification of highly specific signals, often nested within multiple sensory dimensions, as when vision is amplified over other senses or color is amplified over motion. Although, on the one hand, it seems likely that each of these neuromodulators interacts with multiple forms of selective attention, on the other hand, it seems less likely that they are uniquely involved in the selective component of selective attention (see the section Future Issues).

Acetylcholine

Systemic increases in Ach activity are known to enhance selective visual attention in normal human subjects (Warburton & Rusted 1993, Furey et al. 2008). Within cortical areas, basal forebrain stimulation enhances sensory signals within the somatosensory (Tremblay et al. 1990), auditory (Metherate & Ashe 1993), and visual cortices (Goard & Dan 2009), thus providing a means by which Ach release can increase perceptual performance globally and perhaps augment attention selection by other circuit mechanisms. Although these effects appear to be achieved largely via metabotropic muscarinic receptors (mAchRs), the extent to which Ach's role in attention is achieved via mAchRs, ionotropic nicotinic receptors (nAchRs), or both, remains unclear. Studies in rodents suggest that the processing of sensory signals within posterior areas might be influenced by the interaction of the PFC with ascending cholinergic projections, and this interaction appears to depend on nAchRs (Guillem et al. 2011). Indeed, within the primary visual cortex (area V1), gain control appears to be achieved largely by nAchRs (Disney et al. 2007). However, Thiele and colleagues (Herrero et al. 2008) found evidence that mAchRs play a specific role in the modulation of visual cortical responses during selective attention. They recorded visual responses of V1 neurons in monkeys performing a covert attention task and found that iontophoretic application of Ach augmented the attentional modulation of V1 responses. In addition, they found that application of scopolamine, a mAchR antagonist, reduced the attentional modulation, but application of the nAchR antagonist, mecamylamine, had no effect. More recent neurophysiological evidence in monkeys suggests that basal forebrain Ach interacts with the amygdala to direct spatial attention according to motivational factors (Peck & Salzman 2014). Combined, the above evidence demonstrates the important role of Ach-mediated activity, operating via mAchRs, nAchRs, or both, in the control of sensory activity during selective attention.

Dopamine

The effect of DA on selective attention appears to be achieved via its effects on the PFC (Noudoost & Moore 2011a,b). DA can alter the strength and reliability of converging glutamatergic synapses (Seamans & Yang 2004). However, this modulatory influence can exhibit an inverted U–shaped property wherein optimal DA levels lead to peak effects on synaptic efficacy and reduced effects at levels above or below optimal (Vijayraghavan et al. 2007). This complex property of DA neuromodulation appears consistent with hypotheses about a dopaminergic dysfunction in attentional disorders such as attention deficit hyperactivity disorder (ADHD) (Arnsten 2011). ADHD patients not only exhibit perceptual deficits (Mason et al. 2003) but also show evidence of abnormal PFC DA (Ernst et al. 1998).

Several rodent studies have implicated PFC DA in the control of attention (e.g., Chudasama & Robbins 2004). However, many of the behavioral paradigms utilized in rodents do not clearly involve a selective processing component in their task design (e.g., Kim et al. 2016), and thus they do not clearly distinguish between behavioral vigilance and selective attention. Recent work in primates suggests a basis by which changes in PFC DA can alter selective attention. Noudoost & Moore (2011a,b) studied the impact of manipulating DA-mediated activity within the FEF by injecting sub-microliter volumes of D1 and D2 receptor agonists and antagonists into discrete FEF sites. Following injections of a D1 receptor antagonist, visual targets presented within the affected part of space were more likely to be chosen by the monkey as targets for saccades than during control trials. Manipulation of D2 receptor activity had no effect. Thus, the manipulation increased saccadic target selection. In addition, the manipulation produced an enhancement in the gain of visually driven responses in V4 during passive fixation. D1 manipulation effectively elicited correlates of covert attention within the extrastriate cortex in the absence of a behavioral task. Importantly, similar injections of a D2 agonist into FEF sites resulted in target selection effects equivalent to those of the D1 antagonist. However, only the latter produced attention-like effects within V4. Thus, the control of attention and target selection by the FEF appears to be dissociable at the level of DA receptors.

Norepinephrine

In contrast to the extensive range of studies on the roles of Ach and DA in selective attention, less is understood about the role of NE. Past work has generally associated NE with behavioral arousal rather than selective attention (Berridge & Waterhouse 2003). Noradrenergic neurons within the LC respond selectively to salient sensory stimuli (Foote et al. 1980, Grant et al. 1988), and stimulation of the LC can modulate sensory responses in awake animals (Devilbiss et al. 2006). However, other studies indicate that LC activity does not simply reflect stimulus-driven salience but rather depends heavily on the task relevance of stimuli. For example, LC neurons respond with robust phasic bursts to the presentation of learned targets, but they respond only weakly when nontargets are presented (Aston-Jones & Cohen 2005). Thus, noradrenergic modulation may contribute to more than mediation of the influence of arousal state on sensory responses. This view may be consistent with the known benefits of noradrenergic drugs in ADHD (Arnsten et al. 2007) and the finding that blockade of α2A NE receptors impairs response inhibition (Ma et al. 2003) and increases hyperactivity (Ma et al. 2005) in monkeys. Nonetheless, as with Ach and DA, further studies are needed to determine the degree to which noradrenergic modulation is necessary and sufficient for attentional selection.

ASSESSING ATTENTIONAL DYSFUNCTIONS

A fundamental issue facing the study of neural mechanisms of attention is how to define and quantify dysfunctions in selective attention. For future studies aimed at identifying the neural mechanisms causally related to the filtering of behaviorally relevant visual information, the need to answer this question will only grow in importance. Subsequent attempts to pinpoint the neurons, neural circuits, and neural computations that uniquely confer on the nervous system the capacity to distinguish a target from distracters will need to determine more definitively the behavioral phenotypes that reflect a loss in that capacity rather than a loss in some other function. Because attention appears to be defined most specifically by the benefits observed in the processing of relevant sensory information, it is reasonable to posit that one should expect the loss of those benefits, rather than a deficit in some aspect of sensory processing, when attentional mechanisms are absent.

Several models have been proposed to account for the effects of attention on visual signals (Desimone & Duncan 1995, Reynolds et al. 2000, Lee & Maunsell 2009, Reynolds & Heeger 2009). These models provide a framework for understanding the interaction between attentional control and the encoding of visual information, thus allowing one to potentially distinguish between deficits in either process. Each model involves an interaction between attentional gain control and the competition inherent in visual processing. For example, although a representation with higher stimulus drive will tend to exert greater suppression on its competitors than one with lower stimulus drive, attention to one stimulus or the other is expected to mitigate (or exacerbate) that effect. But crucially, when attention is held constant, decreases in the strength of a representation can be brought about not only by reduced competitiveness with the representations of other stimuli but also by reduced stimulus drive, including reduced drive due to brain damage. This loss in stimulus drive should result in a competitive disadvantage at locations within intact maps. As a result, because stimulus drive and attention both interact competitively, the above models suggest that altering stimulus drive in such a way should affect the magnitude of neural responses in a manner that is consistent with a loss of attention, even when attention is functioning normally. Thus, even when attentional gain remains intact, a diminution in the strength of visual input could be sufficient to produce a distracter-dependent deficit (Squire et al. 2013). Unfortunately, distracter dependency is often used to define a loss in attentional function (e.g., De Weerd et al. 1999, Wardak et al. 2006, Lovejoy & Krauzlis 2010). Such a definition may thus be overly broad in many cases (Desimone & Duncan 1995) and may lead to a difficulty in distinguishing between the role of brain structures in visual attention and their role in visual processing, as in the case of V4 (e.g., Schiller & Lee 1991, De Weerd et al. 1999), and their possible role in response selection, as in the case of the SC (Zénon & Krauzlis 2012). Thus, rather than assessing the effect of distracters on perceptual performance as a means of probing attentional dysfunctions, it may be best for future studies to instead assess the potential of attentional cues to produce benefits in the perception of particular stimuli, whether such cues are top-down or bottom-up.

CONCLUDING REMARKS

In this review, we have discussed the aspects and types of visual selective attention, how they alter processing of stimuli by neurons within the visual system, what is currently known about the causal basis of selective attention, and how to assess attentional dysfunctions. We hope it will be apparent to the reader how incomplete current knowledge is about the neural circuitry underlying the selective processing of visual information, particularly when considering the variety of ways in which visual information can be selectively processed. Our goal has been to highlight the comparison between aspects of attention for which much progress has been made (e.g., spatial attention) and aspects for which little progress has been made (e.g., feature-based and bottom-up attention). Although it would certainly be convenient if different aspects of attention were controlled by common, or even homologous, mechanisms, this clearly is not the case, at least in the primate visual system. Thus, as we highlight in the section Future Issues, future studies need to focus on identifying the specific neural mechanisms that underlie each unique aspect of visual selective attention. However, we suspect that such progress is forthcoming.

FUTURE ISSUES

1. What are the relative contributions of the parietal and prefrontal cortices to bottom-up and top-down attention?

2. Is the modulation of visual responses during attentional deployment necessary and sufficient for the perceptual benefits observed in behavior?

3. What is the precise role of particular neuromodulators in selective attention?

4. Aside from gaze-control mechanisms, what is the role, if any, of other effector systems (e.g., reaching) in selective visual attention?

5. What is the precise relationship between mechanisms signaling reward and motivation and (other) mechanisms controlling selective visual attention?

DISCLOSURE STATEMENT

The authors are not aware of any affiliations, memberships, funding, or financial holdings that might be perceived as affecting the objectivity of this review.

ACKNOWLEDGMENTS

We thank R.F. Squire, N.A. Steinmetz, and B. Noudoost for their contributions. This work was supported by NIH EY014924.

LITERATURE CITED

Armstrong KM, Chang MH, Moore T. 2009. Selection and maintenance of spatial information by frontal eye field neurons. *J. Neurosci.* 29:15621–29

Armstrong KM, Fitzgerald JK, Moore T. 2006. Changes in visual receptive fields with microstimulation of frontal cortex. *Neuron* 50:791–98

Armstrong KM, Moore T. 2007. Rapid enhancement of visual cortical response discriminability by microstimulation of the frontal eye field. *PNAS* 104:9499–504

Arnsten AF. 2011. Catecholamine influences on dorsolateral prefrontal cortical networks. *Biol. Psychiatry* 69(12):e89–99

Arnsten AF, Scahill L, Findling RL. 2007. Alpha2-adrenergic receptor agonists for the treatment of attention-deficit/hyperactivity disorder: emerging concepts from new data. *J. Child Adolesc. Psychopharmacol.* 17:393–406

Aston-Jones G, Cohen JD. 2005. An integrative theory of locus coeruleus-norepinephrine function: adaptive gain and optimal performance. *Annu. Rev. Neurosci.* 28:403–50

Averbeck BB, Latham PE, Pouget A. 2006. Neural correlations, population coding and computation. *Nat. Rev. Neurosci.* 7:358–66

Azouz R, Gray CM. 2003. Adaptive coincidence detection and dynamic gain control in visual cortical neurons in vivo. *Neuron* 37:513–23

Balan PF, Gottlieb J. 2006. Integration of exogenous input into a dynamic salience map revealed by perturbing attention. *J. Neurosci.* 26:9239–49

Baldauf D, Desimone R. 2014. Neural mechanisms of object-based attention. *Science* 344:424–27

Baruni JK, Lau B, Salzman CD. 2015. Reward expectation differentially modulates attentional behavior and activity in visual area V4. *Nat. Neurosci.* 18:1656–63

Bashinski HS, Bacharach VR. 1980. Enhancement of perceptual sensitivity as the result of selectively attending to spatial locations. *Percept. Psychophys.* 28:241–48

Beck DM, Kastner S. 2005. Stimulus context modulates competition in human extrastriate cortex. *Nat. Neurosci.* 8:1110–16

Berridge CW, Waterhouse BD. 2003. The locus coeruleus-noradrenergic system: modulation of behavioral state and state-dependent cognitive processes. *Brain Res. Brain Res. Rev.* 42:33–84

Bichot NP, Heard MT, DeGennaro EM, Desimone R. 2015. A source for feature-based attention in the prefrontal cortex. *Neuron* 88:832–44

Bichot NP, Rossi AF, Desimone R. 2005. Parallel and serial neural mechanisms for visual search in macaque area V4. *Science* 308:529–34

Bichot NP, Schall JD. 1999. Effects of similarity and history on neural mechanisms of visual selection. *Nat. Neurosci.* 2:549–54

Bichot NP, Schall JD. 2002. Priming in macaque frontal cortex during popout visual search: feature-based facilitation and location-based inhibition of return. *J. Neurosci.* 22:4675–85

Bisley JW, Goldberg ME. 2010. Attention, intention, and priority in the parietal lobe. *Annu. Rev. Neurosci.* 33:1–21

Born S, Ansorge U, Kerzel D. 2012. Feature-based effects in the coupling between attention and saccades. *J. Vis.* 12:27

Briggs F, Mangun GR, Usrey WM. 2013. Attention enhances synaptic efficacy and the signal-to-noise ratio in neural circuits. *Nature* 499:476–80

Bruce CJ, Goldberg ME. 1985. Primate frontal eye fields. I. Single neurons discharging before saccades. *J. Neurophysiol.* 53:603–35

Buffalo EA, Fries P, Landman R, Buschman TJ, Desimone R. 2011. Laminar differences in gamma and alpha coherence in the ventral stream. *PNAS.* 108:11262–67

Buffalo EA, Fries P, Landman R, Liang H, Desimone R. 2010. A backward progression of attentional effects in the ventral stream. *PNAS.* 107:361–65

Burrows BE, Moore T. 2009. Influence and limitations of popout in the selection of salient visual stimuli by area V4 neurons. *J. Neurosci.* 29:15169–77

Burrows BE, Zirnsak M, Akhlaghpour H, Wang M, Moore T. 2014. Global selection of saccadic target features by neurons in area V4. *J. Neurosci.* 34:6700–6

Buschman TJ, Miller EK. 2007. Top-down versus bottom-up control of attention in the prefrontal and posterior parietal cortices. *Science* 315:1860–62

Cardin JA, Carlén M, Meletis K, Knoblich U, Zhang F, et al. 2009. Driving fast-spiking cells induces gamma rhythm and controls sensory responses. *Nature* 459:663–67

Carrasco M. 2011. Visual attention: the past 25 years. *Vis. Res.* 51:1484–525

Cavanaugh J, Wurtz RH. 2004. Subcortical modulation of attention counters change blindness. *J. Neurosci.* 24:11236–43

Chelazzi L, Duncan J, Miller EK, Desimone R. 1998. Responses of neurons in inferior temporal cortex during memory-guided visual search. *J. Neurophysiol.* 80:2918–40

Chelazzi L, Miller EK, Duncan J, Desimone R. 1993. A neural basis for visual search in inferior temporal cortex. *Nature* 363:345–47

Chudasama Y, Robbins TW. 2004. Dopaminergic modulation of visual attention and working memory in the rodent prefrontal cortex. *Neuropsychopharmacology* 29:1628–36

Churan J, Guitton D, Pack CC. 2012. Perisaccadic remapping and rescaling of visual responses in macaque superior colliculus. *PLOS ONE* 7:e52195

Cohen MR, Maunsell JH. 2009. Attention improves performance primarily by reducing interneuronal correlations. *Nat. Neurosci.* 12:1594–600

Cohen MR, Maunsell JH. 2010. A neuronal population measure of attention predicts behavioral performance on individual trials. *J. Neurosci.* 30:15241–53

Cohen MR, Maunsell JH. 2011. Using neuronal populations to study the mechanisms underlying spatial and feature attention. *Neuron* 70:1192–204

Connor CE, Gallant JL, Preddie DC, Van Essen DC. 1996. Responses in area V4 depend on the spatial relationship between stimulus and attention. *J. Neurophysiol.* 75:1306–8

Connor CE, Preddie DC, Gallant JL, Van Essen DC. 1997. Spatial attention effects in macaque area V4. *J. Neurosci.* 17:3201–14

Constantinidis C, Steinmetz MA. 2005. Posterior parietal cortex automatically encodes the location of salient stimuli. *J. Neurosci.* 25:233–38

Corbetta M, Miezin FM, Dobmeyer S, Shulman GL, Petersen SE. 1991. Selective and divided attention during visual discriminations of shape, color, and speed: functional anatomy by positron emission tomography. *J. Neurosci.* 11:2382–402

Corbetta M, Shulman GL. 2002. Control of goal-directed and stimulus-driven attention in the brain. *Nat. Rev. Neurosci.* 3:201–15

Crovitz HF, Daves W. 1962. Tendencies to eye movement and perceptual accuracy. *J. Exp. Psychol.* 63:495–98

De Weerd P, Peralta MR 3rd, Desimone R, Ungerleider LG. 1999. Loss of attentional stimulus selection after extrastriate cortical lesions in macaques. *Nat. Neurosci.* 2:753–58

Desimone R, Duncan J. 1995. Neural mechanisms of selective visual attention. *Annu. Rev. Neurosci.* 18:193–222

Deubel H, Schneider WX. 1996. Saccade target selection and object recognition: evidence for a common attentional mechanism. *Vis. Res.* 36:1827–37

Devilbiss DM, Page ME, Waterhouse BD. 2006. Locus ceruleus regulates sensory encoding by neurons and networks in waking animals. *J. Neurosci.* 26:9860–72

Disney AA, Aoki C, Hawken MJ. 2007. Gain modulation by nicotine in macaque V1. *Neuron* 56:701–13

Downing CJ. 1988. Expectancy and visual-spatial attention: effects on perceptual quality. *J. Exp. Psychol. Hum. Percept. Perform.* 14:188–202

Duhamel JR, Colby CL, Goldberg ME. 1992. The updating of the representation of visual space in parietal cortex by intended eye movements. *Science* 255:90–92

Egeth HE, Yantis S. 1997. Visual attention: control, representation, and time course. *Annu. Rev. Psychol.* 48:269–97

Einhäuser W, Rutishauser U, Koch C. 2008. Task-demands can immediately reverse the effects of sensory-driven saliency in complex visual stimuli. *J. Vis.* 8:2.1–19

Ekstrom LB, Roelfsema PR, Arsenault JT, Bonmassar G, Vanduffel W. 2008. Bottom-up dependent gating of frontal signals in early visual cortex. *Science* 321:414–17

Ernst M, Zametkin AJ, Matochik JA, Jons PH, Cohen RM. 1998. DOPA decarboxylase activity in attention deficit hyperactivity disorder adults. A [fluorine-18]fluorodopa positron emission tomographic study. *J. Neurosci.* 18:5901–7

Fecteau JH, Munoz DP. 2006. Salience, relevance, and firing: a priority map for target selection. *Trends Cogn. Sci.* 10:382–90

Ferrier D. 1886. *The Functions of the Brain*. London: Smith, Elder & Co.

Fischer B, Boch R. 1981. Enhanced activation of neurons in prelunate cortex before visually guided saccades of trained rhesus monkeys. *Exp. Brain Res.* 44:129–37

Foote SL, Aston-Jones G, Bloom FE. 1980. Impulse activity of locus coeruleus neurons in awake rats and monkeys is a function of sensory stimulation and arousal. *PNAS* 77:3033–37

Fries P. 2009. Neuronal gamma-band synchronization as a fundamental process in cortical computation. *Annu. Rev. Neurosci.* 32:209–24

Fries P, Reynolds JH, Rorie AE, Desimone R. 2001. Modulation of oscillatory neuronal synchronization by selective visual attention. *Science* 291:1560–63

Fries W. 1984. Cortical projections to the superior colliculus in the macaque monkey: a retrograde study using horseradish peroxidase. *J. Comp. Neurol.* 230:55–76

Furey ML, Pietrini P, Haxby JV, Drevets WC. 2008. Selective effects of cholinergic modulation on task performance during selective attention. *Neuropsychopharmacology* 33:913–23

Ganmor E, Landy MS, Simoncelli EP. 2015. Near-optimal integration of orientation information across saccades. *J. Vis.* 15:8

Goard M, Dan Y. 2009. Basal forebrain activation enhances cortical coding of natural scenes. *Nat. Neurosci.* 12:1444–49

Goldberg ME, Bisley JW, Powell KD, Gottlieb J. 2006. Saccades, salience and attention: the role of the lateral intraparietal area in visual behavior. *Prog. Brain Res.* 155:157–75

Goldberg ME, Bushnell MC. 1981. Behavioral enhancement of visual responses in monkey cerebral cortex. II. Modulation in frontal eye fields specifically related to saccades. *J. Neurophysiol.* 46:773–87

Goodale MA, Milner AD. 1992. Separate visual pathways for perception and action. *Trends Neurosci.* 15:20–25

Grant SJ, Aston-Jones G, Redmond DE Jr. 1988. Responses of primate locus coeruleus neurons to simple and complex sensory stimuli. *Brain Res. Bull.* 21:401–10

Guillem K, Bloem B, Poorthuis RB, Loos M, Smit AB, et al. 2011. Nicotinic acetylcholine receptor β2 subunits in the medial prefrontal cortex control attention. *Science* 333:888–91

Hamker FH. 2005a. The emergence of attention by population-based inference and its role in distributed processing and cognitive control of vision. *Comput. Vis. Image Underst.* 100:64–106

Hamker FH. 2005b. The reentry hypothesis: the putative interaction of the frontal eye field, ventrolateral prefrontal cortex, and areas V4, IT for attention and eye movement. *Cereb. Cortex* 15:431–47

Hamker FH, Zirnsak M. 2006. V4 receptive field dynamics as predicted by a systems-level model of visual attention using feedback from the frontal eye field. *Neural. Netw.* 19:1371–82

Hamker FH, Zirnsak M, Calow D, Lappe M. 2008. The peri-saccadic perception of objects and space. *PLOS Comput. Biol.* 4:e31

Handy TC, Kingstone A, Mangun GR. 1996. Spatial distribution of visual attention: perceptual sensitivity and response latency. *Percept. Psychophys.* 58:613–27

Hawkins HL, Hillyard SA, Luck SJ, Mouloua M, Downing CJ, Woodward DP. 1990. Visual attention modulates signal detectability. *J. Exp. Psychol. Hum. Percept. Perform.* 16:802–11

Hegdé J, Felleman DJ. 2003. How selective are V1 cells for pop-out stimuli? *J. Neurosci.* 23:9968–80

Heinze HJ, Mangun GR, Burchert W, Hinrichs H, Scholz M, et al. 1994. Combined spatial and temporal imaging of brain activity during visual selective attention in humans. *Nature* 372:543–46

Herrero JL, Roberts MJ, Delicato LS, Gieselmann MA, Dayan P, Thiele A. 2008. Acetylcholine contributes through muscarinic receptors to attentional modulation in V1. *Nature* 454:1110–14

Herrmann K, Montaser-Kouhsari L, Carrasco M, Heeger DJ. 2010. When size matters: Attention affects performance by contrast or response gain. *Nat. Neurosci.* 13:1554–59

Herwig A, Weiss K, Schneider WX. 2015. When circles become triangular: how transsaccadic predictions shape the perception of shape. *Ann. N. Y. Acad. Sci.* 1339:97–105

Hillyard SA. 1993. Electrical and magnetic brain recordings: contributions to cognitive neuroscience. *Curr. Opin. Neurobiol.* 3:217–24

Hoffman JE, Subramaniam B. 1995. The role of visual attention in saccadic eye movements. *Percept. Psychophys.* 57:787–95

Hu Y, Zylberberg J, Shea-Brown E. 2014. The sign rule and beyond: boundary effects, flexibility, and noise correlations in neural population codes. *PLOS Comput. Biol.* 10:e1003469

Ipata AE, Gee AL, Gottlieb J, Bisley JW, Goldberg ME. 2006. LIP responses to a popout stimulus are reduced if it is overtly ignored. *Nat. Neurosci.* 9:1071–76

Itti L, Koch C. 2001. Computational modelling of visual attention. *Nat. Rev. Neurosci.* 2:194–203

Jazayeri M, Movshon JA. 2007. A new perceptual illusion reveals mechanisms of sensory decoding. *Nature* 446:912–15

Jonikaitis D, Theeuwes J. 2013. Dissociating oculomotor contributions to spatial and feature-based selection. *J. Neurophysiol.* 110:1525–34

Joseph JS, Chun MM, Nakayama K. 1997. Attentional requirements in a 'preattentive' feature search task. *Nature* 387:805–7

Jüttner M, Röhler R. 1993. Lateral information transfer across saccadic eye movements. *Percept. Psychophys.* 53:210–20

Kaiser M, Lappe M. 2004. Perisaccadic mislocalization orthogonal to saccade direction. *Neuron* 41:293–300

Kastner S, Ungerleider LG. 2001. The neural basis of biased competition in human visual cortex. *Neuropsychologia* 39:1263–76

Kim J, Wasserman E, Edward A, Castro L, Freeman JH. 2016. Anterior cingulate cortex inactivation impairs rodent visual selective attention and prospective memory. *Behav. Neurosci.* 130:75–90

Knierim JJ, van Essen DC. 1992. Neuronal responses to static texture patterns in area V1 of the alert macaque monkey. *J. Neurophysiol.* 67:961–80

Kowler E, Anderson E, Dosher B, Blaser E. 1995. The role of attention in the programming of saccades. *Vis. Res.* 35:1897–916

Lamme VA. 1995. The neurophysiology of figure-ground segregation in primary visual cortex. *J. Neurosci.* 15:1605–15

Latto R, Cowey A. 1971. Visual field defects after frontal eye-field lesions in monkeys. *Brain Res.* 30:1–24

Lee J, Maunsell JH. 2009. A normalization model of attentional modulation of single unit responses. *PLOS ONE* 4:e4651

Lovejoy LP, Krauzlis RJ. 2010. Inactivation of primate superior colliculus impairs covert selection of signals for perceptual judgments. *Nat. Neurosci.* 13:261–66

Luck SJ, Chelazzi L, Hillyard SA, Desimone R. 1997. Neural mechanisms of spatial selective attention in areas V1, V2, and V4 of macaque visual cortex. *J. Neurophysiol.* 77:24–42

Luck SJ, Woodman GF, Vogel EK. 2000. Event-related potential studies of attention. *Trends Cogn. Sci.* 4(11):432–40

Luo TZ, Maunsell JH. 2015. Neuronal modulations in visual cortex are associated with only one of multiple components of attention. *Neuron* 86:1182–88

Lynch JC, Hoover JE, Strick PL. 1994. Input to the primate frontal eye field from the substantia nigra, superior colliculus, and dentate nucleus demonstrated by transneuronal transport. *Exp. Brain Res.* 100:181–86

Ma CL, Arnsten AF, Li BM. 2005. Locomotor hyperactivity induced by blockade of prefrontal cortical α_2-adrenoceptors in monkeys. *Biol. Psychiatry* 57:192–95

Ma CL, Qi XL, Peng JY, Li BM. 2003. Selective deficit in no-go performance induced by blockade of prefrontal cortical α_2-adrenoceptors in monkeys. *NeuroReport* 14:1013–16

Martin KA, Schröder S. 2016. Phase locking of multiple single neurons to the local field potential in cat V1. *J. Neurosci.* 36:2494–502

Martínez-Trujillo JC, Treue S. 2004. Feature-based attention increases the selectivity of population responses in primate visual cortex. *Curr. Biol.* 14:744–51

Mason DJ, Humphreys GW, Kent LS. 2003. Exploring selective attention in ADHD: visual search through space and time. *J. Child Psychol. Psychiatry* 44:1158–76

Maunsell JH, Cook EP. 2002. The role of attention in visual processing. *Philos. Trans. R. Soc. Lond. B Biol. Sci.* 357:1063–72

Maunsell JH, Treue S. 2006. Feature-based attention in visual cortex. *Trends Neurosci.* 29:317–22

McAdams CJ, Maunsell JH. 1999. Effects of attention on the reliability of individual neurons in monkey visual cortex. *Neuron* 23:765–73

McAdams CJ, Maunsell JH. 2000. Attention to both space and feature modulates neuronal responses in macaque area V4. *J. Neurophysiol.* 83:1751–55

McAlonan K, Cavanaugh J, Wurtz RH. 2008. Guarding the gateway to cortex with attention in visual thalamus. *Nature* 456:391–94

Metherate R, Ashe JH. 1993. Nucleus basalis stimulation facilitates thalamocortical synaptic transmission in the rat auditory cortex. *Synapse* 14:132–43

Mitchell JF, Sundberg KA, Reynolds JH. 2007. Differential attention-dependent response modulation across cell classes in macaque visual area V4. *Neuron* 55:131–41

Mitchell JF, Sundberg KA, Reynolds JH. 2009. Spatial attention decorrelates intrinsic activity fluctuations in macaque area V4. *Neuron* 63:879–88

Moore T. 1999. Shape representations and visual guidance of saccadic eye movements. *Science* 285:1914–17

Moore T, Armstrong KM. 2003. Selective gating of visual signals by microstimulation of frontal cortex. *Nature* 421:370–73

Moore T, Armstrong KM, Fallah M. 2003. Visuomotor origins of covert spatial attention. *Neuron* 40:671–83

Moore T, Chang MH. 2009. Presaccadic discrimination of receptive field stimuli by area V4 neurons. *Vis. Res.* 49:1227–32

Moore T, Fallah M. 2001. Control of eye movements and spatial attention. *PNAS* 98:1273–76

Moore T, Tolias AS, Schiller PH. 1998. Visual representations during saccadic eye movements. *PNAS* 95:8981–84

Moran J, Desimone R. 1985. Selective attention gates visual processing in the extrastriate cortex. *Science* 229:782–84

Motter BC. 1994a. Neural correlates of attentive selection for color or luminance in extrastriate area V4. *J. Neurosci.* 14:2178–89

Motter BC. 1994b. Neural correlates of feature selective memory and popout in extrastriate area V4. *J. Neurosci.* 14:2190–99

Mountcastle VB, Andersen RA, Motter BC. 1981. The influence of attentive fixation upon the excitability of the light-sensitive neurons of the posterior parietal cortex. *J. Neurosci.* 1:1218–25

Müller HJ, Geyer T, Zehetleitner M, Krummenacher J. 2009. Attentional capture by salient color singleton distractors is modulated by top-down dimensional set. *J. Exp. Psychol. Hum. Percept. Perform.* 35:1–16

Müller HJ, Humphreys GW. 1991. Luminance-increment detection: capacity-limited or not? *J. Exp. Psychol. Hum. Percept. Perform.* 17:107–24

Müller JR, Philiastides MG, Newsome WT. 2005. Microstimulation of the superior colliculus focuses attention without moving the eyes. *PNAS* 102:524–29

Nakamura K, Colby CL. 2002. Updating of the visual representation in monkey striate and extrastriate cortex during saccades. *PNAS* 99:4026–31

Navalpakkam V, Itti L. 2007. Search goal tunes features optimally. *Neuron* 53:605–17

Nothdurft HC, Gallant JL, Van Essen DC. 1999. Response modulation by texture surround in primate area V1: correlates of "popout" under anesthesia. *Vis. Neurosci.* 16:15–34

Noudoost B, Chang MH, Steinmetz NA, Moore T. 2010. Top-down control of visual attention. *Curr. Opin. Neurobiol.* 20:183–90

Noudoost B, Moore T. 2011a. Control of visual cortical signals by prefrontal dopamine. *Nature* 474:372–75

Noudoost B, Moore T. 2011b. The role of neuromodulators in selective attention. *Trends Cogn. Sci.* 15:585–91

Ogawa T, Komatsu H. 2006. Neuronal dynamics of bottom-up and top-down processes in area V4 of macaque monkeys performing a visual search. *Exp. Brain Res.* 173:1–13

Peck CJ, Salzman CD. 2014. The amygdala and basal forebrain as a pathway for motivationally guided attention. *J. Neurosci.* 34:13757–67

Pessoa L, Kastner S, Ungerleider LG. 2003. Neuroimaging studies of attention: from modulation of sensory processing to top-down control. *J. Neurosci.* 23:3990–98

Pollatsek A, Rayner K, Henderson JM. 1990. Role of spatial location in integration of pictorial information across saccades. *J. Exp. Psychol. Hum. Percept. Perform.* 16:199–210

Posner MI. 1980. Orienting of attention. *Q. J. Exp. Psychol.* 32:3–25

Prinzmetal W, Taylor N. 2006. Color singleton pop-out does not always poop out: an alternative to visual search. *Psychon. Bull. Rev.* 13:576–80

Reynolds JH, Chelazzi L. 2004. Attentional modulation of visual processing. *Annu. Rev. Neurosci.* 27:611–47

Reynolds JH, Heeger DJ. 2009. The normalization model of attention. *Neuron* 61:168–85

Reynolds JH, Pasternak T, Desimone R. 2000. Attention increases sensitivity of V4 neurons. *Neuron* 26:703–14

Rizzolatti G, Riggio L, Dascola I, Umiltá C. 1987. Reorienting attention across the horizontal and vertical meridians: evidence in favor of a premotor theory of attention. *Neuropsychologia* 25:31–40

Rolfs M, Carrasco M. 2012. Rapid simultaneous enhancement of visual sensitivity and perceived contrast during saccade preparation. *J. Neurosci.* 32:13744–52

Ross J, Morrone MC, Burr DC. 1997. Compression of visual space before saccades. *Nature* 386:598–601

Ruff DA, Cohen MR. 2014. Attention can either increase or decrease spike count correlations in visual cortex. *Nat. Neurosci.* 17:1591–97

Sàenz M, Buracâs GT, Boynton GM. 2002. Global effects of feature-based attention in human visual cortex. *Nat. Neurosci.* 5:631–32

Sàenz M, Buracâs GT, Boynton GM. 2003. Global feature-based attention for motion and color. *Vis. Res.* 43:629–37

Salinas E, Sejnowski TJ. 2001. Correlated neuronal activity and the flow of neural information. *Nat. Rev. Neurosci.* 2:539–50

Schafer RJ, Moore T. 2007. Attention governs action in the primate frontal eye field. *Neuron* 56:541–51

Schafer RJ, Moore T. 2011. Selective attention from voluntary control of neurons in prefrontal cortex. *Science* 332:1568–71

Schall JD, Morel A, King DJ, Bullier J. 1995. Topography of visual cortex connections with frontal eye field in macaque: convergence and segregation of processing streams. *J. Neurosci.* 15:4464–87

Schiller PH, Lee K. 1991. The role of the primate extrastriate area V4 in vision. *Science* 251:1251–53

Scolari M, Serences JT. 2009. Adaptive allocation of attentional gain. *J. Neurosci.* 29:11933–42

Seamans JK, Yang CR. 2004. The principal features and mechanisms of dopamine modulation in the prefrontal cortex. *Prog. Neurobiol.* 74:1–58

Sheinberg DL, Logothetis NK. 2001. Noticing familiar objects in real world scenes: the role of temporal cortical neurons in natural vision. *J. Neurosci.* 21:1340–50

Shepherd M, Findlay JM, Hockey RJ. 1986. The relationship between eye movements and spatial attention. *Q. J. Exp. Psychol. A* 38:475–91

Shin S, Sommer MA. 2012. Division of labor in frontal eye field neurons during presaccadic remapping of visual receptive fields. *J. Neurophysiol.* 108:2144–59

Siegle JH, Pritchett DL, Moore CI. 2014. Gamma-range synchronization of fast-spiking interneurons can enhance detection of tactile stimuli. *Nat. Neurosci.* 17:1371–79

Soltani A, Koch C. 2010. Visual saliency computations: mechanisms, constraints, and the effect of feedback. *J. Neurosci.* 30:12831–43

Sommer MA, Wurtz RH. 2006. Influence of the thalamus on spatial visual processing in frontal cortex. *Nature* 444:374–77

Spitzer H, Desimone R, Moran J. 1988. Increased attention enhances both behavioral and neuronal performance. *Science* 240:338–40

Squire RF, Noudoost B, Schafer RF, Moore T. 2013. Prefrontal contributions to visual selective attention. *Annu. Rev. Neurosci.* 36:451–66

Sridharan D, Steinmetz NA, Moore T, Knudsen EI. 2014. Distinguishing bias from sensitivity effects in multialternative detection tasks. *J. Vis.* 14:16

Stanton GB, Bruce CJ, Goldberg ME. 1995. Topography of projections to posterior cortical areas from the macaque frontal eye fields. *J. Comp. Neurol.* 353:291–305

Stanton GB, Goldberg ME, Bruce CJ. 1988. Frontal eye field efferents in the macaque monkey: II. Topography of terminal fields in midbrain and pons. *J. Comp. Neurol.* 271:493–506

Steinmetz NA, Moore T. 2014. Eye movement preparation modulates neuronal responses in area V4 when dissociated from attentional demands. *Neuron* 83:496–506

Thompson KG, Bichot NP. 2005. A visual salience map in the primate frontal eye field. *Prog. Brain Res.* 147:251–62

Thompson KG, Biscoe KL, Sato TR. 2005. Neuronal basis of covert spatial attention in the frontal eye field. *J. Neurosci.* 25:9479–87

Tolias AS, Moore T, Smirnakis SM, Tehovnik EJ, Siapas AG, Schiller PH. 2001. Eye movements modulate visual receptive fields of V4 neurons. *Neuron* 29:757–67

Treisman AM, Gelade G. 1980. A feature-integration theory of attention. *Cogn. Psychol.* 12(1):97–136

Treisman AM, Sato S. 1990. Conjunction search revisited. *J. Exp. Psychol. Hum. Percept. Perform.* 16:459–78

Tremblay N, Warren RA, Dykes RW. 1990. Electrophysiological studies of acetylcholine and the role of the basal forebrain in the somatosensory cortex of the cat. II. Cortical neurons excited by somatic stimuli. *J. Neurophysiol.* 64:1212–22

Treue S, Martínez-Trujillo JC. 1999. Feature-based attention influences motion processing gain in macaque visual cortex. *Nature* 399:575–79

Umeno MM, Goldberg ME. 1997. Spatial processing in the monkey frontal eye field. I. Predictive visual responses. *J. Neurophysiol.* 78:1373–83

Vijayraghavan S, Wang M, Birnbaum SG, Williams GV, Arnsten AF. 2007. Inverted-U dopamine D1 receptor actions on prefrontal neurons engaged in working memory. *Nat. Neurosci.* 10:376–84

von Helmholtz H. 1925 (1867). *Treatise on Physiological Optics*, transl. JPC Southall. New York: Dover (from German)

Walker MF, Fitzgibbon EJ, Goldberg ME. 1995. Neurons in the monkey superior colliculus predict the visual result of impending saccadic eye movements. *J. Neurophysiol.* 73:1988–2003

Wang F, Chen M, Yan Y, Zhaoping L, Li W. 2015. Modulation of neuronal responses by exogenous attention in macaque primary visual cortex. *J. Neurosci.* 35:13419–29

Warburton DM, Rusted JM. 1993. Cholinergic control of cognitive resources. *Neuropsychobiology* 28:43–46

Wardak C, Ibos G, Duhamel JR, Olivier E. 2006. Contribution of the monkey frontal eye field to covert visual attention. *J. Neurosci.* 26:4228–35

Welch K, Stuteville P. 1958. Experimental production of unilateral neglect in monkeys. *Brain* 81:341–47

White AL, Rolfs M, Carrasco M. 2013. Adaptive deployment of spatial and feature-based attention before saccades. *Vis. Res.* 85:26–35

Wolfe JM. 1994. Guided Search 2.0: a revised model of visual search. *Psychon. Bull. Rev.* 1:202–38

Wurtz RH, Mohler CW. 1976. Enhancement of visual responses in monkey striate cortex and frontal eye fields. *J. Neurophysiol.* 39:766–72

Zénon A, Krauzlis RJ. 2012. Attention deficits without cortical neuronal deficits. *Nature* 489:434–37

Zhao M, Gersch TM, Schnitzer BS, Dosher BA, Kowler E. 2012. Eye movements and attention: the role of pre-saccadic shifts of attention in perception, memory and the control of saccades. *Vis. Res.* 1:40–60

Zirnsak M, Hamker FH. 2010. Attention alters feature space in motion processing. *J. Neurosci.* 30:6882–90

Zirnsak M, Lappe M, Hamker FH. 2010. The spatial distribution of receptive field changes in a model of peri-saccadic perception: predictive remapping and shifts towards the saccade target. *Vis. Res.* 50:1328–37

Zirnsak M, Moore T. 2014. Saccades and shifting receptive fields: anticipating consequences or selecting targets? *Trends Cogn. Sci.* 18:621–28

Zirnsak M, Steinmetz NA, Noudoost B, Xu KZ, Moore T. 2014. Visual space is compressed in prefrontal cortex before eye movements. *Nature* 507:504–7

Learning, Reward, and Decision Making

John P. O'Doherty, Jeffrey Cockburn,* and Wolfgang M. Pauli*

Division of Humanities and Social Sciences and Computation and Neural Systems Program, California Institute of Technology, Pasadena, California 91125; email: jdoherty@caltech.edu

Annu. Rev. Psychol. 2017. 68:73–100

First published online as a Review in Advance on September 28, 2016

The *Annual Review of Psychology* is online at psych.annualreviews.org

This article's doi:
10.1146/annurev-psych-010416-044216

*These authors contributed equally to this review.

Keywords

model based, model free, instrumental, Pavlovian, cognitive map, outcome valuation

Abstract

In this review, we summarize findings supporting the existence of multiple behavioral strategies for controlling reward-related behavior, including a dichotomy between the goal-directed or model-based system and the habitual or model-free system in the domain of instrumental conditioning and a similar dichotomy in the realm of Pavlovian conditioning. We evaluate evidence from neuroscience supporting the existence of at least partly distinct neuronal substrates contributing to the key computations necessary for the function of these different control systems. We consider the nature of the interactions between these systems and show how these interactions can lead to either adaptive or maladaptive behavioral outcomes. We then review evidence that an additional system guides inference concerning the hidden states of other agents, such as their beliefs, preferences, and intentions, in a social context. We also describe emerging evidence for an arbitration mechanism between model-based and model-free reinforcement learning, placing such a mechanism within the broader context of the hierarchical control of behavior.

Contents

INTRODUCTION

All organisms, including humans, face the fundamental challenge of the need to interact effectively with the environment in a manner that maximizes the prospects of obtaining the resources needed to survive and procreate while minimizing the prospect of encountering situations leading to harm. Organisms have evolved a variety of strategies to solve this problem. Accumulating evidence suggests that these distinct strategies coexist in the human brain. In this review, we outline evidence for the existence of these multiple systems of behavioral control and describe how they can be either interdependent or mutually interfering depending on the situation. We establish the role that predictions play in guiding these different behavioral systems and consider how these systems differ in the ways in which they develop their predictions. Finally, we evaluate the possibility that an additional system, used for performing learning and inference in social contexts, is present in the human brain.

Multiple Strategies for Behavioral Control

Perhaps one of the most fruitful questions that may be answered by an understanding of the brain's varied control strategies is whether behavior is motivated by the onset of a stimulus or is directed toward a goal outcome. Historically, habitual responses that are elicited by the perception of a stimulus regardless of the action's consequences (Thorndike 1898) have been contrasted with goal-directed actions that are deliberatively dispatched to achieve a goal (Tolman 1948). Theory and evidence have resolved arguments as to whether human (and animal) behavior is ruled by one strategy or the other by suggesting that both types of behavioral control coexist. In the following sections, we outline some of the behavioral evidence in support of multiple strategies for behavioral control.

Stimulus-Driven Control

Stimulus-driven control refers to a class of behaviors that are expressed in response to the onset of an unanticipated external stimulus. Because these behaviors are instigated by a particular stimulus or class of stimuli, they are cognitively efficient, automatic, and rapidly deployed. However, because they are initiated without consideration of the organism's goals or subsequent outcomes, stimulus-driven behaviors can suffer from being overly rigid, especially in a volatile environment.

Reflexes are perhaps the most primitive form of adaptive response to environmental challenges. Reflexes are stereotyped in that sensory stimuli have innate (unlearned) activating tendencies; thus, reflexes do not depend on synaptic plasticity and are often implemented at the level of the spinal cord and brainstem (Thibodeau & Patton 1992). Reflexes are thought to have a long evolutionary history because they are present in organisms from the simplest, such as bacteria, to the most complex, such as humans, and because analogous motor reflexes to the same stimulus are present across species. Examples of reflexes include the withdrawal reflex that comes from touching a hot surface, the startle response that is elicited in response to sudden stimuli, and the salivatory response to the presentation of food. Reflexes are considered advantageous. For example, the withdrawal reflex helps to avoid tissue damage, the startle response facilitates successful escape responses, and the salivary response aids in the consumption and digestion of food.

Reflexes are fundamentally reactive in that an unanticipated triggering stimulus elicits a preprogrammed response. However, being able to issue responses in a prospective manner, in anticipation of an event that requires a response, provides significant advantages. For example, digestion can be aided by producing saliva prior to the arrival of food, and personal harm may be avoided by steering clear of a hot surface without having to reflexively retreat from it. Pavlovian conditioning, also referred to as classical conditioning, is a means by which an organism can learn to make predictions about the subsequent onset of behaviorally significant events and leverage these predictions to initiate appropriate anticipatory behaviors (Pavlov 1927). As is the case for reflexes, Pavlovian learning is present in many invertebrates, including insects such as *Drosophila* (Tully & Quinn 1985) and even sea slugs (*Aplysia*; Walters et al. 1981), but also in vertebrates, including humans (Davey 1992).

The type of behavior emitted in response to the stimulus depends on the form of outcome the stimulus is paired with (Jenkins & Moore 1973). For instance, a cue paired with the subsequent delivery of food will result in the acquisition of a salivary response, whereas a cue paired with aversive thermal heat will elicit avoidance behavior. Different classes of Pavlovian conditioned responses have been identified. Some are almost identical to the unconditioned responses elicited by the stimuli that trigger them, but other conditioned Pavlovian responses are more distinct. For example, in addition to salivating in response to a food predictive cue, animals also typically orient toward the site of anticipated food delivery (Konorski & Miller 1937).

Although the adaptive advantages of anticipatory behavior are clear, Pavlovian learning is limited to learning about events that occur independent of the organism's behavior. In other words, Pavlovian learning may help an organism prepare for the arrival of food, but it won't help that organism procure its next meal. To increase the possibility of being able to actively attain rewards, many organisms are also equipped with instrumental conditioning, a mechanism that allows them to learn to perform specific yet arbitrary behavioral responses (such as a lever press) in a specific context. In the simplest form of instrumental conditioning, specific stimulus–response patterns are acquired by virtue of the extent to which a particular response gives rise to positive (i.e., the receipt of a reward) or negative (i.e., avoidance of an aversive outcome) reinforcement. This strategy provides significant benefits in terms of cognitive efficiency, speed, and accuracy; however, these benefits come at a cost. Critically, the execution of this class of behavior does not involve an anticipation of a particular outcome (Thorndike 1898); thus, behavior can become habitual, making it difficult to flexibly adjust the behavior should outcome valuation suddenly change. Thus, to the organism's potential detriment, habits may persist even if their outcomes are no longer beneficial. This persistence is suggested to give rise to various forms of addiction (Everitt & Robbins 2016).

Goal-Directed Control

Goal-directed control refers to a class of instrumental behaviors that appear to be motivated by and directed toward a specific outcome. Whereas stimulus-driven control can be thought of as retrospective in that it depends on integrating past experience, goal-directed control may be thought of as prospective in that it leverages a cognitive map of the decision problem to flexibly revalue states and actions (Tolman 1948). Leveraging this map in conjunction with the organism's internal goals facilitates a highly flexible control system, allowing the organism to adapt to changes in the environment without having to resample environmental contingencies directly. However, the necessity of interrogating a cognitive map in order to generate a behavioral plan makes goal-directed control cognitively demanding and slow.

Goal-directed control has been experimentally distinguished from habitual behavior in a study involving training an animal to perform unique actions (e.g., pressing a lever or pulling a chain) in order to obtain unique food outcomes, then devaluing one of the outcomes by pairing it with illness (Balleine & Dickinson 1991). If the animal is behaving in a goal-directed manner, it should be less likely to elicit the action that had been associated with the now-devalued outcome. Indeed, some animals (Dickinson 1985) and humans (Valentin et al. 2007) have been shown to exhibit goal-directed control.

Evidence for the Coexistence of Multiple Control Systems

Although Dickinson & Balleine (1994) demonstrated that rats are capable of performing in a goal-directed manner, Dickinson et al. (1995) also showed that those same animals may also exhibit habitual tendencies. For example, after animals were exposed to extensive training, they were found to persistently elicit responses associated with devalued outcomes (Dickinson et al. 1983). These findings led to the proposal that animals were no longer sensitive to the value of the outcome, but that their behavior was instead driven by the stimulus that had been paired with response. Thus, reward schedules and degree of experience guide, at least in part, the control strategy deployed by the animal. Dickinson et al. (1983) concluded that both habitual and goal-directed systems of control are present in rodents and that these two systems manifest themselves in behavior under different circumstances. Using a similar overtraining manipulation to that performed in rodents, Tricomi et al. (2009) showed that humans also exhibit reduced outcome sensitivity consistent with the behavioral expression of habit.

Even though the distinction between habitual and goal-directed control is often conceptualized and investigated within the context of instrumental behavior, there is tentative evidence that a similar distinction can be made for Pavlovian behavior. Critically, the core criterion to distinguish habitual from goal-directed behavior in the instrumental domain is also present for conditioned Pavlovian responses: Some Pavlovian responses are more sensitive (Dayan & Berridge 2014) than others to outcome value (Nasser et al. 2015). Nevertheless, Pavlovian conditioned responses are often considered to be habitual in a manner analogous to habits in the instrumental domain; this conception of Pavlovian responses gives rise to the prevalent assumption that incremental synaptic plasticity implements the acquisition of Pavlovian contingencies (Rescorla & Wagner 1972). However, this form of habitual Pavlovian conditioning cannot account for findings showing altered patterns in the conditioned response immediately after devaluation and prior to any resampling of the environment's contingencies (Dayan & Berridge 2014). Despite the evidence for the existence of distinct habitual and goal-directed strategies within Pavlovian learning, the majority of the research on multiple control systems has been performed using instrumental conditioning; we also focus on instrumental conditioning in the remainder of this review, although we revisit the Pavlovian case in the section Model-Free and Model-Based Pavlovian Learning.

Why Multiple Systems?

Given that all of the different strategies for controlling behavior that we have described, from reflexes to goal-directed behavior, seem to be present in humans, a natural question follows: Why have all of these systems continued to coexist simultaneously? In other words, why are humans still endowed with the capacity for less flexible Pavlovian reflexes when they have machinery enabling more flexible goal-directed actions instead? One explanation could be that these behavioral control systems coexist because evolutionary adaptation occurred incrementally. The adaptations allowing goal-directed actions may simply have occurred through the addition of new brain circuitry without the refurbishment or repurposing of control systems already in place, similar to adding a modern extension to an older building. However, this seems unlikely given the inefficiencies (both biologically and functionally) associated with adopting a multicontroller strategy in the absence of some additional benefit.

A second, more compelling possible explanation for the coexistence of multiple behavioral control systems is that the brain's control systems share mutually beneficial interdependencies. Evolutionarily recent regions may depend on the computations performed by more primal regions. Primal regions may also take advantage of the experience that comes with more complex control strategies, as well as more evolutionarily recently developed brain regions, which afford powerful domain-general computational functions to existing decision-making strategies. In other words, primal control systems could offer the scaffolding required for more advanced control systems, and the strategic guidance of advanced systems could help primal systems build adaptive associations more efficiently. Indeed, theoretical work (Sutton 1990) has demonstrated that stimulus-driven learning can be significantly improved when guided by a goal-directed system, and experimental work suggests that these interactions take place in the human brain (Doll et al. 2011).

Yet another benefit of multiple behavioral control systems is rooted in the mutually exclusive challenges faced by most organisms. Each system offers a different solution for the trade-off between accuracy, speed, experience, and (computational) efficiency. Goal-directed control typically moves an organism toward goal satisfaction more reliably than other systems, but its flexibility is cognitively demanding and deployment is relatively slow. A goal-directed strategy could offer significant advantages to a predator stalking its prey but prove ruinous for the prey when a swift retreat is required. Conversely, although stimulus-driven behaviors may not always meet an organism's current needs, particularly in a volatile environment, they can be deployed quickly and require less computational resources because they rely on simple stimulus–response associations rather than a rich cognitive map.

The environment presents complex challenges to survival, the range of which demand mutually exclusive strategies to tackle them in an adaptive manner. Organisms stand to gain the best of all worlds by preserving and adaptively deploying multiple control strategies that meet these challenges. However, before we can begin to understand how the brain handles the coexistence of these different forms of behavior, we first need to consider computational theories of value-based decision making, learning, and action selection to fully grasp the nature of the computations implemented in partially separable networks of brain areas.

ALGORITHMS FOR LEARNING AND DECISION MAKING

A central notion in most (e.g., Balleine et al. 2009, Camerer et al. 2005, Glimcher et al. 2013, Padoa-Schioppa & Assad 2006, Platt & Glimcher 1999, Rangel et al. 2008) but not all (see Gigerenzer & Gaissmaier 2011, Strait et al. 2014) theories of value-based decision making as applied to the brain is that, to establish which option to take, an agent must first compute a representation of the expected value or utility that will follow from selecting a particular option. This computation facilitates a comparative process, allowing the agent to identify and pursue the option leading to the greatest expected value. The idea that agents can compare options based on expected value has motivated a search for neural representations of value predictions in the brain, an endeavor that has been enormously fruitful (for some caveats, see O'Doherty 2014). Value signals have been found in a range of brain regions, including the amygdala, orbitofrontal cortex (OFC), ventromedial prefrontal cortex (vmPFC), and ventral and dorsal striata, as well as in a number of other brain areas such as the parietal, premotor, and dorsal frontal areas.

Reinforcement Learning

Evidence for value signals in the brain raises the question of how such signals could be learned or acquired in the first place. The seminal work of Schultz and colleagues (1997) has provided insight into a potential mechanism; they found that the phasic activity of dopamine neurons encodes a prediction error, which signals the difference between expected and actual rewards. Referred to as a reward prediction error (RPE), phasic dopamine activity has been shown to resemble, both in signature and function, a signal used by computational reinforcement learning (RL) algorithms to support learning (Montague et al. 1996, Sutton 1988). This type of learning signal allows an agent to improve its prediction of what to expect from the environment by continually adjusting those predictions toward what actually occurred. The fact that dopamine neurons send dense projections to the striatum and elsewhere has given rise to proposals that RPE signals carried by phasic dopamine facilitate neural plasticity associated with the acquisition of value predictions in these target areas.

Model-Free and Model-Based Reinforcement Learning

A flurry of interest followed the realization that abstract learning theories from computer science could be applied to better understand the brain at a computational level within a RL framework (Doya 1999). In particular, Daw and colleagues (2005) proposed that the distinction between habitual and goal-directed control could be accounted for in terms of two distinct types of RL mechanisms.

When learning is mediated via RPE signals, value is ascribed by integrating across past reinforcement. Predictive value acquired via this mechanism does not include the agent's motivation at the time of reinforcement, nor does it track the identity of the reinforcer itself. Thus, a controller that learns via RPE signals would be expected to behave in a manner that is insensitive to immediate changes in outcome values, similar to the devaluation insensitivity associated with habits. In essence, this model-free learning strategy (so called because it does not depend on a model of the environment) gives rise to value representation that resembles stimulus-based association.

To account for goal-directed control, Daw and colleagues (2005) proposed that the agent encodes an internal model of the decision problem consisting of the relevant states and actions and, critically, the transition structure among them. This map of the decision process supports flexible online value computation by considering the current expected value of outcomes and integrating into these expected values the knowledge of how to procure them. Critically, value can be flexibly constructed at each decision point as part of an online planning procedure, making the agent immediately sensitive to changes in outcome values. This type of cognitive model–driven RL process is known, perhaps somewhat confusingly (because the terms were originally coined in the computer science literature), as model-based RL (Kuvayev & Sutton 1996).

NEUROCOMPUTATIONAL SUBSTRATES

Formal RL algorithms depend on well-defined learning signals and representations. Therefore, by asking how these are implemented in the brain, we can move toward a better understanding of the brain's computational composition. In the following sections, we outline some of the key representations and signals associated with various forms of RL and discuss their neural correlates. **Figure 1** illustrates the main brain regions and functions discussed in these sections.

The Cognitive Model: Multiple Maps, Multiple Regions

A model-based agent depends on a cognitive map of the task space encoding the environment's relevant features and the relationships among them (Tolman 1948). Electrophysiological recordings from place cells in the hippocampus have provided the most well-characterized evidence for the encoding of a cognitive map, especially in the spatial domain (e.g., O'Keefe & Dostrovsky 1971). Activity in these cells can represent the animal's trajectory during a spatial decision-making task, consistent with the theory that place cell representations play a role in model-based planning (Pfeiffer & Foster 2013) and that place cells are recruited in correspondence with future spatial locations the animal is considering (Johnson & Redish 2007). Others have suggested that the hippocampus might play a more general role in encoding a cognitive map, possibly in the encoding of relationships between stimuli and outcomes, identity and category membership information about objects (Eichenbaum et al. 1999), or even maps of social hierarchy in humans (Tavares et al. 2015).

Although evidence suggests that the hippocampus encodes information relevant to a cognitive map, the hippocampus does not always seem to be necessary for goal-directed choices in simple action–outcome learning tasks (Corbit & Balleine 2000). Wilson et al. (2014) used computational modeling to account for various behavioral effects of orbitofrontal lesions in the extant literature and to suggest that the OFC is involved in signaling the current location of the animal in an abstract task space, especially when that state is not immediately observable (i.e., when task states must be inferred or maintained). Neuroimaging studies have revealed evidence that outcome identity is represented in the OFC in response to stimuli predictive of those outcomes (Howard et al. 2015). This representation may be a mechanism through which the expected value of a particular stimulus or state could be computed. Although this possibility is still a matter of debate, the bulk of the evidence suggests that the OFC seems to be less involved in encoding information about

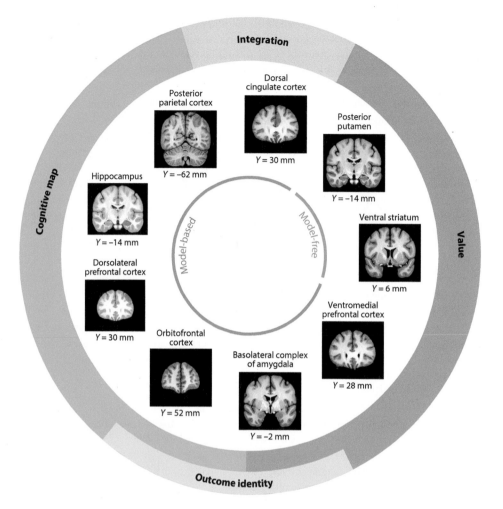

Figure 1

Schematic mapping specific neuroanatomical loci to the implementation of different functions underlying model-based and model-free control. Model-based control depends on a cognitive map of state space and integration of different aspects of a decision, such as effort and estimation uncertainty, as well as the value and the identity of goals or outcomes. Model-free control depends on learning about the value of responses in the current state, based on the history of past reinforcement. The inner circle identifies regions involved in model-based and model-free control, and the outer circle identifies specific subfunctions implemented by particular brain regions, based on the evidence to date as discussed in this review. The objective of this figure is to orient the reader to the location of the relevant brain regions rather than to provide a categorical description of the functions of each region or an exhaustive list of the brain regions involved in reward-related behavior. The neuronal substrates of prediction errors and the loci of arbitration mechanisms are omitted from this figure for simplicity. Y coordinates of coronal brain slices represent their distance from the commissures along the posterior (negative values) to anterior (positive values) axis.

actions than it is in encoding information about stimuli and outcomes (for a review, see Rangel & Hare 2010). Ultimately, the OFC's role in state encoding and in outcome associations may service computations associated with the expected value based on stimulus–stimulus associations.

However, goal-directed action selection demands some form of action representation as well as a representation of the state transitions afforded by performing actions. Evidence has indicated that regions of the posterior parietal cortex, such as the lateral intraparietal sulcus, play an important role in perceptual decision making, a critical aspect of state identification (e.g., Shadlen & Newsome 2001). Notably, neurons in the posterior parietal cortex have been implicated in the encoding of information about stimulus category membership, which could be important for establishing current and future potential states (Freedman & Assad 2006). Indeed, work by Doll et al. (2015) has shown that the category of a prospective stimulus appears to engage these regions of the brain. Critically, neurons in the posterior parietal cortex are implicated in the encoding of associations between arbitrary stimuli; these associations indicate the implementation of specific actions (Dorris & Glimcher 2004). A region of the inferior parietal lobule has also been found to play an important role in the encoding of information pertinent to the distribution of outcomes associated with an action, as well as information about the relative probability of obtaining an outcome contingent on performing a particular action compared to not performing that action (Liljeholm et al. 2011, 2013). Together, these findings suggest a role for the posterior parietal cortex in encoding a cognitive map or, more specifically, in encoding the transitions between states contingent on specific actions.

The presence of cognitive maps in the brain raises the question of how such maps are acquired in the first place. One possible mechanism is a state prediction error (SPE), which signals the discrepancy between an expected state transition and the transition that actually did occur. This SPE can then be used to adjust state transition expectations. In essence, SPEs are similar to RPEs but are used not to learn about reward expectation but to learn state expectations. Gläscher et al. (2010) used fMRI while participants learned a two-step Markov decision problem to find evidence for SPEs in the posterior parietal cortex and dorsolateral prefrontal cortex. These SPE signals were present in both a latent learning task phase, during which participants were guided through the task in the absence of reward, and an active phase, during which reward, and therefore RPEs, were also present. SPEs in the posterior parietal cortex and dorsolateral prefrontal cortex are therefore candidates for the signal underpinning learning of a cognitive model involving actions.

The presence of multiple candidate areas engaged in encoding some form of a cognitive map raises the question of which representations are necessary or sufficient for model-based learning and control. The nature of the cognitive map representation that is used may depend to a great extent on the type of decision problem. Perhaps, a task that has an ostensibly spatial component will necessarily recruit a spatial cognitive map in the hippocampus, whereas decision problems that involve selection among possible motor actions will depend to a greater extent on action codes in the posterior parietal cortex. However, precisely how these various maps might be leveraged by the brain in support of model-based learning and control remains to be determined.

Outcome Valuation During Decision Making

To choose among actions in a model-based manner, an agent needs to determine the value of different available outcomes. Electrophysiological studies in both rodents and monkeys have revealed neuronal activity in the amygdala and OFC related to conditioned stimuli associated with appetitive unconditioned stimuli, such as a sweet taste or juice reward (Schoenbaum et al. 1998), and aversive unconditioned stimuli, such as an aversive flavor, air puff, or eyelid shock (Applegate et al. 1982, Pascoe & Kapp 1985, Paton et al. 2006, Salzman & Fusi 2010, Salzman et al. 2007, Schoenbaum et al. 1998). Furthermore, human imaging studies have revealed responses in the amygdala, ventral striatum, and OFC in response to conditioned stimuli that are predictive of the subsequent delivery of appetitive and aversive outcomes such as tastes and odors (Gottfried et al. 2002, 2003; O'Doherty et al. 2002; Tobler et al. 2006).

During Pavlovian conditioning, many of these brain areas are involved in triggering Pavlovian conditioned responses. The central nucleus of the amygdala projects to lateral hypothalamic and brainstem nuclei involved in implementing conditioned autonomic reflexes (LeDoux et al. 1988). The ventral striatum sends projections via the globus pallidus to motor nuclei in the brainstem, such as the pedunculopontine nucleus (Groenewegen & Berendse 1994, Winn et al. 1997). This projection pattern is compatible with a possible role for the ventral striatum in triggering conditioned skeletomotor reflexes, such as approach and avoidance behavior, as well as consummatory responses. As we discuss in the section Action Valuation and Planning, the output of this network of brain areas is also taken into consideration by a separate network of brain areas when organisms have to choose among different actions in order to gain a desired outcome. First, we explore in greater detail the representations and signals carried by some of these areas.

Value signals have been found in both the OFC and the vmPFC. Electrophysiological recordings in area 13 of the central OFC of nonhuman primates revealed that neurons in this area encode the value of differing amounts of juice on offer (Padoa-Schioppa & Assad 2006). The activity of some of these neurons correlated with the subjective value of each of the two outcomes on offer, whereas other neurons correlated with the subjective value of the outcome that was ultimately chosen. Rodent studies have found similar results, with value signals associated with expected delivery of an outcome being present in the rodent OFC (McDannald et al. 2011, Schoenbaum et al. 1998). Other neurophysiological studies of monkeys have reported neuronal responses correlating with the value of prospective outcomes throughout the OFC and in other brain regions, including the lateral prefrontal and anterior cingulate cortices (Lee et al. 2007, Seo et al. 2007, Smith et al. 2010, Wallis & Miller 2003). Interestingly, neurons in the lateral prefrontal cortex have been found to respond in a manner consistent with the outcome value associated with novel stimuli whose value must be inferred from the outcome of the previous trial, suggesting that these value representations are sensitive to higher-order task structure (Pan et al. 2014). The human vmPFC seems to encode similar representations. Activity in the vmPFC was found to correlate with trial-by-trial variations in the amount participants were willing to pay (WTP) for offered goods (Plassmann et al. 2007). A follow-up experiment comparing value representations for foods, which participants would pay to obtain or avoid, revealed vmPFC activity proportional to the value of goods with positive values and decreasing activity scaling with negative values (Plassmann et al. 2010).

Organisms are forced to choose not only among rewards of varying probability and magnitude but also among rewards that differ in type. Organisms may cope with this issue by representing and comparing outcome values in a common currency. Indeed, activity in overlapping regions of the vmPFC correlated with the subjective value of three distinct categories of goods in a WTP task: food items, nonfood consumer items, and money (Chib et al. 2009). Levy & Glimcher (2012) found evidence for a common currency in the vmPFC by giving participants explicit choices between different types of goods, specifically money versus food, and by demonstrating that activation levels scaled according to the common currency value for both types of good. Although these findings are consistent with the notion of a common currency, they could also be the result of averaging nonoverlapping value representations across individual subjects if there is sufficient spatial variance in these representations among individuals. Using a paradigm similar to that of Chib et al. (2009), McNamee et al. (2013) probed for distributed voxel patterns encoding outcome value and category by training multivariate pattern classifiers on each type of good. A circumscribed region of the vmPFC above the orbital surface was found to exhibit a general value code whereby a classifier trained on the value of one class of goods (e.g., foods) could successfully decode the value of goods from a different category (e.g., consumer goods). In addition to general value codes, value codes specific to particular categories of good were also found along the medial orbital surface, a finding that is consistent with the idea that these regions represent value in a preliminary category-specific form that is then converted into a common currency in more dorsal parts of the vmPFC. Interestingly, no region was found to uniquely encode the distributed value of monetary items, which were only found to be represented in the vmPFC, perhaps because money is a generalized reinforcer that can be exchanged for many different types of goods.

Taken together, these findings support the existence of a common currency in the vmPFC in which the value of various outcomes are proportionally scaled in accordance with subjective value irrespective of the category from which they are drawn. In the following section, we consider how other information relevant to model-based computations is encoded.

Outcome Valuation After a Decision Has Been Made

In addition to evaluating outcomes while forming a decision, an organism also has to evaluate an outcome once it has been received. Extensive evidence implicates the vmPFC and adjacent parts of the OFC in the response to experienced outcomes, including monetary rewards (Knutson et al. 2001, O'Doherty et al. 2001, Smith et al. 2010); taste, odor, and flavor (de Araujo et al. 2003a,b; Rolls et al. 2003); attractive faces (O'Doherty et al. 2003a); and the aesthetic value of abstract art (Kirk et al. 2009). These outcome representations are also strongly influenced by changes in underlying motivational states. The vmPFC and OFC show decreasing responses to food, odor, or even water outcomes as motivational states change from hungry or thirsty to satiated, paralleling changes in the subjective pleasantness of the stimulus (de Araujo et al. 2003a,b; O'Doherty et al. 2000; Rolls et al. 2003; Small et al. 2001). Not only are such representations modulated as a function of changes in internal motivational state, but value-related activity in this region is also influenced by cognitive factors, such as the provision of price information or even the mere use of semantic labels (de Araujo et al. 2005, Plassmann et al. 2008). Thus, the online computation of outcome values in the vmPFC and OFC is highly flexible and influenced by a variety of internal and external factors.

Action Valuation and Planning

Once an organism has determined the value of different outcomes, it must often determine the value of available actions based on how likely they are to lead to a desired outcome. To calculate these so-called model-based action values, a decision-making agent must be armed with a cognitive map that will enable the retrieval of probability distributions over the future states or outcomes that can be attained. The model-free computation of action value, i.e., computation without any consideration of state transitions or of which outcome might be achieved, is discussed in the section Neurobiological Substrates of Model-Free Action Selection.

One strategy for calculating model-based action values involves iteration over states, actions, and state transitions. Given that model-based action values depend on arithmetic computations accounting for quantity and probability, brain systems traditionally associated with working memory, such as the lateral prefrontal cortex (Miller & Cohen 2001), as well as parts of the parietal cortex implicated in numerical cognition (Platt & Glimcher 1999), are likely to be involved. It therefore seems reasonable to hypothesize that regions of the frontal and parietal cortices play a fundamental role in the computation of model-based action values. In a result that is at least partly consistent with this possibility, Simon & Daw (2011) reported increasing activity in the dorsolateral prefrontal and anterior cingulate cortices as a function of the depth of model-based planning during a spatial navigation task. In addition, areas of the posterior parietal cortex are also important in action planning. Distinct neuronal populations seem to be specialized for planning particular actions (such as saccades versus reaching movements), and these neurons appear to be specifically involved in encoding action trajectories and representing the target state of the action trajectories in both monkeys (Andersen et al. 1997, Cohen & Andersen 2002, MacKay 1992) and humans (Desmurget et al. 1999).

In rodents, several studies have produced evidence for a distinct network of brain areas supporting goal-directed behavior. Evidence from these studies indicates that the prelimbic cortex, as well as the dorsomedial striatum in the basal ganglia, to which the prelimbic cortex projects, are involved in the acquisition of goal-directed responses. Studies in rodents show that lesions to these areas impair action–outcome learning, rendering the rodent's behavior permanently stimulus-driven (Baker & Ragozzino 2014, Balleine & Dickinson 1998, Ragozzino et al. 2002, Yin et al. 2005). Although the prelimbic cortex is involved in the initial acquisition of goal-directed learning, this region does not appear to be essential for the expression of goal-directed actions after acquisition (Ostlund & Balleine 2005). In contrast, the dorsomedial striatum appears to be necessary for both acquisition and expression of goal-directed behavior (Yin et al. 2005).

Some researchers have argued that the rodent prelimbic cortex and dorsomedial striatum correspond to the primate vmPFC and caudate nucleus, respectively (Balleine & O'Doherty 2009). Indeed, in addition to representing the value of the different outcomes on offer (as discussed in the previous section), activity in the vmPFC also tracks instrumental contingencies, i.e., the causal relationship between an action and an outcome, sensitivity to which has also been shown to be associated with goal-directed control in rodent studies (Liljeholm et al. 2011, Matsumoto et al. 2003). Contingency manipulations have also implicated the caudate nucleus in goal-directed behavior in nonhuman primates (Hikosaka et al. 1989) and humans (Liljeholm et al. 2011). Furthermore, activity in the vmPFC has been found to track the current incentive value of an instrumental action such that, following devaluation, activity decreases for an action associated with a devalued outcome relative to an action associated with a still-valued outcome (de Wit et al. 2009, Valentin et al. 2007). Interestingly, the strength of the connection between the vmPFC and dorsomedial striatum as measured with diffusion tensor imaging has been shown to correlate with the degree of goal-directed behavioral expression across individuals (de Wit et al. 2012).

Once action values have been computed, they can be compared at decision points. Although several studies have reported evidence for prechoice action values, few studies have determined whether or not such action-value representations are computed in a model-based or model-free manner. Studies in rodents and monkeys report action-value signals in the dorsal striatum, as well as in areas of the dorsal cortex, including the parietal and supplementary motor cortices (Kolb et al. 1994, Lau & Glimcher 2008, Platt & Glimcher 1999, Samejima et al. 2005, Sohn & Lee 2007, Whitlock et al. 2012, Wilber et al. 2014). Human fMRI studies report evidence that putative action-value signals are present in areas of the dorsal cortex, including the supplementary motor, lateral parietal, and dorsolateral cortices (Hare et al. 2011, Morris et al. 2014, Wunderlich et al. 2009).

Little is known about how organisms integrate the range of variables that appear to influence action selection. One candidate region for the site of this integration is the dorsomedial prefrontal cortex. In monkeys, Hosokawa and colleagues (2013) found that some neurons in the anterior cingulate cortex are involved in encoding an integrated value signal that summed over expected costs and benefits for an action. Hunt et al. (2014) also implicated a region of the dorsomedial prefrontal cortex in encoding integrated action values. Together, these preliminary findings support the possibility that action valuation involves an interaction between multiple brain systems and that goal-value representations in the vmPFC are ultimately integrated with action information in dorsal cortical regions to compute an overall action value.

Neurobiological Substrates of Model-Free Action Selection

The canonical learning signal implicated in model-free value learning is the RPE, which is thought to be encoded by the phasic activity of midbrain dopamine neurons (Schultz et al. 1997). Evidence indicates that reward-related prediction errors also play a role in learning in humans. Numerous fMRI studies have reported correlations between RPE signals from RL models and activity in the striatum and midbrain nuclei known to contain dopaminergic neurons during Pavlovian and instrumental learning paradigms (D'Ardenne et al. 2008, O'Doherty 2004, O'Doherty et al. 2003b, Pauli et al. 2015, Wittmann et al. 2005).

Other evidence suggests that the dorsal striatum is critical for learning the stimulus–response associations underlying habitual behavior. In rodents, lesions of the posterior dorsolateral striatum have been found to render behavior permanently goal-directed such that, after overtraining, these animals fail to express habits (Yin et al. 2004, 2006). Tricomi et al. (2009) demonstrated a link between increasing activity in the human posterior striatum as a function of training and the emergence of habitual control as assessed with a reinforcer devaluation test. Wunderlich et al. (2012) reported that activity in this area correlated with the value of overtrained actions (which might be expected to favor habitual control) compared to actions whose values had been acquired more recently. Others have reported putative model-free value signals in the posterior putamen (Horga et al. 2015).

The phasic activity of dopamine neurons is causally related to learning of instrumental actions via dopamine-modulated plasticity in target areas of these neurons, such as the dorsolateral striatum (Faure et al. 2005, Schoenbaum et al. 2013, Steinberg & Janak 2013). Human fMRI studies of motor sequence learning have reported an increase in activity in the posterior dorsolateral striatum as sequences become overlearned. For instance, participants who successfully learn to perform instrumental actions for reward show significantly stronger prediction error signals in the dorsal striatum than those who fail to learn instrumental actions (Schönberg et al. 2007), and the administration of drugs that modulate dopamine function, such as L-3,4-dihydroxyphenylalanine (L-DOPA) or dopaminergic antagonists, influences the strength of learning of instrumental associations accordingly (Frank et al. 2004). Other studies focusing on both model-based and model-free value signals have also found evidence for model-free signals in the posterior putamen (Doll et al. 2015, Lee et al. 2014). However, model-free signals have also been reported across a number of cortical areas (Lee et al. 2014). Moreover, differences in the strength of the connectivity between the right posterolateral striatum and the premotor cortex across individuals is associated with differences in the degree to which individuals show evidence of habitual behavior in a task in which goal-directed and habitual responses are placed in conflict (de Wit et al. 2012).

Other Decision Variables: Effort and Uncertainty

One variable that is likely to play an important role during decision making is the amount of effort, whether cognitive or physical, involved in performing a particular action. Clearly, all else being equal, it is better to exert as little effort as possible, but occasions may arise in which effortful actions yield disproportionately greater rewards. Although effort studies are scarce, there is evidence that the effort associated with performing an action is represented in parts of the dorsomedial prefrontal cortex alongside other areas such as the insular cortex (Prévost et al. 2010). Additional studies in rodents suggest that the anterior cingulate cortex plays a critical role in effortful behavior (Hillman & Bilkey 2012, Walton et al. 2009).

Two forms of uncertainty, expected and estimation uncertainty, may also be relevant factors at the time of decision. The most pertinent form of expected uncertainty for decision making is risk, or the inherent stochasticity of the environment that remains even when the contingencies are fully known. Expected uncertainty regarding different options is useful information to access at the point of decision making because risk preference might vary over time depending on motivational and other contextual factors. Studies have revealed activity correlating with expected uncertainty in a number of cortical and subcortical brain regions, including the insular cortex, inferior frontal gyrus, and dorsal striatum (Critchley et al. 2001, Huettel et al. 2006, Paulus et al. 2003, Yanike & Ferrera 2014).

In contrast to risk, estimation uncertainty corresponds to uncertainty in the estimate of the reward distribution associated with a particular action or state. For example, the first time an action is sampled in a particular context, estimation uncertainty is high; it will decrease as that action is repeated and the precision of the reward distribution's estimate increases. Estimation uncertainty can also be leveraged to balance the trade-off between exploration and exploitation by allowing the agent to target actions that are relatively undersampled. Neural representations of estimation uncertainty have been reported in the anterior cingulate cortex (Payzan-LeNestour et al. 2013), and uncertainty signals (which may or may not correspond to estimation uncertainty) associated with exploration have also been reported in the frontopolar cortex (Badre et al. 2012, Daw et al. 2006, Yoshida & Ishii 2006).

Model-Free and Model-Based Pavlovian Learning

In this section, we turn our attention to the computations that underpin acquisition and expression of Pavlovian conditioned responses. As described in the section Neurobiological Substrates of Model-Free Action Selection, model-free RL has been proposed as a mechanism to underpin learning in at least appetitive Pavlovian conditioning. However, similar to the predictions in the instrumental domain, a model-free RL account of Pavlovian conditioning would be expected to produce conditioned responses that are devaluation insensitive. Nevertheless, many conditioned Pavlovian responses are strongly devaluation sensitive (Dayan & Berridge 2014). This discrepancy has led to suggestions that model-based learning mechanisms might also apply in the case of Pavlovian conditioning (Dayan & Berridge 2014, Prévost et al. 2013).

We might expect such a system to depend on a cognitive model that maps the relationship between different stimuli, that is, a model that encodes stimulus–stimulus association likelihoods. One might expect the mechanism for model-based Pavlovian conditioning to be similar to that involved in model-based instrumental control, with the exception that there is no need for the model to represent action contingencies. Sensory preconditioning represents one piece of behavioral evidence in favor of the existence of a model-based Pavlovian learning mechanism that depends on the formation of stimulus–stimulus associations. In sensory preconditioning, two cues are repeatedly paired together in the absence of reward. Following this, one of the cues is paired with reward. Rescorla (1980) found that, under these conditions, the cue that had not been paired with reward also spontaneously elicited appetitive conditioned responses (Rescorla 1980).

This result raises the question of which brain areas are involved in encoding stimulus–stimulus associations. The hippocampus and the OFC, which we have examined in the context of their role in encoding a cognitive map, are strong candidates. Representations in these two brain regions are perhaps not action dependent but do encode relationships between stimuli, as would be needed by a model-based Pavlovian mechanism. Indeed, consistent with this proposal, both the hippocampus and OFC are implicated in sensory preconditioning (Jones et al. 2012, Holland & Bouton 1999, Wimmer & Shohamy 2012). Researchers have also found that the amygdala encodes information about context, stimulus identity, and reward expectation (Salzman & Fusi 2010). Moreover, Prévost et al. (2013) used a Pavlovian reversal learning paradigm to provide evidence for expected value signals in the human amygdala that were better captured by a model-based algorithm than by a number of model-free learning alternatives.

Two distinct forms of Pavlovian appetitive conditioning, sign tracking and goal tracking, can be distinguished in rodents (Boakes 1977, Hearst & Jenkins 1974, Jenkins & Moore 1973). Sign-tracking animals orient to the cue that predicts the subsequent reward, whereas goal-tracking animals orient to the location where the outcome is delivered. A recent behavioral study has revealed a correlation between the extent to which animals manifest sign-tracking behavior and the extent to which these animals show evidence of devaluation insensitivity in their behavior, suggesting that sign tracking may be a model-free conditioned response (Nasser et al. 2015). Consistent with dopamine's involvement in model-free Pavlovian conditioning, RPE signals in the nucleus accumbens core have been associated with sign tracking. Animals selectively bred to be predominantly sign trackers show phasic dopamine release in the nucleus accumbens, whereas animals bred to be predominantly goal trackers do not show clear phasic dopaminergic activity during learning (Flagel et al. 2007). Furthermore, a recent study has found evidence to suggest that phasic dopaminergic activity associated with a conditioned stimulus may in fact be devaluation insensitive, as would be predicted by a model-free algorithm. Specifically, rats were conditioned to associate a cue with an aversive salt outcome. Following induction of a salt appetite, dopamine neurons showed increased phasic activity following the receipt of the (now-valued) salt outcome, consistent with model-based control. However, consistent with a model-free RL mechanism, phasic responses to the cue predicting salt did not show any such increase until after the animal had a chance to be exposed to the outcome, suggesting that dopamine activity in response to the cue was not immediately updated to reflect the current value of the associated outcome (Cone et al. 2016). These findings suggest that in Pavlovian conditioning, dopaminergic prediction errors may be involved in model-free but not model-based learning.

INTERACTION AMONG BEHAVIORAL CONTROL SYSTEMS

Having considered evidence regarding the existence of multiple control systems in the brain and reviewed ideas and emerging evidence about the possible neural computations underpinning each of these systems, we briefly consider in the following sections how these systems interact. There is evidence to suggest that stimulus-driven, goal-directed, and noninstrumental systems may sometimes interact in an adaptive manner whereby each system exerts complementary influences on behavior in a manner beneficial for the agent. Alternatively, in some instances these systems can interact in a maladaptive manner, leading to pernicious behavioral outcomes.

Interactions Between Goals and Habits

Habitual and goal-directed control systems may interact to provide a strategy that is both flexible and cognitively efficient by supporting hierarchical decomposition of the task at hand. Building on theoretical work demonstrating the computational benefits of encapsulating behavioral invariance in the form of a selectable option (Sutton et al. 1999), studies have begun to probe whether the brain leverages its varied control systems to implement a similar hierarchical decomposition (Botvinick 2012, Botvinick et al. 2009). Evidence from human fMRI studies shows that higher levels of abstraction progressively engage more anterior regions of frontal cortex, suggesting a hierarchical organization of abstraction along a rostral–caudal axis (Badre & D'Esposito 2007, Donoso et al. 2014, Koechlin et al. 2003). Other studies have reported signals consistent with hierarchical event structuring (Schapiro et al. 2013) and prediction errors (Diuk et al. 2013, Ribas-Fernandes et al. 2011). Although the most common depiction of hierarchical control positions the habitual system as subservient to the goal-directed system (Dezfouli & Balleine 2013), other work suggests that the goal-directed system can also be deployed in the service of a habitually selected goal (Cushman & Morris 2015).

The brain's multiple control systems may also facilitate learning. Situations in which control is assigned to the goal-directed system in the early stages of behavioral acquisition may be examples of adaptive interactions between systems. Once the problem space has been sufficiently sampled, behavioral control transitions to the habitual system, thereby freeing up cognitive resources that would otherwise be allocated to the goal-directed system. The complementary nature of the interactions between these systems is such that, even though the goal-directed system is in the driving seat during early learning, the habitual system is given the opportunity to learn a model-free policy because it is exposed to the relevant stimulus associations.

However, there is a downside to this training interaction. Once behavior is under the control of the habitual system, it may guide the agent toward an unfavorable course of action under circumstances in which environmental contingencies have shifted or the agent's goals have changed. Alternatively, errors in goal-directed representations may inculcate inappropriate biases into the stimulus-driven system's learned values (Doll et al. 2011). Numerous examples of maladaptive interactions exist in the realm of psychiatric disease. For instance, habits for abuse of a drug may persist even if the goal of the individual is to stop taking the drug (Everitt & Robbins 2016). Overeating or compulsive behaviors may also be examples of the habitual system exerting inappropriate and ultimately detrimental control over behavior (Voon et al. 2015). The capacity to effectively manage conflicting policy suggestions by the goal-directed and habitual systems likely varies across individuals and may even relate to underlying differences in the neural circuitry, perhaps indicative of differing levels of vulnerability to the emergence of compulsive behavior (de Wit et al. 2012).

Interactions with Pavlovian Predictions

The Pavlovian system can also interact with systems involved in instrumental behavior, a class of interactions referred to as Pavlovian-to-instrumental transfer (PIT) (Lovibond 1983). PIT effects are typically manifested as increased instrumental response vigor in the presence of a reward predicting a Pavlovian conditioned stimulus (Estes 1943). One can make a distinction between general and specific PIT. General PIT refers to circumstances in which a Pavlovian cue motivates increased instrumental responding irrespective of the outcome associated with the Pavlovian cue. Conversely, outcome-specific PIT effects modulate responding when both the Pavlovian cue and instrumental action are associated with the same outcome (Corbit & Balleine 2005, Holland & Gallagher 2003, Rescorla & Solomon 1967).

In a normative relationship between incentives and instrumental response, the provision of higher incentives should result in increased effort and response accuracy, thereby enabling more effective action implementation. However, Pavlovian effects on instrumental responding can also promote maladaptive behavior in circumstances in which PIT effects continue to exert an energizing effect on instrumental actions associated with a devalued outcome (Holland 2004, Watson et al. 2014; although see Allman et al. 2010). This suggests that PIT effects selectively involve the habitual system. Thus, Pavlovian cues may intervene in the interplay between goals and habits by actively biasing behavioral control toward the habitual system.

Furthermore, under certain circumstances, increased incentives can paradoxically result in less-efficacious instrumental performance, an effect known as choking that has been linked to dopaminergic regions of the midbrain (Chib et al. 2014, Mobbs et al. 2009, Zedelius et al. 2011).

For example, Ariely et al. (2009) offered participants in rural India the prospect of winning large monetary amounts relative to their average monthly salaries. Compared to a group offered smaller incentive amounts, the performance of the high-incentive group was much impaired, suggesting the counterintuitive effect of reduced performance in a situation in which the motivation to succeed is high. Numerous theories have been proposed to account for choking effects, reflecting various possible forms of interactions between different control systems. One theory is that choking effects reflect a maladaptive return of behavioral control to the goal-directed system in the face of large potential incentives in a situation in which the habitual system is better placed to reliably execute a skilled behavior. Although some results support this hypothesis (Lee & Grafton 2015), others support an alternative account whereby Pavlovian effects elicited by cues could engage Pavlovian skeletomotor behaviors, such as appetitive approach or aversive withdrawal, that interfere with the performance of the habitual skilled motor behavior (Chib et al. 2012, 2014). More than one of these ideas could hold true, as behavioral choking effects may have multiple causes arising from maladaptive interactions between these systems.

Arbitration Between Behavioral Control Mechanisms

The presence of distinct control systems burdens the brain with the problem of how to apportion control among them. An influential hypothesis is that there exists an arbitrator that determines the influence each system has over behavior based on a number of criteria (Daw et al. 2005). One important factor in this hypothesis is the relative accuracy of the systems' predictions concerning which action should be selected; all else being equal, behavior should be controlled by the system with the most accurate prediction (Daw et al. 2005). Using the computational distinction between model-based and model-free RL, Lee et al. (2014) found evidence for the existence of an arbitration processes in the ventrolateral prefrontal cortex and frontopolar cortex that assigns behavioral control as a function of system reliability. Connectivity between the arbitration areas and the regions of the brain encoding habitual but not goal-directed action values was also found to be modulated as a function of the arbitration process. Consistent with a default model-free strategy, it is better to delegate control to the more-efficient stimulus-driven system; however, when the arbitration system detects that a goal-directed policy is warranted, then it may achieve this through active inhibition of the habitual system, leaving the model-based system free to control behavior. In addition to predictive accuracy, other relevant variables include the amount of cognitive effort required (FitzGerald et al. 2014) and the potential benefits that can be accrued by implementing a model-based strategy (Pezzulo et al. 2013, Shenhav et al. 2013).

Much less is known about how arbitration occurs between Pavlovian and instrumental systems. Changes in cognitive strategies or appraisal implemented via the prefrontal cortex can influence the likelihood of both aversive and appetitive Pavlovian conditioned responses, perhaps via down-regulation of the amygdala and ventral striatum (Delgado et al. 2008a,b; Staudinger et al. 2009). This type of top-down process could be viewed as a form of arbitration, in which Pavlovian control policies are downweighted in situations in which goal-directed control is deemed to be more beneficial. However, the nature of the computations mediating this putative arbitration process is not well understood. Clearly, given that Pavlovian behaviors are often advantageous in time-critical situations when the animal's survival may be at stake, it would be reasonable for at least certain types of Pavlovian predictions to have immediate access to behavior without having to wait for the arbitration process to mediate. Therefore, it seems plausible to expect that, perhaps as with the habitual system, arbitration operates only to inhibit Pavlovian behavior when it is deemed to be inappropriate or irrelevant. One might also predict that any such arbitration process would happen at a slower timescale relative to the more rapid response time available to the Pavlovian system. Therefore, traces of initial Pavlovian control might become manifest in behavior even in situations in which the arbitration system subsequently implements an inhibition of the Pavlovian system.

Neural Systems for Learning and Inference in a Social Context

Thus far, we have considered the involvement of multiple systems in controlling reward-related behavior but have given scant attention to the type of behavioral context in which these systems are engaged. A particularly challenging problem faced by humans and many other animals is the need to learn from and ultimately behave adaptively to conspecifics. Succinctly put, the problem is working out how to conduct oneself in social situations. A full consideration of this issue is beyond the scope of this review. However, we can briefly consider the question of whether value-based action selection in social contexts depends on similar or distinct control systems and neural circuitry as those involved in value-based action selection in nonsocial contexts.

One of the simplest ways to extend the framework we have discussed to the social domain is to apply this framework to the mechanisms underlying observational learning, which allow an agent to learn about the value of stimuli or actions not through direct experience but instead through observing the behavior of another agent. Several studies have revealed the engagement of brain regions including the ventral and dorsal striata and the vmPFC in observational learning (Burke et al. 2010, Cooper et al. 2012). For example, Cooper et al. (2012) found evidence for prediction error signals in the striatum when participants were learning about the value of actions through observing another agent. These preliminary findings suggest that, at least for some forms of observational learning, the brain relies on similar neural mechanisms and circuitry for learning through observation as it does when learning through direct experience. There is also evidence to suggest that, during a number of social situations in which it is necessary to learn from the actions being taken by others, the brain may rely on similar circuitry and updating signals as those known to be involved in model-based RL (Abe & Lee 2011, Liljeholm et al. 2012, Seo et al. 2009).

However, in some social situations, the brain may engage additional circuitry that has been implicated in mentalizing or theory of mind (Frith & Frith 2003, 2006). For instance, Hampton et al. (2008) found that when participants engage in a competitive game against a dynamic opponent, activity in the posterior superior temporal sulcus and dorsomedial prefrontal cortex is related to the updating of a higher-order inference about the strategic intentions of that opponent. Relatedly, Behrens et al. (2008) examined a situation in which it was useful for participants to learn about the reliability of a confederate's recommendations about what actions to take because the confederate's interests sometimes lay in deceiving the subject. Neural activity corresponding to an update signal for such an estimate was found in the anterior medial prefrontal cortex, as well as in a region of the temporoparietal junction. Similarly, Boorman et al. (2013a,b) found evidence for updating signals related to learning about another individual's expertise on a financial investment task in the temporoparietal junction and dorsomedial frontal cortex. Suzuki et al. (2015) found evidence for the representation of beliefs about the likely future actions of a group of individuals in the posterior superior temporal sulcus and, moreover, found that this activity was specifically engaged when performing in a social as compared to a nonsocial context.

Taken together, these findings suggest that, although learning and making decisions in a social context often depends on similar brain circuitry as that used when learning in nonsocial contexts, additional distinct circuitry is deployed to facilitate socially relevant tasks, such as inferring the internal mental states of others, when knowledge about relevant features of another agent is necessary.

CONCLUSIONS AND FUTURE DIRECTIONS

Although much remains to be explored, the past few decades have brought considerable advances in our understanding of the neural and computational mechanisms underlying learning, reward, and decision making. Merging formal work in computational intelligence and empirical research in cognitive neuroscience has allowed considerable headway not only in understanding the algorithms embodied by the brain but also in illuminating how the brain navigates the trade-offs between different strategies for controlling reward-related behavior. Long-standing theoretical arguments as to whether behavior is habitual or goal-directed have been assuaged by demonstrations that the brain has maintained multiple strategies for behavioral control, each offering advantages and disadvantages that may be leveraged across a range of potential circumstances.

As a result of these advances, new unresolved issues have emerged. In this article, we have reviewed evidence from both animal and human studies indicating that a goal-directed (model-based) system guides behavior in some circumstances but that other situations favor a habitual (model-free) strategy. Factors such as task familiarity, task complexity, and reward contingencies may influence the trade-off between these two systems; however, work remains to be done regarding other variables that might influence how various strategies are deployed. Factors such as incentives (the benefits of favoring one strategy over another), cognitive capacities (the brain's awareness of its own limitations), and social context may play a role in system deployment. Whether or not Pavlovian drives factor into the arbitration scheme used to determine behavioral control also remains unknown.

Furthermore, we understand little regarding the mechanisms through which system arbitration is instantiated. We have presented evidence suggesting that the brain adopts a computationally efficient model-free strategy by default but that this can be interrupted by a more flexible goal-directed strategy if needed. However, this evidence raises the question of what the model-based system is doing when it is not favored for control: Is the model-based system passively working in the background, waiting to be called back into activity, or has it moved offline to conserve resources? If the latter, how is it brought back online in a sensible way? We must also ask what the model-free system is doing when the model-based system takes control. There is evidence to suggest that the model-based system can shape the model-free system's value representations, but we know very little about this relationship. Does the model-free system passively learn about choices and experiences governed by the model-based system, or can the model-based system tutor the model-free system more directly and, if so, how might this be operationalized?

The bulk of our discussion has focused on behavioral control with respect to what can be labeled as exploitive action selection: identifying and moving toward the most rewarding options in the environment. However, this is only one half of what is commonly referred to as the explore/exploit trade-off. Almost nothing is known about the role played by the brain's varied control systems with respect to exploration. Given the exploitive advantages that come with having multiple control strategies, some of which we have outlined in this review, at one's disposal, are similar benefits offered to the domain of exploration? Does the brain take advantage of the computational efficiencies offered by the model-free system to direct exploration, or does the novelty and complexity inherent to exploration demand a model-based strategy? Perhaps multiple strategies are deployed in a collaborative fashion to tackle the many facets of exploration in an efficient way. Issues pertinent to the brain's engagement with exploratory decision making are ripe for both theoretical and experimental research.

Finally, we briefly touched upon the role played by the brain's control systems in a social context. However, the nature of these additional learning and inference signals and how they interact with other control systems is not yet fully understood. Value signals in the vmPFC and anterior cingulate cortex do reflect knowledge of strategic information, and the information needed to modify the value signals to reflect this knowledge appears to arrive via inputs from the mentalizing network (Hampton et al. 2008, Suzuki et al. 2015). Whether these mentalizing-related computations can be considered a fourth system for guiding behavior or, instead, a module that provides input into the model-based system is an open question. Moreover, how the brain decides when or whether the mentalizing system should be engaged in a particular situation is currently unknown, although it is tempting to speculate that an arbitration process may play a role.

This, of course, is only a small sample of many questions the field of decision neuroscience is poised to tackle. Although pursuit of these issues will deepen our basic understanding of the brain's functional architecture, of equal importance will be our ability to apply these concepts toward our understanding of cognitive impairments and mental illness (Huys et al. 2016, Maia & Frank 2011, Montague et al. 2012). Despite many advances and huge incentives, and perhaps in testament to the complexity of the problem, reliable and effective treatments are scarce. By building on a functional understanding of the brain's learning and control strategies, their points of interaction, and the mechanisms by which they manifest, novel treatments (whether behavioral, chemical, or mechanistic) may be able to help millions of people lead more fulfilling lives.

DISCLOSURE STATEMENT

The authors are not aware of any affiliations, memberships, funding, or financial holdings that might be perceived as affecting the objectivity of this review.

ACKNOWLEDGMENTS

This work was supported by a National Institutes of Health (NIH) Conte Center grant for research on the neurobiology of social decision making (P50MH094258-01A1), NIH grant number DA033077-01 (supported by OppNet, NIH's Basic Behavioral and Social Science Opportunity Network), and National Science Foundation grant number 1207573 to J.O.D.

LITERATURE CITED

Abe H, Lee D. 2011. Distributed coding of actual and hypothetical outcomes in the orbital and dorsolateral prefrontal cortex. *Neuron* 70(4):731–41

Allman MJ, DeLeon IG, Cataldo MF, Holland PC, Johnson AW. 2010. Learning processes affecting human decision making: an assessment of reinforcer-selective Pavlovian-to-instrumental transfer following reinforcer devaluation. *J. Exp. Psychol. Anim. Behav. Process.* 36(3):402–8

Andersen RA, Snyder LH, Bradley DC, Xing J. 1997. Multimodal representation of space in the posterior parietal cortex and its use in planning movements. *Annu. Rev. Neurosci.* 20:303–30

Applegate CD, Frysinger RC, Kapp BS, Gallagher M. 1982. Multiple unit activity recorded from amygdala central nucleus during Pavlovian heart rate conditioning in rabbit. *Brain Res.* 238(2):457–62

Ariely D, Gneezy U, Loewenstein G, Mazar N. 2009. Large stakes and big mistakes. *Rev. Econ. Stud.* 76(2):451–69

Badre D, D'Esposito M. 2007. Functional magnetic resonance imaging evidence for a hierarchical organization of the prefrontal cortex. *J. Cogn. Neurosci.* 19(12):2082–99

Badre D, Doll BB, Long NM, Frank MJ. 2012. Rostrolateral prefrontal cortex and individual differences in uncertainty-driven exploration. *Neuron* 73(3):595–607

Baker PM, Ragozzino ME. 2014. Contralateral disconnection of the rat prelimbic cortex and dorsomedial striatum impairs cue-guided behavioral switching. *Learn. Mem.* 21(8):368–79

Balleine BW, Daw ND, O'Doherty JP. 2009. Multiple forms of value learning and the function of dopamine. See Glimcher et al. 2013, pp. 367–85

Balleine BW, Dickinson A. 1991. Instrumental performance following reinforcer devaluation depends upon incentive learning. *Q. J. Exp. Psychol. Sect. B* 43(3):279–96

Balleine BW, Dickinson A. 1998. Goal-directed instrumental action: contingency and incentive learning and their cortical substrates. *Neuropharmacology* 37(4–5):407–19

Balleine BW, O'Doherty JP. 2009. Human and rodent homologies in action control: corticostriatal determinants of goal-directed and habitual action. *Neuropsychopharmacology* 35(1):48–69

Behrens TEJ, Hunt LT, Woolrich MW, Rushworth MFS. 2008. Associative learning of social value. *Nature* 456(7219):245–49

Boakes RA. 1977. Performance on learning to associate a stimulus with positive reinforcement. In *Operant-Pavlovian Interactions*, ed. H Davis, HMB Burwitz, pp. 67–97. London: Wiley

Boorman ED, O'Doherty JP, Adolphs R, Rangel A. 2013a. The behavioral and neural mechanisms underlying the tracking of expertise. *Neuron* 80(6):1558–71

Boorman ED, Rushworth MF, Behrens TE. 2013b. Ventromedial prefrontal and anterior cingulate cortex adopt choice and default reference frames during sequential multi-alternative choice. *J. Neurosci.* 33(6):2242–53

Botvinick MM. 2012. Hierarchical RL and decision making. *Curr. Opin. Neurobiol.* 22(6):956–62

Botvinick MM, Niv Y, Barto AC. 2009. Hierarchically organized behavior and its neural foundations: a RL perspective. *Cognition* 113(3):262–80

Burke CJ, Tobler PN, Baddeley M, Schultz W. 2010. Neural mechanisms of observational learning. *PNAS* 107(32):14431–36

Camerer C, Loewenstein G, Prelec D. 2005. Neuroeconomics: How neuroscience can inform economics. *J. Econ. Lit.* 43:9–64

Chib VS, De Martino B, Shimojo S, O'Doherty JP. 2012. Neural mechanisms underlying paradoxical performance for monetary incentives are driven by loss aversion. *Neuron* 74(3):582–94

Chib VS, Rangel A, Shimojo S, O'Doherty JP. 2009. Evidence for a common representation of decision values for dissimilar goods in human VmPFC. *J. Neurosci.* 29(39):12315–20

Chib VS, Shimojo S, O'Doherty JP. 2014. The effects of incentive framing on performance decrements for large monetary outcomes: behavioral and neural mechanisms. *J. Neurosci.* 34(45):14833–44

Cohen YE, Andersen RA. 2002. A common reference frame for movement plans in the posterior parietal cortex. *Nat. Rev. Neurosci.* 3(7):553–62

Cone JJ, Fortin SM, McHenry JA, Stuber GD, McCutcheon JE, Roitman MF. 2016. Physiological state gates acquisition and expression of mesolimbic reward prediction signals. *PNAS* 113(7):1943–48

Cooper JC, Dunne S, Furey T, O'Doherty JP. 2012. Human dorsal striatum encodes prediction errors during observational learning of instrumental actions. *J. Cogn. Neurosci.* 24(1):106–18

Corbit LH, Balleine BW. 2000. The role of the hippocampus in instrumental conditioning. *J. Neurosci.* 20(11):4233–39

Corbit LH, Balleine BW. 2005. Double dissociation of basolateral and central amygdala lesions on the general and outcome-specific forms of Pavlovian-instrumental transfer. *J. Neurosci.* 25(4):962–70

Critchley HD, Mathias CJ, Dolan RJ. 2001. Neural activity in the human brain relating to uncertainty and arousal during anticipation. *Neuron* 29(2):537–45

Cushman F, Morris A. 2015. Habitual control of goal selection in humans. *PNAS* 112(45):13817–22

D'Ardenne K, McClure SM, Nystrom LE, Cohen JD. 2008. BOLD responses reflecting dopaminergic signals in the human ventral tegmental area. *Science* 319(5867):1264–67

Davey GCL. 1992. Classical conditioning and the acquisition of human fears and phobias: a review and synthesis of the literature. *Adv. Behav. Res. Ther.* 14(1):29–66

Daw ND, Niv Y, Dayan P. 2005. Uncertainty-based competition between prefrontal and dorsolateral striatal systems for behavioral control. *Nat. Neurosci.* 8(12):1704–11

Daw ND, O'Doherty JP, Dayan P, Seymour B, Dolan RJ. 2006. Cortical substrates for exploratory decisions in humans. *Nature* 441(7095):876–79

Dayan P, Berridge KC. 2014. Model-based and model-free Pavlovian reward learning: revaluation, revision, and revelation. *Cogn. Affect. Behav. Neurosci.* 14(2):473–92

de Araujo IET, Kringelbach ML, Rolls ET, McGlone F. 2003a. Human cortical responses to water in the mouth, and the effects of thirst. *J. Neurophysiol.* 90(3):1865–76 de Araujo IET, Rolls ET, Kringelbach ML, McGlone F, Phillips N. 2003b. Taste-olfactory convergence, and the representation of the pleasantness of flavour, in the human brain. *Eur. J. Neurosci.* 18(7):2059–68

de Araujo IET, Rolls ET, Velazco MI, Margot C, Cayeux I. 2005. Cognitive modulation of olfactory processing. *Neuron* 46(4):671–79

de Wit S, Corlett PR, Aitken MR, Dickinson A, Fletcher PC. 2009. Differential engagement of the VmPFC by goal-directed and habitual behavior toward food pictures in humans. *J. Neurosci.* 29(36):11330–38

de Wit S, Watson P, Harsay HA, Cohen MX, Vijver I van de, Ridderinkhof KR. 2012. Corticostriatal connectivity underlies individual differences in the balance between habitual and goal-directed action control. *J. Neurosci.* 32(35):12066–75

Delgado MR, Li J, Schiller D, Phelps EA. 2008a. The role of the striatum in aversive learning and aversive prediction errors. *Philos. Trans. R. Soc. Lond. B Biol. Sci.* 363(1511):3787–800

Delgado MR, Nearing KI, Ledoux JE, Phelps EA. 2008b. Neural circuitry underlying the regulation of conditioned fear and its relation to extinction. *Neuron* 59(5):829–38

Desmurget M, Epstein CM, Turner RS, Prablanc C, Alexander GE, Grafton ST. 1999. Role of the posterior parietal cortex in updating reaching movements to a visual target. *Nat. Neurosci.* 2(6):563–67

Dezfouli A, Balleine BW. 2013. Actions, action sequences and habits: evidence that goal-directed and habitual action control are hierarchically organized. *PLOS Comput. Biol.* 9(12):e1003364

Dickinson A. 1985. Actions and habits: the development of behavioural autonomy. *Philos. Trans. R. Soc. Lond. B Biol. Sci.* 308(1135):67–78

Dickinson A, Balleine B. 1994. Motivational control of goal-directed action. *Anim. Learn. Behav.* 22(1):1–18

Dickinson A, Balleine B, Watt A, Gonzalez F, Boakes RA. 1995. Motivational control after extended instrumental training. *Anim. Learn. Behav.* 23(2):197–206

Dickinson A, Nicholas DJ, Adams CD. 1983. The effect of the instrumental training contingency on susceptibility to reinforcer devaluation. *Q. J. Exp. Psychol. Sect. B* 35(1):35–51

Diuk C, Tsai K, Wallis J, Botvinick M, Niv Y. 2013. Hierarchical learning induces two simultaneous, but separable, prediction errors in human basal ganglia. *J. Neurosci.* 33(13):5797–805

Doll BB, Duncan KD, Simon DA, Shohamy D, Daw ND. 2015. Model-based choices involve prospective neural activity. *Nat. Neurosci.* 18(5):767–72

Doll BB, Hutchison KE, Frank MJ. 2011. Dopaminergic genes predict individual differences in susceptibility to confirmation bias. *J. Neurosci.* 31(16):6188–98

Donoso M, Collins AGE, Koechlin E. 2014. Foundations of human reasoning in the prefrontal cortex. *Science* 344(6191):1481–86

Dorris MC, Glimcher PW. 2004. Activity in posterior parietal cortex is correlated with the relative subjective desirability of action. *Neuron* 44(2):365–78

Doya K. 1999. What are the computations of the cerebellum, the basal ganglia and the cerebral cortex? *Neural Netw.* 12(7–8):961–74

Eichenbaum H, Dudchenko P, Wood E, Shapiro M, Tanila H. 1999. The hippocampus, memory, and place cells: Is it spatial memory or a memory space? *Neuron* 23(2):209–26

Estes WK. 1943. Discriminative conditioning. I. A discriminative property of conditioned anticipation. *J. Exp. Psychol.* 32(2):150–55

Everitt BJ, Robbins TW. 2016. Drug addiction: updating actions to habits to compulsions ten years on. *Annu. Rev. Psychol.* 67(1):23–50

Faure A, Haberland U, Condé F, Massioui NE. 2005. Lesion to the nigrostriatal dopamine system disrupts stimulus-response habit formation. *J. Neurosci.* 25(11):2771–80

FitzGerald THB, Dolan RJ, Friston KJ. 2014. Model averaging, optimal inference, and habit formation. *Front. Hum. Neurosci.* 8:457

Flagel SB, Watson SJ, Robinson TE, Akil H. 2007. Individual differences in the propensity to approach signals versus goals promote different adaptations in the dopamine system of rats. *Psychopharmacol. Berl.* 191(3):599–607

Frank MJ, Seeberger LC, O'Reilly RC. 2004. By carrot or by stick: cognitive RL in parkinsonism. *Science* 306(5703):1940–43

Freedman DJ, Assad JA. 2006. Experience-dependent representation of visual categories in parietal cortex. *Nature* 443(7107):85–88

Frith CD, Frith U. 2006. The neural basis of mentalizing. *Neuron* 50(4):531–34

Frith U, Frith CD. 2003. Development and neurophysiology of mentalizing. *Philos. Trans. R. Soc. Lond. B Biol. Sci.* 358(1431):459–73

Gigerenzer G, Gaissmaier W. 2011. Heuristic decision making. *Annu. Rev. Psychol.* 62(1):451–82

Gläscher J, Daw N, Dayan P, O'Doherty JP. 2010. States versus rewards: dissociable neural prediction error signals underlying model-based and model-free RL. *Neuron* 66(4):585–95

Glimcher PW, Camerer CF, Fehr E, Poldrack RA, eds. 2013. *Neuroeconomics: Decision Making and the Brain.* London: Academic

Gottfried JA, O'Doherty J, Dolan RJ. 2002. Appetitive and aversive olfactory learning in humans studied using event-related functional magnetic resonance imaging. *J. Neurosci.* 22(24):10829–37

Gottfried JA, O'Doherty J, Dolan RJ. 2003. Encoding predictive reward value in human amygdala and OFC. *Science* 301(5636):1104–7

Groenewegen HJ, Berendse HW. 1994. Anatomical relationships between the prefrontal cortex and the basal ganglia in the rat. In *Motor and Cognitive Functions of the Prefrontal Cortex*, ed. AM Thierry, J Glowinski, PS Goldman-Rakic, Y Christen, pp. 51–77. Berlin/Heidelberg: Springer

Hampton AN, Bossaerts P, O'Doherty JP. 2008. Neural correlates of mentalizing-related computations during strategic interactions in humans. *PNAS* 105(18):6741–46

Hare TA, Schultz W, Camerer CF, O'Doherty JP, Rangel A. 2011. Transformation of stimulus value signals into motor commands during simple choice. *PNAS* 108(44):18120–25

Hearst E, Jenkins HM. 1974. *Sign-Tracking: The Stimulus-Reinforcer Relation and Directed Action.* Madison, WI: Psychon. Soc.

Hikosaka O, Sakamoto M, Usui S. 1989. Functional properties of monkey caudate neurons. I. Activities related to saccadic eye movements. *J. Neurophysiol.* 61(4):780–98

Hillman KL, Bilkey DK. 2012. Neural encoding of competitive effort in the anterior cingulate cortex. *Nat. Neurosci.* 15(9):1290–97

Holland PC. 2004. Relations between Pavlovian-instrumental transfer and reinforcer devaluation. *J. Exp. Psychol. Anim. Behav. Process.* 30(2):104–17

Holland PC, Bouton ME. 1999. Hippocampus and context in classical conditioning. *Curr. Opin. Neurobiol.* 9(2):195–202

Holland PC, Gallagher M. 2003. Double dissociation of the effects of lesions of basolateral and central amygdala on conditioned stimulus-potentiated feeding and Pavlovian-instrumental transfer. *Eur. J. Neurosci.* 17(8):1680–94

Horga G, Maia TV, Marsh R, Hao X, Xu D, et al. 2015. Changes in corticostriatal connectivity during RL in humans. *Hum. Brain Mapp.* 36(2):793–803

Hosokawa T, Kennerley SW, Sloan J, Wallis JD. 2013. Single-neuron mechanisms underlying cost-benefit analysis in frontal cortex. *J. Neurosci.* 33(44):17385–97

Howard JD, Gottfried JA, Tobler PN, Kahnt T. 2015. Identity-specific coding of future rewards in the human orbitofrontal cortex. *PNAS* 112(16):5195–200

Huettel SA, Stowe CJ, Gordon EM, Warner BT, Platt ML. 2006. Neural signatures of economic preferences for risk and ambiguity. *Neuron* 49(5):765–75

Hunt LT, Dolan RJ, Behrens TEJ. 2014. Hierarchical competitions subserving multi-attribute choice. *Nat. Neurosci.* 17(11):1613–22

Huys QJM, Maia TV, Frank MJ. 2016. Computational psychiatry as a bridge from neuroscience to clinical applications. *Nat. Neurosci.* 19(3):404–13

Jenkins HM, Moore BR. 1973. The form of the auto-shaped response with food or water reinforcers. *J. Exp. Anal. Behav.* 20(2):163–81

Johnson A, Redish AD. 2007. Neural ensembles in CA3 transiently encode paths forward of the animal at a decision point. *J. Neurosci.* 27(45):12176–89

Jones JL, Esber GR, McDannald MA, Gruber AJ, Hernandez A, et al. 2012. OFC supports behavior and learning using inferred but not cached values. *Science* 338(6109):953–56

Kirk U, Skov M, Hulme O, Christensen MS, Zeki S. 2009. Modulation of aesthetic value by semantic context: an fMRI study. *NeuroImage* 44(3):1125–32

Knutson B, Fong GW, Adams CM, Varner JL, Hommer D. 2001. Dissociation of reward anticipation and outcome with event-related fMRI. *Neuroreport* 12(17):3683–87

Koechlin E, Ody C, Kouneiher F. 2003. The architecture of cognitive control in the human prefrontal cortex. *Science* 302(5648):1181–85

Kolb B, Buhrmann K, McDonald R, Sutherland RJ. 1994. Dissociation of the medial prefrontal, posterior parietal, and posterior temporal cortex for spatial navigation and recognition memory in the rat. *Cereb. Cortex* 4(6):664–80

Konorski J, Miller S. 1937. On two types of conditioned reflex. *J. Gen. Psychol.* 16(1):264–72

Kuvayev L, Sutton R. 1996. Model-based RL with an approximate, learned model. *Proc. Yale Worksh. Adapt. Learn. Syst., 9th, June 10–12, New Haven, CT*, pp. 101–5. New Haven, CT: Dunham Lab., Yale Univ.

Lau B, Glimcher PW. 2008. Value representations in the primate striatum during matching behavior. *Neuron* 58(3):451–63

LeDoux JE, Iwata J, Cicchetti P, Reis DJ. 1988. Different projections of the central amygdaloid nucleus mediate autonomic and behavioral correlates of conditioned fear. *J. Neurosci.* 8(7):2517–29

Lee D, Rushworth MFS, Walton ME, Watanabe M, Sakagami M. 2007. Functional specialization of the primate frontal cortex during decision making. *J. Neurosci.* 27(31):8170–73

Lee SW, Shimojo S, O'Doherty JP. 2014. Neural computations underlying arbitration between model-based and model-free learning. *Neuron* 81(3):687–99

Lee TG, Grafton ST. 2015. Out of control: Diminished prefrontal activity coincides with impaired motor performance due to choking under pressure. *NeuroImage* 105:145–55

Levy DJ, Glimcher PW. 2012. The root of all value: a neural common currency for choice. *Curr. Opin. Neurobiol.* 22(6):1027–38

Liljeholm M, Molloy CJ, O'Doherty JP. 2012. Dissociable brain systems mediate vicarious learning of stimulus-response and action-outcome contingencies. *J. Neurosci.* 32(29):9878–86

Liljeholm M, Tricomi E, O'Doherty JP, Balleine BW. 2011. Neural correlates of instrumental contingency learning: differential effects of action-reward conjunction and disjunction. *J. Neurosci.* 31(7):2474–80

Liljeholm M, Wang S, Zhang J, O'Doherty JP. 2013. Neural correlates of the divergence of instrumental probability distributions. *J. Neurosci.* 33(30):12519–27

Lovibond PF. 1983. Facilitation of instrumental behavior by a Pavlovian appetitive conditioned stimulus. *J. Exp. Psychol. Anim. Behav. Process.* 9(3):225–47

MacKay WA. 1992. Properties of reach-related neuronal activity in cortical area 7A. *J. Neurophysiol.* 67(5):1335–45

Maia TV, Frank MJ. 2011. From RL models to psychiatric and neurological disorders. *Nat. Neurosci.* 14(2):154–62

Matsumoto K, Suzuki W, Tanaka K. 2003. Neuronal correlates of goal-based motor selection in the prefrontal cortex. *Science* 301(5630):229–32

McDannald MA, Lucantonio F, Burke KA, Niv Y, Schoenbaum G. 2011. Ventral striatum and OFC are both required for model-based, but not model-free, RL. *J. Neurosci.* 31(7):2700–5

McNamee D, Rangel A, O'Doherty JP. 2013. Category-dependent and category-independent goal-value codes in human vmPFC. *Nat. Neurosci.* 16(4):479–85

Miller EK, Cohen JD. 2001. An integrative theory of prefrontal cortex function. *Annu. Rev. Neurosci.* 24(1):167–202

Mobbs D, Hassabis D, Seymour B, Marchant JL, Weiskopf N, et al. 2009. Choking on the money: Reward-based performance decrements are associated with midbrain activity. *Psychol. Sci.* 20(8):955–62

Montague PR, Dayan P, Sejnowski TJ. 1996. A framework for mesencephalic dopamine systems based on predictive Hebbian learning. *J. Neurosci.* 16(5):1936–47

Montague PR, Dolan RJ, Friston KJ, Dayan P. 2012. Computational psychiatry. *Trends Cogn. Sci.* 16(1):72–80

Morris RW, Dezfouli A, Griffiths KR, Balleine BW. 2014. Action-value comparisons in the dorsolateral prefrontal cortex control choice between goal-directed actions. *Nat. Commun.* 5:4390

Nasser HM, Chen Y-W, Fiscella K, Calu DJ. 2015. Individual variability in behavioral flexibility predicts sign-tracking tendency. *Front. Behav. Neurosci.* 9:289

O'Doherty J, Kringelbach ML, Rolls ET, Hornak J, Andrews C. 2001. Abstract reward and punishment representations in the human OFC. *Nat. Neurosci.* 4(1):95–102

O'Doherty J, Rolls ET, Francis S, Bowtell R, McGlone F, et al. 2000. Sensory-specific satiety-related olfactory activation of the human OFC. *Neuroreport* 11(4):893–97

O'Doherty J, Winston J, Critchley H, Perrett D, Burt DM, Dolan RJ. 2003a. Beauty in a smile: the role of medial orbitofrontal cortex in facial attractiveness. *Neuropsychologia* 41(2):147–55

O'Doherty JP. 2004. Reward representations and reward-related learning in the human brain: insights from neuroimaging. *Curr. Opin. Neurobiol.* 14(6):769–76

O'Doherty JP. 2014. The problem with value. *Neurosci. Biobehav. Rev.* 43:259–68

O'Doherty JP, Dayan P, Friston K, Critchley H, Dolan RJ. 2003b. Temporal difference models and reward-related learning in the human brain. *Neuron* 38(2):329–37

O'Doherty JP, Deichmann R, Critchley HD, Dolan RJ. 2002. Neural responses during anticipation of a primary taste reward. *Neuron* 33(5):815–26

O'Keefe J, Dostrovsky J. 1971. The hippocampus as a spatial map. Preliminary evidence from unit activity in the freely-moving rat. *Brain Res.* 34(1):171–75

Ostlund SB, Balleine BW. 2005. Lesions of medial prefrontal cortex disrupt the acquisition but not the expression of goal-directed learning. *J. Neurosci.* 25(34):7763–70

Padoa-Schioppa C, Assad JA. 2006. Neurons in the OFC encode economic value. *Nature* 441(7090):223–26

Pan X, Fan H, Sawa K, Tsuda I, Tsukada M, Sakagami M. 2014. Reward inference by primate prefrontal and striatal neurons. *J. Neurosci.* 34(4):1380–96

Pascoe JP, Kapp BS. 1985. Electrophysiological characteristics of amygdaloid central nucleus neurons during Pavlovian fear conditioning in the rabbit. *Behav. Brain Res.* 16(2–3):117–33

Paton JJ, Belova MA, Morrison SE, Salzman CD. 2006. The primate amygdala represents the positive and negative value of visual stimuli during learning. *Nature* 439(7078):865–70

Pauli WM, Larsen T, Collette S, Tyszka JM, Seymour B, O'Doherty JP. 2015. Distinct contributions of ventromedial and dorsolateral subregions of the human substantia nigra to appetitive and aversive learning. *J. Neurosci.* 35(42):14220–33

Paulus MP, Rogalsky C, Simmons A, Feinstein JS, Stein MB. 2003. Increased activation in the right insula during risk-taking decision making is related to harm avoidance and neuroticism. *NeuroImage* 19(4):1439–48

Pavlov I. 1927. *Conditioned Reflexes: An Investigation of the Physiological Activity of the Cerebral Cortex.* London: Oxford Univ. Press

Payzan-LeNestour E, Dunne S, Bossaerts P, O'Doherty JP. 2013. The neural representation of unexpected uncertainty during value-based decision making. *Neuron* 79(1):191–201

Pezzulo G, Rigoli F, Chersi F. 2013. The mixed instrumental controller: using value of information to combine habitual choice and mental simulation. *Front. Psychol.* 4:92

Pfeiffer BE, Foster DJ. 2013. Hippocampal place-cell sequences depict future paths to remembered goals. *Nature* 497(7447):74–79

Plassmann H, O'Doherty J, Rangel A. 2007. OFC encodes willingness to pay in everyday economic transactions. *J. Neurosci.* 27(37):9984–88

Plassmann H, O'Doherty J, Shiv B, Rangel A. 2008. Marketing actions can modulate neural representations of experienced pleasantness. *PNAS* 105(3):1050–54

Plassmann H, O'Doherty JP, Rangel A. 2010. Appetitive and aversive goal values are encoded in the medial OFC at the time of decision making. *J. Neurosci.* 30(32):10799–808

Platt ML, Glimcher PW. 1999. Neural correlates of decision variables in parietal cortex. *Nature* 400(6741):233–38

Prévost C, McNamee D, Jessup RK, Bossaerts P, O'Doherty JP. 2013. Evidence for model-based computations in the human amygdala during Pavlovian conditioning. *PLOS Comput. Biol.* 9(2):e1002918

Prévost C, Pessiglione M, Météreau E, Cléry-Melin M-L, Dreher J-C. 2010. Separate valuation subsystems for delay and effort decision costs. *J. Neurosci.* 30(42):14080–90

Ragozzino ME, Ragozzino KE, Mizumori SJ, Kesner RP. 2002. Role of the dorsomedial striatum in behavioral flexibility for response and visual cue discrimination learning. *Behav. Neurosci.* 116(1):105–15

Rangel A, Camerer C, Montague PR. 2008. A framework for studying the neurobiology of value-based decision making. *Nat. Rev. Neurosci.* 9(7):545–56

Rangel A, Hare T. 2010. Neural computations associated with goal-directed choice. *Curr. Opin. Neurobiol.* 20(2):262–70

Rescorla RA. 1980. Simultaneous and successive associations in sensory preconditioning. *J. Exp. Psychol. Anim. Behav. Process.* 6(3):207–16

Rescorla RA, Solomon RL. 1967. Two-process learning theory: relationships between Pavlovian conditioning and instrumental learning. *Psychol. Rev.* 74(3):151–82

Rescorla RA, Wagner AR. 1972. A theory of Pavlovian conditioning: variations in the effectiveness of reinforcement and nonreinforcement. In *Classical Conditioning II: Current Research and Theory*, ed. AH Black, WF Prokasy, pp. 64–99. New York: Appleton-Century-Crofts

Ribas-Fernandes JJF, Solway A, Diuk C, McGuire JT, Barto AG, et al. 2011. A neural signature of hierarchical RL. *Neuron* 71(2):370–79

Rolls ET, Kringelbach ML, De Araujo IET. 2003. Different representations of pleasant and unpleasant odours in the human brain. *Eur. J. Neurosci.* 18(3):695–703

Salzman CD, Fusi S. 2010. Emotion, cognition, and mental state representation in amygdala and prefrontal cortex. *Annu. Rev. Neurosci.* 33:173–202

Salzman CD, Paton JJ, Belova MA, Morrison SE. 2007. Flexible neural representations of value in the primate brain. *Ann. N. Y. Acad. Sci.* 1121(1):336–54

Samejima K, Ueda Y, Doya K, Kimura M. 2005. Representation of action-specific reward values in the striatum. *Science* 310(5752):1337–40

Schapiro AC, Rogers TT, Cordova NI, Turk-Browne NB, Botvinick MM. 2013. Neural representations of events arise from temporal community structure. *Nat. Neurosci.* 16(4):486–92

Schoenbaum G, Chiba AA, Gallagher M. 1998. OFC and basolateral amygdala encode expected outcomes during learning. *Nat. Neurosci.* 1(2):155–59

Schoenbaum G, Esber GR, Iordanova MD. 2013. Dopamine signals mimic reward prediction errors. *Nat. Neurosci.* 16(7):777–79

Schönberg T, Daw ND, Joel D, O'Doherty JP. 2007. Reinforcement learning signals in the human striatum distinguish learners from nonlearners during reward-based decision making. *J. Neurosci.* 27(47):12860–67

Schultz W, Dayan P, Montague PR. 1997. A neural substrate of prediction and reward. *Science* 275(5306):1593–99

Seo H, Barraclough DJ, Lee D. 2007. Dynamic signals related to choices and outcomes in the dorsolateral prefrontal cortex. *Cereb. Cortex* 17(Suppl. 1):110–17

Seo H, Barraclough DJ, Lee D. 2009. Lateral intraparietal cortex and RL during a mixed-strategy game. *J. Neurosci.* 29(22):7278–89

Shadlen MN, Newsome WT. 2001. Neural basis of a perceptual decision in the parietal cortex (Area LIP) of the rhesus monkey. *J. Neurophysiol.* 86(4):1916–36

Shenhav A, Botvinick MM, Cohen JD. 2013. The expected value of control: an integrative theory of anterior cingulate cortex function. *Neuron* 79(2):217–40

Simon DA, Daw ND. 2011. Neural correlates of forward planning in a spatial decision task in humans. *J. Neurosci.* 31(14):5526–39

Small DM, Zatorre RJ, Dagher A, Evans AC, Jones-Gotman M. 2001. Changes in brain activity related to eating chocolate. *Brain* 124(9):1720–33

Smith DV, Hayden BY, Truong T-K, Song AW, Platt ML, Huettel SA. 2010. Distinct value signals in anterior and posterior VmPFC. *J. Neurosci.* 30(7):2490–95

Sohn J-W, Lee D. 2007. Order-dependent modulation of directional signals in the supplementary and pre-supplementary motor areas. *J. Neurosci.* 27(50):13655–66

Staudinger MR, Erk S, Abler B, Walter H. 2009. Cognitive reappraisal modulates expected value and prediction error encoding in the ventral striatum. *NeuroImage* 47(2):713–21

Steinberg EE, Janak PH. 2013. Establishing causality for dopamine in neural function and behavior with optogenetics. *Brain Res.* 1511:46–64

Strait CE, Blanchard TC, Hayden BY. 2014. Reward value comparison via mutual inhibition in VmPFC. *Neuron* 82(6):1357–66

Sutton RS. 1988. Learning to predict by the methods of temporal differences. *Mach. Learn.* 3(1):9–44

Sutton RS. 1990. RL architectures for animats. *Proc. Int. Conf. Simul. Adapt. Behav., 1st, From Animals to Animats, Cambridge, MA*, pp. 288–96. Cambridge, MA: MIT Press

Sutton RS, Precup D, Singh S. 1999. Between MDPs and semi-MDPs: a framework for temporal abstraction in RL. *Artif. Intell.* 112:181–211

Suzuki S, Adachi R, Dunne S, Bossaerts P, O'Doherty JP. 2015. Neural mechanisms underlying human consensus decision-making. *Neuron* 86(2):591–602

Tavares RM, Mendelsohn A, Grossman Y, Williams CH, Shapiro M, et al. 2015. A map for social navigation in the human brain. *Neuron* 87(1):231–43

Thibodeau GA, Patton KT. 1992. *Structure & Function of the Body*. St. Louis, MO: Mosby Year Book. 9th ed.

Thorndike EL. 1898. Animal intelligence: an experimental study of the associative processes in animals. *Psychol. Rev. Monogr. Suppl.* 2(4):1–109

Tobler PN, O'Doherty JP, Dolan RJ, Schultz W. 2006. Human neural learning depends on reward prediction errors in the blocking paradigm. *J. Neurophysiol.* 95(1):301–10

Tolman EC. 1948. Cognitive maps in rats and men. *Psychol. Rev.* 55(4):189–208

Tricomi E, Balleine BW, O'Doherty JP. 2009. A specific role for posterior dorsolateral striatum in human habit learning. *Eur. J. Neurosci.* 29(11):2225–32

Tully T, Quinn WG. 1985. Classical conditioning and retention in normal and mutant *Drosophila melanogaster*. *J. Comp. Physiol.* 157(2):263–77

Valentin VV, Dickinson A, O'Doherty JP. 2007. Determining the neural substrates of goal-directed learning in the human brain. *J. Neurosci.* 27(15):4019–26

Voon V, Derbyshire K, Rück C, Irvine MA, Worbe Y, et al. 2015. Disorders of compulsivity: a common bias towards learning habits. *Mol. Psychiatry* 20(3):345–52

Wallis JD, Miller EK. 2003. Neuronal activity in primate dorsolateral and orbital prefrontal cortex during performance of a reward preference task. *Eur. J. Neurosci.* 18(7):2069–81

Walters ET, Carew TJ, Kandel ER. 1981. Associative learning in *Aplysia*: evidence for conditioned fear in an invertebrate. *Science* 211(4481):504–6

Walton ME, Groves J, Jennings KA, Croxson PL, Sharp T, et al. 2009. Comparing the role of the anterior cingulate cortex and 6-hydroxydopamine nucleus accumbens lesions on operant effort-based decision making. *Eur. J. Neurosci.* 29(8):1678–91

Watson P, Wiers RW, Hommel B, de Wit S. 2014. Working for food you don't desire. Cues interfere with goal-directed food-seeking. *Appetite* 79:139–48

Whitlock JR, Pfuhl G, Dagslott N, Moser M-B, Moser EI. 2012. Functional split between parietal and entorhinal cortices in the rat. *Neuron* 73(4):789–802

Wilber AA, Clark BJ, Forster TC, Tatsuno M, McNaughton BL. 2014. Interaction of egocentric and world-centered reference frames in the rat posterior parietal cortex. *J. Neurosci.* 34(16):5431–46

Wilson RC, Takahashi YK, Schoenbaum G, Niv Y. 2014. OFC as a cognitive map of task space. *Neuron* 81(2):267–79

Wimmer GE, Shohamy D. 2012. Preference by association: how memory mechanisms in the hippocampus bias decisions. *Science* 338(6104):270–73

Winn P, Brown VJ, Inglis WL. 1997. On the relationships between the striatum and the pedunculopontine tegmental nucleus. *Crit. Rev. Neurobiol.* 11(4):241–61

Wittmann BC, Schott BH, Guderian S, Frey JU, Heinze H-J, Düzel E. 2005. Reward-related fMRI activation of dopaminergic midbrain is associated with enhanced hippocampus-dependent long-term memory formation. *Neuron* 45(3):459–67

Wunderlich K, Dayan P, Dolan RJ. 2012. Mapping value based planning and extensively trained choice in the human brain. *Nat. Neurosci.* 15(5):786–91

Wunderlich K, Rangel A, O'Doherty JP. 2009. Neural computations underlying action-based decision making in the human brain. *PNAS* 106(40):17199–204

Yanike M, Ferrera VP. 2014. Representation of outcome risk and action in the anterior caudate nucleus. *J. Neurosci.* 34(9):3279–90

Yin HH, Knowlton BJ, Balleine BW. 2004. Lesions of dorsolateral striatum preserve outcome expectancy but disrupt habit formation in instrumental learning. *Eur. J. Neurosci.* 19(1):181–89

Yin HH, Knowlton BJ, Balleine BW. 2005. Blockade of NMDA receptors in the dorsomedial striatum prevents action-outcome learning in instrumental conditioning. *Eur. J. Neurosci.* 22(2):505–12

Yin HH, Knowlton BJ, Balleine BW. 2006. Inactivation of dorsolateral striatum enhances sensitivity to changes in the action-outcome contingency in instrumental conditioning. *Behav. Brain Res.* 166(2):189–96

Yoshida W, Ishii S. 2006. Resolution of uncertainty in prefrontal cortex. *Neuron* 50(5):781–89

Zedelius CM, Veling H, Aarts H. 2011. Boosting or choking—how conscious and unconscious reward processing modulate the active maintenance of goal-relevant information. *Conscious. Cogn.* 20(2):355–62

Reinforcement Learning and Episodic Memory in Humans and Animals: An Integrative Framework

Samuel J. Gershman[1] and Nathaniel D. Daw[2]

[1] Department of Psychology and Center for Brain Science, Harvard University, Cambridge, Massachusetts 02138; email: gershman@fas.harvard.edu

[2] Princeton Neuroscience Institute and Department of Psychology, Princeton University, Princeton, New Jersey 08544

Annu. Rev. Psychol. 2017. 68:101–28

First published online as a Review in Advance on September 2, 2016

The *Annual Review of Psychology* is online at psych.annualreviews.org

This article's doi:
10.1146/annurev-psych-122414-033625

Keywords

reinforcement learning, memory, decision making

Abstract

We review the psychology and neuroscience of reinforcement learning (RL), which has experienced significant progress in the past two decades, enabled by the comprehensive experimental study of simple learning and decision-making tasks. However, one challenge in the study of RL is computational: The simplicity of these tasks ignores important aspects of reinforcement learning in the real world: (*a*) State spaces are high-dimensional, continuous, and partially observable; this implies that (*b*) data are relatively sparse and, indeed, precisely the same situation may never be encountered twice; furthermore, (*c*) rewards depend on the long-term consequences of actions in ways that violate the classical assumptions that make RL tractable. A seemingly distinct challenge is that, cognitively, theories of RL have largely involved procedural and semantic memory, the way in which knowledge about action values or world models extracted gradually from many experiences can drive choice. This focus on semantic memory leaves out many aspects of memory, such as episodic memory, related to the traces of individual events. We suggest that these two challenges are related. The computational challenge can be dealt with, in part, by endowing RL systems with episodic memory, allowing them to (*a*) efficiently approximate value functions over complex state spaces, (*b*) learn with very little data, and (*c*) bridge long-term dependencies between actions and rewards. We review the computational theory underlying this proposal and the empirical evidence to support it. Our proposal suggests that the ubiquitous and diverse roles of memory in RL may function as part of an integrated learning system.

Contents

INTRODUCTION

Reinforcement learning (RL) is the process by which organisms learn by trial and error to predict and acquire reward. This is challenging from a computational point of view because actions have long-term effects on future reward (e.g., failing to save may lead to penury later in life, drinking stagnant water may slake thirst at the expense of later illness). Furthermore, these deferred consequences may depend critically on other, subsequent actions and events: for example, getting admitted to college pays off only if one manages to graduate. This sequential dependency greatly compounds the classic curse of dimensionality (Bellman 1957) by extending it over time. Clearly, biological organisms cannot try every possible sequence of actions. By making certain simplifying assumptions about the structure of the environment, computer scientists have designed efficient algorithms that are guaranteed to find the optimal behavioral policy. The discovery that the brain itself uses one (indeed several) of these algorithms is one of the great success stories of modern cognitive and computational neuroscience.

Two decades of research have buttressed this account with converging evidence from behavioral, neural, and computational studies. Beginning in the 1990s, celebrated work on RL focused on a dopaminergic and striatal system for simple, incremental learning of action values, known as model-free learning (Houk et al. 1995, Montague et al. 1996, Schultz et al. 1997). Later work has extended this view to encompass additional processes for more deliberative, so-called model-based evaluation (Daw et al. 2005, Dolan & Dayan 2013). This expansion of our understanding of RL increases the computational capability of the theories—allowing them, for instance, to choose more effectively in novel or changed circumstances—and also situates them in relation to a broader framework of research in the cognitive neuroscience of memory. Model-based learning formalizes how organisms employ knowledge about the world—maps or models of task contingencies—in the service of evaluating actions. These results parallel research on multiple memory systems, e.g., distinguishing a striatal procedural learning system from a hippocampal declarative one (Eichenbaum & Cohen 2004, Poldrack et al. 2001), each of which possesses several properties that echo their decision-making counterparts. The emerging relationship between RL and the memory systems that likely subserve it has been illuminating for the study of both.

Despite this success, we are still far from understanding how real-world RL works, either cognitively or computationally. In this review, we suggest that these two questions have a common answer.

Cognitively, research on RL has long embraced procedural learning and semantic memory (in the sense of knowledge of facts about the world that are typically viewed as abstracted from many experiences, such as the map of a well-explored maze). However, this research has had limited contact with another prominent sort of memory: episodic memories connecting different aspects of individual events that the organism experienced at a particular time and place (Tulving 1972). Such traces seem, in principle, relevant to decisions; one goal of this review is to clarify what specific advantages they might confer.

Computationally, biological RL is still greatly hobbled by the restrictive formal assumptions that underpin it. With few exceptions, the kinds of experimental tasks that have been used to study RL are quintessentially toy problems: They are designed to isolate certain computations in a well-controlled setting but do not grapple with the complexity of many decision problems faced by organisms in their natural environments. In particular, (a) real state spaces are high-dimensional, continuous, and partially observable; this implies that (b) data are relatively sparse and, indeed, precisely the same situation will never be encountered twice; furthermore, (c) rewards depend on the long-term consequences of actions in ways that violate the probabilistic independence assumptions that make RL tractable.

Intuitively, these implications can be understood by considering the problem of investing in the stock market. The state of the stock market is high-dimensional and continuous, such that any given state is unlikely to be repeated (i.e., the market history sparsely samples the state space). Furthermore, the long-term consequences of an investment decision depend on forces that are only partially observable (e.g., the strategies of other investors). The kinds of algorithms that have been imputed to the brain break down when confronted with this sort of real-world complexity. Because organisms clearly find a way to cope with this complexity, we are left with the conundrum that much of our understanding about RL in the brain may in fact be irrelevant to important aspects of how organisms naturally behave.

In this review, we suggest that one computational answer to this conundrum is to use a set of algorithmic approaches—those based on nonparametric (kernel- or instance-based) estimation methods—that are different from and complementary to those typically examined in cognitive neuroscience. Nonparametric methods are statistically well-suited for dealing with sparse, arbitrarily structured, trial-unique data. Moreover, because they ultimately base their estimates on records of individual events, they may also clarify the missing links between decision making and episodic memory. These links are relatively underexplored, though they relate to a number of other ideas and make connections with other empirical literatures, which therefore form the balance of our review. The most important idea [building on the work of Lengyel & Dayan (2007)] is that episodic memory could provide detailed and temporally extended snapshots of the interdependency of the actions and outcomes originating from individual experiences; this information may be a reliable guide to decision making precisely in situations in which classical algorithms break down. Episodic memory may thus enable organisms to (a) efficiently approximate value functions over complex state spaces, (b) learn with very little data, and (c) bridge long-term dependencies between actions and rewards.

In the following sections, we review the current conception of RL in neuroscience and psychology and lay out the main arguments, both theoretical and empirical, that make this conception at best incomplete. We then describe a theoretical framework for augmenting RL with additional systems based on nonparametric estimation, which we tentatively identify with episodic memory. We consider the computational implications of this approach and review the available evidence related to this framework and its connection to earlier ideas.

REINFORCEMENT LEARNING: THE CURRENT PICTURE

We begin this section with a brief overview of the standard algorithmic solutions to the RL problem and then review behavioral and neural evidence that the brain implements these algorithms (for more extensive reviews of this material, see Dolan & Dayan 2013, Niv 2009; see also a trilogy of textbook chapters, Daw 2013, Daw & O'Doherty 2013, Daw & Tobler 2013). Our goal in this review is mainly to motivate a more prospective review of the possible connections with additional areas of research.

Markov Decision Processes

In machine learning, RL concerns the study of learned optimal control, primarily in multistep (sequential) decision problems (Bertsekas & Tsitsiklis 1996, Sutton & Barto 1998). Most classic work on this subject concerns a class of tasks known as Markov decision processes (MDPs). MDPs are formal models of multistep decision tasks, including spatial navigation, games such as Tetris, and scheduling problems such as those in factories; if some game-theoretic aspects of the opponent's behavior are neglected, then they can also roughly model multistep multiplayer games such as chess. The goal of RL is typically to learn, by trial and error, to make optimal choices in an initially unknown MDP.

Formally, MDPs are expressed in terms of discrete states s, actions a, and numeric rewards r. Much of the research in psychology and neuroscience surrounding these models concerns the tricky relationship between these formal objects and real-world situations, behaviors, and outcomes. Informally, states are like situations in a task (e.g., locations in a spatial maze), actions are like behavioral choices (turn left or right), and rewards are a measure of the utility obtained in some state (a high value for food obtained at some location, if one is hungry).

An MDP consists of a series of discrete time steps, in which the agent observes some state s_t of the environment, receives some reward r_t, and chooses some action a_t. The agent's goal is to choose actions at each step so as to maximize the expected cumulative future rewards, discounted (exponentially by decay factor $\gamma < 1$) for delay, i.e., the sum $r_t + \gamma r_{t+1} + \gamma^2 r_{t+2} + \ldots$ of future rewards.

Thus, the goal is to maximize not the immediate reward of an action but instead the cumulative reward (the return), summed over all future time steps. Actions influence longer-run reward expectancy because, in an MDP, each successor state s_{t+1} is drawn from a probability distribution $P(s_{t+1} \mid s_t, a_t)$ that depends on the current state and action; rewards at each step are generated according to a probability distribution $P(r_t \mid s_t)$ that depends on the current state. Informally, this means that the agent navigates the states (like positions in a maze) and harvests rewards by choosing actions. Each action not only affects the current reward but, by affecting the next state, also sets the stage for subsequent rewards. Conversely, because the consequences of an action for cumulative reward depend also on subsequent states and actions, choosing optimally can be quite involved.

What makes these problems nevertheless tractably solvable is the eponymous feature of MDPs, the Markov conditional independence property: At any time step t, all future states and rewards depend only on the current state and action via the probability distributions given above. Thus, importantly, conditional only on the present state and action, all future events are independent of all preceding events. This permits a recursive expression for the state-action value function (the sum of future rewards expected for taking some action in some state, the quantity that is the goal of optimization):

$$Q_\pi(s_t, a_t) = r_t + \gamma \sum_{s_{t+1}} P(s_{t+1} \mid s_t, a_t) Q_\pi(s_{t+1}, \pi(s_{t+1})). \tag{1}$$

Equation 1 is a form of the Bellman equation (Bellman 1957), versions of which underlie most classical RL algorithms. Here, it says that the expected future reward for taking action a_t in state s_t (then following some policy π thereafter) is given by the sum of two terms, the current reward and the second term, which stands in for all the remaining rewards $\gamma r_{t+1} + \gamma^2 r_{t+2} + \ldots$. The insight is that this sum is itself just the value Q of the subsequent state, averaged over possible successors according to their probability.

One of the chief problems of RL is how to choose advantageously given the deferred consequences of one's actions. One way to solve this problem is to focus on predicting those consequences via learning to estimate $Q_\pi(s_t, a_t)$ (or some closely related quantity) from experience with rewards, states, and actions in the MDP. Given a good estimate of the value function, you can choose the action with the best return simply by comparing values across candidate actions. Many RL algorithms rely on variations on this basic logic. (We omit some details related to the dependence of Q on the continuation policy π; for our purposes, imagine that by learning Q and choosing according to it, we gradually improve our prevailing action selection policy, which in turn drives an updated Q until we arrive at the best policy.)

Model-Based and Model-Free Algorithms

There are two main classes of algorithms for RL based on Equation 1; these classes focus on either the left- or right-hand side of the equal sign in that equation. The first approach is based on estimating the one-step reward and state transition distributions $P(r_t \mid s_t)$ and $P(s_{t+1} \mid s_t, a_t)$, which together are known as an internal model of the MDP. Notably, these concern only immediate events: which rewards or states directly follow other states and are thus easy to learn from local experience, essentially by counting. Given these, it is possible to iteratively expand the right-hand side of Equation 1 to compute the state-action value for any state and candidate action. Algorithms for doing this, such as value iteration, essentially work by mental simulation, enumerating the possible sequences of states that are expected to follow a starting state and action, summing the rewards expected along these sequences, and using the learned model to keep track of their probability (for a detailed presentation, see Daw & Dayan 2014).

This approach is known as model-based learning due to its reliance on the internal model. Its main advantage is the simplicity of learning, but its main disadvantage is that this simplicity is offset by computational complexity at choice time because producing state-action values depends on extensive computation over many branching possible paths.

The second class of algorithms eschews learning a world model and instead learns a table of long-run state-action values Q (the left-hand side of Equation 1) directly from experience. The discovery of algorithms for accomplishing such model-free RL [in particular, the family of temporal-difference (TD) learning algorithms; Sutton 1988] was a major advance in machine learning that continues to provide the foundation for modern applications (e.g., Mnih et al. 2015).

Briefly, these algorithms use experienced states, actions, and rewards to approximate the right-hand side of Equation 1 and average these to update a table of long-run reward predictions.

More particularly, many algorithms are based on the temporal difference reward prediction error occasioned by comparing the value $Q(s_t, a_t)$ to a sample computed one time step later:

$$\delta_t = r_t + \gamma \, Q(s_{t+1}, a_{t+1}) - Q(s_t, a_t). \tag{2}$$

When the value function is well estimated, this difference should on average be zero [because $Q(s_t, a_t)$ should in expectation equal $r_t + \gamma \, Q(s_{t+1}, a_{t+1})$, according to Equation 1]. When the error is nonzero, stored Qs can be updated to reduce it.

Choice is, accordingly, much simpler using model-free algorithms than using model-based algorithms because the long-run values are already computed and need only be compared to find the best action. However, these computational savings come at the cost of inflexibility and less-efficient learning.

Model-Free Learning in the Brain

The initial and still the most-celebrated success of RL theory in neuroscience was the observation that the firing of dopamine neurons in the midbrain of monkeys behaving for reward resembles the reward prediction error of Equation 2 (Houk et al. 1995, Montague et al. 1996, Schultz et al. 1997), suggesting that the brain may use this signal for RL. The trial–trial fluctuations in this signal track the model quite precisely (Bayer & Glimcher 2005) and can also be measured in rodents using both physiology and voltammetry (Cohen et al. 2012, Hart et al. 2014). A similar signal can also be measured in the ventral striatum (an important dopamine target) in humans using fMRI (e.g., Hare et al. 2008). Although fMRI measurements are not specific to the underlying neural causes, dopaminergic involvement in these prediction error correlates is suggested by the finding that these correlates are modulated by dopaminergic medication (Pessiglione et al. 2006) and by Parkinson's disease (Schonberg et al. 2010), which is marked by the relatively selective degeneration of dopaminergic nuclei.

Many researchers believe that dopamine drives learning about actions by modulating plasticity at its targets, notably medium spiny neurons in striatum (Frank et al. 2004). Via their projections to other basal ganglia nuclei (and ultimately to the motor cortex), these neurons drive elicitation and withholding of behavior (Alexander & Crutcher 1990). Accordingly, Parkinson's disease and dopamine replacement therapy in humans modulate learning in RL tasks (Frank et al. 2004, Shohamy et al. 2005). More temporally specific optogenetic elicitation and suppression of dopaminergic responses in rodents also drives learning in tasks specifically designed to isolate error-driven learning (Parker et al. 2016, Steinberg et al. 2013). These studies refine an earlier literature using less-selective electrical or pharmacological stimulation of the systems; notably, drugs of abuse invariably agonize dopamine as a common link of effect. This suggests that the reinforcing effects of these drugs are ultimately driven by the same RL mechanisms discussed in this review (Everitt & Robbins 2005, Redish 2004).

The behavioral experiments discussed above mainly involve nonsequential decision tasks such as one-step bandit tasks, in which a subject repeatedly chooses between a set of actions (e.g., different slot machines) and receives reward or punishment. Indeed, the trial-by-trial dependency of choices on rewards in such tasks is quantitatively consistent with the pattern predicted by error-driven learning in both monkeys (Lau & Glimcher 2005) and humans (Seymour et al. 2012). However, model-free learning according to Equation 2 makes more specific and characteristic predictions about the progression of learning across states in multistep, sequential tasks. The predicted patterns have been confirmed in humans (Daw et al. 2011, Fu & Anderson 2008), although not exclusively. Indeed, long before the advent of the neurophysiological models, behavioral psychologists had established that basic TD learning cannot by itself explain a number of learning effects, a point we examine in the next section.

Model-Based Learning in the Brain

Although model-free and model-based algorithms both ultimately converge to the optimal value predictions (under various technical assumptions and in the theoretical limit of infinite experience in a fixed MDP; e.g., Bertsekas & Tsitsiklis 1996), they differ in the trial-by-trial dynamics by which they approach the solution. One difference between model-free and model-based algorithms is the fact that, because the model-free algorithms learn long-run action values by sampling them directly along experienced trajectories, they can in some cases fail to integrate information encountered in different trajectories (e.g., separate trials or task stages).

This basic insight has been investigated using tasks involving staged sequences of experience that are ordered in such a way as to defeat a model-free learner. For instance, in latent learning (Gläscher et al. 2010, Tolman 1948) and a similar task called sensory preconditioning (Brogden 1939, Wimmer & Shohamy 2012), organisms are first preexposed to the state-action contingencies in an environment without any rewards (e.g., by exploring a maze), then subsequently learn that reward is available at a particular location.

For a model-based learner, this experience has the effect of teaching them first the transition function $P(s_{t+1} \mid s_t, a_t)$, i.e., the map of the maze, and then, separately, the reward function $P(r_t \mid s_t)$. Together, this information enables them in a subsequent probe phase to navigate to the reward from any location by evaluating Equation 1. However, for a model-free learner, the preexposure stage teaches them nothing useful for the probe (only that Q is everywhere zero); in particular, because they don't separately learn a representation of the map of the maze (the state transition distribution), they must learn the navigation task from scratch when reward is introduced.

Humans and even rodents can, at least under some circumstances, successfully integrate these experiences, demonstrated in this case by facilitated navigation learning in groups who received the preexposure (Gläscher et al. 2010, Tolman 1948). These results and logically similar ones involving studying whether animals require additional experience to adjust their decisions following changes in reward value (e.g., outcome devaluation) or task contingencies (e.g., introduction of blockades or shortcuts, contingency degradation) have been taken as a rejection of model-free RL as a complete account of behavior (Daw et al. 2005, Dickinson & Balleine 2002).

However, the same types of experiments actually do support the predictions of model-free learning mechanisms such as TD because, under other circumstances, organisms fail, as the theories predict, to integrate well- (but separately) learned information about contingencies and rewards. For instance, following overtraining on lever pressing for food, rodents will press the lever even after the outcome is devalued by satiety (Adams 1982), although less thoroughly trained animals can successfully adjust. In psychology, these two sorts of behaviors (incapable and capable of integration, respectively) are known as habitual and goal-directed. Lesion studies in rodents suggest that they are dependent on discrete networks in the brain, involving different parts of the frontal cortex and striatum (for a review, see Daw & O'Doherty 2013).

Altogether, the predictions of model-free learning and the prediction error theories of dopamine are well matched to habitual behavior but fail to account for the additional category of goal-directed behavior and the ability of organisms to integrate experiences. This deficiency led to the suggestion that the latter behavior might be understood in terms of model-based learning operating alongside the model-free system and competing to control behavioral output (Daw et al. 2005). This proposal put hitherto looser ideas about deliberative behavior and cognitive maps on more equal quantitative footing with the more specific neurocomputational theories of habitual learning, enabling further investigation of its properties.

For instance, with more specific characterizations of both sorts of learning, it is possible to dissociate trial-by-trial behavioral adjustments and neural correlates of decision variables like Q

associated with either model-based or model-free learning in multistep decision tasks (e.g., two-step, three-state MDPs; Daw et al. 2011). Experiments using this technique have verified that signatures of both types of learning coexist in humans. Their prevalence can be manipulated situationally (Otto et al. 2013a,b), varies across individuals (e.g., with symptoms of compulsive disorders such as drug abuse) (Gillan et al. 2016), and tracks prospective representation of future states measured in fMRI at the time of choice (consistent with choice-time evaluation via mental simulation) (Doll et al. 2015). Research using elaborate multistep decision tasks has also begun to shed light on the computational shortcuts by which the brain manages to compute the expected reward (Cushman & Morris 2015, Dezfouli & Balleine 2013, Diuk et al. 2013, Huys et al. 2015, Solway & Botvinick 2015).

Less is known about the neural circuits supporting putatively model-based behavior. Particularly in human neuroimaging, there appears to be more overlap between neural signals associated with model-based and model-free learning than might have been expected on the basis of lesion work. For instance, prediction error signals in human striatum (Daw et al. 2011) and rodent dopamine neurons (Sadacca et al. 2016) both reflect integrated, model-based valuations. (This is surprising because those signals provide the foundation for the standard model-free account.) Such results might suggest that the systems interact more cooperatively in the intact than the lesioned brain, that model-based computations are built in part by leveraging phylogenetically earlier model-based circuitry, that there is more of a continuum between them, or that the integration of value that is taken as a signature of model-based computation is actually heterogeneous and may occur via a number of different mechanisms at different times (Gershman et al. 2014, Shohamy & Daw 2015, Wimmer & Shohamy 2012).

Other data point to the hippocampus as an important player in model-based RL. The model-free versus model-based distinction appears to track a similar dichotomy in the study of multiple memory systems, which in broad terms distinguishes a rigid striatal procedural learning system from a more flexible declarative memory system associated with the hippocampus (Gabrieli 1998, Knowlton et al. 1996, Squire 1992). Many of the particular aspects of hippocampal function also suggest it as a candidate site for world models as envisioned in RL. For example, the hippocampus has been viewed as a seat of the cognitive maps useful for spatial navigation (O'Keefe & Nadel 1978). Perhaps the most directly suggestive data concerning a potential neural circuit for model-based evaluation also come from spatial navigation tasks, in which representations of place cells in the rodent hippocampus appear to run ahead of the animal during navigation and at choice points (Johnson & Redish 2007, Pfeiffer & Foster 2013). This prospective activity has been suggested to instantiate a search of future trajectories to support model-based evaluation (e.g., decision-time computation in Equation 1). However, this phenomenon has yet to be specifically linked to choice behaviors (such as latent learning or other integrative tasks) that demonstrate model-based evaluation.

In addition to spatial navigation, the hippocampus is also associated with more abstract relational information reminiscent of the state transition function (Eichenbaum & Cohen 2004, Shohamy & Wagner 2008). However, perhaps the most well-known function of the hippocampus is the formation of episodic memories, which are long-term, autobiographical snapshots of particular events. This function has also been linked to prospective construction of imagined future episodes for planning or other decisions (Schacter et al. 2012). It has not, however, received as much attention in RL. Below, we argue that it may underlie some decisions that appear to be model-based. The relationship between these seemingly disparate aspects of hippocampal memory function is a deep conceptual issue that has given rise to ongoing debate in the cognitive neuroscience of memory.

Computational Shortcomings of the Current Picture

The computational and neural mechanisms described in the two sections above appear to be reasonably well-supported, albeit with some uncertainty related to the neural implementation of world modeling and integrative evaluation. However, the ways in which these mechanisms could scale up to real-world tasks remain unclear. Not only are the tasks that have been studied in the laboratory small and artificial but, more importantly, the very assumptions that allow RL to work well in these sorts of tasks are inapplicable to many richer real-world settings.

Many of the problems with the current conception of RL arise from the definition of the state s_t. Laboratory experiments typically involve at most a handful of discrete states and actions, which are clearly signaled to the subjects and designed to satisfy the Markov conditional independence property. Real-world sensations rarely meet these conditions. The typical sensory experiences of an organism are both too vast and too impoverished to serve as s_t in algorithms based on Equation 1. They are too vast because they are continuous and high-dimensional, such that effective learning requires identifying the subset of relevant dimensions and generalizing appropriately across situations that will never exactly recur (Niv et al. 2015).

Real-world sensations are also too impoverished because, despite the extraneous detail in one's immediate sensory observations, they rarely satisfy the Markov property; other information observed in the past but not currently observable affects future state and reward expectancies. Immediate sensations routinely fail to satisfy the Markov property in real-world tasks; for example, the property is violated whenever two different locations look similar enough to be indistinguishable (state aliasing) during navigation or when there are long-run dependencies between day-to-day events, such as when someone tells you they'll be back tomorrow at noon for lunch. If the Markov property fails to hold for some putative state s, it is not possible to decompose the state-action value via the Bellman equation (Equation 2).

Of course, extensive machine learning work exists on ways to cope with some of these circumstances. Particularly relevant for neuroscience is the theory of partially observable Markov decision processes (POMDPs) (Kaelbling et al. 1998), which treats Markov violations as arising from latent states that would satisfy the Markov property but can be only indirectly (and perhaps ambiguously) observed. With training, one can learn to infer the identity of these states (which may indeed provide part of a theoretical basis for state representation for RL; Daw et al. 2006; Gershman et al. 2010, 2015; Rao 2010), but only after having done so is one in a firm position to learn action values. In the following sections, we consider mechanisms that might be applicable to earlier stages in the learning process and might also be flexible and able to adapt in the face of ongoing learning about how to define the state, which dimensions are relevant, and how to infer latent aspects.

EPISODIC MEMORY FOR NONPARAMETRIC VALUE FUNCTION APPROXIMATION

If the current computational conception of RL is incomplete, how can progress be made? One approach is to further examine what the brain's memory systems might suggest about RL.

Existing RL theories have recognized the links between RL and what is known in memory research as procedural memory (for model-free policies or action values), as well as semantic declarative memories (for world maps or models). Strikingly, these quantities, such as procedural knowledge of how to ride a bike or semantic knowledge of what a typical breakfast might contain, all represent statistical summaries extracted from a series of events. In contrast, a predominant focus of research in memory concerns memory for one-shot events, from word lists to autobiographical events such as your 30th birthday party or what you had for breakfast this morning. The remainder of this review considers how memories for individual events might serve RL and, in particular, why these memories might help theories of RL to escape some of their previous weaknesses and the restrictive assumptions under which they operate.

Though an interesting computational object in the abstract, one-shot memories are not unique to long-term episodic memory. For instance, working memory clearly plays a role in maintaining and manipulating information briefly, as is the case for phone numbers. This type of memory is also discussed in our review. However, we mainly consider long-term episodic memory, which, apart from having a number of appealing computational features for RL, is also associated with the hippocampus, which has other mnemonic roles already implicated in model-based RL. (Although we are not yet in a position to entirely reconcile these functions, it is nevertheless clear that episodic aspects are conspicuously lacking from the current conception of RL.)

Psychologically, episodic memory is associated with detailed autobiographical memories, such as what you had for breakfast this morning, that link many different sensory features of an experience at a particular time and place (Tulving 1972). Computationally, for the purpose of this review, we would stress the notion of a record of an individual event (like a trial in a task) and the connection between many aspects of that event, including multiple sensory dimensions and sensations experienced sequentially. Below, we reason about what sort of advantages episodic memories might confer on an organism's decision making and argue that these memories are well suited to the situations poorly handled by the mechanisms considered above and well linked to another class of estimation algorithm.

For this explanation, we build on an earlier proposal by Lengyel & Dayan (2007), who suggested that episodic memories could be used to record and later mimic previously rewarding sequences of states and actions, a process they dubbed episodic control. In this review, we suggest a somewhat different computational rationale for a similar idea, which we call episodic RL, in which episodic memories are used to construct estimates of the state or state-action value function (rather than for extracting policies, i.e., action sequences, directly). These evaluations can then be compared to derive choice policies in the usual way.

The previous section identified two difficulties with existing algorithms in real-world circumstances. First, the space of situations (states) is vast, and which features or dimensions of it are relevant to value prediction are not typically known in advance. Second, many RL systems harness the recursive structure of the Bellman equation, but the Markov assumptions that underpin this recursive structure are invalid in many real-world environments (e.g., when there are long-term dependencies). Memory for individual episodes can help ameliorate these problems by allowing the later construction of a nonparametric approximation of the value function that need not precommit at the time of encoding to averaging with respect to particular relevant sensory dimensions or to reliance on the Bellman equation for a particular choice of state.

To understand what this means, recall that the value of a state represents the cumulative future reward over a (possibly infinitely long) trajectory. Model-free algorithms store and update a running average of this value, whereas model-based algorithms compute the value on the fly using estimates of the reward and transition functions. These approaches are parametric in the sense that they estimate a set of parameters that specify the value function (cached values in the case of model-free control, model parameters in the case of model-based control). Once these parameters have been estimated, the raw data can be discarded.

Episodic RL keeps the raw data in memory and approximates state values by retrieving samples from memory. Intuitively, this works because the value of a state can be approximated simply by summing rewards collected along a remembered trajectory initiated in that state or averaging such sums across several such trajectories. Because these trajectories are individual and temporally extended, they capture arbitrary long-range, non-Markovian dependencies among events. More-over, as discussed below, this procedure allows for flexible and adaptive generalization in terms of what counts as a similar state for the purpose of forecasting value in novel circumstances.

Episodic RL is nonparametric in the sense that it does not rely on a fixed, parameterized form of the value function. The effective complexity of the approximation (i.e., the number of episodes) grows as more data are observed. This approach is similar to that of a well-developed literature in statistics and machine learning on nonparametric estimation (for a textbook treatment, see Wasserman 2006) and a more specialized set of applications of these techniques to value estimation in the RL setting (e.g., Engel et al. 2005, Ormoneit & Sen 2002).

Formalization of Episodic Reinforcement Learning

The simplest implementation of episodic RL (**Figure 1**) is to store individual trajectories in memory and, when a familiar state is encountered, retrieve the set of trajectories that have followed each candidate action in that state, averaging the rewards subsequently obtained to estimate the value of each action. Formally,

$$Q_\pi(s_1, a) = E_\pi\left[\sum_{n=1}^{N} \gamma^{n-1} r_n \mid s_1, a\right] \approx \frac{1}{M}\sum_{m=1}^{M} R_m,$$

where M is the number of retrieved trajectories, R_m is the cumulative discounted return for each trajectory, and π is the prevailing policy. This approach works reasonably well when the state space is small and sequences are not deep. However, there are several problems with this implementation when applied to more general environments (e.g., with large state spaces and long planning horizons). First, because it seems likely that only relatively short trajectories can be stored in memory (much work in memory concerns the segmentation of events between episodes; e.g., Ezzyat & Davachi 2011), episodic RL may tend to be myopic, neglecting long-term future events due to truncation of the trace. Computationally, estimates of long-run reward based on sample trajectories also have large variance as the horizon grows longer because increasing numbers of random events intervene along the way (Kearns & Singh 2000). Second, in complex or continuous state spaces, states may be rarely, if ever, revisited; thus, the controller needs a mechanism for generalization to new states.

The first problem can be addressed by combining episodic RL with the Bellman equation. Consider an agent who retrieves a set of trajectories M starting with action a in state s_1 and ending N time steps later in some state s_{mN}, which may differ for each episode m. The value of this state can be expressed as follows:

$$Q_\pi(s_1, a) = \frac{1}{M}\sum_{m=1}^{M}\left[R_m + \gamma^N \sum_s P(s_{N+1} = s \mid s_{mN}, \pi(s_{mN})) Q_\pi(s_{N+1}, \pi(s_{N+1}))\right].$$

The first term in this equation represents the expected return from an episode of length N and the second term represents the expected return after that trace has terminated. The second term could be computed using model-based or model-free value estimates or by chaining together a sequence of episodes. Combining these terms allows episodic RL to correctly take into account the long-term consequences of a finite trajectory. Notably, the individual sequences capture arbitrary long-run dependencies among events (up to their length), and a Markovian assumption is invoked only to knit them together. It is also possible to knit together shorter sequences or, in the limit, individual state transitions themselves, each drawn from a set of sample episodes (Ormoneit & Sen 2002), to the extent the Markovian assumption can be relied upon. Unlike traditional

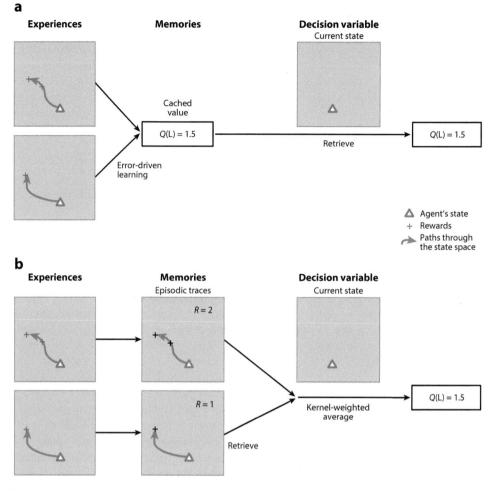

a

Experiences   Memories   **Decision variable**
Current state

Cached
value

$Q(\text{L}) = 1.5$

Error-driven
learning

Retrieve

$Q(\text{L}) = 1.5$

△ Agent's state
+ Rewards
⟶ Paths through
the state space

b

Experiences   **Memories**   **Decision variable**
Episodic traces   Current state

$R = 2$

$R = 1$

Kernel-weighted
average

$Q(\text{L}) = 1.5$

Retrieve

Figure 1

Schematic representation of different approaches to value computation. (*a*) In model-free reinforcement learning, individual experiences are integrated into a cached value, which is then used to compute action values in a new state. Only cached values are stored in memory; individual experiences are discarded. (*b*) In episodic reinforcement learning, individual experiences, along with their associated returns, are retained in memory and retrieved at choice time. Each episodic trace is weighted by its similarity to the current state according to a kernel function. This kernel-weighted average implements a nonparametric value estimate. $Q(\text{L})$ is the value of taking the left action.

model-free approaches (Sutton 1988), the decision of how heavily to rely on the Markovian assumption need not be made when experience is first acquired but instead can be made later, at choice time, when it is used to compute decision variables. Thus, this decision can be informed by additional experience in the interim.

The process of chaining episodes bears a striking resemblance to the use of options in hierarchical RL (Botvinick et al. 2009). Options are policies that have specific initiation and termination conditions; when one option terminates, another option is invoked. Just as options allow an agent to build reusable subroutines out of primitive actions, episodes allow an agent to reuse past experience. In fact, episodic retrieval may be one way in which options are created.

The second problem—generalization—can be addressed by allowing values to be smooth interpolations of episodes. Specifically, the expected return of a trajectory can be estimated by

$$E_\pi \left[\sum_{n=1}^N \gamma^{n-1} r_n \mid s_1, a \right] \approx \frac{\sum_{m=1}^M R_m K(s_1, s_{m1})}{\sum_{m=1}^M K(s_1, s_{m1})},$$

where M is the number of retrieved memory traces, s_{m1} is the initial state of the trajectory stored in memory trace m, and R_m is the return for the trajectory. The kernel function $K(s_1, s_{m1})$ measures the similarity between the current and retrieved states. The kernel function can also be defined over state-action or state-action-reward tuples. Such generalization is important for the purposes of choice because it allows an agent to estimate the value of taking a particular action in novel circumstances or in continuous state spaces. Again, an important feature of this model is that the kernel function K need not be fixed at the time of initial learning but can be shaped by subsequent experience before the episodes are used to guide choice. This contrasts with traditional generalization based on parametric function approximation schemes, such as neural networks, which amount to averaging values over some area of the state space at encoding time (e.g., Sutton & Barto 1998).

The appropriate kernel depends on the structure of the state space. For example, in a smooth, real-valued state space, a commonly used kernel is the Gaussian:

$$K(s, s') = \exp \left(-\frac{\|s - s'\|^2}{2\sigma^2} \right),$$

where the bandwidth parameter σ^2 governs the smoothness of the value function approximation; a smaller bandwidth induces sharper generalization gradients and, in the limit, produces no generalization (i.e., a pure episodic memory). The optimal bandwidth decreases with the number and increases with dispersion of episodes (Wasserman 2006). Intuitively, the bandwidth provides a form of regularization, preventing the kernel estimate from overgeneralizing. Kernels can also be defined over discrete state spaces, as well as structured objects like graphs, grammars, and trees (Gärtner et al. 2004), and an analogous parameterization of bandwidth can sometimes be specified.

Kernel-based approaches to RL fit well with similar approaches applied to other areas of cognition (Jäkel et al. 2009). Exemplar models of memory, categorization, object recognition, and function learning can be interpreted as forms of kernel density estimation. Of particular relevance is Gilboa & Schmeidler's (2001) case-based decision theory, which (as we discuss in the section Case-Based Decision Theory and Decision by Sampling) applies kernel density estimation to decision problems. Research on machine learning has demonstrated the efficacy of kernel-based approaches (Ormoneit & Sen 2002), although relatively little work has compared the computational and statistical trade-offs of these approaches with those of conventional model-based and model-free RL.

Reinforcement Learning and Memory for Individual Episodes

The framework outlined in the previous section and the predecessor proposal by Lengyel & Dayan (2007) suggest that RL behavior should, under some circumstances, be driven by memory for individual episodes distinct from the aggregate statistics of these episodes that would be employed by a model-based or model-free learner. The empirical literature directly supporting these predictions is, at present, fairly sparse, mostly because the sorts of behavioral tasks most commonly used in studies of RL do not easily lend themselves to addressing these issues. Two limitations of these tasks contribute to these deficiencies.

First, unlike studies of categorization—in which subjects render judgments about many unique stimuli and exemplar-based models reminiscent of our framework have long been successful (Nosofsky 1986)—most laboratory studies of RL consist of many repetitions of essentially identical trials. Thus, there has been little, experimentally or psychologically, to differentiate episodes and few objectively predictable features other than temporal recency to govern which episodes subjects might retrieve. Second, although some of the most interesting features of nonparametric episodic evaluation (like RL evaluation in general) occur during the evaluation of sequential decision tasks, existing work relevant to these ideas has mostly taken place in repeated choice-reward bandit tasks without sequential structure. However, some supporting evidence does exist.

Recently, Collins & Frank (2012) proposed a model, as well as an associated experimental task to test it, that argued that many trial-by-trial choices in RL tasks in humans were driven by a small set of memories of previous events held in working memory rather than incremental running averages of the sort associated with model-free (and model-based) RL. This idea bears some resemblance to the current episodic RL proposal (although focusing on a different memory system as the store). In support of this theory, the researchers found that increasing the number of stimuli (the set size) or time delays between state visits in a bandit-like task slowed learning, a finding inconsistent with standard RL models but well explained by a model that uses a limited memory buffer over stimulus history to determine action values. Individuals with a genetic polymorphism associated with higher levels of prefrontal dopamine exhibited greater retention of previous stimulus history in the action values. Further work using this task has shown that schizophrenic patients have a selective impairment in the working memory component of RL (Collins et al. 2014) consistent with the observation of reduced prefrontal dopamine levels in schizophrenia.

This mechanism does not fully coincide with episodic evaluation as we have described it. First, the task is deterministic and the state space discrete, so aspects of generalization and averaging over noisy outcomes are not exercised. Second, we [and other theorists, such as Zilli & Hasselmo (2008)] have assumed that, for an episode-based RL system to be useful over longer delays (including retaining learning from, for example, one day to the next) and larger state spaces, it likely must involve the episodic memory system of the hippocampus rather than short-term working memory.

Other work on bandit tasks, in this case with stochastic outcomes, has been carried out by Erev and colleagues (e.g., Erev et al. 2008). These investigators have argued that many aggregate features of subjects' choice preferences are best explained by a model that maintains individual trial outcomes rather than running averages. According to the model, which can be thought of as an instance of episodic RL, subjects evaluate bandits on the basis of a small sample (e.g., one or two) of particular rewards previously received from them, although not always (as would be predicted by running averages) the most recent ones. The statistics of decision variables implied by such sampling explain a variety of features of preferences in these tasks, such as sensitivity to risk and loss.

One issue standing in the way of examining this sort of model is the basic similarity of all trials in a bandit task to one another. Other research has integrated incidental trial-unique images with bandit tasks to begin to gain leverage over individual episodes. For example, Bornstein et al. (2015) found that using these images to remind subjects of previous trials influenced their subsequent action immediately after the reminder: If a past action resulted in a reward, then a reminder of that trial induced subjects to repeat it, whereas if the action resulted in a loss, then a reminder induced subjects to avoid it. This manipulation might be understood as influencing memory retrieval in episodic RL.

Wimmer et al. (2014) investigated a similar manipulation using fMRI. In this study, episodic memory for the trial-unique objects (tested after the experiment) covaried negatively with the influence of reward history on decisions at encoding time such that better (subsequently measured) episodic memory was associated with weaker feedback-driven learning. This negative effect of successful episodic encoding was also associated with an attenuated striatal prediction error signal and increased connectivity between the hippocampus and the striatum. One possible interpretation of this result in terms of episodic RL is that, because the trial-unique objects were entirely incidental to the task, episodic evaluation mechanisms (to the extent that they were engaged) effectively injected uncontrolled noise into the evaluation process, obscuring both reward-driven choice behavior and associated striatal signals.

Overcoming State Aliasing

One advantage of episodic RL is its robustness: State values can be validly estimated by remembered trajectories even when the Markov properties do not hold within the trajectory. That is, a set of returns following some current state s_1 validly estimate its long-term value even if there are arbitrary long-range dependencies across the events within the sample trajectories. However, this property only partly solves the problems of state representation. In particular, if the starting state s_1 does not itself satisfy the Markov property (that is, if outcomes following s_1 depend on events that happened prior to s_1 but aren't reflected in it), then the set of returns matching s_1 will not reflect this additional information. This will introduce additional noise in even episodic value estimates.

Violations of this assumption can occur when states are aliased: If multiple states are indistinguishable on the basis of the current observation, then the value is not conditionally independent of the agent's history given the current observation. Work on this problem again looks to memory (in this case, short-term working memory) to disambiguate the state by augmenting it with appropriate recent stimulus history. For example, if you received instructions to turn left after the second traffic light, the value of a left turn is not specified simply by whether you are at a traffic light but by the trajectory preceding it. This dependence is eliminated, though, if you can remember how many traffic lights you passed. In other words, the number of traffic lights is a sufficient statistic for your history, and storing it in memory allows you to incorporate it into the state representation and validly apply standard RL algorithms. The main problem here is how much and what sort of history to store.

This insight is the basis of several computational models of the ways in which working memory aids RL. Dopamine functions as a gating signal in the prefrontal cortex, allowing phasic bursts of dopamine to transiently increase the gain of prefrontal neurons, making them more responsive to afferent input (Cohen et al. 2002). Importantly, Braver & Cohen (2000) demonstrated that TD learning could be used to adaptively gate relevant information into working memory, excluding irrelevant distractors. In essence, this work treated the evaluation (via RL) and selection of cognitive actions (inserting and removing items from working memory) in the same way as the selection of motor actions, providing an integrative explanation of dopamine's role in both cognitive and motor control. O'Reilly & Frank (2006) extended this idea by showing how adaptive gating could be realized in a biologically detailed model of prefrontal–basal ganglia interactions. Further insight was provided by Todd et al. (2008), who articulated how adaptive gating could be understood as a normative computational solution to partial observability.

The challenge that all of these models seek to address is discovering which particular past events need to be retained in working memory and for how long. It is noteworthy that Todd et al.'s (2008) model discovers these long-run relationships by leveraging a form of TD value estimation known as TD(λ), in which all previously visited states are eligible for updating on every time step; this variant of the algorithm is statistically related to the evaluation of state values by episodic sample trajectories (Sutton & Barto 1998). This suggests that episodic memory might also be useful for the same purpose. From the perspective of an episodic RL model, learning of this sort, in effect, allows the organism to figure out under what circumstances to apply the Markov property. This understanding can then be applied, going forward, to computing values using the experience stored in episodic traces. In keeping with a recurring theme of this review, one advantage of this understanding, relative to state learning models such as Todd et al.'s (2008), is that action values need not be relearned from new experience, only recomputed as the understanding of the state space evolves.

Approximating Value Functions Over Complex State Spaces

As discussed above, raw memory traces are of limited use when making decisions in novel situations because they generalize poorly. To use a previous example, exactly counting the number of traffic lights will fail if one is forced to take a detour; in this case, it is necessary to use a value function approximation that degrades gracefully with deviations from the stored memory traces. This limitation has motivated the use of kernel methods that allow some degree of generalization.

In studies of RL, this problem is typically addressed as a question of value function approximation: How does an agent approximate the function $Q(s, a)$ over (potentially continuous and high-dimensional) states? Much work in computational neuroscience has been devoted to trying to understand how these issues play out in the brain. Proposed architectures typically implement linear or nonlinear parametric approximations, e.g., taking $Q(s, a)$ to be approximated by a weighted sum of a set of basis functions defined over the state space. However, it is unclear whether such parametric approximations can scale up to real-world problems, in which the appropriate feature space is elusive. One approach pursued in machine learning has been to develop complex architectures, such as deep neural networks, which can learn to discover good parametric representations from a large amount of training data (Mnih et al. 2015). However, this approach does not seem to provide a complete account of human performance, which can in certain cases be effective after observing a very small amount of data (e.g., Griffiths et al. 2010, Lee et al. 2014). This ability is partly attributable to strong inductive biases that guide learning (Griffiths et al. 2010). Another factor may be the brain's use of kernel methods that generalize from sparse training examples to new testing situations in a way that captures the underlying structure of the state space.

Intuitively, a good kernel assigns high similarity to states that have similar values, allowing the value function approximation to average across the rewards in these states while abstaining from averaging over states with different values. In the literature on biological reinforcement learning, these issues of generalization have mainly been discussed in terms of selecting an appropriate set of basis functions for parametric (linear) value function approximation (e.g., Foster et al. 2000, Ludvig et al. 2008), but exactly the same considerations apply to the choice of kernel for nonparametric generalization. A particular advantage of the latter is that the kernel is used at choice time rather than at encoding time, so it can be learned or adapted by subsequent experience, as in many of the schemes discussed below.

In spatial domains, appropriate generalization can be given a concrete, geometric interpretation. For example, a Gaussian kernel defined over Euclidean spatial coordinates would incorrectly predict that standing outside a bank vault is highly valuable. This mistake is the result of failing to encode the fact that getting inside the vault has low probability. Geometric boundaries induce discontinuities in an otherwise smooth value function, and such discontinuities can be encoded by representing similarity in terms of geodesic distance (the shortest path along the connectivity graph of the space). This principle extends beyond physical space to arbitrary feature spaces (Mahadevan 2007, Tenenbaum et al. 2000).

Gustafson & Daw (2011) suggested that place cells in the hippocampus (conceived by them as basis functions rather than approximation kernels) encode a geodesic spatial metric, as evidenced by

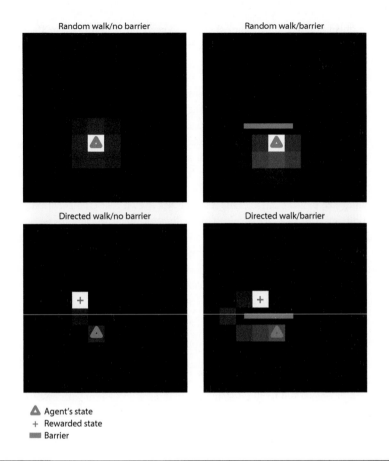

Random walk/no barrier

Random walk/barrier

Directed walk/no barrier

Directed walk/barrier

▲ Agent's state
+ Rewarded state
▬ Barrier

Figure 2

Comparison of the successor representation in different environments. Each image shows the successor representation for the state indicated by the green triangle. The rewarded state is indicated by a red cross. The left column shows an open field. The right column shows a field with a barrier, indicated by the blue line. The top row shows the successor representation for an undirected or random walk induced by a policy that moves through the state space randomly. The bottom row shows the results for a directed policy that moves deterministically along the shortest path to the reward.

systematic spatial distortions in geometrically irregular environments. This idea was extended by Stachenfeld et al. (2014), who argued that a geodesic spatial metric in the hippocampus might arise from a more general predictive representation known as the successor representation (SR) (Dayan 1993). In particular, each state (e.g., spatial location) can be represented in terms of the expected future occupancy of successor states (see **Figure 2** for an illustration). Distance measured in terms of the SR captures the key properties of geodesic distance because passing through boundaries is very unlikely and thus the expected future occupancy is low. The SR goes beyond geodesic distance by also incorporating spatial distortions induced by changes in behavioral policy. An important computational virtue of the SR is that it renders value computation trivial: The value of a state is simply the sum of expected future occupancies for each successor state weighted by the expected reward in that state.

Instead of a basis function for encoding a parametric value approximation, one can think of the SR (or the geodesic distance function) as a particular choice of kernel that encodes the underlying structure of the state space. The Bellman equation implies that states and their successors will tend to have similar values, and thus the SR is a good kernel precisely because it is predictive. The SR can be learned directly from state transitions using TD methods (Dayan 1993, Stachenfeld et al. 2014) and therefore provides a plausible mechanism for adapting the kernel function, with learning, to arbitrary state spaces.

Another aspect of kernel design pertains to multidimensional state spaces: In many real-world tasks, only some of the dimensions are relevant for task performance, necessitating some form of selective attention applied to the feature space. In the kernel view, selective attention would manifest as a distortion of the similarity structure between states depending on the task at hand. This idea has been embodied in several influential exemplar models of categorization, which posit that error-driven learning shapes the mapping from feature inputs to similarity (Kruschke 1992, Love et al. 2004). Related ideas have begun to be explored in RL tasks (Gershman et al. 2010, Niv et al. 2015, Vaidya & Fellows 2015). This research has shown that classical attention areas in the parietal and prefrontal cortices are involved in credit assignment to stimulus features on the basis of reward history. Although researchers have offered an account of this phenomenon in terms of model-free RL, it is possible that the same dimensional attention filter impinges on the kernel used by episodic RL. Again, this would be advantageous because applying the attentional filter at choice time rather than at encoding time reduces the need for relearning values once appropriate dimensional attention is discovered.

Learning with Sparse Data

Another advantage of various sorts of episodic estimation is that they can succeed (relatively speaking) in the extreme low-data limit when model-based and model-free learning fail, as demonstrated in simulations by Lengyel & Dayan (2007). This analysis is consistent with evidence for a shift in behavioral control from the hippocampus to the striatum over the course of training in a variety of tasks (Packard & McGaugh 1996, Poldrack et al. 2001), although these tasks do not specifically isolate an episodic RL strategy.

Some evidence suggests that the hippocampus plays a special role in one-shot learning in decision tasks. Lee et al. (2014) found that humans could learn a novel stimulus-reward outcome after a single observation, and this rapid learning selectively recruited the hippocampus. Rapid learning was also associated with increased coupling between the hippocampus and ventrolateral prefrontal cortex, which was interpreted as evidence supporting an earlier hypothesis that the ventrolateral prefrontal cortex acts as a metacontroller arbitrating between different RL systems (Lee et al. 2014).

The statistically minded reader may object that nonparametric approximations such as kernel density estimation are typically less data-efficient than parametric methods, which is paradoxical in light of our claim that such approximations may be utilized in the low-data limit. It is true that strong parametric assumptions (such as the Markovian assumption) can offer an inductive bias to guide and discipline inference, but this bias is only useful to the extent that the assumptions are correct. Given the twin problems of high dimensionality and state aliasing in the natural environment, it may well be that standard parametric assumptions can only be relied upon if they are validated and tuned by an initial learning phase that identifies relevant dimensions and stimulus history. Furthermore, although the convergence rate of nonparametric approximations is typically slower, such approximations achieve an asymptotically lower error because of their superior flexibility (Wasserman 2006). This is an example of a bias–variance trade-off (Geman et al. 1992): Nonparametric methods more closely approximate the value function (lower bias) at the expense of poorer generalization (higher variance). The purpose of kernel smoothing is precisely to reduce variance by introducing bias (i.e., regularization). If the value function is itself smooth and this smoothness is well matched to the kernel function, the added bias will be small; as discussed in the previous section, kernel smoothing should be strongest across states with similar expected values, a point that can be made precise using the theory of reproducing kernel Hilbert spaces (Schölkopf & Smola 2002). From this discussion, we can posit that episodic RL should perform relatively well in the low-data limit when the value function cannot be well approximated by a parametric family but the values are nonetheless smooth over the state space in a way that is captured by the kernel.

INTERACTIONS BETWEEN LEARNING SYSTEMS

A central theme in contemporary research on RL is the interplay between multiple learning and control systems (Daw et al. 2005, Dolan & Dayan 2013). Much of this research has focused on the principles guiding competitive interactions between model-free and model-based systems— for instance, under what circumstances is it worth engaging in model-based deliberation versus simply acting according to previously learned model-free preferences (Daw et al. 2005, Keramati et al. 2011)—but the full story is more complex and unsettled, particularly in light of the suggested involvement of episodic memory. First, the possibility of additional influences extends the arbitration questions: When should the brain consult episodes versus plan using a previously learned map or model, and which episodes should be consulted? Second, the influences may interact in ways other than simple competition. For instance, as discussed below in this section, in addition to being used to compute values at decision time, episodes may also be useful for offline training of model-free values, e.g., during sleep. Third, and relatedly, all of these considerations may complicate or confound the working of the model-free and model-based systems as they have previously been conceived. In particular, the cognitive and computational bases for putatively model-based choice are as yet underdetermined, and at least some of what has been taken as model-based behavior may arise from some of these episodic influences.

As we have made clear, episodic RL may well constitute yet another system alongside (or as part of) the model-based and model-free systems. Indeed, in other research, influences of individual episodes on choice may have been mistaken for either model-free or model-based learning, which are typically assumed to instead depend on statistical summaries learned over many episodes. For instance, in one-step bandit choice tasks, memory for individual recent episodes can support trial-by-trial choice adjustment that appears similar to model-free incremental learning of action values (Bornstein et al. 2015, Collins & Frank 2012, Erev et al. 2008).

Episodic influences may also have masqueraded as model-based in a number of ways. For example, in multistep sequential tasks, episodic snapshots of individual trajectories also contain information about the sequential state-state map of the task and may support behavior that has the signatures of map- or model-based choice (Daw et al. 2011, Tolman 1948) without actual use of a statistical world model (e.g., Gershman et al. 2014). Indeed, the idea that planning by mental simulation is supported by episodic rather than (or in addition to) semantic representations is a prominent proposal in the cognitive neuroscience of hippocampal function (Hassabis & Maguire 2009, Schacter et al. 2012).

As we have already described, episodic and model-free RL also appear to compete with each other, much like model-based and model-free RL are thought to. Such competition might be understood as a third system or an episodic aspect to the model-based system. Successful episodic memory on individual trials is negatively correlated with sensitivity to reward history and neural prediction error signals (Wimmer et al. 2014; for contrasting results, see Murty et al. 2016). Interfering effects of episodic memory on reward-guided choice can also be directly induced by adding incidental reminders of past actions (Bornstein et al. 2015). More generally, hippocampal involvement in behavioral control tends to predominate early in training, whereas striatal involvement predominates later in training (Packard & McGaugh 1996, Poldrack et al. 2001).

These competitive interactions fit with the picture of largely independent systems vying for behavioral control, with a metacontroller arbitrating between the three (or two) systems according to their relative efficacy at different points during training. In particular, episodic RL may be primarily useful early in training, when parametric value approximations break down due to the sparsity of data and complexity of the state space (Lengyel & Dayan 2007). In all these respects, episodic RL as we have envisioned it echoes features that have also been attributed to model-based RL. Although it seems unlikely that episodic RL alone can account for all of the manifestations of model-based RL, these two putative systems have not been clearly teased apart in the same way that they (collectively) have been dissociated from model-free learning. Doing so will require more precise identification of influences on behavior and brain activity that are verifiably tied to the retrieval of individual episodes versus statistical summaries of them as in a map or world model. If individual episodes are found to directly contribute to evaluation, then this will necessitate fleshing out the emerging theoretical and experimental account of competition between model-based and model-free influences—broadly speaking, thought to reflect a rational speed–accuracy trade-off induced by spending time recomputing better action values (Keramati et al. 2011)—to also weigh the relative costs and benefits of consulting raw episodes for these recomputations versus a summary model.

The influences of episodic memory may also crosscut the model-based and model-free distinction, complicating the picture still further. For instance, the striatum and hippocampus may interact cooperatively as well as competitively (for a review, see Pennartz et al. 2011). Evidence suggests that replay of memories (Lansink et al. 2009) and oscillatory dynamics (van der Meer & Redish 2011) in the two regions are coordinated. Human neuroimaging studies have demonstrated functional connectivity between the hippocampus and striatum during virtual navigation (Brown et al. 2012) and context-dependent decision making (Ross et al. 2011).

One functional explanation for some of these interactions is that they support synergistic influences of episodic memory on model-free values. Such interactions would further leverage episodic memory for choice (beyond the nonparametric value computation) and also produce choices that might, again, appear to mimic some of the behaviors of a model-based system. Model-free RL is, in its traditional conception, limited to learning from direct experience, which renders it inflexible. For example, separately experiencing different parts of an environment will result in a disjointed model-free value function, in which the consistency of values implied by the Bellman equation is violated at the part boundaries. One of the traditional signatures of a model-based system is the ability to stitch these parts together by using them to build a world model that can then be used to simulate sequences of state transitions and rewards that were never experienced together (Shohamy & Daw 2015). However, another way to achieve the same effect is to feed such ersatz experience to a model-free learner, which can then use it in the same way as it would use actual experience to update its stored values. This can be achieved without even building a world model by simply replaying snippets of experience from episodic memory, interleaved across the otherwise separate experiences. Such a replay mechanism is another way (in addition to nonparametric evaluation) in which episodic memories might influence choice, in this case by driving model-free value learning. This hybrid architecture was originally proposed in the machine learning literature by Sutton (1991), who referred to it as Dyna.

Gershman and colleagues (2014) reported behavioral evidence that valuation in humans is supported by Dyna-like offline replay. In these experiments, participants separately learned different parts of a single MDP and were then given a retrospective revaluation test to see if their decisions reflected an integrated value. The experiment indeed found evidence for revaluation, which has typically been taken as a signature of model-based value computation. However, the experiments showed that the extent of successful revaluation was sensitive to several manipulations designed to affect Dyna-style offline replay but irrelevant to model-based choice (in the sense of just-in-time computation of decision variables by mental simulation at choice time). In particular, revaluation was disrupted by placing people under cognitive load during the learning, rather than during the subsequent choice phase, using a secondary task. The deleterious effects of load could be mitigated simply by giving people a brief period of quiescence (listening to classical music) before the revaluation test, consistent with the operation of an offline simulation process.

Neuroimaging studies (Kurth-Nelson et al. 2015, Wimmer & Shohamy 2012) also demonstrate that successful revaluation in a similar integration task is supported by memories retrieved at learning (rather than choice) time. More generally (though without being linked to decisions or learning), replay of the neural responses to previous experiences has repeatedly been observed in neuronal recordings from the hippocampus during quiet rest, sleep, and even ongoing behavior (Carr et al. 2011, Skaggs & McNaughton 1996). These phenomena suggest that the hippocampus may be a candidate for the neural substrate of replay-based learning. However, in all these cases, including the human experiments, it is not yet wholly clear whether the memories being retrieved are episodic (e.g., in the sense of autobiographical snapshots of individualized events) or reflect more semantic knowledge derived from the statistics of multiple episodes (e.g., a statistical world model).

RELATIONSHIP TO OTHER FRAMEWORKS

Case-Based Decision Theory and Decision by Sampling

Research on behavioral economics has explored the role of memory in decision making, focusing on one-shot decision problems rather than the sequential problems on which we have focused. The starting point of this work is a critique of expected utility theory, the cornerstone of neoclassical economics, which assumes that a decision maker will consider all possible states of the world and all possible outcomes so as to average over these in computing expected value. As pointed out by Gilboa & Schmeidler (2001), many real-world situations fit the expected utility framework poorly: The sets of states and outcomes are not readily available to the decision maker. For example, the choice of a nanny would require the enumeration of all possible nanny profiles and all possible consequences of hiring a particular nanny. These sets are, for all practical purposes, infinite. To address this problem, Gilboa & Schmeidler (2001) developed a case-based decision theory (CBDT), drawing upon a venerable tradition in cognitive science (Riesbeck & Schank 1989).

A basic primitive of this theory is the case, consisting of a decision problem, an act, and an outcome. Previously observed cases constitute memories. The decision maker is endowed with a similarity function on decision problems and a utility function on outcomes and is assumed to rank acts for a new decision problem by comparing it to previous cases using the similarity function. This formulation does not require the exhaustive enumeration of states and outcomes, only the retrieval of a subset from memory. Interestingly, the ranking mechanism is a form of kernel-based value estimation, with the similarity function corresponding to a kernel and the cases corresponding to episodes.

The similarity function posited by CBDT effectively determines what memories are available. For simplicity, we can imagine that the similarity is zero for some memories, so that these memories are not retrieved into the available subset, and a constant value for all the retrieved memories. In the most basic form of CBDT, the utility assigned to an act is then proportional to the summed utilities of outcomes stored in the subset of retrieved memories for which the act was chosen. This model has interesting implications for the role played by memory in determining reference points because acts will only be judged with respect to available memories (Simonson & Tversky 1992). For example, Simonsohn & Loewenstein (2006) reported that a household moving to a new city will exhibit dramatically different spending on rent depending on the distribution of rents in their city of origin. In related theoretical work, P. Bordalo, N. Gennaioli, and A. Shleifer (unpublished manuscript) formulated a memory-based model of decision making that allows retrieved memories to influence the decision maker's reference points.

Stewart et al. (2006) took this logic a step further in their decision by sampling theory by arguing that all decision-theoretic quantities (utility, probability, temporal duration, etc.) are based on samples from memory. They demonstrated that the descriptive parameterization of these quantities in prospect theory (Kahneman & Tversky 1979) can be empirically derived from their ecological distribution (a proxy for their availability in memory). For example, Stewart et al. (2006) found that the distribution of credits to bank accounts (a measure of the ecological distribution of gains) is approximately power-law distributed, implying a power-law-revealed utility function under the assumption that the utility function reflects the relative rank of gains. This analysis reproduces the curvature of the utility function proposed by Kahneman & Tversky (1979) on purely descriptive grounds to explain risk aversion; analogous considerations about the relative distribution of debits explain loss aversion.

The idea that subjective utility is computed relative to a memory-based sample has profound implications for models of decision making. It suggests that there is no stable valuation mechanism that consistently obeys the axioms of rational choice. This idea is grounded in a set of psychological principles that extend far beyond economic decisions. Essentially all judgments, ranging from the psychophysics of magnitude, duration, and pain to causal reasoning and person perception, are relative: The same object can be perceived as dramatically different depending on contextual factors that determine a comparison set (Kahneman & Miller 1986, Stewart et al. 2005). This point has not been lost on marketing researchers, who have long recognized the importance of comparison (or consideration) set composition in consumer choice (Bettman 1979, Lynch & Srull 1982, Nedungadi 1990).

Contingent Sampling Models and Instance-Based Learning

Although most economic models have been developed to explain decisions from description (e.g., explicitly described lotteries), RL paradigms typically involve decisions from experience (in which the lottery structure must be learned). Behavioral economists have also studied experiential learning in bandit-like problems in a literature that is largely separate from the study of RL. The most important finding stressed here is that experiential learning often produces striking divergences from description-based decisions (Hertwig & Erev 2009). For example, the classic description-based experiments of Kahneman & Tversky (1979) demonstrated apparent overweighting of rare events, but experience-based experiments have found the opposite phenomenon: underweighting of rare events (e.g., Barron & Erev 2003, Hau et al. 2008). Biele and colleagues (2009) have argued that this underweighting is the result of contingent sampling from memory, in which samples are drawn based on similarity to the current situation. Because rare events are less likely to appear in the sampled set, these events will be relatively neglected. This model can also explain a number of other puzzling behaviors, such as overconfidence (due to a biased estimate of variance from small samples) and inertia (tendency to repeat previous choices; Biele et al. 2009). Gonzalez and colleagues (Gonzalez & Dutt 2011, Gonzalez et al. 2003) have developed closely related instance-based learning models. The important point for the present discussion is that the samples resemble episodes, and the sampling process itself effectively implements a form of kernel smoothing and thus fits into our general framework.

If decisions from experience depend on some form of contingent sampling, then we should expect that memory biases will influence decisions. Ludvig, Madan, and their colleagues (Ludvig et al. 2015, Madan et al. 2014) have shown that the bias to recall extremely positive or negative events is systematically related to risk preferences. In one set of experiments (Madan et al. 2014), individual differences in the tendency to recall extreme events was positively correlated with preference for risky gains and negatively correlated with preference for risky losses. Another experiment (Ludvig et al. 2015) manipulated memory using a priming cue and showed that priming past wins promotes risk seeking. On the theoretical side, Lieder et al. (2014) have shown how a sampling strategy that overweights extreme events is rational when the goal is to minimize the variance of the expected utility estimate from a limited number of samples.

CONCLUSIONS

We have reviewed the current cognitive neuroscience conception of RL, in which model-based and model-free systems compete (and sometimes cooperate) for control of behavior. This dual-system architecture is motivated computationally by the need to balance speed and flexibility, but we have argued that neither system (at least as traditionally conceived) is designed to perform well in high-dimensional, continuous, partially observable state spaces when data are sparse and observations have dependencies over long temporal distances. Unhappily, this situation may be characteristic of many real-world learning problems. A third system—episodic RL—may offer a partial solution to these problems by implementing a form of nonparametric value function approximation. As we have shown, this notion can tie together many disparate observations about the role of episodic memory in RL. Nonetheless, our theory is still largely speculative. We have framed it abstractly to highlight the generality of the ideas, but to make progress the theory must first be more precisely formalized so that it can make quantitative predictions. We expect this to be an exciting frontier for research, both theoretical and experimental, in the near future.

DISCLOSURE STATEMENT

The authors are not aware of any affiliations, memberships, funding, or financial holdings that might be perceived as affecting the objectivity of this review.

ACKNOWLEDGMENTS

The authors are grateful to Daphna Shohamy for longstanding collaborative research underlying many of the ideas in this review and helpful comments on the manuscript. The authors also thank Rahul Bhui for comments on an earlier draft of the manuscript. The authors' research contributing to this review is funded by the National Institute on Drug Abuse, grant number R01DA038891 (N.D.D.); Google DeepMind (N.D.D.); and the Center for Brains, Minds and Machines (CBMM) via National Science Foundation Science and Technology Centers award CCF-1231216 (S.J.G.).

LITERATURE CITED

Adams CD. 1982. Variations in the sensitivity of instrumental responding to reinforcer devaluation. *Q. J. Exp. Psychol.* 34:77–98

Alexander GE, Crutcher MD. 1990. Functional architecture of basal ganglia circuits: neural substrates of parallel processing. *Trends Neurosci.* 13:266–71

Barron G, Erev I. 2003. Small feedback-based decisions and their limited correspondence to description-based decisions. *J. Behav. Decis. Making* 16:215–33

Bayer HM, Glimcher PW. 2005. Midbrain dopamine neurons encode a quantitative reward prediction error signal. *Neuron* 47:129–41

Bellman R. 1957. *Dynamic Programming*. Princeton, NJ: Princeton Univ. Press

Bertsekas DP, Tsitsiklis JN. 1996. *Neuro-Dynamic Programming*. Nashua, NH: Athena Sci.

Bettman JR. 1979. *Information Processing Theory of Consumer Choice*. Boston: Addison-Wesley

Biele G, Erev I, Ert E. 2009. Learning, risk attitude and hot stoves in restless bandit problems. *J. Math. Psychol.* 53(3):155–67

Bornstein AM, Khaw MW, Shohamy D, Daw ND. 2015. What's past is present: Reminders of past choices bias decisions for reward in humans. *bioRxiv* 033910. doi: 10.1101/033910

Botvinick MM, Niv Y, Barto AC. 2009. Hierarchically organized behavior and its neural foundations: a reinforcement learning perspective. *Cognition* 113:262–80

Braver TS, Cohen JD. 2000. On the control of control: the role of dopamine in regulating prefrontal function and working memory. In *Control of Cognitive Processes: Attention and Performance XVIII*, ed. S Monsell, J Driver, pp. 713–37. Cambridge, MA: MIT Press

Brogden W. 1939. Sensory pre-conditioning. *J. Exp. Psychol.* 25:323–32

Brown TI, Ross RS, Tobyne SM, Stern CE. 2012. Cooperative interactions between hippocampal and striatal systems support flexible navigation. *NeuroImage* 60:1316–30

Carr MF, Jadhav SP, Frank LM. 2011. Hippocampal replay in the awake state: a potential substrate for memory consolidation and retrieval. *Nat. Neurosci.* 14:147–53

Cohen JD, Braver TS, Brown JW. 2002. Computational perspectives on dopamine function in prefrontal cortex. *Curr. Opin. Neurobiol.* 12:223–29

Cohen JY, Haesler S, Vong L, Lowell BB, Uchida N. 2012. Neuron-type-specific signals for reward and punishment in the ventral tegmental area. *Nature* 482:85–88

Collins AG, Brown JK, Gold JM, Waltz JA, Frank MJ. 2014. Working memory contributions to reinforcement learning impairments in schizophrenia. *J. Neurosci.* 34:13747–56

Collins AG, Frank MJ. 2012. How much of reinforcement learning is working memory, not reinforcement learning? A behavioral, computational, and neurogenetic analysis. *Eur. J. Neurosci.* 35:1024–35

Cushman F, Morris A. 2015. Habitual control of goal selection in humans. *PNAS* 112:13817–22

Daw ND. 2013. Advanced reinforcement learning. See Glimcher & Fehr 2013, pp. 299–320

Daw ND, Courville AC, Touretzky DS. 2006. Representation and timing in theories of the dopamine system. *Neural Comput.* 18:1637–77

Daw ND, Dayan P. 2014. The algorithmic anatomy of model-based evaluation. *Philos. Trans. R. Soc. Lond. B Biol. Sci.* 369:20130478

Daw ND, Gershman SJ, Seymour B, Dayan P, Dolan RJ. 2011. Model-based influences on humans' choices and striatal prediction errors. *Neuron* 69:1204–15

Daw ND, Niv Y, Dayan P. 2005. Uncertainty-based competition between prefrontal and dorsolateral striatal systems for behavioral control. *Nat. Neurosci.* 8:1704–11

Daw ND, O'Doherty JP. 2013. Multiple systems for value learning. See Glimcher & Fehr 2013, pp. 393–410

Daw ND, Tobler PN. 2013. Value learning through reinforcement: the basics of dopamine and reinforcement learning. See Glimcher & Fehr 2013, pp. 283–98

Dayan P. 1993. Improving generalization for temporal difference learning: the successor representation. *Neural Comput.* 5:613–24

Dezfouli A, Balleine BW. 2013. Actions, action sequences and habits: evidence that goal-directed and habitual action control are hierarchically organized. *PLOS Comput. Biol.* 9:e1003364

Dickinson A, Balleine BW. 2002. The role of learning in the operation of motivational systems. In *Steven's Handbook of Experimental Psychology*, Volume 3: *Learning, Motivation and Emotion*, ed. CR Gallistel, pp. 497–534. New York: John Wiley & Sons. 3rd ed.

Diuk C, Tsai K, Wallis J, Botvinick M, Niv Y. 2013. Hierarchical learning induces two simultaneous, but separable, prediction errors in human basal ganglia. *J. Neurosci.* 33:5797–805

Dolan RJ, Dayan P. 2013. Goals and habits in the brain. *Neuron* 80:312–25

Doll BB, Duncan KD, Simon DA, Shohamy D, Daw ND. 2015. Model-based choices involve prospective neural activity. *Nat. Neurosci.* 18:767–72

Eichenbaum H, Cohen NJ. 2004. *From Conditioning to Conscious Recollection: Memory Systems of the Brain*. Oxford, UK: Oxford Univ. Press

Engel Y, Mannor S, Meir R. 2005. Reinforcement learning with Gaussian processes. *Proc. Int. Conf. Mach. Learn., 22nd, Bonn, Ger.*, pp. 201–8. New York: Assoc. Comput. Mach.

Erev I, Ert E, Yechiam E. 2008. Loss aversion, diminishing sensitivity, and the effect of experience on repeated decisions. *J. Behav. Decis. Making* 21:575–97

Everitt BJ, Robbins TW. 2005. Neural systems of reinforcement for drug addiction: from actions to habits to compulsion. *Nat. Neurosci.* 8:1481–89

Ezzyat Y, Davachi L. 2011. What constitutes an episode in episodic memory? *Psychol. Sci.* 22(2):243–52

Foster DJ, Morris RGM, Dayan P. 2000. A model of hippocampally dependent navigation, using the temporal difference learning rule. *Hippocampus* 10:1–16

Frank MJ, Seeberger LC, O'Reilly RC. 2004. By carrot or by stick: cognitive reinforcement learning in parkinsonism. *Science* 306:1940–43

Fu W-T, Anderson JR. 2008. Solving the credit assignment problem: explicit and implicit learning of action sequences with probabilistic outcomes. *Psychol. Res.* 72:321–30

Gabrieli JD. 1998. Cognitive neuroscience of human memory. *Annu. Rev. Psychol.* 49:87–115

Gärtner T, Lloyd JW, Flach PA. 2004. Kernels and distances for structured data. *Mach. Learn.* 57:205–32

Geman S, Bienenstock E, Doursat R. 1992. Neural networks and the bias/variance dilemma. *Neural Comput.* 4:1–58

Gershman SJ, Blei DM, Niv Y. 2010. Context, learning, and extinction. *Psychol. Rev.* 117:197–209

Gershman SJ, Markman AB, Otto AR. 2014. Retrospective revaluation in sequential decision making: a tale of two systems. *J. Exp. Psychol. Gen.* 143:182–94

Gershman SJ, Norman KA, Niv Y. 2015. Discovering latent causes in reinforcement learning. *Curr. Opin. Behav. Sci.* 5:43–50

Gilboa I, Schmeidler D. 2001. *A Theory of Case-Based Decisions*. Cambridge, UK: Cambridge Univ. Press

Gillan CM, Kosinski M, Whelan R, Phelps EA, Daw ND. 2016. Characterizing a psychiatric symptom dimension related to deficits in goal-directed control. *eLife* 5:e11305

Gläscher J, Daw N, Dayan P, O'Doherty JP. 2010. States versus rewards: dissociable neural prediction error signals underlying model-based and model-free reinforcement learning. *Neuron* 66:585–95

Glimcher PW, Fehr E. 2013. *Neuroeconomics: Decision-Making and the Brain*. Cambridge, MA: Academic

Gonzalez C, Dutt V. 2011. Instance-based learning: integrating sampling and repeated decisions from experience. *Psychol. Rev.* 118:523–51

Gonzalez C, Lerch JF, Lebiere C. 2003. Instance-based learning in dynamic decision making. *Cogn. Sci.* 27:591–635

Griffiths TL, Chater N, Kemp C, Perfors A, Tenenbaum JB. 2010. Probabilistic models of cognition: exploring representations and inductive biases. *Trends Cogn. Sci.* 14:357–64

Gustafson NJ, Daw ND. 2011. Grid cells, place cells, and geodesic generalization for spatial reinforcement learning. *PLOS Comput. Biol.* 7:e1002235

Hare TA, O'Doherty J, Camerer CF, Schultz W, Rangel A. 2008. Dissociating the role of the orbitofrontal cortex and the striatum in the computation of goal values and prediction errors. *J. Neurosci.* 28:5623–30

Hart AS, Rutledge RB, Glimcher PW, Phillips PE. 2014. Phasic dopamine release in the rat nucleus accumbens symmetrically encodes a reward prediction error term. *J. Neurosci.* 34:698–704

Hassabis D, Maguire EA. 2009. The construction system of the brain. *Philos. Trans. R. Soc. Lond. B Biol. Sci.* 364(1521):1263–71

Hau R, Pleskac TJ, Kiefer J, Hertwig R. 2008. The description-experience gap in risky choice: the role of sample size and experienced probabilities. *J. Behav. Decis. Making* 21:493–518

Hertwig R, Erev I. 2009. The description-experience gap in risky choice. *Trends Cogn. Sci.* 13:517–23

Houk JC, Adams JL, Barto AG. 1995. A model of how the basal ganglia generate and use neural signals that predict reinforcement. In *Models of Information Processing in the Basal Ganglia*, ed. JC Houk, JL Davis, DG Beiser, pp. 249–70. Cambridge, MA: MIT Press

Huys QJ, Lally N, Faulkner P, Eshel N, Seifritz E, et al. 2015. Interplay of approximate planning strategies. *PNAS* 112:3098–103

Jäkel F, Schölkopf B, Wichmann FA. 2009. Does cognitive science need kernels? *Trends Cogn. Sci.* 13:381–88

Johnson A, Redish AD. 2007. Neural ensembles in CA3 transiently encode paths forward of the animal at a decision point. *J. Neurosci.* 27:12176–89

Kaelbling LP, Littman ML, Cassandra AR. 1998. Planning and acting in partially observable stochastic domains. *Artif. Intell.* 101:99–134

Kahneman D, Miller DT. 1986. Norm theory: comparing reality to its alternatives. *Psychol. Rev.* 93:136–53

Kahneman D, Tversky A. 1979. Prospect theory: an analysis of decision under risk. *Econometrica* 47:263–91

Kearns MJ, Singh SP. 2000. "Bias-variance" error bounds for temporal difference updates. *Proc. Annu. Conf. Comput. Learn. Theory, 13th, Stanford, CA*, pp. 142–47. New York: Assoc. Comput. Mach.

Keramati M, Dezfouli A, Piray P. 2011. Speed/accuracy trade-off between the habitual and the goal-directed processes. *PLOS Comput. Biol.* 7:e1002055

Knowlton BJ, Mangels JA, Squire LR. 1996. A neostriatal habit learning system in humans. *Science* 273:1399–402

Kruschke JK. 1992. ALCOVE: an exemplar-based connectionist model of category learning. *Psychol. Rev.* 99:22–44

Kurth-Nelson Z, Barnes G, Sejdinovic D, Dolan R, Dayan P. 2015. Temporal structure in associative retrieval. *eLife* 4:e04919

Lansink CS, Goltstein PM, Lankelma JV, McNaughton BL, Pennartz CM. 2009. Hippocampus leads ventral striatum in replay of place-reward information. *PLOS Biol.* 7:e1000173

Lau B, Glimcher PW. 2005. Dynamic response-by-response models of matching behavior in rhesus monkeys. *J. Exp. Anal. Behav.* 84:555–79

Lee SW, Shimojo S, O'Doherty JP. 2014. Neural computations underlying arbitration between model-based and model-free learning. *Neuron* 81:687–99

Lengyel M, Dayan P. 2007. Hippocampal contributions to control: the third way. *Adv. Neural Inf. Process. Syst.*, 20:889–96

Lieder F, Hsu M, Griffiths TL. 2014. The high availability of extreme events serves resource-rational decision-making. *Proc. Ann. Conf. Cogn. Sci. Soc., 36th, Quebec City, Can.*, pp. 2567–72. Wheat Ridge, CO: Cogn. Sci. Soc.

Love BC, Medin DL, Gureckis TM. 2004. SUSTAIN: a network model of category learning. *Psychol. Rev.* 111:309–32

Ludvig EA, Madan CR, Spetch ML. 2015. Priming memories of past wins induces risk seeking. *J. Exp. Psychol. Gen.* 144:24–29

Ludvig EA, Sutton RS, Kehoe EJ. 2008. Stimulus representation and the timing of reward-prediction errors in models of the dopamine system. *Neural Comput.* 20:3034–54

Lynch JG Jr., Srull TK. 1982. Memory and attentional factors in consumer choice: concepts and research methods. *J. Consum. Res.* 9:18–37

Madan CR, Ludvig EA, Spetch ML. 2014. Remembering the best and worst of times: memories for extreme outcomes bias risky decisions. *Psychon. Bull. Rev.* 21:629–36

Mahadevan S, Maggioni M. 2007. Proto-value functions: a Laplacian framework for learning representation and control in Markov decision processes. *J. Mach. Learn. Res.* 8:2169–231

Mnih V, Kavukcuoglu K, Silver D, Rusu AA, Veness J, et al. 2015. Human-level control through deep reinforcement learning. *Nature* 518:529–33

Montague PR, Dayan P, Sejnowski TJ. 1996. A framework for mesencephalic dopamine systems based on predictive Hebbian learning. *J. Neurosci.* 16:1936–47

Murty VP, Feldman Hall O, Hunter LE, Phelps EA, Davachi L. 2016. Episodic memories predict adaptive value-based decision-making. *J. Exp. Psychol. Gen.* 145:548–58

Nedungadi P. 1990. Recall and consumer consideration sets: influencing choice without altering brand evaluations. *J. Consum. Res.* 17:263–76

Niv Y. 2009. Reinforcement learning in the brain. *J. Math. Psychol.* 53:139–54

Niv Y, Daniel R, Geana A, Gershman SJ, Leong YC, et al. 2015. Reinforcement learning in multidimensional environments relies on attention mechanisms. *J. Neurosci.* 35:8145–57

Nosofsky RM. 1986. Attention, similarity, and the identification-categorization relationship. *J. Exp. Psychol. Gen.* 115:39–57

O'Keefe J, Nadel L. 1978. *The Hippocampus as a Cognitive Map*. Oxford, UK: Clarendon Press

O'Reilly RC, Frank MJ. 2006. Making working memory work: a computational model of learning in the prefrontal cortex and basal ganglia. *Neural Comput.* 18:283–328

Ormoneit D, Sen Ś. 2002. Kernel-based reinforcement learning. *Mach. Learn.* 49:161–78

Otto AR, Gershman SJ, Markman AB, Daw ND. 2013a. The curse of planning: dissecting multiple reinforcement-learning systems by taxing the central executive. *Psychol. Sci.* 24:751–61

Otto AR, Raio CM, Chiang A, Phelps EA, Daw ND. 2013b. Working-memory capacity protects model-based learning from stress. *PNAS* 110:20941–46

Packard MG, McGaugh JL. 1996. Inactivation of hippocampus or caudate nucleus with lidocaine differentially affects expression of place and response learning. *Neurobiol. Learn. Mem.* 65:65–72

Parker NF, Cameron CM, Taliaferro JP, Lee J, Choi JY, et al. 2016. Reward and choice encoding in terminals of midbrain dopamine neurons depends on striatal target. *Nat. Neurosci.* 19:845–54

Pennartz CMA, Ito R, Verschure PFMJ, Battaglia FP, Robbins TW. 2011. The hippocampal-striatal axis in learning, prediction and goal-directed behavior. *Trends Neurosci.* 34:548–59

Pessiglione M, Seymour B, Flandin G, Dolan RJ, Frith CD. 2006. Dopamine-dependent prediction errors underpin reward-seeking behaviour in humans. *Nature* 442:1042–45

Pfeiffer BE, Foster DJ. 2013. Hippocampal place-cell sequences depict future paths to remembered goals. *Nature* 497:74–79

Poldrack RA, Clark J, Pare-Blagoev E, Shohamy D, Moyano JC, et al. 2001. Interactive memory systems in the human brain. *Nature* 414:546–50

Rao RP. 2010. Decision making under uncertainty: a neural model based on partially observable Markov decision processes. *Front. Comput. Neurosci.* 4:146

Redish AD. 2004. Addiction as a computational process gone awry. *Science* 306:1944–47

Riesbeck CK, Schank RC. 1989. *Inside Case-based Reasoning*. Mahwah, NJ: Lawrence Erlbaum Assoc.

Ross RS, Sherrill KR, Stern CE. 2011. The hippocampus is functionally connected to the striatum and orbitofrontal cortex during context dependent decision making. *Brain Res.* 1423:53–66

Sadacca BF, Jones JL, Schoenbaum G. 2016. Midbrain dopamine neurons compute inferred and cached value prediction errors in a common framework. *eLife* 5:e13665

Schacter DL, Addis DR, Hassabis D, Martin VC, Spreng RN, Szpunar KK. 2012. The future of memory: remembering, imagining, and the brain. *Neuron* 76:677–94

Schölkopf B, Smola AJ. 2002. *Learning with Kernels: Support Vector Machines, Regularization, Optimization, and Beyond*. Cambridge, MA: MIT Press

Schonberg T, O'Doherty JP, Joel D, Inzelberg R, Segev Y, Daw ND. 2010. Selective impairment of prediction error signaling in human dorsolateral but not ventral striatum in Parkinson's disease patients: evidence from a model-based fMRI study. *NeuroImage* 49:772–81

Schultz W, Dayan P, Montague PR. 1997. A neural substrate of prediction and reward. *Science* 275:1593–99

Seymour B, Daw ND, Roiser JP, Dayan P, Dolan R. 2012. Serotonin selectively modulates reward value in human decision-making. *J. Neurosci.* 32:5833–42

Shohamy D, Daw ND. 2015. Integrating memories to guide decisions. *Curr. Opin. Behav. Sci.* 5:85–90

Shohamy D, Myers CE, Grossman S, Sage J, Gluck MA. 2005. The role of dopamine in cognitive sequence learning: evidence from Parkinson's disease. *Behav. Brain Res.* 156:191–99

Shohamy D, Wagner AD. 2008. Integrating memories in the human brain: hippocampal-midbrain encoding of overlapping events. *Neuron* 60:378–89

Simonson I, Tversky A. 1992. Choice in context: tradeoff contrast and extremeness aversion. *J. Mark. Res.* 29:281–95

Simonsohn U, Loewenstein G. 2006. Mistake #37: the effect of previously encountered prices on current housing demand. *Econ. J.* 116:175–99

Skaggs WE, McNaughton BL. 1996. Replay of neuronal firing sequences in rat hippocampus during sleep following spatial experience. *Science* 271:1870–73

Solway A, Botvinick MM. 2015. Evidence integration in model-based tree search. *PNAS* 112:11708–13

Squire LR. 1992. Memory and the hippocampus: a synthesis from findings with rats, monkeys, and humans. *Psychol. Rev.* 99:195–231

Stachenfeld KL, Botvinick M, Gershman SJ. 2014. Design principles of the hippocampal cognitive map. *Adv. Neural Inf. Process. Sys.* 27:2528–36

Steinberg EE, Keiflin R, Boivin JR, Witten IB, Deisseroth K, Janak PH. 2013. A causal link between prediction errors, dopamine neurons and learning. *Nat. Neurosci.* 16:966–73

Stewart N, Brown GD, Chater N. 2005. Absolute identification by relative judgment. *Psychol. Rev.* 112:881–911

Stewart N, Chater N, Brown GD. 2006. Decision by sampling. *Cogn. Psychol.* 53:1–26

Sutton RS. 1988. Learning to predict by the methods of temporal differences. *Mach. Learn.* 3:9–44

Sutton RS. 1991. Dyna, an integrated architecture for learning, planning, and reacting. *ACM SIGART Bull.* 2:160–63

Sutton RS, Barto AG. 1998. *Reinforcement Learning: An Introduction.* Cambridge, MA: MIT Press

Tenenbaum JB, De Silva V, Langford JC. 2000. A global geometric framework for nonlinear dimensionality reduction. *Science* 290:2319–23

Todd MT, Niv Y, Cohen JD. 2008. Learning to use working memory in partially observable environments through dopaminergic reinforcement. *Adv. Neural Inf. Process. Sys.* 21:1689–96

Tolman EC. 1948. Cognitive maps in rats and men. *Psychol. Rev.* 55:189–208

Tulving E. 1972. Episodic and semantic memory 1. In *Organization and Memory*, ed. E Tulving, W Donaldson, pp. 381–402. New York: Academic

Vaidya AR, Fellows LK. 2015. Ventromedial frontal cortex is critical for guiding attention to reward-predictive visual features in humans. *J. Neurosci.* 35:12813–23

van der Meer MA, Redish AD. 2011. Theta phase precession in rat ventral striatum links place and reward information. *J. Neurosci.* 31:2843–54

Wasserman L. 2006. *All of Nonparametric Statistics.* Berlin: Springer Science & Business Media

Wimmer GE, Braun EK, Daw ND, Shohamy D. 2014. Episodic memory encoding interferes with reward learning and decreases striatal prediction errors. *J. Neurosci.* 34:14901–12

Wimmer GE, Shohamy D. 2012. Preference by association: how memory mechanisms in the hippocampus bias decisions. *Science* 338:270–73

Zilli EA, Hasselmo ME. 2008. Modeling the role of working memory and episodic memory in behavioral tasks. *Hippocampus* 18:193–209

Social Learning and Culture in Child and Chimpanzee

Andrew Whiten

Centre for Social Learning and Cognitive Evolution, School of Psychology and Neuroscience, University of St. Andrews, St. Andrews KY16 9JP, United Kingdom; email: aw2@st-andrews.ac.uk

Annu. Rev. Psychol. 2017. 68:129–54

The *Annual Review of Psychology* is online at psych.annualreviews.org

This article's doi: 10.1146/annurev-psych-010416-044108

Keywords

culture, tradition, social learning, imitation, chimpanzees, primates

Abstract

A few decades ago, we knew next to nothing about the behavior of our closest animal relative, the chimpanzee, but long-term field studies have since revealed an undreamed-of richness in the diversity of their cultural traditions across Africa. These discoveries have been complemented by a substantial suite of experimental studies, now bridging to the wild through field experiments. These field and experimental studies, particularly those in which direct chimpanzee–child comparisons have been made, delineate a growing set of commonalities between the phenomena of social learning and culture in the lives of chimpanzees and humans. These commonalities in social learning inform our understanding of the evolutionary roots of the cultural propensities the species share. At the same time, such comparisons throw into clearer relief the unique features of the distinctive human capacity for cumulative cultural evolution, and new research has begun to probe the key psychological attributes that may explain it.

Contents

INTRODUCTION

Social learning is learning from others, as opposed to learning through one's own efforts, which is variously described as individual, personal, or asocial learning. Social learning can in turn give rise to traditions, or cultures, in which what is learned from others spreads to create enduring features of groups or populations. These cultures may be further transmitted from generation to generation.

The human propensity for social learning and culture pervades our lives. An enormous amount of the information encoded in our brains is assimilated from the culture in which we develop, ranging from our language to our social customs, technology, and other forms of material culture. Our species has developed a distinctive capacity for cumulative culture, such that over the generations, repeated cycles of innovation were incorporated into cultures that became progressively more sophisticated, underpinning the enormous evolutionary success of our species (Henrich 2015, Pagel 2012, Whiten et al. 2011). The achievements of our cumulative cultures have allowed human communities to spread across all major land masses around the world, whereas our nearest primate relatives, chimpanzees, have become restricted to pockets of their tropical forest niche in Africa.

Nevertheless, the remarkable human propensity for culture did not spring out of nowhere; research in recent decades has revealed much that it shares with the African apes and other species, providing unique insights into culture's evolutionary roots. An exponentially growing corpus of research has even documented the basic phenomena of social learning and culture across large swathes of the animal kingdom (Galef & Whiten 2017, Hoppitt & Laland 2013, Whiten et al. 2011). This research has largely focused on primates (Whiten 2012), particularly our closest living primate relative, the chimpanzee (Whiten 2010, 2011); hence the focus of the present comparative review.

The comparative study of social learning and culture is of considerable scientific importance for two main reasons. The first is anthropocentric, driven by our natural curiosity to uncover the evolutionary origins of our own distinctive human capacity for culture. Of course chimpanzees are not our ancestors, but features of social learning discovered to be shared between ourselves and our closest living relatives can be used to reconstruct the likely nature of social learning and culture in our shared ape ancestors. In the case of chimpanzees and their sister species bonobos, the combination of DNA, together with other molecular similarities between our species, and the fossil record suggests these ancestors lived in African forests 6 to 7 million years ago (Hara et al. 2012). The logic of this comparative approach to reconstructing the origins of our cultural cognition can be extended back through evolutionary time, from the origins of the great ape family that also includes gorillas and orangutans, around 14 or so million years ago (Hara et al. 2012), to ever more remote ancestries shared with all other mammals, all other vertebrates, and so on (Dawkins 2005). The other side of this coin is that comparative research simultaneously identifies those features unique to each species and so clarifies exactly what it is that evolved to make each distinctive since the time of common ancestry, such as the unique flowering of cumulative culture we witness in humans.

Another important scientific rationale for the comparative approach to cultural cognition lies in its broader implications for biology at large. Social learning and culture instantiate a "second inheritance system" (Whiten 2005, p. 52) built on the shoulders of the primary genetic inheritance system that provides the foundation of the evolutionary process. Inheritance via social learning has the potential for much more rapid behavioral adaptation than inheritance via genetic change, so our discoveries about such social inheritance across an increasing diversity of species transform our understanding of how the extended processes of evolution work (Mesoudi et al. 2006, Whiten et al. 2011). Chimpanzees remain particularly important from this perspective, because as reviewed below, much evidence suggests they display the most elaborate cultural profile among nonhuman animals.

COMPLEMENTARY METHODOLOGICAL APPROACHES TO PRIMATE AND HUMAN CULTURE AND SOCIAL LEARNING

Nonhuman primate (henceforth "primate") research on social learning and culture has come from two main contexts: from the wild and from captive environments (the latter are sometimes tagged as "the lab" but often encompass large naturalistic enclosures, from research institutes to zoos and sanctuaries). The work conducted from these two differing perspectives has not uncommonly been presented as at loggerheads, with field studies argued to provide the only ecologically valid context for recording nonartifactual behavior (e.g., Boesch 2012) or the lab the only environment permitting tight control of the experiments deemed crucial in distinguishing the operation of social from individual learning (e.g., Galef 1990). Historically, most researchers have tended to fall into one camp or the other, but some have recognized the ideal complementarity the two contexts offer and have tackled questions about the nature of primate culture from these dual perspectives (Biro et al. 2003, Matsuzawa et al. 2001). Moreover, field experiments on the topic have begun to provide a productive bridge between the two approaches. In this review, I emphasize what I see as essential and complementary contributions that flow from these differing strands of research effort.

Field research on the great apes was long thought to be too dangerous or difficult to contemplate (one early adventurer sat in a cage in gorilla forests, and saw little!); thus, early research was mostly with captive apes. This research contributed important foundational findings. Of the 60 studies of primate social learning tabulated by Tomasello & Call (1997, table 9.2), 13 were conducted more than a century ago, and 4 of them were with chimpanzees [the most famous was pioneered by Yerkes (1916)]. Studies of home-raised chimpanzees, in particular by Hayes & Hayes (1952), provided a wealth of observations of apparently spontaneous social learning (brushing one's teeth, applying lipstick) and experimental evidence of imitation (such as a trained "do this" request to—successfully—copy novel motor patterns) (Whiten & Ham 1992).

By contrast, 50 years ago we still knew virtually nothing of chimpanzee behavior in the wild. When multiple field sites across Africa at last began to generate long-term behavioral records, it became apparent that chimpanzees in different parts of Africa behaved in different ways. This finding culminated in international collaborative projects to systematically assess this variation and its potential cultural bases; these projects are summarized further below. This achievement might be thought to be more in the realm of anthropology than psychology, yet in my view it offers the most vital foundation to any psychological study of social learning, whatever the species. We need to begin with the nature of culture as it plays out and functions within a species' natural ecology and everyday life; more refined analyses can follow but make little sense unless we have an adequate picture of the cultural landscape of wild chimpanzees' everyday lives. In any case, research in the wild has extended to sophisticated statistical hypothesis testing and a handful of pioneering field experiments.

Research on human culture has likewise applied a diversity of methodological approaches, ranging from immersive and participant explorations by some cultural anthropologists to a variety of more "scientific" methods of a stripe more familiar to readers of this journal. These include direct, quantitative observations of everyday life that parallel those referred to above for primates, arguably particularly important for peoples living hunter-gatherer modes of life, for these observations offer inferences about the major component of recent human evolution during which our ancestors lived only by such means (Hewlett et al. 2011). Field experiments have recently supplemented such observations (Berl & Hewlett 2015).

In the case of human culture, we additionally have archaeological remains that permit the direct reconstruction of the course of some elements of cumulative cultural evolution, back to the beginnings of the Stone Age 2 to 4 million years ago (Harmand et al. 2015, Stout 2011). Human cultures diversified regionally and began to display their own forms of evolution as cumulative cultures blossomed, and these phenomena have been studied by yet other methods that include the kinds of phylogenetic analysis invented by biologists to study the evolution of organisms (e.g., Atkinson 2011, Currie & Mace 2011).

The psychological processes underlying human social learning and cultural transmission have been studied for more than a century (Whiten & Ham 1992) and through a great diversity of approaches; most studies have focused on childhood as the period of greatest cultural uptake, but some also extend into adulthood. Productive cross-fertilization between the approaches and theories of comparative and developmental psychology has increased over the past 15 years (Nielsen & Haun 2016, Nielsen et al. 2012, Want & Harris 2002). Moreover, in a literature search for truly comparative studies of social learning applying similar methods to two or more species, Galef & Whiten (2017) found only a handful of examples across comparative psychology generally, yet as many as 24 covering direct and indirect chimpanzee/child comparisons [see **Table 1** and **Supplemental Table 1** (follow the **Supplemental Material link** in the online version of this article or at **http://www.annualreviews.org**)]. Accordingly, I visit and extend this corpus further below.

A FRAMEWORK FOR COMPARING CULTURE AND CULTURAL COGNITION ACROSS SPECIES

Social learning and culture are complex phenomena, and any scientific comparison between species must accordingly dissect them to achieve any depth of analysis. A hierarchical analysis (illustrated in **Figure 1**) I recently developed as a comparative endeavor has also been embraced in a sister

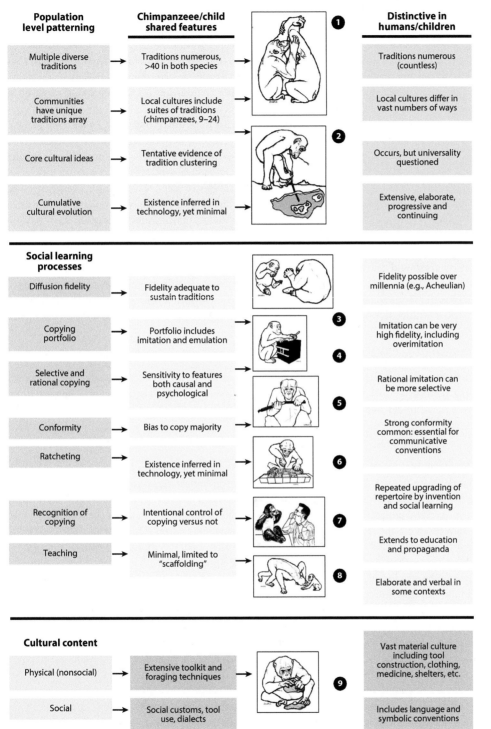

Population level patterning

Population level patterning	Chimpanzeee/child shared features		Distinctive in humans/children
Multiple diverse traditions	Traditions numerous, >40 in both species		Traditions numerous (countless)
Communities have unique traditions array	Local cultures include suites of traditions (chimpanzees, 9–24)		Local cultures differ in vast numbers of ways
Core cultural ideas	Tentative evidence of tradition clustering		Occurs, but universality questioned
Cumulative cultural evolution	Existence inferred in technology, yet minimal		Extensive, elaborate, progressive and continuing

Social learning processes

Social learning processes			
Diffusion fidelity	Fidelity adequate to sustain traditions		Fidelity possible over millennia (e.g., Acheulian)
Copying portfolio	Portfolio includes imitation and emulation		Imitation can be very high fidelity, including overimitation
Selective and rational copying	Sensitivity to features both causal and psychological		Rational imitation can be more selective
Conformity	Bias to copy majority		Strong conformity common: essential for communicative conventions
Ratcheting	Existence inferred in technology, yet minimal		Repeated upgrading of repertoire by invention and social learning
Recognition of copying	Intentional control of copying versus not		Extends to education and propaganda
Teaching	Minimal, limited to "scaffolding"		Elaborate and verbal in some contexts

Cultural content

Cultural content			
Physical (nonsocial)	Extensive toolkit and foraging techniques		Vast material culture including tool construction, clothing, medicine, shelters, etc.
Social	Social customs, tool use, dialects		Includes language and symbolic conventions

Figure 1

Features of culture shared by chimpanzees, humans including children, and (by inference) the common chimpanzee/human ancestor, and features of culture distinctive in humans. Features (rows) are nested under three main headings. Images represent examples discussed in detail in the text. For further explanation of each numbered image, see **Supplemental Text** (follow the **Supplemental Material link** in the online version of this article or at **http://www.annualreviews.org**). Adapted from Whiten (2011), with permission.

discipline, cultural anthropology (Jordan 2015). The scheme initially identifies three dimensions along which species may be compared and contrasted (**Figure 1**). The first concerns the patterning of traditions over space (regional cultures) and time (historical change) and hence includes the topic of cumulative culture. Distinct animal taxa, such as humans, dolphins, and songbirds, show identifiable commonalities in such large-scale patterning despite great differences in the action patterns that populate the patterns. Such patterning could instead show interesting variation, as indeed it appears to do in the case of human cumulative culture.

Another feature concerns the content of culturally transmitted traditions. At different levels of analysis, species may either share or differ in such content, as in the significant repertoire of tool use inherited by chimpanzees as well as humans, or vocal dialects recorded in songbirds, whales, and humans.

The third division focuses on similarities and variations in the social learning processes involved, such as imitation and teaching. As for the other divisions, cross-species similarities can exist in social learning processes despite variation in the other two dimensions that concern the behavioral contents of traditions and their distributions over time and space. Social learning processes may strike the reader as the most clearly psychological of these three foci of analysis, but the relevance of the others should not be neglected; the particular content of a tradition (language, for example, or stone-tool knapping) also has a psychological dimension, and the larger-scale patterning of traditions in time and space incorporates both causes and consequences of cultural learning and content. In the following sections, I address each of the three divisions and key subcomponents in turn.

THE PATTERNING OF TRADITIONS IN TIME AND SPACE

I first focus principally on chimpanzee findings because knowledge in the apes has been hard won only in recent decades and has often surprised us, in contrast with all we know about human culture from scientific research and from ourselves being immersed in the phenomena.

Multiple and Diverse Traditions

When the realization dawned that chimpanzee behavior may differ culturally across Africa, as human behavior is known to vary regionally, primatologists began to build charts of candidate regional traditions (Boesch & Tomasello 1998, Goodall 1986, McGrew 1992). These early explorations were eventually followed by a systematic analysis based on an explicit collaboration between the research groups responsible for the longest-term field studies (Whiten et al. 1999, 2001). The first of these focused on the six longest-running sites that together could collate 150 years of observations; the second analysis included three additional medium-term sites. Each of a long list of candidate traditions, consensually defined, was coded by the groups according to whether it was common at their site or absent without apparent ecological explanation. This process identified 39 putative cultural variants that were habitual or customary in at least one community yet absent in one or more other communities. This is an unprecedented number of variants for all but human societies; indeed, most studies identifying animal traditions have tended to report just a single one, such as the regional dialects of songbirds. The chimpanzee portfolio also widely spanned the species' behavioral repertoire, incorporating foraging techniques; tool use for feeding, comfort, hygiene and communication; and social and sexual gambits. Accordingly, the first commonality identified between humans and chimpanzees is that a substantial and diverse portion of the adult behavioral repertoire is derived from cultural inheritance. Such a state of affairs is thus inferred to have characterized our shared ancestry (Whiten 2011).

Local Cultures Defined by Distinctive Arrays of Traditions

A corollary to the discovery of numerous traditions is that each community is unique: Identifying a set of the relevant behavioral habits of any one individual chimpanzee can mean that its regional origin can be deduced, as can be done for a human being whose cultural attributes are scrutinized. This constitutes a second commonality.

Cultural complexity that comes close to matching both of these two features has been identified in studies of another great ape, the Asian orangutan (Krützen et al. 2011, van Schaik et al. 2003). The authors concluded that local cultures composed of diverse, multiple traditions constitute a characteristic that evolved 14 to 15 million years ago in the ancestors we share with all the great apes (Whiten & van Schaik 2007).

Concern exists about whether the behavioral differences among wild ape communities inferred to be cultural could instead be due to genetic variation across Africa or to environmental factors that are subtle and as yet undetected. Indeed, genetic differences between chimpanzee communities across Africa are correlated with differences in the putative cultural profile of the communities (Langergraber et al. 2011). However, this is a pattern we should expect because until recent times, when long-distance travel (e.g., by sea) made it possible for dispersing human groups to leapfrog past others, geographically and culturally distant communities were expected to be genetically more different, and thus the same would be predicted for apes. In addition, Lycett et al. (2010) examined the particular branching (phylogenetic) structure of putative cultural variants of chimpanzees distributed across study sites and found them incompatible with genetic species structure. Kamilar & Atkinson (2014) further extended these findings, revealing nested relationships between human communities' behavioral commonalities that apparently are diagnostic of cultural diffusion, and finding similar patterns in chimpanzees (but not in orangutans, perhaps because they have smaller networks).

Additional evidence that refutes genetic explanations comes from a variety of other sources. Such evidence includes one of the most striking regional variations: Across a large swath of far West Africa, natural stone and wooden hammers are customarily used to open hard-shelled fruits, but these tools are absent in other regions, despite availability of the needed raw materials. This variation clearly does not reflect genetic preparedness because experiments have shown that East African chimpanzees are perfectly capable of learning the technique if they witness another chimpanzee performing it (Fuhrmann et al. 2014, Marshall-Pescini & Whiten 2008a, Whiten 2015). Luncz & Boesch (2014) have further shown that despite their frequent gene exchange, the chimpanzees in neighboring communities display group-specific preferences in stone versus wooden tool selection, an intriguing finding given that females typically migrate as adults and so must conform to local customs for the group variants to be maintained.

Further evidence that chimpanzees can develop and sustain different traditions in different groups comes from studies incorporating multiple captive groups. For example, some but not all groups in an African sanctuary developed local traditions that included hammering hard-shelled fruits to break them (Rawlings et al. 2014), using a specific style of mutual grooming (handclasp; van Leeuwen et al. 2012), and most bizarre of all, poking a grass leaf into one ear and leaving it there, which serves no apparent function (van Leeuwen et al. 2014a,b). Neither genetic nor environmental differences can explain these variants. The spread of an incipient new tradition, using moss as a sponge to get water from a hole, has now also been documented (Hobaiter et al. 2014). Additional experimental evidence concerning the transmission of traditions is reviewed further below in a discussion of the underlying social learning abilities.

Linkage of Traditions Through Core Cultural Ideas

Cultural anthropologists have argued that elements of culture, such as ideas, memes, and traditions, are not particulate (the way traditions are treated in the discussion above, in which "39 putative cultural variants" are enumerated) but instead may be linked together through some core cultural cognitions (Levine 1984). Because the evidence for such phenomena in anthropology is typically linguistic, this issue is much more difficult to address for nonverbal creatures. However, the findings from recent experimental studies with wild chimpanzees may be relevant. In these studies, holes too small for chimpanzee fingers were drilled in fallen logs and filled with honey in two chimpanzee communities in different parts of Uganda. Chimpanzees in one of these communities (Kanyawara) habitually use stick tools to extract various resources, but stick tool use has long been known to be (unusually) absent in the repertoire of the second group (Budongo), although they use other tool materials, including masticated leaves as sponges to get water out of natural holes (Hobaiter et al. 2014, Whiten et al. 1999). When faced with the honey-filled holes, chimpanzees from each community responded differently (Gruber et al. 2009). Those at Kanyawara gathered sticks and quite efficiently dipped these into the holes so they could then lick off the honey. Budongo chimpanzees, by contrast, made and applied the kind of leaf sponges normally used to extract water, a much less efficient approach. The problem really required stick use, but the Budongo chimpanzees appeared to be "stuck" on their local, habitual technique. Indeed, when in a follow-up study leafy sticks were provided near the holes, Kanyawara chimpanzees promptly stripped the leaves off to make a stick tool, whereas the Budongo chimpanzees stripped the leaves off and used just the leaves for their habitual sponging approach (Gruber et al. 2011). The authors' conclusion (and the title of their paper) was, accordingly, that "Wild chimpanzees rely on their cultural knowledge to solve an experimental honey acquisition task" (Gruber et al. 2009), an explanation that seems in accord with the notion that core cultural cognitions may pervade multiple contexts. This is, of course, a small-scale candidate for this effect in comparison with human examples, such as the contrast between an emphasis on independence and analytical thinking in Western cultures and an emphasis on collectivism and holism in the East (Nisbett et al. 2001).

Cumulative Culture

All authors working in the field of comparative cultural cognition now acknowledge that wild chimpanzees as a species have been shown to display numerous traditions together with unique multitradition local cultures, as outlined above, but conclusions about whether species other than humans display cumulative culture are more diverse. It is commonly stated that only humans have cumulative culture (e.g., Henrich 2015, Tennie et al. 2009). My own view is that this conclusion is premature and that chimpanzees do show some limited evidence of cumulative culture. The magnitude of the species differences in this respect is of course massive, but I suggest that we see initial significant signs of cumulation in chimpanzees, and it would have been from such beginnings that our special human capacities evolved.

Boesch (2012) proposes several candidate cases of small-scale cumulation in chimpanzees. In an example I judge to be currently the most impressive, chimpanzees in the central Congo region have been filmed approaching clearings where they will fish not horizontally in termite mounds as is seen in several communities, but instead extract termites from nests several feet beneath the surface (Sanz et al. 2009). To do this, the chimpanzees first push a stout stick downward into the earth, doing so forcefully and often using their foot to assist in a manner similar to digging with a spade. Having thus created a subterranean tunnel, they prepare fresh, slim stems, which they brought to the site in anticipation, by stripping one end through their teeth to make a comb that will better elicit biting by the termites. The chimpanzees then carefully insert the prepared stem down the long tunnel and withdraw it to nibble off the termites that are biting the brush end. We have no documentation of the history of this elaborate sequence, just as for most of those sequences used in weapon and trap making by human hunter-gatherers, but the cumulative history of the latter is not in doubt, and it likewise seems unimaginable that chimpanzees could have built up this sequential fishing procedure in a single generation. It seems quite miraculous that the chimpanzees know a technique that will extract these termites from deep in the earth; it seems highly plausible that the technique started with termites close to the surface and has evolved over generations into the more elaborate form we see today.

Such candidate cases pale in comparison to the pace and scope of cumulation we have witnessed in recent phases of human history, but they are important to recognize if we are to properly understand the underlying cultural cognition of both species. Moreover, cumulative culture of any significant magnitude is a relatively recent phenomenon along the evolutionary line from the time of our shared ancestor up to the emergence of modern humans. For a long time, the first archaeological evidence for the beginnings of the stone age came at 2.6 million years (Semaw et al. 2003), but new evidence appears to push this back to perhaps 3.3 million years (Harmand et al. 2015); nevertheless, the cumulative step from flaked cobbles to discriminably more advanced, symmetrically shaped Acheulean blades did not come until around 1.8 million years. That procedure then endured, with only minimal progressive change, for another million years or so before the next noticeable cumulative steps took place (Stout 2011), despite hominid brain sizes already being midway between those of chimpanzees and modern humans. Although chimpanzee cumulative culture appears minimal, it is relevantly comparable to perhaps the greater part of the six to seven million years or so of our unique hominin evolutionary pathway. I review potential explanations for the contrast between chimpanzees and modern humans in the capacity for cumulative culture in the social learning section below.

SOCIAL LEARNING PROCESSES

Chimpanzees are both our closest living relatives, with whom we shared our last nonhuman ancestor, and the species that, along with humans, has been the subject of the greatest number of studies of social learning; such studies have often led the way in comparative psychology's exploration of new dimensions in the nature and scope of animal culture. These two observations are not unrelated. This corpus of research probes the psychological mechanisms and processes that make possible the scope of culture in the two species that was outlined in the sections above. Relevant studies include those concerned with fidelity of cultural transmission, different grades of social learning, selective factors modulating what is copied and from whom, conformist copying, teaching, and capacities underwriting cumulative cultural evolution.

The intrinsic interest in chimpanzees is one reason why chimpanzees are represented in an unusually high proportion of studies in which one species is closely compared with another; these comparisons are centered mainly on humans, although in some cases other great ape species are included. **Supplemental Table 1** summarizes 24 such studies, including a set collated in Galef & Whiten's (2017) chapter (see **Table 1** for comparative studies published from 1993 to 2015). The following discussion draws on these as well as other studies that do not offer direct comparisons between species in the same paper. Interested readers may also find it helpful to consult Whiten et al. (2004) for a similar summary of the 31 articles on great ape social learning published since those listed in Tomasello & Call's (1997) book, which covered all such papers up to 1996.

Table 1 Comparative social learning studies with children and (other) apes, 1993–2015. Studies are listed chronologically by publication date. (See Supplemental Table 1 for further details.)

Direct comparisons of child and ape social learning studies	
Reference	**Title**
Nagell et al. 1993	Processes of social learning in the tool use of chimpanzees (*Pan troglodytes*) and human children (*Homo sapiens*)
Tomasello et al. 1993b	Imitative learning of actions on objects by children, chimpanzees and enculturated chimpanzees
Call & Tomasello 1995	The use of social information in the problem-solving of orangutans (*Pongo pygmaeus*) and human children (*Homo sapiens*)
Carpenter et al. 1995	Joint attention and imitative learning in children, chimpanzees and enculturated chimpanzees
Whiten et al. 1996	Imitative learning of artificial fruit processing in children (*Homo sapiens*) and chimpanzees (*Pan troglodytes*)
Call et al. 2005	Copying results and copying actions in the process of social learning: chimpanzees (*Pan troglodytes*) and human children (*Homo sapiens*)
Horner & Whiten 2005	Causal knowledge and imitation/emulation switching in chimpanzees (*Pan troglodytes*) and children (*Homo sapiens*)
Tennie et al. 2006	Push or pull: imitation versus emulation in great apes and human children
Horner et al. 2006	Faithful replication of foraging techniques along cultural transmission chains by chimpanzees and children
Herrmann et al. 2007	Humans have evolved specialized skills of social cognition: the cultural intelligence hypothesis
Horner & Whiten 2007	Learning from others' mistakes? Limits on understanding of a trap-tube task by young chimpanzees and children
Hopper et al. 2008	Observational learning in chimpanzees and children studied through "ghost" conditions
Buttelmann et al. 2008	Rational tool use and tool choice in human infants and great apes
Tennie et al. 2009	Ratcheting up the ratchet: on the evolution of cumulative culture
Haun et al. 2012	Majority-biased transmission in chimpanzees and human children, but not orangutans
Dean et al. 2012	Identification of social and cognitive processes underlying human cumulative culture
van Leeuwen et al. 2014a	Human children rely more on social information than chimpanzees do
Haun et al. 2014	Children conform to the behavior of peers; other great apes stick with what they know
Vale et al. 2014	Public information use in chimpanzees (*Pan troglodytes*) and children (*Homo sapiens*)
Claidière et al. 2015	Selective and contagious prosocial resource donation in capuchin monkeys, chimpanzees and humans

Ape experiments with earlier (or later) child studies explicitly compared to them		
Ape reference	**Child studies compared**	**Title**
Call & Tomasello 1994	Nagell et al. 1993	The social learning of tool use by orangutans
Whiten et al. 2005a	Flynn & Whiten 2012, Hopper et al. 2010, Whiten & Flynn 2010	Conformity to cultural norms of tool use in chimpanzees
Tomasello & Carpenter 2005	Bellagamba & Tomasello 1999, Carpenter et al. 1998, Meltzoff 1995	The emergence of social cognition in three young chimpanzees
Marshall-Pescini & Whiten 2008b	Whiten et al. 2009	Chimpanzees (*Pan troglodytes*) and the question of cumulative culture: an experimental approach
Buttelmann et al. 2007	Gergely et al. 2002	Enculturated chimpanzees imitate rationally

Fidelity in Transmission: Cultural Diffusion Studies

One of the most commonly cited explanations for the gulf between the cultural achievements of humans and chimpanzees concerns the relative copying fidelity of the two species. One prominent version of this explanation was promoted by Tomasello and colleagues in a series of publications [from Tomasello et al. (1993a,b) to Tennie et al. (2009)]. A dichotomy was initially drawn between two social learning processes that have driven much comparative research, especially concerning apes. One learning process was imitation, defined as the copying of others' actions. Imitation had already been studied in comparative and developmental psychology for much of the prior century. The other process, emulation, was newer and highlighted by Tomasello (1990) following a study in which chimpanzees had failed to imitatively copy a tool-use sequence displayed by a conspecific retrieving food, yet showed they had learned something of the function of the stick tool by the way they directed it at the target (Tomasello et al. 1987). Tomasello described this as emulation: recreating the desirable results of another's actions rather than their form. Emulation could thus be considered to lie between imitation and the simple and widespread forms of social learning known as stimulus (with regard to objects) and local (with regard to locations) enhancement, in which all that is socially acquired is the locus of attention displayed by others.

It has been suggested that the often high-fidelity action copying of which children are capable is what permits cumulative culture, because this is what is needed to maintain each progressive step up the cultural ratchet, whereas in the case of emulation the learners have to generate an action sequence of their own to achieve the desirable results they learned about. A considerable corpus of studies has offered support for this hypothesis (e.g., Call et al. 2005, Nagell et al. 1993), and much of it has been reviewed (and debated) by Tennie et al. (2009) and Whiten et al. (2009). For example, Herrmann et al. (2007) presented young children, chimpanzees, and orangutans with modeled behavior patterns and reported that in contrast to the results of other tests revealing often quite similar levels of physical cognition, only the children showed significant evidence of imitating the model.

However, Herrmann et al. (2007) employed only human models, such that the apes faced a model of a different species, whereas children could copy a human adult. Other types of studies have come to different conclusions regarding fidelity of transmission; these are broadly classed as diffusion or transmission studies and have been reviewed up to 2008 for human subjects by Mesoudi & Whiten (2008), for other species by Whiten & Mesoudi (2008), and for both categories in the period since by Whiten et al. (2016). These studies go beyond the classic social learning experimental design that asks, "What does B learn from model A?" to a design that is more appropriate for investigating cultural transmission because whole micropopulations are involved. In the first controlled experiment of this kind with chimpanzees, Whiten et al. (2005a,b) trained one chimpanzee how to use a stick tool to extract food from a foraging box (termed panpipes) using one method (termed lift) and then reunited her with her group; similarly, a model trained to use an alternative method (termed poke) was seeded back into her own group. It was found that these alternative techniques spread differentially in the groups in which they were seeded and became incipient, recognizably different traditions (**Figure 2**). Indeed, although some corruption occurred, with some individuals discovering the alternative technique, it was found that two months later these individuals had tended to reconverge on the technique most common in their group. This experimental design does not discriminate between imitation and emulation but rather suggests that chimpanzees have the capacity to transmit and sustain with adequate fidelity the kinds of alternative tradition inferred from the observations in the wild outlined above.

This design has been labeled open diffusion because it leaves open who will watch the models and who will (or will not) copy what they do. In a more controlled alternative, the diffusion chain, just one observer witnesses the model, then after mastering the task (however they do it) the observer becomes the model for the next observer, and so on along a chain. Horner et al. (2006) applied this approach to both children and chimpanzees and found fidelity along the chains for both (along chains of 10 children; chains of just 6 chimpanzees were used because of the challenging pragmatics of such maneuvering with captive apes). Other variants on these experiments at two different sites confirmed that chimpanzees can express adequate fidelity in sustaining multiple-tradition cultures (Whiten et al. 2007) (**Figure 2**).

The panpipes open-diffusion chimpanzee experiment outlined above has also been repeated with young children in small nursery groups (Flynn & Whiten 2012, Whiten & Flynn 2010). This generated more complex results, with both similarities to and differences from the chimpanzee findings. Initially there was similarity in that two recognizably different incipient traditions were established already on day 1 of the study, as tool-use skills spread across the groups. However, children were quicker than chimpanzees to discover the alternative technique and also invented a third intermediate one. These innovations could in turn be shown to spread by social learning, with

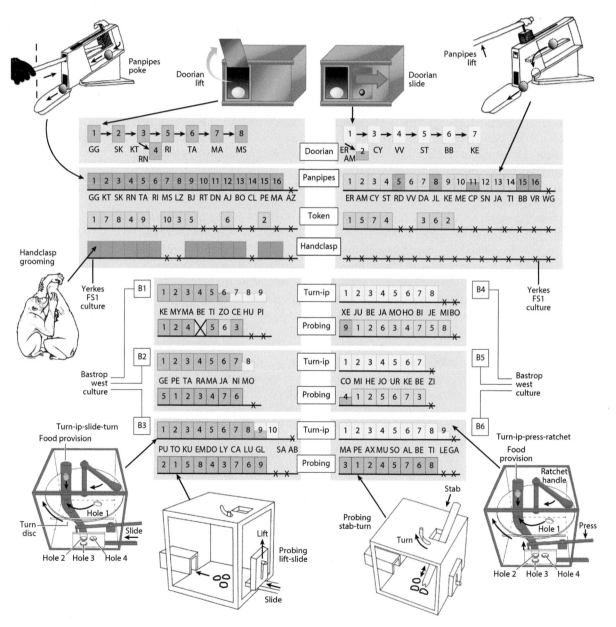

a majority of children being social learners and a minority the innovators who either modified what they learned from others or, more rarely, invented a technique quite different from the one they had learned. This particular child/chimpanzee comparison is thus sobering in that it shows greater fidelity in the chimpanzees than in the children; however, this was surely not because children are inherently less able to faithfully copy but rather that they could independently master the task better and were more ready to innovate. One lesson is thus that in making such comparisons, the level of challenge in the task for each species can be a critical factor in the resulting picture of fidelity of transmission that each presents.

Fidelity in Transmission: Imitation and Emulation

These findings leave unanswered the question of the imitation and emulation profile that truly characterizes each of the two species. Hopper et al. (2007) tackled this issue in the panpipes studies with chimpanzees through a ghost experiment. In this approach, the usual results of a model's actions are recreated without any model present, so the conditions for emulation are available but do not permit imitation. In the ghost experiment, the lift technique, which involves lifting up a blockage to release the food reward, was performed by surreptitious operation of fishing line above the device. No chimpanzees learned from this ghost experiment, in marked contrast with how well chimpanzees had acquired the behavior from seeing it modeled in the earlier diffusion study. This suggests that chimpanzees are limited in their ability to learn merely from object movements [Tomasello (1998) had once suggested such emulation might occur if the wind blew an object instead of the mother moving it] and instead need to watch the actions of a model, consistent with imitative social learning (Hopper et al. 2015).

However, in these ghost studies, there is no active model, even in a refinement of the method in which a passive conspecific is included in the scenario (Hopper et al. 2008). An ingenious alternative accordingly offered by Tennie et al. (2010) involved first showing participant chimpanzees that pouring water from a bottle into a cylinder could make a peanut inside rise to the top of the cylinder so it could be retrieved. However, no bottle was provided for the chimpanzees. Some chimpanzees responded by fetching water from their drinker in their mouths and spitting it into the cylinder, which when repeated delivered the peanut. This action is true emulation because it involves the chimpanzee recreating a desirable result by using a means different from that shown by a model. It does not show that chimpanzees are limited to emulation, but it does identify one context in which they can take this approach, contrasting with the negative results from the ghost experiments.

Horner & Whiten (2005) challenged the dichotomy of child-imitators and chimpanzee-emulators in a different way. These investigators conceptualized the distinction as more of a

Figure 2

Spread of experimentally seeded, multiple traditions generating four chimpanzee "cultures." At each location [Yerkes (*a*) and Bastrop (*b*)], alternative techniques were experimentally seeded in a single individual, and all spread locally. Each two-letter code represents a single chimpanzee, and color-coding corresponds to the technique seeded in the first individual in each case. (*a*) At Yerkes, lift versus slide methods (first row) were seeded to open a door for access to "doorian" fruit; these techniques spread as a diffusion chain (Horner et al. 2006). In the second row, poke versus lift panpipes techniques spread in an open (unconstrained) diffusion (Whiten et al. 2005a,b). The third row illustrates a bucket versus a pipe posting option for tokens in an open diffusion (Bonnie et al. 2007). Handclasp grooming (fourth row) arose and spread spontaneously only in the Yerkes FS1 community. (*b*) At Bastrop, techniques included (first row) actions termed turn-ip-slide-turn versus turn-ip-press-ratchet and (second row) probe lift-slide versus probe stab-turn used to extract food from two different devices; each technique spread to a second group (third and fourth rows; groups B2 and B5) and then to a third group (fifth and sixth rows; B3 and B6) (Whiten et al. 2007). Numbers indicate order of acquisition. Figure based on data in, and adapted with permission from, Whiten et al. (2007).

continuum, and to test this notion they structured an experiment in which young chimpanzees and children watched a familiar model extract a reward from either an opaque or a transparent box. In the case of the opaque box, the model first used a stick tool to open a hole in the top, rammed the tool in several times, then opened a second hole on the side and inserted the stick to bring out the reward and share it. The transparent box was identical, but when the stick was rammed in the top, it was perfectly visible that it merely tapped on a horizontal partition and could not affect what happened on later insertion of the tool into the lower hole. Accordingly, it was predicted that an intelligent imitator like a child would likely imitate the whole sequence in the opaque condition but would prefer a more emulative response with the transparent box, omitting the actions directed at the top hole.

In the experiment, the chimpanzees made this distinction and produced much more complete copies of what they had seen, including ramming the stick in the top hole, in the opaque condition than in the transparent condition. Thus, rather than producing only emulation (omitting actions on the top hole) or mindlessly "aping" all of the actions (not discriminating between the two conditions), the chimpanzees showed flexibility of social learning, switching between emulative responses and those in which they imitated the sequence with the opaque box. An interesting and surprising finding was that the children tended to copy all actions faithfully in both conditions, a response now known as overimitation.

Overimitation

Lyons et al. (2007) coined the term overimitation after having amply replicated the effect with a transparent puzzle box and other manipulable artifacts and failing in several efforts to encourage 3- to 5-year-old children to behave "more sensibly." For example, Lyons and colleagues offered training episodes in which children were encouraged to identify visibly, causally unnecessary action components, such as stroking a feather on a jar before unscrewing the top, and advised children, "Remember, don't do anything silly and extra. Only do the things you have to do, okay?"—all to no avail. Whiten et al. (2005b; see also Horner & Whiten 2005) suggested that the effect might represent a rule of thumb ("copy all, correct later") that was typically productive for children when learning from competent adults and others. Lyons et al. (2007) went further to posit an "automatic encoding mechanism" whereby young children automatically interpret adult actions on unfamiliar objects as causally effective, a functional disposition given that the child is surrounded by a vast array of mysterious objects, the causal workings of which are at least initially quite opaque.

Overimitation has since been confirmed and further explored in numerous studies that have identified the phenomenon in several quite different cultures (Berl & Hewlett 2015, Nielsen et al. 2014) and also extended its age range. The foundational studies were with preschool children, and it was initially anticipated that the effect would dissipate as children matured in their cognition. In fact, the reverse was found, with adolescents (Nielsen & Tomaselli 2010) and then adults (McGuigan et al. 2011; **Figure 3**) displaying an even more pronounced effect. Lyons et al. (2011) have provided further evidence in support of the operation of a causal encoding function, but other studies have suggested that in many contexts a social function may be served through building bonds by being more like others; complying with others' assumed wishes; or acquiring cultural conventions, norms, and ritual procedures (Hoehl et al. 2014, Kenward et al. 2011, Keupp et al. 2013, Nielsen et al. 2008).

It is customarily stated that overimitation is a distinctive human property that is not seen in apes, but this statement hinges only on the original findings of Horner & Whiten (2005) and one other study (Nielsen & Widjojo 2011) that clearly begs for more replication and elaboration. An effect perhaps akin to overimitation was reported by Price et al. (2009), who completed a

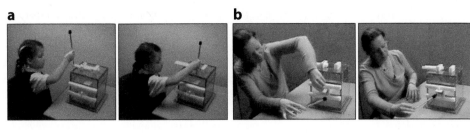

Figure 3

Sequence of models' actions in an overimitation study. Photos illustrate (*a*) a child model performing the causally irrelevant actions of shifting a bolt to access the top hole and then inserting a stick tool, and (*b*) an adult model performing subsequent causally necessary actions to reveal the lower hole and then inserting a stick tool to retrieve a reward. Stills from video presentations used with permission from McGuigan et al. (2011).

study showing that chimpanzees exposed to a model joining two sticks to make a long rake to pull in food were more likely than nonobserving individuals to learn this technique. A handful of these controls did, however, work out the stick-joining option themselves. Testing the cognitive flexibility of successful chimpanzees later by offering closer food items that did not require use of the long rake tool, Price et al. (2009) discovered that the social learners were more likely than the individual learners to persist in the stick-joining technique they had acquired by observation. Arguably, this is at least "overcopying" and indicates some of the potency of social learning we see in the case of overimitation.

Selective and Rational Social Learning

Although copying others can be a productive and safe way to learn, it can also lead one stray if what is copied happens to be maladaptive. Accordingly, we may predict that evolutionary and developmental processes will refine selective biases about when, from whom, and even how best to copy, depending on context. One example of chimpanzees' selectivity was demonstrated in the transparent box experiment of Horner & Whiten (2005), although in that case it contrasted with lack of selectivity in children. However, other studies have demonstrated a range of forms of selectivity in children's social learning (Price et al. 2016, Wood et al. 2013). Many investigators have examined this selectivity in the realm of language, revealing the bases over which children learn to trust (or not trust) the verbal testimonies they hear (Harris 2012), so direct comparisons with apes do not apply. However, comparisons are feasible in other domains.

One example lies in what has been called rational imitation. Gergely et al. (2002) repeated Meltzoff's (1998) dramatic demonstration that human infants can be so imitative as to copy an adult bizarrely bowing down his head instead of using his hand to switch on a light, and they included a new condition in which a model wrapped a blanket round herself, preventing use of her hands. Imitation was more rare in this condition. The conclusion drawn was that even by age one, infants' theory of action is sufficiently sophisticated to recognize that the blanket means using one's head would make sense, whereas without the blanket, using one's head must be intentional and worth copying.

Buttelmann et al. (2007, 2008) have since adapted this paradigm for apes and have expanded it such that the unusual actions are done not only with the head but also with the foot or by sitting on objects to make them light up or make a sound, again either in hands-free or hands-occupied (e.g., wrapped by a blanket or holding a box) conditions. In their work with enculturated chimpanzees (i.e., intimately reared by humans), these authors found rational biases in apes that were similar to those identified in children.

Other biases concern from whom it is best to learn. Incidental observations that chimpanzees might be attending and learning from higher-ranked individuals led Horner et al. (2010) to have high- and low-ranked models post tokens in different receptacles to obtain rewards; they showed that the higher-ranked model's choice was preferentially copied by others. The adaptive benefit of such a bias is likely to be that high rank is a marker of having access to the best resources as well as being correlated with overall biological fitness, so such an individual is a good one to copy—an effect akin to copying prestigious individuals in the case of humans (Henrich & Gil-White 2001). Kendal et al. (2015) have provided complementary evidence, from social learning dynamics in chimpanzee groups, of biases to copy both dominant and already-knowledgeable individuals.

Effects similar to the latter have also been documented in experiments with children [reviewed by Wood et al. (2013) and Price et al. (2016)]. For example, Zmyj et al. (2010) showed that even in infancy, the more competent of two models will be preferentially copied. Age appears to be a cue to this factor, with a number of experiments showing that adults are more likely to be copied than child peers (McGuigan et al. 2011, Rakoczy et al. 2010); however, in play contexts this bias may be reversed (Zmyj et al. 2012), which is an additional measure of the subtlety of selective learning rules in play. Such subtleties suggest a somewhat paradoxical contrast with the lack of selectivity that is the hallmark of overimitation and, at least at first sight, the phenomenon of conformity (Whiten 2013), which is discussed in the next section.

Conformity

Conformity was first made famous by work in social psychology, notably that by Asch (1956), who arranged that a visibly incorrect choice would be given by all but one adult (the subject) in a group of individuals asked in turn to make a simple perceptual judgment about relative line length. Approximately 30% of the participants conformed to the expressed group judgment by stating the same preference as others in the face of quite clearly visible evidence to the contrary. The effect was later investigated in children, with Walker & Andrade (1996) reporting as many as 85% of 3- to 5-year-olds conforming in an Asch-like scenario, which reduced steadily with age to only 9% in 12- to 14-year-olds; by contrast, approximately 20% of 3- to 4-year-olds in a more recent study by Corriveau & Harris (2010) did so, but here the other children were shown only on video.

As noted above, in the panpipes study of Whiten et al. (2005a,b), chimpanzees that discovered the nonseeded solution tended to return later to the group norm—the seeded method—which thus suggested an effect akin to that demonstrated in the Asch paradigm, insofar as the chimpanzees knew of both options and appeared to veer to the norm just because it was the most commonly seen. However, van Leeuwen & Haun (2014) note that this does not exclude a tendency to return to one's first-learned technique, and these authors are skeptical of the existing evidence for this kind of conformity adduced for primates or indeed any nonhuman animals.

The panpipes study had not set out to test for conformity. The first study to do so for the lower-level question of whether naïve chimpanzees (i.e., individuals not needing to overturn existing personal preferences) would favor copying a majority was conducted by Haun et al. (2012), who arranged that subjects saw three conspecifics posting tokens in one of three receptacles, whereas just one conspecific did so three times in a different receptacle. Like children in the same experiment, when chimpanzees decided which receptacle to post their token in to gain reward, they tended to prefer the receptacle chosen by three different chimpanzees. However, this did not require any switching of preference. Haun et al. (2014) did present this dilemma, with individuals first learning a reward location preference, then witnessing three conspecifics choosing a different location. Here, just over half of the 2-year-old children switched to conform to this location, whereas only 1 of 12 chimpanzees tested did so.

In the wild, however, there is different evidence suggesting conformity. Luncz & Boesch (2014) and Luncz et al. (2015) identified subtle but significant differences in the seasonal preference in adjacent communities for different tool materials for cracking nuts. The authors argue that both genetic and ecological explanations for these differences can be discounted, leaving cultural transmission as the inferred cause. The local preferences were also shown by females, who have immigrated from neighboring communities and hence are inferred to have conformed to the new local norms they have experienced, a tendency documented as one female migrated and gradually converged on local patterns (Luncz & Boesch 2014). It is possible that such biases are brought into play when individuals face uncertainty, as is the case in immigrating to a new community and home range, and other cases of conformity recently reported in other primates (van de Waal et al. 2013) and birds (Aplin et al. 2015a,b) fit this pattern.

A somewhat different notion of conformity has been thought important by other researchers who focus on human cultural dynamics. Boyd & Richerson (1985) have defined conformity as an exaggerated tendency to copy the majority. If 80% of individuals in a community express a preference for option A over option B, then immigrants would show this level of conformist transmission if the probability of their opting for A was significantly greater than 0.8, an important effect because, as the authors' modeling has shown, such a tendency would reinforce in-group cultural homogeneity and intergroup cultural diversity. Evidence that humans behave in this way is mixed (Claidière & Whiten 2012), but Morgan et al. (2015) have demonstrated such behavior in young children—again, interestingly, especially in contexts of uncertainty. The use of a large population of marked individuals recently provided evidence of such a conformist effect in birds (Aplin et al. 2015a,b), but to my knowledge there is no primate literature as yet, possibly in part because of the large sample sizes needed.

Cultural Ratcheting and Conservatism

The gulf between the minimal evidence for cumulative culture in primates and the vast cumulative cultural achievements of humans was acknowledged previously in this review. Can this difference be explained at the level of the social learning processes available? Just a handful of studies have so far sought to examine chimpanzee responses in experimental scenarios that offer some opportunities for cumulative cultural change. In the first exploration, Marshall-Pescini & Whiten (2008b) presented young chimpanzees with boxes containing nuts and honey and modeled opening a small hatch in each box, dipping in a small stick, and then licking the honey off it. This action was shown to be socially learned through contrasts with an asocial control sample. Participants were then shown a more complex option that involved inserting the tool into a space to release the lid so that all of the honey and nuts inside became available. Chimpanzee subjects did not learn the complex option once they had acquired the simpler dipping method, whereas two control individuals who had not acquired the dipping method did manage, by exploration, to arrive at the more complex technique. Young children presented with the same scenarios (but gaining prizes other than honey and nuts) did tend to show cultural ratcheting, first learning the simple probing technique and then building on this knowledge to master the levering method of opening the lid (Whiten et al. 2009). Thus what appeared to be limiting the chimpanzees was a marked conservatism, which also has been described in studies in which chimpanzees stuck to inefficient methods despite the presence of models displaying more efficient ones (Hrubesch et al. 2008).

Marshall-Pescini & Whiten (2008b) suggested that this conservatism might have been associated with a readiness to accept a satisficing payoff from the dipping technique. However, this hypothesis was not supported in a later study by Dean et al. (2012) in which chimpanzees and children (and capuchins) were presented with a puzzle box that offered scope for cumulative cultural progress through three levels, at each of which improved rewards could be gained by implementing progressively more challenging manipulations. Children typically progressed through more levels than did the other primates, and in particular, the primates did not benefit by learning from the rare conspecifics that succeeded at the higher levels; thus, the primates failed to display cumulation. In this respect the results concur with earlier ones documenting conservatism (outlined above). However, Dean et al. (2012) also implemented a condition in which participants could no longer obtain rewards at the lowest level. This condition clearly prevented any satisficing operations, yet most of the chimpanzees still failed to show cumulative progress despite occasional modeling of the higher-level techniques by other members of their group.

Dean et al. (2012) compared behavioral profiles of the species and found that children showed a number of behavioral differences to which superior achievements in cumulative progress might be attributed. These differences included spontaneous teaching, prosocial sharing of rewards, and a greater likelihood of matching the behavioral methods they saw successful children already using. It is not possible to discriminate which, if any, of these play a causal role; it may be that all act in concert to make the behavioral difference. To complicate the picture, some studies have experimentally manipulated these variables to test their importance. Caldwell & Millen (2009), for example, ran experiments in which small groups of young adults attempted to make paper planes that flew as far as possible, with potential cumulative cultural progress afforded by removing and adding new members to create chains of overlapping memberships. Information transfer was constrained in different conditions to allow only teaching, only imitative copying, or only emulation (because only the results of groups' actions were witnessed). It was found that chains operating under the latter constraint did as well as those in which teaching was offered or imitation of models was allowed. Similar results have been reported using a different paradigm (Zwinner & Thornton 2016). However, Wasielewski (2014) has argued that different results are to be expected with significantly more complex and challenging activities, and she has explored approaches that may confirm this hypothesis.

Reflexive Recognition of Transmission Processes

A distinctive way in which imitation has been studied in apes is the "Do-as-I-do" approach pioneered by Hayes & Hayes (1952). In this method, the ape first learns to attempt to copy what a trainer does via a set of training actions, upon a request such as "Do this," and is then tested with a battery of relatively novel actions. Custance et al. (1995) replicated the Hayes & Hayes (1952) study in a more rigorous, objectively coded fashion using a battery of 48 novel acts with two young chimpanzees; Call (2001) did likewise with an enculturated orangutan, recording 58% full imitations and 32% partial imitations of this substantial battery. What I emphasize here is that these apes could "learn the game," which required them to recognize what it is to imitate. Interestingly, several intensive efforts to train monkeys to do this have failed (see Whiten et al. 2004), suggesting that achievement of this reflexive recognition of the imitation process may be distinctive to the great ape mind. Young children do this, of course, in playing the "Simon says" game, which is effectively a "Do-as-I-do" procedure.

In the case of children, teaching perhaps comes into this general category. Whiten & Flynn (2010) and Dean et al. (2012) have noted that in the course of their experiments on social learning in groups of children, some children spontaneously began to teach other children what they had learned. Children thus not only come to benefit from imitating and being taught, but also explicitly recognize these processes and what they can achieve, and they apply the processes prosocially to other children. Chimpanzees can come to recognize at least the imitation side of this process.

Teaching

In countries with well-articulated educational systems, teaching looms large in conceptions of the processes whereby culture is transmitted. Informal teaching is often to be observed in the home and other segments of children's lives. However, over past decades anthropologists have often remarked on the lack of explicit teaching in hunter-gatherer societies, in which there are constant daily opportunities to learn simply by direct observation (reviewed in Whiten et al. 2003). It remains possible that the lack of explicit teaching may reflect a lack of systematic observation and quantification, and Hewlett et al. (2011) have argued as much in the context of their pioneering observations of the natural history of cultural transmission in the hunter-gatherers of the African Congo Basin. A broader conception of teaching converges with this newer picture (Kline 2015, Kline et al. 2013).

However, little comparable teaching has been described in wild chimpanzees, beyond an often patchy tolerance of youngsters as they become involved in activities such as nut cracking and are allowed to take and use their mother's hammer materials and nuts (Boesch 2012). This finding contrasts with the fact that evidence of teaching, in the functional sense of incurring a cost to support some aspects of development, exists among certain other animal taxa (Thornton & Raihani 2008), as illustrated in the structured ways that adult meerkat caretakers bring scorpions for pups to practice with, disabling and recovering the scorpions in ways adapted to the different stages of handling competence in the pups (Thornton & McAuliffe 2006). It may be that there is particular pressure on this kind of support for predatory species, such as felines and meerkats, whose young have to make a major developmental leap from being fed by their mothers to succeeding in the challenging pursuit of prey capture and killing. Hoppitt et al. (2008) suggest that by contrast, apes have well-articulated observational learning mechanisms and a long period of immaturity in which to learn skills that can be mastered in a more gradual stepwise fashion, such as opening difficult foods and fishing for invertebrate prey with tools.

CULTURAL CONTENTS

Much of the discussion of what makes human culture special focuses on the phenomenon of cumulative culture and the social learning processes that make it possible. However, a large part of what makes human and chimpanzee cultures look so different is surely the particular behavioral and material content of those cultures, which may profoundly affect the psychological nature of the cultural transmission processes themselves. For example, in language acquisition a child assimilates material with its own unique recursive and syntactic structure, semantics, and pragmatics; there is no direct counterpart in what a young chimpanzee assimilates. The material cultures of even those nomadic hunter-gatherers who can carry all their possessions on their back include such categories as medicines, multicomponent constructed tools, weapons and traps, clothing, fire, musical instruments, and jewelry and other adornments, together with all of the know-how that allows items to be made and their functions served. Aside from language, social customs may include nonverbal gestures and rituals, dance, music and song, religion, social customs and rules, and institutions such as marriage.

This is not to say that no overlaps in content exist between humans and other apes, but comparisons must be at an appropriate level of abstraction. Thus, at a very broad level, one can recognize a commonality between humans and chimpanzees in the possession of a material culture involving both a diversity of types of tool materials and a diversity of related technological functions. Within these functions one can further recognize more particular commonalities at the level of tool use for foraging, for comfort (e.g., leaf mats), and for hygiene (e.g., wipes for body fluids).

CONCLUDING DISCUSSION

Despite the millennia of human history over which we have shared the planet with our closest animal relative, until only a few decades ago we had scarcely any inkling that chimpanzees had the richness of cultural traditions that recent sustained fieldwork, coupled with scientific collaboration, has uncovered. Newly discovered putative traditions are regularly reported. Discoveries in Africa have been complemented by cultural diffusion experiments that have confirmed the social transmission capacities suggested by the field research, and in both these lines of research the chimpanzee studies have repeatedly pioneered approaches later followed by studies of other primate and nonprimate species, including a significant number with human children. Together, these studies have shown that chimpanzees and other apes have extensive, multiple-tradition cultures that shape significant parts of their lives and profoundly affect the nature of development, phenomena shared with our own species and thus pointing to an ancient ancestry. The same is true for numerous aspects of the underlying social learning processes outlined above and summarized in **Figure 1**.

However, I end by pointing out that developmental and comparative research has discovered that this is all part of a larger picture, one that delineates a cluster of sociocognitive features that underwrite humanity's remarkable evolutionary success, yet as for culture and social learning, foundations have been uncovered by primate research. The other pillars of this sociocognitive complex include mind reading (aka theory of mind), language, and egalitarian dispositions coupled with forms of cooperation, unprecedented in primates, that are crucial adaptations in the hunter-gatherer way of life (Whiten & Erdal 2012). Human cumulative culture supports each of these and is in turn facilitated by them. Roots of each can be discerned through recent primate research, but it is likely that it is the way in which the positive feedbacks among them create a uniquely deep social mind that has made our species such a formidable presence on the planet.

DISCLOSURE STATEMENT

The author is not aware of any affiliations, memberships, funding, or financial holdings that might be perceived as affecting the objectivity of this review.

ACKNOWLEDGMENTS

The author is grateful for the support of grant ID40128, "Exploring the Evolutionary Foundations of Cultural Complexity, Creativity and Trust," from the John Templeton Foundation during the writing of this review.

LITERATURE CITED

Aplin LM, Farine DR, Morand-Ferron J, Cockburn A, Thornton A, Sheldon BC. 2015a. Experimentally induced innovations lead to persistent culture via conformity in wild birds. *Nature* 518:538–41

Aplin LM, Farine DR, Morand-Ferron J, Cockburn A, Thornton A, Sheldon BC. 2015b. Counting conformity: evaluating the units of measurement in frequency-dependent social learning. *Anim. Behav.* 110:e5–8

Asch SE. 1956. Studies of independence and conformity: 1. A minority of one against a unanimous majority. *Psychol. Monogr.* 70:1–70

Atkinson Q. 2011. Phonemic diversity supports a serial founder effect model of language expansion from Africa. *Science* 332:346–49

Bellagamba F, Tomasello M. 1999. Re-enacting intended acts: comparing 12- and 18-month-olds. *Infant Behav. Dev.* 22:277–82

Berl R, Hewlett B. 2015. Cultural variation in the use of overimitation by the Aka and Ngandu of the Congo Basin. *PLOS ONE* 10:e0120180

Biro D, Inoue-Nakamura N, Tonooka R, Yamakoshi G, Sousa C, Matsuzawa T. 2003. Cultural innovation and transmission of tool use in wild chimpanzees: evidence from field experiments. *Anim. Cogn.* 6:213–23

Boesch C. 2012. *Wild Cultures*. Cambridge, UK: Cambridge Univ. Press

Boesch C, Tomasello M. 1998. Chimpanzee and human cultures. *Curr. Anthropol.* 39:591–614

Bonnie KE, Horner V, Whiten A, de Waal FBM. 2007. Spread of arbitrary customs among chimpanzees: a controlled experiment. *Proc. R. Soc. B* 274:367–72

Boyd R, Richerson PJ. 1985. *Culture and the Evolutionary Process*. Chicago: Univ. Chicago Press

Buttelmann D, Carpenter M, Call J, Tomasello M. 2007. Enculturated chimpanzees imitate rationally. *Dev. Sci.* 10:31–38

Buttelmann D, Carpenter M, Call J, Tomasello M. 2008. Rational tool use and tool choice in human infants and great apes. *Child Dev.* 79:609–26

Caldwell CA, Millen AE. 2009. Social learning mechanisms and cumulative cultural evolution: Is imitation necessary? *Psychol. Sci.* 20:1478–83

Call J. 2001. Body imitation in an enculturated orangutan (*Pongo pygmaeus*). *Cybern. Syst.* 32:97–119

Call J, Carpenter M, Tomasello M. 2005. Copying results and copying actions in the process of social learning: chimpanzees (*Pan troglodytes*) and human children (*Homo sapiens*). *Anim. Cogn.* 8:151–63

Call J, Tomasello M. 1994. The social learning of tool use by orangutans. *Hum. Evol.* 9:297–313

Call J, Tomasello M. 1995. The use of social information in the problem-solving of orangutans (*Pongo pygmaeus*) and human children (*Homo sapiens*). *J. Comp. Psychol.* 109:308–20

Carpenter M, Akhtar N, Tomasello M. 1998. Fourteen- through 18-month-old infants differentially imitate intentional and accidental actions. *Infant Behav. Dev.* 21:315–30

Carpenter M, Tomasello M, Savage-Rumbaugh S. 1995. Joint attention and imitative learning in children, chimpanzees and enculturated chimpanzees. *Soc. Dev.* 4:217–37

Claidière N, Whiten A. 2012. Integrating the study of conformity and culture in humans and non-human animals. *Psychol. Bull.* 138:126–45

Claidière N, Whiten A, Mareno MC, Messer EJE, Brosnan SF, et al. 2015. Selective and contagious prosocial resource donation in capuchin monkeys, chimpanzees and humans. *Sci. Rep.* 5:7631

Corriveau KH, Harris PL. 2010. Preschoolers (sometimes) defer to the majority in making simple perceptual judgments. *Dev. Psychol.* 46:437–45

Currie TE, Mace R. 2011. Mode and tempo in the evolution of socio-political organization: reconciling "Darwinian" and "Spencerian" evolutionary approaches in anthropology. *Philos. Trans. R. Soc. B* 366:1108–17

Custance DM, Whiten A, Bard KA. 1995. Can young chimpanzees (*Pan troglodytes*) imitate arbitrary actions? Hayes and Hayes 1952 revisited. *Behaviour* 132:837–59

Dawkins R. 2005. *The Ancestor's Tale*. London: Weidenfield & Nicolson

Dean LG, Kendal RL, Schapiro SJ, Thierry B, Laland KN. 2012. Identification of social and cognitive processes underlying human cumulative culture. *Science* 335:1114–18

Flynn EG, Whiten A. 2012. Experimental "microcultures" in young children: identifying biographic, cognitive and social predictors of information transmission. *Child Dev.* 83:911–25

Fuhrmann D, Ravignani A, Marshall-Pescini S, Whiten A. 2014. Synchrony and motor mimicking in chimpanzee observational learning. *Sci. Rep.* 4:5283

Galef BG Jr. 1990. Traditions in animals: field observations and laboratory analyses. In *Interpretation and Explanation in the Study of Behaviour: Interpretation, Intentionality and Communication*. Vol. 1: *Comparative Perspectives*, ed. M Bekoff, D Jamieson, pp. 74–95. Boulder, CO: Westview

Galef BG Jr., Whiten A. 2017. The comparative psychology of social learning. In *APA Handbook of Comparative Psychology*, ed. J Call. Washington, DC: Am. Psychol. Assoc. In press

Gergely G, Bekkering H, Kiraly I. 2002. Rational imitation in preverbal infants. *Nature* 415:755

Goodall J. 1986. *The Chimpanzees of Gombe*. Cambridge, MA: Belknap

Gruber T, Muller MN, Reynolds V, Wrangham R, Zuberbuhler K. 2011. Community-specific evaluation of tool affordances in wild chimpanzees. *Sci. Rep.* 1:128

Gruber T, Muller MN, Strimling P, Wrangham R, Zuberbuhler K. 2009. Wild chimpanzees rely on cultural knowledge to solve an experimental honey acquisition task. *Curr. Biol.* 19:1846–52

Hara Y, Imanishi T, Satta Y. 2012. Reconstructing the demographic history of the human lineage using whole-genome sequences from human and three great apes. *Genome Biol. Evol.* 4:1133–45

Harmand S, Lewis JE, Feibel CS, Lepre CJ, Prat S, et al. 2015. 3.3-Million-year-old stone tools from Lomekwi 3, West Turkana, Kenya. *Nature* 521:310–15

Harris PL. 2012. *Trusting What You're Told: How Children Learn From Others*. Cambridge, MA: Havard Univ. Press

Haun DB, Rekers Y, Tomasello M. 2012. Majority-biased transmission in chimpanzees and human children, but not orangutans. *Curr. Biol.* 22:727–31

Haun DBM, Rekers Y, Tomasello M. 2014. Children conform to the behavior of peers; other great apes stick with what they know. *Psychol. Sci.* 25:2160–67

Hayes KJ, Hayes C. 1952. Imitation in a home-reared chimpanzee. *J. Comp. Physiol. Psychol.* 45:450–59

Henrich J. 2015. *The Secret of Our Success: How Culture Is Driving Human Evolution, Domesticating Our Species and Making Us Smarter*. Princeton, NJ: Princeton Univ. Press

Henrich J, Gil-White FJ. 2001. The evolution of prestige: freely conferred deference as a mechanism for enhancing the benefits of cultural transmission. *Evol. Hum. Behav.* 22:165–96

Herrmann E, Call J, Hernandez-Loreda MV, Hare B, Tomasello M. 2007. Humans have evolved specialized skills of social cognition: the cultural intelligence hypothesis. *Science* 317:1360–66

Hewlett BS, Fouts HN, Boyette AH, Hewlett BL. 2011. Social learning among Congo Basin hunter-gatherers. *Philos. Trans. R. Soc. B* 366:1168–78

Hobaiter C, Poiso T, Zuberbühler K, Hoppit W, Gruber T. 2014. Social network analysis shows direct evidence for social learning of tool use in wild chimpanzees. *PLOS Biol.* 12:e1001960

Hoehl S, Zettersten M, Schleihauf H, Gratz S, Pauen S. 2014. The role of social interaction and pedagogical cues for eliciting and reducing overimitation in preschoolers. *J. Exp. Child Psychol.* 122:122–33

Hopper LM, Flynn EG, Wood LAN, Whiten A. 2010. Observational learning of tool use in children: investigating cultural spread through diffusion chains and learning mechanisms through ghost displays. *J. Exp. Child Psychol.* 106:82–97

Hopper LM, Lambeth SP, Schapiro SJ, Whiten A. 2008. Observational learning in chimpanzees and children studied through "ghost" conditions. *Proc. R. Soc. B* 275:835–40

Hopper LM, Lambeth SP, Schapiro SJ, Whiten A. 2015. The importance of witnessed agency in chimpanzee social learning of tool use. *Behav. Process.* 112:120–29

Hopper LM, Spiteri A, Lambeth SP, Schapiro SJ, Horner V, Whiten A. 2007. Experimental studies of traditions and underlying transmission processes in chimpanzees. *Anim. Behav.* 73:1021–32

Hoppitt WJE, Brown GE, Kendal R, Rendell L, Thornton A, et al. 2008. Lessons from animal teaching. *Trends Ecol. Evol.* 23:486–93

Hoppitt WJE, Laland KN. 2013. *Social Learning: An Introduction to Mechanisms, Methods and Models*. Princeton, NJ: Princeton Univ. Press

Horner V, Proctor D, Bonnie KE, Whiten A, de Waal FBM. 2010. Prestige affects cultural learning in chimpanzees. *PLOS ONE* 5:e10625

Horner V, Whiten A. 2005. Causal knowledge and imitation/emulation switching in chimpanzees (*Pan troglodytes*) and children (*Homo sapiens*). *Anim. Cogn.* 8:164–81

Horner V, Whiten A. 2007. Learning from others' mistakes? Limits on understanding of a trap-tube task by young chimpanzees and children. *J. Comp. Psychol.* 121:12–21

Horner V, Whiten A, Flynn E, de Waal FBM. 2006. Faithful replication of foraging techniques along cultural transmission chains by chimpanzees and children. *PNAS* 103:13878–83

Hrubesch C. Preuschoft S, van Schaik C. 2008. Skill mastery inhibits adoption of observed alternative solutions among chimpanzees (*Pan troglodytes*). *Anim. Cogn.* 12:209–16

Jordan P. 2015. *Technology as Human Social Tradition: Cultural Transmission Among Hunter-Gatherers*. Oakland: Univ. Calif. Press

Kamilar JM, Atkinson QD. 2014. Cultural assemblages show nested structure in humans and chimpanzees but not orangutans. *PNAS* 111:111–15

Kendal RM, Hopper LM, Whiten A, Brosnan SF, Lambeth SP, et al. 2015. Chimpanzees copy dominant and knowledgeable individuals: implications for cultural diversity. *Evol. Hum. Behav.* 36:65–72

Kenward B, Karlsson M, Persson J. 2011. Over-imitation is better explained by norm learning than by distorted causal learning. *Proc. R. Soc. B* 278:1239–46

Keupp S, Behne T, Rakoczy H. 2013. Why do children overimitate? Normativity is crucial. *J. Exp. Child Psychol.* 116:392–406

Kline MA. 2015. How to learn about teaching: an evolutionary framework for the study of teaching behaviour in humans and other animals. *Behav. Brain Sci.* 38:e31

Kline MA, Boyd R, Henrich J. 2013. Teaching and life history of cultural transmission in Fijian villages. *Hum. Nat.* 24:351–74

Krützen M, Willems EP, van Schaik CP. 2011. Culture and geographic variation in orangutan behavior. *Curr. Biol.* 21:1808–12

Langergraber KE, Boesch C, Inoue E, Inoue-Murayama M, Mitani JC, et al. 2011. Genetic and "cultural" similarity in chimpanzees. *Proc. R. Soc. B* 277:408–16

Levine RA. 1984. Properties of culture: an ethnographic view. In *Culture Theory: Essays on Mind, Self and Emotion*, ed. RA Schweder, RA Levine, pp. 67–87. Cambridge, UK: Cambridge Univ. Press

Luncz LV, Boesch C. 2014. Tradition over trend: Neighboring chimpanzee communities maintain differences in cultural behaviour despite frequent immigration of adult females. *Am. J. Primatol.* 76:649–57

Luncz LV, Wittig RM, Boesch C. 2015. Primate archaeology reveals cultural transmission patterns in wild chimpanzees (*Pan troglodytes verus*). *Philos. Trans. R. Soc. B* 370:20140348

Lycett SJ, Collard M, McGrew WC. 2010. Are behavioral differences among wild chimpanzee communities genetic or cultural? An assessment using tool-use data and phylogenetic methods. *Am. J. Phys. Anthropol.* 142:461–67

Lyons DE, Damrosch DH, Lin JK, Macris DM, Keil FC. 2011. The scope and limits of overimitation in the transmission of artefact culture. *Philos. Trans. R. Soc. B* 366:1158–67

Lyons DE, Young AG, Keil FC. 2007. The hidden structure of overimitation. *PNAS* 104:19751–56

Marshall-Pescini S, Whiten A. 2008a. Social learning of nut-cracking behaviour in East African sanctuary-living chimpanzees (*Pan troglodytes schweinfurthii*). *J. Comp. Psychol.* 122:186–94

Marshall-Pescini S, Whiten A. 2008b. Chimpanzees (*Pan troglodytes*) and the question of cumulative culture: an experimental approach. *Anim. Cogn.* 11:449–56

Matsuzawa T, Biro D, Humle T, Inoue-Nakamura N, Tonooka R, Yamakoshi G. 2001. Emergence of culture in wild chimpanzees: education by master-apprenticeship. In *Primate Origins of Human Cognition and Behaviour*, ed. T Matsuzawa, pp. 557–74. Berlin: Springer-Verlag

McGrew WC. 1992. *Chimpanzee Material Culture*. Cambridge, UK: Cambridge Univ. Press

McGuigan N, Makinson J, Whiten A. 2011. From over-imitation to super-copying: Adults imitate causally irrelevant aspects of tool use with higher fidelity than young children. *Br. J. Psychol.* 102:1–18

McGuigan N, Whiten A, Flynn E, Horner V. 2007. Imitation of causally-opaque versus causally-transparent tool use by 3- and 5-year-old children. *Cogn. Dev.* 22:353–64

Meltzoff AN. 1988. Infant imitation after a 1-week delay: long-term memory for novel acts and multiple stimuli. *Dev. Psychol.* 24:470–76

Meltzoff AN. 1995. Understanding the intentions of others: re-enactment of intended acts by 18-month-old children. *Dev. Psychol.* 31:838–50

Mesoudi A, Whiten A. 2008. The multiple roles of cultural transmission experiments in understanding human cultural evolution. *Philos. Trans. R. Soc. B* 363:3489–501

Mesoudi A, Whiten A, Laland KN. 2006. Towards a unified science of cultural evolution. *Behav. Brain Sci.* 29:329–83

Morgan TJH, Laland KN, Harris PL. 2015. The development of adaptive conformity in young children: effects of uncertainty and consensus. *Dev. Sci.* 18:511–24

Nagell K, Olguin RS, Tomasello M. 1993. Processes of social learning in the tool use of chimpanzees (*Pan troglodytes*) and human children (*Homo sapiens*). *J. Comp. Psychol.* 107:174–86

Nielsen M, Haun D. 2016. Why developmental psychology is incomplete without comparative and cross-cultural perspectives. *Philos. Trans. R. Soc. B* 371:20150071

Nielsen M, Mushin I, Tomaselli K, Whiten A. 2014. Where culture takes hold: "overimitation" and its flexible deployment in Western, Aboriginal and Bushmen children. *Child Dev.* 85:2169–84

Nielsen M, Simcock G, Jenkins L. 2008. The effect of social engagement on 24-month-olds' imitation from live and televised models. *Dev. Sci.* 5:722–31

Nielsen M, Subiaul F, Galef BG Jr., Zentall TR, Whiten A. 2012. Social learning in humans and non-human animals: theoretical and empirical dissections. *J. Comp. Psychol.* 126:109–13

Nielsen M, Tomaselli K. 2010. Over-imitation in Kalahari Bushman children and the origins of human cultural cognition. *Psychol. Sci.* 21:729–36

Nielsen M, Widjojo E. 2011. Failure to find over-imitation in captive orangutans (*Pongo pygmaeus*): implications for our understanding of cross-generation information transfer. In *Developmental Psychology*, ed. J Håkansson, pp. 153–67. New York: Nova Sci.

Nisbett R, Peng K, Choi I, Norenzayan A. 2001. Culture and systems of thought: holistic versus analytic cognition. *Psychol. Rev.* 108:291–310

Pagel M. 2012. *Wired for Culture: Origins of the Human Social Mind.* New York: Norton

Price EE, Lambeth SP, Schapiro SJ, Whiten A. 2009. A potent effect of observational learning on chimpanzee tool construction. *Proc. R. Soc. B* 276:3377–83

Price EE, Wood LA, Whiten A. 2016. Adaptive cultural transmission biases in children and nonhuman primates. *Infant. Behav. Dev.* In press

Rakoczy H, Hamann K, Warneken F, Tomasello M. 2010. Bigger knows better: Young children selectively learn rule games from adults rather than from peers. *Br. J. Dev. Psychol.* 28(4):785–98

Rawlings B, Davila-Ross M, Boysen ST. 2014. Semi-wild chimpanzees open hard-shelled fruits differently across communities. *Anim. Cogn.* 17:891–99

Sanz C, Call J, Morgan D. 2009. Design complexity in termite-fishing tools of chimpanzees (*Pan troglodytes*). *Biol. Lett.* 5:293–96

Semaw S, Rogers MJ, Quade J, Renne PR, Butler RF, et al. 2003. 2.6-Million-year-old stone tools and associated bones from OGS-6 and OGS-7, Gona, Afar, Ethiopia. *J. Hum. Evol.* 45:169–77

Stout D. 2011. Stone toolmaking and the evolution of human culture and cognition. *Philos. Trans. R. Soc. B* 366:1050–59

Tennie C, Call J, Tomasello M. 2006. Push or pull: imitation versus emulation in great apes and human children. *Ethology* 112:1159–69

Tennie C, Call J, Tomasello M. 2009. Ratcheting up the ratchet: on the evolution of cumulative culture. *Philos. Trans. R. Soc. B* 364(1528):2405–15

Tennie C, Call J, Tomasello M. 2010. Evidence for emulation in chimpanzees in social settings using the floating peanut task. *PLOS ONE* 5:e10544

Thornton A, McAuliffe K. 2006. Teaching in wild meerkats. *Science* 313:227–29

Thornton A, Raihani NJ. 2008. The evolution of teaching. *Anim. Behav.* 75:1823–36

Tomasello M. 1990. Cultural transmission in the tool use and communicatory signaling of chimpanzees? In *"Language" and Intelligence in Monkeys and Apes: Comparative Developmental Perspectives*, ed. ST Parker, K Gibson, pp. 274–311. Cambridge, UK: Cambridge Univ. Press

Tomasello M. 1998. Emulation learning and cultural learning. *Behav. Brain Sci.* 21:703–4

Tomasello M, Call J. 1997. *Primate Cognition.* Oxford, UK: Oxford Univ. Press

Tomasello M, Carpenter M. 2005. The emergence of social cognition in three young chimpanzees. *Monogr. Soc. Res. Child Dev.* 70(1):vii–132

Tomasello M, Davis-Dasilva M, Camak L, Bard K. 1987. Observational learning of tool-use by young chimpanzees. *Hum. Evol.* 2:175–83

Tomasello M, Kruger AE, Ratner H. 1993a. Cultural learning. *Behav. Brain Sci.* 16:595–652

Tomasello M, Savage-Rumbaugh S, Kruger AC. 1993b. Imitative learning of actions on objects by children, chimpanzees and enculturated chimpanzees. *Child Dev.* 64:1688–705

Vale GL, Flynn EG, Lambeth SP, Schapiro SJ, Kendal RL. 2014. Public information use in chimpanzees (*Pan troglodytes*) and children (*Homo sapiens*). *J. Comp. Psychol.* 128:215–23

van de Waal E, Borgeaud C, Whiten A. 2013. Potent social learning and conformity shape a wild primate's foraging decisions. *Science* 340(6131):483–85

van Leeuwen EJC, Call J, Haun DBM. 2014a. Human children rely more on social information than chimpanzees do. *Biol. Lett.* 10(11):20140487

van Leeuwen EJC, Cronin K, Haun DBM. 2014b. A group-specific arbitrary tradition in chimpanzees (*Pan troglodytes*). *Anim. Cogn.* 17(6):1421–25

van Leeuwen EJC, Cronin KA, Haun DBM, Mundry R, Bodamer MD. 2012. Neighbouring chimpanzee communities show different preferences in social grooming behaviour. *Proc. R. Sci. B* 279:4362–67

van Leeuwen EJC, Haun DBM. 2014. Conformity without majority? The case for demarcating social from majority influences. *Anim. Behav.* 96:187–94

van Schaik CP, Ancrenaz M, Borgen G, Galdikas B, Knott CD, et al. 2003. Orangutan cultures and the evolution of material culture. *Science* 299:102–5

Walker MB, Andrade MG. 1996. Conformity in the Asch test as a function of age. *Br. J. Soc. Psychol.* 136:367–72

Want SC, Harris PL. 2002. How do children ape? Applying concepts from the study of non-human primates to the developmental study of "imitation" in children. *Dev. Sci.* 5:1–14

Wasielewski H. 2014. Imitation is necessary for cumulative cultural evolution in an unfamiliar, opaque task. *Hum. Nat.* 25:161–79

Whiten A. 2005. The second inheritance system of chimpanzees and humans. *Nature* 437:52–55

Whiten A. 2010. Ape behaviour and the origins of human culture. In *Mind the Gap: Tracing the Origins of Human Universals*, ed. P Kappeler, J Silk, pp. 429–50. Berlin: Springer-Verlag

Whiten A. 2011. The scope of culture in chimpanzees, humans and ancestral apes. *Philos. Trans. R. Soc. B* 366:997–1007

Whiten A. 2012. Primate social learning, traditions and culture. In *The Evolution of Primate Societies*, ed. J Mitani, J Call, P Kappeler, R Palombit, J Silk, pp. 681–99. Chicago: Univ. Chicago Press

Whiten A. 2013. Social cognition: making us smart, or sometimes making us dumb? Overimitation, conformity, non-conformity and the transmission of culture in ape and child. In *Navigating the Social World: What Infants, Children, and Other Species Can Teach Us*, ed. M Banaji, S Gelman, pp. 150–54. New York: Oxford Univ. Press

Whiten A. 2015. Experimental studies illuminate the cultural transmission of percussive technology in *Homo* and *Pan. Philos. Trans. R. Soc. B* 370:20140359

Whiten A, Caldwell CA, Mesoudi A. 2016. Cultural diffusion in humans and other animals. *Curr. Opin. Psychol.* 8:15–21

Whiten A, Custance DM, Gomez JC, Teixidor P, Bard KA. 1996. Imitative learning of artificial fruit processing in children (*Homo sapiens*) and chimpanzees (*Pan troglodytes*). *J. Comp. Psychol.* 110:3–14

Whiten A, Erdal D. 2012. The human socio-cognitive niche and its evolutionary origins. *Philos. Trans. R. Soc. B* 367:2119–29

Whiten A, Flynn EG. 2010. The transmission and evolution of experimental "microcultures" in groups of young children. *Dev. Psychol.* 46:1694–709

Whiten A, Goodall J, McGrew WC, Nishida T, Reynolds V, et al. 1999. Cultures in chimpanzees. *Nature* 399:682–85

Whiten A, Goodall J, McGrew WC, Nishida T, Reynolds V, et al. 2001. Charting cultural variation in chimpanzees. *Behaviour* 138:1489–525

Whiten A, Ham R. 1992. On the nature and evolution of imitation in the animal kingdom: reappraisal of a century of research. *Adv. Study Behav.* 21:239–83

Whiten A, Hinde RA, Stringer CB, Laland KN. 2011. Culture evolves. *Philos. Trans. R. Soc. B* 366:938–48

Whiten A, Horner V, de Waal FBM. 2005a. Conformity to cultural norms of tool use in chimpanzees. *Nature* 437:737–40

Whiten A, Horner V, Litchfield CA, Marshall-Pescini S. 2004. How do apes ape? *Learn. Behav.* 32:36–52

Whiten A, Horner V, Marshall-Pescini SRJ. 2003. Cultural panthropology. *Evol. Anthropol.* 12:92–105

Whiten A, Horner V, Marshall-Pescini S. 2005b. Selective imitation in child and chimpanzee: a window on the construal of others' actions. In *Perspectives on Imitation: From Neuroscience to Social Science*, ed. S Hurley, N Chater, pp. 263–83. Cambridge, MA: MIT Press

Whiten A, McGuigan H, Hopper LM, Marshall-Pescini S. 2009. Imitation, over-imitation, emulation and the scope of culture for child and chimpanzee. *Philos. Trans. R. Soc. B* 364:2417–28

Whiten A, Mesoudi A. 2008. An experimental science of culture: animal social diffusion experiments. *Philos. Trans. R. Soc. B* 363:3477–88

Whiten A, Spiteri A, Horner V, Bonnie KE, Lambeth SP, et al. 2007. Transmission of multiple traditions within and between chimpanzee groups. *Curr. Biol.* 17:1038–43

Whiten A, van Schaik CP. 2007. The evolution of animal "cultures" and social intelligence. *Philos. Trans. R. Soc. B* 362:603–20

Wood LA, Kendal RL, Flynn EG. 2013. Whom do children copy? Model-based biases in social learning. *Dev. Rev.* 33:341–46

Yerkes RM. 1916. *The Mental Life of Monkeys and Apes.* Delmar, NY: Scholars' Facsim. Repr.

Zmyj N, Buttelmann D, Carpenter M, Daum MM. 2010. The reliability of a model influences 14-month-olds' imitation. *J. Exp. Child Psychol.* 106(4):208–20

Zmyj N, Daum MM, Prinz W, Nielsen M, Aschersleben G. 2012. Fourteen-month-olds' imitation of differently aged models. *Infant Child Dev.* 21(3):250–66

Zwinner E, Thornton A. 2016. Cognitive requirements of cumulative culture: Teaching is useful but not essential. *Sci. Rep.* 5:16781

Survival of the Friendliest: *Homo sapiens* Evolved via Selection for Prosociality

Brian Hare

Department of Evolutionary Anthropology and Center for Cognitive Neuroscience, Duke University, Durham, North Carolina 27708; email: b.hare@duke.edu

Annu. Rev. Psychol. 2017. 68:155–86

First published online as a Review in Advance on October 12, 2016

The *Annual Review of Psychology* is online at psych.annualreviews.org

This article's doi: 10.1146/annurev-psych-010416-044201

Keywords

cognitive evolution, domestication, human evolution, self-domestication, social cognition

Abstract

The challenge of studying human cognitive evolution is identifying unique features of our intelligence while explaining the processes by which they arose. Comparisons with nonhuman apes point to our early-emerging cooperative-communicative abilities as crucial to the evolution of all forms of human cultural cognition, including language. The human self-domestication hypothesis proposes that these early-emerging social skills evolved when natural selection favored increased in-group prosociality over aggression in late human evolution. As a by-product of this selection, humans are predicted to show traits of the domestication syndrome observed in other domestic animals. In reviewing comparative, developmental, neurobiological, and paleoanthropological research, compelling evidence emerges for the predicted relationship between unique human mentalizing abilities, tolerance, and the domestication syndrome in humans. This synthesis includes a review of the first a priori test of the self-domestication hypothesis as well as predictions for future tests.

Contents

"Man in many respects may be compared with those animals which have long been domesticated."

—Charles Darwin (1871)

INTRODUCTION

Darwin viewed the evolution of human intelligence and morality as the greatest challenge for his theory of evolution through natural selection (Darwin 1871). This remains the case today (MacLean et al. 2012). Our language and cultural cognition allows for cooperation and technology more complex than anything seen in nonhumans, yet our neurobiology, psychology, and genome are remarkably similar to other apes (Somel et al. 2013). A complete theory of human cognitive evolution needs to explain how these shared traits evolved into new forms of human cognition. To meet Darwin's challenge, we must identify derived cognitive features that evolved in our lineage and support our unique phenotype. Then we must identify the process by which these traits arose (Hare 2007, 2011). Adding to this challenge are discoveries suggesting that at least 10 different species evolved within the genus *Homo*. Modern theories of human cognitive evolution must now contend with growing evidence that *Homo sapiens* is just one among many human species that evolved. It is no longer enough to point out what makes us human. We must also determine what allowed our species to outlast as many as five other large-brained human species that shared the planet with us, some perhaps until as recently as 27 kya (Wood & Boyle 2016).

    This article reviews the latest research suggesting that early-emerging cooperative-communicative skills are responsible for unique features of human cognition and that our psychology evolved in large part due to selection for prosociality (i.e., positive but potentially selfishly motivated acts as opposed to antisocial interactions; Eisenberg et al. 1983). Comparisons of mentalizing skills between apes reveal that among apes, only human infants develop cooperative-communicative skills that facilitate human forms of cultural cognition; however, domestic dogs

kya: thousands of years ago

possess some social skills that resemble those seen in human infants. Research with experimentally domesticated foxes and bonobos shows how selection for prosociality can lead to increases in the cooperative-communicative flexibility observed in dogs and infants. This comparative developmental work provides the basis for the self-domestication hypothesis, which proposes that unique human psychology evolved as part of a larger domestication syndrome that converges with other domesticated animals.

HSD: human self-domestication hypothesis

The human self-domestication hypothesis (HSD) draws on comparative, developmental, fossil, and neurobiological evidence to show that late human evolution was dominated by selection for intragroup prosociality over aggression. As a result, modern humans possess traits consistent with the syndrome associated with domestication in other animals (**Table 1**). The HSD suggests this selective pressure also led to enhanced cooperation in intergroup conflicts. The hypothesis proposes that the reduced emotional reactivity that results from self-domestication and increased self-control created a unique form of human tolerance allowing the expression of more flexible social skills only observed in modern humans. Expanded developmental windows like those seen in domesticated animals allow this unique form of human tolerance and social cognition to develop and left *H. sapiens* as the last human standing (**Figure 1**).

PAN VERSUS *HOMO* SOCIAL UNDERSTANDING

Our ability to mentalize, or attribute mental states to others, is the foundation of cultural cognition (Herrmann et al. 2007). Humans develop the ability to recognize what others perceive, feel, intend, and know. Children begin in infancy to recognize that others can have mental states and even false beliefs that can differ from their own or reality. As adults, we rely on our ability to infer others' unobservable thoughts based on observable social cues and context. Our ability to reason about the minds of others allows for everything from imitation to deception, group coordination, teaching, and language acquisition (Seyfarth & Cheney 2014, Tomasello 2009b). Given the central role of these skills in human social cognition, tremendous energy has been focused on testing whether they are shared with other animals or are a derived feature of human cognition (Hare 2011).

Apes Take Others' Perspectives and Cooperate Flexibly

Beginning in the 1970s, chimpanzees (*Pan troglodytes*) quickly became central to studies of mental attribution because they provided a powerful phylogenetic test. The skills we share with chimpanzees were probably present in our last common ancestor, but the skills found only in humans help explain our explosive evolutionary success.

Initial research on chimpanzee theory of mind was as methodologically flawed as it was pioneering. It was only after researchers began taking an ecological approach to cognition that major advances were made in our understanding of chimpanzee mentalizing (Hare 2001, Whiten 2013). Chimpanzees failed to solve visual perspective-taking problems by cooperating and communicating with humans. However, they solved similar problems when placed in competition against each other. A series of competitive experiments show that chimpanzees are skilled at taking the perspective of others based on their current and previous perceptual experience (Hare 2011).

This led to more powerful methods using larger samples that also showed these skills in noncompetitive contexts (MacLean & Hare 2012). These spontaneous measures of social cognition ruled out the potential for simple behavior reading or learning within the experiment (Hare 2011; although see Povinelli & Vonk 2004).

Several studies have suggested that chimpanzees understand what others know, but there remains no compelling evidence for explicit false belief understanding in any animal, including great

Table 1 Evidence for domestication syndrome in modern humans

	Dog versus wolf[a]	Experimental fox versus control fox[a]	Bonobo versus chimpanzee[a]	Holocene humans versus Lower Paleolithic humans
Aggression	Lower-intensity inter- and intragroup aggression in feral dogs	Experimental but not control foxes are nonaggressive toward humans	Lower intensity inter- and intragroup aggression in bonobos	Intragroup tolerance allows and is favored due to demographic pressure in Holocene humans (Cieri et al. 2014, Henrich 2015)
Physiology	Dogs show a muted stress response when interacting with humans	Higher basal serotonin and lower corticosteroids in experimental foxes	Bonobos have more a passive coping response to social stress	Holocene humans exhibit morphologically inferred reductions in neonatal androgens and pubertal testosterone levels and increased brain serotonin and oxytocin availability (Cieri et al. 2014, Nelson et al. 2011)
Morphology	Dogs show reduced cranial capacity and depigmentation of the coat	Experimental foxes show a feminized skull and depigmentation of the coat	Bonobos show reduced cranial capacity, feminized faces, and depigmentation of lips and tail tufts	Holocene humans exhibit a modest reduction in cranial capacity, feminized faces, globular cranial development, and depigmentation of the sclera (Cieri et al. 2014, Hublin et al. 2015, Tomasello et al. 2007)
Prosocial behavior	Dogs are more attracted to humans than to conspecifics	Experimental foxes are more attracted to and interested in playing and interacting with humans as adults	Bonobos exhibit more play and sociosexual behavior as adults, voluntarily share food, and are more food tolerant	Holocene humans exhibit extreme levels of intragroup food sharing, helping, and social bonding (Kramer 2014, Warneken 2015)
Expanded developmental window	Period of socialization with humans begins earlier and lasts longer in dogs; dogs retain the juvenile vocal repertoire into adulthood	Period of socialization with humans begins earlier and lasts longer in experimental foxes; experimental foxes retain the juvenile vocal repertoire into adulthood	Nonreproductive sociosexual behaviors that create tolerance emerge early and last throughout adulthood in bonobos; cognitive skills related to spatial memory and social inhibition exhibit delayed development in bonobos	Holocene humans exhibit early-emerging social cognition and graded brain development with extreme delays in synaptic pruning of cortical regions (Casey & Caudle 2013, Somel et al. 2009, Wobber et al. 2014)
Social cognition	Dogs are more sensitive to human social cues	Experimental foxes are more sensitive to human social cues	Bonobos attend to eyes and exploit a human's gaze more and show increased cooperative flexibility	Holocene humans exhibit increases in cooperative communication, cultural ratcheting, and coordinated defense against out-groups, as well as expanded social networks (Cieri et al. 2014, Hare 2011)

[a]Nonhuman comparisons are based on Hare et al. (2012).

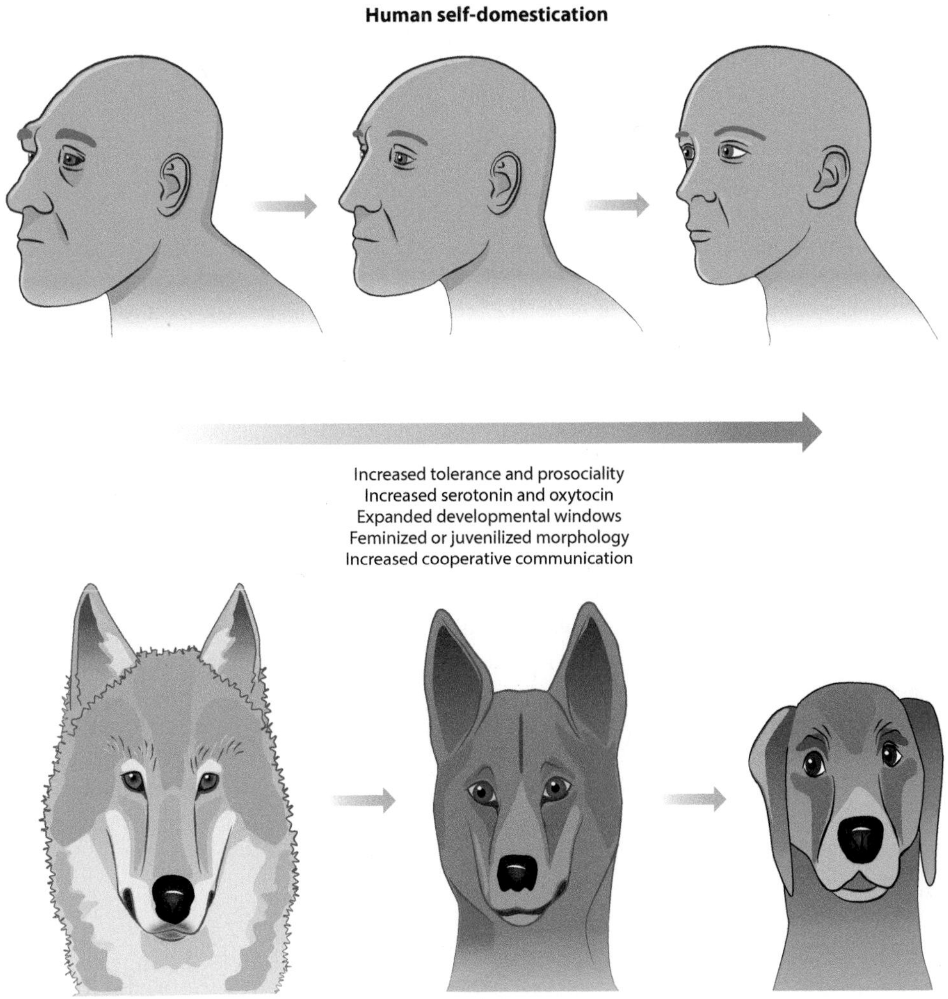

Human self-domestication

Increased tolerance and prosociality
Increased serotonin and oxytocin
Expanded developmental windows
Feminized or juvenilized morphology
Increased cooperative communication

Figure 1

Homo sapiens evolved, in part, as a result of selection for increased in-group prosociality during the Paleolithic, leading to a variety of morphological, physiological, and cognitive changes also observed in domestic animals such as *Canis familiaris*.

apes (Hare 2011, Martin & Santos 2016). Further studies have shown that, in many contexts, chimpanzees behave similarly to human children when they attribute intentions to others. For example, chimpanzees are more patient with an experimenter who is unable to share food than with one who is clearly unwilling (Call et al. 2004).

These social cognitive skills are also applied flexibly to a number of cooperative situations. Chimpanzees can solve novel instrumental problems that require cooperation and helping (Hare & Tan 2012, Melis et al. 2010). They know when they need to recruit help, which potential helper is most skilled, and what leverage they have to negotiate between equal and unequal payoffs (Melis et al. 2006a, 2008, 2009). Chimpanzees are also capable of taking different roles in collaborative tasks (Melis & Tomasello 2013).

Taken together, chimpanzees are flexible in assessing what others perceive and intend. Although chimpanzees are skilled cooperators and take other's perspectives in noncompetitive contexts, it was initially easier to demonstrate many of their theory of mind skills in competitive tasks (Hare 2011).

Only Human Apes Cooperatively Communicate

Despite the social flexibility of chimpanzees, there are meaningful gaps in their understanding of and tolerance for others. Several studies show that, although chimpanzees can cooperate or communicate, they struggle to do both (Bullinger et al. 2014, Herrmann & Tomasello 2006, Melis et al. 2009). Central to this phenomenon is their inability to spontaneously and flexibly use gestures to find hidden food (Hare 2011). Human infants begin using other's gestures and producing them in their first year of life. Infants become part of the cultural world of adults by developing an understanding of the intention behind novel and arbitrary gestures. In contrast, while nonhuman apes can slowly learn to use cooperative-communicative gestures, it is extremely difficult for them to generalize what they learn to a new or arbitrary gestural signal (Call et al. 1998, Hare & Tomasello 2005b, Herrmann et al. 2007, MacLean & Hare 2015a; although see De Waal et al. 2008). This limitation is made worse by the inability of chimpanzees to remain tolerant during cooperative activities. Although chimpanzees are skilled at using other chimpanzees as social tools, cooperation breaks down when the reward for joint effort becomes easily monopolized (MacLean & Hare 2013). Chimpanzees are constrained in their ability to inhibit intolerance toward potential cooperative partners even when they know they cannot solve a problem alone. Only a small minority of chimpanzee dyads within a group are tolerant enough to work for sharable food and no dyad can cooperate once rewards require active sharing or turn taking (Hare et al. 2007, Melis et al. 2006b). This intolerance and inflexibility in cooperative-communicative contexts likely prevent chimpanzees from sharing intentions and building on previous innovations in a process known as cultural ratcheting (Hare 2011).

THE DOMESTICATION OF DOG SOCIAL COGNITION

Domestic dogs are more skillful at using human gestures than nonhuman apes (Hare et al. 2002). Dogs follow the direction of a human gaze or point to locate hidden food or toys. If a human points to one of two locations, dogs are more likely to search where a human has indicated. Dogs can even spontaneously use novel and arbitrary gestures to help direct their search for objects or food. Several controls rule out the possibility that these searches in response to human gestures are reflexive or based on olfactory cues (Hare & Tomasello 2005b). Another similarity between dogs and infants is that both commit the A not B search error when directed by a human in the classic Piagetian task. Like human children in this task, dogs search in a hiding location that has repeatedly been baited in the past over a new location they observe being baited (Topál et al. 2009). Dogs are also the only nonhumans capable of fast mapping. In a way similar to the way young children learn words, several border collies have acquired hundreds of object labels using the principle of exclusion after single interactions with each new toy (Kaminski et al. 2004). Dogs seem to understand the cooperative-communicative intent of human signals in ways resembling those of the youngest human infants. This raises the question of how such a distantly related species can show skills that are crucial to human social cognitive development (Kaminski & Marshall-Pescini 2014). Comparisons of canids have revealed an important process by which social cognition evolves.

Dogs Are Wolves Prepared to Cooperatively Communicate

Dogs do not need intensive exposure to humans to begin using our gestures. Dog puppies also show skill at using basic human gestures (Hare et al. 2002). Although variance exists among individual dogs, as a species, dogs rely on human gestures even as puppies (Hare et al. 2010, Stewart et al. 2015, Wobber et al. 2009). Dogs did not inherit this early-emerging pattern from wolves. The skills of wolves at reading human gestures are more similar to those of nonhuman apes than to those of dogs. To develop skills in reading human gestures, wolves require intensive human socialization during a short critical period; as the window of socialization closes, they show little skill at understanding humans without explicit training as adults (Gacsi et al. 2005, Hare et al. 2002, Viranyi et al. 2008). Unlike dogs and infants, wolves do not commit the socially mediated A not B error (Topál et al. 2009). The independence of wolves from humans also means that when faced with an impossible task, they continue to try to solve the problem without help, whereas dogs quickly look to a human for help (Miklósi et al. 2003).

Foxes Selected for Friendliness Cooperatively Communicate

Because the early-emerging skill at reading gestures is not observed in wolves, the unusual social skills of dogs probably appeared during domestication (Hare et al. 2010). This hypothesis was tested by examining the cooperative-communicative abilities of an experimental line of foxes that had been intensively selected to be attracted to and nonaggressive toward people for 45 generations (Trut 1999). The experimental line was compared to a control line bred randomly for how they respond to humans. As a result of this selection, the experimental line is highly prosocial toward humans and exhibits a suite of phenotypic traits known as the domestication syndrome (**Table 1**). In comparison to the control line, the experimental foxes show the expected increases in approach toward humans. However, they also show a high frequency of traits not intentionally selected, including physiological, morphological, developmental, and behavioral changes also seen in domestic animals. This domestication syndrome includes increased brain serotonin levels and reductions in hypothalamic-pituitary-adrenal axis reactivity. Morphologically, the experimental foxes show increased frequencies of piebald coats, star mutations (white spots on the forehead), shorter muzzles, feminized faces, floppy ears, and curly or shortened tails (Trut et al. 2009). Developmentally, most traits in the experimental foxes appear to relate to expanded developmental windows. Experimenters can socialize experimental foxes earlier in development and the period of socialization remains open for much longer (i.e., similar to that of dogs) (Belyaev et al. 1985). Adult experimental foxes use juvenilized vocalizations and social behaviors such as tail wagging far more frequently when approached by humans than adult control foxes do (Gogoleva et al. 2008). When tested on the same cognitive measures of cooperative-communication used with apes, dogs, and wolves, fox kits from the experimental line are more skilled than same-age control kits. The experimental foxes spontaneously use basic human gestures in two different paradigms and perform similarly to dog puppies of the same age. Controls demonstrate that the experimental and control foxes are similarly motivated even though only the experimental line responded to human gestures. Although the experimental line was never selected (or even evaluated) on the basis of their cooperative-communicative abilities with humans, experimental kits perform like dog puppies when responding to human gestures (Hare et al. 2005).

The foxes' performance with human gestures supports the hypothesis that dogs' social skills evolved not only during domestication but also as a result of it. The fox experiment demonstrates that selection on emotional reactivity changes not only temperament but also a suite of unrelated phenotypic traits as a correlated by-product of this selection. The more flexible skills of cooperating and communicating with humans probably represent another of the by-products of this selection for friendliness. Foxes, like most mammals, use the social cues of conspecifics, but due to selection for prosocial interactions with humans, these old cognitive skills are applied in a new interaction with a new social partner (Hare & Tomasello 2005a).

Less reactive temperament likely replaced fear with an attraction to humans as selection acted on developmental pathways. Shifts in development, especially early in fetal development, can alter emotional reactivity and are thought to create a cascade of unselected consequences throughout the phenotype (Price & Langen 1992, West-Eberhard 2003, Wilkins et al. 2014). For example, the neural crest hypothesis suggests that the domestication syndrome is a result of changes in the migration pattern of melanocytes during neural crest formation, which simultaneously affects neurohormone levels, pigmentation, and morphology early in development (Wilkins et al. 2014), although not in a universal pattern across domestic mammals (Sanchez-Villagra et al. 2016).

Dog Self-Domestication

Based on the fox findings, it might be that dog cognition also evolved as a by-product of selection on emotional reactivity. However, in the case of dog evolution, natural selection acted on the temperament of wolves. Wolves with a temperament allowing them to approach human settlements showed higher reproductive success and favored self-domestication (as do species adapting to urban environments today; Ditchkoff et al. 2006). A population of wolves able to exploit the new niche of scavenging food remains and feces became more tolerant of humans and could be discriminated from other wolves due to morphological traits associated with the domestication syndrome. This new interaction with humans allowed old cognitive abilities to be expressed in a new context and resulted in more flexible social problem solving with humans. As the constraint of temperament was lifted, heritable variance in these newly revealed social skills may have been targeted by selection (Wobber et al. 2009). Thus began the most successful interspecific cooperative-communicative relationship in mammalian evolutionary history (Hare et al. 2010, Hare & Woods 2013; although see Udell et al. 2010). This led to a bond so strong that exogenous administration of oxytocin in dogs also modulates increases in mutual gaze, physical contact, and endogenous oxytocin expression in the humans with which they interact (Nagasawa et al. 2015). Not only have the emotional systems of dogs evolved but they have also hijacked our emotional systems for at least 15,000 years (MacLean & Hare 2015b).

BONOBO SELF-DOMESTICATION

The experimental foxes and dog self-domestication both imply that natural selection can lead to increases in prosocial over aggressive behavior, which can in turn lead to domestication syndrome (**Table 1**). The self-domestication hypothesis predicts that natural selection would also have shaped other species for increases in prosociality. Bonobos (*Pan paniscus*), one of our two closest living relatives, have been identified as a likely candidate for self-domestication (Wrangham & Pilbeam 2002).

Sexual Selection of Friendlier Male Apes

Bonobos differ from chimpanzees in their aggressive behavior (Hare et al. 2012). No bonobo has ever been observed to kill another bonobo (although for a potential exception see Wilson et al. 2014). Unlike chimpanzees, male bonobos do not coerce females, commit infanticide, or target their own mothers for aggression. Also unlike chimpanzees, male bonobos do not form coalitions with one another within their groups but instead rely on their mother's status to gain access to females (Surbeck et al. 2011). Finally, unlike chimpanzees, male bonobos do not participate in border patrols or lethal raids into neighboring territories.

Hare et al. (2012) proposed that male bonobos evolved to be more prosocial through sexual selection. Living in a richer and more predictable ecology, unrelated female bonobos formed bonds that allowed them to respond to male aggression in a way that female chimpanzees cannot. Although wild female chimpanzees rarely support other females when they are targeted by aggressive males, similar coercion by male bonobos is met by female coalitionary defense (Tokuyama & Furuichi 2016). Similarly, female bonobos do not tolerate male aggression toward juveniles and infants (Hare & Yamamoto 2015, Walker & Hare 2016). According to the self-domestication hypothesis, bonobos evolved to be less aggressive because females were able to express a preference for less aggressive males.

A Priori Tests of Bonobo Self-Domestication

After Wrangham & Pilbeam (2002) initially proposed that bonobos could be a candidate for self-domestication, a number of a priori tests examined whether derived features of the bonobo phenotype fit the expected pattern of domestication syndrome (**Table 1**).

Hare et al. (2012) reviewed the evidence that differences between bonobo and chimpanzee prosocial behavior, physiology, morphology, development, and cognition support self-domestication. Bonobos are more tolerant than chimpanzees when sharing food because bonobos use sex and play to reduce social tension when conflicts arise (Hare et al. 2007; although see Jaeggi et al. 2010). Bonobos also voluntarily share food. When given the choice of either eating preferred food before their morning meal or opening a one-way door to allow another bonobo to share the food, bonobos prefer to eat together. When bonobos can choose to open a door for either a group member or a stranger, they prefer to share with another bonobo with which they have never physically interacted (Tan & Hare 2013). This level of xenophilia contrasts with the xenophobia that chimpanzees show toward strangers (Wilson et al. 2014).

The unusual sharing observed in bonobos is modulated by their physiological response to social stress. Before a dyad of male bonobos is released into a room with food, they show increases in cortisol, associated with a stress response, but not testosterone, typically associated with agonism. The increase of cortisol in male bonobos promotes tolerance by creating a passive coping style that encourages social contact to reduce anxiety through sociosexual behavior (likely by releasing the anxiolytic oxytocin). Chimpanzee males show the exact opposite response. The testosterone reactivity seen in chimpanzee males reduces the potential for tolerance because it primes them for competition as they strive for higher status (Van Honk et al. 2010, Wobber et al. 2010a).

Neurobiologically, bonobos resemble animals that show increased serotonin levels and concomitant reductions in anxiety and aggression as the first sign of domestication (i.e., Agnvall et al. 2015, Plyusnina et al. 1991). Although levels of serotonin in the cerebrospinal fluid have not been directly measured due to the obvious ethical concerns, postmortem neuroanatomical studies have found that bonobos have twice the density, relative to chimpanzees, of serotonergic axons in the basal and central nuclei of the amygdala (Rilling et al. 2011, Stimpson et al. 2015). This is a pattern consistent with a species where social frustration is less likely to lead to aggression (Bernhardt 1997).

Morphologically, bonobos show features associated with self-domestication, including reduced cranial size, canine dimorphism, and depigmentation of the lips and tail tufts. Bonobos also show evidence of an expanded window of social development for behaviors involved in generating tolerance. Bonobos exhibit early-emerging sociosexual behaviors that are used in infancy to mitigate the risk of social conflict while sharing food. They also retain nonreproductive sociosexual and play behaviors into adulthood that act to maintain tolerance. In contrast, chimpanzees show no sociosexual behavior in infancy, only demonstrating this behavior during reproductive bouts as adults (Wobber & Hare 2015, Woods & Hare 2011).

Cognitively, bonobos illustrate the connections between temperament, tolerance, and social cognition. Temperamentally, bonobos are more cautious and observant toward novelty than other apes, with the exception of human children (Herrmann et al. 2011). Although bonobos do not differ from chimpanzees in their use of human cooperative-communicative gestures, they are more sensitive to human gaze direction (MacLean & Hare 2015a). Bonobos are more likely to co-orient in response to a shift in a human's gaze direction or to respond appropriately to their intentions in action (Herrmann et al. 2010). Eye tracking comparisons between bonobos and chimpanzees show that bonobos focus more on the eyes of people whereas chimpanzees tend to focus on the mouths of the same people (Kano et al. 2015). Bonobos also show more flexibility than chimpanzees in instrumental cooperative tasks that require feeding tolerance. Whereas even the most experienced chimpanzee cooperators fail to cooperate to obtain monopolizable food, experimentally naïve bonobos succeed. Even when small amounts of prized food (four apple pieces) are placed in one easily monopolizable location, bonobos cooperate and, on average, split the reward in half. The temperament of bonobos, which is conflict averse and uses social interaction to ease tension, allows them to solve more cooperative problems with a wider range of social partners than chimpanzees (Hare et al. 2007).

Bonobos also show developmental delay across a number of cognitive domains related to foraging and feeding competition—they are particularly uninhibited in social contexts as a result (Rosati & Hare 2012, Wobber et al. 2010b). This lack of inhibition likely presents a major constraint on the cooperative-communicative abilities of bonobos relative to humans. Hare et al. (2012) interpret these and other a priori tests as overwhelming support for bonobo self-domestication. This raises the possibility that other apes may have been affected by the same process during selection for increased prosociality.

THE INFLUENCE OF HUMAN TEMPERAMENT ON MENTALIZING

Studies of nonhuman apes suggest that cooperative-communicative forms of mentalizing evolved in our genus and are important to our cognitive sophistication. These studies also show that tolerance is a constraint on cooperation and communication in nonhumans. In bonobos, dogs, and foxes, natural or artificial selection for prosociality has led to increases in tolerance and social cognitive flexibility in association with the domestication syndrome.

On the basis of this type of comparative work, Hare & Tomasello (2005a,b) proposed the emotional reactivity hypothesis. This hypothesis suggests that human levels of cooperative communication were a result of an increase in social tolerance generated by a decrease in emotional reactivity. Without tolerance, advanced computational or social cognitive abilities would not be of much use because individuals could not share the benefits of joint effort. According to this hypothesis, an increase in tolerance in humans allowed inherited cognitive skills to be expressed in new social situations. Selection could then act directly on revealed variance in these newly expressed cognitive abilities.

Taking advantage of individual differences in human responses to novel or startling situations (Kagan & Snidman 2009), Wellman and colleagues conducted an a priori test of the predicted relationship between emotional reactivity and theory of mind development in human infants (Wellman et al. 2011). Children were observed for their interactions with others and then tested on false belief tasks. Consistent with the hypothesis, infants with the least aggressive and most socially reserved temperaments show the earliest expression of the false belief understanding that supports cooperative forms of communication—including language (Lane et al. 2013, Mink et al. 2014, Wellman et al. 2011). Related findings come from an fMRI study of adults. After being provoked in a competition game, women who were highly reactive in a startle test showed the least activity in the temporal parietal junction (TPJ), medial prefrontal cortex (mPFC), and precuneus (PC) when deciding how to punish other women. These highly reactive women had the least activity in the cortical hubs of the brain's mentalizing network. In contrast, even after being provoked, women with low reactivity had high activity in their mentalizing network. Low reactivity led to more tolerance of provocation and more mentalizing (Beyer et al. 2014).

TPJ: temporal parietal junction

mPFC: medial prefrontal cortex

PC: precuneus

Individual differences in this temperament–social cognition axis supports the idea that changes in human social cognition relied on shifts in the hormonal and subcortical profiles (e.g., amygdala reactivity) linked to temperament. Evolutionary shifts in hormonal or neuropeptide expression or receptivity are evolutionarily labile and, as demonstrated in domesticated animals, can dramatically alter prosociality and are believed to produce a cascade of correlated phenotypic effects.

Because human and nonhuman social behavior are modulated by neurohormones, a number of hormones and neuropeptides are potential targets for prosocial selection. Serotonin, testosterone, and oxytocin are among the most important interactants mediating aggressive behavior (Kuepper et al. 2010, Montoya et al. 2012). In experimental animal populations selected for friendliness toward humans, increases in brain levels of serotonin are the first physiological sign of reduced emotional reactivity and aggression (Agnvall et al. 2015, Plyusnina et al. 1991). Exogenous serotonin in people (i.e., citalopram) increases harm avoidance and cooperative behavior during moral dilemmas and cooperative economic games (Crockett et al. 2010, Wood et al. 2006). Low testosterone is related to male prosociality and parental care (Burnham 2007). Exogenously administered oxytocin in humans reduces aggression directed toward in-group members compared to individuals from out-groups (De Dreu & Kret 2016). Selection for increased prosociality could have readily acted on any of these hormones to increase tolerance through decreased emotional reactivity. The changes in developmental pathways needed to alter emotional reactivity can then have widespread effects throughout the phenotype, including effects on social cognition.

THE HUMAN SELF-DOMESTICATION HYPOTHESIS

The HSD builds on the work of Hare & Tomasello (2005b) and Hare et al. (2012) by proposing that modern humans were selected for prosociality. This hypothesis is inspired by the unusual level of intragroup tolerance and cooperation in modern humans and the link between temperament and social cognition demonstrated in animals and humans. The HSD predicts evidence for (*a*) selection for prosocial behavior linked to derived human cooperative-communicative abilities and (*b*) the domestication syndrome in our morphology, physiology, development, and cognition, as seen in other self-domesticated species (**Table 1**) (Wrangham 2014).

Evolutionary shifts in hormonal profiles related to tolerance and cooperation should be identifiable by using the morphological signatures of these changes found in the fossil record as well as by using genetic comparisons (see **Table 2**). The HSD goes beyond the emotional reactivity hypothesis proposed by Hare & Tomasello (2005b) in recognizing the likelihood that interaction between subcortical and cortical pathways led to unprecedented human tolerance. The HSD predicts that humans have reduced reactivity that increases the reward for social interactions, but it also predicts that, unlike any other domestic species, human tolerance is also due to massive increases in inhibition. The HSD suggests that it is this self-control combined with reduced reactivity that creates the human-specific adaptation for more flexible tolerance and unique forms of human social cognition.

The HSD may play a role in explaining three major moments in human cognitive evolution: (*a*) the initial appearance of the human adaptive package in *Homo erectus*, (*b*) increases in brain

Table 2 Morphological signals of increased tolerance and cooperative-communicative abilities in *Homo sapiens*

Image	Morphological trait	Changes indicated	Time of appearance	Reference
	Reduction in brow ridge and facial length	Reduced pubertal androgens and less despotic behavior in males	Middle/Upper Paleolithic	Cieri et al. 2014
	2nd digit to 4th digit length ratio (2D4D)	Reduced prenatal androgens and increased sensitivity to social cues	After the split from Neanderthals	Nelson et al. 2011
	White sclera	Increases in oxytocin and mutual gaze	Predicted: after the split from Neanderthals	Tomasello et al. 2007
	Globular cranial development	Early emergence of social cognition and the brain's social network	After the split from Neanderthals	Hublin et al. 2015
	Extended synaptic pruning	Late onset of adult self-control	Predicted: after the split from Neanderthals	Casey 2015
	Absolute brain size increase	Increase in self-control and social tolerance	Predicted: beginning with the appearance of genus *Homo*	MacLean et al. 2014

size between 2 million years ago and 80 kya, and (*c*) the lag between reaching the lower range of modern human brain size 500 kya and the expression of full-blown modern cultural behavior approximately 50 kya. Although all three moments are touched on in this review, the focus is largely on HSD as an explanation for the paradox of behavioral modernity in late human evolution (i.e., the temporal gap between the appearance of human morphology and the consistent expression of modern behavior). This is where the HSD currently provides the most testable predictions. In the following sections, I review an initial a priori test of the core predictions of the HSD and then examine morphological, physiological, and developmental evidence that can be interpreted in favor of the HSD being an explanation of the appearance of modern human behavior in the Later Stone Age/Upper Paleolithic.

The First A Priori Test of Human Self-Domestication

Largely based on artifacts in the fossil record, researchers have inferred that behavioral modernity (i.e., the persistent establishment of behaviors requiring extremely flexible forms of causal reasoning, episodic memory, symbolic thought, etc.; McBrearty & Brooks 2000) and cultural diversity did not occur for several hundred thousand years after human brain size reached within the lower end of the current modern range (Holloway 2015; although see Schoenemann 2006). Cieri et al. (2014) explored the possibility that the explosion of cultural artifacts beginning around 80 kya occurred due to selection for temperament that allowed more cooperative communication and promoted rapid transmission of innovations.

Both theoretical models and ethnographic studies suggest that the modern toolkit was a product of demographic expansion (Henrich 2015). Before the Upper Paleolithic, *H. sapiens* transitioned from a low-density distribution to a larger, high-density distribution across a greater range of ecologies. This created a larger network of innovators and resulted in the technology revolution of the Upper Paleolithic.

The challenge for this hypothesis is explaining the sudden appearance of cultural ratcheting as competition for scarce resources increased with population density (Cieri et al. 2014). Without extreme levels of social tolerance, this type of competition would not only impede the social transmission of innovations but also prevent prosocial interactions (i.e., Aureli & De Waal 1997, Horner 2010). Cieri et al. (2014) predicted that an increase in tolerance and demographic pressure allowed a wider network of demonstrators to interact and learn from each other. This allowed existing cognitive skills to be expressed in a wider range of contexts across a broader social network.

Both testosterone and serotonin affect craniofacial morphology during development. Large pubertal spikes in testosterone are associated with an enlargement in the suborbital torus, or brow ridges, and elongated upper faces (Cieri et al. 2014). When facial features are manipulated in photos, people judge the exaggerated facial features produced by pubertal testosterone as being more aggressive and less trustworthy (e.g., Wilson & Rule 2015). Serotonin also plays a role in the early human fetal development of craniofacial morphology, although the mechanism is less well understood. Women taking selective serotonin reuptake inhibitors such as citalopram (an antidepressant medication) have an increased risk of giving birth to infants with reduced cranial size (Alwan et al. 2007). These craniofacial changes in humans echo those in domesticated animals and bonobos, in which an increase in serotonin and reduction in testosterone are associated with facial feminization and reduced cranial capacity (Hare et al. 2012).

Cieri et al. (2014) compared brow ridge size and facial width and length in fossil humans and modern humans. They predicted increasingly hypoandrogenized facial features across late human evolution. They also predicted reduced cranial capacity in Holocene humans, as observed in other domesticated animals.

In 13 modern human fossil crania from the Middle Stone Age and Middle Paleolithic (prior to 80 kya), 41 Later Stone Age/Upper Paleolithic (38–10 kya) crania, and more than 1,300 Holocene (less than 10 kya) crania, a temporal decrease in brow ridge size and the length of the face was observed. The brow ridge projection index of the Middle Stone Age sample was 1.5 standard deviations above that of the Late Stone Age sample and as much as 3.0 standard deviations above the Holocene samples. This difference was present in both the hunter-gatherer and agricultural subsamples within the recent human sample.

Facial length followed a similar pattern, with substantial facial shortening after 80 kya. The most extreme facial shortening was in modern hunter-gatherers. Agriculturalists seem to regress and develop slightly longer faces than hunter-gatherers. Replicating previous analysis, modern hunter-gatherers and agriculturalists both had smaller cranial capacity than the Late Stone Age humans (Leach 2003, Zollikofer & Ponce de Leon 2010).

It is also important to note that while Cieri et al. (2014) confined their analysis to modern humans, these results would have been far more extreme if they included similar comparisons to *Homo neanderthalensis* and *Homo heidelbergensis*. Although both archaic human species had similar-sized brains compared to *H. sapiens*, their faces are far more masculinized than the oldest modern humans (Churchill 2014).

Other biomarkers suggest reduced intrasexual competition and androgen exposure in modern humans. Compared to Neanderthals and other hominins, the 2D4D ratio, the relative length of the second digit to the fourth digit (i.e., the index and ring fingers), of modern humans suggests low prenatal androgen exposure in utero (McIntyre et al. 2009, Nelson et al. 2011). In mammalian testes, comparisons of gene expression profiles across development also suggest pedomorphism in human testis development. Human gene expression is more similar to adolescent mice than to chimpanzees that have gene expression profiles similar to other species with high levels of intrasexual competition (Saglican et al. 2014).

Fossil evidence suggests craniofacial feminization occurred just as cultural ratcheting was pushing us toward behavioral modernity. When human populations became increasingly connected and concentrated at high densities during the Holocene, human brains were reduced in size, which in other species is associated with an increase in serotonin. Although brain size generally increased during the evolution of *Homo*, there was a modest reduction in brain size late in human evolution that resembles reductions in domesticated animals. The 2D4D digit ratio and testis development support a shift in intrasexual competition and androgen exposure. The more masculinized 2D4D pattern in Neanderthals suggests this shift occurred late in human evolution.

The observed morphological changes in modern humans support the HSD. Selection likely modulated tolerance with increased serotonin levels and a reduction in androgen exposure. Males in particular must have been less aggressive in dominance interactions. The new level of tolerance resulted in old cognitive abilities being used more flexibly in new social contexts. Any heritable variance in these new skills, revealed when the constraint of intolerance was lifted, could then become the direct target of selection.

The Eye of Cooperative Communication

In the past two decades, another morphological signal of human cognitive evolution has been discovered. Of the dozens of primate species examined, only humans fail to produce eye-sclera pigment (Kobayashi & Kohshima 1997, 2001). All primates except humans pay a metabolic cost to hide the social information contained in the direction of their gaze by producing melanin (Kobayashi & Kohshima 2001). Humans have white sclera and an elongated eye shape that contrasts with the surrounding facial pigment and advertises the direction of our attention. Individual differences in levels of sclera melanin in nonhuman apes suggest heritable variability across hominoids (Mayhew & Gómez 2015).

Humans show an early-emerging and subconscious preference for eyes with white sclera that persists into adulthood. Infants show a preference for looking at white sclera in their first weeks (Farroni et al. 2004). Infants prefer to look at faces with white sclera and dark pupils over eyes with an inverted pattern of coloration (i.e., black sclera, white pupils) (Farroni et al. 2005). Children prefer stuffed animals with white rather than darkened sclera. Adults share this preference but are unaware that their attraction is driven by the presence of white sclera (Segal et al. 2016, Whalen et al. 2004). By 7 months old, infants rely on white eye sclera to encode emotional cues using the same cortical network observed in adults (Grossmann et al. 2008, Jessen & Grossmann 2014).

Comparisons between human infants and nonhuman apes show that, although all species follow gaze direction, only humans prioritize eye direction over facial direction when coorienting to another's gaze. The increased reliance of infants over other apes on eye gaze is probably facilitated by our white sclera (Tomasello et al. 2007).

Our visible eyes provide information about eye direction and cues of mutual gaze that seem crucial to our unique forms of learning, cooperation, and communication (Grossmann 2016). Joint attention, which allows children to learn the association between labels and objects, relies on a child's ability to follow an adult's line of gaze (Tomasello 2009a, Tomasello & Farrar 1986). Mutual gaze is critical to the formation of shared intentions—a central psychological mechanism allowing for the development of unique human forms of cooperative communication (Tomasello et al. 2005).

White sclera may increase the potential for joint attention by enhancing eye-blink synchronization. When eye blinking is synchronized, humans improve the coordination of their subsequent motor activities. This synchronization is thought to lead to a Hebbian association (i.e., neural synchronization) between the activity in the inferior frontal gyrus of two people locked in mutual gaze. This interneural synchronization may prime other regions of the brain's social network and facilitate shared intentions between individuals (Koike et al. 2016). White sclera may serve to increase the likelihood and length of this synchronization.

Visible eyes also promote cooperative behavior in humans. People donate more in a public goods game when they are watched by a robot with large eyes. Subjects whose computer screens display a robot with oversized white sclera donate ~30% more to the public good than those without the robot on their screens (Burnham & Hare 2007). When a picture of human eyes was placed above a public bicycle rack or on a paper leaflet, bike theft was eliminated and littering reduced. In the controls without the eye manipulation, more bikes were stolen and there was more littering (Bateson et al. 2015, Nettle et al. 2012).

Eyes with white sclera favor expression of prosocial behavior. Visible human eyes facilitate cooperation by signaling the potential for social sanctions or reputational consequences. These signals probably affect human cooperation subconsciously (Burnham & Hare 2007; although see Fehr & Schneider 2010, Jessen & Grossmann 2014).

Depigmentation of human sclera may be a by-product of self-domestication because selection against aggression alters melanin expression. Furthermore, scleral tissue originates from the neural crest (Seko et al. 2008, Wilkins et al. 2014). If shifts in melanocyte migration of scleral tissue produced variance in white sclera as a result of self-domestication, selection could subsequently act directly on any heritable variance (West-Eberhard 2003).

Given the role of neuropeptides and hormones in mediating human gaze behavior, prosociality and white sclera likely coevolved. In particular, oxytocin is known to modulate mutual gaze and increase attention to the eyes of others in humans (Gamer et al. 2010, Guastella et al. 2008). In experiments in which human males examined only the eye region of people making different emotional expressions, exogenous administration of oxytocin improved the ability of the participants to infer the other person's affective state (Domes et al. 2013, Meyer-Lindenberg et al. 2011).

Effects of exogenous oxytocin seem specific to improving social memory of faces rather than to improving memory more generally (Rimmele et al. 2009). Oxytocin also facilitates bonding of parent and offspring through touch and mutual gaze (Baribeau & Anagnostou 2015, Carter 2014). This may explain increases in trust during cooperative games in subjects that have been given intranasal oxytocin (Kosfeld et al. 2005). The role of mutual gaze and oxytocin in the human–dog bond demonstrates that this effect even extends to human–animal interactions (Nagasawa et al. 2015, Waller et al. 2013).

STS: superior temporal sulcus

The HSD predicts that increasing oxytocin levels, receptor densities, or receptor responsiveness in the brain was a crucial step in promoting the evolution of human prosociality (Baribeau & Anagnostou 2015). These increases would have promoted the use of eye gaze and favored the evolution of white sclera, allowing the close interactions that led to the social bonding and cooperative communication necessary for the expression of modern human behavior.

Like-Me Psychology Drove Paleolithic Self-Domestication

Humans are helpful or hurtful toward others based on perceived similarity to themselves. As adults, this like-me psychology manifests itself as in-group favoritism across a variety of contexts and cultures (Mullen et al. 1992). This favoritism results in a high degree of tolerance toward in-group members that facilitates unique forms of collaboration and conformity (Burton-Chellew & West 2012, Kurzban et al. 2015). In contrast, ostracism and lethal aggression among hunter-gatherers primarily targets nonconformist or out-group members (Boehm et al. 1993, Wrangham 1999). This type of antisocial or agonistic response is facilitated by the readiness of humans to dehumanize out-group members or those that dehumanize their own in-group (Hodson et al. 2014, Kteily et al. 2016).

This in-group versus out-group preference appears early in development, which suggests that humans are prepared for social discrimination based on like-me preferences (Bloom 2013, Mahajan & Wynn 2012). The latest neurobiological evidence and evolutionary models suggest that intragroup prosociality can explain our paradoxical kindness and cruelty toward others. Selection for in-group prosociality drove late human self-domestication and, as a correlated by-product, is responsible for extreme forms of out-group aggression.

Spontaneous sharing and helping develops early in infancy along with an in-group bias (Hamlin & Wynn 2011, Hamlin et al. 2007, Kinzler et al. 2011, Warneken 2015, Warneken et al. 2007). Nine-month-old infants prefer puppets that help another puppet who shares the child's food preference but also prefer puppets that harm another puppet with a dissimilar food preference (Hamlin et al. 2013). In sharing games, children as young as 5 years old prefer to share with in-group members, whereas 6-year-olds are more willing to pay a cost to punish selfish out-group members than in-group members (Engelmann et al. 2013, Jordan et al. 2014). Children also seem selective in enforcing norms depending on a violator's group affiliation (Schmidt et al. 2012). This early-emerging expression of in-group bias supports the idea that we are biologically prepared to support in-group cooperation and communication.

The neurobiology of this like-me psychology is also present in adults. A cortical network allows for the attribution of mental states and is built from regions specialized in social decision making (Adolphs 2009, Carter & Huettel 2013). Brain imaging using fMRI scans shows involvement of the mPFC, TPJ, and superior temporal sulcus (STS) in tasks requiring subjects to model the intentions, emotions, and beliefs of others (Amodio & Frith 2006, Harris & Fiske 2009). Ventral areas of the mPFC also show activity when people think about their own thoughts or emotions about others (Cikara et al. 2014b).

This cortical network allows people to compare their own thoughts and feelings to those of others and is central to generating both compassionate and dehumanizing responses. When other humans are perceived as having good intentions (being warm) and having the capability to carry them out (being competent), the mPFC is heavily involved in modulating empathic responses. In contrast, the mPFC becomes less active when people are shown photos of individuals perceived as incompetent and cold (i.e., homeless people, drug addicts), and the amygdala and insula that encode disgust become the most active regions (Harris & Fiske 2006, Rilling et al. 2008a).

When subjects were allowed to punish in-group and out-group members for norm violations, punishment of in-group members was less likely and was associated with heightened activity and connectivity between the mPFC and TPJ. Mentalizing regions become more active, suggesting that people were justifying their groupmates' infractions; the same regions were not as active when out-group members made the same transgression (Baumgartner et al. 2012). When there is decreased activity in this mentalizing network, people are able to dehumanize others and are less likely to show empathy, tolerance, or prosociality (Baumgartner et al. 2012, Cikara et al. 2014a, Fiske et al. 2007, Harris & Fiske 2009, Waytz et al. 2012).

The neuropeptide oxytocin is the strongest candidate for explaining the human-unique pattern of empathy and dehumanization. Oxytocin not only increases eye contact and social bonding in humans but also exaggerates in-group favoritism. Adults given oxytocin are more likely to humanize in-group rather than out-group members by attributing human-unique emotions to the in-group members and showing increased positive evaluations of them (De Dreu et al. 2011). Men who are given oxytocin are three times more likely to donate money to their group rather than keep it for themselves (De Dreu et al. 2010). In economic games, intranasal oxytocin also reduces the likelihood of men to cooperate with out-group members when they become a threat to in-group members (De Dreu 2012, De Dreu et al. 2010, De Dreu & Kret 2016). Increased in-group bonds appear to drive larger defensive responses against potential threats from out-group members.

These results probably occur because of oxytocin's influence on the brain's social network, which allows for mentalizing and empathy. Immunohistochemistry suggests the presence of oxytocin receptors in the cingulate cortex and amygdala and perhaps even the frontal cortex (Boccia et al. 2013). Intranasal oxytocin also increases the resting-state connectivity between the amygdala and the mPFC (Sripada et al. 2013). This may cause a blunted mPFC response in individuals competing on behalf of in-group members against an out-group. Consistent with this idea, lower mPFC reactivity has been observed during competitions that increased people's willingness to harm out-group competitors (Cikara et al. 2014a). This is consistent with a subcortical system heavily impacted by serotonin and oxytocin, which both mediate the strength of the response in the brain's social cortex.

Selection for prosociality, which results in a reduced androgen profile and increases in serotonin (or receptor densities) as suggested by Cieri et al. (2014), is expected to facilitate oxytocin expression and binding (Baribeau & Anagnostou 2015). Sex steroids, including testosterone, affect the binding of oxytocin and vasopressin. Whereas testosterone facilitates vasopressin binding, oxytocin and testosterone are antagonistic. The production of oxytocin probably depends on serotonin receptor activity and generates a positive feedback loop, whereas serotonin increases in the presence of oxytocin.

The effects of oxytocin are mediated through serotonin neurons (Baribeau & Anagnostou 2015). This suggests that oxytocin's dependence on serotonin and interactions with testosterone altered its expression or reception over the past 80,000 years. The HSD predicts that the in-group bonds of our species coevolved with out-group distrust due to changes in the serotonergic and androgen systems that allowed oxytocin to have a greater impact on cortical regions related to social decision making.

Although intergroup lethal aggression is likely a conserved trait (Gomez et al. 2016, Wilson et al. 2014, Wrangham & Glowacki 2012, Wrangham et al. 2006), evolutionary modeling supports the idea that any intensification of out-group aggression could be a by-product of selection for intragroup prosociality late in human evolution. If each behavior evolves in isolation, the payoff is not as adaptive. If they emerge simultaneously, in-group favoritism in combination with out-group hostility is a highly successful strategy (Choi & Bowles 2007). The interaction of oxytocin, serotonin, and testosterone suggests a way in which enhanced in-group prosociality and out-group aggression may have coevolved.

Ethnographic analysis also supports the idea that humans show a shift in social structure consistent with self-domestication and the coevolution of parochialism. Hunter-gatherers' intragroup interactions are best described as a reverse dominance hierarchy. Group members work together to defend each other against any individual trying to monopolize power in the group. This suggests that the most aggressive group members would be at a selective disadvantage. Aggression occurs, but ostracism and lethal aggression are levied against those who do not conform to the more egalitarian social system (Boehm et al. 1993). These bonded egalitarian groups would have been more successful in outcompeting other hominin species or human out-groups.

Humans became kinder and crueler as a result of selection for intragroup prosociality. Selection acted on neurohormonal channels that tune subcortical regions to be more or less reactive and subsequently influence the identity of those perceived as like us or not. Just as oxytocin bonds parent to offspring, making parents capable of extreme defensive aggression, our species became similarly protective of our in-group members against out-group threats.

Self-Control: The Unique Feature of Human Self-Domestication

Increases in brain size are the defining characteristic of evolution in our genus and a morphological signal of increased tolerance through self-control. Larger brains are associated with increased self-control. Self-control supports executive function and allows cortical regions to govern subcortical regions. The effects of self-control thus include inhibiting aggressive responses in favor of prosocial reactions (MacLean 2016). This effect contrasts with high or low subcortical reactivity that may sacrifice inhibition, as in bonobos and some dog populations (Bray et al. 2015, Wobber et al. 2010b).

A large-scale phylogenetic study (MacLean et al. 2014) suggests the relationship between brain size and self-control. An average of 15 individuals from 36 species of mammals and birds ($N >$ 550) were tested for their ability to spontaneously inhibit a prepotent response in two different tasks. The first task presented subjects with food in a transparent tube. A correct response required inhibiting the urge to reach directly for the food and instead taking a detour by reaching through one of the tube's open ends. The second task gave subjects the Piagetian A not B task, which requires inhibiting perseverative search errors by choosing where food is hidden as opposed to where it was repeatedly hidden in the past.

Absolute brain size predicted performance across species. In more than 20 primate species, there was no link between performance and ecological variables such as social complexity or frugivory. Instead, brain size was the best predictor of inhibition. Brain size explained up to 70% of the variance in self-control across primate species (MacLean et al. 2014). This indicates that increases in absolute brain size in humans were likely accompanied by increases in self-control.

MacLean et al. (2014) suggest that the relationship between brain size and self-control in primates exists due to the unique scaling relationship between neuron densities in primates. Unlike other taxa, which show reduced neuron densities in larger-brained animals, primate neuron numbers scale isometrically with brain size. In primates, larger brains have the same densities of neurons, leading to exponential growth in potential networks between them (Azevedo et al. 2009). As the total number of neurons increase, primate brains become more modular, which may create new neural networks (Kaas 2000, Rilling et al. 2008b). Human brains take this primate trend to its extreme (Herculano-Houzel 2012). Thus brain size, neural numbers, and self-control can evolve as by-products of selection for body size (although see Grabowski et al. 2016). Simply becoming larger to avoid predation or to promote thermoregulation would also increase self-control and trigger a positive evolutionary feedback loop during early human evolution (e.g., perhaps as seen between the small- and large-brained representatives of early *Homo*; Wood & Boyle 2016). Initial increases in self-control probably increased energetic productivity through more flexible solutions using ancient cognitive skills in new ways.

Cooking is a strong candidate for the initial trigger of this evolutionary feedback loop. Nonhuman apes prefer cooked food and have many of the cognitive prerequisites for cooking (Warneken & Rosati 2015, Wobber et al. 2008). A slight increase in self-control would have brought the energetic payoffs of cooking within reach (Wrangham 2009). Investing in expensive brain tissue would increasingly produce benefits as human energetic productivity expanded with more sophisticated cognitive abilities (Berbesque et al. 2016). These benefits would have led to the modern human energy budget, which is beyond anything seen in other primates. As a result, foragers would have higher reproductive rates and larger brains than any other ape (Pontzer et al. 2016). The cognitive by-product hypothesis is supported by fossil data interpreted to show brain size in our lineage scaling allometrically with body size until approximately 600 kya. According to this view, human brains became disproportionately large only in the last half million years (Hublin et al. 2015).

The HSD predicts that increases in self-control as a result of an increase in brain size steadily drove the evolution of tolerance and social cognitive skills. Late in human evolution, selection for in-group tolerance intensified and acted on our emotional axis, which, together with preexisting self-control, created unprecedented levels of social tolerance. Over the past 100,000 years, humans began to outcompete other hominins through the cooperation and communication that resulted from this increase in in-group bonding, tolerance, and cooperation.

Self-Domestication Through Evolutionary Development

It is important to consider the mechanism that selection might have targeted to produce these changes during human evolution. The HSD predicts that the evolution of developmental pathways is the unifying mechanism leading to the social cognition, temperament, and self-control that create unique human intragroup tolerance.

The widening of developmental windows is a common consequence of domestication. In domesticated animals, ancestral behavioral traits appear earlier and persist for longer (Trut et al. 2009). This heterochrony suggests that a similar shift in human development provided the mechanism for increases in tolerance and cooperative communication. Comparative and neurobiological work provides evidence of cognitive ontogeny consistent with the prediction that the human developmental window extended both earlier and later for cognition related to increased tolerance and cooperative communication.

Humans have unique early-emerging social cognition that facilitates participation in cultural forms of learning and is supported by a pattern of secondary altriciality and globular brain development. Longitudinal comparisons between age-matched human infants and nonhuman apes across a range of cognitive skills have revealed shifts in human cognitive development.

Wobber et al. (2014) published the first comparison that uses a longitudinal design to compare the cognitive development of two dozen bonobos and chimpanzees to a similar sample of age-matched children. Each subject was tested on the same battery of cognitive tasks each year between 2 and 4 years old. The battery was based on tasks used by Herrmann et al. (2007) and included social and nonsocial problem-solving tasks.

Contrary to models predicting slower cognitive development in humans relative to other ape species (e.g., Charnov & Berrigan 1993), 2-year-old children are more skilled than nonhuman apes in social tasks requiring cooperation and communication. Performance in these tasks is near ceiling levels in humans by age 4, whereas the other apes show little development by this same age. The same 2-year-old human infants perform at a similar level to the other apes in nonsocial tasks (i.e., tool properties, numerosity, spatial memory, etc.).

This provides powerful evidence for specialized and early-emerging social cognition, which becomes the scaffolding for subsequent social learning in human infants (Herrmann et al. 2007). Early-emerging social skills allow human infants to cooperate and communicate with others and access all forms of cultural knowledge.

Fossil evidence provides a clue to when this early-emerging social neurocognitive network might have evolved. The most prominent feature of human brain maturation is secondary altriciality or helplessness in human newborns. Human brains are born at 25% their adult volume compared to other apes born with 45% of adult brain volume (Zollikofer & Ponce de Leon 2010). This extreme level of postpartum brain development gives unusual influence to social input during brain development (e.g., eye contact, motherese, etc.). Social interactions can influence the structure and organization of brain development during postnatal brain growth and probably facilitate the early-emerging social skills observed by Wobber et al. (2014).

Morphologically, the most unique feature of the human skull is its globular shape (Zollikofer & Ponce de Leon 2010). Analysis of globularization shows that this shape change occurs early in development and is largely a result of the maintenance of fetal brain growth rates until the eruption of the deciduous teeth at around 30 months old. By 4 years of age, synaptic densities begin to peak, the brain approaches adult size, and more than 60% of a child's metabolism is directed toward brain growth (Hublin et al. 2015, Kuzawa et al. 2014). The globular shape that is produced by the extension of exaggerated growth rates is largely driven by expansion in the brain's parietal region, which includes the PC and TPJ (Bruner et al. 2016, Gunz et al. 2012). This globular expansion is facilitated by elevated levels of white matter development in the human infant PFC relative to those of chimpanzees (Sakai et al. 2011). There is also evidence that the brain's cortical social network (i.e., the TPJ, STS, and mPFC) becomes increasingly active in infants during this period of globular brain development (Grossmann 2015). Globularization has also been linked to changes in the development of the neural crest as well as to a set of candidate genes that show signs of positive selection in humans (Benitez-Burraco et al. 2016).

All of the brain regions leading to globular expansion are also involved in human social cognition, including the attribution of mental states to others. This raises the possibility that globular growth in the fossil record signals the evolution of early-emerging social cognition.

Fossil studies have provided estimates for the appearance of secondary altriciality and globular brain development. In comparing the crania of infant *Homo erectus*, *H. neanderthalensis*, and *H. sapiens*, researchers have found that *H. erectus* infants were born with a more developed brain than those of later hominins. Secondary altriciality is thought to have evolved in the common ancestor of Neanderthals and modern humans. In contrast, globular development was not seen in *H. neanderthalensis*, suggesting that it is a unique feature of our species (Hublin et al. 2015). These studies support the idea of an early window of social cognitive development associated with a derived strategy of brain maturation that evolved uniquely in *H. sapiens*.

Although social cognitive skills develop early, synaptic pruning in cortical regions involved in executive function develops late. Human infants show similar levels of self-control to other apes until early childhood. It is not until around 6 years old that children show more inhibition than nonhuman apes (Herrmann et al. 2015, Vlamings et al. 2010).

Even adolescent humans have lower self-control than adults. Adolescents engage in higher-risk behaviors while showing greater aversion to social punishment (Casey & Caudle 2013). These trends are associated with the final stages of synaptic pruning in cortical regions thought to be involved in executive control and inhibition (Casey 2015). Synaptic pruning in regions of the PFC related to self-control are only complete in our mid-20s. Only when these self-control networks are complete do adults become more risk averse and less sensitive to failure (Casey 2015). As the human brain increased in size, the process of synaptic pruning probably became increasingly pedomorphic. Brain myelination and white matter show a similar pattern of delayed development. Chimpanzees and macaques complete myelination at sexual maturity, but this same process is not complete in humans until our mid-20s (Somel et al. 2013).

Genetic comparisons also support the theory of a widened developmental window in humans. Comparisons of gene expression in macaques, chimpanzees, and humans reveal that a host of genes in humans are expressed at either an accelerated or delayed rate (Somel et al. 2009). The largest changes in the developmental timing of brain gene expression was observed in the human PFC as compared both to other areas of the human brain and to the chimpanzee PFC. Human synaptic genes in the PFC do not show peak expression until up to 5 years of age, whereas the peak for these same genes is reached after a few months in chimpanzees. This results in a late age for peak synaptic densities in the human PFC (3.5–10 years of age); in contrast, peak densities in the human auditory cortex occur between 6 months and 3.5 years of age, and synaptic elimination begins in the human visual cortex a few months after birth. This graded pattern contrasts with simultaneous peaks in all brain tissue types in macaques. The window of synaptic development is longer in humans because elimination begins later but occurs at a slower pace (Somel et al. 2013).

Research on self-control and synaptic pruning is consistent with an increased window of development in humans as predicted by self-domestication. The HSD predicts that both early-emerging social cognition and delayed adult inhibition will be linked to selection for prosociality and provide a mechanistic explanation for features of HSD.

CONCLUSION

Researchers have frequently made use of the concept of domestication in explaining human evolution (Boas 1911, Gould 1977, Leach 2003, Wrangham 2014). Darwin (1859) began *On the Origin of Species* with a discussion of domestication through artificial selection and spent decades collecting examples of natural variation produced through domestication (Darwin 1868). Domestication was crucial to Darwin's case for evolution through natural selection and led him to consider the possibility of human domestication (Darwin 1871).

It was not until the pioneering work of Dmitry Belyeav and colleagues that the HSD, or the link between selection for prosociality and a wide variety of correlated by-products, was discovered (for a review, see Hare & Woods 2013). These by-products include morphological and physiological changes, increases in cooperative communication, and expanding developmental windows (Belyaev et al. 1985, Hare et al. 2005). Belyaev's experimental domestication of foxes clearly defined the selection pressure, its effects, and the potential developmental mechanisms targeted to produce different domesticated phenotypes. The fox experiments allowed further comparative work to test whether natural selection produced similar results in dogs, bonobos, and humans.

The experiments with foxes and comparisons between dogs and wolves reveal that changes in cooperative-communicative abilities can occur as a by-product of selection for prosociality and against fear and aggression. A priori tests of bonobo self-domestication support the possibility that natural selection causes similar results.

The HSD builds on this comparative work and suggests that selection for prosociality also played a large role in human evolution, especially during the Middle and Upper Paleolithic (**Figure 1**). The first a priori test of this hypothesis found evidence by the Upper Paleolithic for the expected link between increases in cultural artifacts and craniofacial signals of increased tolerance.

Future tests can evaluate the proposed link between the evolution of self-control and emotional reactivity that allows flexible human tolerance and social cognition. Future paleoanthropological, neuroendocrine, and genetic research will be able to further examine links between intragroup cooperative communication, morphology (i.e., eye color), and heterochronic shifts related to early-emerging social cognitive development. Hopefully, the HSD will help energize efforts toward answering the ultimate Darwinian challenge: how our minds evolved and allowed *H. sapiens* to survive as Earth's last remaining human.

SUMMARY POINTS

1. Darwin's greatest evolutionary challenge is identifying derived forms of human cognition and the processes by which they evolved. Given recent evidence of the existence of many large-brained human species within the past 50,000 years, we must answer this challenge for both our genus and our species.

2. Comparisons between human and nonhuman ape infants suggest that the early emergence of cooperative communication provides the developmental foundation for human cultural cognition.

3. Domestic dogs converge with human infants in their ability to use human cooperative-communicative gestures. Experimentally domesticated fox kits show dog-like skills in using human gestures even though these skills were not under selection. An increase in cooperative-communicative ability appears to be a by-product of selection for prosociality over aggression.

4. Comparisons between bonobos and chimpanzees support the hypothesis that natural selection favoring prosociality over aggression can lead to self-domestication. Bonobos share many traits with domesticated animals, including increased flexibility in some cooperative-communicative contexts.

5. The HSD suggests that natural selection for prosociality and against aggression played a large role in human evolution. Over the past 80,000 years, fossil humans show morphological evidence for selection against aggression that coincides with an increase in cultural artifacts in the fossil record.

6. Selection for in-group prosociality drove human self-domestication in the Paleolithic. Changes in oxytocin and eye sclera color provide two possible mechanisms to explain the increases in cooperative communication, increases in in-group cooperation, and intensification of intergroup conflict that evolved as a result of this selection.

7. Evolutionarily labile neurohormones and neuropeptides provide a ready target of selection for prosociality over aggression. However, human tolerance is flexible beyond what can be accounted for by muted subcortical responses alone. Phylogenetic comparisons suggesting a strong link between inhibition and absolute brain size point to the critical role of cortical regions in allowing for human levels of self-control and tolerance.

8. Human self-domestication predicts increased developmental windows for traits relating to increased tolerance and cooperative communication. Early-emerging social cognition, which develops despite secondary altriciality, together with graded synaptic pruning continuing into adulthood, played a central role in the evolution of *H. sapiens*.

FUTURE ISSUES

1. The HSD predicts a strong link between individual differences in temperamental profile and mentalizing abilities. Future studies should continue to find evidence for this relationship early in development, using studies of heritability and cross-cultural comparisons.

2. Self-domestication predicts the appearance of the domestication syndrome, but its expression likely differs across taxa due to phylogenetic distance and different developmental, neurohormonal, or subcortical targets. Traits considered part of the syndrome do not present themselves universally (Sanchez-Villagra et al. 2016). This inconsistent pattern may be the result of multiple pathways to increased prosociality, each of which may generate different sets of correlated by-products. For example, humans and bonobos are hypothesized to be self-domesticated, but humans exhibit lethal aggression and neither hominoid shows the high frequencies of piebalding seen in many other domestic mammals (Wilkins et al. 2014). Tools will be needed to discriminate between selection against different forms of aggression (i.e., defensive, predatory, intragroup, intergroup, etc.) that affect different physiological or developmental mechanisms and may lead to this differential expression of correlated traits (Hare et al. 2012). Future selection experiments that target different forms of aggression or prosociality will provide powerful tests (Sanchez-Villagra et al. 2016).

3. The HSD suggests that the underlying evolutionary genetics behind human white sclera can potentially reveal the time of origin for human forms of cooperative communication (Tomasello et al. 2007). For example, if genetic disorders related to sclera color are discovered, then this could provide a powerful test of the self-domestication hypothesis using comparisons of the human and Neanderthal genomes. Individual variability in scleral whiteness in nonhuman apes may offer another route to genetic clues about the origin of human sclera coloration (Mayhew & Gómez 2015).

4. The HSD predicts that *H. sapiens* have an expanded developmental window. Morphological comparisons of development in *Homo* are based on a few fossil specimens. Future discoveries of additional specimens should support extended fetal levels of brain growth and cranial globularization as well as a slower life history in *H. sapiens*, which would support the hypothesis of gradation in brain development across cortical levels (i.e., late myelination and pruning of the cortex).

5. Selection for prosociality is only associated with reduced rather than increased brain size. Another major force, or multiple forces, must have been at play during early human evolution to drive initial body and brain size increases. Increases in body size to escape predation or better thermoregulate or as a result of the island syndrome may have initially produced tolerance as a by-product of self-control increases occurring with concomitant changes in brain size. Selection could then target any heritable variance in self-control. This alone may be the cognitive trait allowing for an initial shift in human energy productivity (Pontzer et al. 2016). Comparative behavioral ecological studies will likely help test whether similar evolutionary scenarios have played out in other taxa.

6. The cooperative breeding hypothesis might be considered an alternative hypothesis to the HSD (Burkart & van Schaik 2010). Although the two hypotheses will likely prove complementary, it will be important to outline and test their competing predictions (ideally using comparative phylogenetic techniques). For example, cooperative breeding does not make the heterochronic or morphological predictions made by the HSD, but both hypotheses predict increased prosociality. Therefore, the hypotheses might be reconciled. For example, it is conceivable that increases in cooperative breeding during human evolution might have led to sexual selection. Females may have chosen to bond with males who did not aggress toward them but rather toward threats to their joint offspring—leading to human self-domestication.

7. Self-domestication is predicted to play a role in shaping the phenotypes of both island- and urban-living populations (Ditchkoff et al. 2006, Raia et al. 2010). Careful comparisons of island and mainland as well as wild and urban populations will help reveal the ecological conditions that favor self-domestication. These lessons will likely also allow for inferences regarding the ecological conditions that favored human self-domestication.

8. If selection acts on prosociality across a variety of species, shared genetics might produce the observed convergence across some species. Any common genetics discovered could be evaluated in extinct and living humans. This would require genotypic and phenotypic comparisons of different pairs of wild and domestic animals, but initial attempts have not revealed this type of commonality (Albert et al. 2012). Future research can explore new genetic candidates related to neural crest development, cranial globularization, and domestication that might be associated with human self-domestication (Benitez-Burraco et al. 2016). However, the human case may prove exceptionally challenging because human behavioral traits are hyperpolygenic (Chabris et al. 2015).

DISCLOSURE STATEMENT

The author is not aware of any affiliations, memberships, funding, or financial holdings that might be perceived as affecting the objectivity of this review.

ACKNOWLEDGMENTS

I want to thank Richard Wrangham for making the connection between the dog domestication literature and hominoid evolution, both in the case of humans and bonobos. His ideas, discussions, and collaboration inspired this review. I also want to thank James Brooks for help with the reference section and Steve Churchill, Evan MacLean, Jingzhi Tan, Michael Tomasello, Vanessa Woods, and Richard Wrangham for extremely valuable comments that resulted in a much-improved paper.

LITERATURE CITED

Adolphs R. 2009. The social brain: neural basis of social knowledge. *Annu. Rev. Psychol.* 60:693–716

Agnvall B, Katajamaa R, Altimiras J, Jensen P. 2015. Is domestication driven by reduced fear of humans? Boldness, metabolism and serotonin levels in divergently selected red junglefowl (*Gallus gallus*). *Biol. Lett.* 11:20150509

Albert FW, Somel M, Carneiro M, Aximu-Petri A, Halbwax M, et al. 2012. A comparison of brain gene expression levels in domesticated and wild animals. *PLOS Genet.* 8:e1002962

Alwan S, Reefhuis J, Rasmussen SA, Olney RS, Friedman JM. 2007. Use of selective serotonin-reuptake inhibitors in pregnancy and the risk of birth defects. *N. Engl. J. Med.* 356:2684–92

Amodio DM, Frith CD. 2006. Meeting of minds: the medial frontal cortex and social cognition. *Nat. Rev. Neurosci.* 7:268–77

Aureli F, De Waal F. 1997. Inhibition of social behavior in chimpanzees under high-density conditions. *Am. J. Primatol.* 41:213–28

Azevedo FA, Carvalho LR, Grinberg LT, Farfel JM, Ferretti RE, et al. 2009. Equal numbers of neuronal and nonneuronal cells make the human brain an isometrically scaled-up primate brain. *J. Comp. Neurol.* 513:532–41

Baribeau DA, Anagnostou E. 2015. Oxytocin and vasopressin: linking pituitary neuropeptides and their receptors to social neurocircuits. *Front. Neurosci.* 9:335

Bateson M, Robinson R, Abayomi-Cole T, Greenlees J, O'Connor A, Nettle D. 2015. Watching eyes on potential litter can reduce littering: evidence from two field experiments. *PeerJ* 3:e1443

Baumgartner T, Gotte L, Gugler R, Fehr E. 2012. The mentalizing network orchestrates the impact of parochial altruism on social norm enforcement. *Hum. Brain Mapp.* 33:1452–69

Belyaev D, Plyusnina I, Trut L. 1985. Domestication in the silver fox (*Vulpes fulvus Desm*): changes in physiological boundaries of the sensitive period of primary socialization. *Appl. Anim. Behav. Sci.* 13:359–70

Benitez-Burraco A, Theofanopoulou C, Boeckx C. 2016. Globularization and domestication. *Topoi.* doi: 10.1007/s11245-016-9399-7

Berbesque JC, Wood BM, Crittenden AN, Mabulla A, Marlowe FW. 2016. Eat first, share later: Hadza hunter-gatherer men consume more while foraging than in central places. *Evol. Hum. Behav.* 37:281–86

Bernhardt PC. 1997. Influences of serotonin and testosterone in aggression and dominance: convergence with social psychology. *Curr. Dir. Psychol. Sci.* 6:44–48

Beyer F, Munte TF, Erdmann C, Kramer UM. 2014. Emotional reactivity to threat modulates activity in mentalizing network during aggression. *Soc. Cogn. Affect. Neurosci.* 9:1552–60

Bloom P. 2013. *Just Babies: The Origins of Good and Evil.* New York: Crown

Boas F. 1911. *The Mind of Primitive Man: A Course of Lectures Delivered Before the Lowell Institute, Boston, Mass., and the National University of Mexico, 1910–1911.* London: Macmillan

Boccia M, Petrusz P, Suzuki K, Marson L, Pedersen CA. 2013. Immunohistochemical localization of oxytocin receptors in human brain. *Neuroscience* 253:155–64

Boehm C, Barclay HB, Dentan RK, Dupre M-C, Hill JD, et al. 1993. Egalitarian behavior and reverse dominance hierarchy [and comments and reply]. *Curr. Anthropol.* 34:227–54

Bray EE, MacLean EL, Hare BA. 2015. Increasing arousal enhances inhibitory control in calm but not excitable dogs. *Anim. Cogn.* 18:1317–29

Bruner E, Preuss TM, Chen X, Rilling JK. 2016. Evidence for expansion of the precuneus in human evolution. *Brain Struct. Funct.* In press. doi: 10.1007/s00429-015-1172-y

Bullinger AF, Melis AP, Tomasello M. 2014. Chimpanzees (*Pan troglodytes*) instrumentally help but do not communicate in a mutualistic cooperative task. *J. Comp. Psychol.* 128:251–60

Burkart JM, van Schaik CP. 2010. Cognitive consequences of cooperative breeding in primates? *Anim. Cogn.* 13:1–19

Burnham TC. 2007. High-testosterone men reject low ultimatum game offers. *Proc. R. Soc. B Biol. Sci.* 274:2327–30

Burnham TC, Hare B. 2007. Engineering human cooperation. *Hum. Nat.* 18:88–108

Burton-Chellew MN, West SA. 2012. Pseudocompetition among groups increases human cooperation in a public-goods game. *Anim. Behav.* 84:947–52

Call J, Hare B, Carpenter M, Tomasello M. 2004. 'Unwilling' versus 'unable': chimpanzees' understanding of human intentional action. *Dev. Sci.* 7:488–98

Call J, Hare BA, Tomasello M. 1998. Chimpanzee gaze following in an object-choice task. *Anim. Cogn.* 1:89–99

Carter CS. 2014. Oxytocin pathways and the evolution of human behavior. *Annu. Rev. Psychol.* 65:17–39

Carter RM, Huettel SA. 2013. A nexus model of the temporal-parietal junction. *Trends Cogn. Sci.* 17:328–36

Casey BJ. 2015. Beyond simple models of self-control to circuit-based accounts of adolescent behavior. *Annu. Rev. Psychol.* 66:295–319

Experimental evidence linking expanded developmental windows with selection for prosociality.

Casey BJ, Caudle K. 2013. The teenage brain: self control. *Curr. Dir. Psychol. Sci.* 22:82–87

Chabris CF, Lee JJ, Cesarini D, Benjamin DJ, Laibson DI. 2015. The fourth law of behavior genetics. *Curr. Dir. Psychol. Sci.* 24:304–12

Charnov EL, Berrigan D. 1993. Why do female primates have such long lifespans and so few babies? Or life in the slow lane. *Evol. Anthropol. Issues News Rev.* 1:191–94

Choi J-K, Bowles S. 2007. The coevolution of parochial altruism and war. *Science* 318:636–40

Churchill SE. 2014. *Thin on the Ground: Neandertal Biology, Archeology and Ecology.* Hoboken, NJ: John Wiley & Sons

Cieri RL, Churchill SE, Franciscus RG, Tan J, Hare B. 2014. Craniofacial feminization, social tolerance, and the origins of behavioral modernity. *Curr. Anthropol.* 55:419–43

Cikara M, Bruneau E, Van Bavel JJ, Saxe R. 2014a. Their pain gives us pleasure: how intergroup dynamics shape empathic failures and counter-empathic responses. *J. Exp. Soc. Psychol.* 55:110–25

Cikara M, Jenkins AC, Dufour N, Saxe R. 2014b. Reduced self-referential neural response during intergroup competition predicts competitor harm. *Neuroimage* 96:36–43

Crockett MJ, Clark L, Hauser MD, Robbins TW. 2010. Serotonin selectively influences moral judgment and behavior through effects on harm aversion. *PNAS* 107:17433–38

Darwin C. 1859. *On the Origin of Species.* London: Murray

Darwin C. 1868. *The Variation of Animals and Plants under Domestication.* London: Murray

Darwin C. 1871. *The Descent of Man and Selection in Relation to Sex.* London: Murray

De Dreu CK. 2012. Oxytocin modulates cooperation within and competition between groups: an integrative review and research agenda. *Horm. Behav.* 61:419–28

De Dreu CK, Greer LL, Handgraaf MJ, Shalvi S, Van Kleef GA, et al. 2010. The neuropeptide oxytocin regulates parochial altruism in intergroup conflict among humans. *Science* 328:1408–11

De Dreu CK, Greer LL, Van Kleef GA, Shalvi S, Handgraaf MJ. 2011. Oxytocin promotes human ethnocentrism. *PNAS* 108:1262–66

De Dreu CK, Kret ME. 2016. Oxytocin conditions intergroup relations through upregulated in-group empathy, cooperation, conformity, and defense. *Biol. Psychiatry* 79:165–73

De Waal FB, Boesch C, Horner V, Whiten A. 2008. Comparing social skills of children and apes. *Science* 319:569

Ditchkoff SS, Saalfeld ST, Gibson CJ. 2006. Animal behavior in urban ecosystems: modifications due to human-induced stress. *Urban Ecosyst.* 9:5–12

Domes G, Steiner A, Porges SW, Heinrichs M. 2013. Oxytocin differentially modulates eye gaze to naturalistic social signals of happiness and anger. *Psychoneuroendocrinology* 38:1198–202

Eisenberg N, Lennon R, Roth K. 1983. Prosocial development: a longitudinal study. *Dev. Psychol.* 19:846–55

Engelmann JM, Over H, Herrmann E, Tomasello M. 2013. Young children care more about their reputation with ingroup members and potential reciprocators. *Dev. Sci.* 16:952–58

Farroni T, Johnson MH, Menon E, Zulian L, Faraguna D, Csibra G. 2005. Newborns' preference for face-relevant stimuli: effects of contrast polarity. *PNAS* 102:17245–50

Farroni T, Massaccesi S, Pividori D, Johnson MH. 2004. Gaze following in newborns. *Infancy* 5:39–60

Fehr E, Schneider F. 2010. Eyes are on us, but nobody cares: Are eye cues relevant for strong reciprocity? *Proc. R. Soc. Lond. B Biol. Sci.* 277:1315–23

Fiske ST, Cuddy AJ, Glick P. 2007. Universal dimensions of social cognition: warmth and competence. *Trends Cogn. Sci.* 11:77–83

Gacsi M, Gyori B, Miklosi A, Viranyi Z, Kubinyi E, et al. 2005. Species-specific differences and similarities in the behavior of hand-raised dog and wolf pups in social situations with humans. *Dev. Psychobiol.* 47:111–22

Gamer M, Zurowski B, Büchel C. 2010. Different amygdala subregions mediate valence-related and attentional effects of oxytocin in humans. *PNAS* 107:9400–5

Gogoleva S, Volodin J, Volodina E, Trut L. 2008. To bark or not to bark: vocalizations by red foxes selected for tameness or aggressiveness toward humans. *Bioacoustics* 18:99–132

Gomez J, Verdu M, Gonzalez-Megias A, Mendez M. 2016. The phylogenetic roots of human lethal violence. *Nature* 538:233–37

Gould SJ. 1977. *Ontogeny and Phylogeny.* Cambridge, MA: Harvard Univ. Press

The first test of the human self-domestication hypothesis revealing predicted morphological changes in fossil humans.

The earliest evolutionary proposal that humans converge with other domestic animals.

Grabowski M, Costa B, Rossoni D, Marroig G, DeSilva J, et al. 2016. From bigger brains to bigger bodies: the correlated evolution of human brain and body size. *Curr. Anthropol.* 57:174–96

Grossmann T. 2015. The development of social brain functions in infancy. *Psychol. Bull.* 141:1266–87

Grossmann T. 2016. The eyes as windows into other minds: an integrative perspective. *Perspect. Psychol. Sci.* In press

Grossmann T, Johnson MH, Lloyd-Fox S, Blasi A, Deligianni F, et al. 2008. Early cortical specialization for face-to-face communication in human infants. *Proc. Biol. Sci.* 275:2803–11

Guastella AJ, Mitchell PB, Dadds MR. 2008. Oxytocin increases gaze to the eye region of human faces. *Biol. Psychiatry* 63:3–5

Gunz P, Neubauer S, Golovanova L, Doronichev V, Maureille B, Hublin JJ. 2012. A uniquely modern human pattern of endocranial development. Insights from a new cranial reconstruction of the Neandertal newborn from Mezmaiskaya. *J. Hum. Evol.* 62:300–13

Hamlin JK, Mahajan N, Liberman Z, Wynn K. 2013. Not like me = bad: Infants prefer those who harm dissimilar others. *Psychol. Sci.* 24:589–94

Hamlin JK, Wynn K. 2011. Young infants prefer prosocial to antisocial others. *Cogn. Dev.* 26:30–39

Hamlin JK, Wynn K, Bloom P. 2007. Social evaluation by preverbal infants. *Nature* 450:557–59

Hare B. 2001. Can competitive paradigms increase the validity of experiments on primate social cognition? *Anim. Cogn.* 4:269–80

Hare B. 2007. From nonhuman to human mind: What changed and why? *Curr. Dir. Psychol. Sci.* 16:60–64

Hare B. 2011. From hominoid to hominid mind: What changed and why? *Annu. Rev. Anthropol.* 40:293–309

Hare B, Brown M, Williamson C, Tomasello M. 2002. The domestication of social cognition in dogs. *Science* 298:1634–36

Hare B, Melis AP, Woods V, Hastings S, Wrangham R. 2007. Tolerance allows bonobos to outperform chimpanzees on a cooperative task. *Curr. Biol.* 17:619–23

Hare B, Plyusnina I, Ignacio N, Schepina O, Stepika A, et al. 2005. Social cognitive evolution in captive foxes is a correlated by-product of experimental domestication. *Curr. Biol.* 15:226–30

Hare B, Rosati A, Kaminski J, Bräuer J, Call J, Tomasello M. 2010. The domestication hypothesis for dogs' skills with human communication: a response to Udell et al. 2008 and Wynne et al. 2008. *Anim. Behav.* 79:e1–e6

Hare B, Tan J. 2012. How much of our cooperative behavior is human? In *The Primate Mind: Built to Connect with Other Minds*, ed. FBM de Waal, PF Ferrari, pp. 175–93. Cambridge, MA: Harvard Univ. Press

Hare B, Tomasello M. 2005a. The emotional reactivity hypothesis and cognitive evolution: reply to Miklósi and Topál. *Trends Cogn. Sci.* 9:464–65

Hare B, Tomasello M. 2005b. Human-like social skills in dogs? *Trends Cogn. Sci.* 9:439–44

Hare B, Wobber V, Wrangham R. 2012. The self-domestication hypothesis: Evolution of bonobo psychology is due to selection against aggression. *Anim. Behav.* 83:573–85

Hare B, Woods V. 2013. *The Genius of Dogs: Discovering the Unique Intelligence of Man's Best Friend*. London: Oneworld Publ.

Hare B, Yamamoto S. 2015. Moving bonobos off the scientifically endangered list. *Behavior* 152:247–58

Harris LT, Fiske ST. 2006. Dehumanizing the lowest of the low: neuroimaging responses to extreme outgroups. *Psychol. Sci.* 17:847–53

Harris LT, Fiske ST. 2009. Social neuroscience evidence for dehumanised perception. *Eur. Rev. Soc. Psychol.* 20:192–231

Henrich J. 2015. *The Secret of Our Success: How Culture is Driving Human Evolution, Domesticating Our Species, and Making Us Smarter*. Princeton, NJ: Princeton Univ. Press

Herculano-Houzel S. 2012. The remarkable, yet not extraordinary, human brain as a scaled-up primate brain and its associated cost. *PNAS* 109:10661–68

Herrmann E, Call J, Hernández-Lloreda MV, Hare B, Tomasello M. 2007. Humans have evolved specialized skills of social cognition: the cultural intelligence hypothesis. *Science* 317:1360–66

Herrmann E, Hare B, Call J, Tomasello M. 2010. Differences in the cognitive skills of bonobos and chimpanzees. *PLOS ONE* 5:e12438

Herrmann E, Hare B, Cissewski J, Tomasello M. 2011. A comparison of temperament in nonhuman apes and human infants. *Dev. Sci.* 14:1393–405

Experimental evidence that (artificial) selection for prosociality leads to more flexible forms of cooperative communication.

Theoretical review of evidence suggesting bonobos are self-domesticated due to natural selection for increased prosociality.

Herrmann E, Misch A, Hernandez-Lloreda V, Tomasello M. 2015. Uniquely human self-control begins at school age. *Dev. Sci.* 18:979–93

Herrmann E, Tomasello M. 2006. Apes' and children's understanding of cooperative and competitive motives in a communicative situation. *Dev. Sci.* 9:518–29

Hodson G, Kteily N, Hoffarth M. 2014. Of filthy pigs and subhuman mongrels: dehumanization, disgust, and intergroup prejudice. *Test. Psychom. Methodol. Appl. Psychol.* 21:267–84

Holloway RL. 2015. The evolution of the hominid brain. In *Handbook of Paleoanthropology*, ed. W Henke, I Tattersall, pp. 1961–87. Berlin: Springer

Horner V. 2010. *The Cultural Mind of Chimpanzees: How Social Tolerance Can Shape the Transmission of Culture.* Chicago: Univ. Chicago Press

Hublin JJ, Neubauer S, Gunz P. 2015. Brain ontogeny and life history in Pleistocene hominins. *Philos. Trans. R. Soc. Lond. B Biol. Sci.* 370:20140062

Jaeggi AV, Stevens JM, Van Schaik CP. 2010. Tolerant food sharing and reciprocity is precluded by despotism among bonobos but not chimpanzees. *Am. J. Phys. Anthropol.* 143:41–51

Jessen S, Grossmann T. 2014. Unconscious discrimination of social cues from eye whites in infants. *PNAS* 111:16208–13

Jordan JJ, McAuliffe K, Warneken F. 2014. Development of in-group favoritism in children's third-party punishment of selfishness. *PNAS* 111:12710–15

Kaas JH. 2000. Why is brain size so important: design problems and solutions as neocortex gets bigger or smaller. *Brain Mind.* 1:7–23

Kagan J, Snidman N. 2009. *The Long Shadow of Temperament.* Cambridge, MA: Harvard Univ. Press

Kaminski J, Call J, Fischer J. 2004. Word learning in a domestic dog: evidence for "fast mapping". *Science* 304:1682–83

Kaminski J, Marshall-Pescini S. 2014. *The Social Dog: Behavior and Cognition.* Amsterdam, Neth: Elsevier

Kano F, Hirata S, Call J. 2015. Social attention in the two species of *Pan*: bonobos make more eye contact than chimpanzees. *PLOS ONE* 10:e0133573

Kinzler KD, Corriveau KH, Harris PL. 2011. Children's selective trust in native-accented speakers. *Dev. Sci.* 14:106–11

Kobayashi H, Kohshima S. 1997. Unique morphology of the human eye. *Nature* 387:767–68

Kobayashi H, Kohshima S. 2001. Unique morphology of the human eye and its adaptive meaning: comparative studies on external morphology of the primate eye. *J. Hum. Evol.* 40:419–35

Koike T, Tanabe HC, Okazaki S, Nakagawa E, Sasaki AT, et al. 2016. Neural substrates of shared attention as social memory: a hyperscanning functional magnetic resonance imaging study. *NeuroImage* 125:401–12

Kosfeld M, Heinrichs M, Zak PJ, Fischbacher U, Fehr E. 2005. Oxytocin increases trust in humans. *Nature* 435:673–76

Kramer KL. 2014. Why what juveniles do matters in the evolution of cooperative breeding. *Hum. Nat.* 25:49–65

Kteily N, Hodson G, Bruneau E. 2016. They see us as less than human: Metadehumanization predicts intergroup conflict via reciprocal dehumanization. *J. Pers. Soc. Psychol.* 110:343–70

Kuepper Y, Alexander N, Osinsky R, Mueller E, Schmitz A, et al. 2010. Aggression—interactions of serotonin and testosterone in healthy men and women. *Behav. Brain Res.* 206:93–100

Kurzban R, Burton-Chellew MN, West SA. 2015. The evolution of altruism in humans. *Annu. Rev. Psychol.* 66:575–99

Kuzawa C, Chugani H, Grossman L, Lipovich L, Muzik O, et al. 2014. Metabolic costs and evolutionary implications of human brain development. *PNAS* 111:13010–15

Lane JD, Wellman HM, Olson SL, Miller AL, Wang L, Tardif T. 2013. Relations between temperament and theory of mind development in the United States and China: biological and behavioral correlates of preschoolers' false-belief understanding. *Dev. Psychol.* 49:825–36

Leach H. 2003. Human domestication reconsidered. *Curr. Anthropol.* 44:349–68

MacLean EL. 2016. Unraveling the evolution of uniquely human cognition. *PNAS* 113:6348–54

MacLean EL, Hare B. 2012. Bonobos and chimpanzees infer the target of another's attention. *Anim. Behav.* 83:345–53

Theoretical review of fossil hominin ontogeny suggesting unique cranial globularization occurring early in human development.

Large-scale comparative anatomical study among primates first demonstrating unique white sclera in humans.

MacLean EL, Hare B. 2013. Spontaneous triadic engagement in bonobos (*Pan paniscus*) and chimpanzees (*Pan troglodytes*). *J. Comp. Psychol.* 127:245–55

MacLean EL, Hare B. 2015a. Bonobos and chimpanzees exploit helpful but not prohibitive gestures. *Behaviour* 152:493–520

MacLean EL, Hare B. 2015b. Dogs hijack the human bonding pathway. *Science* 348:280–81

MacLean EL, Hare B, Nunn CL, Addessi E, Amici F, et al. 2014. The evolution of self-control. *PNAS* 111:E2140–48

MacLean EL, Matthews LJ, Hare BA, Nunn CL, Anderson RC, et al. 2012. How does cognition evolve? Phylogenetic comparative psychology. *Anim. Cogn.* 15:223–38

Mahajan N, Wynn K. 2012. Origins of "us" versus "them": Prelinguistic infants prefer similar others. *Cognition* 124:227–33

Martin A, Santos LR. 2016. What cognitive representations support primate theory of mind? *Trends Cogn. Sci.* 20:375–82

Mayhew JA, Gómez JC. 2015. Gorillas with white sclera: a naturally occurring variation in a morphological trait linked to social cognitive functions. *Am. J. Primatol.* 77:869–77

McBrearty S, Brooks AS. 2000. The revolution that wasn't: a new interpretation of the origin of modern human behavior. *J. Hum. Evol.* 39:453–563

McIntyre MH, Herrmann E, Wobber V, Halbwax M, Mohamba C, et al. 2009. Bonobos have a more human-like second-to-fourth finger length ratio (2D: 4D) than chimpanzees: a hypothesized indication of lower prenatal androgens. *J. Hum. Evol.* 56:361–65

Melis AP, Hare B, Tomasello M. 2006a. Chimpanzees recruit the best collaborators. *Science* 311:1297–300

Melis AP, Hare B, Tomasello M. 2006b. Engineering cooperation in chimpanzees: tolerance constraints on cooperation. *Anim. Behav.* 72:275–86

Melis AP, Hare B, Tomasello M. 2008. Do chimpanzees reciprocate received favours? *Anim. Behav.* 76:951–62

Melis AP, Hare B, Tomasello M. 2009. Chimpanzees coordinate in a negotiation game. *Evol. Hum. Behav.* 30:381–92

Melis AP, Tomasello M. 2013. Chimpanzees' (*Pan troglodytes*) strategic helping in a collaborative task. *Biol. Lett.* 9:20130009

Melis AP, Warneken F, Hare B. 2010. Collaboration and helping in chimpanzees. In *The Mind of the Chimpanzee: Ecological and Experimental Perspectives*, ed. EV Lonsdorf, SR Ross, T Matsuzawa, pp. 278–393. Chicago: Univ. Chicago Press

Meyer-Lindenberg A, Domes G, Kirsch P, Heinrichs M. 2011. Oxytocin and vasopressin in the human brain: social neuropeptides for translational medicine. *Nat. Rev. Neurosci.* 12:524–38

Miklósi Á, Kubinyi E, Topál J, Gácsi M, Virányi Z, Csányi V. 2003. A simple reason for a big difference. *Curr. Biol.* 13:763–66

Mink D, Henning A, Aschersleben G. 2014. Infant shy temperament predicts preschoolers Theory of Mind. *Infant Behav. Dev.* 37:66–75

Montoya ER, Terburg D, Bos PA, van Honk J. 2012. Testosterone, cortisol, and serotonin as key regulators of social aggression: a review and theoretical perspective. *Motiv. Emot.* 36:65–73

Mullen B, Brown R, Smith C. 1992. Ingroup bias as a function of salience, relevance, and status: an integration. *Eur. J. Soc. Psychol.* 22:103–22

Nagasawa M, Mitsui S, En S, Ohtani N, Ohta M, et al. 2015. Oxytocin-gaze positive loop and the coevolution of human-dog bonds. *Science* 348:333–36

Nelson E, Rolian C, Cashmore L, Shultz S. 2011. Digit ratios predict polygyny in early apes, Ardipithecus, Neanderthals and early modern humans but not in Australopithecus. *Proc. Biol. Sci.* 278:1556–63

Nettle D, Nott K, Bateson M. 2012. 'Cycle thieves, we are watching you': impact of a simple signage intervention against bicycle theft. *PLOS ONE* 7:e51738

Plyusnina I, Oskina I, Trut L. 1991. An analysis of fear and aggression during early development of behaviour in silver foxes (*Vulpes vulpes*). *Appl. Anim. Behav. Sci.* 32:253–68

Pontzer H, Brown MH, Raichlen DA, Dunsworth HM, Hare B, et al. 2016. Metabolic acceleration and the evolution of human brain size and life history. *Nature* 533:390–92

Povinelli DJ, Vonk J. 2004. We don't need a microscope to explore the chimpanzee's mind. *Mind Lang.* 19:1–28

Comparative phylogenetics study (*N* = 36 species, >560 subjects) revealing link between increased inhibition and absolute brain size.

Experimental evidence that young human infants show in-group bias during cooperation.

Price T, Langen T. 1992. Evolution of correlated characters. *Trends Ecol. Evol.* 7:307–10

Raia P, Guarino FM, Turano M, Polese G, Rippa D, et al. 2010. The blue lizard spandrel and the island syndrome. *BMC Evol. Biol.* 10:289

Rilling JK, Dagenais JE, Goldsmith DR, Glenn AL, Pagnoni G. 2008a. Social cognitive neural networks during in-group and out-group interactions. *NeuroImage* 41:1447–61

Rilling JK, Glasser MF, Preuss TM, Ma X, Zhao T, et al. 2008b. The evolution of the arcuate fasciculus revealed with comparative DTI. *Nat. Neurosci.* 11:426–28

Rilling JK, Scholz J, Preuss TM, Glasser MF, Errangi BK, Behrens TE. 2011. Differences between chimpanzees and bonobos in neural systems supporting social cognition. *Soc. Cogn. Affect. Neurosci.* 7:369–79

Rimmele U, Hediger K, Heinrichs M, Klaver P. 2009. Oxytocin makes a face in memory familiar. *J. Neurosci.* 29:38–42

Rosati AG, Hare B. 2012. Chimpanzees and bonobos exhibit divergent spatial memory development. *Dev. Sci.* 15:840–53

Saglican E, Ozkurt E, Hu H, Erdem B, Khaitovich P, Somel M. 2014. Heterochrony explains convergent testis evolution in primates. *bioRxiv* 010553

Sakai T, Mikami A, Tomonaga M, Matsui M, Suzuki J, et al. 2011. Differential prefrontal white matter development in chimpanzees and humans. *Curr. Biol.* 21:1397–402

Sanchez-Villagra M, Geiger M, Schneider R. 2016. The taming of the neural crest: a developmental perspective on the origins of morphological covariation in domesticated mammals. *R. Soc. Open Sci.* 3:160107

Schmidt MF, Rakoczy H, Tomasello M. 2012. Young children enforce social norms selectively depending on the violator's group affiliation. *Cognition* 124:325–33

Schoenemann PT. 2006. Evolution of the size and functional areas of the human brain. *Annu. Rev. Anthropol.* 35:379–406

Segal NL, Goetz AT, Maldonado AC. 2016. Preferences for visible white sclera in adults, children and autism spectrum disorder children: implications of the cooperative eye hypothesis. *Evol. Hum. Behav.* 37:35–39

Seko Y, Azuma N, Takahashi Y, Makino H, Morito T, et al. 2008. Human sclera maintains common characteristics with cartilage throughout evolution. *PLOS ONE* 3:e3709

Seyfarth RM, Cheney DL. 2014. The evolution of language from social cognition. *Curr. Opin. Neurobiol.* 28:5–9

Somel M, Franz H, Yan Z, Lorenc A, Guo S, et al. 2009. Transcriptional neoteny in the human brain. *PNAS* 106:5743–48

Somel M, Liu X, Khaitovich P. 2013. Human brain evolution: transcripts, metabolites and their regulators. *Nat. Rev. Neurosci.* 14:112–27

Sripada CS, Phan KL, Labuschagne I, Welsh R, Nathan PJ, Wood AG. 2013. Oxytocin enhances resting-state connectivity between amygdala and medial frontal cortex. *Int. J. Neuropsychopharmacol.* 16:255–60

Stewart L, MacLean EL, Ivy D, Woods V, Cohen E, et al. 2015. Citizen science as a new tool in dog cognition research. *PLOS ONE* 10:e0135176

Stimpson CD, Barger N, Taglialatela JP, Gendron-Fitzpatrick A, Hof PR, et al. 2015. Differential serotonergic innervation of the amygdala in bonobos and chimpanzees. *Soc. Cogn. Affect. Neurosci.* 11:413–22

Surbeck M, Mundry R, Hohmann G. 2011. Mothers matter! Maternal support, dominance status and mating success in male bonobos (*Pan paniscus*). *Proc. R. Soc. Lond. B Biol. Sci.* 278:590–98

Tokuyama N, Furuichi T. 2016. Do friends help each other? Patterns of female coalition formation in wild bonobos at Wamba. *Anim. Behav.* 119:27–35

Tan J, Hare B. 2013. Bonobos share with strangers. *PLOS ONE* 8:e51922

Tomasello M. 2009a. *Constructing a Language: A Usage-Based Theory of Language Acquisition*. Cambridge, MA: Harvard Univ. Press

Tomasello M. 2009b. *The Cultural Origins of Human Cognition*. Cambridge, MA: Harvard Univ. Press

Tomasello M, Carpenter M, Call J, Behne T, Moll H. 2005. Understanding and sharing intentions: the origins of cultural cognition. *Behav. Brain Sci.* 28:675–91

Tomasello M, Farrar MJ. 1986. Joint attention and early language. *Child Dev.* 57:1454–63

Tomasello M, Hare B, Lehmann H, Call J. 2007. Reliance on head versus eyes in the gaze following of great apes and human infants: the cooperative eye hypothesis. *J. Hum. Evol.* 52:314–20

Comparative genomics and gene expression evidence for expanded developmental window of human brain development.

Topál J, Gergely G, Erdőhegyi Á, Csibra G, Miklósi Á. 2009. Differential sensitivity to human communication in dogs, wolves, and human infants. *Science* 325:1269–72

Trut L. 1999. Early canid domestication: the farm-fox experiment: Foxes bred for tamability in a 40-year experiment exhibit remarkable transformations that suggest an interplay between behavioral genetics and development. *Am. Sci.* 87:160–69

Trut L, Oskina I, Kharlamova A. 2009. Animal evolution during domestication: the domesticated fox as a model. *Bioessays* 31:349–60

Udell MA, Dorey NR, Wynne CD. 2010. What did domestication do to dogs? A new account of dogs' sensitivity to human actions. *Biol. Rev.* 85:327–45

Van Honk J, Harmon-Jones E, Morgan BE, Schutter DJ. 2010. Socially explosive minds: the triple imbalance hypothesis of reactive aggression. *J. Pers.* 78:67–94

Viranyi Z, Gacsi M, Kubinyi E, Topál J, Belenyi B, et al. 2008. Comprehension of human pointing gestures in young human-reared wolves (*Canis lupus*) and dogs (*Canis familiaris*). *Anim. Cogn.* 11:373–87

Vlamings PH, Hare B, Call J. 2010. Reaching around barriers: the performance of the great apes and 3–5-year-old children. *Anim. Cogn.* 13:273–85

Walker S, Hare B. 2016. Bonobo baby dominance: Did female defense of offspring lead to reduced male aggression? In *Bonobos: Unique in Mind, Brain and Behavior*, ed. B Hare, S Yamamoto. Oxford, UK: Oxford Univ. Press. In press

Waller BM, Peirce K, Caeiro CC, Scheider L, Burrows AM, et al. 2013. Paedomorphic facial expressions give dogs a selective advantage. *PLOS ONE* 8:e82686

Warneken F. 2015. Precocious prosociality: Why do young children help? *Child Dev. Perspect.* 9:1–6

Warneken F, Hare B, Melis AP, Hanus D, Tomasello M. 2007. Spontaneous altruism by chimpanzees and young children. *PLOS Biol.* 5:e184

Warneken F, Rosati AG. 2015. Cognitive capacities for cooking in chimpanzees. *Proc. R. Soc. B* 282:20150229

Waytz A, Zaki J, Mitchell JP. 2012. Response of dorsomedial prefrontal cortex predicts altruistic behavior. *J. Neurosci.* 32:7646–50

Wellman HM, Lane JD, LaBounty J, Olson SL. 2011. Observant, nonaggressive temperament predicts theory-of-mind development. *Dev. Sci.* 14:319–26

West-Eberhard MJ. 2003. *Developmental Plasticity and Evolution*. Oxford, UK: Oxford Univ. Press

Whalen PJ, Kagan J, Cook RG, Davis FC, Kim H, et al. 2004. Human amygdala responsivity to masked fearful eye whites. *Science* 306:2061

Whiten A. 2013. Humans are not alone in computing how others see the world. *Anim. Behav.* 86:213–21

Wilkins AS, Wrangham RW, Fitch WT. 2014. The "domestication syndrome" in mammals: a unified explanation based on neural crest cell behavior and genetics. *Genetics* 197:795–808

Wilson JP, Rule NO. 2015. Facial trustworthiness predicts extreme criminal-sentencing outcomes. *Psychol. Sci.* 26:1325–31

Wilson ML, Boesch C, Fruth B, Furuichi T, Gilby IC, et al. 2014. Lethal aggression in *Pan* is better explained by adaptive strategies than human impacts. *Nature* 513:414–17

Wobber V, Hare B. 2015. Behavioral heterochrony. In *Emerging Trends in the Social and Behavioral Sciences: An Interdisciplinary, Searchable, and Linkable Resource*, ed. RA Scott, SM Kosslyn, N Pinkerton. doi: 10.1002/9781118900772

Wobber V, Hare B, Koler-Matznick J, Wrangham R, Tomasello M. 2009. Breed differences in domestic dogs' (*Canis familiaris*) comprehension of human communicative signals. *Interact. Stud.* 10:206–24

Wobber V, Hare B, Maboto J, Lipson S, Wrangham R, Ellison PT. 2010a. Differential changes in steroid hormones before competition in bonobos and chimpanzees. *PNAS* 107:12457–62

Wobber V, Hare B, Wrangham R. 2008. Great apes prefer cooked food. *J. Hum. Evol.* 55:340–48

Wobber V, Herrmann E, Hare B, Wrangham R, Tomasello M. 2014. Differences in the early cognitive development of children and great apes. *Dev. Psychobiol.* 56:547–73

Wobber V, Wrangham R, Hare B. 2010b. Bonobos exhibit delayed development of social behavior and cognition relative to chimpanzees. *Curr. Biol.* 20:226–30

Wood B, Boyle E. 2016. Hominin taxic diversity: fact or fantasy? *Am. J. Phys. Anthropol.* 159:S37–78

Wood RM, Rilling JK, Sanfey AG, Bhagwagar Z, Rogers RD. 2006. Effects of tryptophan depletion on the performance of an iterated Prisoner's Dilemma game in healthy adults. *Neuropsychopharmacology* 31:1075–84

Woods V, Hare B. 2011. Bonobo but not chimpanzee infants use socio-sexual contact with peers. *Primates* 52:111–16

Wrangham RW. 1999. Evolution of coalitionary killing. *Am. J. Phys. Anthropol.* 110:1–30

Wrangham RW. 2009. *Catching Fire: How Cooking Made Us Human.* New York: Basic Books

Wrangham RW. 2014. Did *Homo sapiens* self-domesticate? *Domestication and Human Evolution Video Series,* Cent. Acad. Res. Train. Anthropog., San Diego, CA, Oct. 10. **https://www.youtube.com/watch?v=acOZT240bTA**

Wrangham RW, Glowacki L. 2012. Intergroup aggression in chimpanzees and war in nomadic hunter-gatherers. *Hum. Nat.* 23:5–29

Wrangham RW, Pilbeam D. 2002. African apes as time machines. In *All Apes Great and Small,* ed. BMF Galdikas, NE Briggs, LK Sheeran, GL Shapiro, J Goodall, pp. 5–17. Berlin: Springer

Wrangham RW, Wilson ML, Muller MN. 2006. Comparative rates of violence in chimpanzees and humans. *Primates* 47:14–26

Zollikofer CP, Ponce de Leon MS. 2010. The evolution of hominin ontogenies. *Semin. Cell Dev. Biol.* 21:441–52

Numerical Development

Robert S. Siegler[1,2] and David W. Braithwaite[1]

[1]Department of Psychology, Carnegie Mellon University, Pittsburgh, Pennsylvania 15213;
email: rs7k@andrew.cmu.edu

[2]The Siegler Center for Innovative Learning (SCIL), Beijing Normal University,
Beijing 100875, China

Annu. Rev. Psychol. 2017. 68:187–213

First published online as a Review in Advance on
September 21, 2016

The *Annual Review of Psychology* is online at
psych.annualreviews.org

This article's doi:
10.1146/annurev-psych-010416-044101

Keywords

numerical magnitudes, logarithmic-to-linear shift, rational numbers,
arithmetic, mathematics achievement, conceptual understanding

Abstract

In this review, we attempt to integrate two crucial aspects of numerical
development: learning the magnitudes of individual numbers and learning
arithmetic. Numerical magnitude development involves gaining increasingly
precise knowledge of increasing ranges and types of numbers: from nonsymbolic to small symbolic numbers, from smaller to larger whole numbers, and
from whole to rational numbers. One reason why this development is important is that precision of numerical magnitude knowledge is correlated with,
predictive of, and causally related to both whole and rational number arithmetic. Rational number arithmetic, however, also poses challenges beyond
understanding the magnitudes of the individual numbers. Some of these
challenges are inherent; they are present for all learners. Other challenges
are culturally contingent; they vary from country to country and classroom
to classroom. Generating theories and data that help children surmount the
challenges of rational number arithmetic is a promising and important goal
for future numerical development research.

Contents

INTRODUCTION

Numerical knowledge is of great and increasing importance for success in modern society. Reflecting this pervasive importance, numerical knowledge at age 7 predicts socioeconomic status at age 42, even after controlling for the rearing family's socioeconomic status and the child's IQ, working memory, reading skill, years of education, academic motivation, and other variables (Ritchie & Bates 2013).

Consequential individual differences in numerical knowledge are present even before children reach first grade. The numerical knowledge of kindergartners from low-income backgrounds already lags, on average, at least a year behind that of peers from middle-income families (Jordan et al. 2006). These early differences have long-term consequences: A meta-analysis of six large longitudinal studies in the United States, United Kingdom, and Canada revealed that in all six, numerical knowledge in kindergarten predicted numerical knowledge in fifth grade, even after statistically controlling for a wide range of relevant variables (Duncan et al. 2007). Even more striking, numerical knowledge at age 4 predicts mathematics achievement at age 15 (Watts et al. 2014), again after controlling for numerous relevant variables. Many aspects of cognitive development are fairly stable over time, but the relations between early and later mathematical knowledge are stronger than for other important competencies measured in the same studies, including reading, control of attention, and regulation of emotions (Duncan et al. 2007).

Numerical knowledge is also central to theories of cognitive development. Kant [2003 (1781)] argued that number is an a priori concept, an idea that must be present from birth for people and other animals to function in the world. Evidence collected more than 200 years later supports this insight. Animals as varied as guppies, lions, rats, newborn chickens, and human infants mentally represent the approximate number of objects and events they encounter (Dehaene 2011, Piffer et al. 2013, Rugani et al. 2015).

Piaget (e.g., 1952) also assigned numerical development a prominent place in his theory, devoting his classic book *The Child's Concept of Number*, as well as parts of many other books, to it. Contemporary theories, such as neo-Piagetian (Case & Okamoto 1996), core knowledge (Feigenson et al. 2004), information processing (e.g., Siegler 2006), sociocultural (Goncu & Gauvain 2012), evolutionary (Geary et al. 2015), and dynamic systems (Cantrell & Smith 2013), also emphasize the growth of numerical understanding as central to cognitive development.

Consistent with this theoretical emphasis, numerical development is a thriving research area, one with at least 15 active subareas (Siegler 2016). The focus of the present review is on four especially notable themes that have emerged in recent years and that transcend the boundaries of these subareas:

(*a*) Acquisition of increasingly precise knowledge of the magnitudes of increasing ranges and types of numbers provides a unifying theme for numerical development from infancy to adulthood.

(*b*) Understanding numerical development requires understanding acquisition of knowledge about rational numbers (i.e., fractions, decimals, percentages, and negatives) as well as whole numbers (i.e., 0, 1, 2, 3, etc.).

(*c*) Knowledge of the magnitudes of individual numbers is essential to learning arithmetic.

(*d*) Major goals for future research should include clarifying why understanding rational number arithmetic is so hard for so many people and generating effective instruction in it.

The integrated theory of numerical development provides a structure within which to discuss these themes.

THE INTEGRATED THEORY OF NUMERICAL DEVELOPMENT

Underlying the integrated theory of numerical development is the assumption that increasing understanding of numerical magnitudes is the common core of numerical development, one that affects arithmetic and more advanced mathematics as well (Siegler et al. 2011). The theory can be summarized as follows:

(*a*) People, like many other animals, represent the magnitudes of numbers on a mental number line, a dynamic structure that is first used to represent small whole numbers and then is progressively extended rightward to include larger whole numbers, leftward to include negative numbers, and interstitially to include fractions and decimals. The approximate age ranges during which these changes occur are shown in **Figure 1**.

(*b*) Whole number magnitude representations progress from a compressive, approximately logarithmic distribution to an approximately linear one. Transitions occur earlier for smaller than for larger ranges of whole numbers, corresponding both to the complexity of the numbers and to the ages when children gain experience with them.

(*c*) Development of numerical understanding also involves learning that many properties of whole numbers do not characterize other types of numbers, but that all real numbers have magnitudes that can be represented and ordered on number lines.

(*d*) Knowledge of the magnitudes of both whole and rational numbers is correlated with, and predictive of, learning of arithmetic and more advanced aspects of mathematics.

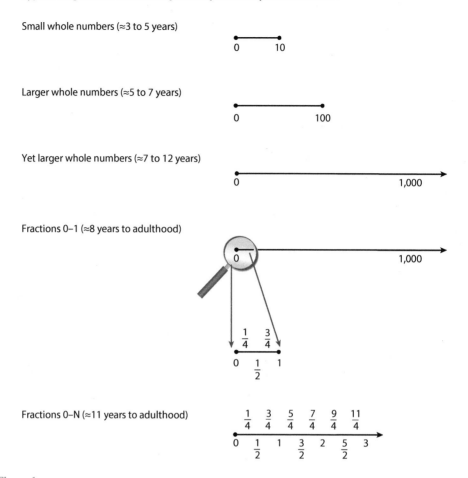

Figure 1

Approximate age ranges of major changes to the sizes and types of symbolic numbers whose magnitudes individuals can represent.

    (*e*) Knowledge of numerical magnitudes is also causally related to learning of arithmetic; interventions that improve knowledge of numerical magnitudes often have positive effects on learning arithmetic.

    The integrated theory, like many other approaches, assumes that numerical magnitudes are represented along a mental number line (for a review of evidence for this assumption, see Hubbard et al. 2005). At least in Western and Far Eastern cultures, the mental number line is usually horizontally oriented, with smaller numbers on the left and larger ones on the right. People are only one of many species that use this organization. For example, after newborn chicks are repeatedly presented a constant number of dots (e.g., 4), they spontaneously associate smaller sets of dots (e.g., 2) with the left side of space and larger sets of dots (e.g., 8) with the right (Rugani et al. 2015).

    One type of evidence for the mental number line is the distance effect: Identification of the larger of two numbers is faster the farther apart the numbers are (Moyer & Landauer 1967). The effect known as SNARC (spatial-numerical association of response codes) provides another type of evidence. When asked which of two numbers is larger, people are faster to indicate "smaller" by pressing a button on their left and to indicate "larger" by pressing a button on their right than with the opposite pairings of side of the body and relative magnitude (e.g., Dehaene et al. 1990). SNARC effects emerge between 5 and 9 years of age: at the lower end of the range when magnitudes are relevant to achieving the goal of the task, and at the higher end when they are irrelevant to the goal (Berch et al. 1999, Hoffmann et al. 2013).

The hypothesis that the mental number line is a dynamic structure that is gradually extended to represent all numerical magnitudes expands the range of ages and types of numbers that can be integrated within a single theory of numerical development. In particular, the integrated theory allows analyses of development to extend from infants' knowledge of nonsymbolic numerical magnitudes (i.e., numbers represented as sets of dots, sequences of tones, etc.) to young children's knowledge of small symbolic whole number magnitudes (i.e., numbers represented by number words or numerals) to older children's knowledge of increasingly large symbolic whole number magnitudes to yet older children's and adults' representations of the magnitudes of symbolic fractions, decimals, and negatives.

One consequence of the focus of the integrated theory on rational as well as whole numbers is to reveal a basic challenge that numerical development poses to children: learning which properties of whole numbers apply to all numbers and which do not. Many properties that are true for all whole numbers do not hold for other types of numbers. Each whole number is represented by a unique symbol within a given symbol system (e.g., 4), but each fraction can be expressed in infinitely many ways (e.g., 1/4, 2/8, 3/12...). All natural numbers (whole numbers other than zero) have unique whole number predecessors and successors, but no decimal does. Multiplying natural numbers never generates a product smaller than either multiplicand, but multiplying rational numbers between 0 and 1 always does. Adding whole numbers never yields an answer smaller than either addend, but adding negatives always does. However, all real numbers share the property that they can be located and ordered on number lines.

A great deal of evidence indicates that numerical magnitude knowledge is related to important mathematical outcomes. For example, such magnitude knowledge correlates positively, and often quite strongly, with children's mathematics achievement in both cross-sectional studies (Ashcraft & Moore 2012, Booth & Siegler 2006, Siegler & Booth 2004) and longitudinal ones (de Smedt et al. 2009, Östergren & Träff 2013). This relation remains present even after controlling for other variables related to mathematics achievement, including IQ, language, nonverbal reasoning, attention, working memory, calculation skill, and reading fluency (Bailey et al. 2012, Jordan et al. 2013).

A basic prediction of the integrated theory is that precision of numerical magnitude knowledge should be correlated with, and predictive of, arithmetic proficiency. This relation is not logically necessary. Children could memorize arithmetic facts and procedures without understanding the magnitudes of the operands (the numbers in problems) and answers. Indeed, many mathematics educators have lamented that rote memorization of arithmetic procedures is exactly what most students do (Cramer et al. 2002, Mack 1995).

In contrast, we hypothesize that many children do use numerical magnitudes to understand arithmetic and that knowledge of numerical magnitudes is much of what makes arithmetic, as well as algebra and other aspects of mathematics, meaningful. For example, when the task is to remember answers to specific arithmetic problems (e.g., $6 \times 4 = 24$), more precise representations of the operands and answer may facilitate recall of the answer, in part by making alternatives implausible (e.g., a child with good magnitude understanding might think of 36 when asked to answer 6×4, because 36 is a multiple of both operands, but might not state it because it seems too big). When the task is to learn arithmetic procedures, accurate magnitude representations make it possible for students to reject procedures that produce implausible answers, leading them to generate and test alternative procedures. For example, when $1/2 + 1/3$ is presented, a child with good knowledge of the magnitudes of individual fractions might initially add the numerators and denominators separately but reject the procedure after seeing that it resulted in an answer ($2/5$) that is smaller than one of the addends.

Thus, the integrated theory predicts that arithmetic facts and procedures will be learned more quickly and completely by children with greater knowledge of the magnitudes of the numbers used in the computations. It also predicts that instruction and other manipulations that improve magnitude understanding will improve arithmetic learning. Due to the pervasiveness of both whole and rational number arithmetic in algebra, trigonometry, and other more advanced areas of mathematics, the theory predicts similar relations between numerical magnitude knowledge and overall math achievement.

DEVELOPMENT OF NUMERICAL MAGNITUDE KNOWLEDGE

The development of numerical magnitude knowledge includes four main changes: generating increasingly precise representations of nonsymbolic magnitudes, connecting symbolic to non-symbolic magnitudes for small whole numbers, accurately representing increasingly large whole numbers, and accurately representing the magnitudes of rational numbers. Siegler (2016) provides an in-depth review of the development of numerical magnitude knowledge; here, we summarize major findings about it.

Development of Whole Number Magnitude Knowledge

Nonsymbolic magnitudes. Infants and many nonhuman animals can discriminate sets of dots or tones that differ in their number but not in dimensions correlated with number, such as summed surface area of dots or duration of tones. With number as well as with many other dimensions, the larger the ratio of number of entities in the sets being compared, the easier is the discrimination. This property of numerical discrimination is known as ratio dependence. Six-month-olds can discriminate 2:1 but not 1.5:1 ratios, and nine-month-olds can discriminate 1.5:1 but not 1.3:1 ratios (Cordes & Brannon 2008). Discrimination between nonsymbolic numerical magnitudes continues to become more precise well beyond infancy, with many adults able to reliably discriminate 1.14:1 ratios (Halberda & Feigenson 2008).

One exception to the ratio dependence of nonsymbolic number discrimination is that discrimination of sets of one to four objects is more accurate, faster, and less variable than would be expected from the ratios alone (Piazza 2011). Interestingly, guppies show the same superiority in discriminating between sets of one to four objects, relative to their usual ratio dependence (Agrillo et al. 2012). This superiority may reflect subitizing, a process that produces quick and automatic perception of small sets of objects or events.

Although precision of discrimination increases with age, the brain areas that most actively process nonsymbolic numerical magnitudes are similar over the course of development. Parts of the intraparietal sulcus (IPS) and dorsolateral prefrontal cortex play major roles in processing nonsymbolic numerical magnitudes from infancy to adulthood (Dehaene 2011).

Small symbolic whole number magnitudes. Nonsymbolic numerical magnitude knowledge provides useful referents for learning the magnitudes represented by symbolic numbers. For example, the spoken word "three" and the Arabic numeral "3" can be mapped onto three dots or fingers. A number of investigators have hypothesized that individual differences in symbolic representations of numerical magnitudes grow out of individual differences in nonsymbolic numerical discrimination (e.g., Halberda et al. 2008, Izard et al. 2008).

Several types of evidence have been cited to support this hypothesis. Ratio dependence like that observed with discrimination of nonsymbolic numerical magnitudes is also evident with discrimination of symbolic numbers (e.g., "Which is bigger, 6 or 8?") (Dehaene 2011). Individual differences in the precision of nonsymbolic magnitude discrimination are predictive of concurrent and future individual differences in discrimination between symbolic magnitudes and are also predictive of symbolic arithmetic and math achievement test scores (e.g., Libertus et al. 2011). Habituation to nonsymbolic numbers generates habituation to equivalent symbolic numbers, as measured by functional magnetic resonance imaging (fMRI) activations (Piazza et al. 2007). Brain areas used to process nonsymbolic and symbolic numbers overlap considerably (Nieder & Dehaene 2009).

Other data, however, have called into question the strength and specificity of the relation between nonsymbolic and symbolic numerical magnitude knowledge. Ratio and distance effects are present not just with nonsymbolic and symbolic numerical stimuli but also with totally nonnumerical tasks, including odor discrimination (Parnas et al. 2013). Relations between the precision of nonsymbolic and symbolic number representations, and between nonsymbolic representations and overall math achievement, have proved far weaker than suggested by early studies (Halberda et al. 2008). Two meta-analyses (Chen & Li 2014, Fazio et al. 2014) found that the average weighted correlation between nonsymbolic magnitude discrimination and overall math achievement was $r = 0.20$ and $r = 0.22$, respectively. An Internet study with more than 10,000 adult participants yielded a relation of $r = 0.21$ (Halberda et al. 2012), and a carefully controlled study with 200 children in each year from first through sixth grade yielded a relation of $r = 0.21$ (Lyons et al. 2014). All of these relations were significant, but all also were weak.

Neural data also have proved more complex than they originally appeared. Symbolic and nonsymbolic numbers are processed in the same general areas of the brain, but processing activities within those areas elicited by corresponding nonsymbolic and symbolic numbers are weakly related (Bulthé et al. 2014, Lyons et al. 2014).

More generally, it is unclear how approximate nonsymbolic representations could contribute to creating precise symbolic understanding of large numbers. No one can consistently discriminate 158 from 159 dots, but everyone who understands the decimal system knows with absolute certainty that 159 is larger than 158.

These data do not imply that knowledge of nonsymbolic numerical magnitudes plays no role in learning the magnitudes of symbolic numbers. It seems likely that toddlers and preschoolers acquire the meaning of small symbolic single-digit numbers by associating them with nonsymbolic representations of the corresponding sets. Consistent with this view, Le Corre & Carey (2007) found that 2- and 3-year-olds learn the magnitudes denoted by the symbolic number words 1 to 4 through a slow process in which they associate first the word "1," then "2," then "3," and then "4" with the corresponding nonsymbolic quantities produced by subitizing.

The process might well extend beyond the subitizing range. Young children frequently put up fingers and count them. The auditory, visual, kinesthetic, and temporal cues that accompany counting of fingers and other objects provide data for associating nonsymbolic quantities with the symbolic numbers that children most often use in counting and adding, that is, the numbers 1 through 10. Consistent with this hypothesis, behavioral data from 4- to 6-year-olds indicate that putting up fingers activates symbolic numbers and answers to addition problems with sums of 10 or less (Siegler & Shrager 1984). Neuroimaging studies provide converging evidence; fMRI data indicate a common neural substrate for finger representations and mental addition and subtraction

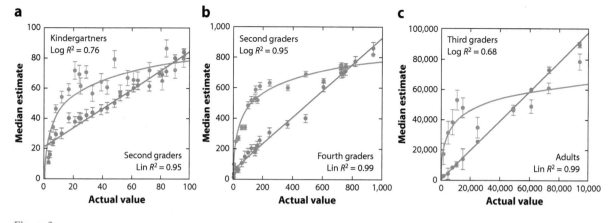

Figure 2

Relations between presented and estimated whole number magnitudes for different ranges of numbers and ages of participants. (*a*) When estimating numbers in the 0 to 100 range, kindergartners generate a logarithmic relation, whereas second graders generate a linear one [adapted from Siegler & Booth (2004) with permission from John Wiley & Sons]. (*b*) With numbers in the 0 to 1,000 range, second graders generate a logarithmic relation and fourth graders a linear one [adapted from Opfer & Siegler (2007) with permission from Elsevier]. (*c*) With numbers in the 0 to 100,000 range, third graders generate a logarithmic relation and adults a linear one [adapted from Thompson & Opfer (2008) with permission from John Wiley & Sons].

with the numbers 1 through 10 for both children and adults (Andres et al. 2012, Berteletti & Booth 2015). Thus, nonsymbolic numerical representations seem to help symbolic numerical magnitude knowledge get off the ground through providing concrete referents for small symbolic whole numbers. Whether individual differences in these representations contribute to individual differences in understanding larger symbolic numerical magnitudes remains an open question.

Large symbolic whole number magnitudes. Children learn about the magnitudes of symbolic whole numbers surprisingly slowly. After children count flawlessly from 1 to 10, they still take a year or more to understand the relative magnitudes of the numbers they are counting (Le Corre & Carey 2007).

Beyond the ages when children have mastered ordinal relations among the symbolic numbers 1 through 10, they represent their magnitudes as increasing in a nonlinear, approximately logarithmic, pattern (**Figure 2**). Illustratively, when 3- and 4-year-olds are asked to perform the number-line estimation task by placing numbers on a line with 0 at the left end, 10 at the right end, and nothing in between, they locate small numbers, such as 2 and 3, much farther apart than larger numbers, such as 8 and 9. In contrast, 5- and 6-year-olds space the two pairs of numbers equally (Berteletti et al. 2010). Thus, between ages 3 and 6 years, children progress from an approximately logarithmic relation to an approximately linear relation between the numbers 1 through 10 and estimates of their magnitudes.

The same developmental sequence recurs at older ages with larger numbers. In the 0 to 100 range, 5- and 6-year-olds generate logarithmically increasing estimates, whereas 7- and 8-year-olds generate linearly increasing ones (Geary et al. 2007, Siegler & Booth 2004). In the 0 to 1,000 range, 7- and 8-year-olds generate logarithmically increasing estimates, but 9- and 10-year-olds generate linearly increasing ones (Booth & Siegler 2006, Thompson & Opfer 2010). Chinese children generate the same developmental progression for each numerical range at younger ages (Siegler & Mu 2008, Xu et al. 2013); children with math learning difficulties generate the same progression at older ages (Reeve et al. 2015). Even in adulthood, the logarithmic representation continues to be seen in transitory processes during number-line estimation, though the final estimates increase linearly (Dotan & Dehaene 2013).

Analogies between smaller and larger orders of magnitude seem to contribute to broadening the range of whole numbers whose magnitudes children represent linearly. Encountering problems presented in ways that highlighted the analogy between smaller and larger numerical ranges—for example, the analogy between the location of 15 on a 0–100 number line and 1,500 on a 0–10,000 number line—led second graders to extend the linear estimation pattern from the 0–100 to the 0–10,000 and the 0–100,000 number lines (Thompson & Opfer 2010). Analogies involving smaller numbers, such as the analogy from 0–100 to 0–1,000 number lines, also have been found to promote generalization of accurate magnitude representations (Opfer & Siegler 2007, Sullivan & Barner 2014).

Development of Rational Number Magnitude Knowledge

Nonsymbolic rational numbers. Development of understanding of nonsymbolic rational number magnitudes, like that of whole number magnitudes, begins in infancy. Six-month-olds can accurately discriminate between two ratios that differ by at least a factor of two. For example, they dishabituate (i.e., look longer) when, after repeated presentations of 2:1 ratios of yellow to blue dots, the ratio of yellow to blue dots switches to 4:1 (McCrink & Wynn 2007). This level of precision matches age peers' discrimination abilities with nonsymbolic whole number displays.

Neuroscience research also points to similarities in whole and rational number processing. Both nonsymbolic and symbolic rational number magnitudes are processed by a fronto-parietal network closely resembling that used to process whole number magnitudes (e.g., Jacob et al. 2012). Neural activations show similar distance effects with fractions as with whole numbers on nonsymbolic numerical magnitude comparison tasks (Ischebeck et al. 2009).

Symbolic rational numbers. The process of acquiring understanding of the magnitudes of symbolic rational numbers starts later, proceeds more slowly, and asymptotes at a lower level than the corresponding process with symbolic whole numbers. Although written fraction notation is usually introduced in early elementary school, connecting written fractions with the magnitudes that they represent remains challenging even for many adults. In several studies, adult community college students correctly answered only 70% to 80% of magnitude comparison problems for fractions with unequal numerators and denominators, where chance was 50% (e.g., Givvin et al. 2011, Schneider & Siegler 2010). This weak performance does not appear to be due to forgetting after years of not studying fractions; middle school students' fraction magnitude comparison accuracy is in the same range (Bailey et al. 2014, Siegler & Pyke 2013).

Acquisition of magnitude knowledge is faster and reaches a higher asymptotic level with fractions from 0 to 1 than for larger fractions, such as fractions from 0 to 5. For example, sixth graders in Belgium had a mean percent absolute error of 9% for fractions between 0 and 1 but 20% for fractions between 0 and 5; the corresponding numbers for peers in the United States were 17% and 26%, and in China 10% and 14% (Torbeyns et al. 2015). Strikingly, second graders' whole number estimates on 0–100 number lines are often more accurate than eighth graders' estimates of fractions on 0–5 number lines (Siegler & Booth 2004, Siegler et al. 2011).

Understanding the magnitudes of symbolically expressed decimals also poses problems for learners. Many fourth to eighth graders predict that, as with whole numbers, longer sequences of digits imply larger numbers (e.g., they think that 0.123 > 0.45) (Lortie-Forgues & Siegler in press, Resnick et al. 1989). Nonetheless, accuracy and speed of numerical magnitude comparison and number-line estimation tend to be greater for decimals than for common fractions (Iuculano & Butterworth 2011).

Alongside the striking differences between development of knowledge of whole and rational numbers are notable similarities. In comparisons of the magnitudes of pairs of fractions or decimals, distance effects are present among both children (Fazio et al. 2014, Iuculano & Butterworth 2011) and adults (Meert et al. 2009, Schneider & Siegler 2010). Moreover, for both symbolic rational and whole numbers, relations are present between precision of magnitude knowledge and arithmetic, as well as between magnitude knowledge and overall mathematics achievement (e.g., Bailey et al. 2015, Torbeyns et al. 2015).

Early individual differences in whole number magnitude knowledge are also predictive of later individual differences in rational number magnitude knowledge. For example, in Bailey and colleagues' (2014) study, 6-year-olds' number-line estimation accuracy with whole numbers predicted their accuracy with fractions at age 13, even after statistically controlling for many relevant variables. Number-line estimation accuracy at age 6 did not predict reading achievement at age 13, which lends discriminant validity to the findings. Similar predictive relations have emerged in other age ranges (Hecht & Vagi 2010, Jordan et al. 2013, Resnick et al. 2016). Causal relations between earlier symbolic whole number magnitude knowledge and later rational number magnitude knowledge remain to be established but may well be present.

DEVELOPMENT OF ARITHMETIC

Nonsymbolic Whole Number Arithmetic

In addition to representing nonsymbolic numerical magnitudes, infants also can perform approximate arithmetic on these representations. Four- to five-month-olds dishabituate when it appears (through trickery) that adding one or two objects to an initial one or two has produced more or fewer objects than the correct number; infants of the same age also dishabituate when shown unexpected subtractive outcomes with similarly small sets (Wynn 1992). Somewhat older infants dishabituate to surprising addition and subtraction outcomes on sets of 5 to 10 objects (McCrink & Wynn 2004).

The neural substrates subserving nonsymbolic arithmetic overlap considerably with those involved in nonsymbolic numerical representations of single sets of objects. In particular, nonsymbolic addition elicits activation in the IPS (Venkatraman et al. 2005), and nonsymbolic addition and subtraction are associated with increased coordinated activity in functionally connected left and right parietal areas, including the IPS (Park et al. 2013).

Symbolic Whole Number Arithmetic

Impressive agreement exists on descriptive features of the development of symbolic whole number arithmetic procedures and concepts (Geary et al. 2017, Verschaffel et al. 2007). The process typically begins at approximately age 3 with counting-based procedures, such as first putting up fingers to represent each addend and then counting from one (the sum strategy), and retrieving from memory the answers to a few small addend problems. Individual preschoolers typically use several distinct counting-based strategies as well as retrieval rather than relying on a single approach. This variable strategy use continues into childhood and adulthood and is present on all four arithmetic operations. Even students attending high-quality universities use strategies other than retrieval to generate answers on 15% to 30% of single-digit problems on all four arithmetic operations (Campbell & Xue 2001, LeFevre et al. 2003).

From early in development, choices among arithmetic strategies are highly adaptive, in the sense of promoting desirable combinations of accuracy and speed (Siegler 1996). In choosing whether to state a retrieved answer or to use a strategy other than retrieval, preschoolers, older children, and adults predominantly use retrieval, the fastest strategy, when they can execute it accurately. They predominantly use slower strategies, such as counting from one or counting-on from the larger addend, when they cannot retrieve accurately. In choosing among strategies other than retrieval, children most often use each backup strategy on the problems where it yields the fastest and most accurate performance relative to available alternatives. For example, 8- to 10-year-olds often subtract by counting up or down, depending on which can be done with fewer counts. They usually count down on $13 - 2$ ("12 is 1, 11 is 2, answer is 11") but usually count up on $13 - 11$ ("12 is 1, 13 is 2, answer is 2") (Siegler 1989).

Along with these commonalities over age of variable strategy use and adaptive strategy choice are large developmental changes. At a general level, arithmetic becomes faster and more accurate. Four sources of this greater speed and accuracy are discovery of new, more effective, strategies; increasing use of the more effective strategies that are already known; faster and more accurate execution of strategies; and increasingly adaptive choices among strategies (Siegler 1996). For example, between ages 5 and 8, children (*a*) discover the addition strategies of counting-on from the larger addend and decomposition (e.g., adding $3 + 9$ by thinking, "$10 + 3 = 13$, $13 - 1 = 12$"); (*b*) increasingly use those relatively efficient strategies and decreasingly use the less efficient strategies of counting from one and guessing; (*c*) execute all strategies more quickly and accurately; and (*d*) generate increasingly adaptive strategy choices.

Beyond these changes in whole number arithmetic procedures, young children also gain considerable conceptual understanding of whole number arithmetic. Five-year-olds discriminate between the validity of strategies that they do not themselves use but that are legitimate (counting-on) and the validity of illegitimate strategies that they also do not use (counting the first addend twice) (Siegler & Crowley 1994). They also gain understanding of the commutative and associative principles (Baroody & Tiilikainen 2003). Moreover, observations of strategy discoveries indicate that children rarely generate conceptually flawed addition strategies under conditions in which they do discover novel correct strategies (Siegler & Jenkins 1989).

One reason for whole number arithmetic strategies being conceptually grounded is that knowledge of earlier learned operations is used to build knowledge of later ones. Knowledge of counting provides a base for learning and understanding addition, and knowledge of addition provides a base for learning and understanding subtraction (as in the previous example of solving $13 - 11$). Addition and subtraction provide a base for understanding multiplication (as when solving 4×3 by adding three fours or four threes) and division (as when solving $12 \div 4$ by adding or subtracting fours while keeping track of the number of fours). Learning of division also benefits from knowledge of multiplication (as when solving $12 \div 4$ by reasoning that if $3 \times 4 = 12$, then $12 \div 4 = 3$).

Another likely reason for children's whole number arithmetic strategies being conceptually grounded is that magnitude knowledge provides a way to check whether answers, and the strategies that yielded them, are reasonable. When asked to verify whether a given answer to a single-digit arithmetic problem is correct, both children and adults are faster to reply "no" when the incorrect answer is far from the correct magnitude (e.g., $5 + 7 = 18$) than when it is close (e.g., $5 + 7 = 14$) (Ashcraft 1995, Campbell & Fugelsang 2001). Similarly, errors generated while solving single-digit arithmetic problems are usually close in magnitude to the correct answer (Siegler 1988).

Understanding does take longer to develop for some arithmetic principles, such as mathematical equality (e.g., $3 + 4 + 5 = \underline{\quad} + 5$) (Alibali & Goldin-Meadow 1993, McNeil 2014) and inversion relations between multiplication and division (e.g., $9 \times 17 \div 17 = $ ____) (Robinson 2016). Moreover, understanding of single-digit procedures is often better than understanding of multidigit arithmetic, as indicated by the existence of buggy subtraction approaches (Brown & Van Lehn 1982) among elementary school students (e.g., answering $308 - 145$ by writing 243, on the logic that the smaller digit in a given column should be subtracted from the larger one, regardless of which number includes the smaller digit in the column). Nonetheless, most children develop substantial understanding of whole number arithmetic.

The cognitive processes that generate both procedural and conceptual development of whole number arithmetic have been modeled in computer simulations (e.g., Shrager & Siegler 1998, Siegler & Araya 2005). These simulations produce changes in thinking that closely resemble those of children along many dimensions. Within the models, development is produced by associating problems with answers and with strategies that produce fast and accurate performance on the problems, freeing of working memory capacity with more efficient strategy execution, and use of goal sketches, a cognitive structure used to evaluate the plausibility of potential new strategies by determining whether they meet the goals viewed as essential for a reasonable strategy for a given task. Together, these processes lead to increasing frequency of retrieval of correct answers, greater use of the more advanced strategies from among existing approaches, increasing knowledge of the types of problems for which each strategy is most effective, and discovery of useful new arithmetic strategies without attempting flawed ones.

Fraction Arithmetic

Knowledge of fraction arithmetic is indispensable for many purposes; students learning physics, chemistry, biology, psychology, economics, statistics, engineering, and many other subjects depend on it. Reflecting this importance, fraction arithmetic was part of more than half of the equations on the reference sheets for the most recent US advanced placement exams in physics and chemistry (College Board 2015). Knowledge of fraction arithmetic also is essential not only in STEM (science, technology, engineering, and mathematics) areas but also in such positions as nurse and pharmacist (e.g., for calculating and evaluating prescribed drug doses), automotive technician, stone mason, carpenter, and tool and die maker (e.g., for adjusting the angles of precision cutting tools) (Davidson 2012, McCloskey 2007, Sformo 2008).

Unfortunately, learning fraction arithmetic is often difficult, and many students do not master it even after the prolonged instruction they typically receive from fourth through eighth grade. Averaging across three recent studies that examined knowledge of all four arithmetic operations, US sixth and eighth graders solved only 59% of fraction arithmetic items (Siegler & Lortie-Forgues 2015, Siegler & Pyke 2013, Siegler et al. 2011). Fraction arithmetic accuracy has been found to improve with age and experience in these and other studies (e.g., Byrnes & Wasik 1991), but adult community college students still err on roughly 20% of problems (e.g., Siegler & Lortie-Forgues 2015, Stigler et al. 2010).

The problem is widely recognized by educators. A nationwide sample of 1,000 US algebra 1 teachers who were asked to rate 15 types of knowledge limitations that interfered with their students' algebra learning rated lack of knowledge of fractions and fraction arithmetic as the second greatest problem (Hoffer et al. 2007). The only knowledge limitation rated as more serious was of the amorphous category "word problems."

Also reflecting widespread recognition of this difficulty were the recommendations of the Common Core State Standards Initiative (CCSSI 2010). These standards, which have been adopted as instructional policy in more than 80% of US states, influence the teaching, textbooks, and standardized achievement tests presented to students (Davis et al. 2013). The CCSSI recommends that rational number arithmetic, and the closely related topics of ratios, rates, and proportions, be emphasized from fourth through eighth grades. However, even after implementation of the CCSSI, children in the United States continue to struggle with rational number arithmetic.

Most fraction arithmetic errors are one of two types. Independent whole number errors (Ni & Zhou 2005) involve performing the arithmetic operation independently on numerators and denominators (e.g., $1/2 + 1/3 = 2/5$). Wrong fraction operation errors involve using subprocedures that are correct within another fraction arithmetic operation but incorrect within the operation in the problem. For example, people often maintain common denominators on fraction multiplication problems (e.g., $3/5 \times 3/5 = 9/5$), an approach that parallels correct fraction addition and subtraction ($3/5 + 3/5 = 6/5$) but is incorrect for multiplication. Both types of errors are common among community college students as well as children (Stigler et al. 2010).

These errors reflect lack of understanding of, or attention to, the magnitudes produced by fraction arithmetic operations. Claiming that $1/2 + 1/3 = 2/5$ implies that adding positive numbers can produce answers that are less than one of the addends. Claiming that $3/5 \times 3/5 = 9/5$ indicates a belief that multiplying two numbers that are less than 1 can result in an answer larger than 1.

This lack of understanding also is apparent in the variability of fraction arithmetic strategies. Within a single session, children often use both correct and incorrect procedures on virtually identical fraction arithmetic problems, for example, $3/5 + 1/4$ and $3/5 + 2/3$ (Siegler & Pyke 2013, Siegler et al. 2011). Children who used both correct and incorrect procedures were more confident when they used the correct procedures, but not overwhelmingly so (mean confidence ratings on a 1 to 5 scale of 4.2 for correct procedures and 3.5 for incorrect procedures).

These findings indicate that many children's fraction arithmetic knowledge includes a mix of correct procedures, incorrect procedures based on incorrect application of whole number knowledge, and incorrect procedures involving subprocedures detached from the fraction arithmetic operation on which they are appropriate. The incorrect procedures often yield answers that violate basic principles, such as when adding two positive numbers yields an answer that is less than one of them. The fraction arithmetic of these children seems to be unconstrained by magnitude knowledge that could be used to eschew procedures that yield implausible answers.

Decimal Arithmetic

Development of decimal arithmetic follows a path similar to that of fraction arithmetic. The most comprehensive data on this development come from Hiebert & Wearne (1985, 1986). Between the first semester of fifth grade and the second semester of ninth grade, accuracy of the 670 children in this study increased from 20% to 80% for addition, 21% to 82% for subtraction, and 30% to 75% for multiplication. Although a great deal of effort has been devoted in the past 30 years to improving rational number arithmetic instruction, students' performance has not changed much. Stigler et al. (2010) reported that community college students correctly answered only approximately 80% of decimal arithmetic problems, and Lortie-Forgues & Siegler (in press) found similar levels of accuracy with sixth and eighth graders.

The largest source of errors in decimal arithmetic is misplacement of the decimal point. This error is often seen on decimal addition and subtraction problems when the operands have unequal numbers of digits to the right of the decimal point. For example, the ninth graders in a study by Hiebert & Wearne (1985) erred on 36% of trials when the problem was $0.86 - 0.3$ but on only 10% of trials when the problem was $0.60 - 0.36$.

Students' difficulty in placing the decimal point in answers also is seen in multiplication and division. For example, Lortie-Forgues & Siegler (in press) reported that 73% of errors, and 34% of answers, to decimal multiplication problems of sixth and eighth graders involved misplacing the decimal point. The most common type of error was of the form $1.23 \times 2.34 = 287.82$, an answer akin to claiming that multiplying two numbers below three yields an answer above 200. Like the correct addition procedure $1.23 + 2.34 = 3.57$, the answer 287.82 leaves the decimal point in the answer two digits to the left of the rightmost digit. As with fraction arithmetic errors, use of such procedures suggests that many students ignore the plausibility of the magnitudes of the answers to decimal arithmetic problems.

RELATIONS BETWEEN KNOWLEDGE OF MAGNITUDES AND ARITHMETIC

Whole Numbers

Individual differences in children's whole number arithmetic competence correlate with individual differences in the precision of their symbolic whole number magnitude knowledge, even after controlling for differences in IQ, working memory, executive function, language, and spatial ability (Booth & Siegler 2008, Fuchs et al. 2010, Linsen et al. 2015). These correlations remain significant into adulthood (Castronovo & Göbel 2012) and are robust compared to correlations between arithmetic and accuracy of nonsymbolic magnitude knowledge (Holloway & Ansari 2009, Skagerlund & Träff 2016). For example, in a study of approximately 1,400 first to sixth graders, symbolic magnitude knowledge predicted unique variance in arithmetic proficiency, but nonsymbolic comparison acuity did not (Lyons et al. 2014). Consistent with the possibility that numerical magnitude knowledge could facilitate arithmetic performance by allowing accurate estimation of correct answers, accuracy of children's symbolic magnitude knowledge predicts their computational estimation (approximate symbolic mental arithmetic) performance (Dowker 1997, Gunderson et al. 2012).

The relation between symbolic arithmetic competence and magnitude knowledge also is evident in neural data. Sensitivity of IPS activation during symbolic magnitude comparison to the ratio of the numbers being compared correlates with children's arithmetic fluency, after controlling for general intelligence (Bugden et al. 2012). Similarly, children who represent numerical magnitudes more precisely show greater sensitivity of parietal response to the sizes of operands and answers in arithmetic problems (Berteletti et al. 2015).

Rational Numbers

As with whole numbers, individual differences in children's knowledge of fraction magnitudes correlate with individual differences in children's fraction arithmetic competence (Byrnes & Wasik 1991, Siegler et al. 2011). These correlations persist across national differences in educational practices (Torbeyns et al. 2015) and after statistically controlling for whole number arithmetic ability, language ability, executive function, working memory, and attentive behavior (Hecht et al. 2003, Siegler & Pyke 2013).

If, as the integrated theory of numerical development asserts, there is developmental continuity in understanding of whole and rational number magnitudes, then whole number magnitude knowledge should also correlate with fraction arithmetic ability. It does (Bailey et al. 2014, Jordan et al. 2013). Strikingly, accuracy of number-line estimation with whole numbers in first grade predicts fraction arithmetic proficiency in seventh grade—a relation fully mediated by fraction magnitude understanding in middle school (Bailey et al. 2014).

EFFECTS OF INTERVENTIONS EMPHASIZING MAGNITUDES ON ARITHMETIC LEARNING

In addition to these individual-difference correlations, experimental evidence indicates that numerical magnitude knowledge is causally related to arithmetic competence.

Whole Number Interventions

If numerical magnitude knowledge is causally related to arithmetic learning, then interventions that produce improvements in numerical magnitude knowledge should also improve arithmetic learning. Ramani and Siegler (e.g., Ramani & Siegler 2008, Siegler & Ramani 2009) produced evidence consistent with this prediction. Their studies examined the effects of playing a numerical board game named "The Great Race" on the numerical knowledge of preschoolers from low-income families. The board in this game has 10 squares labeled with the numbers 1 through 10. Players take turns spinning a spinner that can land on 1 or 2, moving their token forward by the number of spaces indicated on the spinner and saying the numbers in the squares aloud as they proceed. For example, children whose token is on the square labeled 4 and who spin a 2 need to say "5, 6" as they move their token forward. Other children from the same classrooms were randomly assigned to a control group that played the same game, except the children needed to say the colors on the board rather than the numbers. Children who either said a wrong number/color or did not know what number/color to say were helped by the experimenter to state the correct number(s)/color(s). The player whose token first reaches 10 wins.

Playing this game improved children's numerical magnitude knowledge as well as their counting and identification of printed numbers (Ramani & Siegler 2008). Siegler & Ramani (2009) replicated those findings and found that although the game involves no explicit arithmetic problems, children who had played it earlier subsequently learned more from feedback on simple addition problems than did peers who had earlier engaged in other numerical activities, such as counting objects and identifying printed numbers, or children in the previously described control group. The improvements in arithmetic performance included both a higher percent correct answers and answers closer in magnitude to the correct answer.

Other interventions based on the same ideas have yielded similar effects. A 0-to-100 version of "The Great Race" improved kindergartners' magnitude knowledge as well as their understanding of the base-10 system (Laski & Siegler 2014). An eight-week intervention focusing on building number sense and including "The Great Race" as a component improved arithmetic accuracy among kindergartners from low-income communities (Jordan et al. 2012). Similar but distinct games, such as "The Number Race" (Wilson et al. 2006) and "Rescue Calcularis" (Kucian et al. 2011), also have shown positive effects on arithmetic performance in typically developing children and children with developmental dyscalculia, a condition characterized by unusual difficulty with numbers and arithmetic.

Manipulations that activate magnitude knowledge in the context of arithmetic also improve arithmetic learning. In one such study, first graders studied single- and multidigit addition facts either alone or accompanied by analog number-line representations of the magnitudes of addends and sums (Booth & Siegler 2008). On a subsequent posttest, children who had earlier seen the analog magnitude representations recalled the arithmetic answers more accurately. In another study, first graders who practiced an approximate addition task using nonsymbolic numerical magnitudes (dot arrays) subsequently showed superior accuracy and speed at exact symbolic arithmetic, relative to children who practiced nonnumerical tasks (Hyde et al. 2014). Thus, activating knowledge of numerical magnitudes increases addition performance and learning.

Rational Number Interventions

Causal evidence linking rational number magnitude knowledge and rational number arithmetic skill comes from several studies comparing the effects of instruction emphasizing fraction magnitudes to the effects of instruction emphasizing the part-whole interpretation of fractions. This latter interpretation, which is heavily emphasized in US schools, construes fractions as parts of objects or subsets of sets (Kieren 1976). Instruction emphasizing the part-whole interpretation provides children practice with tasks that can be solved by counting a part and the whole, such as choosing whether 3/4, 4/3, 3/7, or 4/7 best represents the fraction of red segments in a circle with three red and four blue segments. Instruction emphasizing magnitudes provides practice with such tasks as fraction number-line estimation and magnitude comparison.

Interventions that focus on fraction magnitudes have yielded greater improvement not only in fraction magnitude knowledge but also in fraction arithmetic (Fuchs et al. 2013, 2014, 2016; Moss & Case 1999). For example, after 12 weeks of participation in Fraction Face-Off!, an intervention emphasizing fraction magnitude knowledge, fourth graders' accuracy at fraction addition and subtraction exceeded that of control students who received, over the same period, a curriculum emphasizing the part-whole interpretation. This finding was especially striking because the curriculum that emphasized magnitudes devoted less explicit instruction in fraction arithmetic procedures (Fuchs et al. 2013, 2014, 2016).

Although improved understanding of fraction magnitudes often facilitates learning of fraction arithmetic, increasing children's magnitude knowledge is sometimes insufficient to produce such learning. In one such case, an intervention that included instruction in fraction magnitudes and approximate arithmetic showed no advantage over a traditional curriculum with respect to learning arithmetic procedures (Gabriel et al. 2012). Moreover, even after the quite successful Fraction Face-Off! intervention, students scored on average only 18 of 41 points on a posttest assessment of fraction arithmetic (Fuchs et al. 2014). This was considerably higher than they had scored on the pretest and considerably higher than scores of a control group, but below 50% in absolute terms. The question is why learning this material is so challenging for so many students.

WHY IS RATIONAL NUMBER ARITHMETIC SO DIFFICULT?

At a general level, the cause of the problems that many children and adults experience in learning fraction and decimal arithmetic is well known: They do not understand the rational number arithmetic operations that they are asked to learn. This lack of understanding of rational number arithmetic is evident in many ways. When asked to estimate the closest whole number to the sum of 12/13 + 7/8, only 24% of the more than 20,000 eighth graders who took a standardized test of math achievement (the National Assessment of Educational Progress, or NAEP) chose 2 (Carpenter et al. 1980). (The response alternatives were 1, 2, 19, 21, and I don't know.) Presenting the same problem in 2014 to eighth graders taking an Algebra 1 course in a fairly affluent suburban school district showed that little had changed in the subsequent 30 years; 27% of the eighth graders in the recent sample correctly answered the problem (Siegler & Lortie-Forgues 2015).

The problem is not unique to fractions. When the NAEP presented the decimal multiplication problem 3.04×5.3, and asked whether 1.6, 16, 160, or 1,600 was closest to the answer, only 21% of eighth graders chose the correct answer, 16; their most common answer was 1,600 (Carpenter et al. 1983). Many high school and college students, preservice teachers, and practicing teachers also lack basic conceptual understanding of rational number arithmetic (Fischbein et al. 1985, Hanson & Hogan 2000, Ma 1999, Siegler & Lortie-Forgues 2015).

Difficulty in learning rational number arithmetic might be thought of as a problem that falls within the field of education more than psychology. We believe, however, that psychological theories, concepts, and analytic techniques are essential for addressing children's difficulties with acquiring this foundational body of knowledge. We also believe that applying knowledge from psychology to challenging real-world problems, including ones in education, provides a valuable test of the utility of our theories and analytic techniques.

As a first step toward the goal of applying psychological theories, concepts, and analytic techniques to the goal of improving children's understanding of rational number arithmetic, we attempt in the remainder of this review to specify sources of difficulty in learning fraction and decimal arithmetic. These sources of difficulty are divided into two categories: inherent and culturally contingent. Inherent sources of difficulty are ones that make understanding rational number arithmetic difficult regardless of the particulars of the society and educational system. Examples include the complex relations among different fraction arithmetic operations and between whole number and fraction arithmetic operations. Culturally contingent sources of difficulty are ones that vary among societies and educational systems. They include teachers' understanding of the material they are teaching, the accuracy and clarity of textbooks in presenting the material, and students' prior knowledge of prerequisites. A more extensive discussion of these issues can be found in Lortie-Forgues et al. (2015); here, we summarize the main points in the analysis.

Inherent Sources of Difficulty of Rational Number Arithmetic

Inaccessibility of rational number magnitudes. For both whole and rational numbers, arithmetic learning is correlated with, and causally related to, knowledge of numerical magnitudes. However, fraction and decimal notations make accessing fraction and decimal magnitudes more difficult than accessing whole number magnitudes. Whole number magnitudes are expressed by a single number, and after age 8 or 9, children access them automatically (Berch et al. 1999, White et al. 2012). In contrast, fraction magnitudes have to be derived from the ratio of two numbers, and even in adulthood, they are usually not accessed automatically (DeWolf et al. 2014).

Accessing most decimal magnitudes is similar to accessing whole number magnitudes (DeWolf et al. 2014). However, this is not the case for decimals with one or more zeros immediately to the right of the decimal point (e.g., 0.012). Indicative of this difficulty, Putt (1995) found that only approximately 50% of US and Australian preservice teachers correctly ordered the magnitudes of five decimals, four of which included one or more zeroes immediately to the right of the decimal point. Hiebert & Wearne (1985) reported similar results regarding decimal magnitude knowledge among US ninth graders. The difficulty of accessing these decimal magnitudes poses an inherent challenge in learning decimal arithmetic.

Opacity of rational number arithmetic procedures. The conceptual basis of standard fraction arithmetic procedures is often far from obvious. Why are equal denominators needed for adding and subtracting but not for multiplying and dividing? Why is the second operand inverted and multiplied by the first when dividing fractions? The most straightforward explanations require knowledge of algebra, a subject that usually is taught after fractions, so that even strong students usually lack such knowledge when they are learning fractions.

Superficially, the conceptual basis of decimal arithmetic is more transparent than that of fraction arithmetic, because the decimal computations resemble those with the corresponding whole number operations. However, considering issues related to placement of the decimal point reveals that understanding decimal arithmetic procedures is more challenging than it first appears.

To understand the complexity, try to explain to someone who does not already understand why 0.123×0.45 yields an answer with five digits to the right of the decimal point. The challenge of providing a clear explanation without recourse to concepts that students lack when they learn about decimal arithmetic, such as negative exponents, seems likely to contribute to difficulty understanding decimal arithmetic.

Complex relations between whole and rational number arithmetic operations. Whole number arithmetic knowledge is often incorrectly generalized to rational number arithmetic. This problem was mentioned above in the context of independent whole number errors with fractions (e.g., $2/3 + 2/3 = 4/6$).

Similarly tempting generalizations from whole number arithmetic lead to incorrect judgments about the direction of effects of multiplying and dividing fractions. Multiplying two natural numbers (whole numbers other than 0) never results in an answer less than either multiplicand, but multiplying two fractions between 0 and 1 always does. Similarly, dividing by a natural number never results in an answer greater than the number being divided, but dividing by a fraction between 0 and 1 always does. However, even after years of experience with fraction multiplication and division, both eighth graders and adults predict that all four fraction arithmetic operations will produce the same direction of effects as with whole numbers, regardless of whether the operands are more than or less than 1 (Siegler & Lortie-Forgues 2015).

Similar overgeneralizations from whole number experience affect decimal arithmetic. With whole number addition and subtraction, aligning the rightmost digits of the numbers in the problem preserves the correspondence of their place values. In contrast, with decimal addition and subtraction, such alignment yields incorrect answers when the numbers of digits to the right of the decimal point differ for the operands. The locations of the decimal point in the operands, rather than the rightmost digits, need to be aligned to correctly add and subtract decimals (i.e., with $0.82 - 0.6$, the "6" needs to be aligned with the "8" rather than with the "2"). Correct mapping is probably made more difficult by the fact that the strategy of aligning the rightmost digit does work when the decimals being added or subtracted have the same number of digits (e.g., $0.82 - 0.64$).

Variable relations among rational number operations. Partial overlaps in subprocedures within different rational number arithmetic operations add to the difficulty of learning rational number arithmetic. For example, when adding or subtracting fractions with the same denominator, the operation is applied only to the numerator, but when multiplying or dividing fractions with the same denominator, the operation must be applied to both numerator and denominator. Perhaps because children generally learn fraction addition and subtraction before fraction multiplication and division, errors of the form $4/5 \times 4/5 = 16/5$ are very common. In one recent study of sixth and eighth graders' fraction arithmetic, 46% of fraction multiplication answers and 55% of fraction division answers involved such errors (Siegler & Pyke 2013). These errors again are easy to understand; if a child does not understand that $4/5 \times 4/5$ means 4/5 of 4/5, and that the answer must therefore be less than 4/5, why not proceed as in fraction addition?

Overgeneralization of decimal addition and subtraction procedures to decimal multiplication and division occurs for similar reasons. On addition and subtraction problems with equal numbers of digits to the right of the decimal point (e.g., $0.5 + 0.7 = 1.2$), the placement of the decimal point relative to the rightmost digit of the addends is maintained. However, with decimal multiplication, the location of the decimal point is determined by the sum of the number of digits in the multiplicands to the right of the decimal point (e.g., $0.5 \times 0.7 = 0.35$ rather than 3.5). Hiebert & Wearne (1985) found that overgeneralization of the rule from addition for placing the decimal point accounted for 76% of sixth graders' multiplication answers. Again, the error is understandable; if a child does not know that 0.5×0.7 means half of 0.7, why shouldn't the answer be 3.5?

Culturally Contingent Sources of Difficulty

Inherent sources of difficulty make learning rational number arithmetic challenging for learners in all cultures. However, the degree to which learners surmount these inherent difficulties depends on several culturally contingent factors.

Teachers' understanding. Understanding a topic is no guarantee of ability to teach it well, but without such understanding, high-quality instruction is unlikely. Consistent with this view, teachers' understanding of rational number arithmetic is strongly related to their knowledge of how to teach it effectively (Depaepe et al. 2015).

Unfortunately, many teachers in Western countries have limited understanding of rational number arithmetic. When asked to illustrate the meaning of a fraction division problem, such as $1\ 3/4 \div 1/2$, only a minority of US and Belgian teachers provided an explanation other than stating the invert-and-multiply algorithm (Depaepe et al. 2015). In contrast, roughly 90% of East Asian teachers provided coherent explanations for the same type of problem (Luo et al. 2011, Ma 1999). Similar national differences were found in those studies in teachers' ability to judge whether multiplication or division was the way to solve a rational number story problem.

Teachers' emphasis on rote memorization. For many years, researchers, associations of math teachers, and national commissions have argued that typical mathematics instruction overemphasizes rote memorization of procedures (e.g., Brownell 1947, Natl. Math. Advis. Panel 2008). Lack of understanding of procedures limits children's initial learning, and the deleterious effects become larger with the passage of time following initial learning (e.g., Reyna & Brainerd 1991). The degree to which teachers emphasize rote memorization of rational number arithmetic procedures may be related to the quality of their understanding of the procedures. Emphasizing rote memorization is one way to avoid the embarrassment of being unable to answer questions about mathematics that some students in the class can answer.

Textbook explanations of limited generality. US textbooks typically explain whole number multiplication as repeated addition (CCSSI 2010). The problem 3×2, for example, could be explained as adding two three times $(2 + 2 + 2)$. This approach has the advantage of grounding understanding of multiplication in understanding of addition, but it also has two limitations. One is that the repeated addition interpretation cannot be straightforwardly applied to multiplication of fractions and decimals. For instance, how to interpret $1/3 \times 3/4$ in terms of repeated addition is not straightforward.

The other limitation is that the repeated addition explanation often leads students to infer that because adding positive numbers always yields an answer larger than either addend, multiplying positive numbers has the same effect. However, this inference is mistaken: Multiplying two numbers between 0 and 1 never yields a product greater than either multiplicand.

The present theoretical emphasis on numerical magnitudes, together with empirical findings about the effectiveness of interventions that emphasize number lines in teaching fractions, suggests alternative instructional approaches that might be more effective. For example, multiplication could be presented as "N of the M's" with whole numbers (e.g., 4 of the 3's) and "N of the M" with fractions (1/3 of the 3/4). Using a number line to represent the 3/4, and then demonstrating that 1/3 of the 3/4 means dividing the segment from 0 to 3/4 into three smaller, equal-sized segments, with the answer being one of them, could help students understand why multiplying fractions less than one yields an answer less than either operand.

A similar point can be made about division. In US textbooks, division is usually introduced as fair sharing (dividing objects equally among people). For example, a teacher or textbook might explain 12 ÷ 4 as 12 cookies shared equally among 4 friends. This interpretation is straightforward with natural numbers but not with rational numbers, at least when the divisor is not a whole number (e.g., what does it mean to share 3/4 of a cookie among 3/8 of a friend?).

Again, the standard explanation is not the only possible one. At least when a larger number is divided by a smaller one, both whole number division and fraction division can be explained straightforwardly as indicating how many times the divisor can go into the dividend (e.g., how many times 8 can go into 32, how many times 3/8 can go into 3/4). Moreover, number lines can be used to illustrate the process in both whole and rational number contexts, which can promote understanding of the shared meaning of multiplication and division with the two types of numbers.

Students' limited prerequisite knowledge. Rational number arithmetic requires mastery of whole number arithmetic. Even adding 1/3 + 2/5 requires five correct single-digit multiplications and additions; fraction arithmetic problems involving multidigit numerators and denominators require far more.

Although much better than their knowledge of rational number arithmetic procedures, many US students' knowledge of whole number arithmetic procedures falls short of the ideal of consistent fast and accurate performance. This leads to a fair number of rational number arithmetic errors. For example, Siegler & Pyke (2013) found that sixth and eighth graders made whole number arithmetic errors on 21% of fraction arithmetic problems. Such computational errors seem likely to interfere with learning of correct rational number procedures because they obscure whether implausible answers are attributable to flawed procedures or to flawed execution of correct procedures.

SUMMARY AND CONCLUSIONS

Prior to the past decade, the field of numerical development focused almost exclusively on infants' and young children's understanding of whole numbers. In recent years, however, the field has expanded greatly to include rational as well as whole numbers and the entire developmental period from infancy to adulthood. Development of numerical magnitude knowledge has provided a unifying theme for this broader field. With age and experience, children gain knowledge of the magnitudes of nonsymbolic numbers; small symbolic whole numbers; larger symbolic whole numbers; and fractions, decimals, and other rational numbers.

A major goal of the present review was to integrate the literature on development of knowledge of numerical magnitudes with the literature on development of arithmetic knowledge. We found that magnitude knowledge was correlated with, predictive of, and causally related to arithmetic competence for both whole and rational numbers. Most individuals eventually achieve relatively good understanding of both whole number magnitudes and whole number arithmetic, but even adults with excellent knowledge of the magnitudes of individual fractions and decimals often have limited understanding of rational number arithmetic. Poor understanding of rational number arithmetic is common not only among students but also among teachers. This problem is especially serious because knowledge of rational number arithmetic is foundational for further mathematics and science learning as well as for a wide range of occupations.

The reasons for many children's and adults' poor understanding of rational number arithmetic include both inherent and culturally contingent sources. One inherent source is the greater difficulty of accessing magnitudes of the operands and answers in fraction and decimal arithmetic problems relative to accessing their magnitudes in whole number arithmetic problems. This greater difficulty reflects the magnitudes of fractions and decimals depending on relations between components (explicitly with fractions, implicitly with decimals) rather than on any single number. Weak knowledge of the magnitudes of rational number operands and answers limits the ability of many children and adults to evaluate the plausibility of answers and the procedures that produce them.

However, the difficulty of learning rational number arithmetic cannot be reduced to poor understanding of rational number magnitudes. Other inherent features of arithmetic with decimals and fractions add to the difficulty of learning. One is that rational number arithmetic procedures are often opaque. For example, it is far from immediately apparent why the invert-and-multiply procedure yields correct answers for fraction division, or why multiplying two decimals that each have two digits to the right of the decimal point must lead to an answer with the decimal point four digits to the left of the rightmost digit. Understanding why these procedures yield correct answers is unlikely without knowledge of algebra, which students rarely have when they are learning fraction and decimal arithmetic. The complex relations between corresponding whole number and rational number arithmetic operations, and of different rational number arithmetic operations to each other (e.g., the relation of fraction addition and subtraction, where common denominators are maintained in the answer, to fraction multiplication and division, where common denominators are not maintained in the answer), add to the inherent difficulty of learning rational number arithmetic. These complex relations lead to tempting but incorrect analogies and obscure correct connections between the same operation with whole and rational numbers.

In the United States and many other Western countries, culturally contingent variables further increase the difficulty of learning rational number arithmetic. Teachers' understanding of rational number arithmetic is often limited, and their instruction often emphasizes rote memorization rather than understanding. Textbook explanations often fail to convey to students the shared meaning of corresponding arithmetic operations with whole and rational numbers. Some students have not fully mastered whole number arithmetic, leading to errors in rational number arithmetic even when the students have chosen the correct procedure.

In sum, investigators have gained considerable knowledge of what develops and how development occurs in numerical development. These gains include increased understanding of the development of both numerical magnitudes and how those magnitudes combine in arithmetic operations for both whole and rational numbers. An important current challenge is to apply this knowledge to facilitate understanding of rational number arithmetic. Attaining this goal will require not only methods for improving learners' knowledge of rational number magnitudes but also effective means for increasing their understanding of the logic underlying rational number arithmetic procedures. Examining the effects of theoretically based interventions designed to improve understanding of rational number arithmetic procedures will provide tests of theories of numerical development as well as useful data for expanding and refining the theories. It will also help surmount the artificial distinction between developmental and educational psychology, to the likely benefit of both fields.

DISCLOSURE STATEMENT

The authors are not aware of any affiliations, memberships, funding, or financial holdings that might be perceived as affecting the objectivity of this review.

ACKNOWLEDGMENTS

This work was supported in part by the Institute of Education Sciences, US Department of Education, through grants R305A150262; R324C100004:84.324C, subaward 23149; and R305B100001 to Carnegie Mellon University. Support was also provided by the Teresa Heinz Chair at Carnegie Mellon University and the Siegler Center for Innovative Learning and Advanced Technology Center, Beijing Normal University. The opinions expressed are those of the authors and do not represent views of the Institute or the US Department of Education.

LITERATURE CITED

Agrillo C, Piffer L, Bisazza A, Butterworth B. 2012. Evidence for two numerical systems that are similar in humans and guppies. *PLOS ONE* 7(2):e31923

Alibali MW, Goldin-Meadow S. 1993. Gesture-speech mismatch and mechanisms of learning: what the hands reveal about a child's state of mind. *Cogn. Psychol.* 25(4):468–523

Andres M, Michaux N, Pesenti M. 2012. Common substrate for mental arithmetic and finger representation in the parietal cortex. *NeuroImage* 62(3):1520–28

Ashcraft MH. 1995. Cognitive psychology and simple arithmetic: a review and summary of new directions. *Math. Cogn.* 1(1):3–34

Ashcraft MH, Moore AM. 2012. Cognitive processes of numerical estimation in children. *J. Exp. Child Psychol.* 111(2):246–67

Bailey DH, Hoard MK, Nugent L, Geary DC. 2012. Competence with fractions predicts gains in mathematics achievement. *J. Exp. Child Psychol.* 113(3):447–55

Bailey DH, Siegler RS, Geary DC. 2014. Early predictors of middle school fraction knowledge. *Dev. Sci.* 17(5):775–85

Bailey DH, Zhou X, Zhang Y, Cui J, Fuchs LS, et al. 2015. Development of fraction concepts and procedures in U.S. and Chinese children. *J. Exp. Child Psychol.* 129:68–83

Baroody AJ, Tiilikainen SH. 2003. Two perspectives on addition development. In *The Development of Arithmetic Concepts and Skills: The Construction of Adaptive Expertise*, ed. AJ Baroody, A Dowker, pp. 75–125. Mahwah, NJ: Erlbaum

Berch DB, Foley EJ, Hill RJ, McDonough-Ryan PM. 1999. Extracting parity and magnitude from Arabic numerals: developmental changes in number processing and mental representation. *J. Exp. Child Psychol.* 74:286–308

Berteletti I, Booth JR. 2015. Perceiving fingers in single-digit arithmetic problems. *Front. Psychol.* 6:226

Berteletti I, Lucangeli D, Piazza M, Dehaene S, Zorzi M. 2010. Numerical estimation in preschoolers. *Dev. Psychol.* 41:545–51

Berteletti I, Man G, Booth JR. 2015. How number line estimation skills relate to neural activations in single digit subtraction problems. *NeuroImage* 107:198–206

Booth JL, Siegler RS. 2006. Developmental and individual differences in pure numerical estimation. *Dev. Psychol.* 42(1):189–201

Booth JL, Siegler RS. 2008. Numerical magnitude representations influence arithmetic learning. *Child Dev.* 79(4):1016–31

Brown JS, Van Lehn K. 1982. Toward a generative theory of "bugs." In *Addition and Subtraction: A Cognitive Perspective*, ed. TP Carpenter, JM Moser, TA Romberg, pp. 117–36. Hillsdale, NJ: Erlbaum

Brownell WA. 1947. The place of meaning in the teaching of arithmetic. *Elem. Sch. J.* 47(5):256–65

Bugden S, Price GR, McLean DA, Ansari D. 2012. The role of the left intraparietal sulcus in the relationship between symbolic number processing and children's arithmetic competence. *Dev. Cogn. Neurosci.* 2(4):448–57

Bulthé J, de Smedt B, Op de Beeck HP. 2014. Format-dependent representations of symbolic and non-symbolic numbers in the human cortex as revealed by multi-voxel pattern analyses. *NeuroImage* 87:311–22

Byrnes JP, Wasik BA. 1991. Role of conceptual knowledge in mathematical procedural learning. *Dev. Psychol.* 27(5):777–86

Campbell JID, Fugelsang J. 2001. Strategy choice for arithmetic verification: effects of numerical surface form. *Cognition* 80(3):B21–30

Campbell JID, Xue Q. 2001. Cognitive arithmetic across cultures. *J. Exp. Psychol.: Gen.* 130(2):299–315

Cantrell L, Smith LB. 2013. Open questions and a proposal: a critical review of the evidence on infant numerical abilities. *Cognition* 128(3):331–52

Carpenter TP, Corbitt M, Kepner H, Lindquist M, Reys R. 1980. Results of the second NAEP mathematics assessment: secondary school. *Math. Teach.* 73:329–38

Carpenter TP, Lindquist MM, Matthews W, Silver EA. 1983. Results of the third NAEP mathematics assessment: secondary school. *Math. Teach.* 76(9):652–59

Case R, Okamoto Y. 1996. The role of central conceptual structures in the development of children's thought. *Monogr. Soc. Res. Child Dev.* 61(1–2):1–295

Castronovo J, Göbel SM. 2012. Impact of high mathematics education on the number sense. *PLOS ONE* 7(4):e33832

CCSSI (Common Core State Stand. Initiat.). 2010. *Common Core State Standards for Mathematics.* Washington, DC: Natl. Gov. Assoc. Cent. Best Pract. Counc. Chief State School Off.

Chen Q, Li J. 2014. Association between individual differences in nonsymbolic number acuity and math performance: a meta-analysis. *Acta Psychol.* 148:163–72

College Board. 2015. *Advanced Placement Physics 1 equations, effective 2015.* New York: College Board. **https://secure-media.collegeboard.org/digitalServices/pdf/ap/ap-physics-1-equations-table.pdf**

Cordes S, Brannon EM. 2008. Quantitative competencies in infancy. *Dev. Sci.* 11(6):803–8

Cramer KA, Post TR, del Mas RC. 2002. Initial fraction learning by fourth- and fifth-grade students: a comparison of the effects of using commercial curricula with the effects of using the rational number project curriculum. *J. Res. Math. Educ.* 33(2):111–44

Davidson D. 2012. Making it in America. *The Atlantic,* Jan./Feb., pp. 65–83

Davis J, Choppin J, McDuffie AR, Drake C. 2013. *Common Core State Standards for Mathematics: middle school mathematics teachers' perceptions.* Rep., Univ. Rochester Warner Cent. Prof. Dev. Educ. Reform, Rochester, NY

de Smedt B, Verschaffel L, Ghesquière P. 2009. The predictive value of numerical magnitude comparison for individual differences in mathematics achievement. *J. Exp. Child Psychol.* 103(4):469–79

Dehaene S. 2011. *The Number Sense: How the Mind Creates Mathematics.* New York: Oxford Univ. Press

Dehaene S, Dupoux E, Mehler J. 1990. Is numerical comparison digital? Analogical and symbolic effects in two-digit number comparison. *J. Exp. Psychol.: Hum. Percept. Perform.* 16(3):626–41

Depaepe F, Torbeyns J, Vermeersch N, Janssens D, Janssen R, et al. 2015. Teachers' content and pedagogical content knowledge on rational numbers: a comparison of prospective elementary and lower secondary school teachers. *Teach. Teach. Educ.* 47:82–92

DeWolf M, Grounds MA, Bassok M, Holyoak KJ. 2014. Magnitude comparison with different types of rational numbers. *J. Exp. Psychol.: Hum. Percept. Perform.* 40(1):71–82

Dotan D, Dehaene S. 2013. How do we convert a number into a finger trajectory? *Cognition* 129(3):512–29

Dowker A. 1997. Young children's addition estimates. *Math. Cogn.* 3(2):140–53

Duncan GJ, Dowsett CJ, Claessens A, Magnuson K, Huston AC, et al. 2007. School readiness and later achievement. *Dev. Psychol.* 43:1428–46

Fazio LK, Bailey DH, Thompson CA, Siegler RS. 2014. Relations of different types of numerical magnitude representations to each other and to mathematics achievement. *J. Exp. Child Psychol.* 123:53–72

Feigenson L, Dehaene S, Spelke E. 2004. Core systems of number. *Trends Cogn. Sci.* 8:307–14

Fischbein E, Deri M, Sainati Nello M, Sciolis Marino M. 1985. The role of implicit models in solving verbal problems in multiplication and division. *J. Res. Math. Educ.* 16(1):3–17

Fuchs LS, Geary DC, Compton DL, Fuchs D, Hamlett CL, Bryant JD. 2010. The contributions of numerosity and domain-general abilities to school readiness. *Child Dev.* 81(5):1520–33

Fuchs LS, Schumacher RF, Long J, Namkung J, Hamlett CL, et al. 2013. Improving at-risk learners' understanding of fractions. *J. Educ. Psychol.* 105(3):683–700

Fuchs LS, Schumacher RF, Long J, Namkung J, Malone A, et al. 2016. Effects of intervention to improve at-risk fourth graders' understanding, calculations, and word problems with fractions. *Elem. Sch. J.* 116(4):625–51

Fuchs LS, Schumacher RF, Sterba SK, Long J, Namkung J, et al. 2014. Does working memory moderate the effects of fraction intervention? An aptitude-treatment interaction. *J. Educ. Psychol.* 106(2):499–514

Gabriel F, Coché F, Szucs D, Carette V, Rey B, Content A. 2012. Developing children's understanding of fractions: an intervention study. *Mind Brain Educ.* 6(3):137–46

Geary DC, Berch DB, Mann-Koepke K. 2015. *Evolutionary Origins and Early Development of Number Processing*, Vol. 1. *Mathematical Cognition and Learning*. San Diego, CA: Elsevier Acad.

Geary DC, Berch DB, Ochsendorf R, Mann-Koepke K. 2017. *Acquisition of Complex Arithmetic Skills and Higher-Order Mathematical Concepts*, Vol. 3. *Mathematical Cognition and Learning*. San Diego, CA: Elsevier Acad. In press

Geary DC, Hoard MK, Byrd-Craven J, Nugent L, Numtee C. 2007. Cognitive mechanisms underlying achievement deficits in children with mathematical learning disability. *Child Dev.* 78(4):1343–59

Givvin KB, Stigler JW, Thompson BJ. 2011. What community college developmental mathematics students understand about mathematics, part II: the interviews. *MathAMATYC Educ.* 2(3):4–18

Goncu A, Gauvain M. 2012. Sociocultural approaches to educational psychology: theory, research, and application. In *APA Educational Psychology Handbook*, Vol. 1. *Theories, Constructs, and Critical Issues*, ed. KR Harris, S Graham, T Urdan, CB McCormick, GM Sinatra, J Sweller, pp. 125–54. Washington, DC: Am. Psychol. Assoc.

Gunderson EA, Ramirez G, Beilock SL, Levine SC. 2012. The relation between spatial skill and early number knowledge: the role of the linear number line. *Dev. Psychol.* 48(5):1229–41

Halberda J, Feigenson L. 2008. Developmental change in the acuity of the "number sense": the approximate number system in 3-, 4-, 5-, and 6-year-olds and adults. *Dev. Psychol.* 44(5):1457–65

Halberda J, Ly R, Wilmer JB, Naiman DQ, Germine L. 2012. Number sense across the lifespan as revealed by a massive Internet-based sample. *PNAS* 109(28):11116–20

Halberda J, Mazzocco MMM, Feigenson L. 2008. Individual differences in non-verbal number acuity correlate with maths achievement. *Nature* 455(7213):665–68

Hanson SA, Hogan TP. 2000. Computational estimation skill of college students. *J. Res. Math. Educ.* 31(4):483–99

Hecht SA, Close L, Santisi M. 2003. Sources of individual differences in fraction skills. *J. Exp. Child Psychol.* 86(4):277–302

Hecht SA, Vagi KJ. 2010. Sources of group and individual differences in emerging fraction skills. *J. Educ. Psychol.* 102(4):843–59

Hiebert J, Wearne D. 1985. A model of students' decimal computation. *Cogn. Instr.* 2(3–4):175–205

Hiebert J, Wearne D. 1986. Procedures over concepts: the acquisition of decimal number knowledge. In *Conceptual and Procedural Knowledge: The Case of Mathematics*, ed. J Hiebert, pp. 199–223. Hillsdale, NJ: Erlbaum

Hoffer TB, Venkataraman L, Hedberg EC, Shagle S. 2007. *Final Report on the National Survey of Algebra Teachers (for the National Mathematics Advisory Panel Subcommittee)*. Washington, DC: US Dep. Educ.

Hoffmann D, Hornung C, Martin R, Schiltz C. 2013. Developing number-space associations: SNARC effects using a color discrimination task in 5-year-olds. *J. Exp. Child Psychol.* 116(4):775–91

Holloway ID, Ansari D. 2009. Mapping numerical magnitudes onto symbols: the numerical distance effect and individual differences in children's mathematics achievement. *J. Exp. Child Psychol.* 103(1):17–29

Hubbard EM, Piazza M, Pinel P, Dehaene S. 2005. Interactions between number and space in parietal cortex. *Nat. Rev. Neurosci.* 6(6):435–48

Hyde DC, Khanum S, Spelke ES. 2014. Brief non-symbolic, approximate number practice enhances subsequent exact symbolic arithmetic in children. *Cognition* 131(1):92–107

Ischebeck A, Schocke M, Delazer M. 2009. The processing and representation of fractions within the brain: an fMRI investigation. *NeuroImage* 47:403–13

Iuculano T, Butterworth B. 2011. Understanding the real value of fractions and decimals. *Q. J. Exp. Psychol.* 64(11):2088–98

Izard V, Dehaene-Lambertz G, Dehaene S. 2008. Distinct cerebral pathways for object identity and number in human infants. *PLOS Biol.* 6(2):e11

Jacob SN, Vallentin D, Nieder A. 2012. Relating magnitudes: the brain's code for proportions. *Trends Cogn. Sci.* 16(3):157–66

Jordan NC, Glutting J, Dyson N, Hassinger-Das B, Irwin C. 2012. Building kindergartners' number sense: a randomized controlled study. *J. Educ. Psychol.* 104(3):647–60

Jordan NC, Hansen N, Fuchs LS, Siegler RS, Gersten R, Micklos D. 2013. Developmental predictors of fraction concepts and procedures. *J. Exp. Child Psychol.* 116(1):45–58

Jordan NC, Kaplan D, Oláh LN, Locuniak MN. 2006. Number sense growth in kindergarten: a longitudinal investigation of children at risk for mathematics difficulties. *Child Dev.* 77(1):153–75

Kant I. 2003 (1781). *The Critique of Pure Reason*. Mineola, NY: Dover

Kieren TE. 1976. On the mathematical, cognitive, and instructional foundations of rational numbers. In *Number and Measurement: Papers from a Research Workshop*, ed. RA Lesh, DA Bradbard, pp. 101–50. Columbus, OH: ERIC/SMEAC

Kucian K, Grond U, Rotzer S, Henzi B, Schönmann C, et al. 2011. Mental number line training in children with developmental dyscalculia. *NeuroImage* 57:782–95

Laski EV, Siegler RS. 2014. Learning from number board games: You learn what you encode. *Dev. Psychol.* 50(3):853–64

Le Corre M, Carey S. 2007. One, two, three, four, nothing more: an investigation of the conceptual sources of the verbal counting principles. *Cognition* 105:395–438

LeFevre JA, Smith-Chant BL, Hiscock K, Dale KE, Morris J. 2003. Young adults' strategic choices in simple arithmetic: implications for the development of mathematical representations. In *The Development of Arithmetic Concepts and Skills: Constructing Adaptive Expertise*, ed. AJ Baroody, A Dowker, pp. 203–28. Mahwah, NJ: Erlbaum

Libertus ME, Feigenson L, Halberda J. 2011. Preschool acuity of the approximate number system correlates with school math ability. *Dev. Sci.* 14(6):1292–300

Linsen S, Verschaffel L, Reynvoet B, De Smedt B. 2015. The association between numerical magnitude processing and mental versus algorithmic multi-digit subtraction in children. *Learn. Instr.* 35:42–50

Lortie-Forgues H, Siegler RS. In press. Conceptual knowledge of decimal arithmetic. *J. Educ. Psychol.*

Lortie-Forgues H, Tian J, Siegler RS. 2015. Why is learning fraction and decimal arithmetic so difficult? *Dev. Rev.* 38:201–21

Luo F, Lo J-J, Leu Y-C. 2011. Fundamental fraction knowledge of preservice elementary teachers: a cross-national study in the United States and Taiwan. *Sch. Sci. Math.* 111(4):164–77

Lyons IM, Price GR, Vaessen A, Blomert L, Ansari D. 2014. Numerical predictors of arithmetic success in grades 1–6. *Dev. Sci.* 17(5):714–26

Ma L. 1999. *Knowing and Teaching Elementary Mathematics: Teachers' Understanding of Fundamental Mathematics in China and the United States*. Mahwah, NJ: Erlbaum

Mack NK. 1995. Confounding whole-number and fraction concepts when building on informal knowledge. *J. Res. Math. Educ.* 26(5):422–41

McCloskey M. 2007. Quantitative literacy and developmental dyscalculias. In *Why Is Math So Hard for Some Children? The Nature and Origins of Mathematical Learning Difficulties and Disabilities*, ed. DB Berch, MMM Mazzocco, pp. 415–29. Baltimore, MD: Paul H. Brookes Publ.

McCrink K, Wynn K. 2004. Large-number addition and subtraction by 9-month-old infants. *Psychol. Sci.* 15(11):776–81

McCrink K, Wynn K. 2007. Ratio abstraction by 6-month-old infants. *Psychol. Sci.* 18(8):740–45

McNeil NM. 2014. A change-resistance account of children's difficulties understanding mathematical equivalence. *Child Dev. Perspect.* 8(1):42–47

Meert G, Grégoire J, Noël M-P. 2009. Rational numbers: componential versus holistic representation of fractions in a magnitude comparison task. *Q. J. Exp. Psychol.* 62(8):1598–616

Moss J, Case R. 1999. Developing children's understanding of the rational numbers: a new model and an experimental curriculum. *J. Res. Math. Educ.* 30(2):122–47

Moyer RS, Landauer TK. 1967. Time required for judgements of numerical inequality. *Nature* 215(5109):1519–20

Natl. Math. Advis. Panel. 2008. *Foundations for Success: The Final Report of the National Mathematics Advisory Panel*. Washington, DC: US Dep. Educ.

Ni YJ, Zhou Y-DD. 2005. Teaching and learning fraction and rational numbers: The origins and implications of whole number bias. *Educ. Psychol.* 40(1):27–52

Nieder A, Dehaene S. 2009. Representation of number in the brain. *Annu. Rev. Neurosci.* 32(1):185–208

Opfer JE, Siegler RS. 2007. Representational change and children's numerical estimation. *Cogn. Psychol.* 55(3):169–95

Östergren R, Träff U. 2013. Early number knowledge and cognitive ability affect early arithmetic ability. *J. Exp. Child Psychol.* 115(3):405–21

Park J, Park DC, Polk TA. 2013. Parietal functional connectivity in numerical cognition. *Cereb. Cortex* 23(9):2127–35

Parnas M, Lin AC, Huetteroth W, Miesenböck G. 2013. Odor discrimination in *Drosophila*: from neural population codes to behavior. *Neuron* 79(5):932–44

Piaget J. 1952. *The Child's Concept of Number.* New York: Norton

Piazza M. 2011. Neurocognitive start-up tools for symbolic number representations. In *Space, Time, and Number in the Brain: Searching for the Foundations of Mathematical Thought*, ed. S Dehaene, E Brannon, pp. 267–85. London: Elsevier

Piazza M, Pinel P, Le Bihan D, Dehaene S. 2007. A magnitude code common to numerosities and number symbols in human intraparietal cortex. *Neuron* 53(2):293–305

Piffer L, Petrazzini MEM, Agrillo C. 2013. Large number discrimination in newborn fish. *PLOS ONE* 8(4):e62466

Putt IJ. 1995. Preservice teachers' ordering of decimal numbers: When more is smaller and less is larger! *Focus Learn. Probl. Math.* 17(3):1–15

Ramani GB, Siegler RS. 2008. Promoting broad and stable improvements in low-income children's numerical knowledge through playing number board games. *Child Dev.* 79(2):375–94

Reeve RA, Paul JM, Butterworth B. 2015. Longitudinal changes in young children's 0–100 to 0–1000 number-line error signatures. *Front. Psychol.* 6:647

Resnick I, Jordan NC, Hansen N, Rajan V, Carrique J, et al. 2016. Developmental growth trajectories in understanding of fraction magnitude from fourth through sixth grade. *Dev. Psychol.* 52(5):746–57

Resnick LB, Nesher P, Leonard F, Magone M, Omanson S, Peled I. 1989. Conceptual bases of arithmetic errors: the case of decimal fractions. *J. Res. Math. Educ.* 20(1):8–27

Reyna VF, Brainerd CJ. 1991. Fuzzy-trace theory and children's acquisition of mathematical and scientific concepts. *Learn. Individ. Differ.* 31(1):27–59

Ritchie SJ, Bates TC. 2013. Enduring links from childhood mathematics and reading achievement to adult socioeconomic status. *Psychol. Sci.* 24(7):1301–8

Robinson KM. 2016. The understanding of additive and multiplicative arithmetic concepts. *Math. Cogn. Learn.* In press

Rugani R, Vallortigara G, Priftis K, Regolin L. 2015. Number-space mapping in the newborn chick resembles humans' mental number line. *Science* 347(6221):534–36

Schneider M, Siegler RS. 2010. Representations of the magnitudes of fractions. *J. Exp. Psychol.: Hum. Percept. Perform.* 36(5):1227–38

Sformo T. 2008. *Practical Problems in Mathematics: For Automotive Technicians.* Clifton Park, NY: Cengage Learn.

Shrager J, Siegler RS. 1998. SCADS: a model of children's strategy choices and strategy discoveries. *Psychol. Sci.* 9(5):405–10

Siegler RS. 1988. Strategy choice procedures and the development of multiplication skill. *J. Exp. Psychol.: Gen.* 117(3):258–75

Siegler RS. 1989. Hazards of mental chronometry: an example from children's subtraction. *J. Educ. Psychol.* 81(4):497–506

Siegler RS. 1996. *Emerging Minds: The Process of Change in Children's Thinking.* New York: Oxford Univ. Press

Siegler RS. 2006. Microgenetic analyses of learning. In *Handbook of Child Psychology*, Vol. 2. *Cognition, Perception, and Language*, ed. W Damon, RM Lerner, D Kuhn, RS Siegler, pp. 464–510. Hoboken, NJ: Wiley. 6th ed.

Siegler RS. 2016. Magnitude knowledge: the common core of numerical development. *Dev. Sci.* 19(3):341–61

Siegler RS, Araya R. 2005. A computational model of conscious and unconscious strategy discovery. In *Advances in Child Development and Behavior*, Vol. 33, ed. RV Kail, pp. 1–42. Oxford, UK: Elsevier

Siegler RS, Booth JL. 2004. Development of numerical estimation in young children. *Child Dev.* 75(2):428–44

Siegler RS, Crowley K. 1994. Constraints on learning in nonprivileged domains. *Cogn. Psychol.* 27(2):194–226

Siegler RS, Jenkins EA. 1989. *How Children Discover New Strategies*. Hillsdale, NJ: Erlbaum

Siegler RS, Lortie-Forgues H. 2015. Conceptual knowledge of fraction arithmetic. *J. Educ. Psychol.* 107(3):909–18

Siegler RS, Mu Y. 2008. Chinese children excel on novel mathematics problems even before elementary school. *Psychol. Sci.* 19(8):759–63

Siegler RS, Pyke AA. 2013. Developmental and individual differences in understanding of fractions. *Dev. Psychol.* 49(10):1994–2004

Siegler RS, Ramani GB. 2009. Playing linear number board games—but not circular ones—improves low-income preschoolers' numerical understanding. *J. Educ. Psychol.* 101(3):545–60

Siegler RS, Shrager J. 1984. Strategy choices in addition and subtraction: How do children know what to do? In *The Origins of Cognitive Skills*, ed. C Sophian, pp. 229–93. Hillsdale, NJ: Erlbaum

Siegler RS, Thompson CA, Schneider M. 2011. An integrated theory of whole number and fractions development. *Cogn. Psychol.* 62(4):273–96

Skagerlund K, Träff U. 2016. Processing of space, time, and number contributes to mathematical abilities above and beyond domain-general cognitive abilities. *J. Exp. Child Psychol.* 143:85–101

Stigler J, Givvin K, Thompson A. 2010. What community college developmental mathematics students understand about mathematics. *MathAMATYC Educ.* 1(3):4–16

Sullivan J, Barner D. 2014. The development of structural analogy in number-line estimation. *J. Exp. Child Psychol.* 128:171–89

Thompson CA, Opfer JE. 2008. Costs and benefits of representational change: effects of context on age and sex differences in magnitude estimation. *J. Exp. Child Psychol.* 101(1):20–51

Thompson CA, Opfer JE. 2010. How 15 hundred is like 15 cherries: effect of progressive alignment on representational changes in numerical cognition. *Child Dev.* 81(6):1768–86

Torbeyns J, Schneider M, Xin Z, Siegler RS. 2015. Bridging the gap: Fraction understanding is central to mathematics achievement in students from three different continents. *Learn. Instr.* 37:5–13

Venkatraman V, Ansari D, Chee M. 2005. Neural correlates of symbolic and non-symbolic arithmetic. *Neuropsychologia* 43(5):744–53

Verschaffel L, Greer B, De Corte E. 2007. Whole number concepts and operations. In *Second Handbook of Research on Mathematics Teaching and Learning*, ed. F Lester, pp. 557–628. Charlotte, NC: Inf. Age

Watts TW, Duncan GJ, Siegler RS, Davis-Kean PE. 2014. What's past is prologue: relations between early mathematics knowledge and high school achievement. *Educ. Res.* 43(7):352–60

White SLJ, Szűcs D, Soltész F. 2012. Symbolic number: the integration of magnitude and spatial representations in children aged 6 to 8 years. *Front. Psychol.* 2:392

Wilson AJ, Revkin SK, Cohen D, Dehaene S. 2006. An open trial assessment of "The Number Race," an adaptive computer game for remediation of dyscalculia. *Behav. Brain Funct.* 2(1):1–16

Wynn K. 1992. Children's acquisition of the number words and the counting system. *Cogn. Psychol.* 24(2):220–51

Xu X, Chen C, Pan M, Li N. 2013. Development of numerical estimation in Chinese preschool children. *J. Exp. Child Psychol.* 116(2):351–66

Gene × Environment Interactions: From Molecular Mechanisms to Behavior

Thorhildur Halldorsdottir[1] and Elisabeth B. Binder[1,2]

[1]Department of Translational Research in Psychiatry, Max Planck Institute of Psychiatry, Munich 80804, Germany; email: binder@psych.mpg.de

[2]Department of Psychiatry and Behavioral Sciences, Emory University School of Medicine, Atlanta, Georgia 30322

Annu. Rev. Psychol. 2017. 68:215–41

First published online as a Review in Advance on September 30, 2016

The *Annual Review of Psychology* is online at psych.annualreviews.org

This article's doi:
10.1146/annurev-psych-010416-044053

Keywords

psychopathology, genomics, epigenetic, gene-by-environment interactions, stress, trauma

Abstract

Gene-by-environment interactions (G × Es) can provide important biological insights into psychiatric disorders and may consequently have direct clinical implications. In this review, we begin with an overview of the major challenges G × E studies have faced (e.g., difficulties replicating findings and high false discovery rates). In light of these challenges, this review focuses on describing examples in which we might begin to understand G × Es on the molecular, cellular, circuit, and behavioral level and link this interaction to altered risk for the development of psychiatric disorders. We also describe recent studies that utilize a polygenic approach to examine G × Es. Finally, we discuss how gaining a deeper understanding of G × Es may translate into a therapeutic practice with more targeted treatments.

Contents

INTRODUCTION

G × E:
gene-by-environment
interaction

It is widely accepted that psychiatric disorders are multifactorial diseases that emerge through the interplay between environmental factors and genetic predisposition. Gene-by-environment interaction (G × E) studies address the extent to which genetic predisposition in combination with environmental determinants shapes the risk for psychiatric disorders (see the sidebar G × E Terminology; **Figure 1**). G × E studies examine the main effects of environmental and genetic determinants as predictors of phenotypes or pathology, as well as whether their joint effects differ from the product of their individual effects. A significant interaction indicates that both independent variables together influence the dependent variable.

Several theoretical models have been proposed to describe G × Es. Among the most prominently used is the diathesis-stress model, which stipulates that genetic vulnerability predisposes an individual to the development of a psychiatric disorder when exposed to adversity. In other words, an individual may be genetically susceptible to a psychiatric disorder, but the disorder

G × E TERMINOLOGY

Before discussing G × Es, it is worthwhile to review commonly used terminology. Genes are small sections of the chromosome that code for RNA molecules and, in consequence, proteins. The human genome is composed of 46 chromosomes, which are long sequences of DNA. The DNA sequence is composed of a chain of the nucleotide bases adenine (A), cytosine (C), guanine (G), and thymine (T). An allele is a variant form of a gene in a specific genetic locus on a chromosome. Humans have two alleles at each genetic locus, one from each parent. Each pair of alleles represents the genotype of a specific gene. Genotypes can be either homozygous, with two identical alleles at a particular locus, or heterozygous, with two differing alleles at a locus. Most G × E studies examine single-nucleotide polymorphisms (SNPs) (see **Figure 1a**). A haplotype is a set of SNPs in close proximity to each other with alleles that are inherited together.

Another important aspect of genetic studies is gene expression, i.e., the way in which DNA is read (see **Figure 1b**). Gene expression occurs via two steps, called transcription (DNA to RNA) and translation (RNA to proteins), within the cell. Cells respond to changes in their environment through these two processes.

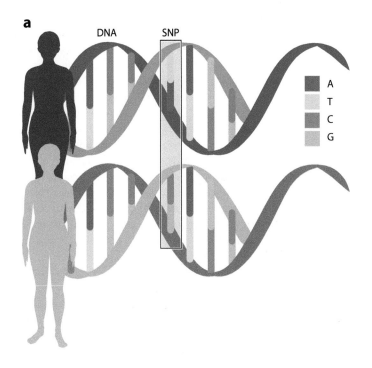

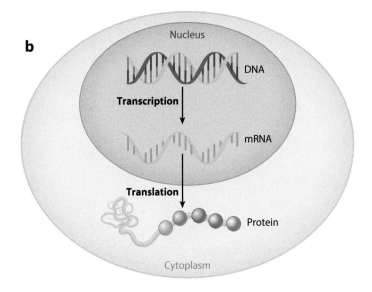

Figure 1

(*a*) The DNA sequence is composed of a chain of the nucleotide bases adenine (A), cytosine (C), guanine (G), and thymine (T). A single-nucleotide polymorphism (SNP) is a variation in a single nucleotide occurring at a certain position, or genetic locus, on a chromosome. Variations at the SNP level account for many of the differences seen across individuals. (*b*) Schematic representation of transcription and translation. Transcription occurs within the nucleus when DNA is copied into RNA and then messenger RNA (mRNA). During translation, information from the mRNA is used to create a protein.

does not develop unless triggered by an environmental stressor. Conversely, individuals without this genetic predisposition do not develop a psychiatric disorder when confronted with adversity. This model has proven very fruitful in stimulating research, and the majority of conducted G × E studies adhere to this model. However, the diathesis-stress model has been criticized for disproportionately focusing on stressors and negative life events and ignoring positive environments (Belsky & Pluess 2009). Among the critics of this model, Belsky and colleagues (2007, Belsky & Pluess 2009) argue that the diathesis-stress model risks misclassifying environmental influences by focusing mainly on negative environmental influences; thus, they propose an alternative, the differential-susceptibility perspective (Belsky et al. 2007, Belsky & Pluess 2009). This model proposes that individuals vary in their susceptibility to environmental influences (both negative and positive) rather than claiming that specific genotypes are inherently good or bad (Belsky et al. 2007, Belsky & Pluess 2009). That is, the genotype can either exacerbate an individual's risk of psychopathology in negative environmental conditions or mitigate the risk of psychopathology in positive environmental conditions. Thus, it is more appropriate to refer to variants for such environmentally dependent genotypes as plasticity variants rather than risk or vulnerability variants because they appear to make individuals more susceptible to both negative and positive environmental influences (see **Figure 2**). As noted above, most G × E studies have limited their analyses to negative environmental risk factors. To represent both perspectives, we point out in this review any G × E studies depicting the differential-susceptibility framework.

G × E studies can provide important biological insights into psychiatric disorders and may consequently have direct clinical implications. It is currently an exciting time for research on the

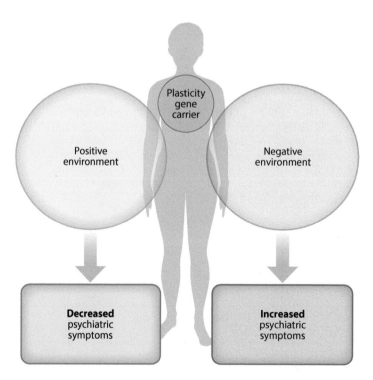

Figure 2

The differential-susceptibility model proposes that genetic predisposition makes an individual more susceptible to both negative and positive environmental conditions and thereby either exacerbates or mitigates the risk of psychiatric symptoms in accordance with the environmental conditions.

genetic underpinnings of psychiatric disorders. New genotyping technologies and analytical tools are emerging, enabling the examination of the effects of genetic variants in multinational collaborations with large sample sizes. At the same time, it is important to view the current literature in light of the methodological challenges that G × E studies have faced. Toward this end, this review begins by discussing some of these challenges associated with G × E studies, namely difficulties replicating findings and high false discovery rates. Due to these challenges, we have selected G × E studies for this review that have moved beyond candidate gene association testing and offer multilevel validation for the interactions detected, including corroborating neuroimaging, endocrine, and molecular findings. Among the new analytical tools, we describe recent studies utilizing a polygenic approach to examine G × Es. Finally, we discuss how gaining a deeper understanding of G × Es may translate into a therapeutic practice with more targeted treatments.

G × E CHALLENGES

As with research in any other field, G × E studies are faced with a number of criticisms and limitations (Dick et al. 2015). In this section, we discuss the major challenges facing the field at present and some of the proposed solutions.

To date, most G × E studies have relied on candidate-gene approaches. In these studies, researchers choose a specific gene of interest on the basis of its biological function in a psychiatric disorder and test whether the association between variation in this gene and the disorder differs across environments. In spite of the hundreds of candidate G × E publications on psychiatric outcomes, few findings are generally accepted by the genetics community because only a small number of interactions have been robustly associated with a psychiatric disorder across multiple studies. This lack of reproducibility is in part because of the small sample sizes (mostly <1,000 participants) in these studies and the resulting lack of power to detect interactions with small effect sizes.

Variation in heritability estimates of psychiatric disorders in different environmental contexts is another complicating factor that increases the difficulty of replication. High heritability indicates that genetic factors account for a large portion of the susceptibility to a particular psychiatric disorder. However, this does not mean that genes cause the disorder. Similarly, it does not imply that the same genetic factors will account for the same amount of variance under all circumstances. Indeed, when environmental or genetic conditions change, so do heritability estimates (Rutter et al. 2006). This poses a methodological challenge to G × E studies, given that heritability is likely to differ across studies when the samples vary in terms of level or range of environmental risk. However, this same variation in heritability estimates underscores the need to examine genetic and environmental determinants jointly. Similarly, findings may also differ on the basis of the operationalization and scaling of measures. Thus, there is a need for high-quality measurement of genetic and environmental factors, along with transparency in the operationalization of variables, to enhance the probability of study findings being replicated (Rutter et al. 2006, Rutter & Pickles 2015).

Candidate-gene approaches have also been criticized for their simplification of genetic models. These studies typically rely on one individual single-nucleotide polymorphism (SNP) or other types of genetic variants such as repeat polymorphisms or a set of variants that explain only a small portion of the genetic variation in psychiatric disorders (Duncan & Keller 2011). Research from both epidemiological and genetic studies, however, indicates that the genetic architecture of psychiatric disorders is highly complex and that psychiatric disorders are polygenic (i.e., involve multiple genes). This combination of low likelihood that a candidate gene accounts for a large portion of the variance, low power, and small effect sizes can lead to high false discovery rates (Duncan & Keller 2011). In addition, G × E studies often account only for confounds using main

SNP:
single-nucleotide polymorphism

effects but not their interaction terms, which may also contribute to spurious associations (Duncan & Keller 2011).

Despite these challenges, we are not claiming that G × Es have only yielded erroneous findings. These challenges do, however, highlight the need to replicate findings and validate them on a mechanistic level. As a starting point for navigating this challenging field, Rutters and colleagues' (2006) recommended strategy has been to focus hypotheses on potential biological pathways that incorporate both genetic and environmental determinants rather than to use an open-ended search for statistical interactions, which would likely result in a high number of false positive findings. They recommend examining genes found to be susceptible to environmental factors rather than genes associated directly with a psychiatric disorder. Hypotheses must be built on the empirical evidence of biological information about the gene and the environmental determinants. The combination of risk-increasing genes and risk-increasing environmental influences likely results in specific pathophysiological disturbances in molecular pathways, which may in turn impact the neural circuits associated with psychopathology. Toward that end, this review focuses on illustrating examples in which we might begin to understand G × E on the molecular, cellular, circuit, and behavioral level and link this interaction to altered risk for the development of psychiatric disorders.

GENE-BY-ENVIRONMENT INTERACTIONS VALIDATED ACROSS MULTIPLE LEVELS

Serotonin Transporter Promoter Polymorphism

Following its initial discovery by Lesch et al. (1996), a polymorphism in the promoter of the serotonin transporter gene (5-HTTLPR) has become one of the most studied polymorphisms in psychological and psychiatric research, including in G × E studies (for an overview of 5-HTTLPR studies, see Caspi et al 2010, Karg et al. 2011, Munafo et al. 2009). The 5-HTTLPR polymorphism is a variation of repeats in the promoter region of the serotonin transporter (the SLC6A4 gene encoding the SERT protein), which is involved in the reuptake of serotonin by brain synapses and is the target of the selective serotonin reuptake inhibitor (SSRI) medications commonly used to treat depression and anxiety disorders. 5-HTTLPR polymorphisms are categorized into short (S) alleles with 14 repeats and long (L) alleles with 16 repeats; the short alleles are associated with lower transporter expression and serotonin uptake (Lesch et al. 1996). Although these are the most common alleles, others have been described and are often specific to certain ethnicities (e.g., Xie et al. 2009). In addition, an SNP within the repeat region has been shown to moderate the functionality of 5-HTTLPR alleles (Hu et al. 2006). A handful of studies have related this polymorphism to the actual binding capacity of SERT in positron emission tomography (PET)-ligand studies or to the abundance of the transporter in postmortem studies, but with inconsistent results (e.g., Cannon et al. 2006, Frankle et al. 2005, Mann et al. 2000).

In the first G × E study involving 5-HTTLPR, Caspi et al. (2003) demonstrated that individuals with one or two copies of the low-expressing S allele of 5-HTTLPR were at greater risk for depression (measured at both the symptomatic and diagnostic level) and exhibited greater suicidality after exposure to stressful life events (both in childhood and adulthood) compared to individuals not carrying this risk allele. In the absence of adverse life events, the polymorphism did not alter risk, a result that is consistent with a large number of studies finding no case/control differences of this polymorphism with the diagnosis of depression per se (for a review, see Karg et al. 2011). This influential article was one of the first to demonstrate genetically driven

SERT: serotonin transporter

SSRI: selective serotonin reuptake inhibitor

5-HTTLPR: serotonin transporter promoter

individual differences in the response to environmental stress and vulnerability to psychopathology. Since this study, *5-HTTLPR* has been found to moderate the relationship between various other environmental stressors and various psychiatric problems, including anxiety, posttraumatic stress disorder (PTSD), suicide attempts, alcohol consumption, eating disorders, substance use, and attention-deficit/hyperactivity disorder (ADHD) (Gibb et al. 2006, Kilpatrick et al. 2007, Koenen et al. 2009, Kranzler et al. 2012, Laucht et al. 2009, Liu et al. 2015, Roy et al. 2007, Stein et al. 2008, Stoltenberg et al. 2012, van der Meer et al. 2014).

PTSD: posttraumatic stress disorder

ADHD: attention deficit hyperactivity disorder

Consistent with the differential-susceptibility perspective, the same genotype (S-allele carriers) has also been found to decrease the risk of psychopathology in enriched environments (Belsky & Pluess 2009, Hankin et al. 2011, Pluess et al. 2010). Specifically, carriers of the *5-HTTLPR* S allele are at greater risk of psychopathology when exposed to stressors, but they display the fewest depressive symptoms when they grew up in a supportive environment or experienced recent positive events (Eley et al. 2004, Taylor et al. 2006).

What mechanisms could confer such differential susceptibility? As described above, *5-HTTLPR* in its environmentally sensitive short form has been associated with lower efficiency of SERT in cell systems compared to its long form. The way this relates to serotonergic signaling in neural circuits is much less clear. Functional brain imaging studies suggest that the polymorphism is associated with an inherently different neural circuit activation during emotion processing. Specifically, differential brain activity in regions involved in emotion processing (e.g., amygdala, cingulate cortex, hypothalamus) has been observed in individuals following exposure to emotional stimuli based on the *5-HTTLPR* genotype (Alexander et al. 2012; Canli et al. 2006; Dannlowski et al. 2007, 2008; Fortier et al. 2010; Hariri et al. 2005; Munafo et al. 2008; Pezawas et al. 2005). For instance, Fortier et al. (2010) found greater regional brain activation in children with the S-allele genotype when watching a sad movie compared to children with the alternate genotype. This altered processing of emotional stimuli may emerge on the behavioral level due to a differential systemic response to stress. In fact, increased neuroticism has been observed in individuals carrying the S allele compared to L-allele carriers (Munafo et al. 2009).

At the endocrine level, enhanced cortisol secretion following an acute stressor has been observed in healthy S-allele carriers with a history of stressful life events but not in individuals homozygous for the L allele with a similar history of stressful events (Alexander et al. 2009). Differences between *5-HTTLPR* genotypes have also been reported in the autonomic nervous system. Specifically, children carrying the L allele have a higher stress-induced increase in salivary α-amylase, which is elicited by the autonomic nervous system, compared to S-allele carriers. This finding suggests differential stress-related autonomic changes in the body based on genotype and an overall sharper recovery following stressor exposure in the L-allele carriers than in the S-allele carriers (Mueller et al. 2012). Taken together, the putative differences in serotonergic neurotransmission, which drive altered activation in various brain regions and differences in stress reactivity, may lead to dysregulated emotional processing of stressors in S-allele carriers and thus cause increased vulnerability to the development of a psychiatric disorder. In-depth knowledge about these mechanisms may also allow more individualized therapeutic interventions, as discussed in the section Implications for Treatment.

Despite the large number of studies conducted on *5-HTTLPR*, the moderating effect of this polymorphism remains controversial. Two meta-analyses have yielded a negative result for the moderation effect of *5-HTTLPR* on the relationship between stressful life events and depression (Munafo et al. 2009, Risch et al. 2009), whereas two more recent meta-analyses supported the moderation findings (Karg et al. 2011, Sharpley et al. 2014). Researchers have explained such incongruent findings in several ways, including heterogeneity of both the measurement of the environmental

HPA: hypothalamic-
pituitary-adrenal

FKBP5: FK506
binding protein-5

GR: glucocorticoid
receptor

mRNA: messenger
RNA

determinants and phenotypes across studies (Caspi et al. 2010, Uher & McGuffin 2008). For example, early-life stress and childhood abuse have consistently been shown to interact with *5-HTTLPR* polymorphisms in predicting depression (Karg et al. 2011). When stressors at other stages of life are examined, the results are less consistent. Other studies indicate that aggregated life stressors at the group level (e.g., living in a dangerous neighborhood), not just the individual level, can moderate G × E findings but are often not accounted for (Kilpatrick et al. 2007, Koenen et al. 2009). Findings have also varied depending on how depression is operationalized. For instance, Uher and colleagues (2011) showed that *5-HTTPLR* moderated the relationship between stressful life events and depression only in patients with persistent depression and not in patients with a single episode of depression. In sum, these findings highlight the importance of careful characterization of the environmental determinant in G × Es, as well as the outcome measure.

FK506 Binding Protein-5 Polymorphisms

Gene variants moderating the stress response and the regulation of the hypothalamic-pituitary-adrenal (HPA) axis are among the most promising candidates for G × E studies in psychiatry (see sidebar The Hypothalamic-Pituitary-Adrenal Axis; **Figure 3**). Among these genes, one of the most comprehensively studied is *FK506 binding protein-5* (*FKBP5*), encoding the protein FKBP51. Within the cell, FKBP51 is a central regulator of stress responsivity because it is part of the steroid receptor complex (Grad & Picard 2007). Glucocorticoid receptor (GR) function, an important part of the stress system (**Figure 3**), is regulated by a large molecular complex that includes chaperones as well as co-chaperones such as FKBP51. When FKBP51 is bound to the GR complex, the receptor has low affinity to cortisol and does not translocate readily to the nucleus (Davies et al. 2002, Wochnik et al. 2005). Importantly, *FKBP5* is also a target of GR activation, and its messenger RNA (mRNA) and protein are induced by cortisol. This creates an ultrashort negative feedback loop in which GR induces FKBP51, which then limits GR activity (Vermeer et al. 2003). This induction of *FKBP5* mRNA and the resulting intracellular regulation of GR activity are moderated by common genetic variants in the *FKBP5* locus. The associated changes in GR sensitivity during the feedback regulation of the HPA axis lead to prolonged stress-related cortisol release in individuals carrying the variant that is associated with higher *FKBP5* mRNA induction

THE HYPOTHALAMIC-PITUITARY-ADRENAL AXIS

Dysregulation in the hypothalamic-pituitary-adrenal (HPA) axis in psychiatric patients has been well documented (Baumeister et al. 2014), making genes associated with the axis attractive targets for G × E researchers.

The HPA axis is central to stress response. When confronted with a stressor, corticotropin-releasing hormone (CRH) is excreted from the paraventricular nucleus of the hypothalamus. CRH acts on the pituitary gland, resulting in the release of adrenocorticotropic hormone (ACTH) from the anterior pituitary. This induces the release of cortisol from the adrenal cortex. Subsequently, ACTH acts on the adrenal glands, stimulating the production and release of glucocorticoids by the adrenal cortices (Vale et al. 1981) (**Figure 3**). Glucocorticoids bind to glucocorticoid receptors (GRs), which inhibit the synthesis and release of CRH in the hypothalamus and of ACTH in the pituitary. This enables a negative feedback regulation, allowing the reduction of HPA axis activation and the restoration of homeostasis once the threat has subsided (Holsboer 2000).

Disruption of this feedback regulation can have long-lasting effects on brain activity and the regulation of the stress hormone system (Bale & Vale 2004). Among the HPA axis–associated genes, *FK506 binding protein-5* (*FKBP5*) and *corticotropin-releasing hormone receptor 1* (*CRHR1*) have received the most attention in G × E studies.

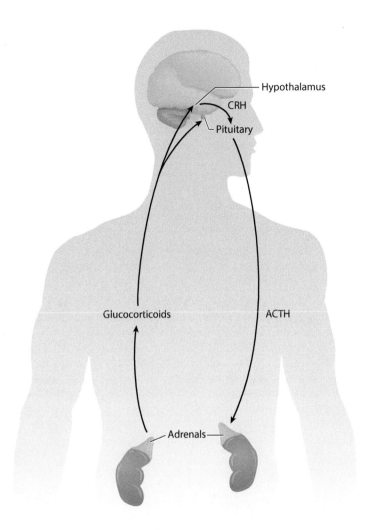

Figure 3

In the hypothalamic-pituitary-adrenal axis, corticotropin-releasing hormone (CRH) is excreted from the paraventricular nucleus of the hypothalamus within minutes of being confronted with a stressor. CRH acts on the pituitary gland, resulting in the release of adrenocorticotropic hormone (ACTH) from the anterior pituitary, which further induces the release of cortisol from the adrenal cortex. Subsequently, ACTH acts on the adrenal glands, stimulating the production and release of glucocorticoids by the adrenal cortices. Of note, CRH and its receptors are also important regulators of the stress response in other, mainly limbic, brain regions.

(Binder et al. 2004, Buchmann et al. 2014, Klengel et al. 2013). This genetic change in the physiologic stress response is associated with an altered risk for psychiatric disorders.

In the case of *FKBP5*, genetic and epigenetic changes must come together (**Figure 4**). Specifically, changes in the DNA methylation of *FKBP5* locus glucocorticoid response elements (GREs; short DNA motifs that can bind to GRs) have been implicated in this additional disinhibition (Klengel et al. 2013). DNA methylation refers to the transfer of a methyl group (CH_3) to any of the millions of cytosine-phosphate-guanosine dinucleotide sites in the human genome. This alters

GRE: glucocorticoid response element

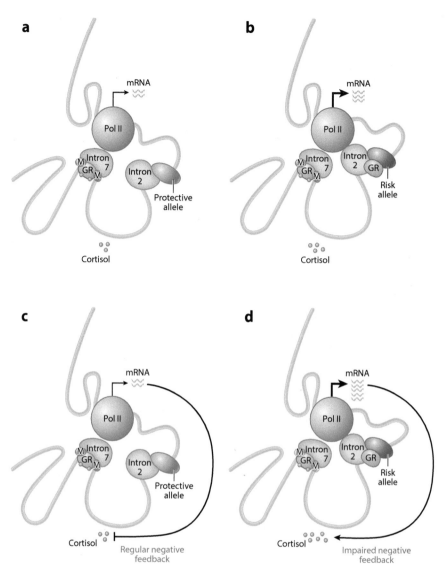

Figure 4

Schematic representation of the interaction of glucocorticoid receptor elements (GREs) in introns 2 and 7 in the rs1360780 single-nucleotide polymorphism of *FKBP5* at the genetic level (*a,b*) and epigenetic level (*c,d*) following exposure to early trauma. (*a*) The protective rs1360780 major allele reduces the interaction between GRE intron 2 and the RNA polymerase II (Pol II), thereby decreasing the production of *FKBP5* messenger RNA (mRNA) in response to glucocorticoid receptor (GR) activation. (*b*) The risk rs1360780 minor allele increases the interaction between GRE intron 2 and the promoter, resulting in increased *FKBP5* induction. In other words, risk-allele carriers have genetically determined higher *FKBP5* mRNA expression and GR resistance. (*c*) When exposed to early trauma, the negative feedback of *FKBP5* in protective allele carriers remains stable. Regular transcriptional activation of *FKBP5* results in the GR terminating the stress response and in regular normalization of cortisol levels once the threat has subsided. (*d*) In contrast, the negative feedback loop is impaired in risk-allele carriers following exposure to childhood trauma. Specifically, early trauma leads to increased activation of *FKBP5*, which in turn results in the reduction of DNA methylation (M) around intron 7 and higher and prolonged cortisol levels. Figure adapted from Klengel & Binder (2015) with permission.

the three-dimensional structure of the DNA and leads to a reduced accessibility of methylated sites to transcriptional regulators (Novik et al. 2002). The likely causal *FKBP5* SNP, rs1360780, is in close proximity to a GRE in intron 2 of the gene (**Figure 4a,b**). Introns are noncoding sections of an RNA transcript that are removed before the RNA molecule is translated into protein but often harbor regions that are important for gene transcription regulation. In the risk-allele conformation, this transcriptional enhancer is in close proximity to the promoter and thus enhances GR signaling in *FKBP5* transcription. This has been associated with an enhanced short feedback on GR sensitivity and a delayed systemic negative feedback on the cortisol response to stress (Klengel et al. 2013). This leads to longer cortisol exposure following stress and, consequently, active demethylation of another GRE (see **Figure 4d**). In fact, binding of the GR to GREs can lead to active demethylation, sensitizing the target to future exposure (Thomassin et al. 2001). The demethylation further derepresses the transcriptional response of *FKBP5* to GR (Klengel & Binder 2015, Sharma et al. 2016). This disruption in regulatory homeostasis is thought to result in long-lasting changes in the neural circuits involved in stress and anxiety regulation via both changes in GR tone and a direct downstream effect of FKBP51 on additional pathways that are highly relevant for neuronal function and synaptic plasticity (Zannas et al. 2016).

GWAS: genome-wide association study

Interactions between *FKBP5* and stressful life events have been found to be associated with a variety of psychiatric disorders and traits, including PTSD, depression, aggression, suicidality, and psychosis, by many studies that include well over 12,000 individuals (for a review, see Zannas et al. 2016). The majority of these studies report a general vulnerability to psychopathology in individuals carrying alleles associated with higher *FKBP5* induction following stress exposure. These findings have largely been proven robust across studies and in different ethnic groups. Importantly, genome-wide association studies (GWASs) and candidate gene case-control association studies have not found a main effect for the gene in predicting psychopathology, indicating that the effect is dependent on environmental influences (Binder et al. 2008, Nievergelt et al. 2015, Solovieff et al. 2014). This suggests that additional mechanisms besides the genetic regulation of *FKBP5* are necessary to trigger the stress interaction effect.

A wealth of evidence from animal and human studies supports the association of high FKBP51 function and psychiatric disorders. In animals, increased FKBP51 function has been associated with increased anxiety, decreased stress coping, delayed fear extinction, and a more dysregulated stress response (Albu et al. 2014, Attwood et al. 2011, Hartmann et al. 2012, O'Leary et al. 2011, Sawamura et al. 2016, Touma et al. 2011). In humans, the alleles with high *FKBP5* reactivity are associated with behavioral risk phenotypes, such as increased dissociation following trauma, increased bias toward threat, and increased intrusions (Cheung & Bryant 2015, Fani et al. 2013, Koenen et al. 2005), as well as a prolonged cortisol response following stress exposure (Buchmann et al. 2014, Ising et al. 2008).

At the circuit level, brain regions associated with emotion processing, inhibition, and memory, including the amygdala and hippocampus, are thought to be involved in *FKBP5*-related vulnerability to psychopathology. Overall, the hippocampus is the brain region with the highest baseline levels of FKBP51 expression, yet it shows little transcriptional reactivity to stress. Other brain regions, such as the amygdala and the hypothalamus, have low baseline levels but show dramatic increases in expression following stress (Scharf et al. 2011). Animal studies have shown that overexpression of FKBP51 in the amygdala increases anxiety behavior and decreases stress coping, and the opposite is true when FKBP51 is blocked in this brain area (Attwood et al. 2011, Hartmann et al. 2015).

Human structural and functional neuroimaging studies also indicate that the *FKBP5* genotype has a major effect on these brain regions (Fani et al. 2013, 2014, 2016; Hirakawa et al. 2016; Holz et al. 2015) and that the interaction with early adversity compounds this effect (Grabe et al.

CRHR1:
corticotropin-releasing
hormone receptor 1

CRH:
corticotropin-releasing
hormone

2016, Holz et al. 2015, Tozzi et al. 2016, White et al. 2012). Increased hippocampal and amygdala activity in response to threat and white matter abnormalities in the posterior cingulum have been observed in risk-allele carriers compared to alternative genotypes (Fani et al. 2013, 2014, 2016; Hirakawa et al. 2016; Holz et al. 2015). Two studies have found that the *FKBP5* risk genotypes interact with childhood neglect to predict increased threat-related activity in the amygdala (Holz et al. 2015, White et al. 2012). Specifically, both studies found that the right amygdala activity increased in parallel with the level of childhood neglect reported by homozygote *rs1360780* risk-allele carrier young adults during an emotional face-matching task, whereas the opposite was true for homozygotes of the protective allele. Heterozygotes exhibited intermediate levels of activity. Holz et al. (2015) also found that homozygote *rs1360780* risk-allele carriers displayed increased amygdala-hippocampus coupling, indicating that *FKBP5* may play a role in emotional memory formation, which may result in the negative emotional memory often seen in depressed patients (Hamilton & Gotlib 2008). Another study indicated that the combination of the *FKBP5* risk allele with a history of childhood abuse may predispose an individual to more widespread structural brain changes in other subcortical and cortical emotion-processing brain regions in addition to the amygdala and hippocampus (Grabe et al. 2016). In particular, Grabe and colleagues (2016) found that minor allele carriers of *FKBP5* rs1360780 exposed to child abuse had reduced gray matter volumes in the bilateral insula, the superior and middle temporal gyrus, and the bilateral anterior cingulate cortex, as well as the hippocampus and amygdala, compared to abused major allele carriers. Although the findings have been less consistent, postmortem studies have shown that *FKBP5* gene and protein expression are reduced in the amygdala of suicide victims compared to controls (Pérez-Ortiz et al. 2013) but increased in the prefrontal cortex of schizophrenia and bipolar patients compared to healthy controls (Sinclair et al. 2013).

These collective multilevel neurobiological findings suggest that an inherent genetic disinhibition of *FKBP5* in several emotion-processing brain regions is associated with increased bias toward threat, enhanced cortisol response, and altered amygdala and hippocampal response to threat. In combination with exposure to trauma in childhood, this genotype results in additional GR-mediated epigenetic disinhibition, which pushes this regulatory circuit over a threshold and leads to disease phenotypes. This result may be due to altered stress-related synaptic plasticity, possibly mediated by the effects of *FKBP5* on relevant pathways (Zannas et al. 2016). In support of this hypothesis, a recent postmortem study comparing PTSD patients and controls suggested that high FKBP51 levels in the orbitofrontal cortex were associated with a decrease in overall dendritic spine density (Young et al. 2015).

Corticotropin-Releasing Hormone Receptor 1

Corticotropin-releasing hormone receptor 1 (CRHR1) is another well-studied gene involved in the regulation of the stress response via the HPA axis. CRHR1 is a guanine nucleotide-binding protein (G-protein) receptor that binds corticotropin-releasing hormone (CRH) and is consequently a major physiological regulator of the HPA axis. The encoded protein plays a key role in the activation of signal transduction pathways involved in the regulation of the stress response (Koob 1999).

The link between genetic variants of both CRH and *CRHR1* and psychopathology has been extensively studied (for a review, see Binder & Nemeroff 2010). In terms of G × Es, *CRHR1* polymorphisms have been shown to predict both risk of and resilience to depressive symptoms in adults who have endured child abuse. More specifically, a haplotype composed of intronic SNPs in the *CRHR1* gene was found to protect against the development of depression in adults with a history of abuse across different ethnic groups (Bradley et al. 2008, Polanczyk et al. 2009). This indicates that genetically determined differences in CRH-mediated neurotransmission may increase or decrease the detrimental effects of child abuse on the stress hormone system and thus influence an individual's susceptibility to developing depressive symptoms in adulthood. Replication of these findings in larger samples is still necessary to rule out false positive associations. Additionally, the ways in which early adversity is assessed may be relevant in the context of this G × E finding given that retrospective self-report of childhood abuse has been found to interact significantly with the gene whereas the prospective assessment of maltreatment has not (Bradley et al. 2008, Polanczyk et al. 2009).

COMT: catechol-O-methyltransferase

Further support for the *CRHR1* findings has come from endocrine and neuroimaging studies. In healthy adults with a history of childhood trauma, Tyrka et al. (2009) showed that individuals carrying the *CRHR1* risk haplotype experienced an increased cortisol response to combined dexamethasone/CRH stimulation but no differences across the genotypes were observed in adults with no history of early trauma. These findings were supported by Heim et al. (2009). Similarly, the *CRHR1* haplotype was found to interact with maltreatment in predicting diurnal regulation of cortisol levels in children (Cicchetti et al. 2011). These findings suggest that *CRHR1* risk-haplotype carriers have a genetic vulnerability to early trauma exposure, which may contribute to a long-lasting increase in CRHR1 signaling and dysregulation in the stress hormone system.

On a circuit level, preclinical studies in rodents have observed altered *CRHR1* mRNA expression and CRH binding in the hypothalamus, amygdala, and other brain regions associated with emotion response (Potter et al. 1994). It is thought that CRH activity at the CRHR1 in extrahypothalamic regions contributes to anxiety and depressive symptoms (Binder & Nemeroff 2010). *CRHR1* risk variants have also been shown to predict differential activation of limbic and cortical areas in emotion paradigms. For example, increased activity in the subgenual cingulate has been observed in depressed homozygote risk-allele carriers (i.e., G carriers) compared to depressed resilience allele carriers (i.e., A carriers) and controls when viewing negative versus neutral words (Hsu et al. 2012). Moreover, deactivation in the hypothalamus, amygdala, and nucleus accumbens was found in the depressed A carriers compared to controls during the same experiment. These findings may suggest biologically different types of depression depending on *CRHR1* genotype (Hsu et al. 2012). Interestingly, both depression and early-life stress were associated with changes in brain activity depending on genotype. Specifically, early-life stress and hypothalamus activation were negatively correlated only in A carriers (Hsu et al. 2012). These findings further support the notion that exposure to early-life stress can differentially impact emotional processing based on *CRHR1* genotype. *CRHR1* genotype–dependent differences have also been observed on a behavioral level with *CRHR1* risk-allele carriers exhibiting increased fear and stress sensitization compared to carriers of the alternative genotype (Starr et al. 2014, Weber et al. 2016).

Catechol-O-Methyltransferase

Although environmental stressors, such as early trauma, are the most common environmental determinant used in G × E studies, several studies suggest genotypic differences in outcomes based on cannabis use. In this and the following section, we review genes found to moderate the relationship between cannabis use and psychotic symptoms and schizophrenia.

Dysregulation in dopaminergic function has been implicated in the pathogenesis of schizophrenia (e.g., Kapur 2003). Cannabis use may also impact dopamine circuits (Colizzi et al. 2016), interacting with genetic variants associated with this system to predict risk for schizophrenia. The *catechol-O-methyltransferase* (*COMT*) gene, located on chromosome 22, encodes an enzyme that metabolizes dopamine and has been linked to schizophrenia.

Caspi and colleagues (2005) reported that a functional *COMT* gene polymorphism had a moderating effect on the increased risk for psychosis in adulthood following cannabis use during

CNR1: cannabinoid receptor type 1

THC: tetrahydrocannabinol

adolescence. They examined a G-to-A missense variation (i.e., one amino acid is altered in the protein product) in which the amino acid valine (Val) substitutes methionine (Met) at codon 158 (Val[158]Met). This variation has been shown to decrease COMT's enzymatic activity and result in a slower breakdown of dopamine. The homozygous Met genotype has been found to have the lowest COMT activity and the homozygous Val genotype the highest, with heterozygous carriers displaying intermediate activity (Männistö & Kaakkola 1999). Caspi et al. (2005) reported that homozygous Val genotype carriers were more likely to develop psychotic symptoms in adulthood after using cannabis during adolescence compared to the homo- and heterozygous Met genotype carriers. These associations have since been replicated, although some studies have yielded null findings for this interaction (Costas et al. 2011; Funke et al. 2005; van Winkel 2011; Zammit et al. 2007, 2011). These findings were further extended by the discovery that the effects of cannabis were dependent on the proportion of THC and cannabidiol (another type of cannabinoid found in cannabis) in the cannabis (Niesink & van Laar 2013, Schubart et al. 2011). A higher concentration of cannabidiol in the cannabis mitigated the risk of the psychotic symptoms associated with cannabis use. Interestingly, two additional studies found a three-way interaction between adolescent cannabis use, the *COMT* gene, and childhood maltreatment (Alemany et al. 2014, Vinkers et al. 2013). In particular, cannabis use and a history of childhood abuse together were associated with increased psychotic symptoms in Val carriers compared to heterozygous or homozygous Met carriers. These genetic differences may increase the impact of cannabis use on dopamine circuits and, consequently, increase the risk for psychotic disorders (Sami et al. 2015).

The cellular and molecular mechanisms by which cannabis use contributes to vulnerability to psychotic symptoms remain unclear (for a review, see Malone et al. 2010). However, neuroimaging studies have provided further support for the relationship between *COMT* Val status and psychotic symptoms (for a review, see Lawrie et al. 2008). For instance, greater activation in the dorsolateral prefrontal cortex and reduced volumes of the prefrontal cortex and temporal lobes have been observed in Val carriers compared to Met carriers (Egan et al. 2001, Ohnishi et al. 2006). In accordance with these brain anomalies, the *COMT* gene variation may also increase cognitive vulnerability to other psychiatric disorders, including depression (Antypa et al. 2013, Craddock et al. 2006). Indeed, the *COMT* gene has been linked to heightened risk of broader personality traits associated with various psychopathologies (Hettema et al. 2015). For example, Val carriers tend to score higher on both introversion and extraversion measures than Met carriers (Hettema et al. 2008, 2015). Furthermore, the *COMT* genotype has been found to moderate the relationship between stressful life events and pathologies other than psychotic symptoms, including aggression, ADHD, and depression (Antypa et al. 2013, Hettema et al. 2015, Hygen et al. 2015, Thapar et al. 2005).

Cannabinoid Receptor Type 1 and Mitogen-Activated Protein Kinase 14

Two other genes, *cannabinoid receptor type 1* (*CNR1*) and *mitogen-activated protein kinase 14* (*MAPK14*), have also been found to moderate the relationship between cannabis use and schizophrenia. The main active component in cannabis, tetrahydrocannabinol (THC), activates cannabinoid receptors such as *CNR1* in the brain. Activation of *CNR1* has been found to induce apoptosis (i.e., the process of programmed cell death) through a complex cascade of kinases (i.e., an enzyme that adds phosphate groups to other molecules) and caspases (i.e., enzymes involved in apoptosis) (Chan et al. 1998, Downer et al. 2003), including *MAPK14* (Derkinderen et al. 2001, Powles et al. 2005). *CNR1* has also been implicated in the regulation of striatal dopamine (Pazos et al. 2005).

The G × E studies involving these gene variants have focused on their moderating effect on cannabis use and brain structure differences in individuals with and without schizophrenia.

Specifically, *CNR1* and *MAPK14* genetic variants have been found to predict greater deficits in white matter volume and cognitive impairment in a subset of patients with schizophrenia and marijuana abuse or dependence compared to individuals with schizophrenia without co-occurring marijuana abuse or dependence (Ho et al. 2011, Onwuameze et al. 2013). Interestingly, one study observed a significant gene–gene (i.e., *CNR1–MAPK14*) interaction influencing brain volume abnormalities in patients with both schizophrenia and a history of cannabis use during adolescence (Onwuameze et al. 2013). This interaction was additive: Patients with co-occurring schizophrenia and marijuana misuse who were carriers of both *CNR1* and *MAPK14* risk-alleles had the greatest deficit in white matter compared to the alternative genotypes. Although these findings are promising, this interaction remains to be expanded to and validated on other biological levels.

PRS: polygenic risk score

MDD: major depressive disorder

Polygenic Approaches

In accordance with Rutter and colleagues' (2006) recommendations, most G × E studies have been conducted using hypothesis-driven candidate genes. However, multiple gene variants likely work together to shape the risk for a psychiatric disorder (Kraft & Aschard 2015). As such, polygenic risk score (PRS) analyses provide an exciting framework for G × E studies. In contrast to hypothesis-driven candidate-gene approaches, polygenic approaches incorporate the contributions of many common genetic variants of small magnitude across the genome. A PRS for an individual is typically calculated by summing the number of alleles for each SNP; this sum is then weighted by the effect size derived from a GWAS. A GWAS involves a systematic examination of whether genotype frequencies for variants across the genome differ between individuals affected with a specific disorder and those who are unaffected. Thus, the PRS represents the additive effect of multiple SNPs, with a higher PRS typically suggesting a greater genetic predisposition toward the psychiatric disorder. Such scores give a much better representation of the genetic risk profile than a single candidate gene. Polygenic analyses have already demonstrated much larger cumulative effect sizes and greater predictive power than single-variant predictors (Bulik-Sullivan et al. 2015, Maier et al. 2015). Additionally, PRSs are not limited to examining disease risk: They also have the potential to investigate behavioral phenotypes, brain activity, and physiological and molecular measures relevant to environmental responses. This will allow a much more detailed exploration of the ways in which the environment interacts with genetic predisposition on different molecular and behavioral levels. This field is rapidly expanding, and new computational advances are emerging to construct PRSs with improved predictive and statistical abilities (e.g., Bulik-Sullivan et al. 2015, Maier et al. 2015). By design, polygenic studies do not point directly to specific genes associated with disease. However, complementary methods, such as gene-set analyses or subsetting using functionally relevant variants that alter gene transcription or DNA methylation or are located in relevant enhancer regions, can be employed to further dissect the potential biological mechanisms underlying such G × Es.

Three studies have examined the interaction between PRSs [based on data from the international Psychiatric Genomics Consortium (PGC) for major depressive disorder (MDD)] and childhood trauma in predicting MDD in independent adult samples (Mullins et al. 2016, Musliner et al. 2015, Peyrot et al. 2014). All three studies reported that the PRS had a significant main effect and examined its interaction with stressful life events. To briefly summarize their findings, Peyrot et al. (2014) and Mullins et al. (2016) reported a significant interaction between the PRS for MDD and childhood trauma in predicting depression. Peyrot and colleagues (2014) found that individuals with a high PRS and a history of childhood trauma were more likely to develop MDD than those with a low PRS and no exposure to trauma. Conversely, Mullins and colleagues (2016) found that individuals with a history of moderate-to-severe childhood trauma had lower

PRSs for MDD than other cases or controls. In explaining their findings, Mullins and colleagues (2016) suggested that childhood trauma is such a strong risk factor that it may override to some extent genetic liability for the disorder. In addition to childhood trauma, Mullins et al. (2016) also examined the interaction between the PRS and stressful life events in adulthood in predicting MDD, which was nonsignificant. In the third study, Musliner et al. (2015) examined the interaction between the PRS for MDD and the occurrence of stressful life events during the previous 2 years in older adults. As in Mullins et al.'s (2016) study, the interaction between stressful life events in adulthood and the PRS was not significant (Musliner et al. 2015). These somewhat discrepant findings highlight the need to further examine both the type and timing of stressful life events in combination with genetic risk for psychopathology.

The studies above investigated PRSs derived from case/control associations but without functional annotation. Investigating PRSs that lead to functional differences in the response to environmental risk factors may, as pointed out by Rutter et al. (2006), be even more likely to lead to promising G × Es. As described in the section *FK506 Binding Protein-5* Polymorphism, the GR plays an important role in regulating gene expression. When an individual is confronted with a stressor, activation of the GR initiates adaptive physiological changes in the body through genome-wide transcriptional changes. As such, genetically determined differences in the transcriptional response to GR activation may contribute to individual differences in response to stressors and thus in susceptibility to psychiatric disorders (Lee & Sawa 2014, Shirazi et al. 2015). Using a stimulated expression quantitative trait locus approach, Arloth et al. (2015) constructed a genetic risk profile score based on genetic variants moderating the immediate transcriptional response to GR activation. The authors identified over 3,000 genetic variants that significantly altered the glucocorticoid-induced transcriptional changes of close to 300 transcripts. The genetic variants that altered the cellular response to stress were significantly enriched among variants associated with MDD and schizophrenia in the large meta-analyses published by the PGC (Ripke et al. 2013, 2014). In an independent sample, the cumulative score of genetic variants associated with both functional changes in the GR response of the transcriptome and risk for MDD predicted abnormal amygdala reactivity during a threat-related task. The findings suggest that genetic variants moderating the immediate cellular response to stress may also be associated with differences in the stress-processing neural circuit and an increased risk for stress-related psychiatric disorders (Arloth et al. 2015).

In addition to polygenic scores in G × E studies, genome-wide gene by environment interaction studies (GWEISs) are another possible unbiased analytical approach and elegant way to preserve power. Dunn and colleagues (2016) recently conducted a GWEIS analysis using social support and stressful life events as environmental determinants of depressive symptoms in over 10,000 women belonging to ethnic minorities. The findings pointed to interesting possible differences between minority groups. Specifically, increased depressive symptoms were observed to co-occur with both higher levels of reported stressful life events and more copies of the major allele of the gene *CEP350* in African American women. However, the same result was not found in a smaller independent replication sample, underscoring the need for large samples in GWEISs. In addition to requiring large sample sizes, GWEISs are based on GWASs in conjunction with environmental determinants and are thus fraught with a number of statistical complexities (e.g., Almli et al. 2014, Aschard et al. 2012). For instance, studies composed of large cohorts incorporating measures of environmental exposure carry the risk of overt and hidden differences in these measures.

IMPLICATIONS FOR TREATMENT

In this section, we discuss how G × E findings may be incorporated into clinical practice. We first define personalized treatment and then describe the current status of treatments for psychiatric disorders and the need to establish neurobiological profiles to advance personalized medicine. We outline G × Es that significantly predict treatment outcomes and discuss how they can be utilized to improve outcomes.

The goals of personalized treatment are to predict an individual's risk of developing a psychiatric disorder, obtain an accurate diagnosis, and determine the most effective and favorable treatment option (Ozomaro et al. 2013). Personalized medicine builds on the assumption that unique characteristics, including clinical presentation, history of environmental influences, and genetic alterations, influence how (and whether) an individual will respond to a certain treatment. This concept has gained considerable attention, likely due to the limitations of our current treatment options and recent advances in genomics. Despite the identification of a number of evidence-based treatments, treatment efficacy for most disorders remains unsatisfactory. As an illustration, approximately 60% of treatment-seeking individuals with depression achieve remission after an initial trial of psychotherapy, pharmacotherapy, or a combination of the two (Gaynes et al. 2009, Holtzheimer & Mayberg 2011, Trivedi et al. 2006). That leaves a staggering 40% of patients who continue to have clinically significant symptoms following the intervention. These relatively low remission rates cause serious individual and public health concerns due to the individual's continued distress, loss of productivity, and heightened risk of suicide.

In an effort to improve treatment outcomes, researchers have sought predictors and moderators to determine what treatment works best for whom. Several studies have examined genetic markers as predictors of response to antidepressants (Garriock et al. 2010, Ising et al. 2009, Keers & Aitchison 2011, Licinio et al. 2004, Porcelli et al. 2012, Uher et al. 2010, Zou et al. 2010) and psychotherapy (Eley et al. 2012, Knuts et al. 2014, Lester et al. 2012, Lonsdorf et al. 2010). However, these findings have been inconsistent (Garriock et al. 2010, GENDEP Investig. et al. 2013, Ising et al. 2009, Uher et al. 2010). Additionally, when a genetic variant has been found to predict treatment outcomes, the effect size of the finding tends to be small and thus not suitable for clinical prediction (Keers & Aitchison 2011). Demographic and clinical characteristics have also proved relatively weak predictors of treatment response (Johnstone et al. 2009, Nanni et al. 2012, Nemeroff et al. 2003). There is, however, evidence suggesting that exposure to stressful life events may differentially predict treatment outcomes (Agnew-Blais & Danese 2016, Nemeroff et al. 2003). For instance, depressed individuals with a history of childhood trauma have been found to respond more favorably to psychotherapy compared to pharmacotherapy (Nemeroff et al. 2003). The collective findings suggest differences in the etiology and pathogenesis of depressed individuals based on their developmental history. These findings also indicate that treatment response may be determined by a combination of factors, such as G × Es.

Several pharmacogenetic G × E studies have been conducted to predict treatment response to antidepressants. Relevant to the genetic variants discussed above, two studies (Keers et al. 2011, Mandelli et al. 2009) found that *5-HTTLPR* moderated the relationship between recent life stress and treatment with SSRIs but not tricyclic antidepressants for depression. In fact, recent life stress predicted poorer treatment outcomes in S-allele carriers compared to L-allele carriers. Conversely, no genotype differences were noted in individuals not exposed to recent life stress. G × Es that are significant for treatment response have also been reported for the *FKBP5* and *CRHR1* polymorphisms (Keers & Uher 2012). However, these findings differ from the *5-HTTLPR* results in that individuals with the risk genotype for depression showed better treatment outcomes than alternative genotypes when exposed to stressors. Homo- or heterozygote minor allele carriers of *FKBP5* or *CRHR1* who had recently been exposed to stressful life events were more likely to respond to antidepressant treatment than individuals with this genotype who had not been exposed to recent life stressors. On the contrary, stressful life events had little effect on treatment response in the respective alternative genotypes. The authors speculated that serotonin signaling and HPA axis dysfunction are two distinct etiological pathways to depression. This might explain why the G × E studies involving the *5-HTTLPR*, *FKBP5*, and *CRHR1* polymorphisms yielded opposite findings in terms of treatment response (Keers & Uher 2012). This hypothesis remains to be tested in future studies.

Interestingly, different genotypes may predict treatment response to psychotherapy than to pharmacotherapy. For instance, Eley and colleagues (2012) found that the S allele of *5-HTTLPR* predicted good cognitive behavioral therapy outcomes in depressed patients, whereas this genotype has been found to negatively predict response to antidepressants (Niitsu et al. 2013, Porcelli et al. 2012). These findings may be in line with the differential-susceptibility model (Belsky & Pluess 2009) mentioned in the Introduction. Individuals with the S allele may be more susceptible to environmental influences and could therefore respond better to changes in the environment brought about by psychotherapy. Indeed, experimental evidence indicates that S-allele carriers benefit more from a supportive environment than do individuals with other genotypes (Brody et al. 2009). Specifically, Brody et al. (2009) examined the differential response of youth to a community-based intervention aimed at increasing nurturing parenting practices and children's compliance and goal-setting. They found that youths carrying the S allele (both homozygote and heterozygote carriers) benefitted more from a family-based intervention designed to reduce risk behaviors in rural African American youths than did L-allele carriers.

Another interesting and potentially clinically relevant study may have identified differential usage of coping strategies as a mechanism for increased internalizing symptoms in children carrying the *5-HTTLPR* S allele (Cline et al. 2015). Specifically, homozygote S-allele carriers exhibited higher levels of internalizing symptoms compared to L-allele carriers. S-allele carriers were also less likely to use distraction coping strategies, particularly after exposure to stressful life events, such as traumatic events and hostile relationships with caregivers. This tendency may, in part, explain the elevated internalizing symptoms in S-allele carriers. In the absence of these distraction strategies, the authors hypothesized that the homozygous S-allele carriers perseverated on negative thoughts about their problems instead of engaging in problem-solving techniques or enlisting social support, thus increasing their risk of developing depressive or anxiety symptoms. Findings such as these can help personalize psychotherapeutic treatment approaches. In particular, identifying skills that individuals are lacking on the basis of genetic and environmental determinants may have important clinical implications for developing effective prevention strategies and interventions.

The current G × E findings highlight the potential clinical utility of environmentally focused preventions and interventions in overcoming genetic predisposition toward developing a psychiatric disorder. These interventions could target specific behavioral domains, as suggested by Cline et al. (2015), but could also target specific neural circuits whose activation is altered in a G × E context. This targeting may be achieved by a combination of diagnostic neuroimaging, genetics, and neurofeedback (Hamilton et al. 2016, Linden et al. 2012, Young et al. 2014). Research suggests that neurofeedback using functional magnetic resonance imaging may be a useful therapeutic option for psychiatric disorders in the future.

CONCLUSIONS

G × Es can shed light on the pathophysiology of psychiatric disorders. These studies describe differing subpopulations within psychiatric disorders on the basis of genotypes and environmental influences, with possibly different molecular pathways and neural circuits mediating risk. This deeper understanding of the underlying pathobiology may allow more targeted prevention and treatment strategies. However, to be successful, several limitations must be overcome and studies in larger cohorts or consortia will be necessary. Importantly, G × E analyses need to be carried out more systematically in longitudinal cohorts with careful mapping of environmental factors so that complex G × Es with multiple environmental factors can be performed. In such studies, deep phenotyping, including endophenotypes at several levels of investigation, and biosampling over several points in time should be performed. We also lack sufficient tools for more mechanistic investigations. Although humanized animal models may allow investigation of specific human variants, models for polygenic risk interactions are needed. For modeling effects on the molecular and cellular level, neurons and brain organoids derived from induced pluripotent stem cells may represent attractive tools. These may allow investigation of the impact of genetic risk factors and environmental mediators (glucocorticoids, monoamines, etc.) in the context of neuronal differentiation and connectivity. In the end, such in-depth G × E analyses may reveal more homogeneous neurobiological diagnostic categories than are provided by our current diagnostic framework, which, in turn, may improve an individual's prognosis through personalized medicine and targeted therapeutic interventions.

DISCLOSURE STATEMENT

E.B. is co-inventor on *FKBP5: a novel target for antidepressant therapy*, European Patent No. EP 1687443 B1, and receives a research grant from Böhringer-Ingelheim for a collaboration on functional investigations of *FKBP5*. T.H. has nothing to disclose.

ACKNOWLEDGMENTS

This review was supported by a European Research Council starting grant, G × E-MOLMECH grant 281338, to E.B.

LITERATURE CITED

Agnew-Blais J, Danese A. 2016. Childhood maltreatment and unfavourable clinical outcomes in bipolar disorder: a systematic review and meta-analysis. *Lancet Psychiatry* 3:342–49

Albu S, Romanowski CP, Letizia Curzi M, Jakubcakova V, Flachskamm C, et al. 2014. Deficiency of FK506-binding protein (FKBP) 51 alters sleep architecture and recovery sleep responses to stress in mice. *J. Sleep Res.* 23:176–85

Alemany S, Arias B, Fatjó-Vilas M, Villa H, Moya J, et al. 2014. Psychosis-inducing effects of cannabis are related to both childhood abuse and COMT genotypes. *Acta Psychiatr. Scand.* 129:54–62

Alexander N, Klucken T, Koppe G, Osinsky R, Walter B, et al. 2012. Interaction of the serotonin transporter-linked polymorphic region and environmental adversity: increased amygdala-hypothalamus connectivity as a potential mechanism linking neural and endocrine hyperreactivity. *Biol. Psychiatry* 72:49–56

Alexander N, Kuepper Y, Schmitz A, Osinsky R, Kozyra E, Hennig J. 2009. Gene–environment interactions predict cortisol responses after acute stress: implications for the etiology of depression. *Psychoneuroendocrinology* 34:1294–303

Almli LM, Duncan R, Feng H, Ghosh D, Binder EB, et al. 2014. Correcting systematic inflation in genetic association tests that consider interaction effects: application to a genome-wide association study of posttraumatic stress disorder. *JAMA Psychiatry* 71:1392–99

Andréasson S, Engström A, Allebeck P, Rydberg U. 1987. Cannabis and schizophrenia: a longitudinal study of Swedish conscripts. *Lancet* 330:1483–86

Antypa N, Drago A, Serretti A. 2013. The role of COMT gene variants in depression: bridging neuropsychological, behavioral and clinical phenotypes. *Neurosci. Biobehav. Rev.* 37:1597–610

Arloth J, Bogdan R, Weber P, Frishman G, Menke A, et al. 2015. Genetic differences in the immediate transcriptome response to stress predict risk-related brain function and psychiatric disorders. *Neuron* 86:1189–202

Aschard H, Lutz S, Maus B, Duell EJ, Fingerlin TE, et al. 2012. Challenges and opportunities in genome-wide environmental interaction (GWEI) studies. *Hum. Genet.* 131:1591–613

Attwood BK, Bourgognon JM, Patel S, Mucha M, Schiavon E, et al. 2011. Neuropsin cleaves EphB2 in the amygdala to control anxiety. *Nature* 473:372–75

Bale TL, Vale WW. 2004. CRF and CRF receptors: role in stress responsivity and other behaviors. *Annu. Rev. Pharmacol. Toxicol.* 44:525–57

Baumeister D, Lightman SL, Pariante CM. 2014. The interface of stress and the HPA axis in behavioural phenotypes of mental illness. *Curr. Top. Behav. Neurosci.* 18:13–24

Belsky J, Bakermans-Kranenburg MJ, Van IJzendoorn MH. 2007. For better and for worse: differential susceptibility to environmental influences. *Curr. Dir. Psychol. Sci.* 16:300–4

Belsky J, Pluess M. 2009. Beyond diathesis stress: differential susceptibility to environmental influences. *Psychol. Bull.* 135:885–908

Binder EB, Bradley RG, Liu W, Epstein MP, Deveau TC, et al. 2008. Association of FKBP5 polymorphisms and childhood abuse with risk of posttraumatic stress disorder symptoms in adults. *JAMA* 299:1291–305

Binder EB, Nemeroff CB. 2010. The CRF system, stress, depression and anxiety-insights from human genetic studies. *Mol. Psychiatry* 15:574–88

Binder EB, Salyakina D, Lichtner P, Wochnik GM, Ising M, et al. 2004. Polymorphisms in FKBP5 are associated with increased recurrence of depressive episodes and rapid response to antidepressant treatment. *Nat. Genet.* 36:1319–25

Bradley RG, Binder EB, Epstein MP, Tang Y, Nair HP, et al. 2008. Influence of child abuse on adult depression: moderation by the corticotropin-releasing hormone receptor gene. *Arch. Gen. Psychiatry* 65:190–200

Brody GH, Beach SRH, Philibert RA, Chen YF, Murry VM. 2009. Prevention effects moderate the association of 5-HTTLPR and youth risk behavior initiation: gene × environment hypotheses tested via a randomized prevention design. *Child Dev.* 80:645–61

Buchmann AF, Holz N, Boecker R, Blomeyer D, Rietschel M, et al. 2014. Moderating role of FKBP5 genotype in the impact of childhood adversity on cortisol stress response during adulthood. *Eur. Neuropsychopharmacol.* 24:837–45

Bulik-Sullivan BK, Loh PR, Finucane HK, Ripke S, Yang J, et al. 2015. LD score regression distinguishes confounding from polygenicity in genome-wide association studies. *Nat. Genet.* 47:291–95

Canli T, Qiu M, Omura K, Congdon E, Haas BW, et al. 2006. Neural correlates of epigenesis. *PNAS* 103:16033–38

Cannon DM, Ichise M, Fromm SJ, Nugent AC, Rollis D, et al. 2006. Serotonin transporter binding in bipolar disorder assessed using [^{11}C]DASB and positron emission tomography. *Biol. Psychiatry* 60:207–17

Caspi A, Hariri AR, Holmes A, Uher R, Moffitt TE. 2010. Genetic sensitivity to the environment: the case of the serotonin transporter gene and its implications for studying complex diseases and traits. *Am. J. Psychiatry* 167:509–27

Caspi A, Moffitt TE, Cannon M, McClay J, Murray R, et al. 2005. Moderation of the effect of adolescent-onset cannabis use on adult psychosis by a functional polymorphism in the catechol-O-methyltransferase gene: longitudinal evidence of a gene × environment interaction. *Biol. Psychiatry* 57:1117–27

Caspi A, Sugden K, Moffitt TE, Taylor A, Craig IW, et al. 2003. Influence of life stress on depression: moderation by a polymorphism in the *5-HTT* gene. *Science* 301:386–89

Chan GC, Hinds TR, Impey S, Storm DR. 1998. Hippocampal neurotoxicity of Δ^9-tetrahydrocannabinol. *J. Neurosci.* 18:5322–32

Cheung J, Bryant RA. 2015. FKBP5 risk alleles and the development of intrusive memories. *Neurobiol. Learn. Mem.* 125:258–64

Cicchetti D, Rogosch FA, Oshri A. 2011. Interactive effects of *corticotropin releasing hormone receptor 1*, serotonin transporter linked polymorphic region, and child maltreatment on diurnal cortisol regulation and internalizing symptomatology. *Dev. Psychopathol.* 23:1125–38

Cline JI, Belsky J, Li Z, Melhuish E, Lysenko L, et al. 2015. Take your mind off it: coping style, serotonin transporter linked polymorphic region genotype (5-HTTLPR), and children's internalizing and externalizing problems. *Dev. Psychopathol.* 27:1129–43

Colizzi M, McGuire P, Pertwee RG, Bhattacharyya S. 2016. Effect of cannabis on glutamate signalling in the brain: a systematic review of human and animal evidence. *Neurosci. Biobehav. Rev.* 64:359–81

Costas J, Sanjuán J, Ramos-Ríos R, Paz E, Agra S, et al. 2011. Interaction between COMT haplotypes and cannabis in schizophrenia: a case-only study in two samples from Spain. *Schizophr. Res.* 127:22–27

Craddock N, Owen MJ, O'Donovan MC. 2006. The catechol-O-methyl transferase (*COMT*) gene as a candidate for psychiatric phenotypes: evidence and lessons. *Mol. Psychiatry* 11:446–58

Dannlowski U, Ohrmann P, Bauer J, Deckert J, Hohoff C, et al. 2008. 5-HTTLPR biases amygdala activity in response to masked facial expressions in major depression. *Neuropsychopharmacology* 33:418–24

Dannlowski U, Ohrmann P, Bauer J, Kugel H, Baune BT, et al. 2007. Serotonergic genes modulate amygdala activity in major depression. *Genes Brain Behav.* 6:672–76

Davies TH, Ning YM, Sánchez ER. 2002. A new first step in activation of steroid receptors: hormone-induced switching of FKBP51 and FKBP52 immunophilins. *J. Biol. Chem.* 277:4597–600

Derkinderen P, Ledent C, Parmentier M, Girault JA. 2001. Cannabinoids activate p38 mitogen-activated protein kinases through CB1 receptors in hippocampus. *J. Neurochem.* 77:957–60

Dick DM, Agrawal A, Keller MC, Adkins A, Aliev F, et al. 2015. Candidate gene-environment interaction research: reflections and recommendations. *Perspect. Psychol. Sci.* 10:37–59

Downer EJ, Fogarty MP, Campbell VA. 2003. Tetrahydrocannabinol-induced neurotoxicity depends on CB1 receptor-mediated c-Jun N-terminal kinase activation in cultured cortical neurons. *Br. J. Pharmacol.* 140:547–57

Duncan LE, Keller MC. 2011. A critical review of the first 10 years of candidate gene-by-environment interaction research in psychiatry. *Am. J. Psychiatry* 168:1041–49

Dunn EC, Wiste A, Radmanesh F, Almli LM, Gogarten SM, et al. 2016. Genome-wide association study (GWAS) and genome-wide by environment interaction study (GWEIS) of depressive symptoms in African American and Hispanic/Latina women. *Depress. Anxiety* 33:265–80

Egan MF, Goldberg TE, Kolachana BS, Callicott JH, Mazzanti CM, et al. 2001. Effect of COMT Val108/158 Met genotype on frontal lobe function and risk for schizophrenia. *PNAS* 98:6917–22

Eley TC, Hudson JL, Creswell C, Tropeano M, Lester KJ, et al. 2012. Therapygenetics: the 5HTTLPR and response to psychological therapy. *Mol. Psychiatry* 17:236–37

Eley TC, Sugden K, Corsico A, Gregory AM, Sham P, et al. 2004. Gene–environment interaction analysis of serotonin system markers with adolescent depression. *Mol. Psychiatry* 9:908–15

Fani N, Gutman D, Tone EB, Almli L, Mercer KB, et al. 2013. FKBP5 and attention bias for threat: associations with hippocampal function and shape. *JAMA Psychiatry* 70:392–400

Fani N, King TZ, Reiser E, Binder EB, Jovanovic T, et al. 2014. FKBP5 genotype and structural integrity of the posterior cingulum. *Neuropsychopharmacology* 39:1206–13

Fani N, King TZ, Shin J, Srivastava A, Brewster RC, et al. 2016. Structural and functional connectivity in post-traumatic stress disorder: associations with FKBP5. *Depress. Anxiety* 33:300–7

Fortier E, Noreau A, Lepore F, Boivin M, Pérusse D, et al. 2010. Early impact of 5-HTTLPR polymorphism on the neural correlates of sadness. *Neurosci. Lett.* 485:261–65

Frankle WG, Narendran R, Huang Y, Hwang DR, Lombardo I, et al. 2005. Serotonin transporter availability in patients with schizophrenia: a positron emission tomography imaging study with [^{11}C]DASB. *Biol. Psychiatry* 57:1510–16

Funke B, Malhotra AK, Finn CT, Plocik AM, Lake SL, et al. 2005. COMT genetic variation confers risk for psychotic and affective disorders: a case control study. *Behav. Brain Funct.* 1:1–19

Garriock HA, Kraft JB, Shyn SI, Peters EJ, Yokoyama JS, et al. 2010. A genomewide association study of citalopram response in major depressive disorder. *Biol. Psychiatry* 67:133–38

Gaynes BN, Warden D, Trivedi MH, Wisniewski SR, Fava M, Rush AJ. 2009. What did STAR*D teach us? Results from a large-scale, practical, clinical trial for patients with depression. *Psychiatr. Serv.* 60:1439–45

Investig GENDEP., Investig MARS., Investig STAR*D. 2013. Common genetic variation and antidepressant efficacy in major depressive disorder: a meta-analysis of three genome-wide pharmacogenetic studies. *Am. J. Psychiatry* 170:207–17

Gibb BE, McGeary JE, Beevers CG, Miller IW. 2006. Serotonin transporter (5-HTTLPR) genotype, childhood abuse, and suicide attempts in adult psychiatric inpatients. *Suicide Life Threat. Behav.* 36:687–93

Grabe HJ, Wittfeld K, Van der Auwera S, Janowitz D, Hegenscheid K, et al. 2016. Effect of the interaction between childhood abuse and rs1360780 of the *FKBP5* gene on gray matter volume in a general population sample. *Hum. Brain Mapp.* 37:1602–13

Grad I, Picard D. 2007. The glucocorticoid responses are shaped by molecular chaperones. *Mol. Cell. Endocrinol.* 275:2–12

Habets P, Marcelis M, Gronenschild E, Drukker M, van Os J. 2011. Reduced cortical thickness as an outcome of differential sensitivity to environmental risks in schizophrenia. *Biol. Psychiatry* 69:487–94

Hamilton JP, Glover GH, Bagarinao E, Chang C, Mackey S, et al. 2016. Effects of salience-network-node neurofeedback training on affective biases in major depressive disorder. *Psychiatry Res. Neuroimaging* 249:91–96

Hamilton JP, Gotlib IH. 2008. Neural substrates of increased memory sensitivity for negative stimuli in major depression. *Biol. Psychiatry* 63:1155–62

Hankin BL, Nederhof E, Oppenheimer CW, Jenness J, Young JF, et al. 2011. Differential susceptibility in youth: evidence that 5-HTTLPR × positive parenting is associated with positive affect 'for better and worse'. *Transl. Psychiatry* 1:e44

Hariri AR, Drabant EM, Munoz KE, Kolachana BS, Mattay VS, et al. 2005. A susceptibility gene for affective disorders and the response of the human amygdala. *Arch. Gen. Psychiatry* 62:146–52

Hartmann J, Wagner KV, Gaali S, Kirschner A, Kozany C, et al. 2015. Pharmacological inhibition of the psychiatric risk factor *FKBP51* has anxiolytic properties. *J. Neurosci.* 35:9007–16

Hartmann J, Wagner KV, Liebl C, Scharf SH, Wang XD, et al. 2012. The involvement of FK506-binding protein 51 (FKBP5) in the behavioral and neuroendocrine effects of chronic social defeat stress. *Neuropharmacology* 62:332–39

Heim C, Bradley B, Mletzko T, Deveau TC, Musselmann DL, et al. 2009. Effect of childhood trauma on adult depression and neuroendocrine function: sex-specific moderation by CRH receptor 1 gene. *Front. Behav. Neurosci.* 3:1–10

Hettema JM, An SS, Bukszar J, Van den Oord EJ, Neale MC, et al. 2008. Catechol-O-methyltransferase contributes to genetic susceptibility shared among anxiety spectrum phenotypes. *Biol. Psychiatry* 64:302–10

Hettema JM, Chen X, Sun C, Brown TA. 2015. Direct, indirect and pleiotropic effects of candidate genes on internalizing disorder psychopathology. *Psychol. Med.* 45:2227–36

Hirakawa H, Akiyoshi J, Muronaga M, Tanaka Y, Ishitobi Y, et al. 2016. FKBP5 is associated with amygdala volume in the human brain and mood state: a voxel-based morphometry (VBM) study. *Int. J. Psychiatry Clin. Pract.* 20:1–10

Ho BC, Wassink TH, Ziebell S, Andreasen NC. 2011. Cannabinoid receptor 1 gene polymorphisms and marijuana misuse interactions on white matter and cognitive deficits in schizophrenia. *Schizophr. Res.* 128:66–75

Holsboer F. 2000. The corticosteroid receptor hypothesis of depression. *Neuropsychopharmacology* 23:477–501

Holtzheimer PE, Mayberg HS. 2011. Stuck in a rut: rethinking depression and its treatment. *Trends Neurosci.* 34:1–9

Holz NE, Buchmann AF, Boecker R, Blomeyer D, Baumeister S, et al. 2015. Role of FKBP5 in emotion processing: results on amygdala activity, connectivity and volume. *Brain Struct. Funct.* 220:1355–68

Hsu DT, Mickey BJ, Langenecker SA, Heitzeg MM, Love TM, et al. 2012. Variation in the corticotropin-releasing hormone receptor 1 (*CRHR1*) gene influences fMRI signal responses during emotional stimulus processing. *J. Neurosci.* 32:3253–60

Hu XZ, Lipsky RH, Zhu G, Akhtar LA, Taubman J, et al. 2006. Serotonin transporter promoter gain-of-function genotypes are linked to obsessive-compulsive disorder. *Am. J. Hum. Genet.* 78:815–26

Hygen BW, Belsky J, Stenseng F, Lydersen S, Guzey IC, Wichstrom L. 2015. Child exposure to serious life events, COMT, and aggression: testing differential susceptibility theory. *Dev. Psychol.* 51:1098–104

Ising M, Depping AM, Siebertz A, Lucae S, Unschuld PG, et al. 2008. Polymorphisms in the *FKBP5* gene region modulate recovery from psychosocial stress in healthy controls. *Eur. J. Neurosc.* 28:389–98

Ising M, Lucae S, Binder EB, Bettecken T, Uhr M, et al. 2009. A genomewide association study points to multiple loci that predict antidepressant drug treatment outcome in depression. *Arch. Gen. Psychiatry* 66:966–75

Johnstone JM, Luty SE, Carter JD, Mulder RT, Frampton C, Joyce PR. 2009. Childhood neglect and abuse as predictors of antidepressant response in adult depression. *Depress. Anxiety* 26:711–17

Kapur S. 2003. Psychosis as a state of aberrant salience: a framework linking biology, phenomenology, and pharmacology in schizophrenia. *Am. J. Psychiatry* 160:13–23

Karg K, Burmeister M, Shedden K, Sen S. 2011. The serotonin transporter promoter variant (5-HTTLPR), stress, and depression meta-analysis revisited: evidence of genetic moderation. *Arch. Gen. Psychiatry* 68:444–54

Keers R, Aitchison KJ. 2011. Pharmacogenetics of antidepressant response. *Expert Rev. Neurother.* 11:101–25

Keers R, Uher R. 2012. Gene–environment interaction in major depression and antidepressant treatment response. *Curr. Psychiatry Rep.* 14:129–37

Keers R, Uher R, Huezo-Diaz P, Smith R, Jaffee S, et al. 2011. Interaction between serotonin transporter gene variants and life events predicts response to antidepressants in the GENDEP project. *Pharmacogenomics J.* 11:138–45

Kilpatrick DG, Koenen KC, Ruggiero KJ, Acierno R, Galea S, et al. 2007. The serotonin transporter genotype and social support and moderation of posttraumatic stress disorder and depression in hurricane-exposed adults. *Am. J. Psychiatry* 164:1693–99

Klengel T, Binder EB. 2015. *FKBP5* allele-specific epigenetic modification in gene by environment interaction. *Neuropharmacol. Rev.* 40:244–46

Klengel T, Mehta D, Anacker C, Rex-Haffner M, Pruessner JC, et al. 2013. Allele-specific FKBP5 DNA demethylation mediates gene-childhood trauma interactions. *Nat. Neurosci.* 16:33–41

Knuts I, Esquivel G, Kenis G, Overbeek T, Leibold N, et al. 2014. Therapygenetics: 5-HTTLPR genotype predicts the response to exposure therapy for agoraphobia. *Eur. Neuropsychopharmacol.* 24:1222–28

Koenen KC, Aiello AE, Bakshis E, Amstadter AB, Ruggiero KJ, et al. 2009. Modification of the association between serotonin transporter genotype and risk of posttraumatic stress disorder in adults by county-level social environment. *Am. J. Epidemiol.* 169:704–11

Koenen KC, Saxe G, Purcell S, Smoller JW, Bartholomew D, et al. 2005. Polymorphisms in FKBP5 are associated with peritraumatic dissociation in medically injured children. *Mol. Psychiatry* 10:1058–59

Koob GF. 1999. Corticotropin-releasing factor, norepinephrine, and stress. *Biol. Psychiatry* 46:1167–80

Kraft P, Aschard H. 2015. Finding the missing gene-environment interactions. *Eur. J. Epidemiol.* 30:353–55

Kranzler HR, Scott D, Tennen H, Feinn R, Williams C, et al. 2012. The 5-HTTLPR polymorphism moderates the effect of stressful life events on drinking behavior in college students of African descent. *Am. J. Med. Genet. B Neuropsychiatr. Genet.* 159:484–90

Laucht M, Treutlein J, Blomeyer D, Buchmann AF, Schmid B, et al. 2009. Interaction between the 5-HTTLPR serotonin transporter polymorphism and environmental adversity for mood and anxiety psychopathology: evidence from a high-risk community sample of young adults. *Int. J. Neuropsychopharmacol.* 12:737–47

Lawrie SM, Hall J, McIntosh AM, Cunningham-Owens DG, Johnstone EC. 2008. Neuroimaging and molecular genetics of schizophrenia: pathophysiological advances and therapeutic potential. *Brit. J. Pharmacol.* 153:S120–24

Lee RS, Sawa A. 2014. Environmental stressors and epigenetic control of the hypothalamic-pituitary-adrenal axis. *Neuroendocrinology* 100:278–87

Lesch KP, Bengel D, Heils A, Sabol SZ, Greenberg BD, et al. 1996. Association of anxiety-related traits with a polymorphism in the serotonin transporter gene regulatory region. *Science* 274:1527–31

Lester KJ, Hudson JL, Tropeano M, Creswell C, Collier DA, et al. 2012. Neurotrophic gene polymorphisms and response to psychological therapy. *Transl. Psychiatry* 2:e108

Licinio J, O'Kirwan F, Irizarry K, Merriman B, Thakur S, et al. 2004. Association of a corticotropin-releasing hormone receptor 1 haplotype and antidepressant treatment response in Mexican-Americans. *Mol. Psychiatry* 9:1075–82

Linden DE, Habes I, Johnston SJ, Linden S, Tatineni R, et al. 2012. Real-time self-regulation of emotion networks in patients with depression. *PLOS ONE* 7:e38115

Liu Y, Garrett ME, Dennis MF, Green KT, Ashley-Koch AE, et al. 2015. An examination of the association between 5-HTTLPR, combat exposure, and PTSD diagnosis among US veterans. *PLOS ONE* 10:e0119998

Lonsdorf TB, Rück C, Bergström J, Andersson G, Öhman A, et al. 2010. The COMTval158met polymorphism is associated with symptom relief during exposure-based cognitive-behavioral treatment in panic disorder. *BMC Psychiatry* 10:99–107

Maier R, Moser G, Chen GB, Ripke S, Coryell W, et al. 2015. Joint analysis of psychiatric disorders increases accuracy of risk prediction for schizophrenia, bipolar disorder, and major depressive disorder. *Am. J. Hum. Genet.* 96:283–94

Malone DT, Hill MN, Rubino T. 2010. Adolescent cannabis use and psychosis: epidemiology and neurodevelopmental models. *Br. J. Pharmacol.* 160:511–22

Mandelli L, Marino E, Pirovano A, Calati R, Zanardi R, et al. 2009. Interaction between SERTPR and stressful life events on response to antidepressant treatment. *Eur. Neuropsychopharmacol.* 19:64–67

Mann JJ, Huang YY, Underwood MD, Kassir SA, Oppenheim S, et al. 2000. A serotonin transporter gene promoter polymorphism (5-HTTLPR) and prefrontal cortical binding in major depression and suicide. *Arch. Gen. Psychiatry* 57:729–38

Männistö PT, Kaakkola S. 1999. Catechol-O-methyltransferase (COMT): biochemistry, molecular biology, pharmacology, and clinical efficacy of the new selective COMT inhibitors. *Pharmacol. Rev.* 51:593–628

Mueller A, Strahler J, Armbruster D, Lesch KP, Brocke B, Kirschbaum C. 2012. Genetic contributions to acute autonomic stress responsiveness in children. *Int. J. Psychophysiol.* 83:302–8

Mullins N, Power RA, Fisher HL, Hanscombe KB, Euesden J, et al. 2016. Polygenic interactions with environmental adversity in the aetiology of major depressive disorder. *Psychol. Med.* 46:759–70

Munafo MR, Brown SM, Hariri AR. 2008. Serotonin transporter (5-HTTLPR) genotype and amygdala activation: a meta-analysis. *Biol. Psychiatry* 63:852–57

Munafo MR, Freimer NB, Ng W, Ophoff R, Veijola J, et al. 2009. 5-HTTLPR genotype and anxiety-related personality traits: a meta-analysis and new data. *Am. J. Med. Genet. B Neuropsychiatr. Genet.* 150:271–81

Musliner KL, Seifuddin F, Judy JA, Pirooznia M, Goes FS, Zandi PP. 2015. Polygenic risk, stressful life events and depressive symptoms in older adults: a polygenic score analysis. *Psychol. Med.* 45:1709–20

Nanni V, Uher R, Danese A. 2012. Childhood maltreatment predicts unfavorable course of illness and treatment outcome in depression: a meta-analysis. *Am. J. Psychiatry* 169:141–51

Nemeroff CB. 1989. Clinical significance of psychoneuroendocrinology in psychiatry: focus on the thyroid and adrenal. *J. Clin. Psychiatry* 50(Suppl. 13–20):21–22

Nemeroff CB, Heim CM, Thase ME, Klein DN, Rush AJ, et al. 2003. Differential responses to psychotherapy versus pharmacotherapy in patients with chronic forms of major depression and childhood trauma. *PNAS* 100:14293–96

Niesink RJ, van Laar MW. 2013. Does cannabidiol protect against adverse psychological effects of THC? *Front. Psychiatry* 4:1–8

Nievergelt CM, Maihofer AX, Mustapic M, Yurgil KA, Schork NJ, et al. 2015. Genomic predictors of combat stress vulnerability and resilience in US Marines: a genome-wide association study across multiple ancestries implicates *PRTFDC1* as a potential PTSD gene. *Psychoneuroendocrinology* 51:459–71

Niitsu T, Fabbri C, Bentini F, Serretti A. 2013. Pharmacogenetics in major depression: a comprehensive meta-analysis. *Prog. Neuropsychopharmacol. Biol. Psychiatry* 45:183–94

Novik KL, Nimmrich I, Genc B, Maier S, Piepenbrock C, et al. 2002. Epigenomics: genome-wide study of methylation phenomena. *Curr. Issues Mol. Biol.* 4:111–28

Ohnishi T, Hashimoto R, Mori T, Nemoto K, Moriguchi Y, et al. 2006. The association between the Val158Met polymorphism of the catechol-O-methyl transferase gene and morphological abnormalities of the brain in chronic schizophrenia. *Brain* 129:399–410

O'Leary JC III, Dharia S, Blair LJ, Brady S, Johnson AG, et al. 2011. A new anti-depressive strategy for the elderly: ablation of FKBP5/FKBP51. *PLOS ONE* 6:e24840

Onwuameze OE, Nam KW, Epping EA, Wassink TH, Ziebell S, et al. 2013. *MAPK14* and *CNR1* gene variant interactions: effects on brain volume deficits in schizophrenia patients with marijuana misuse. *Psychol. Med.* 43:619–31

Ozomaro U, Wahlestedt C, Nemeroff CB. 2013. Personalized medicine in psychiatry: problems and promises. *BMC Med.* 11:132–67

Pazos MR, Nunez E, Benito C, Tolon RM, Romero J. 2005. Functional neuroanatomy of the endocannabinoid system. *Pharmacol. Biochem. Behav.* 81:239–47

Pérez-Ortiz JM, García-Gutiérrez MS, Navarrete F, Giner S, Manzanares J. 2013. Gene and protein alterations of *FKBP5* and glucocorticoid receptor in the amygdala of suicide victims. *Psychoneuroendocrinology* 38:1251–58

Peyrot WJ, Milaneschi Y, Abdellaoui A, Sullivan PF, Hottenga JJ, et al. 2014. Effect of polygenic risk scores on depression in childhood trauma. *Br. J. Psychiatry* 205:113–19

Pezawas L, Meyer-Lindenberg A, Drabant EM, Verchinski BA, Munoz KE, et al. 2005. 5-HTTLPR polymorphism impacts human cingulate-amygdala interactions: a genetic susceptibility mechanism for depression. *Nat. Neurosci.* 8:828–34

Pluess M, Belsky J, Way BM, Taylor SE. 2010. 5-HTTLPR moderates effects of current life events on neuroticism: differential susceptibility to environmental influences. *Prog. Neuropsychopharmacol. Biol. Psychiatry* 34:1070–74

Polanczyk G, Caspi A, Williams B, Price TS, Danese A, et al. 2009. Protective effect of *CRHR1* gene variants on the development of adult depression following childhood maltreatment: replication and extension. *Arch. Gen. Psychiatry* 66:978–85

Porcelli S, Fabbri C, Serretti A. 2012. Meta-analysis of serotonin transporter gene promoter polymorphism (5-HTTLPR) association with antidepressant efficacy. *Eur. Neuropsychopharmacol.* 22:239–58

Potter E, Sutton S, Donaldson C, Chen R, Perrin M, et al. 1994. Distribution of corticotropin-releasing factor receptor mRNA expression in the rat brain and pituitary. *PNAS* 91:8777–81

Powles T, te Poele R, Shamash J, Chaplin T, Propper D, et al. 2005. Cannabis-induced cytotoxicity in leukemic cell lines: the role of the cannabinoid receptors and the MAPK pathway. *Blood* 105:1214–21

Ripke S, Neale BM, Corvin A, Walters JT, Farh KH, et al. 2014. Biological insights from 108 schizophrenia-associated genetic loci. *Nature* 511:421–27

Ripke S, Wray NR, Lewis CM, Hamilton SP, Weissman MM, et al. 2013. A mega-analysis of genome-wide association studies for major depressive disorder. *Mol. Psychiatry* 18:497–511

Risch N, Herrell R, Lehner T, Liang KY, Eaves L, et al. 2009. Interaction between the serotonin transporter gene (*5-HTTLPR*), stressful life events, and risk of depression: a meta-analysis. *JAMA* 301:2462–71

Roy A, Hu XZ, Janal MN, Goldman D. 2007. Interaction between childhood trauma and serotonin transporter gene variation in suicide. *Neuropsychopharmacology* 32:2046–52

Rutter M, Moffitt TE, Caspi A. 2006. Gene–environment interplay and psychopathology: multiple varieties but real effects. *J. Child Psychol. Psychiatry* 47:226–61

Rutter M, Pickles A. 2015. Annual research review: threats to the validity of child psychiatry and psychology. *J. Child Psychol. Psychiatry* 57:398–416

Sami MB, Rabiner EA, Bhattacharyya S. 2015. Does cannabis affect dopaminergic signaling in the human brain? A systematic review of evidence to date. *Eur. Neuropsychopharmacol.* 25:1201–24

Sawamura T, Klengel T, Armario A, Jovanovic T, Norrholm SD, et al. 2016. Dexamethasone treatment leads to enhanced fear extinction and dynamic Fkbp5 regulation in amygdala. *Neuropsychopharmacology* 41:832–46

Scharf SH, Liebl C, Binder EB, Schmidt MV, Müller MB. 2011. Expression and regulation of the *Fkbp5* gene in the adult mouse brain. *PLOS ONE* 6:e16883

Schubart CD, Van Gastel WA, Breetvelt EJ, Beetz SL, Ophoff RA, et al. 2011. Cannabis use at a young age is associated with psychotic experiences. *Psychol. Med.* 41:1301–10

Sharma S, Powers A, Bradley B, Ressler KJ. 2016. Gene × environment determinants of stress- and anxiety-related disorders. *Annu. Rev. Psychol.* 67:239–61

Sharpley CF, Palanisamy SK, Glyde NS, Dillingham PW, Agnew LL. 2014. An update on the interaction between the serotonin transporter promoter variant (*5-HTTLPR*), stress and depression, plus an exploration of non-confirming findings. *Behav. Brain Res.* 273:89–105

Shirazi SN, Friedman AR, Kaufer D, Sakhai SA. 2015. Glucocorticoids and the brain: neural mechanisms regulating the stress response. In *Glucocorticoid Signaling*, ed. J-C Wang, C Harris, pp. 235–52. New York: Springer

Sinclair D, Fillman SG, Webster MJ, Weickert CS. 2013. Dysregulation of glucocorticoid receptor co-factors FKBP5, BAG1 and PTGES3 in prefrontal cortex in psychotic illness. *Sci. Rep.* 3:1–10

Soloviff N, Roberts AL, Ratanatharathorn A, Haloosim M, De Vivo I, et al. 2014. Genetic association analysis of 300 genes identifies a risk haplotype in *SLC18A2* for post-traumatic stress disorder in two independent samples. *Neuropsychopharmacology* 39:1872–79

Starr LR, Hammen C, Conway CC, Raposa E, Brennan PA. 2014. Sensitizing effect of early adversity on depressive reactions to later proximal stress: moderation by polymorphisms in serotonin transporter and corticotropin releasing hormone receptor genes in a 20-year longitudinal study. *Dev. Psychopathol.* 26:1241–54

Stein MB, Schork NJ, Gelernter J. 2008. Gene-by-environment (serotonin transporter and childhood maltreatment) interaction for anxiety sensitivity, an intermediate phenotype for anxiety disorders. *Neuropsychopharmacology* 33:312–19

Stoltenberg SF, Anderson C, Nag P, Anagnopoulos C. 2012. Association between the serotonin transporter triallelic genotype and eating problems is moderated by the experience of childhood trauma in women. *Int. J. Eat. Disord.* 45:492–500

Taylor SE, Way BM, Welch WT, Hilmert CJ, Lehman BJ, Eisenberger NI. 2006. Early family environment, current adversity, the serotonin transporter promoter polymorphism, and depressive symptomatology. *Biol. Psychiatry* 60:671–76

Thapar A, Langley K, Fowler T, Rice F, Turic D, et al. 2005. Catechol O-methyltransferase gene variant and birth weight predict early-onset antisocial behavior in children with attention-deficit/hyperactivity disorder. *Arch. Gen. Psychiatry* 62:1275–78

Thomassin H, Flavin M, Espinas ML, Grange T. 2001. Glucocorticoid-induced DNA demethylation and gene memory during development. *EMBO J.* 20:1974–83

Touma C, Gassen NC, Herrmann L, Cheung-Flynn J, Büll DR, et al. 2011. FK506 binding protein 5 shapes stress responsiveness: modulation of neuroendocrine reactivity and coping behavior. *Biol. Psychiatry* 70:928–36

Tozzi L, Carballedo A, Wetterling F, McCarthy H, O'Keane V, et al. 2016. Single-nucleotide polymorphism of the *FKBP5* gene and childhood maltreatment as predictors of structural changes in brain areas involved in emotional processing in depression. *Neuropsychopharmacology* 41:487–97

Trivedi MH, Rush AJ, Wisniewski SR, Nierenberg AA, Warden D, et al. 2006. Evaluation of outcomes with citalopram for depression using measurement-based care in STAR*D: implications for clinical practice. *Am. J. Psychiatry* 163:28–40

Tyrka AR, Price LH, Gelernter J, Schepker C, Anderson GM, Carpenter LL. 2009. Interaction of childhood maltreatment with the corticotropin-releasing hormone receptor gene: effects on hypothalamic-pituitary-adrenal axis reactivity. *Biol. Psychiatry* 66:681–85

Uher R, Caspi A, Houts R, Sugden K, Williams B, et al. 2011. Serotonin transporter gene moderates childhood maltreatment's effects on persistent but not single-episode depression: replications and implications for resolving inconsistent results. *J. Affect. Disord.* 135:56–65

Uher R, McGuffin P. 2008. The moderation by the serotonin transporter gene of environmental adversity in the aetiology of mental illness: review and methodological analysis. *Mol. Psychiatry* 13:131–46

Uher R, Perroud N, Ng MY, Hauser J, Henigsberg N, et al. 2010. Genome-wide pharmacogenetics of antidepressant response in the GENDEP project. *Am. J. Psychiatry* 167:555–64

Vale W, Spiess J, Rivier C, Rivier J. 1981. Characterization of a 41-residue ovine hypothalamic peptide that stimulates secretion of corticotropin and β-endorphin. *Science* 213:1394–97

van der Meer D, Hartman CA, Richards J, Bralten JB, Franke B, et al. 2014. The serotonin transporter gene polymorphism *5-HTTLPR* moderates the effects of stress on attention-deficit/hyperactivity disorder. *J. Child Psychol. Psychiatry* 55:1363–71

van Winkel R. 2011. Family-based analysis of genetic variation underlying psychosis-inducing effects of cannabis: sibling analysis and proband follow-up. *Arch. Gen. Psychiatry* 68:148–57

Vermeer H, Hendriks-Stegeman BI, van der Burg B, van Buul-Offers SC, Jansen M. 2003. Glucocorticoid-induced increase in lymphocytic FKBP51 messenger ribonucleic acid expression: a potential marker for glucocorticoid sensitivity, potency, and bioavailability. *J. Clin. Endocrinol. Metab.* 88:277–84

Vinkers CH, Van Gastel WA, Schubart CD, Van Eijk KR, Luykx JJ, et al. 2013. The effect of childhood maltreatment and cannabis use on adult psychotic symptoms is modified by the COMT Val[158]Met polymorphism. *Schizophr. Res.* 150:303–11

Weber H, Richter J, Straube B, Lueken U, Domschke K, et al. 2016. Allelic variation in CRHR1 predisposes to panic disorder: evidence for biased fear processing. *Mol. Psychiatry* 21:813–22

White MG, Bogdan R, Fisher PM, Munoz KE, Williamson DE, Hariri AR. 2012. FKBP5 and emotional neglect interact to predict individual differences in amygdala reactivity. *Genes Brain Behav.* 11:869–78

Wochnik GM, Rüegg J, Abel GA, Schmidt U, Holsboer F, Rein T. 2005. FK506-binding proteins 51 and 52 differentially regulate dynein interaction and nuclear translocation of the glucocorticoid receptor in mammalian cells. *J. Biol. Chem.* 280:4609–16

Xie P, Kranzler HR, Poling J, Stein MB, Anton RF, et al. 2009. Interactive effect of stressful life events and the serotonin transporter 5-HTTLPR genotype on posttraumatic stress disorder diagnosis in 2 independent populations. *Arch. Gen. Psychiatry* 66:1201–9

Young KA, Thompson PM, Cruz DA, Williamson DE, Selemon LD. 2015. BA11 FKBP5 expression levels correlate with dendritic spine density in postmortem PTSD and controls. *Neurobiol. Stress* 2:67–72

Young KD, Zotev V, Phillips R, Misaki M, Yuan H, et al. 2014. Real-time FMRI neurofeedback training of amygdala activity in patients with major depressive disorder. *PLOS ONE* 9:e88785

Zammit S, Owen MJ, Evans J, Heron J, Lewis G. 2011. Cannabis, COMT and psychotic experiences. *Br. J. Psychiatry* 199:380–85

Zammit S, Spurlock G, Williams H, Norton N, Williams N, et al. 2007. Genotype effects of *CHRNA7*, *CNR1* and *COMT* in schizophrenia: interactions with tobacco and cannabis use. *Br. J. Psychiatry* 191:402–7

Zannas AS, Wiechmann T, Gassen NC, Binder EB. 2016. Gene-stress-epigenetic regulation of *FKBP5*: clinical and translational implications. *Neuropsychopharmacology* 41:261–74

Zou YF, Wang F, Feng XL, Li WF, Tao JH, et al. 2010. Meta-analysis of *FKBP5* gene polymorphisms association with treatment response in patients with mood disorders. *Neurosci. Lett.* 484:56–61

The Structure of Social Cognition: In(ter)dependence of Sociocognitive Processes

Francesca Happé,[1] Jennifer L. Cook,[2] and Geoffrey Bird[1]

[1]MRC Social, Genetic & Developmental Psychiatry Centre, Institute of Psychiatry, Psychology and Neuroscience, King's College London, London SE5 8AF, United Kingdom;
email: francesca.happe@kcl.ac.uk, geoff.bird@kcl.ac.uk

[2]School of Psychology, University of Birmingham, Birmingham B15 2TT, United Kingdom;
email: j.l.cook@bham.ac.uk

Annu. Rev. Psychol. 2017. 68:243–67

First published online as a Review in Advance on September 21, 2016

The *Annual Review of Psychology* is online at psych.annualreviews.org

This article's doi:
10.1146/annurev-psych-010416-044046

Keywords

social cognition, theory of mind, autism, imitation, empathy

Abstract

Social cognition is a topic of enormous interest and much research, but we are far from having an agreed taxonomy or factor structure of relevant processes. The aim of this review is to outline briefly what is known about the structure of social cognition and to suggest how further progress can be made to delineate the in(ter)dependence of core sociocognitive processes. We focus in particular on several processes that have been discussed and tested together in typical and atypical (notably autism spectrum disorder) groups: imitation, biological motion, empathy, and theory of mind. We consider the domain specificity/generality of core processes in social learning, reward, and attention, and we highlight the potential relevance of dual-process theories that distinguish systems for fast/automatic and slow/effortful processing. We conclude with methodological and conceptual suggestions for future progress in uncovering the structure of social cognition.

Contents

1. WHY IS ESTABLISHING THE IN(TER)DEPENDENCE OF SOCIOCOGNITIVE PROCESSES IMPORTANT?

Few would deny the functional importance of social interaction or the value of scientific study of the processes supporting it. The past few decades have seen a snowballing of interest in the cognitive and neural bases of social processing, much of it motivated by the desire to understand and ameliorate clinical conditions characterized by problems in social interaction. Despite this interest, little agreement exists as to the core sociocognitive processes or their interrelation or independence—we call this the structure of social cognition, which constitutes the focus of this review. We use the term cognition, as Morton & Frith (1995) do, to refer to the level of explanation lying between neural processes and behavior; cognition thus includes emotion. We define social cognition as the processing of stimuli relevant to understanding agents and their interactions.

In contrast to the study of intelligence or personality, little work has examined the factor structure of social cognition. Even limited sampling of recent papers shows how differently authors divide up social cognition. Reviewing work on social cognition in nonhuman animals, Seyfarth & Cheney (2015) propose that the core building blocks comprise individual recognition, knowledge of others' relationships (e.g., dominance), and theory of mind (ToM; i.e., understanding of others' mental states, mentalizing). A recent review of social cognition in schizophrenia (Green et al. 2015, p. 620) focused on "four general social cognitive processes—perception of social cues, experience sharing, mentalizing, and experiencing and regulating emotion." In their comprehensive textbook, *Social Cognition: From Brains to Culture*, Fiske & Taylor (2013) identify 14 domains of social cognition, ranging from more basic concepts such as social attention, encoding of

---

Social cognition: the processing of stimuli relevant to understanding agents and their interactions

Theory of mind (ToM): representing one's own and others' mental states (i.e., mentalizing)

social stimuli, and social memory representations to higher-order social processes such as social decision making, social inference, attitudes, stereotyping, and prejudice. Happé & Frith (2014), reviewing the developmental neuroscience of atypical social cognition, sketched a hypothetical network including at least ten separable components (affiliation, agent identification, emotion processing, empathy, individuals' information store, mental state attribution, self-processing, social hierarchy mapping, social policing, and in-group/out-group categorization). The National Institute of Mental Health's research domain criteria (RDoC) initiative currently divides the domain of social processes (which includes both traditional social psychological processes such as attachment and sociocognitive processes such as animacy perception) into four constructs: affiliation and attachment, social communication, perception and understanding of self, and perception and understanding of others. Little consensus exists across authors as to which processes should be distinguished and which are interrelated. For example, RDoC combine emotions and intentions under the subconstruct of understanding mental states, whereas other authors have claimed these to be dissociable (e.g., Lewis & Todd 2005). RDoC also separate the understanding of self and others, whereas other authors have suggested that, for example, representing own and others' mental states requires common representational mechanisms (e.g., Carruthers 2009).

Does it matter how we divide the space of social cognition or whether we decipher its factor structure? It is helpful to note that these are two independent but complementary endeavors. The first relates to the development of a standard taxonomy and vocabulary of sociocognitive processes. At present, different authors use similar terms differently (e.g., empathy) and different labels for ostensibly similar or overlapping processes (e.g., motor empathy and imitation; cognitive empathy and ToM), leading to misunderstanding and confusion. Loose definitions and a failure to discriminate distinct processes will add to problems of nonreplication and cause difficulties in mapping cognitive to neural processes. Which term is used for a particular process and the dimensions one chooses to group sociocognitive processes are a matter of taste rather than empirical investigation; all that is required is for these terms (for precise and testable processes) to be standardized and applied consistently by researchers.

The second endeavor involves determining the relationship between different sociocognitive abilities; whether, for example, individual differences in emotion recognition predict individual differences in ToM. This question is empirically tractable and will allow sociocognitive ability to be described in terms of a smaller number of factor scores rather than a multitude of scores across different tests of social ability that may or may not measure distinct processes. Furthermore, the identification of latent factors that contribute to performance across a range of sociocognitive tests (as verbal ability contributes to a range of IQ subtests) is likely to aid in mapping sociocognitive processes to neural networks and in identifying the genetic contribution to individual differences. Identification of these factors will make it easier to test causal hypotheses that could be vital to developing, for example, interventions for social impairments, or to understanding the mechanism of putative treatments. Looking forward, having an agreed taxonomy of sociocognitive processes with an understanding of the structure of social cognition would be a starting point for developing a shared protocol of tasks, allowing assessment of specific profiles of ability across sociocognitive processes and across groups. Again, by analogy with intelligence testing, knowing an individual's peaks and troughs across subcomponents of social cognition would allow discrimination of phenocopies (e.g., attachment disorder versus autism), detailed measurement of change (e.g., decline in dementia), test of specificity of treatment effects, and cleaner mapping to neural or genetic bases of social ability.

In the following sections, we largely address the second endeavor, determining the structure of social cognition, since adding a further idiosyncratic taxonomy of sociocognitive abilities to those already in existence would be of little use to the field. This makes our task harder, however,

Empathy: another's affective state mirrored in the self (with recognition that the other is the source of one's state, in some accounts)

Imitation: observation of an action causes the performance of a topographically similar action because very little research has explicitly addressed this subject in large samples of neurotypical adults. As a result, we draw heavily on research addressing social processing in neurodevelopmental disorders, particularly autism spectrum disorder (ASD), the archetypal disorder of social cognition. Although this is a research area rich with relevant data, it should of course be acknowledged that the structure of social cognition in atypical populations may not reflect that in typical populations—due to compensation, for example—but we hope that this research may suggest fruitful methods of investigation in typical individuals (Section 5) as well as other clinical groups (e.g., individuals with acquired lesions). A second difficulty relates to the sheer scope of social cognition—the full range of processes that contribute to social ability has never been delineated, as far as we are aware, and if we were to attempt to list them all, we would likely have little space to do anything else. Therefore, the range of social abilities we discuss is limited and determined by the availability of evidence relating to their in(ter)dependence (much of which is from social neuroscience), the availability of existing reviews of the relevant literature, and our own fields of expertise. This necessarily means that we do not address a vast swath of literature on social ability, but several sections (detailed below) refer to general factors bearing on the structure of social cognition that are of relevance to many, if not all, areas of sociocognitive research.

2. AN OVERVIEW OF OUR APPROACH AND THE CURRENT STATE OF PLAY

In Section 2, we introduce the sociocognitive processes that form the focus of this review (Section 2.1), describe five ways in which sociocognitive processes may be related (Section 2.2), and discuss the types of evidence commonly used to establish the relationship between these processes (Section 2.3).

Section 3 takes four of the five ways in which social processes may be related and reviews literature in which this relationship has been empirically tested. Section 3.1 presents research addressing the relationships among imitation, ToM, and empathy in order to determine whether these three social abilities are unitary or distinct, or whether the development of one of these abilities is necessary for the development of the others. Section 3.2 assesses whether self-other distinction/control may be recruited by a number of sociocognitive processes, explaining correlated ability across seemingly distinct social abilities. Section 3.3 presents a possible example of one sociocognitive process constituting a necessary component of another: the abilities to perceive biological motion and to imitate the actions of others.

Section 4 addresses an issue bearing directly on the question of the factor structure of social cognition: the extent to which social ability relies on domain-specific, possibly modular/modularized (Karmiloff-Smith 1996), processes versus domain-general processes that are recruited for social and nonsocial processing alike. Although the domain specificity and factor structure questions are in principle distinct, if social ability were only to recruit general executive or perceptual processes, for example, one might expect much more overlap among social abilities than if distinct abilities relied on different domain-specific or dedicated modules/processes. Section 4 focuses specifically on the fifth way in which social abilities may be related: assessing whether factors affecting the speed and/or extent of social development are specifically social or whether they merely recruit general learning, attention, and reward mechanisms.

Section 5 addresses how we might make further progress in determining the structure of social cognition. Section 5.1 outlines the available methodologies to address the question and highlights their strengths and limitations. Section 5.2 makes general recommendations that could lead to future progress, focusing on conceptual rather than methodological issues.

Neurotypical: describes an individual who does not display ASD or other neurologically atypical patterns of thought or behavior

Autism spectrum disorder (ASD): a neurodevelopmental disorder characterized by impaired communication and social interaction, and restricted and repetitive interests

Biological motion: the motion profile of animate beings

Domain specific: refers to psychological/neural mechanisms dedicated to the processing of specific content (e.g., social stimuli and information)

2.1. Putative Components of Social Cognition

Potentially, any cognitive process may be called into the service of understanding social agents and social interactions. However, as previously described, this review discusses only a subset of social abilities to illustrate various ways in which different social abilities may be related. These abilities include those related to:

(*a*) Affiliation and social motivation: factors influencing approach tendency and hence quantity of an individual's social interaction.

(*b*) Agent recognition: allowing conspecifics to be individuated.

(*c*) Biological motion perception, action recognition, and imitation: processes underlying the ability to determine which action is being performed by an agent and the reproduction of that action by the self.

(*d*) Emotion recognition: the ability to determine the affective state of another.

(*e*) Empathy: when recognition of another's affective state prompts the recognizer to adopt the same state (with the added requirement that one recognizes that the other is the source of one's state under some accounts).

(*f*) Social attention: the degree of attention paid to social stimuli either due to a conscious choice (endogenous attention) or as a result of automatic capture of attention (exogenous attention).

(*g*) Social learning: learning from other individuals.

(*h*) Theory of mind: the ability to represent one's own mental states (i.e., propositional attitudes, e.g., beliefs) and those of others.

2.2. Types of Relationship Between Components of Social Cognition

Sociocognitive processes may be related in at least five ways.

(*a*) They may actually be synonymous or alternative labels for the same core process. For example, although several authors claim that mirror neurons contribute to action understanding (Gallese & Sinigaglia 2011, Rizzolatti et al. 1996), others have suggested that action understanding is synonymous with either action perception (determining which action has been performed) or ToM (determining the intention driving the action) (Rizzolatti & Sinigaglia 2010).

(*b*) One process may constitute a necessary (sub)component of another. For example, emotion contagion (in which the affective state of another is mirrored in the self) is thought to be a necessary component of empathy under frameworks in which empathy is said to have occurred when the empathizer recognizes that the other is the source of their current emotional state (de Vignemont & Singer 2006).

(*c*) Processes may rely on at least one common process but also have distinct elements. For example, it has been argued that several sociocognitive processes rely on the ability to distinguish representations of the self and others (see Section 3.2). When empathizing with another, one must be able to distinguish between one's own emotional state and that of the other, and when inhibiting the tendency to imitate another, one must be able to distinguish between one's own motor plan and that of the other. Although both imitation inhibition and empathy may require self-other distinction processes, each is likely to recruit additional distinct processes.

(*d*) Two sociocognitive processes may be developmentally associated, due to a direct causal link. This is sometimes referred to as cascading (**Figure 1c**), where, for example, imitation is proposed to be essential for development of ToM. Such cascades are often referred to in theories of atypical developmental; e.g., deficits in social motivation are hypothesized

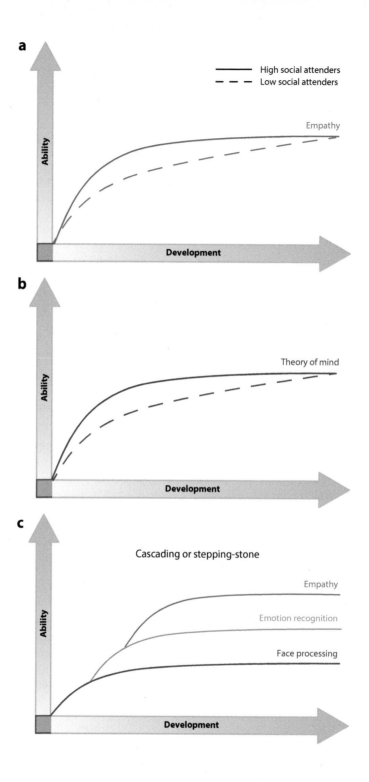

to cause reduced attention to faces, in turn leading to failure of neuronal and cognitive specialization for face processing (Klin & Jones 2008).

(*e*) Two processes may be developmentally associated due to a third factor of importance to both. For example, two processes that are learned through social interaction during development (for example, imitation and empathy) may develop at the same speed/level as a result of an individual's degree of social attention. An individual who is a good social learner may learn to imitate and empathize quickly and thoroughly (**Figure 1*a*,*b***), whereas the opposite may be true of a poor social learner.

2.3. Types of Evidence Currently Used to Establish Relationships

Broadly speaking, researchers interested in the relationships between cognitive components of social processing currently refer to five types of evidence.

(*a*) Single or double dissociation of abilities in developmental or acquired clinical groups: If process *X* is intact but process *Y* is impaired in one group, and process *X* impaired and process *Y* intact in another group, then it is concluded that process *X* is distinct from process *Y*.

(*b*) Neuroimaging data demonstrating overlapping or distinct brain activity during different tasks/processes: Differential activation caused by two different social tasks follows the dissociation logic described above, but common activation of neurological networks by two social processes often prompts the conclusion that the social processes recruit common cognitive mechanisms.

(*c*) Correlations (cross-sectional) between individual differences in two or more sociocognitive processes: Patterns of covariation across individuals have been used to support claims of common mechanisms between processes.

(*d*) Longitudinal associations of individual differences: Covariation within individuals across development has been used to argue for developmental cascading, where the acquisition of one social ability leads to the acquisition of another.

(*e*) Intervention effects: If interventions (psychological, pharmacological, etc.) can differentially affect social abilities, then they are seen as distinct.

3. WHAT DO WE KNOW CURRENTLY ABOUT THE LANDSCAPE OF SOCIAL COGNITION?

In this section, we turn to empirical evidence concerning the factor structure of social cognition. Research directly addressing this question is scarce, but we have sought to illustrate four of the

---

Figure 1

Some sociocognitive abilities are related because of a common factor that is important at some point in the development of each ability. For example, social attention may be important for the development of (*a*) empathy and (*b*) theory of mind; individuals who could be characterized as high social attenders would develop these abilities more quickly than would low social attenders, resulting in a correlation between the two abilities. One should note that if an ability has a critical period (not shown), then an early deficit in one ability (e.g., social attention) may result in a lifelong impact on another ability (e.g., empathy). Although these examples are hypothetical, they serve to illustrate the importance of accounting for development when assessing the factor structure of social cognition: In certain periods of development, abilities that require common processes (e.g., empathy and theory of mind) may be correlated, but this correlation may vanish at different developmental stages. (*c*) Some sociocognitive abilities may be related via a cascading or stepping-stone effect, whereby the development of one ability (e.g., face processing) acts as a stepping-stone for the further development of other abilities (e.g., emotion recognition and empathy).

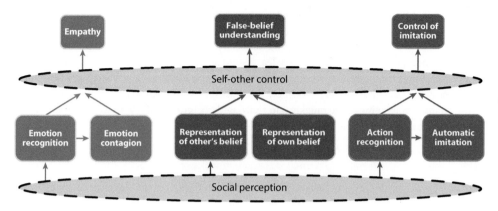

Figure 2

Schematic illustration of two ways in which sociocognitive abilities may be related. In the first hypothesized relationship, some processes may constitute necessary subcomponents of others (e.g., emotion recognition is a necessary subcomponent of empathy). In the second relationship, seemingly distinct sociocognitive functions (e.g., empathy, false-belief understanding, control of imitation) may recruit common subcomponents (e.g., self-other control, social perception). Ovals illustrate common processes, and rectangles represent distinct processes relating to empathy (*red* route), false-belief understanding (*blue*), and control of imitation (*green*).

five ways in which social abilities may be related using examples from the literature. We address the fifth relationship in Section 4.

3.1. Imitation, Empathy, and Theory of Mind: Synonymous, Developmental Cascade, or Distinct?

Although research that attempts to determine the factor structure of social cognition is in its infancy, several sets of social abilities have been examined together, typically because they are associated with psychopathological conditions or because one ability is hypothesized to be either a stepping-stone or subcomponent (**Figure 2**) of the others. All of these motivations underlie research examining imitation, ToM, and empathy together; all three processes have been hypothesized to be impaired in ASD, and imitation has been proposed as a necessary building block for the development of ToM and empathy. Indeed, the concept of empathy has sometimes been extended to include imitation (motor empathy), ToM (cognitive empathy), and affective empathy, and it has been argued that empathizing ability is a primary trait governing individual (and gender) differences in social ability (Baron-Cohen 2009).

Recent evidence, however, does not support a link between these three processes. The idea that imitation leads to the development of ToM and empathy due to the operation of an innate module (Meltzoff & Moore 1977) is not supported by data showing that imitation relies on domain general learning rather than an innate module (Anisfeld 1979, R. Cook et al. 2014, Jones 2009, Ray & Heyes 2011). In addition, McEwen et al. (2007) found that some typically developing children who were reported at age 2 years to show no imitation nonetheless had social skills in the average range at age 8 years. Thus, imitation may not be a vital stepping-stone to later mental state attribution.

The hypothesized links among imitation, ToM, and empathy were bolstered by the discovery of mirror neurons, neurons that fire when actions are both executed and observed (di Pellegrino et al. 1992). These cells are thought to support imitation (Catmur et al. 2009, Heiser et al. 2003) and were originally thought to code the goal of an action (Bonini & Ferrari 2011, Rizzolatti & Craighero 2004, Rizzolatti & Sinigaglia 2010); goal is a nonspecific term commonly construed as the intention behind an action, i.e., a mental state. By coding for own or others' intention, mirror neurons were proposed to provide a neural basis for ToM (Rizzolatti & Sinigaglia 2010).

TPJ: temporoparietal junction

However, more recent evidence calls into question the straightforward interpretation that mirror neurons code the goals of actions and therefore form a connection between own and others' intentions (for summaries, see R. Cook et al. 2014, Cook & Bird 2013). Perhaps most convincingly, a meta-analysis of neuroimaging studies of ToM that set out to determine the contribution of mirror neurons concluded, "The mirror system is not activated and does not aid the mentalizing system in detecting intentionality" (Van Overwalle & Baetens 2009, p. 579).

As mentioned above, one important motivation for hypothesizing the interdependence of imitation, empathy, and ToM has been the claim that all three social processes are affected in ASD. If ASD is characterized by impairments in all three areas, then a parsimonious explanation is that the three are developmentally linked or rely on a common underlying process (online or developmentally) (Colombi et al. 2009, Eckerman & Whitehead 1999, Hobson 1989, Rogers & Pennington 1991).

Again, recent evidence calls into question the claim that ASD is a condition characterized by deficits in imitation and empathy. Studies of automatic imitation (whereby observation of another's action prompts the tendency to produce an identical action) reveal that individuals with ASD have at least a typical, if not increased, tendency to copy simple hand and finger actions (Cook & Bird 2012, Sowden et al. 2016, Spengler et al. 2010) and emotional facial expressions (Press et al. 2010). Deficits in voluntary, nonautomatic imitation in ASD are likely due to nonspecific factors such as attentional control, working memory, and/or pragmatic language understanding (Leighton et al. 2008). In addition, available evidence either is unable to support mirror neuron deficits in ASD (Hamilton 2013) or suggests that abilities that are claimed to depend upon mirror neuron function (e.g., action understanding and prediction) are typical in ASD (Hamilton et al. 2007).

Further evidence from clinical groups also suggests that affective empathy and ToM are distinct and demonstrate a double dissociation. Although ASD does not seem to be directly linked to problems with affective empathy (Bird et al. 2010), most individuals with ASD show impaired ToM (Happé 1994, White et al. 2009). By contrast, individuals with high levels of psychopathic traits demonstrate intact ToM but impaired affective empathy (Jones et al. 2010, Lockwood et al. 2013, Schwenck et al. 2012). Furthermore, meta-analyses of neuroimaging of ToM and empathy in typical and atypical populations have identified reliable but nonoverlapping networks, including the medial prefrontal cortex, temporoparietal junction (TPJ), and precuneus for ToM (Frith & Frith 2010, Saxe et al. 2006) and anterior insula and anterior cingulate cortex for empathy (Singer & Lamm 2009).

3.2. Self-Other Distinction and Control: A Common Factor?

Although imitation, ToM, and empathy appear to be distinct processes, evidence suggests that false-belief attribution (a key test of ToM; tracking a character's mistaken belief), empathy, and the ability to inhibit imitation may call on a common process—that of self-other distinction and control (**Figure 2**). This proposal was originally made by Brass and colleagues (2005), who noted that imitation inhibition caused activation of a neural network commonly seen during ToM tasks. They suggested that this activation may reflect a common process, self-other distinction, that is necessary for both imitation inhibition and ToM. It was argued that in order to inhibit imitation, it is necessary to distinguish between one's own motor intention and that of another, and, at least in classic false-belief tests of ToM, one must be able to distinguish between one's own knowledge states and those of another (inhibiting own true belief to predict behavior based on another's false belief). This explanation was tested in typical individuals and those with ASD (Spengler et al. 2010), who completed a test of imitation inhibition and verbal and nonverbal tests of ToM. Within the ASD group, performance on the imitation inhibition test predicted performance on the verbal ToM test and neural activation in the ToM network when completing the nonverbal ToM task. These measures were not associated in the group of typical adults, which in principle could reflect a meaningful difference between the ways in which typical individuals and those with ASD complete the tasks, but in this case it likely reflects the fact that the tests of ToM were less sensitive to individual differences in typical individuals due to ceiling effects.

The hypothesis of a common self-other distinction process recruited by multiple sociocognitive processes (see **Figure 2**) was tested using two intervention studies in which individuals were trained to inhibit imitation (theorized to increase their ability to distinguish and control representations of the self and others) before completing other sociocognitive tests to identify transfer effects. Santiesteban et al. (2012b) tested the impact of imitation inhibition training on a visual perspective-taking task. It was predicted that the visual perspective-taking task would recruit the same self-other distinction process as ToM and imitation inhibition; in order to represent another's perspective, it must be distinguished from one's own. This prediction was fulfilled—performance on the visual perspective-taking task was improved by imitation inhibition training but not by imitation training, nor by training on a standard Stroop inhibition task closely matched for difficulty. Using a study with a similar design, de Guzman et al. (2016) demonstrated an effect of imitation inhibition training on empathy for pain; the effect was thought to be due to the fact that in order to be empathic, one must be able to distinguish one's own nonpain state from the pained state of the other.

A number of studies using functional magnetic resonance imaging (fMRI) and/or transcranial magnetic stimulation have demonstrated an important role for the TPJ in self-other distinction (Brass et al. 2005; Hogeveen et al. 2015; Santiesteban et al. 2012a, 2015; Sowden & Catmur 2015). In line with these demonstrations, Santiesteban et al. (2012a) used transcranial direct current stimulation to excite the TPJ and showed a corresponding enhancement of the ability to take another individual's perspective. However, Santiesteban et al. (2012a) also showed, in the same individuals, that exciting the TPJ led to a reduction in imitation. Santiesteban et al. (2012a) therefore suggest that the common process may be self-other control rather than distinction, defined as the ability to switch attentional focus between coactivated self- and other-related representations. This ability would allow the selective enhancement of the self and inhibition of the other, or vice versa, according to task demands.

3.3. Biological Motion and Imitation: Constituent Processes?

As listed in Section 2.2, one of the possible ways in which two putative sociocognitive processes might be related is that one constitutes a subcomponent of or a necessary input to another. An example of such a potentially constitutive relationship is between biological motion processing and imitation; a strong argument can be made that one can only imitate another's action if one can accurately perceive the action. Traditionally, biological motion processing and imitation have been treated as distinct topics of inquiry; however, the fact that both abilities are thought to be impaired in individuals with autism has led to their investigation in some depth in this population.

Biological motion, which refers to the movements of other animate beings, has been studied using a variety of stimuli, from animations of moving people (e.g., Pelphrey et al. 2003) to single dots moving with a velocity profile that matches human movement (Dayan et al. 2007). Annaz and colleagues (2012) investigated attention to biological motion in young children with ASD and found that whereas typical children preferentially attended to biological motion, children with ASD showed no such preference. Together with work from other labs (Dawson et al. 1998, Klin et al. 2009), this finding suggests that, unlike typical children, those with ASD do not demonstrate preferential attention to social stimuli. Given that individual differences in some aspects of biological motion processing have been correlated with sociocognitive abilities (Miller & Saygin 2013, Sevdalis & Keller 2011), it has been suggested that atypical attention to biological motion from an early age could be part of a developmental cascade resulting in atypical sociocognitive abilities in ASD (Dawson 1991, Klin et al. 2003).

Reduced attention to biological motion from an early age may be causally related to atypical development of biological motion processing. Annaz and colleagues (2010) demonstrated that between the ages of 5 and 12, typical children improve in their ability to determine human form from biological motion, whereas children with ASD do not (see also Blake et al. 2003), and data from Koldewyn and colleagues (2010) suggest that atypical biological motion processing in ASD extends into adolescence. Though the ability of autistic adults to process biological motion is a matter of debate (Koldewyn et al. 2010, Murphy et al. 2009, Saygin et al. 2010), Kaiser and colleagues (2010) demonstrated that, unlike typical adults, adults with ASD do not exhibit greater visual sensitivity for human motion relative to the motion of a vehicle. Likewise, using stimuli that require only local, not global, motion processing, Cook and colleagues (2009) demonstrated that adults with ASD were less sensitive to perturbations to biological motion compared to typical adults, but they were equally sensitive to perturbations to gravitational motion.

As discussed in Section 3.1, most studies have reported typical automatic imitation in ASD. However, there are some exceptions—and explicating the relationship between imitation and biological motion perception may shed light on these. J. Cook and colleagues (2014a) asked participants to perform horizontal arm movements while observing congruent (horizontal) or incongruent (vertical) arm movements conducted by a virtual reality agent with either human or robot form. For typical individuals, incongruent arm movements conducted by the human, but not the robot avatar, interfered with ongoing action control. In contrast, individuals with ASD were not affected by human or robot movements.

Imitation involves the activation of motor representations upon activation of a visual representation of action. Atypical imitation could therefore be the result of atypical visual biological motion processing. In line with this hypothesis, it is notable that paradigms demonstrating typical imitation in ASD tend to have employed stimuli that rely on apparent motion—stimuli in which still images of body positions are presented and the viewer infers the kinematics of movement (as in a flicker book or traditional cartoon). With such stimuli, the viewer's inferred kinematics are unconstrained and need not necessarily follow the kinematics of typical biological motion. However, some paradigms constrain participants' representation of movement kinematics by showing videos or using live stimuli. For example, the stimuli presented by J. Cook and colleagues (2014a) were animations displayed at a high refresh rate, meaning that the representation of the kinematics of the movement was driven by perceptual input and not inferred by participants. In other words, evidence from the biological motion literature suggests that individuals with ASD may represent the kinematics of movement atypically, and this may have a concomitant effect on imitation if perception of action kinematics is a crucial component of the imitation task.

This literature provides a good example of the importance of considering that some sociocognitive abilities may comprise a constituent component of other abilities. When imitation and biological motion processing are viewed in isolation, it is difficult to explain why imitation appears atypical in some, but not all, situations in autistic individuals. However, if one considers the extent to which an imitation paradigm constrains biological motion processing, then the ambiguity may be resolved.

4. UNIQUELY "SOCIAL" PROCESSING?

As discussed in Section 2, the extent to which social ability relies on domain-specific, possibly modular or modularized processes versus domain-general processes that are recruited for social and nonsocial processing alike has an impact on the question of the factor structure of social cognition. Although the domain specificity and factor structure questions are in principle distinct, if social ability were only to recruit general processes, then one might expect more overlap among social abilities than if distinct abilities relied on distinct domain-specific modules (for a review of this issue within the face-processing literature, see Duchaine & Yovel 2015).

If one accepts that social ability is, to a greater or lesser degree, learned from others over development, then factors affecting the speed and depth of such social learning (i.e., learning from conspecifics) are likely to affect social ability. Assuming that social ability is typically a product of learning from others and individual trial-and-error learning (e.g., learning to imitate may rely on observation of others and on individual learning based on trial-and-error to control one's own actions), then whether social learning is governed by socially specific or domain-general factors will impact the interdependence of social processes. If good individual learners are also good social learners because both types of learning are governed by domain-general factors, then these individuals will excel in all social abilities regardless of the degree to which a particular social ability relies on social, rather than individual, learning. In contrast, if factors affecting social learning are domain specific and distinct from those governing individual learning, then social abilities may dissociate from one another as a function of the degree to which they rely on social versus individual learning. We therefore provide an overview of research examining the domain specificity of social learning (Section 4.1), social reward (Section 4.2), and social attention (Section 4.3). Finally, we discuss the potential relevance of dual-process accounts to the question of domain specificity of sociocognitive processes (Section 4.4).

4.1. Social Learning

A domain-general view is that all learning, including social learning, is governed by the operation of a few general learning principles (e.g., associative and instrumental learning; Heyes & Pearce 2015). Heyes (2012a) presents a summary of the evidence supporting a domain-general view of social learning. Perhaps most important is the finding that social learning covaries with nonsocial learning: In male zebra finches, song complexity (social learning) is correlated with the rate of learning in an extractive foraging task (nonsocial learning) (Boogert et al. 2008). Such correlations are seen not just within species, but also across species, such that species that tend to be good social learners are also good nonsocial learners (Lefebvre & Giraldeau 1996, Reader et al. 2011, Reader & Laland 2002). This correlation between social and nonsocial learning is consistent with the view that there is just one set of domain-general learning principles. Heyes (2012a) also notes that if social learning were an adaptation for social living, it would not be present in solitary species; however, at least two solitary species [the common octopus (Fiorito & Scotto 1992) and the red-footed tortoise (Wilkinson et al. 2010)] are capable of social learning.

By contrast, theoreticians in the domain-specific camp have argued that living in social groups has specifically favored the evolution of social learning: Social learning is an adaptation for social living (Klopfer 1961, Templeton et al. 1999). Neuroimaging studies have demonstrated that social learning and nonsocial learning are associated with activity in dissociable neural networks, thus raising the possibility of distinct and specialized mechanisms. For example, Behrens and colleagues (2008) used fMRI to demonstrate that learning from individual experiences about reward outcomes was associated with activity in a network of brain regions including the ventral striatum and anterior cingulate sulcus, whereas social learning—from an adviser—was associated with activity in a distinct network of brain regions including the TPJ and anterior cingulate gyrus. Further evidence for dissociable mechanisms underlying social learning and nonsocial learning comes from a recent study by J. Cook et al. (2014b) that demonstrated that social and nonsocial learning dissociate with respect to their relationship with social dominance. Whereas social dominance predicted social learning ability, it was not related to ability to learn via nonsocial means. This result is consistent with the domain-specific view that dissociable mechanisms underpin social and nonsocial learning.

With many questions yet to be addressed, the debate concerning the domain specificity of social learning continues. For example, with respect to the neural correlates of social and nonsocial learning, Behrens and colleagues (2009) have argued that although the neural correlates may be dissociable in terms of their spatial location, it may still be the case that the same computational learning mechanisms are employed for both social and nonsocial learning. This issue has been examined using computational modeling approaches in which formal mathematical models of learning are used to model the learning behavior of real individuals. These studies have shown that models developed to explain nonsocial learning can explain social learning (Diaconescu et al. 2014), although in some cases they may need to be modified to adequately explain social behavior (Boorman et al. 2013).

4.2. Social Reward/Motivation

Learning efficiency is affected by reward, and here we review evidence concerning the domain specificity of social reward and the idea of specific social motivation. A number of theories have argued for domain specificity in this area; in particular, several theories suggest that ASD is characterized by a specific deficit in social motivation. The social motivation theory of autism (Chevallier et al. 2012, Dawson 2008) postulates that the starting point for the sociocognitive differences in ASD is that social stimuli and activities are intrinsically less motivating for infants with ASD. For example, Van Etten & Carver (2015) have suggested that reduced social motivation explains reported imitation deficits in ASD (but see Section 3.1). Such a theory implies that reward systems have a modular organization, in which social motivation can be selectively impaired while the processing of other motivational factors (e.g., food or monetary rewards) is spared. Whether a separable social reward system exists, however, is still a matter of debate.

Social reward and motivation are subserved by a network of brain regions including the amygdala, the ventral striatum, and orbital and ventromedial regions of the prefrontal cortex (Chevallier et al. 2012). A long-standing debate in the reward-processing literature concerns whether primary rewards (i.e., rewards essential for the maintenance of homeostasis and reproduction; e.g., food, sex, and shelter) and secondary rewards (i.e., rewards not directly related to survival; e.g., money and power) are processed in common or distinct brain structures (Schultz 2000). Some investigators have speculated that primary and secondary rewards may be represented in phylogenetically distinct brain regions (Knutson & Bossaerts 2007), but the majority of researchers within the decision neuroscience and neuroeconomics fields have argued that both primary and secondary rewards are compared on a common scale in which the unit of comparison is decision value (for a review, see Peters & Büchel 2010). This debate can be extended to encompass social reward: Does one common reward-processing network exist, or is it feasible that social reward processing is subserved by at least partly dissociable neural mechanisms? Sescousse and colleagues (2013) reviewed the human neuroimaging literature concerning the processing of monetary, food, and erotic rewards. They demonstrated that a core set of brain regions, including the striatum, anterior insula/frontal operculum, mediodorsal thalamus, amygdala, and ventromedial prefrontal cortex, is associated with reward processing in an indiscriminate fashion, consistent with the idea of a common reward circuit. In addition, comparative analyses between rewards revealed that some regions are more specifically recruited by one type of reward compared to the others; for example, the bilateral amygdala, the ventral anterior insula, and the extrastriate body area are more robustly activated by erotic than by monetary and food rewards. At face value this result suggests that although all types of rewards recruit core reward-processing mechanisms, different types of rewards may be discriminated on the basis of neural mechanisms outside of the common reward circuit. This result makes it feasible that social reward processing could be subserved by neural mechanisms at least partly dissociable from those related to other rewards. However, it should be noted that it is unclear whether the partially dissociable networks identified by Sescousse et al. (2013) are specifically related to reward processing; for example, the extrastriate body area activation observed in relation to processing of erotic rewards may simply reflect the fact that these stimuli, but not money or food stimuli, contained images of bodies. In other words, differences in neural activation may simply reflect different types of input to a common reward system.

4.3. Social Attention

Objects with social importance are prioritized by attention; social stimuli automatically (exogenously) capture attention rather than requiring deliberate (endogenous) attentional control. Numerous studies demonstrate that infants preferentially attend to face-like stimuli rather than to scrambled or inverted faces (Goren et al. 1975, Morton & Johnson 1991). This preference is maintained throughout the lifetime, such that in human adults attention is rapidly captured by human faces and bodies (Fletcher-Watson et al. 2008, Shah et al. 2013), masked faces are detected more quickly and accurately than are masked objects (Purcell & Stewart 1988), and changes to faces are detected better than are changes to nonface objects (Kikuchi et al. 2009, Salva et al. 2011).

It has been proposed that a subcortical face-detection system, present at birth, underlies this preferential orientation toward faces (Johnson 2005). However, critics have argued that humans are simply biased to attend to top-heavy, as opposed to bottom-heavy, stimuli and that faces fall into this top-heavy stimulus category (Simion et al. 2002). More recent research controlled for top-heavy stimuli and still found a significant bias for attending to face-like stimuli in adult participants (Shah et al. 2013, Tomalski et al. 2009). Humans appear to have a specific, and perhaps innate, bias to attend to stimuli that possess the same orientation and polarity as real-life faces.

Deliberate (or endogenous) attention to social stimuli has been much discussed in theories of ASD (Chawarska et al. 2016). Several developmental accounts (e.g., Chevallier et al. 2012; Dawson 1991; Klin et al. 2003, 2015) trace a pathway from a specific reduction in orientating to social stimuli (due to reduced social motivation or problems of attentional disengagement, for example), through reduced exposure to relevant learning opportunities, to poor social cognition (e.g., ToM). Such theoretical accounts underpin a number of prominent intervention approaches for young children with ASD; these interventions focus on increasing attention to social stimuli and establishing joint attention.

Perhaps the most pertinent evidence regarding these cascade theories comes from studies of infants at high genetic risk of autism (those born into families with a child with ASD); to date, results show little in the everyday social behavior of infants under 12 months of age that discriminates those children who will later receive an ASD diagnosis, and in the lab, attention abnormalities (evident from approximately age 6 months) do not appear to be strongly domain specific (Elsabbagh & Johnson 2016). Claims of sustained abnormalities in attention to social stimuli (e.g., reduced looking at other's eyes, more looking at mouths) in ASD (Klin et al. 2002) did not receive support in a recent review of eye-tracking studies in ASD (Guillon et al. 2014), and at least one study suggests that attention to faces in general and the ratio of eye to mouth fixations may be differentially affected by ASD and alexithymia (the inability to identify and describe one's own emotional state), respectively (Bird et al. 2011). Interestingly, domain-general properties of ostensibly social stimuli (such as point-light displays of biological motion) may determine whether children with ASD pay preferential attention or not; a greater preference for exact predictability or contingency at key stages of development may distinguish children with ASD from typically developing children (Klin et al. 2009).

Alexithymia: the inability to identify and describe one's own emotional state

4.4. Dual-Process Theories and Social Cognition

A broader issue within the domain-specific versus domain-general debate concerns the issue of whether two types of social cognition exist. These types are consistent with classic dual-process theories, which posit two systems: one is cognitively efficient, fast, and automatic [system 1 in Kahneman and colleagues' terminology (Kahneman & Frederick 2002, Stanovich 1999)]; the other is cognitively demanding, slow, controlled, and of limited capacity (system 2). Many instantiations of dual-process theory suggest that system 1 is domain specific and system 2 is domain general (Evans 2008).

This issue has been discussed extensively within the ToM literature (e.g., Apperly & Butterfill 2009, Butterfill & Apperly 2013). The suggestion of two systems for ToM was prompted by the observation that although typical children below the age of 4 years on average do not pass verbal, explicit tests of ToM (as measured by classic false-belief tests), 18-month-old infants pass implicit false-belief paradigms based on eye gaze behavior (Onishi & Baillargeon 2005). A dual-system view of ToM was supported by the finding that individuals with ASD who were able to pass explicit tests of false-belief understanding did not show eye gaze behavior consistent with false-belief understanding on implicit tasks (Senju et al. 2009).

Several authors have claimed to demonstrate automatic, cognitively efficient ToM in typical adults (where it is often labeled implicit mentalizing). For example Samson et al. (2010) introduced the dot perspective task, in which participants are presented with an image of a blue room with red dots on the walls. An avatar faces toward one of the walls, and participants are asked to count the number of dots they can see and to ignore the avatar. Despite this instruction, participants respond faster when the avatar can see the same number of dots that they can see. This consistency effect has been interpreted as evidence for automatic mentalizing: The avatar's visual perspective (i.e., knowledge state) is automatically processed in addition to the participant's own.

The problem with tests of implicit ToM, however, is that it is difficult to establish that the observed effects are a consequence of the automatic representation of mental states (Heyes 2014a,b). For example, Santiesteban and colleagues (Catmur et al. 2016, Santiesteban et al. 2014) demonstrated that the consistency effect could be observed in the dot perspective task when the avatar was replaced with an arrow, a stimulus clearly not appropriate for the attribution of mental states. They argued that the effect observed in the avatar condition was a result of domain-general processes such as attentional orienting, where the avatar's gaze acted as a directional cue, rather than the attribution of mental states to the avatar. A similar debate occurred following the publication of another paper claiming that adults automatically represent an avatar's false belief (Kovács et al. 2010). In a replication and extension of this study, Phillips et al. (2015) demonstrated that the effect was due to an experimental confound.

While the debate surrounding the existence of implicit mentalizing continues, the general principle of separating sociocognitive processes into system 1 and system 2 promises to bear fruit. Perhaps all core social abilities could be accomplished via two routes, one being an automatic, cognitively efficient process that relies in part on heuristics and learned associations, and the other a deliberative reasoning process. If each aspect of social processing can be accomplished via either route, then the relationship between different social abilities may depend on whether the automatic or deliberative route is used to accomplish a particular social goal (and hence, what type of task provides the relevant evidence on interrelations). Presumably, any time the rational, deliberative system 2 route is used, performance will be affected, in part, by individual differences in general processes such as working memory, executive function, and intelligence, and correlations will be observed between different social abilities. As discussed previously, if system 1 processes are learned over development, then factors that determine learning speed (such as social attention, social reward, and social learning ability) will produce associations in the speed of acquisition or extent of learning in each of these processes. By contrast, if system 1 processes rely on dedicated domain-specific modules, then dissociations between different system 1 social abilities are more likely to be seen.

5. HOW CAN WE MAKE FURTHER PROGRESS?

5.1. Available Methodologies

We began our review of the structure of social cognition by contrasting it with the structure of intelligence. Although many in that field would argue that much is still to be determined about the structure of intelligence, the general methodological approach has been successful. Typically, large numbers of participants complete various tests designed to measure some aspect of intelligence, and the relationships among tests are examined with statistical techniques such as factor analysis. The result is the identification of factors that explain performance on those tests. Such an approach would be of obvious benefit when it comes to determining the structure of social cognition. For example, in Section 3.2, we hypothesized that a common ability to distinguish between and select representations of the self and others may be recruited by empathy, ToM, and imitation inhibition. One would therefore expect that a factor analysis of tests assessing these abilities would identify a common factor corresponding to this self-other ability. Such techniques could examine the (in)dependence of a large number of tests of social ability and determine whether evidence exists for factors underlying performance on multiple tests of the sort hypothesized in Section 4, such as social learning ability, social attention, and social motivation.

Such a study, although useful, would not be able to uncover all relationships between different social abilities. One such relationship is where process X is necessary, at a certain developmental stage, in order to develop process Y (the cascading or stepping-stone model) (**Figure 1c**). Such a potential relationship could have been uncovered by the study described in Section 3.1 (McEwan et al. 2007), in which imitation was measured at 2 years of age and social ability was measured in the same individuals at 8 years of age. If all of those who could not imitate at 2 years were socially impaired at 8 years, then one might conclude that the ability to imitate at 2 is necessary to develop appropriate social ability in later childhood. Of course, we could not make that claim solely on the basis of data from such a cross-lagged design—there may be another factor, process Z, that actually determines social ability in later childhood and that also happens to covary with imitation at 2 years of age. Regardless of the inability of cross-lagged designs to demonstrate definitively a causal influence of one process on another, the fact remains that if imitation at 2 years is necessary for appropriate development of other social abilities, then collecting and factor analyzing data from a large group of adults on multiple tests of social ability are unlikely to uncover this developmental relationship because most adults can successfully imitate, leaving little variance in this ability to predict other social abilities.

This issue is an example of a more general problem associated with developmental influences of one process on another. Consider the case of empathy and the recognition of one's own emotions.

In some developmental accounts, the ability to recognize one's own emotion is necessary for the development of empathy. These accounts suggest that infants learn to associate the experience of a state, whether pain, sickness, or joy, with the expression of that state in another. For example, the infant falls and is hurt, and caregivers mimic a pained facial expression and vocalize pain. Over repeated painful experiences, learning will result in a link between the feeling of pain in the self and its expression in another. Several theories suggest that this learning is sufficient for empathy (at least for emotion contagion; e.g., Bird & Viding 2014, Heyes & Bird 2007). After these links have been learned, recognition of one's own emotion may play no further role in the expression of empathy. Under this model, individual differences in empathy and own-emotion recognition will no longer be correlated, meaning the factor analysis strategy using adult data will erroneously conclude that they are unrelated. Although potentially true in adulthood, such a conclusion would not capture the necessary role of recognition of one's own emotion in the development of empathy.

In order to postulate a causal connection between two processes such that one can claim that ability in one sociocognitive domain determines ability in another or that two abilities share common components, one must randomly assign individuals to groups, experimentally increase or decrease social ability in one group, and compare this group following the intervention with another that received a control nonsocial intervention. Such studies are not easy to design, however; one must be extremely careful in ensuring that the control intervention is matched in every way with the social intervention. Although difficult to achieve in practice, such designs are very powerful in determining causality. They are not a panacea, however, and several factors may limit their use. First, if used in adulthood, they are insensitive to the kind of developmental relationships described previously (e.g., imitation at 2 years of age relating to ToM in later childhood). Second, unless several such experiments are performed or extremely subtle (or numerous) control conditions are used, it is hard to determine the process whereby the training is having an effect because it is unclear exactly what is being trained.

Neuroimaging methods, particularly fMRI, have often been used to answer questions about the relationships among different sociocognitive processes. For example, Quirin and colleagues (2013) demonstrated that brain areas coding for dominance relationships did not overlap with those coding for affiliative relationships. Such evidence of dissociation is powerful if a number of design issues are addressed; given tasks equated for sensitivity and difficulty, reliable dissociations are likely to signal processes that are at least partially distinct. Of course, dissociations cannot be claimed on the basis of one study (a lack of evidence that empathy activates TPJ in one study is not the same as evidence that empathy does not activate TPJ) but rather can be made on the basis of multiple studies with appropriate Bayesian statistics.

Studies demonstrating associations between different sociocognitive processes on the basis of shared activation are on shakier ground, however. Such studies find that one process activates a network including region A, and another process activates a more or less distinct network that also includes region A. The problem with this logic is that the unit of analysis common in fMRI studies may contain 7 to 9 million neurons. It is therefore perfectly possible that two processes activate distinct sets of neurons that cannot be distinguished with the existing spatial resolution of fMRI. More promising is a technique known as repetition suppression or fMRI adaptation, which takes advantage of the fact that repetition of a particular stimulus or stimulus class causes a reduction in the signal measured with fMRI. For example, in order to identify which brain areas encode facial identity, one can compare the neural activation elicited by a particular face when it is preceded by the same face to the neural activation elicited when it is preceded by a different face. If an area shows reduced activation to the repetition of the particular face, then it is concluded that the area codes for face identity rather than the mere presence of a face. The cellular mechanisms underlying such reduced activation are unclear (Grill-Spector et al. 2006), but the presence of repetition suppression is thought to reflect the activation of the same population of neurons. At present, this technique has been little used to examine the relationships among different sociocognitive processes, but if the assumption that suppression reflects activation of common neurons holds, it could prove a very powerful technique.

A further class of techniques seeks to find a differential impact of modulators—whether these be drugs, organic or experimental neurological lesions, personality types, or neurodevelopmental disorders—with the aim of demonstrating single or double dissociations. The logic of this approach is simple: If one factor can be shown to modulate sociocognitive process A without affecting sociocognitive process B, and another factor can be shown to modulate process B without affecting A, then we assume A and B are independent. We have already referred to the fact that ASD and psychopathy provide strong evidence for the independence of ToM and empathy; individuals with ASD appear to be impaired at ToM but not empathy, whereas individuals with psychopathy are impaired at empathy but not ToM (Jones et al. 2010). Such dissociations may also be observed with acquired brain lesions: One patient may experience a loss of premorbid ability in a particular social domain whereas another domain is unimpaired, but another patient may have the opposite pattern of deficits. For example, Calder (1996) reported the case of patient D.R., who had a specific impairment in recognizing fear but was able to recognize facial identity, and Tranel et al. (1995) reported a series of patients with acquired prosopagnosia, a deficit in recognizing facial identity, who were still able to recognize emotional facial expressions, including fear.

Although such examples are powerful, their effectiveness rests on the tests of social ability being very finely matched. If one test is speeded and another is not, if one requires holistic processing and another is featural, or if one makes demands on memory and another does not, then dissociations may reflect the differential demands of the tests rather than of the social abilities being tested. Furthermore, dissociations observed in patients with psychiatric or neurodevelopmental conditions or acquired brain lesions may reflect patterns of compensation (over development or in response to brain injury) within an atypical cognitive system. For example, Brewer et al. (2015) demonstrated that emotion recognition and moral reasoning are associated in typical individuals, an association thought to reflect the fact that moral judgments involve a combination of emotional processes, such as empathy, and the application of socially agreed-upon rules arrived at through deductive reasoning (Greene et al. 2001, 2004). In individuals with ASD, however, emotion recognition and moral reasoning are uncoupled, with the hypothesis being that those with ASD rely less on emotional heuristics in decision-making tasks (di Martino et al. 2008).

5.2. Recommendations for Further Progress

As we reviewed the little available literature on the structure of social cognition, it became clear that several factors may be inhibiting progress in this area. First, the vocabulary of sociocognitive ability is highly variable and nonspecific. Happé & Frith (2014) surveyed a multitude of social abilities that still represent only a fraction of the myriad hypothesized social abilities in the literature. The problem is that the relationship between the terms used for different sociocognitive abilities is often not specified, leading to the use of numerous terms that may or may not refer to the same construct. For example, affective ToM, emotion contagion, empathy, emotional mirroring, emotion understanding, and emotional resonance all appear to refer to remarkably similar, or even the same, processes. Therefore, it is difficult to integrate all of these terms into a factor structure of social cognition because they may be synonyms for a single ability. Adopting an agreed-upon lexicon for aspects of social abilities would likely accelerate research in this area and increase the comprehensiveness and utility of meta-analyses relating to these abilities. Such a lexicon is also likely to improve the consistency with which the results of certain tests are interpreted. For example, the Reading the Mind in the Eyes Test (RMET; Baron-Cohen et al. 2001) involves participants being presented with images of the eye region of faces and asked to pick (from four choices) the mental state or emotional term that best describes the image. This task has been claimed to index ToM, empathy, and emotion recognition, but a clear decomposition of task demands, or evidence of differential relationships to performance on other assays of these processes, is lacking. Adopting an agreed-upon lexicon would allow researchers to decide whether ToM, empathy, and emotion recognition are distinct entities and then to determine which is tested by the RMET and other commonly used tasks.

RMET: Reading the Mind in the Eyes Test

A second, potentially important, distinction to be made when determining the structure of social cognition is between the ability to carry out a social computation and the propensity to do so. The paradigmatic case for this distinction is ToM in ASD. When tested on explicit ToM tasks in a laboratory setting, intellectually able adults with ASD often perform at the same level as typical adults. In everyday life, however, individuals with ASD usually exhibit problems interacting with others, difficulties with pragmatic language understanding, and other impairments thought to result from impaired ToM. Assuming laboratory-based tests are sensitive enough to detect a ToM impairment should it exist, then a potential explanation for this discrepancy is that these adults with ASD are able to use ToM but have a reduced propensity to do so (see also Cage et al. 2013).

The distinction between ability and propensity may interact with our third recommendation, that a distinction should be drawn between system 1 and system 2 social processes. If there really are two routes by which a particular social task can be accomplished, then care should be taken to determine how participants are addressing the task: Are they using a fast, automatic, heuristic-based process, or are they instead using a slow, deliberative, rational approach? It may well be that the ability and propensity distinction interacts with the system 1 and system 2 distinction such that differences in propensity reflect the degree to which system 1 processes are automatically engaged during social interaction, whereas ability reflects the degree to which rational deliberative social reasoning (system 2) can produce accurate results.

Finally, there is growing evidence of significant cultural learning in the development of various social abilities (Heyes 2012b, Heyes & Frith 2014). Exposure to literature (Kidd & Castano 2013) and playing video games with a narrative story line (Bormann & Greitemeyer 2015) cause better performance on the RMET, and reading fiction increases self-reported empathy (Bal & Veltkamp 2013). Also, the degree to which mothers use mental state language predicts the development of mental state and emotion understanding in infants from 15 to 33 months of age (Taumoepeau & Ruffman 2006, 2008). The implication of this research is that tests need to be sensitive to participants' cultural background and developmental history. Although this fact has long been acknowledged within social perception research, where there is significant evidence of impaired facial identity recognition with other-race face stimuli, for example (Barkowitz & Brigham 1982, Chance et al. 1975, Chiroro & Valentine 1995, Elliott et al. 2013), it is less often appreciated in other areas of sociocognitive research. For example, although my ToM system may function perfectly in that it enables me to represent the propositional attitudes of others and how attitudes determine their behavior, if my developmental environment consists of a restricted range of individuals (with respect to political or religious affiliation, social class, education level, etc.), then I may frequently fail to infer accurately the mental states of others when in more mixed environments. Happé & Frith (1996), for example, suggested that conduct-disordered children from adverse family backgrounds might have developed a "theory of nasty minds." In everyday life, then, social abilities such as ToM, emotion recognition, and empathy may be determined by the range of minds one has encountered previously and is therefore able to model, as well as the accuracy with which one can determine which model to apply to a particular individual.

DISCLOSURE STATEMENT

The authors are not aware of any affiliations, memberships, funding, or financial holdings that might be perceived as affecting the objectivity of this review.

ACKNOWLEDGMENTS

We are grateful to our students and colleagues for discussion of relevant topics, and to Uta Frith and Essi Viding for their close reading of the manuscript and extremely helpful comments. All errors and opinions are, naturally, our own.

LITERATURE CITED

Anisfeld M. 1979. Interpreting "imitative" responses in early infancy. *Science* 205(4402):214–15

Annaz D, Campbell R, Coleman M, Milne E, Swettenham J. 2012. Young children with autism spectrum disorder do not preferentially attend to biological motion. *J. Autism Dev. Disord.* 42(3):401–8

Annaz D, Remington A, Milne E, Coleman M, Campbell R, et al. 2010. Development of motion processing in children with autism. *Dev. Sci.* 13(6):826–38

Proposes two systems for belief tracking: one efficient but inflexible, the other flexible but cognitively demanding.

Apperly IA, Butterfill SA. 2009. Do humans have two systems to track beliefs and belief-like states? *Psychol. Rev.* 116(4):953–70

Bal PM, Veltkamp M. 2013. How does fiction reading influence empathy? An experimental investigation on the role of emotional transportation. *PLOS ONE* 8(1):e55341

Barkowitz P, Brigham JC. 1982. Recognition of faces: own-race bias, incentive, and time delay. *J. Appl. Soc. Psychol.* 12(4):255–68

Baron-Cohen S. 2009. Autism: the empathizing-systemizing (E-S) theory. *Ann. N. Y. Acad. Sci.* 1156(1):68–80

Baron-Cohen S, Wheelwright S, Hill J, Raste Y, Plumb I. 2001. The "Reading the Mind in the Eyes" Test revised version: a study with normal adults, and adults with Asperger syndrome or high-functioning autism. *J. Child Psychol. Psychiatry* 42(2):241–51

Behrens TEJ, Hunt LT, Rushworth MFS. 2009. The computation of social behavior. *Science* 324(5931):1160–64

Behrens TEJ, Hunt LT, Woolrich MW, Rushworth MFS. 2008. Associative learning of social value. *Nature* 456(7219):245–49

Bird G, Press C, Richardson DC. 2011. The role of alexithymia in reduced eye-fixation in autism spectrum conditions. *J. Autism Dev. Disord.* 41(11):1556–64

Bird G, Silani G, Brindley R, White S, Frith U, Singer T. 2010. Empathic brain responses in insula are modulated by levels of alexithymia but not autism. *Brain J. Neurol.* 133(5):1515–25

Adopting a developmental framework, this article delineates a mechanistic (neuro)cognitive model of empathy.

Bird G, Viding E. 2014. The self to other model of empathy: providing a new framework for understanding empathy impairments in psychopathy, autism, and alexithymia. *Neurosci. Biobehav. Rev.* 47:520–32

Blake R, Turner LM, Smoski MJ, Pozdol SL, Stone WL. 2003. Visual recognition of biological motion is impaired in children with autism. *Psychol. Sci.* 14(2):151–57

Bonini L, Ferrari PF. 2011. Evolution of mirror systems: a simple mechanism for complex cognitive functions. *Ann. N. Y. Acad. Sci.* 1225:166–75

Boogert NJ, Giraldeau L-A, Lefebvre L. 2008. Song complexity correlates with learning ability in zebra finch males. *Anim. Behav.* 76(5):1735–41

Boorman ED, O'Doherty JP, Adolphs R, Rangel A. 2013. The behavioral and neural mechanisms underlying the tracking of expertise. *Neuron* 80(6):1558–71

Bormann D, Greitemeyer T. 2015. Immersed in virtual worlds and minds: effects of in-game storytelling on immersion, need satisfaction, and affective theory of mind. *Soc. Psychol. Personal. Sci.* 6(6):646–52

Brass M, Derrfuss J, von Cramon DY. 2005. The inhibition of imitative and overlearned responses: a functional double dissociation. *Neuropsychologia* 43(1):89–98

Brewer R, Marsh A, Catmur C, Cardinale E, Stoycos S, et al. 2015. The impact of autism spectrum disorder and alexithymia on judgments of moral acceptability. *J. Abnorm. Psychol.* 124(3):589–95

Butterfill SA, Apperly IA. 2013. How to construct a minimal theory of mind. *Mind Lang.* 28(5):606–37

Cage E, Pellicano E, Shah P, Bird G. 2013. Reputation management: evidence for ability but reduced propensity in autism. *Autism Res.* 6(5):433–42

Calder AJ. 1996. Facial emotion recognition after bilateral amygdala damage: differentially severe impairment of fear. *Cogn. J. Neuropsychol.* 13(5):699–745

Carruthers P. 2009. How we know our own minds: the relationship between mindreading and metacognition. *Behav. Brain Sci.* 32(2):121–38

Catmur C, Santiesteban I, Conway JR, Heyes C, Bird G. 2016. Avatars and arrows in the brain. *NeuroImage* 132:8–10

Catmur C, Walsh V, Heyes C. 2009. Associative sequence learning: the role of experience in the development of imitation and the mirror system. *Philos. Trans. R. Soc. B* 364(1528):2369–80

Chance J, Goldstein AG, McBride L. 1975. Differential experience and recognition memory for faces. *J. Soc. Psychol.* 97(2):243–53

Chawarska K, Ye S, Shic F, Chen L. 2016. Multilevel differences in spontaneous social attention in toddlers with autism spectrum disorder. *Child Dev.* 87(2):543–57

Chevallier C, Kohls G, Troiani V, Brodkin ES, Schultz RT. 2012. The social motivation theory of autism. *Trends Cogn. Sci.* 16(4):231–39

Chiroro P, Valentine T. 1995. An investigation of the contact hypothesis of the own-race bias in face recognition. *Q. J. Exp. Psychol. A* 48(4):879–94

Colombi C, Liebal K, Tomasello M, Young G, Warneken F, Rogers SJ. 2009. Examining correlates of cooperation in autism imitation, joint attention, and understanding intentions. *Autism* 13(2):143–63

Cook J, Bird G. 2012. Atypical social modulation of imitation in autism spectrum conditions. *J. Autism Dev. Disord.* 42(6):1045–51

Cook J, Saygin A, Swain R, Blakemore S. 2009. Reduced sensitivity to minimum-jerk biological motion in autism spectrum conditions. *Neuropsychologia* 47(14):3275–78

Cook J, Swapp D, Pan X, Bianchi-Berthouze N, Blakemore S-J. 2014a. Atypical interference effect of action observation in autism spectrum conditions. *Psychol. Med.* 44(4):731–40

Cook JL, den Ouden HEM, Heyes CM, Cools R. 2014b. The social dominance paradox. *Curr. Biol.* 24(23):2812–16

Cook R, Bird G. 2013. Do mirror neurons really mirror and do they really code for action goals? *Cortex* 49(10):2944–45

Cook R, Bird G, Catmur C, Press C, Heyes C. 2014. Mirror neurons: from origin to function. *Behav. Brain Sci.* 37(2):177–92

Dawson G. 1991. A psychobiological perspective on the early socioemotional development of children with autism. In *Rochester Symposium on Developmental Psychopathology*, Vol. 3, ed. S Toth, D Cicchetti, pp. 207–34. Hillsdale, NJ: Erlbaum

Dawson G. 2008. Early behavioral intervention, brain plasticity, and the prevention of autism spectrum disorder. *Dev. Psychopathol.* 20(3):775–803

Dawson G, Meltzoff AN, Osterling J, Rinaldi J, Brown E. 1998. Children with autism fail to orient to naturally occurring social stimuli. *J. Autism Dev. Disord.* 28(6):479–85

Dayan E, Casile A, Levit-Binnun N, Giese MA, Hendler T, Flash T. 2007. Neural representations of kinematic laws of motion: evidence for action-perception coupling. *PNAS* 104(51):20582–87

de Guzman M, Bird G, Banissy MJ, Catmur C. 2016. Self-other control processes in social cognition: from imitation to empathy. *Philos. Trans. R. Soc. B* 371(1686):20150079

de Vignemont F, Singer T. 2006. The empathic brain: how, when and why? *Trends Cogn. Sci.* 10(10):435–41

Diaconescu AO, Mathys C, Weber LAE, Daunizeau J, Kasper L, et al. 2014. Inferring on the intentions of others by hierarchical Bayesian learning. *PLOS Comput. Biol.* 10(9):e1003810

di Martino BD, Harrison NA, Knafo S, Bird G, Dolan RJ. 2008. Explaining enhanced logical consistency during decision making in autism. *J. Neurosci.* 28(42):10746–50

di Pellegrino G, Fadiga L, Fogassi L, Gallese V, Rizzolatti G. 1992. Understanding motor events: a neurophysiological study. *Exp. Brain Res.* 91(1):176–80

Duchaine B, Yovel G. 2015. A revised neural framework for face processing. *Annu. Rev. Vis. Sci.* 1(1):393–416

Eckerman CO, Whitehead H. 1999. How toddler peers generate coordinated action: a cross-cultural exploration. *Early Educ. Dev.* 10(3):241–66

Elliott ES, Wills EJ, Goldstein AG. 2013. The effects of discrimination training on the recognition of white and oriental faces. *Bull. Psychon. Soc.* 2(2):71–73

Elsabbagh M, Johnson MH. 2016. Autism and the social brain: the first-year puzzle. *Biol. Psychiatry* 80(2):94–99

Evans JSBT. 2008. Dual-processing accounts of reasoning, judgment, and social cognition. *Annu. Rev. Psychol.* 59(1):255–78

Fiorito G, Scotto P. 1992. Observational learning in *Octopus vulgaris*. *Science* 256(5056):545–47

Fiske ST, Taylor SE. 2013. *Social Cognition: From Brains to Culture*. London: Sage

Fletcher-Watson S, Findlay JM, Leekam SR, Benson V. 2008. Rapid detection of person information in a naturalistic scene. *Perception* 37(4):571–83

Frith U, Frith C. 2010. The social brain: allowing humans to boldly go where no other species has been. *Philos. Trans. R. Soc. B* 365(1537):165–76

Gallese V, Sinigaglia C. 2011. What is so special about embodied simulation? *Trends Cogn. Sci.* 15(11):512–19

Goren CC, Sarty M, Wu PYK. 1975. Visual following and pattern discrimination of face-like stimuli by newborn infants. *Pediatrics* 56(4):544–49

Green MF, Horan WP, Lee J. 2015. Social cognition in schizophrenia. *Nat. Rev. Neurosci.* 16(10):620–31

Greene JD, Nystrom LE, Engell AD, Darley JM, Cohen JD. 2004. The neural bases of cognitive conflict and control in moral judgment. *Neuron* 44(2):389–400

Greene JD, Sommerville RB, Nystrom LE, Darley JM, Cohen JD. 2001. An fMRI investigation of emotional engagement in moral judgment. *Science* 293(5537):2105–8

Grill-Spector K, Henson R, Martin A. 2006. Repetition and the brain: neural models of stimulus-specific effects. *Trends Cogn. Sci.* 10(1):14–23

Guillon Q, Hadjikhani N, Baduel S, Rogé B. 2014. Visual social attention in autism spectrum disorder: insights from eye tracking studies. *Neurosci. Biobehav. Rev.* 42:279–97

Hamilton AF. 2013. Reflecting on the mirror neuron system in autism: a systematic review of current theories. *Dev. Cogn. Neurosci.* 3:91–105

Hamilton AF, Brindley RM, Frith U. 2007. Imitation and action understanding in autistic spectrum disorders: How valid is the hypothesis of a deficit in the mirror neuron system? *Neuropsychologia* 45(8):1859–68

Happé F, Frith U. 1996. Theory of mind and social impairment in children with conduct disorder. *Br. J. Dev. Psychol.* 14(4):385–98

Happé F, Frith U. 2014. Annual research review: towards a developmental neuroscience of atypical social cognition. *J. Child Psychol. Psychiatry* 55(6):553–77

Happé FGE. 1994. An advanced test of theory of mind: understanding of story characters' thoughts and feelings by able autistic, mentally handicapped, and normal children and adults. *J. Autism Dev. Disord.* 24(2):129–54

Heiser M, Iacoboni M, Maeda F, Marcus J, Mazziotta JC. 2003. The essential role of Broca's area in imitation. *Eur. J. Neurosci.* 17(5):1123–28

Early paper showing reduced orienting to attention-grabbing stimuli (particularly social stimuli) in children with autism.

Uses dissociable deficits revealed by developmental disorders to outline a putative network of sociocognitive abilities.

Heyes C. 2012a. What's social about social learning? *J. Comp. Psychol.* 126(2):193–202

Heyes C. 2012b. Grist and mills: on the cultural origins of cultural learning. *Philos. Trans. R. Soc. B* 367(1599):2181–91

Heyes C. 2014a. False belief in infancy: a fresh look. *Dev. Sci.* 17(5):647–59

Heyes C. 2014b. Submentalizing: I am not really reading your mind. *Perspect. Psychol. Sci.* 9(2):131–43

Heyes C, Bird G. 2007. "Mirroring," association and the correspondence problem. In *Sensorimotor Foundations of Higher Cognition*, ed. Y Rossetti, P Haggard, M Kawato, pp. 461–79. Oxford, UK: Oxford Univ. Press

Heyes C, Pearce JM. 2015. Not-so-social learning strategies. *Proc. R. Soc. B* 282:20141709

Heyes CM, Frith CD. 2014. The cultural evolution of mind reading. *Science* 344(6190):1243091

Hobson P. 1989. Beyond cognition: a theory of autism. In *Autism: Nature, Diagnosis, and Treatment*, ed. G. Dawson, pp. 22–48. New York: Guilford

Hogeveen J, Obhi SS, Banissy MJ, Santiesteban I, Press C, et al. 2015. Task-dependent and distinct roles of the temporoparietal junction and inferior frontal cortex in the control of imitation. *Soc. Cogn. Affect. Neurosci.* 10(7):1003–9

Johnson MH. 2005. Subcortical face processing. *Nat. Rev. Neurosci.* 6(10):766–74

Jones AP, Happé FGE, Gilbert F, Burnett S, Viding E. 2010. Feeling, caring, knowing: different types of empathy deficit in boys with psychopathic tendencies and autism spectrum disorder. *J. Child Psychol. Psychiatry* 51(11):1188–97

Jones SS. 2009. The development of imitation in infancy. *Philos. Trans. R. Soc. B* 364(1528):2325–35

Kahneman D, Frederick S. 2002. Representativeness revisited: attribute substitution in intuitive judgment. In *Heuristics and Biases: The Psychology of Intuitive Judgment*, ed. T Gilovich, D Griffin, D Kahneman, pp. 49–81. New York: Cambridge Univ. Press

Kaiser M, Delmolino L, Tanaka J, Shiffrar M. 2010. Comparison of visual sensitivity to human and object motion in autism spectrum disorder. *Autism Res.* 3(4):191–95

Karmiloff-Smith A. 1996. *Beyond Modularity: A Developmental Perspective on Cognitive Science*. Cambridge, MA: MIT Press

Kidd DC, Castano E. 2013. Reading literary fiction improves theory of mind. *Science* 342(6156):377–80

Kikuchi Y, Senju A, Tojo Y, Osanai H, Hasegawa T. 2009. Faces do not capture special attention in children with autism spectrum disorder: a change blindness study. *Child Dev.* 80(5):1421–33

Klin A, Jones W. 2008. Altered face scanning and impaired recognition of biological motion in a 15-month-old infant with autism. *Dev. Sci.* 11(1):40–46

Klin A, Jones W, Schultz R, Volkmar F. 2003. The enactive mind, or from actions to cognition: lessons from autism. *Philos. Trans. R. Soc. B* 358(1430):345–60

Klin A, Jones W, Schultz S, Volkmar F, Cohen D. 2002. Visual fixation patterns during viewing of naturalistic social situations as predictors of social competence in individuals with autism. *Arch. Gen. Psychiatry* 59(9):809–16

Klin A, Lin D, Gorrindo P, Ramsay G, Jones W. 2009. Two-year-olds with autism orient to non-social contingencies rather than biological motion. *Nature* 459(7244):257–61

Klin A, Shultz S, Jones W. 2015. Social visual engagement in infants and toddlers with autism: early developmental transitions and a model of pathogenesis. *Neurosci. Biobehav. Rev.* 50:189–203

Klopfer PH. 1961. Observational learning in birds: the establishment of behavioral modes. *Behaviour* 17(1):71–80

Knutson B, Bossaerts P. 2007. Neural antecedents of financial decisions. *J. Neurosci.* 27(31):8174–77

Koldewyn K, Whitney D, Rivera SM. 2010. The psychophysics of visual motion and global form processing in autism. *Brain J. Neurol.* 133(Part 2):599–610

Kovács ÁM, Téglás E, Endress AD. 2010. The social sense: susceptibility to others' beliefs in human infants and adults. *Science* 330(6012):1830–34

Lefebvre L, Giraldeau L. 1996. Is social learning an adaptive specialization? In *Social Learning and the Roots of Culture*, ed. CM Heyes, BG Galef, pp. 107–52. San Diego: Academic

Leighton J, Bird G, Charman T, Heyes C. 2008. Weak imitative performance is not due to a functional "mirroring" deficit in adults with autism spectrum disorders. *Neuropsychologia* 46(4):1041–49

Lewis MD, Todd. 2005. Getting emotional: a neural perspective on emotion, intention, and consciousness. *J. Conscious. Stud.* 12(8–9):210–35

Argues that social learning relies on the mechanisms that support individual/asocial learning.

Argues that social learning relies on the mechanisms that support individual/asocial learning.

Argues that domain-general cognitive mechanisms (e.g., attentional orienting) can provide an efficient alternative to mentalizing.

Argues that the modular organization of the mind develops from the process of modularization.

Lockwood PL, Bird G, Bridge M, Viding E. 2013. Dissecting empathy: high levels of psychopathic and autistic traits are characterized by difficulties in different social information processing domains. *Front. Hum. Neurosci.* 7:760

McEwen F, Happé F, Bolton P, Rijsdijk F, Ronald A, et al. 2007. Origins of individual differences in imitation: links with language, pretend play, and socially insightful behavior in two-year-old twins. *Child Dev.* 78(2):474–92

Meltzoff AN, Moore MK. 1977. Imitation of facial and manual gestures by human neonates. *Science* 198(4312):75–78

Miller LE, Saygin AP. 2013. Individual differences in the perception of biological motion: links to social cognition and motor imagery. *Cognition* 128(2):140–48

Morton J, Frith U. 1995. Causal modelling: a structural approach to developmental psychopathology. In *Developmental Psychopathology*, ed. D Cicchetti, D Cohen, pp. 357–90. New York: Wiley

Morton J, Johnson MH. 1991. CONSPEC and CONLERN: a two-process theory of infant face recognition. *Psychol. Rev.* 98(2):164–81

Murphy P, Brady N, Fitzgerald M, Troje N. 2009. No evidence for impaired perception of biological motion in adults with autistic spectrum disorders. *Neuropsychologia* 47(14):3225–35

Onishi KH, Baillargeon R. 2005. Do 15-month-old infants understand false beliefs? *Science* 308(5719):255–58

Pelphrey K, Mitchell T, McKeown M, Goldstein J, Allison T, McCarthy G. 2003. Brain activity evoked by the perception of human walking: controlling for meaningful coherent motion. *J. Neurosci.* 23(17):6819–25

Peters J, Büchel C. 2010. Neural representations of subjective reward value. *Behav. Brain Res.* 213(2):135–41

Phillips J, Ong DC, Surtees ADR, Xin Y, Williams S, et al. 2015. A second look at automatic theory of mind: reconsidering Kovács, Téglás, and Endress (2010). *Psychol. Sci.* 26(9):1353–67

Press C, Richardson D, Bird G. 2010. Intact imitation of emotional facial actions in autism spectrum conditions. *Neuropsychologia* 48(11):3291–97

Purcell DG, Stewart AL. 1988. The face-detection effect: configuration enhances detection. *Percept. Psychophys.* 43(4):355–66

Quirin M, Meyer F, Heise N, Kuhl J, Küstermann E, et al. 2013. Neural correlates of social motivation: an fMRI study on power versus affiliation. *Int. J. Psychophysiol.* 88(3):289–95

Ray E, Heyes C. 2011. Imitation in infancy: the wealth of the stimulus. *Dev. Sci.* 14(1):92–105

Reader SM, Hager Y, Laland KN. 2011. The evolution of primate general and cultural intelligence. *Philos. Trans. R. Soc. B* 366(1567):1017–27

Reader SM, Laland KN. 2002. Social intelligence, innovation, and enhanced brain size in primates. *PNAS* 99(7):4436–41

Rizzolatti G, Craighero L. 2004. The mirror-neuron system. *Annu. Rev. Neurosci.* 27:169–92

Rizzolatti G, Fadiga L, Gallese V, Fogassi L. 1996. Premotor cortex and the recognition of motor actions. *Cogn. Brain Res.* 3(2):131–41

Rizzolatti G, Sinigaglia C. 2010. The functional role of the parieto-frontal mirror circuit: interpretations and misinterpretations. *Nat. Rev. Neurosci.* 11(4):264–74

Rogers S, Pennington B. 1991. A theoretical approach to the deficits in infantile autism. *Dev. Psychopathol.* 3(2):137–62

Salva OR, Farroni T, Regolin L, Vallortigara G, Johnson MH. 2011. The evolution of social orienting: evidence from chicks (*Gallus gallus*) and human newborns. *PLOS ONE* 6(4):e18802

Samson D, Apperly IA, Braithwaite JJ, Andrews BJ, Bodley Scott SE. 2010. Seeing it their way: Evidence for rapid and involuntary computation of what other people see. *J. Exp. Psychol. Hum. Percept. Perform.* 36(5):1255–66

Santiesteban I, Banissy MJ, Catmur C, Bird G. 2012a. Enhancing social ability by stimulating right temporoparietal junction. *Curr. Biol.* 22(23):2274–77

Santiesteban I, Banissy MJ, Catmur C, Bird G. 2015. Functional lateralization of temporoparietal junction—imitation inhibition, visual perspective-taking and theory of mind. *Eur. J. Neurosci.* 42(8):2527–33

Santiesteban I, Catmur C, Hopkins SC, Bird G, Heyes C. 2014. Avatars and arrows: implicit mentalizing or domain-general processing? *J. Exp. Psychol. Hum. Percept. Perform.* 40(3):929–37

Santiesteban I, White S, Cook J, Gilbert SJ, Heyes C, Bird G. 2012b. Training social cognition: from imitation to theory of mind. *Cognition* 122(2):228–35

Training the inhibition of imitation improved perspective-taking abilities arguably via training of self-other control.

Saxe R, Moran JM, Scholz J, Gabrieli J. 2006. Overlapping and non-overlapping brain regions for theory of mind and self reflection in individual subjects. *Soc. Cogn. Affect. Neurosci.* 1(3):229–34

Saygin A, Cook J, Blakemore S. 2010. Unaffected perceptual thresholds for biological and non-biological form-from-motion perception in autism spectrum conditions. *PLOS ONE* 5(10):e13491

Schultz W. 2000. Multiple reward signals in the brain. *Nat. Rev. Neurosci.* 1(3):199–207

Schwenck C, Mergenthaler J, Keller K, Zech J, Salehi S, et al. 2012. Empathy in children with autism and conduct disorder: group-specific profiles and developmental aspects. *J. Child Psychol. Psychiatry* 53(6):651–59

Senju A, Southgate V, White S, Frith U. 2009. Mindblind eyes: an absence of spontaneous theory of mind in Asperger syndrome. *Science* 325(5942):883–85

Sescousse G, Caldú X, Segura B, Dreher J-C. 2013. Processing of primary and secondary rewards: a quantitative meta-analysis and review of human functional neuroimaging studies. *Neurosci. Biobehav. Rev.* 37(4):681–96

Sevdalis V, Keller PE. 2011. Perceiving performer identity and intended expression intensity in point-light displays of dance. *Psychol. Res.* 75(5):423–34

Seyfarth RM, Cheney DL. 2015. Social cognition. *Anim. Behav.* 103:191–202

Shah P, Gaule A, Bird G, Cook R. 2013. Robust orienting to protofacial stimuli in autism. *Curr. Biol.* 23(24):R1087–88

Simion F, Valenza E, Macchi Cassia V, Turati C, Umiltà C. 2002. Newborns' preference for up-down asymmetrical configurations. *Dev. Sci.* 5(4):427–34

Singer T, Lamm C. 2009. The social neuroscience of empathy. *Ann. N. Y. Acad. Sci.* 1156(1):81–96

Sowden S, Catmur C. 2015. The role of the right temporoparietal junction in the control of imitation. *Cereb. Cortex* 25(4):1107–13

Sowden S, Koehne S, Catmur C, Dziobek I, Bird G. 2016. Intact automatic imitation and typical spatial compatibility in autism spectrum disorder: challenging the broken mirror theory. *Autism Res.* 9(2):292–300

Spengler S, Bird G, Brass M. 2010. Hyperimitation of actions is related to reduced understanding of others' minds in autism spectrum conditions. *Biol. Psychiatry* 68(12):1148–55

Stanovich KE. 1999. *Who Is Rational? Studies of Individual Differences in Reasoning*. Hove, UK: Psychol. Press

Taumoepeau M, Ruffman T. 2006. Mother and infant talk about mental states relates to desire language and emotion understanding. *Child Dev.* 77(2):465–81

Taumoepeau M, Ruffman T. 2008. Stepping stones to others' minds: Maternal talk relates to child mental state language and emotion understanding at 15, 24, and 33 months. *Child Dev.* 79(2):284–302

Templeton JJ, Kamil AC, Balda RP. 1999. Sociality and social learning in two species of corvids: the pinyon jay (*Gymnorhinus cyanocephalus*) and the Clark's nutcracker (*Nucifraga columbiana*). *J. Comp. Psychol.* 113(4):450–55

Tomalski P, Csibra G, Johnson MH. 2009. Rapid orienting toward face-like stimuli with gaze-relevant contrast information. *Perception* 38(4):569–78

Tranel D, Damasio H, Damasio AR. 1995. Double dissociation between overt and covert face recognition. *J. Cogn. Neurosci.* 7(4):425–32

Van Etten HM, Carver LJ. 2015. Does impaired social motivation drive imitation deficits in children with autism spectrum disorder? *Rev. J. Autism Dev. Disord.* 2(3):310–19

Van Overwalle F, Baetens K. 2009. Understanding others' actions and goals by mirror and mentalizing systems: a meta-analysis. *NeuroImage* 48(3):564–84

White S, Hill E, Happé F, Frith U. 2009. Revisiting the strange stories: revealing mentalizing impairments in autism. *Child Dev.* 80(4):1097–117

Wilkinson A, Kuenstner K, Mueller J, Huber L. 2010. Social learning in a non-social reptile (*Geochelone carbonaria*). *Biol. Lett.* 6(5):614–16

Toward a Social Psychophysics of Face Communication

Rachael E. Jack and Philippe G. Schyns

Institute of Neuroscience and Psychology, and School of Psychology, University of Glasgow, Glasgow G12 8QB United Kingdom; email: rachael.jack@glasgow.ac.uk

Annu. Rev. Psychol. 2017. 68:269–97

The *Annual Review of Psychology* is online at psych.annualreviews.org

This article's doi:
10.1146/annurev-psych-010416-044242

Keywords

reverse correlation, social communication, facial expressions, culture, social psychophysics

Abstract

As a highly social species, humans are equipped with a powerful tool for social communication—the face. Although seemingly simple, the human face can elicit multiple social perceptions due to the rich variations of its movements, morphology, and complexion. Consequently, identifying precisely what face information elicits different social perceptions is a complex empirical challenge that has largely remained beyond the reach of traditional methods. In the past decade, the emerging field of social psychophysics has developed new methods to address this challenge, with the potential to transfer psychophysical laws of social perception to the digital economy via avatars and social robots. At this exciting juncture, it is timely to review these new methodological developments. In this article, we introduce and review the foundational methodological developments of social psychophysics, present work done in the past decade that has advanced understanding of the face as a tool for social communication, and discuss the major challenges that lie ahead.

Contents

INTRODUCTION

As a species, humans have been immensely successful—they have grown rapidly in number, jour-neyed to and thrived in the most isolated and geographically diverse regions of the planet, and invented medical technologies to control nature (Roberts 2010). One of the main contributing fac-tors to this success is the evolution of humans as socially complex beings; individuals form groups to share labor, knowledge, and resources (Wilson 2012). Consequently, humans are one of the most socially sophisticated species on the planet, engaging in complex interactions to support the functioning of almost every facet of individual lives, including professional, familial, and personal relationships, and wider societal groups such as extended families, neighborhood communities, and workplace environments.

To support these complex social interactions, humans are equipped with a powerful tool—the face (although see also research on voice and body posture, e.g., Atkinson et al. 2004, Belin et al. 2008, Cordaro et al. 2015, Dael et al. 2012, de Gelder 2009, Grezes et al. 2007, Pollick et al. 2001, Roether et al. 2009, Scheiner & Fischer 2011). As a rich source of information, the human face can elicit myriad immediate social judgments—for example, about identity (e.g., Gauthier et al. 1999,

Haxby et al. 2000), gender or sex (e.g., Little et al. 2008, Thornhill & Gangestad 2006), age (e.g., Hummert 2014, Rhodes & Anastasi 2012), race or ethnicity (e.g., O'Toole et al. 1994, Tanaka et al. 2004), physical health (e.g., Grammer & Thornhill 1994, Jones et al. 2012), attractiveness (e.g., Perrett et al. 1998, Rhodes 2006), personality traits (e.g., Krumhuber et al. 2007, Oosterhof & Todorov 2008), sexual orientation (e.g., Freeman et al. 2010, Tskhay et al. 2013), emotions [e.g., Darwin 1999 (1872), Ekman et al. 1969], mental states (e.g., Cunningham et al. 2004, Nusseck et al. 2008), and even religious affiliation (e.g., Rule et al. 2010) and social status (e.g., in pigmentocracies, Telles 2014). In turn, social judgments can have significant consequences for individuals and groups, including influencing employment opportunities (e.g., Johnson et al. 2010), cross-cultural communication barriers (for a review, see Jack 2013), social isolation (e.g., Hawkley & Cacioppo 2007), voting preferences (e.g., Todorov et al. 2005), and sentencing decisions such as the death penalty (e.g., Eberhardt et al. 2006).

So salient is the face in human society that it has remained the object of fascination, admiration, examination, and debate for several centuries and across broad fields including biology, medicine, art, history, philosophy, psychology, anthropology, and law and, more recently, computer vision and social robotics. One of the most enduring and elusive goals across these fields is to understand how the face elicits the spectrum of social judgments that drives the variety of human behaviors described above. However, understanding how complex face information elicits social perception represents a complex empirical challenge that has largely remained beyond the reach of traditional research methods.

With the development of new research methods from an emerging multidisciplinary scientific culture, the field of social face perception is gaining traction on this question. One increasingly fruitful approach is social psychophysics, which has begun to derive law-like principles of social communication that relate variations of specific face information to specific social perceptions. In turn, such laws have the potential to inform the design of socially aware digital agents (e.g., virtual humans, social robots) that can generate realistic behaviors to communicate with and influence the behavior of different human user groups (e.g., students, children, clinical groups, and cross-cultural groups). In this review, we introduce and review the foundational methodological developments of social psychophysics, present work that has advanced understanding of the face as a tool for social communication, and discuss the major challenges ahead.

Social Communication is a System of Information Transmission and Decoding Across a Communication Channel

A useful first step in understanding how the face communicates social information is to appreciate the process of communication itself. Like many other forms of communication (e.g., animal mating calls, bacterial quorum sensing), human social communication involves one individual—the sender—transmitting information across a communication channel, which affects the behavior of another individual—the observer (see, e.g., Dukas 1998) or more precisely, as characterized in Shannon's communication model, the receiver (e.g., Shannon 1948). Although the precise definition of communication, including whether the sender or receiver should benefit from the exchange and the role of sender intention, is widely discussed (e.g., Scott-Phillips 2008), we will first focus on the sending and receiving of information between individuals and then discuss the specific aspects of communication that are relevant to understanding the face as a tool for social interaction.

Specifically, communication begins with a message (e.g., I am happy) being encoded as a form of information, such as a dynamic facial expression pattern. This information pattern is then transmitted via a communication channel to the receiver—in this case, the visual information pattern of a happy facial expression is transmitted through the medium of light (i.e., photons) to the visual system of another human. For communication to succeed, the transmitted information must first be detectable by the receiver. For example, the laws of optics predict that the fine-grained wrinkles around the eyes of a happy facial expression that project onto the receiver's fixed retina are visible only under specific constraints of the communication channel—in this case, relatively short viewing distances. In contrast, a broad smiling mouth revealing the teeth allows detection over longer viewing distances (Smith & Schyns 2009) by virtue of its larger size on the retina. We use viewing distance to illustrate how altering the communication channel—i.e., the distance across which the light-based information pattern must be transmitted—can affect the information that is available to the receiver. We discuss other factors that affect the communication channel (e.g., pose or illumination of the sender's face), including sources of noise in the channel (e.g., haze, occlusion of the face), below.

To decode the transmitted information, the receiver must use their prior knowledge—that is, concepts that are biologically, directly, or vicariously acquired—to extract task-relevant (i.e., diagnostic) information (see, e.g., Schyns 1998). For example, if the receiver aims to detect anger in a given individual (e.g., a spouse or close friend), they might focus their attention specifically on the face regions that reliably indicate anger in this person (e.g., the fixed eyes or tense mouth). The extracted pattern is then compared with a perceptual category that is stored in memory (i.e., a mental representation) and, if it matches, forms the basis of interpreting the message and meaning of the incoming information pattern (e.g., she is angry). Thus, the process of communication involves the human visual system performing the complex task of reducing the varying high-dimensional information impinging the retina (in this example, a complex pattern of face information embedded in a visual scene and transmitted over a variable communication channel) into a smaller set of meaningful categories that are used for adaptive behavior (e.g., spouse, anger, etc.).

In contrast, communication can break down if the transmitted information pattern does not correspond to the receiver's prior knowledge. For example, whereas certain face movements might indicate to a medical professional an underlying neurological condition such as Guillain-Barré syndrome, nonspecialists would derive little meaning from these face-movement patterns. Communication can also break down if the sender and receiver do not associate the information pattern with the same message and meaning. For example, in the United Kingdom, nodding and shaking the head mean yes and no, respectively, but the opposite is true in Bulgaria (see, e.g., Littlewood 2001; for other examples of cross-cultural miscommunication, see Labarre 1947, Morris 1979). Therefore, understanding any system of communication requires identifying which specific information patterns elicit a particular behavior in the receiver, such as the perception that an individual is trustworthy or happy. More specifically, understanding the receiver's stored information patterns—that is, their existing conceptual knowledge or mental representations—and their associated meanings can provide valuable insights into why communication breaks down. For example, comparing the face types associated with the same social message (e.g., trustworthiness or happiness) across cultures could reveal potential sources of miscommunication by showing cultural differences in the expected face movements, morphologies, or complexions.

Understanding the face as a tool for social communication therefore relies on identifying which specific face information elicits different social judgments and, by extension, the different mental representations of individuals in a given culture. However, both endeavors represent a major empirical challenge because (a) the face is a complex visual stimulus in which any dimension of face variation (e.g., movements, morphology, complexion) either individually or in combination could transmit a particular social message, and (b) the detailed mental representations of individuals are generally inaccessible and thus difficult to measure objectively. To further appreciate this challenge, we first detail the complexity of the face as a transmitter of social information before describing both classic and recent approaches used to address these challenges; the latter provide new traction on the issue of understanding mental representations and social face perception.

The Human Face Is a Complex, High-Dimensional Dynamic Information Space

Commensurate with its ability to elicit the perception of multiple intricate social categories, the face comprises several complex dimensions of variation of which three, movement, morphology, and complexion, have mainly been studied. We describe each dimension in turn in this section.

First, the face is equipped with a large number of independent, striated (i.e., voluntarily controlled) muscles that can each be activated individually or in concert to generate observable face movements such as nose wrinkling or smiling. These individual face movements are called Action Units (AUs) in the Facial Action Coding System (FACS) (Ekman & Friesen 1978), which is an objective system that taxonomizes human facial movements (for chimpanzee face movements, see Vick et al. 2007). FACS identifies over 40 AUs, such as the Upper Lid Raiser (AU5), Nose Wrinkler (AU9), and Lip Corner Puller (AU12), each of which can be combined to create complex AU patterns—i.e., facial expressions. Because facial expressions are dynamic, each individual AU can also be activated with specific temporal characteristics, including acceleration, amplitude, peak latency, and deceleration. Thus, considering all biologically plausible combinations of dynamic AUs—that is, the combinatorics of individual AUs that create multiple patterns and the specific temporal dynamics of each AU—the human face is capable of generating a high number of dynamic facial expressions.

Second, genetic variation such as that within and across ethnic groups in turn produces phenotypic variation in face shape and structure (i.e., morphology; see, e.g., Liu et al. 2012). Historically, the field of anthropometry, which aims to characterize the physical size, form, and function of humans, has used the top-down approach of naturalistic observation to identify up to 31 different dimensions of face variation, including jaw width, forehead height, and interpupillary distance (see, e.g., Zacharopoulos et al. 2016). Over the past three decades, rapid technical developments in face measurement have advanced from laser scanning (e.g., Arridge et al. 1985, Hill et al. 1997, Vetter & Troje 1997) to high-resolution digital camera capturing (e.g., Hammond & Suttie 2012, Yu et al. 2012) combined with specialized face-reconstruction algorithms (e.g., Blanz & Vetter 1999) to accurately render 3D face morphologies for scientific use [e.g., illumination (e.g., Braje et al. 1998), viewpoint dependence (e.g., Hill et al. 1995, Johnston et al. 2013), and identity (e.g., Leopold et al. 2001, Troje & Bülthoff 1996)] and computer animation. Thus, based on the several known dimensions of face variation, the number of phenotypically possible face shapes, including those associated with specific medical conditions (for a review, see Winter 1996), is simply huge.

Third, faces also vary in complexion, a dimension that comprises two main dimensions of variation: color, including melanin skin pigmentation and transient pallor or redness, and texture, including wrinkles, scarring, and cutaneous conditions. In the past, melanin skin pigmentation alone has been classified, according to von Luschan's chromatic scale, into 36 different color categories, from very light to olive to very dark (for an example of von Luschan's scale, see Howells 1960); more modern methods using spectrophotometry represent skin color with continuous (L*a*b) color values spanning numerous color categories, including purple, blue, pink, and yellow (see, e.g., Swiatoniowski et al. 2013). In addition, skin texture—i.e., relative smoothness—can vary across different scales, from microrelief lines and pitting or raising to larger, deeper markings, each of which can vary in orientation, location, and density, with specific statistics across different face regions (e.g., Lai et al. 2013).

Finally, as a salient platform for social communication, the face is also regularly adorned in a variety of ways, including cosmetics or painting, tattooing, scarring, jewelry, and hair, which are typically used to indicate social status or group alliances, or to accentuate beauty by enhancing or camouflaging aspects of face morphology or complexion. As a result of the numerous ways in which the face can vary, the 106 billion humans that have ever been born (Haub 2002) have each possessed a unique face that changes transiently throughout the course of each day and in more permanent ways throughout their lifetime.

As illustrated in this section, the face is a complex and variable visual stimulus that, due to recent technical developments, is only now becoming amenable to precise computational characterizations of its information content and thus to rigorous experimental control. Such developments represent a major turning point in the goal of understanding how the face communicates different social information, and identifying within the complex face information space of movements, morphology, and complexion the specific subspaces that elicit specific social perceptions. Before detailing the advantages of these newly developed methods, it is useful to review both the current state of knowledge in the field and one of the classic approaches to addressing this question.

USING THE HUMAN RECEIVER TO UNDERSTAND THE FACE AS A TOOL FOR SOCIAL COMMUNICATION

A glance at any face demonstrates how quickly and apparently effortlessly humans extract face information to make a diverse array of social judgments (see, e.g., Bar et al. 2006, Macrae & Bodenhausen 2000). Commensurate with both the social sophistication of humans and the complexity of the face, the human visual system has coevolved as an efficient and accurate pattern classifier, particularly of social information.

Unsurprisingly then, using the receiver to identify which face information elicits social judgments, as Darwin and many others since have done, has remained one of the most popular methods in the field. One such classic approach involves presenting photographs or videos of real faces and asking receivers to categorize each according to a set of social categories such as basic emotions (e.g., Biehl et al. 1997), personality traits (e.g., Little & Perrett 2007), or health (e.g., Fink et al. 2006). Based on the receiver's responses and the observable or inferred characteristics of the faces, such as certain facial expressions or the person's ethnicity, age, or sex, the receiver's social judgments are then attributed to one or more of these facial characteristics. For example, male faces tend to be perceived as more dominant than female faces (e.g., Burriss et al. 2007)—i.e., the stimulus category male is associated with higher ratings of perceived dominance than the stimulus category female.

However, the capacity of this approach to understand the face as a tool for social communication relies on its implementation, where traditional use of this method typically provides a relatively narrow account. Specifically, the classic approach described above only associates one category label (e.g., male) with another (e.g., dominant) without showing what specific face information communicates dominance (or sexual dimorphism, the category of male or female). Consequently, it does not address the information ontology of the categorization task—i.e., specific information present in male faces that elicits the social perception of dominance. To understand the face as a tool for social communication, information ontologies are of central importance because they functionally link the stimulus (i.e., specific face information) to behavior (i.e., social perception) and thereby provide a lower bound on the information the receiver's brain must process to produce the behavior in question (Schyns et al. 1998, 2009).

Methodological developments designed to address the limitations of such classic approaches and to characterize the information ontologies of social perception have arisen primarily from the field of psychophysics, which aims to measure the relationship between objectively measurable dimensions of a stimulus (e.g., luminance and contrast) and subjective perception (e.g., edge detection). Specifically, psychophysical methods tend to parametrically vary the different dimensions of a stimulus, such as hue and luminance; measure how such variations modulate a given perception, such as color brightness; and derive a law-like model of the relationship using, for example, signal detection theory (Swets et al. 1963) or reverse correlation (Ahumada & Lovell 1971). Thus, psychophysical laws reveal the critical stimulus information that subtends specific perceptions. Another powerful feature of psychophysical methods is that they tend to be data driven—i.e., stimulus information is sampled agnostically (but typically within the limits of biological possibility or theoretical assumptions, a point we discuss below) and tested against the spectrum of a given perception, which typically extends from no perception to perceptual threshold to saturation (e.g., Snodgrass 1975). Adopting such a data-driven approach and making few a priori assumptions about what information will elicit a specific perception therefore allows for a much broader and potentially more informative exploration of a given space of visual information when attempting to identify what information modulates perception. By extension, psychophysical approaches are thus well suited to understanding what specific face information subtends social perception.

However, as illustrated in the section The Human Face is a Complex, High-Dimensional Dynamic Information Space, the human face is a substantially more complex multidimensional stimulus than those typically used in psychophysical experiments on perception, such as a simple Gabor patch image, which comprises only three dimensions of frequency, contrast, and orientation that can each be easily manipulated. How then can a psychophysical approach be expanded to test complex face-movement patterns, morphology, and complexion information against social perception? In the following sections, we review some of the main psychophysical methods that have been developed to successfully address this question.

SOCIAL PSYCHOPHYSICS: DERIVING THE PSYCHOPHYSICAL LAWS OF SOCIAL PERCEPTION

As mentioned in the previous section, psychophysical methods typically sample information from a space with few dimensions and test these samples against perception to derive a psychophysical law. Ideally, a psychophysical law of social face perception would detail the contribution of face movements, morphology, complexion, and their combinations to the perception of different social categories. To achieve this, information-sampling methods have taken three main forms: exposing face information in a stimulus, adding noise to a face stimulus, or generating face information from a model. We describe each using examples in the sections below.

Exposing Face Information to Identify Diagnostic Information

In the field of social face perception, researchers tend to use specific sets of standardized stimuli (e.g., Beaupré et al. 2000, Langner et al. 2010, Lundqvist et al. 1998, Matsumoto & Ekman 1988) to probe different social perceptions and their associated brain activities (Doty et al. 2014). However, classic use of these stimuli cannot identify the information ontology of a social perception—i.e., what stimulus information is driving behavior (or brain activity). To address this limitation, the Bubbles method (Gosselin & Schyns 2001) randomly samples information directly from the stimulus and tests these samples against perception to derive what is typically referred to as a classification image—i.e., an image showing the visual information associated with a given perceptual decision. **Figure 1** demonstrates the procedure using the six classic facial expressions of emotion (see Schyns et al. 2007, Smith et al. 2005).

The rationale of the Bubbles method is that the receiver can only categorize the information samples accurately when they comprise task-relevant (i.e., diagnostic) information; for example,

Exposing information: 3D pixels (2D pixels × spatial frequency bands)

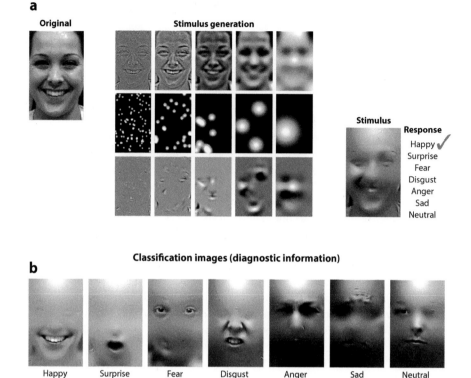

Figure 1

Exposing face information. (*a*) Using the Bubbles method (Gosselin & Schyns 2001), a stimulus (*original*) is decomposed into five nonoverlapping spatial frequency bandwidths, each of which are sampled independently with randomly positioned Gaussian windows (the second row of images shows the windows and the third row shows the resulting samples of face information at each bandwidth). The samples of face information (plus a constant, coarser, nonsampled sixth scale not pictured here) are then summed to produce a stimulus (*stimulus*), which the receiver categorizes according to the six classic emotions (i.e., *happy*, *surprise*, *fear*, *disgust*, *anger*, or *sad*, plus *neutral*); in this example, the response is *happy*. (*b*) To identify the stimulus information required for the accurate categorization of each facial expression of emotion, the image pixels leading to significantly high accuracy at each scale independently are located ($p < 0.05$, greater than 75% correct) and represented in a classification image. Each classification image shows the resulting diagnostic face information for each emotion. Figure adapted from Smith et al. 2005 with permission.

happy is correctly identified because the smiling mouth and the wrinkled eyes are exposed. In contrast, when the random samples do not comprise task-relevant information, the receiver will tend to make an incorrect categorization. Subsequently, by building the relationship between each sampled pixel location at each spatial frequency band and the receiver's correct and incorrect responses (e.g., using correlation, linear regression, or mutual information; see, e.g., Schyns et al. 2011, van Rijsbergen & Schyns 2009), the Bubbles method can reveal the face-information ontology of each categorization task. **Figure 1*b*** shows the information ontologies for the six classic emotions, which comprise smaller subspaces (sets of pixels) of the original image space. For example, recognition of *fear* requires subsets of pixels representing the eyes, *surprise* the open mouth, and *disgust* the wrinkled nose and raised upper lip. Overlap of features between expressions, such as the wide opened eyes in both fear and surprise or the wrinkled corners of the nose in both disgust and anger, predicts their behavioral confusions (Smith et al. 2005). Applying the same method to brain activity data such as electroencephalography sensors or magnetoencephalography sources that each form algorithmic brain networks can also reveal the dynamic flow of these information ontologies in the brain (Ince et al. 2015, Schyns et al. 2007).

Whereas the Bubbles method provides some insight into the content of a receiver's mental representations (i.e., stored information patterns), the information ontology obtained is bound to the actual content of the stimuli used, which can therefore limit the characterization of mental representations. For example, standardized FACS coded facial expressions of fear and disgust systematically elicit significantly lower accuracy in receivers belonging to non-Western cultures (for a review, see Nelson & Russell 2013), which suggests that these particular stimuli do not comprise an information ontology that is close enough to the cultural receiver's mental representations to enable typical recognition performance. An alternative approach to characterizing mental representations is to sample and test face information outside the limits of a specific set of stimuli. How can such information be created? In the following section, we illustrate one method designed to address this question by, seemingly paradoxically, adding pixel noise to a face stimulus.

Adding Pixel Noise to Model New Face Information

As shown in **Figure 2**, adding noise such as random grayscale pixel values (**Figure 2a**) to a neutral face image can create a perceptively different stimulus. In this example, the receiver categorizes the stimulus as expressive (e.g., of anger) if the random pattern formed by the neutral base face plus noise corresponds (by chance) with their mental representation of that facial expression. If it does correspond, then the white noise template on this trial contains information that corresponds with this receiver's mental representation of a specific facial expression (anger). Thus, to visualize the information content of the receiver's mental representations of different facial expressions (e.g., the six classic emotions), each set of noise templates associated with each emotion category response can be averaged to compute classification images. In this case, the classification image is then added to the neutral base face to visualize how the pattern alters the face. The two faces in the center show the resulting representations of *sad* and *anger* for individual receivers. **Figure 2a** also shows the results from individuals of different cultures (i.e., Western, East Asian). Specifically, Westerners required information to be added to both the eye and mouth regions to perceive emotions, whereas East Asians required much more information to be added to the eyes, for example by changing gaze direction (see Jack et al. 2011). A similar approach using structured (Gabor) noise (**Figure 2b**) is used to generate local multiscale random contours on an age-neutral face to estimate, in older and younger adults, the mental representations that underlie their judgments of the chronological age of a face (van Rijsbergen et al. 2014).

Adding noise with more or less intrinsic structure has the advantage of creating for the receiver face information that is not limited to the parameters of an underlying stimulus; this approach also derives the information ontology objectively in a bottom-up manner using the receiver's perceptual response (see the sidebar, Using Noise to Characterize a System; **Figure 3**). In social psychology, this approach has been used successfully to reveal cultural differences in the mental representations of facial expressions of emotion (Jack et al. 2011), aggression in the mental representations of faces of ethnic out-group members amongst prejudiced individuals (Dotsch et al. 2008), the unattractiveness of newly learned female faces in happily partnered males (Karremans et al. 2011), and the homogenization of older adult faces in the mental representations of younger adults (van Rijsbergen et al. 2014). In visual cognition, this approach has also been used fruitfully

Adding noise: 2D pixels

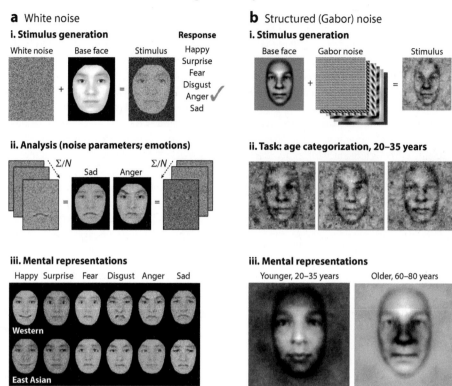

Figure 2

Adding noise to a face. We illustrate two such approaches using (*a*) white noise and (*b*) structured (Gabor) noise. (*a, i*) Adding noise to a neutral base face creates a perceptively different stimulus, which the receiver categorizes according to the six classic emotions if the pattern formed in the stimulus corresponds with their mental representation of that facial expression (in this case, *anger*). (*a, ii*) To identify the face information associated with the perception of each emotion, we compute a classification image by averaging the set of noise templates associated with each emotion category response (in this case, *sad*, outlined in red, and *anger*, outlined in green) and add it to the base face (*central faces*). (*a, iii*) Each face shows a model of an individual receiver's mental representations of each of the six facial expressions of emotion in two cultures: Western (*top row*) and East Asian (*bottom row*). Panel adapted from Jack et al. 2011 with permission. (*b*) Structured (Gabor) noise can also be used to generate local multiscale contours on a neutral base face to identify which face information subtends judgments of chronological age. Panel adapted from van Rijsbergen et al. (2014) with permission.

to estimate mental representations of face identity (e.g., Mangini & Biederman 2004) and even idiosyncratic letter fonts and smiling faces (Gosselin & Schyns 2003).

Such methods have provided several substantial knowledge advances in understanding the social perception of faces and, in the best cases, estimating the information content of mental representations, in itself a feat in cognitive psychology. However, these methods also have several drawbacks. First, estimating the relationship between each individual pixel of the noise template and the receiver's social judgments (see the discussion of the first-order kernel in the sidebar, Using Noise to Characterize a System) typically requires several thousand trials per participant because each pixel is considered a statistically independent parameter to estimate (unless assumptions can be made about the relationship between individual pixels, such as local correlations of

USING NOISE TO CHARACTERIZE A SYSTEM

Volterra (1930) and Wiener (1958) showed that a system F can be reduced to a sum of subsystems F_i if we estimate the kernels (internal functions) f_i of each subsystem by sampling white noise and measuring the system's output response. Imagine we instruct a human that they will see white noise images (of 32×43 pixels) with half of the images comprising a face hidden in the noise. Although their task is to detect the face, only white noise is ever presented. In each experimental trial, the observer uses their expectation of what a face looks like (i.e., their first- and higher-order kernels f_i) and matches this expectation with the incoming white noise. A small positive correlation between the incoming pixel noise and the first-order kernel f_1 of the brain enables the observer to respond with the perception of a face when the input is only noise. We characterize f_1 by computing the correlation between each of the 32×43 pixels (either black or white on each trial) and the detection behavior (face versus no face).

their luminance values). Second, certain face features can be difficult to capture; for example, a deep horizontal wrinkle on the forehead for judgments of older faces would require the unlikely horizontal arrangement of many black and white pixels present on several trials. Rather, a fragment of the horizontal wrinkle is more likely to appear on a given trial, leading the receiver to categorize the face as older. Subsequently, averaging the noise templates associated with older categorizations could result in a horizontal wrinkle across the forehead based on different spatially located wrinkle fragments present in individual trials. Ideally, a full horizontal wrinkle could be revealed using many trials and higher-order analyses of the noise templates—i.e., interactions between two, three, four, or n pixels (see the sidebar Using Noise to Characterize a System, in which pixel order corresponds to kernel order). However, as can be understood intuitively, doing so would be subject to the curse of dimensionality (Bellman 1956) and require a practically impossible number of trials. Nevertheless, first-order analyses, as illustrated in **Figure 2**, can suggest potential candidates for relevant higher-order features, such as deep horizontal wrinkles, that

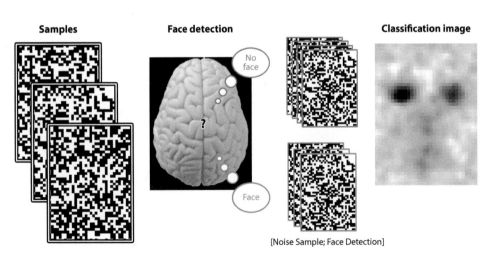

Samples   **Face detection**   **Classification image**

No face

?

Face

[Noise Sample; Face Detection]

Figure 3

The first-order kernel f_1, the classification image that estimates the information content of the face prediction of one typical observer (Smith et al. 2012). The classification image depicts the relationship between single-trial random pixel values (0 or 1) and face detection behavior (face detected or not), schematized as [Noise Sample; Face Detection].

can then be tested for their contribution to social perception (e.g., age judgments) in an explicit experiment.

The above discussion highlights an important consideration for data-driven methods: What information should we sample? For example, rather than sampling individual pixel noise, could we generate information directly from specific higher-order axes of information, such as patterns of face movements, or from multivariate dimensions of 3D face morphology that each constitute a specific hypothesis on the social perception in question (e.g., judgments of personality traits)? The aim of a multivariate approach is to hone in on (and therefore reduce) the relevant parameters for a given perceptual task by capturing the variance of the stimuli in a few axes of information that are tailored to the task at hand. In the following section, we illustrate such an approach using recent methodological developments that can represent and sample higher-order face information such as face movements, morphology, and complexion.

Generating Face Information from Higher-Order Axes of Information

As described in the section The Human Face is a Complex, High-Dimensional Dynamic Information Space, the individual movements of the face, the AUs, can each be animated and combined to create a variety of dynamic facial expressions. To identify which specific dynamic AU patterns communicate specific social messages to individuals in a given culture, psychophysical methods can be used to directly sample the dynamic information space—i.e., dynamic AUs—and test them against perception. **Figure 4** illustrates this method with one example trial.

Compared to classic methods that typically present a limited set of specific facial expression patterns derived from theory, such as FACS-coded facial expressions of emotion, this generative approach allows for a much broader exploration of face-movement patterns as candidates for social communication, including that of emotions (Jack et al. 2012, 2016); mental states such as confusion, interest, and boredom (Chen et al. 2015); and personality traits such as trustworthiness, dominance, and attractiveness (Gill et al. 2014). The above technique of generating face information directly from the higher-order, multivariate information space of dynamic AUs is therefore directly extendable to the multivariate 3D information spaces of face morphology and complexion. **Figure 5** demonstrates the approach using two examples of its application: precisely

---

Figure 4

Generating face information using 4D Action Units (AUs). (*a*) In each experimental trial, a Generative Face Grammar platform (GFG) (Yu et al. 2012) randomly selects a subset of AUs (*red, green, and blue labels*), in this case Upper Lid Raiser (AU5), Nose Wrinkler (AU9), and Upper Lip Raiser (AU10), from a core set of 42 AUs and assigns a random movement to each AU individually using six temporal parameters: onset latency, acceleration, peak amplitude, peak latency, deceleration, and offset latency (*labels over the red curve*). The GFG then combines the randomly activated AUs to produce a photorealistic facial animation (shown with four snapshots across time). As in **Figures 1** and **2**, the receiver categorizes the stimulus as socially meaningful (*disgust*) and rates the intensity of the perceived emotion (strong) when the dynamic pattern correlates with their mental representation of that facial expression. Building a relationship between the dynamic AUs presented in each trial and the receiver's categorical responses produces a mathematical model of each dynamic facial expression of emotion. (*b*) By including the often-neglected but important dimension of dynamics (for a review, see Krumhuber et al. 2013), such an approach can reveal systematic temporal patterns of face movements: for example, that dynamic facial expressions of emotion transmit face movements in an evolving hierarchy over time, characterized by the transmission of shared face movements early in the time course (e.g., Upper Lid Raiser in both *surprise* and *fear*) and different diagnostic face movements later in the time course (e.g., Brow Raiser in *surprise* and Lip Stretcher in *fear*; see Jack et al. 2014).

controlling specific 3D face morphology or complexion associated with different ages, ethnicities, etc. (**Figure 5a–c**) and generating novel identities for a reverse correlation approach (**Figure 5d**).

At this juncture, it is useful to consider the main differences between generating face information directly from a lower-dimensional multivariate space such as dynamic AUs (e.g., 42 AUs × 6 temporal parameters = 252 dimensions) and generating information from a higher-dimensional univariate space such as pixel noise (e.g., 380 × 280 pixel noise = 106,400 dimensions). First, using a lower-dimensional space will require much fewer trials to estimate the face information subtending perception. Second, each dimension of the lower-dimensional space, such as 3D face complexion variations, represents an explicit hypothesis about the information ontology for a

Generating face information: 4D Action Units

a Modelling dynamic facial expressions

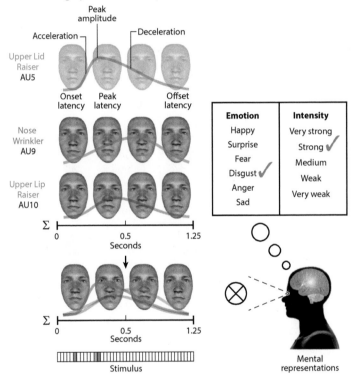

b Hierarchical transmission of face movements over time

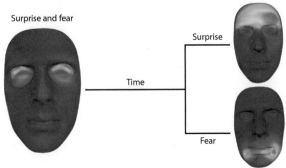

given social perception (e.g., health). Consequently, each resulting psychologically meaningful information subspace—e.g., a specific combination of face color and texture—is bound by the underlying generative information space—e.g., dimensions of 3D face complexion. In contrast, because higher-dimensional noise is not structured, it could in principle reconstruct any face information with sufficiently many trials. However, the curse of dimensionality imposes practical

Generating face information: 3D vertices

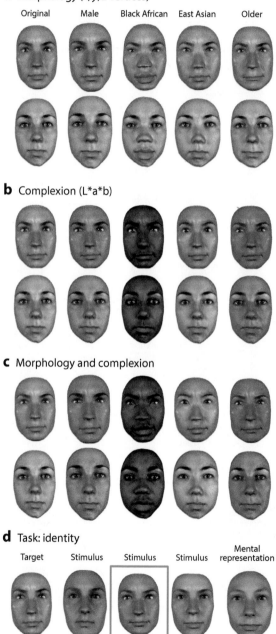

a Morphology (*x, y, z* vertices)

Original Male Black African East Asian Older

b Complexion (L*a*b)

c Morphology and complexion

d Task: identity

Target Stimulus Stimulus Stimulus Mental representation

limitations on what can be accomplished with noise, especially when adding dynamics to model face movements or color for complexion. Thus, when designing an experiment based on such psychophysical information-sampling methods, it is critical to carefully consider the axes of information that should be sampled because each axis (e.g., face movements) is an explicit hypothesis on the information thought to be relevant for a given social perception and will thus bound the models that can be derived.

In the above sections, we have demonstrated three main approaches using the classic reverse correlation method in psychophysics to understand what face information drives social perception. We now discuss the strengths of this approach before addressing some concerns raised about its use.

Advantages of a Data-Driven Approach

Using a data-driven approach provides several advantages. First, psychophysical methods tend to sample information with few a priori assumptions about what face information subtends social judgments. Such an approach makes intuitive sense for the practice of objective investigation and is particularly relevant when studying unfamiliar groups such as different cultures or clinical populations in which existing knowledge is insufficient to provide useful guidance. Consider the scenario of identifying which female physiques are considered desirable in sub-Saharan African cultures. Showing photographs of Coco Chanel or Kate Moss—both Western icons of beauty—to individuals in these cultures would not reveal the sought-after information ontology. Without a more objective, data-driven approach, the female body shapes that are considered desirable in sub-Saharan African cultures—traditionally, clinically obese women—might never even be considered by the Western experimenter (and vice versa). Instead, one approach would be to sample the multivariate variations of 3D human bodies against perceptions of beauty in both cultures (e.g., Mautz et al. 2013). Such an approach could thus be instrumental in bridging the apparently large knowledge gap in psychology arising from the long tradition of empirical and theoretical approaches focused on WEIRD (Western, educated, industrialized, rich, and democratic) cultures (Henrich et al. 2010).

Second, a well-designed information-sampling space, such as one made up of dynamic AUs, multivariate dimensions of 3D face morphology, or color (typically L^*a^*b space), provides a precise visual information space to build rich information ontologies of a variety of social perceptions. Consequently, the resulting information subspaces can reflect a more comprehensive account

←

Figure 5

Generating face information using 3D vertices. This reverse correlation approach has been applied to generate and test (*a*) 3D face morphology, (*b*) complexion, and (*c*) their combinations to (*d*) model the mental representations of face identity. (*a*) Each row of faces shows a different face identity (*original*) that has been transformed using samples of 3D face morphology variation obtained from four different groups (see the labels above each face), with all other dimensions of face variation (i.e., movement and complexion) held constant. (*b*) The same procedure is applied to 3D complexion. (*c*) The 3D face information from panels *a* and *b* is combined, similar to other methods used to model face information associated with personality judgments such as trustworthiness and dominance (e.g., Oosterhof & Todorov 2008). (*d*) Each novel face stimulus (*stimulus*) is created by sampling 3D face morphology variation from the target identity's gender, age, and ethnic group (*target*). In each trial, the receiver selects (*red outline*) the face stimulus that most resembles the target identity based on memory alone. Established statistical procedures such as regression or mutual information, applied to the selected set of face morphologies, provide an estimate of the receiver's mental representation of the target identity (*mental representation*). Methods such as these can therefore be used to precisely generate, control, and test 3D face morphology and/or complexion information subtending judgments of identity (e.g., family resemblance), gender, ethnicity, age, and so on.

of the contribution of face information characterized in quantitative terms, which can support precise, objective analysis and comparison, for example across cultures.

Third, once they are identified, information ontologies behave in a law-like manner. Diagnostic information such as the specific dynamic AU patterns of a positive surprise facial expression in East Asian culture (Jack et al. 2016) could be applied to other East Asian face identities to communicate this social message effectively in this culture. Therefore, one of the main and immediate benefits of developing such generative models is their direct transference to the digital economy via digital agents. For example, social robots and virtual humans are increasingly used in mainstream society to serve a variety of functions, including health care intervention, intelligent tutoring (e.g., social skills training for doctors), companionship, and entertainment (e.g., via the gaming industry) (see, e.g., Morency et al. 2015). Developing and applying such formalisms of face signaling to the design of socially interactive digital agents would allow the generation of realistic and culturally sensitive behaviors with reliable impact on a human user's social judgments (see, e.g., Vinciarelli et al. 2009).

Fourth, the methods outlined above are generic and can thus be used to sample any objectively measureable information space, whether visual, auditory, tactile, olfactory, or gustatory, and to test against almost any form of receiver response, including corresponding sensory perceptions, neural activity (Schyns et al. 2009; for a review, see Wu et al. 2006), or more complex cognitions and behaviors such as approach and avoidance patterns. Sampling combinations of these information spaces can thus further inform the interactive contributions of different sources of information in eliciting a range of behaviors.

CONCERNS RAISED ABOUT REVERSE CORRELATION METHODS

A number of concerns are often raised when psychophysical methods are used to explore social (i.e., high-level) perception. We address these concerns in the following sections.

Why Sample Visual Information? Why Not Instead Increase the Sample Size of Stimuli?

One argument against controlling high-level visual information, as described in this review, is that what can be achieved with reverse correlation methods could also be achieved, in principle, by increasing the number of stimuli used in an experimental design. After all, a typical experimental design implicitly samples visual information by sampling a finite set of stimuli assumed to comprise the visual categories of the design (e.g., classic facial expressions of emotion). If this sampling could be infinite, then by definition it would comprise all the dimensions of variance that can be found in naturalistic stimuli. There is one major flaw with this argument, which makes a practical consequence necessary: Stimulus sets are finite because experimental time is finite. Thus, we cannot test a posteriori all possible dimensions of variance, having collected all possible behavioral or neural responses to all possible stimuli. Instead, increasing the fixed number of stimuli inevitably samples information in an implicit, uncontrolled manner. Consequently, we cannot derive the information ontology of a categorization (including social categorizations) unless we explicitly control and sample visual information.

The Link Between Production and Perception

A commonly raised point is that reverse correlation methods measure the perception but not the production of face information and thus the resulting models of information ontology might only represent a subjective perceptual experience that does not reflect what is actually transmitted by the sender. In addressing this concern, it is worthwhile to revisit some fundamental principles, first of general communication and then specifically of visual perception.

First, such concerns imply that the information pattern transmitted by the sender (e.g., a facial expression of anger) is uncorrelated, either in large part or wholly, with the information patterns that elicit perceptions in the receiver (i.e., the information subset, diagnostic information for anger); in other words, perception and production are two independent processes. Instead, as discussed extensively in human (e.g., Scott-Phillips 2008), animal (e.g., Dukas 1998), and human-made (e.g., Shannon 1948) communication systems, the production and perception of information forms a tightly knit symbiotic relationship in which the capabilities of both sender and receiver shape the ontology of the information patterns that are produced and used for communication. Specifically, if the sender transmits an information pattern that is not meaningful to the receiver (i.e., one that does not correspond to the receiver's prior knowledge), communication tends to break down. Consequently, any such ineffective transmissions will tend to become extinct and replaced with one that is meaningful to the receiver. Thus, the production of information is inextricably shaped by the perceptual and cognitive capabilities of the receiver. One relevant observation from signal phylogeny is that a small discrepancy between the production and the perception of information is necessary for signal evolution (e.g., Arak & Enquist 1993). Thus, precisely identifying and measuring this discrepancy is relevant to further understanding the nature and development of signals for human social communication (although there is also a distinction between signals, cues, and coercion; see, e.g., Dezecache et al. 2013).

Second, long-standing knowledge of human visual perception shows that there is indeed a distinction between what is produced (i.e., transmitted) and what is perceived (i.e., received and decoded). Specifically, the identification of visual events such as objects, faces, or scenes relies only on a subset of the information that is perceptually available to the receiver (i.e., detectable information) (see, e.g., Schyns 1998). Indeed, classic change-blindness experiments provide elegant demonstrations that not all information transmitted in the environment and perceptually available to the receiver is perceived and memorized (e.g., Simons & Rensink 2005). Classic Bubbles experiments have also shown that not all perceptually available information is necessary for accurate perceptual categorization (e.g., Gosselin & Schyns 2002). Thus, understanding communication—e.g., of social categories via the face—requires identifying which subset of the transmitted information subtends the perception of a given social category and so does not necessarily require identifying all that is transmitted (e.g., facial dynamics are unlikely to be necessary for categorizations of ethnicity). Understanding why certain face information is not used for perceptual judgments could further inform the social and biological functions of produced face information, particularly if production is voluntary and costly, as is the case for face movements. For example, a facial expression of disgust might include several different AUs, but accurate perception might only rely on a subset of them (e.g., Nose Wrinkler, Upper Lip Raiser). If only two AUs are necessary and sufficient for accurate recognition, what function, if any, do the others serve? Future work comparing produced face information with the subset that subtends perception could address such questions.

Analyzing Produced Face Information

In research that focuses on facial expressions, one often-cited alternative to using the receiver to characterize their patterns is to record and analyze spontaneously produced facial expressions. Although this approach should provide a useful complement to a perception-based approach, a number of inherent difficulties currently limit its utility.

Facial expression elicitation methods such as film clips (e.g., Gross & Levenson 1995) or images (e.g., Lang et al. 2005) typically generate complex combinations of internal states at different times—for example, a disgusting film could elicit horror, surprise, and anger—with correspondingly complex combinations of face movement patterns over time. How then can this stream of face movements be interpreted? How can the signs of specific internal states (e.g., horror, surprise, or anger) be extracted? Such difficulties are most evident in computer vision, in which automatic detection systems must first be equipped with knowledge of different facial expression patterns to match and categorize incoming information. A common suggestion to decode the complex stream of face movements is to use human receivers—expert pattern classifiers, particularly of social signals—to interpret the produced facial expressions at each time point. Of course, this is exactly the approach of perception-based reverse correlation methods and thus reflects the strength and intuitive simplicity of the approach. Therefore, although analyzing produced facial expressions is clearly a relevant line of investigation, developing a precise knowledge of the dynamic patterns that communicate different social categories is also necessary. One constructive future research direction would be to develop methods that can precisely compare perception-based models of facial expressions with spontaneously produced facial expressions using, for example, automatic decoding of AUs and their temporal parameters.

Ecological Validity

Another common concern about reverse correlation methods is that the face stimuli created by sampling (e.g., Bubbles), adding (e.g., white noise), or generating (e.g., Generative Face Grammar) information lack ecological validity and that using real, unobscured images, videos, or live humans more closely represents genuine social interactions. Although methods that use such stimuli arguably provide a more authentic scenario (while usually not incorporating ecological conditions such as occlusion), they typically cannot identify the information ontology that drives behavior—a point highlighted above in the review of the classic approach to understanding social face perception. Such arguments highlight the ever-present tension between achieving ecological validity and obtaining meaningful results, a point that must be discussed constructively to successfully guide research. We open this discussion by considering some often-cited alternatives and evaluating what they can deliver.

First, in the spirit of a psychophysical approach, one solution is to select images or videos of real faces or to use live humans who vary in one aspect of the face (e.g., skin color) while others are controlled (e.g., facial expression) and then to measure the receiver's response to this variation in the stimulus set (e.g., ratings of attractiveness). However, each real face is a unique identity that necessarily comprises a specific morphology (i.e., shape and structure) that will elicit specific social judgments such as attractiveness, trustworthiness, and dominance (e.g., Oosterhof & Todorov 2008). Consequently, the resulting stimulus set of real faces will inevitably include uncontrolled socially relevant variations that could confound results unless they are fully randomized. Resolving this issue using a finite set of images, videos, or live humans represents a substantial, if not impossible, practical challenge.

A second, often-suggested solution to the problems of using images or videos of real faces or using live humans is to track the receiver's eye movements to study which samples of information are extracted from the stimulus to resolve a given task such as interpreting facial expressions. However, eye movements alone can only index the information in the stimulus that the receiver has fixated and cannot show which information in the fixated content is effectively used for the task (i.e., the diagnostic information). For example, task-relevant information is often extracted extrafoveally (e.g., Blais et al. 2008, Eriksen & James 1986), and not all fixations made during the task are necessary for accurate perception (Hsiao & Cottrell 2008). To address some of these limitations, new eye-tracking methods that separate foveal versus extrafoveal information (e.g., Miellet et al. 2011) or combine eye-tracking data with statistical modeling techniques (e.g., Jack et al. 2009, Peterson & Eckstein 2012) provide the required link between stimulus information and behavior to reveal the diagnostic information. Nevertheless, the use of images, videos, or live humans cannot be used to characterize the information ontology of social perception because these real face stimuli comprise fixed information sources that cannot be flexibly manipulated to correspond to a receiver's mental representations.

Data-Driven Reverse Correlation Methods Are Atheoretical

Data-driven reverse correlation approaches are often described as atheoretical because they make few a priori assumptions about what information will elicit a specific perception. Put more accurately, such methods fundamentally acknowledge that the subspace representing the information ontology of a social category is currently unknown. For example, are judgments of trustworthiness based only on face morphology, or do face movements and complexion also play a role? What about judgments of health or social status? Thus, each dimension of the sampling space (e.g., face movements, morphology, and complexion) in fact forms an explicit hypothesis about the information that is potentially relevant for the social category considered (e.g., trustworthiness, health, social status).

Consequently, the initial challenge of using these methods is to design an information-sampling space that can accurately capture the information ontology for the social category considered. The second challenge is the potential combinatorial explosion of the sampling space used to test against social perceptions—consider, for example, the vastness of a space comprising all variations of face movements, morphology, and complexion. To address these challenges of accuracy and tractability, a creative exercise combining both theoretical and empirical knowledge must be undertaken, first to develop a plausible set of dimensions to sample (e.g., multivariate facial movement patterns to investigate emotion communication) and later to explore how other dimensions (e.g., skin color) might modulate perception. Thus, by using theoretical and empirical knowledge to design and test specific information spaces, the results of data-driven approaches can in turn contribute to the development of existing theories and generate new conceptual advances, thereby both fostering and benefitting from a symbiotic theory–data relationship. In the following sections, we describe some ways to guide the application of psychophysical methods to the high-dimensional and complex stimuli that are typically used in the field of social perception.

GUIDING THE USE OF PSYCHOPHYSICAL METHODS

Understanding Sender and Receiver Capabilities Across a Communication Channel

The initial challenge of applying reverse correlation methods is to design an information-sampling space that could accurately capture the information ontology for a given social category while keeping the problem tractable. In our view, this problem remains possibly the most difficult to solve and still requires considerable creative inputs.

In defining such an information space, the most obvious consideration is the physical constraints of the sender and receiver: the human face and visual system, respectively. In the section The Link Between Production and Perception, we discussed briefly the constraint that the information transmitted by the sender must be at least detectable by the receiver. For example, certain colors and contrasts cannot be distinguished by the human eye, and detailed information is visible only at relatively short viewing distances (see, e.g., Palmer 1999). Thus, aside from the general biological constraints of the human visual system (e.g., the density and functional nature of retinal receptors), one of the major factors affecting receiver capabilities is the communication channel itself: the medium of light across which visual information is transmitted. Similar to the face, the communication channel is itself a space comprised of different dimensions: distances, illumination, pose, and forms of noise such as occlusion and environmental haze, each of which can impact receiver capability. For example, at short viewing distances all six classic emotions—*happy*, *surprise*, *fear*, *disgust*, *anger*, and *sad*—can be accurately identified from the face based on the perceptual availability of specific face-movement patterns (Smith et al. 2005). However, as viewing distance increases, performance decreases for certain emotion categories because the detailed diagnostic information—e.g., the wide-opened eyes for fear—is no longer perceptually available to the receiver (Smith & Schyns 2009). Thus, defining the information-sampling space in accordance with the receiver's capabilities depends critically on the constraints of the communication channel that will be used.

With respect to sender capabilities, if the sender is not capable of successfully transmitting information across a specific communication channel—e.g., using the eye whites to communicate fear across a long viewing distance—or if the face information is biologically implausible—e.g., extremely rapid muscle movements, highly saturated colors, or extremely large eyes or tiny mouths—then this information could be omitted from the sampling space. One notable exception is the exploration of superstimuli: exaggerated forms of a stimulus that can elicit stronger responses in the receiver than the original stimulus, such as highly conspicuous courtship and aggression displays (see, e.g., Tinbergen 1948), and that contribute to signal evolution (e.g., Arak & Enquist 1993). Although superstimuli tend to be beyond the sender's current capabilities, characterizing them still involves identifying, within the original stimulus, the information that elicits a specific response in order to create and test exaggerated versions of the stimulus.

Interactions Between Theory and Data-Driven Approaches

The design of an information-sampling space can also be informed by theoretical considerations. For example, consider the perceptual judgments that might influence mate choice. This behavior likely involves finding an individual who is in good health and has certain desirable behaviors, such as trustworthiness, warmth, or competence. Although good health is probably indicated by genetically determined (i.e., relatively fixed) aspects of the face, such as symmetry and complexion (e.g., Jones et al. 2012), behavioral intentions, such as trustworthiness and warmth, are more likely indicated by voluntarily produced face information such as facial expressions (e.g., Gill et al. 2014).

Thus, the data-driven methods advocated in this review could be used to model the face movement patterns associated with desirable mate behaviors—e.g., trustworthiness, warmth, and competence—thereby reducing the dynamic information space (i.e., dynamic AUs) to a set of dynamic facial expression models. The resulting models could then be combined with other potentially relevant aspects of face information, such as complexion, to derive a bivariate law of social perception relevant for mate choice. Consequently, such an approach can also explore the important question of how voluntary (i.e., face movements) and involuntary (i.e., morphology and complexion) aspects of the face influence the receiver's judgments within an ecological niche. For example, in countries with racial tension, can voluntarily produced facial expressions associated with trustworthiness override the negative stereotype judgments elicited by involuntary facial cues such as skin color?

Exploring the Expanded Social Information Space

In this review, we have described some initial practical steps to exploring how combinations of the complex dimensions of face movements, morphology, and complexion elicit social judgments. Beyond face information, such social judgments could also be influenced by other factors, such as context, the presence (or absence) or other nonverbal information (e.g., body movements or vocalizations), and the communication channel (e.g., short or long viewing distances). As with the dimensions of face variation, each additional potential source of variation nonlinearly increases the complexity of understanding social perception. Thus, although each of these factors might contribute to social perception in some way, it is simply practically impossible to include them all in a full reverse correlation design.

One tractable solution to this problem is to initially model the dimensions that are likely to be most relevant for a given social perception (e.g., face morphology for attractiveness) before adding other potentially relevant dimensions such as body movements, vocalizations, context, and differing communication channels. Consequently, researchers can increasingly refine fundamental models of social perception that capture the main sources of variation, including by demonstrating the robustness of social perception under different conditions (e.g., viewpoint invariance of familiar face recognition). However, this refinement requires sampling a defined and objectively measurable information space. Where no such space exists, one must be created in accordance with existing empirical knowledge or theoretical considerations. For example, although context could be highly relevant for certain social perceptions (see, e.g., Van Bavel et al. 2016), it is not yet well defined or easily measured. In fact, context could be one of the most complex dimensions to test because it spans a broad range of factors, including the social function of the interaction (e.g., cooperation, competition), the current emotional state of sender and/or receiver (e.g., celebrating, mourning), the nature and history of their relationship (e.g., healthy professional, tense spousal), and the physical environment (e.g., hospital, church, workplace, school, outdoors). The challenges of formalizing such knowledge so that it is amenable to sampling indicate that context is one of the most difficult problems in understanding what drives behavior, requiring considerable creative inputs.

CONCLUSION

In this review, we have introduced and reviewed the foundational methodological developments of social psychophysics—a data-driven approach that can estimate the information ontology subtending social perceptions—with a specific focus on face information. In doing so, we have also highlighted the main strengths of this approach, particularly in addressing the limitations of classic approaches in understanding the face as a tool for social communication, one of the longest-standing and most elusive goals in psychology and other fields such as computer vision.

In looking to the future, it is important to consider the historical trajectory of the fields of psychophysics and social face perception and the more recent development of social psychophysics [a term coined by Davis (1963)]. Psychophysics is one of the oldest fields in psychology and long preceded the classic face recognition studies performed in the mid-twentieth century. However, its application to social face perception has developed substantially within the past decade, made possible by rapid advances in technology, such as 3D scanning of faces and computational manipulations of stimuli. Creating stimuli with precise characterization and control of face movements, morphology, and complexion would simply not have been possible prior to such advances and in fact would have likely hindered the development of fundamental knowledge arising from these earlier studies. In the absence of sufficient methodological advances, classic theory-driven approaches such as Darwin's [1999 (1872)] and Ekman's (e.g., Ekman et al. 1969) laid the empirical and theoretical foundations of understanding the face as a tool for social communication. With rapid advances in technology and methods such as those described in this review, new data-driven approaches can build upon this knowledge to drive the field forward.

This exciting juncture represents a major turning point in the field, and several benefits arise from the arrival of mature social psychophysics. Primarily, social psychophysics can deliver the first formal models—psychophysical laws—that detail the precise contribution of face movements, morphology, and complexion to the variety of social perceptions used for social interactions within and across cultures. Psychophysical laws can support the advancement of knowledge in several ways, including the development of new theories of social face perception that unify fragmented lines of research on face movements, morphology, and complexion, which tend to be studied in isolation. Social psychophysics could also address several outstanding questions, including the in-group facial expression recognition advantage (see, e.g., Elfenbein 2015), encoding of in- and out-group faces (e.g., Adams et al. 2010, Young & Hugenberg 2012), the other race effect (see Tanaka 2013), and racial stereotyping (e.g., Bijlstra et al. 2010).

The development of such knowledge could have a significant impact in fields beyond psychology, such as computer vision and social robotics, and in wider society. For example, modern society increasingly demands the use of digital agents for a variety of functions, including day-to-day services (e.g., car rental, supermarket shopping, banking); medical and military training; therapeutic interventions; and communication in cyberspace, often across cultures. To be effective, digital agents must generate signals that reliably produce certain behaviors in human users, such as purchasing healthy foods or feeling empathy toward out-group members. Thus, precisely characterizing the algorithms of social perception—i.e., the psychophysical laws—can inform the design of the digital agents of the future and contribute to the development of the digital economy.

Finally, the shift toward a more symbiotic theory–data relationship that bridges the (at least perceived) traditionally disparate scientific cultures of vision science and social psychology is timely for several reasons. Importantly, such relationships can counter the theoretical and empirical stagnation that can arise from the isolation or perceived hierarchy of scientific cultures. For example, theoretical knowledge is sometimes used to judge the value of empirical data, as when theoretically derived AU patterns are used as a gold standard to measure facial expressions despite their low cross-cultural validity. Consequently, embracing a new scientific culture that recognizes the inherent complementarity of these different fields will encourage novel empirical endeavors, such as testing facial expression patterns or social categories not yet represented by existing theories, and facilitate the importation of new methods and knowledge from other fields to address them.

In conclusion, we stand on the brink of a new scientific horizon that promises an era of genuine creativity and the potential to make significant strides in understanding the face as a tool for social communication. Such advances will facilitate the prominent role that social psychology must play in the burgeoning science of social robotics.

SUMMARY POINTS

1. As one of the most socially sophisticated species on the planet, humans are equipped with a powerful tool for social communication: the face, which, by virtue of its complex variations in movements, morphology, and complexion, can transmit a broad spectrum of social categories from age and sex to social status and trustworthiness. In turn, such perceptions can have significant consequences, including influencing employment opportunities, voting behaviors, and sentencing decisions such as the death penalty.

2. Understanding which aspects of the face information—i.e., specific variations in face movement patterns, morphology, complexion, or their combination—drive social perceptions has long remained a central question in psychology, philosophy, anthropology, and biology and, more recently, computer vision. However, because the face is a complex, high-dimensional dynamic information space, characterizing the information ontologies of social face perception has remained largely beyond the reach of traditional research methods.

3. New data-driven methods developed in the field of psychophysics can help resolve these issues by deriving law-like principles of social communication that relate variations of face information to social perception, thereby revealing the information ontologies of social face perception.

4. Such data-driven psychophysical methods typically sample information that can be transmitted by the sender (e.g., variations of face movements) across a specific communication channel (e.g., long or short viewing distances) and then measure the receiver's response (e.g., perception of emotion).

5. Psychophysical data-driven approaches have several advantages, including enabling a broader exploration of the social information space due to the application of few a priori assumptions about what information drives perception, a precise and formal characterization of the information ontology of social perception, and the capacity to generate information ontologies.

6. Often-raised concerns about data-driven methods include aspects of ecological validity and lack of theoretical grounding.

7. The use of psychophysical methods to understand social perception can be guided by existing empirical knowledge, such as knowledge of sender and receiver capabilities, and theoretical considerations. Thus the field of social psychophysics is well suited to both contribute to and benefit from a mutually beneficial theory–data relationship.

8. The advent of social psychophysics represents an exciting new juncture in the field of human social perception and communication, which has the potential to develop existing theories, generate new conceptual advances, resolve existing questions (e.g., the in-group facial expression recognition advantage, the other race effect, and racial stereotyping), and foster a symbiotic theory–data relationship within a multidisciplinary scientific culture.

9. This framework can also contribute to the development of knowledge that can be transferred to the digital economy via social robots and virtual humans.

FUTURE ISSUES

1. Because data-driven methods can be applied to any objectively measurable stimulus information space (e.g., auditory, visual) and linked to measurable behaviors (e.g., perceptual categories, neural activity, decisions), social psychophysics methods can be further developed to explore the extended social environment (e.g., body movements, vocalizations, contextual factors) and thus refine knowledge of nuanced and complex social perceptions.

2. Data-driven methods also make few a priori assumptions about which information subtends behavior and are therefore well suited to examine social perception in different cultures and atypical groups. Consequently, data-driven approaches could make a significant contribution to advancing knowledge in currently underrepresented non-WEIRD and clinical populations.

3. Law-like principles of social communication have the capacity to generate information ontology, which can be transferred to the digital economy via social robots and virtual humans. Consequently, the field of social psychophysics can inform the design of digital agents of the future so that they can generate realistic behaviors that reliably impact human user engagement.

DISCLOSURE STATEMENT

The authors are not aware of any affiliations, memberships, funding, or financial holdings that might be perceived as affecting the objectivity of this review.

ACKNOWLEDGMENTS

We thank Larry Barsalou and Simon Garrod for their insightful and constructive comments on an earlier draft of this review. P.G.S. and R.E.J. received support from the Economic and Social Research Council (ES/K00607/X/1). P.G.S. received support from the Wellcome Trust (Senior Investigator Award, UK; 107802) and the Multidisciplinary University Research Initiative/Engineering and Physical Sciences Research Council (USA, UK; 172046-01). R.E.J. received support from the British Academy (UK; SG113332) and the Economic and Social Research Council (UK; ES/K001973/1).

LITERATURE CITED

Adams RB, Pauker K, Weisbuch M. 2010. Looking the other way: the role of gaze direction in the cross-race memory effect. *J. Exp. Soc. Psychol.* 46:478–81

Ahumada A, Lovell J. 1971. Stimulus features in signal detection. *J. Acoust. Soc. Am.* 49:1751–56

Arak A, Enquist M. 1993. Hidden preferences and the evolution of signals. *Philos. Trans. R. Soc. Lond. Biol. Sci.* 340:207–13

Arridge S, Moss JP, Linney AD, James DR. 1985. Three dimensional digitization of the face and skull. *J. Maxillofac. Surg.* 13:136–43

Atkinson AP, Dittrich WH, Gemmell AJ, Young AW. 2004. Emotion perception from dynamic and static body expressions in point-light and full-light displays. *Perception* 33:717–46

Bar M, Neta M, Linz H. 2006. Very first impressions. *Emotion* 6:269–78

Beaupré M, Cheung N, Hess U. 2000. *The Montreal set of facial displays of emotion.* Slides, Dep. Psychol., Univ. Quebec Montr.

Belin P, Fillion-Bilodeau S, Gosselin F. 2008. The Montreal Affective Voices: a validated set of nonverbal affect bursts for research on auditory affective processing. *Behav. Res. Methods* 40:531–39

Bellman R. 1956. Dynamic programming and Lagrange multipliers. *PNAS* 42:767–69

Biehl M, Matsumoto D, Ekman P, Hearn V, Heider K, et al. 1997. Matsumoto and Ekman's Japanese and Caucasian Facial Expressions of Emotion (JACFEE): reliability data and cross-national differences. *J. Nonverbal Behav.* 21:3–21

Bijlstra G, Holland RW, Wigboldus DH. 2010. The social face of emotion recognition: evaluations versus stereotypes. *J. Exp. Soc. Psychol.* 46:657–63

Blais C, Jack RE, Scheepers C, Fiset D, Caldara R. 2008. Culture shapes how we look at faces. *PLOS ONE* 3:e3022

Blanz V, Vetter T. 1999. A morphable model for the synthesis of 3D faces. *Proc. Annu. Conf. Comput. Graph. Interact. Techn., 26th, Los Angeles, Aug. 8–13*, pp. 187–94. New York: ACM Press

Braje WL, Kersten D, Tarr MJ, Troje NF. 1998. Illumination effects in face recognition. *Psychobiology* 26:371–80

Burriss RP, Little AC, Nelson EC. 2007. 2D:4D and sexually dimorphic facial characteristics. *Arch. Sex. Behav.* 36:377–84

Chen C, Garrod O, Schyns P, Jack R. 2015. The face is the mirror of the cultural mind. *J. Vis.* 15:928

Cordaro DT, Keltner D, Tshering S, Wangchuk D, Flynn LM. 2015. The voice conveys emotion in ten globalized cultures and one remote village in Bhutan. *Emotion* 16:117–28

Cunningham DW, Kleiner M, Bülthoff HH, Wallraven C. 2004. The components of conversational facial expressions. *Proc. Symp. Appl. Percept. Graph. Vis., 1st, Los Angeles, Aug. 7–8*, pp. 143–50. New York: ACM Press

Dael N, Mortillaro M, Scherer KR. 2012. The body action and posture coding system (BAP): development and reliability. *J. Nonverbal Behav.* 36:97–121

Darwin C. 1999 (1872). *The Expression of the Emotions in Man and Animals*. London: Fontana Press

Davis JA. 1963. Intellectual climates in 135 American colleges and universities: a study in "social psychophysics." *Sociol. Educ.* 37:110–28

de Gelder B. 2009. Why bodies? Twelve reasons for including bodily expressions in affective neuroscience. *Philos. Trans. R. Soc. Biol. Sci.* 364:3475–84

Dezecache G, Mercier H, Scott-Phillips TC. 2013. An evolutionary approach to emotional communication. *J. Pragmat.* 59:221–33

Dotsch R, Wigboldus DH, Langner O, van Knippenberg A. 2008. Ethnic out-group faces are biased in the prejudiced mind. *Psychol. Sci.* 19:978–80

Doty TJ, Japee S, Ingvar M, Ungerleider LG. 2014. Intersubject variability in fearful face processing: the link between behavior and neural activation. *Cogn. Aff. Behav. Neurosci.* 14:1438–53

Dukas R. 1998. *Cognitive Ecology: The Evolutionary Ecology of Information Processing and Decision Making*. Chicago: Univ. Chicago Press

Eberhardt JL, Davies PG, Purdie-Vaughns VJ, Johnson SL. 2006. Looking deathworthy: perceived stereotypicality of Black defendants predicts capital-sentencing outcomes. *Psychol. Sci.* 17:383–86

Ekman P, Friesen W. 1978. *Facial Action Coding System: A Technique for the Measurement of Facial Movement*. Sunnyvale, CA: Consult. Psychol. Press

Ekman P, Sorenson ER, Friesen WV. 1969. Pan-cultural elements in facial displays of emotion. *Science* 164:86–88

Elfenbein HA. 2015. In-group advantage and other-group bias in facial emotion recognition. In *Understanding Facial Expressions in Communication*, ed. MK Mandal, A Awasthi, pp. 57–71. Berlin: Springer

Eriksen CW, James JDS. 1986. Visual attention within and around the field of focal attention: a zoom lens model. *Percept. Psychophys.* 40:225–40

Fink B, Grammer K, Matts PJ. 2006. Visible skin color distribution plays a role in the perception of age, attractiveness, and health in female faces. *Evol. Hum. Behav.* 27:433–42

Freeman JB, Johnson KL, Ambady N, Rule NO. 2010. Sexual orientation perception involves gendered facial cues. *Personal. Soc. Psychol. Bull.* 36:1318–31

Gauthier I, Tarr MJ, Anderson AW, Skudlarski P, Gore JC. 1999. Activation of the middle fusiform 'face area' increases with expertise in recognizing novel objects. *Nat. Neurosci.* 2:568–73

Gill D, Garrod OG, Jack RE, Schyns PG. 2014. Facial movements strategically camouflage involuntary social signals of face morphology. *Psychol. Sci.* 25:1079–86

Gosselin F, Schyns PG. 2001. Bubbles: a technique to reveal the use of information in recognition tasks. *Vis. Res.* 41:2261–71

Gosselin F, Schyns PG. 2002. RAP: a new framework for visual categorization. *Trends Cogn. Sci.* 6:70–77

Gosselin F, Schyns PG. 2003. Superstitious perceptions reveal properties of internal representations. *Psychol. Sci.* 14:505–9

Grammer K, Thornhill R. 1994. Human (*Homo sapiens*) facial attractiveness and sexual selection: the role of symmetry and averageness. *J. Comp. Psychol.* 108:233–42

Grezes J, Pichon S, De Gelder B. 2007. Perceiving fear in dynamic body expressions. *NeuroImage* 35:959–67

Gross JJ, Levenson RW. 1995. Emotion elicitation using films. *Cogn. Emot.* 9:87–108

Hammond P, Suttie M. 2012. Large-scale objective phenotyping of 3D facial morphology. *Hum. Mutat.* 33:817–25

Haub C. 2002. How many people have ever lived on Earth? *Popul. Today* 30:3–4

Hawkley LC, Cacioppo JT. 2007. Aging and loneliness: downhill quickly? *Curr. Dir. Psychol. Sci.* 16:187–91

Haxby JV, Hoffman EA, Gobbini MI. 2000. The distributed human neural system for face perception. *Trends Cogn. Sci.* 4:223–33

Henrich J, Heine S, Norenzayan A. 2010. The weirdest people in the world? *Behav. Brain Sci.* 33:61–83

Hill H, Bruce V, Akamatsu S. 1995. Perceiving the sex and race of faces: the role of shape and colour. *Proc. R. Soc. Lond. Biol. Sci.* 261:367–73

Hill H, Schyns PG, Akamatsu S. 1997. Information and viewpoint dependence in face recognition. *Cognition* 62:201–22

Howells WW. 1960. The distribution of man. *Sci. Am.* 203:113–30

Hsiao JH-W, Cottrell G. 2008. Two fixations suffice in face recognition. *Psychol. Sci.* 19:998–1006

Hummert ML. 2014. Age changes in facial morphology, emotional communication, and age stereotyping. In *The Oxford Handbook of Emotion, Social Cognition, and Problem Solving in Adulthood*, ed. P Verhaeghen, C Hertzog, pp. 47–60. Oxford, UK: Oxford Univ. Press

Ince RA, Van Rijsbergen NJ, Thut G, Rousselet GA, Gross J, et al. 2015. Tracing the flow of perceptual features in an algorithmic brain network. *Sci. Rep.* 5:17681

Jack RE. 2013. Culture and facial expressions of emotion. *Vis. Cogn.* 21:1248–86

Jack RE, Blais C, Scheepers C, Schyns PG, Caldara R. 2009. Cultural confusions show that facial expressions are not universal. *Curr. Biol.* 19:1543–48

Jack RE, Caldara R, Schyns PG. 2011. Internal representations reveal cultural diversity in expectations of facial expressions of emotion. *J. Exp. Psychol. Gen.* 141:19–25. doi: 10.1037/a0023463

Jack RE, Garrod OG, Yu H, Caldara R, Schyns PG. 2012. Facial expressions of emotion are not culturally universal. *PNAS* 109:7241–44

Jack RE, Garrod OGB, Schyns PG. 2014. Dynamic facial expressions of emotion transmit an evolving hierarchy of signals over time. *Curr. Biol.* 24:187–92

Jack RE, Sun W, Delis I, Garrod O, Schyns P. 2016. Four not six: revealing culturally common facial expressions of emotion. *J. Exp. Psychol. Gen.* 145:708–30

Johnson SK, Podratz KE, Dipboye RL, Gibbons E. 2010. Physical attractiveness biases in ratings of employment suitability: tracking down the "beauty is beastly" effect. *J. Soc. Psychol.* 150:301–18

Johnston A, Hill H, Carman N. 2013. Recognising faces: effects of lighting direction, inversion, and brightness reversal. *Perception* 42:1227–37

Jones AL, Kramer RS, Ward R. 2012. Signals of personality and health: the contributions of facial shape, skin texture, and viewing angle. *J. Exp. Psychol. Hum. Percept. Perform.* 38:1353–61

Karremans JC, Dotsch R, Corneille O. 2011. Romantic relationship status biases memory of faces of attractive opposite-sex others: evidence from a reverse-correlation paradigm. *Cognition* 121:422–26

Krumhuber EG, Kappas A, Manstead AS. 2013. Effects of dynamic aspects of facial expressions: a review. *Emot. Rev.* 5:41–46

Krumhuber EG, Manstead AS, Cosker D, Marshall D, Rosin PL, Kappas A. 2007. Facial dynamics as indicators of trustworthiness and cooperative behavior. *Emotion* 7:730–35

Labarre W. 1947. The cultural basis of emotions and gestures. *J. Personal.* 16:49–68

Lai M, I Oruç, Barton JJ. 2013. The role of skin texture and facial shape in representations of age and identity. *Cortex* 49:252–65

Lang PJ, Bradley MM, Cuthbert BN. 2005. *International affective picture system (IAPS): affective ratings of pictures and instruction manual*. Rep. No. A-8, Cent. Study Emot. Atten., Univ. Fla., Gainesville

Langner O, Dotsch R, Bijlstra G, Wigboldus DHJ, Hawk ST, van Knippenberg A. 2010. Presentation and validation of the Radboud Faces Database. *Cogn. Emot.* 24:1377–88

Leopold DA, O'Toole AJ, Vetter T, Blanz V. 2001. Prototype-referenced shape encoding revealed by high-level aftereffects. *Nat. Neurosci.* 4:89–94

Little AC, Jones BC, Waitt C, Tiddeman BP, Feinberg DR, et al. 2008. Symmetry is related to sexual dimorphism in faces: data across culture and species. *PLOS ONE* 3:e2106

Little AC, Perrett DI. 2007. Using composite images to assess accuracy in personality attribution to faces. *Br. J. Psychol.* 98:111–26

Littlewood W. 2001. Cultural awareness and the negotiation of meaning in intercultural communication. *Lang. Aware.* 10:189–99

Liu F, van der Lijn F, Schurmann C, Zhu G, Chakravarty MM, et al. 2012. A genome-wide association study identifies five loci influencing facial morphology in Europeans. *PLOS Genet.* 8:e1002932

Lundqvist D, Flykt A, Öhman A. 1998. *The Karolinska directed emotional faces.* CD-ROM, Dep. Clin. Neurosci., Psychol. Sect., Karolinska Inst., Stockholm

Macrae CN, Bodenhausen GV. 2000. Thinking categorically about others. *Annu. Rev. Psych.* 51:93–120

Mangini M, Biederman I. 2004. Making the ineffable explicit: estimating the information employed for face classifications. *Cogn. Sci.* 28:209–26

Matsumoto D, Ekman P. 1988. *Japanese and Caucasian Facial Expressions of Emotion (JACFEE) and Neutral Faces (JACNeuF).* Slides, Dep. Psychiatry, Univ. Calif., San Francisco

Mautz BS, Wong BB, Peters RA, Jennions MD. 2013. Penis size interacts with body shape and height to influence male attractiveness. *PNAS* 110:6925–30

Miellet S, Caldara R, Schyns PG. 2011. Local Jekyll and global Hyde: the dual identity of face identification. *Psychol. Sci.* 22:1518–26

Morency L-P, Stratou G, DeVault D, Hartholt A, Lhommet M, et al. 2015. *SimSensei demonstration: a perceptive virtual human interviewer for healthcare applications.* Presented at AAAI Conf. Artif. Intell., 29th, Jan. 25–30, Austin, TX

Morris D. 1979. *Gestures, Their Origins and Distribution.* New York: Stein and Day

Nelson NL, Russell JA. 2013. Universality revisited. *Emot. Rev.* 5:8–15

Nusseck M, Cunningham DW, Wallraven C, Bulthoff HH. 2008. The contribution of different facial regions to the recognition of conversational expressions. *J. Vis.* 8:1.1–23

Oosterhof NN, Todorov A. 2008. The functional basis of face evaluation. *PNAS* 105:11087–92

O'Toole AJ, Deffenbacher KA, Valentin D, Abdi H. 1994. Structural aspects of face recognition and the other-race effect. *Mem. Cogn.* 22:208–24

Palmer SE. 1999. *Vision Science: Photons to Phenomenology.* Cambridge, MA: MIT Press

Perrett DI, Lee KJ, Penton-Voak I, Rowland D, Yoshikawa S, et al. 1998. Effects of sexual dimorphism on facial attractiveness. *Nature* 394:884–87

Peterson MF, Eckstein MP. 2012. Looking just below the eyes is optimal across face recognition tasks. *PNAS* 109:E3314–23

Pollick FE, Paterson HM, Bruderlin A, Sanford AJ. 2001. Perceiving affect from arm movement. *Cognition* 82:B51–B61

Rhodes G. 2006. The evolutionary psychology of facial beauty. *Annu. Rev. Psychol.* 57:199–226

Rhodes MG, Anastasi JS. 2012. The own-age bias in face recognition: a meta-analytic and theoretical review. *Psychol. Bull.* 138:146–74

Roberts A. 2010. *The Incredible Human Journey.* London: A&C Black

Roether CL, Omlor L, Christensen A, Giese MA. 2009. Critical features for the perception of emotion from gait. *J. Vis.* 9:15.1–32

Rule NO, Garrett JV, Ambady N. 2010. On the perception of religious group membership from faces. *PLOS ONE* 5:e14241

Scheiner E, Fischer J. 2011. Emotion expression: the evolutionary heritage in the human voice. In *Interdisciplinary Anthropology: Continuing Evolution of Man*, ed. W Welsch, WJ Singer, A Wunder, pp. 105–29. Berlin: Springer

Schyns PG. 1998. Diagnostic recognition: task constraints, object information, and their interactions. *Cognition* 67:147–79

Schyns PG, Goldstone RL, Thibaut JP. 1998. The development of features in object concepts. *Behav. Brain Sci.* 21:1–17, discussion 17–54

Schyns PG, Gosselin F, Smith ML. 2009. Information processing algorithms in the brain. *Trends Cogn. Sci.* 13:20–26

Schyns PG, Petro LS, Smith ML. 2007. Dynamics of visual information integration in the brain for categorizing facial expressions. *Curr. Biol.* 17:1580–85

Schyns PG, Thut G, Gross J. 2011. Cracking the code of oscillatory activity. *PLOS Biol.* 9:e1001064

Scott-Phillips TC. 2008. Defining biological communication. *J. Evol. Biol.* 21:387–95

Shannon CE. 1948. A mathematical theory of communication. *Mob. Comput. Commun. Rev.* 5:3–55

Simons DJ, Rensink RA. 2005. Change blindness: past, present, and future. *Trends Cogn. Sci.* 9:16–20

Smith FW, Schyns PG. 2009. Smile through your fear and sadness. *Psychol. Sci.* 20:1202–8

Smith ML, Cottrell GW, Gosselin F, Schyns PG. 2005. Transmitting and decoding facial expressions. *Psychol. Sci.* 16:184–89

Smith ML, Gosselin F, Schyns PG. 2012. Measuring internal representations from behavioral and brain data. *Curr. Biol.* 22:191–96

Snodgrass JG. 1975. Psychophysics. In *Experimental Sensory Psychology*, ed. B Scharf, pp. 17–67. Glenview, IL: Scott Foresman

Swets JA, Green DM, Shipley EF, Sewall SE, Wasserman AG. 1963. *Signal detection by human observers*. DTIC Doc., Camb. Res. Lab. Electron., Mass. Inst. Technol. **https://dspace.mit.edu/bitstream/handle/1721.1/52270/RLE_QPR_053_XX.pdf?sequence=1**

Swiatoniowski AK, Quillen EE, Shriver MD, Jablonski NG. 2013. Technical note: comparing von Luschan skin color tiles and modern spectrophotometry for measuring human skin pigmentation. *Am. J. Phys. Anthropol.* 151:325–30

Tanaka J. 2013. Introduction. *Vis. Cogn.* 21:1077–80

Tanaka JW, Kiefer M, Bukach CM. 2004. A holistic account of the own-race effect in face recognition: evidence from a cross-cultural study. *Cognition* 93:B1–9

Telles E. 2014. *Pigmentocracies: Ethnicity, Race, and Color in Latin America*. Chapel Hill: Univ. N.C. Press

Thornhill R, Gangestad SW. 2006. Facial sexual dimorphism, developmental stability, and susceptibility to disease in men and women. *Evol. Hum. Behav.* 27:131–44

Tinbergen N. 1948. Social releasers and the experimental method required for their study. *Wilson Bull.* 60:6–51

Todorov A, Mandisodza AN, Goren A, Hall CC. 2005. Inferences of competence from faces predict election outcomes. *Science* 308:1623–26

Troje NF, Bülthoff HH. 1996. Face recognition under varying poses: the role of texture and shape. *Vis. Res.* 36:1761–71

Tskhay KO, Feriozzo MM, Rule NO. 2013. Facial features influence the categorization of female sexual orientation. *Perception* 42:1090–94

Van Bavel JJ, Mende-Siedlecki P, Brady WJ, Reinero DA. 2016. Contextual sensitivity in scientific reproducibility. *PNAS* 113:6454–59

van Rijsbergen N, Jaworska K, Rousselet GA, Schyns PG. 2014. With age comes representational wisdom in social signals. *Curr. Biol.* 24:2792–96

van Rijsbergen NJ, Schyns PG. 2009. Dynamics of trimming the content of face representations for categorization in the brain. *PLOS Comput. Biol.* 5:e1000561

Vetter T, Troje NF. 1997. Separation of texture and shape in images of faces for image coding and synthesis. *JoSAA* 14:2152–61

Vick S-J, Waller BM, Parr LA, Pasqualini MCS, Bard KA. 2007. A cross-species comparison of facial morphology and movement in humans and chimpanzees using the facial action coding system (FACS). *J. Nonverbal Behav.* 31:1–20

Vinciarelli A, Pantic M, Bourlard H. 2009. Social signal processing: survey of an emerging domain. *Image Vis. Comput.* 27:1743–59

Volterra V. 1930. *Theory of Functionals and of Integral and Integro-Differential Equations*. London: Blackie

Wiener N. 1958. *Nonlinear Problems in Random Theory*. Cambridge, MA: MIT Press

Wilson EO. 2012. *The Social Conquest of Earth*. New York: WW Norton & Co.

Winter RM. 1996. What's in a face? *Nat. Genet.* 12:124–29

Wu MC-K, David SV, Gallant JL. 2006. Complete functional characterization of sensory neurons by system identification. *Annu. Rev. Neurosci.* 29:477–505

Young SG, Hugenberg K. 2012. Individuation motivation and face experience can operate jointly to produce the own-race bias. *Soc. Psychol. Personal. Sci.* 3:80–87

Yu H, Garrod OGB, Schyns PG. 2012. Perception-driven facial expression synthesis. *Comput. Graph.* 36:152–62

Zacharopoulos GV, Manios A, Kau CH, Velagrakis G, Tzanakakis GN, de Bree E. 2016. Anthropometric analysis of the face. *J. Craniofac. Surg.* 27:e71–e75

RELATED RESOURCES

Cohen MM. 2006. *Perspectives on the Face*. Oxford, UK: Oxford Univ. Press

Eckstein MP, Ahumada AJ. 2002. Classification images: a tool to analyze visual strategies. *J. Vis.* 2:1. doi: 10.1167/2.1.i

Guilford T, Dawkins MS. 1991. Receiver psychology and the evolution of animal signals. *Anim. Behav.* 42:1–14

Jack RE, Schyns PG. 2015. The human face as a dynamic tool for social communication. *Curr. Biol.* 25:R621–34

MacLin OH, MacLin MK, Peterson D, Chowdhry O, Joshi P. 2001. Social psychophysics: using psychophysics to answer "social" questions with PsychoPro. *Behav. Res. Methods* 41:623–32

Murray RF. 2011. Classification images: a review. *J. Vis.* 11:2

Yost WA, Fay RR. 2012. *Human Psychophysics*, Vol. 3. Berlin: Springer

Social Motivation: Costs and Benefits of Selfishness and Otherishness

Jennifer Crocker,[1] Amy Canevello,[2] and Ashley A. Brown[1]

[1]Department of Psychology, The Ohio State University, Columbus, Ohio 43210; email: crocker.37@osu.edu, brown.5497@osu.edu

[2]Department of Psychology, University of North Carolina, Charlotte, North Carolina 28223; email: acanevel@uncc.edu

Annu. Rev. Psychol. 2017. 68:299–325

First published online as a Review in Advance on June 24, 2016

The *Annual Review of Psychology* is online at psych.annualreviews.org

This article's doi: 10.1146/annurev-psych-010416-044145

Keywords

giving, receiving, selfish, otherish, motivation, well-being, relationships

Abstract

We examine recent evidence on the consequences of selfishness and otherishness for psychological well-being, physical health, and relationships. In the first sections, we consider recent evidence regarding the costs and benefits of giving time, money, and support to others and the costs and benefits of taking or receiving those things from others. Then, because the behaviors of giving and taking can be motivated either by selfish or otherish concerns, we next consider the costs and benefits of the motivation underlying giving and taking. We also examine why and for whom selfishness and otherishness have consequences for psychological well-being, physical health, and relationships. We focus on mechanisms identified in research, including intrapsychic mechanisms such as positive and negative affect, self-esteem and self-efficacy, a sense of meaning and purpose in life, and a sense of connectedness to or isolation from others, as well as interpersonal processes such as reciprocation of support and responsiveness.

Contents

INTRODUCTION

Are people basically selfish, or do they genuinely care about others? This question is at the heart of what it means to be human, and has captured the attention of philosophers, theologians, and social scientists. Nearly four centuries ago, Thomas Hobbes proposed that self-interest is the most fundamental human motivation (Hobbes 1950/1651). Today, most people in Western societies accept the view that people are motivated to pursue their narrow economic and material self-interests, assume that people support policies consistent with their vested interests, and regard behavior that is not self-interested with suspicion (Miller 1999). The assumption of self-interest pervades the social sciences, particularly economics and psychology. In social psychology, which is the subfield of psychology most directly concerned with social relations, many topics of study, theoretical perspectives, and programs of research reflect the assumption of self-interest. For example, research and theory in evolutionary psychology (e.g., Neel et al. 2015), the self (e.g., Alicke & Sedikides 2011), helping behavior (e.g., Cialdini et al. 1987), and close relationships (e.g., Murray et al. 2006) often begin with the explicit or implicit assumption that people are fundamentally or primarily self-centered, self-serving, and self-interested.

Empirical research suggests that this assumption is wrong or at least overstated. Self-interest is at best a weak predictor of attitudes and behavior (Sears & Funk 1990). Although some people are self-interested most of the time (Brunell et al. 2013), and some situations tend to elicit self-interested behavior and motivations in many people (Li et al. 2013), people are also capable of acts of kindness, generosity, and compassion (for reviews, see Mikulincer & Shaver 2010). Humans, like other mammals, have an evolved caregiving system that promotes and motivates caring for their young, who are incapable of surviving on their own. In humans, this capacity to care about others extends beyond caring for one's offspring and kin to caring about and wanting to promote the well-being of friends, acquaintances, and even strangers (e.g., Preston 2013, Sprecher & Fehr 2005). Researchers increasingly study phenomena such as empathy, compassion, and sacrifice that are related to this capacity to care for the well-being of others (see Mikulincer & Shaver 2010). This research suggests that concern for others, or otherishness (Grant 2013), is as much a part of human nature as selfishness (Shaver et al. 2010).

The assumption that selfishness is the fundamental human motivation rests on the view that selfishness is beneficial, whereas otherishness is costly; people are selfish because they benefit from selfishness. In some ways, this is obviously true; people who give their money or time to others have less money or time for themselves, and people who selfishly hoard their money or protect their time tend to have more money or time for themselves. Money, time, and other tangible things tend to be finite resources and therefore often work in zero-sum ways—the more one gives to others, the less one has for oneself.

But many social goods that people give to and take from others are not so clearly finite resources that can be exhausted if spent or accumulated if saved. Emotional support and acts of kindness, for example, may cost no money and needn't take much time. More important, selfishness and otherishness have consequences that extend beyond their impact on how much of these limited resources people have. Psychological well-being, physical health, and interpersonal relationships are all affected by selfishness and otherishness. Furthermore, when shared resources are limited, selfishly taking shared resources hurts everyone in the long run, including the selfish person (Dawes 1980). When these broader consequences are considered, selfishness may have costs, and otherishness may have benefits. Thus, even "costly" giving may ultimately benefit the self, and selfishness may ultimately harm the self.

In the sections that follow, we examine recent evidence on the consequences of selfishness and otherishness for psychological well-being, physical health, and relationships. In the first sections, we consider recent evidence regarding the costs and benefits of giving time, money, and support to others and the costs and benefits of taking or receiving those things from others. Then, because the behaviors of giving and taking can be motivated either by selfish or otherish concerns, we next consider the costs and benefits of the motivation underlying giving and taking.

We also examine why and for whom selfishness and otherishness have consequences for psychological well-being, physical health, and relationships. We focus on mechanisms identified in research, including intrapsychic mechanisms such as positive and negative affect, self-esteem and self-efficacy, a sense of meaning and purpose in life, and a sense of connectedness to or isolation from others, and interpersonal processes such as reciprocation of support and responsiveness.

Otherishness: wanting or striving to benefit others because one cares about their well-being; examples of otherish motivations include empathic concern, compassionate love, compassionate goals, and altruistic motivations for caregiving in close relationships

Selfishness: wanting or striving to benefit the self without regard for the well-being of others; examples of selfish motivations include narcissistic personality characteristics such as entitlement and exploitativeness, dispositional greed, materialism, self-image goals, unmitigated communion, and egoistic reasons for caregiving in close relationships

COSTS AND BENEFITS OF GIVING

Giving is an extremely common social behavior, even in individualistic cultures where the norm of self-interest reigns. In the United States, individuals donated approximately $258 billion to charitable causes in 2015 (Giving Inst. 2015). People are also generous with their time; nearly 63 million people in the United States (about 25% of the total population) spend time volunteering at least once per year (**https://www.volunteeringinamerica.gov/**). Giving does not require a personal connection; people have donated billions of dollars to strangers and outgroup members around the world in response to natural and man-made disasters (Oppenheimer & Olivola 2011). Much giving occurs close to home, in relationships with family members. Although informal caregivers are not paid for their time, the economic value of their contributions was approximately $450 billion in the United States in 2009 (Feinberg et al. 2011).

Giving Can Be Beneficial

Giving to others can be good for psychological health. Research shows that giving one's money or time boosts happiness and psychological well-being. For example, experimental evidence shows that people randomly assigned to spend money on others experience greater happiness than those assigned to spend money on themselves (Dunn et al. 2008a). This phenomenon is not unique to the laboratory; spending more of one's income on others predicts increased happiness over time (Dunn et al. 2008a). Similarly, giving time also promotes happiness and well-being (Mogilner 2010).

The benefits of giving for psychological health extend across the life span. For example, college students who provided social support to their roommates reported decreased symptoms of depression and anxiety across 10 weeks (Crocker et al. 2010). High school students who offered to help strangers reported more positive mood compared to students in a no-help control condition (Yinon & Landau 1987). Even the very young appear to benefit from giving to others—greater happiness was observed in toddlers who gave treats to others compared with those who received treats themselves (Aknin et al. 2012).

Many studies suggest that, especially for the elderly, giving in the form of volunteering has numerous psychological benefits. In elderly samples, volunteering is consistently associated with more positive affect and cheerfulness and less loneliness (e.g., Sarid et al. 2010). Elderly volunteers also report increased happiness, life satisfaction, self-esteem, and mastery over time (Musick & Wilson 2003, Thoits & Hewitt 2001). Volunteering buffers the tendency for increased depression in the elderly (Thoits & Hewitt 2001), even following the death of a spouse (Brown et al. 2008).

Giving can also have benefits for both subjective and objective indicators of physical health and mortality (for a review, see Post 2005). Because younger populations are typically in relatively good health, it is difficult to detect the effects of giving on health in younger samples. In contrast, older people typically suffer from deteriorating health, and thus the effects of giving on health are more easily detected in elderly or chronically ill samples. In comparison with nonvolunteers, elderly volunteers self-report better health over time (Hong & Morrow-Howell 2010). Giving to others is also related to objective measures of health status, including lower systolic and diastolic blood pressure and arterial pressure (Piferi & Lawler 2006). In patients with cardiovascular disease, helping predicts lower risk of subsequent cardiovascular disease events (Heisler et al. 2013). Furthermore, both volunteering and providing support to spouses, relatives, friends, and neighbors predict lower mortality risk (Brown et al. 2003, Heisler et al. 2013).

Giving also promotes relationship development and maintenance. Simple gift giving for holidays and personal events fosters social connection (Aknin & Human 2015). Giving social support predicts increased love, trust, tolerance, commitment, and relationship satisfaction, all of which contribute to the success of close relationships (Cutrona 1996). Giving support is particularly helpful in coping with stressful events—for example, social support provided to partners during a discussion about a personal stressor predicted relationship satisfaction and distress two years later (Pasch & Bradbury 1998).

A recent experiment comparing the effects of acts of kindness toward others with acts of kindness toward the self demonstrates the benefits of giving (Nelson et al. 2016). Participants assigned to perform acts of kindness toward others or toward the world experienced improved emotional, psychological, and social well-being six weeks later, whereas participants assigned to perform acts of kindness toward themselves, or those in a neutral control condition, did not.

These findings suggest that in daily life, giving is often beneficial for givers. It is associated with positive psychological heath, good physical health and decreased mortality, and improved relationships.

Giving Can Be Costly

Alongside research documenting the benefits of giving, a large body of research suggests that giving can have negative effects on psychological, physical, and relationship well-being. Caregiving, or providing care for a close other who has a chronic debilitating illness or condition, is associated with poor psychological health (Pinquart & Sörensen 2003b). For example, meta-analyses of 228 studies suggest that caregiving-related stressors predict more symptoms of depression (Pinquart & Sörensen 2003a). Other meta-analyses demonstrate that, compared to matched noncaregiver controls, caregivers experience greater stress and lower subjective well-being (Pinquart & Sörensen 2003b).

Caregiving is commonly linked to poor physical health. For example, a meta-analysis of 176 studies suggests that caregiver burden is related to lower subjective and objective indicators of physical health (Pinquart & Sörensen 2007). The negative consequences of caregiving for physical health also appear to get under the skin: A meta-analysis of 23 studies demonstrates that caregivers have higher stress hormones and lower antibody response than matched noncaregiver controls (Vitaliano et al. 2003). The negative consequences of this type of giving appear to be long-lasting: Even several years after the death of care recipients, the proinflammatory cytokine (IL-6) profiles of former caregivers did not differ from those of current caregivers (Kiecolt-Glaser et al. 2003). Caregiver stress predicts slower wound healing (Kiecolt-Glaser et al. 1995) and decreased length of telomeres, the protective caps of DNA that are linked to premature aging and greater cancer risk (Damjanovic et al. 2007). These findings have implications for longevity: Older caregivers who felt burdened by their responsibilities had a 63% greater risk of mortality compared to noncaregiving controls (Schulz & Beach 1999).

Caregiving also has costs for relationships. Caregivers of dementia patients report declines in intimacy, communication, and relationship quality (for a review, see Ablitt et al. 2009). A separate review corroborated these findings: Compared to noncaregiver controls, caregivers of spouses with dementia reported less reciprocity with care recipients and fewer shared pleasurable activities (Quinn et al. 2009).

Together, findings from the caregiving literature suggest that being the primary caregiver for an ill or disabled loved one takes a substantial toll on the mental and physical health of the caregiver and may damage the relationship between caregiver and recipient. This type of caregiving occurs under difficult circumstances, and caregivers endure multiple stressors, including the strain of a loved one's functional disabilities (i.e., physical and cognitive disabilities); the demands of caregiving (e.g., providing care and monitoring and attending to recipient's needs; Pinquart & Sörensen 2003a); exposure to a loved one's significant suffering (Monin & Schulz 2009); exposure to a loved one's behavior problems (Pinquart & Sörensen 2003a); and costs to personal and social life, employment, and finances (Brown & Brown 2014). Not surprisingly, those who provide care to chronically ill or debilitated loved ones often feel burdened, with higher levels of caregiving leading to greater burden (Pinquart & Sörensen 2011).

Moderators and Mechanisms

Why do some forms of giving lead to poor outcomes, whereas other forms of giving lead to positive outcomes? A number of mechanisms may explain the benefits of giving. Giving to others may distract people from their own problems, enhance meaning in life, increase self-efficacy and feelings of competence, improve mood (Nelson et al. 2016), and promote a physically active lifestyle (Midlarsky 1991). Most important, giving increases social integration and connection, which bolsters the sense that one is valued by and valuable to others. For example, volunteering is related to lower depression in part because it promotes social integration (Musick & Wilson 2003). Spending money on others leads to happiness because of its positive impact on others (Aknin et al. 2013). Giving time promotes happiness and well-being through strengthened interpersonal connections (Mogilner 2010). Furthermore, giving support increases people's sense that they have value to and can make a difference for others (Krause 2007), leading to a sense of belonging and connectedness (Stillman & Lambert 2013). Giving to others in times of stress contributes to relationship quality and longevity in at least four ways: Giving protects relationships by preventing people from withdrawing from others and isolating themselves; it decreases depressive symptoms that can damage relationships; it prevents conflict from becoming worse; and it promotes closeness, intimacy, and bonding with others (Cutrona 1996).

The negative effects of caregiving may be due to several factors. First, caregiving is often confounded with a range of negative circumstances that endure over time, making it difficult to determine whether the costs associated with caregiving are due to giving per se or to the negative circumstances under which caregiving often takes place. When some of these confounding variables are controlled, the negative effects of caregiving are attenuated, and caregiving is associated with positive outcomes. For example, when controlling for patients' illness status, impairment, and time "on call" for providing care, caregiving is related to greater positive affect (Poulin et al. 2010). In another sample, providing care predicts decreased mortality for elderly caregivers after controlling for a number of factors, including behavioral and cognitive limitations of the recipient, caregiver physical and mental health, and demographic variables such as age, gender, race, education, and income (Brown et al. 2009).

Second, some people perceive caregiving to be a burden, whereas others do not. Independent of the objective circumstances of caregiving noted previously, perceived burden may account for some of the negative consequences of caregiving. Feeling overwhelmed by the demands of caregiving is related to poor mental health (Schwartz et al. 2003). When caregivers perceive less burden, they experience positive aspects of caregiving and better well-being (Hilgeman et al. 2007).

Third, intrinsic versus extrinsic motivation of givers may affect the costs and benefits of giving. Voluntary or freely chosen caregiving may have beneficial effects on the giver, whereas extrinsically motivated, obligatory caregiving may have negative effects. For example, caregivers of dementia patients with more extrinsic motivation feel more burdened, less competent, and more trapped in their caregiving role than do caregivers with less extrinsic motivation (Quinn et al. 2012). Many of the benefits of giving have been demonstrated in situations where the demands of giving are minimal (e.g., spending a small financial windfall on others versus oneself) and freely chosen (e.g., volunteering one's time). Many of the costs of giving have been demonstrated in situations where the demands of giving are heavy and the giving feels obligatory (e.g., caring for an elderly chronically ill or disabled spouse or parent).

Fourth, when caregivers give much more than they receive over the long term, their own psychological and physical needs may go unmet (Quinn et al. 2015). Caregivers who do not have available support, do not seek support, do not practice self-care, or for whom loved ones' needs supersede their own may suffer because their own needs are neglected. When caregivers receive adequate social support, they experience more positive aspects of caregiving (Chen & Greenberg 2004). In particular, caregiving that disrupts social connections may lead to poor psychological, physical, and relational well-being. Caregiving may isolate caregivers from important relationships, resulting in loneliness, which is linked to poor psychological well-being and physical health (Hawkley & Cacioppo 2010). This effect may be exacerbated when the care recipient has physical or emotional limitations that interfere with mutual responsiveness or the recipient's ability to experience or convey gratitude or appreciation to caregivers. Thus, the costs of caregiving may outweigh the benefits when the circumstances of giving prevent givers from feeling that

|

their contributions have value to others and therefore undermine their sense of connection and belonging.

COSTS AND BENEFITS OF RECEIVING

If giving is an extremely common social behavior, then taking should be approximately as common, assuming that what is given must be received. Taking encompasses many distinct behaviors ranging from passive to active, which may have different consequences for psychological, physical, and relational well-being. The most passive form of taking involves being the recipient of something offered by but not requested from others, such as passively receiving gifts or support from others. A more active form of taking involves making requests of others, such as asking for a gift or asking for help or support. An even more active form involves taking without first making a request, such as taking food from someone else's plate or taking found money or objects without prior permission. Most research on the consequences of taking focuses on the more passive forms, particularly receiving gifts, help, or support, and seeking gifts or donations, help, or support.

The majority of studies on receiving have examined effects of receiving social support. Here, researchers have distinguished different types of support. Invisible support involves support of which recipients are unaware (e.g., when one spouse takes care of tasks or problems without informing the other), whereas visible support refers to support that recipients know they have received. Invisible support can be more beneficial to recipients than visible support, but most research has examined visible support (Bolger et al. 2000). Another distinction has been made between received support and perceived available support (Sarason et al. 1990). Perceiving that support is available if needed is clearly related to psychological well-being, physical health, and relational well-being (for a review, see Uchino 2004). Although perceiving that support or other resources are available without actually receiving them can have benefits (Haber et al. 2007), they do not involve actually receiving or taking from others, and therefore we do not include studies of consequences of perceived available support in our review.

What are the costs and benefits of receiving and taking from others? Economists, psychologists, and sociologists have amassed a sizeable literature that describes the circumstances of taking, exploring the roles of communication, group size, reciprocity, altruism, trust, reputation, competition, and cooperation on behavior while playing economic games or encountering hypothetical social dilemmas (e.g., Falk et al. 2007). Surprisingly, this research has largely ignored the consequences of taking for psychological and physical well-being and relationships. However, research on support seeking, which is more active, and on receiving support—such as gifts, benefits, help, or care—from others, which is more passive, has examined the consequences of receiving. Research on these topics suggests that receiving has both costs and benefits (Fisher et al. 1982).

Receiving Can Be Beneficial

Receiving support and responsive care is related to numerous indicators of psychological well-being, including greater positive affect, life satisfaction, and coping, and lower depression and anxiety (for reviews, see Clark & Lemay 2010, Reis et al. 2000). Social support may have its strongest effects when recipients are stressed (Uchino 2004). Receiving social support is related to better quality of life and lower stress (Schwarzer & Knoll 2007) and increased positive mood (Collins & Feeney 2000). Meta-analyses suggest that receiving support protects against depression (Santini et al. 2015).

Receiving is also related to better physical health and delayed mortality (Tay et al. 2013, Uchino 2004), in part because receiving social support is related to more positive health behaviors.

Received social support predicts increased adherence to medical treatment, more fruit and vegetable intake, more exercise, and positive behavior changes related to the management of chronic illness (e.g., smoking cessation in head and neck cancer patients and self-care behaviors related to diabetes; for a review, see Tay et al. 2013). Receiving social support is also related to better cardiovascular, endocrine, and immune function (for a review, see Uchino et al. 1996). Together, these findings may explain associations between received support and overall health and mortality. For example, receiving social support predicted improved physical health six months later in an elderly sample (Cutrona et al. 1986). It also predicts lower incidence and progression of cardiovascular disease and lower incidence of mortality in breast cancer patients (for a review, see Tay et al. 2013).

Receiving support improves relationships; it builds closeness, relationship satisfaction, commitment, trust, and intimacy (for a review, see Clark & Lemay 2010). For example, support received from friends predicts better relationship quality (Deci et al. 2006), and being the recipient of romantic partners' responsiveness plays a key role in the development of intimacy, trust, and love (Laurenceau et al. 2005). Importantly, when people receive support, responsiveness, or other social goods, they tend to reciprocate, either out of adherence to social norms or because they care. This reciprocation creates upward spirals of positive interactions that strengthen relationships (Canevello & Crocker 2010). Receiving may also inspire people to "pay it forward" to others (Gray et al. 2014). Thus, receiving support sparks behaviors that promote both relationship development with the giver and additional giving to third parties.

Although a great deal of research has documented benefits of receiving support, responsiveness, and other social goods, this research must be interpreted with caution because receiving tends to be strongly associated with giving. For example, when people perceive that others are responsive to them, they become more responsive in turn, increasing their self-esteem (Canevello & Crocker 2011). Likewise, when people receive social support, they respond by giving support in return, which predicts decreased symptoms of anxiety and depression (Crocker et al. 2010). This strong tendency to reciprocate the support, help, and responsiveness that one receives from others means that the effects of receiving are often confounded with the effects of giving (Crocker et al. 2010). When recipients reciprocate or pay it forward by giving to others, recipients will experience the benefits of giving. Much of the social support literature assumes that receiving support is the active ingredient that promotes psychological, physical, and relational health. However, because this research often does not measure support given, reciprocated, or paid forward, it cannot ascertain the unique effects of receiving support.

Receiving Can Be Costly

Despite evidence that receiving care, support, and responsiveness from others has a range of benefits, other research suggests that receiving can have costs. People have mixed feelings about seeking and receiving help (Barbee et al. 1998). People in a position to give help often offer it nonspecifically, suggesting that people just ask when they need help. Asking is a powerful yet underappreciated means of obtaining help. People do not like to turn down direct requests for help, yet help seekers underestimate the likelihood that others will comply with their direct requests for help (Flynn & Lake 2008). However, those who suggest that people just ask when they need help underestimate the discomfort that help seekers feel, partly because they fear being turned down (Bohns & Flynn 2010). Indeed, potential help givers often do not like to be asked for help and will avoid situations in which they expect to be asked for help if they can. For example, people sometimes go in a different entrance to a store to avoid a request to donate to the Salvation Army, or leave home when they are forewarned that someone will stop by to request a donation

(Andreoni et al. 2011). In sum, many people dislike both asking and being asked for help, support, or donations.

When people do seek support overtly and directly, they tend to receive appropriate support and benefit from it (Collins & Feeney 2000). However, when people fear that others will not support them and seek support through indirect means, they think that their partners do not understand their problems, are disappointed in them, or make negative or insensitive remarks toward them, and they report lower relationship satisfaction (Don et al. 2013). Furthermore, when people doubt the authenticity or sincerity of the support they receive, they may continue to seek support or reassurance from others, causing others to become annoyed and reject the support seeker, which results in increased depression and relationship difficulties (Joiner et al. 1999).

In sum, interactions that involve help seeking can create discomfort in both the help seeker and the potential helper. Although directly and clearly asking for help is the most effective way to obtain the help one needs, people's fears of being rejected or damaging their relationship make them reluctant to ask directly. For their part, support givers often avoid being asked directly and fail to appreciate how uncomfortable people feel about asking for support, so they offer help vaguely and rely on support seekers to express their needs clearly. As a result, support seekers often fail to receive the support they need, with negative effects on the relationship. The longer-term consequences of asking for help on psychological and physical well-being remain largely unexplored.

Apart from these issues with asking for support, receiving can be costly for psychological well-being. For example, people who focus on receiving gifts during the holiday season experience lower life satisfaction and positive affect and higher negative affect and stress (Kasser & Sheldon 2002). Receiving social support in close relationships is linked to decreased self-esteem, self-competence, and positive mood, and increased negative affect, distress, anxiety, depression, anger, guilt, and feelings of dependence (McClure et al. 2014, Nadler et al. 2010, Shrout et al. 2006). The negative effects of receiving may be particularly detrimental when people perceive that their needs are burdensome to others—recipients who believe that they have become a burden are at heightened risk for suicide and suicidal thoughts (Brown et al. 2009).

Receiving has also been linked to poor physical health. Receiving support is associated with increased mortality (Krause 2007). Furthermore, receiving instrumental support (as compared to other forms of support, such as emotional or informational) contributes to increased risk of death (e.g., Penninx et al. 1997). However, it is worth noting that the larger literatures investigating health outcomes related to receiving suggest that receiving is beneficial for health and mortality (Uchino 2004, Uchino et al. 1996).

Receiving can also have costs for relationships. For example, when people receive support, they report lower relationship equity (McClure et al. 2014) and decreased closeness (Gleason et al. 2008). Furthermore, when people are unhappy with what they have received, for example, an unwanted gift, they see themselves as less similar to the giver and are more pessimistic about the relationship (Dunn et al. 2008b). When support comes with contingencies or threatens self-esteem, recipients are more likely to avoid receiving aid, and when they do receive aid, they quickly repay it (Fisher et al. 1982). Support received under these circumstances can also lead recipients to resent and derogate both the help and the helper (Fisher et al. 1982).

Moderators and Mechanisms

Why is receiving sometimes beneficial and sometimes costly? The consequences of receiving support, help, or aid may depend on the meaning they have for recipients. Receiving can be construed as a signal of indebtedness, dependence, incompetence, weakness, inferiority, or relationship inequality (Bolger et al. 2000, McClure et al. 2014, Nadler et al. 2010). Thus, receiving support may imply something negative about the recipient—dependence, incompetence, or inferiority—and lead recipients to feel distant, isolated, disconnected, or devalued by others. Feelings of incompetence, inferiority, devaluation, and disconnection may in turn prompt recipients to further distance themselves from others, compounding feelings of isolation and loneliness and contributing to poor psychological well-being, physical health, and relationships.

On the other hand, when receiving is interpreted as a signal that others care for, understand, and value the recipient (Gable & Reis 2006), recipients may feel close, connected to, and valued by givers, leading to improved psychological well-being, physical health, and relationships. Thus, receiving support, help, or care can lead recipients to feel valued and connected or inferior and disconnected, accounting for both the positive and negative effects of receiving.

COSTS AND BENEFITS OF OTHERISH MOTIVATION

Our review of research on the consequences of giving and receiving demonstrates that they have mixed effects. Giving can have important benefits for psychological well-being, physical health, and relationships. At times, however, giving feels like a burden, leading to stress, burnout, poor health, and anger and resentment in relationships. Although people sometimes give freely and happily, they often go out of their way to avoid being asked for help or donations, suggesting that giving can be aversive (Cain et al. 2014).

The motivations that energize giving may account for at least some of these mixed findings. A wide range of motivations may prompt giving and taking. For example, people may give for approach or avoidance reasons (Impett et al. 2013) or for intrinsic or extrinsic reasons (Cain et al. 2014). Indeed, research suggests that people often agree to requests for donations or other types of help not because they enjoy giving, but rather because they feel pressure to give (Cain et al. 2014) or feel compelled by social norms to give even when they do not want to (Dunning et al. 2016).

We define otherish motivation as wanting or striving to benefit others because one cares about their well-being. This definition avoids a pitfall that emerged in altruism research, which sometimes defines altruism as aid given to others in distress that is prompted by genuine concern for the well-being of others rather than to gain any benefit or reduce any cost for the self (for a discussion, see Batson 2010). As noted previously, helping or giving to others can boost positive emotions and reduce personal distress. Like reputational boosts or material rewards, these emotional benefits may serve as ulterior motives for giving to others. In addition, people who help others may show self–other overlap, mentally representing the recipient in their self-concepts (Cialdini et al. 1997), suggesting that their motive may be to help themselves rather than others. These and other findings have led some researchers to question whether helping is ever truly altruistic (Cialdini et al. 1987). With our definitions, the costs and benefits of selfish and otherish motivation remain an empirical question rather than part of the definition of the motivation: Both selfish and otherish motivation could have both costs and benefits to the self. People with otherish motivation may sometimes unintentionally hurt others, and people with selfishness motivation may sometimes unintentionally benefit others.

Unlike altruism researchers, laypeople do not seem to discount the good deeds of others as selfishly motivated when those good deeds are prompted by personal distress at the suffering of others or result in positive affect after helping others (Barasch et al. 2014). In a series of studies, Barasch et al. (2014) showed that observers tend to assume that people who help because they expect to feel good after doing so and people who help in order to reduce their own distress about others' suffering genuinely care about the well-being of those they help. Thus, helping in order to obtain or helping that results in emotional benefits signals otherish rather than selfish motivations to perceivers. People who are motivated to give because they expect to feel good about it are judged as having more moral character and more authentic motivation to help than people who are motivated by other types of rewards, such as material or reputational rewards (Barasch et al. 2014, study 6).

These findings may help to better identify otherish motivations. We suspect that people who feel good or expect to feel good about giving to others, as well as those who expect giving to reduce their own distress, genuinely care about the well-being of others; their positive emotions indicate otherish rather than selfish motivations. If so, emotions may help scientists as well as laypeople infer the motivations underlying giving to others.

Consistent with this view, several programs of research suggest that otherish motivation involves a caring emotional response to others. For example, empathic concern is an emotional response, involving feelings such as sympathy, compassion, and tenderness, that motivates helping others in need (Batson 2010). Compassionate love, defined as a kind of love that involves giving of oneself for the good of another, is an emotional state that motivates prosocial behavior (Fehr 2010). Compassionate goals involve the intention to support others "not to obtain something for the self, but out of consideration for the well-being of others" (Crocker & Canevello 2008, p. 557). Research shows that when people have compassionate goals they feel positive other-directed emotions such as love, connection, and empathy (Canevello & Crocker 2015, Crocker & Canevello 2008). Altruistic motivations for caregiving in romantic relationships involve feeling love, concern, and distress when the partner is hurting (Feeney & Collins 2003). Because altruism clearly involves caring about the well-being of others and provides an impetus for prosocial behavior, research that uses measures of these constructs provides the clearest evidence regarding the costs and benefits of otherish motivation.

A number of other measures and constructs also capture otherish motivation, although less precisely. For example, people high in communal orientation feel responsible for others' welfare and both desire and feel obligated to help others when they have a need (Clark et al. 1987). Communally oriented people endorse the norm that people should be helpful and respond noncontingently to others' needs, but their motivations may be either otherish or selfish (Clark & Aragón 2013). Giving that is obligatory or motivated by social norms that one should give to others even if one doesn't want to would not reflect otherish motivation by our definition (Dunning et al. 2016). Communal strength refers to the strength of communal orientation in a particular relationship. A measure of communal strength (Mills et al. 2004) includes items about the costs people would be willing to incur to help a relationship partner, but it does not distinguish selfish, otherish, or normative reasons. Intrinsic life goals, such as aspirations for affiliation and community feeling, refer to what people want for themselves (Grouzet et al. 2005) and likewise may involve selfish or otherish motivation, or both. We suspect that all of these constructs involve otherish motivation, but they may reflect selfish or normative reasons as well.

Benefits of Otherish Motivation

Research on the consequences of otherish motivation suggests that it has many benefits for psychological well-being. Daily diary studies show that people higher in empathic concern for others experience higher well-being (Morelli et al. 2015). Daily diary studies also show that people higher in communal orientation experience higher self-esteem and more positive affect (Le et al. 2013). Furthermore, in the Le et al. (2013) study, the association between communal orientation and well-being was obtained for the otherish aspect of communal orientation (the desire to respond to others' needs), not its selfish aspect (the desire for others to respond to one's own needs).

Compassionate love is linked to positive mood, high self-esteem, and a sense of connectedness to others (Sprecher & Fehr 2006).

Many of these studies are correlational, making it difficult to determine whether otherish motivation predicts increased psychological well-being or psychological well-being predicts increased otherish motivation. Some studies, however, show that otherish motivation predicts improved psychological well-being over time, consistent with (but not conclusively demonstrating) a causal effect of otherish motivation on well-being. For example, compassionate goals to be supportive and constructive and not harmful to others predict decreased symptoms of anxiety and depression (Crocker et al. 2010); less loneliness (Crocker & Canevello 2008); increased self-esteem (Canevello & Crocker 2011); and feeling more peaceful, connected, and clear and less isolated, afraid, and confused (Canevello & Crocker 2015) over time. Giving that focuses on demonstrating caring and belonging is related to fewer depressive symptoms, whereas giving that focuses on providing assistance is associated with more depressive symptoms (Strazdins & Broom 2007). Correlational and longitudinal studies also link intrinsic aspirations (e.g., community, affiliation) with higher well-being and lower distress (Kasser & Ryan 1996, 2001), although as noted, these constructs may have both selfish and otherish components.

Otherish motivations are also associated with better physical health, including reduced mortality. For example, Konrath and colleagues (2012) found that volunteering results in lower mortality, but only when the motive for volunteering is other oriented; people who volunteer for selfish reasons do not live longer than nonvolunteers. Compassionate love in older female spouses is associated with better health outcomes (Rauer et al. 2014).

Perhaps the most pronounced benefits of otherish motivation arise in the domain of interpersonal relationships. For example, compassionate love for one's partner predicts higher marital satisfaction among newlyweds (Reis et al. 2014) as well as higher relationship quality and greater relationship stability overall (Fehr et al. 2014). Additionally, when relationship partners make sacrifices with the goal to make their partner happy, they experience greater personal authenticity, ultimately resulting in better relationship well-being (Impett et al. 2013).

Research by Collins, Feeney, and colleagues demonstrates the positive effects of otherish motivation within relationships. Relationship partners who endorse relatively altruistic motives for providing support within the relationship (e.g., loving the spouse, enjoying helping, wanting to make both the spouse and the self feel good) tend to be more responsive and effective in providing support to their partners (Feeney & Collins 2003). People with relatively altruistic caregiving motives tend to provide more responsive, secure base support for the partner; in other words, people with these otherish motivations are more responsive and supportive of their partner's personal growth, exploration of the environment, and goal striving (Feeney et al. 2013). Over time, the relationship functioning of people with relatively altruistic caregiving motives tends to increase (Feeney & Collins 2003); thus, this otherish motivation predicts benefits for the relationship as a whole as well as for the relationship partner specifically.

Similarly, research on compassionate goals also suggests that otherish motivation has relationship benefits, both for others and for the self. When people have compassionate goals, feelings of closeness, support, and trust within their relationships increase (Crocker & Canevello 2008, Hadden et al. 2014). Furthermore, people with compassionate goals become more secure (less anxious and avoidant) in their relationships over time (Canevello et al. 2013). Compassionate goals predict increased responsiveness to relationship partners, which in turn predicts increased relationship quality for both people (Canevello & Crocker 2010). Compassionate goals also predict increases in perceived social support from family, friends, and relationship partners over the first semester of college, as well as increased social support given to and received from roommates (Crocker & Canevello 2008). In fact, compassionate goals seem to be contagious, such that when people have compassionate goals, their relationship partners develop more compassionate goals over time, which benefits the relationship and each partner specifically (Crocker & Canevello 2012).

Costs of Otherish Motivation

In contrast to the abundant evidence that otherish motivation has benefits for psychological well-being, physical health, and relationships, we were unable to find any evidence that otherish motivation has costs for these outcomes. Perhaps the biggest cost of otherish motivation comes in the form of missed opportunities for personal gain. Otherish people are unlikely to exploit others or take advantage of them. In addition, many people fear that one cost of otherish motivation involves increased vulnerability to exploitation (Gilbert et al. 2011). However, social norms strongly militate against exploitation (Dunning et al. 2016). When people give increased support to their college roommate, the roommate gives increased support in return (Crocker & Canevello 2008). Relationship partners typically reciprocate when people become more responsive to them (Canevello & Crocker 2010). In communal relationships, people do not necessarily reciprocate directly, but rather give support and help in response to others' needs. However, people in communal relationships both expect and find that mutual responsiveness to needs will be reciprocated by relationship partners (Clark & Aragón 2013).

Even in one-time interactions with strangers whom they do not expect to meet, most people do not take advantage of others. For example, in the trust game, often used in behavioral economics, participants are given a sum of money, which they can give to a complete stranger who will invest it for them. In this situation, people generally trust (i.e., give money to the other to invest), even if they are skeptical of the other person's trustworthiness. More remarkably, the investor, who could choose to keep all of the money for him or herself, typically returns at least the amount invested (Johnson & Mislin 2011). Thus, even when people fear being exploited, they often act as if they trust others, and their fears of exploitation are usually unfounded.

Beyond the possibility that one will miss opportunities for personal gain or that one's generosity or trust will be taken advantage of, we did not identify any research showing that otherish motivation has costs for psychological well-being, physical health, or relationships. It is difficult to know whether these costs simply do not exist, or whether they exist in circumstances usually not studied, or if investigators have been more interested in exploring the benefits than the costs of otherish motivation. One possible cost that has not yet been investigated is feelings of sadness when otherish people experience a relationship loss due to death, divorce, or other causes. Research on the relationship benefits of otherish motivation indicates that relationships get closer over time when people have otherish motivation. This increased closeness may predict increased feelings of distress and social pain when relationships are lost (Slotter et al. 2010).

Moderators and Mechanisms

What accounts for the beneficial effects of otherish motivation on psychological well-being, physical health, and relationships? Otherish motivation is associated with positive affect, purpose in life, and satisfaction of psychological needs (e.g., autonomy, competence, and relatedness); prosocial behaviors; and reduced physiological responses to stressful situations; each may account for effects of otherish motivation on these outcomes.

Otherish motivation may provide a strong sense of purpose (Crocker & Canevello 2008), which predicts health behaviors, such as sleep and the use of preventive health care services, as well as health outcomes, such as stroke, myocardial infarction, and even mortality (e.g., Hill & Turiano

2014, Kim et al. 2013). Personal life goals, such as aspirations to have good relationships and contribute to one's community, predict well-being through satisfaction of psychological needs, such as autonomy, relatedness, and competence (Sheldon & Elliot 1999).

Compassionate goals in particular appear to foster a variety of psychological states that predict increased psychological, physical, and relational well-being. For example, people who typically have compassionate goals tend to experience more peaceful, clear, and connected feelings in general. Compassionate goals one day predict increased peaceful, clear, and connected feelings the following day, and when people are higher than their typical level in compassionate goals, they also experience more peaceful, clear, and connected feelings (Canevello & Crocker 2015, Crocker & Canevello 2008). An experimental study showed that people induced to have compassionate goals showed lower adrenocorticotropic hormone and plasma cortisol levels (both of which are linked to physical and mental health problems when persistently elevated) in response to the Trier Social Stress Test compared to three comparison groups who did not have compassionate goals (Abelson et al. 2014).

Otherish motivations also predict improved relationship quality through several mechanisms. When people have compassionate goals, they are more supportive and responsive to their relationship partners, and their partners are more responsive and supportive in return, which predicts increased relationship quality (Canevello & Crocker 2010, Crocker & Canevello 2008). Positive emotions in people with compassionate goals may signal their otherish motivation to relationship partners. In addition, when people have compassionate goals they feel more cooperative with relationship partners and view their relationships in more non-zero-sum ways (Crocker & Canevello 2008), which may predict improved relationship quality, particularly following relationship conflicts. Importantly, otherish motivations predict increased relationship quality in relationship partners as well (Canevello & Crocker 2010, Hadden et al. 2014).

In sum, several mechanisms may account for the benefits to psychological well-being, physical health, and relationships associated with otherish motivation. A unifying thread appears to be the feeling that one is valuable to and valued by others. Furthermore, relationship dynamics such as reciprocation may create upward spirals in relationships when one partner has otherish motivations.

COSTS AND BENEFITS OF SELFISH MOTIVATION

Although people sometimes are motivated by genuine caring about others' well-being, they are also capable of being selfish. Selfish motivations for giving and taking may account for some of their effects on psychological well-being, physical health, and relationships.

We define selfish motivation as the inverse of otherish motivation: wanting or striving to benefit the self without regard for the well-being of others. Selfish motivation occurs in social contexts where behaviors have direct or indirect consequences for others' well-being. Selfish motivation doesn't necessarily mean that people intend to harm others. Selfish people sometimes simply intend to benefit themselves without considering the implications of their actions for the well-being of others or adjusting their actions to take others' well-being into account. At other times, selfish people may intentionally benefit the self at the expense of others.

Perhaps because of the strong assumption by social scientists and laypeople that humans are motivated by self-interest (Miller 1999), the intense debate in the prosocial motivation literature about whether people are ever truly altruistic has not been matched, to our knowledge, by a parallel debate about whether people are ever truly selfish, or a parallel exploration of otherish motivations for giving to and taking from others. If others benefit (e.g., if others receive emotional benefits from giving), is it truly selfish to receive? Can asking for help, support, or donations be motivated by otherishness as well as selfishness? Research plumbing selfish motivations is far scarcer than research plumbing motivations for giving.

Just as emotions can signal to perceivers that prosocial acts are motivated by genuine caring about others' well-being (Barasch et al. 2014), the absence of certain emotions or the presence of others may signal selfish motivations (DeSteno et al. 2010). In particular, we expect that selfish motivation is characterized by the absence of empathic concern or personal distress in response to others' needs and low levels of positive other-focused emotions such as compassion, gratitude, and feelings of love and caring. For example, narcissists, who are self-preoccupied, entitled, and exploitative, tend to be low in empathic concern and rate themselves as low in communal characteristics (Campbell et al. 2006, Jonason & Krause 2013). In contrast, the presence of discomfort or anxiety in social interactions may signal selfish motivations. For example, people motivated to manage the impressions others have of them tend to be anxious, confused, and conflicted (Crocker & Canevello 2008, Leary et al. 2001).

Several constructs in the psychological literature appear to capture selfish motivation. For example, narcissistic personality characteristics, particularly entitlement (Campbell et al. 2004) and exploitativeness (Brunell et al. 2013), reflect selfish motivation. Dispositional greed (Seuntjens et al. 2015), materialism (Kasser et al. 2014), and aspiring for fame and fortune (Kasser & Ryan 1996) generally reflect selfish tendencies, although people can aspire to be wealthy or famous, or loved and community-oriented, for either selfish or otherish reasons (Carver & Baird 1998). In social interactions, impression management and self-image goals (Crocker & Canevello 2008) involve attempts to manage how others view oneself to obtain desired outcomes or avoid undesired outcomes, reflecting selfish inclinations. Unmitigated communion refers to a focus on others to the detriment of the self; people high in unmitigated communion feel compelled to care for others to demonstrate their worth to others and obtain others' care, which reflects selfish motivations (Fritz & Helgeson 1998). Egoistic reasons for caregiving involve providing care and support to relationship partners to obtain benefits for the self, such as looking good to others or feeling in control (Feeney & Collins 2003). Avoidance reasons for sacrificing in relationships appear to involve selfish motivations (e.g., "I do not want my partner to think negatively of me," "I have to sacrifice or my partner will not love me"), although they originally were not conceptualized as selfish (Impett et al. 2013). Finally, both anxious and avoidant attachment insecurities involve selfish motivations along with other qualities (Feeney & Collins 2003). In sum, several constructs involve selfish motivations, although many of the constructs mentioned have other components as well.

Costs of Selfish Motivation

Selfish motivation is clearly related to poor psychological well-being, physical health, and relationships. For example, materialism is associated with lower psychological well-being both cross-sectionally and over time (Kasser et al. 2014). A recent meta-analysis examining data from more than 250 independent samples confirms the robustness of this finding (Dittmar et al. 2014). One of the largest effects in this meta-analysis is the association between materialism and negative self-appraisals (e.g., self-doubt, self-discrepancy, and self-ambivalence). Dispositional greed is associated with lower life satisfaction and higher envy (Krekels & Pandelaere 2015). Self-image goals predict increased symptoms of anxiety and depression over time (Crocker et al. 2010), less emotional clarity and greater emotional confusion (Canevello & Crocker 2015), and greater loneliness (Crocker & Canevello 2008). Similarly, impression management goals are associated with social anxiety, self-handicapping, and even psychotic symptoms (Leary & Kowalski 1990). Unmitigated communion, which reflects selfish motivations for giving to others, is associated with psychological distress (Fritz & Helgeson 1998). Thus, empirical evidence links selfish motivations with poor psychological well-being.

Selfish motivations are linked with poor physical health outcomes as well. A meta-analysis reveals a strong association between materialism and risky health behaviors, including smoking and drinking alcohol (Dittmar et al. 2014). Many studies have also confirmed the association between self-presentational concerns and risky health behavior. For example, college freshmen higher in trait self-presentational concern are more likely to engage in behaviors such as smoking, drinking, reckless driving, and dangerous stunt attempts (Martin & Leary 2001). Self-presentational concerns are also associated with health-damaging behaviors such as failure to wear protective sports equipment, failure to seek medical treatment, and substance abuse (Leary et al. 1994, Martin et al. 2000). Narcissists, who tend to be selfishly motivated, also engage in risky health behaviors (Brunell & Buelow 2015).

Selfish motivations are linked to poor relationship outcomes. For example, people with more egoistic (versus altruistic) caregiving motivations tend to provide low levels of support to their partner, with negative consequences for the partner and for the relationship as a whole. Notably, when people with egoistic caregiving motivations do provide more support, they typically do so in ineffective ways that do not actually address the partner's needs (Feeney & Collins 2003). Similarly, self-image goals are associated with less responsiveness (Canevello & Crocker 2010) and less support provision (Crocker & Canevello 2008) to relationship partners, as well as more interpersonal conflict (Crocker & Canevello 2008). Self-image goals also predict decreased relationship stability via increased relationship avoidance and anxiety (Canevello et al. 2013).

Although some research on selfish motivations and well-being is correlational, making it difficult to distinguish cause from effect, other studies examine predictors of change over time in longitudinal designs, increasing the plausibility of causal associations (Canevello & Crocker 2010, Crocker & Canevello 2008).

Grandiose narcissists provide a puzzling exception to the costs of selfish motivation. People high in trait narcissism report high life satisfaction, well-being, and self-esteem (Rose 2002). Narcissists also seem relatively satisfied with their social relationships. Indeed, trait narcissists typically pursue romantic partners who will increase their own social status and esteem (Campbell 1999) and engage in game playing with their partners to retain greater power and autonomy within their romantic relationships (Rohmann et al. 2012). Although trait narcissists do not report lower relationship satisfaction, they do have difficulty maintaining healthy relationships over time and have a tendency to become aggressive when their self-esteem is threatened (Bushman & Baumeister 1998). The relationship partners of narcissists become dissatisfied over time, perhaps because narcissists have negative views of others, including their relationship partners, and tend to act in arrogant and aggressive ways (Brunell & Campbell 2011). Narcissism has not been linked with long-term physical health problems (for a review, see Konrath & Bonadonna 2014), but it is linked with worse cardiovascular profiles and heightened cortisol and alpha-amylase in response to negative affect (e.g., Cheng et al. 2013).

These findings suggest that narcissists may be unwilling to acknowledge poor psychological well-being, physical health, or relationships because they strive to maintain positive self-views and self-presentations. Thus, narcissists might be doing less well in these domains than they are willing to report. Alternatively, narcissists may simply not care about the quality of their relationships with others (Campbell et al. 2006) and as a result not suffer the negative consequences of selfishness that other people experience. In fact, narcissists acknowledge that narcissism has high social costs, yet they view it as a desirable trait that results in much personal gain (Carlson 2013). Further research is needed to determine why narcissists seem immune to the costs of selfish motivation.

Benefits of Selfish Motivation

Much as being otherish has some seemingly obvious costs, being selfish seemingly has some obvious benefits. Selfish people presumably obtain more resources for themselves at the expense of others. For example, people high in psychological entitlement, interpersonal exploitativeness, and/or dispositional greed make more competitive and fewer cooperative choices in resource allocation tasks, such as the commons dilemma and the dictator game. These competitive choices result in greater gain for the selfish person in the short term, to the detriment of others (Brunell et al. 2013, Seuntjens et al. 2015).

However, in terms of psychological well-being, physical health, and relationships, we have been unable to locate empirical evidence of the benefits of selfish motivation. Thus, although people expect selfish motivation to pay off, this motivation does not actually lead to improved well-being. This is the paradox of self-interested behavior.

Moderators and Mechanisms

What accounts for the negative effects of selfish motivations on psychological well-being, physical health, and relationships? Research suggests several candidate processes. People who are selfishly motivated experience higher negative affect (Canevello & Crocker 2015). Over time, chronic negative affect may undermine psychological well-being and physical health. Selfish motivations may also lead to less meaning and purpose in life, which as noted previously has known associations with psychological and physical health. Selfishness may undermine satisfaction of psychological needs for autonomy, competence, and relatedness (Dittmar et al. 2014). Selfishness may increase feelings of loneliness and disconnection from relationship partners (Canevello & Crocker 2015). Indeed, feeling lonely and isolated may be the unifying theme linking negative affect, decreased meaning and purpose, and unmet psychological needs. As noted previously, social isolation and loneliness have well-established consequences for psychological well-being and physical health. Even people who care for others but are motivated by selfishness may experience decreased connectedness and belongingness.

CONCLUSIONS

Are people basically selfish? People give and take in social relationships; they have the capacity to be both selfish and otherish. Indeed, people are hardwired for both self-interest and other-interest; in the face of threats to existence, the survival of the individual sometimes depends on the human capacity for self-interest. A fight-or-flight motivational system that promotes looking out for oneself can save lives in some circumstances. Yet, the survival of the species depends on the evolved human capacity to care for others. Humans have evolved to live cooperatively in social groups in which people take care of each other. Accordingly, it makes sense that people are psychologically constructed in such a way that giving to others can be rewarding despite its obvious material costs, and selfishness can be costly despite its immediate material benefits. In other words, humans should be psychologically disposed to find benefits in giving that counterbalance the costs, and they should be psychologically disposed to find costs in taking that counterbalance the benefits of selfishness.

Consistent with this hypothesis, research shows that in most circumstances of everyday giving, giving has a range of benefits for psychological well-being, physical health, and relationships. Giving can create a warm glow of happiness, boost self-esteem, increase self-efficacy, and reduce symptoms of depression. It predicts improvements in physical health and even predicts how long people live. It can strengthen social relationships, creating and strengthening social bonds and fostering the sense that one can make a valuable contribution to others. But giving is not universally good for health, well-being, and relationships. When the circumstances of caregiving are excessively burdensome, undermining satisfaction of caregivers' needs, the health, well-being, and relationships of caregivers can suffer.

Taking and receiving, on the other hand, can have negative effects for psychological well-being, physical health, and relationships. Taking and receiving can signal inferiority, dependence, and lack of competence, and they can suggest that one is a burden to others. These processes can create feelings of isolation, social disconnection, and loneliness, which in turn have negative effects on psychological well-being, physical health, and relationships. But taking and receiving are not universally bad. Under some circumstances, asking for and accepting help and receiving support can signal that one has value to others and that one is cared for, creating a sense of belonging and social connection that fosters health, well-being, and relationships.

The mixed consequences of giving and taking may depend on whether they are motivated by selfishness or otherishness. Our review of research on selfish and otherish motivations provides stark evidence consistent with the hypothesis that otherish motivation has benefits, and selfish motivation has costs. Indeed, we located no recent studies demonstrating that otherish motivation has costs or selfish motivation has benefits for psychological well-being, physical health, or relationships. This lack of evidence does not imply that selfishness never has benefits and otherishness never has costs; it may simply reflect a lack of research interest. The widespread assumption that people are fundamentally self-interested may reduce the interest value of research on the benefits of selfishness and the costs of otherishness, perhaps because researchers assume that those benefits and costs are well established.

Apparently, the only people who don't seem to suffer the costs of selfishness are those who truly don't care about the well-being of others or their relationships with others, such as narcissists. Such people are relatively rare, although their numbers may be increasing as cultural beliefs and practices create a "generation me" (Twenge 2006). Indeed, an increase in the prevalence of selfishness in the United States and other countries might lead to increased loneliness and feelings of social disconnection, accounting for parallel increases in depression and anxiety over time (Twenge 2000).

Why is otherishness associated with these benefits, and why is selfishness associated with these costs? Our review points to several candidate mechanisms or processes, including positive affect, increased self-esteem and self-efficacy, a sense of meaning and purpose, and a sense of connection with other people. We suspect that feeling meaningfully connected to others—valuable to them and valued by them—underlies all of these mechanisms. Human social life is interdependent, and human thriving depends critically on creating, maintaining, and strengthening social bonds. Selfish motivation can break mutually supportive connections with others, whereas otherish motivation builds mutually supportive connections with others.

Thus, giving guided by otherish motivation is good for the self in most circumstances. In most social relationships, in most contexts, otherish giving pays, not necessarily in time or money but in good health, psychological well-being, and mutually supportive relationships. Although less studied, taking and receiving guided by otherish motivation may also benefit the self. When people feel gratitude when receiving support, aid, and help, they feel more connected to their benefactors, which may boost well-being and promote good relationships.

In contrast, selfishness does not appear to foster psychological well-being, physical health, or healthy relationships. That is not to say that selfishness is never good for the self. In hostile social environments, or when satisfaction of fundamental needs is endangered, taking and selfish motivation may be necessary. Although selfishness may be essential to survival when other people do not or will not care for one's well-being, it likely does not lead to thriving or optimal well-being.

Research on the costs and benefits of selfishness and otherishness would benefit from careful attention to the measurement of these constructs. As noted, several constructs related to otherishness (e.g., empathic concern, communal orientation) and several constructs related to selfishness (e.g., narcissism, greed) have been studied. Yet, each of these constructs includes additional facets not directly related to otherishness or selfishness. Consequently, it is difficult to determine whether findings regarding these constructs can be ascribed directly to selfishness or otherishness. Understanding of the consequences of these motivations would be speeded by development of more precise measures of selfishness and otherishness.

Our review also points to several gaps in the literature, where sufficient research has not addressed important questions. Most important, research on the costs and benefits of selfishness has not received the same attention or scrutiny as the costs and benefits of otherishness. Perhaps because belief in the norm of self-interest is so pervasive, the benefits of selfishness seem obvious and the costs nonexistent. Research has focused on the more counterintuitive benefits of otherishness. Second, although we now know a great deal about the costs and benefits of giving and taking, and quite a bit about the costs and benefits of selfish and otherish motivation, we know much less about whether selfishness and otherishness are best thought of as personality traits, psychological states, or both. We know little about why people become selfish or otherish and what triggers shifts in the states of selfishness and otherishness. Understanding the triggers of selfishness and otherishness could help improve physical and psychological health and the quality of people's close relationships.

Relatedly, we know relatively little about cultural influences on selfishness and otherishness. People in collectivist cultures may be less selfish because cultural norms dictate giving priority to the goals of the collective over personal goals (Bresnahan et al. 2004, Calderón-Tena et al. 2011). However, cultural differences in otherishness may depend on who the "other" is. People in collectivist cultures may be more otherish toward ingroup members but less otherish toward outgroup members (Yamagishi et al. 2014). We also know little about cultural differences in the costs and benefits of selfishness and otherishness. Selfishness may have greater costs and otherishness may have greater benefits in collectivist cultures because of the strong social norms against selfishness (Kinias et al. 2014).

We also know little about the psychological and interpersonal dynamics of selfishness and otherishness. Behavioral economists have greatly advanced our understanding of giving and taking in financial transactions, but they rarely explore the consequences of these transactions for mood, self-efficacy, self-esteem, or a sense of purpose, meaning, and belonging. We know even less about how selfishness and otherishness in financial transactions affect the development of closeness in interpersonal relationships and their long-term consequences for health and well-being. Social and personality psychologists have begun to explore otherish behavior and motivation in close relationships, but the predictors and consequences of selfishness have received relatively little research attention.

The norm of self-interest shapes psychological research and theory, limiting our understanding of basic psychological phenomena. How would theories and research in evolutionary psychology, the self, helping behavior, and close relationships be altered if they did not begin with the explicit or implicit assumption that people are fundamentally or primarily self-centered, self-serving, and self-interested? By questioning the idea that the default social motivation is selfishness and that otherishness is the exception to the rule, researchers could better understand the costs and benefits of both self-interest and other-interest as well as their interpersonal and societal consequences.

If otherish motivation is as much a part of human nature as selfishness, such a rethinking of the norm of self-interest could lead to a better understanding of what it means to be human and what enables people to thrive.

SUMMARY POINTS

1. People are psychologically constructed in such a way that giving to others can be rewarding despite its obvious material costs, and selfishness can be costly despite its immediate material benefits.

2. Giving has a range of benefits for psychological well-being, physical health, and relationships, but giving is not universally good for health, well-being, and relationships. When the circumstances of caregiving are excessively burdensome, undermining satisfaction of caregivers' needs, the health, well-being, and relationships of caregivers can suffer.

3. Taking, on the other hand, can have negative effects for psychological well-being, physical health, and relationships. Taking can signal inferiority, dependence, and lack of competence, and it can suggest that one is a burden to others. These processes can create feelings of isolation, social disconnection, and loneliness, which in turn have negative effects on psychological well-being, physical health, and relationships.

4. The mixed consequences of giving and taking may depend on whether they are motivated by selfishness or otherishness.

5. Our review of research on selfish and otherish motivations provides stark evidence of the benefits of otherish motivation and the costs of selfish motivation. Indeed, we located no recent studies demonstrating that otherish motivation has costs or selfish motivation has benefits for psychological well-being, physical health, or relationships.

6. Human social life is interdependent, and human thriving depends critically on creating, maintaining, and strengthening social bonds. Selfish motivation can break mutually supportive connections with others, whereas otherish motivation builds mutually supportive connections with others.

FUTURE ISSUES

1. Research on the costs and benefits of selfishness and otherishness would benefit from careful attention to measurement of these constructs.

2. Research on the costs and benefits of selfishness has not received the same attention or scrutiny as the costs and benefits of otherishness.

3. Although we now know a great deal about the costs and benefits of giving and taking, and quite a bit about the costs and benefits of selfish and otherish motivation, we know much less about whether selfishness and otherishness are best thought of as personality traits, psychological states, or both.

4. We know little about why people become selfish or otherish and what triggers shifts in the states of selfishness and otherishness. Understanding the triggers of selfishness and otherishness could help improve physical and psychological health and the quality of people's close relationships.

5. We know relatively little about cultural influences on selfishness and otherishness.

6. We know little about the psychological and interpersonal dynamics of selfishness and otherishness.

ACKNOWLEDGMENTS

We are grateful to Amy Brunell, Belinda Campos, Long Ha, Tao Jiang, Lexi Keaveney, Bonnie Le, Shuqi Li, Yu Niiya, and Michael Poulin for their helpful comments on previous drafts of this manuscript.

LITERATURE CITED

Abelson JL, Erickson TM, Mayer SE, Crocker J, Briggs H, et al. 2014. Brief cognitive intervention can modulate neuroendocrine stress responses to the Trier Social Stress Test: buffering effects of a compassionate goal orientation. *Psychoneuroendocrinology* 44:60–70

Ablitt A, Jones GV, Muers J. 2009. Living with dementia: a systematic review of the influence of relationship factors. *Aging Ment. Health* 13:497–511

Aknin L, Dunn E, Whillans A, Grant A, Norton M. 2013. Making a difference matters: Impact unlocks the emotional benefits of prosocial spending. *J. Econ. Behav. Organ.* 88:90–95

Aknin L, Hamlin JK, Dunn E. 2012. Giving leads to happiness in young children. *PLOS ONE* 7:e39211

Aknin L, Human L. 2015. Give a piece of you: Gifts that reflect givers promote closeness. *J. Exp. Soc. Psychol.* 60:8–16

Alicke MD, Sedikides C. 2011. *Handbook of Self-Enhancement and Self-Protection.* New York: Guilford

Andreoni J, Rao J, Trachtman H. 2011. *Avoiding the Ask: A Field Experiment on Altruism, Empathy, and Charitable Giving.* Cambridge, MA: Natl. Bureau Econ. Res.

Barasch A, Levine EE, Berman JZ, Small DA. 2014. Selfish or selfless? On the signal value of emotion in altruistic behavior. *J. Personal. Soc. Psychol.* 107:393–413

Barbee A, Rowatt T, Cunningham M. 1998. When a friend is in need: feelings about seeking, giving, and receiving social support. In *Handbook of Communication and Emotion: Research, Theory, Applications, and Contexts,* ed. P Andersen, L Guerrero, pp. 281–301. San Diego, CA: Academic

Batson CD. 2010. Empathy-induced altruistic motivation. See Mikulincer & Shaver 2010, pp. 15–34

Bohns VK, Flynn FJ. 2010. "Why didn't you just ask?" Underestimating the discomfort of help-seeking. *J. Exp. Soc. Psychol.* 46:402–9

Bolger N, Zuckerman A, Kessler RC. 2000. Invisible support and adjustment to stress. *J. Personal. Soc. Psychol.* 79:953–61

Bresnahan MJ, Chiu HC, Levine TR. 2004. Self-construal as a predictor of communal and exchange orientation in Taiwan and the USA. *Asian J. Soc. Psychol.* 7:187–203

Brown RM, Brown SL. 2014. Informal caregiving: a reappraisal of effects on caregivers. *Soc. Issues Policy Rev.* 8:74–102

Brown SL, Brown RM, House JS, Smith DM. 2008. Coping with spousal loss: potential buffering effects of self-reported helping behavior. *Personal. Soc. Psychol. Bull.* 34:849–61

Brown SL, Nesse RM, Vinokur AD, Smith DM. 2003. Providing social support may be more beneficial than receiving it: results from a prospective study of mortality. *Psychol. Sci.* 14:320–27

Brown SL, Smith DM, Schulz R, Kabeto MU, Ubel PA, et al. 2009. Caregiving behavior is associated with decreased mortality risk. *Psychol. Sci.* 20:488–94

Brunell AB, Buelow MT. 2015. Narcissism and performance on behavioral decision-making tasks. *J. Behav. Decis. Making.* doi: 10.1002/bdm.1900

Brunell AB, Campbell WK. 2011. Narcissism and romantic relationships: understanding the paradox. In *The Handbook of Narcissism and Narcissistic Personality Disorder: Theoretical Approaches, Empirical Findings, and Treatments,* ed. WK Campbell, JD Miller, pp. 344–50. Hoboken, NJ: Wiley

Brunell AB, Davis MS, Schley DR, Eng AL, van Dulmen MHM, et al. 2013. A new measure of interpersonal exploitativeness. *Front. Psychol.* 4:299

Bushman BJ, Baumeister RF. 1998. Threatened egotism, narcissism, self-esteem, and direct and displaced aggression: Does self-love or self-hate lead to violence? *J. Personal. Soc. Psychol.* 75:219–29

Cain DM, Dana J, Newman GE. 2014. Giving versus giving in. *Acad. Manag. Ann.* 8:505–33

Calderón-Tena CO, Knight GP, Carlo G. 2011. The socialization of prosocial behavioral tendencies among Mexican American adolescents: the role of familism values. *Cultur. Divers. Ethnic Minor. Psychol.* 17:98–106

Campbell WK. 1999. Narcissism and romantic attraction. *J. Personal. Soc. Psychol.* 77:1254–70

Campbell WK, Bonacci AM, Shelton J, Exline JJ, Bushman BJ. 2004. Psychological entitlement: interpersonal consequences and validation of a self-report measure. *J. Personal. Assess.* 83:29–45

Campbell WK, Brunell AB, Finkel EJ. 2006. Narcissism, interpersonal self-regulation, and romantic relationships: an agency model approach. In *Self and Relationships: Connecting Intrapersonal and Interpersonal Processes*, ed. KD Vohs, EJ Finkel, pp. 57–83. New York: Guilford

Canevello A, Crocker J. 2010. Creating good relationships: responsiveness, relationship quality, and interpersonal goals. *J. Personal. Soc. Psychol.* 99:78–106

Canevello A, Crocker J. 2011. Interpersonal goals, others' regard for the self, and self-esteem: the paradoxical consequences of self-image and compassionate goals. *Eur. J. Soc. Psychol.* 41:422–34

Canevello A, Crocker J. 2015. How self-image and compassionate goals shape intrapsychic experiences. *Personal. Soc. Psychol. Compass* 9:620–29

Canevello A, Granillo MT, Crocker J. 2013. Predicting change in relationship insecurity: the roles of compassionate and self-image goals. *Pers. Relatsh.* 20:587–618

Carlson EN. 2013. Honestly arrogant or simply misunderstood? Narcissists' awareness of their narcissism. *Self Identity* 12:259–77

Carver CS, Baird E. 1998. The American dream revisited: Is it what you want or why you want it that matters? *Psychol. Sci.* 9:289–92

Chen F, Greenberg J. 2004. A positive aspect of caregiving: the influence of social support on caregiving gains for family members of relatives with schizophrenia. *Community Ment. Health J.* 40:423–35

Cheng JT, Tracy JL, Miller GE. 2013. Are narcissists hardy or vulnerable? The role of narcissism in the production of stress-related biomarkers in response to emotional distress. *Emotion* 13:1004–11

Cialdini RB, Brown SL, Lewis BP, Luce C, Neuberg SL. 1997. Reinterpreting the empathy-altruism relationship: when one into one equals oneness. *J. Personal. Soc. Psychol.* 73:481–94

Cialdini RB, Schaller M, Houlihan D, Arps K, Fultz J, Beaman AL. 1987. Empathy-based helping: Is it selflessly or selfishly motivated? *J. Personal. Soc. Psychol.* 52:749–58

Clark MS, Aragón OR. 2013. Communal (and other) relationships: history, theory development, recent findings, and future directions. In *The Oxford Handbook of Close Relationships*, ed. JA Simpson, L Campbell, pp. 255–80. New York: Oxford Univ. Press

Clark MS, Lemay EP Jr. 2010. Close relationships. In *Handbook of Social Psychology*, Vol. 2, ed. ST Fiske, DT Gilbert, G Lindzey, pp. 898–940. Hoboken, NJ: Wiley. 5th ed.

Clark MS, Oullette R, Powell MC, Milberg S. 1987. Recipient's mood, relationship type, and helping. *J. Personal. Soc. Psychol.* 53:94–103

Collins NL, Feeney BC. 2000. A safe haven: an attachment theory perspective on support seeking and care giving in close relationships. *J. Personal. Soc. Psychol.* 78:1053–73

Crocker J, Canevello A. 2008. Creating and undermining social support in communal relationships: the role of compassionate and self-image goals. *J. Personal. Soc. Psychol.* 95:555–75

Crocker J, Canevello A. 2012. Consequences of self-image and compassionate goals. In *Advances in Experimental Social Psychology*, Vol. 45, ed. P Devine, A Plant, pp. 229–77. San Diego, CA: Academic

Crocker J, Canevello A, Breines JG, Flynn H. 2010. Interpersonal goals and change in anxiety and dysphoria in first-semester college students. *J. Personal. Soc. Psychol.* 98:1009–24

Cutrona C. 1996. *Social Support in Marriage*. Thousand Oaks, CA: Sage

Cutrona C, Russell D, Rose J. 1986. Social support and adaptation to stress by the elderly. *Psychol. Aging* 1:47–54

Damjanovic AK, Yang Y, Glaser R, Kiecolt-Glaser JK, Nguyen H, et al. 2007. Accelerated telomere erosion is associated with a declining immune function of caregivers of Alzheimer's disease patients. *J. Immunol.* 179:4249–54

Dawes R. 1980. Social dilemmas. *Annu. Rev. Psychol.* 31:169–93

Deci EL, La Guardia JG, Moller AC, Scheiner MJ, Ryan RM. 2006. On the benefits of giving as well as receiving autonomy support: mutuality in close friendships. *Personal. Soc. Psychol. Bull.* 32:313–27

DeSteno D, Bartlett MY, Baumann J, Williams LA, Dickens L. 2010. Gratitude as moral sentiment: emotion-guided cooperation in economic exchange. *Emotion* 10:289–93

Dittmar H, Bond R, Hurst M, Kasser T. 2014. The relationship between materialism and personal well-being: a meta-analysis. *J. Personal. Soc. Psychol.* 107:879–924

Don B, Mickelson K, Barbee A. 2013. Indirect support seeking and perceptions of spousal support: an examination of a reciprocal relationship. *Pers. Relatsh.* 20:655–68

Dunn EW, Aknin LB, Norton MI. 2008a. Spending money on others promotes happiness. *Science* 319:1687–88

Dunn EW, Huntsinger J, Lun J, Sinclair S. 2008b. The gift of similarity: how good and bad gifts influence relationships. *Soc. Cogn.* 26:469–81

Dunning D, Fetchenhauer D, Schlösser T. 2016. The psychology of respect: a case study of how behavioral norms regulate human action. *Adv. Motiv. Sci.* 3:1–34

Falk A, Fehr E, Fischbacher U. 2007. On the nature of fair behavior. *Econ. Inq.* 41:20–26

Feeney BC, Collins NL. 2003. Motivations for caregiving in adult intimate relationships: influences on caregiving behavior and relationship functioning. *Personal. Soc. Psychol. Bull.* 29:950–68

Feeney BC, Collins NL, van Vleet M, Tomlinson JM. 2013. Motivations for providing a secure base: links with attachment orientation and secure base support behavior. *Attachment Hum. Dev.* 15:261–80

Fehr B. 2010. Compassionate love as a prosocial emotion. See Mikulincer & Shaver 2010, pp. 245–65

Fehr B, Harasymchuk C, Sprecher S. 2014. Compassionate love in romantic relationships: a review and some new findings. *J. Soc. Pers. Relatsh.* 31:575–600

Feinberg L, Reinhard SC, Houser A, Choula R. 2011. *Valuing the Invaluable: 2011 Update. The Growing Contributions and Costs of Family Caregiving.* Washington, DC: AARP Policy Inst.

Fisher J, Nadler A, Whitcher-Alagna S. 1982. Recipient reactions to aid. *Psychol. Bull.* 91:27–54

Flynn FJ, Lake VKB. 2008. If you need help, just ask: underestimating compliance with direct requests for help. *J. Personal. Soc. Psychol.* 95:128–43

Fritz HL, Helgeson VS. 1998. Distinctions of unmitigated communion from communion: self-neglect and overinvolvement with others. *J. Personal. Soc. Psychol.* 75:121–40

Gable SL, Reis HT. 2006. Intimacy and the self: an iterative model of the self and close relationships. In *Close Relationships: Functions, Forms and Processes*, ed. P Noller, JA Feeney, pp. 211–25. Hove, UK: Psychol. Press/ Taylor & Francis

Gilbert P, McEwan K, Matos M, Rivis A. 2011. Fears of compassion: development of three self-report measures. *Psychol. Psychother.* 84:239–55

Giving Inst. 2015. *Giving USA Annual Report.* Chicago: Giving Inst. **http://www.givinginstitute.org/ ?page=GUSAAnnualReport**

Gleason MEJ, Iida M, Shrout PE, Bolger N. 2008. Receiving support as a mixed blessing: evidence for dual effects of support on psychological outcomes. *J. Personal. Soc. Psychol.* 94:824–38

Grant AM. 2013. *Give and Take: Why Helping Others Drives Our Success.* New York: Penguin

Gray K, Ward AF, Norton MI. 2014. Paying it forward: generalized reciprocity and the limits of generosity. *J. Exp. Psychol.: Gen.* 143:247–54

Grouzet FME, Kasser T, Ahuvia A, Dols JMF, Kim Y, et al. 2005. The structure of goal contents across 15 cultures. *J. Personal. Soc. Psychol.* 89:800–16

Haber MG, Cohen JL, Lucas T, Baltes BB. 2007. The relationship between self-reported received and perceived social support: a meta-analytic review. *Am. J. Community Psychol.* 39:133–44

Hadden BW, Smith CV, Knee CR. 2014. The way I make you feel: how relatedness and compassionate goals promote partner's relationship satisfaction. *J. Posit. Psychol.* 9:155–62

Hawkley LC, Cacioppo JT. 2010. Loneliness matters: a theoretical and empirical review of consequences and mechanisms. *Ann. Behav. Med.* 40:218–27

Heisler M, Choi H, Piette J, Rosland A, Langa K, Brown S. 2013. Adults with cardiovascular disease who help others: a prospective study of health outcomes. *J. Behav. Med.* 36:199–211

Hilgeman M, Allen R, DeCoster J, Burgio L. 2007. Positive aspects of caregiving as a moderator of treatment outcome over 12 months. *Psychol. Aging* 22:361–71

Hill PL, Turiano NA. 2014. Purpose in life as a predictor of mortality across adulthood. *Psychol. Sci.* 25:1482–86

Hobbes T. 1950/1651. *Leviathan.* New York: Dutton

Hong S, Morrow-Howell N. 2010. Health outcomes of Experience Corps®: a high-commitment volunteer program. *Soc. Sci. Med.* 71:414–20

Impett EA, Javam L, Le BM, Asyabi-Eshghi B, Kogan A. 2013. The joys of genuine giving: approach and avoidance sacrifice motivation and authenticity. *Pers. Relatsh.* 20:740–54

Johnson ND, Mislin AA. 2011. Trust games: a meta-analysis. *J. Econ. Psychol.* 32:865–89

Joiner T, Metalsky G, Katz J, Beach S. 1999. Depression and excessive reassurance-seeking. *Psychol. Inq.* 10:269–78

Jonason PK, Krause L. 2013. The emotional deficits associated with the Dark Triad traits: cognitive empathy, affective empathy, and alexithymia. *Personal. Individ. Differ.* 55:532–37

Kasser T, Rosenblum KL, Sameroff AJ, Deci EL, Niemiec CP, et al. 2014. Changes in materialism, changes in psychological well-being: evidence from three longitudinal studies and an intervention experiment. *Motiv. Emot.* 38:1–22

Kasser T, Ryan RM. 1996. Further examining the American dream: differential correlates of intrinsic and extrinsic goals. *Personal. Soc. Psychol. Bull.* 22:280–87

Kasser T, Ryan RM. 2001. Be careful what you wish for: optimal functioning and the relative attainment of intrinsic and extrinsic goals. In *Life Goals and Well-Being: Towards a Positive Psychology of Human Striving,* ed. P Schmuck, KM Sheldon, pp. 116–31. Ashland, OH: Hogrefe & Huber

Kasser T, Sheldon K. 2002. What makes for a merry Christmas? *J. Happiness Stud.* 3:313–29

Kiecolt-Glaser JK, Marucha PT, Mercado AM, Malarkey WB, Glaser R. 1995. Slowing of wound healing by psychological stress. *Lancet* 346:1194–96

Kiecolt-Glaser JK, Preacher KJ, MacCallum RC, Atkinson A, Malarkey WB, Glaser R. 2003. Chronic stress and age-related increases in the proinflammatory cytokine IL-6. *PNAS* 100:9090–95

Kim ES, Sun JK, Park N, Kubzansky LD, Peterson C. 2013. Purpose in life and reduced risk of myocardial infarction among older U.S. adults with coronary heart disease: a two-year follow-up. *J. Behav. Med.* 36:124–33

Kinias Z, Kim HS, Hafenbrack AC, Lee JJ. 2014. Standing out as a signal to selfishness: culture and devaluation of non-normative characteristics. *Organ. Behav. Hum. Decis. Process.* 124:190–203

Konrath S, Bonadonna JP. 2014. Physiological and health-related correlates of the narcissistic personality. In *Handbook of the Psychology of Narcissism: Diverse Perspectives,* ed. A Besser, pp. 175–213. Hauppauge, NY: Nova Sci.

Konrath S, Fuhrel-Forbis A, Lou A, Brown S. 2012. Motives for volunteering are associated with mortality risk in older adults. *Health Psychol.* 31:87–96

Krause N. 2007. Longitudinal study of social support and meaning in life. *Psychol. Aging* 22:456–69

Krekels G, Pandelaere M. 2015. Dispositional greed. *Personal. Individ. Differ.* 74:225–30

Laurenceau J-P, Barrett LF, Rovine MJ. 2005. The interpersonal process model of intimacy in marriage: a daily-diary and multilevel modeling approach. *J. Fam. Psychol.* 19:314–23

Le BM, Impett EA, Kogan A, Webster GD, Cheng C. 2013. The personal and interpersonal rewards of communal orientation. *J. Soc. Pers. Relatsh.* 30:694–710

Leary MR, Hofmann SG, DiBartolo PM. 2001. Social anxiety as an early warning system: a refinement and extension of the self-presentation theory of social anxiety. In *From Social Anxiety to Social Phobia: Multiple Perspectives,* ed. SG Hofmann, PM DiBartolo, pp. 321–34. Needham Heights, MA: Allyn & Bacon

Leary MR, Kowalski RM. 1990. Impression management: a literature review and two-component model. *Psychol. Bull.* 107:34–47

Leary MR, Tchividijian LR, Kraxberger BE. 1994. Self-presentation can be hazardous to your health: impression management and health risk. *Health Psychol.* 13:461–70

Li Y, Li H, Decety J, Lee K. 2013. Experiencing a natural disaster alters children's altruistic giving. *Psychol. Sci.* 24:1686–95

Martin KA, Leary MR. 2001. Self-presentational determinants of health risk behavior among college freshmen. *Psychol. Health* 16:17–27

Martin KA, Leary MR, Rejeski WJ. 2000. Self-presentational concerns in older adults: implications for health and well-being. *Basic Appl. Soc. Psychol.* 22:169–79

McClure M, Xu J, Craw J, Lane S, Bolger N, Shrout P. 2014. Understanding the costs of support transactions in daily life. *J. Personal.* 82:563–74

Midlarsky E. 1991. Helping as coping. In *Prosocial Behavior*, ed. M Clark, pp. 238–64. Thousand Oaks, CA: Sage

Mikulincer M, Shaver PRR, eds. 2010. *Prosocial Motives, Emotions, and Behavior: The Better Angels of Our Nature.* Washington, DC: Am. Psychol. Assoc.

Miller DT. 1999. The norm of self-interest. *Am. Psychol.* 54:1053–60

Mills J, Clark MS, Ford TE, Johnson M. 2004. Measurement of communal strength. *Pers. Relatsh.* 11:213–30

Mogilner C. 2010. The pursuit of happiness: time, money, and social connection. *Psychol. Sci.* 21:1348–54

Monin J, Schulz R. 2009. Interpersonal effects of suffering in older adult caregiving relationships. *Psychol. Aging* 24:681–95

Morelli SA, Lee IA, Arnn ME, Zaki J. 2015. Emotional and instrumental support provision interact to predict well-being. *Emotion* 15:484–93

Murray SL, Holmes JG, Collins NL. 2006. Optimizing assurance: the risk regulation system in relationships. *Psychol. Bull.* 132:641–66

Musick M, Wilson J. 2003. Volunteering and depression: the role of psychological and social resources in different age groups. *Soc. Sci. Med.* 56:259–69

Nadler A, Halabi S, Harapz-Gorodeisky G, Ben-David Y. 2010. Helping relations as status relations. See Mikulincer & Shaver 2010, pp. 181–200

Neel R, Kenrick DT, White AE, Neuberg SL. 2016. Individual differences in fundamental social motives. *J. Personal. Soc. Psychol.* 110:887–907

Nelson SK, Layous K, Cole SW, Lyubomirky S. 2016. Do unto others or treat yourself? The effects of prosocial and self-focused behavior on psychological flourishing. *Emotion.* 16:850–61

Oppenheimer DM, Olivola CY. 2011. *The Science of Giving: Experimental Approaches to the Study of Charity.* New York: Psychol. Press

Pasch L, Bradbury T. 1998. Social support, conflict, and the development of marital dysfunction. *J. Consult. Clin. Psychol.* 66:219–30

Penninx BW, van Tilburg T, Kriegsman DM, Deeg DJ, Boeke AJ, van Eijk JT. 1997. Effects of social support and personal coping resources on mortality in older age: the Longitudinal Aging Study of Amsterdam. *Am. J. Epidemiol.* 46:510–19

Piferi R, Lawler K. 2006. Social support and ambulatory blood pressure: an examination of both receiving and giving. *Int. J. Psychophysiol.* 62:328–36

Pinquart M, Sörensen S. 2003a. Associations of stressors and uplifts of caregiving with caregiver burden and depressive mood: a meta-analysis. *J. Gerontol. B Psychol. Sci. Soc. Sci.* 58:P112–28

Pinquart M, Sörensen S. 2003b. Differences between caregivers and noncaregivers in psychological health and physical health: a meta-analysis. *Psychol. Aging* 18:250–67

Pinquart M, Sörensen S. 2007. Correlates of physical health of informal caregivers: a meta-analysis. *J. Gerontol. B Psychol. Sci. Soc. Sci.* 62:P126–37

Pinquart M, Sörensen S. 2011. Spouses, adult children, and children-in-law as caregivers of older adults: a meta-analytic comparison. *Psychol. Aging* 26:1–14

Post SG. 2005. Altruism, happiness, and health: It's good to be good. *Int. J. Behav. Med.* 12:66–77

Poulin M, Brown S, Ubel P, Smith D, Jankovic A, Langa K. 2010. Does a helping hand mean a heavy heart? Helping behavior and well-being among spouse caregivers. *Psychol. Aging* 25:108–17

Preston SD. 2013. The origins of altruism in offspring care. *Psychol. Bull.* 139:1305–41

Quinn C, Clare L, McGuinness T, Woods RT. 2012. The impact of relationships, motivations, and meanings on dementia caregiving outcomes. *Int. Psychogeriatr.* 24:1816–26

Quinn C, Clare L, Woods B. 2009. The impact of the quality of relationship on the experiences and wellbeing of caregivers of people with dementia: a systematic review. *Aging Ment. Health* 13:143–54

Quinn C, Clare L, Woods RT. 2015. Balancing needs: the role of motivations, meanings and relationship dynamics in the experience of informal caregivers of people with dementia. *Dementia (Lond.)* 14:220–37

Rauer AJ, Sabey A, Jensen JF. 2014. Growing old together: compassionate love and health in older adulthood. *J. Soc. Pers. Relatsh.* 31:677–96

Reis HT, Collins WA, Berscheid E. 2000. The relationship context of human behavior and development. *Psychol. Bull.* 126:844–72

Reis HT, Maniaci MR, Rogge RD. 2014. The expression of compassionate love in everyday compassionate acts. *J. Soc. Pers. Relatsh.* 31:651–76

Rohmann E, Neumann E, Herner MJ, Bierhoff H-W. 2012. Grandiose and vulnerable narcissism: self-construal, attachment, and love in romantic relationships. *Eur. Psychol.* 17:279–90

Rose P. 2002. The happy and unhappy faces of narcissism. *Personal. Individ. Differ.* 33:379–92

Santini ZI, Koyanagi A, Tyrovolas S, Mason C, Haro JM. 2015. The association between social relationships and depression: a systematic review. *J. Affect. Disord.* 175:53–65

Sarason IG, Pierce GR, Sarason BR. 1990. Social support and interactional processes: a triadic hypothesis. *J. Soc. Pers. Relatsh.* 7:495–506

Sarid O, Melzer I, Kurz I, Shahar D, Ruch W. 2010. The effect of helping behavior and physical activity on mood states and depressive symptoms of elderly people. *Clin. Gerontol.* 33:270–82

Schulz R, Beach S. 1999. Caregiving as a risk factor for mortality: the Caregiver Health Effects Study. *JAMA* 281:2215–19

Schwartz C, Meisenhelder JB, Ma Y, Reed G. 2003. Altruistic social interest behaviors are associated with better mental health. *Psychosom. Med.* 65:778–85

Schwarzer R, Knoll N. 2007. Functional roles of social support within the stress and coping process: a theoretical and empirical overview. *Int. J. Psychol.* 42:243–52

Sears DO, Funk CL. 1990. Self-interest in Americans' political opinions. In *Beyond Self-Interest*, ed. JJ Mansbridge, pp. 147–70. Chicago: Univ. Chicago Press

Seuntjens TG, Zeelenberg M, van de Ven N, Breugelmans SM. 2015. Dispositional greed. *J. Personal. Soc. Psychol.* 108:917–33

Shaver PR, Mikulincer M, Shemesh-Iron M. 2010. A behavioral-systems perspective on prosocial behavior. See Mikulincer & Shaver 2010, pp. 73–91

Sheldon KM, Elliot AJ. 1999. Goal striving, need satisfaction, and longitudinal well-being: the self-concordance model. *J. Personal. Soc. Psychol.* 76:482–97

Shrout PE, Herman CM, Bolger N. 2006. The costs and benefits of practical and emotional support on adjustment: a daily diary study of couples experiencing acute stress. *Pers. Relatsh.* 13:115–34

Slotter EB, Gardner WL, Finkel EJ. 2010. Who am I without you? The influence of romantic breakup on the self-concept. *Personal. Soc. Psychol. Bull.* 36:147–60

Sprecher S, Fehr B. 2005. Compassionate love for close others and humanity. *J. Soc. Pers. Relatsh.* 22:629–51

Sprecher S, Fehr B. 2006. Enhancement of mood and self-esteem as a result of giving and receiving compassionate love. *Curr. Res. Soc. Psychol.* 11:227–42

Stillman TF, Lambert NM. 2013. The bidirectional relationship of meaning and belonging. In *The Experience of Meaning in Life: Classical Perspectives, Emerging Themes, and Controversies*, ed. JA Hicks, C Routledge, pp. 305–15. New York: Springer Sci.

Strazdins L, Broom D. 2007. The mental health costs and benefits of giving social support. *Int. J. Stress Manag.* 14:370–85

Tay L, Tan K, Diener E, Gonzalez E. 2013. Social relations, health behaviors, and health outcomes: a survey and synthesis. *Appl. Psychol. Health Well-Being* 5:28–78

Thoits PA, Hewitt LN. 2001. Volunteer work and well-being. *J. Health Soc. Behav.* 42:115–31

Twenge JM. 2000. The age of anxiety? The birth cohort change in anxiety and neuroticism, 1952–1993. *J. Personal. Soc. Psychol.* 79:1007–21

Twenge JM. 2006. *Generation Me: Why Today's Young Americans Are More Confident, Assertive, Entitled—and More Miserable Than Ever Before.* New York: Free Press

Uchino BN. 2004. *Social Support and Physical Health: Understanding the Health Consequences of Our Relationships.* New Haven, CT: Yale Univ. Press

Uchino BN, Cacioppo JT, Kiecolt-Glaser JK. 1996. The relationship between social support and physiological processes: a review with emphasis on underlying mechanisms and implications for health. *Psychol. Bull.* 119:488–531

Vitaliano P, Zhang J, Scanlan J. 2003. Is caregiving hazardous to one's physical health? A meta-analysis. *Psychol. Bull.* 129:946–72

Yamagishi T, Li Y, Takagishi H, Matsumoto Y, Kiyonari T. 2014. In search of *Homo economicus. Psychol. Sci.* 25:1699–711

Yinon Y, Landau M. 1987. On the reinforcing value of helping behavior in a positive mood. *Motiv. Emot.* 11:83–93

Attitude Strength

Lauren C. Howe[1] and Jon A. Krosnick[2]

[1]Department of Psychology, Stanford University, Stanford, California 94305;
email: lchowe@stanford.edu

[2]Department of Communication, Stanford University, Stanford, California 94305;
email: krosnick@stanford.edu

Annu. Rev. Psychol. 2017. 68:327–51

First published online as a Review in Advance on
September 2, 2016

The *Annual Review of Psychology* is online at
psych.annualreviews.org

This article's doi:
10.1146/annurev-psych-122414-033600

Keywords

attitude, strength, importance, impact, stability

Abstract

Attitude strength has been the focus of a huge volume of research in psychology and related sciences for decades. The insights offered by this literature have tremendous value for understanding attitude functioning and structure and for the effective application of the attitude concept in applied settings. This is the first *Annual Review of Psychology* article on the topic, and it offers a review of theory and evidence regarding one of the most researched strength-related attitude features: attitude importance. Personal importance is attached to an attitude when the attitude is perceived to be relevant to self-interest, social identification with reference groups or reference individuals, and values. Attaching personal importance to an attitude causes crystallizing of attitudes (via enhanced resistance to change), effortful gathering and processing of relevant information, accumulation of a large store of well-organized relevant information in long-term memory, enhanced attitude extremity and accessibility, enhanced attitude impact on the regulation of interpersonal attraction, energizing of emotional reactions, and enhanced impact of attitudes on behavioral intentions and action. Thus, important attitudes are real and consequential psychological forces, and their study offers opportunities for addressing behavioral change.

Contents

INTRODUCTION

The study of attitudes has been central to social psychological theory development since the birth of the field, and psychological insights into attitudes have enjoyed tremendous impact in a wide range of applied settings, including politics, health, marketing, education, and many more. However, the literature on attitudes has had its share of crises. Most importantly, the initial conception of attitudes, developed by scholars in the 1920s and 1930s, viewed them as evaluations, ranging from positive to negative, that efficiently encapsulate prior life experiences and direct thinking and action. Yet, as early as the 1930s, it appeared that attitude might not be as useful a tool for explaining cognition and behavior as had been assumed (LaPiere 1934).

Over the subsequent decades, researchers rescued the concept's apparent utility, pointing out, for instance, the facts that behavior is influenced by many factors other than attitudes (Ajzen & Fishbein 1980), that some people behave more according to their attitudes than do others (Ajzen et al. 1982), and that people act more according to their attitudes in some circumstances than in others (Pryor et al. 1977).

Arguably one of the most valuable advances in the understanding of attitudes was the recognition that attitudes vary in strength. In short, an attitude's strength describes the extent to which an attitude is consequential in shaping thinking and action across situations. Some attitudes are strong and some are weak; strong attitudes have the characteristics that researchers a century ago mistakenly assumed are possessed by all attitudes. In other words, strong attitudes are the attitudes that matter most for an individual's thoughts, intentions, and behavior.

Ignoring the fact that some attitudes are weak risks making assumptions that are counterproductive both for the development of theory and for the successful utilization of the attitude concept in applied settings. Consider, for example, public health professionals, manufacturing companies, political candidates, lobbying groups, and many other individuals and organizations that have spent billions of dollars attempting to change public attitudes to influence behavior. Time and again, such efforts have failed to produce the desired outcomes. One likely explanation for this failure lies with the concept of attitude strength: Attitudes that can be easily changed are weak and unlikely to shape behavior. The attitudes that most powerfully shape behavior are the hardest to change.

Because strong attitudes are resistant to change, efforts to change behavior might ignore such attitudes and focus, instead, on weak attitudes. Fortunately for these efforts, the literature on persuasion points to numerous strategies for changing weak attitudes (Perloff 2013). However, once those attitudes are changed, intervention efforts must not stop. Instead, those new attitudes must be strengthened so that they do not snap back but instead remain behaviorally consequential. A drop of a mixture of glue and catalyst must be put on a new attitude to cement and energize it. In short, the new attitude must be made strong.

But what must be done to make an attitude strong? And what consequences of strength can be expected from such an intervention? Understanding the nature, causes, and consequences of attitude strength may have great value not only for the building of social psychological theory but also for practical applications of that theory.

In this article, we offer a selective review of the accumulating literature on this topic. This is the first *Annual Review of Psychology* article on the topic, and our space limitations preclude a comprehensive review of the huge literature in this area. We have chosen to begin what may become a series of articles on the topic by highlighting the existing theory and research and the remaining questions about one of the most researched strength-related variables: attitude importance. This article offers an opportunity to paint a vivid portrait of what is known about this variable and thereby to set the stage for similar reviews of work on other variables.

Our review focuses on the literature on attitude importance produced since 1995, when the seminal review of research on attitude strength attributes was published (Petty & Krosnick 1995). We begin by offering a brief overview of the concept of attitude strength and discuss its correlates and their structure. We then define attitude importance, explain how it has been measured, outline the proposed theories about its origins and consequences, and review the accumulated empirical evidence in this regard.

DEFINING ATTITUDE IMPORTANCE

Strong attitudes have four features: They are resistant to change, stable over time, influential on cognition, and influential on action (Krosnick & Petty 1995). Over the past three decades, researchers have found different features of attitudes to be related to strength (for a list of these features, see **Table 1**).

Attitude importance is one of the most researched strength-related attitude features. By definition, attitude importance is an individual's subjective judgment of the significance he or she attaches to his or her attitude (e.g., Boninger et al. 1995a). It is most frequently measured by asking participants to report how important the attitude or object is to them, how concerned they are about it, or how much they care about it (Gopinath & Nyer 2009). Some measures assess the relative importance of attitudes, comparing one attitude object's importance to that of another attitude object (e.g., Klar 2014, Ziegler & Schlett 2016). In short, attitude importance reflects the degree of priority a person attaches to an attitude.[1]

To attach personal importance to an attitude is to commit oneself to think about the attitude object, to gather information about it, to use that information as well as one's attitude in making relevant decisions, and to design one's actions according to that attitude. In this sense, attaching personal importance to an attitude represents a substantial commitment, somewhat analogous to

---

[1] Attitude importance is distinct from concepts such as centrality, involvement, ego-involvement, ego-preoccupation, salience, and personal relevance, which have almost always been defined in terms of links between the attitude object and the self (for a review, see Eaton & Visser 2008). These features have also been defined in terms of the degree to which an attitude represents one's important values or is central to one's self-image (Holland et al. 2003, Honaken & Verplanken 2004, Pomerantz et al. 1995), thus distinguishing them from attitude importance.

Table 1 Attitude features related to strength

Feature	Definition
Importance	The degree to which an individual attaches significance to the attitude
Certainty	The individual's level of confidence that his or her evaluation of the attitude object is correct and is clear to him or her
Ambivalence	The degree to which a person holds positive and negative evaluations of the attitude object simultaneously
Accessibility	The likelihood that the attitude will come to mind automatically in relevant situations
Knowledge volume	The amount of information the person has about the attitude object
Extremity	The degree to which the person likes or dislikes the attitude object
Affective–cognitive consistency	The degree to which a person's feelings about the attitude object are evaluatively consistent with his or her thoughts about it
Intensity	The degree to which a person's evaluation of the attitude object activates powerful emotions
Moral conviction	The degree to which the attitude is a strong and absolute belief that something is right or wrong or moral or immoral, or that it reflects core moral values and convictions
Elaboration	The degree of thought one has given to the attitude object's merits and shortcomings
Vested interest	The degree to which the attitude object is perceived to be of personal consequence

taking a job or making a long-term commitment to an interpersonal relationship. Consequently, people seem unlikely to attach personal importance to an attitude lightly. Just as people are misers with regard to cognitive processing (e.g., Fiske & Taylor 2013), they are probably also miserly with their attachments of psychological significance and value to attitudes: Only clear and compelling reasons seem likely to motivate such a psychological investment. High levels of importance are unlikely to emerge unnoticed over time. Rather, deep and lasting concern is likely to be instigated by significant events of which people are well aware. Moreover, the amount of importance a person attaches to an attitude tends to be highly consistent over time (Krosnick et al. 1994).

THEORY

A wealth of research produced from the 1960s through the 1990s has suggested the causes and impacts of attaching importance to an attitude. We summarize this research briefly before moving into a discussion of evidence about attitude importance gathered since 1995.

Causes of Attitude Importance

Attitude importance is thought to be caused by three principal sets of factors: self-interest, social identification, and values (for a review, see Boninger et al. 1995a). First, an attitude may become important to an individual who perceives it to be related to her or his self-interest, that is, to directly affect his or her rights, privileges, or lifestyle in some concrete manner. Second, an attitude may become personally important through social identification with reference groups or reference individuals. Finally, an attitude may become personally important if a person views the attitude object as relevant to her or his basic social and personal values.

Effects of Attitude Importance

Attitude importance is thought to be consequential precisely because of its status as a belief: Perceiving an attitude to be personally important leads people to use that attitude in processing information, making decisions, and taking action (Boninger et al. 1995a). To determine the moment that this subjective perception is most likely to have an impact, it is useful to consider Fazio's (1990) distinction between spontaneous and deliberative processing. He suggested that, on the one hand, people sometimes perform behaviors without actively and effortfully considering relevant attitudes (via spontaneous processing); an extreme example might be a spur-of-the-moment purchase of a candy bar at a supermarket checkout counter. On the other hand, some decisions are made only after very careful consideration of all relevant factors, including attitudes (via deliberative processing); an extreme example would be deciding whether to marry a particular person.

Attitude importance should have its most pronounced effects under the latter conditions, when people can consciously make reference to their beliefs about attitude importance. Importance may have automatic effects on spontaneous processing as well. However, these effects are likely to evolve over time as the result of deliberate choices that people make based on the amount of personal importance they attach to particular attitudes. Thus, whereas Fazio (1990) expected attitude accessibility to have greater effects during spontaneous processing, attitude importance is expected to have greater effects during deliberative processing.

Boninger et al. (1995a) proposed step-wise consequences of holding important attitudes, which are listed in **Table 2**. In addition, social psychological theories suggest that social consequences may result from attaching importance to an attitude. For example, according to balance theory, cognitive imbalance occurs when one dislikes a person who holds an attitude similar to one's own or when one likes a person who holds a contrasting attitude (Heider 1958). According to cognitive dissonance theory, the intensity of the discomfort that results from such inconsistency increases as the personal importance of the attitude increases (e.g., Festinger 1957). Therefore, when an important attitude is involved, the noxious state that results from encountering a person who

Table 2   Proposed consequences of attaching importance to an attitude

Proposed Consequence	Theoretical Cause
Stage 1	
Acquiring information about the topic and thinking deeply about that information	Result of inherent interest in the topic derived from psychological significance attached to the attitude
Selective exposure and selective elaboration	Result of the desire to protect one's attitude by acquiring knowledge that can be used to defend it
Stage 2	
Acquiring a large body of organized knowledge relevant to the important attitude	Result of selective exposure and selective elaboration
High attitude accessibility (attitude comes to mind quickly and automatically when encountering attitude-relevant information)	Result of frequent thought about important attitude
Attitude extremity (holding very positive or very negative, rather than neutral, attitudes)	Result of frequent thought about important attitude
Evaluative consistency between important attitudes and other attitudes and values	Result of frequent thought about this attitude in conjunction with other attitudes and values
Stage 3	
Resistance to attitude change (resulting in attitude stability)	Result of large stores of relevant information and desire to defend the attitude
Behavioral consequences	Result of the high likelihood that important attitudes come to mind automatically and of motivation to express these attitudes and maintain evaluative consistency

Table created using data presented by Boninger et al. (1995a).

holds an attitude that is inconsistent with one's own important attitude should be quite powerful and should demand swift reparation (see Cacioppo & Petty 1981). Because this inconsistency can be resolved by adjusting one's sentiment toward the other person, people probably come to like others whose attitudes are similar to their own important attitudes and to dislike others whose attitudes conflict with their own important attitudes. Unimportant attitudes are less likely to serve as a basis for interpersonal sentiment.

Understanding the logic of important attitudes helps illuminate attitude functioning in important contexts. For instance, attitude importance can help explain the process by which a voter evaluates political candidates. The more important a voter's attitude is toward a policy (e.g., strong gun control laws), the more likely that attitude is to shape evaluations of candidates, for several reasons. First, because important attitudes are frequently subjects of conscious thought, are typically extreme, and are probably extensively linked to other psychological elements (Judd & Krosnick 1989, Krosnick et al. 1993), these attitudes are likely to be highly accessible. Important attitudes are therefore more likely to come to mind as criteria with which to evaluate political candidates. Second, voters with important policy attitudes might be expected to seek out and attend closely to candidates' public statements of their attitudes toward the policy so as to detect differences and to choose between the candidates on that basis. Third, when a citizen recognizes that he or she disagrees with a liked candidate or agrees with a disliked candidate on a policy issue, he or she is unlikely to change his or her own policy attitude. Important attitudes are likely to be highly resistant to change because these attitudes have extensive linkage to other attitudes, beliefs, values, and other psychological elements and because large memory stores of relevant knowledge equip individuals to counter-argue against attitude-challenging information. For these and other reasons following the logic outlined in **Table 2**, attitudes that people consider to be personally important are expected to have substantial impact in the political domain.

EVIDENCE

Causes

Cross-sectional survey data have indicated that, as theorized, self-interest, social identification, and values are all significant predictors of attitude importance (Boninger et al. 1995a; Visser et al. 2016). When participants were asked to explain the amount of importance they attached to an attitude, they most often made reference to self-interest (63% of explanations) and less often referred to social identification (19%) and values (18%) (Boninger et al. 1995a). We present research on these and other causes of attitude importance in the following sections.

Self-interest. Several experiments designed to enhance perceptions of self-interest associated with an attitude have shown consequent increases in the importance of the attitude (Bizer & Krosnick 2001, Boninger et al. 1995a, Stephenson et al. 2001). Correlational studies suggest that perceived self-interest regarding political issues (e.g., the perceived extent to which an issue affects one's life) is linked to greater perceived attitude importance (Holbrook et al. 2016). For instance, the feeling that women's rights directly affect one's own life was associated with greater importance attached to attitudes about women's rights (Lavine et al. 2000, study 1). This holds true in nonpolitical domains as well. For example, more perceived personal benefits of travel (e.g., believing that travel helps one to relax, be healthier, and have fun) are linked to greater importance of attitudes about travel (Chen & Petrick 2014).

Values. Thomsen et al. (2006) asked participants to indicate whether political attitudes (e.g., affirmative action, defense spending) were related to values (freedom, equity). People associated more important sociopolitical attitudes with a greater number of values (Thomsen et al. 2006). When people believe that their attitudes are based on values and general beliefs about how life should be lived, they tend to attach more importance to those attitudes (Lavine et al. 2000, study 1). Furthermore, considering a message in terms of important values increases the personal importance attached to the issue (Blankenship & Wegener 2008). More important attitudes are likely to be those most consistent with a person's values (Honaken & Verplanken 2004, Kemmelmeier et al. 1999).

Particular values predict the amount of importance attached to specific issues. For instance, valuing universalism (e.g., concern for the broader community, social justice) over power (e.g., status, material achievements) predicted greater importance placed on the issue of climate change (Schoenefeld & McCauley 2015). In fact, people who valued power and were presented with information about how global warming would impact their local area (rather than being presented with its global impacts) rated global warming as less personally important, suggesting that values may interact with factors such as the type of persuasive appeal in predicting attitude importance.

Many of the attitudes commonly reported as personally important are religious and moral; in one study, religious and moral convictions were cited by more than 80% of participants as their most important values (Zuwerink Jacks & Cameron 2003). In addition, one survey of a nationally representative sample of US adults found that, regardless of political ideology, respondents tended to see economic issues as more important than social issues (Klar 2014). Only respondents who were extremely socially liberal tended to prioritize social issues more highly, and then only slightly. This may shed light on why economic ideology shaped voting behavior more than did social ideology in the 2012 presidential election.

Social identification. If people believe that an object is relevant to an important reference group's interests, or know that a reference group has taken a strong stance on an issue, then they are more likely to attach importance to this attitude (Lavine et al. 2000, study 1). People report higher attitude importance for issues that have a greater impact on members of their racial or ethnic groups (Holbrook et al. 2016). Surveys of US adults and college students indicate that ethnic and racial minorities hold attitudes toward race relations with more personal importance than Whites (e.g., Garcia et al. 2015). In another study, normative appeals indicating broad support of pro-environmental norms among a reference group (in this case, residents of the same state as the participant) increased the importance of related attitudes (Bolson 2013).

Attitude accessibility. Roese & Olson (1994) proposed that attitude accessibility causes attitude importance: When people are asked to report the amount of personal importance they attach to an attitude, they may do so in part by noting how quickly the attitude comes to mind. People might think that if an attitude comes immediately to mind when they search for it, then it must be important to them. However, if an attitude comes to mind only after they dredge their memory for a while, then people may think that this attitude must not be important to them. This perspective presumes that people sometimes have relatively weak senses of the importance they attach to attitudes and objects (e.g., Bassili 1996) and therefore engage in self-perception-like processes (Bem 1972) to resolve these ambiguities. Roese & Olson (1994) argued that attitude accessibility subsumes attitude importance, such that attitude importance is a judgment completely derivative of attitude accessibility.

To test this claim, Roese & Olson (1994) induced people to express some attitudes repeatedly and others only once. Consistent with previous research, this within-subject manipulation increased the accessibility of the former attitudes. The researchers also found that this manipulation increased the degree of personal importance people reported that they attached to those attitudes.

Furthermore, Roese & Olson (1994) reported that repeated expression significantly increased accessibility when controlling for importance, whereas repeated expression had no significant effect on importance when controlling for accessibility. This evidence would therefore appear to be consistent with the notion that repeated expression increases accessibility, which in turn increases importance. But the test of this hypothesis was accidentally computed incorrectly (see Bizer & Krosnick 2001), and, when Bizer & Krosnick (2001) reconducted the study and computed the tests properly, the results indicated no effect of accessibility on importance. Furthermore, Bizer & Krosnick (2001) analyzed longitudinal survey data to show that attitude accessibility measured at one point in time does not predict subsequent changes in attitude importance.

Ease of retrieval. Haddock et al. (1999) explored the related hypothesis that the ease of information retrieval might influence reports of attitude importance. Specifically, these researchers manipulated the experienced ease of producing attitude-congruent or attitude-incongruent arguments. Some respondents were asked to do a difficult task (listing seven arguments in support of or opposition to a particular policy), and other respondents were asked to do an easier version of the same task (listing only three arguments).

Haddock et al. (1999) expected that the experienced difficulty of generating arguments would influence respondents' perceptions of attitude importance. Having found it very difficult to generate seven arguments consistent with their own opinion, people might reason that if their opinion on this issue were important to them, then they ought to have an easy time generating facts to back up their opinion. However, because it was tough for them to generate these facts, people might reason that perhaps the issue isn't very important to them. In contrast, if people find it easy to generate three supportive arguments, there would be no reason for self-doubt in this regard. Likewise, the experience of easily generating three arguments challenging their own viewpoints might lead people to doubt the validity of their own opinions, thereby reducing perceived importance. If people have difficulty generating seven counterattitudinal arguments, they again have no reason for self-doubt.

However, people who generated three attitude-supportive arguments did not report significantly different importance levels than did people who generated seven attitude-supportive arguments, and people who generated seven counterattitudinal arguments did not manifest higher importance scores than did people who generated only three counterattitudinal arguments. This study offers no evidence that the ease of retrieval of information influences attitude importance.

Public commitment. Gopinath & Nyer (2009, study 2) told their student participants that their university was considering implementing a new, strict grading policy in courses they would be taking in the future. Thus, all participants were subjected to a manipulation that Bizer & Krosnick (2001) showed induces the perception of self-interest being tied to the issue. All participants expressed their attitudes toward this new policy, and a randomly selected half of the participants were asked to consent to those attitudes being made public on a website. Afterward, these participants attached more importance to their attitudes on the issue than did the participants who had not been asked to make their attitudes public. This is consistent with the notion that public commitment to their opinions caused those participants to think more deeply about an issue that had already been made personally important to them, and importance increased more as a result.

Group discussion. Levendusky et al. (2016) asked participants to discuss a political issue (the Keystone XL pipeline) in groups that were either heterogenous or homogenous with respect to political partisanship (i.e., affiliation as either a Democrat or a Republican). Regardless of the partisan composition of the discussion group, talking about the issue increased attitude importance.

In fact, attitude importance increased by nearly a full standard deviation post-discussion. This result offers evidence that participating in discussion about an issue causes deep thought about the topic, which increases attitude importance.

Individual differences. Attitude importance is conceived of as a feature of an attitude, not of a person. That is, it does not seem to be true that, for some people, most or all of their attitudes are personally important, whereas other people hold unimportant attitudes toward almost all objects. Instead, importance appears to vary across objects within individuals, such that an individual is likely to hold some important attitudes and some unimportant attitudes (Krosnick 1988, Krosnick et al. 1994). More important attitudes tend to be more highly heritable (Brandt & Wetherell 2012, Olson et al. 2001). Some evidence suggests that personality variables are associated with attitude importance. For instance, people who have a heightened need to evaluate (i.e., a chronic desire to assess the positive and negative qualities of and form opinions about an object; Jarvis & Petty 1996) tend to report higher importance for many attitudes (Britt et al. 2009). This could occur because being in a chronic state of evaluation leads people to be especially aware of the relevance of an attitude object to their self-interest, social identifications, and values.

In the political domain, attitude importance changes predictably with the life cycle. Specifically, the personal importance assigned to attitudes on policy issues is lowest among the youngest adults, rises as people progress toward middle age, and declines as aging continues (Visser & Krosnick 1998).

Future directions. Although research has uncovered some antecedents of attitude importance, questions remain for future work. For instance, in one study, three of the causes of attitude importance (self-interest, social identification, and values) accounted for only approximately 50% of the variance in attitude importance (Boninger et al. 1995a), suggesting that there are other causes yet to be identified. Specific causes may also prove to be more influential under certain circumstances. For instance, social identification may serve as a more potent predictor of attitude importance when a public commitment to the attitude is made.

In addition, research could explore what leads individuals to place extreme importance on an attitude (i.e., labeling an attitude as extremely rather than very important). Examining individuals who hold extremely important attitudes could explain when and why people make a more significant commitment to certain attitudes and illuminate how attitude importance might be further enhanced.

Crystallization

Strong attitudes are defined as being resistant to change and therefore quite stable over time. The research discussed in this section sheds light on how and why important attitudes evidence these defining features of attitude strength.

Resistance to attitude change. Several studies have shown that important attitudes are unusually resistant to change. An experimentally induced increase in importance (Gopinath & Nyer 2009, study 2) increased resistance to attitude change, and Visser et al. (2016) and Zuwerink Jacks & Devine (1996) found more resistance to attitude change for more important attitudes. Furthermore, Lecheler et al. (2009) showed that more important attitudes were more resistant to framing effects.

Interestingly, this resistance surfaces even in contexts in which people choose to expose themselves to attitude-challenging information. For example, Sevelius & Stake (2003) studied college students who chose to take a course encouraging them to value equal rights for women. Those students who attached more importance to their anti-egalitarian attitudes at the start of the course were more likely to successfully resist changing their attitudes toward equal rights as a result of taking the course.

Important attitudes appear remarkably stable even in the face of plentiful counterattitudinal information. Leeper (2014) assessed participants' initial attitudes toward a healthcare policy. Several weeks later, half of the participants read instructions that emphasized the personal relevance of this policy to participants, and half read instructions emphasizing that this policy would have little direct personal relevance (a manipulation of attitude importance). Participants then browsed news articles that cast this healthcare policy in either a positive or a negative light, presented in a manner similar to an online news site. Participants browsed a site that was either (a) a pro-policy environment, in which two thirds of articles favored the policy and one third did not; (b) an anti-policy environment, in which two thirds of articles opposed the policy and one third favored it; or (c) a mixed environment, in which half of the articles favored the policy and half did not. Although there were no differences in the type of articles that people chose to read based on attitude importance, people who believed this policy was more personally relevant (and thus more important) became more polarized in the direction of their initial attitudes in response to the information they encountered in both the mixed environment and pro-policy environment. However, this same pattern was not found for the anti-policy environment. Furthermore, these individuals tended to become more certain in their attitudes after reviewing the information. In contrast, people who believed the policy to be less personally relevant tended to shift to more moderate opinions and become less certain over time. These results demonstrate that prior attitudes that are held with importance influence the reception of attitude-relevant information, remain strong, and are held with more certainty, regardless of the informational environment.

Why are important attitudes more resistant to change? The studies described in the following four sections shed light on this question. Understanding the processes through which important attitudes become more resistant to change is critical for the science of persuasion, and future research to identify the circumstances under which these processes are most effective (i.e., help create the most crystallized attitudes) is warranted.

Deeper processing. Blankenship & Wegener (2008) found that inducing an increase in the personal importance of an attitude prompted deeper processing of messages. This higher level of elaboration then resulted in increased resistance to change.

Defending important attitudes. People seem highly motivated to defend their important attitudes. Research reveals that people bolster important attitudes even before a persuasive message is encountered (for a review, see Boninger et al. 1995a).

Visser et al. (2016) demonstrated one way in which people defend important attitudes, by asking participants to evaluate a series of pieces of evidence, some of which were proattitudinal and some of which were counterattitudinal. People tended to view the proattitudinal evidence as convincing and of high quality and the counterattitudinal evidence as unconvincing and flawed.

Attitudes that are more important may be more resistant to persuasion because these attitudes are more accessible (Pfau et al. 2003) and thus come to mind more easily when encountering relevant information, automatically inducing cognitive-protective thinking (Zuwerink Jacks & Devine 2000). In contrast, when an attitude is low in importance, people appear to need more time to gather arguments in response to a persuasive attack.

Affective responses. The process of resisting persuasion appears to be more affectively driven among people who hold attitudes with high importance. Some research shows that, when considering a controversial political issue, such as whether people in the military should be allowed to openly disclose their sexual orientation, people holding important attitudes experienced more negative affect (e.g., irritation, anger) and generated more affectively charged negative thoughts in response to their position being attacked, which led them to resist persuasion even by strong arguments (Zuwerink Jacks & Devine 1996, 2000). In addition, people who hold attitudes with importance perceive that they defend these attitudes against persuasive attacks more frequently. When attitudes are more personally important, people recall engaging to a greater extent in a variety of defensive strategies (Zuwerink Jacks & Cameron 2003). To resist persuasion, people who hold attitudes with greater importance may expend more effort counter-arguing or bolstering their own attitudes.

Dissonance processes. Prompting people to remember that an attitude is important to them is particularly effective in preventing attitude change. For instance, reminding people of the importance of their attitudes reduces the attitude change they manifest in response to the experience of cognitive dissonance (Starzyk et al. 2009). Such reminders of importance also prevent trivializing or reducing the importance of these attitudes in response to cognitive dissonance. This may be because people with strong attitudes would feel more discomfort in altering their important attitudes to match their behavior, making this option for reducing dissonance less viable.

Attitude stability. Consistent with the evidence on resistance to attitude change, other studies, involving both political attitudes and self-views, show that more important attitudes are more stable over time (for a review, see Boninger et al. 1995a). Across repeated interviews, people report very similar levels of personal importance attached to an attitude (Krosnick et al. 1994).

Effects on Thinking

A hallmark of strong attitudes is that they influence thought. The research discussed in the following sections explores how attitude importance affects cognitive processes, including people's processing and organization of attitude-relevant information.

Message processing. People who attach importance to attitudes process information related to these attitudes more deeply. For instance, Falk et al. (2012) asked participants to rate their agreement with statements about political topics while in an fMRI scanner. They then did the same from the perspectives of the candidates running for president in 2008 (Barack Obama and John McCain). Among participants who rated an issue as more important, areas in the brain associated with social cognition activated more strongly. These results suggest that attitude importance can motivate social cognition, in line with the view that attitude importance promotes careful thought.

Ciuk & Yost (2016) asked participants to rate how important two environmental issues were to them personally. When evaluating the issue that was less important to them, people tended to rely on party cues over policy information. The opposite pattern was found for the high importance issue, again suggesting that attitude importance may prompt more thoughtful evaluation of messages.

Selective exposure and selective elaboration. People who care deeply about an issue selectively expose themselves to issue-relevant information at the expense of information relevant to unimportant attitudes (M.K. Berent & J.A. Krosnick, unpublished manuscript). Furthermore, people for whom an issue is more important devote more time and effort to thinking about the meaning and implications of new relevant information, which strengthens the representation of this information stored in memory and facilitates recall of it later (M.K. Berent and J.A. Krosnick, unpublished manuscript). People who attach more importance to specific attitudes devote more thought to their attitudes in general, introspecting more about their opinions (Hofmann et al. 2005).

In a series of naturalistic and lab studies, Holbrook et al. (2005) found that people selectively seek more information about and elaborate more upon important issues. This causes people to remember to a greater extent information that is related to a personally important attitude. For instance, when watching a televised presidential debate, people more accurately remembered statements about attitudes that they held with greater importance. However, when the opportunity for elaboration or selective exposure was eliminated, people were not more likely to remember information about a personally important attitude. Lavine et al. (2000, study 3) found that college students who saw a sociopolitical issue as more personally important were more interested in reading information that was congruent with their current attitude, and this preference for proattitudinal information translated into increases in attitude extremity and decreases in ambivalence. Thus, attitude importance may affect information-gathering processes, ultimately leading to more univalent and extreme attitudes. When left to their own devices, people seem to selectively expose themselves more to information related to more important attitudes. Visser et al. (2016) reported similar evidence.

Recent studies further demonstrate the ways in which important political attitudes may be defended through selective exposure processes. Westerwick et al. (2013) told participants that they would have to defend their viewpoints on a variety of issues (e.g., universal healthcare and gun control) against opposing arguments and that prior to doing so, they would have the chance to gather information related to these issues by browsing online search results. The tendency to read information that was consistent with one's prior existing beliefs was particularly pronounced among those who held important attitudes. People who held attitudes with less importance, however, were more likely to read arguments from highly credible sources, regardless of whether these arguments were consistent with their preexisting attitudes.

This result is particularly noteworthy given concerns about the confirmation or congeniality bias, the tendency for people to seek out information that is consistent with preexisting beliefs and avoid information that conflicts with these beliefs (Hart et al. 2009). This bias appears to be enhanced by attitude importance. A meta-analysis of previous research found that other indicators that may relate to attitude importance, such as reporting high personal commitment to an attitude or seeing an attitude as connected to one's personal values, increase the magnitude of this bias (Hart et al. 2009).

One online field study examined people's reading choices while browsing a selection of articles about four political topics (health care, minimum wage, gun control, and abortion) and found that higher attitude importance enhanced confirmation bias (Knobloch-Westerwick et al. 2015). In this study, participants were given the opportunity to browse news articles, presented in an online session as two sets of web search results, including an article about each topic, for two minutes each. Confirmation bias was particularly pronounced during the first half of the browsing period among participants who attached more importance to the topics, suggesting that participants initially focused more on reading attitude-congruent information and avoided attitude-incongruent information when attitude importance was high. These results echo Westerwick et al.'s (2013) findings and suggest that attitude importance may more strongly influence initial information searches and may have less influence during additional exposure to information. This suggestion is particularly meaningful given recent concerns that the accessibility of proattitudinal information on the web and the ability to easily brush past attitude-incongruent information may enhance confirmation bias. In contrast, Knobloch-Westerwick & Meng (2009) found that people who attached more importance to an issue were more likely to seek out exposure to counterattitudinal information and no more likely to seek exposure to proattitudinal information, and Leeper (2014) found that a personal relevance manipulation designed to increase attitude importance did not change information search behavior. Future research could explore moderators that determine the conditions under which attitude importance leads to selective exposure.

Visser et al. (2016) demonstrated that attitude importance is an inherently motivational construct that inspires people to gather some information and avoid other information to prevent challenging their attitudes. Specifically, in procedures adapted from Dawson et al. (2002), participants performed the Wason selection task to test a counterattitudinal assertion. Participants who attached importance to the target attitude were especially motivated to refute the assertion, and this motivation caused them to perform better on the task than participants who attached less importance to the attitude.

Importance also shapes the evaluation of persuasive messages. This includes evaluative measures such as ratings of message effectiveness and source credibility (Zuwerink Jacks & Lancaster 2015). Liu et al. (2016) found evidence for the selective evaluation of attitude-relevant persuasive arguments when attitudes are held with importance. In this study, participants read arguments that were either strong or weak and either incongruent or congruent with their own prior attitudes. When attitudes were more important, participants tended to evaluate strong, attitude-incongruent arguments more critically and were more accepting of weak, attitude-congruent arguments.

Other research has illustrated how the tendency to seek out more information about important attitudes leads to a clustering of attitudes within social networks. Specifically, after the start of the war in Iraq, people who felt that the war was a more personally important issue paid more attention to information about the war. This increased attention led to increased discussion with others of topics relevant to the war, which, in turn, led to the formation of social networks that were more homogenous with respect to these beliefs (Cullum et al. 2011, study 2). It seems likely that attitude importance has additional social consequences, perhaps causing people to distance themselves from others who do not share their opinion. There is some evidence that attitude importance can lead people to more negatively judge sources of messages that conflict with their views, for instance by rating these sources as less competent and less likeable (Zuwerink Jacks & Devine 1996), suggesting that important issues may be particularly socially divisive.

Along with potential social consequences, future research could explore the downstream consequences of the selective exposure and elaboration induced by important attitudes. One might imagine the potential for both positive and negative behavioral impacts of these selective processes. For instance, selective exposure and elaboration might promote depth of knowledge about or activism on important issues, but might also encourage naïve realism or the tendency to be polemical.

Quantity and accuracy of attitude-relevant knowledge. When people are acutely attuned to information that is relevant to policy attitudes they consider personally important, they are likely to accumulate larger stores of this information in their memory. A number of studies have documented such a correlation (e.g., Holbrook et al. 2005). People who report that they consider an attitude to be more important also report that they have more relevant knowledge stored in memory and are able to report more of such knowledge (Krosnick et al. 1993). Furthermore, attitude importance is associated with enhanced accuracy in perceptions of political candidates. In Krosnick's (1990) study, voters who attached more importance to their attitudes on a political issue were more likely to accurately perceive the positions taken on the issue by presidential candidates.

Another set of studies in this area examined systematic bias in perceptions of the distributions of attitudes toward an object in particular groups of people. Campbell (1986) and Krosnick (1992) found that individuals' perceptions of groups' attitudes were less susceptible to the false consensus effect (Ross et al. 1977) when the attitude involved was more important to the individual, and Fabrigar & Krosnick (1995) found that the magnitude of the false consensus effect was unrelated to attitude importance. These studies together support the claim that important attitudes do not bias perceptions more than unimportant ones. This is presumably because people possess more accurate information relevant to important attitudes on which to base their perceptions. Interestingly, people with a greater desire for acceptance by others (M.R. Leary, K.M. Kelly, C.A. Cottrell, & L. Schreindorfer, unpublished manuscript) perceive greater similarity between their own opinions and others' opinions, and they do so to a greater extent when an issue is more important to them (Morrison & Matthes 2011). In light of Fabrigar & Krosnick's (1995) evidence, this finding seems likely to be attributable to the tendency to surround oneself with like-minded others when it comes to important attitudes.

Berent & Krosnick (1995) demonstrated that people are very adept at using knowledge associated with important attitudes. Their study assessed the speed and consistency with which subjects made inferences relevant to political attitudes. For example, subjects were asked whether it was likely that people with particular social characteristics (e.g., old or wealthy) would take certain stands on particular political issues (e.g., favor legalized abortion or oppose gun control laws). As expected, inferences relevant to more important attitudes were made more quickly and more consistently across two occasions.

Selective elaboration inspired by attitude importance is likely to influence the organization of knowledge in memory, which we conceptualize in terms of an associative network framework (Anderson 1983, Collins & Loftus 1975). The process of elaboration involves evaluating new information and relating it to the information already stored in a person's memory. The more a person thinks about a new piece of information, the more likely he or she is to recognize what it has in common with previously stored knowledge. As a result, the person may incorporate new information into existing structures either by linking the information to existing nodes or by creating new nodes. If attitude importance does inspire deeper processing of relevant incoming information, it should also yield more elaborate organization of relevant knowledge in memory. Consistent with this logic, Berent & Krosnick (1995) showed that people who attach more importance to an attitude store relevant information in memory in a more complexly organized format.

Evaluations of people. A great deal of evidence on interpersonal attraction is consistent with the idea that important attitudes shape evaluations of others to a greater extent than unimportant attitudes. People who attach more importance to an attitude tend to exist in social networks that are more attitudinally homogenous and that converge on their own attitude (Visser & Mirabile 2004).

Several studies have explored this hypothesis in evaluations of political candidates. Boyd & Wengrovitz (2005) calculated the frequency with which a survey respondent mentioned a policy issue as a reason to vote for or against a candidate, a reason to like or dislike a political party, or the most important problem facing the country. The more frequently a person mentioned an issue, the more powerfully his or her position on the issue predicted his or her vote choice. Furthermore, some statistical analyses predicting candidate evaluations using attitudes on government policy issues documented greater predictive power for attitudes that were more personally important (Abramowitz 1995, Anand & Krosnick 2003, Carsey & Layman 2006, Fournier et al. 2003, MacInnis & Krosnick 2016, Visser et al. 2003), although some did not (Ansolabehere et al. 2008, Grynaviski & Corrigan 2006).

One exception to this pattern is Grynaviski & Corrigan's (2006) reanalysis of data originally analyzed by Krosnick (1988, 1990). In contrast to Krosnick, Grynaviski & Corrigan (2006) found that attitude importance had no moderating effect on the impact of attitude similarity on liking political candidates. However, Malhotra & Tahk (2011) demonstrated that the analytic method used by Grynaviski & Corrigan (2006) included a flawed assumption, and when that mistake was corrected, Malhotra & Tahk (2011) demonstrated the expected moderating role of attitude importance.

Related evidence shows that people base their votes partly on the past performance of the incumbent in handling various policy issues. The more important the issue is to the voter, the more likely their vote is to be based on the incumbent's performance (Fournier et al. 2003).

Some research indicates that attitude importance can ameliorate the third-person effect, the tendency for individuals to believe that media impacts others more than the self. Lo et al. (2015) found that the more personally concerned people were about a political topic, the more they believed that news coverage of this topic influenced themselves as well as other people.

Attitude importance has consequences within social relationships as well. Familiarity with a partner's attitudes has salubrious benefits, perhaps because attitude familiarity enables a person to better anticipate and influence their partner's behavior, to respond appropriately, and to offer support to their partner, or because partners use the knowledge of these attitudes to maintain a harmonious relationship and avoid conflict (Sanbonmatsu et al. 2011). Other research has suggested that the importance that people attached to their spouse (i.e., responses to the question "How important is your spouse to you?") moderated the relationship between knowledge of one's partner's attitudes and physical health outcomes (Uchino et al. 2013). A stronger correlation between one's own attitudes and one's spouse's ratings of these same attitudes was associated with better interpersonal functioning, as well as better cardiovascular outcomes, but only when the relationship with the spouse was seen as highly important. Thus, spousal importance appears to motivate individuals to act on their knowledge of their partner, providing further evidence that attitude importance strengthens the link between attitude knowledge and behavior.

Attitude accessibility. Several studies have shown that the attitudes that people claim are more personally important to them are also more accessible (Kokkinaki & Lunt 1997, Krosnick 1989, Krosnick & Petty 1995, Krosnick et al. 1993, Lavine et al. 1996, van Herreveld & van der Pligt 2004). Bizer & Krosnick (2001) showed that higher importance causes increased accessibility. People make quicker judgments about attitudes that are important (van Herreveld et al. 2000). The more personally important an attitude is, the more quickly people link the attitude to relevant values, again suggesting that important attitudes are more accessible (Thomsen et al. 2006, van Herreveld & van der Pligt 2004). This enhanced accessibility may relate to other consequences of attitude importance, such as the ability to resist persuasion by counterattitudinal arguments (e.g., Pfau et al. 2003).

Extremity. Tesser (1978) argued that thought about an attitude increases its extremity when the attitude is accompanied by schematically organized knowledge. Therefore, because important attitudes are frequent foci of thought, it is not surprising that more important attitudes tend to be more extreme (for a review, see Tesser et al. 1995).

Some authors have argued that the more important an attitude, the more extremely positive or negative the attitude should be. Liu & Latane (1998a) asserted that when an attitude is unimportant, its positivity or negativity should be determined by the positivity or negativity of the relevant information one has about an object. Slightly positive information should result in slightly more positive attitudes, and vice versa. However, if an issue is highly important, people should be unlikely to adjust their attitudes in response to positive or negative pieces of information unless information against one's position becomes overwhelming and causes a dramatic change in opinion. Thus, moderately extreme opinions that are held with importance should be rare. Evidence consistent with this reasoning has been found using opinions about political issues such as abortion, women's rights, and national health care (Liu & Latane 1998b). Indeed, additional studies found that extremity and importance were slightly-to-moderately correlated with one another (e.g., Britt et al. 2009, Matthes et al. 2010), suggesting that attitude importance may be linked, although not synonymous, with greater attitude extremity.

Consistency between implicit and explicit attitudes. Attitude importance strengthens the consistency between implicit and explicit attitudes (Hofmann et al. 2005, Nosek 2005).[2] In one study, measures of implicit (i.e., the Implicit Association Test) and explicit (e.g., feeling thermometer) attitudes toward the presidential candidates George W. Bush and Al Gore were more highly correlated among people who rated politics and the upcoming presidential election as more important (Karpinski et al. 2005). This was also true for attitudes toward topics outside the political domain, such as one's preference for Coke or Pepsi. This evidence is consistent with the general claim that attaching importance to an attitude enhances the evaluative consistency of that attitude with other cognitive elements.

One study suggests that attitude importance may moderate the relationship between implicit associations and behavior (Hübner et al. 2014). In this study, researchers measured attitude importance regarding organ donation (e.g., agreement with statements such as "organ donation is an important topic to me"). They found that, among people who attached lower importance to organ donation, more positive implicit associations with organ donation predicted a higher likelihood of taking an organ donor card (a measure of behavioral intentions). This relationship was weaker among people who attached more importance to organ donation, and explicit attitudes toward organ donation instead predicted behavior for these individuals. The same pattern was evident for two other attitude strength measures that were assessed (cognitive elaboration and attitude certainty). This evidence is consistent with the theory that attitude importance is linked with deliberate, thoughtful processes in decision-making. Implicit associations may be relied on as a source of information to direct behavior only in the absence of attitude strength. Interestingly, research measuring the implicit importance of exercise (using an implicit association test that asked participants to associate words related to exercise and rest with words related to importance and unimportance) found that implicit exercise importance predicted excessive exercise-related behavior (Forrest et al. 2016).

Emotions. Visser et al. (2016) reported that attitude importance inspires powerful emotions. Specifically, participants reported that they were more likely to experience negative emotions if they were to (a) learn that the government was enacting a policy contrary to an important attitude they hold or (b) listen to a counterattitudinal speech relevant to an important attitude that contained arguments they found difficult to refute. Miller et al. (2016) reported the same finding.

Attitude importance also appears to affect a person's satisfaction with life. For example, Britt et al. (2011) assessed people's overall attitude importance, meaning a person's individual tendency to hold attitudes with personal importance across a number of different attitude objects. The more an individual held attitudes with personal importance, the higher his or her sense of meaning in life, suggesting that attaching importance to issues to a greater extent may be a way in which people find a sense of purpose. Attaching importance across many attitude objects is also associated with a greater sense of coherence and a feeling that one's own purpose in life is clear (Britt et al. 2009).

---

[2]Nosek's (2005) measure of attitude importance included some items that may reflect attitude certainty (e.g., participants' perceptions of how stable their attitude is); whether this should be considered an attribute of attitude certainty or importance is an open question.

Attitude Measurement

Many scholars have speculated that people who hold important attitudes on an issue are most likely to report the same attitude regardless of how the attitude question is worded or structured in a survey (for a review, see Krosnick & Schuman 1988). Consistent with this logic is evidence regarding the impact of offering or omitting a middle alternative (e.g., keeping things as they currently are) between two polar opposite viewpoints (e.g., making divorce laws stricter than they currently are and making divorce laws less strict than they currently are). Krosnick & Schuman (1988), Bishop (1990), and Bassili & Krosnick (2000) found that people for whom attitudes were highly important were relatively immune to the offer or omission of the middle alternative in such questions. In contrast, people whose attitudes were low in importance were especially likely to be attracted to the middle alternative when it was offered.

Lavine et al. (1998) presented evidence suggesting that another type of response effect was not regulated by attitude importance. In their study, people were first asked a series of context questions and a target attitude was then measured. The context questions were designed to promote either liberal or conservative responses to the target attitude question. Lavine et al. (1998) found that attitude importance did not moderate the impact of the earlier questions. Likewise, Bassili & Krosnick (2000) found that attitude importance did not moderate question order effects or acquiescence response bias.

However, Bassili & Krosnick (2000) did find that attitude importance moderated the impact of a question wording manipulation in an experiment asking people whether speeches against democracy should be forbidden or allowed. People who assigned the issue low importance were more affected. This response effect has been attributed to a shift in the perceived extremity of the response options (Hippler & Schwarz 1986), and this moderation by importance may be similar to the moderation of middle alternative effects.

Effects on Action

Among the most important goals of attitude research are the prediction and explanation of behavior. As is to be expected, a number of studies have found greater attitude–behavior consistency among people for whom the attitude was more personally important. Importance increases attitude–behavior correspondence regarding product choice; when products are seen as personally important, attitudes are more predictive of behavior (Kokkinaki & Lunt 1997). In addition, job satisfaction is more strongly predictive of positive work-related behavior (e.g., helping others, fulfilling responsibilities) when employees consider work to be more important (Ziegler & Schlett 2016).

On its own, attitude importance motivates attitude-congruent action. Holding environmental attitudes with more importance predicts environmentally friendly purchasing behavior (Bolsen 2013). In addition, viewing travel as more personally important predicts travel behavior, perhaps because of the positive association between important attitudes toward travel and the frequency of discussing future travel and attending to information about future vacations (Chen & Petrick 2014).

Attitude importance appears to enhance the likelihood of attitude-expressive behavior (e.g., writing letters or making phone calls to newspapers or government representatives; Krosnick & Telhami 1995, Miller et al. 2016, Schuman & Presser 1981). More important attitudes on political issues predict more self-reported political action on these issues (Holbrook et al. 2016). Interestingly, attitude importance and certainty appear to interact to predict expressive behavior (e.g., writing letters or attending meetings about a topic, donating money) such that these behaviors are most common when both certainty and importance are high (Visser et al. 2003). Likewise, Visser et al. (2016) found that attitude importance was most likely to inspire attitude-expressive behavior among people who were knowledgeable about the issue. Furthermore, importance and certainty appear to interact with the amount of money an individual has available when predicting financial attitude-expressive behaviors, such as contributions to lobbying groups dedicated to advocating policies consistent with an individual's preferences (Visser et al. 2003). Attitude importance is especially likely to inspire attitude-expressive behaviors among people who perceive a threat that the government may take action to implement policies toward which they hold negative attitudes (Miller et al. 2016).

Attitude importance shapes behavior during elections. For instance, attaching high personal importance to a policy issue inspires people to try to convince others to vote for a particular candidate (Visser et al. 2003). People whose attitudes toward candidates are held with more importance are more likely to register to vote and to actually cast a vote, and they show higher correspondence between attitudes toward and votes for a candidate (Farc & Sagarin 2009, Krosnick et al. 1994, Visser et al. 2003).

The importance of one's political identities can also increase behavior that is supportive of that identity. For instance, people for whom their identity as a political independent is important are more likely to be engaged in politics than those who regard this identity as less important (Klar 2013). Identity importance thus seems to function similarly to attitude importance, heightening engagement in relevant behaviors. This has also been shown in domains beyond political engagement (for a summary, see Klar 2013). For instance, the importance of one's identity as a blood donor predicts future blood donations (Charng et al. 1988), and the importance of one's identity as a volunteer predicts participation as a volunteer (Grube & Piliavin 2000).

People are reluctant to voice their opinions on an issue if they believe those opinions are out of step with those of the perceived majority, but this suppression of opinion expression is less pronounced among people who attach more importance to the issue. These individuals are inclined to express their opinions regardless of others' opinions (Glynn & Park 1997).

Surprisingly, Nederhof (1989) and Franc (1999) found no relation between attitude importance and the consistency of attitudes with behavioral intentions. However, a reanalysis of Franc's (1999) data revealed the expected moderation, though it was monotonically nonlinear and went undetected by Franc's analytic approach, which looked only for a linear relation (C.J. Bryan and J.A. Krosnick, unpublished manuscript). Furthermore, the expected moderating relation has been documented in other studies, including studies regarding engagement in behaviors such as recycling and eating a low-fat diet (Costarelli & Colloca 2007), voting intentions (Visser et al. 2003), and complying with speed zones during boating (Jett et al. 2013).

Why does attitude importance strengthen the link between attitudes and behavior? Future research could help explore the pathways by which important attitudes increase attitude-congruent behavior. A desire for consistency may motivate people to act in line with attitudes that they have expressed, or attitude importance may bolster knowledge and increase a sense of efficacy in the performance of these actions.

DIMENSIONALITY OF ATTITUDE IMPORTANCE

Although generally treated as a unitary construct, attitude importance may be multidimensional, with multiple functional bases. Attitude importance arising from the recognition of a connection between an attitude object and one's core values may be distinct in terms of its phenomenology and consequences from attitude importance arising from the perception of a link between an attitude object and one's material interests. Furthermore, both may be distinct from attitude importance arising from the perception that one's reference groups or individuals view an attitude as important. Each may inspire discrete motivations: to protect the attitude that expresses one's core values, to hold the correct attitude toward the object that impinges on one's self-interest, and to remain in step with important individuals and groups with regard to the attitudes they deem important.

In an experimental investigation, Boninger et al. (1995a,b) found evidence inconsistent with the multidimensional view of attitude importance. They found that manipulations of one of the causal antecedents of importance reverberated through participants' cognitive structures, impacting other antecedents of importance. Specifically, increasing the degree to which an attitude impinged on participants' material interests also led them to view the attitude as more closely linked to their core values. This suggests that the causal antecedents of attitude importance are related to one another and that changes in one can result in changes in others. This evidence challenges the notion that the causal underpinnings of attitude importance are discrete and lead cleanly to distinct types of importance. Instead, an attitude that is outcome relevant may come to be seen as value relevant as well.

Nevertheless, conclusions on this matter should be drawn with caution given the dearth of empirical evidence. Additional research addressing this issue seems warranted. We contend, also, that the critical issue to be explored is not the factor structure of these various types of attitude importance but rather whether these types of importance arise from distinct causal antecedents and whether they set into motion different cognitive and behavioral consequences. To the extent that they do, differentiating among them is important.

IMPLICATIONS

As demonstrated in this review, much is known about the origins and consequences of attitude importance, and these insights have many interesting implications. For example, consider public health. Public health officials have increasingly come to recognize that many of the leading causes of death in the United States could be drastically reduced if Americans made a few simple changes in their behavior. In fact, an investigation published in the *Journal of the American Medical Association* concluded that approximately half of deaths in the United States can be attributed to a small number of preventable behaviors such as smoking, inactivity, poor diet, and alcohol consumption (Mokdad et al. 2004). Because of this, public health advocates have increasingly turned to the social and behavioral sciences for insight into behavior modification.

In some cases, people already possess positive attitudes toward healthy behaviors and negative attitudes toward unhealthy behaviors. However, these health-positive attitudes do not always manifest themselves in the relevant health behaviors (see, e.g., Fisher & Fisher 1992). The challenge for public health advocates, then, involves strengthening such existing attitudes. Making an attitude personally important, so that it becomes crystallized and motivates and guides thinking and action, is one way to accomplish this. Simply convincing people to enjoy exercise, for example, is not enough—making that attitude important to people is necessary to produce the desired outcome: changes in behavior and, consequently, health status.

The case of AIDS in the United States provides an excellent illustration. Initially, public health officials assumed that if they could educate people about the disease and how to avoid it, the appropriate behaviors would follow (Helweg-Larsen & Collins 1997). Thus, they launched a massive public education campaign to increase the amount of knowledge people had about the disease (for a review, see Fisher & Fisher 1992). This campaign was tremendously successful— surveys show that virtually all US adults now know what AIDS is, have some sense of how it is transmitted, and know what steps can be taken to avoid exposure (DiClemente et al. 1990, Rogers et al. 1993). Yet such educational campaigns often yielded virtually no reliable effects on behavior (e.g., Mann et al. 1992). Creating attitude strength was necessary, and one means of accomplishing this is to inspire people to attach personal importance to the attitude.

Attitude importance is also valuable in the arena of politics. Political events occur every day, and only a small selection of these events is conveyed to the US public through the news media. Data are provided to the nation in convenient and discrete packages in the morning paper and on the evening news. Between these doses of information, Americans have personal experiences that, in one way or another, touch on the world of politics. From this stream of data, experienced personally and received indirectly through reporters, each citizen must select what to attend to, what to think about, what to store in memory, and what to act on in the future. This is especially true during presidential election campaigns, when the volume of political information to which one has access is even greater than usual. To understand the forces that drive Americans' political behavior, particularly during elections, we must understand the processes by which information is gathered and integrated. According to the evidence reviewed in this article, attitude importance can help illuminate how this process unfolds.

The results of research on attitude importance have a number of interesting implications for an understanding of US politics and presidential elections. For example, it seems likely that, when deciding for whom to vote, citizens base their judgments on a few salient criteria, important policy attitudes among them. Thus, people seem to employ a sensible strategy that minimizes the cognitive costs of deriving candidate evaluations while maximizing subjective expected utility.

Candidates may also attempt to manipulate the importance of voters' policy attitudes by prompting individuals to recognize an issue as related to their material self-interests, significant reference groups or individuals, or cherished values. By increasing the importance of voters' attitudes regarding a policy toward which a candidate's attitude is favored by a majority of the public, normally inconsequential attitudes may be called into action in the voting booth.

CONCLUSION

Attitude importance and other strength-related attitude features offer much promise. We look forward to more research further clarifying the causes and consequences of these attitude attributes and illuminating the mechanisms by which they exert their effects.

DISCLOSURE STATEMENT

The authors are not aware of any affiliations, memberships, funding, or financial holdings that might be perceived as affecting the objectivity of this review.

LITERATURE CITED

Abramowitz AI. 1995. It's abortion, stupid: policy voting in the 1992 presidential election. *J. Polit.* 57:176–86

Ajzen I, Fishbein M. 1980. *Understanding Attitudes and Predicting Social Behavior*. Englewood Cliffs, NJ: Prentice-Hall

Ajzen A, Timko C, White JB. 1982. Self-monitoring and the attitude-behavior relation. *J. Personal. Soc. Psychol.* 42:426–35

Anand S, Krosnick JA. 2003. The impact of attitudes toward foreign policy goals on public preferences among presidential candidates: a study of issue publics and the attentive public in the 2000 US presidential election. *Pres. Stud. Q.* 33:31–71

Anderson CA. 1983. Imagination and expectation: the effect of imagining behavioral scripts on personal intentions. *J. Personal. Soc. Psychol.* 45:293–305

Ansolabehere S, Rodden J, Snyder JM. 2008. The strength of issues: using multiple measures to gauge preference stability, ideological constraint, and issue voting. *Am. Polit. Sci. Rev.* 102(2):215–32

Bassili JN. 1996. Meta-judgmental versus operative indexes of psychological attributes: the case of measures of attitude strength. *J. Personal. Soc. Psychol.* 71(4):637–53

Bassili JN, Krosnick JA. 2000. Do strength-related attitude properties determine susceptibility to response effects? New evidence from response latency, attitude extremity, and aggregate indices. *Polit. Psychol.* 21(1):107–32

Bem DJ. 1972. Self-perception theory. In *Advances in Experimental Social Psychology*, ed. L Berkowitz, pp. 1–62. San Diego, CA: Academic

Berent MK, Krosnick JA. 1995. The relation between political attitude importance and knowledge structure. In *Political Judgment: Structure and Process*, ed. M Lodge, K McGraw, pp. 91–109. Ann Arbor: Univ. Mich. Press

Bishop GF. 1990. Issue involvement and response effects in public opinion surveys. *Public Opin. Q.* 54:209–18

Bizer GY, Krosnick JA. 2001. Exploring the structure of strength-related attitude features: the relation between attitude importance and attitude accessibility. *J. Personal. Soc. Psychol.* 81(4):566–86

Blankenship KL, Wegener DT. 2008. Opening the mind to close it: Considering a message in light of important values increases message processing and later resistance to change. *J. Personal. Soc. Psychol.* 94(2):196–213

Bolsen T. 2013. A light bulb goes on: norms, rhetoric, and actions for the public good. *Polit. Behav.* 35(1):1–20

Boninger DS, Krosnick JA, Berent MK. 1995a. Origins of attitude importance: self-interest, social identification, and value relevance. *J. Personal. Soc. Psychol.* 68(1):61–80

Boninger DS, Krosnick JA, Berent MK, Fabrigar L. 1995b. The causes and consequences of attitude importance. See Petty & Krosnick 1995, pp. 159–90

Boyd RW, Wengrovitz SM. 2005. *The elusive concept of issue publics: issue salience in American elections.* Presented at Annu. Meet. Int. Soc. Political Psychol., 28th, Toronto, Canada

Brandt MJ, Wetherell GA. 2012. What attitudes are moral attitudes? The case of attitude heritability. *Soc. Psychol. Personal. Sci.* 3(2):172–79

Britt TW, Millard MR, Sundareswaran PT, Moore D. 2009. Personality variables predict strength-related attitude dimensions across objects. *J. Personal.* 77(3):859–82

Britt TW, Pusilo CL, McKibben ES, Kelley C, Baker AN, Nielson KA. 2011. Personality and strength-related attitude dimensions: between and within person relationships. *J. Res. Personal.* 45(6):586–96

Cacioppo JT, Petty RE. 1981. Effects of extent of thought on the pleasantness ratings of P-O-X trials: evidence for three judgmental tendencies in evaluating social situations. *J. Personal. Soc. Psychol.* 40(6):1000–9

Campbell JD. 1986. Similarity and uniqueness: the effects of attribute type, relevance, and individual differences in self esteem and depression. *J. Personal. Soc. Psychol.* 50:281–94

Carsey TM, Layman GC. 2006. Changing sides or changing minds? Party identification and policy preferences in the American electorate. *Am. J. Polit. Sci.* 50(2):464–77

Charng HW, Piliavin JA, Callero PL. 1988. Role identity and reasoned action in the prediction of repeated behavior. *Soc. Psychol. Q.* 51(4):303–17

Chen C, Petrick JF. 2014. The roles of perceived travel benefits, importance, and constraints in predicting travel behavior. *J. Travel Res.* 55:509–22

Ciuk DJ, Yost BA. 2016. The effects of issue salience, elite influence, and policy content on public opinion. *Polit. Commun.* 33(2):328–45

Collins AM, Loftus EF. 1975. A spreading activation theory of semantic processing. *Psychol. Rev.* 82:407–28

Costarelli S, Colloca P. 2007. The moderation of ambivalence on attitude-intention relations as mediated by attitude importance. *Eur. J. Soc. Psychol.* 37(5):923–33

Cullum JG, Okdie BM, Harton HC. 2011. When my country is at war: Issue importance and interpersonal influence lead Iraq War attitudes to cluster within social networks. *Soc. Influ.* 6(4):231–48

Dawson E, Gilovich T, Regan DT. 2002. Motivated reasoning and performance on the Wason selection task. *Personal. Soc. Psychol. Bull.* 28:1379–87

DiClemente RJ, Forrest KA, Mickler S. 1990. College students' knowledge and attitudes about AIDS and changes in HIV-preventive behaviors. *AIDS Educ. Prev.* 2(3):201–12

Eaton AA, Visser PS. 2008. Attitude importance: understanding the causes and consequences of passionately held views. *Soc. Personal. Psychol. Compass* 2(4):1719–36

Fabrigar LR, Krosnick JA. 1995. Attitude importance and the false consensus effect. *Personal. Soc. Psychol. Bull.* 21(5):468–79

Falk EB, Spunt RP, Lieberman MD. 2012. Ascribing beliefs to ingroup and outgroup political candidates: neural correlates of perspective-taking, issue importance and days until the election. *Phil. Trans. R. Soc. B* 367:731–43

Farc MM, Sagarin BJ. 2009. Using attitude strength to predict registration and voting behavior in the 2004 U.S. presidential elections. *Basic Appl. Soc. Psychol.* 31(2):160–73

Fazio RH. 1990. Multiple processes by which attitudes guide behavior: the MODE model as an integrative framework. *Adv. Exp. Soc. Psychol.* 23:75–109

Festinger L. 1957. *A Theory of Cognitive Dissonance.* Stanford, CA: Stanford Univ. Press

Fisher JD, Fisher WA. 1992. Changing AIDS risk behavior. *Psychol. Bull.* 111(3):455–74

Fiske ST, Taylor SE. 2013. *Social Cognition: From Brains to Culture.* Thousand Oaks, CA: Sage Publications

Forrest LN, Smith AR, Fussner LM, Dodd DR, Clerkin EM. 2016. Using implicit attitudes of exercise importance to predict explicit exercise dependence symptoms and exercise behaviors. *Psychol. Sport Exerc.* 22:91–97

Fournier P, Blais A, Nadeau R, Gidengil E, Nevitte N. 2003. Issue importance and performance voting. *Polit. Behav.* 25:51–67

Franc R. 1999. Attitude strength and the attitude-behavior domain: magnitude and independence of moderating effects of different strength indices. *J. Soc. Behav. Personal.* 14(2):177–95

Garcia RL, Bergsieker HB, Shelton JN. 2015. Racial attitude (dis)similarity and liking in same-race minority interactions. *Group Process. Intergr. Relat.* 2015:1368430215612224

Glynn CJ, Park E. 1997. Reference groups, opinion intensity, and public opinion expression. *Int. J. Public Opin. Res.* 9(3):213–32

Gopinath M, Nyer PU. 2009. The effect of public commitment on resistance to persuasion: the influence of attitude certainty, issue importance, susceptibility to normative influence, preference for consistency and source proximity. *Intern. J. Res. Market* 26(1):60–68

Grube JA, Piliavin JA. 2000. Role identity, organizational experiences, and volunteer performance. *Personal. Soc. Psychol. Bull.* 26(9):1108–19

Grynaviski JD, Corrigan BE. 2006. Specification issues in proximity models of candidate evaluation (with issue importance). *Polit. Anal.* 14(4):393–420

Haddock G, Rothman AJ, Reber R, Schwarz N. 1999. Forming judgments of attitude certainty, intensity, and importance: the role of subjective experiences. *Personal. Soc. Psychol. Bull.* 25:771–82

Hart W, Albarracín D, Eagly AH, Brechan I, Lindberg MJ, Merrill L. 2009. Feeling validated versus being correct: a meta-analysis of selective exposure to information. *Psychol. Bull.* 135(4):555–88

Heider F. 1958. *The Psychology of Interpersonal Relations.* New York: Wiley

Helweg-Larsen M, Collins BE. 1997. A social psychological perspective on the role of knowledge about AIDS in AIDS prevention. *Curr. Dir. Psychol. Sci.* 6(2):23–26

Hippler HJ, Schwarz N. 1986. Not forbidding isn't allowing: the cognitive basis of the forbid-allow asymmetry. *Public Opin. Q.* 50:87–96

Hofmann W, Gschwendner T, Schmitt M. 2005. On implicit-explicit consistency: the moderating role of individual differences in awareness and adjustment. *Eur. J. Personal.* 19(1):25–49

Holbrook AL, Berent MK, Krosnick JA, Visser PS, Boninger DS. 2005. Attitude importance and the accumulation of attitude-relevant knowledge in memory. *J. Personal. Soc. Psychol.* 88:749–69

Holbrook AL, Sterrett D, Johnson TP, Krysan M. 2016. Racial disparities in political participation across issues: the role of issue-specific motivators. *Polit. Behav.* 38:1–32

Holland RW, Verplanken B, van Knippenberg A. 2003. From repetition to conviction: attitude accessibility as a determinant of attitude certainty. *J. Exp. Soc. Psychol.* 39(6):594–601

Honaken P, Verplanken B. 2004. Understanding attitudes towards genetically modified food: the role of values and attitude strength. *J. Consum. Policy* 4:401–20

Hübner G, Mohs A, Peterson LE. 2014. The role of attitude strength in predicting organ donation behavior by implicit and explicit attitudes. *Open J. Med. Psychol.* 3(5):355–63

Jarvis B, Petty RE. 1996. The need to evaluate. *J. Personal. Soc. Psychol.* 70:172–94

Jett J, Thapa B, Swett R. 2013. Boater speed compliance in manatee zones: examining a proposed predictive model. *Soc. Nat. Resour.* 26:95–104

Judd CM, Krosnick JA. 1989. The structural bases of consistency among political attitudes: the effects of political expertise and attitude importance. In *Attitude Structure and Function*, ed. AR Pratkanis, SJ Breckler, AG Greenwald, pp. 99–128. Hillsdale, NJ: Erlbaum

Karpinski A, Steinman RB, Hilton JL. 2005. Attitude importance as a moderator of the relationship between implicit and explicit attitude measures. *Personal. Soc. Psychol. Bull.* 31(7):949–62

Kemmelmeier M, Burnstein E, Peng K. 1999. Individualism and authoritarianism shape attitudes toward physician-assisted suicide. *J. Appl. Soc. Psychol.* 29(12):2613–31

Klar S. 2013. Identity and engagement among political independents in America. *Polit. Psychol.* 35(4):577–91

Klar S. 2014. A multidimensional study of ideological preferences and priorities among the American public. *Public Opin. Q.* 78(S1):344–59

Knobloch-Westerwick S, Johnson BK, Westerwick A. 2015. Confirmation bias in online searches: impacts of selective exposure before an election on political attitude strength and shifts. *J. Comput. Mediat. Commun.* 20(2):171–87

Knobloch-Westerwick S, Meng J. 2009. Looking the other way: selective exposure to attitude-consistent and counter-attitudinal political information. *Commun. Res.* 36(3):426–48

Kokkinaki F, Lunt P. 1997. The relationship between involvement, attitude accessibility, and attitude-behavior consistency. *Br. J. Soc. Psychol.* 36(4):497–509

Krosnick JA. 1988. Attitude importance and attitude change. *J. Exp. Soc. Psychol.* 24:240–55

Krosnick JA. 1989. Attitude importance and attitude accessibility. *Personal. Soc. Psychol. Bull.* 15(3):297–308

Krosnick JA. 1990. Government policy and citizen passion: a study of issue publics in contemporary America. *Polit. Behav.* 12:59–92

Krosnick JA. 1992. The impact of cognitive sophistication and attitude importance on response order effects and question order effects. In *Order Effects in Social and Psychological Research*, ed. N Schwartz, S Sudman, pp. 203–18. New York: Springer-Verlag

Krosnick JA, Berent MK, Boninger DS. 1994. Pockets of responsibility in the American electorate: findings of a research program on attitude importance. *Polit. Commun.* 11(4):391–411

Krosnick JA, Boninger DS, Chuang YC, Berent MK, Carnot CG. 1993. Attitude strength: one construct or many related constructs? *J. Personal. Soc. Psychol.* 65(6):1132–51

Krosnick JA, Petty RE. 1995. Attitude strength: an overview. See Petty & Krosnick 1995, pp. 1–24

Krosnick JA, Schuman H. 1988. Attitude intensity, importance, and certainty and susceptibility to response effects. *J. Personal. Soc. Psychol.* 54(6):940–52

Krosnick JA, Telhami S. 1995. Public attitudes toward Israel: a study of the attentive and issue publics. *Int. Stud. Q.* 39(4):535–54

LaPiere RT. 1934. Attitudes versus action. *Soc. Forces* 13(2):230–37

Lavine H, Borgida E, Sullivan J. 2000. On the relationship between attitude involvement and attitude accessibility: toward a cognitive-motivational model of political information processing. *Polit. Psychol.* 21(1):81–106

Lavine H, Borgida E, Sullivan J, Thomsen C. 1996. The relationship of national and personal issue salience to attitude accessibility on foreign and domestic policy issues. *Polit. Psychol.* 17(2):293–316

Lavine H, Huff JW, Wagner SH, Sweeney D. 1998. The moderating influence of attitude strength on the susceptibility to context effects. *J. Personal. Soc. Psychol.* 75(2):359–73

Lecheler S, de Vreese CH, Slothuus R. 2009. Issue importance as a moderator of framing effects. *Commun. Res.* 36(3):400–25

Leeper TJ. 2014. The informational basis for mass polarization. *Public Opin. Q.* 78(1):27–46

Levendusky MS, Druckman JN, McLain A. 2016. How group discussions create strong attitudes and strong partisans. *Res. Polit.* 3:1–6

Liu C, Lee H, Huang P, Chen H, Sommers S. 2016. Do incompatible arguments cause extensive processing in the evaluation of arguments? The role of congruence between argument compatibility and argument quality. *Br. J. Soc. Psychol.* 107:179–98

Liu J, Latane B. 1998a. The catastrophic link between the importance and extremity of political attitudes. *Polit. Behav.* 20(2):105–26

Liu J, Latane B. 1998b. Extremization of attitudes: Does thought and discussion-induced polarization cumulate? *Basic Appl. Soc. Psychol.* 20(2):103–10

Lo V, Wei R, Lu H, Hou H. 2015. Perceived issue importance, information processing, and third-person effect of news about the imported U.S. beef controversy. *Int. J. Public Opin. Res.* 27(3):341–60

MacInnis B, Krosnick JA. 2016. The impact of candidates' statements about global warming on electoral success in 2008 to 2015: evidence using five methodologies. In *Explorations in Political Psychology*, ed. JA Krosnick, IC Chiang, T Stark. New York: Psychol. Press. In press

Malhotra N, Tahk AM. 2011. Specification issues in assessing the moderating role of issue importance: a comment on Grynaviski and Corrigan 2006. *Polit. Anal.* 19(3):342–50

Mann J, Tarantola DJM, Netter TW. 1992. The HIV pandemic: status and trends. In *AIDS in the World*, ed. J Mann, D Tarantola, pp. 11–108. Cambridge, MA: Harvard Univ. Press

Matthes J, Rios Morrison K, Schemer C. 2010. A spiral of silence for some: attitude certainty and the expression of political minority opinions. *Commun. Res.* 37(6):774–800

Miller JM, Krosnick JA, Holbrook AL, Tahk A, Dionne A. 2016. The impact of policy change threat on financial contributions to interest groups. In *Explorations in Political Psychology*, ed. JA Krosnick, IC Chiang, T Stark. New York: Psychol. Press. In press

Mokdad AH, Marks JS, Stroup DF, Gerberding JL. 2004. Actual causes of death in the United States, 2000. *J. Am. Med. Assoc.* 291(10):1238–45

Morrison KR, Matthes J. 2011. Socially motivated projection: Need to belong increases perceived opinion consensus on important issues. *Eur. J. Soc. Psychol.* 41(6):707–19

Nederhof AJ. 1989. Self-involvement, intention certainty and attitude-intention consistency. *Br. J. Soc. Psychol.* 28:123–33

Nosek B. 2005. Moderators of the relationship between implicit and explicit evaluation. *J. Exp. Psychol. Gen.* 134(4):565–84

Olson JM, Vernon PA, Harris JA, Jang KL. 2001. The heritability of attitudes: a study of twins. *J. Personal. Soc. Psychol.* 80(6):845–60

Perloff RM. 2013. *The Dynamics of Persuasion: Communication and Attitudes in the 21st Century*. New York: Routledge

Petty RE, Krosnick JA. 1995. *Attitude Strength: Antecedents and Consequences*. Mahwah, NJ: Erlbaum

Pfau M, Roskos-Ewoldsen D, Wood M, Yin S, Cho J, et al. 2003. Attitude accessibility as an alternative for how inculcation confers resistance. *Commun. Monogr.* 70(1):39–51

Pomerantz EM, Chaiken S, Tordesillas RS. 1995. Attitude strength and resistance processes. *J. Personal. Soc. Psychol.* 69(3):408–19

Pryor JB, Gibbons FX, Wicklund RA, Fazio RH, Hood R. 1977. Self-focused attention and self-report validity. *J. Personal.* 45:513–27

Roese NJ, Olson T. 1994. Attitude importance as a function of repeated attitude expression. *J. Exp. Soc. Psychol.* 30(1):39–51

Rogers TF, Singer E, Imperio J. 1993. The polls: poll trends. AIDS—an update. *Public Opin. Q.* 57:92–114

Ross L, Greene D, House P. 1977. The "false consensus effect": an egocentric bias in social perception and attribution processes. *J. Exp. Soc. Psychol.* 13:279–301

Sanbonmatsu DM, Uchino BN, Birmingham W. 2011. On the importance of knowing your partner's views: Attitude familiarity is associated with better interpersonal functioning and lower ambulatory blood pressure in daily life. *Ann. Behav. Med.* 41:131–37

Schoenefeld JJ, McCauley MR. 2015. Local is not always better: the impact of climate information on values, behavior, and policy support. *J. Env. Stud. Sci.* 2015. doi: 10.1007/s13412-015-0288-y

Schuman H, Presser S. 1981. *Questions and Answers in Attitude Surveys: Experiments on Question Form, Wording, and Context*. New York: Academic

Sevelius J, Stake J. 2003. The effect of prior attitudes and attitude importance on attitude change and class impact in women's and gender studies. *J. Appl. Soc. Psychol.* 33(11):2341–53

Starzyk KB, Fabrigar LR, Soryal AS, Fanning JJ. 2009. A painful reminder: the role of level and salience of attitude importance in cognitive dissonance. *Personal. Soc. Psychol. Bull.* 35(1):126–37

Stephenson MT, Benoit WL, Tschida DA. 2001. Testing the mediating role of cognitive responses in the elaboration likelihood model. *Commun. Stud.* 52(4):324–37

Tesser A. 1978. Self-generated attitude change. In *Advances in Experimental Social Psychology*, ed. L Berkowitz, pp. 298–338. New York: Academic

Tesser A, Martin L, Mendolia M. 1995. The impact of thought on attitude extremity and attitude-behavior consistency. See Petty & Krosnick 1995, pp. 73–92

Thomsen C, Lavine H, Kounios J. 2006. Social value and attitude concepts in semantic memory: relational structure, concept strength, and the fan effect. *Soc. Cogn.* 14(3):191–225

Uchino BN, Sanbonmatsu DM, Birmingham W. 2013. Knowing your partner is not enough: Spousal importance moderates the link between attitude familiarity and ambulatory blood pressure. *J. Behav. Med.* 36(6):549–55

van Herreveld F, van der Pligt J. 2004. Attitudes as stable and transparent constructions. *J. Exp. Soc. Psychol.* 40(5):666–74

van Herreveld F, van der Pligt J, de Vries NK, Andreas S. 2000. The structure of attitudes: attribute importance, accessibility and judgment. *Br. J. Soc. Psychol.* 39(3):363–80

Visser PS, Krosnick JA. 1998. Development of attitude strength over the life cycle: surge and decline. *J. Personal. Soc. Psychol.* 75(6):1389–410

Visser PS, Krosnick JA, Norris CJ. 2016. Attitude importance and attitude-relevant knowledge: motivator and enabler. In *Explorations in Political Psychology*, ed. JA Krosnick, IC Chiang, T Stark. New York: Psychol. Press. In press

Visser PS, Krosnick JA, Simmons JP. 2003. Distinguishing the cognitive and behavioral consequences of attitude importance and certainty: a new approach to testing the common-factor hypothesis. *J. Exp. Soc. Psychol.* 39(2):118–41

Visser PS, Mirabile RR. 2004. Attitudes in the social context: the impact of social network composition on individual-level attitude strength. *J. Personal. Soc. Psychol.* 87(6):779–95

Westerwick A, Kleinman SB, Knobloch-Westerwick S. 2013. Turn a blind eye if you care: impacts of attitude consistency, importance, and credibility on seeking of political information and implications for attitudes. *J. Commun.* 63(3):432–53

Ziegler R, Schlett C. 2016. An attitude strength and self-perception framework regarding the bi-directional relationship of job satisfaction with extra-role and in-role behavior: the doubly moderating role of work certainty. *Front. Psychol.* 7:1–17

Zuwerink Jacks J, Cameron KA. 2003. Strategies for resisting persuasion. *Basic Appl. Soc. Psychol.* 25(2):145–61

Zuwerink Jacks J, Devine PG. 1996. Attitude importance and resistance to persuasion: It's not just the thought that counts. *J. Personal. Soc. Psychol.* 70(5):931–44

Zuwerink Jacks J, Devine PG. 2000. Attitude importance, forewarning of message content, and resistance to persuasion. *Basic Appl. Soc. Psychol.* 22(1):19–29

Zuwerink Jacks J, Lancaster LC. 2015. Fit for persuasion: the effects of nonverbal delivery style, message framing, and gender on message effectiveness. *J. Appl. Soc. Psychol.* 45:203–13

How Power Affects People: Activating, Wanting, and Goal Seeking

Ana Guinote[1,2]

[1]Department of Experimental Psychology, University College London, London WC1H 0AP,
United Kingdom; email: a.guinote@ucl.ac.uk

[2]Leadership Knowledge Center, Nova School of Business and Economics, Lisbon,
Portugal 1099-032

Annu. Rev. Psychol. 2017. 68:353–81

First published online as a Review in Advance on
September 21, 2016

The *Annual Review of Psychology* is online at
psych.annualreviews.org

This article's doi:
10.1146/annurev-psych-010416-044153

Keywords

social power, dominance, approach motivation, goal seeking,
self-regulation, corruption

Abstract

Sociocognitive research has demonstrated that power affects how people
feel, think, and act. In this article, I review literature from social psychology,
neuroscience, management, and animal research and propose an integrated
framework of power as an intensifier of goal-related approach motivation. A
growing literature shows that power energizes thought, speech, and action
and orients individuals toward salient goals linked to power roles, predispositions, tasks, and opportunities. Power magnifies self-expression linked to
active parts of the self (the active self), enhancing confidence, self-regulation,
and prioritization of efforts toward advancing focal goals. The effects of
power on cognitive processes, goal preferences, performance, and corruption are discussed, and its potentially detrimental effects on social attention,
perspective taking, and objectification of subordinates are examined. Several
inconsistencies in the literature are explained by viewing power holders as
more flexible and dynamic than is usually assumed.

Contents

"The fundamental concept in social science is power, in the same sense in which energy is the fundamental concept in physics." —Bertrand Russell (1938, p. 10)

INTRODUCTION

Power is admired and fought over by those who desire it and often feared by those who lack it. It is ubiquitous and affects the fate of many. Unsurprisingly, power has attracted the attention of ancient and modern philosophers, policy makers, and scholars from various disciplines. In psychology, there has been a substantial increase in research on social power since Keltner et al.'s (2003) review proposing that power activates the behavioral approach system (BAS; see Gray 1990, Gray & McNaughton 2000). This activation may have a wide range of consequences for the thoughts, feelings, and actions of power holders, giving this theory great explanatory power.

This article discusses research published since Keltner et al. (2003) examining how power affects people. In so doing, it revisits this and other theories of power [e.g., Fiske's (1993) theory of power as control; Guinote's (2007a–c) situated focus theory of power] and proposes an integrated

Social power: the ability to control or influence another's thoughts, feelings, or behaviors framework, according to which power energizes thought, speech, and action and intensifies wanting and goal seeking. Power triggers a readiness to think, speak, and act, increasing the vigor and frequency of output (i.e., energizing or activating people) in domains that individuals deem important. Power also brings clarity of focus and eagerness of desire (wanting), as well as drive to work toward desires and aims (goal seeking). In this framework, activating, wanting, and goal seeking among the powerful reflect a stimulated BAS associated with the pursuit of goals. BAS activation among power holders is associated with their desire to have a prompt impact on the social environment and advance their work-role priorities or personal inclinations.

Power-related approach motivation is accompanied by prioritization of important goals and enhanced self-regulation rather than, as has been suggested, hedonic tone or reward seeking and consumption (see Berridge 2007, Salamone & Correa 2002). The perspective taken in this article differs from approach motivation conceptions that associate power with positive affect and reward seeking (Keltner et al. 2003). Instead, this review suggests that people in power typically have strong agendas and more readily act upon their goals. Furthermore, power affects cognitive processes in ways that facilitate self-expression, action, and goal pursuit (Galinsky et al. 2003; Guinote 2007a,b; Overbeck & Park 2006). Enhanced activation, wanting, and goal seeking among power holders have downstream consequences for performance, corruption, and social behavior.

This review is informed by research in the fields of social psychology, cognitive neuroscience, leadership, and management, as well as animal behavior. The focus is on the powerful, although some of the consequences of being powerless are also considered. Although this review primarily discusses the ways in which power affects people, it also addresses the question of who rises to power. Individuals who rise to power often exercise influence in a goal-oriented manner similar to that of individuals who have power. Therefore, their behavior is also approach motivated.

This article begins with conceptual definitions, methods, and theories of power. It revisits Keltner et al.'s (2003) approach motivation theory of power, considering recent developments in the neuroscience of appetitive behavior. Subsequently, it discusses empirical evidence for the framework of power as activating, wanting, and seeking, as well as the effects of having power on cognitive processes. Literature concerning the links between power and the self demonstrates that power potentiates the development of a positive self-concept, independent self-construal, and expression of the active self. This discussion is followed by a section dedicated to goal pursuit and the types of desires and aims sought by people in power. The question of whether power corrupts is also discussed. A subsequent section analyzes how power affects social behavior. This section is followed by concluding considerations.

> **Goals:** mental representations of desired end states that a person seeks to attain
>
> **Approach motivation:** the energization of behavior oriented toward positive or desired objects, events, and possibilities

CONCEPTS, METHODS, AND THEORIES OF POWER

What Is Power?

The word power derives from the Latin word *potere*, meaning to be able. Although the etymology of the word locates it in the person, power is a relational concept and is dependent upon a person's perceptions of his or her levels of control relative to another's [Dahl 1957 (2007), Parsons 1963]. Power results from a negotiation of a shared reality and often involves the creation of shared meanings, ideologies, and identities (Haslam et al. 2010, Hogg 2001, Parsons 1963).

Consistent with Russell's (1938) analogy of energy in the natural sciences, power cannot be reduced to a single form. At a macro level, organizations may generate economic, religious, political, or military power, phenomena described in the elite theories of political science and sociology (e.g., Mills 1999). At a middle level, membership in social groups, such as ethnicity, gender, and social class, also affects control over resources and the attainment of influential social positions

(Keltner et al. 2003). For example, only 4% of CEOs at S&P 500 companies are women (Catalyst 2016). Power also emerges at a group level, often in association with leadership roles (i.e., roles that involve influence geared toward the attainment of group goals; Northouse 2015). Finally, power asymmetries occur at the micro level, such as in families and intimate relationships (e.g., Laurin et al. 2016).

Social power has most frequently been conceptualized in terms of the ability to control or influence another's thoughts, feelings, or behaviors in meaningful ways (Fiske 1993, French & Raven 1959, Thibaut & Kelley 1959, Vescio et al. 2003). However, given the multiple levels of the social structure at which power occurs, and the complexity of power relations, there are various definitions of power. Conceptions of power may be categorized according to three major types: asymmetric interdependence, control over outcomes, and sociofunctional relations in groups.

Some scholars have defined power on the basis of the first category, asymmetric interdependence, or the actual or potential ability to influence another. For instance, Weber [1914 (1978), p. 152] defined power as "the probability that one actor within a social relationship will be in a position to carry out his own will despite resistance." Dahl [1957 (2007), p. 202] considered that "A has power over B to the extent that he can get B to do something that B would not otherwise do." This potential to influence others derives from the possession of valued resources.

The diversity of factors contributing to power processes led French & Raven (1959) to develop an encompassing classification of tactics used to assert power, which they called power bases: coercive (e.g., punishment), reward (e.g., support), legitimate (e.g., shared beliefs about obedience), expert (e.g., knowledge), referent (e.g., religious identification), and informational (e.g., persuasion). In informal, medical, and organizational contexts, soft means, such as reward or expertise, are more effective and trigger greater adherence than harsh means. Harsh means are seen more often in formal structures and are typically used by people in the higher echelons of power. Recently, power bases have been reclassified into social control (harsh bases) and influence (soft bases) (Fiske & Berdahl 2007). Influence is commonly seen in prestige- or status-based hierarchies and is marked by deference and appreciation.

Conceptions of power based on influence rely on observed or inferred potential behavior. However, this conflates structural aspects of tangible control with the targets' psychological reactions and desire to comply (Fiske & Dépret 1996). To solve this issue, some scholars have defined power in terms of the second category, control over valued outcomes (Emerson 1962, Fiske & Dépret 1996, Keltner et al. 2003), which implies that one person, the power holder, has a resource that is valued by another person, who is therefore dependent on the power holder (Emerson 1962). Power holders can affect the thoughts, feelings, or behavior of subordinates (Keltner et al. 2003, Vescio et al. 2003).

Conceptions of the third category, sociofunctional relations, are concerned with the origins and functions of power. From an evolutionary perspective, power emerged to help advance the needs of groups (Maner & Case 2016, Van Vugt et al. 2008). A review of ethnographic accounts of the past 150 years (Boehm 2009) revealed that power structures had already emerged in small hunting and gathering societies to facilitate peacekeeping and performance of religious rituals and to deal with problems of group movement and intergroup rivalries in ancestral environments (Van Vugt et al. 2008).

Functional perspectives draw on legitimized power structures that contribute to collective goals (Parsons 1963). In this conception, people have power only if others recognize (i.e., consent to) it. Social identity perspectives (Ellemers et al. 2004, Haslam et al. 2010, Hogg 2001) claim that power arises from group processes. The effectiveness of leaders depends on their ability to stimulate a shared group identity (Haslam et al. 2010), and groups create power through coordination and social influence. In spite of the ubiquity of legitimized power in society, being powerless is tolerated rather than desired. It conflicts with the basic human need for control and autonomy (Fiske & Berdahl 2007, Lammers et al. 2016, Pratto 2015). Therefore, subordinates generally attempt upward mobility.

Dominance: motivated behavior aimed at increasing power in relation to others, often through assertive and confident actions

Methods and Measures in Power Research

Sociocognitive research on social power has been carried out via experimental, quasi-experimental, and correlational methodologies. Manipulations involving roles that control another's outcomes have been common since Kipnis' (1972, 1976) studies. For example, Fiske & Dépret (1996) asked participants to make decisions about internship applicants. The powerful group was told that their decisions would have a 30% impact on final decisions, and the control group was told they would have no impact. Other procedures have asked participants to enact manager and subordinate roles in the laboratory; managers were paid a fixed amount and subordinates were paid according to the managers' evaluations of their outputs (e.g., Guinote 2007c). Studies have also used episodic recall of a past event in which the participant was powerful, powerless, or in a neutral (control) position (e.g., Galinsky et al. 2003).

Economic games that create resource inequalities (e.g., ultimatum and dictator) and negotiation tasks have contributed to the understanding of power (De Dreu & Van Kleef 2004, Kim et al. 2005, Magee et al. 2007, Schilke et al. 2015). The various manipulations of power generally have similar effects. In addition, studies have used testosterone administration (Mehta & Josephs 2010) as a way to manipulate power-related states.

Researchers have widely examined individual differences in dominance using questionnaire measures such as the California Personality Inventory (Gough 1987) and the Personal Sense of Power Scale (Anderson et al. 2012). Studies have also relied on employee participants who occupy managerial or subordinate positions within organizations (e.g., Guinote & Phillips 2010). Finally, the implicit need for power has been assessed with projective measures (Schultheiss et al. 2005).

Theories of Power

Scientists, philosophers, and political analysts have long associated power with free will, volition, and agency. In short, it is argued that power gives people the ability to act at will [e.g., Weber 1914 (1978)]. This ability derives from reduced resistance and constraint. This article reviews literature demonstrating a different perspective: that power changes people. It affects motivation, cognition, and self-regulation in ways that facilitate carrying out one's aims and desires. In the next sections, prior theories of power are discussed, then an integrated framework is presented.

Fiske's functionalist theory of power. A systematic investigation of the motivational and cognitive underpinnings of power holders emerged after developments in social cognition, with work done by Fiske and colleagues on the links between social attention and motivation (e.g., Fiske & Neuberg 1990). According to the continuum model of impression formation (Fiske & Neuberg 1990), humans are tacticians who deploy their limited cognitive resources in line with their motivations. Interpersonal (or outcome) dependency triggers deliberative processes and raises social attention to predict another's actions. The power as control model (Fiske 1993) proposes that power decreases social attention because power holders are overloaded with other priorities, are not dependent on others, or have a dominant personality and do not want to pay attention.

The proposed framework of power as activation, wanting, and seeking draws on Fiske's central assumption that the role of cognition is to serve action (Fiske 1992) and that attention follows motivation (Fiske & Neuberg 1990). As is discussed below, the present framework provides a broader examination of how power affects the person, including their cognition, affect, and behavior.

Approach motivation theory of power. The dominant paradigm in power research of the past decade has been the approach–inhibition theory of power proposed by Keltner et al. (2003). Based on the notion that people in power live in reward-rich environments and have more opportunities, Keltner et al. (2003) proposed that power activates the BAS (e.g., Gray 1990). The BAS triggers preferential attention to rewards, positive affect, automatic cognition, and disinhibited behavior. In contrast, lack of power is associated with punishment, constraint, and threats, and it activates the behavioral inhibition system (Gray & McNaughton 2000). This system functions as an alarm that inhibits ongoing behavior, triggers vigilance, and produces negative affect.

Expanding on Keltner et al.'s (2003) theory, the model developed in this article relies on one specific part of the BAS: wanting and seeking of salient goals. Goals can be, but are most frequently not, hedonic. Goals linked to power roles or personal dispositions tend to have priority over seeking pleasurable experiences through sex, food, and other positive stimuli.

Situated focus theory of power. The situated focus theory of power (Guinote 2007a) argues that power leads to situated behavior driven by the prioritization of salient goals and constructs. At the cognitive level, power affords flexibility and the use of selective processing strategies that focus on the desires, affordances, and aims deemed relevant in a given context while neglecting irrelevant ones. This processing style enables prompt decisions and actions on a moment-to-moment basis.

The framework developed in this article retains the notions of situated behavior, prioritization, selective processing, and flexibility from the situated focus theory of power, expanding them to encompass the BAS as an intensifier that facilitates thought, speech, and action and assists sustained effort during the pursuit of goals. Although the situated focus theory of power is primarily a cognitive approach with proximal motivational units (e.g., goals), the framework of power as activation, wanting, and seeking encompasses a more general motivational system linked to the energization of behavior consistent with neuroscientific developments on appetitive behavior, as well as to developments in motivational science (Kruglanski et al. 2012).

Other theories. Smith & Trope (2006) argued that power increases social distance, triggering abstract thinking, which allows individuals to focus on primary information and extract the gist from information (see below). Others have theorized the existence of intermediate mechanisms, suggesting that power elevates self-esteem (De Cremer & Van Dijk 2005, Hofstede et al. 2002, Wang 2015, Wojciszke & Struzynska-Kujalowicz 2007) and confidence in one's judgments (Briñol et al. 2007, Fast et al. 2012, Tost et al. 2012). These factors act as proximal mechanisms that are consistent with most conceptual perspectives on social power and contribute to the increased decisiveness and agency of people in positions of authority.

UNDERSTANDING POWER THROUGH THE LENSES OF ACTIVATING, WANTING, AND GOAL SEEKING

The BAS has most frequently been conceptualized as a system that is activated in the presence of positive stimuli (e.g., food, sex; Gray 1990). People with an active BAS experience positive affect in the presence of positive possibilities and events, and they eagerly pursue these rewarding opportunities (Carver & White 1994, Gray & McNaughton 2000). The BAS is implicated in reinforcement learning and in various forms of addiction (Alcaro et al. 2007).

The first premise of the framework in this article is that power leads to activation, energizing thought, speech, and action in ways that are consistent with the BAS. Activation is a neurobiological mechanism that facilitates responses and is common to all types of approach-oriented states (Alcaro et al. 2007, Berridge 2007).

Power Triggers a Generalized Approach

A great deal of evidence supports the claim that power triggers a generalized approach orientation. Power sparks optimism and confidence (Fast et al. 2009), authentic self-expression (Anderson & Berdahl 2002, Guinote et al. 2002, Kraus et al. 2011), action (Galinsky et al. 2003), and disinhibited behavior (Gonzaga et al. 2008) while decreasing vigilance (Willis et al. 2011) and worries about threats or losses (Inesi 2010, Keltner et al. 2003). Power holders and dominant people often experience positive affective states, such as happiness and interest (Anderson & Berdahl 2002, Berdahl & Martorana 2006, Langner & Keltner 2008, Schmid Mast et al. 2009). However, evidence regarding the links between power and affect is mixed (Galinsky et al. 2003, Smith & Bargh 2008, Weick & Guinote 2008). Elevated positive affect could occur primarily in the context of interactions (see Petkanopoulou et al. 2016).

Direct measures of approach, which do not conflate psychological states correlated with approach motivation (e.g., positive affect, optimism) with the underlying motivation itself, also show enhanced generalized approach motivation among the powerful. Support for this theory stems from studies of motor responses (Maner et al. 2010, Smith & Bargh 2008), self-report (Lammers et al. 2010, Smith & Bargh 2008), and left hemispheric brain dominance (Boksem et al. 2012, Wilkinson et al. 2010). For example, in one study (Maner et al. 2010), power-primed participants responded to auditory signals by pressing keys that implied approach movements toward the body or avoidance movements away from the body. High levels of power facilitated approach movements. Similarly, a large survey of employees revealed enhanced approach motivation among the powerful (Lammers et al. 2010). This evidence suggests that power holders have a readiness to move forward toward desired ends, even when the direction of behavior is unspecified.

Neuropsychological Developments in Approach Motivation Research

Most research on appetitive behavior has been conducted in relation to rewards (see Alcaro et al. 2007, Hamid et al. 2016). Therefore, the motivational system underlying appetitive behavior has been linked to reward processing and hedonic tone (Berridge 2007). Power research is no exception (Anderson & Berdahl 2002, Galinsky et al. 2003, Keltner et al. 2003, Magee et al. 2007). However, the overuse of the term reward has recently been criticized. Salamone & Correa (2012, p. 473) pointed out that "the word 'reward' seems to be used as a general term that refers to all aspects of appetitive learning, motivation and emotion, including both conditioned and unconditioned aspects; this usage is so broad as to be essentially meaningless." It has become apparent that approach motivation is not monolithic (Alcaro et al. 2007, Carver & White 1994). For instance, Corr & Cooper (2016) identified four BAS factors: reward interest, goal-drive persistence, reward reactivity, and impulsivity.

Examinations of the neural correlates of appetitive behavior have propelled new insights. Pathways of the brain associated with reward processing (involving a cortico–basal ganglia–thalamic loop) are also responsive to prediction errors, salient nonrewards, and a variety of positive objects, possibilities, and events (e.g., music or shopping; Alcaro et al. 2007, Salamone & Correa 2002). To explain this diversity, Salamone & Correa (2002, 2012) developed a model of facilitation of responses. This model considers two classes of incentive motivation: liking (reward pleasure) and wanting. Wanting involves "appetite to consume" and "working to obtain" motivational stimuli and to "overcome response constraints, activation for engaging in vigorous instrumental actions" (Salamone & Correa 2002, p. 17). Wanting occurs through the release of the neurotransmitter dopamine, which is produced in the basal ganglia of the brain (Hamid et al. 2016). Dopamine is said to signal the value of work, balance energy levels, and sustain behavior directed at desired end states.

Similarly, Berridge (2007) associated wanting with incentive salience and activation (effort, arousal, and vigor), and Alcaro et al. (2007) posited an instinctual emotional appetitive state seeking system that drives exploratory and approach behavior. In this conception, seeking is rewarding per se without the need for consummatory activity and sensory reward. Together, this work shows that approach motivation entails activation and seeking of a variety of desired experiences and is stronger during expectation than consumption. In the model proposed in this article, the term activation is used to denote increased energy, vigor, and effort, which facilitate responses and sustain goal-directed behavior (see also Kruglanski et al. 2012). Wanting refers to focus and the desire to achieve, and seeking refers to the implementation of courses of action geared toward attaining one's aims and desires.

Critics of the dominant reward-seeking models of approach motivation also focus on the role of positive affect. New evidence has cast doubt on the proposed links between approach motivation and positive affect (e.g., anger involves approach; Carver & Harmon-Jones 2009). Compared to others, approach-motivated individuals can become more frustrated, angry, or depressed if their aims are thwarted (Carver 2004).

Given these advances, two questions arise. First, are power holders primarily concerned with seeking pleasure and reward (hedonic tone) or with wanting and seeking desires and aims? Second, is power associated with indulgence and poor self-regulation or with volition and effective goal striving? Evidence regarding these questions is discussed below.

POWER AS ACTIVATING, WANTING, AND GOAL SEEKING: EMPIRICAL EVIDENCE

Most research on social power has been behavioral. However, animal studies have found that the creation of hierarchies affects activity in dopaminergic pathways of the brain associated with motivation (e.g., Kaplan et al. 2002, Morgan et al. 2002). For instance, Morgan et al. (2002) first housed monkeys individually and found that they had similar dopamine levels. Later, the monkeys were housed in groups and hierarchies emerged. Dominant monkeys had increased levels of dopamine. When given the opportunity, subordinates self-administered more cocaine (i.e., a reward) than dominant monkeys. These findings support the links between power and approach motivation. However, they do not support the hypothesis that high rank triggers reward seeking.

In this section, I propose that power increases activation levels and wanting and seeking of desired ends. Furthermore, similar tendencies are already observed in individuals, particularly dominant people, seeking power. A framework based on activation, wanting, and seeking therefore helps us understand the acquisition of emerging and appointed power, as well as the effects of power on people.

Who Rises to Power? Energized Wanting and Seeking Power

The trait that most predicts upward mobility is dominance. Dominance refers to motivated behavior aimed at increasing power in relation to others, and it is associated with forceful, assertive, and confident actions (Gough 1987, Guinote & Chen 2016). Dominant individuals have strong agendas, particularly in seeking power. They deploy a great deal of effort and energy to prevail over and influence others.

In social encounters, dominant people are energized. They are assertive and decisive, and they speak and interrupt others more often (Anderson & Kilduff 2009, Mast 2002). The assertiveness of dominant people creates the impression of competence, even when they are not necessarily more competent than others. This, in turn, affords power to the dominant person (see Anderson & Kilduff 2009, Guinote et al. 2015).

At the hormonal level, testosterone, a steroid hormone, has long been associated with trait dominance. People with high baseline levels of testosterone eagerly and effortfully seek power (Josephs et al. 2006, Mazur & Booth 1998). High levels of testosterone predict features associated with the model of power as activation and seeking, such as longer stare duration, greater amount of talking, and use of expansive postures. However, the relationship between testosterone and dominant behavior depends on the presence of psychological stress and the hormone cortisol (Mehta & Josephs 2010). When cortisol is high, the links between testosterone and power-seeking behavior are blocked. Moreover, the relationship between testosterone and dominance is reciprocal, such that the acquisition of status or power increases testosterone levels (Mazur & Booth 1998), whereas a decrease of status and power diminishes testosterone (Josephs et al. 2006, Schultheiss et al. 2005).

Within the Big Five model of personality (a model that describes personality along the dimensions of extraversion, conscientiousness, openness to experience, neuroticism, and agreeableness; see Costa & McCrae 1995), extroversion is the trait that most contributes to power emergence (Ellemers et al. 2004, Judge et al. 2002). Extraversion refers to the tendency to be sociable, assertive, and active and to experience positive emotions (Costa & McCrae 1995). Extroverts are influential in spontaneous interactions (e.g., Guinote & Chen 2016) and in organizations (see Judge et al. 2002). The extroversion trait has two facets, increased activity level and assertiveness, related to approach-related activation and wanting (Costa & McCrae 1995). As is the case for dominance, the high frequency of output (activation) and conviction in one's desires and opinions (wanting) in extroversion affords power, though extroverts do not necessarily seek power.

Being competent and skilled also affords power. In particular, intelligence was initially considered a good predictor of power emergence. However, a meta-analysis revealed that this relationship is weak ($r = 0.27$; Judge et al. 2004). Instead, people who appear intelligent attain power more easily ($r = 0.60$; Judge et al. 2004). Judge et al. (2004, p. 548) concluded that "it is possible [...] that leadership status is afforded to those who effectively manage a reputation for intelligence." Finally, being empathetic and being a good listener increase leadership potential (Guinote & Chen 2016, Keltner et al. 2010). Importantly, power emergence is often dependent on having a combination of skills (e.g., intelligence and extroversion) and being able to respond to situational demands (Dinh & Lord 2012).

The literature suggests, therefore, that power is most frequently gained through implicit social influence and the creation of a shared reality. Power is readily conferred to individuals who have visible skills or attributes that contribute (or appear to contribute) to the solution of group problems. Power is also conferred to people with dominant or extroverted personalities who spend a great deal of time and effort on presenting ideas and persuading and influencing others. Dominance is frequently associated with energized behavior, conviction, and persuasion rather than with the use of force and threat traditionally associated with dominance (see Mazur & Booth 1998). Under these circumstances, power is consented to, at least in part, because dominant individuals are perceived to add value to groups (see Keltner et al. 2010, Van Vugt et al. 2008). Dominant individuals thus tend to be popular and emerge as leaders because they appear competent, though they are less liked than people with high status, who are socially prominent because they command respect and admiration. The emergence of power is a relational phenomenon often involving skill, effort, strategy, and inference processes among actors. This contrasts with static conceptions concerning the impact of personality traits, styles, and situations on the emergence of power and leadership.

Power Energizes Thought, Speech, and Action

Although the efforts of dominant people are, at first, directed toward the goal of acquiring power, once people have power, they can direct their efforts toward the pursuit of other goals. Thus, power becomes a means to the pursuit of goals, typically those associated with organizational roles and personal inclinations. To effectively pursue these goals, power holders deploy high levels of activation, wanting, and seeking.

Power holders are expected to be energetic and decisive (Allen et al. 2015). For instance, three quarters of British Members of Parliament considered decisiveness the most important attribute of a Prime Minister (for comparison, 32% considered honesty important; Allen et al. 2015). Although decisiveness is often seen as a skill of the particular individuals who emerge as leaders, psychological research shows that the mere fact of having power increases decisiveness. This is demonstrated in elevated verbal production, fast decision making and action, and perseverance (Guinote 2007c). These attributes derive from increased activation levels, which facilitate spontaneous responses and sustain effort during goal-directed action.

Verbal production. Reid & Ng (1999, p. 119) explain that "Language is a communication medium for turning a power base into influence." In organizations, people with power spend up to two thirds of their time in communication with subordinates. Powerful people speak their minds, speak first, and speak more than others (e.g., Guinote et al. 2002, Hall et al. 2005). They also speak more loudly and interrupt others more often. In competitive debates, power holders tend to make the opening arguments (Magee et al. 2007).

In addition to increasing response speed and output, possession of power engages cognitive processes that aid social influence. People in power seek to influence others through linguistic and paralinguistic means that convey confidence, decisiveness, and competence (Kacewicz et al. 2013). Observations of communication in teaching contexts and organizations, eyewitness testimony, and experimental conditions found that, compared to the powerless, powerful people use more plural (we) than singular (I) pronouns (Kacewicz et al. 2013) and tend to use fewer disclaimers (e.g., "I don't really know"), hesitations, hedges ("sort of," "maybe"), tag questions ("it is very cold out today, isn't it"), and intensifiers (e.g., "so;" Reid & Ng 1999, Thomas et al. 2004). Together, these means of verbal communication effectively affect perceptions of status and power in observers, increasing persuasion and ability to attain desired ends (wanting and seeking).

Energized thought and action. Power holders make fast decisions and act promptly. This quick decision making is accompanied by increased cardiovascular efficiency in challenging situations, which provides physical resources for action (Scheepers et al. 2012, Schmid & Schmid Mast 2013). Galinsky et al. (2003) demonstrated that power leads to action regardless of the type of action. For instance, participants with power more readily moved an annoying object (a fan) compared to subordinates (see also Fast et al. 2009). Power holders make faster decisions regarding courses of action and are faster at initiating goal pursuit (Guinote 2007c). In negotiations, power holders generally make the first offers (Magee et al. 2007). Altogether, this research shows an increased readiness to decide and act among the powerful, consistent with the perspective of power as activation.

Power Intensifies Wanting and Goal Seeking

One premise of the framework developed in this article is that power intensifies the wanting and seeking of desired end states. Power gives people clarity of focus and single-mindedness, which help them approach goals without distraction. This focused state is triggered by the desires and aims of people in power, fueled by an overactive BAS. Power holders utilize effortful strategies involving self-regulation (i.e., managing their responses) to attain their aims, even in domains unrelated to power (Galinsky et al. 2003, Guinote, 2007c). A power advantage can be seen across all phases of goal-oriented activity, from setting goals, to initiating goal pursuit, to striving until successful completion (Guinote 2007c).

When they encounter difficulties, people often disengage from goal pursuit. This is not the case for powerful people (DeWall et al. 2011, Guinote 2007c). DeWall et al. (2011) found that participants in power were less depleted after a demanding task compared to others. Power holders also resort to more means to reach their goals compared to subordinates (Guinote 2007c). Organizational literature, including a meta-analysis of 142 studies (Seibert et al. 2011), has long documented that having control at work, one ingredient of power, increases proactive engagement and productivity. Together, this research indicates that people in power eagerly want desired outcomes and engage in self-regulatory processes that help these desires materialize.

Does power enhance performance? The enhanced goal orientation of people in power begs the question of whether power increases effectiveness outside the domain of influence. Power is often beneficial for individual task performance; however, findings are nuanced. With fewer concerns about the ways others evaluate them, high-power people perform better in social contexts, such as in interviews and self-presentations (Guinote et al. 2002, Lammers et al. 2013, Schmid & Schmid Mast 2013). They more frequently express their needs and desires and persuade others to adopt their goals, which helps advance their agendas (Guinote et al. 2002, Laurin et al. 2016, Magee et al. 2007).

Power holders gain important advantages by being quick to act, being the first to intervene, and persevering. For instance, power holders in negotiations often make the first offer, which serves as an anchor that affords them better deals (Magee et al. 2007). Powerful people also perform better on a range of complex tasks. Experimental studies have shown that they generate better arguments (Weick & Guinote 2008) and complete a higher proportion of anagrams correctly (DeWall et al. 2011). Women assigned to a power condition (compared to control) perform math calculations better, showing less interference and better working memory, as seen in the related neural activity (Harada et al. 2012, Van Loo & Rydell 2013). Women who are given power also perform better on visual rotation tasks than powerless women (Nissan et al. 2015).

However, power does not always improve performance. Power is more beneficial under pressure and when stakes are higher (Kang et al. 2015). Power does not facilitate action and performance when power holders dislike tasks (DeWall et al. 2011). Furthermore, power can decrease judgment accuracy when power holders are overconfident or not motivated, which has been documented in the social domain (Fiske & Berdahl 2007, Nissan et al. 2015). Finally, when people in power work together in panels and committees, they often have conflicts and their individual (as well as the group's) performance deteriorates (Hildreth & Anderson 2016). To conclude, there is a power advantage in performance across many contexts and tasks, but the links between power and performance are nuanced and depend on the task and the motivation to complete it.

POWER AND COGNITION

Studies of the traits leading to leadership and power have been common and popular; however, they have not satisfactorily explained the behavior of powerful people, giving way to process approaches in organizational research (Dinh & Lord 2012, Lord & Maher 2002). Simultaneously, sociocognitive experimental research has helped explain how power affects the mind (Guinote 2007b, Smith et al. 2008).

People in power eagerly seek desired outcomes and are facilitated in this seeking by enhanced beliefs about the self and the use of cognitive strategies that optimize important goals. However, to be decisive and ready to intervene, people in positions of authority often compromise accuracy, engaging in quick decision making based on gut feelings and other shortcuts (see Fiske 1993, Keltner et al. 2003, Weick & Guinote 2008). Thus, an examination of power and cognition must consider the specific situation in which power is exercised.

Power and the Self: Positive Self-Concept, Independence, and Magnified Active Self

Having power affects how individuals perceive their attributes, how they evaluate themselves, and how they see themselves independently in relation to others. These effects of power on the self facilitate prompt decision making and agency, allowing individuals to respond in ways that are self-sufficient.

Positive and independent self-concept. Power affects the beliefs people have about themselves. It boosts confidence or conviction about their abilities and opinions, as well as other self-enhancing beliefs, which are middle-level mechanisms that facilitate prompt decision making and exercise of influence. Both field and experimental studies have found increased confidence among the powerful (Briñol et al. 2007, Fast et al. 2012, Scholl & Sassenberg 2014). Power holders take less advice from others (See et al. 2011, Tost et al. 2012) and conform less to others' opinions (Galinsky et al. 2008). Greater confidence leads power holders to validate prior experiences or salient thoughts that they have in mind (Briñol et al. 2007, Guinote et al. 2012), enabling them to make swift decisions and take rapid action.

Power holders have a high sense of control, even in domains unrelated to their power roles (Scholl & Sassenberg 2014). Van Dijke & Poppe (2006) and Lammers et al. (2016) found that people seek power mainly to increase control over their own lives. This increased sense of control plays a causal role in power holders' optimism and action orientation (Fast et al. 2009). Furthermore, with enhanced perceived control, powerful people perceive the self as an independent, self-sufficient entity (independent self-construal). In contrast, powerless people resort to relationships as a means to enhance control, are more communal, and have an interdependent self-construal (see Fiske & Dépret 1996, Guinote et al. 2015, Guinote & Chen 2016).

Power also elevates self-esteem (Fast et al. 2009, Hofstede et al. 2002, Wojciszke & Struzynska-Kujalowicz 2007). For instance, an investigation involving 1,814 participants in managerial positions across 15 countries found that managers rated themselves higher on positive managerial traits compared to the average of managers in their countries (Hofstede et al. 2002). People in power have a sense of superiority in various other domains. For instance, they overestimate their own height (Duguid & Goncalo 2012) while perceiving others as smaller than they really are (Yap et al. 2013; see also Schubert 2005).

Magnified active self. Power changes the person holding it in multiple ways. In addition to affecting the self-concept by enhancing confidence, perceived control, and self-esteem, the framework developed in this article proposes that increased activation and wanting intensify the expression of the active self (Guinote & Chen 2016). This proposal is based on the notion that the self is not monolithic (Markus & Nurius 1986, Wheeler et al. 2007). The active or working self is the part of the overall self-knowledge that is currently accessible and active in a person's working memory (Markus & Nurius 1986). Power holders' increased activation, wanting, and seeking magnify the behavior expression of the active self. This contributes to a frequent expression of predispositions, which are chronically accessible and active in many contexts, as well as other temporarily accessible subsets of the self (see Guinote & Chen 2016, Guinote et al. 2012).

A great deal of evidence shows that people in power promptly express their desires, thoughts, or emotions (Berdahl & Martorana 2006, Chen et al. 2001, Guinote et al. 2002). For instance, Guinote et al. (2002) assigned participants to powerful or powerless groups and videotaped them while they introduced themselves and worked together. Observers, who were unaware of power relations, rated the members of the powerful group as more variable along several personality traits compared to the members of the powerless group because participants in power manifested more fully their idiosyncratic nature. Other studies found that powerful people are more authentic and that they connect more and act more in line with their true desires (Berdahl & Martorana 2006, Kraus et al. 2011, Wang 2015).

Does this mean that power liberates people from constraints, so that they consistently behave in trait-consistent ways? Put differently, does power increase trait–behavior consistency? Decades of research seeking to understand how the traits of leaders affect behavior in organizational contexts have not produced satisfactory answers (for a summary, see Lord & Maher 2002). Therefore, researchers have performed investigations of self-expression across different situations (Chen et al. 2009, Dinh & Lord 2012, Guinote 2008).

Network and process models of personality (see Dinh & Lord 2012), the active self model (Markus & Nurius 1986, Wheeler et al. 2007), and dynamic views of personality have pointed out that people often exhibit second-nature traits that are situationally relevant and help advance goals (known as free traits; Little 2008). These conceptions have led to a new understanding of the ways power affects the self. This understanding explains both stability and variability in the behavior of people in authority positions. Consistent with the situated focus theory of power (see Guinote 2007a), power enhances the expression of any traits, states, or desires that emerge as individuals interact with the environment. Therefore, power holders often act in more expressive and variable ways across different situations. Consistent with this notion, Dinh & Lord (2012, p. 654) stressed that "intrapersonal variability across situations has important consequences for understanding leadership processes, which implies that leadership might be best understood at the *event*, rather than at the *person*-level of analysis."

Because dispositions, values, and power roles are chronically accessible, they often guide the behavior of people in power, contributing to stability. However, temporarily activated aims and desires also readily guide the behavior of people in power, contributing to variability. In the following sections, the chronically accessible recurrent goals of people in power are described, followed by a discussion of situational, temporary influences on self-expression.

Wanting Is Linked to Prioritization and Selective Attention

Power holders prioritize their effort toward salient desires and aims while neglecting secondary ones (Guinote 2007a, Overbeck & Park 2006, Smith & Trope 2006). To illustrate this, a study led participants in the high power condition to make decisions about regulations that would allegedly affect other students (versus the control condition, in which decisions would not affect other students); they were then asked to predict when they would submit coursework due two weeks later (Weick & Guinote 2010). Those in power (versus the control) were more likely to underestimate the time needed to complete the coursework (demonstrating planning fallacy). This result was driven by an overly narrow focus of attention on the focal goal and neglect of other interfering goals and events. Enhanced prioritization of salient goals among power holders involves focus and ranking of action plans. However, power does not necessarily affect the importance of one's goals (Schmid & Schmid Mast 2013).

Selective attention and thought. Power holders allocate their attentional resources selectively according to their motivations and active goals (Guinote 2007b, Overbeck & Park 2006, Smith & Trope 2006, Vescio et al. 2003, Whitson et al. 2013). This idea is consistent with the "motivational tunnel vision" associated with approach states (McGregor et al. 2010, p. 134), with Fiske's (1993; Fiske & Neuberg 1990) motivational account of social attention, and with the situated focus perspective of power and selective attention (Guinote 2007a,b). For instance, in one study (Guinote 2008), participants were asked to describe either a social or a work day and to read work and social information. Powerful (compared to powerless) participants paid more attention to work (versus social) information on a work day and to social (versus work) information on a leisure day. Their attention and behavior were more variable across situations associated with different goals.

Power holders often use rules of thumb to make decisions; however, this tendency is less pronounced when the task at hand is important (Min & Kim 2013). They balance their effort depending on their motivation and the task. In contrast, powerless people more consistently deliberate (Fiske & Dépret 1996). Scholl & Sassenberg (2014, 2015) found that power diminishes forethought (e.g., "What would happen if") before solving a task or making a decision, unless forethought is beneficial for the upcoming task. In contrast, after failure on a project, power increases self-focused counterfactuals (e.g., "If only I had done things differently"). This, in turn, contributes to better future planning. Overall, these findings reconcile contradictory claims arguing that power holders are cognitive misers (Keltner et al. 2003) or that they are competent information processors (Guinote 2007b, Smith & Trope 2006). Power holders are generally competent and efficient information processors who flexibly apply more or fewer cognitive resources depending on the task at hand and their motivation.

Cognitive control. Several studies have examined whether power affects distractibility and the ability to ignore task-irrelevant information, and they have found an advantage for powerful compared to powerless participants (DeWall et al. 2011, Guinote 2007b, Schmid et al. 2015, Smith et al. 2008). Being powerless impairs central executive functions, although power does not enhance these functions (Smith et al. 2008). Nevertheless, power heightens some forms of cognitive control (DeWall et al. 2011, Harada et al. 2012, Schmid et al. 2015). Using event-related potentials and process dissociation analyses, Schmid et al. (2015) found that power increases cognitive control by facilitating the link between conflict detection and the regulative processes that implement actions. The authors concluded that power facilitates goal pursuit through enhanced controlled processing (see also Guinote 2007b). This research shows that power promotes some cognitive processes facilitative of the pursuit of one's aims and desires and also enables strategies for quick decision making and action.

Flexibility, Creativity, and Reliance on Gut Feelings

To thrive in the long term, groups and organizations must innovate and respond to a constantly changing environment. Those in power control innovation and vision. When facing organizational or environmental changes, they must make quick decisions and intervene rapidly (Dane & Pratt

2007). Therefore, power holders often rely on gut feelings and tend to be attuned to environmental inputs.

Power holders also need to think flexibly. In organizational contexts, this attribute has been praised in times of change and uncertainty and has been considered the mark of a good leader. However, experimental work has shown that power changes people and that the mere fact of having power enhances flexibility, reliance on experiential information, and ability to think abstractly into the future.

Situational tuning and flexibility. Organizational studies show that emergent leaders have greater behavioral flexibility and ability to respond to environmental inputs compared to other individuals. For instance, using a rotation paradigm, Zaccaro et al. (1991) found that emergent leaders were more likely than other people to recognize and act upon different situational demands, an attribute that the researchers called response flexibility.

According to the situated focus theory of power (Guinote 2007a), power enhances the ability to discern and respond to environmental inputs in a flexible manner, given opportunities for action or for the advancement of power holders' goals. Experimental work shows that power increases situational tuning and cognitive flexibility. For example, people in power are more likely than powerless people to vary their social attentional strategies depending on the task at hand and the context (Guinote 2007a, 2008; Overbeck & Park 2006; Vescio et al. 2003).

Creativity. Creativity is a skill associated with cognitive flexibility. Organizational studies reveal that feeling empowered is important to creative process engagement (Zhang & Bartol 2010). Similarly, induced power increases creativity (Duguid & Goncalo 2015, Galinsky et al. 2008, Gervais et al. 2013). For example, participants with power generated more novel product names compared to control participants (Galinsky et al. 2008, Gervais et al. 2013). However, Gervais et al. (2013) found that power holders utilize their creative potential only when creativity aids the task at hand, a finding that is consistent with the situated focus perspective.

Reliance on experiential information. Gut feelings and cognitive experiences can inform judgments and contribute to quick decision making. Reliance on these experiential sources of information is associated with insight (Kounios & Beeman 2009) and is an asset for managers under time pressure and in unstable environments (Dane & Pratt 2007). Unsurprisingly, managers often rely on intuitive processes in corporate decision making, especially if they are senior (Dane & Pratt 2007).

Reliance on experiential information could result solely from the managers' predispositions and experience. However, induced power, as well as organizational power and trait dominance, all increase reliance on subjective experiences. For example, studies have shown that power holders are more likely to use the ease or difficulty of retrieving information as a cue to help them make judgments (known as ease of retrieval; Weick & Guinote 2008) and that powerful female participants rely more on their perceived levels of arousal (e.g., heart rate) when making judgments about the attractiveness of male models. When people have expertise, such reliance is not necessarily inaccurate, and power seems to license individuals to use experiential information.

Power also increases the use of motor experiences in the construction of aesthetic judgments (motor fluency; Woltin & Guinote 2015). For instance, Woltin & Guinote (2015) found that after training extraocular muscles to perform certain eye movements used to scan the environment, high-power participants reported liking more moving stimuli that engaged the trained muscles (versus other stimuli) compared to control and powerless participants.

Abstraction. People in positions of authority must provide vision and think abstractly. Consequently, power triggers abstract representations of events, plans, and concepts (Smith & Trope 2006, Nissan et al. 2015). For example, participants in a powerful (versus control) condition focused more on the gist of words presented in a memory task (Smith & Trope 2006), and power holders used more abstract language when describing events (Guinote et al. 2002, Magee et al. 2010). In the framework developed in this review, abstract thinking helps balance between power holders' tendency for prompt responses to salient goals and more abstract, long-term desires and aspirations.

THE GOALS OF POWERFUL PEOPLE

People in power focus their attention clearly on goal priorities. What goals, then, do powerful people seek to accomplish? Since the Greek philosophers Antisthenes and Plato in the fourth–fifth centuries BC, power has been associated with abuse and selfish behavior. According to Lord Acton's [1887 (1997), pp. 335–36] aphorism, "power corrupts, and absolute power corrupts absolutely." Yet others argue that power can be used for good or evil depending on the person (Chen et al. 2001, Clegg et al. 2006). How can these views be reconciled? A consideration of the active self helps address this question. Goals linked to power holders' predispositions, roles, and tasks at hand are linked to the parts of the self that are active and so explain variability. This section discusses research showing that power magnifies the active self, increasing the focus on salient goals. Within this framework, power holders' common goals and the links between power and corruption are also addressed.

Goals Linked to Power Roles, Tasks, and Predispositions

Power energizes people during the pursuit of salient activities, projects, and aims linked to their roles, tasks, affordances, and predispositions. Among the various goals held by people in power, those related to their roles tend to have priority. An investigation of 21 groups in 15 countries asked business managers to list important goals (Hofstede et al. 2002). Growth of the business was consistently ranked first, followed by continuity of business. In Yukl et al.'s (2002) taxonomy of leaders' goals, task goals concerning the efficiency of the use of resources, people, and product operations appear as the primary concerns. The prioritization of goals related to power roles is found also in experimental research showing that the more power people have, the more they identify with their roles (Joshi & Fast 2013a). These findings are consistent with the notion that power often triggers a sense of responsibility (see Chen et al. 2001, Sassenberg et al. 2014).

Experimental research shows that people in power are more agentic and more readily act in ways that are called for by the task at hand. For example, compared to other people, power holders act in more benevolent ways in prosocial tasks and in more selfish ways in tasks that highlight the opportunity for personal gains (Galinsky et al. 2003). Temporarily accessible goals associated with the active self are pursued energetically by power holders.

The preexisting inclinations of powerful actors are chronically accessible and often guide their behavior (Chen et al. 2001, Guinote et al. 2012). Chen et al. (2001) showed that people who adhere to tit-for-tat rules act in more self-interested ways when in power, whereas communally oriented individuals become more prosocial. A similar tendency was found for attributes associated with social responsibility, such as moral identity (DeCelles et al. 2012), and a variety of other predispositions (e.g., Côté et al. 2011, Guinote et al. 2012, Schmid Mast et al. 2009). For example, a study conducted in 73 organizations found that CEOs who scored high on social responsibility (e.g., a preference for moral and legal conduct and a concern for others and for obligations) engaged in ethical leadership, which was then related to increased effectiveness of management and followers' optimism (De Hoogh & Den Hartog 2008).

Exercising and Maintaining Power

People in positions of authority are oriented toward causing an impact in the social environment and maintaining appropriate levels of power. These power goals are necessary for role effectiveness and lead, for example, to increased communication and strategic language use, as discussed in the section Verbal Production.

The motivation on the part of power holders to maintain hierarchical differences becomes particularly visible when power is threatened. For example, when power is perceived as unfair (i.e., illegitimate) or is unstable, powerful people feel threatened, are less efficient (Lammers et al. 2008, Rodriguez-Bailon et al. 2000), and become more vigilant toward others' emotions (Stamkou et al. 2016). Subjective lack of power among the powerful has similar effects (Bugental & Happaney 2004, Fast & Chen 2009, Stamkou et al. 2016). Correlational and experimental evidence shows that subjectively powerless caregivers (e.g., teachers) exhibit high arousal and less effectiveness and use more punishment (see Bugental 2010). That is, perceived losses of power trigger the threat reactivity seen in inefficient and authoritarian power use.

Power enhances personal control and resources (Fast et al. 2009, Van Dijke & Poppe 2006), which motivates some people to seek power and to avoid relinquishing it once they have gained it (Ratcliff & Vescio 2013). Together, this work shows that maintaining power is important for power holders, who monitor their relative power and respond to threats with harsh power assertion.

State-Dependent Reward Seeking

As Salamena & Correa (2002) pointed out in the field of neuroscience, in research on power the usage of the word reward has become so broad as to be essentially meaningless. However, some evidence suggests that power can intensify reward seeking (e.g., seeking food, sex, and other pleasures). Consistent with the framework of power as salient goal seeking, this occurs especially when basic needs are thwarted, during hedonic consumption, and for hedonistic people. For example, powerful participants who were hungry ate more food in a tasting task compared to their powerless counterparts (Guinote 2010). In another study, power holders ate more appetizing food (chocolates) and less distasteful food (radishes) than those who lacked power. Similarly, power can be associated with infidelity and heightened sexual perceptions (Kunstman & Maner 2011, Lammers et al. 2011). Crucially, some evidence suggests that, when given a choice between immediate smaller rewards, such as money, and larger, later rewards, people in power prefer to delay gratification (Joshi & Fast 2013b). This contrasts with the choices of people with hyperactive reward systems, who tend to prefer immediate rewards (McClure et al. 2004).

Does Power Corrupt?

Power holders can use their advantaged positions to satisfy their needs (Pratto 2015). In politics, corporations, and public service, people in the higher echelons often seek to accumulate resources and personal prestige (Ashforth & Anand 2003). These individuals frequently focus on increasing their payouts while neglecting others' payouts. These tendencies can be observed early in ontogeny: Compared to their low-rank counterparts, five-year-old children who were in a high-rank position gave fewer stickers to a child in need (Guinote et al. 2015). This was true regardless of whether rank was determined by dominance or was experimentally induced.

Similarly, power holders often enforce personal values. For instance, the more power CEOs have, the more they implement corporate actions linked to personal political ideologies (Chin et al. 2013). Power holders may also use deceptive tactics, such as making promises and breaking them later.

The self-serving behavior of power holders is linked to feelings of legitimacy and self-entitlement (e.g., Ashforth & Anand 2003, De Cremer & Van Dijk 2005). People in power contribute more to groups; therefore, they feel deserving and are not always aware of their own violation of fairness principles. Self-serving biases and impulses are automatic and common (Ross et al. 1977). To override them, one needs self-control. However, people in power do not always have the resources or desire to exercise self-control to overcome these biases (Fiske & Berdahl 2007).

Nevertheless, the links between power and corruption are moderated by a number of factors and can be reversed depending on predispositions and context (Guinote & Chen 2016). These moderating factors include power stability, intergroup conflict (Maner & Case 2016), national culture (Kopelman 2009, Torelli & Shavitt 2010), organizational culture (Ashforth & Anand 2003), moral identity (DeCelles et al. 2012), the task (Galinsky et al. 2003), and the predispositions of people in power (Sassenberg et al. 2014). In many situations, people in authority positions sacrifice their interests to serve their groups (Hoogervorst et al. 2012, Ratcliff & Vescio 2013). This is more pronounced in collectivistic cultures, which associate power with social responsibility (socialized power), whereas in individualistic cultures power is seen in terms of self-interested opportunities (personalized power; Torelli & Shavitt 2010; see also Sassenberg et al. 2014). These findings are consistent with the notion that power facilitates the pursuit of salient goals, which can be linked to the predispositions of the person, cultural influences, or the situation.

In summary, the behavior of people in power is best understood through the lens of the active self and salient goals, taking the person and the situation into consideration. Typically, power holders are guided by their roles, predispositions, the task at hand, and their cultural inclinations. They also express themselves more, making common self-serving biases more easily noticed. In addition, these biases can be amplified by a sense of entitlement, a desire to maintain the hierarchy, and greater exposure to self-serving opportunities. When responsible uses of power are more likely due to individual predispositions or to organizational or national culture, self-serving behavior is less common.

POWER IN THE SOCIAL WORLD

The prioritized pursuit of institutional or personal goals that is typical for people in power has downstream consequences for the ways they attend and relate to others. In organizations, managers often focus too narrowly on organizational targets, in particular profit, at the expense of relational goals and the employees' needs (Hofstede et al. 2002, Pfeffer 2007). Consequently, up to two-thirds of employees in any organization consider their immediate supervisor the strongest source of stress at work (Hogan et al. 2010). Ironically, neglecting employees markedly reduces organizational profit and the commitment and well-being of subordinates (Pfeffer 2007).

The following section discusses common social inclinations of powerful people, boundary conditions, and how a perspective centering on goal seeking and the active self can incorporate different findings in power research. These findings are linked to social attention, judgment and decision making, perspective taking, and objectification of subordinates.

Social Attention, Perspective Taking, and Objectification of Subordinates

Since Fiske's 1993 article, it has become apparent that power holders are often socially inattentive. Fiske and colleagues (e.g., Fiske 1993, Goodwin et al. 2000) have reasoned that people in power are generally not motivated to or cannot pay attention to the personal attributes of subordinates. This is consistent with the notion proposed in this review that the attention of powerful people is geared primarily toward their salient goals, often the task at hand. Thus, they are more prone to neglect other people (Fiske & Berdahl 2007).

Fiske and colleagues found that, compared to control participants, participants in power seek less diagnostic and personal information about subordinates. In one study (Fiske & Dépret 1996), powerful and control participants judged the suitability of White and Latino internship applicants who were described with stereotypic and nonstereotypic attributes. Power increased attention (reading time) to stereotypic attributes (see Goodwin et al. 2000, Schmid & Amodio 2016).

Other studies have shown that power decreases the ability to recognize the emotions of other people (Galinsky et al. 2006, Gonzaga et al. 2008, Nissan et al. 2015; for contrasting results, see Schmid Mast et al. 2009). Negotiators with power are less motivated to be accurate than their partners, asking more leading questions and fewer diagnostic questions (De Dreu & Van Kleef 2004). This is associated with decreased trust in others (Inesi et al. 2012, Schilke et al. 2015). Power also decreases the ability to take another's vantage point (Galinsky et al. 2006). For example, in one study, participants were first primed with either power or lack of power. They were then invited to draw the letter E on their forehead. Compared to powerless participants, power-primed participants were more likely to draw the letter from their own vantage point rather than from that of the observer. Nevertheless, this does not mean that powerful people are less accurate in their social judgments than other people. Evidence regarding the accuracy of power holders' judgments and recall is mixed. A power disadvantage is more pronounced in studies involving life interactions than in other types of studies (Hall et al. 2015). In addition, power holders are often more accurate than powerless individuals about task-relevant attributes of the targets.

Power holders often rely on socially shared stereotypes and negative attitudes toward disadvantaged groups. When unsupervised, negative attitudes can automatically influence judgments, and power holders may not deploy the resources to or may not want to correct for their automatic biases. Guinote et al. (2010) found that having power increases implicit prejudice against disadvantaged groups. Schmid & Amodio (2016) corroborated these findings. Similarly, powerful participants deny the humanness of others more often, attributing fewer unique human attributes to them (e.g., Gwinn et al. 2013). Finally, elevated power diminishes concern for others and empathy for their suffering (Van Kleef et al. 2008).

In spite of the evidence discussed above, the judgments of people in power are influenced by their salient goals and are therefore malleable. If concentrating on organizational or self-focused goals can be detrimental to social attention, the activation of person-centered goals can neutralize or reverse this tendency. Power holders are socially attentive when predispositions (e.g., Chen et al. 2001, Schmid Mast et al. 2009, Vescio et al. 2003) and situational goals (Guinote 2008; Overbeck & Park 2001, 2006) are oriented toward others. For instance, Vescio et al. (2003) found that people in power use stereotypes only when enacting certain leadership styles. Overbeck & Park (2006) found that power holders in simulated people-centered organizations paid more attention to subordinates compared to those in product-centered organizations.

Gruenfeld et al. (2008) found that high-power people evaluate others more positively if they are instrumental for their goals (i.e., they objectify others). Crucially, this bias is linked to the presence of an active goal, suggesting that goals strongly influence the attention and judgments of people in power. Similarly, when others signal their potential for satisfying chronic needs and desires, such as sexual needs, power holders tend to objectify them. For instance, compared to men and women who lack power, those in power show enhanced selective attention to sexualized images of the opposite gender, identifying them better even if they are difficult to see (e.g., inverted; Civile & Obhi 2016).

Other studies (e.g., Weick & Guinote 2008) found that subjective experiences, such as the ease of retrieving group attributes, affect stereotype use more strongly among power holders compared to other people. Research shows that the social judgments of people in power are constructed on a moment-to-moment basis and depend on the goals and states of the power holders. Given that people in power frequently have nonsocial priorities, the tendency to dehumanize others and be socially inattentive is an enduring risk (see Fiske 1993, Keltner et al. 2003).

Social Behavior

Power holders' propensity for quick decisions and actions can magnify common egocentric biases, leading to a disproportionate focus on their own needs and desires. Generally, in interpersonal relations, power holders sacrifice their interests for those of their partners less often than vice versa (Danescu-Niculescu-Mizil et al. 2012, Laurin et al. 2016, Righetti et al. 2015). Power holders are also more likely to expect to be treated with fairness and are more sensitive to unfair treatment, such as violations of distributive justice, compared to people who lack power (Sawaoka et al. 2015). When communicating, those with power display less language coordination (i.e., mimic others' choices of word classes less) (Danescu-Niculescu-Mizil et al. 2012) compared to their powerless counterparts. In close relationships, dominant and powerful people tend to lead partners to adopt their goals (Laurin et al. 2016).

Nevertheless, people who see power as a responsibility sacrifice their time and resources to benefit others (e.g., Chen et al. 2001, Galinsky et al. 2003, Guinote et al. 2012, Hoogervorst et al. 2012, Sassenberg et al. 2014). When in power, benevolent people are helpful and socially attentive (Chen et al. 2001, Côté et al. 2011, DeCelles et al. 2012, Guinote et al. 2012). Similarly, feelings of group belonging (Hoogervorst et al. 2012), as well as reminders of fairness (Guinote et al. 2012), can block the expression of immediate selfish impulses, increasing power holders' prosocial orientation.

Accountability effectively mitigates power abuse in educational (Ingersoll 2009), organizational, and political arenas (Grant & Keohane 2005) and in experimental conditions (Rus et al. 2012). For example, Oc et al. (2015) conducted a multiround dictator game in which participants distributed resources between themselves and others. Being powerful increased self-serving biases. However, candid feedback from recipients led to fairer distributions, whereas compliant feedback increased self-serving behavior.

CONCLUSIONS

Research over the past 15 years supports the notion that power activates one specific component of approach motivation, that associated with the pursuit of goals. Power energizes people, gives a clear focus, and facilitates seeking or working to obtain salient goals. Power holders spend a great deal of time and effort trying to influence others, promptly intervening, and seeking opportunities to pursue their aims and desires.

As this review shows, power holders successfully attain their desires and aims not only because they can act at will with less resistance [Weber 1914 (1978)] but also because of enhanced self-regulation (DeWall et al. 2011, Guinote 2007c). Powerful people allocate their attentional resources selectively in accordance with their priorities. They tune in to information that is goal relevant and selectively ignore other information (Guinote 2007a,b,c; Overbeck & Park 2006). In addition, they have a greater ability to be creative and flexible and to think abstractly, attributes that are an asset when dealing with complex problems that require innovation and vision of the future. However, to be decisive and readily impact the social environment, power holders often choose to compromise and use fast and frugal decision-making strategies, such as reliance on subjective experiences and gut feelings (Guinote 2010, Weick & Guinote 2008).

Power can be used for good or evil, depending on power roles, the person, and the environment. Consistent with the situated focus theory of power (Guinote 2007a, 2010), power intensifies the active self and helps people strive for salient goals. Common goals of power holders are linked to their roles, predispositions, ideologies, or opportunities and to the task at hand.

Keltner et al.'s (2003) reward- and affect-based theory has dominated more than a decade of psychological research on power. This theory has great explanatory power and has guided research in new directions, producing many valuable insights. The framework presented in this review is consistent with basic tenets of Keltner et al.'s (2003) approach theory of power. However, it departs from the original conception that linked power to reward seeking and positive affect (hedonic tone). The present framework reconciles this theory with Fiske's (1993) sociocognitive paradigm of social attention, which was prominent between 1993 and 2003. Specifically, it incorporates Fiske's functionalist perspective, linking motivation to attention, and proposes that the goal priorities of power holders, fueled by approach motivation, explain the effects of power on social perception. At the same time, the framework explains malleability among power holders and research inconsistencies, opening new avenues for the understanding and prevention of the dark side of power.

Nearly 50 years after the first experimental studies on power and corruption (Kipnis 1972, Zimbardo 1971), evidence continues to testify to the danger of power abuse. The framework of power as activation, wanting, and seeking suggests that this occurs because power intensifies egocentric biases but only to the extent that these are unsupervised and accessible. If organizational goals, culture, and the predispositions of people in power are communally oriented, power holders will primarily benefit their teams and organizations (Chen et al. 2001). Ethical and servant leaders typically do so (Sassenberg et al. 2014).

If power aids social assertion and the quest for priorities, it often does so at the risk of neglecting secondary goals, in particular the needs and perspectives of other people (Fiske & Berdahl 2007, Galinsky et al. 2006). More than two decades after the first discoveries in social cognition linking power to stereotyping (Fiske 1993), related tendencies continue to be uncovered. This includes decreased perspective taking, decreased perception of humanness in others, elevated implicit prejudice, and objectification. Prosocial predispositions and cultural or situational reminders of person-centered goals ameliorate or even reverse these tendencies.

Given the potential negative effects of power in the social domain, what can be done? The research suggests ways of mitigating power abuse and fostering social responsibility. In appointed positions of power, considering predispositions and selecting ethical candidates are important to avoid future abuse. In addition, training can effectively increase social responsibility in powerful people (McClelland & Burnham 1995). Finally, citizens of organizations and communities can influence power holders through norms and culture that associate power with responsibility (Sassenberg et al. 2014, Torelli & Shavitt 2010). Although in nonhuman primate species subordinates often form alliances to challenge power through force (Boehm 2009), in human societies alliances without the use of force and the creation of meaning and shared identities are also influential (Hogg 2001, Parsons 1963). For instance, as a group, subordinates can resort to shared symbolic means, such as culture, to influence power holders. Lastly, reminders of social obligations and accountability have proven successful mechanisms to control power abuse and the neglect of subordinates' needs.

SUMMARY POINTS

1. People who rise to power are typically confident and assertive; many display visible competencies and skills that can help solve organizational or group problems.

2. Having power generally energizes thought, speech, and action. People with power make quicker decisions and speak and act more compared to others, especially on issues that are important to them.

3. Powerful people are goal oriented. They have clarity of focus (wanting) and work toward obtaining (seeking) desired goals.

4. Power affects cognitive strategies, increasing prioritization, selective attention to goal-relevant information, flexibility, and creativity. Nevertheless, power also licenses people to rely on gut feelings and heuristic information processing in domains that are deemed less important or when power holders feel confident and expert.

5. Power increases self-expression. Power holders are more likely to manifest their thoughts, emotions, and predispositions.

6. Power can magnify the expression of common egocentric biases, increasing self-serving behavior. This is often accentuated by feelings of entitlement and deservingness.

7. By increasing freedom to act at will and decreasing accountability, power tends to increase corruption. However, the links between power and corruption depend on personal predispositions and situational factors such as culture. Socially responsible people exercise power ethically.

8. The goal orientation of power holders has downstream consequences for social behavior, often leading to the use of stereotypes, prejudice, and the objectification of subordinates.

FUTURE ISSUES

1. Power is a relational phenomenon, yet little is known about the role of subordinates in power dynamics.

2. Future research must further examine power-related processes across cultures to determine whether the research findings apply also to non-Western cultures.

3. More experimental research investigating power at the group level is necessary to determine how groups affect the exercise of power. Examples of group-level questions are: How do power holders think and act in high power groups (e.g., panels, committees) compared to less powerful groups? How do the gender and ethnic compositions of groups and their leaders affect the exercise of power?

4. Sociocognitive experimental research could develop a better methodology to examine the impact of predispositions and the situation on the ways in which power is exercised, for example by using rotation paradigms that vary the constitution of groups and tasks.

5. Sociocognitive research could further examine power holders' dynamic uses of automatic and controlled processes. This would contribute to the understanding of performance and decision making and clarify controversies regarding when power holders are cognitive misers and when they are efficient processors.

6. The physiological, cardiovascular, and neural correlates of power must be further investigated to determine the biosocial underpinnings of power.

DISCLOSURE STATEMENT

The author is not aware of any affiliations, memberships, funding, or financial holdings that might be perceived as affecting the objectivity of this review.

ACKNOWLEDGMENTS

Preparation of this review was supported by the British Academy, grant number SG132223, and the Daedalus Trust, grant number 520180 F67. The author is grateful for the comments on an earlier draft provided by Marcin Bukowski, Andrew Elliot, Christos Halkiopoulos, Robert Josephs, Merek Kofta, Joris Lammers, Kai Sassenberg, Marianne Schmid Mast, Annika Scholl, Kathleen Vohs, and Guillermo Willis. Thanks are also due to Liyin Sun for assistance.

LITERATURE CITED

Acton JEED. 1887 (1972). Letter to Mandell Creighton, April 5, 1887. In *Essays on Freedom and Power*, ed. G Himmelfarb, pp. 335–36. Gloucester, MA: P. Smith

Alcaro A, Huber R, Panksepp J. 2007. Behavioral functions of the mesolimbic dopaminergic system: an affective neuroethological perspective. *Brain Res. Rev.* 56(2):283–321

Allen N, Angers H, Bhogal A, Ching C, Davidian S, et al. 2015. British MPs on British PMs: parliamentary evaluations of prime ministerial success. *Politics* 35(2):111–27

Anderson C, Berdahl JL. 2002. The experience of power: examining the effects of power on approach and inhibition tendencies. *J. Pers. Soc. Psychol.* 83(6):1362–77

Anderson C, John OP, Keltner D. 2012. The personal sense of power. *J. Pers.* 80(2):313–44

Anderson C, Kilduff GJ. 2009. Why do dominant personalities attain influence in face-to-face groups? The competence-signaling effects of trait dominance. *J. Pers. Soc. Psychol.* 96(2):491–503

Ashforth BE, Anand V. 2003. The normalization of corruption in organizations. *Res. Organ. Behav.* 25:1–52

Berdahl JL, Martorana P. 2006. Effects of power on emotion and expression during a controversial group discussion. *Eur. J. Soc. Psychol.* 36(4):497–509

Berridge KC. 2007. The debate over dopamine's role in reward: the case for incentive salience. *Psychopharmacology* 191(3):391–431

Boehm C. 2009. *Hierarchy in the Forest: The Evolution of Egalitarian Behavior*. Cambridge, MA: Harvard Univ. Press

Boksem MA, Smolders R, De Cremer D. 2012. Social power and approach-related neural activity. *Soc. Cogn. Affect. Neurosci.* 7(5):516–20

Briñol P, Petty RE, Valle C, Rucker DD, Becerra A. 2007. The effects of message recipients' power before and after persuasion: a self-validation analysis. *J. Pers. Soc. Psychol.* 93(6):1040–53

Bugental DB. 2010. Paradoxical power manifestations: power assertion by the subjectively powerless. In *The Social Psychology of Power*, ed. A Guinote, TK Vescio, pp. 209–30. New York: Guilford Press

Bugental DB, Happaney K. 2004. Predicting infant maltreatment in low-income families: the interactive effects of maternal attributions and child status at birth. *Dev. Psychol.* 40:234–43

Carver CS. 2004. Negative affects deriving from the behavioral approach system. *Emotion* 4(1):3–22

Carver CS, Harmon-Jones E. 2009. Anger is an approach-related affect: evidence and implications. *Psychol. Bull.* 135(2):183–204

Carver CS, White TL. 1994. Behavioral inhibition, behavioral activation, and affective responses to impending reward and punishment: the BIS/BAS scales. *J. Pers. Soc. Psychol.* 67(2):319–33

Catalyst. 2016. *Women CEOs of the S&P 500*. New York: Catalyst, updated July 1. **http://www.catalyst.org/knowledge/women-ceos-sp-500**

Chen S, Langner CA, Mendoza-Denton R. 2009. When dispositional and role power fit: implications for self-expression and self–other congruence. *J. Personal. Soc. Psychol.* 96(3):710–27

Chen S, Lee-Chai AY, Bargh JA. 2001. Relationship orientation as a moderator of the effects of social power. *J. Pers. Soc. Psychol.* 80(2):173–87

Chin MK, Hambrick DC, Treviño LK. 2013. Political ideologies of CEOs: the influence of executives' values on corporate social responsibility. *Adm. Sci. Q.* 58(2):197–232

Civile C, Obhi SS. 2016. Power, objectification, and recognition of sexualized women and men. *Psychol. Women Q.* 40(2):199–212

Clegg SR, Courpasson D, Phillips N. 2006. *Power and Organizations*. Thousand Oaks, CA: Pine Forge Press

Corr PJ, Cooper AJ. 2016. The Reinforcement Sensitivity Theory of Personality Questionnaire (RST-PQ): development and validation. *Personal. Individ. Differ.* 89:60–64

Costa PT Jr., McCrae RR. 1995. Domains and facets: hierarchical personality assessment using the Revised NEO Personality Inventory. *J. Pers. Assess.* 64(1):21–50

Côté S, Kraus MW, Cheng BH, Oveis C, Van der Löwe I, et al. 2011. Social power facilitates the effect of prosocial orientation on empathic accuracy. *J. Pers. Soc. Psychol.* 101(2):217–32

Dahl R. 1957 (2007). The concept of power. *Syst. Res.* 2(3):201–15

Dane E, Pratt MG. 2007. Exploring intuition and its role in managerial decision making. *Acad. Manag. Rev.* 32(1):33–54

Danescu-Niculescu-Mizil C, Lee L, Pang B, Kleinberg J. 2012. Echoes of power: language effects and power differences in social interaction. *Proc. Int. Conf. World Wide Web, 21st, Lyon, Fr.*, pp. 699–708. New York: ACM

De Cremer D, Van Dijk E. 2005. When and why leaders put themselves first: leader behaviour in resource allocations as a function of feeling entitled. *Eur. J. Soc. Psychol.* 35(4):553–63

De Dreu CK, Van Kleef GA. 2004. The influence of power on the information search, impression formation, and demands in negotiation. *J. Exp. Soc. Psychol.* 40(3):303–19

De Hoogh AH, Den Hartog DN. 2008. Ethical and despotic leadership, relationships with leader's social responsibility, top management team effectiveness and subordinates' optimism: a multi-method study. *Leadersh. Q.* 19(3):297–311

DeCelles KA, DeRue DS, Margolis JD, Ceranic TL. 2012. Does power corrupt or enable? When and why power facilitates self-interested behavior. *J. Appl. Psychol.* 97(3):681–89

DeWall CN, Baumeister RF, Mead NL, Vohs KD. 2011. How leaders self-regulate their task performance: evidence that power promotes diligence, depletion, and disdain. *J. Pers. Soc. Psychol.* 100(1):47–65

Dinh JE, Lord RG. 2012. Implications of dispositional and process views of traits for individual difference research in leadership. *Leadersh. Q.* 23(4):651–69

Duguid MM, Goncalo JA. 2012. Living large: the powerful overestimate their own height. *Psychol. Sci.* 23(1):36–40

Duguid MM, Goncalo JA. 2015. Squeezed in the middle: the middle status trade creativity for focus. *J. Pers. Soc. Psychol.* 109(4):589–603

Ellemers N, De Gilder D, Haslam SA. 2004. Motivating individuals and groups at work: a social identity perspective on leadership and group performance. *Acad. Manag. Rev.* 29(3):459–78

Emerson RM. 1962. Power-dependence relations. *Am. Sociol. Rev.* 27:31–41

Fast NJ, Chen S. 2009. When the boss feels inadequate: power, incompetence, and aggression. *Psychol. Sci.* 20(11):1406–13

Fast NJ, Gruenfeld DH, Sivanathan N, Galinsky AD. 2009. Illusory control: a generative force behind power's far-reaching effects. *Psychol. Sci.* 20(4):502–8

Fast NJ, Sivanathan N, Mayer ND, Galinsky AD. 2012. Power and overconfident decision-making. *Organ. Behav. Hum. Decis. Process.* 117(2):249–60

Fiske ST. 1992. Thinking is for doing: portraits of social cognition from daguerreotype to laserphoto. *J. Pers. Soc. Psychol.* 63(6):877–89

Fiske ST. 1993. Controlling other people: the impact of power on stereotyping. *Am. Psychol.* 48(6):621–28

Fiske ST, Berdahl J. 2007. Social power. In *Social Psychology: A Handbook of Basic Principles*, Vol. 2, ed. AW Kruglanski, T Higgins, pp. 678–92. New York: Guilford

Fiske ST, Dépret E. 1996. Control, interdependence and power: understanding social cognition in its social context. *Eur. Rev. Soc. Psychol.* 7(1):31–61

Fiske ST, Neuberg SL. 1990. A continuum of impression formation, from category-based to individuating processes: influences of information and motivation on attention and interpretation. *Adv. Exp. Soc. Psychol.* 23:1–74

French JRP, Raven B. 1959. The bases of social power. In *Studies in Social Power*, ed. D Cartwright, pp. 150–67. Ann Arbor: Univ. Michigan Inst. Soc. Res.

Galinsky AD, Gruenfeld DH, Magee JC. 2003. From power to action. *J. Pers. Soc. Psychol.* 85(3):453–66

Galinsky AD, Magee JC, Gruenfeld DH, Whitson JA, Liljenquist KA. 2008. Power reduces the press of the situation: implications for creativity, conformity, and dissonance. *J. Pers. Soc. Psychol.* 95(6):1450–66

Galinsky AD, Magee JC, Inesi ME, Gruenfeld DH. 2006. Power and perspectives not taken. *Psychol. Sci.* 17(12):1068–74

Gervais SJ, Guinote A, Allen J, Slabu L. 2013. Power increases situated creativity. *Soc. Influ.* 8(4):294–311

Gonzaga GC, Keltner D, Ward D. 2008. Power in mixed-sex stranger interactions. *Cogn. Emot.* 22(8):1555–68

Goodwin SA, Gubin A, Fiske ST, Yzerbyt VY. 2000. Power can bias impression processes: stereotyping subordinates by default and by design. *Group Process. Intergroup Relat.* 3(3):227–56

Gough HG. 1987. *California Psychology Inventory Administrator's Guide*. Palo Alto, CA: Consult. Psychol. Press

Grant RW, Keohane RO. 2005. Accountability and abuses of power in world politics. *Am. Polit. Sci. Rev.* 99(1):29–43

Gray JA. 1990. Brain systems that mediate both emotion and cognition. *Cogn. Emot.* 4(3):269–88

Gray JA, McNaughton N, eds. 2000. *The Neuropsychology of Anxiety: An Enquiry into the Function of the Septo-Hippocampal System*. Oxford, UK: Oxford Univ. Press. 2nd ed.

Gruenfeld DH, Inesi ME, Magee JC, Galinsky AD. 2008. Power and the objectification of social targets. *J. Pers. Soc. Psychol.* 95(1):111–27

Guinote A. 2007a. Behaviour variability and the situated focus theory of power. *Eur. Rev. Soc. Psychol.* 18(1):256–95

Guinote A. 2007b. Power affects basic cognition: increased attentional inhibition and flexibility. *J. Exp. Soc. Psychol.* 43(5):685–97

Guinote A. 2007c. Power and goal pursuit. *Pers. Soc. Psychol. Bull.* 33(8):1076–87

Guinote A. 2008. Power and affordances: when the situation has more power over powerful than powerless individuals. *J. Pers. Soc. Psychol.* 95(2):237–52

Guinote A. 2010. In touch with your feelings: Power increases reliance on bodily information. *Soc. Cogn.* 28(1):110–21

Guinote A, Chen S. 2016. Power as active self: acquisition and use of power. In *The Oxford Handbook of Personality and Social Psychology*, ed. K Deaux, M Snyder. Oxford, UK: Oxford Univ. Press. In press

Guinote A, Cotzia I, Sandhu S, Siwa P. 2015. Social status modulates prosocial behavior and egalitarianism in preschool children and adults. *PNAS* 112(3):731–36

Guinote A, Judd CM, Brauer M. 2002. Effects of power on perceived and objective group variability: evidence that more powerful groups are more variable. *J. Pers. Soc. Psychol.* 82(5):708–21

Guinote A, Phillips A. 2010. Power can increase stereotyping: evidence from managers and subordinates in the hotel industry. *Soc. Psychol.* 41:3–9

Guinote A, Weick M, Cai A. 2012. Does power magnify the expression of dispositions? *Psychol. Sci.* 94(6):956–70

Guinote A, Willis GB, Martellotta C. 2010. Social power increases implicit prejudice. *J. Exp. Soc. Psychol.* 46(2):299–307

Gwinn JD, Judd CM, Park B. 2013. Less power = less human? Effects of power differentials on dehumanization. *J. Exp. Soc. Psychol.* 49(3):464–70

Hall JA, Coats EJ, LeBeau LS. 2005. Nonverbal behavior and the vertical dimension of social relations: a meta-analysis. *Psychol. Bull.* 131(6):898–924

Hall JA, Schmid Mast MS, Latu IM. 2015. The vertical dimension of social relations and accurate interpersonal perception: a meta-analysis. *J. Nonverbal Behav.* 39(2):131–63

Hamid AA, Pettibone JR, Mabrouk OS, Hetrick VL, Schmidt R, et al. 2016. Mesolimbic dopamine signals the value of work. *Nat. Neurosci.* 19(1):117–26

Harada T, Bridge DJ, Chiao JY. 2012. Dynamic social power modulates neural basis of math calculation. *Front. Hum. Neurosci.* 6(350):115–27

Haslam SA, Reicher SD, Platow MJ. 2010. *The New Psychology of Leadership: Identity, Influence and Power*. New York: Psychol. Press

Hildreth JAD, Anderson C. 2016. Failure at the top: how power undermines collaborative performance. *J. Pers. Soc. Psychol.* 110(2):261–86

Hofstede G, Van Deusen CA, Mueller CB, Charles TA, Bus. Goals Netw. 2002. What goals do business leaders pursue? A study in fifteen countries. *J. Int. Bus. Stud.* 33:785–803

Hogan J, Hogan R, Kaiser RB. 2010. Management derailment. *APA Handb. Ind. Organ. Psychol.* 3:555–75

Hogg MA. 2001. A social identity theory of leadership. *Pers. Soc. Psych. Rev.* 5(3):184–200

Hoogervorst N, De Cremer D, Van Dijke M, Mayer DM. 2012. When do leaders sacrifice? The effects of sense of power and belongingness on leader self-sacrifice. *Leadersh. Q.* 23(5):883–96

Inesi ME. 2010. Power and loss aversion. *Organ. Behav. Hum. Decis. Process* 112(1):58–69

Inesi ME, Gruenfeld DH, Galinsky AD. 2012. How power corrupts relationships: cynical attributions for others' generous acts. *J. Exp. Soc. Psychol.* 48(4):795–803

Ingersoll RM. 2009. *Who Controls Teachers' Work? Power and Accountability in America's Schools.* Cambridge, MA: Harvard Univ. Press

Josephs RA, Sellers JG, Newman ML, Mehta PH. 2006. The mismatch effect: when testosterone and status are at odds. *J. Pers. Soc. Psychol.* 90(6):999–1013

Joshi PD, Fast NJ. 2013a. I am my (high-power) role: power and role identification. *Pers. Soc. Psychol. Bull.* 39(7):898–910

Joshi PD, Fast NJ. 2013b. Power and reduced temporal discounting. *Psychol. Sci.* 24(4):432–38

Judge TA, Bono JE, Ilies R, Gerhardt MW. 2002. Personality and leadership: a qualitative and quantitative review. *J. Appl. Psychol.* 87(4):765–80

Judge TA, Colbert AE, Ilies R. 2004. Intelligence and leadership: a quantitative review and test of theoretical propositions. *J. Appl. Psychol.* 89(3):542–52

Kacewicz E, Pennebaker JW, Davis M, Jeon M, Graesser AC. 2013. Pronoun use reflects standings in social hierarchies. *J. Lang. Soc. Psychol.* 33(2):125–47

Kang SK, Galinsky AD, Kray LJ, Shirako A. 2015. Power affects performance when the pressure is on: evidence for low-power threat and high-power lift. *Pers. Soc. Psychol. Bull.* 41(5):726–35

Kaplan JR, Manuck SB, Fontenot MB, Mann JJ. 2002. Central nervous system monoamine correlates of social dominance in cynomolgus monkeys (*Macaca fascicularis*). *Neuropsychopharmacology* 26:431–43

Keltner D, Gruenfeld D, Galinsky A, Kraus MW. 2010. Paradoxes of power: dynamics of the acquisition, experience, and social regulation of social power. In *The Social Psychology of Power*, ed. A Guinote, T Vescio, pp. 177–208. New York: Guilford Press

Keltner D, Gruenfeld DH, Anderson C. 2003. Power, approach, and inhibition. *Psychol. Rev.* 110(2):265–84

Kim PH, Pinkley RL, Fragale AR. 2005. Power dynamics in negotiation. *Acad. Manag. Rev.* 30(4):799–822

Kipnis D. 1972. Does power corrupt? *J. Pers. Soc. Psychol.* 24(1):33–41

Kipnis D. 1976. *The Powerholders.* Chicago: Univ. Chicago Press

Kopelman S. 2009. The effect of culture and power on cooperation in commons dilemmas: implications for global resource management. *Organ. Behav. Hum. Decis. Process* 108(1):153–63

Kounios J, Beeman M. 2009. The *Aha*! moment: the cognitive neuroscience of insight. *Curr. Dir. Psychol. Sci.* 18(4):210–16

Kraus MW, Chen S, Keltner D. 2011. The power to be me: Power elevates self-concept consistency and authenticity. *J. Exp. Soc. Psychol.* 47(5):974–80

Kruglanski AW, Bélanger JJ, Chen X, Köpetz C, Pierro A, Mannetti L. 2012. The energetics of motivated cognition: a force-field analysis. *Psychol. Rev.* 119(1):1–20

Kunstman JW, Maner JK. 2011. Sexual overperception: power, mating motives, and biases in social judgment. *J. Pers. Soc. Psychol.* 100(2):282–94

Lammers J, Dubois D, Rucker DD, Galinsky AD. 2013. Power gets the job: Priming power improves interview outcomes. *J. Exp. Soc. Psychol.* 49(4):776–79

Lammers J, Galinsky AD, Gordijn EH, Otten S. 2008. Illegitimacy moderates the effects of power on approach. *Psychol. Sci.* 19(6):558–64

Lammers J, Stoker JI, Jordan J, Pollmann M, Stapel DA. 2011. Power increases infidelity among men and women. *Psychol. Sci.* 22(9):1191–97

Lammers J, Stoker JI, Rink F, Galinsky AD. 2016. To have control over or to be free from others? The desire for power reflects a need for autonomy. *Pers. Soc. Psychol. Bull.* 42(4):498–512

Lammers J, Stoker JI, Stapel DA. 2010. Power and behavioral approach orientation in existing power relations and the mediating effect of income. *Eur. J. Soc. Psychol.* 40(3):543–51

Langner CA, Keltner D. 2008. Social power and emotional experience: actor and partner effects within dyadic interactions. *J. Exp. Soc. Psychol.* 44(3):848–56

Laurin K, Fitzsimons GM, Finkel EJ, Carswell KL, Van Dellen MR, et al. 2016. Power and the pursuit of a partner's goals. *J. Pers. Soc. Psychol.* 110(6):840–68

Little BR. 2008. Personal projects and free traits: personality and motivation reconsidered. *Soc. Personal. Psychol. Compass* 2(3):1235–54

Lord RG, Maher KJ. 2002. *Leadership and Information Processing: Linking Perceptions and Performance*. Abingdon, UK: Routledge

Magee JC, Galinsky AD, Gruenfeld DH. 2007. Power, propensity to negotiate, and moving first in competitive interactions. *Pers. Soc. Psychol. Bull.* 33(2):200–12

Magee JC, Milliken FJ, Lurie AR. 2010. Power differences in the construal of a crisis: the immediate aftermath of September 11, 2001. *Pers. Soc. Psychol. Bull.* 36(3):354–70

Maner JK, Case CR. 2016. Dominance and prestige: dual strategies for navigating social hierarchies. *Adv. Exp. Soc. Psychol.* 54:129–80

Maner JK, Kaschak MP, Jones JL. 2010. Social power and the advent of action. *Soc. Cogn.* 28(1):122–32

Markus H, Nurius P. 1986. Possible selves. *Am. Psychol.* 41(9):954–69

Mast MS. 2002. Dominance as expressed and inferred through speaking time. *Hum. Commun. Res.* 28(3):420–50

Mazur A, Booth A. 1998. Testosterone and dominance in men. *Behav. Brain Sci.* 21(3):353–63

McClelland DC, Burnham DH. 1995. Power is the great motivator. *Harv. Bus. Rev.* 73(1):126–39

McClure SM, Laibson DI, Loewenstein G, Cohen JD. 2004. Separate neural systems value immediate and delayed monetary rewards. *Science* 306(5695):503–7

McGregor I, Nash K, Mann N, Phills CE. 2010. Anxious uncertainty and reactive approach motivation (RAM). *J. Pers. Soc. Psychol.* 99(1):133–47

Mehta PH, Josephs RA. 2010. Testosterone and cortisol jointly regulate dominance: evidence for a dual-hormone hypothesis. *Horm. Behav.* 58(5):898–906

Mills CW. 1999. *The Power Elite*. Oxford, UK: Oxford Univ. Press

Min D, Kim JH. 2013. Is power powerful? Power, confidence, and goal pursuit. *Int. J. Res. Mark.* 30(3):265–75

Morgan D, Grant KA, Gage HD, Mach RH, Kaplan JR, et al. 2002. Social dominance in monkeys: dopamine D2 receptors and cocaine self-administration. *Nat. Neurosci.* 5(2):169–74

Nissan T, Shapira O, Liberman N. 2015. Effects of power on mental rotation and emotion recognition in women. *Pers. Soc. Psychol. Bull.* 41(10):1425–37

Northouse PG. 2015. *Leadership: Theory and Practice*. Thousand Oaks, CA: Sage

Oc B, Bashshur MR, Moore C. 2015. Speaking truth to power: the effect of candid feedback on how individuals with power allocate resources. *J. Appl. Psychol.* 100(2):450–63

Overbeck JR, Park B. 2001. When power does not corrupt: superior individuation processes among powerful perceivers. *J. Pers. Soc. Psychol.* 81(4):549–65

Overbeck JR, Park B. 2006. Powerful perceivers, powerless objects: flexibility of powerholders' social attention. *Organ. Behav. Hum. Decis. Process* 99(2):227–43

Parsons T. 1963. On the concept of political power. *Proc. Am. Phil. Soc.* 107(3):232–62

Petkanopoulou K, Willis GB, Rodríguez-Bailón R. 2016. The emotional side of power(lessness). In *Coping with Lack of Control in a Social World*, ed. M Bukowski, GA Fristche, A Guinote, M Kofa. Abingdon, UK: Taylor & Francis. In press

Pfeffer J. 2007. Human resources from an organizational behavior perspective: some paradoxes explained. *J. Econ. Perspect.* 21(4):115–34

Pratto F. 2015. On power and empowerment. *Brit. J. Soc. Psychol.* 55(1):1–20

Ratcliff NJ, Vescio TK. 2013. Benevolently bowing out: the influence of self-construals and leadership performance on the willful relinquishing of power. *J. Exp. Soc. Psychol.* 49(6):978–83

Reid SA, Ng SH. 1999. Language, power, and intergroup relations. *J. Soc. Issues* 55(1):119–39

Righetti F, Luchies LB, van Gils S, Slotter EB, Witcher B, Kumashiro M. 2015. The prosocial versus proself power holder: how power influences sacrifice in romantic relationships. *Personal. Soc. Psychol. Bull.* 41(6):779–90

Rodríguez-Bailón R, Moya M, Yzerbyt V. 2000. Why do superiors attend to the negative stereotypic information about their subordinates? Effects of power legitimacy on social perception. *Eur. J. Soc. Psychol.* 30:651–71

Ross L, Greene D, House P. 1977. The "false consensus effect": an egocentric bias in social perception and attribution processes. *J. Exp. Soc. Psychol.* 13(3):279–301

Rus D, Van Knippenberg D, Wisse B. 2012. Leader power and self-serving behavior: the moderating role of accountability. *Leadersh. Q.* 23(1):13–26

Russell B. 1938. *Power: A New Social Analysis*. New York: Routledge

Salamone JD, Correa M. 2002. Motivational views of reinforcement: implications for understanding the behavioral functions of nucleus accumbens dopamine. *Behav. Brain Res.* 137(1):3–25

Salamone JD, Correa M. 2012. The mysterious motivational functions of mesolimbic dopamine. *Neuron* 76(3):470–85

Sassenberg K, Ellemers N, Scheepers D, Scholl A. 2014. "Power corrupts" revisited: the role of construal of power as opportunity or responsibility. In *Power, Politics, and Paranoia: Why People Are Suspicious of Their Leaders*, ed. JW Van Prooijen, P Van Lange, pp. 73–87. Cambridge, UK: Cambridge Univ. Press

Sawaoka T, Hughes BL, Ambady N. 2015. Power heightens sensitivity to unfairness against the self. *Personal. Soc. Psychol. Bull.* 41(8):1023–35

Scheepers D, de Wit F, Ellemers N, Sassenberg K. 2012. Social power makes the heart work more efficiently: evidence from cardiovascular markers of challenge and threat. *J. Exp. Soc. Psychol.* 48(1):371–74

Schilke O, Reimann M, Cook SO. 2015. Power decreases trust in social exchange. *PNAS* 112(42):12950–55

Schmid PC, Amodio DM. 2016. Power effects on implicit prejudice and stereotyping: the role of intergroup face processing. *Soc. Neurosci.* 24:1–14

Schmid PC, Kleiman T, Amodio DM. 2015. Power effects on cognitive control: turning conflict into action. *J. Exp. Psychol. Gen.* 144(3):655–63

Schmid PC, Schmid Mast M. 2013. Power increases performance in a social evaluation situation as a result of decreased stress responses. *Eur. J. Soc. Psych.* 43(3):201–11

Schmid Mast M, Jonas K, Hall JA. 2009. Give a person power and he or she will show interpersonal sensitivity: the phenomenon and its why and when. *J. Pers. Soc. Psychol.* 97(5):835–50

Scholl A, Sassenberg K. 2014. Where could we stand if I had. . .? How social power impacts counterfactual thinking after failure. *J. Exp. Soc. Psychol.* 53:51–61

Scholl A, Sassenberg K. 2015. Better know when (not) to think twice: how social power impacts prefactual thought. *Pers. Soc. Psychol. Bull.* 41(2):159–70

Schubert TW. 2005. Your highness: vertical positions as perceptual symbols of power. *J. Pers. Soc. Psychol.* 89(1):1–21

Schultheiss OC, Wirth MM, Torges CM, Pang JS, Villacorta MA, Welsh KM. 2005. Effects of implicit power motivation on men's and women's implicit learning and testosterone changes after social victory or defeat. *J. Pers. Soc. Psychol.* 88(1):174–88

See KE, Morrison EW, Rothman NB, Soll JB. 2011. The detrimental effects of power on confidence, advice taking, and accuracy. *Organ. Behav. Hum. Decis. Process.* 116(2):272–85

Seibert SE, Wang G, Courtright SH. 2011. Antecedents and consequences of psychological and team empowerment in organizations: a meta-analytic review. *J. Appl. Psychol.* 96(5):981–1003

Smith PK, Bargh JA. 2008. Nonconscious effects of power on basic approach and avoidance tendencies. *Soc. Cogn.* 26(1):1–24

Smith PK, Jostmann NB, Galinsky AD, Van Dijk WW. 2008. Lacking power impairs executive functions. *Psychol. Sci.* 19(5):441–47

Smith PK, Trope Y. 2006. You focus on the forest when you're in charge of the trees: power priming and abstract information processing. *J. Pers. Soc. Psychol.* 90(4):578–96

Stamkou E, van Kleef GA, Fischer AH, Kret ME. 2016. Are the powerful really blind to the feelings of others? How hierarchical concerns shape attention to emotions. *Personal. Soc. Psychol. Bull.* 42(6):755–68

Thibaut JW, Kelley HH. 1959. *The Social Psychology of Groups*. New York: Wiley

Thomas L, Singh I, Peccei JS. 2004. *Language, Society and Power: An Introduction*. New York: Psychol. Press

Torelli CJ, Shavitt S. 2010. Culture and concepts of power. *J. Pers. Soc. Psychol.* 99(4):703–23

Tost LP, Gino F, Larrick RP. 2012. Power, competitiveness, and advice taking: why the powerful don't listen. *Organ. Behav. Hum. Decis. Process.* 117(1):53–65

Van Dijke M, Poppe M. 2006. Striving for personal power as a basis for social power dynamics. *Eur. J. Soc. Psychol.* 36(4):537–56

Van Kleef GA, Oveis C, Van der Löwe I, LuoKogan A, Goetz J, Keltner D. 2008. Power, distress, and compassion: turning a blind eye to the suffering of others. *Psychol. Sci.* 19(12):1315–22

Van Loo KJ, Rydell RJ. 2013. On the experience of feeling powerful: perceived power moderates the effect of stereotype threat on women's math performance. *Pers. Soc. Psychol. Bull.* 39(3):387–400

Van Vugt M, Hogan R, Kaiser RB. 2008. Leadership, followership, and evolution: some lessons from the past. *Am. Psychol.* 63(3):182–96

Vescio TK, Snyder M, Butz DA. 2003. Power in stereotypically masculine domains: a Social Influence Strategy X Stereotype Match model. *J. Pers. Soc. Psychol.* 85(6):1062–78

Wang YN. 2015. Authenticity and relationship satisfaction: two distinct ways of directing power to self-esteem. *PloS ONE* 10(12):e0146050

Weber M. 1914 (1978). *Economy and Society: An Outline of Interpretive Sociology.* Berkeley, CA: Univ. Calif. Press

Weick M, Guinote A. 2008. When subjective experiences matter: Power increases reliance on the ease of retrieval. *J. Pers. Soc. Psychol.* 94(6):956–70

Weick M, Guinote A. 2010. How long will it take? Power biases time predictions. *J. Exp. Soc. Psychol.* 46(4):595–604

Wheeler SC, DeMarree KG, Petty RE. 2007. Understanding the role of the self in prime-to-behavior effects: the active-self account. *Pers. Soc. Psychol. Rev.* 11(3):234–61

Whitson JA, Liljenquist KA, Galinsky AD, Magee JC, Gruenfeld DH, Cadena B. 2013. The blind leading: Power reduces awareness of constraints. *J. Exp. Soc. Psychol.* 49(3):579–82

Wilkinson D, Guinote A, Weick M, Molinari R, Graham K. 2010. Feeling socially powerless makes you more prone to bumping into things on the right and induces leftward line bisection error. *Psychon. Bull. Rev.* 17(6):910–14

Willis GB, Rodríguez-Bailón R, Lupiáñez J. 2011. The boss is paying attention: Power affects the functioning of the attentional networks. *Soc. Cogn.* 29(2):166–81

Wojciszke B, Struzynska-Kujalowicz A. 2007. Power influences self-esteem. *Soc. Cogn.* 25(4):472–94

Woltin KA, Guinote A. 2015. I can, I do, and so I like: from power to action and aesthetic preferences. *J. Exp. Psychol. Gen.* 144(6):1124–36

Yap AJ, Mason MF, Ames DR. 2013. The powerful size others down: the link between power and estimates of others' size. *J. Exp. Soc. Psychol.* 49(3):591–94

Yukl G, Gordon A, Taber T. 2002. A hierarchical taxonomy of leadership behavior: integrating a half century of behavior research. *J. Leadersh. Organ. Stud.* 9(1):15–32

Zaccaro SJ, Foti RJ, Kenny DA. 1991. Self-monitoring and trait-based variance in leadership: an investigation of leader flexibility across multiple group situations. *J. Appl. Psychol.* 76(2):308–15

Zhang X, Bartol KM. 2010. Linking empowering leadership and employee creativity: the influence of psychological empowerment, intrinsic motivation, and creative process engagement. *Acad. Manag. J.* 53(1):107–28

Zimbardo PG. 1971. *The Power and Pathology of Imprisonment.* Hearings before House Comm. Judic., Subcomm. 3, 92 Congr., 1st Sess. on Correction, Part II, Prisons, Prison Reform and Prisoner's Rights: California, Congr. Rec. (Serial No. 15), Oct. 25

The Psychology of Close Relationships: Fourteen Core Principles

Eli J. Finkel,[1] Jeffry A. Simpson,[2]
and Paul W. Eastwick[3]

[1]Department of Psychology and Kellogg School of Management, Northwestern University, Evanston, Illinois 60208; email: finkel@northwestern.edu

[2]Department of Psychology, University of Minnesota, Minneapolis, Minnesota 55455; email: simps108@umn.edu

[3]Department of Psychology, University of California, Davis, California 95616; email: eastwick@ucdavis.edu

Annu. Rev. Psychol. 2017. 68:383–411

First published online as a Review in Advance on September 1, 2016

The *Annual Review of Psychology* is online at psych.annualreviews.org

This article's doi: 10.1146/annurev-psych-010416-044038

Keywords

relationship science, core principles, attachment theory, interdependence theory, culinary approach

Abstract

Relationship science is a theory-rich discipline, but there have been no attempts to articulate the broader themes or principles that cut across the theories themselves. We have sought to fill that void by reviewing the psychological literature on close relationships, particularly romantic relationships, to extract its core principles. This review reveals 14 principles, which collectively address four central questions: (*a*) What is a relationship? (*b*) How do relationships operate? (*c*) What tendencies do people bring to their relationships? (*d*) How does the context affect relationships? The 14 principles paint a cohesive and unified picture of romantic relationships that reflects a strong and maturing discipline. However, the principles afford few of the sorts of conflicting predictions that can be especially helpful in fostering novel theory development. We conclude that relationship science is likely to benefit from simultaneous pushes toward both greater integration across theories (to reduce redundancy) and greater emphasis on the circumstances under which existing (or not-yet-developed) principles conflict with one another.

Contents

[R]elationships with other humans are both the foundation and the theme of the human condition: We are born into relationships, we live our lives in relationships with others, and when we die, the effects of our relationships survive in the lives of the living, reverberating throughout the tissue of their relationships.

—Ellen Berscheid (1999, pp. 261–262)

INTRODUCTION

Poets, novelists, and philosophers have long recognized the centrality of relationships to human existence. Yet the coalescence of an integrated science devoted to understanding human relationships dates back only to the 1980s. Today, relationship science is an interdisciplinary field that employs diverse empirical methods to understand the initiation, development, maintenance, and dissolution of interpersonal relationships. This field addresses the structure and trajectory of relationships, how relationships operate, and how relationship outcomes are influenced by both the personal characteristics that people bring to their relationships and the broader context in which relationships are embedded. Relationship scientists investigate many types of relationships, but the primary emphasis is on close relationships—those characterized by "strong, frequent, and diverse interdependence that lasts over a considerable period of time" (Kelley et al. 1983, p. 38)—especially well-established romantic relationships.[1] In her classic article on the "greening of relationship science," Berscheid (1999) discussed the growing coherence and influence of relationship science on myriad scholarly fields, presciently forecasting the growth of a

---

[1] Close relationships researchers investigate a wide range of relationships, even within the subcase of romantic relationships. Although there are main effect differences across relationship types (Kurdek 2005), the available evidence suggests that "the processes that regulate relationship functioning generalize across gay, lesbian, and heterosexual couples" (Kurdek 2004, p. 880). Thus, we have no reason to believe that the 14 principles discussed below qualitatively differ across different romantic relationship arrangements. As such, and because the vast majority of research has examined heterosexual romantic relationships, our examples focus on the heterosexual case.

flourishing discipline in the twenty-first century (see also Campbell & Simpson 2013, Reis 2007).

Researchers have written many reviews of the close relationships literature, including in previous volumes of the *Annual Review of Psychology* (e.g., Clark & Reis 1988, Gottman 1998). In this review, we focus on the major theories that guide research in relationship science, with a particular emphasis on those deriving from social and personality psychology. We seek to understand what assumptions these theories share, the extent to which they align or conflict, and how they could be augmented and complemented. Toward those ends, we attempt to extract from the literature a set of core principles for understanding close relationships and illustrate how articulating and organizing these core principles can promote theory refinement and development.

MAJOR THEORIES IN RELATIONSHIP SCIENCE

Relationship science has produced many strong theories, two of which—interdependence theory and attachment theory—have been especially influential. Interdependence theory, which began as a game-theoretic model of dyadic interaction, traces its roots to Thibaut & Kelley's (1959) book *The Social Psychology of Groups*. This theory was first applied to close relationships in the 1970s (Kelley 1979, Levinger & Snoek 1972) and became a dominant theory of such relationships in the 1980s (Kelley et al. 1983, Rusbult 1983). According to interdependence theory, social situations vary along several dimensions, and this variation influences relationship processes and outcomes (Kelley et al. 2003). For example, situations in which a man is more (versus less) dependent on his girlfriend for rewarding experiences should increase the extent to which he monitors her behavior for signs that she loves and is committed to him. His high level of dependence puts him in a low-power position unless she is also highly dependent upon him. High levels of mutual dependence typically promote cooperative behavior when partners have corresponding interests but conflictual behavior when they have noncorrespondent interests.

Attachment theory, which initially focused on infant–caregiver relationships, traces its roots to Bowlby's (1969, 1973, 1980) trilogy on attachment, separation, and loss. The theory was adapted to explain the nature of close relationships between adults in the 1980s (Hazan & Shaver 1987), and it joined interdependence theory as a dominant model of adult relationships in the 1990s (Hazan & Shaver 1994). According to attachment theory, people develop emotional bonds with significant others (usually romantic partners in adulthood) and are motivated to maintain these bonds over time (Mikulincer & Shaver 2007). People seek proximity to their primary attachment figure, especially when they are stressed, ill, or afraid, and rely on the psychological security provided by this person when pursuing challenging activities that can promote mastery and personal growth. Individuals vary along two dimensions of attachment insecurity: (*a*) anxiety, the extent to which they need reassurance that their attachment figures love and will stay with them, and (*b*) avoidance, the extent to which they are uncomfortable with emotional intimacy and being vulnerable. Secure individuals, who score low on both dimensions, typically display the most constructive relationship processes and have the most positive relationship outcomes.

Several other theoretical perspectives have also been influential in relationship science, including risk regulation theory (Murray et al. 2006), self-expansion theory (Aron et al. 2013), the communal/exchange model (Clark & Mills 2011), the interpersonal process model of intimacy (Reis & Shaver 1988), and the vulnerability-stress-adaptation model (Karney & Bradbury 1995). The existence of such theories, along with many others, is a major strength of relationship science: These theories have fruitfully guided thousands of empirical investigations into how people think, feel, and behave in close relationships.

Nevertheless, it is not obvious how, or whether, these theories cohere and what qualities they have in common. Some theories overlap in intended ways. For example, risk regulation theory (Murray et al. 2006) deliberately combines elements of attachment theory and interdependence theory. Other theories overlap in underappreciated ways. For example, the ideal standards model (Simpson et al. 2001) focuses on standards, whereas the suffocation model (Finkel et al. 2014a) focuses on expectations, two constructs that are almost synonymous in interdependence theory. Still other theories discuss processes that are rarely articulated elsewhere. For example, the emphasis in the vulnerability-stress-adaptation model on stressors external to the relationship (Karney & Bradbury 1995) is neglected in most other theories (but see Hill 1949, McCubbin & Patterson 1983). Relationship science is fortunate to have this rich assemblage of theories, but their collective depiction is murky because the degree to which the field's core principles complement, circumscribe, overlap with, or conflict with one another remains unclear.[2]

EXTRACTING PRINCIPLES: A CULINARY METAPHOR

The primary goal of this review is to articulate the principles that cut across many of the theories in relationship science. Consider a culinary metaphor in which each theory is a dish (e.g., a curry) composed of discrete ingredients (e.g., a grain, a protein, a vegetable, several spices). We set ourselves the task of extracting the core principles—the basic ingredients—and determining which principles emerge repeatedly across different theories. Our approach, in other words, involves temporarily setting the theories aside in order to identify and organize a set of core principles that characterize relationship science in general. Subsequently, we illustrate how theorists might use these principles in theory refinement and novel theory development.

In general, the goal of the extraction process is not to replace current theories, nor to generate a comprehensive list of every theoretical idea ever introduced within the relevant research domain. Rather, the goal is to identify the key—most widespread and influential—principles that have influenced theory development and hypothesis generation in the field. This assessment can help determine whether and how various theories align, perhaps through redundancy or by emphasizing different features of a phenomenon (akin to the proverbial blind men examining different parts of an elephant). Additionally, it fills the theoretical pantry with the main ingredients required for the theory development (cooking) process.

In applying this culinary approach to relationship science, we began by examining psychologically oriented handbook volumes, textbooks, and review articles to identify the major theories and models within the research domain and to extract an initial list of core principles. We then obtained feedback from 16 leading relationship scientists in psychology to refine this initial list, ultimately producing the 14 core principles discussed below (see **Table 1**).

Each principle is described at a fairly high level of abstraction so that it can align with multiple theories; our goal is to capture the general thrust of how each theory characterizes a given principle, even if there is minor variation across theories in the principle's precise specification. Each principle can be used to develop empirical hypotheses, but no one principle specifies how particular constructs should be operationalized (i.e., there is no gold-standard measure required by a particular principle). Reflecting the current state of the field, the principles exist at somewhat

---

[2]The evolutionary psychology of human mating (Buss 2008) developed alongside mainstream relationship science. By and large, however, these two fields have developed in parallel. They address some overlapping topics but tend to employ different research methods and exhibit modest cross-fertilization of ideas (see Durante et al. 2016, Eastwick 2016). Toward the end of this review (see Optimizing Relationship Science: Theoretical Cohesion Versus Conflict), we address some ways in which relationship science could benefit from greater incorporation of ideas from evolutionary psychology.

Table 1 The 14 principles extracted from the psychology literature on relationship science

Set[a]	Number	Name	Definition
1	1	Uniqueness	Relationship outcomes depend not only on the specific qualities of each partner but also on the unique patterns that emerge when the partners' qualities intersect
	2	Integration	Opportunities and motivations for interdependence tend to facilitate cognitive, affective, motivational, or behavioral merging between partners
	3	Trajectory	The long-term trajectories of relationship dynamics are affected by each partner's continually updated perceptions of the couple's relationship-relevant interactions and experiences
2	4	Evaluation	People evaluate their relationships and partners according to a set of positive and negative constructs, which tend to be moderately negatively correlated
	5	Responsiveness	Responsive behaviors promote relationship quality for both the self and the partner
	6	Resolution	The manner in which partners communicate about and cope with relationship events affects long-term relationship quality and stability
	7	Maintenance	Partners in committed relationships exhibit cognitions and behaviors that promote the relationship's persistence over time, even if doing so involves self-deceptive biases
3	8	Predisposition	People bring certain basic qualities of personality and temperament to their relationships, some of which influence their own and their partners' relationship wellbeing
	9	Instrumentality	People bring certain goals and needs to their relationships, and the dynamics between the two partners affect the extent to which they succeed in achieving these goals and meeting these needs
	10	Standards	People bring certain standards to their relationships and tend to experience greater relationship wellbeing when their relationships exceed these standards
4	11	Diagnosticity	Situations vary in the extent to which they afford opportunities to evaluate a partner's true goals and motives regarding the relationship
	12	Alternatives	The presence of attractive alternatives to a current relationship—including the option of not being in a relationship at all—threatens relationship quality and persistence
	13	Stress	High demands external to the relationship predict worse relationship outcomes, especially if the demands exceed the two partners' (individual or combined) resources for coping
	14	Culture	Relationships are embedded in social networks and a cultural milieu—including norms, practices, and traditions—that shape the nature and trajectory of those relationships

[a]Set refers to the four major theoretical questions that the principles address: (1) What is a relationship? (2) How do relationships operate? (3) What tendencies do people bring to their relationships? (4) How does the context affect relationships?.

different levels of analysis. Some, for example, apply to a person at a single moment in time, whereas others apply to a person in general or across time; some imply a particular causal process (e.g., responsive behaviors increase relationship quality), whereas others specify only that a construct accounts for variance in a process or outcome (e.g., culture accounts for variance in the quality of relationship functioning).[3] Consistent with the culinary metaphor, most theories incorporate or address only some of the 14 principles, in the same way that specific dishes do not use all the ingredients in the pantry; it is unlikely that a cogent theory could incorporate all 14 principles, especially at this rather early stage of the field's development.

By necessity, our extraction process involved many subjective judgments. For example, what counts as a theory? Which theories are most relevant to relationship science? Is a given principle

---

[3]All of the principles we discuss can be disconfirmed, though it may be easier to disconfirm principles that specify a particular causal process than principles that specify that a construct should predict an outcome in general.

sufficiently core to warrant inclusion? Thus, we make no claim that our conclusions reflect the absolute truth regarding the key principles that define relationship science from a psychological perspective; other scholars might make different decisions or draw different conclusions about the discipline's core principles. However, the subjectivity of this approach does not render the conclusions arbitrary. The conclusions are constrained by the theories in our research domain, which means that all competent extraction efforts ought to generate principles that are reasonably compatible with one another. We hope that our synthesis starts a dialogue about the core principles that anchor relationship science and about how these principles might be used both to refine current theories and to generate new ones.

THE CORE PRINCIPLES OF RELATIONSHIP SCIENCE

Once we extracted the 14 principles (see **Table 1**), we embedded them within a sensible, albeit post hoc, organizational structure. We settled on a four-set structure in which each set was built around a central theoretical question in relationship science: (*a*) What is a relationship? (*b*) How do relationships operate? (*c*) What tendencies do people bring to their relationships? (*d*) How does the context affect relationships? **Figure 1** depicts an organizational framework for conceptualizing the 14 principles within this four-set structure.

Set 1: What Is a Relationship?

Relationship scientists have written extensively about the definitions of terms such as close and relationship (e.g., Berscheid & Regan 2005, Kelley et al. 1983). One pervasive concept that characterizes all attempts to define close relationships is that partners are dependent on one another to obtain good outcomes and facilitate the pursuit of their most important needs and goals (see Finkel

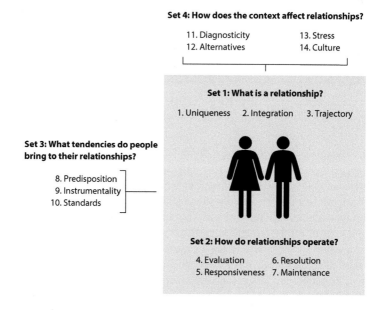

Figure 1

A psychological perspective of the core principles in relationship science. Although the image depicts a heterosexual couple, the available evidence suggests that all 14 core principles generalize to other relationship structures, including those involving gay men or lesbians (see Footnote 1). Picture credit: Pixabay.

& Simpson 2015). Beyond these broad definitional efforts, theories have extensively explored the nature of close relationships. Set 1 contains three core principles that address how and why a relationship becomes more than the sum of its parts (the uniqueness principle), the merging of two partners into a single psychological entity (the integration principle), and the way relationships change over time (the trajectory principle).

Uniqueness. *Relationship outcomes depend not only on the specific qualities of each partner but also on the unique patterns that emerge when the partners' qualities intersect.*

According to relationship scientists, a relationship functions as its own entity that is distinct from and irreducible to the two constituent partners (Berscheid 1999). For example, even if two individuals tend to be low self-disclosers, their idiosyncratic personal characteristics may mesh in a unique way that leads both of them to self-disclose a great deal to each other. From a statistical standpoint, uniqueness effects are evident in the degree of relationship variance in social relations model studies and in actor × partner interaction effects in actor–partner interdependence model studies (Kenny & Kashy 2011).

Various theories address the uniqueness principle in distinct ways, with most emphasizing certain characteristics of relationship partners or specific interpersonal outcomes. Interdependence theory (Kelley et al. 2003) proposes that the qualities of each partner influence how the two partners interact in particular situations and, consequently, the outcomes they reap from those interactions. Transactive goal dynamics theory (Fitzsimons et al. 2015) argues that successful goal attainment depends on features of the self (e.g., a man's desire to lose weight) in conjunction with those of the partner (e.g., his wife's training as a dietician). Relational regulation theory (Lakey & Orehek 2011) posits that the extent to which social interaction successfully regulates affect, behavior, and cognition depends on the idiosyncratic traits, preferences, and personal tastes of each partner (e.g., the two partners find it soothing if she plays guitar while he cooks).

There are many empirical examples of uniqueness. For example, relationship variance explains most of the total variance in perceptions of mate value and long-term attraction, indicating that beauty (as well as other desirable qualities of a mate) really is largely in the eye of the beholder (Eastwick & Hunt 2014). Mutuality of commitment—the degree to which both partners report comparable levels of commitment to the relationship—predicts unique variance in relationship wellbeing above and beyond the two partners' levels of commitment (Drigotas et al. 1999). Capitalization discussions—in which one partner attempts to savor positive news with the other (Gable & Reis 2010)—tend to be especially difficult and unsatisfying if the person sharing the news is high in attachment anxiety and the partner is high in attachment avoidance (Shallcross et al. 2011). Depressive symptoms during the transition to parenthood are particularly pronounced when highly neurotic individuals have highly disagreeable spouses (Marshall et al. 2015). In short, relationships cannot be understood fully by studying main effects involving the two partners; consideration of the unique dyadic context generated by the two partners is also required.

Integration. *Opportunities and motivations for interdependence tend to facilitate cognitive, affective, motivational, or behavioral merging between partners.*

In many close relationships, the psychological boundaries that separate partners are blurry, making it difficult to discern where one partner ends and the other begins. The self component in terms such as self-concept and self-regulation takes on a less individualistic focus. Consider the self-concept, which is often deeply embedded in and possibly altered by close relationships (Andersen & Chen 2002). As a relationship develops and the desire to maintain it increases, an individual's self-concept usually becomes increasingly intertwined with the partner and relationship. In unstructured relationship thought-listing tasks, for example, higher relationship commitment predicts greater spontaneous use of plural pronouns such as we, us, and our (Agnew et al. 1998). Individuals also become confused about whether they or their partner has a given attribute (e.g., extraversion), as illustrated by research showing that participants are slower and less accurate when making me/not me decisions under time pressure if either they or their partner possesses the relevant attribute than if neither or both of them do (Mashek et al. 2003). Similar effects are also found in newly formed relationships when an individual desires high interdependence with his or her potential partner (Slotter & Gardner 2009). Perhaps due to this merging of identities, the tendency for individuals to exhibit self-enhancing biases generalizes to their close (but not nonclose) relationship partners (Sedikides et al. 1998).

Self-regulation is also embedded within close relationships. According to transactive goal dynamics theory (Finkel et al. 2016, Fitzsimons et al. 2015), relationship partners form a single self-regulating unit that involves a complex web of goals, pursuits, and outcomes. The optimal unit of analysis for understanding goal dynamics is the dyad or group, not the individual. For instance, Alice might set a goal for John, such as losing weight; she might then pursue this goal by buying healthier snacks, or John might pursue it by forgoing desserts. Alice might also set a goal for herself, such as submitting a work project on time, which John helps her pursue by doing some solo parenting so she can complete her project. Depending on how efficiently partners coordinate their goals and pursuits, goal interdependence can either bolster or undermine each person's goal success. When goal coordination is strong, partners can achieve a level of goal success that would have been impossible if they were single or had a less compatible partner. In fact, research has shown that individuals assigned to think about ways in which their romantic partner is helpful in their pursuit of a goal work less hard at pursuing that goal (Fitzsimons & Finkel 2011), which frees resources for other goal pursuits.

When performing joint tasks, people who desire a communal rather than an exchange relationship tend to behave in ways that obscure rather than accentuate their independent contributions, which makes overall performance function as a shared dyadic contribution rather than as a combination of two independent contributions. Even at a physiological level, the line separating close relationship partners is fuzzy (Beckes & Coan 2011, IJzerman et al. 2015, Sbarra & Hazan 2008). Romantic partners performing laboratory interaction tasks, for example, exhibit increased alignment over time in their respiratory sinus arrhythmia (a biomarker of feeling safe), an effect that is stronger among individuals who are more satisfied with their relationship (Helm et al. 2014).

Trajectory. *The long-term trajectories of relationship dynamics are affected by each partner's continually updated perceptions of the couple's relationship-relevant interactions and experiences.*

Relationships change over time. Close relationships models from the 1960s and 1970s posited that change reflected a normative series of stages or filters. For example, the intersection model of pair relatedness (Levinger & Snoek 1972) proposes that relationship partners move through stages of escalating interdependence as they become aware of each other, interact, and eventually form a relationship characterized by a couple-level identity. The relational development model (Knapp et al. 2014) suggests that couples move through a series of stages both when beginning a relationship (e.g., initiating, then intensifying, then bonding) and when ending a relationship (e.g., differentiating, then stagnating, then terminating). Shifts between stages are often marked by transitions— turning points where partners' levels of commitment become explicit (Loving et al. 2009) or life events that change the relationship, such as the transition to parenthood (Rholes et al. 2011).

Other models focus on how specific relationship constructs ebb and flow across time. According to social penetration theory (Altman & Taylor 1973), relationship partners develop intimacy as they gradually increase the depth and breadth of their self-disclosures. Attachment theorists propose that the three behavioral systems associated with pair-bonding develop at different rates, with the sexual mating system being particularly important early in a relationship and the attachment and caregiving systems taking on greater importance once the relationship has become established (Zeifman & Hazan 2008). Interdependence theorists have focused on how the situations encountered by a given couple produce relationship-specific behavioral tendencies, which often become reified as injunctive norms (Thibaut & Kelley 1959). For example, if one partner likes action films and the other likes screwball comedies, the couple might develop a strong turn-taking norm, which would not exist in couples in which partners had identical film preferences. People also update their internal working models over time (Bretherton & Munholland 2008). Research has confirmed that events that produce feelings of greater attachment security lead to changes in partner-specific attachment models (e.g., expectations that one's current partner is reliable), which subsequently change global attachment models (e.g., expectations that partners in general are reliable) (Fraley 2007, Pierce & Lydon 2001).

Many of the events and experiences that cause relationships to change occur in simple, ordinary interactions and commonplace situations. Indeed, relational regulation theory (Lakey & Orehek 2011) suggests that people's perceptions of social support originate mainly from everyday conversations and shared activities with partners rather than in response to major life stressors. Consequently, relationship outcomes are challenging to predict before a relationship begins, even if one has considerable knowledge of each partner's personal characteristics (Finkel et al. 2012). The ReCAST model (Eastwick et al. 2016) posits that relationships that turn out to be long-term, committed relationships are often indistinguishable from those that turn out to be short-term and casual in the early stages as two people get to know each other. Long-term and short-term relationships prove difficult to differentiate primarily because people do not know if they want to be in a committed relationship with a specific person until they can fully gauge the relationship's emotional and sexual chemistry. However, relationships do not remain unpredictable forever: Once relationship partners progress to advanced relationship stages (e.g., marriage), latent strengths and vulnerabilities presage whether partners' evaluations of relationship quality will remain high or deteriorate (Lavner et al. 2012).

Set 2: How Do Relationships Operate?

Besides examining existential and temporal features of relationships, relationship scientists also investigate how individuals think, feel, and behave with regard to their experiences and interactions with their partners. Set 2 encompasses four core principles, which address how individuals evaluate their partners and relationships (the evaluation principle); how partners respond to each other's needs (the responsiveness principle); how partners react dyadically to conflict and other important relationship events (the resolution principle); and how partners (typically) manage to sustain their relationship, despite challenges (the maintenance principle).

Evaluation. *People evaluate their relationships and partners according to set of positive and negative constructs, which tend to be moderately negatively correlated.*

People constantly evaluate the world around them, and their relationships and partners are no exception. Most people make relationship evaluations on separable positivity and negativity dimensions (Gable & Reis 2001); researchers have used this two-dimensional conceptualization to examine the effects of ambivalence—simultaneous highly positive and highly negative evaluations—on relationship processes and outcomes (e.g., Uchino et al. 2013).

Typically, however, individuals who evaluate a relationship more positively also evaluate it less negatively, so most evaluative variables are bipolar and labeled according to their positive endpoint (e.g., satisfaction, commitment, trust, etc.). Each of these constructs has its own definition, timecourse, and measure, and various theoretical perspectives have attempted to explain how and why these constructs are related or distinct.

According to the triangular theory of love (Sternberg 1986), for example, love has three elements, which can be present or absent to varying degrees: intimacy (warm feelings of connectedness), passion (romantic and sexual attraction), and commitment (the decision to maintain the relationship). Other scholars have focused on the timecourse of passion and intimacy, finding that passion is a function of the first derivative of intimacy over time: When intimacy is increasing, passion is high; when it is stable (regardless of its level), passion is low (Rubin & Campbell 2012). These and other positive evaluative constructs are conceptually distinct, but they are often positively correlated, sometimes quite highly. Although six of the major evaluative constructs in relationship science—commitment, trust, love, passion, intimacy, and satisfaction—are distinct, they share considerable variance and form a single, broad dimension reflecting overall relationship quality (Fletcher et al. 2000a,b).

Most and perhaps all of these constructs include not only reflective/consciously accessible components but also impulsive/automatic components (Murray et al. 2013). Using distinct measurement approaches (e.g., explicit versus implicit priming), both kinds of components can be assessed; depending on the context, either explicit or implicit measures may account for more of the variance in predicting a given relationship process or outcome (Banse & Kowalick 2007, McNulty et al. 2013).

Responsiveness. *Responsive behaviors promote relationship quality for both the self and the partner.*

Individuals' assessments of relationship quality are strongly influenced by their interactions with their partners, including their degree of mutual responsiveness—the extent to which they are "cognizant of, sensitive to, and behaviorally supportive of" each other's core needs and values (Reis 2007, p. 9; see also Clark & Lemay 2010, Reis & Clark 2013). Studies have confirmed that partners' responsive behaviors across a wide range of negative and positive experiences predict greater personal and relationship wellbeing (Debrot et al. 2012, Gable et al. 2012), above and beyond the positive effects of other more general forms of support (Otto et al. 2015).

This emphasis on responsiveness to the partner's core needs and values indicates that one cannot be responsive by simply learning a set of techniques and applying them in all situations (Finkel et al. 2014b). Rather, responsiveness requires tailoring one's actions to the unique needs of one's partner in a particular situation. Consider this classic example: Having someone immediately repay your favor is responsive if you want an exchange relationship with him or her, but it is unresponsive if you desire a communal relationship (Clark & Mills 1979).

When individuals believe their partner is responsive to their needs, they typically feel good about themselves and are more willing to place themselves in emotionally vulnerable positions, which can enhance the quality of their relationship (Murray et al. 2006). People vary, of course, in how comfortable they are being emotionally vulnerable, an individual difference that influences not only how responsive they are but also how they are likely to react to responsive behavior from their partner. When in a support-provision role, insecurely attached individuals tend to provide less responsive support when their partners are upset (Feeney & Collins 2001, Simpson et al. 1992). When in a support-recipient role, such individuals report feeling greater insecurity and display relationship-destructive behaviors, although receiving more responsive support tailored to their needs buffers them from experiencing these adverse states (Lemay & Dudley 2011, Simpson & Overall 2014). Responsiveness, in other words, plays a crucial role—frequently in conjunction with the partners' individual qualities—in social support contexts in which one partner helps the other cope with negative experiences or stressors. The extent to which individuals perceive that they have high-quality support available predicts greater wellbeing and better health outcomes (Robles et al. 2014).

Responsiveness is also important in capitalization situations (Gable & Reis 2010) in which responsive reactions typically involve active, constructive behaviors such as excitement or enthusiasm (Feeney & Collins 2015). These reactions often yield positive outcomes, such as increases in the discloser's positive mood or self-esteem, which in turn lead the discloser to feel closer to the responsive partner. Conversely, passive or destructive responses such as apathy or envy signal a lack of responsiveness and frequently elicit distancing responses from disclosers.

Resolution. *The manner in which partners communicate about and cope with relationship events affects long-term relationship quality and stability.*

Certain relational events stand out, reverberating with psychological resonance for one or both partners. These events may be commonplace, such as the fifteenth fight over chores in a month, or infrequent, such as the birth of a child. The ways in which these events affect a relationship often hinge on how both partners behave in response to them (Overall & McNulty 2017).

The range of these resonant events is vast, but because negative relational events have stronger consequences for relationship wellbeing than do positive events (Gottman 1998), conflictual interaction tends to be especially significant. Communication often becomes fraught during conflict, and relationship satisfaction and stability largely depend on how partners construe and respond to each other's behavior. In addition, the effectiveness and pace with which partners recover from conflict episodes independently predict relationship satisfaction and stability (e.g., Gottman & Levenson 1999).

The response options to conflict reside within a constructive/destructive × active/passive behavioral space (Rusbult et al. 1982; for a similar model, see Overall & McNulty 2017). Responses within this space have downstream effects on relationship quality; active/constructive responses, for example, tend to predict higher satisfaction and lower breakup likelihood (Rusbult et al. 1982). Observational research has documented four conflict-relevant behavioral patterns that forecast relationship distress and propensity to divorce: globally criticizing your partner's personality, responding defensively to your partner's criticism, conveying the belief that your partner is beneath you, and refusing to engage with your partner's concerns (Gottman 1998).

Major relationship problems must sometimes be directly addressed to resolve persistent, nagging issues that, if left unattended, could further destabilize the relationship. For example, compared to partners who are more passive or destructive, partners who directly and openly confront major problems in active, constructive ways experience greater distress during and immediately following conflict discussions, but they and their partners are more likely to resolve these problems and have happier relationships over time (Overall et al. 2009). It appears that direct opposition is beneficial when serious problems must be addressed and when partners can make changes, but it is often harmful when partners do not have the traits or skills to be adequately responsive to one another (Overall & McNulty 2017). Indirect (i.e., passive) cooperative communication, on the other hand, appears to be harmful when major problems must be resolved but can be beneficial when (*a*) problems are minor, (*b*) things cannot be changed, or (*c*) one or both partners are too defensive to resolve the problem effectively.

Forgiveness research has revealed that the ways in which both partners behave and react following major interpersonal transgressions alter how resolution unfolds. If, for example, transgressors make stronger amends and victims forgive them more wholeheartedly following a major relationship transgression, victims tend to develop greater self-respect and clearer self-views (Luchies et al. 2010), which should result in better and more constructive interactions later on. Indeed, the expression of greater forgiveness by the victim predicts more constructive patterns of marital conflict resolution and greater long-term relationship stability across time (Fincham et al. 2004). If, however, transgressors fail to make adequate amends or are verbally aggressive, victims who are highly (versus modestly) forgiving tend to respect themselves less and feel less satisfied in the marriage (Luchies et al. 2010, McNulty 2008).

Maintenance. *Partners in committed relationships exhibit cognitions and behaviors that promote the relationship's persistence over time, even if doing so involves self-deceptive biases.*

Forgiveness is one of many processes that protect and promote relationships over time; these processes are collectively called relationship maintenance mechanisms. Many of these mechanisms involve a transformation process in which partners override their immediate self-interests in favor of behaviors that are more beneficial to the partner or the relationship (Kelley & Thibaut 1978). One of the most robust predictors of the tendency to enact relationship maintenance mechanisms is relationship commitment, which emerges from feelings of satisfaction and investment in the relationship and from the belief that the alternatives to involvement in the relationship are less desirable (Le & Agnew 2003). Greater relationship commitment, in turn, is associated with en-acting relationship-maintaining cognitions and behaviors, such as perceiving one's relationship as better than others' (including in the sexual arena; see de Jong & Reis 2015), ignoring or men-tally derogating romantic alternatives, making sacrifices to benefit the relationship, and forgiving partner transgressions (Rusbult et al. 2001).

Some of the relationship-promoting effects of commitment stem from motivated biases. For example, the positive association of commitment with perceptions that one's relationship is better than others' relationships is stronger when one's relationship is threatened (Rusbult et al. 2000). The negative association of commitment with the assessment of romantic alternatives as desirable is stronger when alternatives are objectively more appealing; in fact, the negative association disappears when alternatives are objectively unappealing, presumably because they do not threaten the relationship and do not require derogation (Johnson & Rusbult 1989, Simpson et al. 1990). Similarly, although romantically unattached men tend to find a novel woman more desirable when she is at the most fertile stage of her ovulatory cycle, men who are involved in a committed romantic relationship show the opposite pattern (Miller & Maner 2010). That is, men in relationships actually find a woman other than their partner less attractive when she is highly fertile, presumably because she is especially tempting and threatening to their existing relationship and they are therefore motivated to perceive her negatively.

When engaged in relationship maintenance activities, one partner's commitment becomes more closely tied to the other's trust (Wieselquist et al. 1999). It is, after all, fairly easy to trust someone who forgives your transgressions and derogates attractive alternatives. Trust, in turn, is associated with less monitoring of the partner's behavior as the trusting individual develops more faith that the partner has his or her best interests at heart (Holmes & Rempel 1989). Indeed, individuals who place greater trust in their partners exhibit relationship-promoting biases in which they misremember their partner's relationship transgressions as being more benign than they actually were (Luchies et al. 2013).

Relationship scientists have also drawn from other theoretical frameworks to identify rela-tionship maintenance mechanisms. For example, research has shown that positive illusions about the partner predict salutary relationship outcomes over time (Murray et al. 2011), and making more generous attributions about the causes of a partner's behavior predicts higher relationship satisfaction (Bradbury & Fincham 1990). Of course, reality does act as a constraint on an individ-ual's rose-colored glasses (Fletcher & Kerr 2010, West & Kenny 2011), and biases may be more or less pronounced depending on the specific features of a situation. For example, the strength of a person's positive biases is more pronounced when he or she is pursuing important relationship goals rather than deliberating about which goals to pursue (Gagné & Lydon 2004). Relationship-promoting effects are also found when partners engage in novel and arousing (rather than merely pleasant) activities with each other (Aron et al. 2000) and when they adopt the perspective of a neutral, benevolent third party when thinking about relationship conflict (Finkel et al. 2013).

Set 3: What Tendencies Do People Bring to Their Relationships?

Thus far, our discussion has focused predominantly on relationship functioning. We have largely sidestepped both the normative or idiosyncratic tendencies that individuals bring to their relationships (Set 3) and the contextual factors that might influence relationship processes (Set 4). Set 3 contains three core principles that address how and why relationship functioning is influenced by the partners' personality qualities (the predisposition principle), their needs and goals (the instrumentality principle), and the benchmarks they use to evaluate the relationship (the standards principle).

Predisposition. *People bring certain basic qualities of personality and temperament to their relationships, some of which influence their own and their partners' relationship wellbeing.*

The most basic tendencies that people bring to their relationships are tied to their personality and temperament. The effects of personal strengths (e.g., high self-esteem, attachment security, approach goals) or vulnerabilities (e.g., neuroticism, rejection sensitivity, avoidance goals) can be amplified by events that transpire within relationships or in the wider environment. For example, John, who has low self-esteem and adopts avoidance goals in his relationship (e.g., avoiding conflict), may not worry much about the status of his relationship with Alice if they are getting along well and everything is fine at work. However, when either the relationship or work generates stress, his personal vulnerabilities may rise to the fore and make him think, feel, and behave in relationship-damaging ways, which adversely affect Alice and their later interactions (Gable & Impett 2012, Murray et al. 2006).

Several relationship theories are relevant to the predisposition principle. Attachment theory (Bowlby 1973), for instance, proposes that the ways in which an individual is treated by significant others (attachment figures) across the course of his or her life—and especially during childhood—produce internal working models of the self and others, which then guide how he or she thinks, feels, and behaves in later interpersonal contexts, particularly stressful ones. Securely attached individuals, who have received nurturing and sensitive care, develop positive models of the self and others and, therefore, behave more positively and constructively toward their partners (Mikulincer & Shaver 2007), especially when one or both of them are upset (Collins & Feeney 2004, Simpson et al. 1992). Anxiously attached individuals, who have received unpredictable or inconsistent care, develop negative models of the self (viewing themselves as unworthy of love), which motivates them to be hypervigilant to signs that their partner might be pulling away. Avoidantly attached individuals, who have been rebuffed or rejected, develop negative models of others (viewing others as uncaring), which motivates them to keep their attachment systems deactivated by being self-reliant, especially in stressful situations (Simpson & Rholes 2012).

The predisposition principle is prominent in other theories and bodies of research, as well. For example, according to evolutionary models of social development (reviewed in Simpson & Belsky 2016), stressful circumstances (e.g., early unpredictable environments) result in poorer parenting, which creates enduring vulnerabilities (e.g., attachment insecurity) that eventually affect the quality and stability of an individual's romantic relationships years later (Szepsenwol et al. 2016). According to the communal/exchange model (Clark & Mills 2011), people who bring greater communal strength to a relationship typically provide benefits to their partners that are costly to themselves. According to the intimacy process model (Reis & Shaver 1988), the degree to which an individual discloses important personal information to his or her partner—and how the partner then perceives this information and reacts to it—is shaped by the unique motives, needs, goals, and fears (the working models) that each partner brings to the relationship (Laurenceau et al. 1998). Certain personality traits—especially neuroticism, which develops early in life—predict a host of negative relationship outcomes later in life (McNulty 2013).

Instrumentality. *People bring certain goals and needs to their relationships, and the dynamics between the two partners affect the extent to which they succeed in achieving these goals and meeting these needs.*

Beyond personality differences, people also bring many needs and goals to relationships. Some of these motivational elements are species typical. Attachment theory, for example, contends that humans have an innate need to develop attachment bonds (Bowlby 1969), whereas self-expansion theory suggests that humans have an innate need to expand the self (Aron et al. 2013). Applications of self-determination theory in the domain of relationships indicate that people look to their significant others to help them achieve their innate psychological needs for autonomy, competence, and relatedness (La Guardia et al. 2000). Other goals, such as the desire to reduce carbohydrate consumption, are more idiosyncratic. Relationship scientists investigate the ways in which relationships influence how much individuals are able to fulfill these needs and achieve their goals.

One foundational need relevant to the formation and maintenance of close relationships is attachment, the need to establish an emotionally close relationship that fosters feelings of security (Baumeister & Leary 1995, Bowlby 1969). Attachment theory's central idea is that human adults (in contrast to adults of our closest genetic relatives, chimpanzees and bonobos) evolved to form deep, long-term emotional attachments with other adults, presumably because such bonds promoted survival of our species' altricial infants ancestrally (Eastwick 2009, Finkel & Eastwick 2015, Fletcher et al. 2015). Human adults also seek out their primary attachment figures (e.g., romantic partners) for subsidiary attachment-related needs, such as comfort when they are upset or strength when pursuing challenging goals (Feeney & Collins 2015). Brain imaging research reveals that people subjected to physical pain exhibit stronger reductions in the activation of neural systems supporting emotional and behavioral threat responses when they are randomly assigned to hold their spouse's hand, especially if they have a higher-quality marriage (Coan et al. 2006). Other studies demonstrate that merely viewing a photo of one's romantic partner when enduring physical pain activates brain regions linked to safety signaling, especially among those who believe their partner is highly supportive (Eisenberger et al. 2011).

Close others influence an individual's goal pursuit processes in diverse ways. For example, when the opportunity arises, people tend to outsource their goal-related activities to their significant others, which may reduce the effort they exert when pursuing their goals (Fitzsimons & Finkel 2011), and they draw closer to those who help them achieve their high-priority goals (Fitzsimons & Shah 2008). As noted in the section Integration, above, the degree to which goal interdependence bolsters or undermines an individual's goal success is partially determined by how effectively partners can coordinate, such as by pooling and efficiently allocating their goal-relevant resources across the many goals that both partners possess (Fitzsimons et al. 2015). When things go well, partners not only achieve better goal-related outcomes on a daily basis but also move toward their ideal selves across time (Rusbult et al. 2009).

Close others also play a major role in existential outcomes. Perhaps the most remarkable evidence of this is that both marital status (married versus single) and marital quality (higher versus lower) predict lower morbidity and mortality rates (Holt-Lunstad et al. 2010, Robles et al. 2014).

Standards. *People bring certain standards to their relationships and tend to experience greater relationship wellbeing when their relationships exceed these standards.*

A third tendency that people bring to relationships is their personal standards, a construct that assumes a prominent role in many relationship theories. Thibaut & Kelley (1959) express this idea in their concept of comparison level (CL), which refers to individuals' overall assessments of the outcomes they believe they deserve in a particular relationship. According to interdependence theory (Kelley & Thibaut 1978, Thibaut & Kelley 1959) and its offshoots (Rusbult 1983), people are more satisfied with a relationship when the outcomes (rewards minus costs) it provides exceed their CL.

Many domain-specific relationship theories also focus on standards or on similar concepts, such as expectations, ideals, or preferences. For example, the triangular theory of love posits that greater relationship quality is indexed by smaller discrepancies between an individual's ideal level of each component of love (intimacy, passion, commitment) and the actual amount of love that he or she experiences in each component (Sternberg 1986). The ideal standards model (Simpson et al. 2001) claims that individuals should experience higher relationship quality when they perceive greater alignment between their ideals for particular traits in a romantic partner (warmth/loyalty, vitality/attractiveness, and status/resources) and their partner's actual traits. The suffocation model (Finkel et al. 2014a,b) suggests that people have varied historically in the degree to which they expect their spouses to fulfill needs that are low (e.g., safety) versus high (e.g., self-actualization) in Maslow's hierarchy of needs; the extent to which their relationships meet these expectations is theorized to predict marital quality more strongly for higher-level than lower-level needs.

High standards bode poorly for relationship wellbeing when they are unattainable (McNulty 2016a,b); people tend to be less happy when their actual partners and relationships do not fulfill their lofty standards. Conversely, high standards bode well for relationship wellbeing when such standards motivate individuals to engage in behaviors that improve relationship outcomes, such as when molding a less-than-ideal partner into an ideal one (Murray et al. 1996). Although high standards often motivate prorelationship cognitions and behaviors in people who have strong relationship skills, they also produce disappointment in those with poor relationship skills (McNulty & Karney 2004).

People sometimes deviate from strict veridicality when comparing their standards with reality. For example, people who are in a relationship characterized by aggression but nonetheless remain committed to the relationship adopt more tolerant standards for partner aggression (Arriaga et al. 2016). In addition, an individual's ideal partner preferences change over time to match the desirable qualities possessed by his or her current partner (Fletcher et al. 2000a,b; Neff & Karney 2003). People also have difficulty comparing, on a trait-by-trait basis, the concrete features of a flesh-and-blood partner with their abstract standards. Consequently, the match between ideals and a partner's traits is typically irrelevant to relationship outcomes if ideals are measured on single traits (e.g., attractiveness) isolated from the partner's complete suite of traits (Eastwick et al. 2014a,b).

Set 4: How Does the Context Affect Relationships?

Consistent with classic person × situation models (e.g., Lewin 1936), the close relationships literature complements its analysis of the tendencies that people bring to their relationships with an analysis of the situational and contextual factors that influence relationship processes and outcomes (McNulty 2016a,b). Set 4 includes four core principles, which range from the micro to the macro level of analysis. These principles address how and why partners navigate situations in which their interests diverge (the diagnosticity principle), how they respond to appealing alternatives (the alternatives principle), how stressors affect relationship dynamics (the stress principle), and how the broader social network and culture influence relationship dynamics (the culture principle).

Diagnosticity. *Situations vary in the extent to which they afford opportunities to evaluate a partner's true goals and motives regarding the relationship.*

Some situations provide better opportunities than others for revealing a partner's relationship-relevant goals and motives. For example, an individual's behavior in noncorrespondent situations such as strain tests—in which a good outcome for one partner produces a bad outcome for the other partner—can reveal his or her relationship goals, motives, and orientations more clearly than does his or her behavior in correspondent situations (Holmes 1981, 2002; Kelley & Thibaut 1978). If John agrees to quit his dream job and leave his friends and family so Alice can pursue her dream job in a faraway city, his willingness to make these sacrifices reveals how much he cares about her and is committed to their relationship. Alice's ability to make relatively unambiguous attributions about John's motives would have been diminished if the situation were more correspondent, as would be the case if he disliked his current job and did not have close social ties where they were living. Because highly noncorrespondent situations allow individuals to demonstrate their willingness to make significant sacrifices for their partner and relationship, such prorelationship behavior from one partner tends to promote the other partner's trust (Shallcross & Simpson 2012, Wieselquist et al. 1999), among other relationship benefits (Simpson 2007).

Diagnostic situations are central to several theories in relationship science. According to interdependence theory (Holmes 1981, 2002; Rusbult & Van Lange 2003), when relationship partners find themselves in noncorrespondent situations such as strain tests, the partner being asked to make a sacrifice must try to set aside his or her personal desires and transform his or her motivation to do what is best for the partner and relationship. He or she must then coordinate plans and actions with his or her partner to help achieve the partner's important goals. This explains why strain tests in particular are such powerfully diagnostic situations: They leave little attributional ambiguity regarding the extent and nature of the sacrificing partner's transformation of motivation. But if partners fail strain tests because they do not engage in prorelationship transformation of motivation, relationships run the risk of becoming unstable (Rusbult et al. 2001).

Diagnosticity is also a key element of both the risk regulation model (Murray et al. 2006) and the mutual responsiveness model (Murray & Holmes 2009). Individuals are typically motivated to connect emotionally with their partners while protecting the self from excessive vulnerability. Compared to correspondent situations, noncorrespondent situations highlight the fundamental conflict between (*a*) seeking connection and allowing the self to be vulnerable and (*b*) protecting the self and avoiding potential rejection. This is a basic conflict that both partners must struggle to resolve because relationships cannot fully develop unless the two of them are willing to take leaps of faith (Murray et al. 2006) and reciprocally disclose intimate information (Reis & Shaver 1988), actions that make them vulnerable to possible exploitation (Cavallo et al. 2009).

Alternatives. *The presence of attractive alternatives to a current relationship—including the option of not being in a relationship at all—threatens relationship quality and persistence.*

The existence and extent of options that make it desirable for an individual to leave an existing relationship play a vital role in interdependence theory (Kelley & Thibaut 1978, Thibaut & Kelley 1959) and the investment model (Rusbult 1983). Specifically, the comparison level for alternatives (CL_{Alt}) concept reflects the outcomes that individuals would experience in their best alternative to being in the current relationship, including being single. Interdependence theorists hypothesize that relationship stability is more closely aligned with CL_{Alt} (the extent to which a person can achieve better outcomes in another relationship) than with CL (the extent to which a person's current relationship outcomes exceed his or her standards). That is, CL_{Alt} determines the extent to which a person is dependent on his or her partner to achieve his or her needs, goals, and other desirable outcomes.

Most CL_{Alt} studies have emphasized individuals' subjective (rather than objective) perceptions of the degree to which current alternatives are appealing. Research has shown, for example, that the better people perceive their alternatives to be, the more likely their relationships are to dissolve (Le et al. 2010). Research has also tested this association using experimental manipulations: When participants are randomly assigned to believe that their own sex is in the numerical minority (versus majority), they report lower relationship quality with their current partners, presumably because the abundance of opposite-sex people suggests that better options may be available (Kim 2013).

Most relationship models characterize desirable alternatives as threats that individuals should be motivated to ignore, downplay, or derogate to mitigate negative effects on their relationships (Durante et al. 2016, Lydon & Karremans 2015). This process is evident in controlled, conscious responses to attractive alternatives, such as the explicit evaluation of the desirability of opposite-sex alternative partners (Johnson & Rusbult 1989, Simpson et al. 1990). However, it is also evident in automatic, spontaneous responses, such as the amount of time individuals spend looking at attractive alternatives (Maner et al. 2009, Miller 1997) or displaying affiliative nonverbal behaviors in response to them (Karremans & Verwijmeren 2008).

Some theoretical analyses linked to these findings adopt an evolutionary perspective. Pairbonds most likely evolved in humans because such relationships offer adaptive benefits for offspring (Eastwick 2009). However, it takes considerable time and energy to cultivate a strong pair-bond, which suggests that the derogation process may be an evolved adaptation that motivates committed romantic partners to train their attention on each other to preserve the existing pair-bonded relationship (Maner et al. 2008). The process of derogating desirable alternatives is also consistent with cognitive dissonance perspectives: Once people have made a difficult-to-reverse choice (e.g., committing to a partner), they become motivated to perceive nonchosen alternatives as less desirable (Brehm 1956).

However, in some cases, people can sustain committed relationships while also pursuing sexual, even loving, relationships with other partners, as in the case of polyamory, a relationship structure in which individuals have "consensual loving and romantic relationships with more than one partner" (Conley et al. 2012, p. 126). In fact, polyamorous relationships may be stable precisely because people do not construe their additional sexual partners as true alternatives that would replace a current partner.

Stress. *High demands external to the relationship predict worse relationship outcomes, especially if the demands exceed the two partners' (individual or combined) resources for coping.*

Beyond the immediate situation and romantic alternatives, external factors, especially stressors, can also affect relationship functioning. It is difficult to sustain a high-quality relationship when confronting acute or chronic stress external to the relationship (Karney & Bradbury 1995). A broad spectrum of stressors—including job loss, financial strain, incarceration, chronic illness, infertility, and natural disasters—predicts myriad adverse relationship outcomes, including low satisfaction and breakup (Karney & Neff 2015, Randall & Bodenmann 2009).

Research has shown that some couples manage stress better than others. One major factor in explaining this variation is the level of coping-relevant resources (Hill 1949, McCubbin & Patterson 1983). According to stress buffering perspectives (Cohen & Wills 1985), the adverse effects of stressors are especially strong if such resources are low, as is the case when the couple lacks sufficient money or when one or both partners feel psychologically depleted due to work-related stress. However, among couples who have good problem-solving skills, navigating moderate levels of stress early on strengthens the relationship over time, as long as they responded to those stressors effectively (Neff & Broady 2011).

The most influential framework for conceptualizing the impact of stress on relationship functioning is Karney & Bradbury's (1995) vulnerability-stress-adaptation model, which emphasizes the role of interpersonal processes in mediating the effects of stress and resources on relationship outcomes. According to this model, stress exerts its adverse influence on relationship processes and outcomes via two routes (Karney & Neff 2015). First, stress alters how much time partners have for each other and how they use that time. Partners who encounter high levels of stress have less time to engage in tasks that might increase emotional or physical intimacy, and they use more of their winnowed time dealing with stressful, challenging situations (Neff & Karney 2009). Second, stress depletes the self-regulatory resources that partners need to respond constructively to relationship challenges (Repetti 1989). Partners whose self-regulatory resources have been depleted are especially prone to retaliation in response to provocation (Finkel et al. 2009), and the subjective experience of self-regulatory depletion mediates the association of stress with both negative marital behaviors and diminished marital satisfaction (Buck & Neff 2012). These effects are particularly strong when individuals are tempted to lash out at their partners but are smaller or nonexistent in the absence of such temptation (Finkel et al. 2012).

Culture. *Relationships are embedded in social networks and a cultural milieu—including norms, practices, and traditions—that shape the nature and trajectory of those relationships.*

As we broaden the contextual lens to consider cultural and subcultural effects on relationships, we turn to social ecological models, which posit that environmental contexts have nested layers (e.g., Bronfenbrenner 1986). More specifically, individuals live within social networks of friends and family whose approval or disapproval of a given relationship might affect its trajectory. These social networks are themselves embedded in cultural contexts consisting of norms, values, and scripts, and relationships are also shaped by these socially shared constructs. Finally, cultures are embedded in national and historical contexts that can cause relationships to differ across time and place.

At the level of the social network, approval from friends and family members predicts greater relationship satisfaction and stability (Felmlee 2001). In some cases, friends and family members may engage in specific behaviors that help a relationship flourish or flounder; in other cases, simply hearing a loved one's positive reaction about one's current partner can reduce uncertainty and increase the likelihood of investing more in the relationship (Sprecher 2011).

People also share knowledge about sexual scripts and norms within the local culture, which subsequently guide behavior (Simon & Gagnon 2003). Fraternity membership, for example, predicts the extent to which sexual activity is part of the script that undergraduates use when describing a typical date (Bartoli & Clark 2006), and norms about appropriate sexual behaviors vary as a function of regional levels of education and religiosity (Laumann et al. 1994).

Finally, relationships can be influenced by the national and historical context. For example, the degree to which individuals are willing to engage in casual sexual activity is linked to national indicators such as the rate of infectious diseases and women's economic power (Schaller & Murray 2008, Schmitt et al. 2005). People in the United States expect their marriage to help them fulfill certain needs, but these needs have varied over time; Americans were especially likely to prioritize needs like safety and food production circa 1800, needs like intimacy and sexual fulfillment circa 1900, and needs like self-discovery and self-expression circa 2000 (Finkel et al. 2014a). The rise of the postindustrial economy in Western cultures during the second half of the twentieth century facilitated a "grand gender convergence" (although certainly not an equalization) in men's and women's social roles (Goldin 2014), which profoundly influenced relationship dynamics, especially in marriages (Finkel et al. 2014a).

Evolutionary models of culture connect these different context levels to specific psychological processes. Transmitted cultural models, for instance, explore how and why people share beliefs, practices, and knowledge, usually emphasizing the processes of adopting, changing, and improving these products of shared culture (Richerson & Boyd 2005). As an example, college administrators frequently hold workshops that increase students' sensitivity to issues surrounding sexual consent and that change how the students engage in sexual behavior. Evoked cultural models posit that encountering a particular environmental cue that was prevalent in our ancestral past, such as the presence versus absence of a responsive caregiver (Simpson & Belsky 2016), triggers adaptive cognitive and behavioral responses. For example, environments containing more pathogens may trigger preferences for romantic partners who carry genes associated with better health (Gangestad et al. 2006). These two forms of culture may influence psychological functioning in tandem or independently (Eastwick 2013).

COMBINING THE PRINCIPLES TO REFINE OR DEVELOP THEORIES

Scholars can use these 14 core principles from the psychological literature on relationships (see **Figure 1** and **Table 1**) to clarify and refine existing theories and perhaps generate new ones. Using the metaphoric terminology of the culinary approach, the cook (the theorist) can canvas the pantry (the collection of principles) for particular ingredients (specific principles), prepare the recipe (select and arrange the ingredients), and then cook the dish (develop the theory).

Refining Existing Theories

To refine an existing theory, theorists might first map each of the 14 principles onto a theory, retaining the principles that overlap or fit with this theory and setting aside those that do not. Theorists can then determine whether the addition of one or more of the extra principles—those that were not part of the original theory—might broaden the explanatory power of the theory enough to offset the additional complexity that comes with including more principles.

We illustrate this process using transactive goal dynamics theory (Finkel et al. 2016, Fitzsimons et al. 2015). We focus on this theory because we are familiar with it and because it was developed within the past few years, which means that there are few published articulations of the core principles. Transactive goal dynamics theory contains elements of integration (Principle 2), evaluation (Principle 4), responsiveness (Principle 5), predisposition (Principle 8), instrumentality (Principle 9), and alternatives (Principle 12). Specifically, it proposes that: (*a*) relationship partners form a shared system of goal pursuits (integration), (*b*) subjective assessments of relationship commitment predict increased merging (evaluation), (*c*) goal success is maximized when partners support each other in ways tailored to each partner's idiosyncratic goals and needs (responsiveness), (*d*) each partner has certain skills and preferences that can be leveraged for optimal goal functioning at the dyadic level (predisposition), (*e*) partners influence each other's degree of goal success (instrumentality), and (*f*) the relationship is more likely to continue if it results in goal success that exceeds what the two partners would otherwise experience (alternatives). In short, we can formulate much of the content of transactive goal dynamics theory with just these six ingredients.

As with most theories, transactive goal dynamics theory also contains important elements that do not rise to the level of a core principle. For example, one tenet of the theory is that stronger goal interdependence in a relationship should predict poorer goal-related recovery following a breakup. Such idiosyncratic elements are crucial in defining the unique terrain that a given theory seeks to address.

Transactive goal dynamics theory, however, leaves eight core principles unused. Thus, a scholar seeking to refine or expand the theory might consider whether adding any additional principles might benefit or improve the theory enough to offset the complexity of doing so, or whether incorporating additional principles might generate novel hypotheses. For example, transactive goal dynamics theory is not a theory of goal content; it primarily takes the two partners' goals as a given rather than investigating how or why they adopted these particular goals. By adding the perspective of culture (Principle 14), a theorist might wonder whether the goal contents that people bring to their relationships—for example, the desired level or type of interdependence in the relationship—differ in important ways across cultural or historical contexts and whether such variation has implications for relationship quality and longevity. This analysis might lead to the novel hypothesis that emotional responsiveness is more important for such outcomes in the twenty-first century United States than in Jane Austen's England (Light & Fitzsimons 2014).

Generating New Theories

Other scholars might want to use the principles not to refine or expand an existing theory but to guide theory development in a bottom-up manner. Although this process can begin in various ways (e.g., one might start with observations about relationship dynamics in the surrounding world), it is likely to entail a systematic consideration of whether each of the principles can inform thinking, which would lead to the generation of new insights and hypotheses. For example, a scholar might wish to develop a new theoretical perspective on the circumstances under which sexual intercourse draws partners closer together versus pushes them apart. Merely looking at the list of core principles will not yield a new theoretical perspective, but it might be a productive first step. A scholar can consider whether each principle is likely to yield a deeper, better, or more nuanced understanding of a topic and can then explore how the most relevant principles interrelate in theoretically interesting ways. To facilitate this process, he or she might generate a path diagram that specifies precisely how the variables should interrelate, including processes such as mediation, moderation, and feedback loops. Because the principles are cast at a relatively high level of abstraction, they can be exported readily to different research domains. For example, the researcher might find it easier to apply two or three principles—rather than an entire theory of relationships—to an existing evolutionary perspective on how sex affects relationship partners.

OPTIMIZING RELATIONSHIP SCIENCE: THEORETICAL COHESION VERSUS CONFLICT

What has this exercise taught us? Among other things, we have learned that there are few instances in which a notable principle used in one theory clearly conflicts with a notable principle used in another.[4] Many relationship scientists recall interdependence theorists whispering the objection

---

[4]One reason for this cohesion may be the abstract nature of the 14 principles. When different theories operationalize, test, and combine constructs associated with specific principles in novel ways, they may generate different or competing predictions. For example, although scholars agree that the principle of standards (Principle 10) matters, there is debate about the circumstances under which standards influence relationship outcomes (Eastwick et al. 2014a,b; Schmitt 2014). There could also be conflict

that attachment theory is too focused on individual differences. However, as attachment theory complemented research on individual differences with research on normative attachment processes (Mikulincer & Shaver 2007), the whispers dissipated. Many currently prominent relationship models derive specific hypotheses on the basis of ideas borrowed from different theories. When developing the risk regulation model, for example, Murray and colleagues (2006) extracted several key features of interdependence theory and attachment theory, combined them in novel ways, and added new theoretical components to generate an important process model that tied together several major ideas in the field.

In many ways, such strong theoretical cohesion is marvelous. Although relationship scientists have many theories and models that address distinct relationship processes, we appear to have something approximating a consensual theoretical paradigm. This paradigm, which encompasses the 14 principles reviewed above, is compelling and generative. Recent edited volumes (e.g., Simpson & Campbell 2013) and journal special issues (e.g., Finkel & Simpson 2015) indicate that relationship science is thriving.

However, there are also downsides to having such a cohesive discipline. Science often benefits from competition between conflicting ideas. Although it is pleasant to work in an environment characterized by consensus, it sometimes takes friction to generate forward motion. We believe that the current theoretical paradigms in relationship science are excellent, but the field might benefit from some theoretical conflicts—alternative accounts that might sharpen and hone one another. For example, our field could explore whether the dominant view that people are best served by being in a secure relationship with a romantic partner is misguided, at least under some circumstances, such as when close friends provide a better option (DePaulo & Morris 2005). We could also reexamine the widespread, albeit implicit, assumption that relationship stability is a good outcome (with abusive relationships being one exception) and breakups are a bad outcome. Perhaps we could challenge this dominant view by examining the circumstances under which people are best served by leaving their relationship or seeking to trade up for a partner who is more compatible. Revisiting broad questions and assumptions such as these accentuates the fact that many relationship scientists have focused quite heavily on the life cycle of one relationship rather than the multiple relationships that many people develop throughout their lives.

Evolutionary psychology, for example, potentially poses some serious challenges to certain theories and models in relationship science, particularly in the realm of mate selection. The evolutionary psychology of human mating adopts foundational assumptions that differ from many of those in relationship science (Durante et al. 2016, Eastwick 2016). In particular, evolutionary perspectives highlight not only the adaptive value of strong pair-bonds but also the potential adaptive value of behaviors such as sexual infidelity, trading up, and stalking (Buss & Shackelford 1997). If a scholar extracted the core principles in the evolutionary psychological literature on mating, one of these principles might be that people evolved to seek opportunistic copulations outside of long-term, committed relationships. The hypotheses that follow from this principle seem to fundamentally conflict with hypotheses that follow from the maintenance principle discussed above (Durante et al. 2016). If ancestral humans enjoyed a survival advantage from such relationship-destructive behaviors, how can relationship scientists reconcile this with the field's strong emphasis on the benefits—including the survival benefits—of exclusive romantic relationships (Holt-Lunstad et al. 2010, Robles et al. 2014)? And if humans are best served by having

---

at the level of abstraction of the 14 principles, but our extensive literature review unearthed minimal evidence of any such conflict within relationship science.

accurate insights about their partner's romantic attraction to others so that they can guard against mate poaching, why do they shield themselves from the truth precisely in those circumstances when the threat of one's partner's extrarelationship temptation is strongest (Johnson & Rusbult 1989, Simpson et al. 1995)?

By posing these and other questions, evolutionary psychology directly challenges some of the foundational assumptions and principles in relationship science. If those assumptions and principles withstand the challenge, the current relationship science paradigm will be solidified. If they do not, it will need to be altered. Regardless of the outcome, our discipline will benefit.

CONCLUSION

Relationship science has come a long way in a relatively short period of time. It has become a rich discipline characterized by strong theories and highly generative research paradigms. According to our analysis, the field has 14 core principles that address what a relationship is, how relationships operate, what tendencies people bring to their relationships, and how contextual factors affect relationship processes and outcomes. At present, the major theories in our field largely align and rarely conflict.

As we look to the future, it will be interesting to see whether various theories gradually merge into a single, unified theory of relationships or whether some major disagreements will enter mainstream relationship science. As the field continues to mature, it is likely to benefit from simultaneous trends toward greater theoretical unification on the one hand and greater theoretical disagreement on the other. Such trends should refine, deepen, and extend our understanding of how and why relationships function as they do in daily life, potentially providing clinicians and policymakers with more effective tools for helping people achieve deeper and more fulfilling relationships.

SUMMARY POINTS

1. This review presents the first attempt to discern the core principles that cut across the major theories in relationship science, especially the theories within psychology.

2. This review of the major theories used a novel procedure called the culinary approach, which seeks to extract the core principles (the basic theoretical building blocks or ingredients) from a given discipline and address how theorists can use them to refine existing theories or develop new theories.

3. Applying the extraction process to relationship science revealed 14 core principles, which help to answer four basic questions in the literature: (*a*) What is a relationship? (*b*) How do relationships operate? (*c*) What tendencies do people bring to their relationships? (*d*) How does the context affect relationships?

4. The literature review revealed a cohesive discipline with few notable conflicts among the core theoretical principles.

5. We suggest that relationship science would benefit from both (*a*) greater recognition of the principle-level overlap or redundancy across theories and (*b*) greater effort to adopt novel perspectives on relationship dynamics, ideally perspectives that raise important challenges to the dominant paradigm.

DISCLOSURE STATEMENT

The authors are not aware of any affiliations, memberships, funding, or financial holdings that might be perceived as affecting the objectivity of this review.

ACKNOWLEDGMENTS

The authors, who contributed equally to this review, thank Galen Bodenhausen, Jim McNulty, and Nickola Overall for their insightful feedback on a previous draft, as well as the 16 leading relationship scientists who provided constructive feedback on an early outline of this paper.

LITERATURE CITED

Agnew CR, Van Lange PA, Rusbult CE, Langston CA. 1998. Cognitive interdependence: commitment and the mental representation of close relationships. *J. Personal. Soc. Psychol.* 74:939–54

Altman I, Taylor DA. 1973. *Social Penetration: The Development of Interpersonal Relationships.* New York: Holt, Rinehart and Winston

Andersen SM, Chen S. 2002. The relational self: an interpersonal social-cognitive theory. *Psychol. Rev.* 109:619–45

Aron A, Lewandowski GW Jr., Mashek D, Aron EN. 2013. The self-expansion model of motivation and cognition in close relationships. See Simpson & Campbell 2013, pp. 90–115

Aron A, Norman CC, Aron EN, McKenna C, Heyman RE. 2000. Couples' shared participation in novel and arousing activities and experienced relationship quality. *J. Personal. Soc. Psychol.* 78:273–84

Arriaga XB, Capezza NM, Daly CA. 2016. Personal standards for judging aggression by a relationship partner: How much aggression is too much? *J. Personal. Soc. Psychol.* 110:36–54

Banse R, Kowalick C. 2007. Implicit attitudes towards romantic partners predict well-being in stressful life conditions: evidence from the antenatal maternity ward. *Int. J. Psychol.* 42:149–57

Bartoli AM, Clark MD. 2006. The dating game: similarities and differences in dating scripts among college students. *Sex. Cult.* 10:54–80

Baumeister RF, Leary MR. 1995. The need to belong: desire for interpersonal attachments as a fundamental human motivation. *Psychol. Bull.* 117:497–529

Beckes L, Coan JA. 2011. Social baseline theory: the role of social proximity in emotion and economy of action. *Soc. Personal. Psychol. Compass* 5:976–88

Berscheid E. 1999. The greening of relationship science. *Am. Psychol.* 54:260–66

Berscheid E, Regan P. 2005. *The Psychology of Interpersonal Relationships.* New York: Prentice-Hall

Bowlby J. 1969. *Attachment and Loss*, Vol. 1: *Attachment.* New York: Basic Books

Bowlby J. 1973. *Attachment and Loss*, Vol. 2: *Separation: Anxiety and Anger.* New York: Basic Books

Bowlby J. 1980. *Attachment and Loss*, Vol. 3: *Loss.* New York: Basic Books

Bradbury TN, Fincham FD. 1990. Attributions in marriage. Review and critique. *Psychol. Bull.* 107:3–33

Brehm JW. 1956. Postdecision changes in the desirability of alternatives. *J. Abnorm. Soc. Psychol.* 52:384–89

Bretherton I, Munholland KA. 2008. Internal working models in attachment relationships: elaborating a central construct in attachment theory. In *The Handbook of Attachment: Theory, Research, and Clinical Applications*, ed. J Cassidy, PR Shaver, pp. 102–27. New York: Guilford

Bronfenbrenner U. 1986. Ecology of the family as a context for human development: research perspectives. *Dev. Psychol.* 22:723–42

Buck AA, Neff LA. 2012. Stress spillover in early marriage: the role of self-regulatory depletion. *J. Fam. Psychol.* 26:698–708

Buss DM. 2008. *The Evolution of Desire: Strategies of Human Mating.* New York: Basic Books. 2nd ed.

Buss DM, Shackelford TK. 1997. From vigilance to violence: mate retention tactics in married couples. *J. Personal. Soc. Psychol.* 72:346–61

Campbell L, Simpson A. 2013. The blossoming of relationship science. See Simpson & Campbell 2013, pp. 3–10

Cavallo J, Fitzsimons GM, Holmes JG. 2009. Taking chances in the face of threat: romantic risk regulation and approach motivation. *Personal. Soc. Psychol. Bull.* 35:737–51

Clark MS, Lemay EP. 2010. Close relationships. In *Handbook of Social Psychology*, ed. ST Fiske, DT Gilbert, G Lindzey, pp. 898–940. New York: Wiley

Clark MS, Mills J. 1979. Interpersonal attraction in exchange and communal relationships. *J. Personal. Soc. Psychol.* 37:12–24

Clark MS, Mills JR. 2011. A theory of communal (and exchange) relationships. *Handb. Theor. Soc. Psychol.* 1:232–50

Clark MS, Reis HT. 1988. Interpersonal processes in close relationships. *Annu. Rev. Psychol.* 39:609–72

Coan JA, Schaefer HS, Davidson RJ. 2006. Lending a hand: social regulation of the neural response to threat. *Psychol. Sci.* 17:1032–39

Cohen S, Wills TA. 1985. Stress, social support, and the buffering hypothesis. *Psychol. Bull.* 98:310–57

Collins NL, Feeney BC. 2004. Working models of attachment affect perceptions of social support: evidence from experimental and observational studies. *J. Personal. Soc. Psychol.* 87:363–83

Conley TD, Ziegler A, Moors AC, Matsick JL, Valentine B. 2012. A critical examination of popular assumptions about the benefits and outcomes of monogamous relationships. *Personal. Soc. Psychol. Rev.* 17:124–41

de Jong DC, Reis HT. 2015. We do it best: commitment and positive construals of sex. *J. Soc. Clin. Psychol.* 34:181–202

Debrot A, Cook WL, Perrez M, Horn AB. 2012. Deeds matter: daily enacted responsiveness and intimacy in couples' daily lives. *J. Fam. Psychol.* 26:617–27

DePaulo BM, Morris WL. 2005. Singles in society and in science. *Psychol. Inq.* 16:57–83

Drigotas SM, Rusbult CE, Verette J. 1999. Level of commitment, mutuality of commitment, and couple well-being. *Pers. Relat.* 6:389–409

Durante KM, Eastwick PW, Finkel EJ, Gangestad SM, Simpson JA. 2016. Pair-bonded relationships and romantic alternatives: toward an integration of evolutionary and relationship science perspectives. *Adv. Exp. Soc. Psychol.* 53:1–74

Eastwick PW. 2009. Beyond the Pleistocene: using phylogeny and constraint to inform the evolutionary psychology of human mating. *Psychol. Bull.* 135:794–821

Eastwick PW. 2013. Cultural influences on attraction. See Simpson & Campbell 2013, pp. 161–82

Eastwick PW. 2016. The emerging integration of close relationships research and evolutionary psychology. *Curr. Dir. Psychol. Sci.* 25:183–90

Eastwick PW, Hunt LL. 2014. Relational mate value: consensus and uniqueness in romantic evaluations. *J. Personal. Soc. Psychol.* 106:726–51

Eastwick PW, Keneski E, Morgan TA, McDonald M. 2016. *What do short-term and long-term relationships look like? Building the Relationship Coordination and Strategic Timing (ReCAST) model.* Work. Pap., Dep. Psychol., Univ. Calif. Davis. **http://papers.ssrn.com/sol3/papers.cfm?abstract_id = 2820704**

Eastwick PW, Luchies LB, Finkel EJ, Hunt LL. 2014a. The many voices of Darwin's descendants: reply to Schmitt 2014. *Psychol. Bull.* 140:673–81

Eastwick PW, Luchies LB, Finkel EJ, Hunt LL. 2014b. The predictive validity of ideal partner preferences: a review and meta-analysis. *Psychol. Bull.* 140:623–65

Eisenberger NI, Master SL, Inagaki TK, Taylor SE, Shirinyan D, et al. 2011. Attachment figures activate a safety signal-related neural region and reduce pain experience. *PNAS* 108:11721–26

Feeney BC, Collins NL. 2001. Predictors of caregiving in adult intimate relationships: an attachment theoretical perspective. *J. Personal. Soc. Psychol.* 80:972–94

Feeney BC, Collins NL. 2015. A new look at social support: a theoretical perspective on thriving through relationships. *Personal. Soc. Psychol. Rev.* 19:113–47

Felmlee DH. 2001. No couple is an island: a social network perspective on dyadic stability. *Soc. Forces* 79:1259–87

Fincham FD, Beach SRH, Davila J. 2004. Forgiveness and conflict resolution in marriage. *J. Fam. Psychol.* 18:72–81

Finkel EJ, DeWall CN, Slotter EB, McNulty JK, Pond RS Jr., Atkins DC. 2012. Using I³ theory to clarify when dispositional aggressiveness predicts intimate partner violence perpetration. *J. Personal. Soc. Psychol.* 102:533–49

Finkel EJ, DeWall CN, Slotter EB, Oaten M, Foshee VA. 2009. Self-regulatory failure and intimate partner violence perpetration. *J. Personal. Soc. Psychol.* 97:483–99

Finkel EJ, Eastwick PW. 2015. Attachment and pairbonding. *Curr. Opin. Behav. Sci.* 3:7–11

Finkel EJ, Eastwick PW, Karney BR, Reis HT, Sprecher S. 2012. Online dating: a critical analysis from the perspective of psychological science. *Psychol. Sci. Public Interest* 13:3–66

Finkel EJ, Fitzsimons GM, vanDellen MR. 2016. Self-regulation as a transactive process: reconceptualizing the unit of analysis for goal setting, pursuit, and outcomes. In *Handbook of Self-Regulation*, ed. KD Vohs, RF Baumeister, pp. 264–82. New York: Guilford. 3rd ed.

Finkel EJ, Hui CM, Carswell KL, Larson GM. 2014a. The suffocation of marriage: climbing Mount Maslow without enough oxygen. *Psychol. Inq.* 25:1–41

Finkel EJ, Larson GM, Carswell KL, Hui CM. 2014b. Marriage at the summit: response to the commentaries. *Psychol. Inq.* 25:120–45

Finkel EJ, Simpson JA, eds. 2015. Relationship science. *Curr. Opin. Psychol.* 1(Spec. Issue). Amsterdam: Elsevier

Finkel EJ, Slotter EB, Luchies LB, Walton GM, Gross JJ. 2013. A brief intervention to promote conflict-reappraisal preserves marital quality over time. *Psychol. Sci.* 24:1595–601

Fitzsimons GM, Finkel EJ. 2011. Outsourcing self-regulation. *Psychol. Sci.* 22:369–75

Fitzsimons GM, Finkel EJ, vanDellen MR. 2015. Transactive goal dynamics. *Psychol. Rev.* 122:648–73

Fitzsimons GM, Shah JY. 2008. How goal instrumentality shapes relationship evaluations. *J. Personal. Soc. Psychol.* 95:319–37

Fletcher GJ, Kerr PS. 2010. Through the eyes of love: reality and illusion in intimate relationships. *Psychol. Bull.* 136:627–58

Fletcher GJO, Simpson JA, Campbell L, Overall NC. 2015. Pair-bonding, romantic love, and evolution: the curious case of *Homo sapiens*. *Perspect. Psychol. Sci.* 10:20–36

Fletcher GJO, Simpson JA, Thomas G. 2000a. Ideals, perceptions, and evaluations in early relationship development. *J. Personal. Soc. Psychol.* 79:933–40

Fletcher GJO, Simpson JA, Thomas G. 2000b. The measurement of perceived relationship quality components: a confirmatory factor analytic approach. *Personal. Soc. Psychol. Bull.* 26:340–54

Fraley RC. 2007. A connectionist approach to the organization and continuity of working models of attachment. *J. Personal.* 75:1157–80

Gable SL, Gosnell CL, Maisel NC, Strachman A. 2012. Safely testing the alarm: close others' responses to personal positive events. *J. Personal. Soc. Psychol.* 103:963–81

Gable SL, Impett EA. 2012. Approach and avoidance motives and close relationships. *Soc. Personal. Psychol. Compass* 6:95–108

Gable SL, Reis HT. 2001. Appetitive and aversive social interaction. In *Close Romantic Relationships: Maintenance and Enhancement*, ed. JH Harvey, A Wenzel, pp. 169–94. Mahwah, NJ: Lawrence Erlbaum Assoc.

Gable SL, Reis HT. 2010. Good news! Capitalizing on positive events in an interpersonal context. *Adv. Exp. Soc. Psychol.* 42:195–257

Gagné FM, Lydon JE. 2004. Bias and accuracy in close relationships: an integrative review. *Personal. Soc. Psychol. Rev.* 8:322–38

Gangestad SW, Haselton MG, Buss DM. 2006. Evolutionary foundations of cultural variation: evoked culture and mate preferences. *Psychol. Inq.* 17:75–95

Goldin C. 2014. A grand gender convergence: its last chapter. *Am. Econ. Rev.* 104:1091–119

Gottman JM. 1998. Psychology and the study of marital processes. *Annu. Rev. Psychol.* 49:169–97

Gottman JM, Levenson RW. 1999. Rebound from marital conflict and divorce prediction. *Fam. Process.* 38:287–92

Hazan C, Shaver P. 1987. Romantic love conceptualized as an attachment process. *J. Personal. Soc. Psychol.* 52:511–24

Hazan C, Shaver PR. 1994. Attachment as an organizational framework for research on close relationships. *Psychol. Inq.* 5:1–22

Helm JL, Sbarra DA, Ferrer E. 2014. Coregulation of respiratory sinus arrhythmia in adult romantic partners. *Emotion* 14:522–31

Hill R. 1949. *Families under Stress: Adjustment to the Crises of War Separation and Reunion.* New York: Harper & Brothers

Holmes JG. 1981. The exchange process in close relationships: microbehavior and macromotives. In *The Justice Motive in Social Behavior*, ed. MJ Lerner, SC Lerner, pp. 261–84. New York: Plenum

Holmes JG. 2002. Interpersonal expectations as the building blocks of social cognition: an interdependence theory perspective. *Pers. Relat.* 9:1–26

Holmes JG, Rempel JK. 1989. Trust in close relationships. In *Review of Personality and Social Psychology*, Vol. 10, *Close Relationships*, ed. C Hendrick, pp. 187–220. Thousand Oaks, CA: Sage

Holt-Lunstad J, Smith TB, Layton JB. 2010. Social relationships and mortality risk: a meta-analytic review. *PLOS Med.* 7:e1000316

IJzerman H, Coan JA, Wagemans FM, Missler MA, Van Beest I, et al. 2015. A theory of social thermoregulation in human primates. *Front. Psychol.* 6:464

Johnson DJ, Rusbult CE. 1989. Resisting temptation: devaluation of alternative partners as a means of maintaining commitment in close relationships. *J. Personal. Soc. Psychol.* 57:967–80

Karney BR, Bradbury TN. 1995. The longitudinal course of marital quality and stability: a review of theory, method, and research. *Psychol. Bull.* 118:3–34

Karney BR, Neff LA. 2015. Couples and stress: how demands outside a relationship affect intimacy within the relationship. See Simpson & Campbell 2013, pp. 664–84

Karremans JC, Verwijmeren T. 2008. Mimicking attractive opposite-sex others: the role of romantic relationship status. *Personal. Soc. Psychol. Bull.* 34:939–50

Kelley HH. 1979. *Personal Relationships: Their Structures and Processes.* Hillsdale, NJ: Erlbaum

Kelley HH, Berscheid E, Christensen A, Harvey JH, Huston TL, et al. 1983. *Close Relationships.* New York: Freeman

Kelley HH, Holmes JG, Kerr NL, Reis HT, Rusbult CE, Van Lange PAM. 2003. *An Atlas of Interpersonal Situations.* New York: Cambridge Univ. Press

Kelley HH, Thibaut JW. 1978. *Interpersonal Relations: A Theory of Interdependence.* New York: Wiley

Kenny DA, Kashy DA. 2011. Dyadic data analysis using multilevel modeling. In *The Handbook of Advanced Multilevel Analysis*, ed. J Hox, JK Roberts, pp. 335–70. London: Taylor & Francis

Kim JS. 2013. *The influence of local sex ratio on romantic relationship maintenance processes.* PhD Thesis, Univ. Minn., Minneapolis, MN

Knapp ML, Vangelisti AL, Caughlin JP. 2014. *Interpersonal Communication and Human Relationships.* Boston: Allyn & Bacon. 7th ed.

Kurdek LA. 2004. Are gay and lesbian cohabiting couples really different from heterosexual married couples? *J. Marriage Fam.* 66:880–900

Kurdek LA. 2005. What do we know about gay and lesbian couples? *Curr. Dir. Psychol. Sci.* 14:251–54

La Guardia JG, Ryan RM, Couchman CE, Deci EL. 2000. Within-person variation in security of attachment: a self-determination theory perspective on attachment, need fulfillment, and well-being. *Personal. Soc. Psychol.* 79:367–84

Lakey B, Orehek E. 2011. Relational regulation theory: a new approach to explain the link between perceived social support and mental health. *Psychol. Rev.* 118:482–95

Laumann EO, Gagnon J, Michael R, Michaels S. 1994. *The Social Organization of Sexuality: Sexual Practices in the United States.* Chicago: Univ. Chicago Press

Laurenceau J-P, Feldman Barrett LA, Pietromonaco PR. 1998. Intimacy as an interpersonal process: the importance of self-disclosure and perceived partner responsiveness in interpersonal exchanges. *J. Personal. Soc. Psychol.* 74:1238–51

Lavner JA, Bradbury TN, Karney BR. 2012. Incremental change or initial differences? Testing two models of marital deterioration. *J. Fam. Psychol.* 26:606–16

Le B, Agnew CR. 2003. Commitment and its theorized determinants: a meta-analysis of the investment model. *Pers. Relat.* 17:37–57

Le B, Dove NL, Agnew CR, Korn MS, Mutso AA. 2010. Predicting nonmarital romantic relationship dissolution: a meta-analytic synthesis. *Pers. Relat.* 17:377–90

Lemay EP Jr., Dudley KL. 2011. Caution: fragile! Regulating the interpersonal security of chronically insecure partners. *J. Personal. Soc. Psychol.* 100:681–702

Levinger G, Snoek JD. 1972. *Attraction in Relationship: A New Look at Interpersonal Attraction*. Morristown, NJ: Gen. Learn. Press

Lewin K. 1936. *Principles of Topological Psychology*. New York: McGraw-Hill

Light AE, Fitzsimons GM. 2014. Contextualizing marriage as a means and a goal. *Psychol. Inq.* 25:88–94

Loving TJ, Gleason MEJ, Pope MT. 2009. Transition novelty moderates daters' cortisol responses when talking about marriage. *Pers. Relat.* 16:187–203

Luchies LB, Finkel EJ, McNulty JK, Kumashiro M. 2010. The doormat effect: when forgiving erodes self-respect and self-concept clarity. *J. Personal. Soc. Psychol.* 98:734–49

Luchies LB, Wieselquist J, Rusbult CE, Kumashiro M, Eastwick PW. 2013. Trust and biased memory of transgressions in romantic relationships. *J. Personal. Soc. Psychol.* 104:673–94

Lydon JE, Karremans JC. 2015. Relationship regulation in the face of eye candy: a motivated cognition framework for understanding responses to attractive alternatives. *Curr. Opin. Psychol.* 1:76–80

Maner JK, Gailliot MT, Miller SL. 2009. The implicit cognition of relationship maintenance: inattention to attractive alternatives. *J. Exp. Soc. Psychol.* 45:174–79

Maner JK, Rouby DA, Gonzaga GC. 2008. Automatic inattention to attractive alternatives: the evolved psychology of relationship maintenance. *Evol. Hum. Behav.* 29:343–49

Marshall E, Simpson JA, Rholes WS. 2015. Personality, communication, and depressive symptoms across the transition to parenthood: a dyadic longitudinal investigation. *Eur. J. Personal.* 29:216–34

Mashek DJ, Aron A, Boncimino M. 2003. Confusions of self with close others. *Personal. Soc. Psychol. Bull.* 29:382–92

McCubbin HI, Patterson JM. 1983. Family transitions: adaptation to stress. In *Stress and the Family: Coping with Normative Transitions*, Vol. 1, ed. HI McCubbin, CR Figley, pp. 5–25. New York: Brunner-Mazel

McNulty JK. 2008. Forgiveness in marriage: putting the benefits into context. *J. Fam. Psychol.* 22:171–75

McNulty JK. 2013. Personality and relationships. See Simpson & Campbell 2013, pp. 535–52

McNulty JK. 2016a. Highlighting the contextual nature of interpersonal relationships. *Adv. Exp. Soc. Psychol.* 54:247–315

McNulty JK. 2016b. Should spouses be demanding less from marriage? A contextual perspective on the implications of interpersonal standards. *Personal. Soc. Psychol. Bull.* 42:444–57

McNulty JK, Karney BR. 2004. Positive expectations in the early years of marriage: Should couples expect the best or brace for the worst? *J. Personal. Soc. Psychol.* 86:729–43

McNulty JK, Olson MA, Meltzer AL, Shaffer MJ. 2013. Though they may be unaware, newlyweds implicitly know whether their marriage will be satisfying. *Science* 342:1119–20

Mikulincer M, Shaver PR. 2007. *Attachment in Adulthood: Structure, Dynamics, and Change*. New York: Guilford Press

Miller RS. 1997. Inattentive and contented: relationship commitment and attention to alternatives. *J. Personal. Soc. Psychol.* 73:758–66

Miller SL, Maner JK. 2010. Evolution and relationship maintenance: Fertility cues lead committed men to devalue relationship alternatives. *J. Exp. Soc. Psychol.* 46:1081–84

Murray SL, Gomillion S, Holmes JG, Harris B, Lamarche V. 2013. The dynamics of relationship promotion: controlling the automatic inclination to trust. *J. Personal. Soc. Psychol.* 104:305–34

Murray SL, Griffin DW, Derrick JL, Harris B, Aloni M, Leder S. 2011. Tempting fate or inviting happiness? Unrealistic idealization prevents the decline of marital satisfaction. *Psychol. Sci.* 22:619–26

Murray SL, Holmes J. 2009. The architecture of interdependent minds: a motivation-management theory of mutual responsiveness. *Psychol. Rev.* 116:908–28

Murray SL, Holmes JG, Collins NL. 2006. Optimizing assurance: the risk regulation system in relationships. *Psychol. Bull.* 132:641–66

Murray SL, Holmes JG, Griffin DW. 1996. The self-fulfilling nature of positive illusions in romantic relationships: Love is not blind, but prescient. *J. Personal. Soc. Psychol.* 71:1155–80

Neff LA, Broady EF. 2011. Stress resilience in early marriage: Can practice make perfect? *J. Personal. Soc. Psychol.* 101:1050–67

Neff LA, Karney BR. 2003. The dynamic structure of relationship perceptions: differential importance as a strategy of relationship maintenance. *Personal. Soc. Psychol. Bull.* 29:1433–46

Neff LA, Karney BR. 2009. Stress and reactivity to daily relationship experiences: how stress hinders adaptive processes in marriage. *J. Personal. Soc. Psychol.* 97:435–50

Otto AK, Laurenceau JP, Siegel SD, Belcher AJ. 2015. Capitalizing on everyday positive events uniquely predicts daily intimacy and well-being in couples coping with breast cancer. *J. Personal. Soc. Psychol.* 29:69–79

Overall NC, Fletcher GJO, Simpson JA, Sibley CG. 2009. Regulating partners in intimate relationships: the costs and benefits of different communication strategies. *J. Personal. Soc. Psychol.* 96:620–39

Overall NC, McNulty JK. 2017. What type of communication during conflict is beneficial for intimate relationships? *Curr. Opin. Psychol.* 13:1–5

Pierce T, Lydon JE. 2001. Global and specific relational models in the experience of social interactions. *J. Personal. Soc. Psychol.* 80:613–31

Randall AK, Bodenmann G. 2009. The role of stress on close relationships and marital satisfaction. *Clin. Psychol. Rev.* 29:105–15

Reis HT. 2007. Steps toward the ripening of relationship science. *Pers. Relat.* 14:1–23

Reis HT, Clark MS. 2013. Responsiveness. See Simpson & Campbell 2013, pp. 400–23

Reis HT, Shaver PR. 1988. Intimacy as an interpersonal process. In *Handbook of Personal Relationships: Theory, Research, and Interventions*, ed. S Duck, pp. 367–89. Chichester: Wiley

Repetti RL. 1989. Effects of daily workload on subsequent behavior during marital interaction: the roles of social withdrawal and spouse support. *J. Personal. Soc. Psychol.* 57:651–59

Rholes WS, Simpson JA, Kohn JL, Wilson CL, Martin AM, et al. 2011. Attachment orientations and depression: a longitudinal study of new parents. *J. Personal. Soc. Psychol.* 100:567–86

Richerson PJ, Boyd R. 2005. *Not by Genes Alone: How Culture Transformed Human Evolution*. Chicago: Univ. Chicago Press

Robles TF, Slatcher RB, Trombello JM, McGinn MM. 2014. Marital quality and health: a meta-analytic review. *Psychol. Bull.* 140:140–87

Rubin H, Campbell L. 2012. Day-to-day changes in intimacy predict heightened relationship passion, sexual occurrence, and sexual satisfaction: a dyadic diary analysis. *Soc. Psychol. Personal. Sci.* 3:224–31

Rusbult CE. 1983. A longitudinal test of the investment model: the development (and deterioration) of satisfaction and commitment in heterosexual involvements. *J. Personal. Soc. Psychol.* 45:101–17

Rusbult CE, Finkel EJ, Kumashiro M. 2009. The Michelangelo phenomenon. *Curr. Dir. Psychol. Sci.* 18:305–9

Rusbult CE, Olsen N, Davis JL, Hannon P. 2001. Commitment and relationship maintenance mechanisms. In *Close Romantic Relationships: Maintenance and Enhancement*, ed. JH Harvey, A Wenzel, pp. 87–113. Mahwah, NJ: Erlbaum

Rusbult CE, Van Lange P. 2003. Interdependence, interaction, and relationships. *Annu. Rev. Psychol.* 54:351–75

Rusbult CE, Van Lange PA, Wildschut T, Yovetich NA, Verette J. 2000. Perceived superiority in close relationships: why it exists and persists. *J. Personal. Soc. Psychol.* 79:521–45

Rusbult CE, Zembrodt IM, Gunn LK. 1982. Exit, voice, loyalty and neglect: responses to dissatisfaction in romantic involvements. *J. Personal. Soc. Psychol.* 43:1230–42

Sbarra DA, Hazan C. 2008. Coregulation, dysregulation, self-regulation: an integrative analysis and empirical agenda for understanding adult attachment, separation, loss, and recovery. *Personal. Soc. Psychol. Rev.* 12:141–67

Schaller M, Murray DR. 2008. Pathogens, personality, and culture: Disease prevalence predicts worldwide variability in sociosexuality, extraversion, and openness to experience. *J. Personal. Soc. Psychol.* 95:212–21

Schmitt DP. 2014. On the proper functions of human mate preference adaptations: comment on Eastwick, Luchies, Finkel, and Hunt 2014. *Psychol. Bull.* 140:666–72

Schmitt DP, Alcalay L, Allensworth M, Allik J, Ault L, et al. 2005. Sociosexuality from Argentina to Zimbabwe: a 48-nation study of sex, culture, and the strategies of human mating. *Behav. Brain Sci.* 28:247–311

Sedikides C, Campbell WK, Reeder GD, Elliot AJ. 1998. The self-serving bias in relational context. *J. Personal. Soc. Psychol.* 74(2):378–86

Shallcross S, Howland M, Bemis J, Simpson JA, Frazier P. 2011. Not "capitalizing" on social capitalization interactions: the role of attachment insecurity. *J. Fam. Psychol.* 25:77–85

Shallcross S, Simpson JA. 2012. Trust and responsiveness in strain-test situations: a dyadic perspective. *J. Personal. Soc. Psychol.* 102:1031–44

Simon W, Gagnon JH. 2003. Sexual scripts: origins, influences and changes. *Qual. Sociol.* 26:491–97

Simpson JA. 2007. Psychological foundations of trust. *Curr. Dir. Psychol. Sci.* 16:264–68

Simpson JA, Belsky J. 2016. Attachment theory within a modern evolutionary framework. In *The Handbook of Attachment: Theory, Research, and Clinical Applications*, ed. J Cassidy, PR Shaver, pp. 91–116. New York: Guilford. 3rd ed.

Simpson JA, Campbell L. 2013. *The Oxford Handbook of Close Relationships*. New York: Oxford Univ. Press

Simpson JA, Fletcher GJO, Campbell L. 2001. The structure and function of ideal standards in close relationships. In *Blackwell Handbook of Social Psychology: Interpersonal Processes*, ed. GJO Fletcher, MS Clark, pp. 86–106. Malden, MA: Blackwell Publishers

Simpson JA, Gangestad SW, Lerma M. 1990. Perception of physical attractiveness: mechanisms involved in the maintenance of romantic relationships. *J. Personal. Soc. Psychol.* 59:1192–201

Simpson JA, Ickes W, Blackstone T. 1995. When the head protects the heart: empathic accuracy in dating relationships. *J. Personal. Soc. Psychol.* 69:629–41

Simpson JA, Overall NC. 2014. Partner buffering of attachment insecurity. *Curr. Dir. Psychol. Sci.* 23:54–59

Simpson JA, Rholes WS. 2012. Adult attachment orientations, stress, and romantic relationships. *Adv. Exp. Soc. Psychol.* 45:279–328

Simpson JA, Rholes WS, Nelligan JS. 1992. Support-seeking and support-giving within couples in an anxiety-provoking situation: the role of attachment styles. *J. Personal. Soc. Psychol.* 62:434–46

Slotter EB, Gardner WL. 2009. Where do you end and I begin? Evidence for anticipatory, motivated self-other integration between relationship partners. *J. Personal. Soc. Psychol.* 96:1137–51

Sprecher S. 2011. The influence of social networks on romantic relationships: through the lens of the social network. *Pers. Relat.* 18:630–44

Sternberg RJ. 1986. A triangular theory of love. *Psychol. Rev.* 93:119–35

Szepsenwol O, Griskevicius V, Simpson JA, Young ES, Fleck C, Jones RE. 2016. The effect of predictable early childhood environments on sociosexuality in early adulthood. *Evol. Behav. Sci.* In press

Thibaut JW, Kelley HH. 1959. *The Social Psychology of Groups*. New York: Wiley

Uchino BN, Bosch JA, Smith TW, Carlisle M, Birmingham W, et al. 2013. Relationships and cardiovascular risk: perceived spousal ambivalence in specific relationship contexts and its links to inflammation. *Health Psychol.* 32:1067–75

West TV, Kenny DA. 2011. The truth and bias model of judgment. *Psychol. Rev.* 118:357–78

Wieselquist J, Rusbult C, Foster C, Agnew C. 1999. Commitment, prorelationship behavior, and trust in close relationships. *J. Personal. Soc. Psychol.* 77:942–66

Zeifman D, Hazan C. 2008. Pairbonds as attachments: reevaluating the evidence. In *The Handbook of Attachment: Theory, Research, and Clinical Applications*, ed. J Cassidy, PR Shaver, pp. 436–55. New York: Guilford

Moving Beyond Correlations in Assessing the Consequences of Poverty

Greg J. Duncan,[1] Katherine Magnuson,[2] and Elizabeth Votruba-Drzal[3]

[1] School of Education, University of California, Irvine, California 92697;
email: gduncan@uci.edu

[2] School of Social Work, University of Wisconsin, Madison, Wisconsin 53706;
email: kmagnuson@wisc.edu

[3] Department of Psychology, University of Pittsburgh, Pittsburgh, Pennsylvania 15260;
email: evotruba@pitt.edu

Annu. Rev. Psychol. 2017. 68:413–34

First published online as a Review in Advance on September 14, 2016

The *Annual Review of Psychology* is online at psych.annualreviews.org

This article's doi: 10.1146/annurev-psych-010416-044224

Keywords

poverty, family stress, family investments, causal effects

Abstract

In the United States, does growing up in a poor household cause negative developmental outcomes for children? Hundreds of studies have documented statistical associations between family income in childhood and a host of outcomes in childhood, adolescence, and adulthood. Many of these studies have used correlational evidence to draw policy conclusions regarding the benefits of added family income for children, in particular children in families with incomes below the poverty line. Are these conclusions warranted? After a review of possible mechanisms linking poverty to negative childhood outcomes, we summarize the evidence for income's effects on children, paying particular attention to the strength of the evidence and the timing of economic deprivation. We demonstrate that, in contrast to the nearly universal associations between poverty and children's outcomes in the correlational literature, impacts estimated from social experiments and quasi-experiments are more selective. In particular, these stronger studies have linked increases in family income to increased school achievement in middle childhood and to greater educational attainment in adolescence and early adulthood. There is no experimental or quasi-experimental evidence in the United States that links child outcomes to economic deprivation in the first several years of life. Understanding the nature of socioeconomic influences, as well as their potential use in evidence-based policy recommendations, requires greater attention to identifying causal effects.

Contents

INTRODUCTION

The term poverty brings to mind many images and has been used to describe contrasting contexts of scarcity. Poverty typically refers to a lack of economic resources but is sometimes defined more broadly as social exclusion. Mention of poverty often evokes images of poor children from economically developing countries, for whom family life consists of struggles to survive on little, if any, consistent income. Conditions of such severe economic deprivation can compromise children's basic health and development. Yet, even in a nation as wealthy as the United States, poverty characterizes the living conditions of a substantial number of its children. The overall economic conditions of the United States have cycled between growth and recession, but even extensive economic growth has failed to lift millions of children out of poverty.

Measuring poverty in terms of economic resources is complicated because it requires defining both the types of economic resources that should be counted as income and the minimum threshold below which families have insufficient economic resources. In the 1960s, the US federal government developed a method for generating a dollar amount that, if greater than annual income, could be used to designate a family as poor. The resulting definition of poverty has been used for both determining social program eligibility and tracking trends in poverty rates.

In 2014, approximately 15.5 million US children—more than one in five—lived in poor families (DeNavas-Walt & Proctor 2015), meaning that their family income was less than approximately $24,000 for a family of two parents and two children. Since the 1960s, child poverty rates have ranged between 14% and 22%, with higher rates of poverty occurring during periods of economic decline. But this average masks important differences: Poverty rates are higher for younger than for older children, and rates for children of color are nearly 2.5 times higher than those for white children. Most US children who experience poverty do so for a short time, usually only a year or two out of their childhood. However, nearly 10% of children experience persistent poverty throughout childhood (Ratcliffe & McKernan 2012).

Developmental psychology has a long-standing interest in understanding how conditions of economic scarcity affect developmental processes. Part of this attention is driven by a desire to understand how variation in child-rearing environments and experiences gives rise to differences in child development; another part comes from a desire to improve the life chances of economically

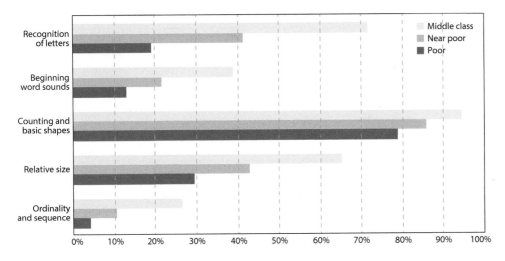

Figure 1

Rates of kindergarten proficiencies for poor, near-poor, and middle-class children, calculated by the authors from data collected by the Early Childhood Longitudinal Study, Kindergarten from 1998 to 1999. Poor children belong to a family with income below the official US poverty threshold. Near-poor children belong to a family with income between one and two times the poverty line. Middle-class children belong to a family with income greater than twice the poverty line.

disadvantaged children by developing better social policies and programs. The existing body of research thus tries to describe both the extent to which poverty affects children and the processes behind these influences.

Correlational evidence shows that poor children fare worse than their more affluent peers, especially with respect to schooling and educational outcomes. Poor children begin formal schooling well behind their more affluent peers in terms of classroom and academic skills, and they never close these gaps during subsequent school years. On average, poor US children have lower levels of kindergarten reading and math skills than their more economically advantaged peers (**Figure 1**). Moreover, when compared with individuals whose families had incomes of at least twice the poverty line during their early childhood, adults who were poor as children completed two fewer years of schooling, earned less than half as much, worked far fewer hours per year, received more food stamps, and were nearly three times as likely to report poor health (**Table 1**).

Such large differences in life chances raise the possibility that poverty itself plays an influential role in shaping development. However, poverty is associated with a constellation of disadvantages that may themselves be harmful to children, including low levels of parental education and living with a single parent. Indeed, sociologists have long argued for the importance of socioeconomic status—the social status and prestige that is derived from a wide set of economic and social conditions—rather than parental income alone. Thus, it is critical to determine whether poverty itself affects development or whether other, correlated aspects of social disadvantage and status are key. Doing so will contribute to a more comprehensive understanding of how environments shape human development and strengthen our capacity to develop policies, programs, and interventions that support healthy physical and psychological development. For this reason, we focus in this review on characterizing the ways in which poverty and the living conditions related to poverty affect children's development. Although we recognize the rich tradition of descriptive studies that characterize the life chances of poor children, we highlight findings from studies that can identify the causal effects of economic disadvantage on child development.

Table 1   Adult (age 30–37) outcomes by poverty status between the prenatal year and age five

Adult outcome	Early childhood income below the official US poverty line (mean or percent)	Early childhood income between one and two times the poverty line (mean or percent)	Early childhood income more than twice the poverty line (mean or percent)
Completed schooling	11.8 years	12.7 years	14.0 years
Earnings[a]	$17,900	$26,800	$39,700
Annual work hours	1,512	1,839	1,963
Food stamps[a]	$896	$337	$70
Poor health	13%	13%	5%
Arrested (men only)	26%	21%	13%
Nonmarital birth (women only)	50%	28%	9%

[a]Earnings and food stamp values are in 2005 dollars.
Table based on data presented in Duncan et al. (2010).

In suggesting that more attention be paid to the causal nature of the associations, we are primarily interested in probabilistic, rather than deterministic, causal associations. Poverty does not always affect all families, or even affect all families that experience negative outcomes from poverty, in the same way. Poverty is best understood as an insufficient, nonredundant part of a condition, which is itself unnecessary but is sufficient for the occurrence of the effect (Mackie 1974). A good analogy is a piece of paper and a match causing a fire. The match and paper are both nonredundant and together give rise to a causal chain of events that leads to the creation of fire. These factors do not constitute the only way in which fire can be created, nor can either alone create fire. However, we would agree that both the match and the paper are causal agents within a condition that makes fire. Thus, we consider family poverty or low income to be part of a sufficient constellation of related factors that create conditions which cause adverse family and child outcomes (see also Cook 2014).

What are the important conditions that, in combination with poverty, are the key causal agents of adverse outcomes? These conditions are best understood by considering the downstream effects of income on family processes. For example, a bag containing a thousand dollars that sits in a family's closet would not have a causal effect on children's outcomes. However, if the money is used to pay overdue bills or buy more nutritious food and thus reduces the parent's psychological distress, then we would identify income as a causal agent in the condition of poverty alleviation. This type of causal thinking is important because it helps us to consider whether a policy that increases family income but does not directly target other characteristics of the family environment would enhance child and adult development.

An understanding of how the timing of poverty intersects with developmental processes is particularly important in considering how poverty shapes child development. Few studies focus on the timing of economic hardship across childhood and adolescence, in part because longitudinal studies rarely track children and their economic contexts across a variety of childhood stages. However, emerging research in neuroscience and developmental psychology suggests that poverty early in a child's life may be particularly harmful. Not only does the astonishingly rapid development of young brains leave children sensitive and vulnerable to environmental conditions during this stage of development, but the family context dominates their everyday lives (as opposed to schools or peers, which have a greater effect on older children). For this reason, we focus our review of existing literature not only on whether poverty affects children but also on whether effects differ as a function of the developmental timing of economic deprivation.

Although our review focuses specifically on poverty, we use the terms poverty and low income synonymously. The official US poverty thresholds ensure consistency in tracking poverty rates over time and are used to determine eligibility for many means-tested programs, but there is no evidence that these precise dollar thresholds meaningfully differentiate families' economic needs. Indeed, evidence suggests that improving the incomes of families both just below and just above the poverty line will have positive effects similar to those of pushing families across the thresholds. However, income increases do appear to matter more for lower- than for higher-income children. This has been demonstrated in studies considering links between income and children's development across a broader spectrum of the income distribution (e.g., Loken et al. 2012). Accordingly, our review focuses on theoretical and empirical evidence of the effects of low family incomes on children rather than on how differences in income affect children residing in middle class or wealthy families.

WHY POVERTY MAY HINDER HEALTHY DEVELOPMENT

What are the consequences of growing up in a poor household? Economists, sociologists, developmental psychologists, and neuroscientists emphasize different pathways by which poverty can influence children's development. The three main theoretical approaches describing these causal processes are the family and environmental stress perspective, the resources and investment perspective, and the cultural perspective. In addition, neuroscience is beginning to provide a fourth approach by documenting functional and structural differences in brain architecture that correlate with both family economic conditions and child development. These frameworks are grounded in different disciplinary backgrounds and vary in the extent to which they focus on socioeconomic status (SES) in general rather than on income, poverty, or any other single component of SES (e.g., parental education, occupational prestige). Nevertheless, these frameworks overlap and are complementary. Although developed primarily in the United States, each theory has cross-national and cross-cultural applications.

Family and Environmental Stress Perspective

Economically disadvantaged families experience more stressors in their everyday environments than do more affluent families, and these disparities may affect children's development (Evans 2004). The family stress model was first developed by Glen Elder (1974; Elder et al. 1985) to explain the influence of economic loss during the Great Depression on children. Other researchers have further developed this model and applied it to families facing sudden economic downturn in rural farming communities (Conger & Elder 1994) and to single parent families (Brody & Flor 1997), as well as to ethnically diverse urban families (Mistry et al. 2002).

According to this perspective, poor families face significant economic pressure as they struggle to pay bills and purchase important goods and services, and they are thus forced to cut back on daily expenditures. This economic hardship is coupled with other stressful life events that are more prevalent in the lives of poor than nonpoor families and creates high levels of psychological distress, including depressive and hostile feelings, in poor parents (Kessler & Cleary 1980, McLeod & Kessler 1990). Psychological distress spills over into marital and coparenting relationships. As couples struggle to make ends meet, their interactions tend to become more hostile and conflicted. This leads them to withdraw from each other (Brody et al. 1994, Conger & Elder 1994). Parents' psychological distress and conflict, in turn, are linked to parenting practices that are, on average, more punitive, harsh, inconsistent, and detached and less nurturing, stimulating, and responsive to children's needs. Such lower-quality parenting elevates children's physiological stress responses and ultimately harms children's development (McLoyd 1990).

Although, historically, work in this field has focused on the family as the primary conduit of stress, theoretical and empirical work conducted in the past two decades has extended this perspective to consider stress in the broader environment. Compared with their more affluent peers, poor children are more likely to live in housing that is crowded, noisy, and characterized by structural defects such as a leaky roof, rodent infestation, or inadequate heating (Evans 2004, Evans et al. 2001). Poor families are more likely to reside in neighborhoods characterized by high rates of violence and crime and such other neighborhood risk factors as boarded-up houses, abandoned lots, and inadequate municipal services.

The schools that low-income children attend are more likely to be overcrowded and have structural problems (e.g., excessive noise and poor lighting and ventilation) compared with the schools attended by more affluent children. Economically disadvantaged children are also exposed to higher levels of air pollution from parental smoking, traffic, and industrial emissions (Clark et al. 2014, Miranda et al. 2011). These environmental conditions in the lives of low-income children create physiological and emotional stress that may impair socioemotional, physical, cognitive, and academic development (Evans 2004). For example, childhood poverty heightens a child's risk for lead poisoning, which has been linked to ill health, problem behavior, and neurological disadvantages that may persist through adolescence and beyond (Grandjean & Landrigan 2006).

Evidence from the field of psychoneuroimmunology suggests that the experience of chronic elevated physiological stress responses may interfere with the healthy development of children's stress response system as well as the regions of the brain responsible for self-regulation. Researchers have documented the harmful effects of such stress on animal brain development. Exposure to stress and the elevation of stress hormones such as cortisol negatively influence animals' cognitive functioning, leading to impairments in brain structures such as the hippocampus, which is important for memory (McEwen 2000). Nonexperimental studies have found that low-income children have significantly higher levels of stress hormones than their more advantaged counterparts and that early childhood poverty is associated with increased allostatic load, a measure of physiological stress (Lupien et al. 2001, Turner & Avison 2003).

These higher levels of physiological stress relate to decreased cognitive and immunological functioning; the latter has long-term implications for a host of inflammatory diseases later in life (Miller et al. 2011). For example, recent work has linked the body's stress response system to brain regions that support cognitive skills, such as executive functioning and self-regulation (Blair et al. 2011). The same study also found that heightened salivary cortisol, an indicator of elevated stress, partially accounts for the association between poverty on the one hand and parenting and children's executive functioning on the other (Blair et al. 2011). Thus, disparities in stress exposure and related stress hormones may partially explain why poor children have lower levels of academic achievement, as well as poorer health later in life.

An emerging body of literature within the family stress perspective suggests that there are important individual differences in children's susceptibility to stressful environmental influences, which may affect how income impacts children's development (e.g., Raver et al. 2013). Ellis et al. (2011) argue that children differ in their sensitivity to environmental contexts for biological or physiological reasons, such that some children are more reactive to both positive and negative environments than other children. This framework, which is termed differential susceptibility, raises the question of whether children who are more susceptible to contextual influences are more likely to be affected by either the adversity created by poverty or the positive environment created by affluence. Empirical support for such an association is found in a small number of studies that consider how cortisol, a measure of temperamental reactivity, interacts with poverty to predict children's executive functioning skills (Obradović et al. 2016, Raver et al. 2013). However, additional research is needed to more fully understand differential sensitivity to environments and how this may interact with poverty to affect children.

Although the biological links between low income and stress are compelling, no methodologically strong study has linked poverty and prolonged elevated stress reactions in children. Some quasi-experimental studies have examined these connections in mothers. A study of the expansions of the Earned Income Tax Credit (EITC), which provides refundable tax credits to low-income working families, used data from the National Health Examination and Nutrition Survey (Evans & Garthwaite 2014) to determine whether increased EITC payments were associated with improvements in maternal health. Between 1993 and 1996, the generosity of the EITC increased sharply, particularly for mothers with two or more children. If income matters for maternal stress, we should see a bigger improvement for children and mothers in low-income families with two children when compared to low-income mothers with a single child. Indeed, the study found that, when compared with mothers with just one child, low-income mothers with two or more children reported larger improvements in mental health, as well as reductions in stress-related biomarkers. An earlier study of the effects of increases in the Canadian Child Benefit, which is similar to a tax credit, also found improvements in maternal mental health among low-income women (Milligan & Stabile 2011).

The family stress perspective has seen major conceptual and empirical advances in the past two decades. A narrow focus on parental mental health and parenting has been extended to incorporate additional stressors that poor children encounter in their everyday environments. In addition, neurobiological evidence has begun to document the potential harmful effects of chronic elevated stress on children's development. Increasingly methodologically rigorous studies suggest linkages between expansion of income supports and reductions in maternal stress. We expect that theoretical and empirical research will continue to benefit from an explosion in neuroscience-based findings shedding light on connections among economic resources, physiological stress responses, behavior, and development.

Resource and Investment Perspective

Although pioneered and championed by economists, household production theory has played a central role in how social scientists and developmental psychologists conceive of family influences on child development. Whereas psychologists have focused on how parent–child interactions affect developmental processes, economists have challenged scholars to think about the many ways parents use economic resources to support healthy development. Gary Becker's (1991) *A Treatise on the Family* posits that child development is produced from a combination of endowments and parental investments. Endowments include genetic predispositions and the values and preferences that parents instill in their children. Parents' preferences, such as the importance they place on education and their orientation toward the future, combined with their resources, shape parental investments.

Economists argue that time and money are the two basic resources that parents draw upon when they invest in their children. For example, investments in high-quality child care and education, housing in good neighborhoods, and rich learning experiences enhance children's development, as do investments of parents' time. Links among endowments, investments, and children's development appear to differ according to the domain of development (e.g., achievement, behavior, health). Characteristics of the children also affect the level and type of investments that parents make in their offspring (Becker 1991, Foster 2002). For example, if a young child is talkative and

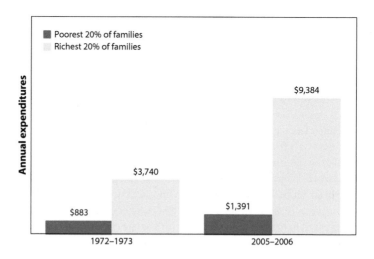

Figure 2

Family enrichment expenditures on children. Calculations are based on data from the Consumer
Expenditure Surveys (presented in Duncan & Murnane 2011a,b). Amounts are in 2012 dollars.

enthusiastic about learning, parents are more likely to purchase children's books or take the child
to the library.

Becker's (1991) household production theory suggests that children from poor families lag behind their economically advantaged counterparts in part because their parents have fewer resources
to invest in them. Compared with more affluent parents, poor parents are less able to purchase
inputs for their children, including books and educational materials at home, high-quality child
care settings and schools, and safe neighborhoods. Economically disadvantaged parents may also
have less time to invest in their children owing to higher rates of single parenthood, nonstandard
work hours, and less flexible work schedules. This, too, may have negative consequences for children. Evidence suggests that the amount of cognitive stimulation in the home environment varies
with changes in family income (Votruba-Drzal 2006).

According to data from the Consumer Expenditure Surveys (**http://www.bls.gov/cex/**), low-
income families in 1972–1973 spent approximately $850 (in 2011 dollars) per year per child on
child enrichment resources such as books, computers, high-quality child care, summer camps, and
private school tuition. Higher-income families spent more than $3,500, already a substantial dif-
ference (**Figure 2**; Duncan & Murnane 2011a). By 2005–2006, low-income families had increased
their expenditures to more than $1,300, but high-income families had increased theirs much more,
to more than $9,000 per child per year. The differences in spending between the two groups al-
most tripled in the intervening years. The largest spending differences were for activities such as
music lessons, travel, and summer camps (Kaushal et al. 2011). Nonexperimental studies suggest
that differences in the quality of the home environments of poorer and more advantaged children
account for a substantial portion of the association between poverty and children's educational
achievement. Thus, economists contend that family income matters to children because it enables
parents to buy many things that support their children's learning and healthy development.

The family stress and investment pathways are complemented by insights from cognitive psychology and by behavioral economic studies of cognitive resources and decision making under
conditions of scarcity. Enhanced family income may create more enriching and less stressful family
environments by reducing the cognitive load that parents face (Gennetian & Shafir 2015). Studies

show that conditions of scarcity place demands on limited cognitive resources, directing attention to some problems at the expense of others (Mani et al. 2013). Research, much of which has been conducted in developing countries, has found that making economic decisions under a variety of conditions of scarcity reduces adults' subsequent behavioral self-control and renders them less able to regulate their own behavior to pursue longer-term goals (Mullainathan & Shafir 2013). The many daily tasks that require poor adults to make complicated decisions and evaluate consequential trade-offs deplete their cognitive resources, increasing the likelihood that subsequent decisions will favor more impulsive and counterproductive choices.

Cultural Perspective

Sociological theories about the ways in which the norms and behavior of poor families and communities affect children were integrated into Oscar Lewis's (1969) culture of poverty model. Drawing from field work with poor families in Latin America, Lewis argued that the poor were economically marginalized and had no opportunity for upward mobility. Individuals responded to their marginalized position with maladaptive behavior and values. The resulting culture of poverty was characterized by weak impulse control and an inability to delay gratification, as well as feelings of helplessness and inferiority—conditions unlikely to change in response to a social program that might boost family income by several thousand dollars. These adaptations manifested in high levels of female-headed households, sexual promiscuity, crime, and gangs. Although Lewis acknowledged that these behaviors emerged in response to structural factors, he theorized that such values and behaviors were transmitted to future generations, and therefore they became a cause of poverty:

> By the time slum children are age six or seven they have usually absorbed the basic values and attitudes
> of their subculture and are not psychologically geared to take full advantage of changing conditions or
> increased opportunities. (Lewis 1966, p. xlv)

Cultural explanations for the effects of poverty on children have thus suggested that high levels of nonmarital childbearing, joblessness, female-headed households, criminal activity, and welfare dependency among the poor were likely to be transmitted from parents to children. From the mid-1980s through the 1990s, scholars expanded the scope of this argument by paying closer attention to the origins of cultural and behavioral differences. For example, some researchers emphasized the role of individual choice in the face of the liberal welfare state's perverse incentives rewarding single-mother households and joblessness among men (e.g., Mead 1986). Others have stressed the importance of structural and economic factors, including the concentration of neighborhood poverty, the social isolation of poor inner-city neighborhoods, and the deindustrialization of urban economies (Massey 1990; Wilson 1987, 1996). They contend that these structural factors negatively affect community norms and influence the behavior of inner-city adults and their children.

A common criticism of culture of poverty explanations is that they fail to differentiate the behavior of individuals from their values and beliefs (Lamont & Small 2008). Evidence suggests that disadvantaged individuals hold many middle-class values and beliefs, but circumstances make it difficult for them to behave accordingly. For example, one study showed that poor Black women value marriage and recognize the benefits of raising children in a two-parent household (Edin & Kefalas 2005). However, their low wages, as well as Black men's high rates of unemployment and incarceration, lead poor women to conclude that marriage is out of their reach.

Traditional views of the culture of poverty do not account for this disconnect between values and behaviors. Incarnations of the cultural perspective over the past two decades argue that it is important to take culture seriously not because the fundamental values and beliefs of the poor differ from those of the middle classes but because it is important to understand the heterogeneity in the worldviews created by the living conditions that poor individuals experience. More specifically, focusing on how conditions and experiences give rise to limited worldviews facilitates an examination of how poverty may constrain the range of choices and productive pathways available to low-income families (Lamont & Small 2010).

Annette Lareau's (2003) qualitative study of family management strategies identifies other differences between the cultural child-rearing repertoires of high- and low-income families, including the degree to which middle-class parents manage their children's lives and working-class and poor parents leave children to play and otherwise organize their activities on their own:

> In the middle class, life was hectic. Parents were racing around from one activity to another.... Because there were so many activities, and because they were accorded such importance, child's activities determined the schedule for the entire family.... [In contrast, in working class and poor families,] parents tend to direct their efforts toward keeping children safe, enforcing discipline, and, when they deem it necessary, regulating their behavior in certain areas.... Thus, whereas middle-class children are often treated as a project to be developed, working class and poor children are given boundaries for their behavior and then allowed to grow. (Lareau 2003, pp. 35, 66–67)

These middle-class child-rearing patterns are called concerted cultivation and involve providing stimulating learning activities and social interactions that parents believe will promote their children's social and cognitive development. In contrast, the natural growth perspective of working-class and poor parents often stops at providing basic supports (e.g., food, shelter, comfort). Such differences in cultural repertoires provide a distinct advantage to middle-class children and contribute to the intergenerational transmission of social class.

These cultural theories extend the resource and investment perspectives discussed above. Class-related differences in the parenting practices of the families studied by Lareau arise, in part, from income differences that enable some to support a much broader repertoire of activities for their children. However, some of the differences arise from divergent beliefs or worldviews about how children succeed and the best kinds of parenting practices for children. Once these beliefs are adopted, they are unlikely to change in response to policy-relevant changes in family income.

DEVELOPMENTAL PERSPECTIVES: POVERTY ACROSS CHILDHOOD AND ADOLESCENCE

Theoretical perspectives on the effects of family poverty on children have focused on how poverty shapes children's environments rather than on processes operating within the child. Attention to within-child processes, however, suggests the importance of greater specification of the implicated developmental processes and greater attention to the developmental timing of poverty. For some children, poverty persists throughout childhood; however, for most children, poverty lasts for shorter periods of time. The developmental perspective leads to the hypothesis that for some outcomes, the timing of economic disadvantage during childhood and adolescence may matter for children's development. The fields of economics and developmental neuroscience have provided conceptual arguments and, to a lesser extent, empirical evidence for the importance of development in the earliest years of children's lives. The field of developmental neuroscience suggests that both the stress response processes (discussed in the section Family and Environmental Stress) and the more general development of brain circuitry early in life may be important mechanisms driving the effects of poverty and related environments on children.

Economists Cunha & Heckman (2007) posit a cumulative model of the production of human capital that allows for the possibility of differing childhood investment stages, as well as roles for the past effects of cognitive and socioemotional skills on the future development of those skills. In this model, children have endowments from birth of cognitive potential and temperament that reflect a combination of genetic and prenatal environmental influences. The Cunha & Heckman (2007) model highlights the interactive nature of skill building and investments from families, preschools and schools, and other agents. It suggests that human capital accumulation results from self-productivity—skills developed in earlier stages bolstering the development of skills in later stages—as well as the dynamic complementary process that results when skills acquired prior to a given investment increase the productivity of that investment. These two principles are combined in the hypothesis that skill begets skill. This model predicts that economic deprivation in early childhood creates disparities in school readiness and early academic success that widen over the course of childhood.

Developmental neuroscience has contributed to the understanding of the developmental timing of poverty by arguing that early environments, especially adverse environments, play an especially important role in shaping early brain development (Rosenzweig 2003). Some studies have focused on family socioeconomic status generally or on income specifically as an important dimension of early contexts (Brito & Noble 2014, Hackman & Farah 2009, Noble et al. 2015a). In contrast to the social science literature, these studies focus on specific cognitive skills and, increasingly, on direct measures of brain function and structure. This innovation is critical because differences in neural circuitry are often evident at an early age, well before general cognitive or behavioral differences can be detected (Fox et al. 2010), and can thus serve as an early indicator of the development of cognitive disparities. Moreover, neuroscience provides an explanatory framework for the physiological mechanisms early in life that lead to lower cognitive skills and other observed behavioral differences later in life. Distinct brain circuits support discrete cognitive skills, and differentiating between these underlying neural systems may point to different causal pathways and avenues for intervention. Specifically, one of the key pathways linking early childhood SES to adult outcomes encompasses the developmental assembly and long-term functioning of particular brain circuits, namely, circuits that are important for cognitive and emotional control functions and self-regulatory behaviors that impact a range of adult processes.

Neuroscience studies have documented SES-based differences in language use, memory, executive function, and socioemotional processing. Socioeconomic disparities in neurocognitive skills have been reported beginning in toddlerhood and continuing throughout adolescence. Electrophysiological and brain imaging research offers evidence that, for children, family socioeconomic disadvantage predicts indicators of brain function hypothesized to reflect the delayed development of the prefrontal cortex. In turn, delayed development of the prefrontal cortex can affect neurocognitive abilities, such as selective attention, reading and language acquisition, decision making, and higher-order cognition. SES-based differences have also been found in the volume, structure, and function of brain regions that support these skills in studies of older children and adolescents using magnetic resonance imaging techniques (Hanson et al. 2013; Kim et al. 2013; Noble et al. 2012a,b, 2015a,b). Noble et al. (2015a,b) reported associations between family income and the size of the brain's surface beginning at age three, particularly in regions supporting children's language and executive functioning; this association was strongest among the most disadvantaged families.

Neuroscience studies suggest that the early experience of poverty may shape children's brain development and that such mechanisms may underlie observed differences in subsequent cognitive skills, behavior, school completion, and achievement. However, despite the specificity and rigor of brain measurement, these descriptive studies of small samples support neither causal inference nor population generalizability. The data and methods typically rely on comparing low-income children with their higher-income counterparts and, at best, control for only a small handful of other characteristics. Thus, it is hard to know whether income is a causal agent in producing the differences in brain structure or function or whether income is just confounded with other conditions that matter.

Additional support for the idea that poverty in early childhood may be particularly pernicious for children's development comes from intensive programs aimed at providing early care and educational experiences for high-risk infants and toddlers. The best known are the Abecedarian program, a full-day, center-based, educational program for children who are at high risk for school failure, starting in early infancy and continuing until school entry; and the Perry Preschool program, which provided one or two years of intensive center-based education for preschoolers (Duncan & Magnuson 2013). Both of these programs have generated long-term improvements in subsequent education, criminal behavior, and employment—outcomes that are strongly associated with poverty, although the general pattern of effects from other early childhood education programs is more modest.

Although income in early childhood may matter the most for early brain development, several studies suggest that economic circumstances experienced later in childhood and adolescence may also be important (Akee et al. 2010, Maynard & Murnane 1979). For example, economic and sociological studies demonstrate that income increases may also be beneficial for low-income adolescents and young adults, particularly when used to help pay for postsecondary schooling. Although Pell Grants and other sources of financial aid drive down the net costs of college for low-income students, the costs of enrollment in public four-year colleges have increased faster than grants have. In contrast, the costs of attendance at a public community college have not increased over the past two decades for students from low-income families because the amount of aid has expanded to cover the higher price. Of course, many low-income students and their parents either lack awareness of the aid that is available or are discouraged by the extremely complex federal financial aid application form (Bettinger et al. 2012).

Additional evidence highlighting the potential importance of family economic circumstances in middle childhood and adolescence comes from studies in social and health psychology suggesting that poverty, and economic inequality more generally, may affect children by creating social distance that imposes harmful intrapsychic costs (Boyce et al. 2012, Odgers et al. 2015). Heberle & Carter (2015) argue that poor individuals may experience status anxiety related to their membership in a low-status group within a highly stratified and unequal society. Thus, the psychological costs of poverty may be exacerbated when the economic and social distance between low-income and higher-income peers is greater. Heberle & Carter (2015) further suggest that the developmental task of forming a sense of self in relation to others may make poor children's anxiety derived from social status especially harmful during middle childhood and adolescence. Similarly, Odgers (2015) argues that low-income children attending schools with affluent peers may be doubly disadvantaged because they are directly affected by both their families' poverty and upward social comparisons that will negatively shape their internal attributions, behavior, and health. Odgers et al. (2015) argue that low-income children who are not exposed to as many affluent peers will not experience the harmful effects of upward comparison. Thus, one important factor in understanding whether poverty has adverse effects on aspects of children's development is the salience of their poverty as determined by their social distance from affluent peers.

However, the empirical support for this proposition remains limited. Odgers et al. (2015) finds that low-income boys have higher levels of antisocial behavior in neighborhoods in England that are of mixed economic status compared with boys who are in more economically segregated neighborhoods. This pattern does not hold true for girls, and more generally, it is not clear to what extent this pattern is generalizable across contexts. For example, descriptive portraits of children's achievement and behavior at school entry do not find that poor children residing in neighborhoods with low rates of poverty have worse behavior or lower achievement than poor children residing in neighborhoods with concentrated poverty (S. Wolf, K. Magnuson, and R. Kimbro, unpublished manuscript). Of course, it is possible that the harm from upward social comparison is more prominent in particular contexts or for children during particular developmental periods. More work is necessary to better understand whether and under what conditions these risks of upward social comparison may occur and to consider whether these risks are offset by access to the improved economic, institutional, and social resources often afforded to low-income children by greater economic integration (Reardon & Owens 2014).

Finally, economic conditions in middle childhood and adolescence may be important if stereotype threat comes into play. Stereotype threat refers to the risk of conforming to negative stereotypes about the group with which an individual identifies. In the case of identification by social class, the argument is that when the contexts experienced by children make social class highly salient, low-income children are more likely to conform to the stereotype of poor children as demonstrating lower achievement (Croizet & Claire 1998). The empirical evidence related to status anxiety and stereotype is suggestive but not extensive enough to draw clear conclusions. Moreover, the work to date describes relevant intraindividual processes but does not articulate how these processes interface with developmental processes. For example, are the harmful effects of upward social comparison most detrimental when children are developing their beliefs about self-efficacy in early middle childhood or during adolescence, when their understanding of how others view poor individuals becomes more complete and possibly negative?

Both theory and correlational evidence suggest that the effects of economic deprivation on children may depend on when in childhood or adolescence that deprivation is experienced. Numerous neuroscience studies have found that brain structure and function vary by income level early in childhood, suggesting that early deprivation might be especially important, a result confirmed in some life-cycle correlational studies. Both social psychological literature and the increase in out-of-pocket costs for college suggest that adolescence may also be a period in which development is sensitive to income fluctuations.

ASSESSING CAUSAL CONSEQUENCES OF POVERTY: METHODS AND RESULTS

Studying how poverty affects children and families is challenging. The most important construct of interest, poverty, is expensive to manipulate, leaving the researcher little choice but to use observational data to disentangle whether and how poverty influences the developmental processes and outcomes of children. However, because poor and nonpoor children differ in so many ways, it is hard to argue that the differences between low-income children and their more affluent peers are due only to income.

Studies aimed at estimating the influence of income on child development differ in their methodological rigor. At one end are correlational studies that analyze associations between family income and child outcomes, with few adjustments for confounding factors. These studies are common, particularly in neuroscience, but are likely to be plagued by biases that lead to overestimates of the causal impacts of income. At the other end are large social policy experiments in which families are randomly assigned to receive additional income. If implemented correctly, experiments provide unbiased estimates of income effects. However, experimental studies are exceedingly rare and sometimes condition their income support on behavior such as full-time work, which may exert its own influence on child development. Quasi-experiments, in which income changes are beyond the control of families, are almost as reliable as experiments. The Evans &

Garthwaite (2014) EITC expansion study is an example of quasi-experimental research based on policy changes that increase the generosity of programs like the EITC. In this case, the larger increase in payments for two or more as opposed to one child created income variation that was beyond the control of recipient families.

School Achievement and Attainment

The differences in academic skills and attainment between poor and nonpoor children have been well documented and described. The focus on these outcomes reflects both the somewhat greater ease of measuring them, using test scores of academic performance and completed schooling, and their importance in social science theories about intergenerational social mobility and status attainment. However, the large body of longitudinal and observational studies varies considerably in the extent to which they address threats to causal inference. In a review, Haveman & Wolfe (1995) conclude that, in studies conducted prior to 1995, growing up in poverty is consistently related to lower education-related outcomes. However, they also point out that these studies suffered from numerous shortcomings, including the lack of a common framework to guide the choice of model specification, and as a result the inclusion of variables often appears to be ad hoc.

The strongest experimental evidence in the literature relates income increases to children's school achievement and attainment. The only large-scale randomized interventions to alter family income directly were the US Negative Income Tax Experiments, which were conducted between 1968 and 1982 to identify the influence of guaranteed income on parents' labor force participation. Three of the sites (Gary, Indiana, and rural areas in North Carolina and Iowa) measured impacts on achievement gains for children in elementary school; significant impacts were found in two of the three sites (Maynard 1977, Maynard & Murnane 1979). In contrast, no achievement differences were found for adolescents and young adults. Impacts on school enrollment and attainment for youth were more uniformly positive, with both the Gary site and a fourth site in New Jersey reporting increases in school enrollment, high school graduation rates, or years of completed schooling. Teachers rated student comportment through eighth grade in the rural sites in North Carolina and Iowa; results showed improvements in North Carolina but not in Iowa. Taken together, this pattern of findings suggests that income may be more important for the school achievement of preadolescents than that of adolescents. In contrast, income may matter more for the completed schooling of adolescents and young adults. However, the small sample sizes and high rates of missing school achievement data make it difficult to draw firm conclusions from this work, in which an understanding of the effects of income supplements on children was not one of the primary goals of the research.

A second body of evidence on the importance of family income comes from experimental welfare reform evaluation studies undertaken during the 1990s to incentivize parental employment by providing wage supplements to working-poor parents. Moreover, some of these studies measured the test scores of at least some children who had not yet entered school when the programs began. One study analyzed data from seven random-assignment welfare and antipoverty policies, all of which increased parental employment; only some of these policies increased family income (Morris et al. 2005). The combined impacts of higher income and more maternal work on children's school achievement varied markedly by the children's age. Treatment-group children who were between the ages of four and seven when the programs took effect, many of whom made the transition into elementary school after the programs began, scored significantly higher on achievement tests than their control-group counterparts. A sophisticated statistical analysis of the data on these younger children suggests that a $3,500 annual income boost is associated with a gain in achievement scores of about one fifth of a standard deviation (Duncan et al. 2011).

In contrast to the positive findings for younger children, the achievement of older children (ages 8 to 11) did not appear to benefit from the income and employment programs, and the achievement of children who were 12 and 13 seemed to be hurt by the programs' efforts to increase family income and parental employment. These results may be explained by maternal employment forcing teens to take on child care responsibilities that interfered with their school work (Gennetian et al. 2002).

Two quasi-experimental studies have focused on expansions in tax credits and a third on casino disbursements as sources of positive income shocks. Studies of expansions to the EITC in the mid-1990s (Dahl & Lochner 2012) and National Child Benefit program across Canadian provinces (Milligan & Stabile 2011) found evidence that increased tax income coincided with modestly higher achievement scores during middle childhood among low-income families. A third quasi-experimental study examined the impact of the opening of a casino by a Native American tribal government in North Carolina, which distributed approximately $6,000 annually to each adult member of the tribe (Akee et al. 2010). A comparison of Native American youth with non-Native American youth, before and after the casino opened, found that receipt of casino payments for approximately six years increased the school attendance and high school graduation rates of poor Native American youth. Achievement test scores were not available in these data, nor were data available on children under the age of nine.

Related evidence on income effects comes from evaluations of programs providing conditional cash transfer (CCT) payments to low-income families. First tested in developing countries as a way to incentivize children's continued schooling and medical care, CCTs distribute cash to mothers only when they engage in targeted behavior such as well-baby visits or their children meet school attendance goals (Fiszbein et al. 2009). Many of the programs tested in developing countries produced significant improvements in children's development, education, and health. It is unclear whether the improvements are caused by the increased income or the structure of CCTs, which provide incentive payments that directly offset the specific and large opportunity cost of the desired behavior.

In the United States, the evaluation of Opportunity New York City, a CCT program aimed at reducing family poverty and economic hardship, showed no impacts on children's school test scores after two years of participation (Riccio et al. 2010, 2013). Possible explanations for the null effects include the complexity of the payment schedule, the diversity and complexity of behaviors targeted by the intervention, implementation difficulties, the small amount of cash support relative to the high cost of living in New York, and the fact that the children were older than those enrolled in many other income studies.

Two lessons emerge from these experimental and quasi-experimental studies. First, achievement gains are selective and depend on the children's age when income gains were received. Elementary school students and children making the transition into school generally demonstrated the most consistent achievement increases. For adolescents, the achievement changes were mixed, with different studies finding positive, null, and even negative impacts for achievement outcomes. Second, in the case of adolescents and young adults, income appears to affect educational attainments, such as high school graduation, and completed years of schooling rather than test scores. Given the high costs of postsecondary education, the effect of family income on completed schooling is not surprising.

Behavior and Mental Health

In addition to lagging behind their economically advantaged peers when it comes to academic achievement and educational attainment, low-income children are typically rated by their parents and teachers as having more behavior problems than more affluent children. This is reflected in elevated levels of externalizing problems, such as aggression and acting out, and internalizing problems, such as depression and anxiety. In adolescence, poverty is related to higher rates of nonmarital fertility and criminal activity. For example, compared with children whose families had incomes of at least twice the poverty line during their early childhood, poor males are more than twice as likely to be arrested. For females, poverty is associated with a more than fivefold increase in the likelihood of bearing a child out of wedlock prior to age 21 (Duncan et al. 2010; **Table 1**). Again, the extent to which these correlations reflect causal impacts remains uncertain.

As is the case for studies of achievement, most poverty-related studies of behavior have been correlational in nature and have varied in the extent to which they have addressed the challenges of identifying causal effects. Using longitudinal data from nationally representative and diverse samples, links have been found between low income and several dimensions of psychological functioning, including internalizing and externalizing behaviors, antisocial behavior, inadequate self-regulation, and poor mental health (Blau 1999, Mistry et al. 2002, Votruba-Drzal 2006). For example, 7.8% of poor parents versus 4.6% of nonpoor parents rated their children as having difficulties with emotions, concentration, behavior, or getting along with others (Simpson et al. 2005). However, these associations are not consistently replicated in studies that hold constant related disadvantages, such as family structure and parental education (Duncan & Brooks-Gunn 1997, Duncan et al. 2010, Mayer 1997). For example, Dearing et al. (2006) examined within-child associations between family income and behavior of young children and found significant negative effects of lower family income on externalizing behavior, especially for children who live in chronically poor households, but not on internalizing behavior.

Few studies have employed rigorous experimental or quasi-experimental designs to study children's psychological and behavioral health. An important exception is the above-cited study by Akee and colleagues (2010) that compared Native American children with non-Native American children before and after a casino opened on tribal land. They found that receipt of casino payments reduced criminal behavior, drug use, and behavioral disorders including depression, anxiety, and other emotional disorders such as conduct or oppositional disorders. This study of adolescents provides a compelling research design and suggests that income may play a causal role in at least some aspects of adolescent mental health.

Associations between income and dimensions of children's behavioral functioning tend to be less consistent and less robust in studies that employ more rigorous methodological approaches and analytical techniques (Reiss 2013). However, the most compelling quasi-experimental study to date shows that income is strongly linked to improvements in behavioral disorders. This suggests that, to the extent that there are causal connections between income and behavior in childhood, these connections may be selective, with some evidence suggesting that there are stronger associations between income and externalizing, rather than internalizing, problems.

However, it is important to note that few studies have been able to differentiate between these subtypes of problem behavior or look carefully at the timing of poverty across childhood. The global measures of child behavior problems that are commonly found in large nationally representative data tend to rely more heavily on items that assess externalizing problems, such as aggression and oppositional behavior, rather than those assessing internalizing problems, including depression and anxiety. Additionally, research in the field of developmental psychopathology has shown that internalizing and externalizing disorders follow different developmental courses as children age (Lewis & Rudolph 2014). Externalizing problems tend to peak during early childhood and then subside as children age, with a second period of elevation for some children in adolescence. Prevalence of problem internalizing behaviors tends to be low throughout early and middle childhood, with increases occurring during the transition into adolescence. Yet most studies examine children only in one age range or, more commonly, collapse the data across developmental stages (e.g., Blau 1999, D'Onofrio et al. 2009). This may obscure important associations, and research would benefit from increased attention to these differences in developmental trajectories, as well as to unique associations between poverty and particular dimensions of children's behavioral functioning.

Childhood Poverty and Development into Adulthood

Studies examining the long-term effects of childhood poverty have begun to appear in the past decade. Some have examined associations between poverty (e.g., family income in early childhood, middle childhood, and adolescence) and achievement and behavioral functioning into adulthood. Like other observational studies, these analyses face challenges in identifying causal effects, but their findings establish that early childhood income predicts adult outcomes. For example, Duncan et al. (2010) and Ziol-Guest et al. (2012) use data from the Panel Study of Income Dynamics (PSID) on individuals born in the early years of the study, for whom adult outcomes were collected when they were in their 30s. The PSID measures income in every year of a child's life from the prenatal period through age 15, making it possible to measure poverty experiences and family income early in life (from the prenatal period through the fifth year of life in one study and through the first year in the other) as well as later in childhood and in adolescence. Analysis of these data indicates that for families with average early childhood incomes below $25,000, an annual boost to family income during early childhood (from birth to age five) is associated with increased adult work hours and a rise in earnings, as well as with reductions in receipt of food stamps (but not receipt of Aid to Families with Dependent Children and Temporary Assistance for Needy Families benefits for female children). Family income in other childhood stages was never significantly related to adult earnings and work hours.

As discussed in the section Cultural Perspective, children raised in low-income households also have higher rates of arrest and incarceration in adulthood than their affluent counterparts (Bjerk 2007, Duncan et al. 2010). Duncan and colleagues (2010) found that boys living in poverty during the first five years of life were more than twice as likely to be arrested as boys who had family incomes over twice the poverty threshold (28% versus 13%). However, taking into account the variety of ways in which poor families differ from wealthier families reduced the associations to statistical insignificance. Thus, it is questionable whether elevations in criminal activity can be attributed to poverty per se rather than to the range of social disadvantages associated with poverty.

When it comes to socioeconomic variability in important adult behaviors, such as arrests, nonmarital childbearing, and educational attainment, the timing of income seems to be important, with income in adolescence more strongly related to adult behavior than is income in earlier life stages. Importantly, few studies have assessed these linkages, so additional research is necessary to confirm these findings; the use of compelling quasi-experimental research designs is especially important.

IMPLICATIONS FOR RESEARCH

A vitally important question in this research field is to what extent variability in household income actually causes differences in children's development. There are many early intervention or enrichment programs designed to promote child development, and most of the program evaluations employ random assignment of subjects to treatment and control groups. Why not adopt the same strategy to assess the causal impact of the components of SES? We should not resign ourselves to the conclusion that SES cannot be manipulated because policies can change individual components of SES, in particular income.

Our review has described several instances of developmental studies taking advantage of ongoing random assignment policy evaluations in which boosting family income is an important component of the experimental manipulation. Several found that both test-based and teacher reports of achievement were affected by these policies. Health and behavioral outcomes were less frequently examined (and often less well measured).

Ongoing data collections involving the measurement of child and adolescent outcomes might be able to take advantage of quasi-experimental manipulation of income. As reviewed in the section Assessing Causal Consequences of Poverty: Methods and Results, several studies have taken advantage of ongoing data collection efforts measuring children's achievement to assess the impacts of changes in the generosity of income support policies such as the US EITC and the Canadian National Child Benefit. Other natural experiments are possible, as indicated by the studies by Akee and colleagues (2010, 2015) that linked data on child outcomes from the Great Smokey Mountain Study of Youth to the timing of the introduction of a casino by a tribal government in North Carolina.

International scholarship estimating causal effects has surpassed efforts by US scholars. Researchers have implemented field studies of CCTs and unconditional cash transfers in many developing countries (Fiszbein et al. 2009). The main outcomes of interest in these studies are often economic and material conditions, which are not traditionally of interest in psychological studies; however, attention is increasingly being paid to the use of these experiments to understand how poverty and conditions of economic standing affect individuals and families. To significantly advance our understanding of how developmental processes are affected by economic conditions, we must be willing to undertake more ambitious studies rather than to rely on methods and samples of convenience.

An alternative, if somewhat expensive, strategy would be to launch an experimental developmental study devoted to assessing the impact of the manipulation of income. Suppose low-income families with newborns were recruited into a five-year study of early child development and randomly assigned to treatment or control groups. The study provides control families nominal monthly payments (say $20) and experimental families much larger monthly payments of a scale associated with policies such as the EITC (say $333 per month, or $4,000 per year). The $3,760 annual difference between the treatment and control groups constitutes a substantial income increase for a family with an income near the poverty line. Quasi-experimental studies suggest that this income increase might be sufficient to boost test scores by approximately 0.20–0.25 of a standard deviation, and a simple power calculation shows that approximately 1,000 cases would be sufficient to provide 80% power to detect an effect of this size (given expected attrition) on outcomes. Rigorous laboratory measures of children's cognitive and brain development, as well as measures of health, stress, and behavior, could be gathered at approximately age three. Careful thought would need to be given to whether more sophisticated measures of brain functioning might be expected to change by at least 0.20 SD. This approach would also help one to better understand how poverty reduction improves brain functioning; one could measure elements of family context expected to link poverty to child development, including parent stress, family expenditures, routines and time use, parenting practices, and child care arrangements.

A large-scale poverty reduction study would not be without challenges and complications, but the potential reward of understanding how and to what extent poverty affects developmental processes would be invaluable to the field. This reorientation of the field, with the resulting goal of studying experimentally or quasi-experimentally induced variation in poverty and economic resources, would vastly increase both the specificity and the certainty of our knowledge about how income affects neurocognitive development (Duncan & Magnuson 2012). This approach would resolve lingering questions about the importance of income in the constellation of potential causal factors leading to disadvantage. Perhaps even more importantly, it would also advance policy discussion by providing a way to better assess the consequences of decisions that might increase or decrease the incomes of parents with young children.

DISCLOSURE STATEMENT

G.D. and K.M. have a proposal under review for a randomized controlled trial to test the impact of income supplements on the cognitive development of young children.

ACKNOWLEDGMENTS

Portions of this article were adapted from a more general review of socioeconomic status that the authors wrote for the *Handbook of Child Psychology and Developmental Science* (Duncan et al. 2015) and from Duncan et al. (2014).

LITERATURE CITED

Akee RKQ, Copeland WE, Keeler G, Angold A, Costello EJ. 2010. Parents' incomes and children's outcomes: a quasi-experiment using transfer payments from casino profits. *Am. Econ. J. Appl. Econ.* 2(1):86–115

Akee R, Simeonova E, Costello EJ, Copeland W. 2015. *How does household income affect child personality traits and behaviours?* Work. Pap. No. 21562, Natl. Bur. Econ. Res.

Becker GS. 1991. *A Treatise on the Family.* Cambridge, MA: Harvard Univ. Press

Bettinger EP, Long BT, Oreopoulos P, Sanbonmatsu L. 2012. The role of application assistance and information in college decisions: results from the H&R Block FAFSA experiment. *Q. J. Econ.* 127(3):1205–42

Bjerk D. 2007. Measuring the relationship between youth criminal participation and household economic resources. *J. Quant. Criminol.* 23(1):23–39

Blair C, Granger DA, Willoughby M, Mills-Koonce R, Cox M, et al. 2011. Salivary cortisol mediates effects of poverty and parenting on executive functions in early childhood. *Child Dev.* 82(6):1970–84

Blau DM. 1999. The effect of income on child development. *Rev. Econ. Stat.* 81(2):261–76

Boyce WT, Obradović J, Bush NR, Stamperdahl J, Kim YS, Adler N. 2012. Social stratification, classroom climate, and the behavioral adaptation of kindergarten children. *PNAS* 109(Suppl. 2):17168–73

Brito NH, Noble KG. 2014. Socioeconomic status and structural brain development. *Front. Neurosci.* 8:276. doi: 10.3389/fnins.2014.00276

Brody GH, Flor DL. 1997. Maternal psychological functioning, family processes, and child adjustment in rural, single-parent, African American families. *Dev. Psychol.* 33(6):1000–11

Brody GH, Stoneman Z, Flor D, McCrary C, Hastings L, Conyers O. 1994. Financial resources, parent psychological functioning, parent co-caregiving, and early adolescent competence in rural two-parent African-American families. *Child Dev.* 65(2):590–605

Clark LP, Millet DB, Marshall JD. 2014. National patterns in environmental injustice and inequality: outdoor NO_2 air pollution in the United States. *PLOS ONE* 9(4):1–8

Conger RD, Elder GH Jr. 1994. *Families in Troubled Times: Adapting to Change in Rural America.* New York: A. de Gruyter

Cook TD. 2014. Generalizing causal knowledge in the policy sciences: external validity as a task of both multiattribute representation and multiattribute extrapolation. *J. Policy Anal. Manag.* 33(2):527–36

Croizet JC, Claire T. 1998. Extending the concept of stereotype threat to social class: the intellectual underperformance of students from low socioeconomic backgrounds. *Personal. Soc. Psychol. Bull.* 24(6):588–94

Cunha F, Heckman J. 2007. The technology of skill formation. *Am. Econ. Rev.* 97(2):31–47

Dahl GB, Lochner L. 2012. The impact of family income on child achievement: evidence from the earned income tax credit. *Am. Econ. Rev.* 102(5):1927–56

Dearing E, McCartney K, Taylor BA. 2006. Within-child associations between family income and externalizing and internalizing problems. *Dev. Psychol.* 42(2):237–52

DeNavas-Walt C, Proctor BD. 2015. *Income and poverty in the United States: 2014.* Curr. Popul. Rep. P60-252, US Census Bur., Washington, DC. **https://www.census.gov/content/dam/Census/library/publications/2015/demo/p60-252.pdf**

D'Onofrio BM, Goodnight JA, Van Hulle CA, Rodgers JL, Rathouz PJ, et al. 2009. A quasi-experimental analysis of the association between family income and offspring conduct problems. *J. Abnorm. Child Psychol.* 37(3):415–29

Duncan GJ, Brooks-Gunn J, eds. 1997. *Consequences of Growing Up Poor.* New York: Russell Sage Found.

Duncan GJ, Magnuson K. 2012. Socioeconomic status and cognitive functioning: moving from correlation to causation. *Wiley Interdiscip. Rev. Cogn. Sci.* 3(3):377–86

Duncan GJ, Magnuson K. 2013. Investing in preschool programs. *J. Econ. Perspect.* 27(2):109–32

Duncan GJ, Magnuson K, Votruba-Drzal E. 2014. Boosting family income to promote child development. *Future Child.* 24(1):99–120

Duncan G, Magnuson K, Votruba-Drzal E. 2015. Children and socioeconomic status. In *Handbook of Child Psychology and Developmental Science,* Vol. 4: *Ecological Settings and Processes in Developmental Systems,* ed. MH Bornstein, T Leventhal, pp. 534–73. New York: Wiley

Duncan GJ, Morris PA, Rodrigues C. 2011. Does money really matter? Estimating impacts of family income on young children's achievement with data from random-assignment experiments. *Dev. Psychol.* 47(5):1263–79

Duncan GJ, Murnane RJ. 2011a. Introduction: the American dream, then and now. See Duncan & Murnane 2011b, pp. 3–23

Duncan GJ, Murnane RJ, eds. 2011b. *Whither Opportunity? Rising Inequality, Schools, and Children's Life Chances.* New York/Chicago: Russell Sage Found./Spencer Found.

Duncan GJ, Ziol-Guest KM, Kalil A. 2010. Early-childhood poverty and adult attainment, behavior, and health. *Child Dev.* 81(1):306–25

Edin K, Kefalas M. 2005. *Promises I Can Keep: Why Poor Women Put Motherhood Before Marriage.* Berkeley, CA: Univ. California Press

Elder GH Jr. 1974. *Children of the Great Depression.* Chicago, IL: Univ. Chicago Press

Elder GH Jr., Nguyen TV, Caspi A. 1985. Linking family hardship to children's lives. *Child Dev.* 56(2):361–75

Ellis BJ, Boyce WT, Belsky J, Bakermans-Kranenburg MJ, van Ijzendoorn MH. 2011. Differential susceptibility to the environment: an evolutionary-neurodevelopmental theory. *Dev. Psychopathol.* 23(1):7–28

Evans GW. 2004. The environment of childhood poverty. *Am. Psychol.* 59(2):77–92

Evans WN, Garthwaite CL. 2014. Giving mom a break: the impact of higher EITC payments on maternal health. *Am. Econ. J. Econ. Policy* 6(2):258–90

Evans GW, Saltzman H, Cooperman JL. 2001. Housing quality and children's socioemotional health. *Environ. Behav.* 33(3):389–99

Fiszbein A, Schady NR, Ferreira FH. 2009. *Conditional cash transfers: reducing present and future poverty.* World Bank Policy Res. Rep., World Bank, Washington, DC

Foster EM. 2002. How economists think about family resources and child development. *Child Dev.* 73(6):1904–14

Fox SE, Levitt P, Nelson CA. 2010. How the timing and quality of early experiences influence the development of brain architecture. *Child Dev.* 81(1):28–40

Gennetian LA, Duncan GJ, Knox VW, Vargas WG, Clark-Kauffman E, London AS. 2002. *How welfare and work policies for parents affect adolescents: a synthesis of research.* MDRC Rep., New York, NY. **http://www.mdrc.org/sites/default/files/full_394.pdf**

Gennetian LA, Shafir E. 2015. The persistence of poverty in the context of financial instability: a behavioral perspective. *J. Policy Anal. Manag.* 34(4):904–36

Grandjean P, Landrigan PJ. 2006. Developmental neurotoxicity of industrial chemicals. *Lancet* 368(9553):2167–78

Hackman D, Farah MJ. 2009. Socioeconomic status and the developing brain. *Trends Cogn. Sci.* 13:65–73. doi:10.1016/j.tics.2008.11.003

Hanson JL, Hair N, Shen DG, Shi F, Gilmore JH, et al. 2013. Family poverty affects the rate of human infant brain growth. *PLOS ONE* 8(12):e80954

Haveman R, Wolfe B. 1995. The determinants of children's attainments: findings and review of methods. *J. Econ. Lit.* 33(4):1829–78

Heberle AE, Carter AS. 2015. Cognitive aspects of young children's experience of economic disadvantage. *Psychol. Bull.* 141(4):723–46

Kaushal N, Magnuson K, Waldfogel J. 2011. How is family income related to investments in children's learning? See Duncan & Murnane 2011b, pp. 187–206

Kessler RC, Cleary PD. 1980. Social class and psychological distress. *Am. Sociol. Rev.* 45(3):463–78

Kim P, Evans GW, Angstadt M, Ho SS, Sripada CS, et al. 2013. Effects of childhood poverty and chronic stress on emotion regulatory brain function in adulthood. *PNAS* 110(46):18442–47

Lamont M, Small ML. 2008. How culture matters for poverty: enriching our understanding of poverty. In *The Colors of Poverty: Why Racial and Ethnic Disparities Persist*, ed. AC Lin, DR Harris, pp. 76–102. New York: Russell Sage Found.

Lamont M, Small ML. 2010. Cultural diversity and anti-poverty policy. *Int. Soc. Sci. J.* 61(199):169–80

Lareau A. 2003. *Unequal Childhoods: Race, Class, and Family Life*. Berkeley: Univ. Calif. Press

Lewis M, Rudolph K. 2014. *Handbook of Developmental Psychopathology*. New York: Springer

Lewis O. 1966. *La Vida: A Puerto Rican Family in the Culture of Poverty—San Juan and New York*. New York: Random House

Lewis O. 1969. The culture of poverty. In *On Understanding Poverty: Perspectives from the Social Sciences*, ed. DP Moynihan, pp. 187–200. New York: Basic Books

Loken KV, Mogstad M, Wiswall M. 2012. What linear estimators miss: the effects of family income on child outcomes. *Am. Econ. J. Appl. Econ.* 4(2):1–35

Lupien SJ, King S, Meaney MJ, McEwen BS. 2001. Can poverty get under your skin? Basal cortisol levels and cognitive function in children from low and high socioeconomic status. *Dev. Psychol.* 13(3):653–76

Mackie JL. 1974. *The Cement of the Universe: A Study of Causation*. Oxford, UK: Clarendon Press

Mani A, Mullainathan S, Shafir E, Zhao J. 2013. Poverty impedes cognitive function. *Science* 341(6149):976–80

Massey DS. 1990. American apartheid: segregation and the making of the underclass. *Am. J. Sociol.* 96:329–57

Mayer SE. 1997. *What Money Can't Buy: Family Income and Children's Life Chances*. Cambridge, MA: Harvard Univ. Press

Maynard RA. 1977. The effects of the rural income maintenance experiment on the school performance of children. *Am. Econ. Rev.* 67(1):370–75

Maynard RA, Murnane RJ. 1979. The effects of a negative income tax on school performance: results of an experiment. *J. Hum. Resour.* 14(4):463–76

McEwen BS. 2000. The neurobiology of stress: from serendipity to clinical relevance. *Brain Res.* 886(1):172–89

McLeod JD, Kessler RC. 1990. Socioeconomic status differences in vulnerability to undesirable life events. *J. Health Soc. Behav.* 31(2):162–72

McLoyd VC. 1990. The impact of economic hardship on black families and children: psychological distress, parenting, and socioemotional development. *Child Dev.* 61(2):311–46

Mead LM. 1986. *Beyond Entitlement: The Social Obligations of Citizenship*. New York: Free Press

Miller GE, Chen E, Parker KJ. 2011. Psychological stress in childhood and susceptibility to the chronic diseases of aging: moving toward a model of behavioral and biological mechanisms. *Psychol. Bull.* 137(6):959–97

Milligan K, Stabile M. 2011. Do child tax benefits affect the well-being of children? Evidence from Canadian child benefit expansions. *Am. Econ. J. Econ. Policy* 3(3):175–205

Miranda ML, Edwards SE, Keating MH, Paul CJ. 2011. Making the environmental justice grade: the relative burden of air pollution exposure in the United States. *Int. J. Environ. Res. Public Health* 8(6):1755–71

Mistry RS, Vandewater EA, Huston AC, McLoyd VC. 2002. Economic well-being and children's social adjustment: the role of family process in an ethnically diverse low-income sample. *Child Dev.* 73(3):935–51

Morris P, Duncan GJ, Clark-Kauffman E. 2005. Child well-being in an era of welfare reform: the sensitivity of transitions in development to policy change. *Dev. Psychol.* 41:919–32

Mullainathan S, Shafir E. 2013. *Scarcity: Why Having Too Little Means So Much*. New York: Time Books

Noble KG, Engelhardt LE, Brito NH, Mack LJ, Nail EJ, et al. 2015a. Socioeconomic disparities in neurocognitive development in the first two years of life. *Dev. Psychobiol.* 57(5):535–51

Noble KG, Grieve SM, Korgaonkar MS, Engelhardt LE, Griffith EY, et al. 2012a. Hippocampal volume varies with educational attainment across the life-span. *Front. Hum. Neurosci.* 6:307

Noble KG, Houston SM, Brito NH, Bartsch H, Kan E, et al. 2015b. Family income, parental education and brain structure in children and adolescents. *Nat. Neurosci.* 18(5):773–78

Noble KG, Houston SM, Kan E, Sowell ER. 2012b. Neural correlates of socioeconomic status in the developing human brain. *Dev. Sci.* 15(4):516–27

Obradović J, Portilla XA, Ballard PJ. 2016. Biological sensitivity to family income: differential effects on early executive functioning. *Child Dev.* 87(2):374–84

Odgers CL. 2015. Income inequality and the developing child: Is it all relative? *Am. Psychol.* 70(8):722–31

Odgers CL, Donley S, Caspi A, Bates CJ, Moffitt TE. 2015. Living alongside more affluent neighbors predicts greater involvement in antisocial behavior among low-income boys. *J. Child Psychol. Psychiatry* 56(10):1055–64

Ratcliffe CE, McKernan SM. 2012. *Child poverty and its lasting consequence.* Low-Income Work. Fam. Pap. 21, Urban Inst., Washington, DC. **http://www.urban.org/sites/default/files/alfresco/publication-pdfs/412659-Child-Poverty-and-Its-Lasting-Consequence.PDF**

Raver CC, Blair C, Willoughby M. 2013. Poverty as a predictor of 4-year-olds' executive function: new perspectives on models of differential susceptibility. *Dev. Psychol.* 49(2):292–304

Reardon SF, Owens A. 2014. 60 years after *Brown*: trends and consequences of school segregation. *Annu. Rev. Sociol.* 40(1):199–218

Reiss F. 2013. Socioeconomic inequalities and mental health problems in children and adolescents: a systematic review. *Soc. Sci. Med.* 90:24–31

Riccio J, Dechausay N, Greenberg D, Miller C, Rucks Z, Verma N. 2010. *Toward reduced poverty across generations: early findings from New York City's conditional cash transfer program.* MDRC Rep., New York, NY. **http://www.mdrc.org/sites/default/files/FamRewards2010ONYC%20FULL%20Report%20REd%202-18-16.pdf**

Riccio J, Dechausay N, Miller C, Nuñez S, Verma N, Yang E. 2013. *Conditional cash transfers in New York City: the continuing story of the Opportunity NYC-Family Rewards Demonstration.* MDRC Rep., New York, NY. **http://www.mdrc.org/sites/default/files/Conditional_Cash_Transfers_FR%202-18-16.pdf**

Rosenzweig MR. 2003. Effects of differential experience on the brain and behavior. *Dev. Neuropsychol.* 24(2–3):523–40

Simpson GA, Bloom B, Cohen RA, Blumberg S, Bourdon KH. 2005. U.S. children with emotional and behavioral difficulties: data from the 2001, 2002, and 2003 National Health Interview Surveys. *Adv. Data* 23(360):1–13

Turner RJ, Avison WR. 2003. Status variations in stress exposure: implications for the interpretation of research on race, socioeconomic status, and gender. *J. Health Soc. Behav.* 44(4):488–505

Votruba-Drzal E. 2006. Economic disparities in middle childhood development: Does income matter? *Dev. Psychol.* 42(6):1154–67

Wilson WJ. 1987. *The Truly Disadvantaged: The Inner City, the Underclass, and Public Policy.* Chicago: Univ. Chicago Press

Wilson WJ. 1996. *When Work Disappears: The World of the New Urban Poor.* New York: Knopf

Ziol-Guest KM, Duncan GJ, Kalil A, Boyce WT. 2012. Early childhood poverty, immune-mediated disease processes, and adult productivity. *PNAS* 109(Suppl.):17289–93

Culture Three Ways: Culture and Subcultures Within Countries

Daphna Oyserman

Department of Psychology, University of Southern California, Los Angeles, California 90089-1061; email: oyserman@usc.edu

Annu. Rev. Psychol. 2017. 68:435–63

First published online as a Review in Advance on September 21, 2016

The *Annual Review of Psychology* is online at psych.annualreviews.org

This article's doi: 10.1146/annurev-psych-122414-033617

Keywords

culture as situated cognition, cultural fluency, culture priming, honor, cultural mindset

Abstract

Culture can be thought of as a set of everyday practices and a core theme—individualism, collectivism, or honor—as well as the capacity to understand each of these themes. In one's own culture, it is easy to fail to see that a cultural lens exists and instead to think that there is no lens at all, only reality. Hence, studying culture requires stepping out of it. There are two main methods to do so: The first involves using between-group comparisons to highlight differences and the second involves using experimental methods to test the consequences of disruption to implicit cultural frames. These methods highlight three ways that culture organizes experience: (*a*) It shields reflexive processing by making everyday life feel predictable, (*b*) it scaffolds which cognitive procedure (connect, separate, or order) will be the default in ambiguous situations, and (*c*) it facilitates situation-specific accessibility of alternate cognitive procedures. Modern societal social-demographic trends reduce predictability and increase collectivism and honor-based go-to cognitive procedures.

Contents

INTRODUCTION

> The worlds in which different societies live are distinct worlds, not merely the same world with different words attached.
>
> —Edward Sapir 1929, p. 209

> Nothing evades our attention so persistently as that which is taken for granted.
>
> —Gustav Ichheiser 1949, p. 1

Culture can be defined as the part of the environment made by humans. It is the set of meanings that a group in a time and place come to adopt or develop, and these meanings facilitate smooth social coordination, clarify group boundaries, and provide a space for innovation (e.g., Geertz 1984, Markus et al. 1996, Oyserman 2011, Packer & Cole 2016). The possibility that people who live in different places not only act and think differently but also have different minds has been considered at least since ancient times, when Herodotus reported on the practices of the people he saw in his far-flung travels (Jahoda 2014). The possibility that people act differently in different places and might even have different minds has two implications for cultural psychologists. The first is that the questions that seem relevant differ in different places and as a result the theories developed to answer questions that seem pressing in one place may not be meaningful in other places (Kruglanski & Stroebe 2012). The second implication is that the field of psychology needs to do a better job of documenting whether a theory that is developed and tested in one place is useful for making predictions elsewhere (Kruglanski & Stroebe 2012).

Noticing culture requires some way of stepping out of it in order to gain perspective on it. The promise of cultural psychology is that making this effort matters because it results in new insights that matter, regardless of whether one is a cultural psychologist. However, because all of life takes place within culture, as Ichheiser (1949) notes, it is easy to fail to see that a cultural lens exists and instead to think that there is no lens at all—just reality.

Figure 1 depicts how culture might matter to a great extent when viewed from outside and be almost entirely unnoticed, thus seeming not to matter at all, when viewed from within. Colored rows describe processes and white rows describe the associative networks that are probabilistically cued as a result of activation of the particular cues that are part of these networks. People typically live in one context, not many; as a result, perception, judgment, and behavior (**Figure 1**, *top row, blue*) seem to flow directly from cues (**Figure 1**, *bottom row, orange*) rather than being the probabilistic result of intermediate processes. Culture feels like reality—not like an interpretation of reality (Morris et al. 2015b, Mourey et al. 2015). Cultural psychology focuses on the universal mechanisms (that is, the probabilistic intermittent processes) by which the everyday cues that are particular to a society, time, and place are interpreted to form perception, judgment, and behavior.

As depicted in **Figure 1**, cues, which can be features of the immediate situation or chronically or momentarily activated information in memory, are interpreted via associative knowledge networks that include social, emotional, physiological, and other content (**Figure 1**, *third row from bottom, red*). These knowledge networks activate one or another cultural mindset that includes relevant content, procedures, and goals (**Figure 1**, *third row from top, brown*). Which cultural mindset is activated is a probabilistic function of how central the cue is to the knowledge network, which cultural mindset has been most recently activated, and which cultural mindset is most typically activated.

This probabilistic process is largely understudied because psychologists operating and testing their theories within one culture are likely to fail to notice culture operating at all, assuming that their perspective is reality rather than, for example, individualism (but see Lun & Bond 2013, Machery 2010). If an activated individualistic cultural mindset is not noticed at all, psychologists may infer that culture matters in other settings but not in Western settings with educated and well-off participants. Even if psychologists in these settings infer that an individualistic cultural mindset is activated, they are likely to assume that this mindset is chronically activated. Only by directly examining the likelihood that a particular contextual cue activates an individualistic, a collectivistic, or an honor mindset can psychologists unpack the probabilistic process by which a particular cultural mindset is activated. However, research on this topic will likely begin to emerge because of changes in modern societies as a result of immigration, differential fertility of groups within societies, and increased social stratification (e.g., Frey 2015, Grusky & MacLean 2016).

These trends are important because, as detailed below, each is likely to lead to an increased propensity for activation of collectivistic and honor culture mindsets, even in wealthy modern societies currently assumed to have chronically activated individualistic mindsets. These trends thus imply that collectivism and honor will become more salient in wealthy modern societies (e.g., Mesoudi et al. 2016, Nowak et al. 2016). These trends involve both the possibility of a general shift toward collectivism and honor throughout these societies and the likelihood of a shift toward collectivism and honor in subcultures within these societies. The development of subcultures is predicted both from increased immigration and segmented assimilation of new immigrants into particular parts of the host society and from increased wage inequality within the host society, as articulated in sociological (Portes & Zhou 1993) and political science (Grusky & MacLean 2016) frameworks.

These processes of increased collectivism and honor are the result of sociodemographic changes: Wealthy countries are experiencing low fertility, higher migration, and either increasing (e.g., Australia, Canada, the United States) or flat (e.g., Germany, France, the Netherlands) wage inequality (Grusky & MacLean 2016). An exception to these general trends is Japan: Although Japan is experiencing low fertility, it is neither a target of large-scale migration nor a site of

Individualism: independence; propensity to interpret ambiguous experiences as being about autonomy and process for a discrete, main point

Honor: face; propensity to interpret ambiguous experiences as being about reputation-respect and process for rank and relative position

Collectivism: interdependence; propensity to interpret ambiguous experiences as being about belongingness-connection and process for relationships and group membership

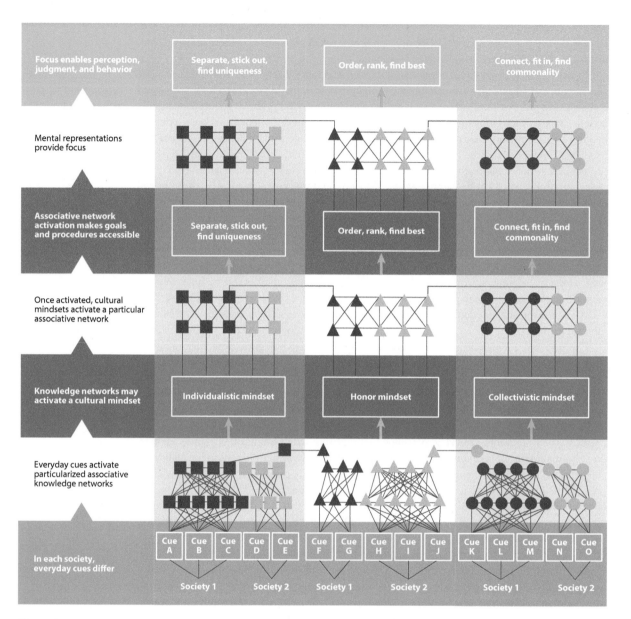

Figure 1

The universal mechanisms, specific cues (UMSC) model. The UMSC model articulates a probabilistic understanding of the brain-culture interface. Because processing is fundamentally associative, whether an initial cue results in a predicted response is highly dependent on the associations that come to mind at each stage. The process is considered from the bottom up. (*Orange row*) The UMSC model proposes that each society includes everyday cues. (*First white row*) These cues activate associative knowledge networks that are specific to the particular society. (*Red row*) The nodes in these networks can activate an individualistic mindset, an honor mindset, or a collectivistic mindset. (*Second white row*) Once one of these cultural mindsets is activated, it cues an associative network. (*Brown row*) The associative network makes mindset-congruent contents, goals, and procedures accessible. (*Third white row*) The result is activation of congruent associative networks, which probabilistically increase accessibility. (*Blue row*) As a result of spreading activation, mindset-congruent actions, perceptions, emotions, and cognitive procedures are ready for use. Figure adapted with permission from Oyserman et al. (2014).

increasing wage inequality (Grusky & MacLean 2016, PricewaterhouseCoopers 2015). In wealthy countries other than Japan, low fertility combined with migration and higher fertility among newcomers means that diversity is higher among the younger generation (e.g., Frey 2015). Wage inequality is likely to increase both the salience of social class as a subcultural frame (e.g., Grusky & MacLean 2016) and the salience of collectivism (e.g., Stephens et al. 2014) and honor (e.g., Nowak et al. 2016).

The idea of subcultures within cultures makes intuitive sense, even though whether something is identified as a culture or a subculture depends in large part on the question being addressed. Take the example of American culture: There can be no definitive answer to the question of whether there is a single American culture or many American subcultures, or whether American culture is really a subculture within modern, postindustrialized, educated, wealthy Western culture (e.g., Bellah 1985, Henrich et al. 2010, Swidler 1986). Each of these formulations is true in some way and each differs in their utility in addressing questions about culture depending on the level of analysis the question requires.

The idea of subculture also makes sense when considering categories such as race-ethnicity, religion, and social class as groups that are experienced as fixed and are linked to placement in the social hierarchy (also called caste-like groups; Bourdieu 1984, Lewis 1966). These caste-like groups are central to everyday understanding of what culture is (Spencer 2014). Though often relegated to studies of stereotyping, caste-like groups have been fruitfully rediscovered by cultural psychologists who are attempting to predict when cultural messages from larger culture will be experienced as matching or mismatching in-group messages and with what consequences (e.g., Oyserman et al. 1995; for reviews, see Oyserman 2007, 2015; Stephens et al. 2014).

TWO WAYS TO STUDY CULTURE

Cultural psychologists use two different methods to step out of culture in order to study it. The first and by far the most common method is to use between-group comparisons to identify differences that might be due to culture or subculture (e.g., Henrich et al. 2010, Rychlowska et al. 2015). The second method is to use experimental techniques to observe the consequences of disruptions to implicit cultural frames (e.g., Oyserman 2011, Oyserman et al. 2014). Both methods are compatible with the premise that culture and humans coevolved (Kurzban & Neuberg 2005, Legare & Nielsen 2015).

Each method is useful in addressing some questions and not others. Consider the between-group comparison method. This method elucidates differences between groups but cannot test assertions about what these differences mean. Finding a difference in one between-group comparison, while interesting, may or may not generalize to other comparisons (e.g., Henrich et al. 2010, Machery 2010, Matsumoto 1999). Moreover, the between-group comparison method carries the risk of reifying differences as large, inherent, deeply rooted, and fixed, yet coevolution does not imply that current between-group differences are fixed, that comparison groups generalize to populations, or that otherwise hidden cultural themes will not emerge if context changes (e.g., Ceci et al. 2010).

The alternative to the between-group comparison method is the experimental method, which entails either activating a particular cultural mindset or activating disjuncture between culturally grounded expectations and actual experience (Oyserman in press). This method thus provides a way to articulate and test a possibility not testable in the between-group comparison method, which is that between-group differences provide a lens to see generally available but differentially accessible features of the human mind (Oyserman et al. 2014). As detailed in the following sections, the experimental method, unlike the between-group comparison method, can test whether observed

Between-group comparison method: attribution of group-based differences in features, behaviors, or traits to culture; the most common method of studying culture

Experimental method: testing of group-based differences attributed to culture by manipulating the predicted proximal active ingredients; the alternative method of studying culture differences between and within groups imply differences in the accessibility (what is usually activated) or in the availability (what can be activated) of cultural values, norms, and meaning-making schemas.

Thus, rather than think of one method as competing with the other, it is more useful to consider each method as capable of addressing some questions and not others. Moreover, neither method can fully address the question of whether a theory has universal applicability—that would require sampling from all peoples, times, and places that have ever existed, which is impossible (Henrich et al. 2010). Whether or not this is a problem depends on perspective: Psychologists typically study the living and, in the same vein, cultural psychology focuses on currently existing cultures.

THREE WAYS THAT CULTURE SHAPES EXPERIENCE

Particular practices: anthropology-based way of describing culture focusing on the everyday, expected, and ordinary; what people do, and when and how they do it

Core themes: group-based differences, typically individualism (independence), collectivism (interdependence), or honor (face); most common psychological way of describing culture

Cultural psychologists use three operationalizations of culture to highlight different aspects of how culture shapes the meaning people make of their everyday experiences. First, culture can be thought of as the particular practices of a group; knowing these practices makes everyday life feel predictable and frees up cognitive resources. These practices include mundane things such as what the rules for public transportation are—whether one can eat and drink, for example—and whether these rules can be broken (Morris et al. 2015b, Mourey et al. 2015, Zou et al. 2009). Second, culture can be thought of as a particular core theme—individualism, collectivism, or honor—that scaffolds what and how people think about ambiguous situations (Oyserman 2011). Third, culture can be thought of as a set of core themes that vary in their accessibility depending on situational cues. For example, even if collectivism is a group's core theme, people can make sense of the world through an individualistic or honor lens (Oyserman 2015, Oyserman & Lee 2008).

Each operationalization highlights a different aspect of what culture is and does. Each is vital because it makes accessible for study something that other operationalizations do not and because the assumptions and methods connected to it are suitable for a particular kind of prediction about culture's consequences. Some operationalizations highlight the situated, dynamic nature of culture's instantiation in norms, values, and self-concept, and others highlight the stable nature of culture. By combining operationalizations, it is possible to make predictions about when cultural change, whether the result of immigration or migration, will be experienced as additive (a both/and experience of multiple cultures merging) and when it will be experienced as subtractive (an either/or experience of competing loyalty). Each way of considering culture highlights different aspects of both the content (what people think about) and the process (how thinking itself proceeds) of culture, as detailed in the following sections.

Particular Practices

A particular practices formulation highlights culture's effects on prediction and the consequences of mismatch between prediction and observation on processing style—whether thinking entails systematic, effortful reasoning or remains automatic and effortless (Mourey et al. 2015, Oyserman et al. 2014). The unique predictions from this formulation are depicted in **Figure 2** as a prediction-observation match-mismatch model of culture.

The prediction-observation match-mismatch model provides insight into when people are likely to shift to systematic processing. Being a part of a culture means knowing, implicitly, how things are likely to unfold, and, as outlined in **Figure 2**, when observations match implicit cultural expectations, there is no need to reason carefully because everything is as it should be. However, if observations mismatch implicit cultural expectations, something might be amiss, calling for careful reasoning—that is, systematic or reflective reasoning rather than associative or reflexive

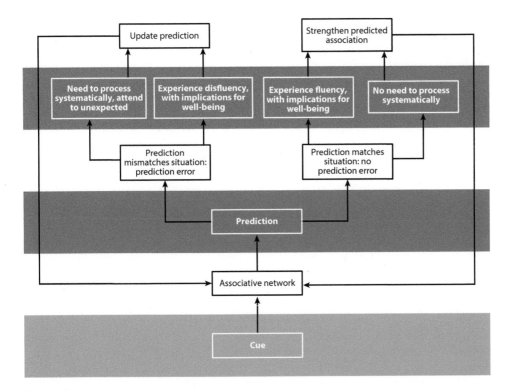

Figure 2

The prediction-observation match-mismatch model articulates how the brain updates and, by implication, why fit between personal and societal style and between prediction and experience influences both processing style in the moment and well-being over time. Note that in spite of high sensitivity to context, acculturation is difficult, and not fitting into a society's typical cultural style can be undermining of well-being. Starting at the bottom, an environmental cue (*orange row*) activates an associative network (*first white row*), which in turn generates predictions about the situation. If predictions (*red row*) match the situation, no error response is generated (*second white row, right side*), fluency is experienced (*brown row, right side*), and associative processing is task focused. If predictions (*red row*) mismatch the situation, an error response is generated (*second white row, left side*), and disfluency is experienced (*brown row, left side*), cuing systematic processing to attend to the unexpected. In cases both of experienced fluency and of experienced disfluency, the associative network is updated (*top white row*). In the case of fluency, the update is to strengthen an existing prediction (*top white row, right side*). In the case of disfluency, the update is to add new information (*top white row, left side*). Note that systematic processing to attend to the unexpected (*brown row, left side*) may or may not improve prediction at the next round since the reason an unexpected situation was encountered cannot be ascertained from registering that an unexpected situation was encountered. The general process model can also be used to understand the process by which fit and misfit between cultural norm and personal style can yield consequences for well-being. Figure adapted with permission from Oyserman et al. (2014).

reasoning. Findings with Chinese and American participants support the core prediction of the role of cultural fluency and disfluency. People from both countries reason more systematically in culturally disfluent, as compared to fluent, cultural contexts (Mourey et al. 2015). This formulation is congruent with models that highlight the importance of social norms in predicting how culture matters (Morris et al. 2015b, Zou et al. 2009). However, instead of what people think the norms are, the focus is on what happens to reasoning when norms are violated versus when they are upheld.

Core Theme

A core theme formulation highlights culture's effects on norms, values, self-concept, and cognitive procedures used to process information—people use a variety of procedures in their everyday lives, but in ambiguous situations, core cultural theme matters (Miyamoto 2013). The core theme formulation is depicted in **Figure 1** in the three columns. The networks in each column are differentially dense to depict differences in chronic accessibility of each core theme between societies. For simplicity, the two societies in **Figure 1** are labeled simply 1 and 2. When a theme is core, the cognitive procedure associated with it is likely to come to mind when another procedure is not specified by contextual cues. As a result, depending on how associative networks respond to cues, a particular procedure—exclusion based (e.g., contrast, pull apart), inclusion based (e.g., assimilate, connect), or ordering based (e.g., hierarchical)—is more or less likely to be applied (Miyamoto 2013; Novin & Oyserman 2017; Oyserman et al. 2009; D. Oyserman & S. Novin, unpublished data).

The core theme formulation focuses on processing style (i.e., exclude, include, or order) and asks which people are likely to use which style to process information (Miyamoto 2013, Spencer-Rodgers et al. 2010). Each of these styles can involve the application of rules and, as a result, systematic reasoning or can proceed at low-level associative levels; thus, processing style is distinct from cognitive style, which is the focus of the particular practices formulation of culture. The two core cultural themes that have been the focus of research to date are individualism and collectivism, also termed independence and interdependence; their associated processing styles are sometimes termed analytic and holistic reasoning, respectively (Miyamoto 2013). A number of processing style differences between individualistic (independent) and collectivist (interdependent) mindsets have been documented. A chronically activated individualistic mindset (analytic) entails processing for a decontextualized main point (e.g., a rule), whereas a chronically activated collectivistic mindset (holistic) entails processing for related connections (e.g., family resemblance). Findings from between-group comparisons (e.g., between Japan and the United States or between China and the United States) support the prediction that there is a match between processing style and dominant cultural theme. That is, Chinese people are more likely to describe a visual scene in terms of all of its elements. In contrast, Americans are more likely to identify individual and specific parts. Japanese people are more likely to make mistakes when trying to reproduce line segments while ignoring the context in which they saw them. In contrast, Americans are more likely to make mistakes when trying to reproduce the relative size of line segments while recalling the context in which they saw them (Miyamoto 2013).

Variable Accessibility

A variable accessibility formulation highlights that each of the core themes is available, though differentially accessible, across cultures and subcultures (Oyserman & Lee 2008). The variable accessibility formulation is depicted in **Figure 1** as the propensity of getting from a particular cue (A to O) in a society to a particular perception, judgment, or behavior. As can be seen (for example, by looking at cues A to C in Society 1), these cues typically activate knowledge structures that turn on an individualistic mindset. However, as shown in **Figure 1**, the final outcome of activation of a knowledge structure is probabilistic. That is, the outcome depends on a variety of factors, including whether a knowledge structure has been recently activated or not and how central a particular cue is to a knowledge structure. For example, a cue might typically activate an individualistic mindset, but whether or not it does at any particular time is probabilistic. Thus, as depicted by the link between squares and triangles and the link between triangles and circles in **Figure 1**, a cue that typically activates an individualistic or a collectivistic mindset might activate a different mindset under particular circumstances.

The variable accessibility formulation provides insight into when people are likely to use one or another processing style (Oyserman 2011, Oyserman & Lee 2008, Oyserman et al. 2016). Findings support the prediction that momentarily activated cultural mindsets influence processing style. In these studies, Asian participants can be made to process like American participants and the reverse, implying that cultural mindsets that are not chronically activated can be momentarily activated (e.g., Oyserman 2011). For example, on divided attention tasks in which context information must be ignored, Koreans and Americans guided to use a collectivistic mindset do worse than Koreans and Americans guided to use an individualistic mindset (Oyserman et al. 2009). Although prior research has focused on basic cognitive processing, emerging research suggests that activating a cultural mindset influences the performance of complex reasoning tasks as well (D. Oyserman, S. Novin, B. Lam, S.X. Chen, E. Newman, & V. Yan, manuscript under review). Collectivistic mindsets cue processing for connection whereas individualistic mindsets cue processing for main points, and evidence indicates that honor mindsets cue processing for order (D. Oyserman, S. Novin, & V. Yan, unpublished data).

CULTURE AS INHERENT MEANING: PARTICULAR PRACTICES

As detailed in **Figures 1** and **2**, thinking about how culture matters starts with the fact that each culture has a particular set of practices (e.g., Geertz 1984, Triandis et al. 1973) that activates core themes (e.g., honor-face, individualism-independence, and collectivism-interdependence) (e.g., Markus et al. 1996, Nisbett & Cohen 1996, Oyserman et al. 2002a). Having cultural expertise means knowing how "we" think, what "we" value, and how "we" do things (e.g., Oyserman 2011, Swidler 1986). Thinking occurs in culture, and culture structures what seems obvious, normative, and real.

From within a culture, cultural expertise is transparent—it is experienced as if it is reality itself. Hence, culturally laden concepts are not experienced as concepts but as something real (e.g., Geertz 1984, Triandis 2007). Given this transparency of culture, people typically assume that others see the world as they do, and if others say they do not have the same perspective, then their alternative perspectives seem funny, strange, or deviant (e.g., Ichheiser 1949, Oyserman 2011, Triandis 2007). This naïve realism (i.e., the experience of one's own perspective as reality) aspect of culture can contribute to between-group tensions. For example, in the United States, liberal and conservative Americans experience their own beliefs as inherently superior to others' beliefs (Toner et al. 2013).

Because "thinking is for doing" and "doing" cues relevant thinking (e.g., Fiske & Taylor 2013), it is instructive to learn that activating a cultural mindset is associated with particular neural responsivity in preparation for action (e.g., Wang et al. 2013). Importantly, neural activity does not imply endorsement—culture's effects do not actually require that culturally sanctioned interpretations be endorsed, just that they be assumed to be the way that others in one's group experience the world (e.g., Morris et al. 2015b, Mourey et al. 2015). That is, just as stereotypes can influence perception among people who do not explicitly endorse stereotype content (e.g., Bigler & Clark 2014), some of culture's effects may be due to illusions of universality or what has been termed pluralistic ignorance (Allport 1924, O'Gorman 1986).

Naïve realism means that culture's presence will go unnoticed until things do not unfold as culturally expected (e.g., Mourey et al. 2015, Oyserman 2011). One method used to see culture in action is to examine the consequences of perturbing cultural expectations. Telltale signs that something did not fit one's cultural frame include a shift to systematic reasoning, a reduced sense of inherence (the feeling that things are as they ought to be), and an increased desire to defend the traditional values of one's culture (Mourey et al. 2015; Y. Lin & D. Oyserman, unpublished manuscript). As shown in **Figure 2**, when observations match cultural expectations, there is no need to shift to systematic processing, but when cultural expectations are not met, higher-level processing is necessary.

The particular practices formulation builds on dual-processing models of reasoning, which distinguish between two neurally distinct processing systems (Chaiken & Trope 1999, Lieberman 2007). The effortless, reflexive system involves associative links that are turned on via spreading activation; the effortful, reflective system involves systematic and sequential processing of information (Lieberman 2007, Strack & Deutsch 2004). The reflexive system is always at work, whereas the reflective system becomes active when one has the time, resources, and desire to consider carefully (e.g., Strack & Deutsch 2004). Reflexive reasoning feels inherent, intuitive, spontaneous, and effortless—"I just feel it in my gut"; in contrast, reflective reasoning feels effortful because it requires one to think about and apply a set of rules or explicit strategies to problem solve—"I know it in my head."

Because reflexive processing seems to occur without intention or effort, its products have been called natural assessments (Tversky & Kahneman 1983) that are immediately available as bases for choice and action. Examples of natural assessments are abstract properties such as similarity, causal propensity, surprisingness, affective valence (e.g., whether something is good or bad), and mood (Kahneman & Frederick 2002). Applying this to culture yields the following principle: The reflexive system characterizes culture as a natural assessment, whereas the reflective system characterizes culture as a set of current practices. Thus, when the reflexive system is activated, people automatically infer that what is culturally normative is the way things naturally should be and morally ought to be. In contrast, when the reflective system is activated, people may take into account or choose to ignore cultural values and norms. In the reflective system, gaps between personal and cultural norms can be reasoned through.

Because the reflexive system is always working and produces judgments that feel inherent to the situation, people inside a cultural frame are unlikely to notice the need for correction—they experience perception (**Figure 1**, *top row, blue*) as flowing directly from cues (**Figure 1**, *bottom row, orange*). People with other things on their mind (i.e., under cognitive load) often process only reflexively unless they are motivated to do otherwise. Moreover, because the reflexive system is not deactivated when the reflective system is activated, culture is always experienced as a natural and immediate basis for choice and action. Thus, even though the reflective system provides choices, people often experience their culture-based responses as emerging from inherent features of the situation and fail to notice cultural processes at work. **Figure 2** shows the processes of processing reflexively and reflectively. Note that reflexive thinking is the result of a match and reflective thinking of a mismatch between observation and expectation.

When cultural scripts (i.e., expectations) are preserved, reflexive processing will likely be the default, but when cultural scripts are disrupted, the mismatch between expectations and observations can lead to a switch to reflective processing. For example, in one experiment, participants were given a set of word problems to solve (Mourey et al. 2015). Each problem had two characteristics: First, it was correctly solvable using a simple rule (which rule should be used differed between problems); second, an alternative, incorrect solution came immediately to mind upon reading the problem. The correct, rule-based solution was evidence of reflective processing, whereas the incorrect but seemingly obvious solution was evidence of reflexive processing. Participants were randomly assigned to a condition: They saw the problems on a screen with either a pink border, a black border, or a white border (no border) and saw the problems either on Valentine's Day or a week later. Participants who saw the pink border on Valentine's Day (the culturally expected color for the day, as compared to black or no color) were more likely to use reflexive, heuristic processing, which undermined test performance. A week later, however, pink had no cultural significance and had no effect on reasoning skills. Parallel effects were found for disruptions of the cultural scripts for funerals (expressions of sadness being expected and happiness being unexpected) and weddings (a white dress being expected and a dress in another color being unexpected). Participants read obituaries or looked at wedding pictures and later performed a separate cognitive task. Disruption shifted processing to reflective reasoning and improved performance. Sticking to the cultural script keeps processing reflexive. For example, on Chinese New Year, the color red is culturally expected and the color black is not; this holds true, of course, only if the holiday is part of one's cultural frame. Chinese participants proceeded reflexively by choosing more food when given red-bordered rather than black-bordered plates, but only on Chinese New Year; the plate border had no effect on American participants for whom there was no associative link between Chinese New Year and red (Mourey et al. 2015). Another set of studies focused on the experienced naturalness of reflexive thinking. For example, in these studies, Chinese participants scored lower on essentialist beliefs if presented with Chinese New Year greetings in black rather than in red (Cimpian & Salomon 2014), an effect that disappeared when it was no longer Chinese New Year (Y. Lin & D. Oyserman, unpublished manuscript).

As has been discussed, mismatch and the consequent shift to reflective thinking shift processing, as well. However, this may or may not change the outcome of reasoning. To understand this somewhat abstract distinction, let us consider how this can play out in a classroom student-teacher interaction. Suppose a teacher witnesses a student behaving in a particular manner. The seemingly natural and automatic implications of this behavior will be culture bound, differing depending on the content that composes the associative network firing for the teacher at that moment. Teachers with different cultural scripts as to how students should behave and what misbehavior means— e.g., whether it signals exuberance or lack of respect for the teacher—would arrive at different conclusions about what the behavior means. Each interpretation would be experienced as natural, and teachers are likely to experience the student's behavior as expressing something essential about the student, whether that essence is biological, social, or something else (Baron 2014).

Say this content includes "male," "African American," and "respect." Although an African American teacher may see the student's behavior as fitting in the normal range of youthful exuberance and therefore either not indicating misbehavior at all or, if indicating misbehavior, not indicating a lack of respect, a white teacher may see the same student's behavior differently. A white teacher might experience the behavior as outside the normal range of behavior and as indicating a lack of respect for the teacher—and thus as a cause for disciplinary action (Wright 2015). Say that the white teacher is highly motivated to consider each student individually or was expecting behavior within the normal range of behavior; in either case, he or she might experience mismatch with expectations and switch to reflective reasoning. Unfortunately, shifting to reflective thinking will not necessarily change the conclusion a teacher draws. For example, suppose the student's behavior is unexpected and cues a cultural stereotype about African American males as dangerous. Reflective thinking is rule-based reasoning, but the rule itself matters. If the rule that comes to mind is to maintain control, then the result of reflective processing, the need to maintain order, might be the same as the result of reflexive processing. In contrast, if the rule that comes to the teacher's mind is to avoid stereotyping, then the teacher may notice the possibility that he or she would experience the behavior itself differently if it was not exhibited by an African American male student. In that case, the reflective processing might result in reframing the behavior as exuberance.

SOCIAL AND DEMOGRAPHIC TRENDS

A criticism of psychological research is that psychologists tend to study students and that both research participants and researchers themselves are typically wealthy, Westernized, and educated, hailing from the United States, other English-speaking countries, and the European

Union (Henrich et al. 2010). Note that Henrich and colleagues (2010) include as Westernized any society with Western-style education, including Japan, Korea, and China (Henrich et al. 2010). This might mean that psychological theories are limited either because the questions they address are chiefly relevant to people in these countries or because, even though the questions are of general importance, the answers that theories provide to these questions only fit people from this subset of the world. Henrich and colleagues' (2010) recommendation, which is to study the few nonmodernized peoples to really understand culture, is one possible next step. An alternative, as outlined here, is to consider how psychological theory and research can benefit from identifying who psychologists are typically trying to generalize to and where these people are located.

Fertility, Population Growth, and Immigration and Linked Cultural Themes of Honor and Collectivism

Even though psychological theorizing is meant to provide explanations for human behavior, the methods of psychological research are limited to study of the present—they do not lend themselves to the study of the past since data are typically obtained from living humans rather than from secondary analyses of other kinds of data. Before dismissing psychological research as narrowly built on students, it is useful to consider who the students in modern societies with Western-style education—including the United States, the European Union, China, and India—are likely to be. As noted in the first section below, due to fertility, population changes, and immigration in the United States and the European Union, student samples are more likely to yield an increasingly diverse snapshot that includes individualistic, collectivistic, and honor mindsets. However, before assuming that this diversity is sufficient, it is useful to consider which societies have the largest and the most rapidly growing populations and what psychological theorizing is needed to make predictions for people in these societies. These issues are tackled next.

The United States and the European Union. The United States and the European Union, the regions associated with individualism, have a combined population of 830 million people. Education is compulsory through secondary school, and most people attend some form of post-secondary training (though not all graduate; 44% of 25- to 34-year-old Americans and Europeans hold postsecondary degrees) (Will 2014).

These individuals form the basis of most psychological research and are likely to be the population to which psychological research can most easily generalize. Thus, it is useful to consider who these people are. Although it is largely not discussed by psychologists (perhaps because effects have not yet been felt on the student subject pools psychologists rely on), the United States and European Union are rapidly diversifying (Chamie 2012, Eur. Comm. 2007, Frey 2015, Hackett 2015, PricewaterhouseCoopers 2015, Rebala & Wilson 2015). These trends are straightforward: Majority groups are aging and have low birthrates, minority group are younger and have higher birthrates, and immigration is bringing people from different regions of the world (e.g., Frey 2015). Immigrants to the European Union (since World War II) are primarily from Turkey, North Africa, and the Middle East (Eur. Comm. 2007, Hackett 2015). Immigrants to the United States (since 1965) are primarily from Mexico, Central and South America, and Asia (China, India, Frey 2015).

By 2020, American psychologists who use students as their participants—though they are often trying to generalize to people more generally—will have diverse subject pools. Since 2011, most children born in the United States have been "minorities," and demographers estimate that by 2020, most Americans under 18 will be "minorities" (Frey 2015). In the United States, minority status is associated with social class; Mexican heritage is associated with lower educational attainment, and Asian heritage is associated with higher educational attainment (Frey 2015, US Census 2011). Lack of college education is associated with collectivism (Stephens et al. 2007, 2014, 2016). In addition, religious traditions associated with cultures of honor are brought by Catholic immigrants (from Mexico and Central and South America) to the United States and by Muslim immigrants (from Turkey, the Middle East, and Africa) to the European Union (Cohen & Varnum 2016, Hackett 2015, Nowak et al. 2016, Pew Res. Cent. 2011, Rebala & Wilson 2015). This means that psychologists who are not interested in culture will be less likely to obtain monocultural participants and are thus more likely than in the past to be able to test the generalizability of their theories.

What does this imply? Just as a psychology that includes only male participants is less robust than one that includes both male and female participants even if gender is not the focus of research, a psychology that includes more culturally diverse participants is more robust than monoculturally based research even if culture is not the focus of research. Increased diversity in student populations may or may not support relevant subgroup analyses but will at least ensure that theories are less likely to be tested in monocultural samples. At the same time, rapid demographic changes mean that failures to replicate results based on theories that apply only to one core cultural theme will increase, which may push psychologists not previously interested in culture to consider its effects.

The most populous countries and biggest contributors to population growth. If psychologists are not interested in culture but do care if their theories generalize, then testing whether theories hold in the world's two most populous countries—China and India (with a combined population of 2.6 billion people)—should matter. In both of these countries, Internet-based subject pools are becoming increasingly available for testing generalizability. Other countries with large populations (in descending order, Indonesia, Brazil, Pakistan, and Nigeria, with a combined population of 920 million people) are assumed to be high in honor and collectivism but are rarely included in research.

These six countries are also responsible for most of the world's population growth and so will constitute an increasing proportion of the world's population (Chamie 2012). Their populations are young (e.g., median age is 27 in India and 18 in Nigeria) and in some cases, skewed male (e.g., in India and China) (CIA 2015). Youths are particularly concentrated in Sub-Saharan Africa, the Middle East, and North Africa—areas also home to the Sunni-Shiite religious divide (Yousef 2003). Half of Nigerians and most Indonesians and Pakistanis are Muslim; Indonesia, Pakistan, and India (three high-growth countries) are home to about one-third of the world's Muslims (CIA 2015). Given this geographic concentration, it might be useful to consider the place-based implications of religion even though this aspect of religion is not widely studied by cultural psychologists focused on religion, religiosity, and belief in a deity (e.g., Atran & Norenzayan 2004; Cohen 2009, 2015; Cohen & Rozin 2001). Culturally, Islam is associated with honor and obedience (Ahlberg 2014). Cultures of honor highlight a particular form of masculinity that is focused on male agency (e.g., Nisbett & Cohen 1996, Novin & Oyserman in press). A population with an abundance of youths is associated with innovation and economic growth if, at the same time, the proportion of the population that is beyond working years also declines (Bloom & Williamson 1998, Brake 2013); otherwise, it is associated with political upheaval, violence, and a shift to dictatorships (Urdal 2006, Weber 2013). At the same time, in some settings, an abundance of young men is associated with higher marriage rates and greater paternal investment in children (Griskevicius et al. 2012). Given the place-based link between Islam and an abundance of youths, future research examining the effects of cultural contact is needed.

Income and Wealth Inequality: Social Class

Modernity theory predicts that inequality in wealth and income is due to an inadequate supply of skilled labor; that by increasing education, societies reduce inequality; and that social mobility reduces the centrality of social class (e.g., Inglehart 1997). Thus, countries that provide free and high-quality education should see less income and wealth inequality because more people can vie for top educational slots. To the extent that education facilitates social movement and reduces economic segregation, these countries should also see less hardening of class-based subcultures. Otherwise, spatial and social segregation should increase and social classes should become more distinct and well formed. Indeed, recent analyses suggest that inequality is increasing in some wealthy countries. Thus, in contrast to other wealthy countries (e.g., Germany, France), in the United States, Australia, and Canada, inequality in wages and income has rebounded since the 1970s (Grusky & MacLean 2016). In these three countries, the richest 1% holds concentrated wealth whereas wages have stagnated or declined for those without college degrees and, even in families with college-educated earners, family time to support socialization of children has declined (Grusky & MacLean 2016). To maintain their standard of living, both parents (or multiple family members) must work (Grusky & MacLean 2016). At the same time, the recreational and cultural facilities and school systems in these countries, which were once publicly funded institutional supports for upward mobility, are increasingly subject to market forces. Taken together, these changes suggest less support for upward mobility and reduced availability of public spaces in which the rich and poor mix—a rising segregation of experience that may yield class-based homophily (Grusky & MacLean 2016).

Grusky & MacLean (2016) argue that the one reason for differences among countries is cultural. That is, in culturally individualistic countries such as the United States, Canada, and Australia, the wealthy have used an aspect of individualism—free-market ideology—to legitimize both inequality and reduced institutional support for mobility. Opportunities for mobility require access to education. In the United States, Canada, and Australia, the wealthy have used two strategies that at first glance seem congruent with individualism but that function to undermine mobility. These strategies are commodification—requiring payment for, rather than supplying free access to, public services (such as education, health care, and child care)—and localization—requiring that local entities support services that are public. Payment and localization may seem congruent with individualism (because opportunities are of one's own or one's proximal group's making), but if the means for getting ahead requires money, then the poor cannot get ahead because they do not have the money to pay either as individuals or as local communities. In this way, free-market ideology masks the opportunity-reducing consequence for the poor of commodification and localization. At the same time, it masks the opportunity-increasing consequences for the wealthy of artificially reducing supply and increasing demand for the particular set of skills that the wealthy have and the less-educated lack.

A number of different theories predict that if social class is experienced as fixed but justified, the poor will come to feel that they are to blame for their situation. Justification can be rooted in individualism and free-market ideologies, as Grusky & MacLean (2016) argue, or collectivism, as Stephens and colleagues (2007, 2014, 2016) and others (Na & Chan 2016) suggest. Both fit early formulations of the experience of poverty as stigma—a shameful, embarrassing character flaw leading to loss of face (Lewis 1966). At the same time, if blocked opportunities are experienced as illegitimate, then fixed social classes can produce political instability. Indeed, in the United States evidence indicates that social class matters in ways that parallel the cultural literature on social power (e.g., Oyserman 2006). Like low power, low social status due to low social class is associated with focusing on concrete details rather than the big picture, and with making adjustments and fitting in rather than taking charge (Oyserman 2006). Low social class is associated with seeing oneself as connected to others and seeing one's competencies in terms of how to be part of a team—how to fit in (e.g., Stephens et al. 2016).

PLACE-BASED GROUP MEMBERSHIP AND CORE CULTURAL THEME

Culture can be operationalized as a set of structures and institutions, values, traditions, and ways of engaging with the social and nonsocial world that are transmitted across generations in a certain time and place (e.g., Shweder & LeVine 1984). One's place within a society and the social networks within which one is embedded should influence the structural and institutional aspects of a culture to which one has access (Oyserman & Uskul 2008). At the individual level, this affects the norms, policies, and practices one is exposed to. Hence, whether immigration triggers cultural change for migrants depends in part on whether social networks in the new context differ from networks in the old one (Oyserman & Uskul 2008) and on how many people are arriving at the same place at the same time (Rychlowska et al. 2015).

Comparing Groups: But Which Ones?

Comparing groups is the most common way in which cultural psychologists study culture. But determining which groups should be compared and what group comparisons imply is not straight-forward. Cultural psychology's promise is to provide the means to test when and how culture matters and the methods to test the applicability of findings and theories developed in one culture for other cultures. One possible way to answer this question is to test theories against earlier historical times or among the small number of people currently living in preliterate, nonagricultural, hunter-gatherer societies (Henrich et al. 2010). Alternatively, psychologists might limit their theorizing to people living in developing and industrialized societies, many of whom have gone to school and can read and write. Indeed, one of the important triumphs of modern cultural psychology has been to decouple cultural differences from differences in economic development. Hence, rather than return to studying culture by studying hunter-gatherer societies, cultural psychologists have much to gain by unpacking the active ingredients of culture.

Psychologists are typically less concerned with whether their results generalize to the Hadza, one of the few living people who live in nonagricultural, hunter-gatherer societies (Finkel 2009), than they are that their theories fail to predict the behavior of Japanese, Chinese, or Indian individuals. The Hadza are central for some questions, such as, "What is human and separate from the adaptations that come from modernity, Western-style education, and industrialization?" For such questions, showing stability of effects from Korea to Canada is trivial, and the Hadza are needed. Clearly, testing whether a theory fits Ghanaians, Germans, and Guatemalans is not the same as asking if a theory is relevant to all people who ever lived (Ceci et al. 2010). Although this question sometimes should be asked, it might be best to leave it aside. After all, generalization at this level is problematic at best, as even the animals used in animal research may not represent animals well (Machery 2010). Instead, it might be better to be more modest in what psychology and cultural psychology can do and focus on whether a theory's generalizability is likely to be moderated or mediated by some active ingredient of culture existing in modern societies.

The question of which active ingredients to look for, although still open to new suggestions, seems to currently focus on individualism, collectivism, and honor or face. This was not always the case. In the first *Annual Review of Psychology* article about culture, Triandis and colleagues (1973) summarized and interpreted results of research documenting place-based differences in seemingly basic cognitive processes. They showed that participants from educated, Westernized societies were more susceptible to the Müller-Lyer illusion (which is that the length of line segment seems to vary when shown in the context of arrowheads) than were participants from nonmodern societies. They explained that the source of the illusion was that participants lived in contexts with carpentered edges that yielded practice in using angles as depth cues. But what did this difference imply about culture?

Individualism and Collectivism

An enormous leap forward in addressing these goals came through simplified rubrics for studying culture that did not depend on differences in economic development and education levels. Arguably, the first to provide a simplifying rubric focused on modern societies was Hofstede (1983), who analyzed differences in preferences for working conditions and training in matched samples of employees from a single multinational firm across countries and regions at two points in time. Eventually, more than 50 countries and three regions of the world were included, with a total of 116,000 responses (Hofstede 2001). Hofstede synthesized the pattern of responses and proposed a small set of factors to describe cultures. The first factor was individualism as opposed to collectivism; this factor provided a way of organizing a huge array of between-group differences. Other proposed factors (masculinity-femininity, power distance, uncertainty avoidance, and long-term/short-term time orientation) subsequently turned out to relate to the individualism factor (Hofstede 2001).

Individualism-collectivism (also termed independent and interdependent self-construals) as a factor articulated a seemingly ubiquitous tension between belongingness and autonomy and suggested that this tension might carry over from features of the environment to norms, values, and ways of relating to others and of defining the self (e.g., Brewer 1991). It yielded a rapid explosion of comparative studies (for a meta-analysis, see Oyserman et al. 2002a). Comparisons were supported in part by Hofstede's work, which allowed researchers to attribute between-group differences to individualism and collectivism. The psychological transformation of this element of culture came in large part through the efforts of Harry Triandis (e.g., Trafimow et al. 1991, Triandis 1989) and Hazel Markus (e.g., Markus & Kitayama 1991, Markus & Oyserman 1989). By the 1990s, culture had come to mean individualism and collectivism for much of psychology; this was lauded as an important advance and remains the case (for reviews, see Oyserman et al. 2002a,b; Oyserman & Lee 2008; Taras et al. 2014; Vargas & Kemmelmeier 2013). The possibility that individualism-collectivism provides a way to organize groups and that it predicts differences in values, self-concepts, and ways thinking and engaging with others has been tested meta-analytically (for values) and with quantified syntheses (for self-concept, relationality, and cognitive process) (e.g., Oyserman et al. 2002a).

This formulation and the studies that come from it have proven invaluable in documenting one particular way in which culture matters. Seven *Annual Review of Psychology* articles on culture over the past 20 years were organized using a between-group formulation of culture based on individualism and collectivism and independent and interdependent self-construals. By synthesizing studies using group-based contrasts and either assessing or assuming differences in self-construal, culture was linked to personality, human development, cognition, children's social competence, and neuroscience (Han et al. 2013, Kitayama & Uskul 2011, Lieberman 2007, Miller et al. 2009, Morris et al. 2015a, Stephens et al. 2014, Triandis et al. 1973).

Indeed, people from modern collectivistic societies showed increased susceptibility to the Müller-Lyer illusion compared to those from modern individualistic societies (Krishna et al. 2008). These findings contrast with those of Triandis and colleagues (1973), who compared people from modern and premodern societies. To understand when and under which circumstances people from modern collectivistic cultures are sensitive to contextual information, emerging research focuses on each stage of information processing. Also being explored is the extent to which findings based on research with Chinese participants generalize to other high-interdependence groups (e.g., Russians, Central Europeans). Some research findings clearly do generalize (e.g., Kühnen et al. 2001, Oyserman et al. 2002a), but other findings may not. For example, the finding that Chinese tend to have a tolerance for inconsistency that is higher than that of Americans might be specifically attributed to Chinese dialectical thinking rather than to collectivism (Spencer-Rodgers et al. 2010).

New research moving beyond comparisons of Americans or Canadians with Chinese or Japanese would provide building blocks for future meta-analyses to separate results that generalize from results based on more specific differences in each culture and subculture. Moreover, in spite of the continued dominance of an individualism-collectivism focus, researchers are beginning to branch out to consider other ways to operationalize what culture is and how it matters.

Honor

Constant vigilance is required to maintain honor, which involves concerns about reputation and respect, being taken seriously, and not being pushed around by others. Face, which involves concerns about worth and reputation in the eyes of others, also requires vigilance. Although face loss typically is associated with embarrassment, retribution can be sought if face was wrongly impugned. Both honor and face are often connected to collectivistic societies (Leung & Cohen 2011) and to minority race and lower social class within the United States (e.g., Kubrin & Weitzer 2003, Stephens et al. 2016).

Disputes about honor, which require a personal response and cannot be resolved by turning to authority, are concentrated in poor urban and minority neighborhoods in the United States (Kubrin & Weitzer 2003). Parents in these contexts teach and socialize to show honor—esteem and respect for authorities (Dixon et al. 2008). Indeed, honor culture thrives in contexts in which central authority is weak and social institutions are ineffective such that the police, courts, and other authorities cannot be assumed to provide redress from wrongdoing (Nisbett & Cohen 1996, Nowak et al. 2016). Honor culture is geographically located—indeed, the Middle East, Mediterranean regions, Latin America, and the southern United States are described as honor societies more so than Northern Europe and the northern United States (Gregg 2007, Mosquera et al. 2002).

Ethnographic, laboratory, and field experiments provide support for some aspects of this theoretical framework; for example, experiments show that differences in honor values are related to responses to insults (Cohen et al. 1996). However, in the United States, when honor is brought to mind, it influences perception even when honor values are not endorsed; for example, when an honor lens is used, people perceive more potent figures as more likely to be male (Novin & Oyserman in press).

When migrants from honor cultures enter new societies, they are likely to carry honor culture with them. However, whether honor culture will continue to thrive in the new setting likely depends on a number of factors. A first factor, as noted in the section on culture as inherent meaning, is that people may continue to assume honor norms exist and act in ways that fit these norms even when they personally do not endorse them. This implies stability of honor culture over time. A second factor to consider, however, is that whether or not honor responses make sense depends on the effectiveness of social institutions in one's local context (Nowak et al. 2016). This implies that some settings provide a better fit for honor cultures than others. The idea that honor, aggression, and weak social institutions feed on each other is useful in considering social movements in Islamic societies, often described as honor cultures. Consider Boko Haram, ISIS, and Al Qaeda; each thrives in weakened or failed states in which the central government cannot punish wrongdoing. Each also weakens alternative social institutions (e.g., educational systems) as well as trust in the central government to punish wrongdoing. As these examples highlight, honor culture thrives in contexts with weak social institutions; at the same time, honor culture weakens these institutions when it gains a foothold. A third factor to consider is the place within a host society into which migrants from honor societies enter. This idea is highlighted in segmented assimilation theory (Portes & Zhou 1993). That is, migrants do not assimilate into all of their host society; rather, they assimilate into that segment of it that they live in, and this segment is often one in which public institutions are weak—poor neighborhoods with high crime rates, high joblessness, and low academic attainment. Segmented assimilation and marketization theory (Grusky & MacLean 2016) converge in predicting that waves of immigrants who enter these segments of their host cultures will need to fend for themselves. In these conditions, cultures of honor will be maintained from the source culture and are likely to take hold in the host culture as well (Nowak et al. 2016).

Remaining Questions

As described in the preceding sections, the focus on core themes has yielded important progress in understanding culture's consequences and how subcultures matter. This progress has been made in spite of a number of theoretical questions and practical issues that still remain (for a review, see Oyserman & Uskul 2008).

Disjunctures. One question is whether individualism and collectivism at the societal-structural level can be assumed to be the same as individualism and collectivism at the personal-individual level (e.g., Kitayama & Uskul 2011). Interesting results are produced at the societal level of analysis (e.g., Bond & Smith 1996). Yet the societal and personal levels are clearly not the same, as can be seen by studies showing effects of disjuncture between the two (Zou et al. 2009). Individuals who differ from their national norms experience lower well-being (Lun & Bond 2013) and less satisfaction with their personal life (Fulmer et al. 2010) and social relationships (Friedman et al. 2010). It is less stressing to move to a new culture if one's personal propensities match the new culture's core theme (Cross 1995). In organizations, cultural misfit has more negative consequences for productivity than does misfit in terms of dissimilarity in race-ethnicity or gender (Elfenbein & O'Reilly 2007).

Knowing what is normative or valued in one's society provides an interpretive lens through which to understand experiences with others and what is likely or expected in social interchange (Fiske & Taylor 2013). In this way, core themes influence perception and experience regardless of whether one personally endorses them (Zou et al. 2009) and whether most people actually endorse that theme. Therefore, a theme may be perceived as core long after it no longer is, or even if it never was, core. This has been termed the illusion of universality or pluralistic ignorance (for a review, see O'Gorman 1986).

Operationalization. Also open to debate is which countries form good bases for extrapolation of effects due to independent-interdependent self-construal or individualism-collectivism (Matsumoto 1999), which personal-level markers of culture should be used (candidates are values, norms, implicit norms, and self-construals), and how markers should be measured. For example, the most common way to assess self-construal is to use Kuhn & McPartland's (1954) Twenty Statements Test, in which open-ended responses must be content coded (Oyserman et al. 2002a). Initial work showed that people who were members of minority religious affiliation groups were more likely to describe themselves in terms of social category memberships (e.g., "I am a man," "I am a student," "I am a football player"; Kuhn & McPartland, p. 72). An early study clearly showed the promise of this measure for cross-cultural work: Bond & Cheung (1983) found that Chinese and American students differed in the frequency that aspirations were part of their self-descriptions and that Japanese students were not much different from American students. Subsequent coding in cross-cultural contexts counted the number of responses that referred to individuating traits and aspirations and those that referred to group memberships or relationships (e.g., Bond & Cheung 1983, Gardner et al. 1999, Trafimow, et al. 1991).

Results, which were predicted to show more use of personal attributes in individualistic societies, are mixed. Indeed, a quantified synthesis of results of cross-national comparison of self-construal, mostly using the Twenty Statements Test, yielded small and heterogeneous effects (Oyserman et al. 2002b). A more recent review of the self-construal literature highlights that this heterogeneity of effects was not an artifact of the studies available at that time (Cross et al. 2010). On the one hand, both the small size of the effect and its heterogeneity might reflect a reality, and this might not be a problem. After all, chronic small and heterogeneous differences in self-concept structure across societies might be consequential. On the other hand, it is possible that the actual average between-country difference is larger but that the true effect is masked either by the common operationalization of self-concept structure into responses on the Twenty Statements Test or by variability in content coding responses to the task. Finally, it is possible that between-country comparisons show culture-level differences that are not fully attributable to differences in independent and interdependent self-concepts.

Active ingredients. Researchers are also divided on whether the active ingredient in studies involving individualism and collectivism or independent-dependent self-construals is one factor or two. Can a person think of him- or herself as both connected to others and separate from others? Do societies support both autonomy and connection? These questions are both theoretical and empirical, and evidence on both sides has been presented (Oyserman et al. 2002a,b; Oyserman & Lee 2008; Taras et al. 2014; Vargas & Kemmelmeier 2013). Because the issue involves theoretical constructs, it cannot be resolved in the abstract, and which formulation is used depends on the questions being addressed, as highlighted in the next section.

VARIABLE ACCESSIBILITY: CULTURE AS HUMAN UNIVERSAL WITH CORE THEMES

Cultures' core themes of individualism, collectivism, and honor can also be thought of as underlying human culture and as essential to human survival (e.g., Boyd & Richerson 1985, Oyserman 2011). As noted in the section on cultural inherence, cultural knowledge provides predictability. Lack of environmental predictability is stressful in itself, yielding increased vigilance and increased threat sensitivity in ambiguous contexts (for a review, see Miller et al. 2009). Beyond predictability, human culture evolves to provide working solutions to three basic problems—sustaining the group over time, organizing relationships, and facilitating individual welfare (e.g., Oyserman 2011, Schwartz & Bardi 2001). These basic problems require that people join together, cooperate with an in-group, regulate themselves to fit in, and be motivated to initiate and invest in problem solving (e.g., Boyd et al. 2011; Boyd & Richerson 1985, Johnson & Earle 2000, Oyserman 2011). Culture provides a means to stick together with others to create and share resources and solutions to the problems that arise from sticking together—from managing relationships to minimize dangerous conflict, to clarifying group boundaries—without which it may be unclear with whom to share and from whom shared resources can be expected.

Resolving how to do these things results in a series of "good enough" solutions—solutions that are not the best or most efficient solution, just better than no solution (e.g., Cohen 2001).

This means that the initial formulation of a solution may be relatively haphazard in that a variety of solutions could have been pursued. Once a good enough solution is attained, it is likely to be relatively stable, and change will be incremental, even if alternatives are available (Argote et al. 1995, Chang et al. 2011, Cohen 2001). Once developed, cultural solutions permeate all aspects of behavior and provide a blueprint or outline for how one is to behave and what one can expect of others across a variety of situations. Cultural solutions become meaning-making frameworks that both constrain and enable perception and reasoning (Nisbett & Norenzayan 2002, Shweder 1984). This permeation makes cultures sticky because once absorbed, no single specific element can be excised.

Population-specific genetic sensitivities (Way & Lieberman 2010) and historic differences in the dominance of one or the other of these basic problems have been used to explain societal focus on individualism, collectivism, and honor (e.g., Kitayama & Uskul 2011, Segall et al. 1990). For example, ecologies differ in harshness of climate (Van de Vliert 2010), environmental pathogens (Fincher et al. 2008), means of production (herding, farming, or fishing; Kitayama & Uskul 2011, Segall et al. 1990), and whether wheat or rice is the staple crop (Talhelm et al. 2014). Societies also differ in when their frontiers were settled, what their core philosophies are, and how well their central governments function to punish wrongdoers (Nowak et al. 2016). All of these historic antecedents are plausible roots of culture: Cultures develop in places, and the specific practices developed in a place are bound up with the specific demands of the ecological niche in which people find themselves (e.g., Kendal et al. 2011).

Yet at the same time, each cultural theme addresses adaptations to group living, and group living is basic to human survival (Boyd & Richerson 2005, Kurzban & Neuberg 2005). Living together requires that people have guides to coordinate and organize relationships, clarify group boundaries, and reward innovation so that it can be imitated or exploited. Evolutionarily, membership in a group is essential; humans need groups to survive (Cohen 2001, 2009). This would imply that people are sensitive to social categories, to social validation versus ostracism, and to cues about when to innovate and do one's own thing (e.g., Legare & Nielsen 2015, Oyserman 2011). Indeed, social allegiances are tightly monitored, social rejection is highly stressful, and social inclusion and physical contact are highly protective (Cohen et al. 2015, Murphy et al. 2013).

Thus, an alternative to the core themes approach to culture is needed. Rather than theorizing that cultures differ in whether particular knowledge networks or cultural mindsets are available for use, it makes more sense to posit that societal cultures differ in the likelihood that each cultural mindset is cued and in the particular ways each is instantiated (Oyserman 2011, Oyserman et al. 2014). What this would imply, as articulated in **Figure 1**, is twofold. First, whether an individualistic, collectivistic, or honor mindset is activated depends on features of the environment and the interaction between these features and their implications. This interaction is a function of the spreading activation of associative knowledge networks. Second, whether a particular experience or observation requires a shift to reflective processing depends on this same interaction. Thus, both the variable activation and the particular practices model of culture build on dual-process models of cognition. These models predict that people do not have a fixed core cultural theme through which they always make sense of their world; instead they have a form of each of the core cultural themes available as cultural mindsets. Situated cues may influence which cultural theme is momentarily activated as a cultural mindset. Third, the particular practices associated with each cultural mindset are likely to be idiosyncratic to a particular time and place. This formulation focuses attention on the (often nonconscious) impact of social contexts, human artifacts, physical spaces, tasks, and language on what and how people think (Oyserman 2011).

These predictions are supported in an emerging body of research. The same differences that have been shown in between-group comparisons have also been shown using situated activation methods. People guided to use a collectivistic mindset automatically take context into account, whether they are Korean or American. The reverse is also true: People guided to use an individualistic mindset automatically focus on main points, whether they are Chinese or American (for a summary, see Oyserman 2011). Both Chinese and Americans can be guided to process for contextual cues, undermining performance on lower-level and complex cognitive tasks if task demands require generating rules and ignoring purposefully extraneous detail (D. Oyserman, S. Novin, B. Lam, S.X. Chen, E. Newman, & V. Yan, manuscript under review). Cross-national effects are replicated for US groups—European Americans, Asian Americans, African Americans, etc. (Oyserman et al. 2009). Complex cognitive performance improves if the activated cultural mindset matches task demands and is undermined if the activated cultural mindset mismatches task demands, in accordance with the process model depicted in **Figure 1**. In contrast to the results of studies in which a cultural mindset is momentarily activated, the results of studies using between-group comparisons capture the effect of whichever cultural mindset is on one's mind at the moment of the test. These studies are inherently less interpretable than they are often assumed to be because the cultural mindset on one's mind at the moment may be the chronically activated mindset or may be the cultural mindset unintentionally activated by some feature of the research context. Although fewer studies exist that compare participants with no activated cultural mindset (control) to participants with an activated mindset, these studies generally support the prediction that a momentarily activated cultural mindset may be either similar to or different from the chronically activated mindset (Oyserman & Lee 2008). Hence, between-group effects do not contradict the prediction that each cultural mindset is available for use, even though it may not be accessible (activated) in the moment.

Just as situations carry cues that probabilistically activate cultural mindsets linked to specific mental procedures, they also carry cues that probabilistically activate experienced cultural match and mismatch, which are linked to either remaining in the reflexive or switching to the reflective reasoning system. Match-mismatch cues are culture rich—as situations unfold, they either follow or deviate from culture-based expectations. Deviations matter because they mark that something is not going as assumed and thus trigger higher-level processing (Mourey et al. 2015). Given the nature of priming, effects are assumed to occur in part outside of conscious awareness and to be multiply determined, so that awareness of the prime should not necessarily undermine the effect. Whether a mismatch is experienced and whether it implies the need to defend one's cultural values should depend, in part, on whether cultural merging is experienced positively as an addition or negatively as a subtraction from one's cultural values.

CONCLUSION

As the world becomes a more heterogeneous place, one of the critical advances of cultural psychology has been to document that cultures can be classified according to the incorporation of a main theme: individualism, collectivism, or honor (face). From this perspective, being acculturated means knowing what is important and which lens to use to make sense of experiences. At the same time, culture is more than a single core theme; it is a detailed, rich, and particularized set of norms and implicit assumptions about how everyday life will unfold, which can be applied to everyday life. From this perspective, being acculturated means knowing how things are likely to unfold within one's society, so that systematic processing is not needed to get through the mundane details of the day. Finally, because each society includes the capacity to activate and access each core theme, psychologists can examine the moderating effects of each, both within and across societies. By focusing attention on differences in which questions seem interesting and in how constructs are operationalized, cultural psychology highlights two issues that are often otherwise overlooked and are important to psychologists whether or not they are interested in culture. The first issue is that what is experienced as central, important, and in need of explanation need not be universal. The second issue is that conceptual rather than exact replication of research is critical in understanding the robustness of a psychological theory because the particular practices associated with the core concepts that a theory identifies are likely to differ between times and places such that operationalization of a core concept must be sensitive to a society's practices.

SUMMARY POINTS

1. Culture is three things: a set of everyday practices, a core chronically accessible theme (individualism, collectivism, or honor/face), and the capacity to understand each of these themes when they are activated. Together, these factors of culture yield a broad set of predictions about culture's consequences.

2. Culture is the lens through which experience is interpreted, but because it is pervasive, it is easy to fail to notice one's own culture and mistake it for unmediated reality. People are always embedded in culture, so studying culture requires stepping out of it. Otherwise, it is difficult to see culture: One's own cultural lens feels like reality and not like a lens at all.

3. Psychological theorizing might be culture bound. Psychologists are just as likely as other people to fail to notice culture. Taking a cultural perspective means understanding that a theory developed and tested in one culture may or may not apply to other cultures. Hence, psychologists cannot assume that theories developed and tested in one culture apply to other cultures without articulating and testing culture's potential moderating function.

4. Group-based comparisons are the most common way to study culture and are a useful first step. A group-based approach makes sense: People live in groups, and cultural practices are transmitted within groups over time, so group membership might be a simple, concrete marker for culture. Using a group-based approach to culture facilitates the inclusion of culture in sampling, making it easier to examine whether a psychological theory developed and tested in one group generalizes to another. A group-based approach also forces a deeper understanding of what a psychological theory predicts. After all, groups may differ in how best to operationalize a basic process predicted by a theory rather than in whether the theory itself applies.

5. Distinguishing culture from subculture is not a precise science. Instead, whether a group constitutes a culture or a subculture depends on perspective. For example, the United States is both a subculture within industrialized, Western-educated, individualistic wealthy societies and a culture on its own. Whether it makes sense to talk about a nation, a state, or a group as a culture depends on the specific comparisons and predictions being made.

6. Modern societal social-demographic trends mean that the United States and other societies are becoming more diverse. This increasing diversity means that these societies will be more likely to include a mix of perspectives—individualism, collectivism, and honor or face—and that everyday life is more likely to be experienced as unpredictable. Psychologists (both cultural psychologists and those with other interests) are just beginning to consider what the implications are for societies, well-being, and psychological theories.

7. Experimental methods are an important additional tool in testing predictions about culture; they address the limitations of the group-based approach and facilitate development of refutable theories about how culture works. To use these methods, researchers must operationalize the abstract idea of culture into specific active ingredients and randomize participants to conditions that differ in their implications for these ingredients. For example, participants can view pictures, unscramble sentences, read a paragraph, or circle words in a text. Researchers predict that these brief tasks will cue the cultural mindset and to-be-tested processing style. Because experimental methods are not dependent on between-group comparisons, they can test the assumption that differences in outcomes are due to differences in activated cultural mindsets or practices.

8. Culture organizes experience in three ways. First, by providing a set of particular practices or ways that "we" do things, culture shields reflexive processing by making everyday life feel predictable to in-group members. Second, by highlighting a main theme, culture scaffolds which cognitive procedure—connect, separate, or order—will be the default in ambiguous situations. Third, by structuring working solutions to universal human needs, culture facilitates situation-specific accessibility of each of the culture-derived cognitive procedures (connecting, separating, and ordering).

FUTURE ISSUES

1. Though much research has already been done on two active ingredients of culture (individualism and collectivism), the cognitive consequences of the third active ingredient (honor or face) are only just now beginning to be explored. Research to date has mostly focused on demonstrating that effects can be found. Having taken this important first step of providing evidence that a phenomenon of interest exists, the next steps will entail developing refutable predictions about the active ingredients of culture and consequences in everyday life. An example is emerging research on the consequences of match and mismatch between the demands of a task and the salient cultural mindset and how this match and mismatch might predict when cultural merging is experienced as additive and when it is experienced as subtractive.

2. What we actually mean by culture continues to be an important topic of research. By contrasting views of individualism and collectivism within industrialized, wealthy, developed, and educated groups, psychologists were able to study culture separate from economic and developmental issues. An alternative is to contrast nonmodern and modern societies, asking whether psychological theories (e.g., about motivation and fairness) developed and tested in modern societies predict behavior in nonmodern ones. The argument is that by studying samples from countries that are developed, industrialized, and relatively wealthy and have Westernized education systems, psychologists are missing a lot of what culture does. The approach of contrasting societies moves away from defining active ingredients of culture and instead highlights the possibilities of understanding how culture may have coevolved with the brain by turning to nonmodern living individuals (albeit few) and historic records. New methods for research, including the use of big data analytic techniques and data from historical records, will be useful for moving these ideas forward.

3. Emerging themes are the consequences of match and mismatch and of juncture and disjuncture between individual propensities and social-structural themes and between expectations and observations. A small literature is beginning to examine the consequences for level of processing, experience of meaning, and well-being of match and mismatch between expectation and observation and of juncture versus disjuncture between dominant social-structural themes and personal propensities. This literature updates an older literature on culture shock and moves beyond a core-theme approach to culture.

4. A significant area for future work is the reconnection of culture to social and demographic trends. Cultural psychology has in some regards been a silo, separate from political science, sociology, racial and ethnic, and poverty research, and a focus on connecting these areas of research and drawing policy implications is emerging. This focus is important because prior and current theorizing and research on racial-ethnic minorities, social class, and poverty across these fields yields insights into psychological processes as yet untested but nevertheless relevant to cultural psychologists and to psychology more generally. Future directions include experimental tests of when cultural mindsets (collectivism, individualism, and honor) predict effects and when effects are better predicted by match-mismatch, juncture-disjuncture consequences.

DISCLOSURE STATEMENT

The author is not aware of any affiliations, memberships, funding, or financial holdings that might be perceived as affecting the objectivity of this review.

LITERATURE CITED

Ahlberg N. 2014. Forced migration and Muslim rituals: an area of cultural psychology? *Scr. Inst. Donneriani Abo.* 15:117–30

Allport FH. 1924. *Social Psychology.* Boston: Houghton Mifflin

Argote L, Ingram P, Levine JM, Moreland RL. 1995. Knowledge transfer in organisations: learning from the experience of others. *Organ. Behav. Hum. Decis. Process.* 82:1–8

Atran S, Norenzayan A. 2004. Religion's evolutionary landscape: counterintuition, commitment, compassion, communion. *Behav. Brain Sci.* 27:713–30

Baron AS. 2014. Is the inherence heuristic simply WEIRD? *Behav. Brain Sci.* 37:481

Bellah RN. 1985. *Habits of the Heart: Individualism and Commitment in American Life.* Berkeley: Univ. Calif. Press

Bigler RS, Clark C. 2014. The inherence heuristic: a key theoretical addition to understanding social stereotyping and prejudice. *Behav. Brain Sci.* 37:483–84

Bloom DE, Williamson JG. 1998. Demographic transitions and economic miracles in emerging Asia. *World Bank Econ. Rev.* 12:419–55

Bond MH, Cheung T-S. 1983. College students' spontaneous self-concept: the effect of culture among respondents in Hong Kong, Japan, and the United States. *J. Cross-Cult. Psychol.* 142:153–71

Bond R, Smith PB. 1996. Culture and conformity: a meta-analysis of studies using Asch's (1952b, 1956) line judgment task. *Psychol. Bull.* 119:111–37

Bourdieu P. 1984. *Distinction: A Social Critique of the Judgement of Taste.* New York: Harvard Univ. Press

Boyd R, Richerson PJ. 1985. *Culture and the Evolutionary Process.* Chicago: Univ. Chicago Press

Boyd R, Richerson PJ. 2005. Solving the puzzle of human cooperation. In *Evolution and Culture*, ed. S Levinson, pp. 105–32. Cambridge, MA: Mass. Inst. Technol. Press

Boyd R, Richerson PJ, Henrich J. 2011. The cultural niche: why social learning is essential for human adaptation. *PNAS* 108:10918–25

Brake M. 2013. *Comparative Youth Culture: The Sociology of Youth Cultures and Youth Subcultures in America, Britain and Canada.* New York: Routledge

Brewer MB. 1991. The social self: on being the same and different at the same time. *Pers. Soc. Psychol. Bull.* 17:475–82

Ceci SJ, Kahan DM, Bramanc D. 2010. The WEIRD are even weirder than you think: Diversifying contexts is as important as diversifying samples. *Behav. Brain Sci.* 33:87–88

CIA (Central Intell. Agency). 2015. *The World Factbook 2014–15.* Washington, DC: Gov. Print. Off.

Chaiken S, Trope Y, eds. 1999. *Dual-Process Theories in Social Psychology.* New York: Guilford

Chamie J. 2012. For better planning, watch global demographic trends. *YaleGlobal Online.* **http://www.yaleglobal.yale.edu/content/better-planning-watch-global-demographic-trends**

Chang L, Mak MCK, Li T, Wu BP, Chen BB, Lu HJ. 2011. Cultural adaptations to environmental variability: an evolutionary account of East-West differences. *Educ. Psychol. Rev.* 23:99–129

Cimpian A, Salomon E. 2014. The inherence heuristic: an intuitive means of making sense of the world, and a potential precursor to psychological essentialism. *Behav. Brain Sci.* 37:461–80

Cohen AB. 2009. Many forms of culture. *Am. Psychol.* 64:194–204

Cohen AB. 2015. Religion's profound influences on psychology morality, intergroup relations, self-construal, and enculturation. *Curr. Dir. Psychol.* 24:77–82

Cohen AB, Rozin P. 2001. Religion and the morality of mentality. *J. Pers. Soc. Psychol.* 81:697–710

Cohen AB, Varnum ME. 2016. Beyond East versus West: social class, region, and religion as forms of culture. *Curr. Opin. Psychol.* 8:5–9

Cohen D. 2001. Cultural variation: considerations and implications. *Psychol. Bull.* 127:451–71

Cohen D, Nisbett RE, Bowdle BF, Schwarz N. 1996. Insult, aggression, and the southern culture of honor: an "experimental ethnography." *J. Pers. Soc. Psychol.* 70:945–59

Cohen S, Janicki-Deverts D, Turner RB, Doyle WJ. 2015. Does hugging provide stress-buffering social support? A study of susceptibility to upper respiratory infection and illness. *Psychol. Sci.* 26:135–47

Cross SE. 1995. Self-construals, coping, and stress in cross-cultural adaptation. *J. Cross-Cult. Psychol.* 26:673–97

Cross SE, Hardin EE, Gercek-Swing B. 2010. The what, how, why, and where of self-construal. *Pers. Soc. Psychol. Rev.* 15:142–79

Dixon SV, Graber JA, Brooks-Gunn J. 2008. The roles of respect for parental authority and parenting practices in parent-child conflict among African American, Latino, and European American families. *J. Fam. Psychol.* 22:1–10

Elfenbein HA, O'Reilly CA. 2007. Fitting in: the effects of relational demography and person-culture fit on group process and performance. *Group Organ. Manag.* 32:109–42

Eur. Comm. 2007. *Europe's Demographic Future: Facts and Figures on Challenges and Opportunities.* Luxembourg: Eur. Communities. **http://www2.warwick.ac.uk/fac/soc/csgr/green/foresight/demography/2007_ec_europes_demographic_future_facts_and_figures_on_challenges_and_opportunities.pdf**

Fincher CL, Thornhill R, Murray DR, Schaller M. 2008. Pathogen prevalence predicts human cross-cultural variability in individualism/collectivism. *Proc. R. Soc. Lond. Biol. Sci.* 275:1279–85

Finkel M. 2009. The Hadza. *National Geographic.* **http://ngm.nationalgeographic.com/2009/12/hadza/finkel-text**

Fiske ST, Taylor SE. 2013. *Social Cognition: From Brains to Culture.* Thousand Oaks, CA: Sage

Frey W. 2015. *Diversity Explosion: How New Racial Demographics Are Remaking America.* Washington, DC: Brookings Inst.

Friedman M, Rholes WS, Simpson J, Bond M, Diaz–Loving R, Chan C. 2010. Attachment avoidance and the cultural fit hypothesis: a cross–cultural investigation. *Pers. Relatsh.* 17:107–26

Fulmer CA, Gelfand MJ, Kruglanski AW, Kim-Prieto C, Diener E, et al. 2010. On "feeling right" in cultural contexts: how person-culture match affects self-esteem and subjective well-being. *Psychol. Sci.* 21:1563–69

Gardner WL, Gabriel S, Lee AY. 1999. "I" value freedom, but "we" value relationships: Self-construal priming mirrors cultural differences in judgment. *Psychol. Sci.* 10:321–26

Geertz C. 1984. From the native's point of view. See Shweder & LeVine 1984, pp. 23–36

Gregg GS. 2007. *Culture and Identity in a Muslim Society*. Oxford, UK: Oxford Univ. Press

Griskevicius V, Tybur JM, Ackerman JM, Delton AW, Robertson TE, White AE. 2012. The financial consequences of too many men: sex ratio effects on saving, borrowing, and spending. *J. Pers. Soc. Psychol.* 102:69–80

Grusky D, MacLean A. 2016. The social fallout of a high-inequality regime. *Ann. Am. Acad. Polit. Soc. Sci.* 6631:33–52

Hackett C. 2015. *5 facts about the Muslim population in Europe*. Pew Res. Cent., Washington, DC. **http://www.pewresearch.org/fact-tank/2016/07/19/5-facts-about-the-muslim-population-in-europe/**

Han S, Northoff G, Vogeley K, Wexler BE, Kitayama S, Varnum ME. 2013. A cultural neuroscience approach to the biosocial nature of the human brain. *Annu. Rev. Psychol.* 64:335–59

Henrich J, Heine SJ, Norenzayan A. 2010. The weirdest people in the world? *Behav. Brain Sci.* 33:61–83

Hofstede G. 1983. National cultures in four dimensions: a research-based theory of cultural differences among nations. *Int. Stud. Manag. Organ.* 13:46–74

Hofstede G. 2001. *Culture's Consequences: Comparing Values, Behaviors, Institutions, and Organizations Across Nations*. Thousand Oaks, CA: Sage. 2nd ed.

Ichheiser G. 1949. Misunderstandings in human relations: a study in false social perception. *Am. J. Sociol.* 552:1–72

Inglehart R. 1997. *Modernization and Postmodernization: Cultural, Economic, and Political Change in 43 Societies*. Princeton, NJ: Princeton Univ. Press

Jahoda G. 2014. On relations between ethnology and psychology in historical context. *Hist. Hum. Sci.* 27:3–21

Johnson AW, Earle TK. 2000. *The Evolution of Human Societies: From Foraging Group to Agrarian State*. Stanford, CA: Stanford Univ. Press

Kahneman D, Frederick S. 2002. Representativeness revisited: attribute substitution in intuitive judgment. In *Heuristics and Biases: The Psychology of Intuitive Judgment*, ed. T Gilovich, D Griffin, D Kahneman, pp. 49–81. New York: Cambridge Univ. Press

Kendal J, Tehrani JJ, Odling-Smee J. 2011. Human niche construction in interdisciplinary focus. *Philos. Trans. R. Soc. B* 366:785–92

Kitayama S, Uskul AK. 2011. Culture, mind, and the brain: current evidence and future directions. *Annu. Rev. Psychol.* 62:419–49

Krishna A, Zhou R, Zhang S. 2008. The effect of self-construal on spatial judgments. *J. Consum. Res.* 35:337–48

Kruglanski AW, Stroebe. 2012. The making of social psychology. In *Handbook of History of Social Psychology*, ed. A Kruglanski, W Stroebe, pp. 3–17. New York: Psychol. Press

Kubrin CE, Weitzer R. 2003. Retaliatory homicide: concentrated disadvantage and neighborhood culture. *Soc. Problems* 50:157–80

Kuhn MH, McPartland TS. 1954. An empirical investigation of self-attitudes. *Am. Sociol. Rev.* 19:68–76

Kühnen U, Hannover B, Roeder U, Shah AA, Schubert B, et al. 2001. Cross-cultural variations in identifying embedded figures comparisons from the United States, Germany, Russia, and Malaysia. *J. Cross-Cult. Psychol.* 32:366–72

Kurzban R, Neuberg S. 2005. Managing ingroup and outgroup relationships. In *The Handbook of Evolutionary Psychology*, ed. DM Buss, pp. 653–75. Hoboken, NJ: Wiley

Legare CH, Nielsen M. 2015. Imitation and innovation: the dual engines of cultural learning. *Trends Cogn. Sci.* 19:688–99

Leung AKY, Cohen D. 2011. Within-and between-culture variation: individual differences and the cultural logics of honor, face, and dignity cultures. *J. Pers. Soc. Psychol.* 100:507–26

Lewis O. 1966. The culture of poverty. *Sci. Am.* 2154:3–10

Lieberman M. 2007. Social cognitive neuroscience: a review of core processes. *Annu. Rev. Psychol.* 58:259–89

Lun VMC, Bond MH. 2013. Examining the relation of religion and spirituality to subjective well-being across national cultures. *Psychol. Relig. Spiritual.* 5:304–15

Machery E. 2010. Explaining why experimental behavior varies across cultures: a missing step in "the weirdest people in the world?" *Behav. Brain Sci.* 33:101–2

Markus HR, Kitayama S. 1991. Culture and the self: implications for cognition, emotion, and motivation. *Psychol. Rev.* 98:224–53

Articulates why social class may become a subculture in the United States versus other wealthy countries.

Articulates the problematics of studying culture as a between-group comparison rather than a human universal.

Suggests that one role of learning culture is to be able to fit in.

Markus HR, Kitayama S, Heiman R. 1996. Culture and "basic" psychological principles. In *Social Psychology: Handbook of Basic Principles*, ed. ET Higgins, AW Kruglanski, pp. 857–913. New York: Guilford

Markus HR, Oyserman D. 1989. Gender and thought: the role of the self-concept. In *Gender and Thought: Psychological Perspectives*, ed. M Crawford, M Gentry, pp. 100–27. New York: Springer

Matsumoto D. 1999. Culture and self: an empirical assessment of Markus and Kitayama's theory of independent and interdependent self–construals. *Asian J. Soc. Psychol.* 2:289–310

Mesoudi A, Magid K, Hussain D. 2016. How do people become WEIRD? Migration reveals the cultural transmission mechanisms underlying variation in psychological processes. *PLOS ONE* 11:1

Miller G, Chen E, Cole SW. 2009. Health psychology: developing biologically plausible models linking the social world and physical health. *Annu. Rev. Psychol.* 60:501–24

Miyamoto Y. 2013. Culture and analytic versus holistic cognition: toward multilevel analyses of cultural influences. *Adv. Exp. Soc. Psychol.* 47:131–88

Morris MW, Chiu CY, Liu Z. 2015a. Polycultural psychology. *Annu. Rev. Psychol.* 66:631–59

Morris MW, Hong YY, Chiu CY, Liu Z. 2015b. Normology: integrating insights about social norms to understand cultural dynamics. *Organ. Behav. Hum. Decis. Process.* 129:1–13

Mosquera PMR, Manstead AS, Fischer AH. 2002. Honor in the Mediterranean and Northern Europe. *J. Cross-Cult. Psychol.* 33:16–36

Mourey JA, Lam BC, Oyserman D. 2015. Consequences of cultural fluency. *Soc. Cogn.* 33:308–44

Murphy ML, Slavich GM, Rohleder N, Miller GE. 2013. Targeted rejection triggers differential pro- and anti-inflammatory gene expression in adolescents as a function of social status. *Clin. Psychol. Sci.* 1:30–40

Na J, Chan MY. 2016. Subjective perception of lower social-class enhances response inhibition. *Pers. Individ. Differ.* 90:242–46

Nisbett RE, Cohen D. 1996. *Culture of Honor: The Psychology of Violence in the South. New Directions in Social Psychology.* Boulder, CO: Westview

Nisbett RE, Norenzayan A. 2002. Culture and cognition. In *Steven's Handbook of Experimental Psychology*, Vol. 2: *Memory and Cognitive Processes*, ed. H Pashler, D Medin, pp. 561–97. Hoboken, NJ: Wiley. 3rd ed.

Novin S, Oyserman D. In press. Honor as cultural mindset: Activated honor mindset affects subsequent judgment and attention in mindset congruent ways. *Front. Psychol.*

Nowak A, Gelfand MJ, Borkowski W, Cohen D, Hernandez I. 2016. The evolutionary basis of honor cultures. *Psychol. Sci.* 271:12–24

O'Gorman HJ. 1986. The discovery of pluralistic ignorance: an ironic lesson. *J. Hist. Behav. Sci.* 22:333–47

Oyserman D. 2006. High power, low power, and equality: culture beyond individualism and collectivism. *J. Consum. Psychol.* 164:352–56

Oyserman D. 2007. Social identity and self-regulation. In *Social Psychology: Handbook of Basic Principles*, ed. AW Kruglanski, ET Higgins, pp. 432–53. New York: Guilford. 2nd ed.

Oyserman D. 2011. Culture as situated cognition: cultural mindsets, cultural fluency, and meaning making. *Eur. Rev. Soc. Psychol.* 22:164–214

Oyserman D. 2015. Culture as situated cognition. In *Emerging Trends in the Social and Behavioral Sciences: An Interdisciplinary, Searchable, and Linkable Resource*, ed. R Scott, S Kosslyn. Hoboken, NJ: John Wiley & Sons. doi: 10.1002/9781118900772

Oyserman D. In press. What does a priming perspective reveal about culture: culture-as-situated-cognition. *Curr. Opin. Psychol.*

Oyserman D, Coon H, Kemmelmeier M. 2002a. Rethinking individualism and collectivism: evaluation of theoretical assumptions and meta-analyses. *Psychol. Bull.* 128:3–73

Oyserman D, Gant L, Ager J. 1995. A socially contextualized model of African American identity: possible selves and school persistence. *J. Pers. Soc. Psychol.* 696:1216

Oyserman D, Kemmelmeier M, Coon H. 2002b. Cultural psychology, a new look: reply to Bond (2002), Fiske (2002), Kitayama (2002), and Miller (2002). *Psychol. Bull.* 128:110–17

Oyserman D, Lee SWS. 2008. Does culture influence what and how we think? Effects of priming individualism and collectivism. *Psychol. Bull.* 134:311–42

Oyserman D, Novin S, Flinkenflögel N, Krabbendam L. 2014. Integrating culture-as-situated-cognition and neuroscience prediction models. *Cult. Brain* 2:1–26

Suggests a different approach to understanding how culture works, via assumed norms governing others' beliefs.

Shows downstream effects of mismatch between reality and culturally embedded expectations or implicit norms.

Shows the dynamics of when honor culture is likely to spread, stabilize, and retreat.

Articulates why between-group and experimental approaches are both necessary to understand culture's consequences.

Oyserman D, Sorensen N, Reber R, Chen SX. 2009. Connecting and separating mindsets: culture as situated cognition. *J. Pers. Soc. Psychol.* 97:217–35

Oyserman D, Uskul AK. 2008. Individualism and collectivism: societal-level processes with implications for individual-level and society-level outcomes. In *Multilevel Analysis of Individuals and Cultures*, ed. F van de Vijver, D van Hemert, Y Poortinga, pp. 145–73. Mahwah, NJ: Erlbaum

Packer M, Cole M. 2016. Culture in development. In *Social and Personality Development: An Advanced Textbook*, ed. MH Bornstein, ME Lamb, pp. 67–124. New York/London: Psychol. Press. 7th ed.

Pew Res. Cent. 2011. *Regional Distribution of Christians*. Washington, DC: Pew Res. Cent. **http://www. pewforum.org/2011/12/19/global-christianity-regions/**

Portes A, Zhou M. 1993. The new second generation: segmented assimilation and its variants. *Ann. Am. Acad. Polit. Soc. Sci.* 530:74–96

PricewaterhouseCoopers LLP. 2015. *Global Annual Review 2014: Demographic and Social Change.* **http://www. pwc.com/gx/en/issues/megatrends/demographic-and-social-change-norbert-winkeljohann.jhtml**

Rebala P, Wilson C. 2015. Growth of Muslim populations in Europe map. *Time Online.* **http://www. time.com/3670892/muslims-europe-map**

Rychlowska M, Miyamoto Y, Matsumoto D, Hess U, Gilboa-Schechtman E, et al. 2015. Heterogeneity of long-history migration explains cultural differences in reports of emotional expressivity and the functions of smiles. *PNAS* 112:E2429–36

Sapir E. 1929. The status of linguistics as a science. *Language* 5:207–14

Schwartz S, Bardi A. 2001. Value hierarchies across cultures: taking a similarities perspective. *J. Cross-Cult. Psychol.* 32:268–90

Segall MH, Dasen PR, Berry JW, Poortinga YH. 1990. *Human Behavior in Global Perspective: An Introduction to Cross-Cultural Psychology.* Elmsford, NY: Pergamon

Shweder RA. 1984. Preview: a colloquy of culture theorists. In *Culture Theory: Essays on Mind, Self, and Emotion*, ed. RA Shweder, RA LeVine, pp. 1–26. New York: Cambridge Univ. Press

Shweder RA, LeVine RA, eds. 1984. *Culture Theory: Essays on Mind, Self, and Emotion.* New York: Cambridge Univ. Press

Spencer S. 2014. *Race and Ethnicity: Culture, Identity, and Representation.* New York: Routledge

Spencer-Rodgers J, Williams MJ, Peng K. 2010. Cultural differences in expectations of change and tolerance for contradiction: a decade of empirical research. *Pers. Soc. Psychol. Rev.* 143:296–312

Stephens NM, Dittmann AG, Townsend SSM. 2016. Social class and models of competence: how gateway institutions disadvantage working-class Americans and how to intervene. In *Handbook of Competence and Motivation*, ed. C Dweck, A Elliot, D Yeager. New York: Guilford Press. In press

Stephens NM, Markus HR, Phillips LT. 2014. Social class culture cycles: how three gateway contexts shape selves and fuel inequality. *Annu. Rev. Psychol.* 65:611–34

Stephens NM, Markus HR, Townsend SS. 2007. Choice as an act of meaning: the case of social class. *J. Pers. Soc. Psychol.* 93:814–30

Strack F, Deutsch R. 2004. Reflective and impulsive determinants of social behavior. *Pers. Soc. Psychol. Rev.* 8:220–47

Swidler A. 1986. Culture in action: symbols and strategies. *Am. Sociol. Rev.* 51:273–86

Talhelm T, Zhang X, Oishi S, Shimin C, Duan D, et al. 2014. Large-scale psychological differences within China explained by rice versus wheat agriculture. *Science* 344:603–8

Taras V, Sarala R, Muchinsky P, Kemmelmeier M, Singelis TM, et al. 2014. Opposite ends of the same stick? Multi-method test of the dimensionality of individualism and collectivism. *J. Cross-Cult. Psychol.* 45:213–45

Toner K, Leary MR, Asher MW, Jongman-Sereno KP. 2013. Feeling superior is a bipartisan issue: extremity (not direction) of political views predicts perceived belief superiority. *Psychol. Sci.* 24:2454–62

Trafimow D, Triandis HC, Goto SG. 1991. Some tests of the distinction between the private self and the collective self. *J. Pers. Soc. Psychol.* 60:649–55

Triandis HC. 1989. The self and social behavior in differing cultural contexts. *Psychol. Rev.* 96:506–20

Triandis HC. 2007. Culture and psychology: a history of their relationship. In *Handbook of Cultural Psychology*, ed. S Kitayama, D Cohen, pp. 59–76. New York: Guilford

Articulates how the ways in which host countries take in immigrants has implications for how immigration shapes host culture.

Articulates how the effects of a history of rapid population change can be transmitted over time.

Triandis HC, Malpass RS, Davidson AR. 1973. Psychology and culture. *Annu. Rev. Psychol.* 24:355–78

Tversky A, Kahneman D. 1983. Extensional versus intuitive reasoning: the conjunction fallacy in probability judgment. *Psychol. Rev.* 90:293–315

Urdal H. 2006. A clash of generations? Youth bulges and political violence. *Int. Stud. Q.* 50:607–29

U.S. Census. 2011. Educational attainment in the United States. **http://www.census.gov/hhes/socdemo/education/data/cps/2011/tables.html**

Van de Vliert E. 2010. Climato-economic origins of variation in ingroup favoritism. *J. Cross-Cult. Psychol.* 42:494–515

Vargas JH, Kemmelmeier M. 2013. Ethnicity and contemporary American culture: a meta-analytic investigation of horizontal-vertical individualism-collectivism. *J. Cross-Cult. Psychol.* 44:2:195–222

Wang C, Oyserman D, Liu Q, Li H, Han S. 2013. Accessible cultural mindset modulates default mode activity: evidence for the culturally situated brain. *Soc. Neurosci.* 8:203–16

Way B, Lieberman M. 2010. Is there a genetic contribution to cultural differences? Collectivism, individualism and genetic markers of social sensitivity. *Soc. Cogn. Affect. Neurosci.* 5:203–11

Weber H. 2013. Demography and democracy: the impact of youth cohort size on democratic stability in the world. *Democratization* 20:335–57

Will M. 2014. U.S. trails in college graduation in global study. Lag also cited in preschool enrollment. *Education Week.* **http://www.edweek.org/ew/articles/2014/09/17/04oecd.h34.html**

Wright AC. 2015. *Teachers' perceptions of students' disruptive behavior: the effect of racial congruence and consequences for school suspension.* Work. Pap., Dep. Econ., Univ. Calif., Santa Barbara. **https://aefpweb.org/sites/default/files/webform/41/Race%20Match,%20Disruptive%20Behavior,%20and%20School%20Suspension.pdf**

Yousef T. 2003. Youth in the Middle East and North Africa: demography, employment, and conflict. In *Youth Explosion in Developing World Cities: Approaches to Reducing Poverty and Conflict in an Urban Age*, ed. BA Ruble, JS Tulchin, DH Varat, LM Hanley. Washington, DC: Woodrow Wilson Int. Cent. Scholars, Comp. Urban Stud. Proj.

Zou X, Tam KP, Morris MW, Lee SL, Lau I, Chiu CY. 2009. Culture as common sense: perceived consensus versus personal beliefs as mechanisms of cultural influence. *J. Pers. Soc. Psychol.* 97:579–97

Learning from Errors

Janet Metcalfe

Department of Psychology, Columbia University, New York, NY 10027;
email: jm348@columbia.edu

Annu. Rev. Psychol. 2017. 68:465–89

First published online as a Review in Advance on
September 14, 2016

The *Annual Review of Psychology* is online at
psych.annualreviews.org

This article's doi:
10.1146/annurev-psych-010416-044022

Keywords

errorless learning, generation effect, hypercorrection effect, feedback,
after-action review (AAR), error management training (EMT), formative
assessment, reconsolidation, prediction error

Abstract

Although error avoidance during learning appears to be the rule in American classrooms, laboratory studies suggest that it may be a counterproductive strategy, at least for neurologically typical students. Experimental investigations indicate that errorful learning followed by corrective feedback is beneficial to learning. Interestingly, the beneficial effects are particularly salient when individuals strongly believe that their error is correct: Errors committed with high confidence are corrected more readily than low-confidence errors. Corrective feedback, including analysis of the reasoning leading up to the mistake, is crucial. Aside from the direct benefit to learners, teachers gain valuable information from errors, and error tolerance encourages students' active, exploratory, generative engagement. If the goal is optimal performance in high-stakes situations, it may be worthwhile to allow and even encourage students to commit and correct errors while they are in low-stakes learning situations rather than to assiduously avoid errors at all costs.

Contents

INTRODUCTION

Nobody wants to make errors in a situation that counts. The consequences of committing such errors can be devastating. If one is performing a piano solo before an audience, controlling a nuclear reactor, taking SATs, making a medical decision, fighting on a battlefield, or giving a lecture, the last thing one wants is an error. This review is not directed at the question of whether errors, in a situation that counts, are good—of course they are not. Rather, the question is how, during initial learning and during practice and preparation for a test that counts, one can best get to a state of performance that is optimal and in which errors will not inadvertently occur just when one needs them least and when they will do the most damage. Should one commit, explore, examine, analyze, and correct errors during learning and practice sessions, or should one avoid errors at all stages of learning?

It might seem intuitive that if one does not want errors on the test that counts, then one should avoid errors at all stages of learning. In this view, committing errors should make those errors more salient and entrench them into both the memory and the operating procedures of the person who makes them. Exercising the errors should make the errors themselves stronger, thus increasing their probability of recurrence. Such a view, which is consistent with a number of the oldest and most well established theories of learning and memory (Bandura 1986, Barnes & Underwood 1959, Skinner 1953), suggests that errors are bad and should be avoided at all costs.

In keeping with these views, Ausubel (1968) warned of the dangers of errors in the learning process and suggested that allowing people to make errors encourages them to practice incorrect and inefficient approaches that will cause trouble because they are difficult to overwrite later with correct approaches. He used this reasoning to argue against an exploratory learning strategy, which by its very nature would mean that incorrect paths and faulty approaches and solutions would be encountered and entertained by the learner. Ausubel (and others) feared that with active exploratory learning, these false starts and errors would be learned and would make learning of the correct solutions and procedures more difficult, if not impossible. Accordingly, active exploratory learning was to be avoided.

Similarly, Bandura (1986, p. 47) urged that learners should be "spared the costs and pain of faulty effort" and that they should instead receive the needed step-by-step guidance that results in flawless behavior from the outset. Feedback should focus only on the correct execution of tasks and should take the form of positive social reinforcement, with errors—if any—being ignored. Indeed, errors can have a detrimental effect for people who have particular neurological deficits; this topic is discussed in further detail below. However, a fear of errors typically diverts learning from highly productive generative strategies, and an error avoidance strategy is even more pernicious because generating errors—as long as corrective feedback is given—is actually beneficial to learning.

ENCOURAGING VERSUS DISCOURAGING ERRORS IN THE CLASSROOM

It is not clear how important the worry about avoiding errors has been in shaping American teaching strategies. It is extremely difficult to obtain accurate data concerning what and how teachers teach, let alone to manipulate that teaching in a manner that would allow confident inferences to be made. However, Stevenson & Stigler (1994; see also Stigler & Hiebert 2009) and their colleagues conducted a landmark study in which they were able to videotape lessons in grade 8 mathematics classrooms in a variety of countries, including the United States, Taiwan, China, and Japan. Of most interest, given that Japan is by far outstripping the United States in math scores, is the striking difference in the teaching methods used in those two countries. Although there may be many other reasons for the differences in math scores, one highly salient difference is whether or not teachers engage with students' errors. Videotapes show that, in the United States, set procedures for doing particular kinds of problems are explicitly taught. These correct procedures are rehearsed and emphasized; errors are avoided or ignored. The students are not passive in American classrooms. A teacher may ask for student participation in repeating, for example, a procedure for borrowing when subtracting. When asking a question such as, "Can you subtract 9 from 5?" to prompt students to answer, "No, you have to borrow to make the 5 a 15," the teacher may fail to even acknowledge the deviant child who says, "Yes. It's negative 4." If the response does not fit with the procedure being exercised, it is not reinforced. Errors (as well as deviant correct answers) are neither punished nor discussed but are disregarded. Praise is given, but only for the "correct" answer.

As Stevenson & Stigler (1994) pointed out, praise curtails discussion and serves mainly to reinforce the teacher's role as the authority who bestows rewards. It does not empower students to think, criticize, reconsider, evaluate, and explore their own thought processes. By way of contrast, in Japan praise is rarely given. There, the norm is extended discussion of errors, including the reasons for them and the ways in which they may seem plausible but nevertheless lead to the incorrect answer, as well as discussion of the route and reasons to the correct answer. Such in-depth discussion of the thought processes underlying both actual and potential errors encourages exploratory approaches by students.

Instead of beginning with teacher-directed classwork and explication, Japanese students first try to solve problems on their own, a process that is likely to be filled with false starts. Only after these (usually failed) attempts by students does teacher-directed discussion—interactively involving students and targeting students' initial efforts and core mathematical principles—occur. It is expected that students will struggle and make errors, insofar as they rarely have available a fluent procedure that allows them to solve the problems. Nor are students expected to find the process of learning easy. But the time spent struggling on their own to work out a solution is considered a crucial part of the learning process, as is the discussion with the class when it reconvenes to share the methods, to describe the difficulties and pitfalls as well as the insights, and to provide feedback on the principles at stake as well as the solutions.

As Stevenson & Stigler (1994, p. 193) note, "Perhaps because of the strong influence of behavioristic teaching, which says conditions should be arranged so that the learner avoids errors and makes only a reinforceable response, American teachers place little emphasis on the constructive use of errors as a teaching technique. Learning about what is wrong may hasten understanding of why the correct procedures are appropriate, but errors may also be interpreted as failure. And Americans, reluctant to have such interpretations made of their children's performance, strive to avoid situations where this might happen."

The Japanese active learning approach well reflects the fundamental ideas of a learning-from-errors approach. Engaging with errors is difficult, but difficulty can be desirable for learning (Bjork 2012). In comparison with approaches that stress error avoidance, making training more challenging by allowing false starts and errors followed by feedback, discussion, and correction may ultimately lead to better and more flexible transfer of skills to later critical situations.

ERROR GENERATION AND MEMORY FOR CORRECT RESPONSES IN THE LAB

Considerable research now indicates that engagement with errors fosters the secondary benefits of deep discussion of thought processes and exploratory active learning and that the view that the commission of errors hurts learning of the correct response is incorrect. Indeed, many tightly controlled experimental investigations have now shown that in comparison with error-free study, the generation of errors, as long as it is followed by corrective feedback, results in better memory for the correct response. Oddly, the researchers who have investigated these processes usually refer to errors as "unsuccessful retrieval," leaving ambiguous whether a mistake was produced or whether the learner had just neglected to generate the correct response.

Early studies by Izawa (1967, 1970) showed that multiple unsuccessful retrieval attempts led to better memory for the correct feedback than did a procedure producing fewer incorrect responses.

Kane & Anderson (1978) showed similar results: Attempting the generation of the last word of the sentence, even if what was generated was wrong, led to enhanced correct performance compared to reading the sentence correctly from the outset. Slamecka & Fevreiski (1983) asked people to remember near antonyms, such as trivial-vital or oscillate-settle. Even failed attempts (followed by feedback containing the correct answer) improved later recall of the correct answers over simply reading the correct answer. Kornell et al. (2015) have conducted a recent investigation of the same issue and have reached similar conclusions.

People rarely produced explicit mistakes in the early experiments. The majority of so-called retrieval failures were omission rather than commission errors. However, when Slamecka & Fevreiski (1983) specifically analyzed the effect of commission as compared to omission errors, they found that commission errors, as long as they were semantically related to the target, resulted in better later recall of the correct answer.

Kornell et al. (2009) conducted the first definitive study that directly compared the effect of producing versus not producing a commission error. The cue and the to-be-remembered target word in most of the experiments in their study were slightly related word pairs. They compared a condition in which the answer, or target, was simply given to participants, with no intervening error generation (the no-error condition), to one in which the participants were asked to guess the answer first and nearly always produced an error before being given the correct answer to study (the error-generation condition). The experiment was carefully controlled to ensure that the amount of time spent studying the correct answer was equated across conditions. Kornell et al. (2009) also eliminated from consideration any instances in which the person did not generate an error in the error-generation condition. This happened less than 10% of the time. The surprising finding, which has now been replicated many times, was that on the final test, participants remembered the correct answers considerably better when they had generated an error than when they had not. It appears, then, that error generation is not inevitably bad and to be avoided at all costs. Indeed, error generation appears to foster learning (see **Figure 1**).

A flurry of replications quickly followed. For example, Huelser & Metcalfe (2012) found a beneficial effect of error generation as long as the errors people produced were not completely unrelated to the target. They found no benefit with unrelated pairs—a finding that was replicated by Grimaldi & Karpicke (2012) and by Knight et al. (2012) and that is consistent with Slamecka &

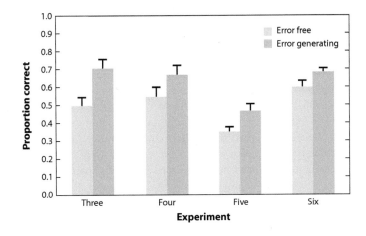

Figure 1

Proportion of correct responses following error-generating and error-free study. Figure adapted with permission from Kornell et al. (2009).

Fevreiski's (1983) earlier analysis. Similarly, Kang et al. (2011) found no effect when participants had absolutely no idea what the answers to factual questions might be but were nevertheless forced to guess. It appears that to be beneficial, the guess needs to be somewhat informed rather than a shot in the dark. Interestingly, in the related-pair case in which a large beneficial effect of committing errors was found, the participants were metacognitively unaware of the benefit. Even immediately after they had experienced the task and had evidenced a benefit of 20% (i.e., roughly the difference between a C− and an A, if it had been a course grade), participants thought that the error-free condition had resulted in better recall (Huelser & Metcalfe 2012). This lack of awareness of the benefits of error generation may contribute to the aversion to errors in the American teaching style evinced in Stigler's work.

In a more educationally realistic study, Richland et al. (2009) found that error generation was related to enhanced memory for material from reading passages. In their study, material from the passage was tested before participants had a chance to read the passage, resulting in participants generating many errors. However, later correct memory for the material that had been pretested in this way was greatly enhanced. More recently, instead of using simple word pairs, Kornell et al. (2015) used general information as their stimuli, asking people either to try to generate the responses (resulting in many mistakes) or to read the question and correct answer. In this situation, too, generation of the error helped later memory for the correct response. Thus, it appears that generating an error, if it is related in any way to the correct response, enhances rather than impairs memory for the correct answer.

Feedback to Errors

When people have made an error, corrective feedback is crucial (Anderson et al. 1971; Butler & Roediger 2008; Hancock et al. 1992; Kornell & Metcalfe 2013; Lhyle & Kulhavy 1987; Metcalfe & Kornell 2007; Metcalfe et al. 2007, 2009; Pashler et al. 2005). It is not enough to simply tell learners whether they were right or wrong. People get virtually no benefit unless the feedback they receive provides the correct answer, as Pashler et al. (2005) showed (and see Bangert-Drowns et al. 1991, Moreno 2004). Furthermore, people need to understand and pay attention to the feedback. Many studies showing a lack of benefit from feedback (and some showing a lack of benefit from committing errors) fail to ensure that the feedback is processed. When the correct answer is made available, though, and people appreciate that the answer is correct as well as why that answer is correct, they are able to integrate that information into memory and improve performance (Anderson et al. 1971).

Furthermore, Metcalfe et al. (2009) showed that the feedback did not have to be given within moments of error commission to be effective. They contrasted a condition in which people were given the feedback immediately upon error commission with one in which it was delayed by up to a week (and they controlled for lag until test, which was one week from feedback in both conditions, so the amount of time until the test did not differ in the two conditions). In both the immediate and delayed feedback conditions, participants were required to attend to the feedback, insofar as they were instructed to type the answer into the computer. The study found that college students performed equally well in the immediate and delayed feedback conditions, whereas children in grades 3 to 5 did better when the feedback was delayed. Interestingly, Kulik & Kulik (1988) noted that whether delayed or immediate feedback produced better results differed between studies conducted in the classroom and those in the laboratory. Lab studies tended to show that delayed feedback was better, whereas classroom studies favored immediate feedback. They concluded, however, that the real difference between these studies was whether the learners paid attention to the feedback. Students in the classroom are highly engaged in knowing the answers to questions right after taking a test. They pay attention to the feedback when it is given immediately. However, their interest flags with a long delay, especially if the feedback is cursory. If the teacher needs or wants to delay feedback (to allow for conscientious scoring, for example), it seems clear that the students' interest in the questions needs to be reignited, and the presentation of the corrective feedback needs to be engaging.

When feedback is elaborative or scaffolded, its beneficial effects are also increased (Finn & Metcalfe 2010). The provision of feedback can be, as it is in the Japanese classrooms, extensive and hence very helpful in allowing students to understand the underlying constructs and to generalize to new situations. Feedback provides an opportunity for exploring and deeply analyzing the principles underlying the problems, the answers, and the reasoning leading to the answers—be they right or wrong. Siegler (1995) conducted a particularly interesting study illustrating the importance of focusing students' attention on the reasoning underlying the feedback. He had three conditions: (a) a feedback-only condition; (b) an explain-own-reasoning condition, in which the children were asked, "Why do you think that?"; and, most effectively, (c) an explain-the-correct reasoning condition, in which the students, after having been given the corrective feedback, were asked, "How do you think I knew that?" As Siegler (2002, p. 40) noted, "Having the children explain another person's correct reasoning has the advantage of both discovery and didactic approaches to instruction. It is like discovery-oriented approaches in that it requires the child to generate a relatively deep analysis of a phenomenon without being told how to do so. It is like didactic approaches in that it focuses the child's attention on the correct reasoning. Thus, it combines some of the efficiency of didactic instruction with some of the motivating properties of discovery."

Sources of Errors

Another fundamental question concerns whether the source of an error modulates its efficacy for learning. The literature indicates that although self-generating an error and being exposed to externally presented irrelevant information may seem similar on the surface, important differences may exist. For example, Grimaldi & Karpicke (2012) showed that error generation, as opposed to merely being presented the correct response (in a paradigm like that of Kornell et al. 2009), had a beneficial effect on later memory for the correct answer. However, when instead of having the participant generate an error, the experimenter presented an incorrect word during what would have been the generation period, memory for the correct answer was harmed. Furthermore, it was also harmful to restrict what the person had to generate as an error (a constrained alternative). A similar phenomenon has been observed with self-generated as compared to experimenter-presented mistaken items when people were in tip-of-the-tongues states. Kornell & Metcalfe (2006) noted that self-generated errors (which, typically, the participants knew were not the correct answers) did not block retrieval of the correct answer, as opposed to when no incorrect answer was produced. In contrast, when experimenter-presented incorrect answers were given while people were in tip-of-the-tongue states, the incorrect answers harmed retrieval of the correct answer in comparison with having nothing presented (Smith & Blankenship 1991). Determining how self-generated wrong answers differ from experimenter-presented wrong items may be important for understanding why error generation helps. It is possible that self-generated errors tap into the person's own semantic memory structure and thus can serve as mediators to help the person get to the correct answer. Externally imposed distracting items may fail to take advantage of an individuals' internal mental structure and thus fail to serve the mediational role. Such items may simply be distracting.

What happens if a person observes another person—say, a fellow student—make an error that is then followed by feedback? Does this exposure have the same beneficial effect as self-generating one's own error, or is it like being exposed to irrelevant experimenter-presented distractions? This is an interesting question with practical implications, but it is an issue that research has not yet addressed.

CONFIDENCE IN ERRORS

Errors Versus Guesses

The critic may argue that perhaps the people in the experiments described above did not really believe in their responses: They were just generating guesses, not genuine errors. Perhaps there is no benefit to generating errors when people really endorse their errors and have strong beliefs that they are correct. The data show greater benefit when the errors were related to the target than when they were unrelated, which somewhat offsets this contention. Even so, few classroom teachers would ask students to memorize lists of word pairs such as oscillate-settle or hillside-banker or similar items used in the experiments on error generation. Kornell and colleagues' (2015) experiment with real general-information questions—which showed error-generation benefits in a real-world factual task—helps allay some concerns that benefits may obtain only with guesses and not with real errors.

Nevertheless, we may ask how much belief is enough to make a particular response a genuine error rather than just a guess. In the next section, we review the literature on the relation between individuals' degree of belief, or their confidence in the truth of their answers to general-knowledge questions, and their propensity to correct those answers and remember the corrections when they turn out to be erroneous.

Correcting High-Confidence Versus Low-Confidence Errors

A number of studies have investigated the correction of errors as a function of the individual's confidence in the error. Typically, a factual question is asked of the participant; the individual generates an answer and then rates his or her confidence that the error is correct. Next, feedback is given, in which the correct answer is provided. For example, participants might be given the question, "What kind of music is associated with the Cajuns in Louisiana?" Participants then give an answer (perhaps "jazz") and rate their confidence in the correctness of the answer they produced. Finally, participants are given the correct answer (in this case, "zydeco"). In contrast to the predictions of a variety of theories that suggest that responses in which one is highly confident should be particularly difficult to overwrite, the high-confidence errors are more likely to be corrected on the retest than are errors endorsed with lower confidence (e.g., Butler et al. 2008, 2011; Butterfield & Mangels 2003; Butterfield & Metcalfe 2001, 2006; Cyr & Anderson 2013; Eich et al. 2013; Fazio & Marsh 2009, 2010; Iwaki et al. 2013; Kulhavy et al. 1976; Metcalfe et al. 2012; Metcalfe & Finn 2011, 2012; Sitzman & Rhodes 2010; Sitzman et al. 2015). This hypercorrection effect occurs both with immediate retest and when the retest is given at a considerable delay (Butler et al. 2011, Butterfield & Mangels 2003, Metcalfe & Miele 2014). A strong degree of belief in the truth of one's errors makes them more, rather than less, susceptible to being correctable.

Explanations of the Hypercorrection Effect

A number of associative theories of memory and of the relation of memory to confidence seem to indicate that the hypercorrection effect should not be found; indeed, perhaps even the reverse should be observed. Responses that are made with high confidence are those in which the person believes most and are thought to be the strongest in memory (e.g., Ebbesen & Rienick 1998).

As such, they should be most easily accessible and most resistant to interference as well as the most difficult to overwrite or replace with a new response. Certainly, in all data presented to date on the hypercorrection effect, the correlation between confidence in one's first responses and the correctness of those responses is high: The responses in which people are highly confident are nearly always correct, indicating that in general people know what they do and don't know and that their high-confidence responses are strongly and readily retrieved from memory. Most errors that people make are assigned low confidence (and because they are weak, should be easy to overwrite with a new response). People make high-confidence errors only rarely. But if such a high-confidence response were in error, it too—like correct high-confidence responses—should be strong, entrenched, and difficult rather than easy to change. The consistent finding of a hypercorrection effect, whereby high-confidence errors are corrected more readily than low-confidence errors, flies in the face of traditional interference, response hierarchy, and associative theories.

Two nonmutually exclusive factors are central to the hypercorrection phenomenon in young adults, though these are not the only factors at play. The first relates to the surprise individuals experience at being wrong when they were sure they were right. The second relates to the structure of the semantic network surrounding high- as compared to low-confidence errors.

Because they are surprised (and perhaps embarrassed) at having made a mistake on a response they strongly thought was correct, individuals may rally their attentional resources to better remember the correct answer. Several lines of evidence support this surprise/attentional factor. For example, Butterfield & Metcalfe (2006) conducted an experiment designed to evaluate the extent to which one task drew attention from another. Subjects were required to detect when very soft tones occurred while they were doing the general-information error-correction task. Some of the tones were intentionally presented simultaneously with the corrective feedback following high- and low-confidence errors. Participants were more likely to fail to detect the tones that were presented at the time of high-confidence error feedback than those presented at the time of low-confidence error feedback. This result indicates that because participants' attention was captured by the high-confidence error feedback, they had less capacity to detect the tones.

Fazio & Marsh (2009) tested for memory for the surrounding context that accompanied feedback. They showed that the surrounding context of high-confidence error feedback was better remembered than was the surrounding context of low-confidence error feedback, and they interpreted this result as favoring the attentional explanation.

Butterfield & Mangels (2003) used young adult participants in the first event-related brain potential (ERP) study on this paradigm. The most salient result from their study was that participants showed a voltage deflection—the P3a—that past literature on ERPs has linked to surprise reactions in which people rally their attention (Friedman et al. 2001). The literature has also associated this deflection with enhanced memory (Paller et al. 1985). Butterfield & Mangel's (2003) study revealed that there was a confidence-graded P3a when corrective feedback was given, a result that has been replicated and extended by Metcalfe et al. (2015) (see **Figure 2**). The P3a was largest for the feedback to high-confidence errors and smallest for the feedback to low-confidence errors. These results support the contention that high-confidence errors are surprising and that increased attention is paid to corrective feedback to such errors.

Finally, Metcalfe et al. (2012) conducted a study on hypercorrection using event-related functional magnetic resonance imaging. Participants answered questions for several hours, giving their confidence in their answer outside the scanner. Participants then entered the scanner and were presented with questions, their original answers, their original confidence ratings, and finally the correct answer. When the brain activations to the feedback to high- and low-confidence errors were compared, it was found that medial frontal areas that prominently included the anterior cingulate—an area related to surprise, error detection, and attention—were differentially

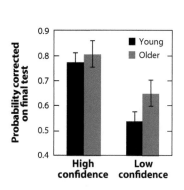
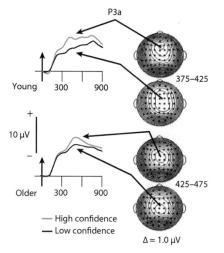

Figure 2

Event-related potentials (ERPs) synchronized to the onset of corrective feedback given to high- and low-confidence errors made by young adults and older adults. The ERP tracings show a prominent P3a to feedback to high-confidence errors. The behavioral results showing the proportion correct on the final test, for both groups as a function of initial error confidence, are shown on the left. Figure adapted with permission from Metcalfe et al. (2015).

activated. Other areas, such as the dorsolateral prefrontal cortex and the temporal parietal junction (see **Figure 3**), were also differentially activated. These results also implicate a surprise-related explanation of the enhanced encoding associated with the feedback to high-confidence errors.

The second factor that has been implicated in the hypercorrection effect is a greater semantic knowledge in the domain of the high-confidence errors than in the low-confidence error domain. Butterfield & Mangels (2003) noted that participant-ascribed familiarity to high- and to

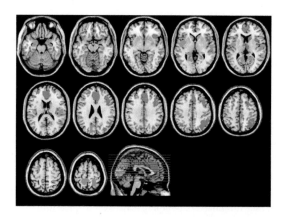

Figure 3

Contrast map of high-confidence errors versus low-confidence errors. Red areas were more active for high-confidence errors, and green areas were more active for low-confidence errors; both areas had an uncorrected threshold of $p < 0.001$. Figure adapted with permission from Metcalfe et al. (2012), © 2012 by the Massachusetts Institute of Technology, **http://www.mitpressjournals.org/doi/abs/10.1162/jocn_a_00228**.

low-confidence responses was differential. Butterfield & Metcalfe (2006) showed that the a priori probability of a correct response was greater for high- than for low-confidence errors.

Latent semantic analysis (Landauer & Dumais 1997) has shown that the similarity of the error to the correct response is higher for high- than for low-confidence errors. This semantic similarity has been found both for young (Metcalfe & Finn 2011) and for older (Eich et al. 2013) adults. Thus, individuals are "closer" in semantic space to the right answer when they produce a high-confidence error than when they produce a low-confidence error.

Furthermore, Metcalfe & Finn (2011) have shown that young adults claim that they "knew it all along" frequently when they receive corrective feedback to high-confidence errors. In Metcalfe & Finn's study, young adults were more likely to produce a second guess that was correct following a high- as compared to a low-confidence error. They were more likely to choose the correct alternative in a multiple-choice test that excluded their original answer if the error had been committed with high confidence. Additionally, young adults required fewer clues to guess the correct answers to questions on which they had made high- as compared to low-confidence errors. These results indicate that familiarity with the domain of the high-confidence error, and plausibly with the answer itself, plays a role in the hypercorrection effect.

Children as well as adults showed these familiarity effects (Metcalfe & Finn 2012). Familiarity effects appear to follow the pattern of hypercorrection, but even so, these effects are probably coupled with the effects of surprise. When a person is highly familiar with a domain of knowledge, it is within that domain that surprise at one's errors is most salient.

EXCEPTIONS

Amnesics and Error-Free Learning

People with amnesia present an exception to the general finding that learning from errors is helpful. In a seminal effort to promote learning in people with severe amnesia, Glisky et al. (1986) devised a procedure called the method of vanishing cues (MVC). MVC was developed on the assumption that errors produce enormous interference in amnesics and hence are particularly disruptive for these patients (see, e.g., Hayman et al. 1993). The idea was to always present sufficient information so that the patient never produced a mistake, allowing them to circumvent the proactive interference while at the same time to benefit from priming. Some of the initial demonstrations of MVC were implemented in attempts to teach deeply amnesic patients definitions of computer terms. The experimenters first exposed the definition for 10 seconds, and if the patient failed to produce the word, the first letter appeared on the computer screen. If the patient still failed to produce the target word after 10 more seconds had elapsed, an additional letter was provided, and so on until the word was produced correctly. Then the computer reversed the procedure, providing one less letter on each subsequent trial. Using this method, K.C., a profoundly amnesic patient, was eventually able to "remember" the previously unlearned semantic terms with no letter cues at all. Other researchers (e.g., Baddeley & Wilson 1994, Hamann & Squire 1995; for a review, see Clare & Jones 2008) have also shown that amnesic patients can benefit from errorless learning. These results, while fascinating in their own right, also have implications for theories seeking to explain why making errors helps later correct performance in neurologically typical participants.

Older Adults and Hypercorrection

Older adults provide a different kind of exception. Although older adults benefit from making errors, their pattern of confidence-related benefits is different from that of younger people. Eich and colleagues' (2013) study in which older adults were compared to young adults revealed a typical hypercorrection effect with young adult participants, but the older adults corrected high-confidence errors only slightly more than low-confidence errors (see also Cyr & Anderson 2013). A hypercorrection experiment with older adults by Sitzman et al. (2015) indicated that they had greater familiarity with the low-confidence corrections than did the younger adults—evoking a preexperimental familiarity explanation. Metcalfe et al. (2015) also presented data indicating that older adults claimed greater familiarity with the correct answers to low-confidence errors than did younger adults. Interestingly, though, their results indicate that the older adults may not have actually relied that much on preexperimental familiarity: In comparison with younger adults, they also showed greater learning of answers with which they were unfamiliar. These authors argued for an attentional explanation of the decreased hypercorrection effect because compared to young adults, the older adults showed a larger attention-related event-related P3a to their low-confidence errors. The older adults not only hypercorrected their high-confidence errors but also did extremely well in correcting their low-confidence errors—errors that young adults tended not to correct.

IMPLICATIONS OF THE HYPERCORRECTION EFFECT

Scientific Understanding

Van Loon et al. (2015) investigated the correction of scientific misconceptions, which is one of the most interesting extensions of the hypercorrection effect. They looked at people's correction of conceptual errors, a highly relevant and ecologically valid situation in which error correction is vital for understanding. They found that although hypercorrection did not occur when students simply read standard texts that presented the correct factual information without emphasis on the conceptual errors, it did occur when the students read what they called refutation texts. In these latter texts, the misconceptions that the students had voiced were explicitly stated and then discussed and refuted. The authors suggested that individuals are surprised when they find that a misconception held with high confidence is, in fact, wrong, and the surprise results in enhanced attention to the refutation.

Lexical Representations

Iwaki et al. (2013) extended the hypercorrection paradigm to the correction of erroneous lexical representations found in language learning. In their study, participants performed a Japanese kanji word-reading task, in which the inscriptions had several possible pronunciations, only one of which was correct. Participants read each word aloud and indicated their confidence in their response before being given visual feedback of the correct response. As in the factual knowledge case, a hypercorrection effect was observed in this lexical representation case. Interestingly, the effect was modulated by participants' evaluation of the practical value of to-be-learned words.

Correcting False Inferences in Episodic Memory

Fazio & Marsh (2010) conducted a study in which participants made erroneous inferences, sometimes with high confidence. For example, individuals were asked to remember statements such as "The clumsy chemist had acid on his coat" or "The karate champion hit the cinder block." Later, the participants often made inferences beyond what was actually given in the statement. For example, they might have recalled, "The clumsy chemist *spilled* acid on his coat," or "The karate champion *broke* the cinder block." The authors asked participants to rate confidence in their answers and then gave feedback concerning the original statement. Interestingly, a hypercorrection effect was found in this ecologically valid situation—the greater participants' confidence was in their wrong answers, the greater the correction upon retest. This study suggests that false episodic memories, in which people often express high confidence, may be open to rectification when the correct information is provided.

THEORIES OF WHY ERRORS ENHANCE LEARNING

As was noted in the introduction, standard interference theory does a poor job of accounting for why generating errors helps later memory for the correct answer. Other theories, though, do better.

Mediation

In seeking to explain why testing helps learning, Pyc & Rawson (2010) and Carpenter (2011) proposed that when individuals are tested, they are likely to generate effective mediational retrieval cues. An interesting possibility is that erroneous responses serve as signposts or stepping-stones rather than as interfering competitors to the correct answer. This conjecture is consistent with the data showing that only errors that are related to the target are effective in aiding later recall. It is also consistent with the idea that the errors have to be self-generated to help. Externally presented items seem, intuitively, much less likely to tap into the individual's own semantic memory structure in such a way that they could later provide a route to the target correct item. Whether such mediation might be entirely semantic or might rely on an episodic-memory component has not been fully explored. However, a position outlined by Jacoby & Wahlheim (2013) suggests the latter.

Recursive Reminding

Jacoby & Wahlheim (2013) discussed the possibility that errors (and other contextual aspects of the encoding situation) have a facilitative effect to the extent that they are related to retrieving the original episodic event in which both the correct answer and the mistake were embedded. The idea is that individuals may be able to remember the context in which they made an error and by so doing think not only of the error itself but also of the surrounding context in which it was made clear that the error had been made and that the correction was the desired answer. This process, which is called recursive reminding, relies on the learner's explicit or episodic memory for the event, including making the mistake and receiving the correction. This explanation of the beneficial effects of errors is particularly attractive in light of the findings that people with amnesia, who have impaired explicit or episodic memory, are harmed by generating errors, whereas people with intact episodic memory benefit from making errors. However, not all data are supportive. The theory would seem to imply that memory for the correct answer should be particularly enhanced if the error is regenerated at time of retrieval. However, Butterfield & Metcalfe (2001) and Metcalfe & Miele (2014) showed that correct recall was independent of error generation at time of retrieval. On the other hand, Wahlheim & Jacoby (2013) showed a positive relation between remembering that there had been a change from what the person had previously thought was the answer, at time of encoding, and later target memory. Clearly, further research is needed to test this promising theory.

Reconsolidation

The reconsolidation framework was formulated within a fear-conditioning paradigm that is entirely different from the present error-correction paradigm (e.g., Dudai 2012, Lee 2008, Nader et al. 2000). The reconsolidation framework has been directed at discovering methods to overcome posttraumatic stress disorder and traumatic conditioned fears (see Schiller et al. 2010) and is compatible with a number of therapies. Despite a difference in domain, striking similarities exist between the reconsolidation framework and the error-correction paradigm.

The basic premise is that in order for a conditioned fear to be altered or eradicated, the dysfunctional response first needs to be evoked. Following fear response retrieval there is a short time window during which the undesirable response can be eradicated or modified and reconsolidated. If the response is not evoked, though, then it stays buried and unchanged. Some similarities between fear conditioning and error correction suggest that applying reconsolidation theory to both domains may be fruitful. The most important of these similarities is the core idea that the undesired response, be it the dysfunctional fear response or the semantic error, needs to be retrieved in order for it to be rendered susceptible to change.

The reconsolidation framework is consistent with the gist of the results of the many studies that have shown that the probability of producing the correct answer is greater when the error was first retrieved in conjunction with the new, overwriting stimulus, as contrasted to when the preexisting error was not evoked and only the correct answer was provided. Interestingly, reconsolidation theory has detailed a number of factors of interest that have not been explored within the semantic error-correction paradigm. First, the temporal window of opportunity for modification of the erroneous response has not been much explored in the semantic memory situation. If such a window exists, then it would be important—for educational reasons—to identify it. Second, in the reconsolidation framework, the more strongly the fear is evoked, the more likely it is to be malleable (Lee 2008). This finding may be analogous to some of the similarity relations seen in the error-correction paradigm and perhaps even to the basic hypercorrection effect, though these relations—and the reasons for them—need to be specified in more detail. Third, in reconsolidation theory, some experiments use neurological agents such as anisomycin, or even electroshock, to eliminate the fear, which raises the issue of the need for unlearning. Does the semantic error need to be obliterated for a new correct response to be learned? Or, as in some theories such as the recursive reminding model and the mediational model (described above), is the continued mental presence of the error actually helpful?

Finally, is the ouster of the dysfunctional response permanent? Within the fear conditioning/animal-learning domain, there is a long history of empirical investigations of extinction methods that later result in spontaneous recovery. With reconsolidation, however, the learning of the new correct response is thought to be permanent. Only a few studies in the error-correction paradigm have investigated the important analogous question of the potential return of the errors (Butler et al. 2011, Metcalfe & Miele 2014), and the results are not yet definitive. The permanence of error correction is clearly a crucial question for the efficacy of this method in education. Further effort is needed to investigate whether the kind of permanent change thought to obtain with reconsolidation is also found in the domain of error correction.

Prediction Error

The notion that the discrepancy between a person's expectation and the actual outcome is crucial for learning—at all levels from perception to cognition and memory—has been postulated in many neurally based computational and machine models of learning (Friston 2005, Rumelhart &

McClelland 1986). In these models, if everything happens just as is expected, no learning need take place. It is only when expectations are violated or when there is prediction error that the network needs to change to accommodate the unexpected results. The greater the prediction error, the greater the learning. This attractive and parsimonious theory is consistent with many of the findings cited above.

Furthermore, prediction error models seem at first blush to be particularly applicable to the hypercorrection situation insofar as the magnitude of the prediction error determines the extent of learning. Intuitively, high-confidence errors seem like big, serious errors. As is evidenced by the ERP and the attentional literatures described above, high-confidence errors preferentially evoke such a surprise/attentional reaction. Thus, this aspect of prediction error models fits nicely.

A problem needs to be solved, however. If predication error is assessed in terms of the representational characteristics of the item that is retrieved as compared to the correct answer—as seems plausible—then it would appear that the magnitude of the prediction error in the high-confidence error case is smaller than it is in the low-confidence error case, and therefore less learning should occur. Latent semantic analysis (Landauer & Dumais 1997) showed that the similarity between the correct answers and high-confidence errors was greater than the similarity between the correct answers and the low-confidence errors (Metcalfe & Finn 2011; for a model of the experimental results based on high similarity rather than high prediction error, see Sitzman et al. 2015). Furthermore, as noted above, when individuals were simply told they were wrong and were asked to make a second guess, they were more likely to come up with the correct answer when they had made a high- rather than a low-confidence error; they were more able to choose the correct answer in a multiple choice test; and they were more likely to complete the answer correctly when given fragmentary cues (Metcalfe & Finn 2011). Prediction error models have tremendous appeal, and they fit with the apparent surprise that people feel when they are highly confident but wrong. However, if the prediction error framework is to seamlessly apply, theoretic resolution is needed for the mismatch between individuals' apparent surprise at being wrong in high-confidence errors and their equally evident nearness to being right. A formal implementation of the prediction error framework to this particular error correction situation—a situation of enormous practical import—could greatly contribute to our understanding of error correction in the real world and to the predication error framework.

SECONDARY BENEFITS OF ENCOURAGING ERRORS

Active Generation Is Beneficial to Memory for Correct Responses

One of the spinoffs of pedagogical techniques that allow or even encourage students to generate errors is that during such active participation students frequently generate the correct responses. Active generation as opposed to passive study (Slamecka & Graf 1978; for a review, see Bertsch et al. 2007) and the related testing effect (e.g., McDaniel et al. 2007; Roediger & Karpicke 2006a,b) both produce large beneficial effects on learning. Allowing students to self-generate induces one of the strongest beneficial effects on learning in the cognitive literature.

Knowledge of Student Errors Helps the Teacher

The nature of the errors that students generate, when they are allowed to do so, can provide crucial information to the teacher. Much research on formative assessment (Black & Wiliam 1998; see also Dunn & Mulvenon 2009) indicates that any assessment that could be potentially used by teachers to focus instruction is of great interest. This perspective, although not specifically dwelling on errors, is highly compatible with the approach taken here: Errors indicate areas of difficulty for students and as such are the very areas on which the instruction should be focused. Errors also provide indications to the teacher of what students are thinking and what diverts them from the correct solution. Understanding students' misunderstanding can help the teacher focus on the aspects of the to-be-learned concepts that need to be clarified.

Consideration of Errors Offsets Overconfidence

Encouraging students to consider ways in which they could be wrong has a metacognitive benefit of helping to train subjective confidence (see Bjork 1994). The many experimental studies investigating the confidence of individuals reveal an overarching finding of overconfidence (for a review, see Dunlosky & Metcalfe 2009): People believe that they have learned and know things when they do not yet know them (Metcalfe 1998). Furthermore, people's confidence affects their study choices and time (Finn 2008, Metcalfe & Finn 2008). When people have high confidence that they have learned materials, they decline further study. Similarly, when they have high confidence on tests, they may leave a question prematurely, possibly committing a correctible mistake. Pervasive overconfidence, then, has a deleterious effect on both study and eventual test performance.

One method that has been found to be effective in offsetting overconfidence is to have people consider possible errors and think about how they could be wrong (Koriat et al. 1980). Note that the tendency of individuals to assume that anything retrieved is correct (and to disregard the possibility of error) fits with the mechanisms used for making metacognitive judgments (see, for example, Koriat 2008, 2012) and underlies the need for training subjective as well as objective experience.

A reflective practice method used in medical schools to improve diagnostic decisions (Mamede & Schmidt 2004, Schiff et al. 2009) has the students imagine that they have already made their diagnosis on a particular case and that treatment and the course of action, based on that diagnosis, have already taken place. Students then learn that the patient has died. Students are asked to reevaluate their diagnosis on the basis of this outcome and, if warranted, to make a different diagnosis. This method of checking is termed a premortem analysis. A similar method referred to as prospective hindsight (Mitchell et al. 1989) uses consideration of a possible erroneous outcome to improve choice selection. It, too, has been shown to have positive effects on performance.

ORIGIN OF THE IDEA THAT ERRORLESS LEARNING IS A GOOD THING

With all of this evidence that generating errors helps learning, one might wonder where we got the idea—so entrenched in our educational system—that error generation is bad? The classic paper on errorless learning is that of Terrace (1963). He showed that pigeons could be taught to discriminatively peck a red circle as opposed to a green circle by being reinforced in such a way that they never pecked the green circle at all, that is, the pigeons performed in an errorless manner. This method involved first contrasting the reinforced red circle with a neutral gray background (rather than with the green circle); the neutral gray background would be flashed very quickly so that the pigeon would have no time to peck it even if it was so inclined. But the on-time was gradually increased, the neutral gray background color was slowly replaced with a very faint green circle that over trials gradually became more intensely green, and finally both the red and the green circle were fully visible for an amount of time sufficient for the pigeon to peck either stimulus. With this method, the pigeon pecked only the red circle, never making the error of pecking the green circle. The contrasting method involved presenting both the red and green circles at full intensity, with sufficient pecking time from the outset but reinforcing only pecking of the red circle, a procedure that evinced many pecks to the green circle (errors) during training.

In developing the errorless method of learning, Terrace was endeavoring to test a theory of the role of inhibition in learning and was not attempting to develop—nor did he claim to have developed—a better way to learn. However, the method was vaunted by others and put to use in Skinner's teaching machines. The consequences of the two procedures differed, though. For example, some complex differences in later extinction depended on whether the bird learned in an errorless or errorful way and on which initial reinforcement schedule was used. It is not clear how these differences would apply to classroom learning. Other differences between errorful and errorless learning were observed, but it was not clear that errorless learning was better, even in this very narrow paradigm.

First, the pigeon's reaction time to the red circles was faster when the learning procedure had been errorful rather than error free (Terrace 1968). This finding is consistent with the idea that learning was stronger, even in this paradigm, in the errorful condition. Second, the pigeons did not show a directional shift in preferences away from the error after having been trained in an errorless manner. Avoidance or inhibition of the error might be considered a desirable repercussion of learning. This favorable concomitant occurred only in the errorful learning condition (Terrace 1966, 1968). Third, the pigeons did not show a contrast effect, whereby the presence of the green stimulus enhanced responding to the red, in the errorless learning condition, though they did show a contrast effect in the errorful learning condition (Terrace 2010). Enhanced responding to the correct answer is desirable. The actual results stemming from the method of errorless learning, then, appear to contrast with the ideological beliefs concerning the desirability of errorless learning, even within the original context of simplified reinforcement learning.

Were there any consequences that may have been unfavorable for errorful learning? The most salient, as emphasized by Skinner, was that the pigeons did not show gross emotional responses to the green circle (S−) when they were taught in an errorless manner: "The pigeon quietly waits for the next appearance of S+" (Terrace 1966, p. 316). By way of contrast, following discrimination learning with errors, the green circle evoked "various emotional responses such as wing flapping and turning away from the stimulus" (p. 316).

EMOTIONAL CONSEQUENCES OF ERRORS

One possible negative consequence of learning with errors is exaggerated emotionality. This section provides an overview of the literature on this issue.

Event-Related Potential Studies

Many studies have examined an ERP termed error-related negativity (ERN), which is produced when individuals make, and recognize that they have made, a simple motor mistake in a paradigm in which participants are told to press a button whenever an X, say, is presented on-screen and to withhold responding if anything else—say a V—is presented. Every now and then participants wrongly hit the button when the V is presented. When they do, an early negative voltage deflection is observed in the event-related tracing (Gehring et al. 1990) that has been thought to be a marker of unpleasant emotion. If individuals are shown an unpleasant picture just before making such an error, the ERN amplitude is increased (Wiswede et al. 2009). If they are anxious, the ERN amplitude is increased (Proudfit et al. 2013). Furthermore, adolescents diagnosed with anxiety disorder show larger ERNs (Ladouceur et al. 2006).

The effects, though, are complex and depend on task expectations. In addition, it is not clear whether the detection of these simple incorrect motor responses are the same as, or even related to, the responses that people have to cognitive errors. Butterfield & Mangels (2003) did report a fronto-central negativity similar to the ERN in the hypercorrection paradigm. This negativity, though, was not correlated in any discernible way with error correction.

A second ERP voltage deflection—the P3a—has also been associated with the correction of high-confidence errors (Butterfield & Mangels 2003, Metcalfe et al. 2015). The rich literature on this ERP deflection shows its relation to novelty, memory, and attention (e.g., Friedman et al. 2001, Paller et al. 1985), and it may have a relation to emotion, insofar as participants' anxiety can sometimes affect the amplitude of this component (Luck & Kappenman 2011). Consistent with the localization results of the ERP studies on the P3a in error correction, a functional magnetic resonance imaging study (Metcalfe et al. 2012) showed anterior cingulate and mid-frontal activation in conjunction with the presentation of corrections to high- as compared to low-confidence errors. However, peak activation was in areas most strongly associated with cognition rather than emotion (as shown in **Figure 3**) (see Bush et al. 2000).

Emotional Consequences of Medical and Police Errors

When the consequences of errors are severe, such as in a misdiagnosis or other medical error, the emotional consequences for the agent can also be severe (Wu 2000). Many published studies (e.g., Delbanco & Bell 2007, Waterman et al. 2007) document extreme and troubling emotional consequences felt by doctors. Similarly, police errors can result in severe emotional consequences (Blum & Poliscar 2004). These are unequivocally mistakes on the test that counts and have terrible consequences for another human being for whom the doctor or the police officer feels responsible. As such, these errors can result in guilt feelings and considerable emotion. However, they are not the kind of errors that occur in an inconsequential practice situation, which is the type we focus on in this review.

Rarely have the emotional consequences of making conceptual or factual mistakes in the field (but not in a life-threatening situation) been studied experimentally, although such consequences have been assumed to exist. One exception was an applied managerial study by Zhao (2011), in which it was found that the effect associated with errors was helpful rather than harmful to learning and motivation.

Personality Differences in Responsivity to Errors

Higgins (1999) has proposed that the regulatory focus of individuals—whether they are primarily prevention focused or promotion focused—is related to their sensitivity to errors (Scholar et al. 2008). People who are promotion focused are concerned with advancement, growth, and achievement and care little about making errors; people who are prevention focused are concerned with safety, security, and responsibility and are concerned not to make mistakes. Within a signal-detection framework, the promotion-focused person is concerned with maximizing hits and to do so is willing to tolerate false alarms (i.e., errors). A prevention-focused person is unwilling to tolerate mistakes, even if it means missing out on opportunities. Although regulatory focus is often seen as a dispositional tendency, it can also be experimentally manipulated. Crowe & Higgins (1997) found that failure on a difficult task was more demotivating for people in the prevention set: They produced fewer solutions in a problem-solving task presumably because they monitored their output more closely, and they were wary of producing errors. In contrast, promotion-focused individuals showed a risky bias. It is not known, however, whether prevention-focused or promotion-focused individuals learn better. Metcalfe & Miele (2014) showed subtle effects of being prevention focused versus promotion focused in the hypercorrection paradigm. Prevention-focused individuals showed a larger hypercorrection effect when they were tested immediately, but the effect did not persist at a delay, and overall, there were no learning differences.

Differences in sensitivity to errors among individuals are proposed in other theories of personality as well. Dweck (2006), in her "implicit theories of intelligence" framework, proposed that people may be classified as being either incremental theorists or entity theorists, depending upon their stance toward the malleability of intelligence. Incremental theorists are growth oriented and believe that intelligence is malleable. They have a distinctly positive attitude toward errors, which, for them, provide an opportunity for learning. This attitude is thought to render them resilient to setbacks and to have beneficial effects on learning. In contrast, entity theorists believe that intelligence is fixed. Errors, for an entity theorist, are a mark of deficient intelligence and to be avoided at all costs. The entity theorist's stance seems consistent with Skinner's original concerns.

Methods to Buffer Potential Negative Emotional Effects

Although a number of studies are relevant to overcoming potentially negative emotional effects of errors on motivation, perhaps the most significant are those that have investigated error management training (EMT), an implementation used in software training (see Keith & Frese 2008). EMT participants are explicitly encouraged to make errors during training and to learn from them. They are also given error management instructions, which tell them to expect errors while they work and emphasize the positive informational feedback of errors for learning. EMT has been contrasted with proceduralized training methods, which mimic conventional training tutorials that have a negative attitude toward errors. In the proceduralized condition, detailed step-by-step instructions on correct task solutions are provided to prevent participants from making errors. To investigate the conditions under which EMT does and does not provide learning benefits, Keith & Frese (2008) conducted a meta-analysis of 24 EMT studies. Most of the studies were in the area of software skills, although three investigated decision-making tasks. The results were highly favorable to EMT, with the beneficial effects being particularly favorable for posttraining transfer. This benefit is important because transfer to a nonidentical situation, rather than just easy fluency during the lesson itself, is essential for education. The meta-analysis also showed that the benefits of EMT were modulated by an attitude that errors can be good and provide an opportunity for learning. Heimbeck et al. (2003) explicitly tested the role of error attitude instructions and found that the beneficial effect of EMT was improved when participants were given instructions designed to counteract the negative emotional connotations of errors.

Similarly, Dweck & Leggett (1988) have shown that an incremental (error-resilient) mindset can be induced, even among people who might otherwise adopt an entity theory and be error averse. Dweck and colleagues (e.g., Blackwell et al. 2007) have shown that learning is thereby enhanced. Finally, work on stereotype threat suggests that minority students may be particularly vulnerable to the emotional consequences of errors. Cohen et al. (2009), though, have created a self-affirmation manipulation that has been shown to reduce such stresses and enhance performance. Thus, although some individuals may experience emotional reactions from making errors, especially if the teaching method is not sensitive, it appears to be possible to offset these potentially negative consequences.

USING ERRORS TO IMPROVE LEARNING

Although few methods that capitalize on people's errors have been implemented in teaching, one interesting example exists: The American armed forces use a battle training method that focuses on errors. After-action review (AAR; sometimes termed hotwashing) is an army training method described by Druckman & Bjork (1994) in a National Academy of Sciences report (see also Morrison & Meliza 1999). The gist is that units of novice trainees engage in an action against a so-called opposing force that is extremely well trained and well versed. The novice unit typically is defeated decisively. The novices then undergo the AAR, in which rank is put aside and everyone is free to voice their view. A trained facilitator is present to provide helpful specialized knowledge and to ensure that everyone participates and that the sessions are nonjudgmental of the people involved. Every misstep is analyzed, and discussion centers around what people should have done and why. The concept is that more is learned from defeat than from victory, as long as the trainees have a chance to consider all of their mistakes and make plans to remedy them, and that such learning is better accomplished in a simulated battle rather than in actual battle. The next time the unit meets the opposing force, performance improves, and this encounter is also followed by an AAR. Only after many such battles, each followed by an AAR, is the unit ready for deployment. Within the military, there is much praise for this method. General Gordon R. Sullivan asserted that the "AAR as an essential part of training is one of the most important training interventions ever" (quoted in Morrison & Meliza 1999, p. 21). "Managed and conducted by those closest to the activity, AARs identify how to correct deficiencies, sustain strengths, and focus on improved performance of specific tasks, activities, events, or programs" (USAID 2006, p. iii). Although there is little experimental research on this method, there appears, nevertheless, to be considerable consensus about its efficacy. Interestingly, the manual on AAR (USAID 2006) cites extensive evidence from the literature on human memory and cognition that provides supportive data for each aspect of the method.

CONCLUSION

An unwarranted reluctance to engage with errors may have held back American education. The behavioral and neurological data reviewed here indicate that, as long as one is not amnesic, making errors can greatly facilitate new learning. Errors enhance later memory for and generation of the correct responses, facilitate active learning, stimulate the learner to direct attention appropriately, and inform the teacher of where to focus teaching. The concern that errors might evoke dysfunctional emotional reactions appears to be exaggerated. Of course, sensitive handling of errors and avoiding gratuitous punishments—verbal or otherwise—is essential. The research reviewed here suggests that teachers and learners alike should be encouraged to be open to mistakes and to actively use them in becoming prepared for the test that counts.

DISCLOSURE STATEMENT

The author is not aware of any affiliations, memberships, funding, or financial holdings that might be perceived as affecting the objectivity of this review.

ACKNOWLEDGMENTS

I am grateful to Robert A. Bjork and Nate Kornell for inspiration. I thank the Institute of Education Science of the US Department of Education for facilitating this work under grant number R305A150467. The views expressed in this review are those of the author.

LITERATURE CITED

Anderson RC, Kulhavy RM, Andre T. 1971. Conditions under which feedback facilitates learning from programmed lessons. *J. Educ. Psychol.* 63:186–88

Ausubel DP. 1968. *Educational Psychology: A Cognitive View*. New York: Holt, Rinehart & Winston

Baddeley A, Wilson BA. 1994. When implicit learning fails: amnesia and the problem of error elimination. *Neuropsychologia* 32:53–68

Bandura A. 1986. *Social Foundations of Thought and Action: A Social Cognitive Theory*. Englewood Cliffs, NJ: Prentice-Hall

Bangert-Drowns RL, Kulik C-LC, Kulik JA, Morgan MT. 1991. The instructional effect of feedback in test-like events. *Rev. Educ. Res.* 61:213–38

Barnes JM, Underwood BJ. 1959. Fate of first-list associations in transfer theory. *J. Exp. Psychol.* 58:97–105

Bertsch S, Pesta BJ, Wiscott R, McDaniel MA. 2007. The generation effect: a meta-analytic review. *Mem. Cogn.* 35:201–10

Bjork RA. 1994. Memory and metamemory considerations in the training of human beings. In *Metacognition: Knowing About Knowing*, ed. J Metcalfe, A Shimamura, pp. 185–205. Cambridge, MA: MIT Press

Bjork RA. 2012. Desirable difficulties perspective on learning. In *Encyclopedia of the Mind*, ed. H Pashler, pp. 242–44. Thousand Oaks, CA: Sage

Black P, Wiliam D. 1998. Assessment and classroom learning. *Assess. Educ.* 5:7–74

Blackwell L, Trzesniewski K, Dweck CS. 2007. Implicit theories of intelligence predict achievement across an adolescent transition: a longitudinal study and an intervention. *Child Dev.* 78:246–63

Blum LM, Poliscar JM. 2004. Why things go wrong in police work. *Police Chief* 71:49–52

Bush G, Luu P, Posner MI. 2000. Cognitive and emotional influences in anterior cingulate cortex. *Trends Cogn. Sci.* 4:215–22

Butler AC, Fazio LF, Marsh EJ. 2011. The hypercorrection effect persists over a week, but high confidence errors return. *Psychon. Bull. Rev.* 18:1238–44

Butler AC, Karpicke JD, Roediger HL. 2008. Correcting a metacognitive error: feedback increases retention of low-confidence correct responses. *J. Exp. Psychol.: Learn. Mem. Cogn.* 34:918–28

Butler AC, Roediger HL. 2008. Feedback enhances the positive effects and reduces the negative effects of multiple-choice testing. *Mem. Cogn.* 36:604–16

Butterfield B, Mangels JA. 2003. Neural correlates of error detection and correction in a semantic retrieval task. *Cogn. Brain Res.* 17:793–817

Butterfield B, Metcalfe J. 2001. Errors committed with high confidence are hypercorrected. *J. Exp. Psychol.: Learn. Mem. Cogn.* 27:1491–94

Butterfield B, Metcalfe J. 2006. The correction of errors committed with high confidence. *Metacogn. Learn.* 1:69–84

Carpenter SK. 2011. Semantic information activated during retrieval contributes to later retention: support for the mediator effectiveness hypothesis of the testing effect. *J. Exp. Psychol.: Learn. Mem. Cogn.* 37:1547–52

Clare L, Jones RSP. 2008. Errorless learning in the rehabilitation of memory impairment: a critical review. *Neuropsychol. Rev.* 18:1–23

Cohen GL, Garcia J, Purdie-Vaughns V, Apfel N, Brzustoski P. 2009. Recursive processes in self-affirmation: intervening to close the minority achievement gap. *Science* 324:400–3

Crowe E, Higgins ET. 1997. Regulatory focus and strategic inclinations: promotion and prevention in decision-making. *Org. Behav. Hum. Decis. Proc.* 69:117–32

Cyr A-A, Anderson ND. 2013. Updating misconceptions: effects of age and confidence. *Psychon. Bull. Rev.* 20:574–80

Delbanco T, Bell SK. 2007. Guilty, afraid, and alone—struggling with medical error. *N. Engl. J. Med.* 357:1682–83

Druckman D, Bjork RA. 1994. *Learning, Remembering, Believing: Enhancing Human Performance*. Washington, DC: Natl. Acad. Press

Dudai Y. 2012. The restless engram: consolidations never end. *Annu. Rev. Neurosci.* 35:227–47

Dunlosky J, Metcalfe J. 2009. *Metacognition*. Thousand Oaks, CA: Sage

Dunn KE, Mulvenon SW. 2009. A critical review of research on formative assessment: the limited scientific evidence of the impact of formative assessment in education. *Pract. Assess. Res. Eval.* 14:1–11

Dweck CS. 2006. *Mindset*. New York: Random House

Dweck CS, Leggett EL. 1988. A social-cognitive approach to motivation and personality *Psychol. Rev.* 95:256–73

Ebbesen EB, Rienick CB. 1998. Retention interval and eyewitness memory for events and personally identifying attributes. *J. Appl. Psychol.* 83:745–62

Eich TS, Stern Y, Metcalfe J. 2013. The hypercorrection effect in younger and older adults. *Aging Neuropsychol. Cogn.* 20:511–21

Fazio LK, Marsh EJ. 2009. Surprising feedback improves later memory. *Psychon. Bull. Rev.* 16:88–92

Fazio LK, Marsh EJ. 2010. Correcting false memories. *Psychol. Sci.* 21:801–3

Finn B. 2008. Framing effects on metacognitive monitoring and control. *Mem. Cogn.* 36:813–21

Finn B, Metcalfe J. 2010. Scaffolding feedback to maximize long-term error correction. *Mem. Cogn.* 38:951–61

Friedman D, Cycowicz Y, Gaeta H. 2001. The novelty P3: an event-related brain potential (ERP) sign of the brain's evaluation of novelty. *Neurosci. Biobehav. Rev.* 25:355–73

Friston K. 2005. A theory of cortical responses. *Philos. Trans. R. Soc. B* 360:815–83

Gehring WJ, Coles MGH, Meyer DE, Donchin E. 1990. The error-related negativity: an event-related brain potential accompanying errors. *Psychophysiology* 27:S34

Glisky EL, Schacter DL, Tulving E. 1986. Learning and retention of computer related vocabulary in memory-impaired patients: method of vanishing cues. *J. Clin. Exp. Neuropsychol.* 8:292–312

Grimaldi PJ, Karpicke JD. 2012. When and why do retrieval attempts enhance subsequent encoding? *Mem. Cogn.* 40:505–13

Hamann SB, Squire LR. 1995. On the acquisition of new declarative knowledge in amnesia. *Behav. Neurosci.* 109:1027–44

Hancock TE, Stock WA, Kulhavy RW. 1992. Predicting feedback effects from response-certitude estimates. *Bull. Psychon. Soc.* 30:173–76

Hayman CA, MacDonald CA, Tulving E. 1993. The role of repetition and associative interference in new semantic learning in amnesia: a case experiment. *J. Cogn. Neurosci.* 5:375–89

Heimbeck D, Frese M, Sonnentag S, Keith N. 2003. Integrating errors into the training process: the function of error management instructions and the role of goal orientation. *Personal. Psychol.* 56:333–61

Higgins ET. 1999. Promotion and prevention as a motivational duality: implications for evaluative processes. In *Dual-Process Theories in Social Psychology*, ed. S Chaiken, Y Trope, pp. 503–25. New York: Guilford

Huelser BJ, Metcalfe J. 2012. Masking related errors facilitates learning, but learners do not know it. *Mem. Cogn.* 40:514–27

Iwaki N, Matsushima H, Kodaira K. 2013. Hypercorrection of high confidence errors in lexical representations. *Percept. Motor Skills* 117:219–35

Izawa C. 1967. Function of test trials in paired-associate learning. *J. Exp. Psychol.* 76:194–209

Izawa C. 1970. Optimal potentiating effects and forgetting-prevention effects of tests in paired-associate learning. *J. Exp. Psychol.* 83:340–44

Jacoby LL, Wahlheim CN. 2013. On the importance of looking back: the role of recursive remindings in recency judgments and cued recall. *Mem. Cogn.* 41:625–37

Kane JH, Anderson RC. 1978. Depth of processing and interference effects in the learning and remembering of sentences. *J. Educ. Psychol.* 70:626–35

Kang SHK, Pashler H, Cepeda NJ, Rohrer D, Carpenter SK, Mozer MC. 2011. Does incorrect guessing impair fact learning? *J. Educ. Psychol.* 131:48–59

Keith N, Frese M. 2008. Effectiveness of error management training: a meta-analysis. *J. Appl. Psychol.* 93:59–69

Knight JB, Ball BH, Brewer GA, DeWitt MR, Marsh RL. 2012. Testing unsuccessfully: a specification of the underlying mechanisms supporting its influence on retention. *J. Mem. Lang.* 66:731–46

Koriat A. 2008. Easy comes, easy goes? The link between learning and remembering and its exploitation in metacognition. *Mem. Cogn.* 36:416–28

Koriat A. 2012. The self-consistency model of subjective confidence. *Psychol. Rev.* 119:80–113

Koriat A, Lichtenstein S, Fischhoff B. 1980. Reasons for confidence. *J. Exp. Psychol.: Hum. Learn. Mem.* 6:107–18

Kornell N, Hays MJ, Bjork RA. 2009. Unsuccessful retrieval attempts enhance subsequent learning. *J. Exp. Psychol.: Learn. Mem. Cogn.* 35:989–98

Kornell N, Klein PJ, Rawson KA. 2015. Retrieval attempts enhance learning, but retrieval success (versus failure) does not matter. *J. Exp. Psychol.: Learn. Mem. Cogn.* 41:283–94

Kornell N, Metcalfe J. 2006. Blockers do not block recall in tip-of-the-tongue states. *Metacogn. Learn.* 1:248–61

Kornell N, Metcalfe J. 2013. The effects of memory retrieval, errors, and feedback on learning. In *Applying Science of Learning in Education: Infusing Psychological Science into the Curriculum*, ed. VA Benassi, CE Overson, CM Hakala. Washington, DC: Am. Psychol. Assoc. Soc. Teach. Psychol. **http://teachpsych.org/ebooks/asle2014/index.php**

Kulhavy RW, Yekovich FR, Dyer JW. 1976. Feedback and response confidence. *J. Educ. Psychol.* 68:522–28

Kulik JA, Kulik C-LC. 1988. Timing of feedback and verbal learning. *Rev. Educ. Res.* 58:79–97

Ladouceur CD, Dahl RE, Birmaher B, Axelson DA, Ryan ND. 2006. Increased error-related negativity (ERN) in childhood anxiety disorder. *J. Child Psychol. Psychiatry* 47:1073–82

Landauer TK, Dumais ST. 1997. A solution to Plato's problem: the latent semantic analysis theory of acquisition, induction, and representation of knowledge. *Psychol. Rev.* 104:211–40

Lee JLC. 2008. Memory reconsolidation mediates the strengthening of memories by additional learning. *Nat. Neurosci.* 11:1264–66

Lhyle KG, Kulhavy RW. 1987. Feedback processing and error correction. *J. Educ. Psychol.* 79:320–22

Luck SJ, Kappenman ES. 2011. *The Oxford Handbook of Event-Related Potential Components*. New York: Oxford Univ. Press

Mamede S, Schmidt HG. 2004. The structure of reflective practice in medicine. *Med. Educ.* 38:1302–8

McDaniel MA, Roediger HL, McDermott KB. 2007. Generalizing test-enhanced learning from the laboratory to the classroom. *Psychon. Bull. Rev.* 14:200–6

Metcalfe J. 1998. Cognitive optimism: self-deception of memory-based processing heuristics. *Pers. Soc. Psychol. Rev.* 2:100–10

Metcalfe J, Butterfield B, Habeck C, Stern Y. 2012. Neural correlates of people's hypercorrection of their false beliefs. *J. Cogn. Neurosci.* 24:1571–83. **http://www.mitpressjournals.org/doi/abs/10.1162/jocn_a_00228**

Metcalfe J, Casal-Roscum L, Radin A, Friedman D. 2015. On teaching old dogs new tricks. *Psychol. Sci.* 12:1833–42

Metcalfe J, Finn B. 2008. Evidence that judgments of learning are causally related to study choice. *Psychon. Bull. Rev.* 15:174–79

Metcalfe J, Finn B. 2011. People's correction of high confidence errors: Did they know it all along? *J. Exp. Psychol.: Learn. Mem. Cogn.* 37:437–48

Metcalfe J, Finn B. 2012. Hypercorrection of high confidence in children. *Learn. Instr.* 22:253–61

Metcalfe J, Kornell N. 2007. Principles of cognitive science in education: the effects of generation, errors and feedback. *Psychon. Bull. Rev.* 14:225–29

Metcalfe J, Kornell N, Finn B. 2009. Delayed versus immediate feedback in children's and adults' vocabulary learning. *Mem. Cogn.* 37:1077–87

Metcalfe J, Kornell N, Son LK. 2007. A cognitive-science based program to enhance study efficacy in a high- and low-risk setting. *Eur. J. Cogn. Psychol.* 19:743–68

Metcalfe J, Miele DB. 2014. Hypercorrection of high confidence errors: Prior testing both enhances delayed performance and blocks the return of the errors. *J. Appl. Res. Mem. Cogn.* 3:189–97

Mitchell DJ, Russo JE, Pennington, N. 1989. Back to the future: temporal perspective in the explanation of events. *J. Behav. Decis. Mak.* 2:25–39

Moreno R. 2004. Decreasing cognitive load for novice students: effects of explanatory versus corrective feedback on discovery-based multimedia. *Instr. Sci.: Int. J. Learn. Cogn.* 32:99–113

Morrison JE, Meliza LL. 1999. *Foundations of the After Action Review Process*. US Army Res. Inst. Behav. Soc. Sci., Spec. Rep. 42. Alexandria, VA: Inst. Def. Anal.

Nader K, Schafe G, LeDoux JE. 2000. Fear memories require protein synthesis in the amygdala for reconsolidation after retrieval. *Nature* 406:722–26

Paller KA, Kutas M, Mayes AR. 1985. An investigation of neural substrates of memory encoding in man. *Psychophysiology* 22:607

Pashler H, Cepeda NJ, Wixted JT, Rohrer D. 2005. When does feedback facilitate learning of words? *J. Exp. Psychol.: Learn. Mem. Cogn.* 31:3–8

Proudfit GH, Inzlicht M, Mennin DS. 2013. Anxiety and error monitoring: the importance of motivation and emotion. *Front. Hum. Neurosci.* 7:636

Pyc MA, Rawson KA. 2010. Why testing improves memory: mediator effectiveness hypothesis. *Science* 330:335

Richland LE, Kao LS, Kornell N. 2009. The pretesting effect: Do unsuccessful retrieval attempts enhance learning? *J. Exp. Psychol. Appl.* 15:243–57

Roediger HL, Karpicke JD. 2006a. Test-enhanced learning: Taking memory tests improves long-term retention. *Psychol. Sci.* 17:249–55

Roediger HL, Karpicke JD. 2006b. The power of testing memory: basic research and implications for educational practice. *Perspect. Psychol. Sci.* 1:181–210

Rumelhart DE, McClelland JL. 1986. *Parallel Distributed Processing*, Vol. 1: *Explorations in the Microstructure of Cognition*. Cambridge, MA: MIT Press

Schiff GD, Hasan O, Kim S, Abrams R, Cosby K, et al. 2009. Diagnostic error in medicine: analysis of 583 physician-reported errors. *Arch. Intern. Med.* 169:1881–87

Schiller D, Monfils M-H, Raio CM, Johnson DC, LeDoux JE, Phelps EA. 2010. Preventing the return of fear in humans using reconsolidation update mechanisms. *Nature* 463:49–53

Scholar AA, Stroessner SJ, Higgins ET. 2008. Responding to negativity: how a risky tactic can serve a vigilant strategy. *J. Exp. Soc. Psychol.* 44:767–74

Siegler RS. 1995. How does change occur: a microgenetic study of number conservation. *Cogn. Psychol.* 28:225–73

Siegler RS. 2002. Microgenetic studies of self-explanation. In *Microdevelopment: A Process-Oriented Perspective for Studying Development and Learning*, ed. N Garnott, J Parziale, pp. 31–58. Cambridge, UK: Cambridge Univ. Press

Sitzman DM, Rhodes MG. 2010. *Does the hypercorrection effect occur when feedback is delayed?* Poster presented at 2010 Psychon. Soc. Annu. Meet., St. Louis, MO

Sitzman DM, Rhodes MG, Tauber SK, Liceralde VR. 2015. The role of prior knowledge in error correction for younger and older adults. *Aging Neuropsychol. Cogn.* 22:502–16

Skinner BF. 1953. *Science and Human Behavior*. New York: MacMillan

Slamecka NJ, Fevreiski J. 1983. The generation effect when generation fails. *J. Verb. Learn. Verb. Behav.* 22:153–63

Slamecka NJ, Graf P. 1978. The generation effect: delineation of a phenomenon. *J. Exp. Psychol.: Hum. Learn. Mem.* 4:592–604

Smith SM, Blankenship SE. 1991. Incubation and the persistence of fixation in problem solving. *Am. J. Psychol.* 104:61–87

Stevenson H, Stigler JW. 1994. *The Learning Gap: Why Our Schools Are Failing and What We Can Learn from Japanese and Chinese Education*. New York: Simon & Schuster

Stigler JW, Hiebert J. 2009. Closing the teaching gap. *Kappan* 91:32–37

Terrace HS. 1963. Discrimination learning with and without errors. *J. Exp. Anal. Behav.* 6:1–27

Terrace HS. 1966. Stimulus control. In *Operant Behavior: Areas of Research and Application*, ed. WK Honig, pp. 271–334. New York: Appleton-Century-Crofts

Terrace HS. 1968. Discrimination learning the peak shift and behavioral contrast. *J. Exp. Anal. Behav.* 11:727–41

Terrace HS. 2010. Defining the stimulus—a memoir. *Behav. Process.* 83:139–53

USAID (US Agency Int. Dev.). 2006. *After-action review. Technical guidance.* PN-ADF-360. Washington, DC: USAID

van Loon MH, Dunlosky J, van Gog T, van Merriënboer JJG, de Bruin ABH. 2015. Refutations in science texts lead to hypercorrections of misconceptions held with high confidence. *Contemp. Educ. Psychol.* 42:39–48

Wahlheim CN, Jacoby LL. 2013. Remembering change: the critical role of recursive remindings in proactive memory. *Mem. Cogn.* 41:1–15

Waterman AD, Garbutt J, Hazel E, Dunagan WC, Levinson W, et al. 2007. The emotional impact of medical errors on practicing physicians in the United States and Canada. *Jt. Comm. J. Qual. Patient Saf.* 33:467–76

Wiswede D, Münte TF, Goschke T, Rüsseler J. 2009. Modulation of the error-related negativity by induction of short-term negative affect. *Neuropsychology* 47:83–90

Wu AW. 2000. Medical error: the second victim. *BMJ* 320:726–27

Zhao B. 2011. Learning from errors: the role of context, emotion, and personality. *J. Org. Behav.* 32:435–63

Mindfulness Interventions

J. David Creswell

Department of Psychology, Carnegie Mellon University, Pittsburgh, Pennsylvania 15213;
email: creswell@cmu.edu

Annu. Rev. Psychol. 2017. 68:491–516

First published online as a Review in Advance on
September 28, 2016

The *Annual Review of Psychology* is online at
psych.annualreviews.org

This article's doi:
10.1146/annurev-psych-042716-051139

Keywords

mindfulness, meditation, review, randomized controlled trial, health

Abstract

Mindfulness interventions aim to foster greater attention to and awareness of present moment experience. There has been a dramatic increase in randomized controlled trials (RCTs) of mindfulness interventions over the past two decades. This article evaluates the growing evidence of mindfulness intervention RCTs by reviewing and discussing (*a*) the effects of mindfulness interventions on health, cognitive, affective, and interpersonal outcomes; (*b*) evidence-based applications of mindfulness interventions to new settings and populations (e.g., the workplace, military, schools); (*c*) psychological and neurobiological mechanisms of mindfulness interventions; (*d*) mindfulness intervention dosing considerations; and (*e*) potential risks of mindfulness interventions. Methodologically rigorous RCTs have demonstrated that mindfulness interventions improve outcomes in multiple domains (e.g., chronic pain, depression relapse, addiction). Discussion focuses on opportunities and challenges for mindfulness intervention research and on community applications.

Contents

INTRODUCTION

> There are few people I know on the planet who couldn't benefit more from a greater dose of awareness.
>
> —Jon Kabat-Zinn (on Bill Moyers, *Healing and the Mind*)

Readers not familiar with mindfulness meditation practices or mindfulness interventions might try a quick exercise: close your eyes for about a minute and maintain an open awareness of the sensations of breathing at your nostrils. There is no need to do anything special, just continuously observe the sensations of breathing in and breathing out at the nostrils with curiosity and interest. Even doing a one-minute mindfulness exercise like this can reveal that our minds are quick to race off to other places. For example, you might have thought about planning dinner tonight, drifted off, or noticed a strong desire to consciously control how you were breathing. Moreover, there is often a rich kaleidoscope of experiences and emotional reactions, including relaxation or agitation, occurring even in a short exercise such as this. Formal mindfulness training exercises, such as learning how to mindfully attend to breathing, form the backbone of many mindfulness interventions. Collectively, mindfulness interventions aim to foster greater awareness of present moment experience, which, as Jon Kabat-Zinn suggests in the quote in the epigraph of this review, may have manifold benefits ranging from enhancing the quality and vividness of our daily life experience to helping us better manage life's slings and arrows.

Interest in mindfulness interventions has increased exponentially over the past three decades. Much of this interest has been fueled by scientific reports and corresponding media coverage describing the potential benefits of mindfulness interventions for a broad array of outcomes, ranging from mental and physical health outcomes (Ludwig & Kabat-Zinn 2008) to cognitive, affective, and interpersonal outcomes (Brown et al. 2015). Mindfulness interventions are also increasingly being integrated into institutional settings—in clinical treatment (Dimidjian & Segal

Mindfulness:
a process of openly attending, with awareness, to one's experience in the present moment

2015), the workplace (Good et al. 2016), schools (Sibinga et al. 2016), the military (Johnson et al. 2014), and prisons (Samuelson et al. 2007), to name only a few. This proliferation of interest in mindfulness interventions has been met by the scientific community with a wide range of reactions, from skepticism to fanaticism. This review evaluates what we have learned from randomized controlled trials (RCTs) of mindfulness interventions in terms of their effects, applications to new populations, putative mechanisms, dosing questions, and potential risks.

RCT: randomized controlled trial

What Is Mindfulness?

There has been a rich scholarly dialogue about how to define mindfulness as a construct. One working definition of mindfulness is a process of openly attending, with awareness, to one's present moment experience. This process of awareness of present moment experience contrasts with much of our daily life experience, in which we often find ourselves unintentionally letting our minds wander (Killingsworth & Gilbert 2010), running on automatic pilot (Bargh & Chartrand 1999), or suppressing unwanted experiences (Kang et al. 2013). Moreover, the mindless states that predominate in our daily life experience have been demonstrated to be undesirable. For example, one study showed that our minds wander approximately 47% of the time and that mind wandering predicts subsequent unhappiness (Killingsworth & Gilbert 2010). In contrast, the capacity to be mindful is associated with higher well-being in daily life (Brown & Ryan 2003).

Mindfulness has been operationalized in many different ways in the scientific literature (for a review, see Quaglia et al. 2015). Two features appear in most definitions of mindfulness. First, mindfulness grounds attention and awareness in one's present moment experience. The present moment experience that one attends to can take many forms, including one's body sensations, emotional reactions, mental images, mental talk, and perceptual experiences (e.g., sounds). Scholars have described this monitoring feature of mindfulness as "watchfulness" or a "lucid awareness of each experience that presents itself" (Bodhi 2011, Brown et al. 2007, Quaglia et al. 2015). Second, many contemporary conceptualizations of mindfulness posit that adopting an attitude of openness or acceptance toward one's experience is critical. This open and accepting attitude consists of attending to experience with a curious, detached, and nonreactive orientation. Importantly, this attitude of acceptance toward experience is not one of passive resignation to one's current circumstances but rather one of inviting in experiences, even if they are difficult.

Although psychological scientists have been interested in mindfulness for the past three decades, this is a thin slice of scholarly work relative to the 2,500-year tradition of scholarship about (and practice of) mindfulness interventions in many Buddhist traditions (Anālayo 2003). Buddhist scholarship has thus informed a great deal of the psychological research on mindfulness and mindfulness interventions, but mindfulness is by no means exclusive to Buddhism or Buddhist contemplative practices. First, most of the mindfulness interventions now tested in the scientific literature are secular in nature. Second, being mindfully aware is not synonymous with being a Buddhist; it is instead a basic feature of being human.[1] As Bhante Gunaratana (2011, p. 146) states in his classic mindfulness training text, "Mindfulness is not limited by any condition. It exists to some extent in every moment, in every circumstance that arises." Similarly, Jon Kabat-Zinn (2003,

---

[1] It is possible that many cultural practices in human history have been developed to help foster mindful awareness (e.g., centering prayer, journaling, surfing, psychotherapy). Indeed, some work suggests that training in tango dancing increases self-reported mindfulness (Pinniger et al. 2012). Many open questions remain about the role of various cultural practices in fostering mindfulness or the ways in which these factors might interact with formal mindfulness training interventions. In one intriguing case in point, cultural anthropologists have described a more mindful culture: The Amazonian Piraha tribe's cultural practices and language are geared toward helping individuals to be more grounded in present moment awareness, and members report high degrees of daily well-being (Everett 2005).

pp. 145–46) has written, "We are all mindful to one degree or another, moment by moment." Thus, we all have the capacity to openly pay attention to our moment-to-moment experience, and this capacity is something that can be developed and deepened by mindfulness interventions.

Although everyone is capable of mindfulness, formal mindfulness intervention exercises can feel quite effortful and challenging at first. This is understandable given that our default methods of attending to experience are commonly letting our minds wander, engaging in self-criticism, ruminating about the past, or worrying about the future. Tellingly, one study showed that participants preferred receiving mild electric shocks over being left alone with their thoughts (Wilson et al. 2014). Formal mindfulness intervention exercises require one to make deliberate efforts to turn toward and sustain attention on moment-to-moment experience. To borrow an expression from cognitive science, this effort of attending to present moment experience may be a desirable difficulty (Bjork & Bjork 2011) such that the effort put forth during mindfulness training exercises can foster insight, learning, and self-regulation skills.

Types of Mindfulness Interventions

Much of the early work on mindfulness interventions used nonrandomized pretest posttest designs; however, beginning in the early 2000s, there was a dramatic increase in RCTs that compare mindfulness interventions to treatment as usual (TAU), wait-list control, or active comparison interventions (see **Figure 1**). This section describes some of the most common types of mindfulness and control interventions used in the scientific literature.

Mindfulness-based stress reduction and related group-based mindfulness interventions. The 8-week mindfulness-based stress reduction (MBSR) program, developed by Jon Kabat-Zinn at the University of Massachusetts Medical School, is perhaps the most well-known mindfulness

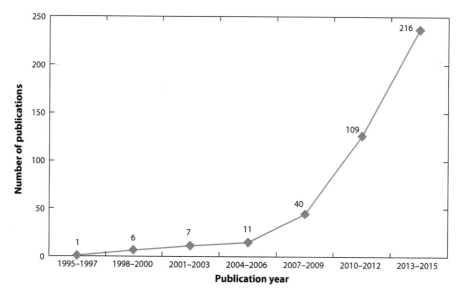

Figure 1

A noncumulative plot of the number of mindfulness randomized controlled trials (RCTs) published during 3-year periods between 1995 and 2015. The data were gathered from a PubMed abstract/title search (in February 2016) of human clinical trial studies using the terms mindfulness and randomized controlled trial.

TAU: treatment as usual

Wait-list control: refers to participants who are randomized to serve as a no-treatment comparison group and placed on a wait list to receive a mindfulness intervention

Mindfulness-based stress reduction (MBSR): an 8-week mindfulness meditation training program that includes weekly classes, daily audio-guided home practice, and a day-long retreat

intervention in the scientific literature (Kabat-Zinn 1982). MBSR consists of weekly 2–2.5-h group-based classes with a trained teacher, daily audio-guided home practice (approximately 45 min/day), and a day-long mindfulness retreat (occurring during week 6 of the 8-week program) (Kabat-Zinn 1990). Much of the MBSR program focuses on learning how to mindfully attend to body sensations through the use of body scans, gentle stretching, and yoga mindfulness exercises, along with discussions and practices geared toward applying mindful awareness to daily life experiences, including dealing with stress. The MBSR program was initially used to treat chronic pain patients (Kabat-Zinn 1982) but has been applied to many other populations of adult patients and community members (Ludwig & Kabat-Zinn 2008).

Over the past three decades, MBSR has stimulated the development of many mindfulness interventions that share the same basic program structure but are modified to treat specific populations or outcomes. These interventions have focused on treating depression [mindfulness-based cognitive therapy (MBCT); e.g., Teasdale et al. 2000] and drug addiction [mindfulness-based relapse prevention (MBRP); e.g., Bowen et al. 2014], fostering healthy eating (Mason et al. 2015), and improving relationship functioning [mindfulness-based relationship enhancement (MBRE); Carson et al. 2004], among other applications (for a review, see Dimidjian & Segal 2015).

Mindfulness intervention retreats and brief interventions. The scientific community has often assumed MBSR and other 8–12-week mindfulness-based programs are the exclusive way to deliver mindfulness training, but there are other evidence-based forms of mindfulness intervention available to researchers and practitioners. Mindfulness meditation residential retreat programs ranging from 3 days to 3 months are a powerful way to deliver intensive and well-controlled doses of mindfulness intervention (Creswell et al. 2016, Rosenberg et al. 2015). Brief mindfulness meditation interventions have also been developed, ranging from 2–3-week programs (Lim et al. 2015, Mrazek et al. 2013) to lab-based 3–4-day mindfulness interventions (Creswell et al. 2014, Zeidan et al. 2011). Finally, brief experimental mindful attention inductions have been developed and tested in the literature (e.g., Broderick 2005, Papies et al. 2015, Schofield et al. 2015, Westbrook et al. 2013). These induction approaches offer a great deal of experimental control but have relatively small and transient effects.

Internet and smartphone application mindfulness interventions. There has been an explosion of Internet- and smartphone-based mindfulness programs hitting the market over the past five years. One example of this trend, the Headspace mindfulness smartphone app, has over two million active users worldwide. Given that so many people are using these programs (which lack, in most cases, access to a well-trained mindfulness teacher), there are important untested questions about the safety and efficacy of these programs. However, these mindfulness intervention programs have a tremendous advantage in that they are inexpensive and portable and can be more easily implemented in harder-to-reach populations that can access the Internet. Although there has been no research on the efficacy of these programs compared to in-person group-based approaches (e.g., MBSR), initial studies suggest that these Internet and smartphone mindfulness interventions may have benefits (e.g., Boettcher et al. 2014, Lim et al. 2015).

Mindfulness-related interventions. The objective of this article is to review mindfulness-based interventions in which the primary goal is to foster mindfulness (e.g., MBSR, MBCT, brief mindfulness meditation training interventions). However, there are also many mindfulness-related interventions which incorporate mindfulness training exercises as one component of a broader treatment program (e.g., acceptance and commitment therapy, dialectical behavior therapy,

Mindfulness-based cognitive therapy (MBCT): an 8-week mindfulness-based program that combines elements of MBSR and CBT

MBRP: mindfulness-based relapse prevention

cognitive behavioral stress management, integrative body–mind training). Initial efficacy evidence suggests that incorporating mindfulness training exercises in these interventions can be beneficial to patients. Space considerations preclude a careful review of these mindfulness-related interventions in this article, but published reviews are available for interested readers (e.g., Hayes et al. 2011).

Control interventions. It is important to consider the comparison groups used in RCT studies of mindfulness interventions (Davidson & Kaszniak 2015), and most published mindfulness intervention RCTs use TAU or wait-list controlled comparison groups. These studies provide a valuable initial evaluation of whether mindfulness interventions have an impact on outcomes above and beyond standard care or no treatment. Researchers have made impressive efforts to develop active treatment comparison programs that control for non-mindfulness-specific treatment factors (e.g., group support, home practice exercises, relaxation, placebo expectancies). These programs provide opportunities to evaluate whether mindfulness interventions have unique treatment effects above and beyond non-mindfulness-specific factors and whether mindfulness interventions can outperform gold-standard active pharmacological or behavioral treatments.

There are many different active treatment programs used as comparisons in the RCT literature on mindfulness interventions. The health enhancement program (HEP) is an 8-week health education and relaxation program that was developed to match MBSR on program components, including group support and education, home practice, and a day-long retreat (MacCoon et al. 2012). Other active group-based interventions ranging from relaxation interventions (Creswell et al. 2016) to targeted health education programs (Morone et al. 2016) have been effectively implemented. The literature on brief mindfulness interventions (consisting of interventions that last 2 weeks or fewer) also offers a number of well-matched active control interventions ranging from attention control training programs (e.g., listening to the same guided mindfulness exercise with the instruction to count the number of verbs) (Koole et al. 2009, Schofield et al. 2015) to placebo conditioning (Zeidan et al. 2015) and health education interventions (Mrazek et al. 2013). One intriguing new approach to brief mindfulness interventions offers sham mindfulness meditation training in which participants are periodically instructed "to take a deep breath as we sit here in mindfulness meditation" without any explicit instructions on how to foster mindful awareness (Zeidan et al. 2015, p. 15,309). This sham mindfulness procedure has been effective in controlling for positive treatment expectancies in studies but does not provide the same pain-relief benefits as actual mindfulness meditation training (Zeidan et al. 2010b, 2015).

EFFECTS OF MINDFULNESS INTERVENTIONS

Mindfulness interventions have been shown to impact a broad range of outcomes in RCTs. Despite this proliferation of work, most mindfulness intervention RCTs have used small samples and lack high-quality pretreatment, posttreatment, and follow-up measures. These methodological limitations make it difficult to draw strong inferences about the validity and reliability of mindfulness intervention effects on many outcomes. However, some areas show quite promising mindfulness intervention RCT effects; these effects are selectively reviewed in the following sections with a focus on recent developments in this active area of scientific inquiry. This review focuses on mindfulness-based intervention RCTs and not on studies of other forms of meditation interventions (e.g., transcendental meditation), cross-sectional studies of expert mindfulness meditators, or correlational studies relating self-report measures of mindfulness to outcomes (for a more general review, see Brown et al. 2007).

Physical Health

The earliest work with the MBSR program was focused on treating chronic pain patients who were not responding well to traditional medical treatments (Kabat-Zinn 1982), demonstrating the long-standing scientific interest in applying mindfulness interventions to the treatment of physical health. Much of the interest in this physical health domain has been guided by views that mindfulness interventions can foster greater body (interoceptive) awareness, promote relaxation, and improve stress management and coping skills, all of which can promote physical health and reduce disease risks. We have formalized a mindfulness stress-buffering account, which posits that stress reduction and resilience pathways explain mindfulness intervention effects on a broad range of physical health outcomes (Creswell & Lindsay 2014). This account is based on the view that learning how to monitor experience with acceptance is an emotion regulation skill learned in mindfulness interventions, which fosters stress resilience and coping under stress. Furthermore, these stress-buffering effects in turn reduce the negative impacts stress has on increasing risk for stress-related disease outcomes. Consistent with this account, a growing number of rigorous RCT studies show that mindfulness interventions impact stress-related physical health outcomes ranging from chronic pain to immune system functioning to disease-specific physical health outcomes.

CBT: cognitive behavioral therapy

Chronic pain. Stress is a powerful trigger for pain symptomatology among chronic pain patients (Schwartz et al. 1994), and early nonrandomized studies showed that MBSR was effective in reducing pain symptoms and dependence on pain-relief medication among chronic pain patients pre-post intervention (Kabat-Zinn 1982, Ludwig & Kabat-Zinn 2008). Several independent well-controlled studies have conceptually replicated and extended this work. Morone and colleagues (2016) showed that MBSR, relative to an active healthy aging program, was effective in reducing self-reported pain disability posttreatment in a large RCT with adults suffering from chronic low-back pain ($N = 282$), although these pain-related benefits were not sustained at the 6-month follow-up assessment. E.L. Garland and colleagues (2014) showed that, relative to an active support group therapy program, an 8-week mindfulness-oriented recovery enhancement (MORE) program reduced pain severity and pain interference among chronic pain opioid-abusing patients posttreatment and at a 3-month follow-up. In a daily diary study of adults with rheumatoid arthritis ($N = 143$), Davis and colleagues (2015) showed that an 8-week mindfulness training program was superior to a cognitive behavioral therapy (CBT) program for pain and an arthritis education program in reducing posttreatment daily-level stress, pain-related catastrophizing, disability, and fatigue. In one of the largest mindfulness intervention RCTs to date ($N = 342$), MBSR reduced functional limitations due to pain among chronic back pain participants at both 4-month and 10-month follow-ups compared to TAU (Cherkin et al. 2016). Although this large RCT study showed that MBSR provided a clinically meaningful improvement in pain management in a greater percentage of participants at follow-up (61%) relative to TAU (44%), there was no evidence in this study that MBSR was superior to a matched CBT program (58%).[2]

Immunity. The immune system plays a central role in protecting the body from a variety of pathogens and infectious agents. Chronic stress impairs several aspects of the immune system's

---

[2]Given the promising evidence for pain management effects of mindfulness intervention, one interesting question is whether these mindfulness pain reduction effects are driven by alterations in pain sensation processing or by fostering the regulation of one's emotional reactivity to pain (i.e., reducing pain unpleasantness). Some initial evidence suggests that mindfulness interventions can modulate both neural sensory and emotional reactivity pain pathways (Zeidan et al. 2011).

functional response, including its capacities to mount antibody responses and to produce lymphocyte proliferative and natural killer cell responses (for a review, see Segerstrom & Miller 2004). Furthermore, stress has been linked to increases in C-reactive protein and interleukin 6, which are circulating markers of inflammation linked with morbidity and accelerated mortality. Mindfulness interventions may potentially modulate these stress-related immune outcomes, and initial RCTs demonstrate promising effects on some immune markers (for a review, see Black & Slavich 2016). For example, several initial well-controlled studies show that mindfulness interventions may reduce markers of proinflammation, including circulating blood markers of C-reactive protein (Malarkey et al. 2013), interleukin 6 (Creswell et al. 2016), and the stress-induced inflammatory skin flare response (Rosenkranz et al. 2013) (although MBSR failed to affect stimulated interleukin 6 responses in rheumatoid arthritis patients; see Zautra et al. 2008). In contrast to inflammatory effects, the evidence of mindfulness interventions' effects on antibody levels or the antibody response to vaccination is mixed (Hayney et al. 2014, Moynihan et al. 2013).

Stress also plays an important role in the acceleration of HIV infection and the development of AIDS, in part by attacking $CD4^+$ T lymphocytes. Three RCTs show that mindfulness interventions can buffer declines in or increase $CD4^+$ T lymphocyte counts in stressed HIV-positive adults at posttreatment and at follow-up time points up to 9 months later (Creswell et al. 2009, Gonzalez-Garcia et al. 2013, SeyedAlinaghi et al. 2012).

Clinical symptoms and disease-specific outcomes. Some of the most encouraging RCT research on the relationship between mindfulness intervention and physical health focuses on whether mindfulness interventions affect clinically relevant measures of health and disease. An initial large RCT ($N = 154$) showed that MBSR may reduce the number of self-reported illness days and the duration of illness over the course of a cold and flu season relative to a no-treatment group (Barrett et al. 2012). However, in this trial, MBSR showed no relative advantage in illness-related outcomes compared to a moderate aerobic exercise program, although there was some evidence that MBSR reduced the total number of acute respiratory infection–related work days missed (16 days) compared to the aerobic exercise (32 days) and no-treatment control (67 days) groups. Some initial large well-controlled RCT studies have also showed that mindfulness interventions (relative to controls) reduce physical symptoms and improve quality of life in fibromyalgia patients (Schmidt et al. 2011), in women with irritable-bowel syndrome (IBS) (Gaylord et al. 2011), and among distressed breast cancer survivors (Carlson et al. 2013). Finally, there is some initial evidence that brief audio-guided mindfulness training practices during light-booth phototherapy can accelerate skin clearing in psoriasis patients; one trial showed a fourfold-faster clearing rate in the mindfulness intervention group relative to TAU (Kabat-Zinn et al. 1998). Some researchers have questioned whether the group training context is necessary for mindfulness intervention benefits, and this psoriasis study joins others that have trained participants individually (with audio-guided mindfulness practices only) and showed benefits independent of a group context (see also Creswell et al. 2014, Zeidan et al. 2011).

Health behaviors. Stress is known to disrupt health behaviors such as sleep, exercise, smoking, and diet, and these stress-related disruptions in health behaviors negatively impact physical health and disease outcomes. Despite these established links, little rigorous empirical work has tested whether mindfulness interventions impact health behaviors. There is some initial RCT evidence that mindfulness interventions can reduce smoking among heavy smokers (Brewer et al. 2011), alter dietary behaviors such as eating sweets (Arch et al. 2016, Mason et al. 2015), and improve self-reported and polysomnographic markers of sleep (although the sleep outcomes evidence is mixed; see Black et al. 2015; Britton et al. 2010, 2012; S.N. Garland et al. 2014).

Interim summary of physical health effects. Several large RCTs provide compelling evidence that mindfulness interventions improve chronic pain management relative to TAU, with some initial evidence that mindfulness interventions may be superior to some active treatments (support groups, health education programs) but not to other treatments (CBT). There is also promising initial evidence that mindfulness interventions may reduce immune markers of proinflammation among stressed individuals and buffer declines in $CD4^+$ T lymphocytes in HIV-infected adults, although large well-controlled trials are needed to evaluate the links between mindfulness and immunity. Mindfulness interventions may reduce symptoms and improve quality of life across a broad range of stress-related conditions (e.g., fibromyalgia, IBS, breast cancer, psoriasis); however, relatively little is currently known about how mindfulness interventions affect health behaviors.

Mental Health

There is a great deal of interest among clinical psychologists in using mindfulness interventions to treat a broad range of mental health outcomes. Indeed, some clinical scientists have posited that mindfulness and acceptance interventions are a third-wave treatment approach, following behavioral and cognitive-behavioral treatment approaches (Hayes et al. 2004). This interest among clinicians has in part been built on views that mindfulness interventions can help individuals notice and regulate the maladaptive thoughts, emotional responses, and automatic behaviors that underlie mental health problems.

Depression relapse. Some of the strongest evidence to date in the mindfulness intervention literature shows that the MBCT program is effective in reducing depression relapse during follow-up periods in at-risk populations. Several RCTs demonstrate that 8-week MBCT is a cost-effective treatment that significantly reduces the risk of depression relapse compared to TAU among individuals who have had three or more previous major depressive episodes in their lifetimes (e.g., Ma & Teasdale 2004, Teasdale et al. 2000). This impressive body of work has made use of careful clinician condition-blinded assessment of depression during long-term follow-up periods ranging from 12 months to 2 years, with studies demonstrating that MBCT reduces depression relapse by approximately 50% relative to TAU during these periods. Furthermore, these MBCT benefits seem to be most pronounced among those at the greatest risk for relapse, such as individuals with four or more previous major depressive episodes (Ma & Teasdale 2004) or individuals who suffered from maltreatment during childhood (Ma & Teasdale 2004, Williams et al. 2014). Many at-risk individuals prefer not to use antidepressant medications (e.g., during pregnancy or to avoid side effect symptoms), and two RCTs indicate that MBCT (with a 4-week taper-off of antidepressant medications during the 8-week program) has depression relapse prevention benefits equivalent with maintenance antidepressant medication treatments during 18–24-month follow-up periods (Kuyken et al. 2015, Segal et al. 2010); however, a recent trial suggests that the combination of MBCT with maintenance antidepressant medication may be optimal (Huijbers et al. 2016).

Depression and anxiety symptoms. The previous section highlights the benefits of offering mindfulness interventions to individuals who are not currently depressed but are at risk for depression relapse; might mindfulness interventions also help individuals with mood disorders who are currently experiencing high levels of anxiety or depressive symptoms? Mindfulness interventions aim to foster an open and accepting awareness of one's thoughts and feelings, including an observant attitude toward the thought patterns and body experiences that occur when

PTSD: posttraumatic stress disorder

one feels acutely anxious or depressed. This process of turning attention and awareness toward these experiences has been posited to help reduce the experiential avoidance, self-judgment, and rumination that are often triggered by acute depression and anxiety (Roemer & Orsillo 2009). Some initial well-controlled studies indicate that MBCT may be effective in reducing depressive symptoms among acutely depressed individuals (e.g., Strauss et al. 2014). In one of the best-controlled trials to date, Eisendrath and colleagues (2016) tested a modified MBCT program for treatment-resistant depression and showed that MBCT reduced depressive symptoms posttreatment compared to a well-matched HEP comparison program in a sample of treatment-resistant depressed patients. These mindfulness intervention effects were specific to reducing depressive symptoms; there were no differences between the MBCT and HEP groups in the depression remission rates posttreatment.

Meta-analyses indicate that mindfulness interventions significantly reduce anxiety among anxiety-disordered populations pre-post intervention but are mixed about whether this effect is greater than that of control programs (Strauss et al. 2014, Vøllestad et al. 2012). Furthermore, there is little evidence that mindfulness interventions are better than CBT interventions for anxiety symptom reduction (Goldin et al. 2016), although some work suggests that MBSR may be more effective for participants with moderate-to-severe dysphoria whereas CBT may be more effective for participants with mild dysphoria in anxiety disorder groups (Arch & Ayers 2013). Trials conducted since these meta-analyses show that mindfulness training may be effective in reducing anxiety symptoms compared to some active treatments. For example, a recent Internet-based mindfulness intervention was effective in reducing anxiety posttreatment compared to a supervised online discussion group program (Boettcher et al. 2014). Hoge and colleagues (2013) also showed that MBSR reduced some measures of anxiety symptoms (including anxiety in response to a laboratory social stress challenge task) compared to an active stress-management education program group in a sample of participants with generalized anxiety disorder (Hoge et al. 2013). Mood disorders are prevalent among individuals with posttraumatic stress disorder (PTSD), and initial well-controlled evidence in Vietnam War veterans indicates that MBSR reduces self-reported and clinician-rated PTSD symptomatology 2 months posttreatment (Polusny et al. 2015).

Addiction and addictive disorders. All humans have experienced cravings at one time or another and have felt the strong pull to act on them with consummatory behaviors such as eating, having sex, or using addictive substances. These behaviors can sometimes spiral out of control into addictions (e.g., to alcohol, gambling, smoking) when engaging in them interferes with daily life functioning or causes harm to the self or others. Mindfulness interventions foster an ability to observe the rise and fall of cravings and the behaviors they encourage and offer the opportunity to meet these experiences with more skillful action. Thus, mindfulness interventions have tremendous potential to address craving, addiction, and addictive disorders (Bowen et al. 2015). Alan Marlatt and colleagues developed an 8-week mindfulness-based relapse prevention (MBRP) program, which integrates mindfulness meditation practices from MBSR with CBT techniques for drug relapse prevention, including practices focused on mindfully attending to cravings (e.g., urge surfing) (Bowen et al. 2009).

Several well-controlled studies suggest that mindfulness interventions impact craving, drug use, and drug relapse rates in at-risk individuals. Mindfully attending to drug cues reduces neural and self-reported craving among smokers (Westbrook et al. 2013), and some initial evidence indicates that mindfulness interventions reduce cravings more than CBT treatment (Garland et al. 2016). Moreover, mindfulness interventions can disrupt the increases in suffering and substance abuse caused by cravings (Witkiewitz & Bowen 2010). Initial RCTs show that mindfulness interventions, compared to TAU or other relapse-prevention programs, reduce substance abuse in at-risk populations. For example, MBRP has been shown to reduce drug use days and reduce the number of legal problems compared to a standard relapse prevention program at a 15-week follow-up among substance-abusing female criminal offenders (Witkiewitz et al. 2014). A 4-week mindfulness training program, compared to a standard 4-week smoking cessation treatment, reduced cigarette use among heavy smokers posttreatment and at 3-month follow-up (Brewer et al. 2011). Finally, in one of the largest trials to date ($N = 286$), Bowen and colleagues (2014) randomly assigned substance-abusing individuals at a treatment facility to either MBRP, a cognitive-behavioral relapse prevention program, or standard treatment (a 12-step program) and monitored their reported substance abuse during a 12-month follow-up period. Compared to the standard 12-step treatment group, both the MBRP and cognitive-behavioral relapse prevention groups demonstrated a 54% reduction in drug relapse and a 59% reduction in relapse to heavy drinking. Interestingly, the cognitive-behavioral relapse prevention program had early advantages in delaying the time to the first drug relapse relative to the MBRP program, but the MBRP program appeared to have long-term advantages at the 12-month follow-up time point in reducing the number of drug use days (Bowen et al. 2014).

Interim summary of mental health effects. Strong RCT evidence indicates that mindfulness interventions reduce depression relapse rates in at-risk individuals and improve the treatment of drug addiction. Specifically, multiple large RCTs indicate that MBCT reliably reduces the risk of depression relapse during follow-up periods among at-risk individuals and that MBRP (relative to standard relapse prevention programs) improves substance abuse outcomes. There are also several well-controlled studies showing that mindfulness interventions can reduce anxiety, depression, and PTSD symptomatology. In the mindfulness interventions literature, the research on mental health outcomes has made the most progress in comparing mindfulness interventions to other gold-standard clinical treatments, and there are some initial suggestions of contexts in which mindfulness interventions offer similar or additional long-term benefits compared to gold-standard treatments (e.g., antidepressant medication, relapse prevention programs, CBT).

Cognitive and Affective Outcomes

Formal mindfulness training practices focus on training multiple features of attention, such as noticing when the mind wanders, repeatedly reorienting attention back to a focus area (e.g., sensations of breathing), developing sustained attention, and learning how to foster an open accepting form of attention so as not to get caught up in thoughts, emotions, or body sensations. One would expect these attention skills to improve attention-related cognitive outcomes, and RCT studies in predominantly healthy young adult samples show that mindfulness interventions improve behavioral measures of sustained attention (Jensen et al. 2012, Jha et al. 2015, Mrazek et al. 2012, Semple 2010, Zeidan et al. 2010a), working memory performance (Jensen et al. 2012, Mrazek et al. 2013, Zeidan et al. 2010a), and problem-solving performance (Mrazek et al. 2013, Ostafin & Kassman 2012). It could be argued that mindfulness interventions might benefit all types of attention-related outcomes (e.g., sustained attention, task switching, working memory). However, in one of the most well-controlled trials to date, Jensen and colleagues (2012) showed that MBSR demonstrated superior benefits on sustained attention and working memory at posttreatment compared to a relaxation group or an incentivized (motivated) control group but no relative advantage on some measures of set shifting or attentional vigilance and effort.

Mindfulness interventions not only train attention but also develop the skill of maintaining an open and accepting attitude toward experience, which may be important for emotion regulation and affective outcomes (Slutsky et al. 2016). As described in the section Mental Health, there is mounting evidence that mindfulness interventions reduce negative affect–related outcomes, such as depression and anxiety symptoms or risk of depression relapse in at-risk individuals. There is also some evidence that mindfulness interventions may reduce self-reported measures of negative affect and improve measures of positive affect in healthy populations. For example, Jain and colleagues (2007) showed that a 4-week MBSR program reduced rumination and increased positive states of mind compared to a 4-week somatic relaxation program during a final exam period in students. However, both the mindfulness and relaxation programs had comparable benefits in reducing self-reported psychological distress at postintervention relative to a no-treatment control group. The RCT studies reviewed in this article provide some examples of the effects of mindfulness intervention on cognitive and affective outcomes; more detailed narrative and meta-analytic reviews of this literature have been published elsewhere (e.g., Arch & Landy 2015, Eberth & Sedlmeier 2012, van Vugt 2015).

Interim summary of cognitive and affective outcomes. Among healthy young adult samples, mounting RCT evidence indicates that mindfulness interventions can improve attention-related outcomes (e.g., sustained attention, working memory) and affective outcomes (e.g., reducing rumination).

Interpersonal Outcomes

Research on how mindfulness interventions impact social and relational outcomes is limited, which is surprising given the extensive anecdotal reports that mindfulness training increases feelings of compassion toward others and can enhance one's close relationships. Indeed, some scholars have argued that kindness and compassion toward others might be a critical marker for evaluating whether mindfulness interventions work (e.g., Grossman 2011), and several lines of research suggest that studies on this topic would be fruitful. First, mindfulness interventions have been shown to improve basic processes associated with better interpersonal functioning outcomes, such as buffering stress and increasing perspective taking (for a theoretical and empirical review, see Karremans et al. 2016). Second, initial RCTs using wait-list control designs suggest that 8-week mindfulness interventions impact social functioning outcomes by, for example, reducing loneliness among older adults (Creswell et al. 2012) and improving relationship satisfaction in adult couples (Carson et al. 2004). In the latter case, Carson and colleagues (2004) conducted one of the first daily diary studies to show that 8-week mindfulness training improved daily reports of relationship satisfaction. Moreover, among mindfulness intervention participants, day-level analyses showed that home mindfulness meditation practice on the first day was significantly associated with higher levels of lagged second- and third-day relationship satisfaction, indicating potentially important daily carry-over benefits of home mindfulness meditation practice.

Mindfulness meditation teachers have long emphasized that mindful awareness can foster insights into the nature of one's suffering and that this understanding naturally gives rise to feelings of compassion toward the self and others (Gunaratana 2011), but little scientific work has attempted to link mindfulness interventions with compassion-related outcomes. Two small RCT studies show that mindfulness meditation training increases compassionate prosocial behaviors such that participants who completed either a 2-week Headspace mindfulness smartphone app intervention or an 8-week group-based mindfulness intervention were more likely to give up their chair to a female confederate on crutches, which was operationalized as a lab-based behavioral measure of compassion (Condon et al. 2013, Lim et al. 2015). This work provides an initial indication that mindfulness interventions increase prosocial outcomes; more research is needed to evaluate whether feelings of compassion mediate these behavioral effects.

It is important to note that mindfulness interventions can be distinguished from compassion (or loving-kindness) meditation programs, which have been receiving more scientific interest in recent years (e.g., Fredrickson et al. 2008). Little is known about the comparative effects of mindfulness versus compassion interventions, but in the above study, Condon et al. (2013) showed that the 8-week mindfulness intervention produced equivalent elevated levels of prosocial behavior at postintervention compared to a well-matched 8-week compassion meditation intervention. One intriguing possibility is that these intervention benefits occurred via dissociable pathways. Loving-kindness meditation practices focus on the explicit generation of positive feelings toward the self and others, whereas mindfulness meditation practices aim to foster an open awareness of experience (as opposed to fostering any specific positive affective states). Thus, one hypothesis is that compassion meditation interventions affect outcomes via positive affect mechanisms, whereas mindfulness interventions affect outcomes through metacognitive awareness and decentering mechanisms (see section Mechanisms of Mindfulness Interventions, below) (Feldman et al. 2010).

Decentering: a mechanism of change involving observing internal experiences from a more objective third-person perspective

Interim summary of interpersonal outcomes. There is currently little mindfulness intervention RCT research on interpersonal outcomes, but initial studies suggest that mindfulness interventions may improve relational outcomes (e.g., relationship satisfaction and prosocial behaviors).

EMBEDDING MINDFULNESS INTERVENTIONS IN INSTITUTIONS AND ACROSS THE LIFE SPAN

First-generation mindfulness intervention studies primarily focused on treating adult patients in clinic settings. Over the past 10 years, there has been a shift toward moving mindfulness intervention RCTs out of the clinic and into institutional settings (e.g., the workplace, schools, prisons, the military, and sport settings) and populations spanning the entire life span (e.g., pregnant women, children, and older adults). High-quality RCT studies are needed to evaluate the safety, efficacy, and effectiveness of mindfulness interventions in these particular contexts. Some initial studies suggest that embedding mindfulness interventions into the workplace (either with group-based or Internet-based training programs) may reduce stress and boost job satisfaction among workers (for a review, see Good et al. 2016). Likewise, mindfulness training programs may be effective in buffering the negative effects of stress in soldiers during high-stress periods (Jha et al. 2010, Johnson et al. 2014).

Initial studies of mindfulness interventions across the life span are also promising. Some pilot RCT evidence shows that mindfulness interventions reduce pregnancy anxiety and depressive symptoms during and following pregnancy (Dimidjian et al. 2016, Guardino et al. 2014). A current trend in research is the development of adapted mindfulness interventions for children, and some initial evidence indicates that classroom mindfulness interventions reduce stress, reduce aggressive behavior, and improve cognitive performance (Flook et al. 2015, Schonert-Reichl et al. 2015, Zenner et al. 2013). In one of the largest RCTs to date ($N = 300$), low-income and predominantly African American urban middle school children were randomly assigned to receive either a classroom-adapted MBSR program or a health education program. At posttreatment, MBSR program participants had greater self-reported improvements in mood, coping, and rumination relative to health education program participants (Sibinga et al. 2016). Finally, in relation to late life, wait-list controlled RCTs also suggest that mindfulness interventions have the potential to improve markers of healthy aging among older adults (e.g., executive function, inflammation) (Creswell et al. 2012, Moynihan et al. 2013).

MECHANISMS OF MINDFULNESS INTERVENTIONS

With high-quality mindfulness intervention RCTs demonstrating promising initial effects on outcomes, there has been growing interest in the mechanisms driving these effects. Mindfulness interventions certainly change a number of processes, including both mindfulness-specific (e.g., acceptance and emotion regulation mechanisms) and non-mindfulness-specific (e.g., positive treatment expectancies) processes (e.g., Creswell et al. 2014). But which mechanistic processes are critical for helping explain the effects of mindfulness intervention on outcomes? In the following sections, I consider some of the psychological and neurobiological mechanisms of mindfulness interventions that have been studied (for some recent reviews, see Brown et al. 2015, Creswell & Lindsay 2014, Hölzel et al. 2011b, Tang et al. 2015).

Psychological Mechanisms

Although a great deal of research has focused on self-reported mindfulness (as measured by questionnaires) as a primary psychological mechanism of change, the evidence is mixed. A recent meta-analysis indicates a moderate positive effect size in mindfulness interventions increasing self-reported mindfulness ($g = 0.53$), and initial evidence in at least 10 studies indicates that increases in self-reported mindfulness statistically mediate improvements in self-reported outcomes, such as reductions in perceived stress or anxiety symptoms (see Visted et al. 2014, table 2). In one example, MBSR was shown to increase self-reported mindfulness compared to an active present-centered group therapy program (without a mindfulness component); these improvements in self-reported mindfulness were associated with decreases in PTSD symptomatology among veterans (Polusny et al. 2015). However, these promising effects are offset by the fact that approximately 50% of mindfulness intervention studies fail to show a significant increase in self-reported mindfulness pre-post intervention (i.e., 37 out of 72 trials in a recent meta-analysis failed to show an increase) (Visted et al. 2014). Furthermore, there is currently limited evidence of mindfulness interventions increasing self-reported mindfulness more than active comparison treatments (e.g., relaxation interventions). Some have argued that there are problems inherent with self-reporting mindfulness that undermine the validity of these measures (e.g., self-reporting is subject to socially desirable responding and retrospective reporting biases, it is difficult to know how attentive and aware one is on a daily basis, the meaning of self-reported mindfulness can change with more formal mindfulness training experiences) (Grossman 2011). Given these concerns, investigators have recently begun to develop and test task-based measures of mindfulness (e.g., Levinson et al. 2013) and second-person mindfulness teacher assessments of mindfulness. Advances in the development of mindfulness measures will likely help clarify the mechanistic role of self-report and behavioral measures of mindfulness in the coming years (for a commentary, see Davidson & Kaszniak 2015).

Mindfulness interventions foster an ability to more objectively observe one's moment-to-moment experience, and this decentered mindset (also described as metacognitive awareness or nonattachment) may be an important psychological mechanism of change. Decentering involves observing internal experiences from a more objective third-person stance (Bernstein et al. 2015), which may help one more effectively decide how one wants to respond to thoughts, emotions, or behaviors (Feldman et al. 2010, Golubickis et al. 2016, Papies et al. 2015). Decentering processes hold promise as an explanation for the mindfulness intervention effects seen in some studies. For example, an early study showed that MBCT improved metacognitive awareness in recovered depressed patients (Teasdale et al. 2002); more recently, well-controlled studies showed that self-reported increases in decentering mediated MBSR treatment effects on anxiety reduction in generalized anxiety disorder patients (Hoge et al. 2014) and MBCT-related decreases in depressive symptoms among individuals at risk for depression relapse (Bieling et al. 2012).

Other psychological and behavioral mechanisms of change have been proposed to explain the effects of mindfulness intervention RCTs, although there are currently few methodologically rigorous mindfulness intervention studies testing these mechanisms in statistical mediation analyses or experiments. These include psychological processes such as acceptance and emotion regulation skills (Hölzel et al. 2011b, Lindsay & Creswell 2015), exposure (Baer 2003), reducing ruminative thoughts (Jain et al. 2007), or changing aspects of one's self-concept (e.g., quieting the egoic self) (Carlson 2013, Golubickis et al. 2016). Finally, formal daily home mindfulness meditation practice has been implicitly assumed to be a behavioral mechanism of change for mindfulness intervention effects (considered in more detail in the section Dosing: How Much Mindfulness Intervention Is Needed for Benefits?), although few well-controlled RCT studies have rigorously evaluated this assumption (Carmody & Baer 2009).

Neurobiological Mechanisms

The effects of mindfulness intervention on outcomes are certainly mediated by the brain, and some initial mindfulness intervention RCT studies have employed structural and functional neuroimaging to evaluate neurobiological mechanisms (for a review, see Tang et al. 2015). Formal mindfulness meditation practices (e.g., mindful awareness of breathing) have been shown to activate a distributed network of brain regions, including the insula, putamen, somatosensory cortex, and portions of the anterior cingulate cortex and prefrontal cortex (Hölzel et al. 2007, Tomasino & Fabbro 2016, Zeidan et al. 2015). Some initial evidence also indicates that mindfulness interventions might structurally alter the brain, increasing gray matter density in the hippocampus (Hölzel et al. 2011a), although well-controlled mindfulness intervention studies are lacking. Despite these advances, little is known about the neural mechanisms linking mindfulness interventions with outcomes.

Our theory of mindfulness as a buffer against stress posits that mindfulness training interventions increase the activity and functional connectivity of prefrontal cortical regions that are important in top-down stress regulation while decreasing the activity and functional connectivity in neural regions that are important in gating the fight-or-flight stress response (e.g., amygdala, subgenual anterior cingulate cortex) (Creswell & Lindsay 2014). We have provided some initial supportive evidence for this neural mechanistic account with a RCT of mindfulness versus relaxation training in stressed unemployed adults (Creswell et al. 2016, Taren et al. 2015). Specifically, we showed that a mindfulness meditation retreat (relative to a well-matched relaxation retreat without a mindfulness component) increased resting-state functional connectivity between the default mode network and the stress regulatory region of the dorsolateral prefrontal cortex while also decreasing stress-related resting-state functional connectivity between the amygdala and the subgenual anterior cingulate cortex. Importantly, we found some initial associations linking these brain changes with reduced stress biomarkers (i.e., cortisol, circulating interleukin 6) at a 4-month follow-up time point (Creswell et al. 2016, Taren et al. 2015).

In addition to neural stress health mechanisms, initial mindfulness intervention studies also link brain changes with affective outcomes. Hölzel and colleagues (2013) showed that MBSR intervention–related increases in ventrolateral prefrontal cortex activity (and amygdala–prefrontal connectivity) during an affect-labeling task were associated with reductions in anxiety symptoms in a sample of patients with generalized anxiety disorder. Zeidan and colleagues (2011, 2015) showed that a brief mindfulness intervention (20 min/day for 4 days) decreased both intensity and unpleasantness ratings given to a noxious thermal pain stimulation to the calf and that the neural mechanisms of these mindfulness-related pain-reduction effects were dissociable from the neural mechanisms driving placebo conditioning effects on pain reduction. In combination, these initial studies suggest that it is possible to identify the putative brain mechanisms that are linked to mindfulness intervention effects, although all of these studies had small sample sizes and focused only on a small subset of the outcomes discussed in the growing mindfulness intervention literature.

DOSING: HOW MUCH MINDFULNESS INTERVENTION IS NEEDED FOR BENEFITS?

One of the most common questions posed by individuals contemplating whether they should enroll in a mindfulness intervention concerns the amount of mindfulness intervention necessary to experience benefits. The current evidence base suggests that even brief mindfulness interventions (e.g., 5–10-min guided mindfulness inductions, 3–4-session mindfulness meditation training) can buffer affective reactivity (e.g., negative affect, craving, pain) and reduce impulsive behaviors immediately following training (Broderick 2005, Papies et al. 2015, Westbrook et al. 2013, Zeidan et al. 2011), although a recent meta-analysis suggests that these brief training effects are small in magnitude ($g = 0.21$) (M. Schumer, E.K. Lindsay, and J.D. Creswell, unpublished manuscript). In contrast, larger doses of mindfulness interventions, such as the 8-week MBSR program, produce moderate-to-large overall effects pre-post training (Baer 2003, Goyal et al. 2014). One illustrative study measured anxiety symptomatology in anxiety disorder patients weekly before, during, and after an MBSR intervention and showed relatively linear declines in anxiety symptoms over the course of the intervention, which were maintained at follow-up (see **Figure 2**)—suggesting a potential dose–response relationship in interventions, with greater doses of mindfulness intervention producing larger scalable effects over the 8-week intervention. However, few published RCTs have tested for mindfulness intervention dose–response relationships (either by experimentally manipulating the intervention dose or by relating measures of class attendance and home mindfulness practice duration with outcomes), which is an area that is in need of more research (see Carmody & Baer 2009).

Different mindfulness intervention teachers recommend a wide range of daily doses of formal mindfulness practice, from 10 min to 1 h or more per day. There is no one-size-fits-all recommendation for how one should dose one's mindfulness intervention training programs. Dosing

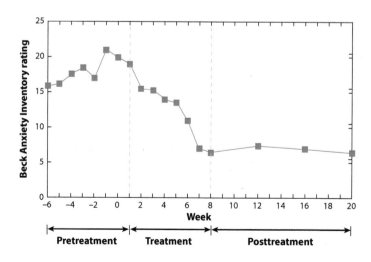

Figure 2

Mean Beck Anxiety Inventory ratings of patients before, during, and after treatment in a mindfulness-based stress reduction program. Figure created using data from Kabat-Zinn et al. (1992).

of mindfulness interventions might follow the same general rules of thumb as dosing aerobic exercise interventions. Larger doses are likely to produce larger effects, the periodicity of the dose is probably important (with regular daily home practice producing larger effects), and there is an upper-bound dose of formal mindfulness intervention that is probably not helpful to participants new to mindfulness practices. Finally, although dosing is important, it is more important for participants to learn how to apply formal mindfulness training skills to stressful or appetitive daily life experiences so that mindfulness skill development can translate into more effective coping.

RISKS OF PARTICIPATING IN MINDFULNESS INTERVENTIONS

Dark night experiences: significant adverse events that can occur with intensive mindfulness meditation interventions

It is not uncommon for participants in mindfulness interventions to report various unpleasant reactions, such as agitation, anxiety, discomfort, or confusion, during formal mindfulness training exercises (although participants also commonly report relaxation and contentment). Indeed, these negative reactions are viewed as an important feature of the psychotherapeutic change process in mindfulness interventions because sustained mindful attention to one's experience is thought to help participants explore and understand the full embodied experience of these reactions, to learn that the experience of these reactions is temporary, and to foster insight into how one reacts to these uncomfortable experiences. These more benign risks aside, there have also been calls to study whether mindfulness interventions can trigger more significant adverse events (Lustyk et al. 2009, Shapiro 1992). For example, a participant who has a life history of trauma might experience the resurfacing of these trauma memories during mindfulness training exercises, potentially triggering a major depressive episode. Researchers have also voiced the concern that individuals who are at risk for psychosis (e.g., schizophrenia) or seizures (e.g., epilepsy) might put themselves at elevated risk for exacerbation of these symptoms if they participate in formal mindfulness exercises (e.g., Walsh & Roche 1979). Currently, there is little empirical published research on the prevalence, type, and severity of these more significant "dark night" experiences with mindfulness interventions. Some observational research suggests that these severe adverse events can occur (albeit infrequently) among individuals going through more intensive residential mindfulness meditation retreats lasting from 2 weeks to 3 months (e.g., Shapiro 1992). The current evidence-based mindfulness interventions (e.g., MBSR, MBCT), which are offered in smaller-spaced doses by trained instructors, carry minimal risks for significant adverse events; furthermore, these mindfulness interventions provide the greatest benefits among high-trauma and high-stress populations (Creswell & Lindsay 2014, Polusny et al. 2015, Williams et al. 2014).

In addition to specific risks and adverse events, it is interesting to consider the possibility that the conscious effort at maintaining awareness on present moment experience might have cognitive costs among individuals who are new to mindfulness interventions. Some studies suggest that training in mindfulness can be initially cognitively depleting. For example, a brief mindful awareness induction was shown to decrease pain tolerance to a cold pressor challenge task, depleting self-regulatory strength (Evans et al. 2014). We also showed that a brief mindfulness meditation training program (25 min/day for 3 consecutive days) buffered psychological perceptions of stress in a laboratory stress challenge task but also increased cortisol reactivity (Creswell et al. 2014). One explanation for this finding is that brief mindfulness training helped foster emotion regulation skills (decreasing psychological stress perceptions) but the extra effort of using a new mindful awareness strategy during a stress task increased cortisol reactivity.

In addition to short-term depleting effects, it is also possible that the cognitive demands of adopting this more reflective awareness of one's present moment experience might disrupt, slow, or bias one's responses on cognitive tasks. Although some initial research indicates that brief mindfulness inductions can reduce evaluative cognitive biases such as the correspondence bias and sunk cost bias (Hafenbrack et al. 2014, Hopthrow et al. 2016), they can also increase false-memory recall (Wilson et al. 2015). Many open questions about how mindfulness interventions affect cognitive processing variables remain.

DISCUSSION

Our scientific understanding of mindfulness interventions has accelerated over the past two decades, and this review provides some selective highlights of this literature. RCTs provide promising evidence that mindfulness interventions can improve mental and physical health, cognitive and affective factors, and interpersonal outcomes. Some of the strongest and most reliable RCT evidence indicates that mindfulness interventions (and particularly 8-week mindfulness programs, such as MBSR and MBCT) improve the management of chronic pain, reduce depression relapse rates in at-risk individuals, and improve substance abuse outcomes. In these RCT studies, there is consistent evidence that mindfulness interventions improve outcomes relative to TAU or no-treatment control groups, some evidence that mindfulness interventions can improve some outcomes relative to other active behavioral treatments (e.g., relaxation or health education programs), and limited evidence for a relative advantage of mindfulness interventions over other gold-standard pharmacological or behavioral treatments (e.g., CBT).[3] However, few RCT studies have been conducted examining mindfulness intervention effects on interpersonal outcomes (Karremans et al. 2016) or in institutional settings beyond medical or psychological clinics, such as prisons, workplaces, or schools; these areas are ripe for high-quality RCT research.

Although this review has focused on some of the higher-quality RCT mindfulness intervention studies, most of the mindfulness intervention literature to date has methodological limitations (e.g., small samples, lack of active control groups, limited use of high-quality measures, nonblinding of outcome assessors) that currently preclude any definitive statements about the efficacy of mindfulness interventions on many outcomes. Two important areas are especially in need of research attention: measuring formal (and informal) mindfulness practices during and after mindfulness interventions and testing for treatment effects at follow-up time points. Regarding the first point, few mindfulness studies carefully measure and report the amount of daily formal mindfulness practices (and the amount of informal mindful awareness practices) completed during mindfulness interventions, even fewer studies measure whether the amount of daily practice statistically mediates outcomes, and almost no studies have reported how much daily practice participants continue to do in the weeks, months, and years following the completion of formal mindfulness intervention programs (see Barkan et al. 2016). RCT studies that include follow-up time point assessments to measure stability of treatment effects are similarly necessary. This review has highlighted some trials that include follow-up assessments and that provide mixed evidence about the maintenance of effects up to two years following intervention. It is currently unclear what factors are important for determining when beneficial effects are observed at follow-up time points after mindfulness interventions (e.g., in 2-year follow-up periods among participants at risk for depressive relapse) or when postintervention treatment effects disappear at follow-up time points (e.g., pain-reduction benefits disappearing at a 6-month follow-up; see Morone et al. 2016). One implicit assumption (that has gone untested) is that sustained daily mindfulness practices drive the maintenance of intervention effects.

---

[3] The comparison of CBT to mindfulness interventions is conceptually curious because some mindfulness interventions are hybridized mindfulness-CBT treatments (e.g., MBCT, MBRP), and it is certainly possible that CBT approaches, which aim to bring awareness to automatic thoughts and their effects on behavior, may increase a form of mindful awareness as a central mechanism of change.

I began this review by recognizing the dramatic growth in our scientific understanding of mindfulness and the wide range, from skepticism to fanaticism, of the response among scientists. In this article, I aim to provide a balanced review of the current mindfulness intervention RCT evidence base, along with a consideration of when and where mindfulness interventions demonstrate benefits, an identification of some possible mechanisms for these effects, and a consideration of their potential risks. There are certainly many contexts in which public interest in the benefits of mindfulness interventions has resulted in some fanaticism and characterization of mindfulness training as a panacea treatment. For example, mindfulness interventions are being integrated into schools and the workplace in the absence of a corpus of high-quality well-controlled RCT studies. Many investigators are using mindfulness interventions in patient populations without regard to the active mechanisms of change for affecting specific outcomes of interest (Dimidjian & Segal 2015). Future research on the mechanisms of mindfulness interventions and specification of how (and for whom) mindfulness interventions work will accelerate our basic and clinical efforts in this area.

As the literature on mindfulness interventions has grown, there have also been skeptics who question the value of mindfulness interventions and the ways they are implemented. Some discussions have considered the risks of mindfulness interventions, such as so-called "dark night" experiences that are potentially triggered by mindfulness training (see section Risks of Participating in Mindfulness Interventions, above). Our current understanding of 8-week mindfulness intervention trials indicates a low prevalence of these significant adverse events, with the side effect profile of most individuals consisting of greater insight, well-being, and self-regulated behavior. Skeptics have also questioned the value of secularized forms of mindfulness interventions (such as MBSR and MBCT) that are stripped of the ethical and compassion-related teachings that are common to many Buddhist forms of mindfulness meditation training (Grossman 2011). More research is needed to evaluate these concerns, but initial work suggests that secular forms of mindfulness meditation training may be just as beneficial as spiritual forms (Feuille & Pargament 2015).

As we begin to develop reliable efficacy indications for mindfulness interventions in RCT studies, it will be important to shift our focus to translating this knowledge into effective and sustainable community mindfulness intervention programs; however, there is currently little effectiveness research in this area (Dimidjian & Segal 2015). Epidemiological work suggests that more affluent, healthy white adults are the ones who are most likely to seek out and use mindfulness practices, whereas mindfulness practices are underutilized among low-income minorities with worse health (Olano et al. 2015). From an effectiveness standpoint, this is problematic because our RCT evidence to date suggests that these more high-stress, low-income, and health-compromised individuals would benefit the most from mindfulness interventions (Creswell & Lindsay 2014). Thus, we need to develop effectiveness studies that carefully consider how we can reach out in the coming years to communities of need with evidence-based, cost-effective, and sustainable mindfulness interventions.

DISCLOSURE STATEMENT

The author is not aware of any affiliations, memberships, funding, or financial holdings that might be perceived as affecting the objectivity of this review.

ACKNOWLEDGMENTS

I want to thank Hayley Rahl, Lauren Simicich, Kasey Creswell, Fadel Zeidan, and the members of the Health and Human Performance Lab at Carnegie Mellon University for help and feedback. Research reported in this publication was supported by two grants from the National Center for

Complementary and Integrative Health (NCCIH) at the National Institutes of Health (NIH) (grants R21AT008493 and R01AT008685). The content is solely the responsibility of the author and does not necessarily represent the official views of the NIH.

LITERATURE CITED

Anālayo. 2003. *Satipaṭṭhāna: The Direct Path to Realization*. Cambridge, UK: Windhorse Publ.

Arch JJ, Ayers CR. 2013. Which treatment worked better for whom? Moderators of group cognitive behavioral therapy versus adapted mindfulness based stress reduction for anxiety disorders. *Behav. Res. Ther.* 51(8):434–42

Arch JJ, Brown KW, Goodman RJ, Della Porta MD, Kiken LG, Tillman S. 2016. Enjoying food without caloric cost: the impact of brief mindfulness on laboratory eating outcomes. *Behav. Res. Ther.* 79:23–34

Arch JJ, Landy LN. 2015. Emotional benefits of mindfulness. See Brown et al. 2015, pp. 208–24

Baer RA. 2003. Mindfulness training as a clinical intervention: a conceptual and empirical review. *Clin. Psychol. Sci. Pract.* 10(2):125–43

Bargh JA, Chartrand TL. 1999. The unbearable automaticity of being. *Am. Psychol.* 54(7):462–79

Barkan T, Hoerger M, Gallegos AM, Turiano NA, Duberstein PR, Moynihan JA. 2016. Personality predicts utilization of mindfulness-based stress reduction during and post-intervention in a community sample of older adults. *J. Altern. Complement. Med.* 22:390–95

Barrett B, Hayney MS, Muller D, Rakel D, Ward A, et al. 2012. Meditation or exercise for preventing acute respiratory infection: a randomized controlled trial. *Ann. Fam. Med.* 10(4):337–46

Bernstein A, Hadash Y, Lichtash Y, Tanay G, Shepherd K, Fresco DM. 2015. Decentering and related constructs: a critical review and metacognitive processes model. *Perspect. Psychol. Sci.* 10(5):599–617

Bieling PJ, Hawley LL, Bloch RT, Corcoran KM, Levitan RD, et al. 2012. Treatment-specific changes in decentering following mindfulness-based cognitive therapy versus antidepressant medication or placebo for prevention of depressive relapse. *J. Consult. Clin. Psychol.* 80(3):365–72

Bjork EL, Bjork RA. 2011. Making things hard on yourself, but in a good way: creating desirable difficulties to enhance learning. In *Psychology and the Real World: Essays Illustrating Fundamental Contributions to Society*, ed. MA Gernsbacher, RW Pew, LM Hough, JR Pomerantz, pp. 56–64. New York: Worth

Black DS, O'Reilly GA, Olmstead R, Breen EC, Irwin MR. 2015. Mindfulness meditation and improvement in sleep quality and daytime impairment among older adults with sleep disturbances: a randomized clinical trial. *JAMA Intern. Med.* 175(4):494–501

Black DS, Slavich GM. 2016. Mindfulness meditation and the immune system: a systematic review of randomized controlled trials. *Ann. N. Y. Acad. Sci.* 1373:13–24

Bodhi B. 2011. What does mindfulness really mean? A canonical perspective. *Contemp. Buddhism* 12(1):19–39

Boettcher J, Åström V, Påhlsson D, Schenström O, Andersson G, Carlbring P. 2014. Internet-based mindfulness treatment for anxiety disorders: a randomized controlled trial. *Behav. Ther.* 45(2):241–53

Bowen S, Chawla N, Collins SE, Witkiewitz K, Hsu S, et al. 2009. Mindfulness-based relapse prevention for substance use disorders: a pilot efficacy trial. *Subst. Abus.* 30(4):295–305

Bowen S, Vietan C, Witkiewitz K, Carroll H. 2015. A mindfulness-based approach to addiction. See Brown et al. 2015, pp. 387–404

Bowen S, Witkiewitz K, Clifasefi SL, Grow J, Chawla N, et al. 2014. Relative efficacy of mindfulness-based relapse prevention, standard relapse prevention, and treatment as usual for substance use disorders: a randomized clinical trial. *JAMA Psychiatry* 71(5):547–56

Brewer JA, Mallik S, Babuscio TA, Nich C, Johnson HE, et al. 2011. Mindfulness training for smoking cessation: results from a randomized controlled trial. *Drug Alcohol Depend.* 119(1):72–80

Britton WB, Haynes PL, Fridel KW, Bootzin RR. 2010. Polysomnographic and subjective profiles of sleep continuity before and after mindfulness-based cognitive therapy in partially remitted depression. *Psychosom. Med.* 72(6):539–48

Britton WB, Haynes PL, Fridel KW, Bootzin RR. 2012. Mindfulness-based cognitive therapy improves polysomnographic and subjective sleep profiles in antidepressant users with sleep complaints. *Psychother. Psychosom.* 81(5):296–304

A large, well-controlled trial showing that MBRP can improve substance abuse outcomes.

Broderick PC. 2005. Mindfulness and coping with dysphoric mood: contrasts with rumination and distraction. *Cogn. Ther. Res.* 29(5):501–10

Brown KW, Creswell JD, Ryan RM, eds. 2015. *Handbook of Mindfulness: Theory, Research, and Practice*. New York: Guilford Publ.

Brown KW, Ryan RM. 2003. The benefits of being present: mindfulness and its role in psychological well-being. *J. Pers. Soc. Psychol.* 84(4):822–48

Brown KW, Ryan RM, Creswell JD. 2007. Mindfulness: theoretical foundations and evidence for its salutary effects. *Psychol. Inq.* 18(4):211–37

Carlson EN. 2013. Overcoming the barriers to self-knowledge: mindfulness as a path to seeing yourself as you really are. *Perspect. Psychol. Sci.* 8(2):173–86

Carlson LE, Doll R, Stephen J, Faris P, Tamagawa R, et al. 2013. Randomized controlled trial of mindfulness-based cancer recovery versus supportive expressive group therapy for distressed survivors of breast cancer. *J. Clin. Oncol.* 31(25):3119–26

Carmody J, Baer RA. 2009. How long does a mindfulness-based stress reduction program need to be? A review of class contact hours and effect sizes for psychological distress. *J. Clin. Psychol.* 65(6):627–38

Carson JW, Carson KM, Gil KM, Baucom DH. 2004. Mindfulness-based relationship enhancement. *Behav. Ther.* 35(3):471–94

Cherkin DC, Sherman KJ, Balderson BH, Cook AJ, Anderson ML, et al. 2016. Effect of mindfulness-based stress reduction versus cognitive behavioral therapy or usual care on back pain and functional limitations in adults with chronic low back pain: a randomized clinical trial. *JAMA* 315(12):1240–49

Condon P, Desbordes G, Miller W, DeSteno D. 2013. Meditation increases compassionate responses to suffering. *Psychol. Sci.* 24(10):2125–27

Creswell JD, Irwin MR, Burklund LJ, Lieberman MD, Arevalo JMG, et al. 2012. Mindfulness-based stress reduction training reduces loneliness and pro-inflammatory gene expression in older adults: a small randomized controlled trial. *Brain Behav. Immun.* 26(7):1095–101

Creswell JD, Lindsay EK. 2014. How does mindfulness training affect health? A mindfulness stress buffering account. *Curr. Dir. Psychol. Sci.* 23(6):401–7

Creswell JD, Myers HF, Cole SW, Irwin MR. 2009. Mindfulness meditation training effects on CD4+ T lymphocytes in HIV-1 infected adults: a small randomized controlled trial. *Brain Behav. Immun.* 23(2):184–88

Creswell JD, Pacilio LE, Lindsay EK, Brown KW. 2014. Brief mindfulness meditation training alters psychological and neuroendocrine responses to social evaluative stress. *Psychoneuroendocrinology* 44:1–12

Creswell JD, Taren AA, Lindsay EK, Greco CM, Gianaros PJ, et al. 2016. Alterations in resting-state functional connectivity link mindfulness meditation with reduced interleukin-6: a randomized controlled trial. *Biol. Psychiatry* 80:53–61

Davidson RJ, Kaszniak AW. 2015. Conceptual and methodological issues in research on mindfulness and meditation. *Am. Psychol.* 70(7):581–92

Davis MC, Zautra AJ, Wolf LD, Tennen H, Yeung EW. 2015. Mindfulness and cognitive-behavioral interventions for chronic pain: differential effects on daily pain reactivity and stress reactivity. *J. Consult. Clin. Psychol.* 83(1):24–35

Dimidjian S, Goodman SH, Felder JN, Gallop R, Brown AP, Beck A. 2016. Staying well during pregnancy and the postpartum: a pilot randomized trial of mindfulness-based cognitive therapy for the prevention of depressive relapse/recurrence. *J. Consult. Clin. Psychol.* 84(2):134–45

Dimidjian S, Segal ZV. 2015. Prospects for a clinical science of mindfulness-based intervention. *Am. Psychol.* 70(7):593–620

Eberth J, Sedlmeier P. 2012. The effects of mindfulness meditation: a meta-analysis. *Mindfulness* 3(3):174–89

Eisendrath SJ, Gillung E, Delucchi KL, Segal ZV, Nelson JC, et al. 2016. A randomized controlled trial of mindfulness-based cognitive therapy for treatment-resistant depression. *Psychother. Psychosom.* 85(2):99–110

Evans DR, Eisenlohr-Moul TA, Button DF, Baer RA, Segerstrom SC. 2014. Self-regulatory deficits associated with unpracticed mindfulness strategies for coping with acute pain. *J. Appl. Soc. Psychol.* 44(1):23–30

Everett D. 2005. Cultural constraints on grammar and cognition in Pirahã: another look at the design features of human language. *Curr. Anthropol.* 46(4):621–46

A theoretical and narrative review of mindfulness and its effects.

A comprehensive review of MBSR and MBCT treatment studies.

A large RCT study showing that MBCT reduces depressive symptoms in treatment-resistant depression.

Feldman G, Greeson J, Senville J. 2010. Differential effects of mindful breathing, progressive muscle relaxation, and loving-kindness meditation on decentering and negative reactions to repetitive thoughts. *Behav. Res. Ther.* 48(10):1002–11

Feuille M, Pargament K. 2015. Pain, mindfulness, and spirituality: a randomized controlled trial comparing effects of mindfulness and relaxation on pain-related outcomes in migraineurs. *J. Health Psychol.* 20(8):1090–106

Flook L, Goldberg SB, Pinger L, Davidson RJ. 2015. Promoting prosocial behavior and self-regulatory skills in preschool children through a mindfulness-based kindness curriculum. *Dev. Psychol.* 51(1):44–51

Fredrickson BL, Cohn MA, Coffey KA, Pek J, Finkel SM. 2008. Open hearts build lives: Positive emotions, induced through loving-kindness meditation, build consequential personal resources. *J. Pers. Soc. Psychol.* 95(5):1045–62

Garland EL, Manusov EG, Froeliger B, Kelly A, Williams JM, Howard MO. 2014. Mindfulness-oriented recovery enhancement for chronic pain and prescription opioid misuse: results from an early-stage randomized controlled trial. *J. Consult. Clin. Psychol.* 82(3):448–59

Garland EL, Roberts-Lewis A, Tronnier CD, Graves R, Kelley K. 2016. Mindfulness-oriented recovery enhancement versus CBT for co-occurring substance dependence, traumatic stress, and psychiatric disorders: proximal outcomes from a pragmatic randomized trial. *Behav. Res. Ther.* 77:7–16

Garland SN, Carlson LE, Stephens AJ, Antle MC, Samuels C, Campbell TS. 2014. Mindfulness-based stress reduction compared with cognitive behavioral therapy for the treatment of insomnia comorbid with cancer: a randomized, partially blinded, noninferiority trial. *J. Clin. Oncol.* 32:1–9

Gaylord SA, Palsson OS, Garland EL, Faurot KR, Coble RS, et al. 2011. Mindfulness training reduces the severity of irritable bowel syndrome in women: results of a randomized controlled trial. *Am. J. Gastroenterol.* 106(9):1678–88

Goldin PR, Morrison A, Jazaieri H, Brozovich F, Heimberg R, Gross JJ. 2016. Group CBT versus MBSR for social anxiety disorder: a randomized controlled trial. *J. Consult. Clin. Psychol.* 84(5):427–37

Golubickis M, Tan LBG, Falben JK, Macrae CN. 2016. The observing self: diminishing egocentrism through brief mindfulness meditation. *Eur. J. Soc. Psychol.* 46:521–27

Gonzalez-Garcia M, Ferrer MJ, Borras X, Muñoz-Moreno JA, Miranda C, et al. 2013. Effectiveness of mindfulness-based cognitive therapy on the quality of life, emotional status, and CD4 cell count of patients aging with HIV infection. *AIDS Behav.* 18(4):676–85

Good DJ, Lyddy CJ, Glomb TM, Bono JE, Brown KW, et al. 2016. Contemplating mindfulness at work: an integrative review. *J. Manag.* 42:114–42

Goyal M, Singh S, Sibinga EM, Gould NF, Rowland-Seymour A, et al. 2014. Meditation programs for psychological stress and well-being: a systematic review and meta-analysis. *JAMA Intern. Med.* 174(3):357–68

Grossman P. 2011. Defining mindfulness by how poorly I think I pay attention during everyday awareness and other intractable problems for psychology's (re)invention of mindfulness: comment on Brown et al. 2011. *Psychol. Assess.* 23(4):1034–40

Guardino CM, Dunkel Schetter C, Bower JE, Lu MC, Smalley SL. 2014. Randomised controlled pilot trial of mindfulness training for stress reduction during pregnancy. *Psychol. Health* 29(3):334–49

Gunaratana BH. 2011. *Mindfulness in Plain English*. New York: Simon & Schuster

Hafenbrack AC, Kinias Z, Barsade SG. 2014. Debiasing the mind through meditation: mindfulness and the sunk-cost bias. *Psychol. Sci.* 25(2):369–76

Hayes SC, Follette VM, Linehan M. 2004. *Mindfulness and Acceptance: Expanding the Cognitive-Behavioral Tradition*. New York: Guilford Press

Hayes SC, Villatte M, Levin M, Hildebrandt M. 2011. Open, aware, and active: contextual approaches as an emerging trend in the behavioral and cognitive therapies. *Annu. Rev. Clin. Psychol.* 7:141–68

Hayney MS, Coe CL, Muller D, Obasi CN, Backonja U, et al. 2014. Age and psychological influences on immune responses to trivalent inactivated influenza vaccine in the meditation or exercise for preventing acute respiratory infection (MEPARI) trial. *Hum. Vaccines Immunother.* 10(1):83–91

Hoge EA, Bui E, Goetter E, Robinaugh DJ, Ojserkis RA, et al. 2014. Change in decentering mediates improvement in anxiety in mindfulness-based stress reduction for generalized anxiety disorder. *Cogn. Ther. Res.* 39(2):228–35

Hoge EA, Bui E, Marques L, Metcalf CA, Morris LK, et al. 2013. Randomized controlled trial of mindfulness meditation for generalized anxiety disorder: effects on anxiety and stress reactivity. *J. Clin. Psychiatry* 74(8):786–92

Hölzel BK, Carmody J, Vangel M, Congleton C, Yerramsetti SM, et al. 2011a. Mindfulness practice leads to increases in regional brain gray matter density. *Psychiatry Res. Neuroimaging* 191(1):36–43

Hölzel BK, Hoge EA, Greve DN, Gard T, Creswell JD, et al. 2013. Neural mechanisms of symptom improvements in generalized anxiety disorder following mindfulness training. *NeuroImage Clin.* 2:448–58

Hölzel BK, Lazar SW, Gard T, Schuman-Olivier Z, Vago DR, Ott U. 2011b. How does mindfulness meditation work? Proposing mechanisms of action from a conceptual and neural perspective. *Perspect. Psychol. Sci.* 6(6):537–59

Hölzel BK, Ott U, Hempel H, Hackl A, Wolf K, et al. 2007. Differential engagement of anterior cingulate and adjacent medial frontal cortex in adept meditators and non-meditators. *Neurosci. Lett.* 421(1):16–21

Hopthrow T, Hooper N, Mahmood L, Meier BP, Weger U. 2016. Mindfulness reduces the correspondence bias. *Q. J. Exp. Psychol.* In press. doi: 10.1080/17470218.2016.1149498

Huijbers MJ, Spinhoven P, Spijker J, Ruhé HG, van Schaik DJF, et al. 2016. Discontinuation of antidepressant medication after mindfulness-based cognitive therapy for recurrent depression: randomised controlled non-inferiority trial. *Br. J. Psychiatry* 208:366–73

Jain S, Shapiro SL, Swanick S, Roesch SC, Mills PJ, Schwartz GE. 2007. A randomized controlled trial of mindfulness meditation versus relaxation training: effects on distress, positive states of mind, rumination, and distraction. *Ann. Behav. Med.* 33(1):11–21

Jensen CG, Vangkilde S, Frokjaer V, Hasselbalch SG. 2012. Mindfulness training affects attention—or is it attentional effort? *J. Exp. Psychol. Gen.* 141(1):106–23

Jha AP, Morrison AB, Dainer-Best J, Parker S, Rostrup N, Stanley EA. 2015. Minds "at attention": mindfulness training curbs attentional lapses in military cohorts. *PLOS ONE* 10(2):e0116889

Jha AP, Stanley EA, Kiyonaga A, Wong L, Gelfand L. 2010. Examining the protective effects of mindfulness training on working memory capacity and affective experience. *Emotion* 10(1):54–64

Johnson DC, Thom NJ, Stanley EA, Haase L, Simmons AN, et al. 2014. Modifying resilience mechanisms in at-risk individuals: a controlled study of mindfulness training in marines preparing for deployment. *Am. J. Psychiatry* 171(8):844–53

Kabat-Zinn J. 1982. An outpatient program in behavioral medicine for chronic pain patients based on the practice of mindfulness meditation: theoretical considerations and preliminary results. *Gen. Hosp. Psychiatry* 4(1):33–47

Kabat-Zinn J. 1990. *Full Catastrophe Living: Using the Wisdom of Your Body and Mind to Face Stress, Pain, and Illness*. New York: Delta

Kabat-Zinn J, Massion AO, Kristeller J, Peterson LG, Fletcher KE, et al. 1992. Effectiveness of a meditation-based stress reduction program in the treatment of anxiety disorders. *Am. J. Psychiatry* 149:936–43

Kabat-Zinn J. 2003. Mindfulness-based interventions in context: past, present, and future. *Clin. Psychol. Sci. Pract.* 10(2):144–56

Kabat-Zinn J, Wheeler E, Light T, Skillings A, Scharf MJ, et al. 1998. Influence of a mindfulness meditation-based stress reduction intervention on rates of skin clearing in patients with moderate to severe psoriasis undergoing phototherapy (UVB) and photochemotherapy (PUVA). *Psychosom. Med.* 60(5):625–32

Kang Y, Gruber J, Gray JR. 2013. Mindfulness and de-automatization. *Emot. Rev.* 5(2):192–201

Karremans JC, Schellekens MPJ, Kappen G. 2016. Bridging the sciences of mindfulness and romantic relationships: a theoretical model and research agenda. *Personal. Soc. Psychol. Rev.* In press. doi: 10.1177/1088868315615450

Killingsworth MA, Gilbert DT. 2010. A wandering mind is an unhappy mind. *Science* 330(6006):932

Koole SL, Govorun O, Cheng CM, Gallucci M. 2009. Pulling yourself together: Meditation promotes congruence between implicit and explicit self-esteem. *J. Exp. Soc. Psychol.* 45(6):1220–26

Kuyken W, Hayes R, Barrett B, Byng R, Dalgleish T, et al. 2015. Effectiveness and cost-effectiveness of mindfulness-based cognitive therapy compared with maintenance antidepressant treatment in the prevention of depressive relapse or recurrence (PREVENT): a randomised controlled trial. *Lancet* 386(9988):63–73

Levinson DB, Stoll EL, Kindy SD, Merry HL, Davidson RJ. 2013. A mind you can count on: validating breath counting as a behavioral measure of mindfulness. *Front. Psychol.* 5:1202

Lim D, Condon P, DeSteno D. 2015. Mindfulness and compassion: an examination of mechanism and scalability. *PLOS ONE* 10(2):e0118221

Lindsay EK, Creswell JD. 2015. Back to the basics: how attention monitoring and acceptance stimulate positive growth. *Psychol. Inq.* 26(4):343–48

Ludwig DS, Kabat-Zinn J. 2008. Mindfulness in medicine. *J. Am. Med. Assoc.* 300(11):1350–52

Lustyk MKB, Chawla N, Nolan RS, Marlatt GA. 2009. Mindfulness meditation research: issues of participant screening, safety procedures, and researcher training. *Adv. Mind Body Med.* 24(1):20–30

Ma SH, Teasdale JD. 2004. Mindfulness-based cognitive therapy for depression: replication and exploration of differential relapse prevention effects. *J. Consult. Clin. Psychol.* 72(1):31–40

MacCoon DG, Imel ZE, Rosenkranz MA, Sheftel JG, Weng HY, et al. 2012. The validation of an active control intervention for Mindfulness Based Stress Reduction (MBSR). *Behav. Res. Ther.* 50(1):3–12

Malarkey WB, Jarjoura D, Klatt M. 2013. Workplace based mindfulness practice and inflammation: a randomized trial. *Brain. Behav. Immun.* 27(1):145–54

Mason AE, Epel ES, Kristeller J, Moran PJ, Dallman M, et al. 2015. Effects of a mindfulness-based intervention on mindful eating, sweets consumption, and fasting glucose levels in obese adults: data from the SHINE randomized controlled trial. *J. Behav. Med.* 39(2):201–13

Morone NE, Greco CM, Moore CG, Rollman BL, Lane B, et al. 2016. A mind-body program for older adults with chronic low back pain: a randomized clinical trial. *JAMA Intern. Med.* 176(3):329–37

Moynihan JA, Chapman BP, Klorman R, Krasner MS, Duberstein PR, et al. 2013. Mindfulness-based stress reduction for older adults: effects on executive function, frontal alpha asymmetry and immune function. *Neuropsychobiology* 68(1):34–43

Mrazek MD, Franklin MS, Phillips DT, Baird B, Schooler JW. 2013. Mindfulness training improves working memory capacity and GRE performance while reducing mind wandering. *Psychol. Sci.* 24(5):776–81

Mrazek MD, Smallwood J, Schooler JW. 2012. Mindfulness and mind-wandering: finding convergence through opposing constructs. *Emotion* 12(3):442–48

Olano HA, Kachan D, Tannenbaum SL, Mehta A, Annane D, Lee DJ. 2015. Engagement in mindfulness practices by U.S. adults: sociodemographic barriers. *J. Altern. Complement. Med.* 21(2):100–2

Ostafin BD, Kassman KT. 2012. Stepping out of history: Mindfulness improves insight problem solving. *Conscious. Cogn.* 21(2):1031–36

Papies EK, Pronk TM, Keesman M, Barsalou LW. 2015. The benefits of simply observing: Mindful attention modulates the link between motivation and behavior. *J. Pers. Soc. Psychol.* 108(1):148–70

Pinniger R, Brown RF, Thorsteinsson EB, McKinley P. 2012. Argentine tango dance compared to mindfulness meditation and a waiting-list control: a randomised trial for treating depression. *Complement. Ther. Med.* 20(6):377–84

Polusny MA, Erbes CR, Thuras P, Moran A, Lamberty GJ, et al. 2015. Mindfulness-based stress reduction for posttraumatic stress disorder among veterans: a randomized clinical trial. *JAMA* 314(5):456–65

Quaglia JT, Brown KW, Lindsay EK, Creswell JD, Goodman RJ. 2015. From conceptualization to operationalization of mindfulness. See Brown et al. 2015, pp. 151–70

Roemer L, Orsillo SM. 2009. *Mindfulness- and Acceptance-Based Behavioral Therapies in Practice (Guides to Individualized Evidence-Based Treatment)*. New York: Guilford Press

Rosenberg EL, Zanesco AP, King BG, Aichele SR, Jacobs TL, et al. 2015. Intensive meditation training influences emotional responses to suffering. *Emotion* 15(6):775–90

Rosenkranz MA, Davidson RJ, MacCoon DG, Sheridan JF, Kalin NH, Lutz A. 2013. *Brain Behav. Immun.* 27:174–84

Samuelson M, Carmody J, Kabat-Zinn J, Bratt MA. 2007. Mindfulness-based stress reduction in Massachusetts correctional facilities. *Prison J.* 87(2):254–68

Schmidt S, Grossman P, Schwarzer B, Jena S, Naumann J, Walach H. 2011. Treating fibromyalgia with mindfulness-based stress reduction: results from a 3-armed randomized controlled trial. *PAIN®*. 152(2):361–69

An early and important review of the mindfulness intervention health literature.

A validation study of the well-matched HEP comparison program for MBSR research studies.

An initial well-controlled RCT showing that MBSR can reduce PTSD symptomatology in veterans.

Schofield TP, Creswell JD, Denson TF. 2015. Brief mindfulness induction reduces inattentional blindness. *Conscious. Cogn.* 37:63–70

Schonert-Reichl KA, Oberle E, Lawlor MS, Abbott D, Thomson K, et al. 2015. Enhancing cognitive and social-emotional development through a simple-to-administer mindfulness-based school program for elementary school children: a randomized controlled trial. *Dev. Psychol.* 51(1):52–66

Schwartz L, Slater MA, Birchler GR. 1994. Interpersonal stress and pain behaviors in patients with chronic pain. *J. Consult. Clin. Psychol.* 62(4):861–64

Segal ZV, Bieling P, Young T, MacQueen G, Cooke R, et al. 2010. Antidepressant monotherapy versus sequential pharmacotherapy and mindfulness-based cognitive therapy, or placebo, for relapse prophylaxis in recurrent depression. *Arch. Gen. Psychiatry* 67(12):1256–64

Segerstrom SC, Miller GE. 2004. Psychological stress and the human immune system: a meta-analytic study of 30 years of inquiry. *Psychol. Bull.* 130(4):601–30

Semple RJ. 2010. Does mindfulness meditation enhance attention? A randomized controlled trial. *Mindfulness* 1(2):121–30

SeyedAlinaghi S, Jam S, Foroughi M, Imani A, Mohraz M, et al. 2012. Randomized controlled trial of mindfulness-based stress reduction delivered to human immunodeficiency virus-positive patients in Iran: effects on CD4$^+$ T lymphocyte count and medical and psychological symptoms. *Psychosom. Med.* 74(6):620–27

Shapiro DH. 1992. Adverse effects of meditation: a preliminary investigation of long-term meditators. *Int. J. Psychosom.* 39(1–4):62–67

Sibinga EMS, Webb L, Ghazarian SR, Ellen JM. 2016. School-based mindfulness instruction: an RCT. *Pediatrics* 137(1):1–8

Slutsky J, Rahl H, Lindsay EK, Creswell JD. 2016. Mindfulness, emotion regulation, and social threat. In *Mindfulness in Social Psychology*, ed. JC Karremans, EK Papies. New York: Routledge. In press

Strauss C, Cavanagh K, Oliver A, Pettman D. 2014. Mindfulness-based interventions for people diagnosed with a current episode of an anxiety or depressive disorder: a meta-analysis of randomised controlled trials. *PLOS ONE* 9(4):e96110

Tang Y-Y, Hölzel BK, Posner MI. 2015. The neuroscience of mindfulness meditation. *Nat. Rev. Neurosci.* 16(4):213–25

Taren AA, Gianaros PJ, Greco CM, Lindsay EK, Fairgrieve A, et al. 2015. Mindfulness meditation training alters stress-related amygdala resting state functional connectivity: a randomized controlled trial. *Soc. Cogn. Affect. Neurosci.* 10(12):1758–68

Teasdale JD, Moore RG, Hayhurst H, Pope M, Williams S, Segal ZV. 2002. Metacognitive awareness and prevention of relapse in depression: empirical evidence. *J. Consult. Clin. Psychol.* 70(2):275–87

Teasdale JD, Segal ZV, Mark J, Ridgeway VA, Soulsby JM, Lau MA. 2000. Prevention of relapse/recurrence in major depression by mindfulness-based cognitive therapy. *J. Consult. Clin. Psychol.* 68(4):615–23

Tomasino B, Fabbro F. 2016. Increases in the right dorsolateral prefrontal cortex and decreases the rostral prefrontal cortex activation after-8 weeks of focused attention based mindfulness meditation. *Brain Cogn.* 102:46–54

van Vugt MK. 2015. Cognitive benefits of mindfulness meditation. See Brown et al. 2015, pp. 190–207

Visted E, Vøllestad J, Nielsen MB, Nielsen GH. 2014. The impact of group-based mindfulness training on self-reported mindfulness: a systematic review and meta-analysis. *Mindfulness* 6(3):501–22

Vøllestad J, Nielsen MB, Nielsen GH. 2012. Mindfulness- and acceptance-based interventions for anxiety disorders: a systematic review and meta-analysis. *Br. J. Clin. Psychol.* 51(3):239–60

Walsh R, Roche L. 1979. Precipitation of acute psychotic episodes by intensive meditation in individuals with a history of schizophrenia. *Am. J. Psychiatry* 136:1085–86

Westbrook C, Creswell JD, Tabibnia G, Julson E, Kober H, Tindle HA. 2013. Mindful attention reduces neural and self-reported cue-induced craving in smokers. *Soc. Cogn. Affect. Neurosci.* 8:73–74

Williams M, Crane C, Barnhofer T, Brennan K, Duggan DS, et al. 2014. Mindfulness-based cognitive therapy for preventing relapse in recurrent depression: a randomized dismantling trial. *J. Consult. Clin. Psychol.* 82(2):275–86

A large RCT showing that a classroom-based mindfulness intervention can improve outcomes in at-risk children.

A comprehensive integrative review of the neuroscience of mindfulness meditation interventions.

The first RCT to show that MBCT can reduce depression relapse in at-risk individuals.

Wilson BM, Mickes L, Stolarz-Fantino S, Evrard M, Fantino E. 2015. Increased false-memory susceptibility after mindfulness meditation. *Psychol. Sci.* 26(10):1567–73

Wilson TD, Reinhard DA, Westgate EC, Gilbert DT, Ellerbeck N, et al. 2014. Just think: the challenges of the disengaged mind. *Science* 345(6192):75–77

Witkiewitz K, Bowen S. 2010. Depression, craving and substance use following a randomized trial of mindfulness-based relapse prevention. *J. Consult. Clin. Psychol.* 78(3):362–74

Witkiewitz K, Warner K, Sully B, Barricks A, Stauffer C, et al. 2014. Randomized trial comparing mindfulness-based relapse prevention with relapse prevention for women offenders at a residential addiction treatment center. *Subst. Use Misuse* 49(5):536–46

Zautra AJ, Davis MC, Reich JW, Nicassario P, Tennen H, et al. 2008. Comparison of cognitive behavioral and mindfulness meditation interventions on adaptation to rheumatoid arthritis for patients with and without history of recurrent depression. *J. Consult. Clin. Psychol.* 76(3):408–21

Zeidan F, Emerson NM, Farris SR, Ray JN, Jung Y, et al. 2015. Mindfulness meditation-based pain relief employs different neural mechanisms than placebo and sham mindfulness meditation-induced analgesia. *J. Neurosci.* 35(46):15307–25

Zeidan F, Johnson SK, Diamond BJ, David Z, Goolkasian P. 2010a. Mindfulness meditation improves cognition: evidence of brief mental training. *Conscious. Cogn.* 19(2):597–605

Zeidan F, Johnson SK, Gordon NS, Goolkasian P. 2010b. Effects of brief and sham mindfulness meditation on mood and cardiovascular variables. *J. Altern. Complement. Med.* 16(8):867–73

Zeidan F, Martucci KT, Kraft RA, Gordon NS, McHaffie JG, Coghill RC. 2011. Brain mechanisms supporting the modulation of pain by mindfulness meditation. *J. Neurosci.* 31(14):5540–48

Zenner C, Herrnleben-Kurz S, Walach H. 2013. Mindfulness-based interventions in schools—a systematic review and meta-analysis. *Front. Psychol.* 5:603

Hidden Wounds? Inflammatory Links Between Childhood Trauma and Psychopathology

Andrea Danese[1,2,3] and Jessie R. Baldwin[1]

[1]MRC Social, Genetic, and Developmental Psychiatry Research Centre, Institute of Psychiatry, Psychology and Neuroscience, Kings College London, London SE5 8AF, United Kingdom; email: andrea.danese@kcl.ac.uk

[2]Department of Child and Adolescent Psychiatry, Institute of Psychiatry, Psychology and Neuroscience, King's College London, London SE5 8AF, United Kingdom

[3]National and Specialist Clinic for Child Traumatic Stress and Anxiety Disorders, South London and Maudsley NHS Foundation Trust, London SE5 8AZ, United Kingdom

Annu. Rev. Psychol. 2017. 68:517–44

First published online as a Review in Advance on August 17, 2016

The *Annual Review of Psychology* is online at psych.annualreviews.org

This article's doi: 10.1146/annurev-psych-010416-044208

Keywords

childhood trauma, maltreatment, psychopathology, psychiatric disorders, inflammation, immunity

Abstract

Childhood trauma is a key risk factor for psychopathology. However, little is known about how exposure to childhood trauma is translated into biological risk for psychopathology. Observational human studies and experimental animal models suggest that childhood exposure to stress can trigger an enduring systemic inflammatory response not unlike the bodily response to physical injury. In turn, these "hidden wounds" of childhood trauma can affect brain development, key behavioral domains (e.g., cognition, positive valence systems, negative valence systems), reactivity to subsequent stressors, and, ultimately, risk for psychopathology. Further research is needed to better characterize the inflammatory links between childhood trauma and psychopathology. Detecting and healing these hidden wounds may help prevent and treat psychopathology emerging after childhood trauma.

Contents

INTRODUCTION

The word trauma comes from the ancient Greek word for wound (τραύμα) related to physical injury. It was only in the late nineteenth century that the word trauma started to acquire a new metaphorical meaning in popular culture. During the Industrial Revolution, Victorian surgeons became puzzled by psychological and physical symptoms appearing in victims of railway accidents who did not have apparent physical wounds (Erichsen 1867). The origins of the symptoms then known collectively as railway spine were hotly debated. The leading German neurologist Hermann Oppenheim suggested that symptoms were caused by undetectable physical damage to the spine or brain (Holdorff 2011). In contrast to this organic explanation and in light of the high prevalence of histories of childhood abuse noted among patients with unexplained somatic and emotional complaints (Briquet 1859), the leading French neurologists Jean-Martin Charcot and Pierre Janet theorized that the symptoms were caused by the idea of the trauma—the subjective perception of intensely distressing experiences—which triggered psychological and physical manifestations (hysteria) (Micale 1995). The Austrian psychiatrist Sigmund Freud further developed Charcot and Janet's psychological theory and popularized the notion that intensely distressing experiences—psychological traumas (and particularly those occurring in childhood)—could have significant impact on psychological development and psychopathology (Freud 1962).

   The influence of such psychological theories (and the later psychoanalytical focus on imagined experiences or fantasies as triggers of hysteria) was so profound that trauma research was long dominated by intrapsychic explanatory models. Although these models have undeniably advanced the psychological understanding of the response to psychological trauma, they have also created significant misunderstandings regarding the nature of many of the resulting symptoms and, at times, a culture of blame. Biological theories on psychological trauma, and particularly childhood trauma, have progressively emerged from experimental animal studies revealing how the body adapts to psychosocial stress (Selye 1936), how peripheral biological mediators of the stress response affect the brain (McEwen et al. 1968), and how the development of the biological response to stress is profoundly shaped by early life stressors (Levine et al. 1957).

In this review, we propose that the links between psychological and physical traumas are not, as it is commonly assumed, only metaphorical. Psychological trauma can trigger similar biological responses as physical trauma (Molina 2005), including the activation of the innate immune system. In particular, we discuss how childhood psychological trauma could affect the development of the innate immune system and thus induce a chronically activated and hyperreactive inflammatory response starting in childhood and persisting into adult life. In turn, elevated inflammation can influence brain development and functioning, thereby impacting the risk for psychopathology. Finally, we suggest that these "hidden wounds" caused by childhood psychological trauma have important clinical and treatment implications.

CHILDHOOD TRAUMA AND PSYCHOPATHOLOGY

Observational Studies in Humans

Much of what we know about childhood trauma comes from investigations of the consequences of childhood maltreatment, a prototypical form of severe and chronic interpersonal stress that includes sexual, physical, and emotional abuse as well as physical and emotional neglect. This prevalent form of childhood trauma affects up to one in five children in high-income countries worldwide and has been consistently associated with heightened risk of mental and physical illness in later life (Gilbert et al. 2009b). Childhood maltreatment predicts both high incidence and poor longitudinal course of several psychiatric disorders. For example, individuals with a history of childhood maltreatment have high lifetime risk of major depression, as well as an earlier age of onset and greater comorbidity (Brown & Harris 1978, Kessler et al. 1997). This link is unlikely to be explained by biased retrospective reports of individuals who were depressed at the time of maltreatment assessment because the retrospective findings are consistent with findings based on official records and prospective measures of maltreatment collected in childhood (Danese et al. 2009). Furthermore, this is also unlikely to be explained by the effects of genetic confounding because the high risk of depression in maltreated individuals was also observed within twin-pairs, that is, differences in depression risk were detected between individuals with the same or similar genes but different sexual abuse histories (Kendler et al. 2000). In addition to the elevated lifetime risk of depression, maltreated individuals with depression often show an unfavorable course of illness characterized by recurrent and persistent episodes (Nanni et al. 2012), which accounts for the largest health burden due to depression. Furthermore, individuals with a history of childhood maltreatment are at high risk of poor response to conventional antidepressant treatment and in particular to combined pharmacological and psychological treatment (Nanni et al. 2012). A history of childhood maltreatment is also highly prevalent in patients with bipolar disorder and, among bipolar patients, predicts unfavorable course of illness and clinical features such as greater severity of manic, depressive, and psychotic symptoms; higher risk of comorbid anxiety disorders and of substance or alcohol use disorders; earlier age of onset; higher risk of rapid cycling; greater number of manic and depressive episodes; and higher risk of suicide attempts (Agnew-Blais & Danese 2016). Childhood maltreatment predicts a heightened incidence of psychotic disorders, including schizophrenia, in later life (Varese et al. 2012). Furthermore, childhood maltreatment is associated with increased risk for incident posttraumatic stress disorder (PTSD) (Widom 1999) and is thought to be related to more complex presentation among patients with PTSD, with symptoms including emotional dysregulation, poor self-concept, and disturbed relationships (complex PTSD) (Maercker et al. 2013).

PTSD: posttraumatic stress disorder

IQ: intelligence quotient

Experimental Studies in Animal Models

In addition to observational studies in humans, experimental studies in animal models have shown that early-life exposure to stressful experiences can cause significant emotional and behavioral abnormalities later in life. Despite the biological and theoretical limitations of using proxy models for human experiences, brain functioning, or behavior (van der Worp et al. 2010), these experimental studies are uniquely placed to address causal inference because of their ability to manipulate the environment and to randomly assign animals to experiences. This is important because individual risk factors of the child and parents, family risk factors, and community risk factors are all associated with increased risk of childhood traumas such as maltreatment (Danese & McCrory 2015). Many of these risk factors [e.g., low intelligence quotient (IQ), family history of mental illness] also predict later psychopathology. These correlated risk factors represent alternative explanations for the link between childhood trauma and later psychopathology and need to be ruled out before inference of causal effects can be drawn (Duncan et al. 2004). Therefore, by manipulating early life experiences independent of the features of individual animals, experimental models can identify unbiased or causal effects of early-life stress. Although experimental studies have stronger internal validity than observational studies, generalization of causal inference from the narrow context of the experiment to the life of living humans requires demonstration (or assumption) that the experiences and physiology in animal models are similar to those of humans (i.e., external or ecological validity).

Building on the pioneering clinical observations of Spitz (1945) and Bowlby (1951) on the effects of maternal separation on psychological development and psychopathology, experimental models in rodents (Francis et al. 1999, Levine et al. 1956) and nonhuman primates (Harlow et al. 1965, Hinde & Spencer-Booth 1971, Sánchez et al. 2001, Suomi 1997) have shown that early-life stress owing to maternal separation or poor maternal care can negatively impact emotional and behavioral development and, thus, impair psychological functioning. Typically, animals experimentally exposed to early-life stress show greater behavioral despair and learned helplessness (depressive-like symptoms measured, for example, through a forced swimming test or tail suspension test in rodents) (Cryan & Holmes 2005), more avoidance behaviors (anxiety-like symptoms measured, for example, through an elevated plus maze or light/dark exploration test) (Cryan & Holmes 2005), and abnormal fear conditioning. Although the effects of experimentally induced early-life stress can vary based on the protocol used and the age and gender of the animals, the overall results of these experimental studies suggest a causal role of early-life stress in later psychopathology.

How Does Childhood Trauma Affect Psychopathology?

Several studies have explored the biological mechanisms underlying the clinical association between childhood trauma and psychopathology. Most of these studies have focused on testing differences in brain and hormonal function between individuals with a history of childhood maltreatment and those without.

Childhood trauma and the brain. To understand how childhood trauma affects the risk of psychopathology, several studies have tested the association of childhood trauma (often assessed through retrospective recall) with neuropsychological tests scores and structural or functional brain imaging measures. A detailed description of brain abnormalities associated with childhood trauma is beyond the scope of this review; several comprehensive reviews can be consulted for more information (Danese & McEwen 2012, Lim et al. 2014, Lupien et al. 2009, McCrory et al. 2010, Nusslock & Miller 2016, Teicher & Samson 2016, Tottenham & Sheridan 2009). The findings in this area can be summarized using the Research Domain Criteria (RDoC) framework (Insel 2014, Kaufman et al. 2015). Brain function abnormalities associated with childhood trauma include, but are not limited to, changes in the domains of cognition, positive valence, and negative valence.

With regard to cognition, childhood maltreatment has been associated with small-to-moderate and pervasive cognitive impairment. Individuals with a history of childhood maltreatment have lower IQ and poorer declarative memory and executive function than individuals with no history of childhood maltreatment (Pechtel & Pizzagalli 2011). Similar cognitive impairment has been described in animals experimentally exposed to early-life stress (Brunson et al. 2005). Deficits in declarative memory may be related to the macroscopic (smaller hippocampal volume) (Danese & McEwen 2012) and microscopic (impaired adult neurogenesis) (Mirescu et al. 2004) hippocampal abnormalities found in adult animals and humans exposed to early-life stress. Furthermore, deficits in executive function may be related to functional or structural prefrontal cortex abnormalities (Danese & McEwen 2012).

With regard to positive valence, childhood maltreatment has been associated with impaired reward processing. Human studies showed that individuals with a history of childhood maltreatment may be less sensitive to reward, as indicated by blunted subjective responses to reward-predicting cues and blunted activation in the basal ganglia during reward anticipation (Dillon et al. 2009, Guyer et al. 2006, Mehta et al. 2010). Consistent with these findings in humans, animals experimentally exposed to early-life stress showed attenuated sucrose preference and attenuated behavioral responses (self-administration) to powerful artificial reinforcers, such as intravenous cocaine or intra-accumbens amphetamine (Matthews & Robbins 2003, Phillips et al. 1994, Pryce et al. 2004).

With regard to negative valence, childhood maltreatment has been associated with heightened threat perception. Compared to nonmaltreated individuals, those with a history of maltreatment have biased perceptual representations of emotions and tend to overidentify threat signals, such as angry faces (Leppänen & Nelson 2009, Pollak & Kistler 2002). Individuals with a history of maltreatment showed selective heightened amygdala activation in response to angry faces, even when these stimuli were presented preattentively (McCrory et al. 2013, Tottenham et al. 2011, van Harmelen et al. 2013), possibly as a result of impaired functional coupling between the subgenual anterior cingulate cortex (sACC) and the amygdala (Herringa et al. 2013). Consistent with findings in humans, animal studies have highlighted the crucial contribution of the early social environment to amygdala development and functioning (e.g., Moriceau & Sullivan 2006).

Childhood trauma and the neuroendocrine response to stress. Although the link between childhood trauma and brain abnormalities provides biological plausibility for the clinical effects described in the previous section, it does not inform about the underlying biological processes that might have triggered changes in the brain and behavior. Studies of proximal biological processes have traditionally focused on abnormalities and changes in the physiology of the hypothalamic-pituitary-adrenal (HPA) axis (Danese & McEwen 2012, Gunnar & Quevedo 2007, Heim & Nemeroff 2001, Lupien et al. 2009). These studies have stemmed from preclinical findings showing that the HPA axis is a key neuroendocrine pathway involved in the biological adaptation to stress (Selye 1936); that peripheral and central HPA axis mediators affect brain function (McEwen et al. 1968); and that early life experiences can significantly shape the development of the HPA axis and, thus, affect its functioning across the life span (Levine et al. 1957). In humans, studies of children

HPA: hypothalamic-pituitary-adrenal

CRH: corticotrophin-releasing hormone

ACTH: adrenocorticotropic hormone

have shown that the experience of maltreatment is associated with chronic activation of the HPA axis. For example, maltreated children with significant emotional problems showed higher average daily cortisol levels across 1 week (Cicchetti & Rogosch 2001). Similarly, maltreated children with PTSD showed higher 24-h urinary free cortisol and daily salivary cortisol levels compared to a healthy comparison group with no maltreatment history (Carrion et al. 2002, De Bellis et al. 1999). Studies of adults reporting a history of maltreatment found consistent results, including evidence of high corticotrophin-releasing hormone (CRH) levels in the cerebrospinal fluid (Carpenter et al. 2004), greater adrenocorticotropic hormone (ACTH) and cortisol response to a laboratory-based acute psychosocial stress test (Heim et al. 2000), and greater ACTH and cortisol response to a pharmacological challenge with the dexamethasone/CRH test (Heim et al. 2008). These human studies highlight that maltreated individuals have elevated baseline cortisol levels and heightened cortisol reactivity in the context of new stressors. HPA axis hyperactivity may emerge as a compensatory mechanism for primary abnormalities due to insufficient functioning of glucocorticoid receptor–mediated signaling, also known as insufficient glucocorticoid signaling. Consistent with the results of human studies, findings from experimental animal models have shown that early-life stress is associated with altered methylation of the glucocorticoid receptor gene, which is linked to insufficient glucocorticoid signaling (Weaver et al. 2004).

Elevated cortisol levels during early development may have toxic effects on brain development and, thus, have long-term effects on brain function and behavior (Danese & McEwen 2012, Gunnar & Quevedo 2007, Heim & Nemeroff 2001, Lupien et al. 2009). Certain brain areas could be more sensitive to the effects of glucocorticoids and, consequently, more likely to be modified by high levels of glucocorticoids. In particular, high levels of cortisol have been associated with shrinkage of the hippocampus and the prefrontal cortex and with hypertrophy and hypermetabolism of the amygdala. Through these direct effects on the brain, high glucocorticoid levels could have long-term effects on the domains of cognition, positive affect, and negative affect described in the previous section (Danese & McEwen 2012, Gunnar & Quevedo 2007, Heim & Nemeroff 2001, Lupien et al. 2009).

Some thought-provoking new interpretations of these findings highlight the role of the links between the HPA axis systems and other stress-sensitive systems, such as the immune system, in shaping trajectories of brain development. On the one hand, the insufficient glucocorticoid signaling found in individuals with a history of childhood maltreatment could bring about systemic inflammation (Heim et al. 2000, Miller et al. 2002, Raison & Miller 2003). In turn, by affecting the immune system, glucocorticoids could exert significant indirect effects on brain development and functioning. On the other hand, inflammation could trigger HPA axis activation (Besedovsky et al. 1986) and induce glucocorticoid resistance (Barnes & Adcock 2009), thereby potentially acting as the original trigger for neuroendocrine abnormalities. The two-way interaction between the HPA axis and inflammation suggests the need for more complex explanatory models for the effects of childhood trauma on the brain and behavior. The potential involvement of the immune system in brain development and psychopathology is described in the following sections.

INFLAMMATION AND PSYCHOPATHOLOGY

Observational Studies in Humans

The association between inflammation and psychopathology has arguably been best illustrated in the case of major depression (Miller & Raison 2015). Initial conceptualizations of this link emerged from the observations that experimental administration of proinflammatory cytokines produces a clinical response resembling major depression (the macrophage theory of depression)

(Smith 1991) and that immune cell profiling of depressed patients is characterized by systemic immune activation (Maes et al. 1992). In response to these observations, several clinical and population studies have measured cytokines and other proinflammatory mediators in depressed individuals and controls. Meta-analysis of these cross-sectional studies suggests that depression is characterized by a small elevation in circulating levels of inflammation biomarkers (Howren et al. 2009). Longitudinal studies suggest that group differences are likely to result from bidirectional associations between depression and inflammation over time (e.g., Matthews et al. 2010). Notably, high inflammation predicts not only the risk of incident depression but also of poor response to treatment (Strawbridge et al. 2015) and an unfavorable course of illness characterized by recurrent episodes (Ford & Erlinger 2004).

CRP: C-reactive protein
LPS: lipopolysaccharide
IL: interleukin

High levels of circulating inflammation biomarkers have also been found in patients with bipolar disorder. Meta-analytical studies show that bipolar disorder is associated with small to moderate elevation in proinflammatory cytokines (Modabbernia et al. 2013) and C-reactive protein (CRP) (Dargél et al. 2015). Elevation in CRP and in some proinflammatory cytokines is also present in euthymic phases. On the basis of these findings, bipolar disorder is increasingly seen as a multisystem inflammatory disease (Leboyer et al. 2012) in which inflammation contributes to the onset of illness as well as its progression (Berk et al. 2011).

The immune contribution to schizophrenia etiopathogenesis has been investigated for over a century (Khandaker et al. 2015). A meta-analytical investigation has shown that circulating levels of proinflammatory cytokines are moderately elevated in patients with both chronic psychosis and first-episode psychosis (Miller et al. 2011). Furthermore, high baseline levels of inflammation predict poor treatment response in first-episode psychosis patients (Mondelli et al. 2015).

Proinflammatory mediators may also play a role in the symptoms of patients with PTSD. Meta-analytical studies show that PTSD patients have a moderate to large elevation in levels of several proinflammatory cytokines, that these associations are not explained by comorbid depression, and that inflammation is related to illness duration (Passos et al. 2015). Genetic (Michopoulos et al. 2015) and longitudinal (Eraly et al. 2014) studies suggest that inflammation is a preexisting vulnerability factor for the development of PTSD in trauma-exposed individuals.

These findings highlight the transdiagnostic links between inflammation and psychopathology. Despite this evidence, published studies have often been based on a case-control design focused on single diagnoses. Notably, this design does not allow a critical evaluation of the nonspecific links between inflammation and psychopathology and may cause overestimation of the unique contribution of inflammation to single diagnoses. Furthermore, this design is unsuitable for the evaluation of the direction of effects or for the comprehensive assessment of potential confounding factors. Therefore, it is important to consider findings from these observational studies alongside results from experimental studies.

Experimental Studies in Animal Models and Humans

Experimental studies in animal models and humans suggest causal effects of inflammation on affective symptoms and disorders. This research began with the recognition that the onset of febrile infectious diseases was linked to a stereotypical pattern of behaviors in animals and humans that was characterized by lethargy, depression, anorexia, and reduction in grooming (Hart 1988). This sickness behavior was recognized as an organized, evolved behavioral strategy to facilitate the role of fever in combating viral and bacterial infections. Building on this initial theory, pharmacological experiments have been undertaken by manipulating an organism's inflammatory state through systemic or central administration of bacterial cell components [e.g., lipopolysaccharide (LPS), also known as endotoxin] or proinflammatory cytokines [e.g., interleukin (IL)-1β and tumor necrosis factor (TNF)-α]. These experiments reproduced sickness behavior in animal models, with symptoms including decreased motor activity (fatigue), social withdrawal, reduced food and water intake, increased slow-wave sleep, and altered cognition (Dantzer et al. 2008). Furthermore, consistent with the role of inflammation in these phenomena, the expression of sickness behavior after LPS stimulation was buffered by administration of the anti-inflammatory cytokine IL-10 and exacerbated in IL-10-deficient mice (Dantzer et al. 2008). Similar findings are now accumulating in humans.

Several experimental studies in humans have tested behavioral changes induced by different proinflammatory compounds. A set of early studies looked at inflammation-related changes in mood and behavior among patients with hepatitis C or cancer that were treated with the proinflammatory cytokine interferon (IFN)-α and were free of depression prior to the beginning of the trial. About half of patients treated with IFN-α developed depressive disorder within weeks of the start of treatment, whereas nearly all treated patients developed neurovegetative symptoms including anorexia, fatigue, psychomotor retardation, and disrupted sleep (Musselman et al. 2001). Consistent with the effects of chronic treatment with IFN-α, acute administration of proinflammatory mediators, such as typhoid vaccination and LPS, can also induce transient depressive-like symptoms (Reichenberg et al. 2001).

Not only can proinflammatory compounds induce depression, but anti-inflammatory medications can have antidepressant effects. A recent meta-analysis of 10 trials with nonsteroidal anti-inflammatory drugs and four trials with cytokine inhibitors found small to moderate antidepressant effects (Köhler et al. 2014). Notably, the meta-analysis also found significant heterogeneity in the effect sizes across trials (Köhler et al. 2014). This latter meta-analytical finding was reinforced by a clinical trial with a potent anti-inflammatory monoclonal antibody that specifically inhibits TNF-α function, commonly known as infliximab (Raison et al. 2013). Treatment with infliximab was not effective overall in a group of treatment-resistant depressed patients. However, infliximab treatment showed some therapeutic effect in the subgroup of depressed patients with high baseline inflammation levels (Raison et al. 2013). These findings highlight the complexity of depression pathophysiology and suggest that inflammation may be an important etiological factor in a large subgroup of depressed patients. Evidence of the treatment effects of anti-inflammatory intervention in other psychiatric conditions is more limited and indirect. For example, a 12-week, randomized, double-blind, placebo-controlled trial of omega-3 polyunsaturated fatty acids, which have complex physiological properties including anti-inflammatory effects, found a reduction in both the risk of progression to psychotic disorders and in psychiatric morbidity over a 7-year follow-up in young people with subthreshold psychotic states (Amminger et al. 2015).

How Does Inflammation Affect Psychopathology?

To complement these clinical studies, much research has focused on the molecular and cellular mechanisms through which inflammation could influence psychopathology. An important discovery in this area came from the evidence that the traditional view that the brain has immune privilege, meaning that the brain is both immunologically inert and immunologically separated from the peripheral immune system, was incorrect (Galea et al. 2007). Researchers increasingly appreciate that the brain immune system actively contributes to normal brain functioning (Yirmiya & Goshen 2011) and that the brain is connected with the peripheral immune system (Dantzer et al. 2008).

The brain immune system and normal brain functioning. The brain has an active immune system that contributes both to surveillance against pathogens and to tissue remodeling.

Consistent with the effects of immunity in other parts of the body, immune activity (and particularly innate immune activity, or neuroinflammation) can be either beneficial or detrimental depending on the level of activation. Low-level activation of the innate immune system in the brain is vital to support tissue remodeling, including molecular (long-term potentiation) and cellular (neurogenesis) mechanisms of brain plasticity. However, both deficient neuroinflammation (e.g., due to immune deficiency or genetic or pharmacological manipulation) and exaggerated neuroinflammation (e.g., due to inflammatory or infectious disorders or, to a lesser extent, psychosocial stress) are associated with symptoms of impaired brain function, such as poor learning and memory (Yirmiya & Goshen 2011). The brain immune system includes specialized cells, such as microglia and T cells, and molecules, such as cytokines.

BBB: blood–brain barrier

CSF: cerebrospinal fluid

BDNF: brain-derived neurotrophic factor

Microglia are macrophage-like cells of myeloid hematopoietic origin that colonize the brain parenchyma during early embryonic development and self-renew locally thereafter (Hanisch & Kettenmann 2007). Microglia continuously scan the surrounding extracellular space for signals of cellular damage or infection. Resting-state microglia play important roles in normal adult brain function, including repairing microdamages [small ischemic events or blood–brain barrier (BBB) lesions], cleaning up cellular debris and inactive or dysfunctional synaptic structures (with overall anti-inflammatory effects), and supporting neurogenesis. In contrast, upon detection of pathogens or inflammatory signals, activated microglia respond by eliminating triggering stimuli through phagocytosis and by producing proinflammatory cytokines, prostaglandins, free radicals, and other mediators. These molecules are helpful in neutralizing a variety of pathogens but can also have neurotoxic effects and suppress neurogenesis.

T cells are cells of lymphoid hematopoietic origin that can migrate to the cerebrospinal fluid (CSF), where they are separated from the brain parenchyma only by the pia mater (in the subarachnoid space) (Kipnis et al. 2012). This vantage point enables T cells to monitor and respond to signals released from the brain into the CSF. T cells, and particularly those that are reactive against brain self-antigens, play a supportive role in learning and memory by stimulating adult neurogenesis. Upon encountering relevant self-antigens, autoreactive T cells produce cytokines (e.g., IL-4) that promote the expression of brain-derived neurotrophic factor (BDNF) by astrocytes and suppress proinflammatory activity in meningeal and parenchymal myeloid cells, including microglia. In contrast, upon detection of pathogens or inflammatory signals, T cells trigger a protective immune response that may have detrimental consequences for brain function.

Cytokines can be produced in the brain by resident cells, including microglia and T cells, in response to local stimuli. Peripheral cytokines can also accumulate in the brain through BBB leaks and the signaling pathways described below (see the following section). Low levels of proinflammatory cytokines support brain plasticity (Yirmiya & Goshen 2011). In particular, low levels of IL-1 play an important role in hippocampus-dependent learning and memory processes, presumably by supporting the induction and maintenance of long-term potentiation. In contrast, high levels of proinflammatory cytokines potentiate neuroinflammation and neurotoxicity, reduce monoaminergic transmission (e.g., by reducing the availability of the precursors or increasing reuptake by presynaptic transporters), stimulate glutamate transmission (e.g., by stimulating glutamate release and inhibiting glutamate reuptake in astrocytes), stimulate the HPA axis–mediated neuroendocrine stress response (with resulting insufficient glucocorticoid signaling after chronic stimulation), inhibit the secretion of BDNF and nerve growth factor, and inhibit cholinergic transmission (Dantzer et al. 2008, Yirmiya & Goshen 2011).

Links between the peripheral immune system and the brain immune system. In the same way that the brain monitors and responds to the external environment and the status of internal organs, it also monitors and responds to the immune system through at least five different pathways

(Dantzer et al. 2008). The neural pathway involves the activation of the afferent fibers of the vagus nerve or the trigeminal nerve by peripherally produced cytokines. The humoral pathway involves the crossing of circulating cytokines into the brain where the BBB is permeable (e.g., the area postrema). The transmembrane pathway involves active transport of cytokines (IL-6, IL-1, TNF-α) through the BBB via saturable carriers. The signal transduction pathway involves stimulation by circulating cytokines of cell surface receptors on astrocytes and on the brain endothelial cells that form the BBB, which, in turn, triggers cytokine production by these cells. Finally, the cellular pathway involves minimal passage of dendritic cells, leukocytes, and lymphocytes via gaps in the epithelial lining of the BBB, the circumventricular organs, and the choroid plexus. Through these pathways, peripheral inflammation can induce neuroinflammation (Dantzer et al. 2008, Perry et al. 2003). For example, peripheral administration of LPS in rodents induces the expression of proinflammatory cytokines in the brain (Breder et al. 1994), the activation of microglia (Monje et al. 2003), and the inhibition of adult neurogenesis (Monje et al. 2003).

The peripheral immune system and abnormal brain functioning. Because the peripheral immune system can affect neuroinflammation, peripheral immune activation can have significant effects on brain functioning. Notably, LPS-induced systemic inflammation affects several domains of brain functioning in humans (Schedlowski et al. 2014). With regard to cognition, peripheral administration of LPS reduces verbal and nonverbal memory functions in humans (Reichenberg et al. 2001). With regard to positive valence systems, peripheral administration of LPS (and also of typhoid vaccine and IFN-α) reduces ventral striatum responses to reward (Capuron et al. 2012, Eisenberger et al. 2010). With regard to negative valence systems, peripheral administration of LPS potentiates amygdala activity in response to socially threatening stimuli (fear faces) (Inagaki et al. 2012), and typhoid vaccine reduces the connectivity of the sACC to the amygdala and increases the activity within the sACC during emotional face processing (Harrison et al. 2009). The specificity of the effects of systemic inflammation on these brain functions is likely due to several factors including the different density of cytokine receptors and different sensitivity to changes in monoamine metabolism in different brain areas. In turn, abnormalities in cognition, reward processing, and threat processing are important putative mediators for the effect of systemic inflammation on behavior.

Long-term effects of early-life immune activation on the brain and behavior. In addition to the broad effect of acute immune stimulation on concurrent measures of brain functioning, immune stimulation during early development can have enduring effects on the brain and behavior. For example, experimental studies found that infection (e.g., by the influenza virus or *Escherichia coli*) and systemic inflammation [e.g., due to synthetic RNA poly(I:C) or LPS] during prenatal or neonatal periods led to stable, long-term impairments in cognition, including deficits in learning, memory, and attention, in rodents (Bilbo & Schwarz 2009, Knuesel et al. 2014, Patterson 2009) and nonhuman primates (Short et al. 2010). Consistent with the evidence in experimental animal models, observational studies in humans have found a link between early-life infection and risks of later neurodevelopmental disorders. For example, some studies, although not all, found an association between prenatal exposure to infection and increased risk of schizophrenia (Khandaker et al. 2013, Mednick et al. 1988) and autism (Atladóttir et al. 2010, Deykin & MacMahon 1979). Furthermore, high levels of systemic inflammation in childhood have been associated with an increased risk of developing depression and psychosis in young adulthood (Khandaker et al. 2014). There are several ways in which early-life immune activation can induce these detrimental effects on the brain, including direct impact on brain development, priming of resident immune cells, and programming of the neuroendocrine response to stress.

The immune system and brain development. The immune system is critical to several aspects of brain development. Although the immune system significantly affects prenatal brain development processes, such as cell proliferation and migration, these effects are beyond the scope of this review and are detailed elsewhere (Boulanger 2009). More relevant to childhood, the immune system also profoundly affects postnatal brain development processes, such as synaptogenesis, synaptic refinement, myelination, and adult neurogenesis (Boulanger 2009). First, synaptogenesis is the formation of synapses between neurons in the nervous system, which begins during fetal life (second trimester) and continues into adulthood. The chemokine CXCL12 and its receptor, CXCR4, regulate axonal elongation and branching and axon pathfinding by modulating neuronal responses to axon guidance cues (e.g., Slit-2, semaphorin 3A, and semaphorin 3C) (Chalasani et al. 2003). Second, synaptic refinement is the activity-dependent modulation of synaptic strength and survival that takes place after birth. Microglia and astrocytes can sense the overall neuronal activity levels and make compensatory changes in synaptic strength by secreting TNF-α. Low synaptic activity induces secretion of TNF-α, which promotes the surface expression of glutamate receptors in neurons, increasing excitability and, thus, synaptic strength (a process known as synaptic scaling). Furthermore, the surface expression of the major histocompatibility complex class I (MHC-I) is necessary for the regulation of both basal synaptic transmission and acute synaptic plasticity. Another activity-dependent mechanism that regulates synaptic survival involves the expression of complement proteins C1q and C3 by synapses that are inactive. Microglia recognize and phagocytize the complement-tagged synapses, thus eliminating them (synaptic pruning) (Boulanger 2009). Third, myelination is the production of myelin by oligodendrocytes, which begins during fetal life (third trimester) and continues into adulthood. Myelin forms an electrically insulating layer around axons to improve the transmission of electrical signals between cells. Microglia secrete proinflammatory mediators and growth factors that are crucial for the survival and functioning of oligodendrocytes and, thus, myelin production (Peferoen et al. 2014). Finally, adult neurogenesis is the process of proliferation and differentiation of neural stem cells that takes place after birth and significantly affects learning and memory. This process can be significantly inhibited by inflammatory mediators in the context of systemic immune activation (Ekdahl et al. 2003, Monje et al. 2003) and can be potentiated by autoreactive T cells (Ziv et al. 2006). Because of these critical effects of the immune system on brain development, postnatal early-life immune activation involving disruption of these fine-tuned processes could exert direct, long-term influence on the brain and behavior. Furthermore, it is possible that early-life immune activation could exert indirect influence by modifying the reactivity of immune cells and the neuroendocrine response to later stimuli.

Early-life immune activation and glial priming. Immune activation in early life can induce long-term functional changes in the microglia. Acute inflammatory stimuli can not only activate microglia (see the section The Brain Immune System and Normal Brain Functioning) but also prime them to show a greater response in the face of subsequent inflammatory stimulation. Compared to rodents with naïve microglia, rodents with primed microglia show heightened production of proinflammatory cytokines in the brain, increased neurotoxicity, and exaggerated fever and sickness behavior in response to subsequent inflammatory stimulation (Perry & Holmes 2014). These priming effects are induced by direct morphological changes and upregulation of cell-surface antigens on glial cells. Furthermore, priming could be due to loss or downregulation of neuronal ligands that inhibit priming or to a reduction in the inhibitory effect of glucocorticoids (see the following section) (Frank et al. 2013, Perry & Holmes 2014). Notably, the long-term priming effects described after early-life exposure to systemic immune activation suggest the potential existence of sensitive periods for microglia priming (Bilbo & Schwarz 2009, Knuesel et al. 2014).

Early-life immune activation and hypothalamic pituitary adrenal axis reactivity. In addition to effects directly mediated by the immune system, early-life immune activation also induces long-term changes in other stress-sensitive systems, such as the HPA axis. Acute immune stimulation elicits activation of both central catecholamines and the HPA axis similar to that seen following stress (Besedovsky et al. 1986, Dunn 2006). Notably, there may be sensitive periods for the programming of HPA axis function by immunity. Research in rodents has shown that early-life immune stimulation with LPS was associated with elevated levels of CRH, greater ACTH and corticosterone responses to restraint stress, decreased negative feedback sensitivity to glucocorticoids, and a reduction in glucocorticoid receptor density across the brain in adult animals (Shanks et al. 1995, 2000). Because these abnormalities in HPA functioning are hallmarks of affective disorders (Pariante & Miller 2001), the immune programming of the HPA axis system could contribute to the effects of early-life immune stimulation on psychopathology.

CHILDHOOD TRAUMA AND INFLAMMATION

Observational Studies in Humans

Because of the association of childhood trauma with abnormal brain and behavioral functioning and the comparable effects of early-life immune activation on these outcomes, we became interested in directly testing the association between childhood trauma and innate immunity in later life. We initially investigated this association in the Dunedin Multidisciplinary Health and Development Study, a birth cohort of 1,037 children born in Dunedin, New Zealand, in 1972–1973 (Danese et al. 2007). Study members had been followed from birth until adulthood through repeated waves of assessment. Crucially, this enabled a longitudinal-prospective assessment of maltreatment experiences as study members grew up, resulting in a cumulative measure of childhood maltreatment that included indicators of maternal rejection, harsh discipline, disruptive caregiver changes, physical abuse, and sexual abuse. We found that cumulative exposure to childhood maltreatment was associated with significant and graded elevation in inflammation levels at the age-32 follow-up (Danese et al. 2007). The association was not sensitive to the particular measure of inflammation used but rather generalized to all inflammation biomarkers available, including CRP, fibrinogen, and white blood cell count, and was independent of key potential confounders, such as low birth weight, disadvantaged socioeconomic conditions of the family, and low IQ. Furthermore, the association was not explained by obvious mediators, such as adult stressors, poor adult health, and unhealthy behaviors, or acute infections at the time of inflammation assessment. Since these initial findings, the association between childhood trauma and adult inflammation has been tested in more than two dozen independent studies, and qualitative and quantitative reviews suggest small but pervasive elevation in inflammation biomarkers among maltreated compared to nonmaltreated individuals (Baumeister et al. 2015, Coelho et al. 2014). Immune abnormalities appeared to be associated not only with maltreatment by adults but also with bullying by peers (Takizawa et al. 2015). Furthermore, immune abnormalities may not be restricted to the innate immune system but may also generalize to impairment in the acquired immune system (Shirtcliff et al. 2009).

In addition to studying the long-term effects of childhood maltreatment, we were interested in testing whether the elevation in inflammation biomarkers in maltreated children was already detectable in childhood years, during sensitive periods of brain development. We investigated this association among a subset of 170 members of the Environmental-Risk (E-Risk) Longitudinal Twin Study, a birth cohort of 2,232 twins born in England and Wales in 1994–1995 (Danese et al. 2011). We compared a group of 12-year-old children for whom we had longitudinal-prospective evidence of maltreatment to a group of nonmaltreated children matched for sex, socioeconomic status, and zygosity. We found that inflammation levels (derived by measuring CRP in dried blood spots) were elevated in maltreated children who developed depression by age 12 compared to controls (Danese et al. 2011). These initial findings were supported and expanded by later studies showing that elevated inflammation levels were detectable among children exposed to adverse events in the first decade of life (Slopen et al. 2013) and among some children with a Child Protective Services–documented history of maltreatment (Cicchetti et al. 2015).

Individuals with a history of childhood maltreatment show not only elevated levels of unstimulated inflammation but also greater proinflammatory responses in the context of subsequent stressors. For example, individuals with a history of childhood maltreatment showed heightened inflammatory responses to a laboratory-based acute psychosocial stress test (Carpenter et al. 2010). Furthermore, maltreated individuals have greater inflammatory responses in the face of daily stressors and caregiving stress in later life (Gouin et al. 2012, Kiecolt-Glaser et al. 2011). Finally, depressed individuals with a history of childhood maltreatment show both elevated unstimulated inflammation levels (Danese et al. 2008) and greater inflammatory responses to acute psychosocial stress (Pace et al. 2006) compared to controls.

Experimental Studies in Animal Models

Experimental animal models have been used to strengthen causal inference for the link between childhood trauma and immune system abnormalities and to investigate more invasive measures of immune functioning. Evidence for the contribution of early experiences to immune development and function has been found in studies of rodents showing that rats handled before weaning showed a lower rate of development of transplanted tumors (Ader & Friedman 1965) and had greater serum antibody titer in response to flagellin, a protein derived from bacterial flagella (Solomon et al. 1968). Several subsequent investigations have explored the association between different types of early-life stressors and multiple immune measures in later life. A detailed account of all these findings is beyond the scope of this paper, but several comprehensive reviews can be consulted for more information (Ganguly & Brenhouse 2015, Hennessy et al. 2010a, Shanks & Lightman 2001). Results are mixed, reflecting, at least in part, the heterogeneity of stressors and immune system measures used. However, several papers have reported significant associations between maternal separation and inflammation. In nonhuman primates, maternal separation led to an immediate and prolonged increase in macrophage activity (Coe et al. 1988) and peer-rearing induced long-term upregulation in proinflammatory gene transcription in monocytes (Cole et al. 2012). In rodents, maternal separation led to an inflammation-mediated increase in core temperature (Hennessy et al. 2010b) and to an increase in proinflammatory cytokines in the plasma (Wieck et al. 2013).

In addition to elevation in peripheral inflammatory biomarkers, early-life stress has also been linked to markers of neuroinflammation. It is currently challenging to study neuroinflammation in humans because only comparatively nonspecific, expensive, and invasive methods, such as positron emission tomography (PET), exist (Bloomfield et al. 2016, Setiawan et al. 2015). However, this type of investigation is possible in experimental animal models, and initial findings suggest early-life stress has significant and potentially sexually dimorphic effects (Ganguly & Brenhouse 2015). Maternal separation is associated with blunted expression of proinflammatory mediators (such as LPS binding protein) in the hippocampus (Wei et al. 2012) and with reduced microglial cell numbers in midbrain areas (Chocyk et al. 2011) in rodent pups at a time when innate immunity is crucial for brain development. Furthermore, maternal separation is associated with greater hippocampal expression of receptors for proinflammatory cytokines (Viviani et al. 2014), greater number and motility of cortical microglial processes (Takatsuru et al. 2015), and greater microglia activation (Brenhouse & Thompson 2015).

Similar to the results of human studies, early-life stress in animal studies is associated not only with high unstimulated inflammation levels but also with greater proinflammatory responses in the context of subsequent stressors. In particular, rodents exposed to maternal separation showed a greater increase in core temperature upon a second separation (Hennessy et al. 2010b), greater cytokine expression in response to subsequent viral infection (Avitsur et al. 2006), and greater cortical microglial activation following subsequent exposure to chronic food-restriction stress (Brenhouse & Thompson 2015).

How Does Childhood Trauma Affect Inflammation?

Childhood trauma may become associated with elevated inflammation levels through several mechanisms, including both narrowly defined biological mechanisms and broader behavioral responses to trauma exposure. In addition, although experimental animal studies do not indicate that genetic factors play a significant role in the association between early-life stress and elevated inflammation levels, genetic influences may nevertheless be important in studies of humans who are not randomly allocated to childhood trauma and have greater genetic heterogeneity. These mechanisms are not mutually exclusive. However, the following sections highlight different mechanisms individually because they could potentially be independently targeted for secondary prevention in traumatized children or adults.

Biological mechanisms. Childhood trauma could be linked with innate immune abnormalities through several biological mechanisms. First, the more traditional view is that childhood trauma is indirectly linked to dysregulated innate immunity because of primary neuroendocrine abnormalities. This view builds on the established association between childhood trauma and HPA axis abnormalities and on the link between insufficient glucocorticoid signaling and inflammation (see the section Childhood Trauma and the Neuroendocrine Response to Stress). Chronic activation of the HPA axis during a sensitive developmental period can induce a compensatory reduction in signaling through epigenetic changes in the glucocorticoid receptor (Weaver et al. 2004), leading to resistance to the anti-inflammatory properties of cortisol. For example, human studies showed that reports of childhood trauma were related to allele-specific DNA demethylation in functional glucocorticoid response elements of the FKBP5 gene, which, in turn, was associated with lower sensitivity of peripheral blood immune cells to the inhibitory effect of glucocorticoids on LPS-induced production of IL-6 in vitro (Klengel et al. 2013). Furthermore, a longitudinal study showed that adolescents from harsh families had declining glucocorticoid sensitivity over time and increasing ex vivo cytokine response to LPS stimulation (Miller & Chen 2010).

Second, childhood trauma may impact immune development because of elevated risk of and susceptibility to infections. On the one hand, traumatized children are more likely to be exposed to physical injury and infections (Gilbert et al. 2009a). On the other hand, childhood trauma might confer vulnerability to infections. Psychological stress in general is known to increase susceptibility to infection (Cohen et al. 1991), and traumatic experiences in children have been associated with recrudescence for latent viral infections (Shirtcliff et al. 2009). In turn, immune activation linked to infections could lead to systemic inflammation.

Third, childhood trauma might affect the colonization and composition of the gut microbiota. In nonhuman primates, maternal separation during the first year of life led to a transient but substantial decrease in fecal lactobacilli (Bailey & Coe 1999). In rats, maternal separation had long-term effects on the composition of the gut microbiota manifested into adult life (O'Mahony et al. 2009). In turn, altered composition of the gut microbiota in early life could affect immune system development and could directly influence brain development by way of inflammatory signal transmission through the vagus nerve or through metabolic changes (Cryan & Dinan 2012).

Behavioral mechanisms. In addition to biological mechanisms, behavioral mechanisms, including abnormal eating and sleeping patterns and psychopathology, could indirectly explain the link between childhood trauma and inflammation in humans. For example, meta-analytical findings and experimental research in animal models show that childhood trauma is linked to a small increase in the risk of obesity (Danese & Tan 2014). In turn, production of proinflammatory cytokines by adipocytes, particularly IL-6, can induce a systemic inflammatory state commonly observed in obese individuals (Gregor & Hotamisligil 2011). Childhood maltreatment may be associated with a thrifty phenotype characterized by increased energy intake and storage and by reduced energy expenditure (Danese & Tan 2014). Several features associated with childhood trauma might increase energy intake, such as impaired reward processing, heightened HPA axis activation, and impaired executive function. Because individuals with a history of childhood trauma may be less sensitive to reward (see the section Childhood Trauma and the Brain), they may engage in more appetitive behaviors, including eating more high-calorie food. Furthermore, because individuals with a history of childhood trauma may have greater HPA activation (see the section Childhood Trauma and the Neuroendocrine Response to Stress) and related unpleasant feelings, they may eat more in an attempt to dampen HPA axis activation. Finally, individuals with a history of childhood trauma may also have impaired inhibitory control (see the section Childhood Trauma and the Brain), which could limit their ability to suppress unwanted behavior in the context of positive or negative reinforcers. In addition to these effects on energy intake, childhood trauma could be linked to reduced energy expenditure. Individuals with a history of childhood trauma may have impaired functioning in hormonal pathways regulating thermogenesis and lipolysis, such as the HPA axis and leptin pathway (see the section Childhood Trauma and the Neuroendocrine Response to Stress) (Danese et al. 2014). Notably, because of the significant overlap between the brain mechanisms involved in obesity and addiction (Volkow & Wise 2005) and the high prevalence of substance and alcohol abuse disorders among individuals with a history of childhood trauma (Dube et al. 2003), more general addiction behaviors could contribute to the link between childhood trauma and inflammation. For example, childhood trauma is associated with an elevated risk of smoking (Anda et al. 1999), which, in turn, can increase circulating inflammatory biomarkers (Shiels et al. 2014). Because they generally occur later in life, addiction behaviors other than overeating are unlikely to significantly contribute to the biological embedding of stress in children. However, they may contribute to the persistence of high inflammation levels in individuals with a history of childhood trauma.

Disruption of sleep patterns is an additional behavioral mechanism through which childhood trauma could induce heightened inflammation levels. Individuals with a history of childhood trauma are at heightened risk of sleep problems (Gregory & Sadeh 2016, Kajeepeta et al. 2015). Notably, the association appears to be stronger for participants with more severe maltreatment experiences (Gregory & Sadeh 2016) and independent of concurrent PTSD or depression diagnoses (Noll et al. 2006). These epidemiological findings are consistent with evidence from experimental animal models, such as decreased total sleep and disruption in sleep architecture found in rodents separated from their mothers in early life (Mrdalj et al. 2013). In turn, experimentally induced sleep deprivation increases the expression of proinflammatory cytokines in humans (Irwin et al. 2006), and sleep loss is associated with elevated inflammation levels in epidemiological studies, particularly in women (Miller et al. 2009).

Childhood trauma may also induce heightened inflammation levels because of related psychopathology. This might happen in a number of ways. A longitudinal study of humans has described bidirectional associations between psychopathology (e.g., depression) and inflammation over time (Matthews et al. 2010) (see the section Inflammation and Psychopathology). This observation suggests that vulnerabilities linked to emotional symptoms, subjective perception of distress, or related behavioral responses could increase inflammation levels over time. First, individuals, particularly women, suffering from depression appear to be more likely than nondepressed individuals to experience high numbers of negative life events to which they had contributed (i.e., dependent events with interpersonal content) (Hammen 2005). These findings of stress generation could be explained by vulnerabilities of the individual (e.g., cognitive or attachment style, personality traits, values, and expectations) and risk factors within their environment (e.g., socioeconomic disadvantage, domestic violence, or parental mental illness), both of which have notable overlap with risk factors for childhood maltreatment (Danese & McCrory 2015). Second, the subjective perception of distress linked to emotional symptoms can lead to chronic stress. This stress could be due, for example, to the persistence of low mood in depression or the recurrent, intrusive nature of PTSD symptoms (Agnew-Blais & Danese 2016, Nanni et al. 2012). Third, individuals who develop psychopathology could engage in behaviors driven by their emotional symptoms. For example, individuals with emotional symptoms may engage in self harm either to relieve distress or, more dramatically, with intent to end their lives (Agnew-Blais & Danese 2016). In turn, chronic stress and physical injury can induce inflammation.

Genetic mechanisms. Although biological and behavioral mechanisms can help us understand why traumatized children have elevated inflammation, it is important to also consider genetic mechanisms, which offer an alternative, noncausal interpretation of this association. It is possible that shared genetic vulnerability underlies the association between childhood trauma and inflammation, a phenomenon known as gene–environment correlation (Jaffee & Price 2007). For example, genetic pathways related to the immune system predict risk for several psychiatric diagnoses (Netw. Pathw. Anal. Subgr. Psychiatr. Genom. Consort. 2015), and early expressions of liability to these conditions, such as emotional dysregulation or oppositional behavior, might increase the risk of maltreatment in childhood.

DOES INFLAMMATION EXPLAIN THE LINK BETWEEN CHILDHOOD TRAUMA AND LATER PSYCHOPATHOLOGY?

We have reviewed several lines of research highlighting the associations between (*a*) childhood trauma and psychopathology, (*b*) inflammation and psychopathology, and (*c*) childhood trauma and inflammation. However, these associations provide only indirect evidence for the inflammatory links between childhood trauma and psychopathology. More direct evidence of the interplay among these three factors may come, for example, from the examination of the analogy of the effects of childhood trauma and inflammation on psychopathology, the synergy between childhood trauma and innate immunity in predicting psychopathology, the specificity of the link between inflammation and psychopathology within groups of traumatized individuals, and the reversibility of the effects of early life stress with anti-inflammatory compounds.

Analogy

It is possible to identify several analogies between the long-term consequences of childhood trauma and early-life immune activation in humans and animal models (Danese & McEwen 2012). As detailed above (see the sections Childhood Trauma and Psychopathology and Inflammation and Psychopathology), both childhood trauma and childhood innate immune activation demonstrate presumably causative associations with a wide range of adult mental health outcomes. Emerging evidence suggests that both could be associated not only with an elevated incidence of psychopathology but also with an unfavorable course of illness and poor response to treatment (Agnew-Blais & Danese 2016, Nanni et al. 2012, Strawbridge et al. 2015). Finally, at a more biological level, childhood trauma and childhood innate immune activation are linked to similar domains of brain function, such as cognition, positive valence, and negative valence.

Synergy

There is evidence of cross-sensitization between childhood stress and immune activation and of interaction between childhood trauma and inflammatory genes. On the one hand, we have summarized the evidence for the sensitization of the innate immune system after childhood trauma, including findings of heightened inflammatory responses in the context of subsequent stressors (see the section Childhood Trauma and Inflammation). In addition, we have reviewed evidence for the sensitization of the biological and behavioral responses to stress after childhood immune activation (see the section Long-Term Effects of Early-Life Immune Activation on the Brain and Behavior) and for the link between higher baseline levels of inflammation and greater stress-induced responses in animal models and humans (Hodes et al. 2014). On the other hand, initial evidence suggests that genetic variation in inflammatory genes could moderate the association between a history of childhood maltreatment and the amygdala response to angry and fearful faces (involving the *IFN-γ* gene) (Redlich et al. 2015) or the association between contextual stress and depression in children (involving the *IL-1B* gene) (Ridout et al. 2014). The evidence of sensitization and of gene–environment interaction involving maltreatment and inflammatory genes indicates that both factors are likely to be on the same causative pathways influencing the brain and behavior.

Specificity

If inflammation helps explain the relationship between childhood trauma and psychopathology, inflammation levels should be higher in psychiatric patients with a history of childhood trauma compared to those without. Several studies have tested and found some support for this hypothesis. For example, members of the Dunedin Study who had depression at the time of the study but no prospectively collected evidence of childhood maltreatment showed only a small and statistically nonsignificant elevation in inflammation levels at 32 years old compared to nonmaltreated and healthy controls (Danese et al. 2008). In contrast, depressed individuals with a history of childhood maltreatment showed a moderate elevation in inflammation biomarkers that reached statistical significance (Danese et al. 2008). Overall, the association between inflammation and depression was no longer significant once the effect of childhood maltreatment was controlled for (Danese et al. 2008). We have observed similar stratified findings among 12-year-old members of the E-Risk Longitudinal Twin Study, in which depressed children with a history of maltreatment already had significant elevation in inflammation levels compared to controls, whereas depressed children without a history of maltreatment did not (Danese et al. 2011). Consistent with these findings, longitudinal analyses found that adolescents with a history of early-life stress had greater increases in both IL-6 and CRP when developing depression compared to counterparts without a history of early-life stress (Miller & Cole 2012). In addition, although adolescents with a history of early-life stressors showed persistently elevated inflammation levels even after the remission of depressive symptoms, their counterparts without a history of early-life stressors showed reductions in inflammation levels as their depressive symptoms abated (Miller & Cole 2012).

Reversibility

Studies in experimental animal models found that administration of medications with anti-inflammatory activity could buffer the effects of early-life stress on the brain and behavior. An experimental model in rats demonstrated that pups separated from their mothers later showed more depressive-like symptoms and lower levels of parvalbumin (a GABAergic marker) in the prefrontal cortex compared to unchallenged pups (Leussis et al. 2012). Notably, these differences between the groups were attenuated in maternally separated rats treated with a cyclo-oxygenase 2 (COX-2) inhibitor, an anti-inflammatory medication (Brenhouse & Andersen 2011), or with IL-10, an anti-inflammatory cytokine (Wieck et al. 2013). In addition to this direct evidence, several other interventions indirectly support the role of anti-inflammatory strategies in buffering the long-term consequences of early-life stress. For example, both physical exercise and anti-depressant medications have anti-inflammatory effects (Gleeson et al. 2011, Hannestad et al. 2011) and have demonstrated an ability to buffer the effects of early-life stress on brain and behavioral outcomes (Harrison & Baune 2014).

Mediation

None of the findings discussed in this review can be taken in isolation as definitive evidence for the mediating role of inflammation in the association between childhood trauma and psychopathology. However, cumulatively, these findings do offer significant support for this role. Formal or direct tests of this mediation hypothesis (MacKinnon et al. 2007) will require new studies with peculiar design features. First, studies aiming to formally test mediation will require comprehensive models including assessment of childhood trauma, inflammation biomarkers, and psychopathology. Second, these studies must minimize bias due to reverse causality by capitalizing on prospectively collected information on childhood trauma and on repeated measures of inflammation and psychopathology (to measure longitudinal changes rather than cross-sectional group differences). Third, future studies must minimize bias due to measurement error, for example by using latent inflammation variables derived from multiple inflammation biomarkers (rather than single measures), by using repeated measures of inflammation to capture the chronicity of the effect, and by measuring inflammation early in life, when the effects on brain development are presumably stronger. Finally, future studies must minimize bias due to omitted variables by measuring and accounting for the effects of factors that either are correlated with childhood trauma (e.g., family socioeconomic status, genetic liability to psychopathology) or can offer alternative explanations for the link between inflammation and psychopathology (e.g., genetic liability to inflammation). Although it may not be possible for any single study to include all these design features, research that includes some of these features will be helpful to advance knowledge about the mediating role of inflammation in the association between childhood trauma and psychopathology.

Broader challenges to understanding the mechanisms underlying this association are linked to the inherent heterogeneity of these measures and the limits of causal inference in complex systems. With regard to heterogeneity, the concept of childhood trauma has been applied to stressful experiences ranging widely from child sexual abuse, to parental loss, to road traffic accidents, but different types of trauma may have different correlates and consequences (Terr 1991). In addition, any individual psychiatric diagnosis will likely arise through different pathways (equifinality), and different psychiatric diagnoses have significant pathophysiological overlap (Cicchetti & Rogosch

2009, Kendler et al. 2003). With regard to causal inference, not all cases of psychopathology are associated with childhood trauma, and not all individuals with a history of childhood trauma develop psychopathology. The nonnecessary and nonsufficient nature of this association is not uncommon (Rothman & Greenland 2005), but it counters any attempts to build rigorous models for mediation analyses. Thus, a better characterization of childhood trauma and its association with psychopathology will provide researchers with a better framework to identify mediation pathways.

CONCLUSION

Our understanding of the response to psychological trauma—and particularly childhood psychological trauma—has come full circle to recognize the truth in the analogy with the response to physical trauma or injury, partly reconciling the debate between Oppenheim and Charcot over the origins of trauma-related symptoms. Childhood psychological trauma is associated with similar biological responses as those triggered by physical injury, including activation of the innate immune system (Molina 2005). Notably, because of its occurrence early in life, childhood psychological trauma could influence immune system development, promoting chronic activation and hyperreactivity of the inflammatory response from childhood into adult life. In turn, these "hidden wounds" of childhood psychological trauma could affect the brain and behavior over the course of an individual's lifetime by influencing brain development, potentiating the neuroendocrine and immune responses to subsequent stressors, and biasing key domains of brain functioning. As discussed in the previous section, this hypothesis needs to be more comprehensively tested in future research. If confirmed, it will provide a useful framework to conceptualize adaptive and maladaptive aspects of the response to childhood trauma and to understand and treat trauma-related psychopathology.

Because the immune abnormalities emerging after early-life stress exposure appear to be broadly conserved across species with comparatively distant common ancestors, it is intriguing to speculate about whether the inflammatory response to childhood trauma could, in some ways, be adaptive. The evolutionary forces that have shaped the inflammatory response to childhood trauma presumably acted in a context in which physical threats were frequent and psychological stress was often coupled with injury and infection. In this context, the inflammatory response to childhood psychological trauma could provide adaptive benefits by promoting survival and enabling reproduction (Danese & McEwen 2012, Nusslock & Miller 2016). The increase in unstimulated inflammation levels and heightened inflammatory reactivity could prepare the body to respond to subsequent injury and infection. The reduction in motor activity linked to impaired positive valence systems could promote recovery after injury and infection by channeling metabolic resources to support the immune response. The increase in threat perception and the behavioral responses to threat linked to potentiation of negative valence systems could prevent subsequent injury through avoidance. In addition, routine encounters with minimally pathogenic organisms in rural environments could inhibit chronic elevation in inflammation biomarkers by inducing regulatory T cells and B cells (McDade 2012, Miller & Raison 2015). To the extent that the modern experience of childhood trauma still involves frequent and unpredictable threats to survival, the inflammatory response in traumatized children and adults may promote adaptive strategies reflecting those evolutionary imperatives. However, when psychological stress is no longer coupled with injury and infection, when the response persists years after the original threat has ceased, when the ecological niche does not allow encounters with minimally pathogenic immunomodulatory organisms, and when priorities shift from short-term goals (survival) to long-term goals (wellbeing and aging), the chronic elevation in inflammatory biomarkers becomes maladaptive because of the associated risk of psychopathology and age-related disease (Danese & McEwen 2012).

With regard to clinical implications, the presence of elevated inflammation could help explain the complex clinical presentations related to childhood trauma and could provide innovative targets for intervention. First, because inflammation affects both basic developmental processes (see the section Long-Term Effects of Early-Life Immune Activation on the Brain and Behavior) and broad neurobiological systems (see the section How Does Inflammation Affect Psychopathology?), elevated inflammation could help explain the transdiagnostic psychological correlates of childhood trauma (Caspi et al. 2014). Second, because inflammation is associated with complex presentations and can impair the response to conventional treatments (Strawbridge et al. 2015), elevated inflammation could help explain the stratified clinical effects of childhood trauma across psychopathology (Agnew-Blais & Danese 2016; Danese et al. 2011, 2008; Nanni et al. 2012). Third, because inflammation not only is associated with psychopathology but also contributes to the pathophysiology of several medical conditions (Danese & McEwen 2012), elevated inflammation could help explain the high rate of medical comorbidities in individuals with a history of childhood trauma (Danese et al. 2009, Taylor 2010). Fourth, with regard to interventions, the evidence that both pharmacological and nonpharmacological anti-inflammatory strategies can reverse the long-term consequences of early-life stress in animal models (see the section Reversibility) suggests that similar strategies might be effective in preventing the onset of clinical outcomes in humans (secondary prevention). Provocative findings in animal models also suggest that harnessing the immune response to self-antigens may contribute to psychological stress resilience (Lewitus & Schwartz 2009). An initial mild stressor can increase lymphocyte trafficking to the brain, which in turn reduces secondary neuronal damage by the microglia and produces autoreactive memory T cells that increase neuroprotection in the face of subsequent stressors (Lewitus & Schwartz 2009). Building on these findings, immunization with CNS-derived peptides has been associated with lower anxiety symptoms in rodents exposed to predator odor (Lewitus & Schwartz 2009). However, this immunization approach has not yet been studied in relation to early-life stress. In addition to strategies directly targeting the immune system, psychosocial interventions might be used to reduce inflammation in traumatized children (Pace et al. 2009) and to decrease psychosocial adversity more generally (Miller et al. 2014), although the impact of commonly used psychosocial interventions with established clinical significance (Danese & McCrory 2015) requires further investigation. Finally, similar anti-inflammatory strategies might be effective in improving treatment response and course of illness in trauma-related psychopathology (tertiary prevention) (Agnew-Blais & Danese 2016, Danese et al. 2008, Nanni et al. 2012, Raison et al. 2013).

In addition to its manifest signs and symptoms (Gilbert et al. 2009a), childhood trauma may leave more hidden wounds: immune abnormalities that have the potential to influence brain development and subsequent behavior. Advances in detecting and healing these hidden wounds may help prevent some of the impairing health problems documented in children exposed to psychological trauma.

DISCLOSURE STATEMENT

The authors are not aware of any affiliations, memberships, funding, or financial holdings that might be perceived as affecting the objectivity of this review.

LITERATURE CITED

Ader R, Friedman SB. 1965. Differential early experiences and susceptibility to transplanted tumor in the rat. *J. Comp. Physiol. Psychol.* 59:361–64

Agnew-Blais J, Danese A. 2016. Childhood maltreatment and unfavourable clinical outcomes in bipolar disorder: a systematic review and meta-analysis. *Lancet Psychiatry* 3:342–49

Amminger GP, Schäfer MR, Schlögelhofer M, Klier CM, McGorry PD. 2015. Longer-term outcome in the prevention of psychotic disorders by the Vienna omega-3 study. *Nat. Commun.* 6:7934

Anda RF, Croft JB, Felitti VJ, Nordenberg D, Giles WH, et al. 1999. Adverse childhood experiences and smoking during adolescence and adulthood. *JAMA* 282(17):1652–58

Atladóttir HO, Thorsen P, Østergaard L, Schendel DE, Lemcke S, et al. 2010. Maternal infection requiring hospitalization during pregnancy and autism spectrum disorders. *J. Autism Dev. Disord.* 40(12):1423–30

Avitsur R, Hunzeker J, Sheridan JF. 2006. Role of early stress in the individual differences in host response to viral infection. *Brain Behav. Immun.* 20(4):339–48

Bailey MT, Coe CL. 1999. Maternal separation disrupts the integrity of the intestinal microflora in infant rhesus monkeys. *Dev. Psychobiol.* 35(2):146–55

Barnes PJ, Adcock IM. 2009. Glucocorticoid resistance in inflammatory diseases. *Lancet* 373(9678):1905–17

Baumeister D, Akhtar R, Ciufolini S, Pariante CM, Mondelli V. 2015. Childhood trauma and adulthood inflammation: a meta-analysis of peripheral C-reactive protein, interleukin-6 and tumour necrosis factor-α. *Mol. Psychiatry* 21:642–49

Berk M, Kapczinski F, Andreazza AC, Dean OM, Giorlando F, et al. 2011. Pathways underlying neuroprogression in bipolar disorder: focus on inflammation, oxidative stress and neurotrophic factors. *Neurosci. Biobehav. Rev.* 35(3):804–17

Besedovsky H, del Rey A, Sorkin E, Dinarello CA. 1986. Immunoregulatory feedback between interleukin-1 and glucocorticoid hormones. *Science* 233(4764):652–54

Bilbo SD, Schwarz JM. 2009. Early-life programming of later-life brain and behavior: a critical role for the immune system. *Front. Behav. Neurosci.* 3:14

Bloomfield PS, Selvaraj S, Veronese M, Rizzo G, Bertoldo A, et al. 2016. Microglial activity in people at ultra high risk of psychosis and in schizophrenia: an [^{11}C]PBR28 PET brain imaging study. *Am. J. Psychiatry* 173(1):44–52

Boulanger LM. 2009. Immune proteins in brain development and synaptic plasticity. *Neuron* 64(1):93–109

Bowlby J. 1951. Maternal care and mental health. *Bull. World Health Organ.* 3(3):355–533

Breder CD, Hazuka C, Ghayur T, Klug C, Huginin M, et al. 1994. Regional induction of tumor necrosis factor alpha expression in the mouse brain after systemic lipopolysaccharide administration. *PNAS* 91(24):11393–97

Brenhouse HC, Andersen SL. 2011. Nonsteroidal anti-inflammatory treatment prevents delayed effects of early life stress in rats. *Biol. Psychiatry* 70(5):434–40

Brenhouse HC, Thompson V. 2015. *Maternal separation increases IBA-1 expression: a microglia activation marker in the prefrontal cortex of adolescent males following a second hit of stress.* Presented at Annu. Meet. Soc. Biol. Psychiatry, 70th, May 14–16, Toronto, Canada (Abstr.)

Briquet P. 1859. *Traite clinique et thérapeutique de l'hystérie.* Paris: J.-B. Baillière et Fils

Brown GW, Harris T. 1978. *Social Origins of Depression: A Study of Psychiatric Disorder in Women.* New York: Free Press

Brunson KL, Kramár E, Lin B, Chen Y, Colgin LL, et al. 2005. Mechanisms of late-onset cognitive decline after early-life stress. *J. Neurosci.* 25(41):9328–38

Capuron L, Pagnoni G, Drake DF, Woolwine BJ, Spivey JR, et al. 2012. Dopaminergic mechanisms of reduced basal ganglia responses to hedonic reward during interferon alfa administration. *Arch. Gen. Psychiatry* 69(10):1044–53

Carpenter LL, Gawuga CE, Tyrka AR, Lee JK, Anderson GM, Price LH. 2010. Association between plasma IL-6 response to acute stress and early-life adversity in healthy adults. *Neuropsychopharmacology* 35(13):2617–23

Carpenter LL, Tyrka AR, McDougle CJ, Malison RT, Owens MJ, et al. 2004. Cerebrospinal fluid corticotropin-releasing factor and perceived early-life stress in depressed patients and healthy control subjects. *Neuropsychopharmacology* 29(4):777–84

Carrion VG, Weems CF, Ray RD, Glaser B, Hessl D, Reiss AL. 2002. Diurnal salivary cortisol in pediatric posttraumatic stress disorder. *Biol. Psychiatry* 51(7):575–82

Caspi A, Houts RM, Belsky DW, Goldman-Mellor SJ, Harrington H, et al. 2014. The p factor: one general psychopathology factor in the structure of psychiatric disorders? *Clin. Psychol. Sci.* 2(2):119–37

Chalasani SH, Sabelko KA, Sunshine MJ, Littman DR, Raper JA. 2003. A chemokine, SDF-1, reduces the effectiveness of multiple axonal repellents and is required for normal axon pathfinding. *J. Neurosci.* 23(4):1360–71

Chocyk A, Dudys D, Przyborowska A, Majcher I, Maćkowiak M, Wędzony K. 2011. Maternal separation affects the number, proliferation and apoptosis of glia cells in the substantia nigra and ventral tegmental area of juvenile rats. *Neuroscience* 173:1–18

Cicchetti D, Handley ED, Rogosch FA. 2015. Child maltreatment, inflammation, and internalizing symptoms: investigating the roles of C-reactive protein, gene variation, and neuroendocrine regulation. *Dev. Psychopathol.* 27:553–66

Cicchetti D, Rogosch FA. 2001. The impact of child maltreatment and psychopathology on neuroendocrine functioning. *Dev. Psychopathol.* 13(4):783–804

Cicchetti D, Rogosch FA. 2009. Equifinality and multifinality in developmental psychopathology. *Dev. Psychopathol.* 8(4):597–600

Coe CL, Rosenberg LT, Levine S. 1988. Prolonged effect of psychological disturbance on macrophage chemiluminescence in the squirrel monkey. *Brain Behav. Immun.* 2(2):151–60

Coelho R, Viola TW, Walss-Bass C, Brietzke E, Grassi-Oliveira R. 2014. Childhood maltreatment and inflammatory markers: a systematic review. *Acta Psychiatr. Scand.* 129(3):180–92

Cohen S, Tyrrell DA, Smith AP. 1991. Psychological stress and susceptibility to the common cold. *N. Engl. J. Med.* 325(9):606–12

Cole SW, Conti G, Arevalo JMG, Ruggiero AM, Heckman JJ, Suomi SJ. 2012. Transcriptional modulation of the developing immune system by early life social adversity. *PNAS* 109(50):20578–83

Cryan JF, Dinan TG. 2012. Mind-altering microorganisms: the impact of the gut microbiota on brain and behaviour. *Nat. Rev. Neurosci.* 13(10):701–12

Cryan JF, Holmes A. 2005. The ascent of mouse: advances in modelling human depression and anxiety. *Nat. Rev. Drug Discov.* 4(9):775–90

Danese A, Caspi A, Williams B, Ambler A, Sugden K, et al. 2011. Biological embedding of stress through inflammation processes in childhood. *Mol. Psychiatry* 16(3):244–46

Danese A, Dove R, Belsky DW, Henchy J, Williams B, et al. 2014. Leptin deficiency in maltreated children. *Transl. Psychiatry* 4(9):e446

Danese A, McCrory E. 2015. Child maltreatment. In *Rutter's Child and Adolescent Psychiatry*, ed. A Thapar, DS Pine, JF Leckman, S Scott, MJ Snowling, E Taylor, pp. 364–75. London: Wiley-Blackwell

Danese A, McEwen BS. 2012. Adverse childhood experiences, allostasis, allostatic load, and age-related disease. *Physiol. Behav.* 106(1):29–39

Danese A, Moffitt TE, Harrington H, Milne BJ, Polanczyk G, et al. 2009. Adverse childhood experiences and adult risk factors for age-related disease: depression, inflammation, and clustering of metabolic risk markers. *Arch. Pediatr. Adolesc. Med.* 163(12):1135–43

Danese A, Moffitt TE, Pariante CM, Ambler A, Poulton R, Caspi A. 2008. Elevated inflammation levels in depressed adults with a history of childhood maltreatment. *Arch. Gen. Psychiatry* 65(4):409–15

Danese A, Pariante CM, Caspi A, Taylor A, Poulton R. 2007. Childhood maltreatment predicts adult inflammation in a life-course study. *PNAS* 104(4):1319–24

Danese A, Tan M. 2014. Childhood maltreatment and obesity: systematic review and meta-analysis. *Mol. Psychiatry* 19(5):544–54

Dantzer R, O'Connor JC, Freund GG, Johnson RW, Kelley KW. 2008. From inflammation to sickness and depression: when the immune system subjugates the brain. *Nat. Rev. Neurosci.* 9(1):46–56

Dargél AA, Godin O, Kapczinski F, Kupfer DJ, Leboyer M. 2015. C-reactive protein alterations in bipolar disorder: a meta-analysis. *J. Clin. Psychiatry* 76(2):142–50

De Bellis MD, Baum AS, Birmaher B, Keshavan MS, Eccard CH, et al. 1999. Developmental traumatology. Part I: biological stress systems. *Biol. Psychiatry* 45(10):1259–70

Deykin EY, MacMahon B. 1979. Viral exposure and autism. *Am. J. Epidemiol.* 109(6):628–38

Dillon DG, Holmes AJ, Birk JL, Brooks N, Lyons-Ruth K, Pizzagalli DA. 2009. Childhood adversity is associated with left basal ganglia dysfunction during reward anticipation in adulthood. *Biol. Psychiatry* 66(3):206–13

Dube SR, Felitti VJ, Dong M, Chapman DP, Giles WH, Anda RF. 2003. Childhood abuse, neglect, and household dysfunction and the risk of illicit drug use: the adverse childhood experiences study. *Pediatrics* 111(3):564–72

Duncan GJ, Magnuson KA, Ludwig J. 2004. The endogeneity problem in developmental studies. *Res. Hum. Dev.* 1(1–2):59–80

Dunn AJ. 2006. Cytokine activation of the HPA axis. *Ann. N. Y. Acad. Sci.* 917(1):608–17

Eisenberger NI, Berkman ET, Inagaki TK, Rameson LT, Mashal NM, Irwin MR. 2010. Inflammation-induced anhedonia: Endotoxin reduces ventral striatum responses to reward. *Biol. Psychiatry* 68(8):748–54

Ekdahl CT, Claasen J-H, Bonde S, Kokaia Z, Lindvall O. 2003. Inflammation is detrimental for neurogenesis in adult brain. *PNAS* 100(23):13632–37

Eraly SA, Nievergelt CM, Maihofer AX, Barkauskas DA, Biswas N, et al. 2014. Assessment of plasma C-reactive protein as a biomarker of posttraumatic stress disorder risk. *JAMA Psychiatry* 71(4):423–31

Erichsen JE. 1867. *On Railway and Other Injuries of the Nervous System*. Philadelphia: Henry C. Lea

Ford DE, Erlinger TP. 2004. Depression and C-reactive protein in US adults: data from the Third National Health and Nutrition Examination Survey. *Arch. Intern. Med.* 164(9):1010–14

Francis D, Diorio J, Liu D, Meaney MJ. 1999. Nongenomic transmission across generations of maternal behavior and stress responses in the rat. *Science* 286(5442):1155–58

Frank MG, Watkins LR, Maier SF. 2013. Stress-induced glucocorticoids as a neuroendocrine alarm signal of danger. *Brain Behav. Immun.* 33:1–6

Freud S. 1962. *The Standard Edition of the Complete Psychological Works of Sigmund Freud*, Vol. IV: *The Interpretation of Dreams (First Part)*. London: Hogarth Press

Galea I, Bechmann I, Perry VH. 2007. What is immune privilege (not)? *Trends Immunol.* 28(1):12–18

Ganguly P, Brenhouse HC. 2015. Broken or maladaptive? Altered trajectories in neuroinflammation and behavior after early life adversity. *Dev. Cogn. Neurosci.* 11:18–30

Gilbert R, Kemp A, Thoburn J, Sidebotham P, Radford L, et al. 2009a. Recognising and responding to child maltreatment. *Lancet* 373(9658):167–80

Gilbert R, Widom CS, Browne K, Fergusson D, Webb E, Janson S. 2009b. Burden and consequences of child maltreatment in high-income countries. *Lancet* 373(9657):68–81

Gleeson M, Bishop NC, Stensel DJ, Lindley MR, Mastana SS, Nimmo MA. 2011. The anti-inflammatory effects of exercise: mechanisms and implications for the prevention and treatment of disease. *Nat. Rev. Immunol.* 11(9):607–15

Gouin J-P, Glaser R, Malarkey WB, Beversdorf D, Kiecolt-Glaser JK. 2012. Childhood abuse and inflammatory responses to daily stressors. *Ann. Behav. Med.* 44(2):287–92

Gregor MF, Hotamisligil GS. 2011. Inflammatory mechanisms in obesity. *Annu. Rev. Immunol.* 29(1):415–45

Gregory AM, Sadeh A. 2016. Annual research review: sleep problems in childhood psychiatric disorders—a review of the latest science. *J. Child Psychol. Psychiatry* 57(3):296–317

Gunnar M, Quevedo K. 2007. The neurobiology of stress and development. *Annu. Rev. Psychol.* 58:145–73

Guyer AE, Kaufman J, Hodgdon HB, Masten CL, Jazbec S, et al. 2006. Behavioral alterations in reward system function: the role of childhood maltreatment and psychopathology. *J. Am. Acad. Child Adolesc. Psychiatry* 45(9):1059–67

Hammen C. 2005. Stress and depression. *Annu. Rev. Clin. Psychol.* 1:293–319

Hanisch U-K, Kettenmann H. 2007. Microglia: active sensor and versatile effector cells in the normal and pathologic brain. *Nat. Neurosci.* 10(11):1387–94

Hannestad J, DellaGioia N, Bloch M. 2011. The effect of antidepressant medication treatment on serum levels of inflammatory cytokines: a meta-analysis. *Neuropsychopharmacology* 36(12):2452–59

Harlow HF, Dodsworth RO, Harlow MK. 1965. Total social isolation in monkeys. *PNAS* 54(1):90–97

Harrison EL, Baune BT. 2014. Modulation of early stress-induced neurobiological changes: a review of behavioural and pharmacological interventions in animal models. *Transl. Psychiatry* 4(5):e390

Harrison NA, Brydon L, Walker C, Gray MA, Steptoe A, Critchley HD. 2009. Inflammation causes mood changes through alterations in subgenual cingulate activity and mesolimbic connectivity. *Biol. Psychiatry* 66(5):407–14

Hart BL. 1988. Biological basis of the behavior of sick animals. *Neurosci. Biobehav. Rev.* 12(2):123–37

Heim C, Ehlert U, Hellhammer DH. 2000. The potential role of hypocortisolism in the pathophysiology of stress-related bodily disorders. *Psychoneuroendocrinology* 25:1–35

Heim C, Mletzko T, Purselle D, Musselman DL, Nemeroff CB. 2008. The dexamethasone/corticotropin-releasing factor test in men with major depression: role of childhood trauma. *Biol. Psychiatry* 63(4):398–405

Heim C, Nemeroff CB. 2001. The role of childhood trauma in the neurobiology of mood and anxiety disorders: preclinical and clinical studies. *Biol. Psychiatry* 49(12):1023–39

Heim C, Newport DJ, Heit S, Graham YP, Wilcox M, et al. 2000. Pituitary-adrenal and autonomic responses to stress in women after sexual and physical abuse in childhood. *JAMA* 284(5):592–97

Hennessy MB, Deak T, Schiml-Webb PA. 2010a. Early attachment-figure separation and increased risk for later depression: potential mediation by proinflammatory processes. *Neurosci. Biobehav. Rev.* 34(6):782–90

Hennessy MB, Deak T, Schiml-Webb PA, Carlisle CW, O'Brien E. 2010b. Maternal separation produces, and a second separation enhances, core temperature and passive behavioral responses in guinea pig pups. *Physiol. Behav.* 100(4):305–10

Herringa RJ, Birn RM, Ruttle PL, Burghy CA, Stodola DE, et al. 2013. Childhood maltreatment is associated with altered fear circuitry and increased internalizing symptoms by late adolescence. *PNAS* 110(47):19119–24

Hinde RA, Spencer-Booth Y. 1971. Effects of brief separation from mother on rhesus monkeys. *Science* 173(3992):111–18

Hodes GE, Pfau ML, Leboeuf M, Golden SA, Christoffel DJ, et al. 2014. Individual differences in the peripheral immune system promote resilience versus susceptibility to social stress. *PNAS* 111(45):16136–41

Holdorff B. 2011. The fight for "traumatic neurosis," 1889–1916: Hermann Oppenheim and his opponents in Berlin. *Hist. Psychiatry* 22:465–76

Howren MB, Lamkin DM, Suls J. 2009. Associations of depression with C-reactive protein, IL-1, and IL-6: a meta-analysis. *Psychosom. Med.* 71(2):171–86

Inagaki TK, Muscatell KA, Irwin MR, Cole SW, Eisenberger NI. 2012. Inflammation selectively enhances amygdala activity to socially threatening images. *NeuroImage* 59(4):3222–26

Insel TR. 2014. The NIMH Research Domain Criteria (RDoC) project: precision medicine for psychiatry. *Am. J. Psychiatry* 171(4):395–97

Irwin MR, Wang M, Campomayor CO, Collado-Hidalgo A, Cole S. 2006. Sleep deprivation and activation of morning levels of cellular and genomic markers of inflammation. *Arch. Intern. Med.* 166(16):1756–62

Jaffee SR, Price TS. 2007. Gene-environment correlations: a review of the evidence and implications for prevention of mental illness. *Mol. Psychiatry* 12(5):432–42

Kajeepeta S, Gelaye B, Jackson CL, Williams MA. 2015. Adverse childhood experiences are associated with adult sleep disorders: a systematic review. *Sleep Med.* 16(3):320–30

Kaufman J, Gelernter J, Hudziak JJ, Tyrka AR, Coplan JD. 2015. The Research Domain Criteria (RDoC) project and studies of risk and resilience in maltreated children. *J. Am. Acad. Child Adolesc. Psychiatry* 54(8):617–25

Kendler KS, Bulik CM, Silberg J, Hettema JM, Myers J, Prescott CA. 2000. Childhood sexual abuse and adult psychiatric and substance use disorders in women. *Arch. Gen. Psychiatry* 57(10):953–59

Kendler KS, Prescott CA, Myers J, Neale MC. 2003. The structure of genetic and environmental risk factors for common psychiatric and substance use disorders in men and women. *Arch. Gen. Psychiatry* 60(9):929–37

Kessler RC, Davis CG, Kendler KS. 1997. Childhood adversity and adult psychiatric disorder in the US National Comorbidity Survey. *Psychol. Med.* 27(5):1101–19

Khandaker GM, Cousins L, Deakin J, Lennox BR, Yolken R, Jones PB. 2015. Inflammation and immunity in schizophrenia: implications for pathophysiology and treatment. *Lancet Psychiatry* 2(3):258–70

Khandaker GM, Pearson RM, Zammit S, Lewis G, Jones PB. 2014. Association of serum interleukin 6 and C-reactive protein in childhood with depression and psychosis in young adult life. *JAMA Psychiatry* 71(10):1121–28

Khandaker GM, Zimbron J, Lewis G, Jones PB. 2013. Prenatal maternal infection, neurodevelopment and adult schizophrenia: a systematic review of population-based studies. *Psychol. Med.* 43(2):239–57

Kiecolt-Glaser JK, Gouin J-P, Weng N-P, Malarkey WB, Beversdorf DQ, Glaser R. 2011. Childhood adversity heightens the impact of later-life caregiving stress on telomere length and inflammation. *Psychosom. Med.* 73(1):16–22

Kipnis J, Gadani S, Derecki NC. 2012. Pro-cognitive properties of T cells. *Nat. Rev. Immunol.* 12(9):663–69

Klengel T, Mehta D, Anacker C, Rex-Haffner M, Pruessner JC, et al. 2013. Allele-specific *FKBP5* DNA demethylation mediates gene–childhood trauma interactions. *Nat. Neurosci.* 16:33–41

Knuesel I, Chicha L, Britschgi M, Schobel SA, Bodmer M, et al. 2014. Maternal immune activation and abnormal brain development across CNS disorders. *Nat. Rev. Neurol.* 10(11):643–60

Köhler O, Benros ME, Nordentoft M, Farkouh ME, Iyengar RL, et al. 2014. Effect of anti-inflammatory treatment on depression, depressive symptoms, and adverse effects: a systematic review and meta-analysis of randomized clinical trials. *JAMA Psychiatry* 71(12):1381–91

Leboyer M, Soreca I, Scott J, Frye M, Henry C, et al. 2012. Can bipolar disorder be viewed as a multi-system inflammatory disease? *J. Affect. Disord.* 141(1):1–10

Leppänen JM, Nelson CA. 2009. Tuning the developing brain to social signals of emotions. *Nat. Rev. Neurosci.* 10(1):37–47

Leussis MP, Freund N, Brenhouse HC, Thompson BS, Andersen SL. 2012. Depressive-like behavior in adolescents after maternal separation: sex differences, controllability, and GABA. *Dev. Neurosci.* 34(2–3):210–17

Levine S, Alpert M, Lewis GW. 1957. Infantile experience and the maturation of the pituitary adrenal axis. *Science* 126(3287):1347

Levine S, Chevalier JA, Korchin SJ. 1956. The effects of early shock and handling on later avoidance learning. *J. Personal.* 24(4):475–93

Lewitus GM, Schwartz M. 2009. Behavioral immunization: immunity to self-antigens contributes to psychological stress resilience. *Mol. Psychiatry* 14:532–36

Lim L, Radua J, Rubia K. 2014. Gray matter abnormalities in childhood maltreatment: a voxel-wise meta-analysis. *Am. J. Psychiatry* 171(8):854–63

Lupien SJ, McEwen BS, Gunnar MR, Heim C. 2009. Effects of stress throughout the lifespan on the brain, behaviour and cognition. *Nat. Rev. Neurosci.* 10(6):434–45

MacKinnon DP, Fairchild AJ, Fritz MS. 2007. Mediation analysis. *Annu. Rev. Psychol.* 58:593–614

Maercker A, Brewin CR, Bryant RA, Cloitre M, van Ommeren M, et al. 2013. Diagnosis and classification of disorders specifically associated with stress: proposals for ICD-11. *World Psychiatry* 12(3):198–206

Maes M, Lambrechts J, Bosmans E, Jacobs J, Suy E, et al. 1992. Evidence for a systemic immune activation during depression: results of leukocyte enumeration by flow cytometry in conjunction with monoclonal antibody staining. *Psychol. Med.* 22(1):45–53

Matthews K, Robbins TW. 2003. Early experience as a determinant of adult behavioural responses to reward: the effects of repeated maternal separation in the rat. *Neurosci. Biobehav. Rev.* 27(1–2):45–55

Matthews KA, Schott LL, Bromberger JT, Cyranowski JM, Everson-Rose SA, Sowers M. 2010. Are there bi-directional associations between depressive symptoms and C-reactive protein in mid-life women? *Brain Behav. Immun.* 24(1):96–101

McCrory EJ, De Brito SA, Kelly PA, Bird G, Sebastian CL, et al. 2013. Amygdala activation in maltreated children during pre-attentive emotional processing. *Br. J. Psychiatry* 202(4):269–76

McCrory EJ, De Brito SA, Viding E. 2010. Research review: the neurobiology and genetics of maltreatment and adversity. *J. Child Psychol. Psychiatry* 51(10):1079–95

McDade TW. 2012. Early environments and the ecology of inflammation. *PNAS* 109(Suppl. 2):17281–88

McEwen BS, Weiss JM, Schwartz LS. 1968. Selective retention of corticosterone by limbic structures in rat brain. *Nature* 220(5170):911–12

Mednick SA, Machon RA, Huttunen MO, Bonett D. 1988. Adult schizophrenia following prenatal exposure to an influenza epidemic. *Arch. Gen. Psychiatry* 45(2):189–92

Mehta MA, Gore-Langton E, Golembo N, Colvert E, Williams SCR, Sonuga-Barke E. 2010. Hyporesponsive reward anticipation in the basal ganglia following severe institutional deprivation early in life. *J. Cogn. Neurosci.* 22(10):2316–25

Micale MS. 1995. Charcot and les névroses traumatiques: scientific and historical reflections. *J. Hist. Neurosci.* 4:101–19

Michopoulos V, Rothbaum AO, Jovanovic T, Almli LM, Bradley B, et al. 2015. Association of CRP genetic variation and CRP level with elevated PTSD symptoms and physiological responses in a civilian population with high levels of trauma. *Am. J. Psychiatry* 172(4):353–62

Miller AH, Raison CL. 2015. The role of inflammation in depression: from evolutionary imperative to modern treatment target. *Nat. Rev. Immunol.* 16(1):22–34

Miller BJ, Buckley P, Seabolt W, Mellor A, Kirkpatrick B. 2011. Meta-analysis of cytokine alterations in schizophrenia: clinical status and antipsychotic effects. *Biol. Psychiatry* 70(7):663–71

Miller GE, Brody GH, Yu T, Chen E. 2014. A family-oriented psychosocial intervention reduces inflammation in low-SES African American youth. *PNAS* 111(31):11287–92

Miller GE, Chen E. 2010. Harsh family climate in early life presages the emergence of a proinflammatory phenotype in adolescence. *Psychol. Sci.* 21(6):848–56

Miller GE, Cohen S, Ritchey AK. 2002. Chronic psychological stress and the regulation of pro-inflammatory cytokines: a glucocorticoid-resistance model. *Health Psychol.* 21(6):531–41

Miller GE, Cole SW. 2012. Clustering of depression and inflammation in adolescents previously exposed to childhood adversity. *Biol. Psychiatry* 72(1):34–40

Miller MA, Kandala N-B, Kivimaki M, Kumari M, Brunner EJ, et al. 2009. Gender differences in the cross-sectional relationships between sleep duration and markers of inflammation: Whitehall II study. *Sleep* 32(7):857–64

Mirescu C, Peters JD, Gould E. 2004. Early life experience alters response of adult neurogenesis to stress. *Nat. Neurosci.* 7(8):841–46

Modabbernia A, Taslimi S, Brietzke E, Ashrafi M. 2013. Cytokine alterations in bipolar disorder: a meta-analysis of 30 studies. *Biol. Psychiatry* 74(1):15–25

Molina PE. 2005. Neurobiology of the stress response: contribution of the sympathetic nervous system to the neuroimmune axis in traumatic injury. *Shock* 24(1):3–10

Mondelli V, Ciufolini S, Belvederi Murri M, Bonaccorso S, Di Forti M, et al. 2015. Cortisol and inflammatory biomarkers predict poor treatment response in first episode psychosis. *Schizophr. Bull.* 41(5):1162–70

Monje ML, Toda H, Palmer TD. 2003. Inflammatory blockade restores adult hippocampal neurogenesis. *Science* 302(5651):1760–65

Moriceau S, Sullivan RM. 2006. Maternal presence serves as a switch between learning fear and attraction in infancy. *Nat. Neurosci.* 9(8):1004–6

Mrdalj J, Pallesen S, Milde AM, Jellestad FK, Murison R, et al. 2013. Early and later life stress alter brain activity and sleep in rats. *PLOS ONE* 8(7):e69923

Musselman DL, Lawson DH, Gumnick JF, Manatunga AK, Penna S, et al. 2001. Paroxetine for the prevention of depression induced by high-dose interferon alfa. *N. Engl. J. Med.* 344(13):961–66

Nanni V, Uher R, Danese A. 2012. Childhood maltreatment predicts unfavorable course of illness and treatment outcome in depression: a meta-analysis. *Am. J. Psychiatry* 169(2):141–51

Netw. Pathw. Anal. Subgr. Psychiatr. Genom. Consort. 2015. Psychiatric genome-wide association study analyses implicate neuronal, immune and histone pathways. *Nat. Neurosci.* 18(2):199–209

Noll JG, Trickett PK, Susman EJ, Putnam FW. 2006. Sleep disturbances and childhood sexual abuse. *J. Pediatr. Psychol.* 31(5):469–80

Nusslock R, Miller GE. 2016. Early-life adversity and physical and emotional health across the lifespan: a neuroimmune network hypothesis. *Biol. Psychiatry* 80:23–32

O'Mahony SM, Marchesi JR, Scully P, Codling C, Ceolho A-M, et al. 2009. Early life stress alters behavior, immunity, and microbiota in rats: implications for irritable bowel syndrome and psychiatric illnesses. *Biol. Psychiatry* 65(3):263–67

Pace TWW, Mletzko TC, Alagbe O, Musselman DL, Nemeroff CB, et al. 2006. Increased stress-induced inflammatory responses in male patients with major depression and increased early life stress. *Am. J. Psychiatry* 163(9):1630–33

Pace TWW, Negi LT, Adame DD, Cole SP, Sivilli TI, et al. 2009. Effect of compassion meditation on neuroendocrine, innate immune and behavioral responses to psychosocial stress. *Psychoneuroendocrinology* 34(1):87–98

Pariante CM, Miller AH. 2001. Glucocorticoid receptors in major depression: relevance to pathophysiology and treatment. *Biol. Psychiatry* 49(5):391–404

Passos IC, Vasconcelos-Moreno MP, Costa LG, Kunz M, Brietzke E, et al. 2015. Inflammatory markers in post-traumatic stress disorder: a systematic review, meta-analysis, and meta-regression. *Lancet Psychiatry* 2(11):1002–12

Patterson PH. 2009. Immune involvement in schizophrenia and autism: etiology, pathology and animal models. *Behav. Brain Res.* 204(2):313–21

Pechtel P, Pizzagalli DA. 2011. Effects of early life stress on cognitive and affective function: an integrated review of human literature. *Psychopharmacology* 214(1):55–70

Peferoen L, Kipp M, van der Valk P, van Noort JM, Amor S. 2014. Oligodendrocyte-microglia cross-talk in the central nervous system. *Immunology* 141(3):302–13

Perry VH, Holmes C. 2014. Microglial priming in neurodegenerative disease. *Nat. Rev. Neurol.* 10(4):217–24

Perry VH, Newman TA, Cunningham C. 2003. The impact of systemic infection on the progression of neurodegenerative disease. *Nat. Rev. Neurosci.* 4(2):103–12

Phillips GD, Howes SR, Whitelaw RB, Robbins TW, Everitt BJ. 1994. Isolation rearing impairs the reinforcing efficacy of intravenous cocaine or intra-accumbens *d*-amphetamine: impaired response to intra-accumbens D1 and D2/D3 dopamine receptor antagonists. *Psychopharmacology* 115(3):419–29

Pollak SD, Kistler DJ. 2002. Early experience is associated with the development of categorical representations for facial expressions of emotion. *PNAS* 99(13):9072–76

Pryce CR, Dettling AC, Spengler M, Schnell CR, Feldon J. 2004. Deprivation of parenting disrupts development of homeostatic and reward systems in marmoset monkey offspring. *Biol. Psychiatry* 56(2):72–79

Raison CL, Miller AH. 2003. When not enough is too much: the role of insufficient glucocorticoid signaling in the pathophysiology of stress-related disorders. *Am. J. Psychiatry* 160(9):1554–65

Raison CL, Rutherford RE, Woolwine BJ, Shuo C, Schettler P, et al. 2013. A randomized controlled trial of the tumor necrosis factor antagonist infliximab for treatment-resistant depression: the role of baseline inflammatory biomarkers. *JAMA Psychiatry* 70(1):31–41

Redlich R, Stacey D, Opel N, Grotegerd D, Dohm K, et al. 2015. Evidence of an IFN-γ by early life stress interaction in the regulation of amygdala reactivity to emotional stimuli. *Psychoneuroendocrinology* 62:166–73

Reichenberg A, Yirmiya R, Schuld A, Kraus T, Haack M, et al. 2001. Cytokine-associated emotional and cognitive disturbances in humans. *Arch. Gen. Psychiatry* 58(5):445–52

Ridout KK, Parade SH, Seifer R, Price LH, Gelernter J, et al. 2014. Interleukin 1B gene (*IL1B*) variation and internalizing symptoms in maltreated preschoolers. *Dev. Psychopathol.* 26(4 Pt. 2):1277–87

Rothman KJ, Greenland S. 2005. Causation and causal inference in epidemiology. *Am. J. Public Health* 95(Suppl. 1):S144–50

Sánchez MM, Ladd CO, Plotsky PM. 2001. Early adverse experience as a developmental risk factor for later psychopathology: evidence from rodent and primate models. *Dev. Psychopathol.* 13(3):419–49

Schedlowski M, Engler H, Grigoleit J-S. 2014. Endotoxin-induced experimental systemic inflammation in humans: a model to disentangle immune-to-brain communication. *Brain Behav. Immun.* 35:1–8

Selye H. 1936. A syndrome produced by diverse nocuous agents. *Nature* 138(3479):32

Setiawan E, Wilson AA, Mizrahi R, Rusjan PM, Miler L, et al. 2015. Role of translocator protein density, a marker of neuroinflammation, in the brain during major depressive episodes. *JAMA Psychiatry* 72(3):268–75

Shanks N, Larocque S, Meaney MJ. 1995. Neonatal endotoxin exposure alters the development of the hypothalamic-pituitary-adrenal axis: early illness and later responsivity to stress. *J. Neurosci.* 15(1 Pt. 1):376–84

Shanks N, Lightman SL. 2001. The maternal-neonatal neuro-immune interface: Are there long-term implications for inflammatory or stress-related disease? *J. Clin. Investig.* 108(11):1567–73

Shanks N, Windle RJ, Perks PA, Harbuz MS, Jessop DS, et al. 2000. Early-life exposure to endotoxin alters hypothalamic-pituitary-adrenal function and predisposition to inflammation. *PNAS* 97(10):5645–50

Shiels MS, Katki HA, Freedman ND, Purdue MP, Wentzensen N, et al. 2014. Cigarette smoking and variations in systemic immune and inflammation markers. *J. Natl. Cancer Inst.* 106:dju294

Shirtcliff EA, Coe CL, Pollak SD. 2009. Early childhood stress is associated with elevated antibody levels to herpes simplex virus type 1. *PNAS* 106(8):2963–67

Short SJ, Lubach GR, Karasin AI, Olsen CW, Styner M, et al. 2010. Maternal influenza infection during pregnancy impacts postnatal brain development in the rhesus monkey. *Biol. Psychiatry* 67(10):965–73

Slopen N, Kubzansky LD, McLaughlin KA, Koenen KC. 2013. Childhood adversity and inflammatory processes in youth: a prospective study. *Psychoneuroendocrinology* 38(2):188–200

Smith RS. 1991. The macrophage theory of depression. *Med. Hypotheses* 35(4):298–306

Solomon GF, Levine S, Kraft JK. 1968. Early experience and immunity. *Nature* 220(5169):821–22

Spitz RA. 1945. Hospitalism; an inquiry into the genesis of psychiatric conditions in early childhood. *Psychoanal. Study Child* 1:53–74

Strawbridge R, Arnone D, Danese A, Papadopoulos A, Herane Vives A, Cleare AJ. 2015. Inflammation and clinical response to treatment in depression: a meta-analysis. *Eur. Neuropsychopharmacol.* 25(10):1532–43

Suomi SJ. 1997. Early determinants of behaviour: evidence from primate studies. *Br. Med. Bull.* 53(1):170–84

Takatsuru Y, Nabekura J, Ishikawa T, Kohsaka S-I, Koibuchi N. 2015. Early-life stress increases the motility of microglia in adulthood. *J. Physiol. Sci.* 65(2):187–94

Takizawa R, Danese A, Maughan B, Arseneault L. 2015. Bullying victimization in childhood predicts inflammation and obesity at mid-life: a five-decade birth cohort study. *Psychol. Med.* 45(13):2705–15

Taylor SE. 2010. Mechanisms linking early life stress to adult health outcomes. *PNAS* 107(19):8507–12

Teicher MH, Samson JA. 2016. Annual research review: enduring neurobiological effects of childhood abuse and neglect. *J. Child Psychol. Psychiatry* 57:241–66

Terr LC. 1991. Childhood traumas: an outline and overview. *Am. J. Psychiatry* 148(1):10–20

Tottenham N, Hare TA, Millner A, Gilhooly T, Zevin JD, Casey BJ. 2011. Elevated amygdala response to faces following early deprivation. *Dev. Sci.* 14(2):190–204

Tottenham N, Sheridan MA. 2009. A review of adversity, the amygdala and the hippocampus: a consideration of developmental timing. *Front. Hum. Neurosci.* 3:68

van der Worp HB, Howells DW, Sena ES, Porritt MJ, Rewell S, et al. 2010. Can animal models of disease reliably inform human studies? *PLOS Med.* 7(3):e1000245

van Harmelen A-L, van Tol M-J, Demenescu LR, van der Wee NJA, Veltman DJ, et al. 2013. Enhanced amygdala reactivity to emotional faces in adults reporting childhood emotional maltreatment. *Soc. Cogn. Affect. Neurosci.* 8(4):362–69

Varese F, Smeets F, Drukker M, Lieverse R, Lataster T, et al. 2012. Childhood adversities increase the risk of psychosis: a meta-analysis of patient-control, prospective- and cross-sectional cohort studies. *Schizophr. Bull.* 38(4):661–71

Viviani B, Boraso M, Valero M, Gardoni F, Marco EM, et al. 2014. Early maternal deprivation immunologically primes hippocampal synapses by redistributing interleukin-1 receptor type I in a sex dependent manner. *Brain Behav. Immun.* 35:135–43

Volkow ND, Wise RA. 2005. How can drug addiction help us understand obesity? *Nat. Neurosci.* 8(5):555–60

Weaver ICG, Cervoni N, Champagne FA, D'Alessio AC, Sharma S, et al. 2004. Epigenetic programming by maternal behavior. *Nat. Neurosci.* 7(8):847–54

Wei L, Simen A, Mane S, Kaffman A. 2012. Early life stress inhibits expression of a novel innate immune pathway in the developing hippocampus. *Neuropsychopharmacology* 37(2):567–80

Widom CS. 1999. Posttraumatic stress disorder in abused and neglected children grown up. *Am. J. Psychiatry* 156(8):1223–29

Wieck A, Andersen SL, Brenhouse HC. 2013. Evidence for a neuroinflammatory mechanism in delayed effects of early life adversity in rats: relationship to cortical NMDA receptor expression. *Brain Behav. Immun.* 28:218–26

Yirmiya R, Goshen I. 2011. Immune modulation of learning, memory, neural plasticity and neurogenesis. *Brain Behav. Immun.* 25(2):181–213

Ziv Y, Ron N, Butovsky O, Landa G, Sudai E, et al. 2006. Immune cells contribute to the maintenance of neurogenesis and spatial learning abilities in adulthood. *Nat. Neurosci.* 9(2):268–75

Adjusting to Chronic Health Conditions

Vicki S. Helgeson and Melissa Zajdel

Department of Psychology, Carnegie Mellon University, Pittsburgh, Pennsylvania 15213;
email: vh2e@andrew.cmu.edu

Annu. Rev. Psychol. 2017. 68:545–71

The *Annual Review of Psychology* is online at
psych.annualreviews.org

This article's doi:
10.1146/annurev-psych-010416-044014

Keywords

chronic illness, adjustment, personality, social environment

Abstract

Research on adjustment to chronic disease is critical in today's world, in
which people are living longer lives, but lives are increasingly likely to be
characterized by one or more chronic illnesses. Chronic illnesses may deteriorate, enter remission, or fluctuate, but their defining characteristic is that
they persist. In this review, we first examine the effects of chronic disease
on one's sense of self. Then we review categories of factors that influence
how one adjusts to chronic illness, with particular emphasis on the impact
of these factors on functional status and psychosocial adjustment. We begin with contextual factors, including demographic variables such as sex
and race, as well as illness dimensions such as stigma and illness identity.
We then examine a set of dispositional factors that influence chronic illness adjustment, organizing these into resilience and vulnerability factors.
Resilience factors include cognitive adaptation indicators, personality variables, and benefit-finding. Vulnerability factors include a pessimistic attributional style, negative gender-related traits, and rumination. We then turn to
social environmental variables, including both supportive and unsupportive
interactions. Finally, we review chronic illness adjustment within the context
of dyadic coping. We conclude by examining potential interactions among
these classes of variables and outlining a set of directions for future research.

Contents

INTRODUCTION

In 1900, the average life expectancy in the United States was 47 years. By 2013, it was 79 years (Cent. Dis. Control Prev. 2013). Major reasons for this leap included better nutrition, better health care, and the development of vaccines. As the life span lengthened, people were no longer as likely to die from infectious diseases, such as tuberculosis, influenza, pneumonia, and diphtheria, but were more likely to acquire and die from chronic diseases, such as heart disease, cancer, emphysema, and cerebrovascular disease. However, today's leading causes of mortality are not always fatal; instead, people live for long periods of time with chronic disease. Today, about 85.6 million people in the United States are living with some form of cardiovascular disease or the aftereffects of stroke (Mozaffarian et al. 2015), 14.5 million people have a history of or are living with cancer (Am. Cancer Soc. 2016), and 29.1 million people have diabetes (Cent. Dis. Control Prev. 2014). People live for years if not decades with numerous other chronic diseases, including arthritis, HIV infection, osteoporosis, and multiple sclerosis. The defining feature of a chronic disease is that it is persists, although conditions may deteriorate, advance, fluctuate, or be characterized by remissions. Chronic diseases are often managed by a variety of behaviors executed by the patient as opposed to the physician, such as taking medication, monitoring diet, exercising, and following up with health care professionals. These behaviors are expected to control or inhibit disease progression and to minimize disease side effects and disruptions to daily living. The prevalence of chronic disease and its impact on quality of life necessitate an understanding of how individuals adjust to chronic medical conditions.

In this review, we first examine the effects of chronic disease on one's sense of self. Then, we examine categories of factors that influence how one adjusts to chronic disease. These include (*a*) contextual factors, such as demographic variables and dimensions of illness; (*b*) personality variables, which can be classified as resilience factors (e.g., self-esteem, mastery, optimism) or vulnerability factors (e.g., pessimistic attribution style, gender-related traits of unmitigated agency and unmitigated communion, rumination, avoidance); (*c*) social environmental variables, including social integration, social support, social conflict, and social control; and (*d*) dyadic coping. In describing the research that has linked each of these sets of factors to disease adjustment, we discuss various attempts to explicate these relations. Because these factors do not act in isolation, we also examine several interactionist frameworks that cut across categories in order to predict adjustment. Finally, we conclude by outlining a set of directions for future research in this area.

We note at the outset that several lines of investigation are not addressed in this review. We do not discuss research on chronic pain, nor do we focus specifically on terminal illness. This review focuses on work that has been conducted on adult populations rather than pediatric populations. Intervention research in this area is plentiful but beyond the scope of this review.

EFFECTS OF CHRONIC DISEASE ON THE SELF

Adjustment to chronic disease can be understood by distinguishing between disease and illness: Disease refers to the undesirable biological processes that affect individuals, whereas illness refers to the person's experience of the disease, including its psychological and social effects (Charmaz & Rosenfeld 2010). In some sense, the American Psychological Association and other organizations have acknowledged this distinction by requiring the use of language that separates the illness from the self. That is, phrases such as cancer patients and terms such as diabetics have been replaced by phrases such as people with cancer and people with diabetes. We recognize that persons are not necessarily defined by disease.

The examination of how individuals adjust to chronic disease extends beyond the physical symptoms associated with the disease to include how the individual perceives, assesses, and adapts to these symptoms. The presence of a chronic illness alters an individual's sense of self, as the previously held healthy identity is replaced by an illness identity that includes physical impairments, emotional reactions to physical symptoms, and cognitive constructions of the illness (Charmaz & Rosenfeld 2010). A chronic illness heightens one's awareness of the body, challenges previously held beliefs about the self, influences relationships with others, and may alter an individual's plans for the future. Thus, an individual with a chronic illness must learn how the sense of self can accommodate the illness. Chronic illness also undermines the stability of the self by introducing a degree of uncertainty into life (Charmaz 1995, Charmaz & Rosenfeld 2010).

One aspect of the self that may be threatened by chronic disease is one's gender role or sexuality. For example, many cancers require surgical treatment that can threaten gender-related self-image. A study of men with prostate cancer showed that one-third reported feelings of diminished masculinity since treatment (Zaider et al. 2012). This sense of diminished masculinity was related to greater worries about sexual functioning, controlling for actual level of sexual functioning. Among women with breast cancer, those who were highly invested in their appearance reported greater distress prior to surgery and greater distress over the next year, and those who were highly invested in having their body intact showed more adjustment difficulties, including problems with attractiveness and sexual desirability (Carver et al. 1998). In a study that compared heterosexual women and lesbians with breast cancer, lesbians evidenced less sexual concern and less concern about appearance (Arena et al. 2007).

An individual can restore a sense of self by both altering the concept of the self and adjusting daily behaviors to accommodate physical impairments and symptoms (Charmaz 1995). However, this adjustment process does not happen at a single point in time; it is a continuous process that is re-experienced every time a new physical impairment or deterioration occurs (Charmaz 1995). The extent to which an illness disrupts the sense of self and the severity of that disruption can change over time as individuals gain distance from the initial event and learn to integrate previously absent physical limitations into a new sense of identity (Charmaz 1995, Charmaz & Rosenfeld 2010). Thus, adjustment to chronic disease is affected by many factors, including the nature of the illness, the sex of the person experiencing the illness, personality variables, and characteristics of the social environment. We examine each of these factors in this article.

ADJUSTMENT TO CHRONIC DISEASE: CONTEXTUAL FACTORS

A number of characteristics of both individuals and illnesses influence how one adjusts to chronic disease. In this section, we review some of the factors that have received the most research attention, specifically sex, social class, and race or ethnicity. A relatively unexplored area of research is sexual orientation and gender identity. With the exception of HIV and breast cancer, research on chronic illness among LGBT persons is sparse (Jowett & Peel 2009).

Sex

Many studies have examined whether the sex of the person with a chronic disease is related to adjustment. For example, studies of people with type 2 diabetes have shown that women report poorer psychosocial adjustment, more depressive symptoms, and greater physical limitations compared to men (e.g., Iida et al. 2010). Similarly, studies of cancer (Baider et al. 1989) and heart disease (Hunt-Shanks et al. 2009) have shown that women adjust more poorly than men. There are exceptions, however, as one study showed that men with heart failure reported poorer health perceptions than women did (Macabasco-O'Connell et al. 2010).

There are many reasons for these sex differences. First, sex differences in disease adjustment are confounded by sex differences in morbidity among people without chronic disease. That is, in the general population, women perceive worse health, report more functional limitations, and have higher rates of depressive symptoms than men (for a review, see Helgeson 2012). Second, there are often sex differences in disease severity that could account for sex differences in disease adjustment. In the area of coronary heart disease, for example, women have more severe disease than men at diagnosis (Bucholz et al. 2014).

Among couples, the sex of the partner has implications for adjustment to chronic disease. A meta-analytic review of the literature on distress in couples coping with cancer showed that women were more distressed than men whether they were patients or partners of patients (Hagedoorn et al. 2008). Because women are more distressed than men in general, however, these studies cannot discern whether the distress is due to being female, being a spouse of a person with a chronic illness, or a combination of the two. One reason that female spouses could become particularly distressed is emotional contagion (Segrin et al. 2005). Patient distress may be more directly translated to spouse distress when spouses are female than when they are male.

Social Class

A great deal of research has linked lower socioeconomic status (SES) or lower social class to poorer adjustment to chronic disease. For example, low-income individuals with coronary heart disease were more likely to experience a significant decline in their ability to perform the activities of daily life over 5 years compared to higher-income individuals (Sin et al. 2015). Individuals with chronic obstructive pulmonary disease (COPD) at the lowest levels of income were at higher risk of hospital-based care, had more severe disease, and visited the emergency room more frequently compared to individuals at higher levels of income (Eisner et al. 2011).

There are several explanations as to why SES would be related to poor disease adjustment. The chronic stress inherent in the lives of low-SES individuals, including environmental hazards, noise pollution, and crime, may account for SES effects on health (Matthews & Gallo 2011). These same chronic stressors likely also impact psychosocial adjustment to chronic disease. Psychological distress has been identified as a potential link between SES and health, although findings from the literature supporting the mediating role of stress and distress have been mixed (Matthews & Gallo 2011). There is clearer evidence that the lack of positive psychosocial resources, such as perceived control and optimism, accounts for some of the relation between low SES and poor adjustment to chronic disease (Matthews & Gallo 2011).

Race and Ethnicity

There is a large body of literature on racial and ethnic health disparities in the prevalence of and mortality from chronic disease (for reviews, see Mays et al. 2007, Mensah et al. 2005), but fewer studies examine how adaptation to chronic disease varies across races or ethnicities. Compared to White persons, Black persons report greater diabetes-related distress and greater interference from diabetes with daily life (Hausmann et al. 2010). Among those with heart failure, non-Whites report poorer health perceptions compared to Whites (Macabasco-O'Connell et al. 2010), and non-White persons with heart disease show a greater deterioration in functioning over 5 years compared to White persons (Sin et al. 2015).

Making these simple comparisons is easy, but it is more difficult to identify the reasons for these differences. Perceived severity may account for some of these differences, as, compared to White persons, Black persons are diagnosed with cancer at a later stage (Warner et al. 2012), have worse metabolic control of diabetes (Kirk et al. 2006), and have more severe heart disease (Cooper et al. 2000).

Adherence is another prominent explanatory variable. Compared to White persons, Black persons reported lower rates of medication adherence among patients with heart failure (Dickson et al. 2015) and hypertension (Kressin et al. 2007) and more missed appointments in a study of adults with diabetes (Schectman et al. 2008). In a survey by a medical management organization of more than 6,000 people with diabetes, Black persons were less likely to use preventive services, were less likely to monitor their diet, and reported lower levels of exercise compared to White persons (Oster et al. 2006).

There may also be racial and ethnic differences in the way people respond to disease. In a sample of women with breast cancer, Hispanic women used less approach coping (acceptance, active coping, and positive reframing) and more avoidance coping (denial and behavioral disengagement) compared to non-Hispanic Whites (Umezawa et al. 2012). Black persons are more likely than White persons to turn to religion to cope with chronic disease (Harper et al. 2013). Black persons also have a general mistrust of the medical system that may impact their coping as well as adherence, as indicated by in-depth interviews with Black persons with diabetes (Peek et al. 2010). These interviews revealed that Black persons believe physicians are more likely to be domineering with them and less likely to share information with them, which leads to a general mistrust of physicians. Thus, Black persons are less inclined to share symptoms and health concerns with their physician. There is also evidence that Black persons have more negative beliefs about medication compared to Whites. In a survey of 806 persons with diabetes, adjusting for age, income, gender, and health literacy, Black persons were more likely than White persons to believe that prescription medication can be addictive, that prescription medication can do more harm than good, and that it is good to stop using medication once in a while (Piette et al. 2010).

Social support does not clearly account for racial differences in disease adjustment. In studies of adults with diabetes, one showed that Black persons reported more diabetes-related social support than Whites (Hausmann et al. 2010), whereas another showed no differences in social support across Whites, Latinos, and Blacks (Rees et al. 2010). A nationally representative survey showed that non-Hispanic Whites reported more interactions with friends than Black persons but that Black persons reported more fictive kin (people not related by blood but treated like family) relationships and more interactions with family members than non-Hispanic Whites (Taylor et al. 2013). Thus, a clear support deficit does not exist among racial and ethnic minorities that accounts for poor adjustment outcomes.

One difficulty in examining the effects of race on disease outcomes is that race and ethnicity are often confounded with SES. There is some evidence that race differences in adjustment to chronic disease can be partly accounted for by SES and that SES is the more powerful predictor of adjustment. For example, in one study, the race effect on COPD outcomes disappeared after controlling for SES (Eisner et al. 2011).

Illness Dimensions

Several dimensions of a chronic disease may be linked to adjustment. The Illness Perceptions Questionnaire was developed to identify these dimensions (Moss-Morris et al. 2002). A meta-analytic review of the literature using this instrument showed that three dimensions were strongly linked to nearly all indictors of illness adjustment (Hagger & Orbell 2003). Illness consequences (i.e., perceiving that the illness has major consequences for one's life) and illness identity (i.e., identifying that one has the illness itself, as well as the symptoms people associate with the illness) were associated with poor psychological and physical adjustment. By contrast, illness controllability (i.e., perceiving personal control over aspects of the illness) was associated with good psychological and physical adjustment. In a study of young adults with type 1 diabetes, perception of control over the illness was related to fewer treatment-related problems 5 years later, whereas perception of illness consequences was related to multiple indicators of poor diabetes adjustment (Rassart et al. 2015).

Stigma associated with a chronic illness also contributes to poorer adjustment (Charmaz & Rosenfeld 2010). Stigma has been linked to poor mental health (for a review, see Mak et al. 2007), and it interferes with treatment adherence (Bogart et al. 2015). Research on chronic illness among LGBT persons has identified discrimination by health care professionals and homophobia among potential support providers as barriers to effective treatment and impediments to adjustment (Jowett & Peel 2009). Perceived stigma is most strongly linked to poor outcomes, especially low self-esteem, when the stigma is perceived as legitimate and is internalized. When perceived stigma is internalized, it can be translated into feelings of shame and self-blame (Browne et al. 2013). Internalized homophobia has been linked to poor adjustment to breast cancer among lesbians (McGregor et al. 2001). However, if people reject the stigma, reactions range from anger to advocacy and empowerment to indifference. Certain dimensions of an illness influence the likelihood that the illness is stigmatized by others. For example, illnesses that are perceived as controllable and preventable, including lung cancer (Chapple et al. 2004), HIV/AIDS (Mahajan et al. 2008), and type 2 diabetes (Schabert et al. 2013), are associated with greater social stigma.

Disease adjustment is also influenced by the extent to which the illness is tied to one's self-concept. Illness centrality reflects the extent to which a person defines himself or herself in terms of the illness. Research on women with breast cancer found that illness centrality was related to poor psychological well-being, but this relation depended on illness valence (Helgeson 2011).

Illness centrality was related to poor psychological well-being only for individuals who viewed their illness in especially negative terms.

The impact of chronic disease on adjustment depends on whether the illness exists in isolation from other chronic diseases. People with chronic disease frequently face multiple chronic conditions (Parekh & Barton 2010), which makes adjustment more challenging as the individual has to adapt to the medical regimens required by each disease as well as any unique disease-specific psychosocial concerns. For example, in the Third National Health and Nutrition Examination Survey, 42.3% of individuals who were diagnosed with type 2 diabetes were also diagnosed with chronic kidney disease (Afkarian et al. 2013). Those with chronic kidney disease also have significantly more cardiovascular disease risk factors than those without chronic kidney disease, indicating the possibility of future comorbidity (Foster et al. 2013). These data indicate that it is highly likely that individuals with chronic disease are adjusting to multiple conditions.

In addition to comorbid physical disease, one of the most significant impediments to optimal adjustment to chronic disease is mental health status, particularly depression and anxiety. Depression is extremely common among those with chronic physical disease (Soo et al. 2009) and interferes with disease management (Hare et al. 2013). Thus, chronic illness adjustment is shaped by the presence of additional comorbid physical and mental health conditions.

ADJUSTMENT TO CHRONIC DISEASE: RESILIENCE AND VULNERABILITY FACTORS

The risk and resistance framework (Wallander et al. 1989) can be used to understand what factors play a role in disease adjustment. This framework is an expansion of the stress and coping model and has been used to understand adaptation to chronic physical disorders (Wallander & Varni 1992, 1998). Chronic physical disorders are conceptualized as an ongoing strain. Risk factors impede adjustment, whereas resistance factors facilitate adjustment. Risk and resistance factors include both intrapersonal factors such as personality and interpersonal factors such as the social environment. We begin this section by examining resistance or resilience factors and then turn to risk or vulnerability factors. Rather than provide an exhaustive review of all the resilience and vulnerability factors that have been investigated, we highlight the ones for which large bodies of literature exist in the context of chronic illness.

Resilience Factors

In the context of chronic illness, resilience is defined "as the ability to maintain normal levels of psychological well-being, or to return rapidly to prediagnosis levels" (Moskowitz 2010, p. 466). A number of studies have linked measures of resilience to good illness adjustment (for a review, see Moskowitz 2010). Rather than being a specific variable, resilience is often inferred from the relations between positive dispositional variables and good illness adjustment. In this section we discuss some of those positive frameworks.

Cognitive adaptation theory. One resilience framework that has been used to study disease adjustment is cognitive adaptation theory (Taylor 1983, Taylor & Brown 1988). According to cognitive adaptation theory, traumatic events, such as the onset of a chronic illness, threaten one's assumptions about the self and the world, and successful adjustment requires the restoration of these assumptions. There is evidence that those who have faced trauma or chronic disease view the world somewhat differently than those who have not. In a study that compared victims of trauma to nonvictims, victims perceived themselves and the world more negatively than did nonvictims

(Janoff-Bulman 1989). In the area of chronic illness, a study that compared 5-year breast cancer survivors to an age-matched healthy control group showed that survivors perceived the world as less controllable and more random than did healthy controls but did not perceive any differences in personal control over their daily lives compared to controls (Tomich & Helgeson 2002).

Restoration of these positive beliefs about the self and the world seems to be associated with successful adaptation to chronic disease. Specifically, finding ways to enhance views of the self (e.g., by making downward comparisons), finding ways to reestablish one's sense of control, and maintaining an optimistic outlook through adversity have been linked to good psychological and physical adjustment to disease (for a review, see Taylor et al. 2000). Helgeson (2003a,b) utilized this theory to examine adjustment to heart disease and found that a cognitive adaptation index composed of self-esteem, mastery, and optimism predicted positive adjustment to disease and reduced likelihood of a recurrent event 4 years later. A longitudinal study of women with breast cancer identified distinct trajectories of mental and physical functioning over 4 years and showed that cognitive adaptation indicators (e.g., self-image, optimism, perceived control) distinguished trajectories in the predicted direction (Helgeson et al. 2004b).

Many studies focus on specific resilience factors rather than all three components of cognitive adaptation theory. A wealth of studies on perceived control show positive links to disease adjustment (Rassart et al. 2015) and better treatment adherence (Gonzalez et al. 2015). The related construct of self-efficacy, which is typically operationalized as feeling capable of controlling aspects of treatment regimen and disease outcomes, is related to better adherence and better health (Guertin et al. 2015) and explains the link between depressive symptoms and poor adherence (Tovar et al. 2015).

One of the potential limitations of cognitive adaptation theory with respect to chronic disease is that the health threat persists and individuals may face disease progression, setbacks, or recurrent events that further challenge beliefs about the self and world. Several studies have tested whether cognitive adaptation indicators continue to predict positive disease adjustment in the face of recurrent health threats. In a study of people who had been treated with angioplasty for heart disease, cognitive adaptation indicators continued to predict positive disease adjustment in the presence of a recurrent event—sometimes showing even stronger beneficial associations (Helgeson 1999). One possibility is that recurrent events imply a more severe health threat, and cognitive adaptation indicators are more potent in the face of more severe disease.

By contrast, a study that compared women with breast cancer who had and had not sustained a recurrence within 5 years of diagnosis showed that beliefs about control over illness at diagnosis were related to poorer physical and mental functioning for women who sustained a recurrence but were unrelated to outcomes for those who remained disease-free (Tomich & Helgeson 2006). Rather than argue that these findings refute an entire body of research on cognitive adaptation theory, the investigators argued that there might be boundary conditions on the theory and that the controllability of the illness is one such condition. In addition, whereas many of the previous studies examined a general sense of control or mastery, which may continue to be adaptive under severe circumstances, this study focused specifically on perceptions of control over the cancer. Other research on women with recurrent breast cancer found no links between control over the disease and adjustment (Carver et al. 2000).

A variety of pathways may connect cognitive adaptation indicators to positive disease adjustment. Positive health behavior is an obvious one. As described above, people characterized by control, optimism, and self-esteem are more likely to adhere to treatment recommendations and reduce risk behavior. A second possibility is social support. It may be easier for network members to provide support to those who have a positive outlook in regard to their disease and are taking actions to promote their health. In fact, research has shown that depression drives network members away (Iida et al. 2010, Rassart et al. 2015).

Personality. One approach to the relation between resilience and disease adjustment focuses on the so-called big five personality traits: conscientiousness, neuroticism, openness to experience, extraversion, and agreeableness. However, not all of these traits can be conceptualized as resilience. Of the five, the strongest links to chronic illness adjustment have been found for conscientiousness (a resilience factor) and neuroticism (a vulnerability factor). Conscientiousness has predicted good adjustment in studies of adults with diabetes (Lawson et al. 2010, Rassart et al. 2014) and people with multiple sclerosis (Bruce et al. 2010), whereas neuroticism has been associated with poor adjustment in adults with type 1 diabetes (Lawson et al. 2010), poor health-related quality of life among persons with chronic kidney disease (Poppe et al. 2012), and poor adherence among adults with multiple sclerosis (Bruce et al. 2010). Coping has been implicated in the relation between these personality traits and disease adjustment. One study showed that those who were high in neuroticism and low in conscientiousness engaged in avoidant coping, which was then linked to poor adjustment (Rassart et al. 2014). Another study showed that the relation between neuroticism and poor health outcomes was explained by a lack of acceptance (Poppe et al. 2012).

Optimism has also received substantial attention with respect to adjustment to chronic disease. Optimism has been linked to better psychological and physical adjustment to coronary artery disease, cancer, and AIDS (for a review, see Rasmussen et al. 2006). In this case, as well, a primary explanation has been coping strategies. People who are optimistic are more likely to engage in positive coping strategies, such as positive reappraisal, acceptance, and problem-focused coping, and less likely to engage in maladaptive strategies, such as avoidance (Carver et al. 2010). Optimists are also more likely to re-engage with new goals when other goals become unattainable.

Mindfulness, or the ability to attend to the present moment in a nonjudgmental way, is a personality variable that has received increasing attention over the past few years and has been linked to disease adjustment. In a cross-sectional study of adults with multiple sclerosis, mindfulness was related to higher quality of life (Schirda et al. 2015). The ability to regulate emotions mediated the association. Mindfulness has also been linked to psychological health among other diseased populations (for a review, see Keng et al. 2011).

Personality characteristics linked to sex, referred to as gender-related traits, have been investigated in the context of chronic illness. Gender-related traits are typically understood in terms of communion and agency. An agentic or instrumental orientation involves a focus on the self, whereas a communal or an expressive orientation involves a focus on others (Bakan 1966). Agency has been linked conceptually and empirically to being male, whereas communion has been linked conceptually and empirically to being female (Bakan 1966). Agency has been associated with good adjustment to chronic diseases (Helgeson 2012). Potential explanations for this association center on self-esteem and social support. In studies of men with prostate cancer, self-esteem and the ability to express emotions mediated the relations between agency and positive health outcomes. Communion, by contrast, is typically linked to good relationship outcomes but is unrelated to disease adjustment (Helgeson 2012, Helgeson & Fritz 2000).

Benefit-finding. One way that people respond to stressful life events, including the onset of chronic disease, is by construing benefits. This response has been widely documented among people with cancer, for example (for a review, see Stanton et al. 2006). Deriving benefits from adversity was one of the features of the original version of cognitive adaptation theory (see the section Cognitive Adaptation Theory) (Taylor 1983) and later became the basis for Tedeschi & Calhoun's (1995) theory of posttraumatic growth (PTG).

Numerous studies have examined the relation between benefit-finding and disease adjustment, and findings have been mixed (Stanton et al. 2006, Tomich & Helgeson 2004). A meta-analytic review of the literature confirmed the mixed relations, showing that benefit-finding was related to reduced depression and more positive well-being, but also to more intrusive thoughts about the illness (Helgeson et al. 2006). It was unrelated to anxiety and global distress.

Although the theory of PTG suggests that growth will facilitate adjustment to disease, it does not specify that growth will be related to reduced psychological distress—at least in the short term. To the extent that people make positive life changes as a result of traumatic events, one would expect growth to be related to positive health outcomes. However, making major life changes is stressful, which may lead growth experiences to be related to negative outcomes, especially if the life changes are still ongoing. In fact, Tedeschi & Calhoun (1995) noted that growth occurs in the context of highly distressing events, which means that PTG may co-occur with distress. This may explain why the link between PTG and good outcomes is more likely to be found when a longer period of time has passed since the stressor onset (Helgeson et al. 2006).

One issue that researchers have wrestled with is the validity of PTG reports (Park & Helgeson 2006). Especially in cross-sectional studies, it is difficult to know whether PTG is a consequence of coping or a coping strategy in and of itself. People may be experiencing actual changes in their lives since the onset of the illness, or people may be construing benefits from adversity as a way to reduce their distress and cope with the illness (McFarland & Alvaro 2000). A study of people who underwent bone marrow transplants showed that patients perceived a decrease in distress from before to after the transplant, but actual distress levels did not change between the two points in time (Widows et al. 2005). Instead, after the transplant people overestimated how distressed they were prior to the transplant.

It is difficult to distinguish perceived growth from actual growth, as the latter requires information about a person prior to the stressor, in this case prior to the onset of the chronic illness. One of the strongest studies to date to distinguish between perceived and actual growth involved college students from four universities who were followed over time to determine who did and did not sustain a major stressor (Frazier et al. 2009). Among those who sustained a stressor, results revealed that perceived growth was unrelated to actual growth (i.e., actual changes in domains from before to after the stressor) and that perceived growth was related to an increase in distress from before to after the stressor. This study not only called into question the veridicality of a person's reports of PTG but also suggested that PTG was used to cope with distress. However, this study did not involve people with chronic disease. In an attempt to address the issue in the case of breast cancer, 5-year breast cancer survivors were compared to a carefully matched control group of women who responded to a stressful event they had experienced in the past 5 years (Tomich et al. 2005). As predicted, survivors reported more benefits from breast cancer than controls did with respect to their major stressor, but survivors also reported more adverse effects of their stressor compared to controls. There were no group differences in overall psychological distress. In a 10-year follow-up study of this same sample, the validity of growth reports was examined by comparing patient reports to reports by significant others of changes patients had experienced (Helgeson 2010). There was little corroboration of patient growth from significant others, and significant others reported that survivors had sustained fewer benefits than the survivors themselves reported. Taken collectively, the evidence for the validity of PTG reports is mixed at best.

One way that these mixed findings have been reconciled is by use of the two-component model of growth, in which the constructive and transformative form of growth is distinguished from the dysfunctional and deceptive form of growth (for a review, see Zoellner & Maercker 2006). The idea that there are adaptive and maladaptive aspects of growth reports is consistent with research that has shown growth to be linked to both adaptive (e.g., problem-focused) and maladaptive (e.g., avoidant) coping strategies. For example, a study of people undergoing bone marrow transplants for cancer found that PTG was related to positive reappraisal and problem solving as well as avoidance coping (Widows et al. 2005). The mixed findings from cross-sectional studies might be due to the inclusion of both groups of people—those who are characterized by the functional and those who are characterized by the dysfunctional forms of growth. Longitudinal studies might be more likely to reflect the more constructive form of growth.

Goals. One way that people may successfully adjust to chronic disease is to disengage from unattainable goals and reengage with more attainable goals (for reviews, see Rasmussen et al. 2006, Wrosch et al. 2013). A study of women with breast cancer demonstrated the importance of both processes. Women who disengaged from some goals and reengaged with new goals showed the greatest increases in positive affect over a 3-month period (Wrosch & Sabiston 2013). This effect appeared to be mediated by physical activity. In a study of older adults, those who had greater functional disabilities were more depressed only if they had difficulty with goal disengagement (Dunne et al. 2011). Whereas goal disengagement buffered the adverse effects of functional disabilities, goal reengagement did not predict outcomes.

The implications of goals for adjustment to chronic illness might be better understood within a developmental framework. According to socioemotional selectivity theory, people select their goals based on where they are in their life span (Carstensen 2006). In a test of this theory, women with metastatic breast cancer were compared to a healthy control group and asked to identify goals (Sullivan-Singh et al. 2015). Women with breast cancer reported goals with a more limited time perspective (e.g., enjoy present moment, spend time with those close to them) than the comparison group, and these goals predicted positive adjustment for women with breast cancer.

Other resistance factors. In addition to the factors described above, other factors have been linked to good disease adjustment outcomes. For example, illness acceptance has been linked to better psychological health among patients hospitalized for chronic medical conditions (heart disease, cancer, kidney disease), and illness acceptance mediates the link between hospital stress and subjective well-being (Karademas et al. 2009). Research on emotion regulation shows links to disease adjustment, such that the avoidance and inhibition of emotion are associated with poor illness adjustment outcomes, whereas the confrontation and expression of emotion are associated with good illness adjustment outcomes (for a review, see de Ridder et al. 2008). Emotional expression has been linked to good adjustment outcomes, but the effects of emotional expression depend on timing with respect to the stressor, the controllability of the stressor, the supportiveness of the social environment, and personality variables (for a review, see Stanton & Low 2012). Rather than elaborate on all of the possible resistance factors, we refer the reader to the references listed in this section.

Vulnerability Factors

Researchers have also examined a set of factors that predispose a person to have more difficulties adjusting to chronic disease. These vulnerability factors include a pessimistic attributional style and two gender-related traits, unmitigated agency and unmitigated communion. Some specific coping styles can also be considered vulnerability factors. In the following sections, we discuss two of these coping styles, avoidant coping and rumination.

Pessimistic attributional style. A person who attributes negative outcomes to stable, global, and internal factors, while also attributing positive outcomes to unstable, specific, and external factors, is characterized by a pessimistic attributional style. Given that chronic illness is a negative outcome, it would not be surprising if those characterized by a pessimistic attributional style have more difficulty adjusting to chronic disease. This turns out to be the case. Two studies assessed pessimistic attributional style prior to a health event and found links to negative adjustment outcomes years later. In a study of people who had total knee replacement, pessimistic attributional style assessed prior to surgery predicted more severe pain and poorer knee function 2 years later (Singh et al. 2010). A pessimistic attributional style identified prior to heart transplant predicted increased depressive symptoms 4 years post transplant (Jowsey et al. 2012). In addition, a pessimistic attributional style has been implicated in the development of physical diseases such as lung cancer (e.g., Novotny et al. 2010).

Negative gender-related traits. Bakan (1996) distinguished agency from its counterpart, unmitigated agency, which reflects a focus on the self to the exclusion of others. Unmitigated agency consists of an overly inflated view of the self and a disregard for and hostile orientation toward others (Helgeson 1994). Numerous studies have linked unmitigated agency to poor adjustment to disease (for a review, see Helgeson & Fritz 2000). One explanation for this link is a reluctance to seek help. For example, a study of persons with heart disease showed that unmitigated agency was linked to longer delays before seeking help for a first heart attack (for a review, see Helgeson 2012, Helgeson & Fritz 2000). A second explanation is difficulty with emotional expression. In a study of men with prostate cancer, difficulties with emotional expression accounted for the relation between unmitigated agency and poor functioning (Helgeson & Lepore 1997). A third explanation involves self-efficacy. In another study of men with prostate cancer, unmitigated agency was related to feeling less capable of controlling illness demands, which was then linked to increased distress and more functional difficulties (Helgeson & Lepore 2004). Finally, a fourth explanation is noncompliance with physician instructions (Helgeson & Fritz 2000).

Taken collectively, many of these explanations as to why people who score high on unmitigated agency evidence poor disease adjustment have to do with poor connections to the social environment—being unable or unwilling to reveal vulnerabilities, unable to seek help, and unresponsive to the help that is offered. Unmitigated agency is related to conflictual interactions with network members (Helgeson & Fritz 2000, Helgeson 2012). A study of persons with advanced cancer showed that unmitigated agency interacted with social support such that social support was related to decreased distress only among persons who scored low on unmitigated agency (Hoyt & Stanton 2011). This is evidence that those who score high on unmitigated agency may not reap the benefits of support.

Although Bakan (1966) never explicitly used the term unmitigated communion, he described the destructive effects of high levels of communion not mitigated by agency. Helgeson (1994) developed a measure of unmitigated communion, which reflects a focus on others to the exclusion of the self. Unmitigated communion consists of overinvolvement in others and self-neglect (Fritz & Helgeson, 1998) and has been linked to poor adjustment to disease among women with breast cancer, women with rheumatoid arthritis, and adults with heart disease (for reviews, see Helgeson & Fritz 1998, Helgeson 2012). The primary mechanism linking unmitigated communion to psychological distress in diseased populations is interpersonal stress. Those characterized by unmitigated communion take on others' problems as their own and become overly involved in and affected by those problems. Another mechanism is poor health care. Because those characterized by unmitigated communion place others' needs before their own, they do not always adhere to physician instructions (for a review, see Helgeson & Fritz 2000). Finally, one study has shown that unmitigated communion is linked to poor adjustment to breast cancer via cognitive adaptation indicators (Helgeson 2003a). Specifically, unmitigated communion was related to low self-esteem, poor body image, lower optimism, and a greater reliance on external sources of control.

Avoidance. A great deal of research links avoidant coping to poor adjustment to a variety of chronic illnesses and medical conditions (for a review, see Stanton et al. 2007). Studies have shown that avoidant coping is linked to increased depression and anxiety among women with breast cancer (Donovan-Kicken & Caughlin 2011) and to a decline in marital satisfaction among their partners (Kraemer et al. 2011). Avoidant coping has also been linked to negative affect in patients with heart failure (Nahlen & Saboonchi 2010). One reason for the links between avoidance and poor outcomes may be lack of social support. People who avoid talking about the illness may not be able to solicit support from network members. One study showed that self-blame and a failure to seek support explained the link between illness avoidance and increased distress (Donovan-Kicken & Caughlin 2011). Rather than as a predictor variable, research is more likely to examine avoidance as a mediator variable linking other variables discussed in this review to outcomes. For example, avoidant coping mediates the link between optimism and good health, as optimists engage less in avoidance (Carver et al. 2010).

Rumination. Nolen-Hoeksema (1987) developed a model of rumination and depression that suggested that people who respond to environmental stressors by ruminating have worse outcomes. Rumination consists of thinking about the causes, consequences, and symptoms associated with stressful events. Nolen-Hoeksema and colleagues (2008) suggested that rumination was related to increases in negative affect or depression by (*a*) interfering with problem solving that would have the potential to reduce depression; (*b*) increasing the accessibility of other negative thoughts and feelings, which reinforces depression; and (*c*) leading to difficulties with support networks that would otherwise be potentially helpful.

Some researchers have proposed that rumination mediates the link between chronic disease and depression and that rumination plays a critical role in the maintenance of depression among those who are chronically ill (Soo et al. 2009). Rumination may be one way in which individuals think about their disease and attempt to reconcile how their chronically ill self fits with their previously healthy self—the distorted sense of identity discussed by Charmaz & Rosenfeld (2010). Rumination about anger has been linked to perceiving greater disease severity independent of objective severity in persons with cardiac disease (Leon et al. 2010) and also to increased production of endothelin-1, a peptide and vasoconstrictor, which contributes to atherosclerosis (Fernandez et al. 2010). Rumination can also predict delays in seeking treatment for breast cancer (Lyubomirsky et al. 2006).

ADJUSTMENT TO CHRONIC DISEASE: SOCIAL ENVIRONMENT

As noted in the introduction to this review, most, if not all, chronic diseases require some form of self-management. Many of these self-care behaviors take place in an interpersonal context; that is, the social environment can influence whether the person with chronic disease adheres to the prescribed regimen.

To address how social network members influence regimen adherence, researchers conducted focus groups with White and Black adults aged 65 or older with a variety of chronic diseases and asked them to identify positive and negative social support strategies (Gallant et al. 2007). Participants identified more positive than negative factors and distinguished between direct and indirect strategies. Instrumental support, defined in terms of specific task assistance, was considered a direct strategy, whereas emotional support, in the form of encouragement, was more of an indirect strategy that motivated the person to take care of him- or herself. There were also direct and indirect negative strategies. Direct negative tactics included providing unwanted advice or discouraging good health behavior, whereas an example of an indirect negative tactic was failing to alter one's diet to make it easier for the patient to adhere to his or her own diet. In this section, we review the links between illness adjustment and the positive and negative (and direct and indirect) strategies employed by network members.

Social Support

Historically, the literature on social support has identified three main support functions: emotional, instrumental, and informational (House & Kahn 1985, Thoits 1985). Emotional support is defined as the communication of caring and concern, including listening, being there, empathizing, reassuring, and comforting. Informational support is defined as the provision of information to guide or advise, and instrumental support is defined as the provision of concrete assistance or aid. Despite these distinctions, the vast majority of research employs measures that average across multiple kinds of support or focuses on emotional support specifically.

Social support indices that combine across different support functions have been related to better adjustment to chronic illness. Social support has also been linked to better illness self-management (for a review, see Magrin et al. 2015). Social support is especially critical when the regimen is complex, which is the case with diabetes (King et al. 2010). Daily diary studies have linked support on a daily basis to greater physical activity among persons with type 2 diabetes (Khan et al. 2013) and to happier mood, better dietary adherence, and increased exercise in persons with newly diagnosed type 2 diabetes (Helgeson et al. 2016).

The vast majority of research has focused on emotional support and has shown links to disease adjustment; other kinds of support are not nearly as often the subject of investigation (Uchino 2004). The data concerning the relation between instrumental support and disease adjustment have been more mixed. Although instrumental support in the form of concrete assistance can reduce the burden of disease management, it can also communicate that support is needed and that one cannot manage the disease on one's own. To the extent that instrumental support reduces self-efficacy, it will not be linked to good adjustment outcomes, at least in the long term. A daily diary study of adults with newly diagnosed type 2 diabetes showed that daily fluctuations in partner emotional support were linked to daily fluctuations in happy mood, exercise, and dietary adherence (Helgeson et al. 2016), but patient reports of partner instrumental support were not related to mood or self-care behavior. However, partner reports of providing instrumental support were related to better patient mood. The authors suggested that patients may benefit from partner assistance when they are unaware of it, a finding consistent with the literature on invisible support, which is the idea that support provided but not perceived is most strongly connected to health (Bolger et al. 2000). Support received but not perceived does not induce feelings of incompetence or undermine feelings of self-efficacy.

Support providers are most often assumed to be family but may also be friends and health care professionals. LGBT persons may rely less on family and more on friends for support compared to heterosexual persons (Arena et al. 2007).

The most effective support matches the demands of the stressor (optimal matching) (Cutrona & Russell 1990) or the characteristics of the person (Martire et al. 2002). Cutrona & Russell (1990) argued that emotional support is most effective in the case of uncontrollable stressors, in which the need to feel loved, comforted, and accepted is highest, and that instrumental or informational support is most effective in the case of controllable stressors, in which the need for information and assistance to help prevent or solve problems is highest. Their literature review supported this theory. Personal characteristics may also affect who benefits from instrumental support. In two studies of persons with osteoarthritis, Martire and colleagues (2002, 2011) found that instrumental support in the form of physical assistance was related to good adjustment outcomes among people for whom independence was not central to their self-concepts but was related to poor adjustment outcomes among people for whom independence was central to their self-concepts.

The support-buffering hypothesis (Cohen & Wills 1985) suggests that support is especially beneficial under conditions of high stress. A number of studies have supported this theory. In a study of gynecologic cancer survivors, social support was most strongly related to reduced cancer-specific intrusive thoughts for those under conditions of high stress (Carpenter et al. 2010). In a study of LGB persons who were chronically ill, caregiver relationship quality buffered the effect of discrimination on depression (Fredriksen-Goldsen et al. 2009). In a study of adults with diabetes, cognitive impairment was associated with poor glycemic control, but this effect was reduced under conditions of high social support (Okura et al. 2009).

There are many explanations for the link between social support and good disease adjustment. Cognitive processing has been postulated as one mechanism by which social support is connected to good disease adjustment, in particular reduced psychological distress. In a study of men with prostate cancer, indicators of cognitive processing, such as intrusive thoughts about the illness and searching for meaning or understanding in the illness, accounted for the relation between social support and better mental health (Roberts et al. 2006). Social network members may help individuals process their disease, which then leads to better adjustment. Adherence is another mechanism, as people who have access to social support are more likely to enact positive health behaviors (Cohen 1988). It has also been suggested that social support increases self-esteem, provides one with a sense of identity, and enhances perceptions of control over one's environment (Cohen 1988), all of which have implications for disease adjustment. In a study of persons with end-stage renal disease, social support was linked to increased self-esteem, which in turn decreased depression and increased optimism (Symister & Friend 2003).

Unsupportive Social Interactions

Supportive interactions are not the only way in which network members can influence disease adjustment. Network members may behave in negative ways, either intentionally or unintentionally (Gallant et al. 2007). Studies that distinguish the supportive from the unsupportive behaviors of network members often find that unsupportive behaviors show even stronger links to health outcomes (Helgeson et al. 2015).

Several mechanisms for the relations between unsupportive behavior and poor adjustment have been examined. A study of women with breast cancer suggested that avoidance is a primary mechanism in this relationship (Manne & Glassman 2000). That is, when network members behave in unsupportive ways—whether intentional or not—people may respond by both cognitive (avoiding thinking about the cancer) and behavioral (avoiding dealing with the cancer) avoidance. In addition, when network members are critical or fail to offer needed help, self-efficacy may be undermined (Manne & Glassman 2000).

Social constraints. One specific kind of unsupportive social interaction is known as social constraint. Social constraints appear when network members make it more difficult for persons with chronic disease to discuss their illness by avoiding illness discussions, changing the subject when illness comes up, or acting uncomfortable when illness is discussed. In a study of men with prostate cancer, social constraints by family and friends were related to poorer mental and physical functioning (Eton et al. 2001) and were also associated with more avoidant thinking, which accounted for the link between social constraints and poorer mental health (Lepore & Helgeson 1998). Social constraints have also functioned as a moderator variable, such that intrusive thoughts about cancer are more strongly linked to poor mental health among those who report high levels of social constraints from network members. A recent innovative study of women with breast cancer used an electronically activated recorder device to record couples' naturalistic conversations over a weekend and showed the benefits of illness discussion when constraints were low. Specifically, illness discussions with their spouses were related to lower levels of intrusive and avoidance thoughts in patients, presumably because the discussions were reciprocal and partners were responsive and encouraged patient disclosure (Robbins et al. 2014).

Conflict. Other studies have assessed directly unsupportive behaviors in terms of criticism and conflict and show links between these behaviors and poor outcomes. A study of women with breast cancer showed that unsupportive partner behavior was related to both patient and partner distress (Manne et al. 2014). Avoidant coping mediated the association, such that unsupportive partner behavior was linked to greater patient and partner behavioral disengagement (e.g., withdrawal) and greater patient mental disengagement (e.g., distraction). A study of adults with type 2 diabetes showed that unsupportive family behavior was linked to poor glycemic control, and poor adherence mediated this association (Mayberry & Osborn 2012). In both of these studies, unsupportive behavior was connected to poor outcomes by undermining active coping to address the illness.

Overprotective behavior. A well-intentioned but unhelpful behavior in the context of chronic illness is overprotective behavior. Network members who engage in overprotective behavior are trying to be helpful, but their efforts backfire. Overprotective spouse behavior has been associated with decreased improvement in glycemic control following a treatment program for adults with diabetes (Hagedoorn et al. 2006).

Social Control

Social control in the context of chronic disease has been defined as "attempts to induce needed changes in the health behavior of a partner who has been unable or unwilling to make such changes" (Franks et al. 2006, p. 312). Social control includes network members reminding, if not urging, the patient to enact a health behavior. According to the dual effects hypothesis (Lewis & Rook 1999), social control benefits patient health behavior but at a cost to patient mental health. That is, patients may respond to these control efforts by enacting the appropriate health behavior but be distressed over the interaction, the health behavior, or both, and feel a threat to self-efficacy.

However, the evidence for the dual effects hypothesis is equivocal, as the data concerning the relations of social control to health behaviors and affect have been mixed (Helgeson et al. 2004a, Lewis & Rook 1999). The primary reason for the inconsistent findings is that social control is an umbrella term that captures a variety of distinct strategies. One distinction is between positive and negative social control tactics. Positive strategies have been defined as motivating and encouraging (which have some conceptual overlap with emotional support as described above), whereas negative strategies involve pressure, criticizing, and nagging (Fekete et al. 2006, Stephens et al. 2010). Even this distinction has not always proved useful. In one study, the positive and negative strategies were positively correlated and combined into a single index, obscuring the distinction (August et al. 2013).

A more useful distinction, at least on the surface, is the distinction between persuasion and pressure strategies, with persuasion being the gentler, more acceptable form of control and pressure being the more direct, overtly controlling behavior. These two strategies, however, also seem to be positively correlated (Martire et al. 2013), and findings have been inconsistent across studies. A study of couples in which one person had knee replacement therapy for osteoarthritis showed that both persuasion and pressure predicted better adherence but were differentially related to affect (i.e., pressure related to negative affect and persuasion related to positive affect) (Stephens et al. 2009), whereas another study of the same population showed that persuasion was unrelated to physical activity but pressure was related to decreased activity among males only (Martire et al. 2013). Persuasion and pressure have also been studied in the context of couples in which one person has type 2 diabetes. In this case, both diet-related pressure and persuasion were related to decreases in dietary adherence (Stephens et al. 2013). Thus, it is not clear that either of these social control strategies is effective in changing behavior. Social control has been linked to poor outcomes through a reduction in self-efficacy or feelings of personal control (Helgeson et al. 2004a).

DYADIC COPING

Although the vast majority of research on adjustment to chronic illness examines the effects of individual factors, whether one's personality or the perception of one's social environment, on patient adjustment, it is increasingly recognized that chronic illness takes place in an interpersonal context. The illness affects not only the person but also the social environment, and a prominent member of the social environment is the spouse or romantic partner (Gamarel & Revenson 2015). The partner not only is affected by the illness but also has the potential to affect the patient's adaptation. The well-being of patients and partners is intertwined (Segrin et al. 2005).

To address these issues, several theorists have developed the construct of dyadic coping (Bodenmann 1997, Lyons et al. 1998). As the traditional nuclear family declines, dyads may extend beyond romantic partners to involve friends, children, and other relatives, but, to date, studies of dyadic coping have focused on romantic partners. The construct has been conceptualized and measured in several different ways, but the core ideas are that illness is a shared health threat that affects both patients and partners and that both patients and partners are involved in managing the illness (Gamarel & Revenson 2015). One approach to studying dyadic coping has been to examine how couples interact as they deal with the stressor (Bodenmann 1997). In this case, dyadic coping refers to either the management of a stressor that affects the couple directly, such as the loss of a child, or the management of a stressor that primarily affects one partner but is communicated and transferred to the other partner, as is the case with chronic illness. Bodenmann (2005) distinguishes between four kinds of dyadic coping: positive or common dyadic coping, in which both partners are directly affected and work symmetrically; supportive dyadic coping, in which one person is primarily affected and the other assists; delegated communal coping, in which one partner is affected and the other takes over several tasks to reduce stress; and negative dyadic coping, in which the partner attempts to help the actor cope but does so ineffectively, such as through hostility, ambivalence, or superficial dyadic coping. Of these strategies, the clearest health benefits are associated with common dyadic coping (e.g., Rottman et al. 2015).

Dyadic coping has also been discussed by Berg & Upchurch (2007) within a developmental framework. They outline four categories of dyadic coping with chronic illness: uninvolvement (patient copes individually), support (spouse provides emotional or instrumental support), collaboration (joint problem-solving), and control (spouse dominates and tries to control patient's behavior). In a daily diary study of men with prostate cancer, collaborative coping was related to more positive emotions in both husbands and wives (Berg et al. 2008). These effects were partly mediated by the couple's perception that they were dealing effectively with the illness.

Revenson (1994) has examined dyadic coping from the perspective of coping congruence, or use of the same coping strategies by couples. There is some evidence that couples who demonstrate coping congruence have better outcomes. In a study of couples in which one member did or did not have a chronic illness, couples who were congruent in terms of active coping had higher marital adjustment (Badr 2004). Congruence in other kinds of coping, such as protective buffering and avoidance coping, were not associated with marital adjustment. Researchers have concluded that congruence in adaptive coping strategies may enhance adjustment to chronic illness, whereas congruence in maladaptive coping strategies does not (Berg & Upchurch 2007).

Finally, dyadic coping has been conceptualized in terms of communal coping, as described by Lyons et al. (1998). They defined communal coping as occurring when "one or more individuals perceive a stressor as 'our' problem (a social appraisal) versus 'my' or 'your' problem (an individualistic appraisal), and activate a process of shared or collaborative coping" (Lyons et al. 1998, p. 583). Thus, in the case of chronic illness, communal coping involves both shared illness appraisal and collaboration. The shared illness appraisal has been examined by a number of studies that have focused on communal language, or what has become known as we language, and has shown links to good outcomes. For example, in a study of persons with heart failure, spouse we-talk predicted positive changes in patients' symptoms and general health over 6 months (Rohrbaugh et al. 2008). We-talk also predicted greater success in quitting smoking following an intervention for persons with heart or lung disease (Rohrbaugh et al. 2012). In our work, we distinguished between patient explicit communal coping (i.e., self-report) and patient implicit communal coping (i.e., pronoun usage) and found that explicit communal coping was related to better patient relationship quality, greater support received from partners, and reduced partner distress (V.S. Helgeson, B. Jakubiak, H. Seltman, L.R.M. Hausmann, & M. Korytkowski, unpublished manuscript). Partner implicit communal coping was related to reduced patient distress and better patient self-care behavior. These results suggest that communal coping may be beneficial for both relationships and health, but that the effects of explicit measures differ from those of implicit measures. Patients may benefit especially from partner communal coping efforts that are less obvious. We also coded communal coping from couples' behavioral interactions and found that behavioral measures of communal coping were more strongly related to relationship quality, support receipt, patient distress, and patient self-care than were self-report measures (Zajdel et al. 2016).

INTERACTIONS AMONG RESISTANCE, VULNERABILITY, AND DYADIC FACTORS

The literature on adjustment to chronic disease has become increasingly sophisticated in recognizing that the factors discussed in this review do not act in isolation of one another. Studies show that personality variables interact with social environmental variables to predict outcomes, as, for example, independence centrality interacts with instrumental support to predict adjustment (Martire et al. 2002, 2011). It may be that people with more interdependent self-construals benefit more from social support. In a study of people recently diagnosed with type 2 diabetes, the relations between supportive and unsupportive behavior and mood were stronger for people who scored high on unmitigated communion compared to those who scored low (Helgeson et al. 2016). Thus, persons characterized by unmitigated communion may be more strongly affected by the social environment.

Interactions also occur among social environmental variables. Social support and social conflict may have a synergistic effect on outcomes. Research has shown that supportive and unsupportive behaviors interact in such a way that unsupportive behavior is related to poor outcomes only in the absence of supportive behavior (Manne et al. 2003). A study of patients with colorectal cancer found that the link between current helpful and unhelpful spouse behavior and adjustment depended on past levels of support (Hagedoorn et al. 2011). Current supportive and unsupportive behaviors were linked to good and poor relationship satisfaction, respectively, only when past levels of support were low. When past levels of support were high, current spouse behavior was less likely to be linked to outcomes.

A NOTE ON INTERVENTIONS

It is beyond the scope of this article to review research on interventions in the case of adjustment to chronic disease (for reviews, see Bohlmeijer et al. 2010, Faller et al. 2013, Martire et al. 2010). However, we would like to note that interventionists are increasingly recognizing that individual variables affect the outcome of an intervention. Some studies have found that personal resources or resilience factors (e.g., optimism, self-efficacy) interact with a psychosocial intervention, such that those with fewer resources receive the most benefit (Helgeson et al. 2000, Scheier et al. 2007). Vulnerability factors also interact with interventions, such that those who are most vulnerable are more likely to benefit. For example, a psychoeducational intervention for men with prostate cancer showed that men who lacked a college education reaped more benefits than college graduates (Lepore et al. 2003). Studies have also found that social environmental resources moderate the benefits of a psychosocial intervention, such that those with less adequate social support benefit more from the intervention (Helgeson et al. 2000).

FUTURE DIRECTIONS

Future research in the area of chronic disease must recognize that the personal and social factors that influence adjustment to chronic illness do not act in isolation from one another. With demographic variables, in particular, it is important to take an intersectional approach. Intersectionality refers to the ideas that sex, race, ethnicity, social class, age, gender identity, and religion cannot be examined independently of one another and that a focus on a single category is limiting because there is overlap among categories (Cole 2009). For example, a focus on gender in chronic illness will leave much to be desired in understanding how a poor young Black woman adjusts to chronic disease. Intersectionality requires attendance to the diversity within social categories, as well as the observation that there are commonalities across categories that are often viewed quite differently. Some of these commonalities have to do with status and power. This is an important direction for future research on adjustment to chronic illness to pursue.

The literature increasingly recognizes that chronic illness has an interpersonal context. However, much of that research has emphasized the spousal relationship to the exclusion of other relationships, such as relationships with adult children, parents, friends, and extended family. Research on LGBT persons with chronic illness has shown that the primary caregiver is just as likely to be a friend as a partner (e.g., Fredriksen-Goldsen et al. 2009), although ethnicity strongly influenced the relationship of the caregiver to the chronically ill person. For instance, among Fredriksen-Goldsen et al.'s (2009) subjects, 86% of African American patients' caregivers were friends, but 100% of Hispanic patients' caregivers were partners. Understanding the diversity of caregiver relationships is important for extending the research beyond the study of White middle-class couples, as two-parent families and marriage are more common among White people than ethnic minorities. Research has shown that extended family is more prevalent in the lives of Black individuals as opposed to White individuals, and these relationships may have the potential to impact a patient's adjustment process.

Future research should also address the incorporation of time into studies of chronic disease. Convenience samples study people at a single point in time or follow people over time from an arbitrary starting point. Other studies examine how people initially adapt to the onset of chronic disease. Studies that examine people prior to and following chronic illness are lacking, undoubtedly due to the difficulty in obtaining such samples. However, large longitudinal data sets are increasingly available for researchers to draw on to examine this question. The time course of chronic illness is important not only for understanding psychological and physical health changes over time but also for understanding whether predictor variables are more or less potent at different stages of illness. For example, the literature on PTG shows that benefits increase with time since diagnosis. Sophisticated longitudinal data analytic methods, such as trajectory analysis, may help to address these questions.

Ecological momentary assessment methods have become more common in the area of chronic disease. These methods help to determine what happens on a daily basis and to identify proximal antecedents to adjustment and proximal outcomes from psychological and physical changes. More sophisticated technological advances, including mobile devices and electronically activated recorders, may help advance our understanding of how people are coping with chronic illness in their natural environments.

CONCLUSION

In this review, we have discussed how chronic disease affects the sense of self and how successful adaptation requires both assimilation and accommodation processes. Adjustment to disease is influenced by contextual factors such as demographic variables and the dimensions of the illness; resilience factors such as self-esteem, optimism, and control; vulnerability factors such as unmitigated agency, unmitigated communion, and rumination; positive social environmental variables such as emotional and instrumental support; negative social environmental variables such as social constraints and social control; and forms of dyadic coping. Each of these factors has unique contributions to functional status and adjustment, as well as to more complicated synergistic effects. Common mechanisms that link resilience factors to disease adjustment include positive health behavior changes, elicitation of social support, increased adaptive coping (e.g., problem-focused coping, positive reappraisal), and enhanced self-efficacy. Common mechanisms linking vulnerability factors to poor disease adjustment include failure to enact appropriate health behavior changes, decreases in self-efficacy, and avoidant coping. Future research in this area would benefit from a more process-oriented approach that takes into consideration the course of chronic disease through time, pinpointing the specific factors that have the strongest effects at each stage of illness.

DISCLOSURE STATEMENT

The authors are not aware of any affiliations, memberships, funding, or financial holdings that might be perceived as affecting the objectivity of this review.

ACKNOWLEDGEMENTS

The authors acknowledge the support of National Institutes of Health grants DP3 DK103999, R01 DK095780, and R01 DK060586, which support work on adjustment to chronic disease.

LITERATURE CITED

Afkarian M, Sachs MC, Kestenbaum B, Hirsch IB, Tuttle KR, et al. 2013. Kidney disease and increased mortality risk in type 2 diabetes. *J. Am. Soc. Nephrol.* 24:302–8

Am. Cancer Soc. 2016. *Cancer Facts & Figures 2016*. Atlanta, GA: Am. Cancer Soc.

Arena PL, Carver CS, Antoni MH, Weiss S, Ironson G, Duran RE. 2007. Psychosocial responses to treatment for breast cancer among lesbian and heterosexual women. *Women Health* 44:81–102

August KJ, Rook KS, Franks MM, Stephens MAP. 2013. Spouses' involvement in their partners' diabetes management: associations with spouse stress and perceived marital quality. *J. Fam. Psychol.* 27:712–21

Badr H. 2004. Coping in marital dyads: a contextual perspective on the role of gender and health. *Pers. Relatsh.* 11:197–211

Baider LA, Perez T, Kaplan De-Nour A. 1989. Gender and adjustment to chronic disease: a study of couples with colon cancer. *Gen. Hosp. Psychiatry* 11:1–8

Bakan D. 1966. *The Duality of Human Existence*. Chicago: Rand McNally

Berg CA, Upchurch R. 2007. A developmental-contextual model of couples coping with chronic illness across the adult life span. *Psychol. Bull.* 133:920–54

Berg CA, Wiebe DJ, Butner J, Bloor L, Bradstreet C, et al. 2008. Collaborative coping and daily mood in couples dealing with prostate cancer. *Psychol. Aging* 23:505–16

Bodenmann G. 1997. Dyadic coping: a systemic-transactional view of stress and coping among couples: theory and empirical findings. *Eur. Rev. Appl. Psychol.* 47:137–40

Bodenmann G. 2005. Dyadic coping and its significance for marital functioning. In *Couples Coping with Stress: Emerging Perspectives on Dyadic Coping*, ed. T Revenson, K Kayser, G Bodenmann, pp. 33–49. Washington, DC: Am. Psychol. Assoc.

Bogart LM, Wagner GJ, Green HD, Mutchler MG, Klein DJ, McDavitt B. 2015. Social network characteristics moderate the association between stigmatizing attributions about HIV and non-adherence among Black Americans living with HIV: a longitudinal assessment. *Ann. Behav. Med.* 49:865–72

Bohlmeijer E, Prenger R, Taal E, Cuijpers P. 2010. The effects of mindfulness-based stress reduction therapy on mental health of adults with a chronic medical disease: a meta-analysis. *J. Psychosom. Res.* 68:539–44

Bolger N, Zuckerman A, Kessler RC. 2000. Invisible support and adjustment to stress. *J. Pers. Soc. Psychol.* 79:953–61

Browne JL, Ventura A, Mosely K, Speight J. 2013. 'I call it the blame and shame disease': a qualitative study about perceptions of social stigma surrounding type 3 diabetes. *BMJ Open* 3:e003384

Bruce JM, Hancock LM, Arnett P, Lynch S. 2010. Treatment adherence in multiple sclerosis: association with emotional status, personality, and cognition. *J. Behav. Med.* 33:219–27

Bucholz EM, Butala NM, Rathore SS, Dreyer RP, Lansky AJ, Krumholz HM. 2014. Sex differences in long-term mortality after myocardial infarction: a systematic review. *Circulation* 130:757–67

Carpenter KM, Fowler JM, Maxwell GL, Andersen BL. 2010. Direct and buffering effects of social support among gynecologic cancer survivors. *Ann. Behav. Med.* 39:79–90

Carstensen LL. 2006. The influence of a sense of time on human development. *Science* 312:1913–15

Carver CS, Harris S, Lehman J, Durel L, Antoni M, et al. 2000. How important is the perception of personal control? Studies of early stage breast cancer patients. *Pers. Soc. Psychol. Bull.* 26:139–49

Carver CS, Pozo-Kaderman C, Price AA, Noriega V, Harris SD, et al. 1998. Concern about aspects of body image and adjustment to early stage breast cancer. *Psychosom. Med.* 60:168–74

Carver CS, Scheier MF, Segerstrom SC. 2010. Optimism. *Clin. Psychol. Rev.* 30:879–89

Cent. Dis. Control Prev. 2013. Deaths: final data for 2013. *Natl. Vital Stat. Rep.* 64(2):1–119

Cent. Dis. Control Prev. 2014. *National Diabetes Statistics Report: Estimates of Diabetes and Its Burden in the United States*. Atlanta, GA: US Dep. Health Hum. Serv.

Chapple A, Ziebland S, McPherson A. 2004. Stigma, shame, and blame experienced by patients with lung cancer: qualitative study. *Br. Med. J.* 328:1470

Charmaz K. 1995. The body, identity, and self: adapting to impairment. *Sociol. Q.* 36:657–80

Charmaz K, Rosenfeld D. 2010. Chronic illness. In *The New Blackwell Companion to Medical Sociology*, ed. WC Cockerham, pp. 312–33. Oxford, UK: Wiley-Blackwell

Cohen S. 1988. Psychosocial models of the role of social support in the etiology of physical disease. *Health Psychol.* 7:269–97

Cohen S, Wills TA. 1985. Stress, social support, and the buffering hypothesis. *Psychol. Bull.* 98:310–57

Cole ER. 2009. Intersectionality and research in psychology. *Am. Psychol.* 64:170–80

Cooper R, Cutler J, Desvigne-Nickens P, Fortmann SP, Friedman L, Thom T. 2000. Trends and disparities in coronary heart disease, stroke, and other cardiovascular diseases in the United States: findings of the National Conference on Cardiovascular Disease Prevention. *Circulation* 102:3137–47

Cutrona CE, Russell DW. 1990. Type of social support and specific stress: toward a theory of optimal matching. In *Social Support: An Interactional View*, ed. BR Sarason, IG Sarason, GR Pierce, pp. 319–66. Oxford, UK: Wiley

de Ridder D, Geenen R, Kuijer R, van Middendorp H. 2008. Psychological adjustment to chronic disease. *Lancet* 372:246–55

Dickson VV, Knafl GJ, Wald J, Riegel B. 2015. Racial differences in clinical treatment and self-care behaviors of adults with chronic heart failure. *J. Am. Heart Assoc.* 4:e001561

Donovan-Kicken E, Caughlin J. 2011. Breast cancer patients' topic avoidance and psychological distress: the mediating role of coping. *J. Health Psychol.* 16:596–606

Dunne E, Wrosch C, Miller GE. 2011. Goal disengagement, functional disability, and depressive symptoms in old age. *Health Psychol.* 30:763–70

Eisner MD, Blanc PD, Omachi TA, Yelin EH, Sidney S, et al. 2011. Socioeconomic status, race and COPD health outcomes. *J. Epidemiol. Community Health* 65:26–34

Eton DT, Lepore SJ, Helgeson VS. 2001. Early quality of life in localized prostate cancer: an examination of treatment-related, demographic, and psychosocial factors. *Cancer* 92:1451–59

Faller H, Schuler M, Richard M, Heckl U, Weis J, Kuffner R. 2013. Effects of psycho-oncologic interventions on emotional distress and quality of life in adult patients with cancer: systematic review and meta-analysis. *J. Clin. Oncol.* 31:782–93

Fekete EM, Stephens MAP, Druley JA, Greene KA. 2006. Effects of spousal control and support on older adults' recovery from knee surgery. *J. Fam. Psychol.* 20:302–10

Fernandez AB, Soufer R, Collins D, Soufer A, Ranjbaran H, Burg MM. 2010. Tendency to angry rumination predicts stress-provoked endothelin-1 increase in patients with coronary artery disease. *Psychosom. Med.* 72:348–53

Foster MC, Rawlings AM, Marrett E, Neff D, Willis K, et al. 2013. Cardiovascular risk factor burden, treatment, and control among adults with chronic kidney disease in the United States. *Am. Heart J.* 166:150–56

Franks MM, Stephens MAP, Rook KS, Franklin BA, Keteyian SJ, Artinian NT. 2006. Spouses' provision of health-related support and control to patients participating in cardiac rehabilitation. *J. Fam. Psychol.* 20:311–18

Frazier P, Tennen H, Gavian M, Park C, Tomich P, Tashiro T. 2009. Does self-reported posttraumatic growth reflect genuine positive change? *Psychol. Sci.* 20:912–19

Fredriksen-Goldsen KI, Kim H-J, Muraco A, Mincer S. 2009. Chronically ill midlife and older lesbians, gay men, and bisexuals and their informal caregivers: the impact of the social context. *Sex. Res. Soc. Policy* 6:52–64

Fritz HL, Helgeson VS. 1998. Distinctions of unmitigated communion from communion: self-neglect and overinvolvement with others. *J. Pers. Soc. Psychol.* 75:121–40

Gallant MP, Spitze GD, Prohaska TR. 2007. Help or hindrance? How family and friends influence chronic illness self-management among older adults. *Res. Aging* 29:375–409

Gamarel KE, Revenson TA. 2015. Dyadic adaptation to chronic illness: the importance of considering context in understanding couples' resilience. In *Couple Resilience: Emerging Perspectives*, ed. K Skerrett, K Fergus, pp. 83–105. New York: Springer Sci. Bus. Media

Gonzalez JS, Shreck E, Psaros C, Safren SA. 2015. Distress and type 2 diabetes-treatment adherence: a mediating role for perceived control. *Health Psychol.* 34:505–13

Guertin C, Rocchi M, Pelletier LG, Emond C, Lalande G. 2015. The role of motivation and the regulation of eating on the physical and psychological health of patients with cardiovascular disease. *J. Health Psychol.* 20:543–55

Hagedoorn M, Dagan M, Puterman E, Hoff C, Meijerink JWHJ, et al. 2011. Relationship satisfaction in couples confronted with colorectal cancer: the interplay of past and current spousal support. *J. Behav. Med.* 34:288–97

Hagedoorn M, Sanderman R, Bolks HN, Tuinstra J, Coyne JC. 2008. Distress in couples coping with cancer: a meta-analysis and critical review of role and gender effects. *Psychol. Bull.* 134:1–30

Hagedoorn M, Van Yperen NW, Coyne JC, van Jaarsveld CHM, Ranchor AV, et al. 2006. Does marriage protect older people from distress? The role of equity and recency of bereavement. *Psychol. Aging* 21:611–20

Hagger MS, Orbell S. 2003. A meta-analytic review of the common-sense model of illness representations. *Psychol. Health* 18:141–84

Hare D, Toukhsati S, Johansson P, Jaarsma T. 2013. Depression and cardiovascular disease: a clinical review. *Eur. Heart J.* 35:1365–72

Harper FWK, Nevedal A, Eggly S, Francis C, Schwartz K, Albrecht TL. 2013. "It's up to you and God": understanding health behavior change in older African American survivors of colorectal cancer. *Trans. Behav. Med.* 3:97–103

Hausmann LRM, Ren D, Sevick MA. 2010. Racial differences in diabetes-related psychosocial factors and glycemic control in patients with type 2 diabetes. *Patient Prefer. Adherence* 4:291–99

Helgeson VS. 1994. Relation of agency and communion to well-being: evidence and potential explanations. *Psychol. Bull.* 116:412–28

Helgeson VS. 1999. Applicability of cognitive adaptation theory to predicting adjustment to heart disease after coronary angioplasty. *Health Psychol.* 18:561–69

Helgeson VS. 2003a. Cognitive adaptation, psychological adjustment, and disease progression among angioplasty patients: 4 years later. *Health Psychol.* 22:30–38

Helgeson VS. 2003b. Unmitigated communion and adjustment to breast cancer: associations and explanations. *J. Appl. Soc. Psychol.* 33:1643–61

Helgeson VS. 2010. Corroboration of growth following breast cancer: 10 years later. *J. Soc. Clin. Psychol.* 29:546–74

Helgeson VS. 2011. Survivor centrality among breast cancer survivors: implications for well-being. *Psycho-Oncology* 20:517–24

Helgeson VS. 2012. Gender and health: a social psychological perspective. In *Handbook of Health Psychology*, ed. A Baum, T Revenson, J Singer, pp. 519–37. New York: Psychol. Press

Helgeson VS, Cohen S, Schulz R, Yasko J. 2000. Group support interventions for people with cancer: Who benefits from what? *Health Psychol.* 19:107–14

Helgeson VS, Fritz HL. 1998. A theory of unmitigated communion. *Personal. Soc. Psychol. Rev.* 2:173–83

Helgeson VS, Fritz HL. 2000. The implications of unmitigated agency and unmitigated communion for domains for problem behavior. *J. Personal.* 68:1031–57

Helgeson VS, Lepore SJ. 1997. Men's adjustment to prostate cancer: the role of agency and unmitigated agency. *Sex Roles* 37:251–67

Helgeson VS, Lepore SJ. 2004. Quality of life following prostate cancer: the role of agency and unmitigated agency. *J. Appl. Soc. Psychol.* 34:2559–85

Helgeson VS, Mascatelli K, Reynolds K, Becker DJ, Escobar O, Siminerio LM. 2015. Friendship and romantic relationships among emerging adults with and without type 1 diabetes. *J. Pediatr. Psychol.* 40:359–72

Helgeson VS, Mascatelli K, Seltman H, Korytkowski M, Hausmann LRM. 2016. Implications of supportive and unsupportive behavior for couples with newly diagnosed diabetes. *Health Psychol.* In press

Helgeson VS, Novak SA, Lepore SJ, Eton DT. 2004a. Spouse social control efforts: relations to health behavior and well-being among men with prostate cancer. *J. Soc. Pers. Relatsh.* 21:53–68

Helgeson VS, Reynolds K, Tomich P. 2006. A meta-analytic review of benefit finding and growth. *J. Consult. Clin. Psychol.* 74:797–816

Helgeson VS, Snyder P, Seltman H. 2004b. Psychological and physical adjustment to breast cancer over 4 years: identifying distinct trajectories of change. *Health Psychol.* 23:3–15

House JS, Kahn RL. 1985. Measures and concepts of social support. In *Social Support and Health*, ed. S Cohen, SL Syme, pp. 83–108. Orlando, FL: Academic

Hoyt MA, Stanton AL. 2011. Unmitigated agency, social support, and psychological adjustment in men with cancer. *J. Personal.* 79:259–76

Hunt-Shanks T, Blanchard C, Reid RD. 2009. Gender differences in cardiac patients: a longitudinal investigation of exercise, autonomic anxiety, negative affect and depression. *Health Med.* 14:375–85

Iida M, Stephens MAP, Rook KS, Franks MM, Salem JK. 2010. When the going gets tough, does support get going? Determinants of spousal support provision to type 2 diabetic patients. *Pers. Soc. Psychol. Bull.* 36:780–91

Janoff-Bulman R. 1989. Assumptive worlds and the stress of traumatic events: applications of the schema construct. *Soc. Cogn.* 7:113–36

Jowett A, Peel E. 2009. Chronic illness in non-heterosexual contexts: an online survey of experiences. *Fem. Psychol.* 19:454–74

Jowsey S, Cutshall S, Colligan R, Stevens S, Kremers W, et al. 2012. Seligman's theory of attributional style: optimism, pessimism, and quality of life after heart transplant. *Prog. Transplant.* 22:49–55

Karademas EC, Tsagaraki A, Lambrou N. 2009. Illness acceptance, hospitalization stress and subjective health in a sample of chronic patients admitted to hospital. *J. Health Psychol.* 14:1243–50

Keng S-L, Smoski MJ, Robins CJ. 2011. Effects of mindfulness on psychological health: a review of empirical studies. *Clin. Psychol. Rev.* 31:1041–56

Khan CM, Stephens MAP, Franks MM, Rook KS, Salem JK. 2013. Influences of spousal support and control on diabetes management through physical activity. *Health Psychol.* 32:739–47

King DK, Estabrooks PA, Glasgow RE, Osuna D, Toobert DJ, et al. 2010. Self-efficacy, problem solving, and social-environmental support are associated with diabetes self-management behaviors. *Diabetes Care* 33:751–53

Kirk JK, D'Agostino RB, Bell RA, Passmore LV, Bonds DE, et al. 2006. Disparities in HbA1c levels between African-American and non-Hispanic white adults with diabetes. *Diabetes Care* 29:2130–36

Kraemer LM, Stanton AL, Meyerowitz BE, Rowland JH, Ganz PA. 2011. A longitudinal examination of couples' coping strategies as predictors of adjustment to breast cancer. *J. Fam. Psychol.* 25:963–72

Kressin NR, Wang F, Long J, Bokhour BG, Orner MB, et al. 2007. Hypertensive patients' race, health beliefs, process of care, and medication adherence. *J. Gen. Intern. Med.* 22:768–74

Lawson VL, Bundy C, Belcher J, Harvey JN. 2010. Mediation by illness perceptions of the effect of personality and health threat communication on coping with the diagnosis of diabetes. *Br. J. Health Psychol.* 15:623–42

Leon TC, Nouwen A, Sheffield D, Jaumdally R, Lip GYH. 2010. Anger rumination, social support, and cardiac symptoms in patients undergoing angiography. *Br. J. Health Psychol.* 15:841–57

Lepore SJ, Helgeson VS. 1998. Social constraints, intrusive thoughts, and mental health after prostate cancer. *J. Soc. Clin. Psychol.* 17:89–106

Lepore SJ, Helgeson VS, Eton DT, Schulz R. 2003. Improving quality of life in men with prostate cancer: a randomized controlled trial of group education interventions. *Health Psychol.* 22:443–52

Lewis MA, Rook KS. 1999. Social control in personal relationships: impact on health behaviors and psychological distress. *Health Psychol.* 18:63–71

Lyons RF, Mickelson KD, Sullivan MJL, Coyne JC. 1998. Coping as a communal process. *J. Soc. Pers. Relatsh.* 15:579–605

Lyubomirsky S, Kasri F, Chang O, Chung I. 2006. Ruminative response styles and delay of seeking diagnosis for breast cancer symptoms. *J. Soc. Clin. Psychol.* 25:276–304

Macabasco-O'Connell A, Crawford MH, Stotts N, Stewart A, Froelicher ES. 2010. Gender and racial differences in psychosocial factors of low-income patients with heart failure. *Heart Lung J. Acute Crit. Care* 39:2–11

Magrin ME, D'Addario M, Greco A, Miglioretti M, Sarini M, et al. 2015. Social support and adherence to treatment in hypertensive patients: a meta-analysis. *Ann. Behav. Med.* 49:307–18

Mahajan AP, Sayles JN, Patel VA, Remien RH, Szekeres G, Coates TJ. 2008. Stigma in the HIV/AIDS epidemic: a review of the literature and recommendations for the way forward. *AIDS* 22:S67–79

Mak WWS, Poon CYM, Pun LYK, Cheung SF. 2007. Meta-analysis of stigma and mental health. *Soc. Sci. Med.* 65:245–61

Manne SL, Glassman M. 2000. Perceived control, coping efficacy, and avoidance coping as mediators between spouses' unsupportive behaviors and cancer patients' psychological distress. *Health Psychol.* 19:155–64

Manne SL, Kashy DA, Siegel S, Myers Virtue S, Heckman C, Ryan D. 2014. Unsupportive partner behaviors, social-cognitive processing, and psychological outcomes in couples coping with early stage breast cancer. *J. Fam. Psychol.* 28:214–24

Manne SL, Ostroff J, Sherman M, Glassman M, Ross S, et al. 2003. Buffering effects of family and friend support on associations between partner unsupportive behaviors and coping among women with breast cancer. *J. Soc. Pers. Relatsh.* 20:771–92

Martire LM, Schulz R, Helgeson VS, Small BJ, Saghafi EM. 2010. Review and meta-analysis of couple-oriented interventions for chronic illness. *Ann. Behav. Med.* 40:325–42

Martire LM, Stephens MAP, Druley JA, Wojno W. 2002. Negative reactions to received spousal care: predictors and consequences of miscarried support. *Health Psychol.* 21:167–76

Martire LM, Stephens MAP, Mogle J, Schulz R, Brach J, Keefe FJ. 2013. Daily spousal influence on physical activity in knee osteoarthritis. *Ann. Behav. Med.* 45:213–23

Martire LM, Stephens MAP, Schulz R. 2011. Independence centrality as a moderator of the effects of spousal support on patient well-being and physical functioning. *Health Psychol.* 30:651–55

Matthews KA, Gallo LC. 2011. Psychological perspectives on pathways linking socioeconomic status and physical health. *Annu. Rev. Psychol.* 62:501–30

Mayberry LS, Osborn CY. 2012. Family support, medication adherence, and glycemic control among adults with type 2 diabetes. *Diabetes Care* 35:1239–45

Mays VM, Cochran SD, Barnes NW. 2007. Race, race-based discrimination, and health outcomes among African Americans. *Annu. Rev. Psychol.* 58:201–25

McFarland C, Alvaro C. 2000. The impact of motivation on temporal comparisons: coping with traumatic events by perceiving personal growth. *J. Pers. Soc. Psychol.* 79:327–43

McGregor BA, Carver CS, Antoni MH, Weiss S, Yount SE, Ironson G. 2001. Distress and internalized homophobia among lesbian women treated for early stage breast cancer. *Psychol. Women Q.* 25:1–9

Mensah GA, Mokdad AH, Ford ES, Greenlund KJ, Croft JB. 2005. State of disparities in cardiovascular health in the United States. *Circulation* 111:1233–41

Moskowitz JT. 2010. Positive affect at the onset of chronic illness: planting the seeds of resilience. In *Handbook of Adult Resilience*, ed. JW Reich, AJ Zautra, JS Hall, pp. 465–83. New York: Guilford

Moss-Morris R, Weinman J, Petrie KJ, Horne R, Cameron LD, Buick D. 2002. The Revised Illness Perception Questionnaire (IPQ-R). *Psychol. Health* 17:1–16

Mozaffarian D, Benjamin EJ, Go AS, Arnett DK, Blaha MJ, et al. 2015. Heart disease and stroke statistics—2016 update: a report from the American Heart Association. *Circulation* 132:e1–323

Nahlen C, Saboonchi F. 2010. Coping, sense of coherence and the dimensions of affect in patients with chronic health failure. *Eur. J. Cardiovasc. Nurs.* 9:118–25

Nolen-Hoeksema S. 1987. Sex differences in unipolar depression: evidence and theory. *Psychol. Bull.* 101:259–82

Nolen-Hoeksema S, Wisco BE, Lyubomirsky S. 2008. Rethinking rumination. *Perspect. Psychol. Sci.* 3:400–24

Novotny P, Colligan RC, Szydlo DW, Clark MM, Rausch S, et al. 2010. A pessimistic explanatory style is prognostic for poor lung cancer survival. *J. Thorac. Oncol.* 5:326–32

Okura T, Heisler M, Langa KM. 2009. Association between cognitive function and social support with glycemic control in adults and diabetes mellitus. *J. Am. Geriatr. Soc.* 57:1816–24

Oster NV, Welch V, Schild L, Gazmararian JA, Rask K, Spettell C. 2006. Differences in self-management behaviors and use of preventive services among diabetes management enrollees by race and ethnicity. *Dis. Manag.* 9:167–75

Parekh AK, Barton MB. 2010. The challenge of multiple comorbidity for the US health care system. *J. Am. Med. Assoc.* 303:1303–4

Park C, Helgeson VS. 2006. Growth following highly stressful life events: current status and future directions. *J. Consult. Clin. Psychol.* 74:791–96

Peek ME, Odoms-Young A, Quinn MT, Gorawara-Bhat R, Wilson SC, Chin MH. 2010. Race and shared decision-making: perspectives of African-Americans with diabetes. *Soc. Sci. Med.* 71:1–9

Piette JD, Heisler M, Harand A, Juip M. 2010. Beliefs about prescription medications among patients with diabetes: variation across racial groups and influences on cost-related medication underuse. *J. Health Care Poor Underserved* 21:349–61

Poppe C, Crombez G, Hanoulle I, Vogelaers D, Petrovic M. 2012. Mental quality of life in chronic fatigue is associated with an accommodative coping style and neuroticism: a path analysis. *Qual. Life Res.* 21:1337–45

Rasmussen HN, Wrosch C, Scheier MF, Carver CS. 2006. Self-regulation processes and health: the importance of optimism and goal adjustment. *J. Personal.* 74:1721–47

Rassart J, Luyckx K, Berg CA, Bijttebier P, Moons P, Weets I. 2015. Psychosocial functioning and glycemic control in emerging adults with type 1 diabetes: a 5-year follow-up study. *Health Psychol.* 34:1058–65

Rassart J, Luyckx K, Klimstra TA, Moons P, Groven C, Weets I. 2014. Personality and illness adaptation in adults with type 1 diabetes: the intervening role of illness coping and perceptions. *J. Clin. Psychol. Med. Settings* 21:41–55

Rees CA, Karter AJ, Young BA. 2010. Race/ethnicity, social support, and associations with diabetes self-care and clinical outcomes in NHANES. *Diabetes Educ.* 36:435–45

Revenson TA. 1994. Social support and marital coping with chronic illness. *Ann. Behav. Med.* 16:122–30

Robbins ML, Lopez AM, Weihs KL, Mehl MR. 2014. Cancer conversations in context: naturalistic observation of couples coping with breast cancer. *J. Fam. Psychol.* 28:380–90

Roberts KJ, Lepore SJ, Helgeson VS. 2006. Social-cognitive correlates of adjustment to prostate cancer. *Psycho-Oncology* 14:183–92

Rohrbaugh MJ, Mehl MR, Varda S, Reilly ES, Ewy GA. 2008. Prognostic significance of spouse *we* talk in couples coping with heart failure. *J. Consult. Clin. Psychol.* 78:781–89

Rohrbaugh MJ, Shoham V, Skoyen JA, Jensen M, Mehl MR. 2012. *We*-talk, communal coping, and cessation success in a couple-focused intervention for health-compromised smokers. *Fam. Process* 51:107–21

Rottman N, Hansen DG, Larsen PV, Nicolaisen A, Flyger H, et al. 2015. Dyadic coping within couples dealing with breast cancer: a longitudinal, population-based study. *Health Psychol.* 34:486–95

Schabert J, Browne JL, Mosely K, Speight J. 2013. Social stigma in diabetes: a framework to understand a growing problem for an increasing epidemic. *Patient Patient-Cent. Outcomes Res.* 6:1–10

Schectman JM, Schorling JB, Voss JD. 2008. Appointment adherence and disparities in outcomes among patients with diabetes. *J. Gen. Intern. Med.* 23:1685–87

Scheier MF, Helgeson VS, Schulz R, Colvin S, Berga S, et al. 2007. Moderators of interventions designed to enhance physical and psychological functioning among younger women with early stage breast cancer. *J. Clin. Oncol.* 25:5710–14

Schirda B, Nicholas JA, Prakash RS. 2015. Examining trait mindfulness, emotion dysregulation, and quality of life in multiple sclerosis. *Health Psychol.* 34:1107–15

Segrin C, Badger TA, Meek P, Lopez AM, Bonham E, Sieger A. 2005. Dyadic interdependence on affect and quality-of-life trajectories among women with breast cancer and their partners. *J. Soc. Pers. Relatsh.* 22:673–89

Sin NL, Yaffe K, Whooley MA. 2015. Depressive symptoms, cardiovascular disease severity, and functional status in older adults with coronary heart disease: the heart and soul study. *J. Am. Geriatr. Soc.* 63:8–15

Singh JA, O'Byrne MM, Colligan RC, Lewallen DG. 2010. Pessimistic explanatory style: a psychological risk factor for poor pain and functional outcomes two years after knee replacement. *J. Bone Joint Surg.* 92(6):799–806

Soo H, Burney S, Basten C. 2009. The role of rumination in affective distress in people with a chronic physical illness: a review of the literature and theoretical formulation. *J. Health Psychol.* 14:956–66

Stanton AL, Bower JE, Low CA. 2006. Posttraumatic growth after cancer. In *Handbook of Posttraumatic Growth: Research and Practice*, ed. L Calhoun, R Tedeschi, pp. 138–75. Mahwah, NJ: Erlbaum

Stanton AL, Low CA. 2012. Expressing emotions in stressful contexts: benefits, moderators, and mechanisms. *Curr. Dir. Psychol. Sci.* 21:124–28

Stanton AL, Revenson TA, Tennen H. 2007. Health psychology: psychological adjustment to chronic disease. *Annu. Rev. Psychol.* 58:565–92

Stephens MAP, Fekete EM, Franks MM, Rook KS, Druley JA, Greene KA. 2009. Spouses' use of pressure and persuasion to promote osteoarthritis patients' medical adherence after orthopedic surgery. *Health Psychol.* 28:48–55

Stephens MAP, Franks MM, Rook KS, Iida M, Hemphill RC, Salem JK. 2013. Spouses' attempts to regulate day-to-day dietary adherence among patients with type 2 diabetes. *Health Psychol.* 32:1029–37

Stephens MAP, Rook KS, Franks MM, Khan C, Iida M. 2010. Spouses' use of social control to improve diabetic patients' dietary adherence. *Fam. Syst. Health* 28:199–208

Sullivan-Singh SJ, Stanton AL, Low CA. 2015. Living with limited time: socioemotional selectivity theory in the context of health adversity. *J. Pers. Soc. Psychol.* 108:900–16

Symister P, Friend D. 2003. The influence of social support and problematic support on optimism and depression in chronic illness: a prospective study evaluating self-esteem as a mediator. *Health Psychol.* 22:123–29

Taylor RJ, Chatters LM, Woodward AT, Brown E. 2013. Racial and ethnic differences in extended family, friendship, fictive kin and congregational informal support networks. *Fam. Relat.* 62:609–24

Taylor SE. 1983. Adjustment to threatening events: a theory of cognitive adaptation. *Am. Psychol.* 38:1161–73

Taylor SE, Brown J. 1988. Illusion and well-being: a social psychological perspective on mental health. *Psychol. Bull.* 103:193–210

Taylor SE, Kemeny ME, Reed GM, Bower JE, Gruenewald TL. 2000. Psychological resources, positive illusions, and health. *Am. Psychol.* 55:99–109

Tedeschi R, Calhoun L. 1995. *Trauma and Transformation: Growing in the Aftermath of Suffering.* Thousand Oaks, CA: Sage

Thoits PA. 1985. Social support and psychological well-being: theoretical possibilities. In *Social Support: Theory, Research, and Applications*, ed. IG Sarason, BR Sarason, pp. 51–72. Dordrecht, Neth.: Martinus Nijhoff

Tomich P, Helgeson VS. 2002. Five years later: a cross-sectional comparison of breast cancer survivors with healthy women. *Psycho-Oncology* 11:154–69

Tomich P, Helgeson VS. 2004. Is finding something good in the bad always good? Benefit finding among women with breast cancer. *Health Psychol.* 23:16–23

Tomich P, Helgeson VS. 2006. Cognitive adaptation theory and breast cancer recurrence: Are there limits? *J. Consult. Clin. Psychol.* 74:980–87

Tomich P, Helgeson VS, Nowak Vache E. 2005. Perceived growth and decline following breast cancer: a comparison to age-matched controls 5-years later. *Psycho-Oncology* 14:1018–29

Tovar E, Rayens MK, Gokun Y, Clark M. 2015. Mediators of adherence among adults with comorbid diabetes and depression: the role of self-efficacy and social support. *J. Health Psychol.* 20:1405–15

Uchino BN. 2004. *Social Support and Physical Health: Understanding the Health Consequences of Relationships.* New Haven, CT: Yale Univ. Press

Umezawa Y, Lu Q, You J, Kagawa-Singer M, Leake B, Maly RC. 2012. Belief in divine control, coping, and race/ethnicity among older women with breast cancer. *Ann. Behav. Med.* 44:21–32

Wallander JL, Varni JW. 1992. Adjustment in children with chronic physical disorders: programmatic research on a disability-stress-coping model. In *Stress and Coping in Child Health*, ed. A La Greca, L Siegel, J Wallander, C Walker, pp. 279–98. New York: Guilford Press

Wallander JL, Varni JW. 1998. Effects of pediatric chronic physical disorders on child and family adjustment. *J. Child Psychol. Psychiatry* 39:29–46

Wallander JL, Varni JW, Babani L, Banis HT, Wilcox KT. 1989. Family resources as resistance factors for psychological maladjustment in chronically ill and handicapped children. *J. Pediatr. Psychol.* 14:157–73

Warner ET, Tamimi RM, Hughes ME, Ottesen RA, Wong Y-N, et al. 2012. Time to diagnosis and breast cancer stage by race/ethnicity. *Breast Cancer Res. Treat.* 136:813–21

Widows MR, Jacobsen PB, Booth-Jones M, Fields KK. 2005. Predictors of posttraumatic growth following bone marrow transplantation for cancer. *Health Psychol.* 24:266–73

Wrosch C, Sabiston CM. 2013. Goal adjustment, physical and sedentary activity, and well-being and health among breast cancer survivors. *Psycho-Oncology* 22:581–89

Wrosch C, Scheier MF, Miller GE. 2013. Goal adjustment capacities, subjective well-being, and physical health. *Soc. Personal. Psychol. Compass* 7:847–60

Zaider T, Manne SL, Nelson C, Mulhall J, Kissane D. 2012. Loss of masculine identity, marital affection, and sexual bother in men with localized prostate cancer. *J. Sex. Med.* 9:2724–32

Zajdel M, Helgeson VS, Seltman H, Korytkowski M, Hausmann LRM. 2016. *Communal coping in type 2 diabetes: a multi-method approach*. Presented at Annu. Meet. Soc. Behav. Med., March 30–Apr. 2, Washington, DC

Zoellner T, Maercker A. 2006. Posttraumatic growth in clinical psychology—a critical review and introduction of a two component model. *Clin. Psychol. Rev.* 26:626–53

Health Behavior Change: Moving from Observation to Intervention

Paschal Sheeran,[1] William M.P. Klein,[2]
and Alexander J. Rothman[3]

[1]Department of Psychology and Neuroscience, University of North Carolina, Chapel Hill, North Carolina 27599; email: psheeran@email.unc.edu

[2]Behavioral Research Program, National Cancer Institute, Bethesda, Maryland 20892

[3]Department of Psychology, University of Minnesota, Minneapolis, Minnesota 55455

Annu. Rev. Psychol. 2017. 68:573–600

First published online as a Review in Advance on September 8, 2016

The *Annual Review of Psychology* is online at psych.annualreviews.org

This article's doi:
10.1146/annurev-psych-010416-044007

Keywords

experimental medicine, interventions, trials, theory, construct, correlational data

Abstract

How can progress in research on health behavior change be accelerated? Experimental medicine (EM) offers an approach that can help investigators specify the research questions that need to be addressed and the evidence needed to test those questions. Whereas current research draws predominantly on multiple overlapping theories resting largely on correlational evidence, the EM approach emphasizes experimental tests of targets or mechanisms of change and programmatic research on which targets change health behaviors and which techniques change those targets. There is evidence that engaging particular targets promotes behavior change; however, systematic studies are needed to identify and validate targets and to discover when and how targets are best engaged. The EM approach promises progress in answering the key question that will enable the science of health behavior change to improve public health: What strategies are effective in promoting behavior change, for whom, and under what circumstances?

Contents

INTRODUCTION: A VIEW FORWARD

Over the past three decades, there have been tremendous advances in our understanding of the basic processes that shape people's behavior. We have come to recognize that different systems can regulate behavior (e.g., reflection versus impulse; Strack & Deutsch 2004), that different classes of cognitions shape and are shaped by behavior (i.e., implicit versus explicit cognition; Gawronski & Payne 2011), and that these processes unfold within a complex social world [e.g., relationships (Smith & Christakis 2008); discrimination (Pascoe & Smart Richman 2009)]. At the same time, it has only become more apparent that rates of morbidity and mortality depend critically on people's behavior (e.g., Mokdad et al. 2004, Yoon et al. 2014). National and international mandates to improve public health rely on changes in a broad array of behaviors, from diet and physical activity to tobacco and substance use to adherence to treatment and screening guidelines. Thus, efforts to meet these mandates depend upon intervention strategies effectively and efficiently modifying people's behavior (Rothman et al. 2015). However, when faced with the challenge of pursuing these mandates, interventionists and policy makers are left with more questions than answers as they grapple with limited theoretical and empirical guidance about what intervention strategy to use to modify a specific behavior and whether the intervention strategy is more or less effective for particular types of people or under particular conditions.

Given this challenge, researchers are increasingly recognizing the need for new approaches that can forge tighter links between advances in basic behavioral sciences and innovation in the design and delivery of strategies to improve public health (Czajkowski et al. 2015, Klein et al. 2015). The development of interdisciplinary research teams provides one valuable strategy because it facilitates communication about and use of information that too often remains siloed within a given discipline or area of study (Hall et al. 2012). However, there is also a need for an approach that shapes how basic and applied behavioral scientists specify the questions that need to be addressed and how they pursue the evidence needed to test those questions. To address this need, this review adopts the approach used to discern the mechanisms underlying treatments for disease (Bernard 1957) and advocates for an experimental medicine (EM) approach to research on health behavior change (Riddle et al. 2015). We first describe the EM approach, how it differs from traditional efficacy trials, and how it relates to other research frameworks. We devote the body of the review to evaluating the theories, constructs, and evidence used in health behavior change research from an EM perspective. Finally, we offer directions for future research that are informed by an EM analysis of the current state of the field.

THE EXPERIMENTAL MEDICINE APPROACH

The EM approach offers a vantage point on what programs of research need to be undertaken, why research questions need to be tackled experimentally, and how different research programs can be marshaled to forge a more cumulative science of health behavior change. EM involves four steps, beginning with the identification of factors that relate to behavior and are potentially modifiable and that thus qualify as targets for interventions to change health behaviors (i.e., **Figure 1**, Path A). The second step is the validation of those targets by developing assays (measures) of the targets and assessing when, how, and to what extent those targets elicit behavior change (**Figure 1**, Path B). The third step tests different intervention strategies to determine how target engagement, the desired change in targets, can be maximized (**Figure 1**, Path C). Findings from studies following Paths B and C provide researchers with a firm foundation from which to pursue the final step, full tests or randomized controlled trials (RCTs) to determine whether an intervention strategy or a set of strategies changes behavior via their effects on specified targets (Path D). The EM approach can be contrasted with traditional efficacy trials (Path X), which are principally concerned with whether, not how, interventions promote health behavior change and often either fail to obtain target assays or omit analyses of target engagement or target validation.

Efficacy trial: an experimental test of the impact of an intervention strategy on a health behavior or outcome that may eschew issues of target engagement

Targets: constructs that serve as mechanisms of action for health behavior change

Assays: measures of targets in experimental medicine

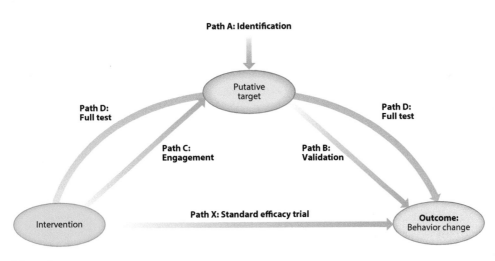

Figure 1

The experimental medicine (EM) approach to health behavior change. The EM approach specifies that research on health behavior change should proceed along four paths. Path A identifies putative targets, which are modifiable factors that may cause the behavior. Path B validates those targets by developing assays (i.e., measures) and testing the extent to which change in behavior accrues from manipulating the targets. Path C assesses the impact of different manipulations on the extent to which the target changes to discover how best to engage the target. Path D tests whether an intervention changes behavior because the intervention engaged the target and engaging the target changed the behavior. Whereas standard efficacy trials (Path X) often test only whether an intervention changes a behavior, the EM approach allows researchers to test both whether and why an intervention is effective. Figure adapted from Riddle et al. (2015).

Consider medication adherence as an example. Decades of research have established that rates of adherence to prescribed medication are suboptimal; however, interventions to improve adherence have been largely unsuccessful (e.g., Nieuwlaat et al. 2014). Interviews and surveys indicate that forgetting is the reason offered by most patients for failing to take their medication (e.g., Khatib et al. 2014). An EM approach to this problem might begin by identifying remembering to take one's medication as the target. The development of target assays (i.e., measures of remembering) might involve assessing whether patients have specified a particular opportunity for taking their medication each day (Gollwitzer & Sheeran 2006) or measuring the accessibility of this opportunity and the strength of its association with taking one's medication using a lexical decision task (Webb & Sheeran 2008). To validate this target, the researchers could test whether manipulating remembering (e.g., by mentally rehearsing the link between the relevant opportunity and taking one's medication) leads to improved adherence (Path B). Testing target engagement (Path C) involves assessing the impact of different strategies designed to enhance remembering to take one's medication. For instance, one could compare a pill box, a daily text message reminder, and the formation of an implementation intention [an if-then plan that specifies if this (opportunity) then this (response)] (Gollwitzer 1999). The data generated by these tests of Paths B and C enable researchers to undertake an RCT that tests, for example, the impact of implementation intentions on medication adherence via increased accessibility of the opportunity and stronger links between the opportunity and the behavior (Path D). A standard efficacy trial approach (Path X), by contrast, would make the leap from identifying forgetting as the reason for nonadherence to testing the effects of an intervention strategy (e.g., a text-based reminder system) on rates of adherence without testing the specific steps underlying any impact of the intervention. Thus, crucial information is not obtained or reported. For instance, if the intervention is unsuccessful, it cannot be determined whether this failure is due to the validity of the target (e.g., motivation to avoid side effects rather than forgetting explains nonadherence in this sample) or the strategy used to engage the target (e.g., the intervention did not increase the accessibility of the opportunity or strengthen the opportunity–behavior association). Furthermore, even if the intervention is successful, the investigators will have little information about why the intervention was effective and thus have limited guidance for subsequent efforts to refine or disseminate this intervention.

By emphasizing mechanisms of change, the EM approach unites basic research on behavior change with applied research that tests interventions to change health behaviors in clinical or field settings. Basic research is integrated into the larger process of studying health behavior change. Applied research focuses on Path D rather than Path X and can thus contribute rigorous tests of basic mechanistic processes that explain why interventions prove effective (or not). The EM approach promises that the production of knowledge about what targets to adopt and how they are best engaged will become more cumulative and efficient: Lessons can be learned from tests of Paths B, C, and D that cannot be learned from standard efficacy trials. Moreover, knowledge gained from tests in one domain can be applied to other health behaviors (e.g., strategies that improve remembering to take one's medication could also prove valuable in promoting flu vaccination or cancer screening) (Klein et al. 2016).

The EM approach to research on health behavior change underlies research frameworks such as the National Institutes of Health (NIH) stage model (Onken et al. 2014) and the NIH Science of Behavior Change initiative (SOBC) (Riddle et al. 2015) and is consistent with the Obesity-Related Behavioral Intervention Trials (ORBIT) model for developing behavioral treatments (Czajkowski et al. 2015), the United Kingdom's National Institute for Health and Care Excellence (2007) guidelines for behavior change, and methods such as the Multiphase Optimizations Strategy (MOST) (Collins et al. 2005, 2011) and Sequential Multiple Assignment Randomized Trial designs (SMART) (Lei et al. 2012). The EM approach and these other approaches are each characterized by their responsiveness to the theoretical and practical challenges that underlie the development of effective intervention strategies. They engage with the practical challenges posed by the question of what intervention strategy to use for which person at what time or context and do so through a programmatic emphasis on experimentation. These approaches also recognize that our theories must provide more precise specifications than most current theories do. If we are to develop interventions that can effectively address the major challenges in public health, then our theories need to specify which mechanism of action to engage, what manipulations can elicit changes in that mechanism of action, and for whom and under what conditions these mechanisms and manipulations do and do not work.

The EM approach offers a useful lens through which to view the current state of research on health behavior change. In particular, EM invites reflection upon the progress of research concerning each of the paths specified in **Figure 1** and profitable directions for future work. In relation to Path A, we ask what targets are identified by contemporary health behavior theories and whether theories specify the parameters of target effects (i.e., what targets should be valid for different kinds of behaviors, samples, and contexts). We also discuss how targets are characteristically measured and offer evidence explaining why experiments are needed for target validation (Path B). We discuss the role of taxonomies of behavior change techniques (BCTs) and new trial designs in improving what can be learned from standard efficacy trials. Competitive tests of target engagement (Path C) and full tests (Path D) appear to be infrequent, and we discuss the implications of this dearth both for establishing targets and techniques and for developing new ones. The key message of the EM approach is that theoretical and empirical work that links change techniques to targets and targets to behavioral outcomes can move the discipline from observation to intervention and thus advance public health in domains such as adherence, tobacco use, alcohol abuse, vaccination, and suicide.

TARGETS SPECIFIED BY HEALTH BEHAVIOR THEORIES

Multiple Overlapping Theories and Targets

Health behaviors are "overt behavioral patterns, actions or habits that relate to health maintenance, to health restoration and to health improvement" (Gochman 1997, p. 3). Health behavior theories are a family of psychological models that have been used to understand and predict health behaviors (see the sidebar Health Behavior Theories). Numerous overlapping theories of health behavior have been developed or coopted since the inception of the health belief model (Rosenstock 1966). These theories include but are not limited to protection motivation theory (Rogers 1983), the extended parallel process model (Witte 1992), social cognitive theory (e.g., Bandura 1998), the transtheoretical model (Prochaska et al. 1992), the theory of reasoned action (Fishbein & Ajzen 1975), the theory of planned behavior (Ajzen 1991), and the prototype/willingness model (Gibbons et al. 1998) (for overviews of these theories, see Avishai-Yitshak & Sheeran 2017, Conner & Norman 2015, Glanz et al. 2008, Salovey et al. 1998). Typically, new theories are developed by adding new constructs to those specified by previous theories (for definitions of these constructs, see the appendix). For instance, protection motivation theory extends the health belief model by including (*a*) fear as a component of threat appraisal, alongside perceived risk and perceived severity of disease, and (*b*) self-efficacy as a component of coping appraisal, alongside beliefs about costs and benefits of action. Similarly, the theory of reasoned action has been extended by the inclusion of perceived behavioral control as an additional predictor of intentions and behavior (to form the theory of planned behavior) or by the inclusion of social prototypes and behavioral willingness (to form the prototype/willingness model). Thus, theoretical development has primarily involved

HEALTH BEHAVIOR THEORIES

The sheer volume of theories relevant to health behavior change presents a formidable challenge for testing and integrating new targets. For example, Michie et al. (2014) identified 83 theories comprising more than 1,000 constructs. Listed below are 17 frequently cited health behavior theories that represent both classic and contemporary research.

Classic Theories

- Health belief model (Rosenstock 1966)
- Protection motivation theory (Rogers 1983)
- Extended parallel process model (Witte 1992)
- Social cognitive theory (e.g., Bandura 1998)
- Transtheoretical model (Prochaska et al. 1992)
- Theory of planned behavior (Ajzen 1991)
- Control theory (e.g., Carver & Scheier 1982, Powers 1973)

Theories Developed During the 1990s

- Information-motivation-behavioral skills model (Fisher & Fisher 1992),
- Implementation intentions theory (Gollwitzer 1993, 1999)
- Health action process approach (e.g., Schwarzer 2008)
- Prototype/willingness model (Gibbons et al. 1998)

Recent Developments

- Temporal self-regulation theory (Hall & Fong 2007)
- Theories concerned with implicit processes, including Hofmann et al.'s (2008) adaptation of the reflective-impulsive model (Strack & Deutsch 2004) to health behaviors, Borland's (2013) CEOS theory, habit theory (Wood & Neal 2007), the nudge framework (Thaler & Sunstein 2008), and Papies' (2016) model of health goal priming

The targets specified by these theories are defined in the appendix Targets Specified by Health Behavior Theories, and the overlap among the theories and targets is illustrated in **Table 1.**

expanding the number of constructs in a theory rather than identifying when and how those constructs are most influential.

Piecemeal theoretical development has been accompanied by the use of a wide variety of terms to characterize essentially the same construct. Evaluation of the likely outcomes of performing health behaviors is termed attitude in the theories of reasoned action and planned behavior, outcome expectancies in the health action process approach, costs and benefits in the health belief model, and pros and cons in the transtheoretical model, and it is captured by the concepts of response efficacy and response costs in protection motivation theory. These different terms are also associated with distinct measures even though there appears to be no difference in their predictive validity (Sheeran et al. 2016).

The use of multiple terms for the same construct belies a different problem, the failure of health behavior theories to embrace important distinctions within constructs. For instance, the distinction between cognitive beliefs (concerning the instrumental consequences of behavior) and affective beliefs (concerning the emotional consequences of performing a behavior) as components

Table 1 Overlap among targets specified by major health behavior theories

Putative targets	Extended parallel process model	Health belief model	Protection motivation theory	Transtheoretical model	Theory of planned behavior	Social cognitive theory	Control theories	Information-motivation-behavior skills	Health action process approach	Prototype/ willingness model	Temporal self-regulation theory	Implementation intentions theory	Implicit process theories
Cognitions about health threat													
Risk perception	✓	✓	✓					✓	✓				
Perceived severity	✓	✓	✓					✓					
Fear or worry	✓		✓										
Cognitions about focal behavior													
Intention	✓		✓		✓	✓		✓	✓	✓	✓	✓	✓
Willingness										✓			
Attitude	✓	✓	✓	✓	✓	✓		✓	✓	✓	✓		✓
Norms					✓	✓		✓	✓	✓			
Self-efficacy	✓	✓	✓	✓	✓	✓		✓	✓	✓	✓	✓	
Social prototypes										✓			

(Continued)

Table 1 (*Continued*)

	Health behavior theories												
Putative targets	Extended parallel process model	Health belief model	Protection motivation theory	Transtheoretical model	Theory of planned behavior	Social cognitive theory	Control theories	Information-motivation-behavior skills	Health action process approach	Prototype/ willingness model	Temporal self-regulation theory	Implementation intentions theory	Implicit process theories
Volitional factors													
If-then plans									✓			✓	
Behavioral skills								✓					
Processes of change				✓									
Progress monitoring							✓						
Executive function											✓		✓
Implicit cognition													
Attentional bias													✓
Implicit attitudes													✓
Approach bias													✓
Implicit goals or norms													✓
Habits											✓		

of attitude is supported by principal component analyses of survey items (e.g., Crites et al. 1994) and cognitive paradigms (Trafimow & Sheeran 1998). Primary studies (e.g., Lawton et al. 2009) and meta-analysis (e.g., Rhodes et al. 2009) indicate that affective beliefs are stronger predictors of health-related intentions and behavior than are cognitive beliefs. However, current health behavior theories do not formally specify affective attitude as a distinct target for intervention (but see Conner & Sparks 2015, Kiviniemi et al. 2007). Similarly, there is a long-standing distinction between injunctive norms (beliefs about what other people think one should do) and descriptive norms (beliefs about what other people themselves do) (see Deutsch & Gerard 1955), but most health behavior theories focus on either injunctive norms (e.g., the theory of planned behavior) or descriptive norms (e.g., the prototype/willingness model), and no theory discusses both types of norms. Several theories (e.g., social cognitive theory) appear to construe norms as mere social consequences (e.g., doing X will lead to approval from others), although evidence suggests that beliefs about social consequences do not capture the impact of norms (e.g., Trafimow et al. 2010).

Decisions about whether constructs are equivalent or distinct encompass larger questions about how to update health behavior theories with new constructs and what evidence is needed to warrant theoretical development. Although theories have developed via the inclusion of new constructs (e.g., the prototype/willingness model), in several instances new constructs for which empirical support seems compelling have not been integrated into health behavior theories. One prominent example is habit (for a review, see Wood & Rünger 2015). Ouellette & Wood (1998) and Webb & Sheeran (2006) found that intentions were good predictors of infrequently performed behaviors (e.g., cancer screening) but observed that the predictive validity of intention was much weaker for behaviors that were performed repeatedly in stable contexts and could thus become habitual (e.g., exercise). This finding suggests that intention may not be the most appropriate target for interventions designed to change habitual behaviors but also indicates that habit formation could be a worthwhile target for interventions designed to promote behavioral maintenance (Rothman et al. 2015). However, despite decades of research on habit, temporal self-regulation theory (Hall & Fong 2007) is the only prominent model of health behavior that makes explicit mention of habit.

Table 1 presents a cross-tabulation of health behavior theories by the targets specified by those theories. Targets can be grouped into four broad categories: cognitions about the health threat (i.e., beliefs about the focal disease or condition), cognitions about the health behavior (i.e., beliefs about the focal behavior), volitional factors (i.e., factors that serve to bolster motivation or promote more effective translation of intentions into action), and implicit cognition (i.e., automatic responses to relevant stimuli). The overlap in the targets specified, especially by classic theories (see the sidebar Health Behavior Theories), is striking. Whether theories emphasize the role of cognitions about the health threat and the behavior (e.g., health belief model) or cognitions about the behavior only (e.g., social cognitive theory) appears to be an important distinction. Classic theories generally do not specify volitional or implicit factors as targets. However, many newer theories make little mention of the role of cognitions about the health threat or the behavior, so it is unclear whether the targets specified by those theories are designed to supplant or complement the targets specified by earlier models. Moreover, the potential for redundancy or synergy among volitional and implicit targets remains to be determined. For example, it is not yet clear whether there is redundancy among implicit targets such that attentional bias, implicit attitudes, and approach bias are not all needed to understand health behavior performance. Evidence of synergy across targets can be seen in studies that combine if-then plans with relevant behavioral skills (e.g., Achtziger et al. 2008, Sheeran et al. 2007), processes of change (e.g., Armitage 2009), and progress monitoring (Harkin et al. 2016) or use if-then plans to compensate for poor executive function (Hall et al. 2014). However, simultaneous tests of multiple targets—both within and between key categories of targets—are relatively rare and constitute an important avenue for future research. The field offers many theories to guide our understanding of (and attempts to change) health behavior, yet there is both too much overlap (in terms of the targets that are identified) and too little overlap (in terms of accumulated knowledge about the relative importance of targets or how targets should be integrated) among theories. This state of affairs makes it difficult for an investigator to make informed choices about which targets to use in interventions.

The Parameters That Regulate Target Effects

Kurt Lewin's admonition that there is nothing more practical than a good theory relies on the existence of good theories (Rothman 2004, Rothman et al. 2013). What should a good theory be able to do? Although there is likely no single answer to this question, efforts to link theory and intervention provide insight into the questions that theories could be fashioned to address. Interventionists need to know what targets to engage, but that alone is not sufficient. Interventions are situated within a multidimensional context characterized by the behavior, the sample, and the setting. Thus, interventionists turn to theories to specify not only the targets for intervention but also the parameters that regulate target effects: For what behavior(s) and sample(s) and in what contexts (the psychological, physical, or social conditions) does engaging the target promote behavior change?

Classic health behavior theories identify a rich array of targets but provide limited guidance regarding the parameters that regulate the impact of targets on behavior. Constructs such as perceived risk, perceived severity, attitudes, norms, and self-efficacy are specified in theories as predictors—directly or indirectly—of behavioral performance irrespective of the focal behavior, sample, or setting. Although theorists would agree that these contextual factors affect the impact of targets and interventionists are advised to conduct initial assessments or focus groups to ascertain the applicability of specific targets, theories have not evolved to provide a priori guidance regarding the relative impact of specific targets (Rothman 2009).

Some theories have begun to offer greater specificity. For example, the prototype/willingness model proposes that behavioral willingness is a stronger predictor of behavior than is behavioral intention when the behavior involves risk (e.g., alcohol or drug use) and among younger people and those having less experience with the behavior (Gibbons et al. 2004). In contrast, behavioral intention is a stronger predictor of behavior than is behavioral willingness when the focus is on protective behaviors (e.g., physical activity) and among older or more experienced people (for a review, see Gerrard et al. 2008). Theories have also begun to delineate the conditions under which explicit (self-reported) attitudes have less of an influence on behavior. For example, according to Hofmann et al.'s (2008) dual process model, when people face impairments in self-control or working memory capacity (due to state or trait factors), the impact of explicit attitudes on health behavior is attenuated. Similarly, investigators have demonstrated that the formation of implementation intentions (i.e., if-then plans) is particularly effective when people are faced with a behavior that is difficult to perform or when they have chronic difficulty regulating their behavior (Gollwitzer & Sheeran 2006).

Theories have also begun to suggest that specific targets might be more influential at different times during the behavior change process. Rothman and colleagues (Rothman 2000, Rothman et al. 2011) have emphasized distinctions between the factors that underlie the initiation versus the maintenance of behavior change. For example, outcome expectations and self-efficacy are thought to be important determinants of behavioral initiation, whereas satisfaction with behavior change is thought to be an important determinant of behavioral maintenance (e.g., Baldwin et al. 2006, Hertel et al. 2008). Furthermore, people's dispositions for promotion or prevention affects their ability to successfully initiate and maintain behavior change (Fuglestad et al. 2008, 2013).

However, even with these advances, health behavior theories remain woefully underspecified. They provide remarkably few direct answers to the questions that emerge when researchers are faced with the challenge of intervening to change behavior: For which behaviors, samples, or settings will engaging a target be particularly effective, and perhaps even more important, under what conditions will target engagement not be effective? Given the scale and scope of empirical work in this area, why have these theories not evolved to answer these questions and address these needs? One important challenge may be the way in which theorists construe evidence of moderation or boundary conditions on effects (Rothman 2013). If a theoretical principle is thought to hold across behaviors, samples, or settings, then empirical evidence concerning boundary conditions could be considered a limitation; the failure to observe the predicted relation under certain conditions is construed as challenging the theory. Given this mind-set, investigators may focus their work on demonstrating that evidence of moderation is the exception rather than on trying to delineate the factors that mark the boundary conditions of the target.

What if investigators were to approach the same studies with an a priori commitment to discovering when or where the principle underlying their work may and may not operate? With this mind-set, obtaining evidence of moderation would not be construed as a limitation or a challenge but as an opportunity to improve the specificity and precision of the theory (McGuire 1989, Rothman & Salovey 2007). Moreover, because investigators would be prepared from the outset to delineate the target's boundary conditions, they would be more likely to make methodological decisions that improve the quality of the evidence generated. In particular, the moderator would be more likely to be measured with a valid and reliable instrument and at the right time within the study design. The investigator would also be more likely to capture the processes that underlie evidence of moderation, linking mediators and moderators both theoretically and statistically.

For example, gender might moderate the effect of an intervention strategy such that it works for women but not men either because gender moderates the effect of the intervention on the target (i.e., Path C) or because gender moderates the effect of the target on the behavioral outcome (i.e., Path B). These two outcomes have distinct implications for both theory and practice (Rothman 2013, Rothman & Baldwin 2012). In the first case, the evidence would indicate that the target may be appropriate for both men and women, but a different strategy is needed to engage that target for men. In the second case, the evidence would indicate that the strategy is able to affect change in the target equally well for men and women, but the target is not an important determinant of the behavior for men. The accumulation of empirical evidence that can distinguish between these two explanations would, over time, provide the evidence base necessary to enhance the specification of our theories. The fact that this approach to moderation has not been fully embraced may help to explain why our theories remain underspecified despite the accumulation of an enormous body of empirical work (Noar & Zimmerman 2005, Weinstein & Rothman 2005).

Target Measurement

An essential precursor to identifying promising targets for interventions to promote behavior change is having reliable and valid target assays. Importantly, the EM approach encourages the development of assays that capture the target at different levels of analysis (e.g., self-report, behavioral, neural, and physiological). Most of the targets specified by health behavior theories are measured using self-report questionnaires. Self-reports have considerable advantages (e.g., ease of use, capacity to survey large numbers of participants) but also well-known limitations (e.g., memory, accessibility, social desirability, and self-presentational bias; for a review, see Podsakoff et al. 2003). Concerns about self-report measures, combined with technological advances in measurement over the past 20 years, highlight the need for and potential to develop new and more reliable target assays. Sensor and wireless technologies allow researchers to capture affective states (e.g., using voice pitch), exposure to social norms (e.g., using online recordings of social interactions), actual rather than perceived barriers (e.g., using GPS codes to determine whether the built environment facilitates physical activity), self-regulatory resources (e.g., using grip strength), attention to health information (e.g., using unobtrusive eye tracking), and health behavior itself (e.g., using accelerometers to measure physical activity). Immersive virtual reality environments (Persky 2011) can capture numerous targets in the context in which behavior takes place, increasing ecological validity. Such observational measures could serve not only to validate self-report assays but also to explain unique variance in health behavior. For example, Falk and colleagues (2010, 2011) observed that neural responses to persuasive messages explained substantial variance in health behavior change even after standard self-report assays were taken into account. Moreover, neural responses to different smoking cessation campaigns predicted the volume of calls to smoking quit lines at the population level, whereas self-reports concerning campaign effectiveness did not (Falk et al. 2012).

The increased ability to capture theoretically important targets with a variety of assays changes not only what can be measured but also when and how often targets can be measured. This progress is important considering that most tests of theories hinge on the measurement of constructs at a single, static moment in time. Researchers might measure participants' intentions to use a condom with a one-time survey—likely at a time when the behavior is not salient—and then use this measure to predict subsequent condom use. If intentions are measured more than once, however, it becomes possible to assay the temporal stability of intention, which is an important determinant of whether or not intention gets translated into action (e.g., Sheeran & Abraham 2003). Fluctuations in cognitions are likely commonplace, as demonstrated by research on the empathy gap (Loewenstein 2005) showing that, when people are in a cold (e.g., satiated) state, they have different intentions and self-efficacy than when they are in a hot (e.g., hungry) state (Nordgren et al. 2008). Moreover, fluctuations may characterize not only scores on the target assay but also how well or under what circumstances the target relates to behavior.

Research on health behavior change also departs from the EM approach by failing to standardize measurement of key targets. Clear medical guidelines exist for measuring blood pressure and concluding whether a single patient's blood pressure is high, low, or normal (Weber et al. 2014). There are no equivalent guidelines for the targets specified by health behavior theories. Fortunately, efforts are underway to address the need for consensual measures of health behavior constructs. The NIH has supported the funding and development of numerous portals that archive reliable, tested, and professionally vetted measures of many different constructs, including targets specified by health behavior theories. Examples include the Patient-Reported Outcomes Measurement Information System (PROMIS) (Carle et al. 2015), the Grid-Enabled Measures (GEM) project (Moser et al. 2011), and the Phenotype Measurement (PhenX) project (Hamilton et al. 2011). The NIH is also working on supporting tools that facilitate the development and use of shared definitions of constructs used across health behavior theories. Taking an EM approach requires thorough and rigorous efforts to assay targets. To this end, the field of health behavior needs to work toward the development of consensual and evidence-driven assays and take full advantage of the many new methods of obtaining target assays at different levels.

THE IMPACT OF TARGET ENGAGEMENT ON HEALTH BEHAVIORS

Evidence concerning the impact of target engagement (Path B) predominantly comes from observational studies that measure targets at one time point and measure health behavior(s) either at the same or a later time. Such correlational data largely support the predictive validity of targets specified by health behavior theories. For example, several meta-analyses indicate that risk perceptions and perceived severity (e.g., Brewer et al. 2007, Milne et al. 2000), intentions and self-efficacy (e.g., McEachan et al. 2011), and implicit attitudes (e.g., Greenwald et al. 2009) each have average correlations of medium-to-large magnitudes with health behaviors. However, there are several reasons why correlational data can be misleading about how much behavior change will accrue from target engagement. The first reason is that the associations typically reported in meta-analyses are bivariate and do not take the influence of alternative targets into consideration. Thus, for example, it is unclear how much variance perceived severity explains in behavior once risk perceptions have been taken into account or how well self-efficacy predicts behavior over and above intention. Greenwald et al. (2009) observed that the average correlation between implicit attitude and behavior was $r_+ \approx 0.18$, controlling for explicit attitude. However, the choice of alternative targets likely plays a role. Explicit attitudes exhibit weaker correlations with health behaviors compared to intention and self-efficacy (e.g., McEachan et al. 2011), and the increment in variance explained by implicit attitude after associations with these targets have been considered remains unclear (Blanton et al. 2016). It is also unclear how large an increment in variance a target would have to explain for researchers to consider the target valid and thus worth engaging in a planned intervention (for a seminal analysis of the problems of drawing inferences from change in R^2, see Trafimow 2004).

The second reason is that past behavior is not typically taken into account. Bivariate correlations do not indicate whether targets predict changes in behavior. To gain insight into this issue, we reanalyzed data from McEachan et al.'s (2011) meta-analysis. The sample-weighted average correlations between intention and behavior, past behavior and intention, and past behavior and current behavior were each of medium-to-large magnitude ($r_+ = 0.40, 0.44,$ and 0.48, respectively; minimum $N = 21,786$). Controlling for past behavior, however, the average correlation between intention and behavior change was only $r_+ = 0.21$, a small-to-medium effect size (Cohen 1992). It seems that the prediction of health behavior change is a good deal more modest than is the prediction of health behavior.

The third reason is that correlational designs cannot rule out the impact of unmeasured (third) variables and are therefore not fit for determining whether engaging a target changes health behaviors (Weinstein 2007). Only experiments permit causal inferences. Experiments have three defining features: (*a*) Participants are randomized to a treatment versus a control or comparison condition, (*b*) the treatment engages the target (i.e., engenders a difference between the treatment versus control condition on the target assay), and (*c*) behavior change or some other outcome is measured in the wake of the intervention (e.g., West et al. 2000). In a series of meta-analyses (Sheeran et al. 2014, 2016; Webb & Sheeran 2006), we leveraged these features of experiments to address the fundamental question that underlies the experimental medicine approach: How much change in behavior accrues from interventions that successfully engage key targets specified by health behavior theories? Findings showed that changing cognitions about the focal threat (risk perception, perceived severity) led to small or small-to-medium changes in health behaviors ($d_+ = 0.25$ and 0.34, respectively). Changing cognitions about the focal behavior also proved effective. Heightening intentions, attitudes, and social norms each had small-to-medium effects on behavior change ($d_+ = 0.36, 0.38$ and 0.36, respectively), whereas increasing self-efficacy had a medium effect ($d_+ = 0.47$). These findings indicate that designing interventions that engage risk perceptions, perceived severity, attitudes, social norms, intentions, or self-efficacy should be effective in promoting health behavior change.

How well do findings from correlational tests of these targets compare to the experimental results? We used Milne et al.'s (2000) meta-analysis of prospective correlational studies to represent the average correlations for risk perception and perceived severity and Sheeran et al.'s

(2016) meta-analysis of 18 previous meta-analyses to represent the average correlations between health behaviors and attitudes, social norms, and self-efficacy. The average correlation between intention and health behavior came from McEachan et al.'s (2011) quantitative review. All effect sizes were converted to Cohen's (1992) d-values for comparison purposes. Overall, correlational studies offered a poor estimate of the impact of targets on health behavior change observed in experimental studies. Correlational tests underestimated the impact of engaging perceived severity ($d_{\text{correlational}} = 0.14$ versus $d_{\text{experimental}} = 0.34$), slightly overestimated the impact of engaging self-efficacy ($d_{\text{correlational}} = 0.58$ versus $d_{\text{experimental}} = 0.47$), and substantially overestimated the impact of engaging attitude ($d_{\text{correlational}} = 0.70$ versus $d_{\text{experimental}} = 0.38$) and intention ($d_{\text{correlational}} = 0.87$ versus $d_{\text{experimental}} = 0.36$). Only in the case of risk perception and norms were the effect sizes from correlational and experimental tests of equivalent magnitude ($d_{\text{correlational}} = 0.24$ and 0.41 versus $d_{\text{experimental}} = 0.25$ and 0.36, respectively). These findings would seem to cast serious doubt on the value of correlational tests for intervention design: How well a target predicts health behavior does not indicate how much change in behavior accrues from engaging that target.

Evidence regarding the effects of several other targets identified in **Table 1** rests primarily on correlational tests. We could locate only a single experiment that engaged implicit attitudes and tested their effects on health behaviors (Hollands et al. 2011). Similarly, relatively few studies have systematically manipulated social prototypes (Gerrard et al. 2006, Rivis & Sheeran 2013) or processes of change (e.g., Armitage 2009). Behavioral skills from the information-motivation-behavioral skills model have been tested in several interventions (e.g., Chang et al. 2014), but it is difficult to disentangle the precise contribution of this target compared to the other targets included in the intervention (e.g., motivation, self-efficacy). Executive function (EF) and habits are expected to moderate the influence of other targets (e.g., intentions) and tend to be measured rather than manipulated in studies of health behavior. One intervention study involving working memory training observed reliable effects on subsequent alcohol consumption (Houben et al. 2011), but the magnitude and mechanisms of EF training effects in adults are the subjects of debate (e.g., Shipstead et al. 2012). Training programs to improve self-control, which EF subserves (Hofmann et al. 2012), do not appear to be effective (Inzlicht & Berkman 2015, Miles et al. 2016).

In contrast, evidence regarding the effects of implicit goals, approach bias, progress monitoring, and if-then plans rests predominantly or exclusively on experimental tests. There are compelling demonstrations of changes in eating behavior immediately following priming of health goals (e.g., Papies & Hamstra 2010, Papies & Veling 2013, Papies et al. 2014) and improvements in hand hygiene following priming of injunctive norms (King et al. 2016). The reliable associations between approach bias and risk behavior observed in correlational studies (e.g., Palfai & Ostafin 2003) have been complemented by inhibitory control training interventions to reduce this bias. A meta-analysis of RCTs reported a small-to-medium effect of training on health behaviors ($d_+ = 0.33$, Allom et al. 2016), although follow-up periods were generally short. Interventions that promote monitoring of goal progress (e.g., via food diaries, pedometers) are highly effective at increasing rates of progress monitoring ($d_+ = 1.98$) and lead to small-to-medium changes in health behaviors ($d_+ = 0.40$) (Harkin et al. 2016). Several meta-analyses indicate that if-then plan interventions are effective in promoting health behaviors (Adriaanse et al. 2011, Bélanger-Gravel et al. 2013, Gollwitzer & Sheeran 2006). If-then plans have proved effective in large-scale public health interventions (e.g., Neter et al. 2014) and, over extended periods, for consequential health behaviors such as pregnancy prevention (Martin et al. 2011) and reducing smoking uptake among adolescents (Conner & Higgins 2010). In sum, there are several reasons to question the adequacy of correlational tests of the impact of target engagement on health behaviors and to advocate for conducting experimental tests instead. Although many of the targets specified by health behavior have been validated by experiment, experimental tests are overdue for several other targets.

LEARNING FROM EFFICACY TRIALS

Numerous successful efficacy trials indicate that interventions are effective in promoting health behavior change (e.g., Diabetes Prev. Progr. Res. Group 2002, Greaves et al. 2011, Lemmens et al. 2008). For understandable reasons, efficacy trials focus on the intervention's ultimate impact on behavior, and it is often not feasible to obtain assays of targets that were engaged by the intervention. The absence of target assays poses a problem, however, as it is not possible to explain why interventions prove successful or unsuccessful; what can be learned from such trials is therefore limited. Two important responses to the issues raised by standard efficacy trials concern the development of taxonomies of BCTs and new approaches to trial designs.

Behavior Change Techniques

Several guidelines indicate that reports of behavior change interventions should specify such important features as the source, recipients, setting, duration, intensity, delivery mode, and fidelity of the intervention, as well as its content (e.g., Boutron et al. 2008, Moher et al. 2001, Davidson et al. 2003, Des Jarlais et al. 2004). Abraham & Michie (2008) pointed out that even though the contents of behavior change interventions constitute the programs' active ingredients, these contents are often poorly specified in the methods section of reports—the generic label behavioral counseling is probably the most notorious example. The first characterization of intervention content was in a meta-analysis of HIV-prevention interventions. Albarracín et al. (2005) identified ten techniques (such as information and attitudinal arguments) and tested whether the presence versus absence of these techniques was associated with changes in condom use. Importantly, this meta-analysis also tested whether techniques engaged respective targets (e.g., information changed knowledge, attitudinal arguments changed attitudes) and whether target engagement led to changes in condom use. Albarracín et al. (2005) were able to present decision trees that designated which techniques were effective for samples that differed in terms of gender, age, ethnicity, and risk status.

Of course, there are more than ten techniques that can be used to change health behaviors, and researchers are generally unable to trace the impact of BCTs through targets to behavioral outcomes in efficacy trials because target assays are not obtained. To formalize matters, Abraham & Michie (2008) offered a taxonomy of 26 BCTs that included clear definitions of each technique and evidence that these techniques could be identified reliably from intervention descriptions. Subsequent refinement and extension of the taxonomy has generated a hierarchical classification of 93 discrete BCTs (Michie et al. 2013).

The development of taxonomies of BCTs has been a boon to research on health behavior change. It has served to focus researchers' attention on the components of the intervention that engender change. BCT taxonomies have also given the field a common language with which to characterize intervention components and have thus facilitated the development, replication, and implementation of behavior change interventions in a manner that was not previously possible. Moreover, coding BCTs from reports of interventions has enabled researchers to compute associations between the use of particular techniques and the effect sizes obtained in RCTs (via metaregression and related techniques). In this way, researchers have been able to determine which BCTs are associated with a larger or smaller effect size and which are unrelated to effect size for various health behaviors (e.g., Bartlett et al. 2014, Dombrowski et al. 2012, Webb et al. 2010). BCT taxonomies thus enable informed comparisons between efficacy trials that involve complex intervention content and offer insights that go beyond the mere assessment of overall effectiveness.

However, efforts to relate BCTs to intervention outcomes face significant practical and conceptual challenges. At the practical level, extensive training is required to code interventions in terms of 93 discrete techniques, and reliability is modest ($\kappa < 0.70$) for approximately 20% of these 93 BCTs (Abraham et al. 2015). Published descriptions of the BCTs used in interventions can also differ markedly from the BCTs coded from the original intervention manuals (Abraham & Michie 2008), which are often difficult to obtain (Abraham et al. 2014). Moreover, coding the BCTs used in the control conditions in addition to those used in the treatment conditions may be crucial for accurate interpretation of BCT associations. This is because the techniques used in the control condition (e.g., usual care) can explain substantial variance in effect sizes, and the BCTs deployed in the treatment condition may explain only a modest increment in the variance after techniques used in the control condition have been taken into account (de Bruin et al. 2010).

Conceptual issues must also be considered. Metaregressions of effect sizes on BCTs have revealed no significant associations between individual BCTs and intervention effectiveness (e.g., Hartmann-Boyce et al. 2014, Michie et al. 2009), which raises difficult questions about whether the coding of BCTs or the techniques themselves are causing the problem. Findings from metaregressions of effect sizes on BCTs can also be at odds with findings from meta-analyses of experimental trials that focus on particular techniques. For example, Michie et al.'s (2009) meta-analysis observed no reliable associations between implementation intentions and weight control behaviors (diet, physical activity), whereas meta-analyses of implementation intention interventions in relation to diet (Adriaanse et al. 2011) and physical activity (Bélanger-Gravel et al. 2013) observed reliable effects. Similar conflict is apparent in data regarding the effectiveness of progress monitoring (see Michie et al. 2009, Harkin et al. 2016). Analyzing the BCTs used in interventions can offer researchers who are planning trials valuable clues about which targets should be engaged and which procedures should be used to engage those targets. However, retrospective cataloging of intervention content and correlational tests of that content via metaregression cannot substitute for experimental studies to validate, engage, and offer full tests of targets.

New Approaches to Trials

Given the goal of specifying which intervention strategy to use for which person at what time or in what context, there is a clear need for approaches to RCTs that not only embrace the complexity of this goal but also strive to address it in an effective and efficient manner. Although there are numerous innovations in approaches to RCTs, we focus on two that are particularly synergistic with the aims of this review: multiphase optimization strategy (MOST) (Collins et al. 2005, 2011) and sequential multiple assignment randomized trial (SMART) designs (Lei et al. 2012). Both approaches demonstrate the ways in which experimentation can offer a more precise understanding of which intervention components should be used (i.e., what works) and under what conditions (i.e., when it works).

Interventions typically include many BCTs, making it difficult to discern the relative contribution that each BCT makes to the desired outcome. MOST provides a framework for assessing the relative contribution of discrete techniques by encouraging investigators to first specify the distinct factors that make up the intervention (consistent with the BCT approach discussed above) and then develop an experimental design that can assess the relative contribution of an identified set of factors on a specified outcome. Through the use of factorial or fractional factorial experiments (see Collins et al. 2005), investigators are able to test competing hypotheses about the relative impact of intervention strategies that are designed to either affect change in the same target (providing insights into which strategy is the most effective way to modify a target) or affect change in different targets (providing insights about which target pathway is the most effective means to modify behavior). Moreover, MOST is amenable to evaluating the effect of parameters of the context in which the intervention is delivered (e.g., neighborhood resources) that may not be specified formally in theory. This should make it easier for investigators to articulate the conditions under which specific intervention targets should and should not be engaged.

Adaptive interventions can respond to the challenge of optimizing intervention strategies to match features of the individual, behavior, and context while also recognizing that the optimal strategy may change over time in response to changes in the person or the situation. Thus, adaptive interventions rely on decision rules that determine which intervention strategies to use at which time and in which sequence on the basis of prespecified factors (e.g., a person's response to an initial intervention strategy). SMART designs provide a framework for developing adaptive interventions by providing an opportunity to rerandomize participants to a subsequent intervention strategy in response to predetermined indicators (Almirall et al. 2014, Lei et al. 2012). Although SMART designs have been used primarily in domains in which response to an initial treatment strategy is poor (e.g., substance use), these designs can address nearly any question regarding the ongoing tailoring or targeting of intervention strategies. For example, all treatment participants could be randomized to an if-then plan intervention (a treatment that requires modest resources). Participants who respond to the treatment could be randomized to no further treatment or to booster if-then plans. Participants who do not respond to the treatment might need a more resource-intensive treatment (e.g., a motivational intervention plus if-then plans). In this way, participants receive the treatment they need, but there are savings in terms of intervention resources and participants' time that would not have been achieved if all participants had received the combined motivation plus if-then planning intervention at the outset. SMART designs thus provide a framework for examining whether there are advantages to engaging specific targets in a particular sequence and have the potential to stimulate significant transformations in current health behavior theories.

COMPETITIVE TESTS OF TARGET ENGAGEMENT

Effective Techniques in Search of Targets

Often, a technique is found to promote behavior change in traditional efficacy trials but the relevant target or mechanism of action linking the technique to behavior change remains unclear. Two prominent techniques in research on health behavior change that exhibit this feature are the question-behavior effect (QBE) and self-affirmation. The QBE is the phenomenon whereby questions about a target behavior (e.g., behavioral intentions) promote performance of that behavior relative to participants who were not asked questions. The QBE has been observed in relation to various health behaviors (e.g., vaccination uptake, cancer screening), and meta-analyses indicate that the effect is robust, albeit of small magnitude (Rodrigues et al. 2015, Wood et al. 2016). Self-affirmation (Steele 1988) involves reflecting upon important values, attributes, or social relations and is usually induced via a writing exercise. Self-affirmation was found by two recent meta-analyses (Epton et al. 2015, Sweeney & Moyer 2015) to reduce defensive resistance to health-risk communications and promote health-related intentions and behavior. Thus, the QBE and self-affirmation are relatively well-established BCTs.

However, we do not always know why or when these techniques are effective. The most likely targets underlying the QBE are attitude accessibility (questioning activates participants' underlying attitudes and so makes it more likely that those attitudes will be translated into action) and dissonance reduction (questioning causes participants to strive to act consistently with their expressed views). However, it is currently unclear whether either, neither, or both of these targets are responsible for the QBE (Wood et al. 2016). The list of possible targets underlying self-affirmation effects is even longer and includes reduced attentional bias, enhanced self-regulatory resources, higher-level temporal construal, improved judgmental confidence, greater feelings of vulnerability, and increased self- or other-directed positive affect (Cohen & Sherman 2014). A better understanding of the conditions under which each of these mechanisms operates will facilitate the productive use of self-affirmation in interventions.

The EM approach suggests that a useful starting point could be competitive tests of target engagement, e.g., studies to compare the impact of QBE or self-affirmation manipulations on their various possible targets (Path C). These studies could, in turn, be followed by a program of research to validate the respective targets identified by the first set of studies (Path B). Competitive tests of target engagement could have both conceptual and practical benefits by explaining the variability in the impact of these techniques on health behaviors. For example, Godin et al. (2008) found that the QBE increased blood donation over one year, whereas a similar study of blood donation by van Dongen et al. (2012) observed no reliable QBE. Similarly, Peterson et al. (2012) found that a self-affirmation intervention increased physical activity among patients following a percutaneous coronary procedure, whereas an equivalent intervention proved ineffective among patients with asthma (Mancuso et al. 2012). In other studies, self-affirmation has been observed to promote behavior change without influencing cognitive responses to the message (e.g., intentions, Wileman et al. 2014) or even to reduce behavior change (e.g., Good et al. 2015). The EM approach suggests that research designed to identify, validate, and engage the relevant target(s) would better advance the field than studies repeatedly testing the behavioral impact of the QBE and self-affirmation. Other BCTs (e.g., use of incentives, mindfulness or self-compassion training, altering plates or utensils) could also benefit from this approach.

Targets in Search of Effective Techniques

In contrast, there is relatively little research on the most effective and efficient ways to engage several important targets that have been shown to elicit change in health behaviors (e.g., risk perception, intentions, self-efficacy). The need to specify techniques that effectively engage such targets presents both an empirical and a theoretical challenge. At the empirical level, competitive tests of target engagement are clearly warranted. An important review by Ashford and colleagues (2010) of self-efficacy for physical activity undertook detailed coding of the techniques used in randomized trials to increase self-efficacy and examined which techniques led to the largest improvements. Their findings showed that vicarious experience and feedback on both past performance and others' performance were the most effective techniques, whereas verbal persuasion, barrier identification, and problem solving actually reduced self-efficacy. Although this work represents a valuable starting point, we cannot rely on retrospective coding and meta-analysis to offer competitive tests. A sustained program of experimental studies that explicitly compare different techniques for engaging targets specified by health behavior theories is needed.

The theoretical challenge is to develop conceptual models of target engagement. Health behavior theories specify what targets should be engaged by interventions but generally have little to say about how these targets can best be engaged. The next generation of health behavior theories should focus on how best to engage targets. Research on health behavior change has long relied on intuition or pilot studies to determine how to engage targets. This approach is insufficient. Theory development and competitive empirical tests need to go hand in hand in order to forge a science of target engagement. Because the amount of change in the target forms the dependent variable in this work, researchers, reviewers, and editors need to recognize the value of research that is explicitly concerned with target change. The promise of the EM approach is that the study of target engagement is a vital part of behavior change research.

MOVING FROM OBSERVATION TO INTERVENTION

EM offers a roadmap for research on health behavior change that could help move the field from observation to intervention. Many researchers already recognize the limitations of standard efficacy trials and see value in full tests that assess whether intervention components engage targets and whether target engagement changes health behaviors. EM shares with other approaches the ideal that full tests should be used to evaluate behavior change interventions, and it also challenges health researchers to examine basic mechanistic processes as part of the trial (Path D). Like these other approaches, EM indicates that different programs of research are needed to provide the foundation upon which full tests can build. Basic research that identifies, measures, and validates targets (Paths A and B) can be the starting point for other programs of research. The techniques used to validate targets in basic research programs may be neither feasible nor acceptable outside of the laboratory, however, and thus research that tests the best ways to maximize target engagement (Path C) is an essential contribution. The EM approach also encourages researchers to look beyond their favorite theory or the behavior at issue and to view the science of behavior change in terms of targets—their identification, assays, validation, and engagement.

The identification and measurement of new targets are likely to come not only from theories but also from advances in technology. Many important determinants of behavior may have simply not found their way into current theories because of difficulties in measuring those targets in the past. Affective processes are a case in point. Whereas self-reports can alter the affect that one is trying to measure (Kassam & Mendes 2013), facial and vocal recognition software may offer unobtrusive insight into what participants are feeling and how that changes over time and in response to new information. Collecting intensive within-person data may offer new insights into when and how targets fluctuate and lead to refinements of our theories. Relatedly, the fact that techniques such as the QBE have proven effective in changing behavior even though respective targets are not precisely identified underlines the role of both rigorous empirical tests and deeper conceptual analysis in identifying new targets.

The EM approach challenges researchers concerned with health behavior change to strive for greater precision and specificity in the research questions we address (Paths A–D), the ways in which we address them (via experimentation, using assays at different levels), and the theories we use. Precise theories of health behavior change will specify whether cognitions about the health threat, cognitions about the focal behavior, volitional factors, and implicit cognition are all needed to understand behavior change and when or under what circumstances these different targets are or are not influential. Precise theories will also be able to specify the dosage of behavior change interventions: how much a target needs to change to generate behavior change (whether there is a linear dose-response relation or a threshold that must be met) and how much engagement is needed to create that change in the target (e.g., one or more face-to-face sessions versus a pencil-and-paper exercise). Courage will be needed to develop precise theories, as precision puts theories at grave danger of refutation (Meehl 1978). The encouragement offered by the EM approach is the promise of substantial progress in research on health behavior change that could meet mandates to improve public health.

APPENDIX: TARGETS SPECIFIED BY HEALTH BEHAVIOR THEORIES

Below we define 23 targets specified by health behavior theories.

- Risk perception is a person's judgment concerning the likelihood of getting a disease or illness (e.g., How likely is it that you will get HIV/AIDS?).

- Perceived severity is a person's belief concerning the seriousness of a disease or illness (e.g., How serious would it be if you got HIV/AIDS?).
- Fear is a negative emotion caused by the possibility of getting a disease or illness (e.g., How afraid are you of getting HIV/AIDS?).
- Threat appraisal is a person's overall estimate of how dangerous a disease or illness is and the output of risk perception, perceived severity, and fear.
- Intention is a person's self-instruction to act in a particular manner (e.g., I intend to use a condom if I have sex with someone new).
- Willingness is a person's inclination to perform an unhealthy behavior given conducive circumstances (e.g., If your partner was extremely attractive and you were using another form of contraception, how likely is it that you would have sex without using a condom?).
- Attitude is a person's overall evaluation of the consequences of performing a behavior (e.g., How good or bad would it be to use a condom if you have sex with a new partner?).
- Norms can be either injunctive or descriptive. An injunctive norm is a person's belief about whether significant others think that he or she should behave in a particular manner (e.g., Most people who are important to me think that I should use a condom if I have sex with someone new). A descriptive norm is a person's belief about how significant others themselves behave (e.g., Most people who are important to me use a condom if they have sex with someone new).
- Self-efficacy is a person's confidence in his or her ability to perform a behavior (e.g., How confident are you that you can use a condom if you have sex with someone new?).
- Perceived behavioral control (PBC) is a person's beliefs about how easy or difficult it is to perform a behavior (e.g., How easy or difficult would it be for you to use a condom if you have sex with someone new?). Although PBC includes both self-efficacy and beliefs about the controllability of the behavior, beliefs about controllability do not predict behavior over and above self-efficacy (e.g., Conner et al. 2016), and PBC and self-efficacy are effectively synonymous.
- Coping appraisal is a person's overall estimate of his or her ability to prevent or manage a disease or illness; the output of self-efficacy and beliefs about whether a recommended behavior is effective in preventing the disease or illness (i.e., response efficacy); and the costs of engaging in the behavior (i.e., response costs). Both response efficacy and response costs can be seen as components of attitude.
- Social prototypes are a person's images of someone who typically engages or does not engage in a particular behavior. Measures of social prototypes involve both judgments of similarity (e.g., How similar are you to the type of person who uses a condom during sex with a new partner?) and evaluations (e.g., How likeable or dislikable is the type of person who uses a condom during sex with a new partner?).
- If-then plans specify cognitive or behavioral responses to good opportunities to act or obstacles that could prevent action and make it more likely that people successfully realize their intentions to perform health behaviors. The plans are so-named because they have the format if (opportunity/obstacle)-then (response).
- Behavioral skills are a person's actual and perceived abilities to undertake the various behaviors relevant to reaching one's goal. In the context of condom use with a new partner, relevant skills include buying, storing, and carrying a condom and negotiating condom use with a sexual partner.
- Processes of change are strategies that a person can use to change behavior. The transtheoretical model specifies ten processes of change comprising both experiential (e.g., developing awareness, using self-reappraisal) and behavioral (e.g., reorganizing one's environment, engaging in substitute activities) strategies.

- Progress monitoring is the practice of comparing one's current standing relative to one's goal. Both features of a behavior (frequency, intensity, duration) and outcomes of a behavior (e.g., weight loss) can be compared.
- Executive function is a set of cognitive abilities that serve to keep thoughts, feelings, and behavior in line with the person's goals. Executive function has three components: response inhibition (overriding unwanted responses), mental flexibility (switching from one rule to another), and working memory (holding relevant information in mind and using it effectively).
- Attentional bias is the extent to which cues related to unhealthy substances (e.g., tobacco, alcohol) capture and hold a person's attention. Attentional bias is typically measured by modifications of the Stroop color-naming task or the visual dot probe task.
- Implicit attitude is a person's automatic affective reactions triggered by a stimulus. Implicit attitudes are typically measured by reaction time tasks such as the implicit association test.
- Approach bias is a person's automatic action tendency to move toward a desired stimulus (e.g., chocolate, tobacco). Approach bias is typically measured using a joystick task that measures how quickly participants move toward versus away from relevant stimuli.
- Implicit goals or norms are desired outcomes or behavioral standards that are primed by features of the context without the person realizing the impact of the priming stimulus on behavior. For example, a poster for a low-fat recipe primed participants to consume fewer snacks (Papies & Hamstra 2010), and placing an image of eyes over a sanitizing dispenser increased rates of hand hygiene among people entering a hospital (King et al. 2016).
- Habit is a person's automatic tendency to repeat a well-practiced behavior in response to cues that led to performance of the behavior in the past. The cues that trigger habit performance can include particular times, places, settings, or people or previous actions in a sequence.

The theories that specify these targets are outlined in the sidebar Health Behavior Theories, and the overlap among the theories and targets is illustrated in **Table 1**.

DISCLOSURE STATEMENT

The authors are not aware of any affiliations, memberships, funding, or financial holdings that might be perceived as affecting the objectivity of this review.

ACKNOWLEDGMENTS

We thank the members of the NCI Cognitive, Affective, and Social Processes in Health Research Workgroup (http://cancercontrol.cancer.gov/brp/casphr/) for discussions regarding the issues addressed in this review, and members of the SOBC Common Fund Program Workgroup (https://commonfund.nih.gov/behaviorchange/) for their work and contributions in implementing and funding research adopting the EM approach to behavior change research. We are grateful for feedback on a previous version of this paper from Allison Farrell from Alex Rothman's lab and Aya Avishai-Yitshak, Katelyn Jones, and Kelsey Eaker from Paschal Sheeran's lab.

LITERATURE CITED

Abraham C, Johnson BT, de Bruin M, Luszczynska A. 2014. Enhancing reporting of behavior change intervention evaluations. *J. Acquir. Immune Defic. Syndr.* 66(Suppl. 3):S293–99

Abraham C, Michie S. 2008. A taxonomy of behavior change techniques used in interventions. *Health Psychol.* 27(3):379–87

Abraham C, Wood CE, Johnston M, Francis J, Hardeman W, et al. 2015. Reliability of identification of behavior change techniques in intervention descriptions. *Ann. Behav. Med.* 49(6):885–900

Achtziger A, Gollwitzer PM, Sheeran P. 2008. Implementation intentions and shielding goal striving from unwanted thoughts and feelings. *Pers. Soc. Psychol. Bull.* 34(3):381–93

Adriaanse MA, Vinkers CDW, De Ridder DTD, Hox JJ, De Wit JBF. 2011. Do implementation intentions help to eat a healthy diet? A systematic review and meta-analysis of the empirical evidence. *Appetite* 56(1):183–93

Ajzen I. 1991. The theory of planned behavior. *Org. Behav. Hum. Dec. Proc.* 50(2):179–211

Albarracín D, Gillette JC, Earl AN, Glasman LR, Durantini MR, Ho MH. 2005. A test of major assumptions about behavior change: a comprehensive look at the effects of passive and active HIV-prevention interventions since the beginning of the epidemic. *Psychol. Bull.* 131(6):856–97

Allom V, Mullan B, Hagger MS. 2016. Does inhibitory control training improve health behavior? A meta-analysis. *Health Psychol. Rev.* 10:168–86

Almirall D, Nahum-Shani I, Sherwood NE, Murphy SA. 2014. Introduction to SMART designs for the development of adaptive interventions: with application to weight loss research. *Transl. Behav. Med.* 4(3):260–74

Armitage CJ. 2009. Is there utility in the transtheoretical model? *Br. J. Health Psychol.* 14(2):195–210

Ashford S, Edmunds J, French DP. 2010. What is the best way to change self-efficacy to promote lifestyle and recreational physical activity? A systematic review with meta-analysis. *Br. J. Health Psychol.* 15(2):265–88

Avishai-Yitshak A, Sheeran P. 2017. Implicit processes and health behavior change. In *The Wiley Encyclopedia of Health Psychology*, ed. K Sweeny, M Robbins. New York: Wiley. In press

Baldwin AS, Rothman AJ, Hertel AW, Linde JA, Jeffery RW, et al. 2006. Specifying the determinants of the initiation and maintenance of behavior change: an examination of self-efficacy, satisfaction, and smoking cessation. *Health Psychol.* 25(5):626–34

Bandura A. 1998. Health promotion from the perspective of social cognitive theory. *Psychol. Health* 13(4):623–49

Bartlett YK, Sheeran P, Hawley MS. 2014. Effective behaviour change techniques in smoking cessation interventions for people with chronic obstructive pulmonary disease: a meta-analysis. *Br. J. Health Psychol.* 19(1):181–203

Bélanger-Gravel A, Godin G, Amireault S. 2013. A meta-analytic review of the effect of implementation intentions on physical activity. *Health Psychol. Rev.* 7(1):23–54

Bernard C. 1957. *An Introduction to the Study of Experimental Medicine*, transl. HC Greene. New York: Dover

Blanton H, Jaccard J, Burrows CN. 2016. To accurately estimate implicit influence on behavior, accurately estimate explicit influences. *Health Psychol.* 35(8):856–60

Borland R. 2013. *Understanding Hard to Maintain Behaviour Change: A Dual Process Approach*. New York: Wiley

Boutron I, Moher D, Altman DG, Schulz KF, Ravaud P. 2008. Extending the CONSORT statement to randomized trials of nonpharmacologic treatment: explanation and elaboration. *Ann. Intern. Med.* 148(4):295–309

Brewer NT, Chapman GB, Gibbons FX, Gerrard M, McCaul KD, et al. 2007. Meta-analysis of the relationship between risk perception and health behavior: the example of vaccination. *Health Psychol.* 26(2):136–45

Carle AC, Riley W, Hays RD, Cella D. 2015. Confirmatory factor analysis of the Patient Reported Outcomes Measurement Information System (PROMIS) adult domain framework using item response theory scores. *Med. Care* 53(10):894–900

Carver CS, Scheier MF. 1982. Control theory: a useful conceptual framework for personality—social, clinical, and health psychology. *Psychol. Bull.* 92(1):111–35

Chang SJ, Choi S, Kim SE, Song M. 2014. Intervention strategies based on Information-Motivation-Behavioral Skills Model for health behavior change: a systematic review. *Asian Nurs. Res.* 8(3):172–81

Cohen GL, Sherman DK. 2014. The psychology of change: self-affirmation and social psychological intervention. *Annu. Rev. Psychol.* 65:333–71

Cohen J. 1992. A power primer. *Psychol. Bull.* 112:155–59

Collins LM, Baker TB, Mermelstein RJ, Piper ME, Jorenby DE, et al. 2011. The multiphase optimization strategy for engineering effective tobacco use interventions. *Ann. Behav. Med.* 41(2):208–26

Collins LM, Murphy SA, Nair VN, Strecher VJ. 2005. A strategy for optimizing and evaluating behavioural interventions. *Ann. Behav. Med.* 30(1):65–73

Conner M, Higgins AR. 2010. Long-term effects of implementation intentions on prevention of smoking uptake among adolescents: a cluster randomized controlled trial. *Health Psychol.* 29(5):529–38

Conner M, McEachan R, Lawton R, Gardner P. 2016. Reasoned action approach to health protection and health risk behaviors. *Ann. Behav. Med.* 50(4):592–612

Conner M, Norman P. 2015. *Predicting Health Behavior*. New York: McGraw-Hill. 3rd ed.

Conner M, Sparks P. 2015. The theory of planned behavior and the reasoned action approach. In *Predicting Health Behavior*, ed. M Conner, P Norman, pp. 142–88. New York: McGraw-Hill. 3rd ed.

Crites SL, Fabrigar LR, Petty RE. 1994. Measuring the affective and cognitive properties of attitudes: conceptual and methodological issues. *Pers. Soc. Psychol. Bull.* 20(6):619–34

Czajkowski SM, Powell LH, Adler N, Naar-King S, Reynolds KD, et al. 2015. From ideas to efficacy: the ORBIT model for developing behavioral treatments for chronic diseases. *Health Psychol.* 34(10):971–82

Davidson KW, Goldstein M, Kaplan RM, Kaufmann PG, Knatterund GL, et al. 2003. Evidence-based behavioral medicine: What is it and how do we achieve it? *Ann. Behav. Med.* 26(3):161–71

de Bruin M, Viechtbauer W, Schaalma HP, Kok G, Abraham C, Hospers HJ. 2010. Standard care impact on effects of highly active antiretroviral therapy adherence interventions: a meta-analysis of randomized controlled trials. *Arch. Intern. Med.* 170(3):240–50

Des Jarlais DC, Lyles C, Crepaz N. 2004. Improving the reporting quality of nonrandomized evaluations of behavioral and public health interventions: the TREND statement. *Am. J. Public Health* 94(3):361–66

Deutsch M, Gerard HB. 1955. A study of normative and informational social influences upon human judgment. *J. Abnorm. Soc. Psychol.* 51:629–36

Diabetes Prev. Progr. Res. Group. 2002. The Diabetes Prevention Program (DPP): description of lifestyle intervention. *Diabetes Care* 25(12):2165–71

Dombrowski SU, Sniehotta FF, Avenell A, Johnston M, MacLennan G, Araújo-Soares V. 2012. Identifying active ingredients in complex behavioural interventions for obese adults with obesity-related co-morbidities or additional risk factors for co-morbidities: a systematic review. *Health Psychol. Rev.* 6(1):7–32

Epton T, Harris PR, Kane R, van Koningsbruggen GM, Sheeran P. 2015. The impact of self-affirmation on health behavior change: a meta-analysis. *Health Psychol.* 34(3):187–96

Falk EB, Berkman ET, Lieberman MD. 2012. From neural responses to population behavior: Neural focus group predicts population-level media effects. *Psychol. Sci.* 23(5):439–45

Falk EB, Berkman ET, Mann T, Harrison B, Lieberman MD. 2010. Predicting persuasion-induced behavior change from the brain. *J. Neurosci.* 30(25):8421–24

Falk EB, Berkman ET, Whalen D, Lieberman MD. 2011. Neural activity during health messaging predicts reductions in smoking above and beyond self-report. *Health Psychol.* 30(2):177–85

Fishbein M, Ajzen I. 1975. *Belief, Attitude, Intention and Behavior: An Introduction to Theory and Research*. Reading, MA: Addison-Wesley

Fisher JD, Fisher WA. 1992. Changing AIDS risk behavior. *Psychol. Bull.* 111(3):455–74

Fuglestad P, Rothman AJ, Jeffery RW. 2008. Getting there and hanging on: the effect of regulatory focus on performance in smoking and weight loss interventions. *Health Psychol.* 27(Suppl. 3):S260–70

Fuglestad PT, Rothman AJ, Jeffery RW. 2013. The effects of regulatory focus on responding to and avoiding slips in a longitudinal study of smoking cessation. *Basic Appl. Soc. Psychol.* 35(5):426–35

Gerrard M, Gibbons FX, Brody GH, Murry VM, Cleveland MJ, Wills TA. 2006. A theory-based dual focus alcohol intervention for pre-adolescents: the Strong African American Families Program. *Psychol. Addict. Behav.* 20:185–95

Gerrard M, Gibbons FX, Houlihan AE, Stock ML, Pomery EA. 2008. A dual-process approach to health risk decision making: the prototype willingness model. *Dev. Rev.* 28(1):29–61

Gibbons FX, Gerrard M, Blanton H, Russell DW. 1998. Reasoned action and social reaction: willingness and intention as independent predictors of health risk. *J. Pers. Soc. Psychol.* 74(5):1164–80

Gibbons FX, Gerrard M, Lune LSV, Wills TA, Brody G, Conger RD. 2004. Context and cognitions: environmental risk, social influence, and adolescent substance use. *Pers. Soc. Psychol. Bull.* 30(8):1048–61

Gawronski B, Payne BK. 2011. *Handbook of Implicit Social Cognition: Measurement, Theory, and Applications*. New York: Guilford Press

Glanz K, Rimer BK, Viswanath K. 2008. *Health Behavior and Health Education: Theory, Research, and Practice.* Hoboken, NJ: Wiley. 4th ed.

Gochman DS. 1997. *Handbook of Health Behavior Research I: Personal and Social Determinants.* New York: Plenum

Godin G, Sheeran P, Conner M, Germain M. 2008. Asking questions changes behavior: mere measurement effects on frequency of blood donation. *Health Psychol.* 27(2):179–84

Gollwitzer PM. 1993. Goal achievement: the role of intentions. In *European Review of Social Psychology*, Vol. 4, ed. W Strobe, M Hewstone, pp. 141–85. New York: Wiley

Gollwitzer PM. 1999. Implementation intentions: strong effects of simple plans. *Am. Psychol.* 54:493–503

Gollwitzer PM, Sheeran P. 2006. Implementation intentions and goal achievement: a meta-analysis of effects and processes. *Adv. Exp. Soc. Psychol.* 38:69–119

Good A, Harris PR, Jessop D, Abraham C. 2015. Open-mindedness can decrease persuasion amongst adolescents: the role of self-affirmation. *Br. J. Health Psychol.* 20(2):228–42

Greaves CJ, Sheppard KE, Abraham C, Hardeman W, Roden M, et al. 2011. Systematic review of reviews of intervention components associated with increased effectiveness in dietary and physical activity interventions. *BMC Public Health* 11(1):119

Greenwald AG, Poehlman TA, Uhlmann EL, Banaji MR. 2009. Understanding and using the Implicit Association Test: III. Meta-analysis of predictive validity. *J. Pers. Soc. Psychol.* 97(1):17–41

Hall KL, Stokols D, Stipelman BA, Vogel AL, Feng A, et al. 2012. Assessing the value of Team Science: a study comparing center- and investigator-initiated grants. *Am. J. Prev. Med.* 42(2):157–63

Hall PA, Fong GT. 2007. Temporal self-regulation theory: a model for individual health behavior. *Health Psychol. Rev.* 1(1):6–52

Hall PA, Zehr C, Paulitzki J, Rhodes R. 2014. Implementation intentions for physical activity behavior in older adult women: an examination of executive function as a moderator of treatment effects. *Ann. Behav. Med.* 48(1):130–36

Hamilton CM, Strader LC, Pratt JG, Maiese D, Hendershot T, et al. 2011. The PhenX Toolkit: Get the most from your measures. *Am. J. Epidemiol.* 174(3):253–60

Harkin B, Webb TL, Chang BPI, Prestwich A, Conner M, et al. 2016. Does monitoring goal progress promote goal attainment? A meta-analysis of the experimental evidence. *Psychol. Bull.* 142(2):198–229

Hartmann-Boyce J, Johns DJ, Jebb SA, Aveyard P, Behav. Weight Manag. Rev. Group. 2014. Effect of behavioural techniques and delivery mode on effectiveness of weight management: systematic review, meta-analysis and meta-regression. *Obes. Rev.* 15(7):598–609

Hertel AW, Finch E, Kelly K, King C, Lando H, et al. 2008. The impact of outcome expectations and satisfaction on the initiation and maintenance of smoking cessation: an experimental test. *Health Psychol.* 27(Suppl. 3):S197–206

Hofmann W, Friese M, Wiers RW. 2008. Impulsive versus reflective influences on health behavior: a theoretical framework and empirical review. *Health Psychol. Rev.* 2(2):111–37

Hofmann W, Schmeichel BJ, Baddeley AD. 2012. Executive functions and self-regulation. *Trends Cogn. Sci.* 16(3):174–80

Hollands GJ, Prestwich A, Marteau TM. 2011. Using aversive images to enhance healthy food choices and implicit attitudes: an experimental test of evaluative conditioning. *Health Psychol.* 30(2):195–203

Houben K, Wiers RW, Jansen A. 2011. Getting a grip on drinking behavior: training working memory to reduce alcohol abuse. *Psychol. Sci.* 22(7):968–75

Inzlicht M, Berkman E. 2015. Six questions for the resource model of control (and some answers). *Soc. Pers. Psychol. Compass* 9(10):511–24

Kassam KS, Mendes WB. 2013. The effects of measuring emotion: Physiological reactions to emotional situations depend on whether someone is asking. *PLOS ONE* 8(6):e64959–8

Khatib R, Schwalm JD, Yusuf S, Haynes RB, McKee M, et al. 2014. Patient and healthcare provider barriers to hypertension awareness, treatment and follow up: a systematic review and meta-analysis of qualitative and quantitative studies. *PLOS ONE* 9(1):e84238

Klein WMP, Grenen EG, O'Connell M, Blanch-Hartigan D, Chou W-YS, et al. 2016. Integrating knowledge across domains to advance the science of health behavior: overcoming challenges and facilitating success. *Trans. Behav. Med.* In press

Klein WMP, Shepperd JA, Suls J, Rothman AJ, Croyle RT. 2015. Realizing the promise of social psychology in improving public health. *Pers. Soc. Psychol. Rev.* 19(1):77–92

King D, Vlaev I, Everett-Thomas R, Fitzpatrick M, Darzi A, Birnbach DJ. 2016. "Priming" hand hygiene compliance in clinical environments. *Health Psychol.* 35(1):96–101

Kiviniemi MT, Voss-Humke AM, Seifert AL. 2007. How do I feel about the behavior? The interplay of affective associations with behaviors and cognitive beliefs as influences on physical activity behavior. *Health Psychol.* 26(2):152–58

Lawton R, Conner M, McEachan R. 2009. Desire or reason: predicting health behaviors from affective and cognitive attitudes. *Health Psychol.* 28(1):56–65

Lei H, Nahum-Shani I, Lynch K, Oslin D, Murphy SA. 2012. A "SMART" design for building individualized treatment sequences. *Annu. Rev. Clin. Psychol.* 8(1):21–48

Lemmens V, Oenema A, Knut IK, Brug J. 2008. Effectiveness of smoking cessation interventions among adults: a systematic review of reviews. *Eur. J. Cancer Prev.* 17(6):535–44

Loewenstein G. 2005. Hot-cold empathy gaps and medical decision-making. *Health Psychol.* 24(Suppl. 4):S49–56

Mancuso CA, Choi TN, Westermann H, Wenderoth S, Hollenberg JP, et al. 2012. Increasing physical activity in patients with asthma through positive affect and self-affirmation. *Arch. Intern. Med.* 172(4):337–43

Martin J, Sheeran P, Slade P, Wright A, Dibble T. 2011. Durable effects of implementation intentions: reduced rates of confirmed pregnancy at 2 years. *Health Psychol.* 30(3):368–73

McEachan RR, Conner M, Taylor NJ, Lawton RJ. 2011. Prospective prediction of health-related behaviours with the theory of planned behaviour: a meta-analysis. *Health Psychol. Rev.* 5(2):97–144

McGuire WJ. 1989. A perspectivist approach to the strategic planning of programmatic scientific research. In *Psychology of Science: Contributions to Metascience*, ed. B Gholson, WR Shadish Jr., RA Neimeyer, AC Houts, pp. 214–45. New York: Cambridge Univ. Press

Meehl PE. 1978. Theoretical risks and tabular asterisks: Sir Karl, Sir Ronald, and the slow progress of soft psychology. *J. Consult. Clin. Psychol.* 46:806–34

Michie S, Abraham C, Whittington C, McAteer J, Gupta S. 2009. Effective techniques in healthy eating and physical activity interventions: a meta-regression. *Health Psychol.* 28(6):690–701

Michie S, Richardson M, Johnston M, Abraham C, Francis J, et al. 2013. The Behavior Change Technique Taxonomy (v1) of 93 hierarchically clustered techniques: building an international consensus for the reporting of behavior change interventions. *Ann. Behav. Med.* 46(1):81–95

Michie S, West R, Campbell R, Brown J, Gainforth H. 2014. *ABC of Behaviour Change Theories.* London: Silverback. 1st ed.

Miles E, Sheeran P, Baird H, Macdonald I, Webb TL, Harris PR. 2016. Does self-control improve with practice? Evidence from a 6-week training program. *J. Exp. Psychol. Gen.* 145:1075–91

Milne S, Sheeran P, Orbell S. 2000. Prediction and intervention in health-related behavior: a meta-analytic review of protection motivation theory. *J. Appl. Soc. Psychol.* 31(1):106–43

Moher D, Schultz KF, Altman DG, CONSORT Group. 2001. The CONSORT statement: revised recommendations for improving the quality of reports of parallel-group randomized trials. *Lancet* 357(9263):1191–94

Mokdad AH, Marks JS, Stroup DF, Gerberding JL. 2004. Actual causes of death in the United States, 2000. *J. Am. Med. Assoc.* 291(10):1238–45

Moser RP, Hesse BW, Shaikh AR, Courtney P, Morgan G, et al. 2011. Grid-enabled measures: using Science 2.0 to standardize measures and share data. *Am. J. Prev. Med.* 40(5):S134–43

Natl. Inst. Health Care Excell. (NICE). 2007. *Behaviour Change: General Approaches.* London: NICE. **http://www.nice.org.uk/Guidance/PH6**

Neter E, Stein N, Barnett-Griness O, Rennert G, Hagoel L. 2014. From the bench to public health: population-level implementation intentions in colorectal cancer screening. *Am. J. Prev. Med.* 46(3):273–80

Nieuwlaat R, Wilczynski N, Navarro T, Hobson N, Jeffery R, et al. 2014. Interventions for enhancing medication adherence. *Cochrane Database Syst. Rev.* 11:CD000011

Noar SM, Zimmerman RS. 2005. Health Behavior Theory and cumulative knowledge regarding health behaviors: Are we moving in the right direction? *Health Educ. Res.* 20(3):275–90

Nordgren LF, van der Pligt J, van Harreveld F. 2008. The instability of health cognitions: Visceral states influence self-efficacy and related health beliefs. *Health Psychol.* 27(6):722–27

Onken LS, Carroll KM, Shoham V, Cuthbert BN, Riddle M. 2014. Reenvisioning clinical science: unifying the discipline to improve the public health. *Clin. Psychol. Sci.* 2(1):22–34

Ouellette JA, Wood W. 1998. Habit and intention in everyday life: the multiple processes by which past behavior predicts future behavior. *Psychol. Bull.* 124(1):54–74

Palfai TP, Ostafin BD. 2003. Alcohol-related motivational tendencies in hazardous drinkers: assessing implicit response tendencies using the modified-IAT. *Behav. Res. Ther.* 41(10):1149–62

Papies EK. 2016. Health goal priming as a situated intervention tool: how to benefit from nonconscious motivational routes to health behavior. *Health Psychol. Rev.* In press

Papies EK, Hamstra P. 2010. Goal priming and eating behavior: enhancing self-regulation by environmental cues. *Health Psychol.* 29(4):384–88

Papies EK, Potjes I, Keesman M, Schwinghammer S, van Koningsbruggen GM. 2014. Using health primes to reduce unhealthy snack purchases among overweight consumers in a grocery store. *Int. J. Obes.* 38(4):597–602

Papies EK, Veling H. 2013. Healthy dining. Subtle diet reminders at the point of purchase increase low-calorie food choices among both chronic and current dieters. *Appetite* 61(1):1–7

Pascoe EA, Smart Richman L. 2009. Perceived discrimination and health: a meta-analytic review. *Psychol. Bull.* 135(4):531–54

Persky S. 2011. Employing immersive virtual environments for innovative experiments in health care communication. *Patient Educ. Couns.* 82(3):313–17

Peterson JC, Charlson ME, Hoffman Z, Wells MT, Wong SC, et al. 2012. A randomized controlled trial of positive-affect induction to promote physical activity after percutaneous coronary intervention. *Arch. Intern. Med.* 172(4):329–36

Podsakoff PM, MacKenzie SB, Lee JY, Podsakoff NP. 2003. Common method biases in behavioral research: a critical review of the literature and recommended remedies. *J. App. Psychol.* 88(5):879–903

Powers WT. 1973. *Behavior: The Control of Perception.* New York: Aldine DeGruyter

Prochaska JO, DiClemente CC, Norcross JC. 1992. In search of how people change: applications to addictive behaviors. *Am. Psychol.* 47(9):1102–14

Rhodes RE, Fiala B, Conner M. 2009. A review and meta-analysis of affective judgments and physical activity in adult populations. *Ann. Behav. Med.* 38(3):180–204

Riddle M, Sci. Behav. Change Work. Group. 2015. News from the NIH: using an experimental medicine approach to facilitate translational research. *Transl. Behav. Med.* 5(4):486–88

Rivis A, Sheeran P. 2013. Automatic risk behavior: direct effects of binge drinker stereotypes on drinking behavior. *Health Psychol.* 32(5):571–80

Rodrigues AM, O'Brien N, French DP, Glidewell L, Sniehotta FF. 2015. The question–behavior effect: genuine effect or spurious phenomenon? A systematic review of randomized controlled trials with meta-analyses. *Health Psychol.* 34(1):61–78

Rogers RW. 1983. Cognitive and physiological processes in fear appeals and attitude change: a revised theory of protection motivation. In *Social Psychophysiology*, ed. J Cacioppo, R Petty, pp. 153–76. New York: Guilford Press

Rosenstock IM. 1966. Why people use health services. *Milbank Mem. Fund Q.* 44:94–124

Rothman AJ. 2000. Toward a theory-based analysis of behavioral maintenance. *Health Psychol.* 19(Suppl. 1):64–69

Rothman AJ. 2004. "Is there nothing more practical than a good theory?": why innovations and advances in health behavior change will arise if interventions are more theory-friendly. *Int. J. Behav. Nutr. Phys. Act.* 1:11

Rothman AJ. 2009. Capitalizing on opportunities to nurture and refine health behavior theories. *Health Educ. Behav.* 36(Suppl. 5):150S–55S

Rothman AJ. 2013. Exploring connections between moderators and mediators: commentary on subgroup analyses in intervention research. *Prev. Sci.* 14(2):189–92

Rothman AJ, Baldwin AS. 2012. A person X intervention strategy approach to understanding health behavior. In *Handbook of Personality and Social Psychology*, ed. K Deaux, M Snyder, pp. 729–52. New York: Oxford Univ. Press

Rothman AJ, Baldwin AS, Hertel AW, Fuglestad P. 2011. Self-regulation and behavior change: disentangling behavioral initiation and behavioral maintenance. In *Handbook of Self-Regulation: Research, Theory, and Applications*, ed. KD Vohs, RF Baumeister, pp. 106–22. New York: Guilford

Rothman AJ, Gollwitzer PM, Grant AM, Neal DT, Sheeran P, Wood W. 2015. Hale and hearty policies: how psychological science can create and maintain healthy habits. *Perspect. Psychol. Sci.* 10(6):701–5

Rothman AJ, Klein WMP, Cameron LD. 2013. Advancing innovations in social/personality psychology and health: opportunities and challenges. *Health Psychol.* 32(5):602–8

Rothman AJ, Salovey P. 2007. The reciprocal relation between principles and practice: social psychology and health behavior. In *Social Psychology: Handbook of Basic Principles*, ed. A Kruglanski, ET Higgins, pp. 826–49. New York: Guilford

Salovey P, Rothman AJ, Rodin J. 1998. Health behavior. In *The Handbook of Social Psychology*, ed. DT Gilbert, ST Fiske, L Gardner, pp. 633–83. New York: McGraw-Hill

Schwarzer R. 2008. Modeling health behavior change: how to predict and modify the adoption and maintenance of health behaviors. *Appl. Psychol. Int. Rev.* 57(1):1–29

Sheeran P, Abraham C. 2003. Mediator of moderators: temporal stability of intention and the intention-behavior relation. *Personal. Soc. Psychol. Bull.* 29(2):205–15

Sheeran P, Aubrey R, Kellett S. 2007. Increasing attendance for psychotherapy: implementation intentions and the self-regulation of attendance-related negative affect. *J. Consult. Clin. Psychol.* 75(6):853–63

Sheeran P, Harris PR, Epton T. 2014. Does heightening risk appraisals change people's intentions and behavior? A meta-analysis of experimental studies. *Psychol. Bull.* 140(2):511–43

Sheeran P, Maki A, Montanaro E, Avishai-Yitshak A, Bryan A, et al. 2016. The impact of changing attitudes, norms, and self-efficacy on health-related intentions and behavior: a meta-analysis. *Health Psychol.* In press

Shipstead Z, Redick TS, Engle RW. 2012. Is working memory training effective? *Psychol. Bull.* 138(4):628–54

Smith KP, Christakis NA. 2008. Social networks and health. *Annu. Rev. Sociol.* 34(1):405–29

Steele CM. 1988. The psychology of self-affirmation: sustaining the integrity of the self. *Adv. Exp. Soc. Psychol.* 21:261–302

Strack F, Deutsch R. 2004. Reflective and impulsive determinants of social behavior. *Personal. Soc. Psychol. Rev.* 8(3):220–47

Sweeney AM, Moyer A. 2015. Self-affirmation and responses to health messages: a meta-analysis on intentions and behavior. *Health Psychol.* 34(2):149–59

Thaler RH, Sunstein CR. 2008. *Nudge: Improving Decisions about Health, Wealth, and Happiness*. New Haven: Yale Univ. Press

Trafimow D. 2004. Problems with change in R^2 as applied to theory of reasoned action research. *Br. J. Soc. Psychol.* 43(4):515–30

Trafimow D, Clayton KD, Sheeran P, Darwish A-FE, Brown J. 2010. How do people form behavioral intentions when others have the power to determine social consequences? *J. Gen. Psychol.* 137:287–309

Trafimow D, Sheeran P. 1998. Some tests of the distinction between cognitive and affective beliefs. *J. Exp. Soc. Psychol.* 34(4):378–97

Van Dongen A, Abraham C, Ruiter RAC, Veldhuizen IJT. 2012. Does questionnaire distribution promote blood donation? An investigation of question–behavior effects. *Ann. Behav. Med.* 45(2):163–72

Webb TL, Joseph J, Yardley LM. 2010. Using the internet to promote health behavior change: a systematic review and meta-analysis of the impact of theoretical basis, use of behavior change techniques, and mode of delivery on efficacy. *J. Med. Internet Res.* 12(1):e4

Webb TL, Sheeran P. 2006. Does changing behavioral intentions engender behavior change? A meta-analysis of the experimental evidence. *Psychol. Bull.* 132(2):249–68

Webb TL, Sheeran P. 2008. Mechanisms of implementation intention effects: the role of intention, self-efficacy, and accessibility of plan components. *Br. J. Soc. Psychol.* 47:373–95

Weber MA, Schiffrin EL, White WB, Mann S, Lindholm LH, et al. 2014. Clinical practice guidelines for the management of hypertension in the community. *J. Clin. Hyperten.* 16:14–26

Weinstein ND. 2007. Misleading tests of health behavior theories. *Ann. Behav. Med.* 33(1):1–10

Weinstein ND, Rothman AJ. 2005. Commentary: revitalizing research on health behavior theories. *Health Educ. Res.* 20(3):294–97

West SG, Biesanz C, Pitts SC. 2000. Causal inference and generalization in field settings: experimental and quasi-experimental designs. In *Handbook of Research Methods in Social and Personality Research*, ed. HT Reis, CM Judd, pp. 40–65. Cambridge, UK: Cambridge Univ. Press

Wileman V, Farrington K, Chilcot J, Norton S, Wellsted DM, et al. 2014. Evidence that self-affirmation improves phosphate control in hemodialysis patients: a pilot cluster randomized controlled trial. *Ann. Behav. Med.* 48(2):275–81

Witte K. 1992. Putting the fear back into fear appeals: the Extended Parallel Process Model. *Commun. Monogr.* 59:329–49

Wood C, Conner MT, Miles E, Sandberg T, Taylor N, et al. 2016. The impact of asking intention or self-prediction questions on subsequent behavior: a meta-analysis. *Personal. Soc. Psychol. Rev.* 20(3):245–68

Wood W, Neal DT. 2007. A new look at habits and the habit-goal interface. *Psychol. Rev.* 114(4):843–63

Wood W, Rünger D. 2015. Psychology of habit. *Annu. Rev. Psychol.* 67(1):89–314

Yoon PW, Bastian B, Anderson RN, Collins JL, Jaffe HW, Cent. Dis. Control Prev. (CDC). 2014. Potentially preventable deaths from the five leading causes of death—United States, 2008–2010. *Morb. Mortal. Wkly. Rep.* 63(17):369–74

Experiments with More Than One Random Factor: Designs, Analytic Models, and Statistical Power

Charles M. Judd,[1] Jacob Westfall,[2] and David A. Kenny[3]

[1] Department of Psychology and Neuroscience, University of Colorado, Boulder, Colorado 80309; email: charles.judd@colorado.edu

[2] Department of Psychology, University of Texas at Austin, Austin, Texas 78712; email: jake.westfall@utexas.edu

[3] Department of Psychological Sciences, University of Connecticut, Storrs, Connecticut 06269; email: david.kenny@uconn.edu

Annu. Rev. Psychol. 2017. 68:601–25

First published online as a Review in Advance on September 28, 2016

The *Annual Review of Psychology* is online at psych.annualreviews.org

This article's doi: 10.1146/annurev-psych-122414-033702

Keywords

experimental design, mixed models, random factors, statistical power, sample size, effect size

Abstract

Traditional methods of analyzing data from psychological experiments are based on the assumption that there is a single random factor (normally participants) to which generalization is sought. However, many studies involve at least two random factors (e.g., participants and the targets to which they respond, such as words, pictures, or individuals). The application of traditional analytic methods to the data from such studies can result in serious bias in testing experimental effects. In this review, we develop a comprehensive typology of designs involving two random factors, which may be either crossed or nested, and one fixed factor, condition. We present appropriate linear mixed models for all designs and develop effect size measures. We provide the tools for power estimation for all designs. We then discuss issues of design choice, highlighting power and feasibility considerations. Our goal is to encourage appropriate analytic methods that produce replicable results for studies involving new samples of both participants and targets.

Contents

INTRODUCTION

Psychologists learn early in their statistical training to use analysis of variance procedures (*t*-tests and ANOVA) to analyze data from designs in which participants respond in various experimental conditions. In these designs and analyses, condition is a fixed factor, whereas participants are a random factor, meaning that the participants used in any particular study are thought to be a sample of participants that might have been used. In analyzing the data from such experiments, one obtains an estimate of the mean condition difference, as well as an estimate of the uncertainty surrounding that difference, by examining the variability across participants (i.e., across the random factor in the design). The goal is to determine whether the mean condition difference, given the variability of participants, is sufficiently large to permit the belief that it would continue to be found with other samples of participants.

However, many questions in psychology do not lend themselves easily to these well-learned analytic approaches. Frequently, research questions demand experiments that involve more than a single random factor across which generalization about condition differences should be sought. For instance, a memory researcher might be interested in memory for word lists under different conditions and wish to reach conclusions that generalize both to other samples of participants and to other samples of words that might have been used. Likewise, a social psychologist might ask participants to respond to faces of individuals coming from two different ethnic or racial categories. Here the goal would be to reach conclusions that generalize both to other participants and to other samples of faces that might have been used. Additionally, consider a clinical psychologist who is interested in showing that a new therapeutic approach for the treatment of depression is more effective than the standard approach. He or she might collect data from patients who are being treated by therapists under either the new or the standard approach. Again, generalization of any differences should reasonably be sought both across other patients and across other therapists that might have been studied.

Because psychological researchers are not routinely trained in the analysis of data from designs, such as those just illustrated, that have multiple random factors, all too often the data from such designs are inappropriately analyzed by collapsing across or ignoring one of the random factors so that the familiar t-tests and ANOVA procedures can be used. For instance, the memory researcher would typically compute a mean score for each participant for the word list as a whole; the social psychologist would compute, for each participant, means across faces within a racial category; and the depression researcher might simply ignore the therapists in the analysis. If the goal is to reach conclusions that generalize to both random factors, then these analyses are likely inappropriate because they have been shown to result in seriously inflated type I statistical errors, leading researchers to claim statistically significant effects that may be unlikely to replicate with different samples of words, faces, or therapists (Clark 1973, Judd et al. 2012). Many failures to replicate experimental results likely stem from this (Westfall et al. 2015).

To remedy these errors, in this review we provide a thorough treatment of the design and analysis of experiments in psychology that have more than one random factor. In such experiments, rather than having a single source of error variation in the data that arises from a single random factor (e.g., participants), there exist multiple sources of error variation arising from multiple random factors (e.g., words as well as participants, faces as well as participants, therapists as well as patients). Given this fact, a more general analytic approach is necessary, in which those multiple sources of random variation are explicitly modeled and estimated. This more general analytic approach relies on what are called generalized linear mixed models (Bolker et al. 2009, Stroup 2012). We provide a thorough treatment of this approach in the context of psychological experimental designs having two random factors.

We begin with the familiar designs involving only one random factor, participants, and a single fixed condition factor having two levels. These are the experimental designs for which the well-learned t-tests and ANOVA procedures are appropriate. We show how these procedures can be recast into the mixed-model framework so that the familiar analyses become special cases of mixed-model analyses.

We then turn to designs having two random factors (which we call participants and targets) and one fixed factor (which we call condition), and present the full mixed model that identifies all the sources of variation in the resulting data. We develop a comprehensive typology of all such designs, including designs in which the two random factors are crossed and designs in which one random factor is nested within the other. For each design, we give specifics about estimation and discuss an effect size estimate that is modeled on Cohen's d (i.e., the standardized mean difference; Cohen 1988) but generalized to the current designs involving two random factors.

Next we develop procedures for the estimation of statistical power in the context of the designs considered, including providing access to a web-based application for power estimation. In light of this, we discuss considerations relating to sample sizes, design choices, and the efficiency of alternative designs.

In the concluding sections of the review, we expand the design possibilities, discussing designs with more than two levels of condition, with multiple fixed factors, with more than two random factors, and with dyadic data.

MIXED MODELS FOR DESIGNS WITH ONE RANDOM AND ONE FIXED FACTOR

We begin with familiar designs in which there is one fixed factor, condition, having two levels, and only one random factor, participants. For instance, imagine that we are interested in task performance under stress. We are comparing the responses of participants under two conditions, with and without stress. In this context, there are two possible designs: participants are in both conditions or participants are in only one condition. The former is typically called a within-participant design, whereas the latter is called a between-participant design (Smith 2014). We refer to the first design as the C design, meaning that participants are crossed with condition, and the second as the N design, meaning that participants are nested within the levels of condition. The standard least-squares analysis for data from the C design is the paired t-test or, equivalently, a repeated-measures ANOVA. For data from the N design, the standard analysis is the independent samples t-test or a between-subject ANOVA.

To recast the analysis of data from these designs into the mixed-model terminology, we first specify the possible sources of variation in the observations from these designs. We assume participants are measured on a single dependent variable, Y_{ik}, where i refers to the individual participant and k to the condition under which the observation is taken. The mixed-model specification of the individual observations can be written as follows:

$$Y_{ik} = \beta_0 + \beta_1 c_{ik} + \alpha_i^P + \alpha_i^{P \times C} c_{ik} + \varepsilon_{ik}. \tag{1}$$

The values of c_{ik} represent condition and are assumed to be contrast- or deviation-coded[1] (i.e., $c_{i1} = 1$ and $c_{i2} = -1$). The terms β_0 and β_1 represent the fixed effects and capture the overall mean response (β_0) and the condition difference in responses (β_1). In the mixed-model terminology, β_0 is the fixed intercept and β_1 is the fixed slope of condition. What makes this a mixed model is that, in addition to these fixed sources of variation in the data, there are multiple sources of variation that are random in the sense that they vary across the participants in the design. The following are the random components of variation in the observations:

$$\text{var}(\alpha_i^P) = \sigma_P^2, \qquad \text{var}(\alpha_i^{P \times C}) = \sigma_{P \times C}^2, \qquad \text{var}(\varepsilon_{ik}) = \sigma_E^2.$$

The variance attributable to participant mean differences is designated as σ_P^2. In the language of mixed models, this is the random variation across participants in their intercepts. The variance attributable to participant differences in the condition effects (i.e., participant-by-condition interaction effects) is $\sigma_{P \times C}^2$. In the language of mixed models, this is the random variation across participants in their condition slopes. And finally, σ_E^2 represents residual random error variation in the observations. These variances are also in the standard ANOVA approach to these designs; the mixed-model specification makes them explicit. Additionally, in the mixed-model specification, a possible covariance is explicitly considered between participant intercepts and their slopes,

$$\text{cov}(\alpha_i^P, \alpha_i^{P \times C}) = \sigma_{P, P \times C},$$

allowing those participants with higher mean responses to have smaller or larger condition differences. This covariance is typically ignored in the standard ANOVA approach.

The mixed model given in Equation 1 can be rewritten to make clear that the α_i^P and $\alpha_i^{P \times C}$ terms represent random variation in the intercepts and slopes across participants:

$$Y_{ik} = \underbrace{(\beta_0 + \alpha_i^P)}_{\text{intercepts}} + \underbrace{(\beta_1 + \alpha_i^{P \times C})}_{\text{slopes}} c_{ik} + \varepsilon_{ik}. \tag{2}$$

Cast this way, we have a linear model with a single predictor variable, c_{ik}, specifying varying intercepts and slopes over and above their fixed (or average) components.

---

[1] Other values could be used for the contrast codes (e.g., +0.5 and −0.5), but the key is that they are centered around zero. We assume +1 and −1 throughout. If dummy coding (+1, 0) is used, the meaning of the model's variance components dramatically changes: the intercept variance becomes the random variance of those scoring zero and not the variance for both groups.

As already specified, the condition effect in the above model is captured by β_1, which equals $(\mu_1 - \mu_2)/2$. Cohen (1988) defined the general standardized effect size d as the raw mean difference divided by the square root of the pooled variance of the observations within the conditions:[2]

$$d = \frac{\mu_1 - \mu_2}{\sqrt{\sigma_P^2 + \sigma_{P \times C}^2 + \sigma_E^2}}.$$

This full model, with all the random components of variation, is estimable only when each participant is crossed with condition (as in the C design) and when there are multiple replicates (i.e., multiple independent observations from each participant in each condition). In the C design with only one replicate (i.e., one observation from each participant in each condition) and in the N design, one can still estimate the fixed effects, but there is a confounding of the three random variance components. Although we do not consider in detail designs with multiple replicates (although see the **Supplemental Appendix**; follow the **Supplemental Material** link in the online version of this article or at **http://www.annualreviews.org/**), we want to provide the details of how one would estimate the full model from such a design if one had such data available. The specifications for the C and N designs become a simple matter of trimming from the full model those variance components that cannot be estimated in those designs.

One important issue in estimating the mixed model is the structure of the data file. In the typical ANOVA approach to data, each participant has one row of data in the data file. For the mixed model estimation, each row of data consists of a single observation taken from a particular participant in a particular condition. For instance, if a given participant were to be observed in both conditions with three replicates in each, then that participant would have six lines of data in the data file.

The code for estimating the mixed model specified above for these data is as follows:

```
SAS:      proc mixed;
          class participant;
          model y = c;
          random intercept c/sub = participant type = un;
          run;
SPSS:     mixed y with c
          /fixed = c
          /print = solution testcov
          /random = intercept c | subject(participant) covtype(un).
R:        model <- lmer(y ~ c + (c|participant))
```

In each case, the fixed effects are specified in the mixed model, modeling the observations as a function of condition. Implicit in the model specification are the intercept and the residual at the level of the individual observation. The code specifies the random components of variance, indicating that both the intercept and the slope for condition are allowed to vary randomly across participants. In the *lme4* package in R, the random components are included by the specification "+ (c|participant)," which indicates that the slope for c (and implicitly the intercept) varies across participants. The "un" option in both SAS and SPSS specifies that the random intercept and slope are allowed to covary, which is implicit in the R code. The resulting output includes the intercept

---

[2] This formula assumes contrast codes of $+1$ and -1, an assumption that we make in defining effect sizes throughout. Given this coding, the intercept–slope covariance does not contribute to the expected within-condition variation (Westfall et al. 2014, appendix). Additionally, the c^2 term in the effect sizes given by Westfall et al. (2014) drops out because $c^2 = 1$.

and slope fixed estimates (along with standard errors) and the variances and covariance of the random intercepts and slopes. Assumptions are that the random effects are distributed normally and that the model residuals are independent across observations (e.g., no carryover or lagged effects).

We turn now to the C and N designs with a single replicate. In these designs, as we have said, the same underlying components of variance contribute to the individual observations, but not all of them are estimable.

Mixed-Model Specification of the C Design

In the C design, with each participant in both conditions, the same fixed effects can be estimated. However, not all of the random components are estimable. More specifically, σ_P^2 can be estimated, but $\sigma_{P \times C}^2$ cannot. Although $\sigma_{P \times C}^2$ still contributes to variation in the observations, it cannot be disentangled from the residual error term σ_E^2. Accordingly, in the mixed model code, one simply eliminates the random variance in participant slopes from the specification, as that source of variation is contained in the error variance. Thus, in this design, one estimates only two random variance components, participant intercepts and residual error.

The general effect size for this design is given as

$$d = \frac{\mu_1 - \mu_2}{\sqrt{\sigma_P^2 + [\sigma_E^2 + \sigma_{P \times C}^2]}}.$$

The denominator of this effect size contains, as before, all three random sources of variation in the observations, but in this case two of these sources are placed in brackets together to indicate the confounding: What is estimated as residual error also includes the variance due to participant slopes.

The test of the condition effect is based on a t-statistic that divides the estimated mean difference between the conditions by its estimated standard error. In this design, the variance components that contribute to the standard error of the treatment difference include the participant slope variance and the residual error variance. The variance attributable to participant intercepts (or means) does not contribute to the standard error of the mean difference between conditions. Cohen (1988) defined what we call the operative effect size as the mean condition difference divided only by those variance components that contribute to its standard error. Accordingly, for the C design, the operative effect size is[3]

$$d_0 = \frac{\mu_1 - \mu_2}{\sqrt{[\sigma_E^2 + \sigma_{P \times C}^2]}}.$$

In any sample of data, the operative effect size is estimated as the mean observed condition difference divided by the square root of the estimated residual error (which contains in it the variance attributable to random participant slopes). The general, rather than operative, effect size is typically reported. We give both to clarify those variance components that do and do not contribute to the standard error of the condition difference.

Mixed-Model Specification of the N Design

In this design—the classic two-group between-subjects design—each participant is observed in only one condition. As a result, the error variance contains all three random components of variance

---

[3]This operative effect size can also be given as $d_O = d \times \frac{1}{\sqrt{1 - \rho_{12}}}$, where ρ_{12} is the correlation between the participants' scores in the two conditions.

(participant intercepts, participant slopes, and residual error). Accordingly, in the mixed-model specification, no random components are estimable except for residual error. In the computer code to estimate and test the model, any reference to random slopes or intercepts due to participants is omitted.

The general effect size for this design is

$$d = \frac{\mu_1 - \mu_2}{\sqrt{\left[\sigma_E^2 + \sigma_P^2 + \sigma_{P \times C}^2\right]}}.$$

As in the general effect size for the C design, the brackets indicate that the variance due to participant intercepts and participant slopes is now part of the residual error variance. This effect size is estimated as the mean observed condition difference divided by the square root of the estimated residual error variance.

Because variances due to both participant intercepts and participant slopes contribute to the estimated residual error in this design, all three components contribute to the standard error for testing the mean condition difference. Accordingly, in this design the operative effect size is identical to the general effect size.

The mixed-model specifications for the C and N designs yield tests of the condition difference that are identical to the comparable standard ANOVA approaches.[4] The difference lies in the structure of the data and the modeling of the sources of variation in the data. The standard ANOVA approach treats the individual participant as the unit of analysis and does not normally make explicit all sources of variation in the data. In contrast, the mixed-model specification treats the individual observations as the unit of analysis and allows multiple simultaneous sources of random variation in the data. For this reason, the mixed-model approach is appropriate for the analysis of data with multiple random factors.

DESIGNS WITH TWO RANDOM AND ONE FIXED FACTOR

With only one random factor, the design alternatives are limited. With two random factors, the design possibilities grow considerably. The random factors may be crossed with each other, or one may be nested within the levels of the other; each random factor may also be crossed with or nested within the levels of the fixed factor. In this section, we lay out all the design possibilities. We continue to refer to the fixed factor as condition, having two levels. We refer to the two random factors as participants and targets. We assume the goal is to estimate and test the condition difference so that inferences can be made to other samples of participants and targets that might have been used.

We start with the most general design, in which all factors are crossed with each other (every participant responds to every target in both conditions) and in which there are multiple replicates (multiple observations taken from each participant in response to each target in each condition). We refer to this as the most general design because it is only in the context of this design that we can define and estimate all the random components of variance contributing to the observations. Thus, only for this most general design can we give the full mixed-model specification and its associated code for estimation. We then provide a general effect size definition as the magnitude of the condition difference relative to all of the random sources of variation in the data.

We turn next to more widely used designs that do not include multiple replicates and in which, therefore, not all of the variance components are estimable. These include both designs

---

[4]Technically, this is true only if ρ_{12}, as defined in footnote 3, is nonnegative.

in which the two random factors are crossed with each other and designs in which one random factor is nested within the other. Accordingly, the designs that we consider, and their mixed-model specifications, bridge two rather disparate literatures devoted to linear mixed models. Designs with crossed random factors have been considered primarily by experimental researchers in psychology and linguistics (Baayen et al. 2008, Clark 1973, Judd et al. 2012); designs with nested random factors have a long history in educational psychology and applied statistics, fields in which they are commonly referred to as multilevel or hierarchical linear models (Hox 2010, Raudenbush & Bryk 2002, Snijders & Bosker 2011).

As was the case for the specific designs with participants as the only random factor that were considered in the previous section, these specific designs differ from the most general design in that only some of the variance components from the full set that contributes to the observations can be estimated. For each design, we give those variance components that are estimable and those that are not and then present the code modifications that are necessary for estimation. All designs permit the testing of condition differences with generalization across both participants and targets. For each design, we also give appropriate design-specific effect sizes.

Mixed-Model Specification and Effect Size for the Most General Design

In this section, we present the full mixed-model specification for designs with the two random factors of participants and targets and the fixed factor of condition having two levels. As discussed in the preceding paragraphs, this full specification requires a design in which all three factors are fully crossed and in which there are multiple replicates. This is the most general design in the sense that only in this design can all of the underlying variance components be estimated. All other designs involving these factors represent modifications of this design in which some of the observations are systematically missing and, accordingly, in which some of the variance components are confounded with each other.

We assume a single dependent variable with variation accruing from a condition difference; a series of random effects attributable to the underlying factors in the design; and, additionally, random error. The full mixed model for the response of the ith participant to the jth target in the kth condition is

$$Y_{ijk} = \beta_0 + \beta_1 c_{ijk} + \alpha_i^P + \alpha_i^{P \times C} c_{ijk} + \alpha_j^T + \alpha_j^{T \times C} c_{ijk} + \alpha_{ij}^{P \times T} + \alpha_{ij}^{P \times T \times C} c_{ijk} + \varepsilon_{ijk} \qquad (3)$$

and the following are the sources of variation in Y_{ijk}:

$$\text{var}\left(\alpha_i^P\right) = \sigma_P^2, \quad \text{var}\left(\alpha_i^{P \times C}\right) = \sigma_{P \times C}^2, \quad \text{cov}\left(\alpha_i^P, \alpha_i^{P \times C}\right) = \sigma_{P, P \times C},$$

$$\text{var}\left(\alpha_j^T\right) = \sigma_T^2, \quad \text{var}\left(\alpha_j^{T \times C}\right) = \sigma_{T \times C}^2, \quad \text{cov}\left(\alpha_j^T, \alpha_j^{T \times C}\right) = \sigma_{T, T \times C},$$

$$\text{var}\left(\alpha_{ij}^{P \times T}\right) = \sigma_{P \times T}^2, \quad \text{var}\left(\alpha_{ij}^{P \times T \times C}\right) = \sigma_{P \times T \times C}^2, \quad \text{cov}\left(\alpha_{ij}^{P \times T}, \alpha_{ij}^{P \times T \times C}\right) = \sigma_{P \times T, P \times T \times C},$$

$$\text{var}(\varepsilon_{ijk}) = \sigma_E^2.$$

As above, β_0 and β_1 in this model represent the fixed effects and capture, respectively, the overall mean response and the condition difference in responses. The other elements in this model are the random effects, the variances and covariances of which are given intuitive interpretations in **Table 1**. To show more clearly the specification of some of these components as random intercept

Table 1 Definitions of random variance and covariance components in the designs considered in this review

Variance or covariance component	Definition
σ_P^2	Participant intercept variance: the extent to which participants have different mean responses
$\sigma_{P \times C}^2$	Participant slope variance: the extent to which the mean difference between conditions varies across participants
$\sigma_{P,P \times C}$	Participant intercept–slope covariance: the extent to which participants with larger mean responses also show larger condition differences
σ_T^2	Target intercept variance: the extent to which targets elicit different mean responses
$\sigma_{T \times C}^2$	Target slope variance: the extent to which the mean difference between conditions varies across targets
$\sigma_{T,T \times C}$	Target intercept–slope covariance: the extent to which targets that elicit larger mean responses also show larger condition differences
$\sigma_{P \times T}^2$	Participant-by-target intercept variance: the extent to which participants show stable, unique patterns of mean responses toward particular targets
$\sigma_{P \times T \times C}^2$	Participant-by-target slope variance: the extent to which the mean difference between conditions varies across different participant–target pairs
$\sigma_{P \times T, P \times T \times C}$	Participant-by-target intercept–slope covariance: the extent to which participant–target pairs with larger mean responses also show larger condition differences
σ_E^2	Residual error variance: the extent to which there is variation in responses not due to the above sources

Variables: C, fixed condition factor; E, error; P, random participant factor; T, random target factor.

components and others as random slope components, we rewrite the mixed model of Equation 3 as

$$Y_{ijk} = \underbrace{(\beta_0 + \alpha_i^P + \alpha_j^T + \alpha_{ij}^{P \times T})}_{\text{intercepts}} + \underbrace{(\beta_1 + \alpha_i^{P \times C} + \alpha_j^{T \times C} + \alpha_{ij}^{P \times T \times C})}_{\text{slopes}} c_{ijk} + \varepsilon_{ijk}. \qquad (4)$$

On the basis of this model and again using Cohen's (1988) specification of the effect size, the following can be defined as the general effect size for this design:[5]

$$d = \frac{\mu_1 - \mu_2}{\sqrt{\sigma_P^2 + \sigma_{P \times C}^2 + \sigma_T^2 + \sigma_{T \times C}^2 + \sigma_{P \times T}^2 + \sigma_{P \times T \times C}^2 + \sigma_E^2}}. \qquad (5)$$

For mixed-model estimation, the data file is again structured so that each individual observation is a row of data. The code for estimating effects for data from this fully crossed design with multiple replicates is as follows:

```
SAS:    proc mixed;
        class participant target;
        model Y = c;
        random intercept c/sub = participant type = un;
        random intercept c/sub = target type = un;
        random intercept c/sub = participant*target type = un;
        run;
```

---

[5] Consistent with footnote 2, we assume contrast code values of +1 and −1. Other values require a slight modification of the effect size denominator. Under the contrast-coding convention, the intercept–slope covariances do not contribute to the expected within-condition variation (Westfall et al. 2014, appendix).

```
SPSS:     mixed y with c
          /fixed = c
          /print = solution testcov
          /random = intercept c | subject(participant) covtype(un)
          /random = intercept c | subject(target) covtype(un)
          /random = intercept c | subject(participant*target) covtype(un).
R:        model <- lmer(y ~ c + (c|participant) + (c|target)
          + (c|participant:target))
```

This code is an extension of the code given above for designs with one random factor (see Mixed Models for Designs with One Random and One Fixed Factor); in this case, it provides for the additional random components of variance in the design: random intercepts and slopes due to participants, those due to targets, and finally those due to the participant-by-target interaction.

As before, not all variance components contribute to the standard error used to test the condition difference in this design. Accordingly, the operative effect size for this fully crossed design with replicates, calculated by dividing the condition mean difference by those components that contribute to its standard error, is:

$$d_0 = \frac{\mu_1 - \mu_2}{\sqrt{\sigma_{P \times C}^2 + \sigma_{T \times C}^2 + \sigma_{P \times T \times C}^2 + \sigma_E^2}}. \tag{6}$$

In the following sections, we systematically define the possible designs that involve two random factors (participants and targets) and a single fixed factor (condition) but that have only a single replicate. All of the designs that we define can be seen as special cases of the most general design considered above but with systematically missing observations. Each design provides an estimate of the fixed effects of interest. In all the designs, the same variance components potentially contribute to the observations, but some of these components are confounded with each other, and thus model specification and effect sizes must be tailored to each particular design.

Design Possibilities

To define the full range of designs that have the three factors of condition, participants, and targets, we must consider the three possible pairs of these factors: condition and participants, condition and targets, and participants and targets. For each pair, the two factors may be crossed or nested. We use C and N to indicate whether the factors in each pair are crossed or nested, respectively. Each design is thus identified by three letters: the first C or N indicates whether participants are crossed with condition or are nested within condition; the second C or N indicates whether targets are crossed with condition or nested within condition; and, finally, the third letter defines whether the two random factors, participants and targets, are themselves crossed or nested. When the two random factors are nested, there are two possibilities: Either targets are nested within participants (meaning that each participant responds to a unique set of targets), or participants are nested within targets (meaning that each target is responded to by a unique set of participants). In the first case, the final letter in the definition of each design is N_P, meaning that participants are the higher-level factor within which targets are nested, and in the second case, in which participants are nested within targets, the final letter in the definition of each design is N_T.

The designs are listed in **Table 2**; each design is identified by the labels defined above. We now further define and illustrate each of these designs. We start with the first column of the table, in which the two random factors, participants and targets, are crossed with each other.

Table 2 Typology of designs with two random factors [participants (P) and targets (T)] and one fixed factor (condition)

How are P and T related to condition?	How are P and T related to each other?		
	P and T crossed	T nested in P	P nested in T
P and T crossed with condition	CCC	CCN_P	CCN_T
P crossed with condition; T nested in condition	CNC	CNN_P	Impossible
P nested in condition; T crossed with condition	NCC	Impossible	NCN_T
P and T nested in condition	NNC	NNN_P	NNN_T

Designs with crossed random factors. The four cells in the first column of **Table 2** define four designs with the final letter C. These designs are illustrated in **Figure 1a**. For ease of depiction, in these matrices the numbers of levels of the random factors are considerably smaller than what they would likely be in any actual study.

The first design, CCC, is the fully crossed design in which every participant responds to every target twice, once in each condition. Imagine a design in which participants make speeded categorization judgments of two computer-altered versions of a set of male faces, one version morphed towards a prototypic White face and the other morphed towards a prototypic Black face. Faces constitute the random target factor. The condition variable refers to the two morphing conditions. Every participant categorizes every face in both its White-morphed version and its Black-morphed version (i.e., condition).

The CNC design is one in which every target is responded to by every participant, but each target is in only one condition. Imagine a variation of the previous example in which participants judge target faces of different races, but in this case the faces judged are actual faces of White and Black individuals rather than morphed versions of faces. Thus, each individual face is either White or Black, so targets are nested within condition. Participants make a speeded categorization judgment of every face, half of which are White and half Black.

In the NCC design, participants are nested within condition and targets are crossed with condition. Imagine that participants complete a series of target judgments either under cognitive load or without such load. Each participant is in only one of the two load conditions. However, every target is judged under both load conditions, albeit by different participants.

In the NNC design, both random factors are nested within condition. Imagine that participants make career likelihood judgments of faces (e.g., "How likely is it that this person is a scientist?"). There are two sets of faces, either male or female, and participants respond only to one set or the other. Gender of target is the condition variable of interest.

Designs with nested random factors. Designs in the second and third columns of **Table 2** have one of the two random factors nested within the other. In the second column, in which targets are nested within participants, each participant has a unique set of targets. In the third column, each target is responded to by its own unique set of participants. These designs are illustrated by the matrices in **Figure 1b**.

The CCN_P and CCN_T designs have one random factor nested within the other, but both of these factors are crossed with condition. The classic nested design from educational research involves students who are nested in classrooms, each taught by a single instructor. In one version of this design, the CCN_P design, the instructors evaluate their students in two different conditions or subjects, math and language. Thus, the instructors are the participants and they evaluate their students (targets) on both subjects. The question is whether the evaluations depend on the subject matter. In the CCN_T design, the students are now the participants and they evaluate their instructor as both a math teacher and a language teacher. Thus, students continue to be nested within

a Designs with crossed P and T random factors

CCC

P \ T	1	2	3	4	5	6
1	AB	AB	AB	AB	AB	AB
2	AB	AB	AB	AB	AB	AB
3	AB	AB	AB	AB	AB	AB
4	AB	AB	AB	AB	AB	AB
5	AB	AB	AB	AB	AB	AB
6	AB	AB	AB	AB	AB	AB

CNC

P \ T	1	2	3	4	5	6
1	A	A	A	B	B	B
2	A	A	A	B	B	B
3	A	A	A	B	B	B
4	A	A	A	B	B	B
5	A	A	A	B	B	B
6	A	A	A	B	B	B

NCC

P \ T	1	2	3	4	5	6
1	A	A	A	A	A	A
2	A	A	A	A	A	A
3	A	A	A	A	A	A
4	B	B	B	B	B	B
5	B	B	B	B	B	B
6	B	B	B	B	B	B

NNC

P \ T	1	2	3	4	5	6
1	A	A	A			
2	A	A	A			
3	A	A	A			
4				B	B	B
5				B	B	B
6				B	B	B

b Designs with nested P and T random factors

CCN_P

P \ T	1	2	3	4	5	6
1	AB	AB				
2			AB	AB		
3					AB	AB

CCN_T

P \ T	1	2	3
1	AB		
2	AB		
3		AB	
4		AB	
5			AB
6			AB

CNN_P

P \ T	1	2	3	4	5	6	7	8
1	A	A	B	B				
2					A	A	B	B

NCN_T

P \ T	1	2
1	A	
2	A	
3	B	
4	B	
5		A
6		A
7		B
8		B

NNN_P

P \ T	1	2	3	4	5	6	7	8
1	A	A						
2			A	A				
3					B	B		
4							B	B

NNN_T

P \ T	1	2	3	4
1	A			
2	A			
3		A		
4		A		
5			B	
6			B	
7				B
8				B

c Other designs (also with crossed P and T random factors)

Replication designs

Counterbalanced

P \ T	1	2	3	4	5	6
1	A	A	A	B	B	B
2	A	A	A	B	B	B
3	A	A	A	B	B	B
4	B	B	B	A	A	A
5	B	B	B	A	A	A
6	B	B	B	A	A	A

R(CCC)

Replication 1

P \ T	1	2	3	4
1	AB	AB	AB	AB
2	AB	AB	AB	AB
3	AB	AB	AB	AB
4	AB	AB	AB	AB

Replication 2

P \ T	5	6	7	8
5	AB	AB	AB	AB
6	AB	AB	AB	AB
7	AB	AB	AB	AB
8	AB	AB	AB	AB

R(NCC)

Replication 1

P \ T	1	2	3	4
1	A	A	A	A
2	A	A	A	A
3	B	B	B	B
4	B	B	B	B

Replication 2

P \ T	5	6	7	8
5	A	A	A	A
6	A	A	A	A
7	B	B	B	B
8	B	B	B	B

R(CNC)

Replication 1

P \ T	1	2	3	4
1	A	A	B	B
2	A	A	B	B
3	A	A	B	B
4	A	A	B	B

Replication 2

P \ T	5	6	7	8
5	A	A	B	B
6	A	A	B	B
7	A	A	B	B
8	A	A	B	B

R(NNC)

Replication 1

P \ T	1	2	3	4
1	A	A		
2	A	A		
3			B	B
4			B	B

Replication 2

P \ T	5	6	7	8
5	A	A		
6	A	A		
7			B	B
8			B	B

Figure 1

Illustrative matrices for all designs having two random factors, participants (P, *rows*) and targets (T, *columns*), and one fixed factor, condition, with two levels (A and B) under which particular observations occur. An empty or blank cell indicates that the observation for a specific combination of participant and target is not collected.

instructors, but these two groups have switched their roles in terms of the design: The instructors elicit responses, and we thus designate them as the targets, whereas the students produce responses, and we thus designate them as the participants. Both random factors are crossed with condition.

In the case of nested random factors where one of the factors is crossed with condition and the other is nested within condition, the higher-order random factor, rather than the lower-order one, must be the factor that is crossed with condition. Accordingly, two of the cells in the second and third columns of **Table 2** define impossible designs. In the CNN_P design, targets are nested within participants, participants are crossed with condition, and targets are nested within condition. Imagine that male participants are each asked to nominate and judge their two closest male and two closest female friends. Thus, each participant has a unique set of targets (friends) who are either male or female (the condition variable). The question is whether participants give systematically different ratings to their nominated male friends than their female friends.

In the NCN_T design, participants are nested within targets, targets are crossed with condition, and participants are nested within condition. In this case, the four friends nominated by each person are recruited as the participants, and they each rate their common (male) friend, the target. Participants (those who do the rating of their common nominating friend) are now nested within gender (their own), but target (the male nominating person who is rated) is crossed with the friends' genders.

The final two designs of **Table 2** are the fully nested designs, NNN_P and NNN_T, in which either targets are nested within participants or the other way around, and both random factors are nested within condition. As an example of the NNN_P design, imagine that male and female participants are recruited, and they nominate and rate as targets two friends of only their own gender. In this case, targets are nested within participants and both participants and targets are either male or female (condition being gender). For the NNN_T design, again imagine that people nominate their two friends, who are, again, the same gender as the nominating person. However, this time, the nominated friends serve as the participants, and they each rate the person who nominated them (target). Participants are now nested within targets and both are nested within condition (gender).

In addition to these designs, there are two final designs, used with some frequency, in which participants and targets are in fact confounded, with just a single target nested within each participant or, equivalently, a single participant nested within each target. Imagine research in which each participant thinks of a single friend and rates him or her, either in one condition only or in both. Thus participant and target are completely confounded, and both can be either crossed with condition or nested within condition. The analysis of this design is formally equivalent to those with one random factor that we considered above. However, in this case the random factor is not participants but the participant–target pair, and random variation in the data accrues from both sources, as well as their interaction.

Other designs. **Table 2** provides a coherent way of defining the possibilities with two random and one fixed, two-level factor. However, other possibilities deserve discussion. These designs are illustrated by the matrices in **Figure 1c**.

First, there is a variation on the fully crossed CCC design that we call the counterbalanced design (Westfall et al. 2014). This is a fully crossed design in the sense that all participants are crossed with all targets and every participant and target occurs in both conditions. Unlike the CCC design, however, each participant responds to each target in just one condition. As shown in **Figure 1c**, participants and targets are divided into two blocks that define the condition under which a specific participant–target pair is observed. In the CCC design, condition, participants, and targets are fully crossed, whereas in the counterbalanced design, condition is confounded with the participant-by-target interaction. As an example, imagine that participants complete a set of math problems, some while under cognitive load and others without load. Every participant does all problems, but the division of the problems between the half that are done under load and the half that are not varies across participants.

Second, there are four designs that we refer to as replication designs in that they replicate some of the designs of **Table 2** with multiple sets of participants and targets. Above, we talked about designs with multiple replicates (meaning multiple observations from the same participant, target, and condition). We mean something entirely different by replication designs, i.e., that an entire previously defined design is replicated more than once with new sets of participants and targets. Consider, for instance, the first row of **Table 2**, in which both participants and targets are crossed with condition. Suppose that, rather than fully crossing participants and targets, we group participants and targets such that each group contains unique participants and unique targets. Within each group, participants and targets are fully crossed, but there are multiple such groups. This design essentially replicates the CCC design many times, with each group of participants and targets constituting one replication. We refer to this design as R(CCC). Again, a replication is defined as a specific group or subset of participants and targets. In **Figure 1c** we have illustrated the R(CCC) design with the number of replications equal to two (and four participants and targets in each replication). As a more extended example, suppose participants are put in groups of four and everyone in a particular group responds to the same four targets twice, once in one condition and once in the second. There might be a total number of 32 participants and 32 targets across the total of eight replications. The advantage of this design over the fully crossed design is that it potentially reduces participant load (i.e., participants do not need to make as many responses) while nevertheless using a large number of targets, which can be important for statistical efficiency reasons considered below (see Power Considerations and Research Design).

The R(CCC) design is the replication design from the first row of **Table 2**. The other three replication designs correspond to the remaining three rows of **Table 2**. These are illustrated in **Figure 1c**, again with only two replications. The R(CNC) design is the CNC design replicated multiple times with different sets of participants and targets; each target occurs in only one condition or the other. The R(NCC) design is the NCC design replicated many times with different sets of participants and targets, in this case with participants nested within condition and targets crossed with condition. And finally, the R(NNC) design is the NNC design with multiple replications of different sets of participants and targets.

These replication designs, with participants crossed with targets in each replication, become the nested designs of the second and third columns of **Table 2** when the number of either participants or targets in each replication equals one. Thus, for instance, the R(CCC) design becomes the CCN_P design if each replication contains only a single participant, responding to the targets that are unique to that replication; it becomes the CCN_T design if each replication has only a single target responded to by the unique set of participants in that replication. The other replication designs also become the nested designs of the third and fourth columns of **Table 2** when the number of either participants or targets in each replication equals one.

Design-Specific Estimation and Effect Sizes

In this section, we discuss the mixed-model specification that estimates the condition difference given all of the random variance components that are estimable in each design. Recall that there are a total of six variance components (and three covariances) that, along with residual error, contribute to the total variation in observations. These are defined in **Table 1**. In the fully crossed design with multiple replicates (i.e., multiple observations from each participant, target, and condition combination) considered earlier, all of these variance components are estimable. Accordingly, we gave the mixed-model code in SAS, SPSS, and R; this code specifies how one estimates the fixed effect of condition and the random variance components. Finally, we also gave the effect sizes for this design; the general effect size is defined as the mean condition differences divided by all six variance components plus the residual variance, and the operative effect size is defined as the mean condition difference divided by only those variance components that contribute to the standard error of the condition difference.

In the second column of **Table 3**, we present the general effect sizes for all of the designs that we have defined. (The third column of this table lists the noncentrality parameters, which are necessary for the computation of statistical power and are discussed in the section below devoted to that subject.) Consistent with our earlier treatment of designs that have participants as the only random factor, the confounding of the variance components in these designs is indicated by brackets in the effect sizes. The denominators of the general effect sizes include, for all designs, all six variance components defined in **Table 1** plus random error variance, but many of these are confounded and not separately estimable. The first variance component within a set of brackets indicates the component that is estimable in the mixed-model specification, and the components that follow within the brackets are those that are confounded with the estimable component. The operative effect sizes for all of the designs are given in the **Supplemental Appendix**. All the information necessary for specifying the appropriate mixed model for each design is implicit in its general effect size. In the **Supplemental Appendix**, we give the code (again in SAS, SPSS, and R) for each of the designs, but the specifics of the code follow from the denominators of each design's general effect size in **Table 3**. The rule is that one specifies as random effects those variance components that are not contained in brackets in the denominator of the effect size or those that appear first in a set of bracketed components. (Note that the residual variance is included in the model by default and does not need to be specified explicitly.)

In the following paragraphs we provide illustrations for a few of the designs of how one goes from the general effect sizes in **Table 3** to the mixed model code given in the **Supplemental Appendix** for each design. We also briefly discuss for each design the estimable components that do not contribute to the standard error of the condition difference, thus highlighting the differences between the general (in **Table 3**) and the operative effect sizes (which are listed in the **Supplemental Appendix**).

The first design we consider is the CCC design. The only use of brackets in the denominator of its general effect size in **Table 3** is $[\sigma_E^2 + \sigma_{P \times T \times C}^2]$, which indicates that the variance attributable to the three-way interaction is confounded with the residual error variance. Accordingly, in modifying the code given in the section Mixed-Model Specification and Effect Size for the Most General Design (the most general design being the crossed design with multiple replicates), one includes all random components except random condition slopes for the participant-by-target interaction. Because participants and targets (and their interaction) are crossed with condition, the intercept variances attributable to these three do not contribute to the standard error of the condition difference, although those components are estimable and should be included in the model.

Second, the NCC design has two sets of brackets in the denominator of its effect size. Variance attributable to the participant by condition interaction is confounded with participant variance, and, additionally, both the participant-by-target interaction and the triple interaction are confounded with the residual error variance. Thus, the code must be modified to estimate only random participant intercepts and random target intercepts and slopes. All estimable components contribute to the standard error of the condition difference in this design except that due to target intercepts.

As a third example, the NCN_T design has three estimable components, those due to target variance, target by condition variance, and residual variance. Thus, the code specifies only those

Table 3 General effect sizes (d) and noncentrality parameters for the designs of Table 2 and Figure 1[a]

Designs	d	Noncentrality parameter
CCC	$\dfrac{\mu_1-\mu_2}{\sqrt{\sigma_P^2+\sigma_{P\times C}^2+\sigma_T^2+\sigma_{T\times C}^2+\left[\sigma_E^2+\sigma_{P\times T\times C}^2\right]}}$	$\dfrac{\mu_1-\mu_2}{2\sqrt{\dfrac{\left[\sigma_E^2+\sigma_{P\times T\times C}^2\right]}{2pq}+\dfrac{\sigma_{P\times C}^2}{p}+\dfrac{\sigma_{T\times C}^2}{q}}}$
CNC	$\dfrac{\mu_1-\mu_2}{\sqrt{\sigma_P^2+\sigma_{P\times C}^2+\left[\sigma_T^2+\sigma_{T\times C}^2\right]+\left[\sigma_E^2+\sigma_{P\times T}^2+\sigma_{P\times T\times C}^2\right]}}$	$\dfrac{\mu_1-\mu_2}{2\sqrt{\dfrac{\left[\sigma_E^2+\sigma_{P\times T}^2+\sigma_{P\times T\times C}^2\right]}{pq}+\dfrac{\sigma_{P\times C}^2}{p}+\dfrac{\left[\sigma_T^2+\sigma_{T\times C}^2\right]}{q}}}$
NCC	$\dfrac{\mu_1-\mu_2}{\sqrt{\left[\sigma_P^2+\sigma_{P\times C}^2\right]+\sigma_T^2+\sigma_{T\times C}^2+\left[\sigma_E^2+\sigma_{P\times T}^2+\sigma_{P\times T\times C}^2\right]}}$	$\dfrac{\mu_1-\mu_2}{2\sqrt{\dfrac{\left[\sigma_E^2+\sigma_{P\times T}^2+\sigma_{P\times T\times C}^2\right]}{pq}+\dfrac{\left[\sigma_P^2+\sigma_{P\times C}^2\right]}{p}+\dfrac{\sigma_{T\times C}^2}{q}}}$
NNC	$\dfrac{\mu_1-\mu_2}{\sqrt{\left[\sigma_P^2+\sigma_{P\times C}^2\right]+\left[\sigma_T^2+\sigma_{T\times C}^2\right]+\left[\sigma_E^2+\sigma_{P\times T}^2+\sigma_{P\times T\times C}^2\right]}}$	$\dfrac{\mu_1-\mu_2}{2\sqrt{\dfrac{2\left[\sigma_E^2+\sigma_{P\times T}^2+\sigma_{P\times T\times C}^2\right]}{pq}+\dfrac{\left[\sigma_P^2+\sigma_{P\times C}^2\right]}{p}+\dfrac{\left[\sigma_T^2+\sigma_{T\times C}^2\right]}{q}}}$
CCN$_P$	$\dfrac{\mu_1-\mu_2}{\sqrt{\sigma_P^2+\sigma_{P\times C}^2+\left[\sigma_T^2+\sigma_{P\times T}^2\right]+\left[\sigma_E^2+\sigma_{T\times C}^2+\sigma_{P\times T\times C}^2\right]}}$	$\dfrac{\mu_1-\mu_2}{2\sqrt{\dfrac{\left[\sigma_E^2+\sigma_{P\times T\times C}^2+\sigma_{T\times C}^2\right]}{2q}+\dfrac{\sigma_{P\times C}^2}{p}}}$
CCN$_T$	$\dfrac{\mu_1-\mu_2}{\sqrt{\left[\sigma_P^2+\sigma_{P\times T}^2\right]+\sigma_T^2+\sigma_{T\times C}^2+\left[\sigma_E^2+\sigma_{P\times C}^2+\sigma_{P\times T\times C}^2\right]}}$	$\dfrac{\mu_1-\mu_2}{2\sqrt{\dfrac{\left[\sigma_E^2+\sigma_{P\times T\times C}^2+\sigma_{P\times C}^2\right]}{2p}+\dfrac{\sigma_{T\times C}^2}{q}}}$
CNN$_P$	$\dfrac{\mu_1-\mu_2}{\sqrt{\sigma_P^2+\sigma_{P\times C}^2+\left[\sigma_E^2+\sigma_T^2+\sigma_{P\times T}^2+\sigma_{T\times C}^2+\sigma_{P\times T\times C}^2\right]}}$	$\dfrac{\mu_1-\mu_2}{2\sqrt{\dfrac{\left[\sigma_E^2+\sigma_{P\times T}^2+\sigma_{P\times T\times C}^2+\sigma_T^2+\sigma_{T\times C}^2\right]}{p}+\dfrac{\sigma_{P\times C}^2}{p}}}$
NCN$_T$	$\dfrac{\mu_1-\mu_2}{\sqrt{\sigma_T^2+\sigma_{T\times C}^2+\left[\sigma_E^2+\sigma_P^2+\sigma_{P\times T}^2+\sigma_{P\times C}^2+\sigma_{P\times T\times C}^2\right]}}$	$\dfrac{\mu_1-\mu_2}{2\sqrt{\dfrac{\left[\sigma_E^2+\sigma_{P\times T}^2+\sigma_{P\times T\times C}^2+\sigma_P^2+\sigma_{P\times C}^2\right]}{p}+\dfrac{\sigma_{T\times C}^2}{q}}}$
NNN$_P$	$\dfrac{\mu_1-\mu_2}{\sqrt{\left[\sigma_P^2+\sigma_{P\times C}^2\right]+\left[\sigma_E^2+\sigma_T^2+\sigma_{P\times T}^2+\sigma_{T\times C}^2+\sigma_{P\times T\times C}^2\right]}}$	$\dfrac{\mu_1-\mu_2}{2\sqrt{\dfrac{\left[\sigma_E^2+\sigma_{P\times T}^2+\sigma_{P\times T\times C}^2+\sigma_T^2+\sigma_{T\times C}^2\right]}{q}+\dfrac{\left[\sigma_P^2+\sigma_{P\times C}^2\right]}{p}}}$
NNN$_T$	$\dfrac{\mu_1-\mu_2}{\sqrt{\left[\sigma_T^2+\sigma_{T\times C}^2\right]+\left[\sigma_E^2+\sigma_P^2+\sigma_{P\times T}^2+\sigma_{P\times C}^2+\sigma_{P\times T\times C}^2\right]}}$	$\dfrac{\mu_1-\mu_2}{2\sqrt{\dfrac{\left[\sigma_E^2+\sigma_{P\times T}^2+\sigma_{P\times T\times C}^2+\sigma_P^2+\sigma_{P\times C}^2\right]}{p}+\dfrac{\left[\sigma_T^2+\sigma_{T\times C}^2\right]}{q}}}$
Counterbalanced	$\dfrac{\mu_1-\mu_2}{\sqrt{\sigma_P^2+\sigma_{P\times C}^2+\sigma_T^2+\sigma_{T\times C}^2+\left[\sigma_E^2+\sigma_{P\times T}^2+\sigma_{P\times T\times C}^2\right]}}$	$\dfrac{\mu_1-\mu_2}{2\sqrt{\dfrac{\left[\sigma_E^2+\sigma_{P\times T}^2+\sigma_{P\times T\times C}^2\right]}{pq}+\dfrac{\sigma_{P\times C}^2}{p}+\dfrac{\sigma_{T\times C}^2}{q}}}$
R(CCC)	Same as CCC	$\dfrac{\mu_1-\mu_2}{2\sqrt{\dfrac{r\left[\sigma_E^2+\sigma_{P\times T\times C}^2\right]}{2pq}+\dfrac{\sigma_{P\times C}^2}{p}+\dfrac{\sigma_{T\times C}^2}{q}}}$
R(CNC)	Same as CNC	$\dfrac{\mu_1-\mu_2}{2\sqrt{\dfrac{r\left[\sigma_E^2+\sigma_{P\times T}^2+\sigma_{P\times T\times C}^2\right]}{pq}+\dfrac{\sigma_{P\times C}^2}{p}+\dfrac{\left[\sigma_T^2+\sigma_{T\times C}^2\right]}{q}}}$
R(NCC)	Same as NCC	$\dfrac{\mu_1-\mu_2}{2\sqrt{\dfrac{r\left[\sigma_E^2+\sigma_{P\times T}^2+\sigma_{P\times T\times C}^2\right]}{pq}+\dfrac{\left[\sigma_P^2+\sigma_{P\times C}^2\right]}{p}+\dfrac{\sigma_{T\times C}^2}{q}}}$
R(NNC)	Same as NNC	$\dfrac{\mu_1-\mu_2}{2\sqrt{\dfrac{2r\left[\sigma_E^2+\sigma_{P\times T}^2+\sigma_{P\times T\times C}^2\right]}{pq}+\dfrac{\left[\sigma_P^2+\sigma_{P\times C}^2\right]}{p}+\dfrac{\left[\sigma_T^2+\sigma_{T\times C}^2\right]}{q}}}$

[a]Brackets indicate the confounding of variance components. All variance components in the noncentrality parameters are defined in **Table 1**. The number of participants is p and the number of targets is q. In replication designs, the number of replications is r.

random components due to target intercepts and slopes, in addition to the implicit residual error term. Target intercept variance, although estimable, does not contribute to the standard error of the condition difference.

At the bottom of the first column of **Table 3**, we indicate that the effect sizes for the four replication designs are identical to those of the parallel designs in which participants and targets are crossed but the design is replicated only once (i.e., all participants get all targets). Thus, for instance, the effect size for the R(CCC) design is identical to that given for the CCC design. The syntax for these designs is also the same as that for the parallel designs with a single replication, although it probably makes sense to include replications in the model as an additional fixed factor (along with the fixed condition-by-replications interaction).

We end this section with a final warning on model specification. We have seen published analyses of designs with crossed random factors of participants and targets that use a mixed model specified as if it were a nested design in which targets are nested within participants (e.g., Toma et al. 2012). Typically in diary studies, for instance, days of measurement are crossed with participants but are treated as nested within them. We suspect this happens because so-called hierarchical or multilevel models have been used in the literature for some time, whereas models for crossed random factors are a more recent development. The misspecification of a crossed design as a nested one essentially amounts to ignoring the random variation in the target factor and thus risks serious inflation of type I errors if in fact there is nonzero target variance (Judd et al. 2012). The lesson is that model specification should follow from the design.

STATISTICAL POWER FOR DESIGNS WITH TWO RANDOM FACTORS

In this section and in the **Supplemental Appendix**, we provide the tools necessary to estimate statistical power for the test of the condition difference for each of the designs that we have covered. We discuss the general approach to power estimation and then provide a web-based application that computes power for all the designs. In earlier work (Westfall et al. 2014), we developed a power application for those designs that involve two crossed random effects. The current application (located online at **http://jakewestfall.org/two_factor_power/**) extends the range of designs treated to all those defined in this review, having both crossed and nested random effects, as well as the replication designs.

Our approach to statistical power estimation is consistent with the general approach laid out by Cohen (1988). One begins by specifying both a null hypothesis of no condition difference and an alternative hypothesis given an anticipated condition difference of some magnitude. Power is defined as the probability of correctly rejecting the null hypothesis when the alternative hypothesis is correct. To compute power, one must specify those variance components that contribute to the standard error of the condition difference for each design; these are given in the denominators of the design-specific operative effect sizes (see the **Supplemental Appendix**). These variance components are then weighted appropriately by the sample sizes involved in the prospective study [total numbers of participants (p) and targets (q) in the design and number of replications (r) in the replication designs] to give what is called the noncentrality parameter for the hypothesized true effect, which is presented in the third column of **Table 3** for each design. One can think of the noncentrality parameter as approximating the average t-statistic that one would obtain if the expected condition difference were found. The denominator of the noncentrality parameter can be thought of as the expected standard error of the condition mean difference. When squared and multiplied by the total number of observations, the denominator is equal to what the ANOVA literature refers to as the expected mean square (EMS) for the condition factor (Winer 1971).

Given degrees of freedom for this noncentrality parameter, power can be computed by examining areas under the noncentral t-distribution, given the multivariate normality assumption of the underlying random effects' distributions. Because the noncentrality parameters pool or combine various relevant variance components, the degrees of freedom of the noncentral t must be approximated. We use the Satterthwaite approximation to estimate the relevant degrees of freedom (Satterthwaite 1946, Welch 1947). Expressions for the approximate degrees of freedom for each design are given in the **Supplemental Appendix**.

We provide a web-based application (**http://jakewestfall.org/two_factor_power/**) that computes power for these designs. The user must identify the specific design used, the numbers of participants and targets,[6] the hypothesized mean difference or effect size, and the relevant variance components. In the application, the user has a choice between two different ways of thinking about the variance components and the effect size. Under the first option, the user inputs the mean difference expected and estimated values for all of the estimable variance components. An often-simpler option is to input what might be thought of as standardized versions of these, including the anticipated effect size (in terms of d) and the relative magnitude of the estimable variance components for each design (the proportion of the total variance in the observations attributable to a particular component of variance). We refer to these relative estimates of the variance components as Variance Partitioning Coefficients (Goldstein et al. 2002), and designate them as V (e.g., V_P for participant intercept variance, $V_{T \times C}$ for target slope variance). By definition, the sum of all the Vs (including residual error) must equal 1.0.

POWER CONSIDERATIONS AND RESEARCH DESIGN

All designs permit an estimate of the condition difference. Therefore, in making a decision about which design to use, the most important considerations are feasibility and statistical power. We discuss the feasibility issues in the section Design Choices: Power and Feasibility Considerations. In this section, we consider those factors influencing the power to detect the anticipated condition difference.

In general, the smaller the variance components that contribute to the noncentrality parameter (or operational effect size) and the larger the relevant sample sizes, the greater the power. In designs with participants as the only random factor, power is determined by the participant variance components and the participant sample size. In the designs that we are now considering, power is determined by the variance components and sample sizes of both participants and targets, although the extent to which these matter varies from design to design. The important point, however, is that we must think in terms of multiple relevant variance components and multiple sample sizes.

To increase power in designs with participants as the only random factor, researchers can either decrease the error variability in the data or increase the number of participants. Both strategies involve costs. The costs associated with increasing the number of participants are obvious. Those associated with decreasing participant variability are less obvious. Selecting participants who are relatively homogeneous on relevant variables related to the outcome should decrease the relevant variance components. Doing so, however, restricts one's ability to generalize observed results to other samples that are not so restricted.

The same considerations hold in thinking about designs with multiple random factors, in which variance components due to targets and their sample size, in addition to those due to participants, figure prominently in determining power. Power often dramatically increases as the number of targets in a design increases. Additionally, if we restrict the variance attributable to targets through pretesting, removing extraneous factors, and other strategies, then power should increase. For instance, it is common in research on face perception to edit target faces to eliminate facial hair and other idiosyncrasies. However, restricting target variance imposes a cost in that one is unable to generalize to samples of targets that are not so restricted. The important point is that the same power considerations apply to the sampling of targets as to the sampling of participants. Larger and more homogeneous samples of both increase power, but these strategies come with costs.

---

[6]In nested and replication designs, care must be exercised in defining the values of p and q for designs. They represent the total numbers of participants and targets in the entire design.

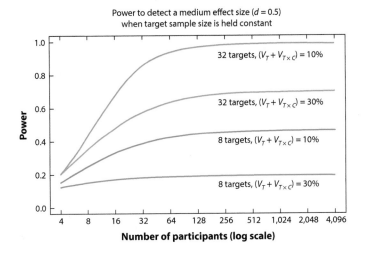

Power to detect a medium effect size ($d = 0.5$)
when target sample size is held constant

Figure 2

Plot of statistical power as a function of the total number of participants for the CNC (P and T crossed, P crossed with C, and T nested in C) design. The number of targets has been set to either 8 or 32. The other variance components are set to the following values: $V_E = 0.3$, $V_P \times T = 0.1$, $V_P \times T \times C = 0$, $V_P = 0.2$, and $V_P \times C = 0.1$. Note that these other variance components affect only the rate at which the power functions converge to their asymptotes; they do not affect the maximum attainable power values, which depend only on the effect size, number of targets, and the target variance components. Abbreviations: C, fixed condition factor; E, error; P, random participant factor; T, random target factor.

Increasing the Sample Sizes

In designs with just one random factor, as the participant sample size increases, power eventually approaches one. However, in many of the designs considered in this review, if the sample size of one of the two random factors is fixed, then increasing the sample size of the other random factor increases power, but generally to a limit of less than one. This is a surprising result; in our experience, many researchers naturally assume that increasing the number of participants in a design will eventually ensure adequate power. When the number of targets in a design is small, power will increase as the participant sample size increases but may asymptote at levels that are quite a bit lower than one. In many designs that involve both participants and targets, the number of targets used is typically substantially smaller than the number of participants [e.g., a meta-analysis by Bond & DePaulo (2008) in one research domain reports on average 80 participants per study but only 12 targets], as researchers may mistakenly think that power is determined only (or primarily) by the sample size of participants.

To illustrate, in **Figure 2** we plot the power to detect a medium effect size of $d = 0.5$ in the CNC design as a function of number of participants under different assumptions about the sample of targets. Varied in the figure are number of targets, 8 or 32, and how much variance is due to targets and their interaction with condition, 10% or 30% of the total variance. When the number of targets is small or when the targets are highly variable, the maximum attainable power in the study can be far less than one.

A similar phenomenon occurs in nested designs (targets within participants or participants within targets), but only for the lower-level factor. For example, if targets are nested within participants so that each participant responds to a unique set of targets, then the maximum attainable power is less than one if the participant sample size is held constant and the target sample size is increased, but power does approach one if the participant sample is increased. The reason for this asymmetry is that increasing the sample size of the higher-level factor necessarily entails increasing the sample size of the lower-level factor, but the reverse is not true.

Assuming that one is able to vary either the participant sample size or the target sample size (or both), which is expected to have a greater effect on statistical power? The answer depends on several factors, including the initial sample sizes, the relative sizes of the participant and target variance components, and the design of the experiment. The definitive answer is contained implicitly in the noncentrality parameters we have given. In the following paragraphs, we offer a few rules of thumb.

First, assuming crossed random factors, the larger the variance components associated with one random factor (relative to the other random factor), the more beneficial it is to increase the sample size of that factor. Thus, if participant mean and slope variances are larger than those due to targets, then increasing the sample size of participants reaps greater benefits than increasing that of targets.

Second, if the sample sizes of targets and participants are substantially different, then there will generally be a greater power benefit to increasing the size of whichever sample is smaller, assuming that both participants and targets have approximately equal associated variance components. For instance, if one sample size is 300 units and the other is 10, then adding an additional 10 units to the larger sample size (for a new total of 310) is unlikely to have as big an effect on statistical power as adding an additional 10 units to the smaller sample size (for a new total of 20).

Third, all else being equal, it is better to increase the sample size of a random factor that is nested within condition than one that is crossed with condition. The reason for this is that when a random factor is nested within condition, the standard error of the condition difference depends on both the intercept and slope variance components of that factor, whereas when the random factor is crossed with condition, only the random slope variance is relevant.

Fourth, in a design in which one random factor is nested within the other (e.g., targets within participants), it is usually more effective to increase the sample size of the higher-level factor (e.g., participants) than that of the factor nested within it (e.g., targets). As discussed above, the maximum attainable power level when increasing the lower-level sample size in a nested design is, in general, less than 1.0. According to this rule, even in smaller studies that do not approach the theoretical maximum power level, power increases more quickly by increasing the higher-level sample size than by increasing the lower-level sample size.

Design Choices: Power and Feasibility Considerations

Power is not the only consideration guiding the choice of design; feasibility issues also figure prominently. We discuss some of those issues in this section.

Although power will often increase dramatically as the target sample size increases, sometimes it is not feasible for participants to respond to a large number of targets. In this case, the best strategy may be to use a design with nested, rather than crossed, random factors. Researchers often assume that a crossed design is more powerful, but in fact it can be shown that for any crossed design, a nested version of the same design—that is, one with the same number of responses per participant and the same relationships between the random factors and condition, but in which every participant receives different targets—is always more powerful. This difference derives simply from the fact that as we move to the nested design there is a dramatic increase in the number of targets even as the number of responses per participant remains constant.

However, nested designs may in some contexts require unreasonable numbers of targets (the number of participants times the number of responses per participant). Consider the CCC design and the CCN$_P$ design. If each of 30 participants gives 15 responses, then the CCC design involves responses to only 15 targets, whereas the CCN_P design involves responses to 450 targets, resulting in a potentially dramatic increase in power if random variance due to targets is present. However, it may simply not be feasible to find so many targets. A reasonable alternative is to consider the R(CCC) design, containing, for instance, three replications of the CCC design, with 10 participants and 15 targets in each, for a total of 45 targets. Each participant still responds only 15 times, but the total number of targets has gone up threefold over the number in the CCC design. Generally speaking, in cases in which each response imposes a considerable burden on participants, it makes sense to increase power by increasing the number of targets across different replications of a design, rather than to limit the number of targets by the use of a design in which all participants respond to the same set of targets (Westfall et al. 2014).

If one has a choice between crossing a random factor with condition and nesting that random factor within condition, then one should always choose to cross the random factor with condition to maximize statistical power. This is because intercept variance due to a random factor contributes to the noncentrality parameter (making it smaller) when that factor is nested within condition, but not when it is crossed with condition. It follows that, if only one random factor is to be crossed with condition, then it is generally better to cross whichever factor has the larger anticipated variance components. Of course, there are feasibility issues that arise in considering whether a random factor can be crossed with condition. Crossing participants with condition raises issues of order and carryover effects, as well as the potential suspicion that participants may develop about the study's purpose. These issues do not arise if the crossed factor is targets.

Finally, if one is using a design with nested random factors and one has the choice of which is the higher-order and which the lower-order factor, then it is always better to choose as the higher-order factor the one with less variance. So, for instance, if participants have larger associated variance components than targets, then a design that nests participants within targets is preferable to one that nests targets within participants. This is true so long as it is feasible to have a reasonable sample size of the higher-level factor.

COMPLICATIONS AND EXTENSIONS

Our designs have assumed only two random factors and one fixed factor having only two levels. We have also assumed that when one factor is nested within another, the nesting is randomly determined. What happens when we go beyond these assumptions? We first discuss the issue of nonrandom nesting and then turn to design extensions.

Nonrandom Nesting

When a random factor is nested within condition, differences attributable to that random factor are confounded with condition differences. With random assignment of levels of the random factor to condition, that confounding can be estimated and dealt with, which is not possible with nonrandom assignment. This is as true of targets as it is of participants. Hence, nonrandom assignment of either participants or targets to condition generally results in bias in estimating condition effects.

When one of the two random factors is nested within the other, either targets within participants or participants within targets, we have assumed random assignment of the nested factor to the levels of the higher-order factor. What happens when this is not the case? For simplicity, we rely on the situation in which targets are nested within participants, but the following considerations apply under the reverse nesting as well. With nonrandom nesting of targets within participants, target differences are confounded with participant differences, resulting in covariances between participant and target intercepts and (perhaps) condition slopes. In many situations, it is likely that such covariances are positive (participants with higher means respond to targets that, on average, have associated higher means). This positive covariance augments the variance components of participants, which generally results in less efficient tests of condition differences. Thus, a power consequence of nonrandom assignment of targets to participants is likely. However, nonrandom assignment of targets to participants does not result in bias in the estimate of the condition difference, so long as participants are crossed with condition or, when they are nested within condition, they have been randomly assigned to condition. In other words, in a fully nested design, nonrandom assignment of the lower-order random factor to levels of the higher-order one (resulting in a nonzero covariance between the random participant and target effects) does not bias the condition difference estimate so long as the higher-order random factor is still randomly assigned to condition levels.

In the replication designs, participants and targets are nested within each replication. We have assumed random assignment of both factors to each replication. If this is not the case, for instance when unique sets of participants and targets come to the experiment intact and constitute the replications, then the replications often should be treated as an additional random factor in the design specification rather than as a fixed factor, as we suggested when we discussed the model specification for these replication designs. In consequence, one must have sufficient numbers of replications, because the sample size of this factor now becomes relevant in determining power.

Design Extensions

As discussed in the previous section, replications in the replication designs should be considered a random factor in the case of nonrandom nesting within replications. Other contexts also require more than two random factors. For instance, priming studies present participants with primes and ask them to respond to subsequently presented targets. In most cases, one should treat both primes and targets, in addition to participants, as random factors. Using principles extracted from what we have covered in this review, we can extend the designs and models to cover these scenarios. Additional random factors lead to additional complexities in specifying the random components of the underlying model, as the number of variance components can increase exponentially if the random factors are all crossed with each other (as in the priming example). Condition slope variance components must be specified in the model for those random factors that are crossed with condition (and their interactions). Accordingly, though the complete model specification is possible, it may be necessary to specify a large number of variance components, leading to possible convergence problems in estimating the parameters of the linear mixed model. The recent literature has recommended specifying the complete underlying model (including all random variances and covariances that are estimable; see Barr et al. 2013), a recommendation with which we generally concur. At the same time, if convergence cannot be achieved in estimating the model, respecification may help by dropping some of the variance components that represent higher-order interactions that might reasonably be expected to be nonexistent (see also Bates et al. 2015).

Our designs also have only one fixed factor, condition, with only two levels. In many experiments there are more fixed factors, generally crossed and often with more than two levels. So long as those fixed factors (and their interactions) are contrast-coded and the effects of those contrasts tested as single-degree-of-freedom tests, additional fixed factors present no further problems other than, again, the complexity of the model to be specified. Intercept and slope variance components must be specified for any random factors that are crossed with those additional fixed factors (and with the interactions of fixed factors).

There may also be continuous covariates that one would like to include in the fixed part of the model. We strongly recommend centering such covariates (Judd et al. 2008). Doing this is necessary to preserve the meaning of the random variance components and fixed parameter estimates (including the condition difference).

Finally, we have assumed completely balanced research designs with no missing data. Mixed-model estimation can generally be accomplished with missing data. However, to have unbiased estimates, it must be assumed that such missing data are randomly lost, a highly dubious assumption. More detail on missing data is contained in the **Supplemental Appendix**.

FROM OUR DESIGNS TO DYADIC DESIGNS

There is extensive literature on what are called dyadic designs (Kenny et al. 2006), in which participants interact with other participants. Dyadic designs are also designs with two random factors. In fact, all of our designs can be viewed as dyadic. This seems most natural when the targets are people; nonetheless, even when the targets are inanimate, each observation involves a dyad or a pair.

One advantage of viewing studies with participants and targets as dyadic designs is that there is an established tradition of quantifying the random sources of variances in the observations from such designs. As we have discussed, having some idea of the relative amount of variance of the different components can be very helpful in planning a study. Designs using the social relations model (SRM) are understood in great detail; the rest of this section describes these designs.

The SRM examines observations taken from actors about partners (Kenny et al. 2006). In the parlance of this review, an actor is a participant and a partner is a target. In the SRM, the variance in the observations is partitioned into actor, partner, and relationship, i.e., actor × partner interaction. In most applications that use the SRM, there is no fixed variable such as condition, so variances due to condition slopes are not present. The traditional focus in an SRM analysis is on the partitioning of variance into actor, partner, and relationship. For instance, Hönekopp (2006) had participants in three studies judge the physical attractiveness of targets' faces using photographs. In the second study, which had 31 actors and 60 targets, he found that 15% of the variance was due to the participant or actor, 26% due to the target or partner, 33% due to the relationship or participant × target interaction, and the remaining 26% due to error. Quite clearly in this study, the two key systematic sources of variance were relationships and partners, and knowledge of these variances would prove useful in planning studies on interpersonal attraction.

Although all the designs in this review can be viewed as dyadic designs, only one of the designs is a SRM design: the CCC design, which is called the half-block design in SRM parlance. In this design, there are actors (i.e., participants), each of whom is paired with the same set of partners (i.e., targets). The prototypical SRM design, however, involves a case in which the actors and partners are the same group of people, and each person is paired with every other person. Such a design is called a round robin design and is not considered in this review (see, however, the extensive discussion in Kenny et al. 2006).

Many dyadic designs, like the round robin design, are reciprocal in the sense that observations accrue from both participant A responding to target B and from participant B responding to target A. In other words, each person serves as both a participant and a target. The CCC design would be a reciprocal design in the following situation: Consider a study in which a sample of men interact with a sample of women; in each interaction, each person states how much he or she likes his or her interaction partner. If we were interested in the effect of gender, then we could view the study as a fully crossed design in which, for the male judge condition, men are the participants and women are the targets, and for the female judge condition, the same women are now the participants and the same men are the targets. This SRM design is referred to as the asymmetric block design.

Other designs that we have considered can be made into reciprocal designs by combining them. For instance, in the example we used for the CCN$_P$ design, the instructors evaluate their students in two different conditions or subjects, math and language; in the CCN$_T$ design, the students evaluate their instructor in math and language. If we obtained data from both students and teachers in the same study, we would have a reciprocal design. Using the parlance developed by Kenny et al. (2006), such a design is a reciprocal one-with-many study. Other designs can also be combined to form reciprocal designs, as is discussed in the **Supplemental Appendix**.

CONCLUSION

In psychology experiments, we frequently ask participants to respond to targets (e.g., faces, words, other people) in various experimental conditions. In such experiments, the interest is in reaching conclusions about condition differences that generalize to other samples of participants and, typically, other samples of targets that might have been used. To permit this, it is essential that the analysis of the resulting data treat both participants and targets as random factors. The failure to do so, collapsing across targets or ignoring the variation they induce, leads to serious bias and, we suggest, failures to replicate experimental effects when other samples of targets are used.

In this review, we provide an exhaustive typology of designs based on the nesting or crossing of three factors (participants, targets, and condition) in such experiments. For each of these designs, we discuss the mixed-model specification that permits unbiased estimates of condition effects while treating both participants and targets as random factors. Additionally, we provide tools to estimate the effect size and statistical power of the condition difference in each design.

We conclude by emphasizing the importance of considering targets as well as participants in determining statistical power. We also discuss considerations that ought to drive the choice among alternative designs. Our hope is that researchers will adopt appropriate designs and analytic models that incorporate target variation and thus permit conclusions that are more likely to replicate with other samples of both participants and targets.

DISCLOSURE STATEMENT

The authors are not aware of any affiliations, memberships, funding, or financial holdings that might be perceived as affecting the objectivity of this review.

ACKNOWLEDGMENTS

We thank Markus Brauer, Leonard Katz, Reinhold Kliegl, Gary McClelland, Dominique Muller, and Vincent Yzerbyt for their helpful comments on drafts of this review.

LITERATURE CITED

Baayen RH, Davidson DJ, Bates DM. 2008. Mixed-effects modeling with crossed-random effects for subjects and items. *J. Mem. Lang.* 59:390–412

Barr DJ, Levy R, Scheepers C, Tily HJ. 2013. Random effects structure for confirmatory hypothesis testing: keep it maximal. *J. Mem. Lang.* 68:255–78

Bates D, Kliegl R, Vasishth S, Baayen H. 2015. Parsimonious mixed models. arxiv:1506.04967v1 [stat.ME]

Bolker BM, Brooks ME, Clark CJ, Geange SW, Poulsen JR, et al. 2009. Generalized linear mixed models: a practical guide for ecology and evolution. *Trends Ecol. Evol.* 24(3):127–35

Bond CF, DePaulo B. 2008. Individual differences in judging deception: accuracy and bias. *Psychol. Bull.* 134:477–92

Clark HH. 1973. The language-as-fixed-effect fallacy: a critique of language statistics in psychological research. *J. Verb. Learn. Verb. Behav.* 12:335–59

Cohen J. 1988. *Statistical Power Analysis for the Behavioral Sciences*. Hillsdale, NJ: Erlbaum

Goldstein H, Browne W, Rasbash J. 2002. Partitioning variation in multilevel models. *Underst. Stat.* 1:223–31

Hönekopp J. 2006. Once more: Is beauty in the eye of the beholder? Relative contributions of private and shared taste to judgments of facial attractiveness. *J. Exp. Psychol. Hum. Percept. Perfor.* 32:199–209

Hox JJ. 2010. *Multilevel Analysis: Techniques and Applications*. New York: Routledge

Judd CM, McClelland RG, Ryan CS. 2008. *Data Analysis: A Model Comparison Approach*. New York: Routledge

Judd CM, Westfall J, Kenny DA. 2012. Treating stimuli as a random factor in social psychology: a new and comprehensive solution to a pervasive but largely ignored problem. *J. Pers. Soc. Psychol.* 103:54–69

Kenny DA, Kashy DA, Cook WL. 2006. *Dyadic Data Analysis*. New York: Guilford Press

Raudenbush SW, Bryk AS. 2002. *Hierarchical Linear Models: Applications and Data Analysis Methods*. Thousand Oaks, CA: Sage

Satterthwaite FE. 1946. An approximate distribution of estimates of variance components. *Biom. Bull.* 2(6):110–14

Smith ER. 2014. Research design. In *Handbook of Research Methods in Social and Personality Psychology*, ed. HT Reis, CM Judd, pp. 27–48. Cambridge, UK: Cambridge Univ. Press

Snijders T, Bosker R. 2011. *Multilevel Analysis: An Introduction to Basic and Advanced Multilevel Modeling*. Thousand Oaks, CA: Sage

Stroup WW. 2012. *Generalized Linear Mixed Models: Modern Concepts, Methods and Applications*. New York: CRC Press

Toma C, Corneille O, Yzerbyt V. 2012. Holding a mirror up to the self: egocentric similarity beliefs underlie social projection in cooperation. *Pers. Soc. Psychol. Bull.* 38:1259–71

Welch BL. 1947. The generalization of 'Student's' problem when several different population variances are involved. *Biometrika* 34:28–35

Westfall J, Judd CM, Kenny DA. 2015. Replicating studies in which samples of participants respond to samples of stimuli. *Pers. Psychol. Sci.* 10:390–99

Westfall J, Kenny DA, Judd CM. 2014. Statistical power and optimal design in experiments in which samples of participants respond to samples of stimuli. *J. Exp. Psychol. Gen.* 143:220–45

Winer BJ. 1971. *Statistical Principles in Experimental Design*. New York: McGraw-Hill

Interactions With Robots: The Truths We Reveal About Ourselves

Elizabeth Broadbent

Department of Psychological Medicine, Faculty of Medical and Health Sciences, The University of Auckland, Auckland 1142, New Zealand; email: e.broadbent@auckland.ac.nz

Annu. Rev. Psychol. 2017. 68:627–52

First published online as a Review in Advance on September 14, 2016

The *Annual Review of Psychology* is online at psych.annualreviews.org

This article's doi: 10.1146/annurev-psych-010416-043958

Keywords

human–robot interaction, uncanny valley, mind perception, anthropomorphism

Abstract

In movies, robots are often extremely humanlike. Although these robots are not yet reality, robots are currently being used in healthcare, education, and business. Robots provide benefits such as relieving loneliness and enabling communication. Engineers are trying to build robots that look and behave like humans and thus need comprehensive knowledge not only of technology but also of human cognition, emotion, and behavior. This need is driving engineers to study human behavior toward other humans and toward robots, leading to greater understanding of how humans think, feel, and behave in these contexts, including our tendencies for mindless social behaviors, anthropomorphism, uncanny feelings toward robots, and the formation of emotional attachments. However, in considering the increased use of robots, many people have concerns about deception, privacy, job loss, safety, and the loss of human relationships. Human–robot interaction is a fascinating field and one in which psychologists have much to contribute, both to the development of robots and to the study of human behavior.

Contents

INTRODUCTION

Robots in science fiction movies are often humanlike. They experience emotions, express opinions, and have motives, and we relate to them easily. Few of us have seen robots in real life, and our ideas about them are often informed by what we see in movies (Broadbent et al. 2010), where robots have minds, are conscious, can love us, can kill us, and can be all but indistinguishable from us. But how close is fiction to reality? How human are robots? Can they really think and feel? Can we love them? Do they really want to take over the world?

Humans have a long history of trying to make artificial versions of ourselves. Leonardo da Vinci designed a mechanical knight in 1495 that was operated by pulleys and could sit, stand, move its arms, and raise its visor (Rosheim 2006). Another well-known example is the Turk, which was built in the late eighteenth century to appear as an automaton that could play chess but was secretly operated by a real human hiding inside its base (Thicknesse 1784). It was not until the middle of the twentieth century that Alan Turing and his contemporaries laid the foundations for modern digital computing and autonomous robots (Turing 1950). An autonomous robot is a machine that can operate and perform tasks by itself without continuous human guidance. The first robot was a digitally operated programmable arm used in the car industry in the 1950s. Since then, industrial robots have burgeoned; they often operate inside safety cages away from humans. Military robots have also been extensively developed for tasks such as surveillance, bomb disposal, and automated weaponry. These kinds of robots are largely seen as tools for humans to use. Over the past 20 years, we have seen an increase in the development of social robots, which are made to

Autonomous robot: a robot that can operate and perform tasks by itself without continuous human guidance interact closely with humans as artificial companions and helpers in our homes, hospitals, schools, shopping malls, and beyond. It is in this application that robots are being made to mimic humans most closely—in looks, mind, emotional expression, and behavior. It is in this area that young roboticists, inspired by the robots portrayed in science fiction, are trying to make robots just like us.

This article delves into the psychology behind our relationships with social robots. It reviews current applications of robots and research on how humans relate to robots, explores concerns about robots, and looks ahead to the future of the field. This article also highlights research on robots that has contributed to our understanding of human behavior. The further we go down the path toward making and interacting with artificial humans, the more truths we learn about ourselves. Computer scientists and engineers have conducted most of the research in this area over the past 20 years, investigating the construction of robots and testing them with humans. However, psychologists have made some important contributions to both theory and methods. Because psychologists have expert knowledge in understanding human behavior, building theoretical models, conducting social science research, and constructing valid and reliable measures, they have much to contribute. Greater involvement by psychologists will help to shape the future development of robots in socially acceptable ways.

CURRENT APPLICATIONS OF SOCIAL ROBOTS

For someone unfamiliar with robots, the first thing to understand is that almost all the robots we see in science fiction are very much a fantasy. Even the robot in the film *Robot & Frank* (Ford 2012), which looks much like the real robot Asimo, made by Honda, has been given far greater abilities in the film than are possessed by the real Asimo. Typical robots that you might see in many robot labs across the world range from simple wheeled robots to mechanical arms, aerial drones, robots that look like animals, and robots that look like humans. **Figure 1** shows some examples of pet-like and humanlike robots.

There are many robots currently in the development phase in robotic labs across the world. Seeing social robots in real life is less common. However, autonomous robots are operating in shopping malls in Japan and Korea. Autonomous robots have also been used in kindergartens in Korea (Hyun et al. 2010). In many developed countries, autonomous robots do vacuum cleaning in houses, and there are a growing number of autonomous companion robots in retirement homes across the developed world. There is even a Japanese hotel staffed by robots, albeit with humans assisting (Rajesh 2015). Roboticists are naturally motivated to make useful robots and ones that will have commercial success. The following sections describe how social robots are currently being used.

Healthcare Robots for Older People

The current demographic trend of increasing numbers of people aged 65 and over is placing strain on healthcare systems (Bloom et al. 2015). Robots have been proposed as one way to help meet some of the healthcare needs of older people (Robinson et al. 2014). The majority of healthcare robots are still in development and have not yet been commercialized, but research has been conducted with various prototypes. Robots are being made to assist with physical tasks (e.g., walking, fetching and carrying, and bathing), cognitive issues (e.g., reminding and playing memory games), health management (e.g., monitoring blood pressure, detecting falls, and encouraging exercise), and psychosocial issues (e.g., providing companionship and entertainment).

One of the best-known commercialized and autonomous social robots is Paro, a Japanese companion robot shaped like a baby harp seal, which can move and make seal noises in response

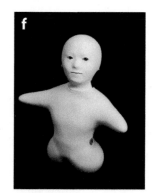

to touch, light, noise, and orientation. Thousands of Paros have been sold across Europe, the United States, and Asia, mainly for use in rest homes for companionship and in dementia care for therapy. Paro has been designed to look cute, with big eyes, big eyelashes, and soft fur. One of the reasons a baby seal was chosen (rather than a more familiar animal like a cat) is that it is relatively easy to meet people's expectations of its behavior. People like to cuddle, stroke, and talk with Paro like they would with a pet animal. A randomized controlled trial found that Paro reduced loneliness and increased social interactions (i.e., talking to the robot and to other people) in a group setting in a rest home or hospital compared to other activities (Robinson et al. 2013). However, responses to Paro were mixed, with some older people liking and engaging with it and others not interacting with it (Robinson et al. 2015, 2016). Analysis of conversations that rest-home residents had with Paro revealed instances in which residents spoke about Paro knowing what was going on, having emotions, and having bodily states (e.g., Paro felt cold or had a rumbling tummy), yet the residents also spoke of Paro as an artificial object. A randomized cluster trial suggested Paro could reduce agitation and depression in people with dementia (Jøranson et al. 2015). Paro was also shown to help address individual problematic behaviors among psychogeriatric patients in a quasi-experimental study (Bemelmans et al. 2015). Paro has been well received by staff in dementia care and relatives of people with dementia (Robinson et al. 2012).

Interviews with people who had healthcare robots in their homes for 6 weeks or more reveal important themes of robot companionship and sociability (Broadbent et al. 2014, Orejana et al. 2015). Two robots, iRobi and Cafero, were used to remind people to take their medications, take blood pressure measurements and pulse oximetry, and provide entertainment and cognitive stimulation. People reported talking to the robot and rubbing its head, feeling not as alone when it was in the house, and missing the robot when it was gone. There were preliminary indications that these healthcare robots could reduce healthcare visits.

Research suggests that the appearance of robots for the care of older people should be matched to the task they perform. People preferred a fluffy robot for companionship but a more mechanical robot for reminding them to take their medication (Broadbent et al. 2009). Practicalities are important because of the size restrictions of people's rooms. The height should not be too intimidating but should be high enough to be seen easily. In interviews with residents of a retirement village, humanlikeness was perceived to be necessary only if it related to the robot's function. For example, a lifting robot need not look human but a telemedicine robot should (Broadbent et al. 2012). Many residents expressed a preference for nonhumanlike robots as they did not want them to replace humans. Voices are also important in robots, with people preferring a more humanlike voice over a more robotic-sounding voice in a healthcare robot (Tamagawa et al. 2011).

These studies show that robots can provide benefits to older people, including reducing loneliness, problematic behaviors, and depression, as well as increasing social interactions with other people. However, some staff and residents in retirement facilities have concerns that robots will take away the jobs of humans and that residents could miss out on human contact (Broadbent et al. 2012). Other concerns include potential harm from accidents with the robot, lack of reliability, incorrect or slow relaying of information to staff, lack of privacy, and navigation difficulties.

Figure 1

Examples of social robots: (*a*) iRobi (Yujin Robot); (*b*) Nao, a humanoid (Aldebaran); (*c*) Pepper, a humanoid (Softbank Corp.); (*d*) Paro, a pet-like robot (Intelligent System Co.); (*e*) Pleo, a pet-like robot (Innvo Labs); (*f*) Telenoid R1 (Osaka University and ATR Hiroshi Ishiguro Laboratory); (*g*) Philip K. Dick, an android (Hanson Robotics); (*h*) Hiroshi Ishiguro and his geminoid (ATR Hiroshi Ishiguro Laboratory).

Robots for Children with Autism

Teleoperated:
a robot that is operated
remotely by a person,
often over the Internet

Engineers and computer scientists are enthusiastic about the use of robots for children with autism spectrum disorder who have difficulty communicating with and understanding other people. The basic reasoning behind this is that robots are simpler to interact with than people are because robots are more predictable, have fewer states, and have a smaller range of actions. Therefore, children with autism may be able to learn about social cues from interactions with robots and then apply this knowledge to social interactions with people. Robots are being developed for several tasks: to elicit behaviors to diagnose autism and to increase prosocial behaviors; to model, teach, or practice skills; and to provide feedback or encouragement (Diehl et al. 2012). However, research to date has only been exploratory. Most studies have been done with a few individuals over only a few days with qualitative methods, no control groups, and limited diagnostic information on the participants. A range of different robots have been used, but these are often controlled by a therapist in the same room and are not autonomous (Scassellati et al. 2012). There have been mixed results with large variability between individuals (Diehl et al. 2012). Only some children show a preference for robots over other toys.

No conclusions can be made with such small sample sizes and methodological limitations. A further difficulty is showing whether children's interactions with robots can be transferred to improve functioning in other situations. One of the strongest clinical studies to date showed no differences in social behaviors (other than eye contact) when children interacted with a robot compared to when they interacted with a human on a collaborative task. Furthermore, the difference in eye contact may have been due to a novelty effect (Simut et al. 2016). Additional well-designed studies conducted in collaboration with clinicians are needed to show whether robot-assisted therapy provides benefits for some children, and psychologists will play an important role in this research.

Telerobotics

Another area of robot development is teleoperation, in which mobile robots can be controlled by humans at a distance. In these cases, the robot is usually acting as a tool by which two humans can communicate with each other or a human can complete a remote task, rather than the robot being a social agent in itself. Several teleoperated robots exist, most of which look like a screen mounted at the top of a pole on a mobile base. However, some teleoperated robots have a more humanlike appearance (Kristoffersson et al. 2013). Teleoperated robots can be used in harsh environments such as space or the sea, for distant communication between people in business teleconferencing, or in telemedicine for specialist doctors to visit patients remotely in a hospital or at home. Technological hurdles, such as lack of network stability, inability to open doors or travel up and down stairs, and difficulties with navigation and docking, still exist for telepresence robots.

The use of telepresence robots has been shown to be beneficial in healthcare. For example, telepresence robots have been used by surgeons for postsurgical ward rounds and found to have similar patient satisfaction ratings as in-person visits (Ellison et al. 2007). Using the robot, doctors were able to make additional postsurgical visits to gastric bypass patients, resulting in significantly shorter hospital stays and cost savings (Gandsas et al. 2007). Similarly, the use of telepresence robots in intensive care allowed neurologists to respond more quickly to nurse pages and was associated with reduced length of patient stay as well as substantial cost savings (Vespa et al. 2007). Using telepresence robots rather than telephones allowed physicians quicker access to critical visual information (minutes rather than hours), enabling faster diagnosis and decision making.

Children with chronic illnesses, such as cancer, can become isolated from their friends due to missing school and being unable to join in with activities. In some cases, technologies can be used to facilitate communication (Liu et al. 2015). Sick children have used telepresence robots to attend school classes. Case studies indicate a mix of positive and negative interactions, but overall the robot can help provide a way to reduce social, emotional, and academic isolation for hospitalized children (Fels et al. 2001).

Minimally invasive robot-assisted surgery is another real-world application in which robots are operated remotely. The da Vinci surgical system is a leader in this field, with more than 500 units sold in 2013 across the United States, Japan, Europe, and other markets at a cost of US$1.5 million each, and revenue is projected to increase (Intuit. Surg. 2016). Despite promises of fewer complications and lower blood loss, a recent meta-analysis of 20 randomized controlled trials showed no differences between robot-assisted surgery and laparoscopic surgery in surgical blood loss, complication rates, or length of hospital stay (Broholm et al. 2016). The only difference was that robot-assisted surgery took longer. In comparison to open surgery, robot-assisted surgery took longer but also resulted in lower blood loss (Broholm et al. 2016). There is limited research on the perceptions and feelings of patients toward these robots.

Humanoid: a robot that has a body shape similar to a human, usually with a head, torso, arms, and legs

Robot-Assisted Recovery from Stroke

Robot therapy following stroke has been shown to improve hand and arm function for patients in all stages of recovery (Basteris et al. 2014). Robots can also help with gait recovery, although whether robot therapy is better than other methods is not clear (Swinnen et al. 2014). Qualitative interviews reveal that patients think robot-assisted therapy has benefits for mobility, with the added convenience of being able to schedule exercises when they like. This increases independence and can improve mood. Indeed, some patients prefer the robot over a human assisting them with the exercises, despite technical and ergonomic difficulties (Cherry et al. 2016). The majority of these robots would not be classed as social because they are wearable and physically assistive and apply forces to the user's limbs. Feedback from patients with stroke consists of comments about how the system could be improved rather than any comments about their sociability (Hughes et al. 2011). However, small studies have investigated more socially assistive hands-off exercise robots for stroke rehabilitation. A closer match between the user's personality (extrovert or introvert) and the rehabilitation robot's behavior (nurturing or challenging exercise instructions) increased the time that people spent interacting with the robots (Tapus et al. 2008). This suggests that social aspects could be utilized to enhance adherence to the interactions of rehabilitation robots.

Education

Robots have been used in education, predominantly in the areas of science and technology but also in foreign language teaching (Mubin et al. 2013). Robots can be used as a tool through which technical skills can be learned, can act as a peer by providing encouragement, or can function as teachers. Robotic kits are often used to engage students in learning about science and technology. Kit types include creative kits in which any kind of robots can be created (such as Lego), kits that come with wheels (e.g., cars) and are most suited to younger users, and kits that come as humanoids and are more suitable for older users (Basoeki et al. 2013). Preliminary evidence suggests that teaching children from low-income families using humanoid robots increases motivation, sense of community, and self-expression more than teaching children using creative-type kits (Han et al. 2015). Robots have also been tested for health education in pilot studies of children. A humanoid robot (Nao) was used in three sessions to administer quizzes either in a motivational way, using self-determination theory (with behaviors to increase competence, autonomy, and relatedness), or in a neutral way (Blanson et al. 2013). Diabetes knowledge increased over time and the children found it fun, especially in the initial sessions. The children mimicked the robot's interaction style, suggesting social modelling was occurring.

Shopping Mall Guides

Robots are being used as guides in public places such as shopping malls and museums. Some of these robots are autonomous in usual use, but in research they are often operated remotely to gain better control over study conditions. Qualitative interviews with people in a Japanese shopping mall that had a guiding-type robot for over three years showed that people based their judgments mainly on the robot's appearance and the way it moved (Sabelli & Kanda 2015). They saw it as a mascot for the mall rather than a utility. Other interviews have shown that a shopping mall robot giving out instructions and flyers is seen by the majority of users to have benefits, including giving clear instructions and being enjoyable and good for children (Satake et al. 2015). Interestingly, 65% said they would prefer such services from a robot rather than a human, with comments indicating that the robot does not judge people based on appearance and treats everyone the same; some respondents also claimed that if the robot was too humanlike, then it would be scary. More than 90% wanted to use the robot again.

CURRENT DIRECTIONS, CONCERNS, AND ETHICAL ISSUES

We will likely continue to see the development of social robots for these applications and others. Governments continue to be concerned about the rising proportion of people aged 65 and over and would like technological solutions to reduce healthcare costs. These governments see robots as useful both in industry and in homes. Europe, for example, has a strategic research agenda for robots, envisioning that they will impact every aspect of work and home, improving safety and service and creating jobs (euRobotics AISBL 2013).

Some researchers are concerned about the use of technology, especially by children. Turkle (2014) argues that we are developing an always-on culture in which children do not develop the capacity to enjoy solitude and devote time to self-reflection. Research suggests that our relationships with mobile devices may come at the cost of relationships with each other, with the presence of cell phones linked to feelings of decreased empathy and closeness during dyadic conversations (Misra et al. 2016). These kinds of concerns are also beginning to arise with robots.

There are concerns that robots are deceiving people about their real nature because robots can only simulate love or friendship. Some philosophers argue that this deception is unethical and may cause harm (Sparrow & Sparrow 2006). Sparrow & Sparrow believe that robots should only be used if cognitively aware people express a preference for robots over humans.

In fact, there is evidence that people do perceive robots to have advantages over humans in some aspects of healthcare; these advantages include increased perseverance, commitment, and availability, as well as decreased distraction from patients, in robots compared to human doctors (Broadbent et al. 2010). A survey of 420 people, including some parents and therapists of children with autism, showed that more than 80% agreed it was ethically acceptable to use robots with children with autism, although approximately half of the respondents did not want the robot to replace therapists and approximately 20% did not want the children to see robots as friends (Coeckelbergh et al. 2016).

Some work suggests that people like the social presence of robots, at least in healthcare. One study showed that 50% of hospital pain clinic patients did not mind the presence of a female humanlike robot in their first consultation with the doctor, 33% preferred the robot's presence, and only 6% preferred its absence (Yoshikawa et al. 2011). When the robot expressed empathy with the patient, this added to its positive effects. Smiling and nodding in synchrony with the patient during the consultation increased the number of patients who preferred the robot to be present to above 50% (Takano et al. 2008). When the robot smiled and nodded in synchrony with the doctor, patients' preference for its presence was 40%.

There are also concerns that, if robots are used as nannies to care for young infants, then infants may not develop linguistically, socially, or emotionally due to insufficient human care (Sharkey & Sharkey 2011). A code of ethics, in which safety, law, and social impact are important components, has been proposed for the use of robots (Lin et al. 2011).

It will be interesting to see how trust of robots develops in the future. A 2015 news article reported Samsung's warning that people should not talk about private matters in front of their smart TVs because the TV's voice recognition software could record and transmit conversations to third parties (BBC News 2015a). This news article also warned of home devices that knew when you were out; this information could possibly be relayed to others. Robots will have the ability to gather even more data about us, which may potentially be hackable or otherwise accessible and useful to others. Another recent news article reported that a talking doll that answers children's questions by looking up answers on the Internet (similar to Siri on the iPhone) could be hacked to say frightening things (BBC News 2015b). The hacking of our robots could potentially create many unsettling new threats.

WHAT MAKING ROBOTS CAN TEACH US ABOUT OURSELVES

Creating Humanlike Robots

Some robots look humanlike; the androids built by Ishiguro & Nishio (2007) are examples. An android is a robot that is highly anthropomorphic in both appearance and behavior. Android science is an interdisciplinary field in which engineers build humanlike robots and cognitive scientists test these robots with humans to discover more about human nature. Using this feedback loop, Ishiguro's ultimate goal is to build androids that can take part in humanlike conversations (Ishiguro & Nishio 2007). Because that is currently impossible, he is building and studying geminoids. A geminoid is a robot built to look exactly like an existing person and teleoperated by a human in a so-called Wizard of Oz fashion. Through teleoperation, a robot can be made to act with the same behaviors, conversational abilities, and personality of a real person. A geminoid has, in effect, an artificial body and a human mind. A geminoid is intended to mirror a specific person; Ishiguro has a geminoid that is a likeness of himself (see **Figure 1**).

One robot, the telenoid, is a teleoperated robot with the minimal features of any human and has been built by Ishiguro and colleagues to possess the essence of humanness (**Figure 1**; Ogawa et al. 2011). It has a head, a face, short arms, and fused legs and is designed to have no gender or age. Its advantage is that it can be operated by anyone and the person interacting with it can perceive any number of variations of age, gender, and personality. The telenoid has received mixed reactions, including fear, from people interacting with it, and people prefer to talk to a real person than a teleoperated telenoid (Ogawa et al. 2011). However, a study of engineering students found that most operators of the robot reported that it could transmit their intentions to a moderate degree and most students interacting with the robot perceived its behavior as moderately sociable (Sorbello et al. 2014).

Even laypeople are beginning to build humanlike robots. One man with little knowledge of engineering or software successfully built a robot in his apartment that looked similar to movie star Scarlett Johansson (Bolton 2016).

Engineers are attempting to make robots look and behave identically to humans in part so that humans can interact with robots on a more intuitive and natural level. However, making robots behave like humans is difficult in many ways, not least due to limitations in technology preventing the production of a humanlike body that can perceive the world as we do and perform the same actions. Nevertheless, engineers are trying to make robots look and behave identically to humans.

Android: a robot with a human appearance (but not that of a specific individual)

Geminoid: a teleoperated robot that is built to resemble a specific human individual

Wizard of Oz: a situation in which people interact with a robot that they think is autonomous but that is secretly being operated by another person

Telenoid: a teleoperated robot designed to have minimal characteristics of a human, usually ageless and genderless with a head, torso, and short limbs

Leaving aside the technical difficulties, there are many complex human behaviors that engineers must first define and then model. To illustrate the complexities of this task and to show that this effort to model human behavior can reveal more about ourselves, I examine two common social behaviors that roboticists are trying to model: social distance and gaze behavior.

The first example of human behavior that roboticists are attempting to model is proxemics, or physical and psychological distancing from others (Mumm & Mutlu 2011). Engineers argue that robots should show appropriate distancing behavior based on human norms to be better integrated into human society. Engineers have first turned to what psychologists and other social scientists have already discovered on this topic, which includes several theoretical models of dyadic interpersonal distancing. Whether approach from one partner results in reciprocal or compensatory distancing can depend on likability. Other factors influencing social distance include gender, culture, and age. When these models are tested in human–robot dyads, people respond to robots in social interactions in similar (although not exactly the same) ways as they respond to humans (Mumm & Mutlu 2011). This research can be applied to allow robots to approach people in socially acceptable ways when handing over objects. To create such behavior, researchers have systematically observed how humans approach each other and created robot models that try to use similar approach behaviors (Avrunin & Simmons 2014). Human participants preferred the approach behaviors of the robot when it used approach paths modelled on human behavior over purely straight-line paths but only when the robot approached people from behind. This illustrates the blending of research into human and robot behavior—first observing how we approach others, then programming the robot to behave the same way, and finally testing whether this modelled behavior in a robot is acceptable to people.

The second example of the attempt to create robots with humanlike appearance and behavior is the development of realistic eye models for robots and computer agents based on human eye appearance and gaze behavior (Ruhland et al. 2015). Human–robot interaction (HRI) researchers have studied head, eye, and body orientation as indicators of level of engagement in a social context (Srinivasan & Murphy 2011). This research has shown that social gaze functions to establish the robot as an agent, to communicate the robot's interest in a person, to signal conversational turn-taking, and to communicate which object the robot is referring to. A variety of different gaze acts, such as long gazes, short glances, gaze aversion, rapid gaze shifts, and eye scanning, as well as head movements, have been studied in robots to determine their effects in interactions with people.

For robots to be social agents, they must not only act in humanlike ways but also be able to perceive and understand human behavior. To create robots that can detect untrustworthy behavior in humans, engineers have studied the behaviors that elicit trust in human–human dyads during cooperative behavior games using both manual and automated coding systems (Lee et al. 2013). This research showed that face touching, arm crossing, leaning back, and hand touching were associated with less trustworthy behavior, and leaning forward, having the arms in the lap, and having an open-armed pose were associated with more trustworthy behavior. This work sheds light on our own tendencies and adds to Ekman's (1989) work on behaviors that indicate deception and lying and to work on emotional expression and trustworthiness (Boone & Buck 2003).

Because robots have limited language abilities, posture and gesture are important means by which robots can convey and detect emotions. Research suggests that people can interpret intended emotions from postural manipulations of robots (Beck et al. 2010). Roboticists have studied the biology of human body schema (self-awareness of body position in space) and applied this to robots, allowing robots to have an awareness of their own body positions (Hoffmann et al. 2010). It has been argued that this type of work can both help give robots new capabilities and also complement psychology and neuroscience research by creating and testing artificial models.

Creating Pet-Like Robots

Pet-like robots, including Paro (a seal), Genibo (a dog), and Pleo (a dinosaur), have been developed for both therapy and play (**Figure 1**). Paro was developed as a therapeutic robot for people with dementia, as described in the section Healthcare Robots for Older People. Genibo was developed in Korea as a toy robot in the form of a bull terrier dog that can understand voice commands such as "sit," respond to patting, wag its tail, bark, and take photos. It is popular in Korea despite its cost. Pleo is a robot in the form of a baby dinosaur developed as a toy that can learn voice commands, sense special food that is held up to it, and react to touch. Pleo has been used with children to study relationships; however, research reveals children's interest is not sustained over time (Fernaeus et al. 2010). Other research includes the addition of a virtual version of Pleo to increase interactions and interest from children (Fernandez-Baena et al. 2015).

To increase the capacity of robots to provide companionship, several design principles have been incorporated into existing artificial pets. These include freedom for the robot to refuse an order, dependency of the robot on its owner to look after it and help it mature over time (to make the human feel responsible for it), juvenile traits in the robot to trigger emotional responses, and emotional exchanges (predominantly via nonverbal modes due to difficulties with speech comprehension) (Kaplan 2001). Pleo has been developed with this maturation concept in mind, as it learns to walk over the first few days with its owner.

To be successful, pet-like robots should display similar kinds of attachment behaviors to those displayed by real animals. Kaplan proposes that Ainsworth's strange situation test (which normally tests a child's attachment to his or her mother) could be used to test a robot's attachment to its owner (Ainsworth & Bell 1970, Kaplan 2001). If the robot displayed appropriate contact-seeking behavior, such as following its owner, and appropriate signaling behavior, such as blinking its lights or beeping toward its owner, then this would indicate to observers that the robot was attached to its owner. To achieve behaviors typical of attachment, the robot could be programmed with a motivational drive to stay with its owner. Like a pet dog, the robot would need to recognize its owner, monitor the presence of the owner during independent activity, and display short-term distress at the owner's absence and short-term happiness on the owner's return. Careful observations of dog behaviors in relation to their owners have shed light on how humans and dogs interact and provided a guide for the development of social robots (Faragó et al. 2014). Proxemics, orientation and gazing behavior, tail wagging, and greeting behavior were particularly important in dog response to owner activity.

STUDYING HOW WE THINK, FEEL, AND BEHAVE TOWARD ROBOTS

The study of HRI is a fairly recent phenomenon. It is a cross-disciplinary field with its origins in the work of computer scientists and engineers as well as sociologists and psychologists. Because robots come in many shapes and sizes and have many applications, the field has a wide scope and researchers are still exploring its boundaries.

Research can be divided into what one could call simulated robot studies and real-world robot studies. Both types of study can contribute to knowledge of human–robot relationships. Simulated studies may employ written descriptions, photographs, or videos of robots instead of real robots or may use robots that aren't autonomous (a Wizard of Oz design). Simulated studies have the advantages of enabling a high degree of control over study manipulations, being quicker, and allowing robots to behave in more humanlike ways than they would normally be able to do. However, simulated designs have the disadvantage that people are under artificial conditions, and thus the results may not generalize to real robots and real-world conditions.

Real-world studies are typically conducted with actual robots in settings such as rest homes or shopping malls. In contrast to simulated studies, real-world robot studies are usually longer, harder to conduct, and much more expensive. They often involve collaborations between psychologists and engineers, and a robot must be built (or bought) and programmed to operate, preferably autonomously. This work is challenging in part because the technology is not as reliable or sophisticated as the researchers would like and because there are often no quick fixes for technological problems away from the laboratory. The robots also have limited capabilities and battery life.

There are advantages to real-world studies, however. First, people are actually interacting with robots, as opposed to watching videos of robots, reading descriptions of robots, or interacting with simulated robots. Second, real-world studies allow relationships to be formed and studied over a much longer period of time in natural environments. They can remove the artificiality of the lab and reduce response bias and novelty effects.

Over the past 50 years, observations of people's real-world behaviors toward technologies such as computers have led to the generation of hypotheses and theories about human behavior. In the next section, I examine several approaches and theories that are relevant to HRI, beginning with a historical perspective.

A Visit to the Uncanny Valley

As early as the 1970s, a relationship was proposed between the humanlikeness of robots and feelings of comfort with them. A positive relationship was proposed, but it had a steep dip in comfort when robots looked almost but not perfectly human (Mori 1970, Mori et al. 2012). This dip is called the uncanny valley and explains feelings of discomfort and unease toward close-to-human robots. These feelings can occur when there is something fundamentally inhuman about a robot despite an otherwise close resemblance. For example, a robot may look humanlike but move in an odd manner or have a hand that is cold and lacks a bonelike structure within (Cabibihan et al. 2015). Mori's original theory likens the feeling of the uncanny valley to the way people feel about interacting with a dead body.

There are mixed findings concerning both the existence of the uncanny valley and its explanations (MacDorman & Chattopadhyay 2016). Some of the variability between studies may be due to differences in the terms used to measure these feelings—including familiarity, comfort, threat, likability, similarity, unease, uncanniness, and eeriness. This is partly because the original paper was in Japanese and there is no direct translation into English. The variation in the types of robot used has also created differences between studies. Robots can vary in many aspects of appearance; furthermore, sometimes only the face is used, whereas other times the whole body is shown.

Some evidence supports the existence of the uncanny valley, with a demonstrated drop in familiarity and a rise in eeriness in the middle of a series of images morphed from a robot face to a human (MacDorman & Ishiguro 2006). However, other work has found people like realistic humanlike robots and found no evidence for a dip in feelings of comfort in the middle of a continuum of faces morphed from cartoonlike to realistic (Hanson et al. 2005). Similarly, there was no evidence for a dip in familiarity or rise in eeriness when a range of robots that varied in humanlikeness were shown in videos (MacDorman 2006).

Factors other than humanlikeness may contribute to robots falling into the uncanny valley. Robots rated equal on humanlikeness were rated differently in strangeness or familiarity, suggesting other variables contribute to these perceptions (MacDorman 2006). Other work supports this conclusion, with a range of design features such as height, bulk, and bipedal form adding to or subtracting from humanlikeness and contributing to the perceived threat or likability of robots (Rosenthal-von der Pütten & Krämer 2014). A study of what makes people appear creepy also found that multiple factors of appearance and behavior contributed to feelings of threat, including unkempt hair, odd dress, and unpredictable behavior (McAndrew & Koehnke 2016). Certain occupations were rated as creepier than others, including clowns, who have distorted human appearance, and taxidermists and funeral directors, who are associated with death.

In terms of theory, ratings of unease toward not-quite-humanlike robots may be explained by evolutionary theory because it could be beneficial to feel revulsion as a defense mechanism to protect against infection from diseased or deceased bodies. Unease toward robots could alternatively be caused by category uncertainty (i.e., wondering whether it is human or not). A similar theory, realism inconsistency, claims that human and nonhuman features are combined in a robot, creating an uncanny effect. Supporting this theory, one study found that a mixture of real and artificial features (e.g., eyes, eyelashes, mouth) in the same face created eeriness to a greater extent than a slow morphing from real to computer animated across all facial features together (MacDorman & Chattopadhyay 2016). Furthermore, a humanlike face with silver skin and empty-looking eyes was rated more eerie than the same face with humanlike skin and eyes (Broadbent et al. 2013). The eyes appear to be particularly important when judging whether a face is alive or not (Looser & Wheatley 2010). Together, this work suggests that conflicting cues are an important component in uncanniness as they may violate our expectations of humans.

The violation of perceptual expectations may occur when a robot looks like but does not act like a human. Video clips of an android (human appearance and mechanical action), a human (human appearance and human action), and a more mechanical robot (mechanical appearance and mechanical action) performing actions were shown to 20 people in a fMRI machine (Saygin et al. 2012). The results suggested greater brain activity in the bilateral anterior intraparietal sulcus (an important part of the action perception system) when viewing the android than when viewing the human and the mechanical robot. This provides support for the predictive coding framework of neural processing, in which brain activity is higher when observed behavior is mismatched with expectations. That is, people expect a human to walk in a humanlike way, so if the android that looks humanlike walks in a mechanical way it violates our expectations, resulting in large feedback error signals in the brain (MacDorman & Chattopadhyay 2016). The study by Saygin and colleagues (2012) also illustrates that robots can be used to study human perceptions of movement.

Robots Change, Challenge, and Reveal Us: The Second Self

In the 1980s, Sherry Turkle studied human–computer relationships from a psychoanalytic perspective and described the insights people gain about themselves through the use of computers. She wrote that the cultural phenomenon that occurred in the early 1980s, in which people likened human experiences, such as memory, to computer processes, allowed a simplified understanding of ourselves (Turkle 2005). Programming computers also fostered a sense of control over the world and could be a form of self-expression in which what you created in programs reflected your personality. Turkle (2005) wrote that the early days of computing taught children about logical thinking and procedures, whereas children now use more sophisticated modern computers on a surface level, and their understanding of how they actually work has been lost. From this perspective, the engineers and scientists who are programming the brains and behaviors of robots are learning more about models of thought processes and behavior than are the people who are interacting with robots on a surface level.

Robots may challenge us by prompting us to become more reflective about ourselves. Turkle (2005) describes the computer as an evocative object that makes us question how we think and what makes up our nature. Similarly, robots prompt questions about what it is to be human and how we differ from robots (Turkle et al. 2006). In addition, Turkle and colleagues (2006) comment that in-depth observations of the different ways children and older adults treat robots can reflect their family situation and that people may project their psychological needs in their interactions with robots. Watching children's interactions with robots can therefore be useful in gaining insights into their personal situations and experiences.

We Mindlessly Apply Social Rules to Robots: The Media Equation

Another pioneering researcher on HRI was Clifford Nass, a computer scientist and sociologist. His seminal work on the media equation informed much of the field of HRI as it is today (Nass & Reeves 1996). Nass & Moon (2000) demonstrated in a series of studies that people treat computers and other technologies as if they were human even though they know this is not the case. This is somewhat irrational, and Nass and colleagues argued that people mindlessly apply social rules to computers. The evidence for this comes from several angles.

First, there is evidence that people use stereotypical social categories, such as gender, ethnicity, and in-group and out-group status, when interacting with computers. For example, just as women are assumed to have more caring competencies and men to have more agentic competencies (Huddy & Terkildsen 1993), computers with a female voice were rated more informative about love and relationships, whereas computers with a male voice were rated more knowledgeable about computers, despite the computers giving identical information (Nass et al. 1997). Similar to findings on racial prejudice (Brown 1995), one study found that people rated computer agents with a face of the same ethnicity as them to be more attractive, trustworthy, persuasive, and intelligent than agents of another ethnicity (Nass & Moon 2000). Moreover, similar to findings on in-group bias exhibited by people toward others (Fu et al. 2012), studies have found that participants with an armband the same color as the computer's screen band rated the computer more highly and conformed to its instructions more than they did if the bands were a different color (Nass et al. 1996, Nass & Reeves 1996).

Second, experiments show that people use overlearned social behaviors, such as politeness, in their interactions with computers. For example, after using a computer, people evaluate its performance more highly if the same computer delivers the rating scale than if another computer delivers the scale or if they rate it with pen and paper (Nass et al. 1999). This result is similar to experimenter bias, in which people try not to offend a human researcher. Another example of a social behavior is reciprocity—we help others who help us. People helped a computer with a task for more time and more accurately if the computer first helped them with a task than if it did not (Fogg & Nass 1997). Reciprocal self-disclosure is also evident in the way people respond to computers. People's responses are more intimate to computers that disclose more about themselves in the initial interaction than to other computers (Moon 2000).

Similar studies have shown that people mindlessly apply social rules to robots as well. In terms of racial prejudice, German participants rated a robot that had a German name and was described as having been developed in Germany as warmer and as having a better design and a greater capacity to experience the world than an identical robot that had been given a Turkish name and was described as having been developed in Turkey (Eyssel & Kuchenbrandt 2012). The participants also reported feeling closer to the German robot. In terms of gender stereotypes, a robot with short hair and flat lips was rated less feminine and more suitable for typically male tasks (e.g., technical work) than an otherwise-identical robot with long hair and shapely lips, which was rated more feminine and more suitable for typically female tasks (e.g., child rearing) (Eyssel & Hegel 2012). Robot gender has been shown to influence participants' behavior as well. For example, people in a museum were more likely to donate money to a robot research lab when the robot asked with a female voice than when it asked with a male voice (Siegel et al. 2009).

Just as people can be polite to computers, people can be polite to robots. In interactions with Nao, some people were polite and tried to help the robot; others, however, called the robot names and enjoyed having power over the robot (Rehm & Krogsager 2013). Similarly, approximately 50% of people greeted a robot receptionist at a university campus in some way (e.g., by typing hello) before the rest of the interaction, and the presence of a greeting predicted a more sociable and polite subsequent conversation with the robot (Lee et al. 2010).

Some research shows that people demonstrate reciprocity toward robots. For example, people's perceptions of a care robot were more positive if the robot asked for help and returned the help with a favor than if the robot did neither of these things (Lammer et al. 2014). In the prisoner's dilemma game, two criminals are faced with a situation in which cooperative behavior (mutual silence) results in a lower prison sentence for both, but betrayal results in the betrayer being set free and a longer prison term for the betrayed. In a repeated version of this game, reciprocal behavior is often employed. In one study, participants demonstrated the same amount of reciprocal behavior toward a robot opponent as they did toward a human opponent (Sandoval et al. 2016). Furthermore, the amount of reciprocity shown toward the robot was higher when the robot showed cooperative behavior in the first round than when it displayed random behavior in the first round.

However, there is evidence that not all reactions to robots are mindless and that there is variation in the degree to which people display social behavior toward robots. One study looking at verbal responses to a talking wheelchair robot suggested that people were not reacting mindlessly to the robot; rather, reactions differed according to people's goals and people were aware of their choices of how to respond (Fischer 2011).

A common approach in HRI research is to recreate experiments from psychology, repeating what the experimenters originally did to test participants' reactions to humans but observing reactions to robots instead. These studies aim to determine whether we behave toward robots in the same ways as we behave toward humans. One such study was based on Milgram's obedience paradigm (Milgram 1963). In this case, rather than asking participants to give increasing levels of electric shock to a human actor, participants were asked to give electric shocks to a robot (Bartneck et al. 2005). The results showed that 100% of the participants shocked the robot to the maximum level, despite the robot's protests and requests to stop the experiment, compared to 65% of the participants in Milgram's original work who shocked the human actor to the maximum level. This suggests that people treat robots differently to humans in some circumstances, perhaps in this case because they did not think the robot could feel pain.

Studies on honesty provide another example of this kind of replication. Research in psychology has shown that the presence of an observer can increase people's honesty, but incentives for cheating can reduce honesty (Covey et al. 1989). In a robot version of this work, participants given incentives to cheat were shown to be less honest when alone compared to when they were accompanied either by a human or by a simple robot (Hoffman et al. 2015). This illustrates that the social presence of robots may make people feel as though they are being watched and increase their honesty in an effect similar to that produced by the presence of humans.

We Perceive the World Through a Human Filter: Anthropomorphism

Anthropomorphism refers to our tendency to see humanlike characteristics, emotions, and motivations in nonhuman entities such as animals, gods, and objects (Epley et al. 2007). Anthropomorphism can be conceptualized and measured in different ways—from a simple rating of humanlikeness on a single-dimension scale to broader and less concrete conceptualizations including mind, emotionality, intention, consciousness, and free will (Waytz et al. 2014).

The tendency of humans to anthropomorphize objects can be explained by the fact that being human is the thing we know best. When trying to understand or interact with an unfamiliar nonhuman agent, people use their knowledge of themselves as a basis for understanding these entities. In other words, being human forms our frame of reference. Our biology is thought to contribute to this tendency, as watching a nonhuman agent perform a humanlike behavior may activate mirror neurons and therefore cause us to experience a similar state (Epley et al. 2007).

Neurophysiological research suggests that we react more to a nonanthropomorphic robot when a human acts socially toward it (Hoenen et al. 2016). In this study, watching a robot vacuum cleaner being verbally harassed triggered more compassion and a greater response in the mirror neuron system than a situation in which the robot was not harassed (Hoenen et al. 2016). The authors interpret this research as showing that observing someone interact socially with a robot can increase perceptions of the robot's social agency.

Our tendency to anthropomorphize increases with the humanlikeness of a nonhuman entity. This may be because the entity is seen as more similar to the self. For example, robots that have a greater number of facial features (nose, mouth, eyes, etc.) are perceived as more humanlike than those with fewer facial features (DiSalvo et al. 2002). Epley et al. (2007) hypothesize that lack of certainty about a nonhuman entity will increase the tendency to anthropomorphize. Experimental work supports this hypothesis by showing that agents described as less predictable are anthropomorphized to a greater extent (Waytz et al. 2010).

Epley and colleagues (2007) also propose that people have an inherent need to be social and that when they are lacking social ties, anthropomorphism of nonhuman entities will help meet this need. This hypothesis was supported by research showing that lonely people had a greater tendency to anthropomorphize a humanlike robot than nonlonely people (Eyssel & Reich 2013). These experiments demonstrate that robots can serve as a way to study the human tendency to anthropomorphize nonhuman objects, as well as to inform us about how we perceive robots.

We Perceive Mind in Robots: Mind Perception

The question of whether robots can think has interested humans since the early days of computing. Alan Turing's (1950) famous imitation game or Turing test reasons that if an interrogator asking questions of a human and a computer is unable to distinguish which is which, then one would have to conclude that the computer was intelligent. Accordingly, the answer to the question of whether robots can think depends on how advanced the technology is and the opinion of the person asking the question.

The question of whether people think that robots can think is different. Perceived mind has been found to consist of two dimensions of mind—the capacity for agency (e.g., self-control, morality, memory, emotion recognition, planning, communication, and thought) and the capacity for experience (e.g., hunger, fear, pain, pleasure, rage, desire, personality, consciousness, pride, embarrassment, and joy) (Gray et al. 2007). In this study, people ascribed different amounts of agency and experience to different kinds of beings: An adult human was perceived as having the most agency and experience, a baby was perceived to have high experience but no agency, and God was perceived to have high agency but no experience. In this way, perceived mind can differ from perceived humanness. No one would argue that a baby is not human, but everyone agrees its mind is not yet fully developed. The robot in Gray et al.'s (2007) study was perceived to have little ability to experience but to have a moderate degree of agency. This suggests that robots are seen by most people to have at least some components of mind.

Different kinds of robots are likely to be perceived as having more or less mind. For example, people who see a video of a robot's head from the front, with a face in view, think the robot has more mind on the experience dimension than people who see the robot's head from behind, with wires in view (Gray & Wegner 2012). Subsequent work on interactions with actual robots has shown that people perceive a robot with a face on its screen as being more humanlike and having both more agency and more experience than a robot with no face at all (Broadbent et al. 2013).

Morality has been linked to perceptions of mind. It has been argued that moral judgments require a dyad in which intention is perceived on the part of an agent and the experience of suffering is perceived on the part of a patient (Gray et al. 2012). Because robots are perceived to have aspects of mind, this begs the question of whether robots should behave morally and be treated morally. In one experiment, children had a social interaction with a Robovie robot (talking, playing, and hugging); the experimenter then interrupted to put the robot in a closet while the robot protested that it was not fair, that it was afraid of the dark, and that it did not want to go in the closet. The majority of the children saw the robot as having thoughts and emotions and as a social agent. All of the children thought it was all right to put a broom in the closet, whereas less than half of the children thought that it was all right to put the robot in the closet and all of them thought it wrong to put a human in the closet (Kahn et al. 2012a). This is in accordance with previous research showing that robots are perceived to have less mind than humans. In another study with undergraduate students, Robovie was programmed to make a mistake in a game; on average, participants rated it only slightly accountable and significantly less accountable than they said they would rate a human for the same mistake (Kahn et al. 2012b).

Research on ethical dilemmas suggests that we think it less wrong for robots to make logical decisions that sacrifice one for the many than for humans to make the same decisions, supporting earlier findings that we attribute different standards to humans and robots (Malle et al. 2015). Furthermore, this suggests perceptions that robots are less capable of feeling emotions than humans but that they have some capacity for cognition. Although the morality of robots is a somewhat philosophical topic, it does have real-world implications for a future in which robots in the real world cause accidents. Who is to blame? The robot? The developer? The owner?

Emotional Attachment to Robots

Studies attempting to assess people's emotional attachment to robots have observed some forms of attachment. Emotional attachment, as measured by positive interactions, perceptions of the robot as having mind, and positive reactions to the robot as a companion, was demonstrated in children interacting with Aibo, a robotic dog designed for companionship, over a short interaction period (Weiss et al. 2009). Evidence suggests that almost all children attribute biology, mental life, sociability, and moral standing to real dogs and fewer, but still the majority, attribute these characteristics to stuffed toy dogs and robotic dogs (Melson et al. 2009). At least 75% of children thought the robotic dog could be their friend. In observations, preschoolers explored the robotic dog more than a soft toy, attempted to interact with it more, and showed greater apprehension towards it, whereas children aged 7–12 showed five times as much affection (through patting, hugging, etc.) for a real dog than for the robotic one. Analysis of themes within online chat forums about Aibo found that owners wrote about the robot having batteries and being an object but also seeming alive and having emotions and personality; owners also described forming an emotional attachment with Aibo (Friedman et al. 2003).

Several studies of robots have explored whether people feel situational empathy for robots when they are harmed. For example, watching a robot expressing fear of losing its memory and then observing it lose its memory induced more empathy than a control condition in which memory was not lost (Seo et al. 2015). Other work using fMRI suggests that people experience similar but weaker late top-down processing of empathy in response to pictures of a robot's finger being cut compared to pictures of a human's finger being cut (Suzuki et al. 2015). Giving more background information about a small bug-like robot increased participants' hesitation to hit it with a mallet (Darling et al. 2015), suggesting empathy was increased when they knew more about the robotic life form.

The display of positive behavior may increase affection toward robots. For example, a robot that expressed encouraging comments was rated higher on a measure of friendship than a robot that expressed more neutral comments (Pereira et al. 2011).

Robots Versus Other Technologies: Physical Embodiment

One interesting question is whether we form different relationships with robots, virtual robot characters (presented as avatars on a screen), and computers. Preliminary evidence suggests that we do. People rated a physical robot that was in the room with them as more watchful and enjoyable than both a simulated robot on a computer and a real robot shown through teleconferencing (Wainer et al. 2006). In another study, children were asked to administer electric shocks to either a physically present robot or a simulated robot on a computer screen, both of whom displayed colored bruises to indicate pain after being shocked; the children were then asked how much they empathized with the robot. Children empathized significantly more with the embodied robot than the computer-simulated robot (Kwak et al. 2013).

People tend to form a closer therapeutic alliance with robots than with computers and to be more compliant with the instructions of robots. In one study, people interacted for a longer time with a diet coach robot than either a diet coach computer or a pen-and-paper diet diary and also rated their alliance with the robot more highly (Kidd & Breazeal 2008). In subsequent work, people were shown to be more likely to follow relaxation instructions from a robot than from a computer tablet with the same software and voice (Mann et al. 2015). People spoke and smiled more at the robot than at the computer and trusted the robot and enjoyed interacting with it more. Their desire to interact with the robot again was higher than their desire to interact with the computer tablet again.

Trust is critical to successful interactions with robots. The concerns people currently have over security and privacy on digital devices (Chin et al. 2012) are likely to transfer to robots. A recent review showed that robot performance factors, such as reliability and failure rate, had large effects on people's trust. Robot attributes, such as personality and anthropomorphism, still had significant but smaller effects on trust (Hancock et al. 2011).

Physical embodiment may result in different physiological reactions to robots than to more machinelike entities. For example, reactions were greater when people were asked to a touch a robot on the eye or on the buttocks than when asked to touch it on the arm (Li et al. 2016). Physiological effects can also be seen in reactions to healthcare robots, with research showing that stroking Paro can reduce blood pressure and heart rate in rest-home and hospital residents (Robinson et al. 2015).

Robot Abuse

The rights of robots themselves and the potential for them to be abused should not be ignored. Studies in shopping malls have shown that children are well behaved toward robots when they are with their parents. However, without adults, groups of children can congregate and abuse the robot—blocking its path, calling it names, kicking it, punching it, ignoring its polite requests for them to stop, and stopping only when they become bored or when parents intervene (Brscić et al. 2015). To reduce robot abuse, the authors demonstrated that the robot's best strategies were avoidance and escape, because attempts by the robot to change verbal behavior or gently push to continue on its way unobstructed were both found to be ineffective.

This finding is not unique; similar bullying behavior by groups of young people has been observed toward an information-type robot in a plaza area (Salvini et al. 2010). Again the robot was not abused when researchers accompanied the robot, only when people thought the robot was alone. Observations of people interacting either alone or in pairs with a small wheeled robot showed that boys aged from seven to the early teens were the most aggressive, sometimes trapping it, covering its eyes, or verbally abusing it (Scheeff et al. 2002). If the robot responded with a fearful or sad facial expression, then the abuse increased, whereas if the robot responded with an angry expression and drove at the boys, then better treatment ensued.

One might reasonably argue that we should not worry about robot abuse if robots cannot suffer in the same way that humans do. However, Whitby (2008) argues that because robots might look humanlike, behave in humanlike ways, and take the role of humans, they are more than just objects. He suggests that we must make some agreement regarding how robots should be treated and how they can be designed to look and behave in order to reduce the risk of maltreatment. Additionally, studying the abuse of robots may allow us to gain insights into human behavior and ways to mitigate the abuse of humans and animals.

CONCLUSIONS AND FUTURE DIRECTIONS

This review has demonstrated that social robots are starting to become more common in our society and can benefit us by providing companionship, increasing communication, and reducing costs, especially in healthcare settings. Engineers are attempting to make robots look and behave like humans and animals so that we feel more comfortable with them. However, robots can also make us feel uncomfortable, especially when their appearance is inconsistently humanlike and thus threatening or when their behavior violates expectations. Interacting with robots can make us question who we are, and we can project our desires onto them. Theories suggest we are wired through a combination of nature and nurture to perceive robots through human filters. We mindlessly interact with robots and other technologies as if they were human and we perceive humanlike characteristics in them, including thoughts and emotions. However, we do not see them as having as much mind as humans do, nor do we ascribe to them the same moral rights and responsibilities as humans. We can experience empathy for and attachment to robot pets but to a lesser degree than live pets. In addition, we feel closer to actual robots than virtual robots or computers, suggesting that physical embodiment is important in our relationships with artificial technologies.

What does this mean for the future? David Levy (2007) argues in his book *Love and Sex with Robots* that people (men in particular) often have few close friends yet crave affection. He argues that people may prefer relationships with robots that are programmed to always be social, smart, and loyal over relationships with unpredictable humans who do not always behave as desired and get upset when we behave badly. Ethicists even argue that the creation of such beings may lead to the breakdown of society because people will prefer to interact with robots rather than each other (Whitby 2008). In some ways, this aligns with Turkle's (2005) comments that the first visitors to Disney's Animal Kingdom were disappointed that the real animals were not as realistic as their animatronic versions at Disney World and had less lifelike behavior. In her work, Turkle (2010) questions the advantages that real animals have over simulated ones and outlines the child's perspective that simulated animals can be better in some situations. She suggests that our relationships with robots make us question the purpose of life itself.

A biddable designer human with none of the bad features of real humans and all of the good features is a tempting promise. But is it possible? It would require an incredible feat of engineering and is not possible with today's technology—battery power, materials, language comprehension, actuators, sensors, etc.—let alone the gaps in our understanding of the human cognition, emotion, and behavior on which the robot needs to be modelled. If we could create superior versions of humans, how would we feel toward these beings? With this question, we come full circle back to the arena of science fiction movies, in which humans and robots live together in strange, tension-filled dramas or in which humans are fighting for their lives.

This discussion opens up the question of what we want to achieve and why. Why are we going beyond building useful robots that can help in difficult environments? We have found that companion robots can provide benefits in contexts in which people have restricted opportunities to socially interact with human companions, animals, or doctors, but how far do we want to go in terms of humanlikeness? Are we building robots because we want to build a perfect human? Yet how can a robot be a perfect human when it is not even human? What is humanness?

Humans have a fundamental tendency to create, and the ultimate creation is another human. Engineers know that they need to understand more about human beings to make humanlike robots, and they are looking to psychology for several reasons: Psychology can help engineers understand and model humans better, perform experiments with appropriate methods, and develop therapeutic robots.

Although the field of HRI is still dominated by engineers and computer scientists, psychologists are beginning to become involved, and the field has rapidly expanded in the past few years. Most research has focused on the technical side of robotics, and more research is needed on the ways humans respond to and work with robots. The research is still in its exploratory phase, and the rapid expansion feels a bit like a runaway train. There is enormous potential for psychologists to contribute to this strangely compelling field. This can be a win-win situation, with the study of human behavior informing the construction of robots and tests with robots informing us about human cognition, emotion, and behavior. What will be the consequences of the human quest to make copies of ourselves? Psychologists have a role to play in helping shape our future and that of our robot companions.

DISCLOSURE STATEMENT

The author is not aware of any affiliations, memberships, funding, or financial holdings that might be perceived as affecting the objectivity of this review.

LITERATURE CITED

Ainsworth MDS, Bell SM. 1970. Attachment, exploration, and separation: illustrated by the behavior of one-year-olds in a strange situation. *Child Dev.* 41:49–67

Avrunin E, Simmons R. 2014. Socially-appropriate approach paths using human data. *Proc. IEEE Int. Symp. Robot Hum. Interact. Commun., 23rd, Edinburgh, Scotl.*, May 25–29, pp. 1037–42. Piscataway, NJ: IEEE

Bartneck C, Rosalia C, Menges R, Deckers I. 2005. Robot abuse—a limitation of the media equation. *Proc. Interact 2005 Workshop Abuse, Rome*, Sept. 12, pp. 54–57. **http://www.agentabuse.org/Abuse_Workshop_WS5.pdf**

Basoeki F, Libera F, Menegatti E, Moro M. 2013. Robots in education: new trends and challenges from the Japanese market. *Themes Sci. Technol. Educ.* 6:51–62

Basteris A, Nijenhuis SM, Stienen AHA, Buurke JH, Prange GB, Amirabdollahian F. 2014. Training modalities in robot-mediated upper limb rehabilitation in stroke: a framework for classification based on a systematic review. *J. Neuroeng. Rehabil.* 11:1–15

BBC News. 2015a. Moment owner told 'Samsung TV is listening'. *BBC News*, Feb. 9. **http://www.bbc.com/news/technology-31297376**

BBC News. 2015b. What did she say? Talking doll Cayla is hacked. *BBC News*, Jan. 30. **http://www.bbc. com/news/technology-31059893**

Beck A, Hiolle A, Mazel A, Cañamero L. 2010. Interpretation of emotional body language displayed by robots. *Proc. Int. Workshop Affect. Interact. Nat. Env., 3rd, Firenze, Italy*, Oct. 25–29, pp. 37–42. New York: ACM

Bemelmans R, Gelderblom GJ, Jonker P, de Witte L. 2015. Effectiveness of robot Paro in intramural psychogeriatric care: a multicenter quasi-experimental study. *J. Am. Med. Dir. Assoc.* 16:946–50

Blanson HOA, Bierman BPB, Janssen J, Neerincx MA, Looije R, et al. 2013. Using a robot to personalise health education for children with diabetes type 1: a pilot study. *Patient Educ. Couns.* 92:174–81

Bloom DE, Chatterji S, Kowal P, Lloyd-Sherlock P, McKee M, et al. 2015. Macroeconomic implications of population ageing and selected policy responses. *Lancet* 385(9968):649–57

Bolton D. 2016. Scarlett Johansson lookalike robot built by Hong Kong man in his flat. *Independent*, Apr. 4. **http://www.independent.co.uk/life-style/gadgets-and-tech/news/scarlett-johansson-robot-hong-kong-ricky-ma-a6967971.html**

Boone RT, Buck R. 2003. Emotional expressivity and trustworthiness: the role of nonverbal behavior in the evolution of cooperation. *J. Nonverb. Behav.* 27:163–82

Broadbent E, Kumar V, Li X, Sollers J, Stafford RQ, et al. 2013. Robots with display screens: A robot with a more humanlike face display is perceived to have more mind and a better personality. *PLOS ONE* 8(8):e72589

Broadbent E, Kuo I, Lee YI, Rabindran J, Kerse N, et al. 2010. Attitudes and reactions to a healthcare robot. *Telemed. e-Health* 16:608–13

Broadbent E, Peri K, Kerse N, Jayawardena C, Kuo I, et al. 2014. Robots in older people's homes to improve medication adherence and quality of life: a randomized cross-over trial. *Proc. Int. Conf. Soc. Robot., Sydney, Australia*, Oct. 27–29, pp. 64–73. Cham, Switz.: Springer

Broadbent E, Tamagawa R, Kerse NM, Knock BW, Patience AA, MacDonald BA. 2009. Retirement home staff and residents' preferences for healthcare robots. *Proc. IEEE Int. Symp. Robot Hum. Interact. Commun., 18th, Toyama, Jpn.*, Sep. 27–Oct. 2, pp. 645–50. Piscataway, NJ: IEEE

Broadbent E, Tamagawa R, Patience A, Knock B, Kerse N, et al. 2012. Attitudes towards health-care robots in a retirement village. *Australas. J. Ageing* 31:115–20

Broholm M, Onsberg HI, Rosenberg J. 2016. Limited evidence for robot-assisted surgery: a systematic review and meta-analysis of randomized controlled trials. *Surg. Laparosc. Endosc. Percutan. Tech.* 26:117–23

Brown R. 1995. *Prejudice: Its Social Psychology*. Oxford, UK: Blackwell

Brscić D, Kidokoro H, Suehiro T, Kanda T. 2015. Escaping from children's abuse of social robots. *Proc. ACM/IEEE Int. Conf. Hum.-Robot Interact., 10th, Portland, OR*, Mar. 2–5, pp. 59–66. New York: ACM

Cabibihan JJ, Joshi D, Srinivasa YM, Chan MA, Muruganantham A. 2015. Illusory sense of human touch from a warm and soft artificial hand. *IEEE Trans. Neural Syst. Rehabil. Eng.* 23:517–27

Cherry CO, Chumbler NR, Richards K, Huff A, Wu D, et al. 2016. Expanding stroke telerehabilitation services to rural veterans: a qualitative study on patient experiences using the robotic stroke therapy delivery and monitoring system program. *Disabil. Rehabil. Assist. Technol.* In press. doi: 10.3109/17483107.2015.1061613

Chin E, Felt AP, Sekar V, Wagner D. 2012. Measuring user confidence in smartphone security and privacy. *Proc. Symp. Usable Priv. Secur., 8th, Washington, DC*, Jul. 11–13. pp. 1–16. New York: ACM

Coeckelbergh M, Pop C, Simut R, Peca A, Pintea S, et al. 2016. A survey of expectations about the role of robots in robot-assisted therapy for children with ASD: ethical acceptability, trust, sociability, appearance, and attachment. *Sci. Eng. Ethics* 22:47–65

Covey MK, Saladin S, Killen PJ. 1989. Self-monitoring, surveillance, and incentive effects on cheating. *J. Soc. Psychol.* 129:673–79

Darling K, Nandy P, Breazeal C. 2015. Empathic concern and the effect of stories in human-robot interaction. *Proc. IEEE Int. Symp. Robot Hum. Interact. Commun., 24th, Kobe, Jpn.*, Aug. 31–Sep. 4, pp. 770–775. Piscataway, NJ: IEEE

Diehl JJ, Schmitt LM, Villano M, Crowell CR. 2012. The clinical use of robots for individuals with Autism Spectrum Disorders: a critical review. *Res. Autism Spect. Dis.* 6:249–62

DiSalvo CF, Gemperle F, Forlizzi J, Kiesler S. 2002. All robots are not created equal: the design and perception of humanoid robot heads. *Proc. Des. Interact. Syst., 4th, London*, Jun. 25–28, pp. 321–26. New York: ACM

Ekman P. 1989. Why lies fail and what behaviors betray a lie. In *Credibility Assessment*, ed. JC Yuille, pp. 71–81. Berlin: Springer

Ellison LM, Nguyen M, Fabrizio MD, Soh A, Permpongkosol S, Kavoussi LR. 2007. Postoperative robotic telerounding: a multicenter randomized assessment of patient outcomes and satisfaction. *Arch. Surg.* 142:1177–81

Epley N, Waytz A, Cacioppo JT. 2007. On seeing human: a three-factor theory of anthropomorphism. *Psychol. Rev.* 114:864

euRobotics AISBL. 2013. *Robotics 2020: strategic research agenda for robotics in Europe*. euRobotics Coord. Action Draft 0v42, 7th Framework Progr., Eur. Comm., Brussels. **https://ec.europa.eu/research/ industrial_technologies/pdf/robotics-ppp-roadmap_en.pdf**

Eyssel F, Hegel F. 2012. (S)he's got the look: gender stereotyping of robots. *J. Appl. Soc. Psychol.* 42:2213–30

Eyssel F, Kuchenbrandt D. 2012. Social categorization of social robots: anthropomorphism as a function of robot group membership. *Br. J. Soc. Psychol.* 51:724–31

Eyssel F, Reich N. 2013. Loneliness makes the heart grow fonder (of robots): on the effects of loneliness on psychological anthropomorphism. *Proc. ACM/IEEE Int. Conf. Hum.-Robot Interact., 8th, Tokyo*, Mar. 3–6, pp. 121–22. Piscataway, NJ: IEEE

Faragó T, Miklósi A, Korcsok B, Száraz J, Gácsi M. 2014. Social behaviours in dog-owner interactions can serve as a model for designing social robots. *Interact. Stud.* 15:143–72

Fels DI, Waalen JK, Zhai S, Weiss P. 2001. Telepresence under exceptional circumstances: enriching the connection to school for sick children. *Proc. Interact 2001, Tokyo*, Jul. 9–13, pp. 617–24. Amsterdam: IOS Press

Fernaeus Y, Håkansson M, Jacobsson M, Ljungblad S. 2010. How do you play with a robotic toy animal? A long-term study of Pleo. *Proc. Int. Conf. Interact. Des. Child., 9th, Barcelona, Spain*, Jun. 9–12, pp. 39–48. New York: ACM

Fernandez-Baena A, Boldú R, Albo-Canals J, Miralles D. 2015. Interaction between Vleo and Pleo, a virtual social character and a social robot. *Proc. Int. Symp. Robot Hum. Interact. Commun., 24th, Kobe, Jpn.*, Aug. 31–Sep. 4, pp. 694–99. Piscataway, NJ: IEEE

Fischer K. 2011. Interpersonal variation in understanding robots as social actors. *Proc. ACM/IEEE Int. Conf. Hum.-Robot Interact., 6th, Lausanne, Switz.*, Mar. 8–11, pp. 53–60. Piscataway, NJ: IEEE

Fogg BJ, Nass C. 1997. How users reciprocate to computers: an experiment that demonstrates behavior change. *Proc. ACM Conf. Hum. Factors Comput. Syst., Atlanta, GA*, Mar. 22–27, pp. 331–32. New York: ACM

Ford C. 2012. *Robot & Frank*, directed by J Schreier. New York: Samuel Goldwyn Films

Friedman B, Kahn PH Jr., Hagman J. 2003. Hardware companions? What online AIBO discussion forums reveal about the human-robotic relationship. *Proc. ACM Conf. Hum. Factors Comput. Syst., Ft. Lauderdale, FL*, Apr. 5–10, pp. 273–80. New York: ACM

Fu F, Tarnita CE, Christakis NA, Wang L, Rand DG, Nowak MA. 2012. Evolution of in-group favoritism. *Sci. Rep.* 2:460–65

Gandsas A, Parekh M, Bleech MM, Tong DA. 2007. Robotic telepresence: profit analysis in reducing length of stay after laparoscopic gastric bypass. *J. Am. Coll. Surg.* 205:72–77

Gray HM, Gray K, Wegner DM. 2007. Dimensions of mind perception. *Science* 315(5812):619

Gray K, Wegner DM. 2012. Feeling robots and human zombies: mind perception and the uncanny valley. *Cognition* 125:125–30. doi: 10.1016/j.cognition.2012.06.007

Gray K, Young L, Waytz A. 2012. Mind perception is the essence of morality. *Psychol. Inq.* 23:101–24

Han J, Park I, Park M. 2015. Outreach education utilizing humanoid type agent robots. *Proc. Int. Conf. Hum.-Agent Interact., 3rd, Daegu, Korea*, Oct. 21–24, pp. 221–22. New York: ACM

Hancock PA, Billings DR, Schaefer KE, Chen JYC, De Visser EJ, Parasuraman R. 2011. A meta-analysis of factors affecting trust in human-robot interaction. *Hum. Factors* 53:517–27

Hanson D, Olney A, Prilliman S, Mathews E, Zielke M, et al. 2005. Upending the uncanny valley. In *Proc. Int. Conf. Assoc. Adv. Artif. Intell., 20th, Pittsburgh, PA*, Jul. 9–13, pp. 1728–29. Palo Alto, CA: AAAI Press

Hoenen M, Lübke KT, Pause BM. 2016. Non-anthropomorphic robots as social entities on a neurophysiological level. *Comput. Hum. Behav.* 57:182–86

Hoffman G, Forlizzi J, Ayal S, Steinfeld A, Antanitis J, et al. 2015. Robot presence and human honesty: experimental evidence. *Proc. ACM/IEEE Int. Conf. Hum.-Robot Interact., 10th, Portland, OR*, Mar. 2–5, pp. 181–88. New York: ACM

Hoffmann M, Marques HG, Arieta AH, Sumioka H, Lungarella M, Pfeifer R. 2010. Body schema in robotics: a review. *IEEE Trans. Auton. Ment. Dev.* 2:304–24

Huddy L, Terkildsen N. 1993. Gender stereotypes and the perception of male and female candidates. *Am. J. Polit. Sci.* 37:119–47

Hughes A, Burridge J, Freeman CT, Donnovan-Hall M, Chappell PH, et al. 2011. Stroke participants' perceptions of robotic and electrical stimulation therapy: a new approach. *Disabil. Rehabil. Assist. Technol.* 6:130–38

Hyun E, Park H, Jang S, Yeon H. 2010. The usability of a robot as an educational assistant in a kindergarten and young children's perceptions of their relationship with the robot. *Korean J. Child Stud.* 31:267–82

Intuit. Surg., Inc. 2016. *Intuitive Surgical, Inc. 2015 annual report*. Annu. Rep., Intuit. Surg., Inc., Sunnyvale, CA. **http://www.annualreports.com/Company/intuitive-surgical-inc**

Ishiguro H, Nishio S. 2007. Building artificial humans to understand humans. *J. Artif. Organs* 10:133–42

Jøranson N, Pedersen I, Rokstad AM, Ihlebæk C. 2015. Effects on symptoms of agitation and depression in persons with dementia participating in robot-assisted activity: a cluster-randomized controlled trial. *J. Am. Med. Dir. Assoc.* 16:867–73

Kahn PH Jr., Kanda T, Ishiguro H, Freier NG, Severson RL, et al. 2012a. "Robovie, you'll have to go into the closet now": children's social and moral relationships with a humanoid robot. *Dev. Psychol.* 48:303–14

Kahn PH Jr., Kanda T, Ishiguro H, Gill BT, Ruckert JH, et al. 2012b. Do people hold a humanoid robot morally accountable for the harm it causes? *Proc. ACM/IEEE Int. Conf. Hum.-Robot Interact., 7th, Boston, MA*, Mar. 5–8, pp. 33–40. New York: ACM

Kaplan F. 2001. Artificial attachment: Will a robot ever pass Ainsworth's strange situation test? *Proc. IEEE-RAS Int. Conf. Humanoid Robot., Tokyo*, Sept. 29–30, pp. 125–32. Piscataway, NJ: IEEE

Kidd CD, Breazeal C. 2008. Robots at home: understanding long-term human-robot interaction. *Proc. IEEE/RSJ Int. Conf. Intell. Robot. Syst., Nice, Fr.*, pp. 3230–35. Piscataway, NJ: IEEE

Kristoffersson A, Coradeschi S, Loutfi A. 2013. A review of mobile robotic telepresence. *Adv. Hum. Comput. Int.* 3:3

Kwak SS, Kim Y, Kim E, Shin C, Cho K. 2013. What makes people empathize with an emotional robot? The impact of agency and physical embodiment on human empathy for a robot. *Proc. IEEE Int. Symp. Robot Hum. Interact. Commun., 22nd, Gyeongju, Korea*, Aug. 29, pp. 180–85. Piscataway, NJ: IEEE

Lammer L, Huber A, Weiss A, Vincze M. 2014. Mutual care: how older adults react when they should help their care robot. *Proc. Int. Symp. Soc. Stud. Artif. Intell. Simul. Behav., 3rd, London*, Apr. 3–4. **http://hobbit.acin.tuwien.ac.at/publications/AISB2014-HRIpaper.pdf**

Lee JJ, Knox B, Breazeal C. 2013. Modeling the dynamics of nonverbal behavior on interpersonal trust for human-robot interactions. *Proc. Spring Symp. Assoc. Adv. Artif. Intell., Palo Alto, CA*, Mar. 25–27, pp. 46–47. Palo Alto, CA: AAAI

Lee MK, Kiesler S, Forlizzi J. 2010. Receptionist or information kiosk: How do people talk with a robot? *Proc. ACM Conf. Comput. Support. Coop. Work, Savannah, GA*, Feb. 6–10, pp. 31–40. New York: ACM

Levy D. 2007. *Love and Sex with Robots: The Evolution of Human-Robot Relationships*. New York: Harper Collins

Li J, Ju W, Reeves B. 2016. Touching a mechanical body: Tactile contact of a human-shaped robot is physiologically arousing. *Proc. Int. Conf. Int. Commun. Assoc., Fukuoka, Jpn.*, June 9–13. In press

Lin P, Abney K, Bekey G. 2011. Robot ethics: mapping the issues for a mechanized world. *Artif. Intell.* 175:942–49

Liu LS, Inkpen KM, Pratt W. 2015. I'm not like my friends: understanding how children with a chronic illness use technology to maintain normalcy. *Proc. ACM Conf. Comput. Support. Coop. Work, Vancouver, Can.*, Mar. 14–18, pp. 1527–39. New York: ACM

Looser CE, Wheatley T. 2010. The tipping point of animacy: how, when, and where we perceive life in a face. *Psychol. Sci.* 21:1854–62

MacDorman KF. 2006. Subjective ratings of robot video clips for human likeness, familiarity, and eeriness: an exploration of the uncanny valley. *Proc. Int. Conf. Cogn. Sci., 5th, Vancouver, Can.*, July 26–29, pp. 26–29. Mahwah, NJ: Lawrence Erlbaum

MacDorman KF, Chattopadhyay D. 2016. Reducing consistency in human realism increases the uncanny valley effect; increasing category uncertainty does not. *Cognition* 146:190–205

MacDorman KF, Ishiguro H. 2006. The uncanny advantage of using androids in cognitive and social science research. *Interact. Stud.* 7:297–337

Malle BF, Scheutz M, Arnold T, Voiklis J, Cusimano C. 2015. Sacrifice one for the good of many? People apply different moral norms to human and robot agents. *Proc. ACM/IEEE Int. Conf. Hum.-Robot Interact., 10th, Portland, OR*, Mar. 2–5, pp. 117–24. New York: ACM

Mann JA, MacDonald BA, Kuo I, Li X, Broadbent E. 2015. People respond better to robots than computer tablets delivering healthcare instructions. *Comput. Hum. Behav.* 43:112–17

McAndrew FT, Koehnke SS. 2016. On the nature of creepiness. *New Ideas Psychol.* 43:10–15

Melson GF, Kahn PH Jr., Beck A, Friedman B. 2009. Robotic pets in human lives: implications for the human-animal bond and for human relationships with personified technologies. *J. Soc. Issues* 65:545–67

Milgram S. 1963. Behavioral study of obedience. *J. Abnorm. Soc. Psych.* 67:371–78

Misra S, Cheng L, Genevie J, Yuan M. 2016. The iPhone effect: the quality of in-person social interactions in the presence of mobile devices. *Environ. Behav.* 48:275–98

Moon Y. 2000. Intimate exchanges: using computers to elicit self-disclosure from consumers. *J. Consum. Res.* 26:323–39

Mori M. 1970. The uncanny valley. *Energy* 7:33–35

Mori M, MacDorman KF, Kageki N. 2012. The uncanny valley [from the field]. *IEEE Robot. Autom. Mag.* 19:98–100

Mubin O, Stevens CJ, Shahid S, Mahmud AA, Dong J. 2013. A review of the applicability of robots in education. *J. Tech. Educ. Learn.* 1:209–15

Mumm J, Mutlu B. 2011. Human-robot proxemics: physical and psychological distancing in human-robot interaction. *Proc. ACM/IEEE Int. Conf. Hum.-Robot Interact., 6th, Lausanne, Switz.*, Mar. 8–11, pp. 331–38. Piscataway, NJ: IEEE

Nass C, Fogg BJ, Moon Y. 1996. Can computers be teammates? *Int. J. Hum.-Comp. Stud.* 45:669–78

Nass C, Moon Y. 2000. Machines and mindlessness: social responses to computers. *J. Soc. Issues* 56:81–103

Nass C, Moon Y, Carney P. 1999. Are respondents polite to computers? Social desirability and direct responses to computers. *J. Appl. Soc. Psychol.* 29:1093–110

Nass C, Moon Y, Green N. 1997. Are machines gender neutral? Gender-stereotypic responses to computers with voices. *J. Appl. Soc. Psychol.* 27:864–76

Nass C, Reeves B. 1996. *The Media Equation: How People Treat Computers, Televisions, and New Media as Real People and Places.* Cambridge, UK: Cambridge Univ. Press

Ogawa K, Nishio S, Koda K, Balistreri G, Watanabe T, Ishiguro H. 2011. Exploring the natural reaction of young and aged person with telenoid in a real world. *J. Adv. Comput. Intell. Intell. Inform.* 15:592–97

Orejana JR, MacDonald BA, Ahn HS, Peri K, Broadbent E. 2015. Healthcare robots in homes of rural older adults. In *Social Robotics*, ed. A Tapus, E Andre, J Martin, F Ferland, M Ammi, pp. 512–52. Berlin: Springer

Pereira A, Leite I, Mascarenhas S, Martinho C, Paiva A. 2011. Using empathy to improve human-robot relationships. In *Human-Robot Personal Relationships*, ed. MH Lamers, FJ Verbeek, pp. 130–38. Berlin: Springer

Rajesh M. 2015. Inside Japan's first robot-staffed hotel. *The Guardian*, Aug. 14. **http://www.theguardian.com/travel/2015/aug/14/japan-henn-na-hotel-staffed-by-robots**

Rehm M, Krogsager A. 2013. Negative affect in human robot interaction—impoliteness in unexpected encounters with robots. *Proc. IEEE Int. Symp. Robot Hum. Interact. Commun., 22nd, Gyeongju, Korea*, Aug. 26–29, pp. 45–50. Piscataway, NJ: IEEE

Robinson HM, Broadbent E, MacDonald B. 2016. Group sessions with Paro in a nursing home: structure, observations and interviews. *Australas. J. Ageing* 35:106–12

Robinson HM, MacDonald BA, Broadbent E. 2014. The role of healthcare robots for older people at home: a review. *Int. J. Soc. Robot.* 6:575–91

Robinson HM, MacDonald BA, Broadbent E. 2015. Physiological effects of a companion robot on blood pressure of older people in residential care facility: a pilot study. *Australas. J. Ageing* 34:27–32

Robinson HM, MacDonald BA, Kerse N, Broadbent E. 2012. Suitability of healthcare robots for a dementia unit and suggested improvements. *J. Am. Med. Dir. Assoc.* 14:34–40

Robinson HM, MacDonald BA, Kerse N, Broadbent E. 2013. The psychosocial effects of a companion robot: a randomized controlled trial. *J. Am. Med. Dir. Assoc.* 14:661–67

Rosenthal-von der Pütten AM, Krämer NC. 2014. How design characteristics of robots determine evaluation and uncanny valley related responses. *Comput. Hum. Behav.* 36:422–39

Rosheim M. 2006. *Leonardo's Lost Robots*. Berlin: Springer

Ruhland K, Peters CE, Andrist S, Badler JB, Badler NI, et al. 2015. A review of eye gaze in virtual agents, social robotics and HCI: behaviour generation, user interaction and perception. *Comput. Graph. Forum* 34:299–26

Sabelli AM, Kanda T. 2015. Robovie as a mascot: a qualitative study for long-term presence of robots in a shopping mall. *Int. J. Soc. Robot.* 8:211–21

Salvini P, Ciaravella G, Yu W, Ferri G, Manzi A, et al. 2010. How safe are service robots in urban environments? Bullying a robot. *Proc. IEEE Int. Symp. Robot Hum. Interact. Commun., 19th, Pisa, Italy*, Sep. 13–15, pp. 1–7. Piscataway, NJ: IEEE

Sandoval EB, Brandsetter J, Bartneck C. 2016. Reciprocity in human-robot interaction: a quantitative approach through the prisoner's dilemma and the ultimatum game. *Int. J. Soc. Robot.* 8:303–17

Satake S, Hayashi K, Nakatani K, Kanda T. 2015. Field trial of an information-providing robot in a shopping mall. *Proc. Int. Conf. Intell. Robot. Syst., Hamburg, Ger.*, Sep. 28–Oct. 2, pp. 1832–39. Piscataway, NJ: IEEE

Saygin AP, Chaminade T, Ishiguro H, Driver J, Frith C. 2012. The thing that should not be: predictive coding and the uncanny valley in perceiving human and humanoid robot actions. *Soc. Cogn. Affect. Neur.* 7:413–22

Scassellati B, Admoni H, Mataric M. 2012. Robots for use in autism research. *Annu. Rev. Biomed. Eng.* 14:275–94

Scheeff M, Pinto J, Rahardja K, Snibbe S, Tow R. 2002. Experiences with Sparky, a social robot. In *Socially Intelligent Agents*, ed. K Dautenhahn, A Bond, L Canamero, B Edmonds, pp. 173–80. Berlin: Springer

Seo SH, Geiskkovitch D, Nakane M, King C, Young JE. 2015. Poor thing! Would you feel sorry for a simulated robot? A comparison of empathy toward a physical and a simulated robot. *Proc. ACM/IEEE Int. Conf. Hum.-Robot Interact., 10th, Portland, OR*, Mar. 2–5, pp. 125–32. New York: ACM

Sharkey A, Sharkey N. 2011. Children, the elderly, and interactive robots. *IEEE Robot. Autom. Mag.* 18:32–38

Siegel M, Breazeal C, Norton MI. 2009. Persuasive robotics: the influence of robot gender on human behavior. *Proc. Int. Conf. Intell. Robot. Syst., St. Louis, MO*, Oct. 10–15, pp. 2563–68. Piscataway, NJ: IEEE

Simut R, Vanderfaeillie J, Peca A, Perre G, Vanderborght B. 2016. Children with Autism Spectrum Disorders make a fruit salad with Probo, the social robot: an interaction study. *J. Autism Dev. Disord.* 46:113–26

Sorbello R, Chella A, C Calí, Giardina M, Nishio S, Ishiguro H. 2014. Telenoid android robot as an embodied perceptual social regulation medium engaging natural human-humanoid interaction. *Robot. Auton. Syst.* 62:1329–41

Sparrow R, Sparrow L. 2006. In the hands of machines? The future of aged care. *Mind. Mach.* 16:141–61

Srinivasan V, Murphy RR. 2011. A survey of social gaze. *Proc. ACM/IEEE Int. Conf. Hum.-Robot Interact., 6th, Lausanne, Switz.*, Mar. 8–11, pp. 253–54. Piscataway, NJ: IEEE

Suzuki Y, Galli L, Ikeda A, Itakura S, Kitazaki M. 2015. Measuring empathy for human and robot hand pain using electroencephalography. *Sci. Rep.* 5:15924

Swinnen E, Beckwée D, Meeusen R, Baeyens J, Kerckhofs E. 2014. Does robot-assisted gait rehabilitation improve balance in stroke patients? A systematic review. *Top. Stroke Rehabil.* 21:87–100

Takano E, Matsumoto Y, Nakamura Y, Ishiguro H, Sugamoto K. 2008. Psychological effects of an android bystander on human-human communication. *Proc. IEEE-RAS Int. Conf. Humanoid Robot., 8th, Daejeon, Korea*, Dec. 1–3, pp. 635–39. Piscataway, NJ: IEEE

Tamagawa R, Watson C, Kuo IH, MacDonald BA, Broadbent E. 2011. The effects of synthesized voice accents on user perceptions of robots. *Int. J. Soc. Robot.* 3:253–62

Tapus A, Tapus C, Mataric MJ. 2008. User–robot personality matching and assistive robot behavior adaptation for post-stroke rehabilitation therapy. *Intell. Serv. Robot.* 1:169–83

Thicknesse P. 1784. *The Speaking Figure and the Automaton Chess-Player, Exposed and Detected*. London: John Stockdale

Turing AM. 1950. Computing machinery and intelligence. *Mind* 49:433–60

Turkle S. 2005. *The Second Self: Computers and the Human Spirit*. Cambridge, MA: MIT Press

Turkle S. 2010. In good company? On the threshold of robotic companions. In *Close Engagements with Artificial Companions: Key Social, Psychological, Ethical and Design Issues*, ed. Y Wilks, pp. 3–10. Amsterdam: John Benjamins Publ.

Turkle S. 2014. Objects of desire. In *What Should We Be Worried About? Real Scenarios that Keep Scientists Up at Night*, ed. J Brockman, pp. 93–97. New York: Harper Perennial

Turkle S, Taggart W, Kidd C, Dasté O. 2006. Relational artifacts with children and elders: the complexities of cybercompanionship. *Connect. Sci.* 18:347–61

Vespa PM, Miller C, Hu X, Nenov V, Buxey F, Martin NA. 2007. Intensive care unit robotic telepresence facilitates rapid physician response to unstable patients and decreased cost in neurointensive care. *Surg. Neurol.* 67:331–37

Wainer J, Feil-Seifer DJ, Shell DA, Matarić MJ. 2006. The role of physical embodiment in human-robot interaction. *Proc. IEEE Int. Symp. Robot Hum. Interact. Commun., 15th, Hatfield, UK*, Sept. 6–8, pp. 117–22. Piscataway, NJ: IEEE

Waytz A, Cacioppo J, Epley N. 2014. Who sees human? The stability and importance of individual differences in anthropomorphism. *Perspect. Psychol. Sci.* 5:219–32

Waytz A, Morewedge CK, Epley N, Monteleone G, Gao J, Cacioppo JT. 2010. Making sense by making sentient: effectance motivation increases anthropomorphism. *J. Pers. Soc. Psychol.* 99:410–35

Weiss A, Wurhofer D, Tscheligi M. 2009. "I love this dog"—children's emotional attachment to the robotic dog AIBO. *Int. J. Soc. Robot.* 1:243–48

Whitby B. 2008. Sometimes it's hard to be a robot: a call for action on the ethics of abusing artificial agents. *Interact. Comput.* 20:326–33

Yoshikawa M, Matsumoto Y, Sumitani M, Ishiguro H. 2011. Development of an android robot for psychological support in medical and welfare fields. *Proc. IEEE Int. Conf. Robot. Biomim., Phuket, Thail.*, Dec. 7–11, pp. 2378–83. Piscataway, NJ: IEEE

Cumulative Indexes

Contributing Authors, Volumes 58–68

Cook TD, 60:607–29
Coplan RJ, 60:141–71
Cosmides L, 64:201–29
Craighead WE, 65:267–300
Creswell JD, 68:491–516
Crocker J, 68:299–325
Csibra G, 66:689–710
Cudeck R, 58:615–37
Curran PJ, 62:583–619
Curry SJ, 60:229–55

D

Danese A, 68:517–44
Davey Smith G, 67:567–85
Davies PG, 67:415–37
Daw ND, 68:101–28
de Waal FBM, 59:279–300
Deary IJ, 63:453–82
den Nieuwenboer NA, 65:635–60
D'Esposito M, 66:115–42
Diamond A, 64:135–68
Dickel N, 62:391–417
Diefendorff JM, 61:543–68
Dijksterhuis A, 61:467–90
Dishion TJ, 62:189–214
Donnellan MB, 58:175–99
Dotsch R, 66:519–45
Druckman D, 67:387–413
Duncan GJ, 68:413–34
Dunkel Schetter C, 62:531–58
Dunlop BW, 65:267–300
Dunlosky J, 64:417–44
Dupré KE, 60:671–92

E

Eastwick PW, 68:383–411
Eby LT, 61:599–622
Echterhoff G, 63:55–79
Ehrhart MG, 64:361–88
Eichenbaum H, 68:19–45
Einarsson EÖ, 61:141–67
Eisenberger NI, 66:601–29
Elliot AJ, 65:95–120
Emberson LL, 66:349–79
Emery NJ, 60:87–113
Erez M, 58:479–514
Erickson KI, 66:769–97
Evans JStBT, 59:255–78
Everitt BJ, 67:23–50

F

Fairchild AJ, 58:593–614
Farah MJ, 63:571–91
Federico CM, 60:307–37
Federmeier KD, 62:621–47
Fingerhut AW, 58:405–24
Finkel EJ, 68:383–411
Finniss DG, 59:565–90
Fivush R, 62:559–82
Floresco SB, 66:25–52
Forstmann BU, 67:641–66
Fouad NA, 58:543–64
Fox NA, 66:459–86
French DC, 59:591–616
Frese M, 66:661–87
Fried I, 63:511–37
Friedman HS, 65:719–42
Frith CD, 63:287–313
Frith U, 63:287–313
Fritz MS, 58:593–614
Fuligni AJ, 66:411–31
Furman W, 60:631–52

G

Gage SH, 67:567–85
Gaissmaier W, 62:451–82
Gallistel CR, 64:169–200
Gallo LC, 62:501–30
Gazzaniga MS, 64:1–20
Geisler WS, 59:167–92
Gelfand MJ, 58:479–514
Gelman SA, 60:115–40
Gershman SJ, 68:101–28
Gervain J, 61:191–218
Gifford R, 65:541–79
Gigerenzer G, 62:451–82
Glover LR, 66:53–81
Glück J, 62:215–41
Goldin-Meadow S, 64:257–83
Golomb JD, 62:73–101
Gonzalez CM, 59:329–60
Goodman GS, 61:325–51
Gosling SD, 66:877–902
Gould E, 61:111–40
Graham JW, 60:549–76
Graham S, 65:159–85
Green DP, 60:339–67
Griffiths TD, 65:743–71
Gross C, 67:693–711
Gross JJ, 58:373–403

H

Grotevant HD, 65:235–65
Grusec JE, 62:243–69
Guinote A, 68:353–81
Gunia BC, 61:491–515;
  67:667–92
Gunnar M, 58:145–73

H

Hall RJ, 61:543–68
Halldorsdottir T, 68:215–41
Hampson SE, 63:315–39
Han S, 64:335–59
Happé F, 68:243–67
Hardt O, 61:141–67
Hare B, 68:155–86
Harring JR, 58:615–37
Haslam N, 65:399–423
Hauser M, 61:303–24
Hawkins EH, 60:197–227
Healey MP, 59:387–417
Heatherton TF, 62:363–90
Heine SJ, 60:369–94
Helgeson VS, 68:545–71
Hennessey BA, 61:569–98
Hensch TK, 66:173–96
Herek GM, 64:309–33
Higgins ET, 59:361–85
Hirst W, 63:55–79
Hodgkinson GP, 59:387–417
Hollins M, 61:243–71
Holsboer F, 61:81–109
Holyoak KJ, 62:135–63
Horn EE, 65:515–40
Hornsey MJ, 65:461–85
Howe LC, 68:327–51
Huston AC, 61:411–37
Hwang E, 61:169–90
Hyde JS, 65:373–98

I

Iacoboni M, 60:653–70
Irwin MR, 66:143–72
Ising M, 61:81–109
Izard CE, 60:1–25

J

Jack RE, 68:269–97
Jetten J, 65:461–85

Johnson EJ, 60:53–85
Jonides J, 59:193–224
Jost JT, 60:307–37
Judd CM, 68:601–25
Judge TA, 63:341–67
Juvonen J, 65:159–85

K

Kammeyer-Mueller JD,
  63:341–67
Kang SK, 66:547–74
Kaplan RM, 64:471–98
Kassam KS, 66:799–823
Kasser T, 67:489–514
Keen R, 62:1–21
Keith N, 66:661–87
Kelley K, 59:536–63
Kelloway EK, 60:671–92
Kelso E, 66:277–94
Keltner D, 65:425–60
Kenny DA, 68:601–25
Kern ML, 65:719–42
Kilduff M, 64:527–47
Kim HS, 65:487–514
Kingdom FAA, 59:143–66
Kish-Gephart JJ, 65:635–60
Kitayama S, 62:419–49;
  64:335–59
Klein WMP, 68:573–600
Knobe J, 63:81–99
Kogan A, 65:425–60
Koob GF, 59:29–53
Kopp CB, 62:165–87
Kornell N, 64:417–44
Kounios J, 65:71–93
Kraiger K, 60:451–74
Kramer AF, 66:769–97
Kraus N, 67:83–103
Krosnick JA, 68:327–51
Kruglanski AW, 58:291–316
Kurzban R, 66:575–99
Kutas M, 62:621–47

L

Lagnado D, 66:223–47
Lakin JL, 64:285–308
Langdon R, 62:271–98
Le Moal M, 59:29–53
Leary MR, 58:317–44
Lee HS, 64:445–69

Lent RW, 67:541–65
Lerner JS, 66:799–823
Leuner B, 61:111–40
Leventhal EA, 59:477–505
Leventhal H, 59:477–505
Levin HS, 65:301–31
Levine EL, 63:397–425
Lewis RL, 59:193–224
Li X, 65:301–31
Li Y, 66:799–823
Lieberman MD, 58:259–89
Lievens F, 59:419–50
Liu Z, 66:631–59
Loewenstein G, 59:647–72
Loftus EF, 68:1–18
Logel C, 67:415–37
Lord RG, 61:543–68
Loughnan S, 65:399–423
Lowenstein AE, 62:483–500
Lustig CA, 59:193–224

M

Macey WH, 64:361–88
MacKenzie SB, 63:539–69
MacKinnon DP, 58:593–614;
  62:299–329
Magnuson K, 68:413–34
Maguire EA, 67:51–82
Maher CP, 61:599–622
Mahon BZ, 60:27–51
Maier MA, 65:95–120
Manuck SB, 65:41–70
Mar RA, 62:103–34
Markus HR, 65:611–34
Martin A, 58:25–45
Martin CL, 61:353–81
Mashek DJ, 58:345–72
Masicampo EJ, 62:331–61
Mason W, 66:877–902
Masten AS, 63:227–57
Mather M, 67:213–38
Matthews KA, 62:501–30
Matzel LD, 64:169–200
Maxwell SE, 59:536–63
Mayer JD, 59:507–36
Mays VM, 58:201–25
McAdams DP, 61:517–42
McArdle JJ, 60:577–605
McCaffery JM, 65:41–70
McDermott JM, 65:235–65
McGaugh JL, 66:1–24

McIntosh AR, 64:499–525
McKay R, 62:271–98
McLemore KA, 64:309–33
Meaney MJ, 61:439–66
Mechoulam R, 64:21–47
Meck WH, 65:743–71
Medin DL, 66:249–75
Mehler J, 61:191–218
Mende-Siedlecki P, 66:519–45
Mermelstein RJ, 60:229–55
Mesquita B, 58:373–403
Metcalfe J, 68:465–89
Milad MR, 63:129–51
Miller DT, 67:339–61
Miller GE, 60:501–24
Miller MI, 66:853–76
Mills KL, 65:187–207
Mišic B, 64:499–525
Monin B, 67:363–85
Moore KS, 59:193–224
Moore T, 68:47–72
Moors A, 67:263–87
Mori S, 66:853–76
Morris MW, 66:631–59
Morris R, 59:451–75
Morris RGM, 61:49–79
Morrison C, 59:55–92
Moscovitch M, 67:105–34
Mukamel R, 63:511–37
Mullen E, 67:363–85
Mulliken GH, 61:169–90
Munafò MR, 67:567–85

N

Nadel L, 67:105–34
Nader K, 61:141–67
Nagayama Hall GC, 60:525–48
Napier JL, 60:307–37
Narayan AJ, 63:227–57
Nee D, 59:193–224
Nesbit JC, 61:653–78
Nichols S, 63:81–99
Niedenthal PM, 63:259–85
Norenzayan A, 67:465–88
Northoff G, 64:335–59
Norton ES, 63:427–52
Norton MI, 60:475–99

O

Ochsner KN, 58:373–403
O'Doherty JP, 68:73–100

Ogle CM, 61:325–51
Oishi S, 65:581–609
ojalehto bl, 66:249–75
Olivola CY, 66:519–45
Olson BD, 61:517–42
Oppenheimer DM, 66:277–94
Orehek E, 58:291–316
Owen AM, 64:109–33
Oyserman D, 68:435–63

P

Palmer SE, 64:77–107
Paluck EL, 60:339–67
Park DC, 60:173–96
Parker LA, 64:21–47
Parker SK, 65:661–91
Pauli WM, 68:73–100
Peissig JJ, 58:75–96
Penn DC, 58:97–118
Pennington BF, 60:283–306
Peplau LA, 58:405–24
Peter J, 67:315–38
Pettersson E, 65:515–40
Pettigrew TF, 67:1–21
Phillips DA, 62:483–500
Phillips LA, 59:477–505
Phillips LT, 65:611–34
Piff PK, 65:425–60
Pine DS, 66:459–86
Pittman TS, 59:361–85
Ployhart RE, 65:693–717
Podsakoff NP, 63:539–69
Podsakoff PM, 63:539–69
Poldrack RA, 67:587–612
Posner MI, 58:1–23
Postle BR, 66:115–42
Povinelli DJ, 58:97–118
Powers A, 67:239–61
Prakash RS, 66:769–97
Pratte MS, 63:483–509
Preacher KJ, 66:825–52
Prentice DA, 67:339–61
Price DD, 59:565–90
Proctor RW, 61:623–51

Q

Qiu A, 66:853–76
Quas JA, 61:325–51
Quevedo K, 58:145–73
Quirk GJ, 63:129–51

R

Rabinowitz AR, 65:301–31
Ratcliff R, 67:641–66
Rausch JR, 59:536–63
Rauschecker AM, 63:31–53
Raver CC, 66:711–31
Recanzone GH, 59:119–42
Ressler K, 67:239–61
Reuter-Lorenz P, 60:173–96
Revenson TA, 58:565–92
Richeson JA, 67:439–63
Rick S, 59:647–72
Rilling JK, 62:23–48
Rissman J, 63:101–28
Robbins P, 63:81–99
Robbins TW, 67:23–50
Roberts RD, 59:507–36
Roediger HL III, 59:225–54
Rosati AG, 66:321–47
Rothbart MK, 58:1–23
Rothman AJ, 68:573–600
Rousseau DM, 67:667–92
Rubin KH, 60:141–71
Ruble DN, 61:353–81
Rünger D, 67:289–314
Ryan AM, 65:693–717

S

Sackett PR, 59:419–50
Salmon DP, 60:257–82
Salthouse T, 63:201–26
Sammartino J, 64:77–107
Samuel AG, 62:49–72
Sanchez JI, 63:397–425
Sandler I, 62:299–329
Sanfey AG, 62:23–48
Santos LR, 66:321–47
Saribay SA, 59:329–60
Sarkissian H, 63:81–99
Sasaki JY, 65:487–514
Sasaki Y, 66:197–221
Saturn SR, 65:425–60
Schippers MC, 58:515–41
Schloss KB, 64:77–107
Schmidt AM, 61:543–68
Schneider B, 64:361–88
Schoenfelder EN, 62:299–329
Schooler JW, 66:487–518
Schyns PG, 68:269–97
Scott RM, 67:159–86

Seyfarth RM, 63:153–77
Shadish WR, 60:607–29
Shamsudheen R, 66:689–710
Shanks DR, 61:273–301
Sharma S, 67:239–61
Shaywitz BA, 59:451–75
Shaywitz SE, 59:451–75
Sheeran P, 68:573–600
Sherman DK, 65:333–71
Shevell SK, 59:143–66
Shi J, 65:209–33
Shiffrar M, 58:47–73
Shukla M, 66:349–79
Siegler RS, 68:187–213
Simpson JA, 68:383–411
Skinner EA, 58:119–44
Slater J, 67:83–103
Sloman SA, 66:223–47
Smallwood J, 66:487–518
Sobel N, 61:219–41
Sommers SR, 67:439–63
Sommers T, 63:81–99
Spencer SJ, 67:415–37
Sporer AK, 60:229–55
Sporns O, 67:613–40
Stanton AL, 58:565–92
Staudinger UM, 62:215–41
Stephens NM, 65:611–34
Sternberg RJ, 65:1–16
Stone AA, 64:471–98
Stuewig J, 58:345–72
Sue S, 60:525–48
Sunstein CR, 67:713–37
Sutter ML, 59:119–42

T

Tangney JP, 58:345–72
Tarr MJ, 58:75–96
Tasselli S, 64:527–47
Teki S, 65:743–71
Tennen H, 58:565–92
Thau S, 60:717–41
Thompson LL, 61:491–515
Tipsord JM, 62:189–214
Todorov A, 66:519–45
Tomasello M, 64:231–55
Tong F, 63:483–509
Tooby J, 64:201–29
Treviño LK, 65:635–60
Trickett EJ, 60:395–419

Tsai KM, 66:411–31
Turk-Browne NB, 62:73–101
Turkheimer E, 65:515–40

U

Uleman JS, 59:329–60
Uskul AK, 62:419–49

V

Vaish A, 64:231–55
Valdesolo P, 66:799–823
Valkenburg PM, 67:315–38
van IJzendoorn MH, 66:381–409
van Knippenberg D, 58:515–41
Vandello JA, 67:515–39
Varnum MEW, 64:335–59
Vogeley K, 64:335–59
Vohs KD, 62:331–61
Voss MW, 66:769–97
Votruba-Drzal E, 68:413–34
Vu KL, 61:623–51

W

Wagenmakers E, 67:641–66
Wagner AD, 63:101–28
Wagner LM, 67:387–413
Walker BM, 58:453–77
Walther JB, 67:315–38
Walumbwa FO, 60:421–49
Wanberg CR, 63:369–96
Wandell BA, 63:31–53
Wang J, 61:491–515
Wang M, 65:209–33
Wang S, 61:49–79
Ward J, 64:49–75
Watanabe T, 66:197–221
Weber TJ, 60:421–49
Weinman J, 59:477–505
Welsh DP, 60:631–52
Werker JF, 66:173–96
West SA, 66:575–99
Westfall J, 68:601–25
Wexler BE, 64:335–59
Whiten A, 68:129–54
Williams JC, 67:515–39
Williams KD, 58:425–52

Winne PH, 61:653–78
Winocur G, 67:105–34
Winter DA, 58:453–77
Wolchik SA, 62:299–329
Wolf M, 63:427–52
Wood J, 61:303–24
Wood W, 67:289–314

Y

Yarkoni T, 67:587–612
Yeatman JD, 63:31–53
Yeshurun Y, 61:219–41
Yousafzai AK, 66:433–57

Z

Zajdel M, 68:545–71
Zane N, 60:525–48
Zhang T, 61:439–66
Zimmer-Gembeck MJ,
  58:119–44
Zirnsak M, 68:47–72

Article Titles, Volumes 58–68